Cyclopedia Of Law And Procedure...

William Mack

roads,[5] streets and alleys in incorporated cities, towns, and villages,[6] and public ways of every description.[7] It accordingly includes not only public ways devoted to vehicular transportation,[8] but also public ways of all kinds, including

a way for vehicles drawn by animals, constituting, respectively, the "*iter*," the "*actus*," and the "*via*" of the Romans. And thus the methods of using public highways expanded with the growth of civilization, until to-day our urban highways are devoted to a variety of uses not known in former times, and never dreamed of by the owners of the soil when the public easement was acquired. Cater *v.* Northwestern Tel. Exch Co., 60 Minn. 539, 543, 63 N. W. 111, 51 Am. St. Rep. 543, 28 L. R. A. 310. And see Boyden *v.* Achenbach, 79 N. C. 539, 541. Highways "are of many kinds, varying with the state of civilization and wealth of the country through which they are constructed, and according to the extent of the traffic to be carried on upon them." Shelby County *v.* Castetter, 7 Ind. App. 309, 33 N. E. 986, 987, 34 N. E. 687.

Nature.— A public highway is a perpetual easement and a freehold estate. Taylor *v.* Pierce, 174 Ill. 9, 11, 50 N. E. 1109; Crete *v.* Hewes, 168 Ill. 330, 332, 48 N. E. 36; Chaplin *v.* Highway Com'rs, 126 Ill. 264, 271, 18 N. E. 765.

The way must be public else it is not a highway (Coulter *v.* Great Northern R. Co., 5 N. D. 568, 67 N. W. 1046, 1050. And see *infra*, II, B, 2, b), although it is the right to travel upon a way by all the world, and not the exercise of the right, which makes the way a highway (*In re* New York, 135 N. Y. 253, 260, 31 N. E. 1043, 31 Am. St. Rep. 825), and a road open to the public is a public road, although one person will be most benefited by it (Galveston, etc., R. Co. *v.* Baudat, 18 Tex. Civ. App. 595, 600, 45 S. W. 939). It is essential to the notion of a highway that its use must be common to all citizens. Sun Printing, etc., Assoc. *v.* New York, 8 N. Y. App. Div. 230, 283, 40 N. Y. Suppl. 607 [*affirmed* in 152 N. Y. 257, 46 N. E. 499, 37 L. R. A. 788]. To constitute a highway, it must be one to which all the people of the state have a common and equal right to travel, and in which they have a common, and at least general, interest to keep unobstructed. Talbott *v.* Richmond, etc., R. Co., 31 Gratt. (Va.) 685, 692. Accordingly the term "public highway" is a tautological expression, since a highway is a passage, road, or street which every citizen has a right to use, and is therefore necessarily public. Walton *v.* St. Louis, etc., R. Co., 67 Mo. 56, 57; Jenkins *v.* Chicago, etc., R. Co., 27 Mo. App. 578, 583. And the public includes strangers as well as inhabitants of the district where the way exists. Mobile, etc., R. Co. *v.* Davis, 130 Ill. 146, 150, 22 N. E. 850; Lynch *v.* Rutland, 66 Vt. 570, 573, 29 Atl. 1015; Slicer *v.* Hyde Park, 55 Vt. 481, 482.

Necessity of practical passage.— The word "highway" imports a practicable passage. It is a contradiction in terms to speak of an impassable highway. Armstrong *v.* St. Louis, 3 Mo. App. 151, 157. And see *infra*, II, B, 2, b.

Cul-de-sac as highway see *supra*, note 1; *infra*, note 50.

Town way as highway see *supra*, note 1.

5. *Indiana.*— State *v.* Moriarty, 74 Ind. 103, 104; Shelby County *v.* Castetter, 7 Ind. App. 309, 33 N. E. 986, 987, 34 N. E. 687.

Iowa.— Chamberlain *v.* Iowa Tel. Co., 119 Iowa 619, 621, 93 N. W. 596; Sachs *v.* Sioux City, 109 Iowa 224, 227, 80 N. W. 336; Stokes *v.* Scott County, 10 Iowa 166, 175.

Missouri.—Walton *v.* St. Louis, etc., R. Co., 67 Mo. 56, 57; Kerney *v.* Barber Asphalt Paving Co., 86 Mo. App. 573, 578; Jenkins *v.* Chicago, etc., R. Co., 27 Mo. App. 578, 583.

Nebraska.— Union Pac. R. Co. *v.* Colfax County, 4 Nebr. 450, 456.

New Jersey.— Vantilburgh *v.* Shann, 24 N. J. L. 740, 744.

New York.— *In re* Burns, 155 N. Y. 23, 28, 49 N. E. 246 [*reversing* 16 N. Y. App. Div. 507, 44 N. Y. Suppl. 930].

Oklahoma.— Southern Kansas R. Co. *v.* Oklahoma City, 12 Okla. 82, 94, 69 Pac. 1050.

Wisconsin.— Herrick *v.* Geneva, 92 Wis. 114, 117, 65 N. W. 1024.

United States.—Abbott *v.* Duluth, 104 Fed. 833, 837 [*affirmed* in 117 Fed. 137, 55 C. C. A. 153].

England.— Reg. *v.* Chart, etc., Upper Half Hundred, L. R. 1 C. C. 237, 239.

New England town way as highway see *supra*, note 1.

Road defined see *infra*, this section, text and notes 12–20.

6. See MUNICIPAL CORPORATIONS, 28 Cyc. 832 *et seq.*

New England town way as highway see *supra*, note 1.

7. See *supra*, this section, text and notes.

8. *Arkansas.*— Arkansas River Packet Co *v.* Sorrels, 50 Ark. 466, 472, 8 S. W. 683.

Connecticut.— Laufer *v.* Bridgeport Traction Co., 68 Conn. 475, 488, 37 Atl. 379, 37 L. R. A. 533.

Kansas.— Burlington, etc., R. Co. *v.* Johnson, 38 Kan. 142, 148, 16 Pac. 125.

Massachusetts.— Harding *v.* Medway, 10 Metc. 465, 469.

Nebraska.— Union Pac. R. Co. *v.* Colfax County, 4 Nebr. 450, 456.

North Carolina.— State *v.* Cowan, 29 N. C. 239, 248.

South Carolina.—State *v.* Harden, 11 S. C. 360, 368; Heyward *v.* Chisolm, 11 Rich. 253, 263.

Tennessee.— State *v.* Stroud, (Ch. App. 1898) 52 S. W. 697, 698.

England.— Reg. *v.* Chart, etc., Upper Half Hundred, L. R. 1 C. C. 237, 239; Reg. *v.* Saintiff, 6 Mod. 255, 4 Vin. Abr. 502, 87 Eng. Reprint 1002.

Canada.— Styles *v.* Victoria, 8 Brit. Col. 406, 414.

generic term for all kinds of ways,[16] and thus includes highways,[17] streets,[18] alleys,[19] and lanes.[20]

II. ESTABLISHMENT, ALTERATION, AND DISCONTINUANCE.

A. Modes of Establishment in General. A highway may be established either by prescription, user, or recognition,[21] by statute or statutory proceedings

communication between one city or town and another." Hutson *v.* New York, 5 Sandf. (N. Y.) 289, 312 [*affirmed* in 9 N. Y. 163, 59 Am. Dec. 526].

The term "public highway" and "public road" are not deemed synonymous in Georgia. Johnson *v.* State, 1 Ga. App. 195, 198, 58 S. E. 265.

Necessity of actual user.—A "road" is a way actually used in passing from one place to another. A mere survey or location of a route for a road is not a road. Brooks *v.* Morrill, 92 Me. 172, 176, 42 Atl. 357.

16. Griffin *v.* Sanborn, 127 Ga. 17, 56 S. E. 71; Windham *v.* Cumberland County Com'rs, 26 Me. 406, 409.

A carriageway is within the term "road." International, etc., R. Co. *v.* Jordan, 1 Tex. App. Civ. Cas. § 859; Terry *v.* McClung, 104 Va. 599, 602, 52 S. E. 355.

A footway is included in the term "road." International, etc., R. Co. *v.* Jordan, 1 Tex. App. Civ. Cas. § 859; Terry *v.* McClung, 104 Va. 599, 602, 52 S. E. 355. And see Kister *v.* Reeser, 98 Pa. St. 1, 4, 42 Am. Rep. 608. A road *prima facie* includes the foot-paths as well as the carriageway. Derby County *v.* Urban Dist., [1896] A. C. 315, 323, 60 J. P. 676, 65 L. J. Q. B. 419, 74 L. T. Rep. N. S. 595. So a sidewalk is part of the road. Manchester *v.* Hartford, 30 Conn. 118, 120.

A bridle path is included in the term "road" in its generic sense. Terry *v.* McClung, 104 Va. 599, 602, 52 S. E. 355.

A driftway is within the term "road." Terry *v.* McClung, 104 Va. 599, 602, 52 S. E. 355.

In all the old acts the word "path" is used as synonymous with the word "road." Singleton *v.* Road Com'rs, 2 Nott & M. (S. C.) 526, 527.

Great road defined see 20 Cyc. 1365.

17. Manchester *v.* Hartford, 30 Conn. 118, 120; Stokes *v.* Scott County, 10 Iowa 166, 175; Dubuque County *v.* Dubuque, etc., R. Co., 4 Greene (Iowa) 1, 14 (per Kinney, J., dissenting); Follmer *v.* Nuckolls County Com'rs, 6 Nebr. 204, 209; People *v.* Buffalo County Com'rs, 4 Nebr. 150, 158; Kister *v.* Reeser, 98 Pa. St. 1, 4, 42 Am. Rep. 608.

18. *Connecticut.*— Manchester *v.* Hartford, 30 Conn. 118, 120.

Iowa.— Chamberlain *v.* Iowa Tel. Co., 119 Iowa 619, 621, 93 N. W. 596; Stokes *v.* Scott County, 10 Iowa 166, 175; Dubuque County *v.* Dubuque, etc., R. Co., 4 Greene 1, 14, 15, per Kinney, J., dissenting.

Minnesota.— Northwestern Tel. Exch. Co. *v.* Minneapolis, 81 Minn. 140, 154, 83 N. W. 527, 86 N. W. 69, 53 L. R. A. 175.

Nebraska.— Follmer *v.* Nuckolls County Com'rs, 6 Nebr. 204, 209; People *v.* Buffalo County Com'rs, 4 Nebr. 150, 158.

Pennsylvania.— Kister *v.* Reeser, 98 Pa. St. 1, 4, 42 Am. Rep. 608.

Texas.— International, etc., R. Co. *v.* Jordan, 1 Tex. App. Civ. Cas. § 859.

Wisconsin.— State *v.* Sheboygan, 111 Wis. 23, 33, 86 N. W. 657, 659.

United States.— Abbott *v.* Duluth, 104 Fed. 833, 837 [*affirmed* in 117 Fed. 137, 55 C. C. A. 153].

To the contrary see Carter *v.* Rahway, 55 N. J. L. 177. 178, 26 Atl. 96; *In re* Woolsey, 95 N. Y. 135, 138; Vanderkar *v.* Rensselaer, etc., R. Co., 13 Barb. (N Y.) 390, 391.

Loose use of terms.— An examination of the authorities will show that the terms "street." "avenue," "road," "public road," "county road," etc., are used loosely and indiscriminately in legislation and judicial decisions relating to public highways, and little reliance can be placed on the particular term used to describe any given way. Undoubtedly the term "street" or "avenue" commonly applies to a public highway in a village, town, or city, and the term "road" to suburban highways. But there may be roads in a city or town and streets and avenues in the country. Murphy *v.* King County, 45 Wash. 587, 591, 88 Pac. 1115.

19. Chamberlain *v.* Iowa Tel. Co., 119 Iowa 619, 621, 93 N. W. 596; Northwestern Tel. Exch. Co. *v.* Minneapolis, 81 Minn. 140, 154, 83 N. W. 527, 86 N. W. 69, 71, 53 L. R. A. 175; State *v.* Sheboygan, 111 Wis. 23, 33, 86 N. W. 657; Abbott *v.* Duluth, 104 Fed. 833, 837 [*affirmed* in 117 Fed. 137, 55 C. C. A. 153].

20. *Connecticut.*— Manchester *v.* Hartford, 30 Conn. 118, 120.

Iowa.— Chamberlain *v.* Iowa Tel. Co., 119 Iowa 619, 623, 93 N. W. 596; Stokes *v.* Scott County, 10 Iowa 166, 175; Dubuque County *v.* Dubuque, etc., R. Co., 4 Greene 1, 14, 15, per Kinney, J., dissenting.

Minnesota.— Northwestern Tel. Exch. Co. *v.* Minneapolis, 81 Minn. 140, 154, 83 N. W. 527, 86 N. W. 69, 53 L. R. A. 175.

Nebraska.— Follmer *v.* Nuckolls County Com'rs, 6 Nebr. 204, 209; People *v.* Buffalo County Com'rs, 4 Nebr. 150, 158.

Pennsylvania.—Kister *v.* Reeser, 98 Pa. St. 1, 4, 42 Am. Rep. 608.

Texas.— International, etc., R. Co. *v.* Jordan, 1 Tex. App. Civ. Cas. § 859.

Wisconsin.— State *v.* Sheboygan, 111 Wis. 23, 33, 86 N. W. 657.

United States.—Abbott *v.* Suluth, 104 Fed. 833. 837 [*affirmed* in 117 Fed. 137, 55 C. C. A. 153].

21. See *infra*, II, B.

user.[57] Hence if the landowner obstructs free travel by means of gates or fences, it ordinarily prevents the public from acquiring a highway by prescription.[58]

e. Hostility of User; Color or Claim of Right; Permissive User — (I) *In General.* Mere user of another's land by the public as for a highway is insufficient of itself to establish a highway by prescription.[59] The user must be adverse and

57. Madison Tp. *v.* Gallagher, 159 Ill. 105, 42 N. E. 316; Chicago *v.* Chicago, etc., R. Co., 152 Ill. 561, 38 N. E. 768; Warren *v.* Jacksonville, 15 Ill. 236, 58 Am. Dec. 610; Toof *v.* Decatur, 19 Ill. App. 204; Missouri, etc., R. Co. *v.* Long, 27 Kan. 684; Devenpeck *v.* Lambert, 44 Barb. (N. Y.) 596; Gaines *v.* Merryman, 95 Va. 660, 29 S. E. 738.

58. *Alabama.*—Whaley *v.* Wilson, 120 Ala. 502, 24 So. 855; Harper *v.* State, 109 Ala. 66, 19 So. 901.

California.— See Smithers *v.* Fitch, 82 Cal. 153, 22 Pac. 935.

Delaware.— Johnson *v.* Stayton, 5 Harr. 448.

Idaho.— See Palmer *v.* Northern Pac. R. Co., 11 Ida. 583, 83 Pac. 947.

Indiana.— Shellhouse *v.* State, 110 Ind. 509, 11 N. E. 484.

Iowa.— Mills *v.* Evans, 100 Iowa 712, 69 N. W. 1043; Gray *v.* Haas, 98 Iowa 502, 67 N. W. 394; Breneman *v.* Burlington, etc., R. Co., 92 Iowa 755, 60 N. W. 176.

Kansas.— State *v.* Cipra, 71 Kan. 714, 81 Pac. 488.

Kentucky.—Louisville, etc., R. Co. *v.* Bailey, 109 S. W. 336, 33 Ky. L. Rep. 179.

Maine.— State *v.* Strong, 25 Me. 297.

Massachusetts.—Aiken *v.* New York, etc., R. Co., 188 Mass. 547, 74 N. E. 929.

Nebraska.— Horn *v.* Williamson, 4 Nebr. (Unoff.) 763, 96 N. W. 178.

New York.— Loughman *v.* Long Island R. Co., 83 N. Y. App. Div. 629, 81 N. Y. Suppl. 1097. See Riley *v.* Brodie, 22 Misc. 374, 50 N. Y. Suppl. 347.

Tennessee.—Whitesides *v.* Earles, (Ch. App. 1901) 61 S. W. 1038.

Texas.— Cunningham *v.* San Saba County, 11 Tex. Civ. App. 557, 32 S. W. 928, 33 S. W. 892.

Washington.— Megrath *v.* Nickerson, 24 Wash 235, 64 Pac. 163; Shell *v.* Poulson, 23 Wash. 535, 63 Pac. 204.

See 25 Cent. Dig. tit. "Highways," § 14.

Gate as allowing travel.— The fact that the landowner places a gate in a fence which he erects across a claimed highway (State *v.* Cipra, 71 Kan. 714, 81 Pac. 488), and leaves it unlocked (Shell *v.* Poulson, 23 Wash. 535, 63 Pac. 204), does not affect the rule stated in the text. And see cases cited *supra*, this note.

However, putting up a fence or barrier across a way does not necessarily, as matter of law, constitute an interruption of the use of the way claimed by prescription, in the absence of evidence of the occasion or circumstances or effect of the act. Weld *v.* Brooks, 152 Mass. 297, 25 N. E. 719. Thus fences with gates erected solely to keep cattle from straying do not defeat prescription. Clark *v.* Hull, 184 Mass. 164, 68 N. E. 60; Sikes *v.* St. Louis, etc., R. Co., 127 Mo. App. 326, 105 S. W. 700; Rhodes *v.* Halvorson, 120 Wis. 99, 97 N. W. 514. So where plaintiff fenced in a part of the originally traveled road, which had been used for seven or eight years, and established a new road in another place, with the intention that the road as changed should be used by the public, and it was so used for eight or nine years, the act of plaintiff, not being hostile to the right of the public, did not interrupt the running of the statute so as to prevent the whole road from becoming a highway by adverse possession. Berry *v.* St. Louis, etc., R. Co., 124 Mo. App. 436, 101 S. W. 714. *Compare* Goelet *v.* Newport, 14 R. I. 295.

Fencing a road after the prescriptive rights of the public have matured is of no effect. Yakima County *v.* Conrad, 26 Wash 155, 66 Pac. 411.

59. *Alabama.*— Gosdin *v.* Williams, 151 Ala. 592, 44 So. 611; Jones *v.* Bright, 140 Ala. 268, 37 So. 79, both holding that the mere use of land for the purpose of a road carries with it no presumption of adverse claim or claim of right to so use it.

Illinois.— Falter *v.* Packard, 219 Ill. 356, 76 N. E. 495.

Iowa.— Davis *v.* Bonaparte, 137 Iowa 196, 114 N. W. 896; Haan *v.* Meester, 132 Iowa 709, 109 N. W. 211; State *v.* Mitchell, 58 Iowa 567, 12 N. W. 598, all decided under a statute providing that the fact of adverse possession must be proved by evidence distinct from and independent of the use. And see Gray *v.* Haas, 98 Iowa 502, 67 N. W. 394.

Kentucky.— Hall *v.* McLeod, 2 Metc. 98, 74 Am. Dec. 400, holding that, where a way is opened as a private passway, it cannot be converted into a highway by the mere use thereof, no matter how long that use may be continued.

Massachusetts.— Fall River Print Works *v.* Fall River, 110 Mass. 428.

North Carolina.— State *v.* Wolf, 112 N. C. 889, 17 S. E. 528.

Vermont.— Emery *v.* Washington, Brayt. 129; Bailey *v.* Fairfield, Brayt. 128.

Virginia.— Terry *v.* McClung, 104 Va. 599, 52 S. E. 355; Com. *v.* Kelly, 8 Gratt. 632.

West Virginia.— State *v.* Dry Fork R. Co., 50 W. Va. 235, 40 S. E. 447; Dicken *v.* Liverpool Salt, etc., Co., 41 W. Va. 511, 23 S. E. 582.

United States.— District of Columbia *v.* Robinson, 180 U. S. 92, 21 S. Ct. 283, 45 L. ed. 440 [*affirming* 14 App. Cas. (D. C.) 512].

See 25 Cent. Dig. tit. "Highways," §§ 10, 11.

The use of a strip of an open common for driving or walking is the exercise of the right in a common, and does not make it a highway by prescription. McKay *v.* Reading,

hostile to the rights of the owner,[60] and under color or claim of right so to use the

184 Mass. 140, 68 N. E. 43; Emerson *v.* Wiley, 7 Pick. (Mass.) 68.

Operation of statute.— Miller Code Iowa, § 2031, providing that the use of land shall not be admitted as evidence of a claim of right, but the fact of adverse possession shall be proved by evidence distinct from and independent of the use, does not apply where a highway had been acquired by prescription before the statute was enacted, it being so declared in section 2036. McAllister *v.* Pickup, 84 Iowa 65, 50 N. W. 556; Baldwin *v.* Herbst, 54 Iowa 168, 6 N. W. 257.

60. *Alabama.*— Jones *v.* Bright, 140 Ala. 268, 37 So. 79; Harper *v.* State, 109 Ala. 66, 19 So. 901.

Colorado.— Lieber *v.* People, 33 Colo. 493, 81 Pac. 270.

Illinois.— Chicago *v.* Galt, 224 Ill. 421, 79 N. E. 701; Falter *v.* Packard, 219 Ill. 356, 76 N. E. 495; Rose *v.* Farmington, 196 Ill. 226, 63 N. E. 631; Chicago *v.* Borden, 190 Ill. 430, 60 N. E. 915; O'Connell *v.* Chicago Terminal Transfer R. Co., 184 Ill. 308, 56 N. E. 355; Illinois Cent. R. Co. *v.* Bloomington, 167 Ill. 9, 47 N. E. 318; Madison Tp. *v.* Gallagher, 159 Ill. 105, 42 N. E. 316; Chicago *v.* Chicago, etc., R. Co., 152 Ill. 561, 38 N. E. 768; Gentleman *v.* Soule, 32 Ill. 271, 83 Am. Dec. 264; Dickerman *v.* Marion, 122 Ill. App. 154; Toof *v.* Decatur, 19 Ill. App. 204.

Indiana.— Baltimore, etc., R. Co. *v.* Seymour, 154 Ind. 17, 55 N. E. 953.

Iowa.— Hougham *v.* Harvey, 40 Iowa 634.

Kansas.— Topeka *v.* Cowee, 48 Kan. 345, 29 Pac. 560.

Massachusetts.— Slater *v.* Gunn, 170 Mass. 509, 49 N. E. 1017, 41 L. R. A. 268; Com. *v.* Coupe, 128 Mass. 63.

Mississippi.— Warren County *v.* Mastronardi, 76 Miss. 273, 24 So. 199, holding that the privilege exercised must be such as to expose the party asserting the right of way to an action, if he wrongfully exercised the privilege.

Nebraska.— Nelson *v.* Sneed, 76 Nebr. 201, 107 N. W. 255; Bleck *v.* Keller, 73 Nebr. 826, 103 N. W. 674; Gehris *v.* Fuhrman, 68 Nebr. 325, 94 N. W. 133; Engle *v.* Hunt, 50 Nebr. 358, 69 N. W. 970.

North Carolina.— State *v.* Fisher, 117 N. C. 733. 23 S. E. 158; State *v.* Wolf, 112 N. C. 889, 17 S. E. 528.

Oregon.— Bayard *v.* Standard Oil Co., 38 Oreg. 438, 63 Pac. 614.

Pennsylvania.— Root *v.* Com., 98 Pa. St. 170, 42 Am. Rep. 614; *In re* Springfield Tp. Road, 14 Montg. Co. Rep. 97.

Washington.— Stohlton *v.* Kitsap County, 49 Wash. 305. 95 Pac. 268; Petterson *v.* Waske, 45 Wash. 307, 88 Pac. 206.

United States.— District of Columbia *v.* Robinson, 180 U. S. 92, 21 S. Ct. 283, 45 L. ed. 440 [*affirming* 14 App. Cas. (D. C.) 512].

See 25 Cent. Dig. tit. "Highways," § 10.

Adverse user of a highway imports an assertion of right, on the part of those traveling the road, hostile to the owner of the land over which the highway runs. St. Andrews Parish Tp. Com'rs *v.* Charleston Min., etc., Co., 76 S. C. 382, 57 S. E. 201. Accordingly a highway is not established where no act of control or dominion over the land was exercised or asserted by the public authorities (Hill *v.* McGinnis, 64 Nebr. 187, 89 N. W. 783. Recognition, maintenance, and repair by public authorities see *infra*, II, B, 2, e, (III)), or where the use was not inconsistent with the use of the land by the owner (Dexter *v.* Tree, 117 Ill. 532, 6 N. E. 506; Heilbron *v.* St. Louis Southwestern R. Co., (Tex. Civ. App. 1908) 113 S. W. 610, 979). So where a city seeks to establish a highway by prescription along a railroad right of way, evidence that the city, during the period it claims adverse user, had recognized the company's right of way as an easement or by title is material and competent. Illinois Cent. R. Co. *v.* Bloomington, 167 Ill. 9, 47 N. E. 318.

Levy of taxes on land in dispute.—While the fact that the municipality has levied and collected taxes or special assessments on the land claimed as a highway within the prescriptive period tends to rebut the claim of adverse user (Illinois Cent. R. Co. *v.* Bloomington, 167 Ill. 9, 47 N. E. 318; Huntington *v.* Townsend, 29 Ind. App. 269, 63 N. E. 36. And see Haan *v.* Meester, 132 Iowa 709, 109 N. W. 211), it is not conclusive against the claim that the land is a highway (Toof *v.* Decatur, 19 Ill. App. 204), especially where the highway did not cover all the tract on which the tax was levied (Cedar Rapids *v.* Young, 119 Iowa 552, 93 N. W. 567). And where the public has already acquired an easement by user in a highway, the listing of the land for taxes and the payment thereof by the owner do not affect the rights of the public in the land. Campau *v.* Detroit, 104 Mich. 560, 62 N. W. 718.

However, it is not always necessary to show some aggressively hostile act by the public, but the adverse character of the user may be presumed from the facts and circumstances of the case. Barnes *v.* Daveck, 7 Cal. App. 220, 487, 94 Pac. 779; Earle *v.* Poat, 63 S. C. 439, 41 S. E. 525 (holding that where the public has for twenty years asserted the right to a way for public purposes, it is sufficient to carry with it an adverse use by the public); Hall *v.* Austin, 20 Tex. Civ. App. 59, 48 S. W. 53 (holding that a highway by prescription may be established without other evidence of the assertion of an adverse claim than that afforded by the nature of the use). And see McAllister *v.* Pickup, 84 Iowa 65, 50 N. W. 556.

Burden of proof.—Where the public claims title to the easement in a highway by user, the burden rests on the state to show adverse possession. State *v.* Fisher, 117 N. C. 733, 23 S. E. 158. And where plaintiff sued for land included in a deed from his father,

land.[61] **A user by license or permission of the owner of the land sought to be impressed with a public easement of travel is not adverse, and affords no basis for prescription,**[62]

which land defendants claimed the prescriptive right to use as a road, plaintiff's evidence of title and that defendants' use of the road had been merely permissive established a *prima facie* case, and placed the burden on defendants to prove their adverse holding. Rose *v.* Stephens, (Ky. 1908) 112 S. W. 676.

Highway prescription acts.— In New York, it seems, the words, "used as public highways," in 1 Rev. St. 521, § 100, declaring that "all roads not recorded which have been or shall have been used as public highways for twenty years or more shall be deemed public highways," do not require the user to be adverse and under such circumstances as would be required to give an individual a right of way by prescription (Speir *v.* Utrecht, 121 N. Y. 420, 24 N. E. 692 [*modifying* 49 Hun 294, 2 N. Y. Suppl. 426]), although a different conclusion seems to have been reached by the courts of some other states having similar statutes (see cases cited *supra*, this note; *infra*, note 61). The user, however, must be like that of highways generally. Speir *v.* Utrecht, *supra*; Buffalo *v.* Delaware, etc., R. Co., 68 N. Y. App. Div. 488, 74 N. Y. Suppl. 343 [*affirmed* in 178 N. Y. 561, 70 N. E. 1097]. The road must be not only traveled upon but kept in repair or taken in charge of or adopted by the public authorities. See *infra*, note 68. And the fact that a portion of the public have traveled over it for more than twenty years does not alone make it a highway. See *supra*, II, B, 2, b.

61. *Alabama.*— Jones *v.* Bright, 140 Ala. 268, 37 So. 79.

Colorado.— Lieber *v.* People, 33 Colo. 493, 81 Pac. 270.

District of Columbia.— District of Columbia *v.* Robinson, 14 App. Cas. 512 [*affirmed* in 180 U. S. 92, 21 S. Ct. 283, 45 L. ed. 440].

Illinois.— Chicago *v.* Galt, 224 Ill. 421, 79 N. E. 701; Falter *v.* Packard, 219 Ill. 356, 76 N. E. 495; Chicago *v.* Borden, 190 Ill. 430, 60 N. E. 915; O'Connell *v.* Chicago Terminal Transfer R. Co., 184 Ill. 308, 56 N. E. 355; Illinois Cent. R. Co. *v.* Bloomington, 167 Ill. 9, 47 N. E. 318; Madison Tp. *v.* Gallagher, 159 Ill. 105, 42 N. E. 316; Chicago *v.* Chicago, etc., R. Co., 152 Ill. 561, 38 N. E. 768; Dexter *v.* Tree, 117 Ill. 532, 6 N. E. 506; Gentleman *v.* Soule, 32 Ill. 271, 83 Am. Dec. 264; Toof *v.* Decatur, 19 Ill. App. 204. See, however, Menard County Road Dist. No. 1 *v.* Beebe, 231 Ill. 147, 83 N. E. 131.

Indiana.— Southern Indiana R. Co. *v.* Norman, 165 Ind. 126, 74 N. E. 896; Shellhouse *v.* State, 110 Ind. 509, 11 N. E. 484.

Iowa.— Fairchild *v.* Stewart, 117 Iowa 734, 89 N. W. 1075; Hougham *v.* Harvey, 40 Iowa 634; State *v.* Tucker, 36 Iowa 485.

Kansas.— Topeka *v.* Cowee, 48 Kan. 345, 29 Pac. 560.

Kentucky.— Louisville, etc., R. Co. *v.* Bailey, 109 S. W. 336, 33 Ky. L. Rep. 179.

Massachusetts.— Slater *v.* Gunn, 170 Mass. 509, 49 N. E. 1017, 41 L. R. A. 268.

Mississippi.— Wills *v.* Reed, 86 Miss. 446, 38 So. 793; Burnley *v.* Mullins, 86 Miss. 441, 38 So. 635; Warren County *v.* Mastronardi, 76 Miss. 273, 23 So. 199.

Nebraska.— Nelson *v.* Sneed, 76 Nebr. 201, 107 N. W. 255; Kansas City, etc., R. Co. *v.* State, 74 Nebr. 868, 105 N. W. 713; Bleck *v.* Keller, 73 Nebr. 826, 103 N. W. 674; Gehris *v.* Fuhrman, 68 Nebr. 325, 94 N. W. 133; Hill *v.* McGinnis, 64 Nebr. 187, 89 N. W 783; Lewis *v.* Lincoln, 55 Nebr. 1, 75 N. W. 154; Engle *v.* Hunt, 50 Nebr. 358, 69 N. W. 970.

Oregon.— Bayard *v.* Standard Oil Co., 38 Oreg. 438, 63 Pac. 614.

Pennsylvania.— Root *v.* Com., 98 Pa. St. 170, 42 Am. Rep. 614.

Tennessee.— Sharp *v.* Mynatt, 1 Lea 375.

Texas.— Cunningham *v.* San Saba County, 1 Tex. Civ. App. 480, 20 S. W. 941.

Wisconsin.— State *v.* Joyce, 19 Wis. 90. See, however, State *v.* Lloyd, 133 Wis. 468, 113 N. W. 964.

See 25 Cent. Dig. tit. "Highways," § 11.

The claim of right must be manifested by acts indicating an intention to enjoy the land as a highway without regard to the wishes of the owner (Rose *v.* Farmington, 196 Ill. 226, 63 N. E. 631; Shellhouse *v.* State, 110 Ind. 509, 11 N. E. 484; State *v.* Green, 41 Iowa 693), as by some appropriate action on the part of the public authorities (Kansas City, etc., R. Co. *v.* State, 74 Nebr. 868, 105 N. W. 713; Hill *v.* McGinnis, 64 Nebr. 187, 89 N. W. 783; Lewis *v.* Lincoln, 55 Nebr. 1, 75 N. W. 154. Recognition, maintenance, and repair by public authorities see *infra*, II, B, 2, e, (III)).

However, it is not always necessary for the public in using a roadway to make proclamation that they are using it under a claim of right, where the right is asserted as flowing from long usage with the knowledge and acquiescence of the owner of the land; but the claim of right may be presumed from the facts and circumstances attending the use. Barnes *v.* Daveck, 7 Cal App. 220, 487, 94 Pac. 779; Rose *v.* Farmington, 196 Ill. 226, 63 N. E. 631; Shellhouse *v.* State, 110 Ind. 509, 11 N. E. 484; State *v.* Green, 41 Iowa 693. An unexplained user of land as a highway by the public for the prescriptive period will be presumed to be under a claim of right, the user being otherwise sufficient. Southern Indiana R. Co. *v.* Norman, 165 Ind. 126, 74 N. E. 896; Hanson *v.* Taylor, 23 Wis. 547. And see Evans *v.* Cook, 111 S. W. 326, 33 Ky. L. Rep. 788.

Effect of levy of taxes on land in dispute see *supra*, note 60.

62. *Alabama.*— Jones *v.* Bright, 140 Ala. 268, 37 So. 79; Harper *v.* State, 109 Ala. 66, 19 So. 901.

California.— Hartley *v.* Vermillion, (1902) 70 Pac. 273, 141 Cal. 339, 74 Pac. 987. And

lands,[77] provided the user is adverse and under claim or color of right,[78] and not by mere license or permission of the landowner,[79] and is such as to put the owner on notice that a highway is claimed as of right,[80] and is otherwise sufficient to establish a highway by prescription.[81]

(v) *USER OF LAND OUTSIDE OF ESTABLISHED HIGHWAY.* An adverse user by the public, by mistake or otherwise, for the requisite period of time, of lands outside of the lines of an established highway is generally held to create a prescriptive right to use such lands as a highway,[82] and after the lapse of the

South Carolina.— Gibson *v.* Durham, 3 Rich. 85.

Washington.— Rice *v.* Pershall, 41 Wash. 73, 82 Pac. 1038.

See 25 Cent. Dig. tit. "Highways," § 16.

77. *Illinois.*— Peotone *v.* Illinois Cent. R. Co., 224 Ill. 101, 79 N. E. 678 (holding that Laws (1887), p. 263, which declares roads used by the public for fifteen years to be public highways, applies to both inclosed and uninclosed roads, but in the latter the acts of the public indicating the location of a highway must be more pronounced than in the former); O'Connell *v.* Chicago Terminal Transfer R. Co., 184 Ill. 308, 56 N. E. 355 (*semble*); Dimon *v.* People, 17 Ill. 416; Shugart *v.* Halliday, 2 Ill. App. 45.

Iowa.— Onstott *v.* Murray, 22 Iowa 457.

Kansas.— State *v.* Horn, 35 Kan. 717, 12 Pac. 148, *semble.*

South Carolina.— State *v.* Toale, 74 S. C. 425, 54 S. E. 608; Kirby *v.* Southern R. Co., 63 S. C. 494, 41 S. E. 765.

Texas.— Hall *v.* Austin, 20 Tex. Civ. App. 59, 48 S. W. 53.

See 25 Cent. Dig. tit. "Highways," § 16.

Where the lands are reclaimed, and the ways thereover are left open for use and are used by the public as highways, these acts may constitute the beginning of a prescriptive right of way, and, if continued for twenty years without interruption, raise the presumption of a grant to the public. Rosser *v.* Bunn, 66 Ala. 89.

Question for jury.— The continuous use by the public for more than ten years of a road along a mountain valley defining its course by natural limits, although it ran through an unfenced country and had never been laid out or recognized by the authorities as a public road, is sufficient to demand the submission to the jury of the right of those using it to a highway by prescription. Hall *v.* Austin, 20 Tex. Civ. App. 59, 48 S. W. 53.

78. *Arkansas.*— Brumley *v.* State, 83 Ark. 236, 103 S. W. 615.

Colorado.— Lieber *v.* People, 33 Colo. 493, 81 Pac. 270.

Illinois.— Ottawa *v.* Yentzer, 160 Ill. 509, 43 N. E. 601.

Maine.— Bethun *v.* Turner, 1 Me. 111, 10 Am. Dec. 36.

South Carolina.— Hutto *v.* Tindall, 6 Rich. 396; Gibson *v.* Durham, 3 Rich. 85.

Texas.— Cunningham *v.* San Saba County, 1 Tex. Civ. App. 480, 20 S. W. 941.

See 25 Cent. Dig. tit. "Highways," § 16.

Fencing highway.— The rule that a public road cannot be established by prescription where it runs over a prairie does not apply where it is fenced on each side. Raven *v.* Travis County, (Tex. Civ. App. 1899) 53 S. W. 355. But fencing is not always necessary to establish a highway over such lands by prescription. Shugart *v.* Halliday, 2 Ill. App. 45; Hall *v.* Austin, 20 Tex. Civ. App. 59, 48 S. W. 53. Fencing as notice of adverse claim see *infra*, II, B, 2, g, (I), note 8.

Presumption as to adverseness of user see *infra*, note 79.

Recognition, maintenance, and repair of road as evidence of existence of highway see *supra*, II, B, 2, e, (III), note 70. Failure to work or recognize road as evidence of non-existence of highway see *supra*, II, B, 2, e, (III), note 72.

79. *Arkansas.*— Brumley *v.* State, 83 Ark. 236, 103 S. W. 615.

Colorado.— Lieber *v.* People, 33 Colo. 493, 81 Pac. 270.

Illinois.— Falter *v.* Packard, 219 Ill. 356, 76 N. E. 495; Rose *v.* Farmington, 196 Ill. 226, 63 N. E. 631; Brushy Mound *v.* McClintock, 150 Ill. 129, 36 N. E. 976.

North Carolina.— Stewart *v.* Frink, 94 N. C. 487, 55 Am. Rep. 619.

Texas.— Cunningham *v.* San Saba County, 1 Tex. Civ. App. 480, 20 S. W. 941.

Washington.— Rice *v.* Pershall, 41 Wash. 73, 82 Pac. 1038; Watson *v.* Adams County Com'rs, 38 Wash. 662, 80 Pac. 201.

See 25 Cent. Dig. tit. "Highways," § 16.

Presumption as to permission.—Where the public use a road through open and unfenced lands without any order of the county court making it a public road, and without any attempt to work it or exercise authority over it as a highway, the presumption is that the use of the road is not adverse to the rights of the owner of the land, but is by his consent. Brumley *v.* State, 83 Ark. 236, 103 S. W. 615. And see Cross *v.* State, 147 Ala. 125, 41 So. 875; Brushy Mound *v.* McClintock, 150 Ill. 129, 36 N. E. 976.

80. See *infra*, II, B, 2, g, (I).

81. See *passim*, II, B, 2.

82. *California.*— Patterson *v.* Munyan, 93 Cal. 128, 29 Pac. 250.

Illinois.— Landers *v.* Whitefield, 154 Ill. 630, 39 N. E. 656 [*overruling dictum* in Manrose *v.* Parker, 90 Ill. 581]; Green *v.* Stevens, 49 Ill. App. 24.

Indiana.— Bales *v.* Pidgeon, 129 Ind. 548, 29 N. E. 34 (holding that where adjoining landowners agree upon their division line, and establish a road supposed to be on the land of one of them, which road for fifty years is used by the subsequent owners of the land and by the public, the road cannot

such,[88] for the requisite period, it becomes such by prescription, the user and recognition generally being referable to a claim and color of right in the public. However, in the absence of statute to the contrary, the public user, as in other cases, must be adverse and under claim or color of right, and not merely by revocable permission of the owner,[89] and otherwise sufficient to establish a highway by prescription;[90] and the land so used must be that described in the defective proceedings.[91] Similarly a highway may be established by prescription over land which the owner has made an ineffectual attempt to dedicate to the public as a highway.[92]

f. Duration of User; Prescriptive Period. The period of time during which the user must continue in order to create a highway by prescription varies in the different states.[93] Anciently prescription implied a claim to an incorporeal hereditament arising from the same having been enjoyed from time immemorial.[94]

v. Stockwell, 84 Mich. 586, 48 N. W. 174, 22 Am. St. Rep. 708; Potter *v.* Safford, 50 Mich. 46, 14 N. W. 694, so holding under statute. See Green *v.* Belitz, 34 Mich. 512.

Minnesota.— Rogers *v.* Aitkin, 77 Minn. 539, 80 N. W. 702.

Missouri.— Harper *v.* Morse, 46 Mo. App. 470; State *v.* Pullen, 43 Mo. App. 620, it being expressly so declared by statute.

Montana.— State *v.* Auchard, 22 Mont. 14, 55 Pac. 361.

Nebraska.— Lydick *v.* State, 61 Nebr. 309, 85 N. W. 70; Beatrice *v.* Black, 28 Nebr. 263, 44 N. W. 189; Langdon *v.* State, 23 Nebr. 509, 37 N. W. 79.

New Hampshire.— Bryant *v.* Tamworth, 68 N. H. 483, 39 Atl. 431.

New York.— See Wakeman *v.* Wilbur, 147 N. Y. 657, 42 N. E. 341 [*reversing* 4 N. Y. Suppl. 938].

Oregon.— Nosler *v.* Coos Bay R. Co., 39 Oreg. 331, 64 Pac. 644; Bayard *v.* Standard Oil Co., 38 Oreg. 438, 63 Pac. 614.

Pennsylvania.— Ide *v.* Lake Tp., 9 Kulp 192.

Wisconsin.— West Bend *v.* Mann, 59 Wis. 69, 17 N. W. 972; Tomlinson *v.* Wallace, 16 Wis. 224, it being expressly so declared by statute.

See 25 Cent. Dig. tit. "Highways," § 17.

Operation of statute.—Wis. Laws (1857), c. 19, embodying the rule stated in the text, although prospective in its operation, applies as well to highways laid out and recorded and opened and worked before its passage as after. Tomlinson *v.* Wallace, 16 Wis. 224 [*overruling* State *v.* Atwood, 11 Wis. 422].

Question for jury.— Under the Wisconsin statutes, notwithstanding informalities may have intervened in laying out a highway, it is proper for the court to submit the question of its legality to the jury upon the record and evidence as to its having been opened and worked. Tomlinson *v.* Wallace, 16 Wis. 224.

88. Elmira Highway Com'rs *v.* Osceola Highway Com'rs, 74 Ill. App. 185; Willow Branch, etc., Highway Com'rs *v.* People, 69 Ill. App. 326; Rogers *v.* Aitkin, 77 Minn. 539, 80 N. W. 702; Tomlinson *v.* Wallace, 16 Wis. 224. And see Wakeman *v.* Wilbur, 147 N. Y. 657, 42 N. E. 341 [*reversing* 4 N. Y. Suppl. 938].

89. Whitesides *v.* Earles, (Tenn. Ch. App. 1901) 61 S. W. 1038.

90. See *passim*, II, B, 2.

91. Watrous *v.* Southworth, 5 Conn. 305; Horn *v.* Williamson, 4 Nebr. (Unoff.) 763, 96 N. W. 178. And see Shell *v.* Poulson, 23 Wash. 535, 63 Pac. 204; Bartlett *v.* Beardmore, 74 Wis. 485, 43 N. W. 492.

However, proof that part of an entire highway the laying out of which was defective has been used by the public for the prescriptive period is evidence of a legal highway as to the part so used, although no distinct act of acceptance by the town be shown. State *v.* Morse, 50 N. H. 9.

Width of highway by prescription under defective proceedings to establish see *infra*, II, B, 6, b, (II).

92. Com. *v.* Henchey, 196 Mass. 300, 82 N. E. 4; Bassett *v.* Harwich, 180 Mass. 585, 62 N. E. 974 [*overruling* in effect Moffatt *v.* Kenny, 174 Mass. 311, 54 N. E. 850].

93. See cases cited *infra*, this note *et seq.*

Period held sufficient see Canday *v.* Lambert, 2 Root (Conn.) 173 (forty years); Smith *v.* Illinois Cent. R. Co., 105 S. W. 96, 31 Ky. L. Rep. 1323 (twenty-five years); Reed *v.* Northfield, 13 Pick. (Mass.) 94, 23 Am. Dec. 662 (forty years); Gulick *v.* Groendyke, 38 N. J. L. 114 (seventy years).

Period held insufficient see Oliphant *v.* Atchison County Com'rs, 18 Kan. 386, five years.

By the law of Scotland, where the English Prescription Act of 1832 is not in force, forty years' user of a road by the public is sufficient to establish the right of user; but evidence of user as of right for a period short of forty years is not sufficient, unless the circumstances are such that the user raises a presumption of prior user of the same character extending over the required period. Edinburgh Magistrates *v.* North British R. Co., 5 F. (Ct. Sess.) 620.

94. Washburn Easem. & Serv. 124. And see Riley *v.* Buchanan, 116 Ky. 625, 76 S. W. 527, 25 Ky. L. Rep. 863, 63 L. R. A. 642; Witt *v.* Hughes, 66 S. W. 281, 23 Ky. L. Rep. 1836; Clark *v.* Hull, 184 Mass. 164, 68 N. E. 60; Com. *v.* Coupe, 128 Mass. 63; Folger *v.* Worth, 19 Pick. (Mass.) 108; Odiorne *v.* Wade, 5 Pick. (Mass.) 421; Hancock *v.* Wyoming Borough, 148 Pa. St. 635, 24 Atl. 88; State *v.* Cumberland, 6 R. I. 496 [*cited* in

user, it must be open and of such a character, and the facts and circumstances must be such, as to put him on notice thereof and of the fact that a public right of travel is claimed.[8] As just intimated, however, actual knowledge is not necessary, but it may be implied from the character of the user and the facts and circumstances of the case.[9]

(II) *INTENT; CONSENT; MISTAKE.* The intent of the landowner and his consent or dissent to the public user of his land are immaterial, standing alone, to the question whether a highway has been established by prescription.[10] The fact that he intends to abandon his land to the public and acquiesces in its use as a highway does not, on the one hand, detract from the hostility of the public's user so as to preclude prescription;[11] nor, on the other hand, does the fact that the owner does not intend to abandon his land, and dissents to its user as a highway, preclude the public from acquiring a highway over it,[12] unless he does some positive act amounting to an interruption of the adverse user.[13] So the fact that the owner's acquiescence in the adverse user is due to a mistaken belief that a highway over the land has been duly established by the public authorities does not defeat the public's prescriptive right thereto.[14]

3. AGAINST WHOM PRESCRIPTION MAY BE ASSERTED.[15] It has been seen that by the better opinion the doctrine of prescription as applied to highways is based, not on the presumption of a lost grant, but on the presumption of an antecedent exercise of the right of eminent domain by the public authorities;[16] and since the exercise of this power is not affected by any legal disability of the landowner,[17] it should follow that a highway may be acquired by prescription over lands owned by a person who is *non sui juris*.[18] Most of the cases in which this question is

110 N. W. 703, 112 N. W. 902; Watson *v.* Adams County, 38 Wash. 662, 80 Pac. 201.

8. O'Connell *v.* Chicago Terminal Transfer R. Co., 184 Ill. 308, 56 N. E. 355; Gentleman *v.* Soule, 32 Ill. 271, 83 Am. Dec. 264; State *v.* Kansas City, etc., R. Co., 45 Iowa 139; State *v.* Wolf, 112 N. C. 889, 17 S. E. 528; Rice *v.* Pershall, 41 Wash. 73, 82 Pac. 1038.

Necessity of fencing as notice.—Where a pass through the mountains was the only available passway to the public, the fact that the public had not fenced it would not bar their acquiring a prescriptive right from the beginning of such use, such fence being unnecessary as notice. Hall *v.* Austin, 20 Tex. Civ. App. 59, 48 S. W. 53. And see *supra*, II, B, 2, e, (IV), note 78.

Presumption of knowledge.—While long continued notoriety of a fact is usually sufficient to raise a presumption that persons affected thereby or interested therein had full notice of the matter, yet in the case of wild and uninclosed land the presumption would not so readily arise, and adding a further circumstance of the non-residence of the owner, or the location of the lands at a distance from his place of residence, the law will not presume that the notorious use as a highway is known to the owner. State *v.* Kansas City, etc., R. Co., 45 Iowa 139. And see Topeka *v.* Cowee, 48 Kan. 345, 29 Pac. 560; Bethum *v.* Turner, 1 Me. 111, 10 Am. Dec. 36; Watson *v.* Adams County, 38 Wash. 662, 80 Pac. 201. See, however, Dimon *v.* People, 17 Ill. 416. *Compare* State *v.* Teeters, 97 Iowa 458, 66 N. W. 754.

Necessity of acts indicating adverse user under claim of right see *supra*, II, B, 2, e, (I), notes 60, 61.

9. Barnes *v.* Daveck, 7 Cal. App. 220, 94 Pac. 779; Chicago *v.* Galt, 224 Ill. 421, 79 N. E. 701. And see cases cited *supra*, note 8.

10. *California.*— Freshour *v.* Hihn, 99 Cal. 443, 34 Pac. 87.

Idaho.— Meservey *v.* Gulliford, 14 Ida. 133, 93 Pac. 780.

Illinois.— Peotone *v.* Illinois Cent. R. Co., 224 Ill. 101, 79 N. E. 678; Madison Tp. *v.* Gallagher, 159 Ill. 105, 42 N. E. 316.

Indiana.— Strong *v.* Makeever, 102 Ind. 578, 1 N. E. 502, 4 N. E. 11 [*overruling* Greene County *v.* Huff, 91 Ind. 333]; McClaskey *v.* McDaniel, 37 Ind. App. 59, 74 N. E. 1023; Brown *v.* Hines, 16 Ind. App. 1, 44 N. E. 655.

Michigan.— Ellsworth *v.* Grand Rapids, 27 Mich. 250.

New York.— Speir *v.* Utrecht, 121 N. Y. 420, 24 N. E. 692; Devenpeck *v.* Lambert, 44 Barb. 596.

See 25 Cent. Dig. tit. "Highways," § 13.

User under revocable license or permission from the owner, however, is insufficient to prescribe a highway. See *supra*, II, B, 2, e, (I).

11. See *supra*, II, B, 2, e, (I).

12. See cases cited *supra*, note 10.

13. See *supra*, II, B, 2, d.

14. State *v.* Waterman, 79 Iowa 360, 44 N. W. 677; Duncombe *v.* Powers, 75 Iowa 185, 39 N. W. 261.

Mistake as to location of established highway see *supra*, II, B, 2, e, (V).

15. **Prescription against sovereign** see *infra*, II, B, 4.

16. See *supra*, II, B, 1.

17. See EMINENT DOMAIN, 15 Cyc. 611.

18. Elliott R. & St. (2d ed.) §§ 177, 180.

tinued,[28] a railroad right of way,[29] a previously established private way,[30] common lands,[31] and lands held by proprietors in common,[32] provided in all these cases that the user is otherwise sufficient to establish a highway by prescription.[33]

5. Effect of Prescription. User of land as a highway for the prescriptive period, the user being otherwise sufficient to establish a highway by prescription,[34] vests an indefeasible right in the public so to use the land,[35] of which right they cannot be divested,[36] save by alteration,[37] vacation,[38] or abandonment [39] of the highway. This right inures to the benefit of any person who has an interest in maintaining the road,[40] and it is not lost by the fact that the principal use of the road has become beneficial to only one person.[41]

6. Character and Extent of Highway — a. Town or County Way. In some of the New England states a county highway, and not a town way, is generally presumed from mere use and enjoyment; [42] but once a town way is duly estab-

34 Kan. 293, 8 Pac. 385, although the road be occupied by an intending homesteader.

State lands.—A highway may be established by prescription over public school lands. Wallowa County *v.* Wade, 43 Oreg. 253, 72 Pac. 793.

Municipal lands.—Although land be set aside for a public square, the public may acquire a highway across it by user. Green County *v.* Huff, 91 Ind. 333.

Saving questions for review.— The objection that a highway cannot be prescribed over lands owned by the United States cannot be raised for the first time on appeal. Parkey *v.* Galloway, 147 Mich. 693, 111 N. W. 348.

28. Coakley *v.* Boston, etc., R. Co., 159 Mass. 32, 33 N. E. 930, *semble.* And see Larry *v.* Lunt, 37 Me. 69.

29. Peotone *v.* Illinois Cent. R. Co., 224 Ill. 101, 79 N. E. 678; Blumenthal *v.* State, 21 Ind. App. 665, 51 N. E. 496; Marino *v.* Central R. Co., 69 N. J. L. 628, 56 Atl. 306, *semble.*

Otherwise by statute in Massachusetts. See Aiken *v.* New York, etc., R. Co., 188 Mass. 547, 74 N. E. 929.

30. *Alabama.*— Harper *v.* State, 109 Ala. 66, 19 So. 901, *semble.*

Illinois.— Madison Tp. *v.* Gallagher, 159 Ill. 105, 42 N. E. 316; Bolo Tp. *v.* Liszewski, 116 Ill. App. 135, both cases so holding under highway prescription acts.

Iowa.— Breneman *v.* Burlington, etc., R. Co., 92 Iowa 755, 60 N. W. 176, *semble.*

Kentucky.— Smythe *v.* Cleary, 11 Ky. L. Rep. 328.

Massachusetts.—Weld *v.* Brooks, 152 Mass. 297, 25 N. E. 719; Com. *v.* Petitcler, 110 Mass. 62; Taylor *v.* Boston Water Power Co., 12 Gray 415.

North Carolina.— Davis *v.* Ramsey, 50 N. C. 236, *semble.*

Wisconsin.— Frye *v.* Highland, 109 Wis. 292, 85 N. W. 351, *semble.*

See 25 Cent. Dig. tit. "Highways," § 15.

As against landowner not a party to suit.—Where part of an alleged way is over a private alley way owned by two in common, the court will not declare the existence of such alleged way unless both the owners of the private way are before the court. In such a case the court would rather presume a license by the absent owner than to declare that the use was adverse without his being heard. South Branch R. Co. *v.* Parker, 41 N. J. Eq. 489, 5 Atl. 641.

There must be clear evidence of a change to a public way in such case. Hall *v.* McLeod, 2 Metc. (Ky.) 98, 74 Am. Dec. 400; Aiken *v.* New York, etc., R. Co., 188 Mass. 547, 74 N. E. 929; Frye *v.* Highland, 109 Wis. 292, 85 N. W. 351. And see Miles *v.* Postal Cable Tel. Co., 55 S. C. 403, 33 S. E. 493; State *v.* McCabe, 74 Wis. 481, 43 N. W. 322.

31. Veale *v.* Boston, 135 Mass. 187 [*distinguished* in McKay *v.* Reading, 184 Mass. 140, 68 N. E. 43 (*citing* Emerson *v.* Wiley, 7 Pick. (Mass.) 68)].

32. Folger *v.* Worth, 19 Pick. (Mass.) 108.

33. See *supra*, II, B, 2, *passim.*

34. **Sufficiency of user** see *supra*, II, B, 2, *passim.*

35. Ft. Wayne *v.* Coombs, 107 Ind. 75, 7 N. E. 743, 57 Am. Rep. 82; Devenpeck *v.* Lambert, 44 Barb. (N. Y.) 596.

Presumptions.— Mere user of land as a highway for the prescriptive period is only *prima facie* evidence of a right so to use it; but the right is conclusively established if the user was adverse and under claim of right and not merely by license of the owner, and also exclusive, continuous, and uninterrupted, and with the owner's knowledge and acquiescence. Washburn Easem. & Serv. 66, 67 [*cited* erroneously in Falter *v.* Packard, 219 Ill. 356, 76 N. E. 495].

Acquisition of highway by prescription subject to peculiar privilege of landowner see *infra*, III, C, 2.

36. Kyle *v.* Kosciusko County, 94 Ind. 115 (by the owner of the fee); Campau *v.* Detroit, 104 Mich. 560, 62 N. W. 718. And see LeRoy *v.* Leonard, (Tenn. Ch. App. 1895) 35 S. W. 884; Yakima County *v.* Conrad, 26 Wash. 155, 66 Pac. 441.

37. See *infra*, II, D, 1, a, (vi).

38. See *infra*, II, D, 2, e.

39. See *infra*, II, D, 3.

40. Hall *v.* Austin, 20 Tex. Civ. App. 59, 48 S. W. 53.

Rights of abutting landowners see *infra*, II, C.

41. Galveston, etc., R. Co. *v.* Baudat, 21 Tex. Civ. App. 236, 51 S. W. 541.

Abandonment by nonuser see *infra*, II, D, 3, b.

42. Stedman *v.* Southbridge. 17 Pick.

8. Pleading[56] **and Evidence.**[57] A defense in ejectment that the *locus in quo* is a highway by prescription must be pleaded in order to be proved.[58] Such a plea is not objectionable as a plea of acquisition of title to land by parol.[59] An allegation that a road had been used as a highway for more than ten years prior to the commencement of the action cannot be treated as definitely describing a longer period than ten years and one day.[60] The pleadings and proof must correspond.[61] Gen-

to trial. Vandever *v.* Garshwiler, 63 Ind. 185.

Pleading and proof; issues; variance.— The only issue to be tried in such a proceeding is whether the alleged highway has existed by user for more than twenty years with the consent of the owners, or has been laid out and not recorded. Vandever *v.* Garshwiler, 63 Ind. 185. Where the petition and evidence agree that there was a highway commencing at the north end of a certain road, but disagree as to the distance of the north end of that road from the named corner of land, such variance will overthrow the proceedings. Washington Ice Co. *v.* Lay, 103 Ind. 48, 2 N. E. 222.

Evidence.— The burden is on petitioner to show affirmatively that none of an objector's land would be unconstitutionally taken. McCreery *v.* Fallis, 162 Ind. 255, 67 N. E. 673. In Rhode Island deeds showing that the lands had become a highway by dedication and had been recognized as such are admissible as tending to show that the lands had been "considered" a highway, within the terms of the statute. Goelet *v.* Newport, 14 R. I. 295.

Questions for jury.— The user or non-user by the public as described in the statute is a question for the jury. Goelet *v.* Newport, 14 R. I. 295.

Viewers need not be appointed in such proceedings. Vandever *v.* Garshwiler, 63 Ind. 185.

Location of road; boundaries; width.— In ascertaining and describing a road which has not been laid out but has become a highway merely by public use for twenty years, the power of the highway commissioners is limited to ascertaining the boundaries of the road according to the actual use of the twenty years and they cannot enlarge the road or change its location with reference to present public convenience. Talmadge *v.* Huntting, 29 N. Y. 447 [*affirming* 39 Barb. 654]; People *v.* Cortland County, 24 Wend. (N. Y.) 491.

Certainty of ascertainment and description. — To entitle a highway to be entered of record, it should be ascertained and described with the same certainty that would be necessary in establishing a highway originally. Stephenson *v.* Farmer, 49 Ind. 234. However, where the survey gives the termini exactly and the line of the road between them by distances and directions from point to point, so that any practical surveyor could easily ascertain and describe the road as it is surveyed, it is sufficient. Higham *v.* Warner, 69 Ind. 549.

Sufficiency of order.— Under R. I. Gen. St. c. 59, §§ 18–21, empowering town councils to declare lands used as highways for twenty years to be public highways, the plat described by section 21 must be made a part of the declaration. Simmons *v.* Providence, 12 R. I. 8.

Conclusiveness of order.— In New York, when the commissioners of highways meet, and, it appearing to them that a certain road has been used as a highway for more than twenty years, order it to be ascertained and recorded, such order is not conclusive on a person claiming that the highway is a private road. Cole *v.* Van Keuren, 4 Hun (N. Y.) 262, 6 Thomps. & C. 480 [*affirmed* in 64 N. Y. 646]. But see Colden *v.* Thurber, 2 Johns. (N. Y.) 424. So in Missouri the refusal of the county court to recognize the existence of a prescriptive highway does not affect its existence as such, or the vested rights of the public therein. State *v.* Wells, 70 Mo. 635; Brown *v.* Kansas City, etc., R. Co., 20 Mo. App. 427.

Appeal; injunction.— Parties aggrieved by the action of the commissioners have their remedy by appeal or by injunction. Gibbons *v.* Copper, 67 Ind. 81.

56. See, generally, Pleading, 31 Cyc. 1.

57. See, generally, Evidence, 16 Cyc. 821, 17 Cyc. 1.

58. Burlew *v.* Hunter, 41 N. Y. App. Div. 148, 58 N. Y. Suppl. 453.

59. Rose *v.* Stephens, (Ky. 1908) 112 S. W. 676, holding that where, in a suit to recover a strip of land used as a road between the lands of plaintiff and defendants, defendants, after pleading a parol agreement between prior owners for the straightening of the line providing that the strip in controversy should be thereafter used as a road for themselves and the owners of more remote land, alleged that for more than fifteen years before suit was brought defendants had occupied the strip in controversy as a public road as a matter of right, such plea was good as a plea of limitations.

60. Meservey *v.* Gulliford, 14 Ida. 133, 93 Pac. 780.

61. Meservey *v.* Gulliford, 14 Ida. 133, 93 Pac. 780, holding that where, in an action to remove an obstruction of a highway, it was alleged that for more than ten years preceding the commencement of the action the road had been traveled by the public, it was error to admit evidence that the road was first traveled more than nineteen years prior to the commencement of the action, and to find that the same had been established by user under a law which did not require such highway to be kept up at public expense, which law had been amended more than thirteen years prior to the commencement of the action so as to require it to be so kept up,

erally speaking the ordinary rules of evidence relating to presumptions and burden of proof,[62] admissibility of evidence,[63] and weight and sufficiency of evi-

and under which amendment the action was brought.

62. See cases cited *infra*, this note.

Generally speaking the burden of proof on an issue whether a highway exists by prescription rests on the party who has the affirmative of the issue, and he must in consequence convince the jury of the existence of all the essential elements of prescription as applied to highways. District of Columbia *v.* Robinson, 14 App. Cas. (D. C.) 512 [*affirmed* in 180 U. S. 92, 21 S. Ct. 283, 45 L. ed. 440]; Shaver *v.* Edgell, 48 W. Va. 502, 37 S. E. 664. It has been held, however, that the unexplained public user of a road as a highway for the prescriptive period raises a presumption of the existence of the other elements of a highway by user, and accordingly shifts the burden of adducing evidence. Chicago *v.* Chicago, etc., R. Co., 152 Ill. 561, 38 N. E. 768; Toof *v.* Decatur, 19 Ill. App. 204.

Adverse user; claim of right; permissive user.— Presumptions and burden of proof as to adverseness of user, claim of right, and permissive user are elsewhere considered. See *supra*, II, B, 2, e, (I), notes 60–62. Presumption as to adverseness of user of wild and unoccupied lands see *supra*, II, B, 2, e, (IV), note 79.

Burden of proof as to legal capacity of landowner see *supra*, note 19.

Presumptions from adverse use for prescriptive period. Antecedent exercise of right of eminent domain see *supra*, II, B, 1. Dedication see *supra*, II, B, 1. And see DEDICATION, 13 Cyc. 434. Grant see *supra*, II B, 1.

Presumption as to width of road see *supra*, II, B, 6, b, (I).

63. Clark *v.* Hull, 184 Mass. 164, 68 N. E. 60 (holding that a coast survey chart made under Act Cong. Feb. 10, 1807 (2 U. S. St. at L. 413, c. 8, § 1), providing for a coast survey, showing the roads within twenty leagues of the shore, is admissible to show the existence of an ancient way); Plummer *v.* Ossipee, 59 N. H. 55 (holding that a selectman's declaration that he directed the removal of a stone by permission of the adjacent landowner is evidence of a use of land for highway purposes by license, and not adversely). And see Miles *v.* Postal Tel. Cable Co., 55 S. C. 403, 33 S. E. 493.

Ancient deeds.— On an issue whether a street was a public way by prescription, an ancient deed describing the lots therein conveyed as being bounded by the street, and referring to a plan showing the lots to be bounded on the street, was admissible to show the origin and location of the street. Bagley *v.* New York, etc., R. Co., 165 Mass. 160, 42 N. E. 571, holding also, on an issue whether a street which crossed a railway was a public way by prescription, that a charge that there was no sufficient evidence of such prescription before the location of the railway, but that, in passing on the question whether there had been twenty years' adverse use after the location of the railway, the jury might consider the condition of things prior to that time — as whether it was then used adversely and under a claim of right — did not authorize the consideration of an ancient deed and plan, which were made before the location of the railway and showed certain lots to be bounded by said street, as evidence of such adverse use. And see Clark *v.* Hull, 184 Mass. 164, 68 N. E. 60.

Defective records of highway.— In order to establish the limitation under Wis. Laws (1857), c. 19, the record of the highway may be admitted in evidence, and it is not necessary to show that the survey followed the precise route named in the petition, that the proper notices were given of the meeting of the commissioners, or that they met pursuant thereto, or that there was an appraisement of damages or compensation made to the landowner. Tomlinson *v.* Wallace, 16 Wis. 224. However, an invalid order laying out a highway is not admissible as a foundation for showing that a certain place is a highway by user, where it does not describe such place as an intended highway and the other evidence shows that there was no intention to lay out a highway at that place; and the admission of such an order and the statement of the trial court to the jury that it was admitted as some evidence of a highway by user is a material error, the jury having found, against a preponderance of the evidence, that the place in question was a highway. Bartlett *v.* Beardmore, 74 Wis. 485, 43 N. W. 492.

Primary and secondary evidence.— Parol testimony tending to prove a highway by prescription may be received without requiring the party first to show that there is no record of such road, or that the record was imperfect or beyond his reach, or the like. The parol evidence is not secondary. Eyman *v.* People, 6 Ill. 4; Mosier *v.* Vincent, 34 Iowa 478; Young *v.* Garland, 18 Me. 409; Brigham City *v.* Crawford, 20 Utah 130, 57 Pac. 842. And see Woburn *v.* Henshaw, 101 Mass. 193, 3 Am. Rep. 333. See, generally, EVIDENCE, 17 Cyc. 465 *et seq.*

Reputation.— A prescriptive highway may be established by reputation or tradition, or the general understanding in the community. Clark *v.* Hull, 184 Mass. 164, 68 N. E. 60; Gage *v.* Pittsfield Tp., 120 Mich. 436, 79 N. W. 687; Wicks *v.* Ross, 37 Mich. 464; Hampson *v.* Taylor, 15 R. I. 83, 8 Atl. 331, 23 Atl. 732; State *v.* Cumberland, 6 R. I. 496.

Width of way.— Evidence of the location of wheel tracks a year or more after the time in question is competent to show the limits of a highway established by user at the time in question, it being found as a matter of fact that the evidence was not too remote. Plummer *v.* Ossipee, 59 N. H. 55. An order made by the highway commissioners after a road has been used as a highway for

dence [64] govern in cases wherein the existence or location of a highway by prescription is in dispute.

C. Establishment by Legislative Act or by Statutory Proceedings [65] — **1. Constitutional Power** [66] — **a. In General.** The state may, in the exercise of the inherent right of eminent domain, appropriate private property for use as a highway,[67] such use being public within the rule that the use for which property may be appropriated by the state must be a public one.[68] And in such case the owner is not deprived of his property without due process of law,[69] provided he is given notice of the proceedings so as to afford him an opportunity to contest the appropriation or to have the amount of his damages fairly determined.[70]

b. Conditions Annexed to Its Exercise [71] — (I) *In General.* Since the power to take property for highway purposes is referable to the right of eminent domain,[72] it follows that the exercise of that power is subject to all the conditions and limitations annexed to the exercise of the right of eminent domain.[73] Furthermore, in appropriating property for a highway, as in other cases, due process of law must be observed.[74]

(II) *Public Use; Public Necessity, Utility, and Convenience* — (A) *In General.* To justify the exercise of the right of eminent domain the pro-

twenty years is admissible to show the width of the highway as manifested by its use as such for twenty years, and that without proof of the commissioners' authority to make it. Ivory *v.* Deer Park, 116 N. Y. 476, 22 N. E. 1080. Since, when the public right rests on usage, it can be no more extensive than the usage itself, evidence of private occupancy is admissible to disprove or qualify the usage. State *v.* Trask, 6 Vt. 355, 27 Am. Dec. 554. Acts of abutting owners in recognition of bounds of highway as evidence see *supra*, II, B, 6, b, (I).

Evidence as to recognition, maintenance, and repair of road by public authorities see *supra*, II, B, 2, e, (III).

Levy of taxes on land in dispute as tending to rebut claim of adverse user see *supra*, II, B, 2, e, (I), note 60.

64. Teeter *v.* Quinn, 62 Iowa 759, 17 N. W. 529; State *v.* Toale, 74 S. C. 425, 54 S. E. 608 (holding that where a well-defined road was laid out through uninclosed woodland and used for more than twenty years by the public as a road, it is some evidence of adverse user); Whitesides *v.* Earles, (Tenn. Ch. App. 1901) 61 S. W. 1038; Whitesides *v.* Green, 13 Utah 341, 44 Pac. 1032, 57 Am. St. Rep. 740.

Evidence held sufficient to take case to jury see Casey *v.* Tama County, 75 Iowa 655, 37 N. W. 138; Clark *v.* Hull, 184 Mass. 164, 68 N. E. 60; Bagley *v.* New York, etc., R. Co., 165 Mass. 160, 42 N. E. 571; Hall *v.* Austin, 20 Tex. Civ. App. 59, 48 S. W. 53.

Evidence as to recognition, maintenance, and repair of road by public authorities see *supra*, II, B, 2, e, (III).

Evidence of change of private way to highway see *supra*, note 30.

Reputation as establishing highway by prescription see *supra*, note 63.

65. **Establishment of:** Free roads of gravel, macadam, etc., or free turnpikes, so-called see *infra*, V, H. Streets and alleys in incorporated cities, towns, and villages see Municipal Corporations, 28 Cyc. 834 *et seq.* Toll-Roads see Toll-Roads.

66. **Constitutional distribution of governmental powers and functions with respect to highways** see Constitutional Law, 8 Cyc. 827, 830 note 88.

Special or local statutes relating to establishment of highways see Statutes, 36 Cyc. 1008.

67. See Eminent Domain, 15 Cyc. 585.

68. See Eminent Domain, 15 Cyc. 578.

69. See Constitutional Law, 8 Cyc. 1126, 1127.

70. See *infra*, II, C, 1, b, (I).

71. **Right of trial by jury** see Eminent Domain, 15 Cyc. 872; Juries, 24 Cyc. 133.

72. Clark *v.* Saybrook, 21 Conn. 313. And see Eminent Domain, 15 Cyc. 585.

73. See, generally, Eminent Domain, 15 Cyc. 543. And see Clark *v.* Saybrook, 21 Conn. 313.

Compensation see *infra*, V, J. And see, generally, Eminent Domain, 15 Cyc. 638 *et seq.*

Necessity that taking be for public use see Eminent Domain, 15 Cyc. 578 *et seq.*, 585, 586. And see *infra*, II, C, 1, b, (II).

Notice and opportunity to be heard see *infra*, II, C, 5, d; II, C, 5, g, (V), (B). And see, generally, Eminent Domain, 15 Cyc. 841 *et seq.*

De minimis.— The fact that the quantity of land proposed to be taken for a highway is very small affords no reason for taking it without legal right. Earl Highway Com'rs *v.* People, 4 Ill. App. 391.

74. See, generally, Constitutional Law, 8 Cyc. 1080 *et seq.*, 1124.

Compensation see *infra*, V, J. And see, generally, Constitutional Law, 8 Cyc. 1124, 1127.

Necessity that taking be for public use see Constitutional Law, 8 Cyc. 1127. And see *infra*, II, C, 1, b, (II).

Notice and opportunity to be heard see *infra*, II, C, 5, d; II, C, 5, g, (V), (B). And

posed use for which the property is sought to be taken must be a public use.[75] It is unquestioned that use for a highway is a public use for which land may be appropriated.[76] Nevertheless the question may arise whether in the particular case the road sought to be laid out would, if established, constitute a highway, and so justify the taking of land therefor. Bearing in mind what has been elsewhere said of the nature and essentials of a highway,[77] it is sufficient to say here that in order to justify the taking of land as for a highway, it is necessary that the road, if laid out, should be subject to a public easement of travel, and be so situated and conditioned as to be susceptible of use as a highway. In the absence of constitutional authority, one man's land cannot be appropriated against his consent for the sole benefit of private individuals.[78] In order to justify the taking of land as for a highway, there must exist a public necessity for the proposed road, and it must be of public utility or convenience.[79]

(B) *As Affected by Termini of Road; Cul-de-Sac.* The character of the place of beginning and ending of a proposed highway has a bearing on the question of the public necessity, utility, or convenience thereof. If the proposed road neither begins nor ends at a preëxisting highway or other public place, it cannot as a rule be established as a highway, since in the nature of the case no public necessity exists for it, and if formally laid out it would not be of public utility or conven-

see, generally, CONSTITUTIONAL LAW, 8 Cyc. 1126.

75. See EMINENT DOMAIN, 15 Cyc. 578.

76. See EMINENT DOMAIN, 15 Cyc. 585.

77. See *supra*, I.

78. See EMINENT DOMAIN, 15 Cyc. 578–586. And see cases cited *infra*, next note.

79. *Indiana.*— Blackman *v.* Halves, 72 Ind. 515. See Sterling *v.* Frick, 171 Ind. 710, 86 N. E. 65, 87 N. E. 237.

Kentucky.— Fletcher *v.* Fugate, 3 J. J. Marsh. 631; Morris *v.* Salle, 19 S. W. 527, 14 Ky. L. Rep. 117.

Maine.— Gay *v.* Bradstreet, 49 Me. 580, 77 Am. Dec. 272.

Maryland.— State *v.* Price, 21 Md. 448.

Michigan.— People *v.* Jackson, 7 Mich. 432, 74 Am. Dec. 729.

New Hampshire.— Gurnsey *v.* Edwards, 26 N. H. 224; Dudley *v.* Cilley, 5 N. H. 558.

New York.— People *v.* East Fishkill Highway Com'rs, 42 Hun 463, 4 N. Y. St. 850 (holding that mandamus will not issue to compel highway commissioners to open a road which would be a benefit to relator alone, and not to the public, although a jury had after due formalities certified to the necessity of such road, and although relator executed a personal undertaking to fence the road and indemnify the town against all damages); Matter of Lawton, 22 Misc. 426, 50 N. Y. Suppl. 408.

Ohio.— Kinney *v.* De Mar, 8 Ohio Cir. Ct. 149, 4 Ohio Cir. Dec. 282, holding that Ohio Act Feb. 19, 1893 (90 Laws 28), making it obligatory on township trustees to appropriate the land of private persons for a highway at the request of certain persons, who have no land through which it is to pass, without giving such trustees the power to determine whether or not such highway and appropriation will be for the public good, is unconstitutional.

Pennsylvania.— *In re* Nescopek Road, 1 Kulp 402; *In re* Brecknock Tp. Road, 2 Woodw. 437.

South Carolina.—Singleton *v.* Road Com'rs, 2 Nott & M. 526.

Vermont.— Woodstock *v.* Gallup, 28 Vt. 587.

See 25 Cent. Dig. tit. "Highways," § 26.

Absolute necessity — Under the Indiana general highway act, limiting the right of viewers to lay out highways to such highways as will in their judgment be of public utility, and declaring a want of public utility a ground of remonstrance, the question of public utility is generally one of fact to be determined in the light of public convenience and interest, but it is not essential that the contemplated road be absolutely necessary to the public. Speck *v.* Kenoyer, 164 Ind. 431, 73 N. E. 896; Fritch *v.* Patterson, 149 Ind. 455, 49 N. E. 380; Green *v.* Elliott, 86 Ind. 53. But in the state of Tennessee, on the other hand, the necessity for the road must be imperative. McWhirter *v.* Cockrell, 2 Head (Tenn.) 9.

Individual advantages.—In deciding whether the public good requires that a highway be laid out, it is proper that individual advantages going to make up the public should be considered by the commissioners. Hopkinton *v.* Winship, 35 N. H. 209. The charter of a bridge company providing that no way should at any time thereafter be located leading from the bridge to a certain place, which "shall be for the necessary convenience of said company, unless the entire cost and expense of building and maintaining such new way . . . shall be defrayed by said company," does not prohibit the location of any way required by common convenience and necessity. Shattuck's Appeal, 73 Me. 318. The fact that one or a few individuals will be most benefited by the proposed highway does not necessarily prevent the establishment of the road. Heath *v.* Sheetz, 164 Ind. 665, 74 N. E. 505; Masters *v.* McHolland, 12 Kan. 17; Heninger *v.* Peery, 102 Va. 896, 47 S. E. 1013. But see *In re* Richmond County Four-Cornered Road, 13 N. Y. Suppl. 458. **Extent of travel as af-**

the road when laid out need not be a thoroughfare.[82] The state line is a proper terminus, although there is no connecting road, existing or proposed, in the other state.[83]

(C) *Determination as to Public Use, Necessity, Utility, and Convenience.*[84] Generally speaking the question of the necessity or expediency of exercising the right of eminent domain is a political question to be determined by the legislature or those to whom it has delegated the power of exercising the right,[85] in the absence of a constitutional or statutory provision investing the courts with jurisdiction to determine it,[86] either in the first instance[87] or by way of reviewing the deter-

82. *Connecticut.*— Goodwin *v.* Wethersfield, 43 Conn. 437; Peckham *v.* Lebanon, 39 Conn. 231.

Iowa.— Johnson *v.* Clayton County, 61 Iowa 89, 15 N. W. 856, holding that a road may be of public utility, although it gives egress to only one person, who has no other public road, and he objects to its establishment; for the public is entitled to a road to reach him, and he has no right to render himself inaccessible.

Kansas.— Masters *v.* McHolland, 12 Kan. 17.

Maryland.— State *v.* Price, 21 Md. 448.

Michigan.— Fields *v.* Colby, 102 Mich. 449, 60 N. W. 1048.

New Hampshire.— See Boston, etc., R. Co. *v.* Folsom, 46 N. H. 64.

New Jersey.— Atkinson *v.* Bishop, 39 N. J. L. 226.

New York.— People *v.* Kingman, 24 N. Y. 559; People *v.* Van Alstyne, 3 Abb. Dec. 575, 3 Keyes 35; Saunders *v.* Townsend, 26 Hun 308. See Hickok *v.* Plattsburgh, 41 Barb. 130.

Texas.— Decker *v.* Menard County, (Civ. App. 1894) 25 S. W. 727.

See 25 Cent. Dig. tit. "Highways," § 27. And see *supra*, I, note 1; II, B, 2, b.

But see *In re* London Britain Road, 13 Lanc. Bar (Pa.) 207; *In re* Roaring Brook Road, 1 Wilcox (Pa.) 263; *In re* Brecknock Tp. Road, 2 Woodw. (Pa.) 437, all holding that a highway cannot end on private land.

Public necessity, utility, or convenience.— A cul-de-sac cannot be established as a highway unless it is a public necessity, or unless it will be of public utility or convenience. Ayres *v.* Richards, 41 Mich. 680, 3 N. W. 179 (holding that the road commissioner cannot establish a highway which is of no practical use to the public or to individuals until extended or connected with some existing or future highway); People *v.* Jackson, 7 Mich. 432, 74 Am. Dec. 729; People *v.* Van Alstyne, 32 Barb. (N. Y.) 131. See, however, Rice *v.* Rindge, 53 N. H. 530.

83. Rice *v.* Rindge, 53 N. H. 530; Crosby *v.* Hanover, 36 N. H. 404.

84. **Notice of hearing on question of expediency, necessity, or utility, as convenience** see *infra*, II, C, 5, d, (I).

85. See EMINENT DOMAIN, 15 Cyc. 629 *et seq.*

Rule applied to highways see Lowndes County *v.* Bowie, 34 Ala. 461; Matter of Whitestown, 24 Misc. (N. Y.) 150, 53 N. Y. Suppl. 397; Fanning *v.* Gilliland, 37 Oreg. 369, 61 Pac. 636, 62 Pac. 209, 82 Am. St. Rep. 758 (holding that the claim in a petition for a public road over private property that it is necessary, and that the property of petitioners cannot be reached by any convenient highway, is not issuable, since the manner of its determination is a legislative question, and since the legislature has provided that the appearance of these facts in the petition shall be sufficient to authorize the court to appoint viewers to lay out the road); Paine *v.* Leicester, 22 Vt. 44.

Discretion of local officers.— Determination of question of necessity, expediency, etc., held to be within the discretion of the local administrative officers see *In re* Conant, 102 Me. 477, 67 Atl. 564; Strahan *v.* Attala County, 91 Miss. 529, 44 So. 857; Howard *v.* Clay County, 54 Nebr. 443, 74 N. W. 953. And see Sackett *v.* Greenwich, 38 Conn. 525; Monterey *v.* Berkshire County, 7 Cush. (Mass.) 394.

Jurisdiction in the first instance is generally vested in local administrative officers. See the statutes of the different states. And see Shattuck's Appeal, 73 Me. 318.

86. See EMINENT DOMAIN, 15 Cyc. 629 *et seq.*

87. Greenburg *v.* International Trust Co., 94 Fed. 755, 36 C. C. A. 471, holding that N. Y. Laws (1892), c. 493, providing for the extending of highways in one town into or through other towns in the same county is not in violation of the state constitution because it confers on certain courts of the state the power to determine the necessity or expediency of such extensions, the highest court of the state having upheld the exercise of such powers by the courts in numerous analogous cases arising under the same constitution.

Intervention of committee.— Under the Connecticut statute, the court to which a petition is made for the laying out of a highway may find with regard to the convenience and necessity of the road without the intervention of a committee. Bridgeport *v.* Hubbell, 5 Conn. 237; Windsor *v.* Field, 1 Conn. 279. So in Massachusetts the appointment of a viewing committee by the court of sessions, in proceedings to lay out a highway, to report an opinion as to the convenience or necessity of the way prayed for, is not required by statute, but is discretionary with the court. Com. *v.* Cambridge, 7 Mass. 158; Com. *v.* Coombs, 2 Mass. 489.

Delegation of jurisdiction.—A general rule of court requiring viewers to report, in proceedings to lay out a new road, whether dam-

2. Lands Subject to Exercise of Power. Subject to certain statutory exemptions, and to certain qualifications with reference to property already devoted to public use, any land susceptible of public travel may be taken for highway purposes.[11]

3. Persons Against Whom Power May Be Exercised.[12] The fact that a person is under legal disability does not prevent the taking of his land for a highway.[13]

4. Establishment by Statute or by Town Vote. It is competent for the legislature to establish a specific highway without the intervention of any inferior agency,[14] and this it sometimes does.[15] In New England a highway over private lands cannot be established simply by town vote.[16]

830 note 88; Eminent Domain, 15 Cyc. 566. And see *infra*, II, C, 5, a.

Effect of delegation.— The power of laying out highways, with necessary bridges over coves and creeks and other highways, has been delegated to the county commissioners, and consequently no special act of the legislature authorizing such a highway is requisite. Groton *v.* Hurlburt, 22 Conn. 178.

11. See Eminent Domain, 15 Cyc. 602 *et seq.*

Burial grounds see Cemeteries, 6 Cyc. 715.

12. **Sovereign** see Eminent Domain, 15 Cyc. 611.

13. See Eminent Domain, 15 Cyc. 611; also *supra*, II, B, 3.

Cases assuming this to be so see *infra*, notes 53, 70.

14. *Georgia.*—Johnson *v.* State, 1 Ga. App. 195, 58 S. E. 265.

New York.— People *v.* McDonald, 4 Hun 187 [*affirmed* in 69 N. Y. 362].

Pennsylvania.— Mahanoy Tp. *v.* Comry, 103 Pa. St. 362.

Rhode Island.— Knowles *v.* Knowles, 25 R. I. 325, 55 Atl. 755.

Washington.— Lewis County *v.* Hays, 1 Wash. Terr. 109.

See 25 Cent. Dig. tit. "Highways," § 37.

Special statutes relating to establishment of highways see Statutes, 36 Cyc. 1008.

15. Lyons *v.* Hinckley, 12 La. Ann. 655 (holding, however, that the Louisiana act of Feb. 7, 1829, relative to roads and levees, establishing a highway on the banks of bayous, etc., does not apply to those streams or bayous running through a high country not subject to overflow, and where the roads are made directly across the country, and not along the winding of the stream); Knowles *v.* Knowles, 25 R. I. 325, 55 Atl. 755 (holding that where the legislature establishes a highway no acceptance is necessary).

However, Kan. Laws (1887), p. 308, c. 215 (since repealed by Kan. Laws (1889), p. 281, c. 188), declaring all section lines in certain counties public highways, did not declare them open for travel. Hanselman *v.* Boan, 71 Kan. 573, 81 Pac. 182. So Nebr. Gen. St. (1873) p. 959, declaring section lines public roads, did not of itself create a lawful highway along such lines, but proper authorities must provide first for the payment of damages for the right of way. Van Wanning *v.* Deeter, 78 Nebr. 284, 112 N. W. 902, 78 Nebr. 282, 110 N. W. 703. Moreover, such statute was so far modified by Nebr. Laws (1879), p. 120 (Comp. St. c. 78), that section lines not used as roads for five years before the passage of the latter act cannot be opened as such without complying with the requirements of that act. Henry *v.* Ward, 49 Nebr. 392, 68 N. W. 518.

Highway or private way.— The general assembly ordered a committee to plat land owned by the state. The certificate of the surveyor on the plat stated that it was a draft of, among other things, a highway, the land of which was not included in the lots. The report of the committee stated that they had laid out a highway to a pond that every lot might have free access in case of drought. It was held that such statement of the reason therefor did not limit the meaning of the word "highway" so as to make it a private way. Knowles *v.* Knowles, 25 R. I. 325, 35 Atl. 755.

Highway over public lands under act of congress see Public Lands, 32 Cyc. 866.

Highway by user.— Statutes declaring roads previously in use to be highways, although not opened pursuant to law, are treated *supra*, II, B, 1; II, B, 2, e, (iii).

16. Burns *v.* Annas, 60 Me. 288 (holding that a way across private lands cannot be established by a town vote of acceptance without any previous location by the selectmen); Kean *v.* Stetson, 5 Pick. (Mass.) 492 (holding that where the selectmen of the several towns are authorized and empowered by statute to lay out ways for the use of their towns, this act is to be done by them independently and without any direction, and therefore a town vote directing the selectmen to lay out a particular town way is unauthorized and improper); Haywood *v.* Charlestown, 34 N. H. 23; State *v.* Newmarket, 20 N. H. 519 (holding, under St. Feb. 8, 1791, prescribing that where there shall be occasion for a new highway, the selectmen are empowered, on application made to them, if they see cause, to lay out the same, that a road was not legally established where a town, at a meeting warned to see if it would instruct the selectmen to lay out such road, voted so to instruct, and the selectmen returned that pursuant to the vote they did lay out the road).

Highway over public lands.—Where a town passed a vote that certain persons, naming them, "have liberty to make a road from," etc., "over the public land, provided they give a deed to the town of their own lands, two

governing the proceedings should be embodied in one statute, but the general rules of procedure, statutory and otherwise, may be looked to in aid of a statute providing for the establishment of highways.[21] The statutes must be complied with by the local authorities, substantially, if not strictly.[22] Questions as to the amendment or repeal of highway statutes are governed by the rules relating to statutes generally.[23] An unconditional repeal of the statute under which a proceeding for the establishment of a highway is pending *ipso facto* abates the proceeding.[24] If the mode of procedure is changed by statute *pendente lite*, the subsequent proceedings should as a rule follow the new procedure.[25]

b. Jurisdiction and Powers Generally of Local Authorities[26] — (I) *IN GENERAL.* The question of what officer or body of officers is invested with the del-

and the articles immediately preceding. Fuselier *v.* Iberia Parish Police Jury, 109 La. 551, 33 So. 597.

Ascertainment and entry of record of highway by user see *supra*, II, B, 7.

Condemnation proceedings in general see EMINENT DOMAIN, 15 Cyc. 805 *et seq.*

Exclusiveness of statutory mode of establishment see supra, II, A; II, B, 1, note 33; II, B, 2, e, (III).

21. Lawrence County *v.* Deadwood, etc., Toll-Road Co., 11 S. D. 74, 75 N. W. 817.

22. Cumberland Valley R. Co. *v.* Martin, 100 Md. 165, 59 Atl. 714; People *v.* Scio Tp. Bd., 3 Mich. 121; McBeth *v.* Trabue, 69 Mo. 642; York County *v.* Fewell, 21 S. C. 106. See also *infra*, II, C, 5, *passim.*

Strict compliance is necessary. Curran *v.* Shattuck, 24 Cal. 427; Hyslop *v.* Finch, 99 Ill. 171; Geneseo Highway Com'rs *v.* Harper, 38 Ill. 103; *In re* Conanta, 102 Me. 477, 67 Atl. 564; Cassidy *v.* Smith, 13 Minn. 129; Delahuff *v.* Reed, Walk. (Miss.) 74; Austin *v.* Allen, 6 Wis. 134. Other cases, on the contrary, hold that a substantial compliance is sufficient. Canyon County *v.* Toole, 8 Ida. 501, 69 Pac. 320; Nickerson *v.* Lynch, 135 Mo. 471, 37 S. W. 128; *In re* Spear's Road, 4 Binn. (Pa.) 174. At any rate if jurisdictional requisites are complied with, a substantial compliance in other respects is sufficient. Town *v.* Blackberry, 29 Ill. 137; Shull *v.* Brown, 25 Nebr. 234, 41 N. W. 186; Howard *v.* Dakota County, 25 Nebr. 229, 41 N. W. 185; Sanford *v.* Webster County, 5 Nebr. (Unoff.) 364, 98 N. W. 822; State *v.* Richmond, 26 N. H. 232. But the requirements conferring jurisdiction must be observed. Wabaunsee County *v.* Muhlenbacker, 18 Kan. 129; *In re* Buffalo, 78 N. Y. 362; Ruhland *v.* Hazel Green, 55 Wis. 664, 13 N. W. 877.

Curative acts see *infra*, II, C, 5, j, (III).

Mandamus to highway officers see MANDAMUS, 26 Cyc. 296 *et seq.*

23. See, generally, STATUTES, 36 Cyc. 1053, 1068.

Repeal of particular statutes see Hutchinson *v.* Lowndes County, 131 Ga. 637, 62 S. E. 1048; Barham *v.* Weems, 129 Ga. 704, 59 S. E. 803; Howell *v.* Chattooga County, 118 Ga. 635, 45 S. E. 241; McGinnis *v.* Ragsdale, 116 Ga. 245, 42 S. E. 492; Casey *v.* Kilgore, 14 Kan. 478; Hurst *v.* Martinsburg, 80 Minn. 40, 82 N. W. 1099; Cook *v.* Vickers, 141 N. C. 101, 53 S. E. 740; *In re* Bucks County Road, 3 Whart. (Pa.) 105; Greene, etc., Tp. Road, 21 Pa. Super. Ct. 418.

24. *Illinois.*— Menard County *v.* Kincaid, 71 Ill. 587.

Maine.— Webster *v.* County Com'rs, 63 Me. 27 (holding that the word "actions," as used in Rev. St. c. 1, § 3, providing that "actions pending at the time of the passage or repeal of an act, shall not be affected thereby," does not include petitions for the location of highways pending before the county commissioners); William *v.* Lincoln County, 35 Me. 345 (*semble*).

Maryland.— Wade *v.* St. Mary's Industrial School, 43 Md. 178.

Pennsylvania.— *In re* Uwchlan Tp. Road, 30 Pa. St. 156; *In re* North Canal St. Road, 10 Watts 351, 36 Am. Dec. 185. And see *In re* Hatfield Tp. Road, 4 Yeates 392.

Virginia.— Terry *v.* McClung, 104 Va. 599, 52 S. E. 355.

See 25 Cent. Dig. tit. "Highways," § 30.

But see Steele *v.* Empsom, 142 Ind. 397, 41 N. E. 822; Burrows *v.* Vandevier, 3 Ohio 383.

If the statute saves pending proceedings there is of course no abatement thereof. Sayres *v.* Gregory, 7 Ind. 633; Schuylkill County's Appeal, 38 Pa. St. 459.

Repeal of statute conferring jurisdiction see *infra*, II, C, 5, b, (I).

Right to recover damages after repeal of statute see *infra*, V, J.

25. Mayne *v.* Huntington County, 123 Ind. 132, 24 N. E. 80; Burrows *v.* Vandevier, 3 Ohio 383; *In re* Hickory Tree Road, 43 Pa. St. 139 (subject, however, to some qualifications); Towamencin Road, 23 Pa. Co. Ct. 113, 15 Montg. Co. Rep. 194; Tuttle *v.* Knox County, 89 Tenn. 157, 14 S. W. 486. And see *In re* Hatfield Tp. Road, 4 Yeates (Pa.) 392. See, however, Wentworth *v.* Farmington, 48 N. H. 207; Boston, etc., R. Co. *v.* Cilley, 44 N. H. 578; Colony *v.* Dublin, 32 N. H. 432.

Saving clause see Baubie *v.* Ossman, 142 Mo. 499, 44 S. W. 338.

But the proceedings are not therefore abated. Mayne *v.* Huntington County, 123 Ind. 132, 24 N. E. 80; Burrows *v.* Vandevier, 3 Ohio 383; *In re* Uwchlan Tp. Road, 30 Pa. St. 156.

Enactment of statute conferring jurisdiction pendente lite see *infra*, II, C, 5, b, (I).

26. **Jurisdiction by consent** see *infra*, II, C, 5, j, (II).

egated power to establish highways depends of course upon the statutes of the particular state.[27] Sometimes the power is delegated to officers whose office is especially created for the purpose;[28] but more commonly it is delegated as an additional power to officers having other functions in the administration of the local government.[29] It has been held that where jurisdiction is conferred on a

Waiver of objections to jurisdiction see *infra*, II, C, 5, j, (II).

27. See the statutes of the different states.

28. See cases cited *infra*, this note.

Highway commissioners or supervisors see State *v.* Canterbury, 28 N. H. 195. Without an order of the quarter sessions, supervisors of the highways have no authority either to open a temporary way for the public in a case of sudden necessity through private property or to correct errors in the opening of an old one. Holden *v.* Cole, 1 Pa. St. 303. The South Carolina act of 1728, authorizing highway commissioners "to make, alter, and keep in repair" the roads, means only such roads as are or shall be laid out by legislative authority, and does not give the commissioners discretionary power to create highways, as the legislature showed, by other and special legislation for the creation of highways, that there was no intention to vest such power in the commissioners. Withers *v.* Claremont County Road Com'rs, 3 Brev. (S. C.) 83.

Highway surveyors.— The word "highway," as used in Mass. St. (1896) c. 417, providing a board of survey for the town of Revere to lay out and establish highways, covers all ways which the public interest requires to be laid out, relocated, altered, or widened by the town authorities, including an avenue in the town. Janvrin *v.* Poole, 181 Mass. 463, 63 N. E. 1066. Surveyors of the highways have power to lay out a road in a newly created township before the town officers can by its terms be elected. Minhinnah *v.* Haines, 29 N. J. L. 388.

29. See cases cited *infra*, this note.

County commissioners or supervisors see Kennedy *v.* Dubuque, etc., R. Co., 34 Iowa 421; Johnson County *v.* Minnear, 72 Kan. 326, 83 Pac. 828; Wells *v.* York County, 79 Me. 522, 11 Atl. 417; Barrickman *v.* Harford County, 11 Gill & J. (Md.) 50; Blackstone *v.* Worcester County, 108 Mass. 68; Foster *v.* Dunklin, 44 Mo. 216 (county court); Gillett *v.* McGonigal, 80 Wis. 158, 49 N. W. 814. Formerly the levy court in Maryland. Williamson *v.* Carnan, 1 Gill & J. (Md.) 184. In Louisiana the police jury. Fuselier *v.* Iberia Parish Police Jury, 109 La. 551, 33 So. 597; Jefferson Police Jury *v.* De Hemecourt, 7 Rob. (La.) 509.

Township committee or supervisors see Carter *v.* Wade, 59 N. J. L. 119, 35 Atl. 649; Lewly *v.* West Hoboken, 54 N. J. L. 508, 24 Atl. 477; Williams *v.* Turner Tp., 15 S. D. 182, 87 N. W. 968.

Town selectmen see Orrington *v.* Penobscot County, 51 Me. 570; Butchers' Slaughtering, etc., Assoc. *v.* Boston, 139 Mass. 290, 30 N. E. 94.

Courts.— In Tennessee the county courts have power to lay out highways. Hydes Ferry Turnpike Co. *v.* Davidson County, 91 Tenn. 291, 18 S. W. 626. But not the circuit courts in Iowa. Kennedy *v.* Dubuque, etc., R. Co., 34 Iowa 421. Police magistrates may lay out roads in Illinois. Goshen Highway Com'rs *v.* Jackson, 165 Ill. 17, 45 N. E. 1000 [*affirming* 61 Ill. App. 381].

As between county supervisors and auditor. — Under Iowa Code (1873), § 937, providing that the auditor shall proceed to establish a highway if no objections or claims for damages are filed before a certain time; and section 939, providing that if objections to the establishment of the highway or claims for damages are filed, the further hearing of the application shall stand continued to the next session of the board of supervisors, the auditor has no authority to establish the highway where a claim for damages is filed before the time specified, although the claim is also paid before that time. Ressler *v.* Hirshire, 52 Iowa 568, 3 N. W. 613. Iowa Acts, 12th Sess. c. 160, § 2, making the auditor clerk of the board of supervisors, his acts "subject however, in all cases, to final review and approval by the Board," does not abridge the authority of the board to establish highways, the "review" embracing the facts, as well as the law, of each case. Brooks *v.* Payne, 38 Iowa 263.

As between county commissioners and public land agent.— The authority to locate roads through public lands selected for settlement being vested by Me. Rev. St. c. 18, § 32, in the county commissioners, the requirement of chapter 5, section 29, that the land agent "cause such roads to be located as the public interests," etc., "shall require," confers on him no authority to locate them. Burns *v.* Annas, 60 Me. 288.

As between selectmen and fire district commissioners.— N. H. Act, July 21, 1887, did not transfer from town selectmen to fire district commissioners the power to lay out highways. Henry *v.* Haverhill, 67 N. H. 172, 37 Atl. 1039.

As between county commissioners and district court see *infra*, II, C, 5, b, (IV).

As between town and selectmen see *supra*, II, C, 4.

Change of statute pendente lite.—Where a statute provided for courts of common pleas, and gave them all the jurisdiction vested in the former court of common pleas and of all actions pending in the several counties, it transferred to such new courts all petitions for highways from county to county pending in the late court. *In re* Wheeler, 7 N. H. 280. Prior to Vt. Acts (1886), No. 20, the selectmen or the county court had no authority to establish highways at grade across a railroad; but while this case was pending on appeal, having been remanded from the supreme court to the county court, said act was passed authorizing the laying of high-

(III) *WHERE ROAD IS WHOLLY OR PARTLY IN ANOTHER COÖRDINATE TERRITORIAL JURISDICTION.* The legislature may confer on the supervisors of one county the power to establish a highway in another county.[35] As a rule, however, if a proposed road lies in two or more counties, the officers of each must take action to establish the highway;[36] and a like rule applies where the proposed road lies in two or more townships.[37]

(IV) *REFUSAL OR NEGLECT OF OFFICERS HAVING PRIMARY POWER.* In New England county commissioners or certain county courts have jurisdiction to lay out a town way in case the town selectmen neglect or refuse to do so.[38]

the county officers have jurisdiction to lay it out (Windham *v.* Litchfield, 22 Conn. 226; Com. *v.* Stockbridge, 13 Mass. 294, holding that the court of sessions have authority to locate a highway on the divisional line between two towns, so that the whole extent of the road shall be divided lengthwise by such line; *In re* Newport, *supra*; Platt *v.* Milton, 55 Vt. 490; Kelley *v.* Danby, *supra*; Kent *v.* Wallingford, 42 Vt. 651, the last two cases further holding that, where a petition prays for a highway extending into two towns in the same county, the county court has original jurisdiction, and this is not taken away by the road's being laid out in one town only), and the selectmen cannot do so (Monterey *v.* Berkshire County *supra*; *In re* Griffin, *supra*).

As between officers of county and municipal corporation.—As a rule the county officers have no power to establish highways wholly (Philbrick *v.* University Place, 106 Iowa 352, 76 N. W. 742; Barker *v.* Wyandotte County, 45 Kan. 681, 698, 26 Pac. 585, 591; Salsbury *v.* Gaskin, 66 N. J. L. 111, 48 Atl. 531; *In re* Verona Borough, etc., Road, 9 Pa. Cas. 114, 12 Atl. 456; *In re* West Liberty, etc., Roads, 20 Pa. Super. Ct. 586) or partly (Shields *v.* Ross, 158 Ill. 214, 41 N. E. 985; Atlantic Coast Electric R. Co. *v.* Griffin, 64 N. J. L. 513, 46 Atl. 1062; Freeman *v.* Price, 63 N. J. L. 151, 43 Atl. 432. *Contra*, Sparling *v.* Dwenger, 60 Ind. 72; *In re* Verona Borough, etc., Road, *supra*; *In re* Chester, etc., Tp. Road, 2 Chest. Co. Rep. 438, 3 Del. Co. 174; *In re* Plymouth Borough, etc., Road, 5 Kulp (Pa.) 115; *In re* Ransom Tp., etc., Road, 2 Lack. Leg. N. (Pa.) 279) within the limits of an incorporated city, town, or village. Proceedings of commissioners of highways attempting to lay out a highway sixty feet wide on land of which half the width was situated in an incorporated city whose charter gave it power to open, alter, and abolish streets, being void as to the land inside the city, was also void as to the half lying outside the city limits, as the statute did not allow a highway less than forty feet wide to be opened by the commissioners. Shields *v.* Ross, *supra*.

35. People *v.* Lake County, 33 Cal. 487.

36. See cases cited *infra*, this note.

Joint action is necessary. State *v.* Wood County Treasurer, 17 Ohio 184.

Separate action.—Where a proposed highway runs from a town in one county into an adjoining town in another county the superior court in each county has power to lay out the portion of the road within its county; and it is not a valid objection to the laying out of the road within one town that the section in the other cannot be laid out by the court of that county, since the complaint and decree can be postponed until after action has been had in the other county, or can be made in such form as to provide for such a contingency. Peckham *v.* Lebanon, 39 Conn. 231. In Indiana where proceedings are instituted for the location of a highway extending into two or more counties, the county board before whom the petition is first filed has jurisdiction. Cooper *v.* Harmon, 170 Ind. 113, 83 N. E. 704. It is not a valid objection to the location of a highway by the county commissioners of one county that the way begins at the end of a town way which extends into another county. Millett *v.* Franklin County, 81 Me. 257, 16 Atl. 897.

37. Mack *v.* Highway Com'rs, 41 Ill. 378; Brewer *v.* Gerow, 83 Mich. 250, 47 N. W. 113, both holding that where the road is to be on the line between two towns, the commissioners of highways of both towns must act jointly.

However, commissioners of highways have the power to locate roads anywhere within the limits of their own towns, without the intervention of the commissioners of highways of adjoining towns. Mack *v.* Highway Com'rs, 41 Ill. 378. And a petitioner may apply for a highway terminating at a town line, and trust to the adjoining town to treat the balance of the way to his farm as a highway, or to his being able to make other satisfactory arrangements as to that part of the road, and he need not apply under the law providing for laying out highways in two or more towns. Matter of Burdick, 27 Misc. (N. Y.) 298, 58 N. Y. Suppl. 759.

New England towns.—In New Hampshire a petition praying that a new highway may be laid out within two towns may be filed in the office of the clerk of the supreme court, or may be presented to the selectmen of such towns acting jointly; and neither such presentation, nor the neglect or refusal of the selectmen to lay out the highway, is necessary to give the court jurisdiction. Lord *v.* Dunbarton, 54 N. H. 405.

38. *Connecticut.*—Waterbury *v.* Darien, 9 Conn. 252, holding also that the averment of neglect and refusal by the selectmen to lay out a highway may be supported by any evidence from which the fact may be fairly inferred.

Maine.—Orrington *v.* Penobscot County, 51 Me. 570.

Massachusetts.—Monterey *v.* Berkshire

In such case the neglect or refusal of the selectmen is a prerequisite to the jurisdiction of the county commissioners or court;[39] and a like rule prevails in

County, 7 Cush. 394; Brown *v.* Essex County, 12 Metc. 208, so holding, although the selectmen, in the petition to them, were requested to discontinue an old way, which they had no authority to do, as well as to lay out a new one.

New Hampshire.— Simpson *v.* Orford, 41 N. H. 228 (holding also that a petition to the court for the laying out of a highway for the accommodation of the public will not be dismissed for any difference between it and the petition to the selectmen, in the order of naming the termini of the route or in describing the route, provided the court can see without any possibility of mistake, from a comparison of the two petitions, that the highway they are asked to lay out is in all respects identical with the one described in the petition to the selectmen); White *v.* Landaff, 35 N. H. 128; *In re* Stratton, 21 N. H. 44 (holding further that the neglect of the selectmen to lay out a road for the space of seven months after presentment of a petition to them, and their separating at the end of that time without adjournment or recording their proceedings, constitute such neglect as will give jurisdiction to the court of common pleas).

Vermont.— Dunn *v.* Pownal, 65 Vt. 116, 26 Atl. 484 (holding further that where, on a petition for the appointment of commissioners to lay out a highway, defendant moved to dismiss on the ground that its selectmen had not at the time of the bringing of such petition refused to lay out a highway, and witnesses were produced by both parties, and trial had by the court, it was error for the court, on disagreeing, not to decide the issues raised, and to adjudge that petitioners were entitled as a matter of right to the appointment of commissioners); Crawford *v.* Rutland, 52 Vt. 412.

See 25 Cent. Dig. tit. "Highways," § 34.

Extent of jurisdiction.— On the neglect or refusal of the selectmen to act, the county commissioners have the same powers, and the performance of the same duties, and none others, that were given to the selectmen under the petition when pending before them; and hence the commissioners can act only within the territorial limits of the town. *In re* Bridport, 24 Vt. 176.

Character of way.— The county commissioners are not restricted in laying out a way, where the selectmen of a town shall unreasonably refuse, to a way exclusively for the benefit of one or more individuals; but the statute is intended to embrace those cases also where the way should be adjudged to be of general benefit. Lisbon *v.* Merrill, 12 Me. 210. The authority conferred on selectmen to lay out town ways for the use of their respective towns is limited to roads having their termini within the town; but it is no objection to such laying out that the road is intended as one link in a chain of continuous roads; that it is for the convenience of the inhabitants only from its connection with some great thoroughfare; and that, when established, it will be for the use of the public generally, as well as of the inhabitants of the town in which it is situated; and if selectmen unreasonably neglect or refuse to lay out such way, the county commissioners may lay out the same; and whether a town way, for the laying out of which application is made to the county commissioners on the refusal of the selectmen to lay it out, is for the use of the town within which it is situated, is a question exclusively within the discretion of the commissioners to decide. Monterey *v.* Berkshire County, 7 Cush. (Mass.) 394. The court of common pleas have jurisdiction of petitions for highways in towns bordering on adjacent states, where the petitions have been presented to the selectmen of such towns and refused by them. The fact that the highway prayed for is only a part of one which may be or has been made in the adjoining states does not affect the jurisdiction. Crosby *v.* Hanover, 36 N. H. 404.

Subsequent action of selectmen.—After the court has acquired jurisdiction by the neglect of selectmen to lay out a road and the filing in court of a petition, it cannot be ousted of such jurisdiction by subsequent action of the selectmen in laying out the road. *In re* Stratton, 21 N. H. 44.

Delay in petitioning court.— The selectmen to whom a petition for a highway was first presented neglected to act upon it while they were in office from December, 1848, until March, 1849, it appearing that their refusal to lay out the highway was recorded Dec. 24, 1849, and petitioners did not file their petition to the court until Dec. 9, 1850. It was held that the delay did not oust the court of its jurisdiction. *In re* Toppan, 24 N. H. 43.

Refusal of town to approve laying out of way by selectmen.—The county commissioners have power to approve and allow of a town way as laid out by the selectmen, leading from one town road to another town road and passing through the land of the applicant under his possession and improvement, if the town shall unreasonably refuse or delay to approve thereof. North Berwick *v.* York County, 25 Me. 69.

Waiver of objections to jurisdiction of county officers see *infra*, II, C, 5, j, (II).

39. Wolcott *v.* Pond, 19 Conn. 597; Plainfield *v.* Packer, 11 Conn. 576 (holding that it must not only be averred in the petition that the selectmen neglected and refused to lay out such highways, but it must appear from the record that such averment is true); Lewiston *v.* Lincoln County, 30 Me. 19 (holding further that the town cannot be said to have delayed or refused to approve the way where the selectmen had made no proper return or report of the laying out of such way); *In re* Newport, 39 N. H. 67 (holding, on a petition asking for the laying out of a new highway in two towns originally pre-

torial jurisdictions, it is generally required that persons of the requisite qualifications from all such jurisdictions shall join in the petition.[43] The qualification

174, 62 N. E. 462, both holding that the commissioners have no jurisdiction unless it is established that twelve of the persons whose names are signed to the petition are freeholders of the county in which the highway is proposed to be located, and that six of them reside in the immediate neighborhood of such highway.

Kansas.— Oliphant *v.* Atchison County, 18 Kan. 386; Wabaunsee County *v.* Muhlenbacker, 18 Kan. 129, both holding that where neither upon the papers nor the proceedings of the county board does it affirmatively appear that at least twelve of the petitioners were householders, resident in the vicinity of the proposed road, and the proceedings are attacked directly by petition in error, the defect is fatal, and the proceedings must be set aside as void. And see Willis *v.* Sproule, 13 Kan. 257.

Kentucky.— Louisville, etc., R. Co. *v.* Gerard, 130 Ky. 18, 112 S. W. 915, holding that the petition must be signed by at least five landowners of the county.

Maine.— Cyr *v.* Dufour, 68 Me. 492, holding that the provision of Rev. St. c. 18, that a petition for laying out a highway must be presented by "responsible persons," is merely directory to the commissioners, and is for the protection of the county against needless costs, if the location is not found to be of common convenience or necessity.

Michigan.—Wilson *v.* Burr Oak Tp. Bd., 87 Mich. 240, 49 N. W. 572, holding that a petition for a highway which does not purport to be signed by freeholders of the township confers no jurisdiction on the commissioner.

Minnesota.— Cassidy *v.* Smith, 13 Minn. 129, holding that the statute requiring the petition to be signed by not less than six legal voters living within a mile of the proposed road must be strictly observed.

Nebraska.— Letherman *v.* Hauser, 77 Nebr. 731, 110 N. W. 745 (holding that the statutory provision that the petition shall be signed by at least ten electors residing within five miles of the road is jurisdictional); Shull *v.* Brown, 25 Nebr. 234, 41 N. W. 186 [*following* Howard *v.* Dakota County, 25 Nebr. 229, 41 N. W. 185] (holding that where a petition for the establishment of a public road is presented to the county clerk under Comp. St. (1887) c. 78, by a greater number of signers than is required by law, and it is accompanied by an affidavit of one of such signers that all the signers are electors of the county in which the establishment of the road is desired, and that they reside within five miles of the proposed road, and is accompanied also with a deposit of money for the purpose of defraying the expenses in case the road should not be established, the county clerk will have jurisdiction to appoint a commissioner, as provided for by section 6 of said chapter, to view the proposed road); Horn *v.* Williamson, 4 Nebr. (Unoff.) 763, 96 N. W. 178 (holding that in the case of a consent road, all persons owning land to be taken must sign the petition).

New York.— People *v.* Warren County, 82 Hun 298, 31 N. Y. Suppl. 248 (holding that a highway commissioner as such cannot apply for a highway); Harrington *v.* People, 6 Barb. 607; People *v.* Eggleston, 13 How. Pr. 123; Brunswick Highway Com'rs *v.* Meserole, 10 Wend. 122.

Oregon.— King *v.* Benton County, 10 Oreg. 512 (holding that the county court has no jurisdiction to act on a petition for a county road signed by persons whose names are not on the notice); Kamer *v.* Clatsop County, 6 Oreg. 238 (holding that an unmarried man who keeps house and employs domestic servants is a householder, within Misc. Laws, c. 50, tit. 1, § 2, calling for a petition by householders for the establishment of a road).

South Dakota.— Kothe *v.* Berlin Tp., 19 S. D. 427, 103 N. W. 657 (holding that Rev. Pol. Code, § 1707, providing for the laying out of a highway on the petition of a specified number of voters owning real estate within one mile of the road, means one mile in a direct line, and not by the usual route of travel); Bockoven *v.* Lincoln Tp., 13 S. D. 317, 83 N. W. 335 (holding that under Comp. Laws, §§ 1296–1298, giving the board of supervisors jurisdiction to lay out highways and award compensation for the land appropriated for that purpose, on the filing of a petition with the board, signed by at least six legal voters who are owners of land or occupants under the homestead or preëmption laws of the United States, or under contract from the state, situated within one mile from the proposed road, a petition signed by ten persons is sufficient, without designating how they held their land, although some of them were not qualified, where it appeared that six of them were competent).

Texas.— Huggins *v.* Hurt, 23 Tex. Civ. App. 404, 56 S. W. 944, holding that under Rev. St. art. 4671, giving commissioners' courts the power, and making it their duty, to lay out and open public roads "when necessary," that court has authority to establish a road on its own motion, and therefore is not without jurisdiction to appoint a jury of view and establish a road on petition of freeholders, because of the persons who sign the petition not exceeding five are freeholders residing in any road precinct through which the road is sought to be established.

Vermont.— Gilman *v.* Westfield, 47 Vt. 20, holding that a highway may be laid and established in one town solely upon the petition of residents thereof, although the only land and premises interested in the construction of the road are situate in an adjoining town.

See 25 Cent. Dig. tit. "Highways," § 41.

Waiver of objections to number or qualifications of petitioners see *infra,* II, C, 5, e, (VII), note 20.

43. Wright *v.* Middlefork Highway Com'rs, 145 Ill. 48, 33 N. E. 876; Warne *v.* Baker,

d. Citation and Notice; [52] **Opportunity to Be Heard; Appearance** — (I) *NECESSITY.* It is generally necessary throughout the United States that some sort of notice of the application for the opening of a highway should be given the owner or occupant of the land to be affected or other persons interested; [53] and in some

1095; Black *v.* Campbell, 112 Ind. 122, 13 N. E. 409; Little *v.* Thompson, 24 Ind. 146; Webster *v.* Bridgewater, 63 N. H. 296; Hays *v.* Jones, 27 Ohio St. 218.

Effect on jurisdiction.— If, after the withdrawal of certain petitioners, the remaining petitioners are less than the required number, the proceeding is properly dismissed. Ralston *v.* Beall, 171 Ind. 719, 30 N. E. 1095. *Contra,* Little *v.* Thompson, 24 Ind. 146.

Effect of remonstrance by petitioner.— In a proceeding under Ohio Act Jan. 27, 1853, as amended by Ohio Act April 16, 1873, jurisdiction once properly attached is not defeated by any number of the petitioners becoming remonstrants against granting the prayer of the petition. Grinnell *v.* Adams, 34 Ohio St. 44. It is otherwise, however, under Ohio Act March 29, 1867, as amended by Ohio Act May 9, 1869. Hays *v.* Jones, 27 Ohio St. 218. However, until a petitioner for a road improvement has indicated in some unmistakable manner his intention to withdraw his consent and become a remonstrator, he may be counted as a petitioner. Dawson *v.* Barron, 9 Ohio S. & C. Pl. Dec. 706.

Waiver.— The right of petitioners to insist, in the circuit court, upon a motion to withdraw their names, made before the county commissioners had decided upon the sufficiency of the petition, is not waived by permitting the remonstrants in the first instance to move in the circuit court to dismiss the petition for want of jurisdiction, and allowing the case to be disposed of on that motion. Black *v.* Campbell, 112 Ind. 122, 13 N. E. 409. However, a request by a part of the signers of a petition for the alteration of a highway to withdraw their names therefrom when made for the first time after the commissioners of highways have passed on the petition comes too late. Tolono Highway Com'rs *v.* Bear, 224 Ill. 259, 79 N. E. 581.

Withdrawal of party by amendment of petition see *infra,* II, C, 5, e, (V), note 11.

Withdrawal of petition see *infra,* II, C, 5, e, (VI).

52. **Notice of proceedings by commissioners, viewers, etc. see** *infra,* II, C, 5, g, (V), (B).

53. *California.*— Curran *v.* Shattuck, 24 Cal. 427, holding that notice, actual or constructive, to the owner of land, of proceedings to lay out a public way across it, is indispensable, whether the statute provides for such notice or not.

Connecticut.— Shelton *v.* Derby, 27 Conn. 414, holding, under the statute with regard to the laying out of highways, which provides that an application to the superior court for a highway shall, unless the parties shall agree on the judgment to be rendered, be referred by the court to a committee, to be heard by them "at such time and place, and with such notice to those interested therein, as said court shall order," that by the term "those interested therein," persons other than those already before the court as parties to the record are intended, persons whose lands might be taken for the highway, or who might be injuriously affected by the laying out of the same, and who have therefore a right to be heard before the committee.

Delaware.— *In re* Jones, 6 Pennew. 463, 70 Atl. 15, holding, however, that service of notice of an intention to apply for the establishment of a public road upon him holding legal title to lands across which the road is to run is sufficient, although another has a life-interest therein, it being unnecessary to serve notice on the life-tenant or tenant in possession.

Illinois.— Frizell *v.* Rogers, 82 Ill. 109; Perry *v.* Bozarth, 95 Ill. App. 566 [*reversed* on other grounds in 198 Ill. 328, 64 N. E. 1075]; Oran Highway Com'rs *v.* Hoblit, 19 Ill. App. 259; North Henderson Highway Com'rs *v.* People, 2 Ill. App. 24.

Indiana.— Ft. Wayne *v.* Ft. Wayne, etc., R. Co., 149 Ind. 25, 48 N. E. 342; Wright *v.* Wells, 29 Ind. 354.

Iowa.— Chicago, etc., R. Co. *v.* Ellithrope, 78 Iowa 415, 43 N. W. 277; Barnes *v.* Fox, 61 Iowa 18, 15 N. W. 581; Alcott *v.* Acheson, 49 Iowa 569 (holding that if the owner of the abutting land be a non-resident, notice of the proposed highway must be served on the occupier); State *v.* Anderson, 39 Iowa 274.

Kansas.— Hughes *v.* Milligan, 42 Kan. 396, 22 Pac. 313; State *v.* Farry, 23 Kan. 731.

Kentucky.— Louisville, etc., R. Co. *v.* Gerard, 130 Ky. 18, 112 S. W. 915; Case *v.* Myers, 6 Dana 330; Morris *v.* Salle, 19 S. W. 527, 14 Ky. L. Rep. 117.

Michigan.— Welch *v.* Hodge, 94 Mich. 493, 54 N. W. 175; Wilson *v.* Burr Oak Tp. Bd., 87 Mich. 240, 49 N. W. 572; Dixon *v.* Port Huron Tp. Highway Com'r, 75 Mich. 225, 42 N. W. 814; Blodgett *v.* Highway Com'rs, 47 Mich. 469, 11 N. W. 275.

Minnesota.— Thompson *v.* Berlin, 87 Minn. 7, 91 N. W. 25 (holding that under Gen. St. (1894) § 1808, providing that when town supervisors receive a petition for laying out a highway they shall cause notice of the time and place for hearing thereon to be served on all occupants of the land through which the highway may pass, the service must be had on the person having the actual possession and control of the land, and not on all who may reside thereon); Cassidy *v.* Smith, 13 Minn. 129. See Lyle *v.* Chicago, etc., R. Co., 55 Minn. 223, 56 N. W. 820.

Missouri.— Monroe *v.* Crawford, 163 Mo. 178, 63 S. W. 373.

Nebraska.— Barry *v.* Deloughrey, 47 Nebr. 354, 66 N. W. 410; State *v.* Otoe County, 6 Nebr. 129, holding that where the inhabitants

son interested, some form of process, such as a summons or an order to show cause,

for the loss or injury occasioned thereby. Neeld's Road Case, 1 Pa. St. 353.

Heirs and legatees must have notice. Sheldon *v.* Derby, 27 Conn. 414 (holding that where the road was laid by the committee over land belonging to the unsettled estate of a deceased person, and the party remonstrating had no other interest than as one of the residuary legatees under the will of deceased and as one of his heirs at law, and the executors were authorized to sell the land and convert it into money, and the interest of the remonstrant under the will was liable to be divested upon a certain contingency, he had a sufficient interest in the land taken to have a right to object to the omission of the notice and to appear and remonstrate against the acceptance of the report); North Henderson Highway Com'rs *v.* People, 2 Ill. App. 24 (holding that where the record shows that a portion of land taken for a highway belongs to certain heirs, one of whom is a non-resident, and no notice is shown to have been given her, and it does not appear that any one is authorized to represent her, and she has never released her claim for damages, the commissioners of highways are justified in refusing to open the road); Boonville *v.* Ormond, 26 Mo. 193 (heirs).

Notice to agent held to be sufficient see *In re* Kimmey, 5 Harr. (Del.) 18 (overseer of non-resident); Pickford *v.* Lynn, 98 Mass. 491. Otherwise see Chase County *v.* Carter, 30 Kan. 581, 1 Pac. 814; Lullamire *v.* Kaufman County, 3 Tex. App. Civ. Cas. § 325, holding that a person who had been looking after land for a non-resident, and preventing persons from cutting timber on it, and who had contracted with the owner to fence the land, but who had no connection with it, was not an agent or attorney of the owner so that service on him, under Tex. Rev. St. art. 4470, in proceedings to establish a public road, of the notice required to be given, was service on the owner.

Trustee.—It is enough that notice be served on one of several trustees who has control of land. *In re* Ralph, 5 Pennew. (Del.) 124, 58 Atl. 1036.

The mortgagor is the proper person to serve with notice (Whiting *v.* New Haven, 45 Conn. 303; Goodrich *v.* Atchison County, 47 Kan. 355, 27 Pac. 1006, 18 L. R. A. 113; Cool *v.* Crommet, 13 Me. 250; Gurnsey *v.* Edwards, 26 N. H. 224), unless the mortgagee is in possession (Cool *v.* Crommet, *supra*; *In re* Parker, 36 N. H. 84, holding also that if the mortgagee in possession holds under a mortgage from a corporation, duly executed, the court will not, in a proceeding for laying out a highway, inquire whether the corporation had authority under its charter to make the mortgage).

A judgment creditor of the owner is not entitled to notice. Gimbel *v.* Stolte, 59 Ind. 446.

Where a highway is laid over a turnpike road, and the easement or franchise of the corporation is taken, it is not necessary to notify the owners of the land over which the turnpike road was established. Peirce *v.* Somersworth, 10 N. H. 369.

Death of owner pendente lite.—Where public notice of a meeting of the county commissioners for the purpose of locating a highway and assessing the damages was given in the manner prescribed by Mass. St. (1828) c. 103, § 3, it was sufficient as against the heirs of a person over whose land the highway was laid out, although such person died four days before the meeting, out of the commonwealth, and none of the heirs resided at that time within the commonwealth, or had actual notice. Taylor *v.* Hampden County, 18 Pick. (Mass.) 309.

A purchaser pendente lite is not entitled to notice. Murphy *v.* Beard, 138 Ind. 560, 38 N. E. 33; Graham *v.* Flynn, 21 Nebr. 229, 31 N. W. 742. *Contra*, Curran *v.* Shattuck, 24 Cal. 427.

Petitioner is not entitled to notice, since he is plaintiff. Graham *v.* Flynn, 21 Nebr. 229, 31 N. W. 742.

Railroad company.—A railroad running over the land of non-residents is such a resident occupier as must be served with notice of the lay-out of a highway over the land. State *v.* Iowa Cent. R. Co., 91 Iowa 275, 59 N. W. 35. Where a railroad company's ownership of a railroad track is not shown by the county transfer book, notice of a report in favor of establishing a road across such track need not be served personally on an officer or agent of the road. State *v.* Chicago, etc., R. Co., 80 Iowa 586, 46 N. W. 741. Iowa Code (1873), § 936, relative to the establishment of highways, declares that "notice shall be served on each owner or occupier of land lying in the proposed highway, or abutting thereon, as shown by the transfer books in the auditor's office, who resides in the county, in the manner provided for service of original notice in actions of law." It was held that where it does not appear that the land proposed to be taken stands in the name of any one as owner on the auditor's books, a railway corporation which is in the open and notorious occupation of the land is entitled to notice, if a resident of the county. Chicago, etc., R. Co. *v.* Ellithrope, 78 Iowa 415, 43 N. W. 277. In the application of the statutes relating to notice of the establishment of highways, a railway company is to be regarded as a resident of any county in which it operates its road or exercises corporate franchises. Chicago, etc., R. Co. *v.* Ellithrope, *supra*; State *v.* Bogardus, 63 Kan. 259, 65 Pac. 251. Land belonging to a railroad company, on which its tracks are laid, is improved property, within the rule of court requiring notice to be given to owners of such property when a highway is proposed to be laid out over it. *In re* Lancaster City Road, 68 Pa. St. 396. A station agent at a depot on the grounds through which the highway is proposed to be laid out is the occupant of such grounds, upon whom notice may be served, under Sanborn & B. Annot. St. Wis.

is necessary.[54] In some of the New England states the town is entitled to notice of a proceeding to lay out a town way.[55] Persons interested likewise have a right to appear and be heard.[56] The authorities are in conflict as to whether persons interested are entitled to notice and a hearing on the question of the expediency or necessity of establishing a road, or of its public utility or convenience.[57]

(II) *FORM AND SUFFICIENCY* — (A) *In General.* A notice substantially conforming to the statutory requisites as to form is generally sufficient.[58] As a rule it should state the names of petitioners for the highway,[59] and the tribunal to whom the application will be made,[60] the time when the application is to be

§ 1267, providing for the service of such notices, or under section 2637, as amended by Laws (1887), c. 552 (2 Sanborn & B. Annot. St. p. 1512), providing for the service of summons in actions against railway companies. State *v.* O'Connor, 78 Wis. 282, 47 N. W. 433.

Township and borough officers.— Pa. Act May 2, 1899 (Pamphl. Laws 176), relating to notice to supervisors in proceedings for opening a road, does not require notice of a proposed opening and construction of a new road to be given to borough officers. *In re* Cornplanter Tp. Road, 26 Pa. Super. Ct. 29. But all the supervisors of the township must be notified. *In re* Chartiers Tp. Road, 30 Pittsb. Leg. J. N. S. (Pa.) 268.

New notice after amendment of petition.— Where a petition for the location of a highway was filed after due notice, and subsequently an amended petition was filed changing the length of the proposed highway from two and one-half to one and three-quarter miles, but no new notice was given, the commissioners had no jurisdiction to determine the matters set forth in the amended petition, since in effect it amounted to a new proceeding. Thrall *v.* Gosnell, 28 Ind. App. 174, 62 N. E. 462.

County line road.— In proceedings to open a highway on the county line, where the petition and notice required by law are not posted in one of the counties, all the proceedings are void for want of jurisdiction. Schuchman *v.* Highway Com'rs, 52 Ill. App. 497.

Constructive notice is sufficient. Stewart *v.* Hines County Police Bd., 25 Miss. 479. And see Curran *v.* Shattrick, 24 Cal. 427.

54. Fletcher *v.* Fugate, 3 J. J. Marsh. (Ky.) 631 (holding that, before appointing viewers of a proposed road, the county court should cause the owners of the land through which the road is to be passed to show cause why it should not be established); Anonymous, 2 T. B. Mon. (Ky.) 91 (holding that to authorize the establishment of a public road it must appear that the owners of the land were summoned or that they appeared in court).

55. Gifford *v.* Norwich, 30 Conn. 35; Baker *v.* Windham, 25 Conn. 597; Plainfield *v.* Packer, 11 Conn. 576; Com. *v.* Cambridge, 7 Mass. 158; Com. *v.* Egremont, 6 Mass. 491; Com. *v.* Sheldon, 3 Mass. 188; Com. *v.* Chase, 2 Mass. 170; Com. *v.* Metcalf, 2 Mass. 118; Drown *v.* Barton, 45 Vt. 33.

However, a town in which no part of a road prayed for lies is not entitled to notice, although it is a party to the petition. Windsor *v.* Field, 1 Conn. 279. And it is not necessary that the towns in the vicinity of those through which a road is to pass, and which may be chargeable under the statute, should be notified of the hearing on the question of laying out the road. Webster *v.* Alton, 29 N. H. 369.

Only the town is entitled to notice of the pendency of a petition against it in court for the laying out of a road. The landowners' rights are secured by notice of hearing thereon. *In re* Toppan, 24 N. H. 43.

56. Shelton *v.* Derby, 27 Conn. 414 (holding that it was not necessary that before being permitted to appear a person interested should give a bond to the town, respondent on the record, to save it harmless from all cost resulting from his appearance, under the statute which provides that any member of a community appearing in and defending a suit brought against the community shall give such bond, since he was appearing in his own name, and to defend his own rights and not in the name or to defend the rights of the town); Storm Lake *v.* Iowa Falls, etc., R. Co., 62 Iowa 218, 17 N. W. 489 (tenant under lease perpetual at his option).

57. Pro.— Walbridge *v.* Cabot, 67 Vt. 114, 30 Atl. 805; Lynch *v.* Rutland, 66 Vt. 570, 29 Atl. 1015; Seifert *v.* Brooks, 34 Wis. 443.

Con.— Lent *v.* Tillson, 72 Cal. 404, 14 Pac. 71; Com. *v.* Cambridge, 7 Mass. 158; People *v.* Smith, 21 N. Y. 595.

58. Stevens *v.* Cerro Gordo County, 41 Iowa 341, holding that a notice that a petition will be presented "for a new road" is in substance a notice of the petition for establishment of a new road, and is therefore sufficient.

59. King *v.* Benton County, 10 Oreg. 512.

However, an immaterial variance between the names on the petition and notice is not a jurisdictional defect, and will not render the proceedings void. Bewley *v.* Graves, 17 Oreg. 274, 20 Pac. 322.

60. Abbott *v.* Scott County, 36 Iowa 354 (holding, however, that notice stating that application will be made to the county auditor, who is *ex officio* clerk of the board of supervisors, or to the board of supervisors, is sufficiently certain, since the effect of notice is that, if the board of supervisors should be in session at the time named, the petition will be presented to them, and that, if not in session, it would be presented to the county auditor); Sweek *v.* Jorgensen, 33 Oreg. 270, 54 Pac. 156 (holding, however, that notice that, at a session of the "county court for —— County," a petition will be pre-

made [61] or when objections must be filed,[62] and the place of application.[63] It should also contain a description of the proposed road.[64] The notice is sometimes required to be signed,[65] but need not be under seal.[66]

(B) *Time.*[67] The statutory provisions as to the time of notice must be strictly observed.[68] It has been held that in computing the time both the day of service and the day of hearing must be excluded.[69]

sented to "said court" to establish a road "within said county" along a certain line in H county, sufficiently shows, as against collateral attack, that the petition is to be presented to the county court of H county).

61. State *v.* Waterman, 79 Iowa 360, 44 N. W. 677.

However, notice of the presentation of a petition to construct a road, stating that the petition would be presented on the first day of the next term of the board of commissioners, "which will be held on the first day of May," is not defective because such term in fact commenced on the "first Monday" in May, all persons being charged with notice of the statutory requirement (Burns Rev. St. Ind. (1901) § 7821) that such board shall meet on the first Monday of each month. Gifford *v.* Baker, 158 Ind. 339, 62 N. E. 690. And notice of an application for surveyors to lay out a road need not set out the precise hour of the day that the application will be made. *In re* Highway, 3 N. J. L. 665. See People *v.* Wallace, 4 Thomps. & C. (N. Y.) 438.

62. Beatty *v.* Beethe, 23 Nebr. 210, 36 N. W. 494, holding that, under Comp. St. (1881) c. 78, § 18, providing that in the location of highways a notice shall be published stating that objections to such highway must be filed by a day named therein, a notice which fails to fix such day gives the county commissioners no jurisdiction.

63. *In re* Public Roads, 5 Harr. (Del.) 174.

64. Butterfield *v.* Pollock, 45 Iowa 257; *In re* Highway, 16 N. J. L. 391, holding that the notice should designate the beginning and the terminating points.

A substantial description is sufficient. Jenkins *v.* Riggs, 100 Md. 427, 59 Atl. 758. Thus, although words may be used which, according to their strict literal meaning, render the description somewhat confused, yet if, on giving them their ordinary signification, and referring to the context, there does not seem to be any want of particularity as to the commencement, termination, or route of the proposed street, it is sufficient. State *v.* Orange, 32 N. J. L. 49. So a notice designating the points of commencement and termination of the highway, and indicating the line of route by intelligible reference to the lines of the congressional subdivisions of the land through which it passes, sufficiently describes the proposed highway. Woolsey *v.* Hamilton County, 32 Iowa 130. And where a notice sufficiently states the starting point and width, the use of the words, "varying so far as is necessary to find suitable ground for making a good and substantial road," will not vitiate the legality of the highway, so far as it actually follows the survey lines. Shepard *v.* Gates, 50 Mich. 495, 15 N. W. 878. And since the statutes do not require that the notice of an application of freeholders for appointment of surveyors to lay out a public road shall state the width of the road, proceedings will not be set aside because the width is not stated in such notice. State *v.* Shreve, 4 N. J. L. 297.

Obvious mistake.— A mistake in the notice respecting the proposed location will not defeat the jurisdiction of the supervisors if it is of such a character that a person would readily discover it. Butterfield *v.* Pollock, 45 Iowa 257.

Variance between notice and petition.— Where the description of a proposed public road in the notice to landowners of the petition for the road does not correspond with the description in the petition, the notice is insufficient. *In re* Parker, 2 Pennew. (Del.) 336, 45 Atl. 347. Variance between location and description in notice see *infra,* II, C, 5, h, (I), (C).

65. *In re* Parker, 2 Pennew. (Del.) 336, 45 Atl. 347; *In re* Road Notices, 5 Harr (Del.) 324; State *v.* Orange, 32 N. J. L. 49; Minard *v.* Douglas County, 9 Oreg. 206. *Contra,* Wright *v.* Wells, 29 Ind. 354; Daugherty *v.* Brown, 91 Mo. 26, 3 S. W. 210. But see Milhollin *v.* Thomas, 7 Ind. 165.

66. State *v.* Chicago, etc., R. Co., 80 Iowa 586, 46 N. W. 741.

67. **Statement of time of application in notice** see *supra,* II, C, 5, d, (II), (A).

68. Dixon *v.* Port Huron Tp. Highway Com'r, 75 Mich. 225, 42 N. W. 814; Anderson *v.* San Francisco, 92 Minn. 57, 99 N. W. 420; Cassidy *v.* Smith, 13 Minn. 129; Ball *v.* Westmoreland, 54 N. H. 103 (holding that the court has no authority to make an order of notice on a petition for laying out or altering a highway, filed in term-time or vacation, returnable during an existing term); Bitting *v.* Douglas County, 24 Oreg. 406, 33 Pac. 981 (holding, under Hill Annot. Laws Oreg. § 4063, providing that notice to establish a county road shall be served by posting in public places, and that it shall be posted thirty days previous to presentation of the petition, that a notice, without date, merely stating that at the next regular term of court a petition would be presented for change in a road, is not sufficient).

69. *In re* Public Roads, 5 Harr. (Del.) 174; Cox *v.* Hartford Tp. Highway Com'r, 83 Mich. 193, 47 N. W. 122; People *v.* Clay Tp. Highway Com'rs, 38 Mich. 247. *Contra,* under S. D. Comp. Laws, § 4805, which provides that the time in which any act provided by law is to be done is computed by excluding the first day and including the last.

(III) *SERVICE* — (A) *In General.* Service of the notice may be made by delivery thereof to the person concerned,[70] or by leaving it at his dwelling-house,[71] or it may be made constructively, as by publication in a newspaper,[72] or by posting a copy of the petition or notice.[73]

Williams *v.* Turner Tp., 15 S. D. 182, 87 N. W. 968.

70. See cases cited *infra*, this note.

Service on infant.— Where a committee appointed by the common pleas reported that a highway sought to be laid out would pass over the land of certain infants, a notice served on the infants themselves of the time and place for hearing the landowners is insufficient, and it was proper for the court, on motion by petitioners, to appoint a guardian *ad litem* for the infants, on whom legal notice might be served of the time and place of hearing. Clarke *v.* Gilmanton, 12 N. H. 515.

Service on town.— In proceedings under Conn. Rev. St. tit. 24, § 22, providing for an application to the superior court for relief by any party aggrieved by the doings of selectmen in laying out a highway, and that the selectmen shall be duly cited to show reason why the relief should not be granted, the town is the party respondent, and service on one of the selectmen is sufficient. Baker *v.* Windham, 25 Conn. 597. And see Plainfield *v.* Packer, 11 Conn. 576.

Sufficiency of service generally.— The fact that the copy of a petition for a highway, and of the clerk's order of notice on the petition, served on the towns, were made and served by petitioner himself, did not render the service insufficient. McClure *v.* Groton, 50 N. H. 49. Where witness saw plaintiff a distance from him, and called to him to come and get a notice of proceedings to open a road, and plaintiff sent his wife after the paper, and she placed it in his hands, there was a valid personal service on plaintiff. Vogt *v.* Bexar County, 16 Tex. Civ. App. 567, 42 S. W. 127. Where the notice by the supervisors of the time and place of meeting to decide on the application for the laying out of a highway is served by reading the notice to those entitled to it it is a personal service. Green *v.* State, 56 Wis. 583, 14 N. W. 620.

71. Winchester *v.* Hinsdale, 12 Conn. 88 (holding that service of a petition for a highway on a town by leaving a copy at the usual place of abode of one of the selectmen is good); Sanborn *v.* Meredith, 58 N. H. 150.

72. State *v.* Chicago, etc., R. Co., 68 Iowa 135, 26 N. W. 37 (holding also that a foreign railroad corporation across whose tracks a highway is being established is not an "owner or occupier . . . who resides in the county," within the meaning of Iowa Code (1873), § 936, requiring written notice of the proposed establishment of a highway, and consequently it is not entitled to notice otherwise than by publication); Wilson *v.* Hathaway, 42 Iowa 173; State *v.* Beeman, 35 Me. 242 (where no mode is pointed out by statute for giving notice); Pawnee County *v.* Storm, 34 Nebr. 735, 52 N. W. 696.

Presumption of notice.— In such case notice is imputed to the person concerned, regardless of his actual knowledge. State *v.* Beeman, 35 Me. 242; East Baltimore Station Methodist Protestant Church *v.* Baltimore, 6 Gill (Md.) 391, 48 Am. Dec. 540. And see Pawnee County *v.* Storm, 34 Nebr. 735, 52 N. W. 696.

Character of newspaper.—Where public notice in road cases is required to be made in two newspapers nearest the road, such publication made in two German newspapers in the German language is not according to law. *In re* Upper Hanover Road, 44 Pa. St. 277.

Affidavit for publication.— In an action by a county to obtain a right of way over land for a highway, the affidavit for the publication of the summons, when the person on whom service is to be made resides out of the state, must state that the proceedings directed by Cal. Pol. Code, §§ 2698–2708, have been had, or no cause of action is shown. Yolo County *v.* Knight, 70 Cal. 430, 11 Pac. 662.

73. Wilson *v.* Hathaway, 42 Iowa 173; Mathewson *v.* Clinton Tp., 8 Pa. Co. Ct. 204, holding that want of personal notice to the owner of seated land will not render void the decree of the court of quarter sessions establishing a road over it, although such notice is required by rule of court, notice by posting advertisements, as required by Pa. Act, Feb. 24, 1845, having been given.

Posting held to be necessary see Frizell *v.* Rogers, 82 Ill. 109; North Henderson Highway Com'rs *v.* People, 2 Ill. App. 24; Anderson *v.* San Francisco, 92 Minn. 57, 99 N. W. 420; Cassidy *v.* Smith, 13 Minn. 129; People *v.* Stedman, 57 Hun (N. Y.) 280, 10 N. Y. Suppl. 787, holding, under a statute which requires every person applying for the laying out of a highway to cause notices in writing to be posted in three of the most public places in the town, specifying as near as possible the proposed route of the highway, etc., that it is not sufficient to deposit such notices in the mail, addressed to the persons whose land is to be affected by the proposed highway.

Both petition and notice must be posted under a statute requiring that petitioners "shall cause a copy of their petition and notice stating when said petition will be presented to the township board to be heard, to be posted." Peed *v.* Barker, 61 Mo. App. 556.

Copies of the notice may be posted under Hill Annot. Laws Oreg. § 4063, providing that a petition for the establishment of a county road shall be accompanied by "proof that notice has been given by advertisement, posted at the place of holding county court, and also in three public places" in the vicinity of the proposed road. Vedder *v.* Marion County, 22 Oreg. 264, 29 Pac. 619.

Posting by county commissioner.—The fact

(IV) *OBJECTIONS AND WAIVER.* Notice of a proceeding to lay out a high-

Laws (1879), c. 89, § 4, which requires the giving of notice to the landowners, and the filing of affidavits of service, with copies of the notice, in the county clerk's office.

Kentucky.— Louisville, etc., R. Co. *v.* Gerard, 130 Ky. 18, 112 S. W. 915, holding that the giving of notice prior to filing the petition is an indispensable jurisdictional fact that must be made to appear in the county court, either by the record or the introduction of evidence.

New Jersey.— State *v.* Shreeve, 15 N. J. L. 57, holding that the court of common pleas have no jurisdiction to appoint surveyors of the highways without due proof that the advertisements have been set up according to law.

See 25 Cent. Dig. tit. "Highways," § 69.

See, however, Pagels *v.* Oaks, 64 Iowa 198, 19 N. W. 905 (holding that under Code (1873), §§ 937, 938, providing that, if the auditor is satisfied that notice has been served and published as required, he shall proceed to establish the road, no filing of an affidavit of publication is necessary to give the county supervisors jurisdiction to establish a highway, and the burden of showing want of notice is on the party objecting thereto); Forster *v.* Winona County, 84 Minn. 308, 87 N. W. 921 (holding that Gen. St. (1894) § 1883, as amended by Gen. Laws (1895), c. 47, providing for roads in more than one county, and directing the presentation of the petition to the judge of the district court in the district in which one of the counties is situated, which must be posted thirty days prior to its presentation at three of the most public places in such district, does not require affidavits of posting to be filed at the time of the presentation of the petition; it is enough if the notices are in fact posted).

By whom made.— In Nebraska proof of posting should be made by the affidavit of the person who posted the notice. State *v.* Otoe County, 6 Nebr. 129. In New Hampshire, however, it is not necessary that the return of service should be made by the person making the service, but any other satisfactory proof of the fact of service is sufficient. Parish *v.* Gilmanton, 11 N. H. 293. In Oregon the proof may be by the affidavit of one of the petitioners, who knows that such notice has been given. Gaines *v.* Linn County, 21 Oreg. 425, 28 Pac. 131.

Oral proof may be given that a person who was inadvertently omitted in the affidavit of service of notice on the landowners through whose property a public road was petitioned for was served with notice. Isaacs' Petition, 1 Pennew. (Del.) 61, 39 Atl. 588.

Necessity of calling witnesses.— To prove that copies of the petition were properly posted, it is not necessary to call as witnesses the parties who posted them. Their *ex parte* affidavits attached to the petition are sufficient. Wells *v.* Hicks, 27 Ill. 343.

The affidavit should state when, where, and by whom the notices were posted. State *v.* Otoe County, 6 Nebr. 129. Howell Annot. St. Mich. § 1298, requires notice of proceedings to lay out a highway to be served on railroad companies by leaving a copy "with the agent in charge of any ticket or freight office of the company," etc. Section 1299 provides that, on service of the notice required by the last section, the person by whom the service was made shall make an affidavit stating the time and manner of service, "and, if upon a railroad company, the fact of such service, and upon whom." It was held that an affidavit showing merely that service was made on a railroad company "by leaving a copy of the notice with their freight agent at Dorr station," without giving his name, or showing that he was in charge of the freight office, is insufficient. Truax *v.* Sterling, 74 Mich. 160, 41 N. W. 885.

Certificate of posting.— Under Ill. Rev. Laws (1874), c. 121, § 71, providing that a copy of a petition for a highway shall be posted up in three of the most public places in the town, and that the posting of any such notice required by the act may be proved by affidavit of the person posting the same, or by other legal evidence, it is not sufficient proof of such posting that at the end of the petition there appears this recital, "I hereby certify this was posted according to law." Frizell *v.* Rogers, 82 Ill. 109.

Affidavit as aided by record.— An affidavit stating that a notice of the intention to petition for the opening of a road was posted more than thirty days before presentation of said petition, and to which a copy of the notice is attached, and which bears a notation purporting to state the date when the notice was posted, such date being more than thirty days prior to the presentation of the petition, when taken in connection with the order of the county court establishing the road, which recites that it appears from proof filed that due notice of the proceeding has been given more than thirty days prior to the presentation of the petition, sufficiently shows that the posting was made at a date more than thirty days before the presentation of the petition. French-Glenn Live-Stock Co. *v.* Harney County, 36 Oreg. 138, 58 Pac. 35. So posting of notice in three public places within the vicinity of the proposed road is sufficiently shown by affidavits designating places where notices were posted, as a barn on the line of road, the barn of V, and a fence at the east end of the road, and the recital, in the journal entry of the court appointing viewers, that it appeared that the notice had been posted in three of the most public places along the line. Sweek *v.* Jorgensen, 33 Oreg. 270, 54 Pac. 156. Record and presumption as to notice see *infra*, II, C, 5, i, (I), (D).

Power to administer oath.— Since Ind. Rev. St. (1842) p. 189, § 52, gives the county auditor power to administer all oaths necessary for the performance of the duties of his office, and since, by virtue of his office, he is clerk of the board of commissioners of high-

way may be waived by a landowner;[76] and if he appears generally and participates in the proceeding he thereby waives the absence of notice or defects therein.[77] So notice may be waived by the consent of the landowner to the laying out of the road.[78] The right to object to the absence of notice is generally regarded as personal.[79]

e. Petition or Other Application — (I) *Necessity.* Unless expressly required

ways, the proof of putting up the notices of an intended application, and that the petition was signed by the requisite number of freeholders, might be made on oath administered by the county auditor. Milhollin *v.* Thomas, 7 Ind. 165.

76. McCown *v.* Hill, (Tex. Civ. App. 1903) 73 S. W. 850 (so holding, although the notice is jurisdictional); Allen *v.* Parker County, 23 Tex. Civ. App. 536, 57 S. W. 703. And see cases cited *infra*, note 77 *et seq.*

77. *California.*— Kimball *v.* Alameda County, 46 Cal. 19.

Indiana.— Fisher *v.* Hobbs, 42 Ind. 276; Daggy *v.* Coats, 19 Ind. 259; Milhollin *v.* Thomas, 7 Ind. 165.

Kansas.— State *v.* Hadeen, 47 Kan. 402, 28 Pac. 203 (holding that, although no notice is given to one of the owners through whose land a highway is laid out, or any finding made that he is a non-resident of the county, the want of jurisdiction is cured by the presentation by him to the county commissioners of a claim for damages in consequence of the opening of the road); Woodson County *v.* Heed, 33 Kan. 34, 5 Pac. 543 (holding that where county commissioners had jurisdiction over the laying out of a road, but not over the person of one landowner, his presentation of a claim for damages after the opening of the road was a waiver of want of jurisdiction).

Kentucky.—Anonymous, 2 T. B. Mon. 91.

Massachusetts.— Hyde Park *v.* Wiggin, 157 Mass. 94, 31 N. E. 693; Copeland *v.* Packard, 16 Pick. 217 (holding that where a party was present at the town meeting when the proceedings of selectmen laying out a road were approved, and objected that he was not allowed sufficient amount of damages, he cannot thereafter object that he had not received sufficient notice of the laying out of such road); *In re* New Salem, 6 Pick. 470.

Michigan.— Page *v.* Boehmer, 154 Mich. 693, 118 N. W. 602, holding that jurisdiction was obtained over a landowner by his participation in the proceedings and taking an appeal.

New Hampshire.— Roberts *v.* Stark, 47 N. H. 223 (holding that if a town files exceptions to the notice and at the same time contests the petition on other grounds, the defect in the notice will be waived); Peavey *v.* Wolfborough, 37 N. H. 286 (holding that objections to the notices, if not taken at the hearing, will be waived).

North Carolina.— Little *v.* May, 10 N. C. 599.

Pennsylvania.— *In re* Corplanter Tp. Road, 26 Pa. Super. Ct. 29, holding that where a borough has actual notice of proceedings to open a road, and its representatives are present at the view, it has no standing subsequently to object that written notice was not served on its officers, and that a duly attested copy of the notice was not filed in the office of the clerk of the quarter sessions.

South Dakota.— Issenhuth *v.* Baum, 11 S. D. 223, 76 N. W. 928.

Texas.— Onken *v.* Riley, 65 Tex. 468, holding that a landowner who was present when a road was laid out through his land by a jury of freeholders appointed by the commissioner's court, and also when their action was confirmed and adopted by the court, cannot object to such road on the ground of want of notice to him of the proceedings for its establishment.

Vermont.— Robinson *v.* Winch, 66 Vt. 110, 28 Atl. 884, holding that want of notice of a hearing by the board of selectmen as to the necessity of a highway is waived by one's appearance at the hearing.

Virginia.— Tench *v.* Abshire, 90 Va. 768, 19 S. E. 779.

See 25 Cent. Dig. tit. "Highways," § 70.

Otherwise unless the occupant consents to the laying out of the road over his land, or accepts damages, or in some way adopts the acts of the supervisors as his own. State *v.* Langer, 29 Wis. 68.

78. Barnes *v.* Fox, 61 Iowa 18, 15 N. W. 581 (*semble*); Crawford *v.* Snowden, 3 Litt. (Ky.) 228 (*semble*); State *v.* Langer, 29 Wis. 68 (*semble*). *Contra*, St. Bartholomew's Parish Lower Bd. Road Com'rs *v.* Murray, 1 Rich. (S. C.) 335.

However, the consent of the proprietors of land where a road is to pass must be given in court, and not to the commissioners appointed to view the road. Crawford *v.* Snowden, 3 Litt. (Ky.) 228.

79. Knox *v.* Epsom, 56 N. H. 14 (holding that persons interested in the laying out of a highway, but who are not by statute entitled to notice of the petition, cannot object to the sufficiency of the notice given to a town which is entitled to notice); Hasler *v.* Hitler, 9 Ohio Dec. (Reprint) 233, 11 Cinc. L. Bul. 246 (holding that where a landowner through whose land the proposed way is to be constructed waives his right to compensation and damages for the taking of such land, persons other than such landowner cannot object that he was not served with notice of the proceedings to lay out such way). But see State *v.* Logue, 73 Wis. 598, 41 N. W. 1061, holding that the fact that a landowner signed the petition for a highway does not dispense with the necessity of notice to the public and other owners, and he may avail himself of want of such notice to impeach the proceedings.

by statute, which is usually the case,[80] it is not necessary to the valid laying out of a highway that there should have been a petition or other application therefor.[81]

(II) *FORMAL REQUISITES.* A petition for the establishment of a highway should be addressed to the court or board having jurisdiction to establish highways.[82] It need not be signed by petitioners,[83] in the absence of a statute to the contrary.[84]

(III) *SUFFICIENCY*[85] — (A) *In General.* A petition for the establishment of a highway should contain all the facts required to be stated therein by statute in order to confer jurisdiction.[86] It is not essential that the petition should follow the exact language of the statute. Language unmistakably indicating its object and purpose will be held sufficient.[87]

80. *Iowa.*— Lehmann *v.* Rinehart, 90 Iowa 346, 57 N. W. 866.

Kansas.— Shaffer *v.* Weech, 34 Kan. 595, 9 Pac. 202; Oliphant *v.* Atchison County, 18 Kan. 386; Hentzler *v.* Bradbury, 5 Kan. App. 1, 47 Pac. 330.

Maine.— Cushing *v.* Webb, 102 Me. 157, 66 Atl. 719.

Maryland.—Barrickman *v.* Harford County, 11 Gill & J. 50.

Massachusetts.— Com. *v.* Cambridge, 7 Mass. 158; Com. *v.* Peters, 3 Mass. 229; Com. *v.* Coombs, 2 Mass. 489.

Nebraska.— Doody *v.* Vaughn, 7 Nebr. 28; State *v.* Otoe County, 6 Nebr. 129; Robinson *v.* Mathwick, 5 Nebr. 252.

New Hampshire.— State *v.* Morse, 50 N. H. 9; Clement *v.* Burns, 43 N. H. 609; State *v.* Rye, 35 N. H. 368; Haywood *v.* Charlestown, 34 N. H. 23; Wiggin *v.* Exeter, 13 N. H. 304; Prichard *v.* Atkinson, 3 N. H. 335.

Oregon.— Johns *v.* Marion County, 4 Oreg. 46.

United States.— Burns *v.* Multnomah R. Co., 15 Fed. 177, 8 Sawy. 543.

See 25 Cent. Dig. tit. "Highways," § 47.

81. Howard *v.* Hutchinson, 10 Me. 335; O'Neil *v.* Walpole, 74 N. H. 197, 66 Atl. 119; Kopecky *v.* Daniels, 9 Tex. Civ. App. 305, 29 S. W. 533; Decker *v.* Menard County, (Tex. Civ. App. 1894) 25 S. W. 727.

In Nebraska the establishment of section-line roads is governed by the special provisions of Road Law, § 46, by which all section lines are declared to be public roads, and may be opened as such whenever, in the judgment of the county boards, the public interest demands, a petition not being essential. Barry *v.* Deloughrey, 47 Nebr. 354, 66 N. W. 410; Rose *v.* Washington County, 42 Nebr. 1, 60 N. W. 352; Howard *v.* Brown, 37 Nebr. 902, 56 N. W. 713; McNair *v.* State, 26 Nebr. 257, 41 N. W. 1099; Throckmorton *v.* State, 20 Nebr. 647, 31 N. W. 232.

In New York it is not necessary to the valid laying out of a highway, that there should have been a written application therefor, but the commissioner may act of his own motion, 1 Rev. St. p. 513, § 55, providing that, whenever the commissioners shall lay out any road either "upon application or otherwise," they shall cause a survey to be made, etc. Marble *v.* Whitney, 28 N. Y. 297; People *v.* Richmond County, 20 N. Y. 252; McCarthy *v.* Whalen, 19 Hun 503 [*affirmed* in 87 N. Y. 148]; Gould *v.* Glass, 19 Barb. 179. *Contra*, Harrington *v.* People, 6 Barb. 607.

82. State *v.* Barlow, 61 Iowa 572, 16 N. W. 733.

However, it is no cause for complaint that the petition runs to the clerk of the board of supervisors instead of the board itself. State *v.* Barlow, 61 Iowa 572, 16 N. W. 733. Nor is a petition fatally defective because it is addressed to the wrong court, where it was filed and indorsed in the proper court, and all subsequent proceedings, including the appointment of viewers, and the confirmation of their report, were made by that court. *In re* Union Tp. Road, 29 Pa. Super. Ct. 573. An omission in the address, not going to the jurisdiction, cannot be taken advantage of by a motion to dismiss. Tucker *v.* Eden, 68 Vt. 168, 34 Atl. 698.

83. Warren *v.* Gibson, 40 Mo. App. 469.

84. Cooper *v.* Harmon, 170 Ind. 113, 83 N. E. 704, holding, however, that the fact that many of the signers of such petition signed their christian names by the initials does not warrant the dismissal of the petition, but merely entitles defendants upon proper motion to have the full christian and surname of each petitioner entered of record.

85. **Sufficiency as against collateral attack** see *infra*, II, C, 5, i, (VI), (F).

86. Canyon County *v.* Toole, 9 Ida. 561, 75 Pac. 609; Randolph *v.* Ætna Highway Com'rs, 8 Ill. App. 128; *In re* Sussex County, etc., Road, 13 N. J. L. 157, holding that it should specify the places where the notices were set up.

Averment of ultimate facts is sufficient. Sullivan *v.* Cline, 33 Oreg. 260, 54 Pac. 154.

87. Stevens *v.* Cerro Gordo County, 41 Iowa 341.

No particular words or form of words are required by the statute in applications to the county commissioners for the location of roads, and the greatest technical accuracy and precision is not to be expected. Windham *v.* Cumberland County, 26 Me. 406. Thus a petition for the appointment of a commissioner "to open a road" sufficiently complies with a statute providing for the "establishment" (Stevens *v.* Cerro Gordo County, 41 Iowa 341; McCollister *v.* Shuey, 24 Iowa 362) or "laying out" (Winooski Lumber, etc., Co. *v.* Colchester, 57 Vt. 538) of a road. Likewise a petition for the appointment of a commissioner to "examine into the expediency of establishing" the road confers jurisdiction un-

(B) *Particular Averments* — (1) QUALIFICATION OF PETITIONERS. Unless required by statute, it is not necessary that the petition should show on its face that petitioners possessed the requisite qualifications.[88] This fact is a matter of evidence to be determined by the board or court on the hearing of the petition.[89]

(2) OWNERSHIP OR OCCUPANCY OF LAND. A petition for the location of a highway is frequently required to give the names of the owners and occupants or agents of all lands over which the proposed road is to run,[90] or, if unknown, it must so state.[91]

(3) UTILITY, NECESSITY, AND CHARACTER OF ROAD. When required by statute, a petition for a highway should aver that the highway is of public utility and necessity.[92] But it is not necessary that the exact language of the statute

der such a statute. State *v.* Pitman, 38 Iowa 252. Nor does jurisdiction fail merely because the word "road" instead of "highway" is used in the petition or in the record, if an examination of the whole will show what description of road was intended. Windham *v.* Cumberland County, *supra.* And see Dartmouth *v.* Bristol County, 153 Mass. 12, 26 N. E. 425. But a petition asking that a highway commencing and terminating at designated points "be ——" not indicating the relief desired, is insufficient to confer jurisdiction on the board to establish a highway. Lehmann *v.* Rinehart, 90 Iowa 346, 57 N. W. 866.

88. *California.*— Humboldt County *v.* Dinsmore, 75 Cal. 604, 17 Pac. 710.

Illinois.— Afton Highway Com'rs *v.* Ellwood, 193 Ill. 304, 61 N. E. 1033, where such qualification appears by recitals in the petition or in the record of the proceedings of the commissioners.

Indiana.—Hall *v.* McDonald, 171 Ind. 9, 85 N. E. 707; Washington Ice Co. *v.* Lay, 103 Ind. 48, 2 N. E. 222; Brown *v.* McCord, 20 Ind. 270. But see Conaway *v.* Ascherman, 94 Ind. 187; Watson *v.* Crowsore, 93 Ind. 220.

Iowa.— Keyes *v.* Tait, 19 Iowa 123.

Kansas.— Wabaunsee County *v.* Muhlenbacker, 18 Kan. 129; Willis *v.* Sproule, 13 Kan. 257.

Missouri.— Snoddy *v.* Pettis County, 45 Mo. 361; Fisher *v.* Davis, 27 Mo. App. 321. But see Jefferson County *v.* Cowan, 54 Mo. 234.

Oregon.— Bewley *v.* Graves, 17 Oreg. 274, 20 Pac. 322.

See 25 Cent. Dig. tit. "Highways," § 51.

But see Nischen *v.* Hawes, 21 S. W. 1049, 15 Ky. L. Rep. 40; Craft *v.* De Soto County, 79 Miss. 618, 31 So. 204; *In re* Sussex County, etc., Road, 13 N. J. L. 157; Howe *v.* Jamaica, 19 Vt. 607; Hewes *v.* Andover, 16 Vt. 510.

89. Humboldt County *v.* Dinsmore, 75 Cal. 604, 17 Pac. 710; Brown *v.* McCord, 20 Ind. 270; Snoddy *v.* Pettis County, 45 Mo. 361; Fisher *v.* Davis, 27 Mo. App. 321.

90. Conaway *v.* Ascherman, 94 Ind. 187; Schmied *v.* Kenney, 72 Ind. 309; Meyers *v.* Brown, 55 Ind. 596 (holding that it is sufficient to allege in the alternative that such persons are owners, occupants, or agents); Vawter *v.* Gilliland, 55 Ind. 278 (holding that the petition is fatally defective where, instead of setting out the full given names of the owners of the land, it gives initials only of the christian names of the individual owners, and the firm-names only of the owners in partnership); Hughes *v.* Sellers, 34 Ind. 337 (holding that it is not a sufficient designation of such owners to say that they are the heirs of a person named); Hays *v.* Campbell, 17 Ind. 430; Milhollin *v.* Thomas, 7 Ind. 165 (holding, however, that the fact that the petition, while stating the owners of the land through which the road would pass, failed to state who occupied the land, will not affect the jurisdiction of the commissioners); Cowing *v.* Ripley, 76 Mich. 650, 43 N. W. 648; Navin *v.* Martin, (Mo. App. 1907) 102 S. W. 61; Mulligan *v.* Martin, 125 Mo. App. 630, 102 S. W. 59; Godchaux *v.* Carpenter, 19 Nev. 415, 14 Pac. 140.

A map accompanying the petition, and showing the names of the landowners, may be considered in determining the sufficiency of the petition. Bennett *v.* Hall, 184 Mo. 407, 83 S. W. 439.

Highway crossing railroad.— Where the route of a proposed highway crosses a railroad, the petition should name the railroad company as one of the owners of the land crossed by it. Lyle *v.* Chicago, etc., R. Co., 55 Minn. 223, 56 N. W. 820. But see Weymouth *v.* York County, 86 Me. 391, 29 Atl. 1100, holding that a petition need not aver the fact that the way will cross a railroad track, although the railroad company must receive notice of the pendency of the petition.

91. Navin *v.* Martin, (Mo. App. 1907) 102 S. W. 61; Mulligan *v.* Martin, 125 Mo. App. 630, 102 S. W. 59

92. Morris *v.* Salle, 19 S. W. 527, 14 Ky. L. Rep. 117.

In Alabama it is held that, although the petition should properly state facts to show the expediency of the road prayed for, yet it is not demurrable for omitting to do so. Lowndes County Com'rs Ct. *v.* Bowie, 34 Ala. 461.

In Indiana, in a petition to locate a highway under Acts (1905), c. 167, § 21, it is not necessary to allege that the proposed highway will be of public utility, or that the cost thereof will be less than the benefits, since it is the duty of the county commissioners to appoint viewers, if the jurisdictional facts exist, and thereafter the matters suggested are to be considered. Cooper *v.* Harmon, 170 Ind. 113, 83 N. E. 704; Conaway

as to convenience and necessity be followed, a substantial allegation thereof being sufficient.[93]

(4) NEGLECT OR REFUSAL OF SELECTMEN TO ESTABLISH ROAD. Under a statute authorizing an application to the county court for a highway from place to place within the same town only where the selectmen neglect or refuse to lay out the same, it has been decided that the averment of such neglect or refusal is indispensable to give the court jurisdiction.[94]

(5) DESCRIPTION OF ROAD. Technical accuracy is not necessary in the description of a proposed line of road.[95] It is sufficient if the description is so definite and certain as to enable persons familiar with the locality to locate the way,[96] and to enable a surveyor to run it.[97] Thus the petition must describe with reasonable certainty the terminal points of the proposed way [98] and its general

v. Ascherman, 94 Ind. 187; Bowers *v.* Snyder, 88 Ind. 302.

93. Plainfield *v.* Packer, 11 Conn. 576 (holding that a petition was sufficient which stated that, in the opinion of petitioners, common convenience and necessity required that a new highway should be laid out between the two places, and that thereby the distance would be greatly lessened, and not only the travel in the immediate neighborhood, but also the general travel, be greatly facilitated); Windsor *v.* Field, 1 Conn. 279 (holding that where a petition for a highway alleged that the old road was "very circuitous, hilly, and on bad ground," and that a new road might be laid out between the same termini "so as to greatly accommodate the public, with little expense to the town, or injury to private property," it was sufficient, under the statute, without alleging that the highway "is wanting," or that it would be of "common convenience or necessity"); Lockwood *v.* Gregory, 4 Day (Conn.) 407 (holding that an application for a highway by petition, under the statute, need not state that the road prayed for would be "of common convenience or necessity," if the facts stated induce such an inference).

94. Torrington *v.* Nash, 17 Conn. 197 (holding that an averment that the "town" neglected and refused to lay out the highway is not equivalent to an averment that the "selectmen" neglected and refused to lay out the highway); Plainfield *v.* Packer, 11 Conn. 576 (holding further that it must appear from the record that the averment is true; otherwise the proceeding is erroneous); Waterbury *v.* Darien, 9 Conn. 252 (holding, however, that the allegation of a special demand or request is unnecessary); Treat *v.* Middletown, 8 Conn. 243; *In re* Kennett, 24 N. H. 139 (holding that an affidavit saying, "I am confident that a petition was presented to the selectmen before any petition was filed in court," is not sufficient alone to prove that fact); *In re* Patten, 16 N. H. 277.

In Maine the petition must allege that the refusal was unreasonable. Goodwin *v.* Sagadahoc County, 60 Me. 328. But a specific statement of all the acts and facts which constitute an unreasonable refusal is unnecessary. True *v.* Freeman, 64 Me. 573.

95. *Illinois.*— Henline *v.* People, 81 Ill. 269.

Indiana.— Adams *v.* Harrington, 114 Ind. 66, 14 N. E. 603.

Maine.— Windham *v.* Cumberland County, 26 Me. 406.

Maryland.— Jenkins *v.* Riggs, 100 Md. 427, 59 Atl. 758.

Michigan.— Page *v.* Boehmer, 154 Mich. 693, 118 N. W. 602.

See 25 Cent. Dig. tit. "Highways," § 53.

A petition for the location of a county road should not be too critically judged, especially where the termini are plainly fixed. Bryant *v.* Penobscot County, 79 Me. 128, 8 Atl. 460.

96. Cushing *v.* Webb, 102 Me. 157, 66 Atl. 719; Page *v.* Boehmer, 154 Mich. 693, 118 N. W. 602.

97. Wells *v.* Rhodes, 114 Ind. 467, 16 N. E. 830; Adams *v.* Harrington, 114 Ind. 66, 14 N. E. 603; Conaway *v.* Ascherman, 94 Ind. 187; McDonald *v.* Wilson, 59 Ind. 54; Fancher *v.* Coffin, 41 Ind. App. 489, 84 N. E. 354; Warren *v.* Brown, 31 Nebr. 8, 47 N. W. 633; Robinson *v.* Winch, 66 Vt. 110, 28 Atl. 884; Shell *v.* Poulson, 23 Wash. 535, 63 Pac. 204.

Descriptions held sufficiently certain see McDonald *v.* Payne, 114 Ind. 359, 16 N. E. 795; Clift *v.* Brown, 95 Ind. 53; Casey *v.* Kilgore, 14 Kan. 478; Acton *v.* York County, 77 Me. 128; Thompson *v.* Trowe, 82 Minn. 471, 85 N. W. 169; People *v.* Taylor, 34 Barb. (N. Y.) 481; State *v.* O'Connor, 78 Wis. 282, 47 N. W. 433.

Descriptions held too uncertain see Hayford *v.* Aroostook County, 78 Me. 153, 3 Atl. 51; Clement *v.* Burns, 43 N. H. 609.

98. *Maine.*— Andover *v.* Oxford County, 86 Me. 185, 29 Atl. 982; Hayford *v.* Aroostook County, 78 Me. 153, 3 Atl. 51; Sumner *v.* Oxford County, 37 Me. 112.

Massachusetts.— Pembroke *v.* Plymouth County, 12 Cush. 351.

New Jersey.— State *v.* Green, 18 N. J. L. 179; State *v.* Hart, 17 N. J. L. 185; *In re* Highway, 16 N. J. L. 391.

Pennsylvania.—*In re* Cornplanter Tp. Road, 26 Pa. Super. Ct. 20; Anderson's Appeal, 25 Leg. Int. 77.

Washington.— Chelan County *v.* Navarre, 38 Wash. 684, 80 Pac. 845.

See 25 Cent. Dig. tit. "Highways," § 54.

The caption of a petition for a road view may be considered in connection with the petition in determining whether the termini and the names of the township and county are

(IV) *Application Relating to Two or More Roads.* In the absence of express statutory authority,[3] some decisions lay down the rule that several distinct highways cannot be prayed for in the same petition,[4] unless they connect with one another [5] or are closely identified and designed to form a system of roads.[6] On the other hand it has been held that while such a proceeding is doubtless irregular, and it may be safer and better to require that a separate petition be filed in each case,[7] such irregularity is not jurisdictional.[8] By the weight of authority a prayer for a new road and the vacation of an old road may be joined in the same petition,[9] where the former is to take the place of the latter.[10]

(V) *Amendments.* The power to allow amendments to petitions in highway cases is well established.[11] This power is comprehensive, and the discretion of the court or board will not be reviewed unless abused.[12] But it will not be construed to extend to allowing the petition to be amended in those particulars upon which the original jurisdiction of the local tribunal depends, after reference to commissioners or viewers and a report made by them,[13] or after the case has been removed into the appellate court.[14] Nor is an amendment permissible which will vary the original purpose of the proceeding.[15] A second petition by

In Indiana, under 1 Rev. St. (1876) pp. 531, 532, § 16, providing that where the road is laid out on the line dividing the land of two individuals, each shall give half of the road, a petition for a highway which describes the highway in several places as "running on the line dividing" the lands of certain named proprietors, without averring that it ran upon or over such lands, or what part of such road passed upon each tract, is sufficient. Hedrick *v.* Hedrick, 55 Ind. 78.

3. See the statutes of the different states.

4. Baker *v.* Ashland, 50 N. H. 27; State *v.* Oliver, 24 N. J. L. 129; *In re* Sadsbury Tp. Roads, 147 Pa. St. 471, 23 Atl. 772. *Compare In re* Highway, 7 N. J. L. 37.

Designation of two routes.— In the absence of a statute permitting it, there is said to be no authority for an application for one road to be laid out in one or another of two designated routes. *In re* Highway, 7 N. J. L. 37.

5. Barry *v.* Deloughery, 47 Nebr. 354, 66 N. W. 410.

6. *In re* Sadsbury Road, 9 Pa. Co. Ct. 521; *In re* West Goshen Roads, 7 Pa. Co. Ct. 250.

In Ohio, where the laying out and construction of a new county road and the improvement of an existing road or roads constitute one continuous road improvement, the proceedings therefor before the county commissioners, under 64 Ohio Laws, p. 80, and the acts amendatory thereof, may be had under the same petition. Putnam County *v.* Young, 36 Ohio St. 288.

7. Banse *v.* Clark, 69 Minn. 53, 71 N. W. 819; Chelan County *v.* Navarre, 38 Wash. 684, 80 Pac. 845.

8. Banse *v.* Clark, 69 Minn. 53, 71 N. W. 819; Chelan County *v.* Navarre, 38 Wash. 684, 80 Pac. 845. And see Hardy *v.* Keene, 54 N. H. 449.

9. Anderson *v.* Wood, 80 Ill. 15; Brown *v.* Roberts, 23 Ill. App. 461 [*affirmed* in 123 Ill. 631, 15 N. E. 30]; Bowers *v.* Snyder, 88 Ind. 302; People *v.* Robertson, 17 How. Pr. (N. Y.) 74. *Contra,* Cox *v.* Hartford Tp. Highways Com'r, 83 Mich. 193, 47 N. W. 122; Shue *v.* Richmond Tp. Highway Com'rs, 41 Mich. 638, 2 N. W. 808.

The consolidation of a proceeding to establish a new road with another to vacate a road, the order of vacation being issued without a view, and after objections thereto duly made, is erroneous, and should be set aside on appeal. Geddes *v.* Rice, 24 Ohio St. 60.

10. Harris *v.* Mahaska County, 88 Iowa 219, 55 N. W. 324.

11. *Indiana.*— Thrall *v.* Gosnell, 28 Ind. App. 174, 62 N. E. 462.

Massachusetts.— Dartmouth *v.* Bristol County, 153 Mass. 12, 26 N. E. 425.

New Hampshire.— Young *v.* Laconia, 59 N. H. 534; *In re* Patten, 16 N. H. 277.

North Carolina.— Pridgen *v.* Anders, 52 N. C. 257.

Pennsylvania.— *In re* Dickinson Tp. Road, 23 Pa. Super. Ct. 34; *In re* East Hempfield Tp. Road, 2 Leg. Chron. 151.

See 25 Cent. Dig. tit. "Highways," § 58.

Illustrations.—Thus it has been held proper to allow an amendment slightly changing the route to be followed (Windham *v.* Litchfield, 22 Conn. 226; Burns *v.* Simmons, 101 Ind. 557, 1 N. E. 72), changing the terminal points (*In re* Upper Mt. Bethel Road, 7 North. Co. Rep. (Pa.) 29), showing ownership of the land affected (Hedrick *v.* Hedrick, 55 Ind. 78; Milhollin *v.* Thomas, 7 Ind. 165; Sisson *v.* Carithers, 35 Ind. App. 161, 72 N. E. 267, 73 N. E. 924), adding (Bronnenburg *v.* O'Bryant, 139 Ind. 17, 38 N. E. 416) or striking out (Webster *v.* Bridgewater, 63 N. H. 296) names, or showing the qualifications of petitioners (Howe *v.* Jamaica, 19 Vt. 607; Hewes *v.* Andover, 16 Vt. 510).

12. Burns *v.* Simmons, 101 Ind. 557, 1 N. E. 72.

13. Dinsmore *v.* Auburn, 26 N. H. 356.

14. Shuey *v.* Stoner, 47 Md. 167; Gilley *v.* Barre, (Vt. 1897) 37 Atl. 1111.

15. Spencer *v.* Graham, 5 Ind. 158 (holding that where there were two sections of a statute in force concerning highways, and a petition was filed for leave to do a certain act, and it was materially defective upon the section on which it was evidently founded, the practice act of 1852 not being in force,

proper parties entitled "supplemental" will be treated as part of the original petition, although not stated to be such.[16]

(VI) *WITHDRAWAL OF PETITION.*[17] A petition for a highway may be withdrawn at any time before the final decision of the tribunal having jurisdiction thereof,[18] unless under the circumstances such action would be contrary to public policy.[19]

(VII) *OBJECTIONS AND WAIVER.* As a general rule, objections not going to the jurisdiction should be made at the first opportunity, or they will be deemed waived.[20] But if the petition is so insufficient as to form no basis for the action of the local tribunal, an objection thereto will be fatal at any stage of the proceeding.[21] Objections to the petition must be specifically stated, or they will be disregarded.[22]

f. Opposition, Remonstrance, or Other Answer;[23] **Demurrer.** The statutes of the several states generally provide for a contest of highway proceedings by the filing of a remonstrance or other answer to the petition;[24] but in Indiana

it was not competent for the court to allow such amendments as would bring it under the other section); Thrall *v.* Gosnell, 28 Ind. App. 174, 62 N. E. 462.

16. *In re* Markley St., 13 Montg. Co. Rep. (Pa.) 120.

17. **Withdrawal of parties** see *supra*, II, C, 5, c, (III).

18. West *v.* Tolland, 25 Conn. 133, holding that a petition for a highway may be withdrawn after the commissioners to whom it has been referred have announced to the parties that they are of opinion that public convenience and necessity do not require such highway to be laid out.

19. Jacobs *v.* Tobiason, 65 Iowa 245, 21 N. W. 590, 54 Am. Rep. 9, holding that proceedings for the establishment of highways are essentially public in their character, and, although instituted on the petition of a private person, are for the benefit of the whole people, and a contract whereby such party agrees to abandon the proceedings is contrary to public policy and void.

20. Dillman *v.* Crooks, 91 Ind. 158; Crossley *v.* O'Brien, 24 Ind. 325, 87 Am. Dec. 329; Fox *v.* Tuftonborough, 58 N. H. 19; Lord *v.* Dunbarton, 55 N. H. 245; Hardy *v.* Keene, 54 N. H. 449; Stevens *v.* Goffstown, 21 N. H. 454.

Objections to the number or qualifications of the petitioners should be made at the first opportunity before the county board. If not made then and there, they will be deemed waived. Bronnenburg *v.* O'Bryant, 139 Ind. 17, 38 N. E. 416; Osborn *v.* Sutton, 108 Ind. 443, 9 N. E. 410; Washington Ice Co. *v.* Lay, 103 Ind. 48, 2 N. E. 222; Forsythe *v.* Kreuter, 100 Ind. 27.

Appearance without making objections to the sufficiency of the petition is a waiver of whatever objections might have been made. Crouse *v.* Whitlock, 46 Ill. App. 260; Washington Ice Co. *v.* Lay, 103 Ind. 48, 2 N. E. 222; Turley *v.* Oldham, 68 Ind. 114; Fisher *v.* Hobbs, 42 Ind. 276; Smith *v.* Goldsborough, 80 Md. 49, 30 Atl. 574; Carpenter *v.* Sims, 3 Leigh (Va.) 675. Filing a remonstrance against granting a petition for the establishment of a highway, without objection to the sufficiency of the petition, waives such objection. Sowle *v.* Cosner, 56 Ind. 276. The reference of a petition for a highway to the commissioners without objection is a waiver of all objections to the form of the petition and preliminary proceedings. Bachelér *v.* New Hampton, 60 N. H. 207.

21. Treat *v.* Middletown, 8 Conn. 243; Hughes *v.* Sellers, 34 Ind. 337; Hays *v.* Campbell, 17 Ind. 430.

A landholder who signs such a petition is not estopped thereby from asserting a judicial defect for lack of sufficient signatures. Stewart *v.* Wyandotte County, 45 Kan. 708, 26 Pac. 683, 23 Am. St. Rep. 746.

22. Osborn *v.* Sutton, 108 Ind. 443, 9 N. E. 410.

23. **Effect of filing of remonstrance by petitioner** see *supra*, II, C, 5, c, (III), note 51.

24. See cases cited *infra*, this note. *Contra*, Logan *v.* Kiser, 25 Ind. 393. And see Irwin *v.* Armuth, 129 Ind. 340, 28 N. E. 702, where a person who was not a party to the proceeding appeared before the board of commissioners and filed a "plea in abatement," alleging that less than six persons signing the petition for the highway resided in the neighborhood thereof, and the board struck out the plea on the ground that the contestant offering it was not a party to the proceeding, and it was held that if contestant had a right to contest the jurisdiction of the board, he had the right without filing any plea whatever, and that the same was properly stricken out.

Who may contest proceeding.—A person through whose lands a proposed road will pass is beneficially interested, and is a proper party to contest the legality of the proceedings for the establishment of the road. Damrell *v.* San Joaquin County, 40 Cal. 154. But if the land assessed does not front the proposed street, or is legally exempt from assessment, the owner cannot competently object. French *v.* East Orange, 49 N. J. L. 401, 8 Atl. 107. And a taxpayer, merely as such, will not be heard in opposition to laying out a highway. He is represented by the town, and his interest is too remote. Burnham *v.* Goffstown, 50 N. H. 560. Under Ind. Rev. St. (1881) § 5023, confining the right to object to the location of a highway as use-

it has been held that no such pleadings as an answer or demurrer are proper in highway proceedings.[25]

g. Commissioners, Viewers, Surveyors, Jurors, and Other Like Officers — (I) *RIGHT TO AND NECESSITY FOR SUCH OFFICERS.*[26] It is generally, although not always, required that a petition for a highway shall be referred to commissioners, viewers, surveyors, jurors, or other like officers, the question depending entirely upon the local statutes.[27]

less to resident freeholders of the county, a remonstrance must show on its face that its signers are such resident freeholders. Wells *v.* Rhodes, 114 Ind. 467, 16 N. E. 830.

Dissent of a majority of the owners of land to be affected by the proposed road defeats the proceedings under some statutes. Lewly *v.* West Hoboken, 54 N. J. L. 508, 24 Atl. 477; French *v.* East Orange, 49 N. J. L. 401, 8 Atl. 107.

Time for remonstrance.— Allegations of a road petition essential to the jurisdiction of the commissioners are to be taken as true if not controverted at the proper stage of the proceedings, which is before reference of the petition. State *v.* Rye, 35 N. H. 368. On petition to the county court for the laying out of a highway, the question of the pendency of a prior petition to the selectmen, and the consequent unlawfulness of an assumption of jurisdiction by such court, may be raised by plea *in limine*, and need not await the appointment of commissioners and determination by them. Crawford *v.* Rutland, 52 Vt. 412.

Grounds of remonstrance.— An owner of land through which a right of way is condemned for a road cannot object on the ground that the land taken occupies the only available route for a contemplated railroad, which, if constructed, would enhance the value of his property. Phillips *v.* Watson, 63 Iowa 28, 18 N. W. 659. And see *infra*, II, C, 5, h.

Sufficiency of averments.— An averment in a remonstrance that the proposed highway would not be of "sufficient public utility" is a negative pregnant, and is equivalent to an admission that it would be of public utility. Wells *v.* Rhodes, 114 Ind. 467, 16 N. E. 830.

Amendments.— Where a remonstrance alleging want of public utility was rejected by the commissioners and circuit court as to that allegation, as not showing that the remonstrants were resident freeholders, the court does not err in refusing to allow the remonstrance to be amended in that respect, there being no reason why the amendment should not have been made in the commissioners' court, and no showing as to what actually occurred there. Wells *v.* Rhodes, 114 Ind. 467, 16 N. E. 830.

Waiver of objections.— Persons may remonstrate on the ground of the inutility of the proposed highway, and also claim damages in the same remonstrance. Schmied *v.* Keeney, 72 Ind. 309; Peed *v.* Brenneman, 72 Ind. 288. But see Fisher *v.* Hobbs, 42 Ind. 276, holding that where, on petition for a highway, a remonstrant over whose lands it would pass appeared in the commissioners' court and filed his claim for damages without objecting to the utility of the road, the objection was thereby waived. In a proceeding to establish a highway, a person filed with the county commissioners two remonstrances: The first relying on the ground that the proposed highway was not of public utility; the second on the ground that it ran through his inclosed land, damaging him to the extent of a sum specified, and asking the appointment of reviewers to assess his damages. It was held that the remonstrances raised no objection to the proposed highway on the ground that it ran through the remonstrator's inclosure of one year's standing without his consent, and that a good way could otherwise be had; and such objection was thereby impliedly waived. Cummins *v.* Shields, 34 Ind. 154.

25. Logan *v.* Kiser, 25 Ind. 393.

26. **Right of trial by jury** see EMINENT DOMAIN, 15 Cyc. 872; JURIES, 24 Cyc. 133.

27. *Georgia.*—Howell *v.* Chattooga County, 118 Ga. 635, 45 S. E. 241, holding that Pol. Code (1895), § 520, providing that on application for any new road the ordinary shall appoint commissioners, who shall make their report that it is laid out conformably to law, is not inconsistent with the alternative road law of 1891, and must be complied with before a new public road can be lawfully established in a county where such alternative road law is operative.

Kansas.— Hughes *v.* Milligan, 42 Kan. 396, 22 Pac. 313, where the general road law of 1868 provides that before a highway can be laid out and opened it is necessary that viewers be appointed, whose duty it is to determine whether the road prayed for is necessary, and also to assess and determine the amount of damages sustained by any person through whose land the road may run, and Laws (1867), c. 67, as amended by Laws (1868–1869), declare section lines in certain counties to be highways, and provide that the provisions of the general road law shall be applicable where damages are claimed under the act, and it was held that the opening of a highway under the provisions of the latter act could be enjoined where no viewers were appointed.

Kentucky.— Louisville, etc., R. Co. *v.* Gerard, 130 Ky. 18, 112 S. W. 915, holding that the provision of St. (1903) § 4296, that when, in proceedings to have a new road opened, exceptions shall be filed by either party, the court shall, unless the parties agree that it may try such issues, impanel a jury to try the issue of fact made by the exceptions, applies to questions of fact growing out of the necessity for opening the road and the amount

ute,[46] and in that event it must be administered in that form.[47] In some states the oath need not be subscribed,[48] or even be in writing.[49] An oath of office of a surveyor is not rendered invalid because of a mistake in the spelling of his name in the body of the oath, where he signed it with his true name.[50] The question as to who may administer the oath is governed by the local statutes.[51]

(E) *Proof of Qualification; Record, Return, Report, Etc.* In order to render the proceedings effective in some jurisdictions it must appear that the commissioners, viewers, etc., were duly sworn;[52] and this is generally required to appear of

Texas.— Davidson *v.* State, 16 Tex. App. 336, holding that where jurors do not take the oath prescribed by statute before acting, the proceedings are void.

Virginia.— Fisher *v.* Smith, 5 Leigh 611.

See 25 Cent. Dig. tit. "Highways," § 89.

See, however, State *v.* Hogue, 71 Wis. 384, 36 N. W. 860, holding that under Const. art. 4, § 28, providing that the legislature may exempt inferior officers from taking an oath, the failure of a special act appointing commissioners to locate a state road to provide for their taking an oath is not fatal, where the general law makes no provision for such an oath.

All acting must be sworn. *In re* Middlesex County, etc., Public Road, 4 N. J. L. 396; *In re* Broad St. Road, 7 Serg. & R. (Pa.) 444.

The failure of the township clerk to transmit the official oaths of the surveyors of highways to the county clerk, however, did not vitiate their election to office, or their appointment by the court of common pleas in a proceeding to establish a road. Bassett *v.* Denn, 17 N. J. L. 432.

46. Huntington *v.* Birch, 12 Conn. 142; Matter of David, 44 Misc. (N. Y.) 192, 89 N. Y. Suppl. 812, holding that Highway Law (Laws (1890), c. 568), § 84, requiring commissioners appointed by a county court to determine the necessity of a highway and to assess the damages to take the constitutional oath of office, means the oath prescribed by Const. art. 13, § 1, requiring, among other things, an oath to support the federal and state constitutions.

47. Keenan *v.* Dallas County Com'rs' Ct., 26 Ala. 568 (holding that the statutory form must be precisely pursued); Molett *v.* Keenan, 22 Ala. 484; State *v.* McLeod County, 27 Minn. 90, 6 N. W. 421 (holding that under Sp. Laws (1879), c. 248, requiring the commissioners appointed thereby to survey, locate, and establish a state road in certain counties, to meet and make oath "that they will faithfully and impartially discharge their duties, as provided by this act, and fairly and impartially assess the damage, if any, they may find to be sustained by owners of land through which said road may run, and then proceed to discharge their duties," an oath taken by the commissioners that "we will faithfully proceed to locate and establish said state road according to the provisions of said act, and according to the best of our abilities," is not sufficient); *In re* Cambria St., 75 Pa. St. 357 (an oath by road viewers faithfully to discharge their duties held not to comply with a statutory requirement that they make oath to perform their duties "impartially and according to the best of their judgment"); *In re* Kidder Tp. Road, 1 Kulp (Pa.) 10 (holding that the oath to be taken by road viewers as prescribed by the general road law must be substantially complied with, or it will be fatal to the proceedings upon exceptions to the report); *In re* Jefferson Tp. Road, 2 Lack. Leg. N. (Pa.) 328 (holding that, the statute having prescribed the form of oath to be taken by road viewers, the courts have no discretion to permit a modification).

Oaths held to be sufficient see Com. *v.* Westborough, 3 Mass. 406 (holding that where a warrant to a locating committee particularly describes their whole duty, an oath "faithfully and impartially to perform the service to which they are appointed," or "faithfully and impartially to discharge the trust reposed in them," is sufficient); *In re* Foster Tp. Road, 1 Kulp (Pa.) 100; *In re* Kidder Tp. Road, 9 Luz. Leg. Reg. (Pa.) 10 (the last two cases holding that under the general road law of 1836 (Brightly's Purdon Dig. p. 1283, pl. 87), requiring viewers of a highway to make oath "to perform their duties impartially according to the best of their judgment," an oath "to perform their duties with impartiality and fidelity" is sufficient).

48. Hays *v.* Parrish, 52 Ind. 132. *Contra*, Hoagland *v.* Culvert, 20 N. J. L. 387; State *v.* Barnes, 13 N. J. L. 268; Fisher *v.* Allen, 8 N. J. L. 301; State *v.* Lawrence, 5 N. J. L. 1000; *In re* Middlesex County, etc., Public Road, 4 N. J. L. 396.

49. Galveston, etc., R. Co. *v.* Baudat, 18 Tex. Civ. App. 595, 45 S. W. 939, holding that the oaths of the members of a jury of view need not be reduced to writing.

50. Hoagland *v.* Culvert, 20 N. J. L. 387.

51. *In re* Lower Merion Tp. Road, 8 Pa. Dist. 581, 15 Montg. Co. Rep. 177 (holding that the Pennsylvania act of Aug. 10, 1864, § 2 (Pamphl. Laws 962), authorizing notaries "to take depositions and affidavits," etc., authorizes them to administer an oath to a road viewer, under the act of June 13, 1836, providing that the oath or affirmation must be administered by a magistrate); *In re* East Penn Tp. Road, 2 Pa. Co. Ct. 453 (holding that under the Pennsylvania act of June 13, 1836, providing that the oath will be administered to the viewers of a highway by any magistrate of the county, or by any one of their number, a viewer who is also a justice of the peace could not administer the oath to himself).

52. Crossett *v.* Owens, 110 Ill. 378; *In re* Ryan Tp. Road, 3 Kulp (Pa.) 76.

or over which the road is proposed to be established;[77] or, it has been held, where he is a taxpayer in the town through which the proposed road runs;[78] or where he is a relative of a person thus interested,[79] or a stock-holder in an interested corporation.[80] So in New England a resident in one of several towns through which it is proposed to run a highway cannot act as commissioner in laying it out.[81]

the establishment or non-establishment of the highway. Chase *v.* Rutland, 47 Vt. 393. However, an interest, to disqualify them, must be shown to be an immediate, direct interest in the laying out the road, as distinguished from that general interest which each citizen has in a highway. Parham *v.* Justices Decatur County Inferior Ct., 9 Ga. 341. It must be a direct interest, and not a remote or supposed advantage or disadvantage. Mitchell *v.* Holderness, 29 N. H. 523.

The fact that two persons are related is no reason why both should not be viewers. Crowley *v.* Gallatin County, 14 Mont. 292, 36 Pac. 313.

77. *Indiana.*— Daggy *v.* Green, 12 Ind. 303.

Maryland.— Cumberland Valley R. Co. *v.* Martin, 100 Md. 165, 59 Atl. 714.

Minnesota.— Kieckenapp *v.* Wheeling, 64 Minn. 547, 67 N. W. 662.

New Jersey.— State *v.* Conover, 7 N. J. L. 203, holding that where a caveat is entered against recording the return of surveyors, and the court, in appointing freeholders to view the road and certify whether they believe the same necessary, appoint, by mistake, a person through whose land the road runs as one of the six freeholders to view the road, and he actually proceeds with the five others to view and advise concerning the same, although he does not actually sign the certificate, the court may set aside the appointment as incautiously made.

Pennsylvania.—*In re* Warrington Tp. Road, 8 Del. Co. 79. But see *In re* Nelson's Mill Road, 2 Leg. Op. 54.

See 25 Cent. Dig. tit. "Highways," § 83.

Otherwise in absence of statute see Danvers *v.* Essex County, 2 Metc. (Mass.) 185; Webster *v.* Washington County, 26 Minn. 220, 2 N. W. 697 (as to adjacent landowners); Foot *v.* Stiles, 57 N. Y. 399; People *v.* Landreth, 1 Hun (N. Y.) 544.

Removal of disqualification by conveyance. — A landowner who has been appointed commissioner may remove his disqualification by conveying his lands before acting. Gray *v.* Middletown, 56 Vt. 53.

78. *In re* New Boston, 49 N. H. 328. *Contra,* Wilbraham *v.* Hampden County, 11 Pick. (Mass.) 322; Parsell *v.* Mann, 30 N. J. L. 530. And see Thompson *v.* Goldthwait, 132 Ind. 20, 31 N. E. 451.

79. *Arkansas.*— Beck *v.* Biggers, 66 Ark. 292, 50 S. W. 514, father-in-law or brother of the principal petitioner.

Kentucky.— Phillips *v.* Tucker, 3 Metc. 69, brother-in-law of a petitioner.

Maine.—*In re* Clifford, 59 Me. 262, uncle of petitioner.

Massachusetts.—Taylor *v.* Worcester County, 105 Mass. 225, brother-in-law of owner of land to be taken.

Pennsylvania.— *In re* Hellam County Road, 6 York Leg. Rec. 149, brother-in-law of a petitioner. But see *In re* Lower Windsor Tp. Road, 29 Pa. St. 18, holding that it is no objection to the competency of a person as viewer that he is related to a person living near the highway and having an interest in the location thereof, but who is not one of the petitioners therefor.

See 25 Cent. Dig. tit. "Highways," § 83.

Contra.— Groton *v.* Hurlburt, 22 Conn. 178, holding also that a statute disqualifying judges and justices of the peace from acting in civil actions by reason of relationship does not apply to the acts of commissioners in surveying and laying out highways, as such acts are not judicial in their character.

However, an engineer is not ineligible because his brother-in-law owns real estate within the limits assessable for the construction of the road laid out, the viewers alone being empowered to make the assessments, and his duty being simply to aid the viewers in the location of the work, and in making estimates of cost, etc. Thompson *v.* Goldthwait, 132 Ind. 20, 31 N. E. 451. So a county commissioner is not disqualified by reason of the fact that his brother and his son are among the petitioners for the highway, in the absence of a showing that such persons have any other than a public interest in the matter. Wilbraham *v.* Hampden County, 11 Pick. (Mass.) 322. Where one of twelve freeholders appointed to view the site of a proposed road and certify as to its necessity was a brother-in-law of a trustee of a church, land of which would be taken if the proposed location were adopted, he was not such "kin to the owner" of the land, within the statute, as to be incapacitated from acting. People *v.* Cline, 23 Barb. (N. Y.) 197. And the fact that a petitioner's wife was aunt of a wife of one of the road viewers is not ground for setting aside their report, where there was no intimacy between petitioner and the viewer. *In re* Sadsbury Road, 9 Pa. Co. Ct. 521.

80. *In re* New Boston, 49 N. H. 328.

81. Mitchell *v.* Holderness, 29 N. H. 523.

However, a county commissioner is not disqualified by reason of being an inhabitant of a town to the line of which the road in question extends, and with a road in which it is intended to connect. Monterey *v.* Berkshire County, 7 Cush. (Mass.) 394. And although a commissioner who resides in one of several towns through which a highway is sought to be laid out is interested in the question whether the way shall be laid out, he is not disqualified, after a board of disinterested commissioners has adjudged that the way is necessary and determined its course, from acting in laying out any section in another town which cannot affect the course of the way within the town in which he resides.

missioners will not be set aside on the ground that the notice to the selectmen and landholders of the hearing was insufficient, in the absence of anything to show that any one was prejudiced;[1] and notice of a view to open or vacate a road has been held necessary to an adjoining property-owner only when his land is affected thereby.[2]

(2) CONTENTS AND SUFFICIENCY. The sufficiency of the notice must of course be determined largely by the statute or order under which the notice is given.[3] The notice should be of the time and place of the meeting of the commissioners and viewers;[4] and both time[5] and place[6] should be specified with particularity. It must describe the starting point of the road to be laid out[7] and the land included in the proposed highway.[8] If in writing, the notice should be authenticated by a responsible signature.[9] In the absence of a provision to the contrary, notice need

is laid out. Kelly *v.* Honea, (Civ. App. 1903) 73 S. W. 846.

1. *In re* Ford, 45 N. H. 400.

2. Matter of Susquehanna River Road, 1 Pearson (Pa.) 59.

3. See cases cited *infra*, this note.

Notice held sufficient see Lawrence *v.* Nahant, 136 Mass. 477; Copeland *v.* Packard, 16 Pick. (Mass.) 217; *In re* Toppan, 24 N. H. 43; Parish *v.* Gilmanton, 11 N. H. 293.

Where the statute requires a notice that the meeting is called "to decide" upon the application, this requirement is not satisfied by a notice of a meeting "to examine and consider" (Austin *v.* Allen, 6 Wis. 134); or by a notice by the town supervisors that they will meet at a certain time and place to take into consideration an application to lay out a highway (Babb *v.* Carver, 7 Wis. 124). See also Fitchburg R. Co. *v.* Fitchburg, 121 Mass. 132.

The notice required by Pennsylvania act of April 15, 1891, providing that notice of the time and place of holding a view for laying out a public road shall be given to the county commissioners, must be actual notice. *In re* Ryon Tp. Road, 4 Pa. Dist. 736.

Extrinsic evidence is inadmissible to explain a notice for the establishment of a highway, respecting the proposed location thereof, in determining the sufficiency of such notice. Butterfield *v.* Pollock, 45 Iowa 257.

Sufficiency of entry of record of notice. — The requirement of Gen. St. (1901) § 6018, that a record of the notice of the meeting of viewers shall be entered in the commissioners' journal, is satisfied by copying the contents of such notice in the journal, no references as to its publication being required. Molyneux *v.* Grimes, (Kan. 1908) 98 Pac. 278.

4. Audubon *v.* Hand, 231 Ill. 334, 83 N. E. 196; Damon *v.* Baldwin Town Bd., 101 Minn. 414, 112 N. W. 536; State *v.* Auchard, 22 Mont. 14, 55 Pac. 361 (holding that it is necessary to jurisdiction that the affidavit show that notice of the place, as well as the time, of the meeting of the viewers was given); State *v.* O'Connor, 78 Wis. 282, 47 N. W. 433. But see Orono *v.* Penobscot County, 30 Me. 302, holding that a notice given by county commissioners of the time and place appointed for viewing the route in relation to the location of a highway need not fix the time and place for hearing the parties.

5. Damon *v.* Baldwin Town Bd., 101 Minn. 414, 112 N. W. 536. See also People *v.* Wallace, 4 Thomps. & C. (N. Y.) 438.

6. Audubon *v.* Hand, 231 Ill. 334, 83 N. E. 196 (holding that the statute means some definite point or locality, and the site of a proposed road one mile long is not such place or locality); Hammon *v.* Highway Com'rs, 38 Ill. App. 237 (holding a notice of the place of meeting as "at the sight of the proposed road in said town" too indefinite, and the proceedings based therein void); Oran Highway Com'rs *v.* Hoblit, 19 Ill. App. 259 (holding that notice of the place of a meeting to examine a proposed route of a highway is insufficient, where it declares that the meeting will be in a certain village, which is composed of a dozen houses, without stating the particular house).

Notice held sufficiently specific as to place see Smith *v.* Hudson Tp. Highway Com'rs, 150 Ill. 385, 36 N. E. 967 (where commissioners of highways gave notice that they would meet at the west end of a proposed road for the purpose of viewing the road); Thompson *v.* Berlin, 87 Minn. 7, 91 N. W. 25; Thompson *v.* Emmons, 24 N. J. L. 45 (holding that notice for a surveyor's meeting "at the house of A" was sufficient without specifying the township, the alleged deficiency not appearing to have prevented any one's attendance); *In re* Mt. Joy Tp. Road, 13 Lanc. L. Rev. (Pa.) 383 (holding that a notice of view is sufficient, although it did not give the proper christian name of the proprietor of the hotel where the viewers met, the surname having been correctly given).

7. Behrens *v.* Melrose Tp. Highway Com'rs, 169 Ill. 558, 48 N. E. 578, holding, however, that a notice of a meeting to finally determine on the laying out of the road is not fatally defective for failing to describe the starting point of the road with certainty, where it refers to the petition, where the route is clearly described, and the party objecting has not been misled.

8. State *v.* O'Connor, 78 Wis. 282, 47 N. W. 433, where, however, a notice was held sufficient which describes the land included in the proposed highway as a portion of the right of way of a railway company, giving the government subdivisions of which it is a part.

9. *In re* Springfield Tp. Road, 6 Del. Co. (Pa.) 94, holding that notice of a road view

not be in writing if the owner is notified personally and attends the survey;[10] but a rule requiring written notice of a road view to be given to the owner or occupier of lands is not complied with by giving verbal notice to a tenant.[11] Notice of the time and place of the surveyors' meeting may be served by the applicants or any other person in their behalf.[12]

(3) MANNER OF GIVING. Personal notice is necessary where required by rule of court [13] or by statute; [14] but under some statutes personal notice is not necessary,[15] notice by posting [16] or by publication or advertisement [17] being held sufficient. And the appointment of commissioners and viewers, and their visiting the ground, have been held to be circumstances of such notoriety as to put all persons on their guard that they may know when to attend court to be heard.[18]

(4) TIME. The notice must be given the number of days before the meeting specified in the statute,[19] or, in the absence of specific provision enacted by the

must be signed by some person, either by the clerk, the viewers, persons interested, or some other responsible person or persons.

A notice of hearing signed by the chairman of the board is sufficient, where the statute does not direct by whom it shall be signed. Peavey *v.* Wolfborough, 37 N. H. 286. And a notice of a meeting of highway commissioners to view the route of a highway, signed "by order of the commissioners, A. B., Chairman," is sufficient over an objection that it does not appear that the notice was issued at a meeting of three or more of the commissioners. Com. *v.* Berkshire County, 8 Pick. (Mass.) 343.

A notice signed by a majority of the committee and duly served on all landholders interested was sufficient. Goodwin *v.* Wethersfield, 43 Conn. 437.

10. Humboldt County *v.* Dinsmore, 75 Cal. 604, 17 Pac. 710.

11. *In re* Clinton Tp. Road, 3 Pa. Co. Ct. 170.

A verbal communication, made by the selectmen to a landowner at the time of hearing on a petition for a new highway, that they had decided to lay out the proposed highway, no return or record of the laying out having then been made, is not sufficient notice of the laying out to limit the time within which such landowner may appeal to sixty days, under N. H. Gen. St. c. 63, § 11. Freeman *v.* Cornish, 52 N. H. 141.

12. State *v.* Atkinson, 27 N. J. L. 420.

13. *In re* Lower Swatara Tp. Road, 6 Pa. Dist. 686.

Personal notice to owners residing out of the state is unnecessary, notice by mail being reasonable notice. Crane *v.* Camp, 12 Conn. 464.

Service held sufficient see *In re* Moreland Tp. Road, 13 Montg. Co. Rep. (Pa.) 71; State *v.* Pierce County Super. Ct., 47 Wash. 11, 91 Pac. 241.

Service held insufficient see Damon *v.* Baldwin Town Bd., 101 Minn. 414, 112 N. W. 536. See also Evans *v.* Santana Live-Stock, etc., Co., 81 Tex. 622, 17 S. W. 232, holding that notice of proceedings by viewers appointed to lay out a road, served on one who is the agent of a corporation, does not bind the corporation, where it does not purport to be notice served on the corporation's agent.

14. Damon *v.* Baldwin Town Bd., 101 Minn. 414, 112 N. W. 536.

15. Murphy *v.* Beard, 138 Ind. 560, 38 N. E. 33; Matter of David, 44 Misc. (N. Y.) 192, 89 N. Y. Suppl. 812; Clayton's Case, 1 Walk. (Pa.) 527.

16. Frizell *v.* Rogers, 82 Ill. 109; Matter of David, 44 Misc. (N. Y.) 192, 89 N. Y. Suppl. 812.

Notice held to be properly posted see People *v.* La Grange Tp. Bd., 2 Mich. 187.

Improper posting see *In re* West Manheim Road, 1 Pa. Dist. 800 (holding that where a rule of court requires notice of the meeting of viewers of a public road to be posted at private dwellings along the route of the proposed road, the posting of the same at a remote blacksmith shop is not sufficient); *In re* West Manchester Tp. Road, 8 York Leg. Rec. (Pa.) 169.

17. Murphy *v.* Beard, 138 Ind. 560, 38 N. E. 33; Freetown *v.* Bristol County, 9 Pick. (Mass.) 46 (holding that publication of a notice by highway commissioners, to all persons interested, of the time and place appointed for viewing a road prayed for, in a newspaper printed within the county, is sufficient); *In re* Sterrett Tp. Road, 114 Pa. St. 627, 7 Atl. 765.

18. Stewart *v.* Hines County Police Bd., 25 Miss. 479; *In re* Baldwin, etc., Road, 3 Grant (Pa.) 62.

In New Hampshire it has been held that the notice of the original petition for a highway is held to be sufficient notice of a hearing of all matters properly and legally arising on that petition from beginning to end, and therefore notice of proceedings by the commissioners need not be given. Chandler *v.* Candia, 54 N. H. 178.

19. Coquard *v.* Bœhmer, 81 Mich. 445, 45 N. W. 996; Detroit Sharpshooters' Assoc. *v.* Hamtramck Highway Com'rs, 34 Mich. 36; Anderson *v.* San Francisco, 92 Minn. 57, 99 N. W. 420; Matter of Niel, 55 Misc. (N. Y.) 317, 106 N. Y. Suppl. 479, where, however, there was held to be a sufficient compliance with the highway law, requiring five days' notice of such application.

In computing the time, the day on which the notice is served and the day of meeting must be excluded. Coquard *v.* Bœhmer, 81 Mich. 445, 45 N. W. 996.

(C) *Adjournments and Continuances.* It is competent for the commissioners or viewers to adjourn, at their discretion, to another time and place,[28] the commissioners being the sole judges of what is a sufficient cause to adjourn;[29] but where the statute limits the number of days for which adjournment may be made, proceedings at a meeting adjourned beyond the time specified are void,[30] the unauthorized adjournment being in effect a denial of the application of the highway.[31] It has been held that the commissioners must give notice of the adjournment to all interested parties;[32] and that if, after a commissioner sits pursuant to a proper notice, he adjourns the hearing to another day without designating the time and place, he thereby loses jurisdiction to proceed further;[33] but other cases hold that all parties originally notified must take notice of such adjournments without any new notice.[34] The omission of commissioners to adjourn from day to day, pending proceedings on a petition for a highway, is an irregularity which is not jurisdictional in its character.[35]

(D) *Proceedings by Part of Commissioners, Viewers, or Other Officers.* Under some of the statutes it is held that a majority of the commissioners or viewers can act in laying out the road.[36] This is so of course where the statute expressly so provides,[37] or even where there is a general statute providing that majorities of boards of this kind can act.[38] Under other statutes it is held that when several persons are authorized to view a road, they must all deliberate and view the proposed road,[39] although a majority may decide[40] or make the report,[41] unless the

an owner or occupant who is not described in such report.

28. *Connecticut.*— Goodwin *v.* Wethersfield, 43 Conn. 437.

Maine.—Orono *v.* Penobscot County, 30 Me. 302; Harkness *v.* Waldo County, 26 Me. 353.

Michigan.— Wilson *v.* Atkin, 80 Mich. 247, 45 N. W. 94.

Minnesota.—Burkleo *v.* Washington County, 38 Minn. 441, 38 N. W. 108.

New Jersey.— State *v.* Vanbuskirk, 21 N. J. L. 86, holding also that the power to adjourn, given to surveyors by Rev. St. p. 520, § 12, is not restricted to the case where only a part meet; but the whole six, when met, may adjourn.

New York.— Brooklyn *v.* Patchen, 8 Wend. 47.

Ohio.— Butman *v.* Fowler, 17 Ohio 101.

Pennsylvania.— *In re* Paradise Tp. Road, 29 Pa. St. 20.

South Dakota.— Issenhuth *v.* Baum, 11 S. D. 223, 76 N. W. 928.

See 25 Cent. Dig. tit. "Highways," § 99.

29. *In re* Hampstead, 19 N. H. 343, holding that where no corruption is surmised, the court will not revise the decision of the commissioners on a motion to adjourn, founded on the state of the weather or of the earth.

30. Wilson *v.* Atkin, 80 Mich. 247, 45 N. W. 94; State *v.* Castle, 44 Wis. 670.

31. State *v.* Castle, 44 Wis. 670.

32. Goodwin *v.* Wethersfield, 43 Conn. 437. See also *In re* Britton, 19 N. H. 445.

33. Dixon *v.* Port Huron Tp. Highway Com'rs, 75 Mich. 225, 42 N. W. 814.

34. Weymouth *v.* York County, 86 Me. 391, 29 Atl. 1100; Westport *v.* Bristol County, 9 Allen (Mass.) 203 (holding that county commissioners may complete the laying out of a highway at an adjourned or subsequent meeting without any new notice, the parties in interest having been previously fully heard); *In re* Peach Bottom Tp. Road, 3 Pennyp. (Pa.) 541.

35. Allison *v.* McDonough County Highway Com'rs, 54 Ill. 170.

36. Hays *v.* Parrish, 52 Ind. 132; Dartmouth *v.* Bristol, 153 Mass. 12, 26 N. E. 425; Jones *v.* Andover, 9 Pick. (Mass.) 146; Hall *v.* Manchester, 40 N. H. 410; *In re* Church St., 49 Barb. (N. Y.) 455.

37. Eatontown Tp. *v.* Wolley, 49 N. J. L. 386, 8 Atl. 517 [*affirmed* in 50 N. J. L. 177, 17 Atl. 1103]; *In re* State Road, 60 Pa. St. 330; *In re* Paradise Tp. Road, 29 Pa. St. 20.

38. Hall *v.* Manchester, 40 N. H. 410, 39 N. H. 295. See also Dartmouth *v.* Bristol County, 153 Mass. 12, 26 N. E. 425.

39. Com. *v.* Ipswich, 2 Pick. (Mass.) 70; State *v.* Shreve, 4 N. J. L. 341; Babcock *v.* Lamb, 1 Cow. (N. Y.) 238; *In re* Paradise Tp. Road, 29 Pa. St. 20; *In re* Pike Tp. Road, 30 Pa. Super. Ct. 644; *In re* Road, etc., Viewers, 8 Pa. Co. Ct. 557; *In re* Plains Tp. Road, 7 Kulp (Pa.) 233; *In re* Butler Tp. Road, 6 Kulp (Pa.) 443; *In re* Ryan Tp. Road, 3 Kulp (Pa.) 158; *In re* Ryan Tp. Road, 3 Kulp. (Pa.) 76.

Where one member does not qualify or act, proceedings of the other two commissioners have been held erroneous. *In re* Wells County Road, 7 Ohio St. 16. *Contra,* Hays *v.* Parrish, 52 Ind. 132. See People *v.* Schellenger, 10 N. Y. Suppl. 947.

40. Babcock *v.* Lamb, 1 Cow. (N. Y.) 238; *In re* State Road, 60 Pa. St. 330; *In re* Paradise Tp. Road, 29 Pa. St. 20; *In re* Pike Tp. Road, 30 Pa. Super. Ct. 644; *In re* Plains Tp. Road, 7 Kulp (Pa.) 233.

41. Bronnenburg *v.* O'Bryant, 139 Ind. 17, 38 N. E. 416; Hays *v.* Parrish, 52 Ind. 132; Jones *v.* Andover, 9 Pick. (Mass.) 146; *In re* Paradise Tp. Road, 29 Pa. St. 20; *In re* New Hanover Tp. Road, 18 Pa. St. 220.

character, as whether it is a town or private way, or whether it is necessary for public or private purposes.[98]

(4) REPORT AS TO DAMAGES AND COST OF ROAD. It is commonly required that the report shall contain a finding as to the damages which would result to property owners from the establishment of the proposed road;[99] and it is sometimes neces-

statute Keenan v. Dallas County Com'rs, Ct., 26 Ala. 568.

In Kentucky the report of road viewers must state the public and private conveniences to result from the proposed road (Winston v. Waggoner, 5 J. J. Marsh. 41; Fletcher v. Fugate, 3 J. J. Marsh. 631; Abney v. Barnett, 1 Bibb 557), and state them specifically (Wood v. Campbell, 14 B. Mon. 422; Peck v. Whitney, 6 B. Mon. 117; Foreman v. Allen, 2 Bibb 581).

In Maine, where the charter of a bridge company (Priv. Laws (1879), c. 128, § 6) provided that no way should at any time thereafter be located leading from said bridge to a certain place, which shall be for the necessary convenience of said company, unless the entire cost thereof be defrayed by said company, it was not sufficient that the committee adjudged the way to be a common convenience and necessity, but they must also adjudge, after due notice to the bridge company, whether the way would be a necessary convenience to the company. Shattuck's Appeal, 73 Me. 318. But under Acts (1832), c. 42, requiring county commissioners in proceedings for the laying out of the road to adjudge the road to be of "common convenience and necessity," it is sufficient if they find it of "convenience and necessity," omitting the word "common" (Cushing v. Gay, 23 Me. 9); and under St. (1821) c. 118, the evidence that a road laid out by the selectmen of a town is for the benefit of the town, or of some one or more individuals in it, is the approval and allowance of it by the town at a legal meeting or of the county commissioners on appeal, and the selectmen therefore need not state that fact in their report (*In re* Limerick, 18 Me. 183).

In New Jersey, in laying out a road, the requirements of the statute that the surveyors shall so lay it "as may appear to them to be most for the public and private convenience," and "in such a manner as to do the least injury to private property," are matters of substance, and the return of the surveyors must show a compliance with them. State v. Lippincott, 25 N. J. L. 434.

In Oregon the viewers, in proceedings under Laws (1903), p. 269 (Road Laws 1903), § 20, to locate a public road from petitioner's residence to another public road, being required by law to locate the road "so as to do the least damage," where this fact appears from their report, it is not necessary that the report show that the road located by them is on the most accessible or desirable route. Kemp v. Polk County, 46 Oreg. 546, 81 Pac. 240.

In Vermont, under Acts (1882), No. 14, providing that commissioners appointed to lay out a highway may make their decision to lay out the road conditional upon payment by petitioners, especially to be benefited, of such sums as they may think proper toward the expense of laying out and building the road, a report showing an unconditional decision by the commissioners that the convenience of individuals and the public good required the road to be laid out, is not affected by the fact that the decision as to convenience and necessity is made conditional upon the payment of part of the expenses by one who was benefited, but who did not sign the petition, although he agreed to make the payments, as it is immaterial at whose expense it was built. Hancock v. Worcester, 62 Vt. 106, 18 Atl. 1041. And a report of commissioners laying out a highway in such manner as to protect a railroad will not be set aside if it imposes no additional burden upon defendant town, the error being only formal. Orcutt v. Bartland, 52 Vt. 612.

98. Christ Church v. Woodward, 26 Me. 172 (holding that the return of the selectmen of the laying out of a way must state whether it is a town or private way, as in the one case the damage is to be paid by the individuals benefited and in the other by the town); *In re* Herrick Tp., etc., Road, 16 Pa. Super. Ct. 579 (holding that the viewers' report should state whether the road is necessary for public or private purposes).

However, a report of viewers that they have laid out a road for public use is a sufficient compliance with the order to state whether it is deemed necessary for a public or private road. *In re* Norriton Tp., etc., Road, 4 Pa. St. 337. So it is a sufficient adjudication that the road is a public one if the viewers say they lay out the road for public use. *In re* App's Tavern Road, 17 Serg. & R. (Pa.) 388. And it is not a sufficient exception to the report of a jury of review in the case of a street that it does not state whether the street be necessary for a public or a private road, where the report adopts and confirms the record of the first jury, in which the street is laid out as a public one. Greenleaf Ct. Case, 4 Whart. (Pa.) 514. Under Pa. Act, June 13, 1836, § 3, requiring the viewers of a road to state in their report whether the road is necessary for a public or private road, the report by viewers that they had laid out and "do return for public use the following road" was sufficient, as showing that it was necessary for a public road. *In re* West Hempfield Tp. Road, 4 Lanc. Bar (Pa.) 7.

99. *Indiana.*— Peed v. Brenneman, 72 Ind. 288.

Massachusetts.— Com. v. Coombs, 2 Mass. 489.

New Hampshire.— *In re* Patten, 16 N. H. 277.

New Jersey.—In laying out a highway over land of any one not an applicant therefor, the

errors and mistakes,[56] it being held that the question of the necessity of a proposed public road must be determined in the duly appointed mode of proceeding by viewers, reviewers, and, in the discretion of the court, re-reviewers; and it is error for the court to determine the question on evidence given before it on appeal from the reports of viewers,[57] the court being held to exercise the same control over commissioners for laying out a road, etc., that it does over arbitrators, and no more, and that it will not review their proceedings by way of appeal.[58] Elsewhere the report of viewers concerning the establishment of a road is held to be designed to aid the court, but not in any manner to control it;[59] and where the view is taken upon the hearing evidence may be introduced in regard to the pro-

In **New Jersey** jurisdiction to determine the necessity of a road is conferred on the surveyors exclusively, and the power to review their determination is lodged exclusively in freeholders who shall be delegated to review their report; and unless the decision of the surveyors shall be reversed by the freeholders, the return of the surveyors is to be recorded without a review by the court. Carpenter *v.* Brown, 53 N. J. L. 181, 20 Atl. 738; Hoffman *v.* Rodman, 39 N. J. L. 252; State *v.* Bishop, 39 N. J. L. 226; State *v.* Justice, 24 N. J. L. 413. The common pleas court has, however, jurisdiction to determine whether the proceedings have been conducted according to the directions of the statute, and may set aside the surveyors' report or the freeholders' certificate for non-conformity with the statutory requirements or illegality in matter of substance, but cannot review the surveyors' determination as to the necessity of the road, nor set aside their return on the ground that their judgment was erroneous. State *v.* Bishop, *supra*.

In **Virginia**, where landowners are summoned under Code (1887), § 949, providing that, on the favorable report of the viewers, if the court be in favor of establishing the road, it shall award process to summon proprietors to show cause against the establishment of the road, the burden of proof is on the landowners to overcome the *prima facie* case made by the report of the viewers. Heininger *v.* Peery, 102 Va. 896, 47 S. E. 1013.

56. *Illinois.*— Cole *v.* Peoria, 18 Ill. 301, where a party was prevented from adducing evidence before the commissioners by reason of the statement of one of them to him that their minds were made up.

New Hampshire.— Thompson *v.* Conway, 53 N. H. 622.

New Jersey.— State *v.* Justice, 24 N. J. L. 413.

Pennsylvania.— *In re* East Franklin Tp. Road, 8 Pa. Co. Ct. 590 (holding that the report of road viewers, so far as it relates to the necessity for the road, is entitled to the same respect as the verdict of a jury, and ought not to be disregarded, save for errors of law apparent on its face or misconduct on the part of viewers); *In re* Berks St., 15 Phila. 381 (holding that the court will not disturb the finding of a road jury before whom all the facts have been properly placed, and by whom the subject has been maturely considered, merely because the evidence might support conclusions somewhat different, and the court does not fully agree with the jury in all their determinations); *In re* Byberry New Road, 6 Phila. 384 (holding that where the report of viewers is not palpably erroneous, the court will not interfere with their finding upon mere allegations of mistake as to facts).

Vermont.— Shattuck *v.* Waterville, 27 Vt. 600, holding that if commissioners appointed by the court upon a petition to lay out a road report adversely, the court can take no further action, and the petition must be dismissed unless improper practices upon the committee are shown.

57. *In re* Ohio, etc., Tp. Road, 166 Pa. St. 132, 31 Atl. 74; Cummings *v.* Kendall County, 7 Tex. Civ. App. 164, 26 S. W. 439, holding that Rev. Civ. St. art. 4361, providing that the commissioners' court may, on their own motion, open new roads, does not authorize the courts to change the report made by the jury of view as to the location of the road, or as to damages, without a hearing, or without complying with article 4360*a*, § 4, which provides for the rejection of the report, and the appointment of another jury.

58. Bushwick, etc., Bridge, etc., Co. *v.* Ebbets, 3 Edw. (N. Y.) 353.

59. Molyneux *v.* Grimes, 78 Kan. 830, 98 Pac. 278 (holding that the provision of Gen. St. (1901) § 6021, that if the viewers report against a proposed road, and the commissioners think the report just, no further preceeding shall be had, implies that the commissioners may establish the road notwithstanding the adverse report, if their opinion is contrary to that of the viewers); Bennett *v.* Greenup County, 17 S. W. 167, 13 Ky. L. Rep. 349; Vedder *v.* Marion County, 28 Oreg. 77, 36 Pac. 535, 41 Pac. 3 (holding that Hill Annot. Laws Oreg. § 4065, providing that, the county court being satisfied that a road sought to be established will be of public utility, the viewers' report being favorable thereto, the court shall cause the report, survey, and plat to be recorded, and the road shall thenceforth be considered a highway, does not make the favorable report of viewers binding on the court); *In re* Blakely Road, 8 Pa. Co. Ct. 592 (holding that where a road is projected almost wholly through a borough not benefited thereby, and is also parallel with another road which would be rendered useless, and the court is not satisfied that the road is necessary, the report of the jury laying it out will be set aside).

reports the court will have regard to the public interest.[90] After reviewers have filed their report in the clerk's office, it is competent for the court, during the same term, to vacate their appointment for sufficient reasons, and to set aside all the proceedings thereon.[91] Where viewers and re-reviewers unanimously favor a road, it will not be refused because two of three reviewers report adversely to its establishment.[92] A report of the jury of review is sufficient if it adopts and confirms the original return of the viewers.[93] Where viewers have recommended a certain width, and this was the width fixed by the court when it confirmed the report nisi, and the re-reviewers report and recommend "the same road, with its courses and distances as reported by the viewers in this case," the omission to attach a copy of the plan reported by the viewers to the report of the re-reviewers is not a fatal defect.[94]

h. Location [95] — (I) *COURSE* — (A) *By Whom Selected.* Local statutes govern the body empowered to select the route of a highway.[96]

(B) *Where Located* — (1) IN GENERAL. Statutes sometimes provide that highways shall be laid out only over vacant[97] private[98] land. While it is true as

see *In re* New Washington Road, 23 Pa. St. 485, where the court confirmed a report of viewers absolutely, and of reviewers *nisi*, on the same day, and it was held that the proceedings were erroneous.

90. *In re* Dallas Road, 7 Luz. Leg. Reg. (Pa.) 147. See also *In re* Aston Tp. Road, 4 Yeates (Pa.) 372, holding that where there have been different views of a road, and separate returns thereon, it is immaterial whether any two returns agree, since the court of sessions is bound to approve such return as will most conduce to the public good and do the least injury to private property.

Burden of proving necessity for road.— Where there is a report of viewers in favor of a proposed road, and a report of reviewers against it, it is a proper cause for a re-review; but, in the absence of such re-review, the court must decide between the two reports, and in such case the burden of showing the necessity for the road rests upon the petitioners therefor. *In re* Hatfield Tp. Road, 1 Pa. Dist. 820.

The difficulty in keeping in proper repair existing roads is sufficient reason for refusing to open a new road where its necessity is doubtful, where there is a report of viewers in favor of a proposed road, and a report of reviewers against it, and no re-review is asked. *In re* Hazle Tp. Road, 6 Kulp (Pa.) 463.

91. *In re* Baldwin Tp., etc., Road, 36 Pa. St. 9.

92. *In re* Manheim Tp. Road, 5 Lanc. Bar (Pa.) Feb. 14, 1874.

93. *In re* Moreland Tp. Road, 13 Montg. Co. Rep. (Pa.) 71.

94. *In re* Stowe Tp. Road, 20 Pa. Super. Ct. 404.

95. Location of streets see MUNICIPAL CORPORATIONS, 28 Cyc. 838.

96. *Connecticut.*—Windham *v.* Litchfield, 22 Conn. 226.

Louisiana.— Calder *v.* Police Jury, 44 La. Ann. 173, 10 So. 726, police juries and jury of freeholders.

Massachusetts.— Lanesborough *v.* Berkshire County, 22 Pick. 278; Merrill *v.* Berkshire, 11 Pick. 269.

North Carolina.— Welch *v.* Piercy, 29 N. C. 365, jury determines line between termini.

Pennsylvania.— *In re* Sadsbury Tp. Roads, 147 Pa. St. 471, 23 Atl. 772 (viewers and not court should designate route); *In re* McConnell's Mill Road, 32 Pa. St. 285 (route for viewers to decide); Com. *v.* Plymouth Tp., 19 Pa. Super. Ct. 408 (supervisors and not viewers).

Rhode Island.— Watson *v.* South Kingstown, 5 R. I. 562, precise course voted by town council and order given to mark out "as may be most advantageous to the public."

Texas.— Ehilers *v.* State, 44 Tex. Cr. 156, 69 S. W. 148, commissioners' court and not overseer may locate road.

See 25 Cent. Dig. tit. "Highways," § 138; and see the statutes of the different states.

Defects cured.— On petition for a public road over private property, designating the exact route desired, the court ordered that the road be laid in accordance with the petition. The viewers appointed by the court thereafter reported that they had laid the road as ordered, and so "as to do the least possible damage to the land over which it passed." It was held that while the order of the court might imply that the road should be laid exactly as called for in the petition, regardless of damage, the report of the viewers that it had been so laid as to cause the least damage cured the defect. Fanning *v.* Gilliland, 37 Oreg. 369, 61 Pac. 636, 62 Pac. 209, 82 Am. St. Rep. 758.

The board having once laid out a road have no power to change it. Farrelly *v.* Kane, 172 Ill. 415, 50 N. E. 118.

97. Fredericks *v.* Hoffmeister, 62 N. J. L. 565, 41 Atl. 722, not through building even of an applicant for a highway.

98. Gist *v.* Owings, 95 Md. 302, 52 Atl. 395 (not through lands owned by the county); Hope Tp. Highway Com'rs *v.* Ludwick, 151 Mich. 498, 115 N. W. 419, 15 L. R. A. N. S. 1170 (not over or into navigable water); *In re* Catawissa Tp., etc., Road,

often have authority to change it.[15] If one through whose land the road would run agrees that it may be run in a given way, it cannot be established in any other way without first summoning the landowner.[16]

(2) FROM REPORT AND ORDER. Ordinarily no change will be permitted in the lay-out from the report of the officers designated.[17]

(II) *LENGTH.* Public roads must be laid out neither shorter [18] nor longer [19] than ordered or petitioned for.

(III) *WIDTH*[20] — (A) *How Fixed.* Statutes sometimes fix the width of public highways,[21] and sometimes leave it to the discretion of the local authorities to fix

out, taken as a whole, answers substantially the description in the application. Covert *v.* Hulick, 33 N. J. L. 307.

Presumption as to materiality of variance. — When the viewers reported only the admission that the street had not been opened according to the draft, "but had been changed to run more at right angles through the property of the petitioner," and it did not appear how much the divergence was, whether material or so slight as to come within the discretion of the proper authorities, there was no error in the confirmation of the report by the court below. Schuylkill County's Appeal, 38 Pa. St. 459.

15. *Connecticut.*— Clark *v.* Middlebury, 47 Conn. 331, selectmen.

Maryland.— Smith *v.* Goldsborough, 80 Md. 49, 30 Atl. 574.

Minnesota.— State *v.* Thompson, 46 Minn. 302, 48 N. W. 1111.

Pennsylvania.— *In re* State St., 8 Pa. St. 485, not confined to course suggested.

Texas.— Kelley *v.* Honea, 32 Tex. Civ. App. 220, 73 S. W. 846.

See 25 Cent. Dig. tit. "Highways," § 139.

Re-reviewers may recommend a route of their own, and return the plan of such route. *In re* Abington Tp. Road, 14 Serg. & R. (Pa.) 31.

16. Lewis *v.* Smith, 1 A. K. Marsh (Ky.) 158.

17. *Alabama.*— Lowndes County Com'rs' Ct. *v.* Bowie, 34 Ala. 461, no discretion left in the order.

Kansas.— Shaffer *v.* Weech, 34 Kan. 595, 9 Pac. 202.

Kentucky.— Com. *v.* Logan, 5 Litt. 286.

New Jersey.—Whittingham *v.* Hopkins, 70 N. J. L. 322, 57 Atl. 402, lay-out deviating more than the width of the road is void.

North Dakota.— Dunstan *v.* Jamestown, 7 N. D. 1, 72 N. W. 899.

Pennsylvania.— Furniss *v.* Furniss, 29 Pa. St. 15, from report of viewers.

See 25 Cent. Dig. tit. "Highways," § 138.

The route but not the termini may be varied by a committee appointed by the court. Goodwin *v.* Hallowell, 12 Me. 271.

Consent of the interested landowners has been held not to authorize a variance. Calder *v.* Chapman, 8 Pa. St. 522. However, a change of twenty feet in the final location of a road from that originally laid out and surveyed, when it appears to have been by the consent of those affected thereby, does not avoid the proceedings upon the objection thereafter made by a landowner whose lines are not affected by the change. Miller *v.* Hamilton County Com'rs, 9 Ohio Dec. (Reprint) 312, 12 Cinc. L. Bul. 152.

Slight changes may be made. Lowndes County Com'rs Ct. *v.* Bowie, 34 Ala. 461 (regarding nature of ground); Riggs *v.* Winterode, 100 Md. 439, 59 Atl. 762 (in course).

18. *California.*— Brannan *v.* Mecklenburg, 40 Cal. 672.

Michigan.— People *v.* Springwells Tp. Bd., 12 Mich. 434.

New Hampshire.— Ford *v.* Danbury, 44 N. H. 388.

New Jersey.— Freeman *v.* Price, 63 N. J. L. 151, 43 Atl. 432 (void where laid out in two unconnected parts); State *v.* Cassedy, 33 N. J. L. 179.

Pennsylvania.— Matter of Twenty-eighth St., 11 Phila. 436.

See 25 Cent. Dig. tit. "Highways," § 140.

Partial lay-out held to be valid see Harkness *v.* Waldo County, 26 Me. 353; Princeton *v.* Worcester County, 17 Pick. (Mass.) 154.

A short difference is immaterial. Riggs *v.* Winterode, 100 Md. 439, 59 Atl. 762.

19. State *v.* Molly, 18 Iowa 525; Anderson's Appeal, 25 Leg. Int. (Pa.) 77; Megrath *v.* Nickerson, 24 Wash. 235, 64 Pac. 163.

Unauthorized extension over land at request of owner held not to vitiate the layout see State *v.* O'Connor, 78 Wis. 282, 47 N. W. 433.

20. **Specification of width in judgment ordering location** see *infra*, II, C, 5, i, (I), (C).

Width of street see MUNICIPAL CORPORATIONS, 28 Cyc. 838.

21. *Iowa.*— Quinn *v.* Baage, 138 Iowa 426, 114 N. W. 205.

Nebraska.— Sanford *v.* Webster County, 5 Nebr. (Unoff.) 364, 98 N. W. 822, that buildings and river-banks extended into highway at certain points is no objection.

New York.— Matter of Adolph, 102 N. Y. App. Div. 371, 92 N. Y. Suppl. 841 [*affirmed* in 186 N. Y. 547, 79 N. E. 1100]; Purdy *v.* Moore, 73 N. Y. App. Div. 615, 76 N. Y. Suppl. 289.

Ohio.— Hays *v.* Lewis, 28 Ohio St. 326.

Vermont.— Bridgman *v.* Hardwick, 67 Vt. 132, 31 Atl. 33.

See 25 Cent. Dig. tit. "Highways," § 147.

The presumption is that the road was laid out of the statutory width (Hentzler *v.* Bradbury, 5 Kan. App. 1, 47 Pac. 330, to minimum legal width; Schenider *v.* Brown Tp., 142 Mich. 45, 105 N. W. 13; McGarry *v.* Runkel, 118 Wis. 1, 94 N. W. 662), or the width of an old road over which it was laid out (*In re*

(C) *Width.*[47] A judgment of lay-out must specify the width of the road[48] as laid,[49] which may be done by proper reference.[50]

(D) *Statement of Jurisdictional Facts; Notice.* The record must affirmatively show jurisdiction,[51] and notice, being jurisdictional, must appear from the

Michigan.— Blodgett *v.* Clam Lake Highway Com'rs, 47 Mich. 469, 11 N. W. 275.

Minnesota.— Sonnek *v.* Minnesota Lake, 50 Minn. 558, 52 N. W. 961, "as near as practicable" to a specified line insufficient.

Missouri.— Peterson *v.* Beha, 161 Mo. 513, 62 S. W. 462, holding that a description of a road as "beginning at a point ten or twelve rods north of the center of section 33," etc., is so uncertain and indefinite as to amount to no description at all.

Montana.— Pagel *v.* Fergus County, 17 Mont. 586, 44 Pac. 86 [*distinguishing* Crowley *v.* Gallatin County, 14 Mont. 292, 36 Pac. 313].

New York.— Matter of De Camp, 19 N. Y. App. Div. 564, 46 N. Y. Suppl. 293 (survey should be incorporated in order); People *v.* Diver, 19 Hun 263 (starting "near" instead of "at" certain objects).

Pennsylvania.— *In re* Hector Tp. Road, 19 Pa. Super. Ct. 124; *In re* Crescent Tp. Road, 18 Pa. Super. Ct. 160; *In re* Dunbar Tp Road, 12 Pa. Super. Ct. 491.

Wisconsin.— Blair *v.* Milwaukee Light, etc., Co., 110 Wis. 64, 85 N. W. 675 (monuments which cannot be located by reference to the order cannot be used to cure ambiguities); Moll *v.* Benckler, 30 Wis. 584; Isham *v.* Smith, 21 Wis. 32.

United States.— Hicks *v.* Fish, 15 Fed. Cas. No. 6,459, 4 Mason 310, from A, as it shall be most convenient, insufficient.

See 25 Cent. Dig. tit. "Highways," § 159.

Description held to be sufficiently certain see Blakeslee *v.* Tyler, 55 Conn. 387, 11 Atl. 291; Harwinton *v.* Catlin, 19 Conn. 520; Green *v.* Bibb County Road Bd., 126 Ga. 693, 56 S. E. 59; Brown *v.* Sams, 119 Ga. 22, 45 S. E. 719; Clifford *v.* Eagle, 35 Ill. 444; Todd *v.* Crail, 167 Ind. 48, 77 N. E. 402; Ruston *v.* Grimwood, 30 Ind. 364; Baker *v.* Gowland, 37 Ind. App. 364, 76 N. E. 1027; People *v.* Milton Highway Com'rs, 37 N. Y. 360; People *v.* Brown, 47 Hun 459; People *v.* Nash, 15 N. Y. Suppl. 29; Woolsey *v.* Tompkins, 23 Wend. 324; Dunstan *v.* Jamestown, 7 N. D. 1, 72 N. W. 899; *In re* Sewickley Tp. Road, 23 Pa. Super. Ct. 170; Bare *v.* Williams, 101 Va. 800, 45 S. E. 331; Tench *v.* Abshire, 90 Va. 768, 19 S. E. 779; Moore *v.* Roberts, 64 Wis. 538, 25 N. W. 564.

Where a road has been used for more than fifty years, uncertainty in the original lay-out will not render it void. Dominick *v.* Hill, 6 N. Y. St. 329. So if the evidence shows that the beginning of the road is marked by a monument fixed by the commissioners who laid out said road, and that its course and boundaries have become well defined by use in accordance with said monuments, and the actual markings made by them, the judgment may be corrected to correspond with such facts, although the commissioners' report itself and the petition may have wrongly stated the distance the starting point is from the center of the section. Peterson *v.* Beha, 161 Mo. 513, 62 S. W. 462.

The judgment will be treated as an entirety usually. Hence if the description is in part defective the lay-out is void. Sonnek *v.* Minnesota Lake, 50 Minn. 558, 52 N. W. 961.

47. See also *supra*, II, C, 5, h, (III).

48. *California.*— Freshour *v.* Hihn, 99 Cal. 443, 34 Pac. 87; Humboldt County *v.* Dinsmore, 75 Cal. 604, 17 Pac. 710.

Illinois.—File *v.* St. Jacob Highway Com'rs, 34 Ill. App. 538. Otherwise after recognition for eighteen years. Pearce *v.* Gilmer, 54 Ill. 25. And see Highway Com'rs *v.* Harrison, 108 Ill. 398.

Missouri.— Snoddy *v.* Pettis County, 45 Mo. 361; State *v.* Parsons, 53 Mo. App. 135.

Nebraska.— Close *v.* Swanson, 64 Nebr. 389, 89 N. W. 1043.

New York.— Matter of King, 42 Misc. 480, 87 N. Y. Suppl. 236.

Pennsylvania.— *In re* Hempfield Tp. Road, 122 Pa. St. 439, 16 Atl. 738; *In re* Boyer's Road, 37 Pa. St. 257; Bliss *v.* Sears, 24 Pa. St. 111; *In re* Shaefferstown Road, 5 Pa. St. 515; *In re* Norriton Tp., etc., Road, 4 Pa. St. 337; *In re* Pitt Tp. Public Road, 1 Pa. St. 356; *In re* Clowe's Road, 2 Grant 129; *In re* Bridgewater Turnpike, etc., Road, 4 Watts & S. 39; *In re* Silverlake Tp. Public Road, 3 Watts & S. 559; *In re* Shamokin Road, 6 Binn. 36.

Vermont.— State *v.* Leicester, 33 Vt. 653.

Canada.— Basterach *v.* Atkinson, 7 N. Brunsw. 439.

See 25 Cent. Dig. tit. "Highways," § 160.

Contra.— Quinn *v.* Baage, 138 Iowa 426, 114 N. W. 205; Clarke *v.* South Kingstown, 18 R. I. 283, 27 Atl. 336; Boston, etc., R. Corp. *v.* Lincoln, 13 R. I. 705.

The width should be fixed at the time of the order (*In re* Whitemarsh Tp. Road, 7 Montg. Co. Rep. (Pa.) 161; *In re* Derry Road, Wilcox (Pa.) 165), and not *nunc pro tunc* (*In re* Lackawanna Tp. Road, 112 Pa. St. 212, 3 Atl. 848; *In re* Lower Allen Tp. Road, 5 Pa. Dist. 764, 18 Pa. Co. Ct. 298).

49. Carlton *v.* State, 8 Blackf. (Ind.) 208 (void where width not defined); Snyder *v.* Plass, 28 N. Y. 465.

50. State *v.* Schilb, 47 Iowa 611; Rose *v.* Kansas City, 128 Mo. 135, 30 S. W. 518; People *v.* Haverstraw, 137 N. Y. 88, 32 N. E. 1111 [*reversing* 20 N. Y. Suppl. 7] (sufficient where center line and width on each side given); *In re* Loretto Road, 29 Pa. St. 350. See, however, Hudson *v.* Voreis, 134 Ind. 642, 34 N. E. 503, holding that a reference to the petition is insufficient where the statute does not require the petition to state the width.

51. *Alabama.*— Russell Com'rs' Ct. *v.* Harver, 25 Ala. 480; Talladega Com'rs' Ct. *v.* Thompson, 18 Ala. 694.

Colorado.— Thatcher *v.* Crisman, 6 Colo.

and a power given to one officer, while the survey is incomplete, to sign for another is ineffectual.[60]

(F) *Conditional in Form.* Exactly to what extent an order establishing a highway may be made conditional does not clearly appear from the cases. Thus it has been held that the court or commissioners may in the exercise of a sound discretion impose as a condition that the expense of location should be borne by petitioners,[61] while, on the other hand, such a condition has been held void,[62] as has been also a provision requiring a town to tend a draw in a bridge and to keep lamps lighted thereon,[63] or attempting to bind the petitioner for the road to construct and maintain a fence to protect the owner through whose land the road will run.[64] But the imposition of unauthorized conditions does not necessarily render void the whole order laying out a road,[65] although an order conditional in form may not be final.[66]

(II) *AMENDMENT NUNC PRO TUNC.* The record of proceedings may be amended *nunc pro tunc* if there be matter of record authorizing it,[67] and where the record is amended in a proper and legal manner it has the same force and effect as though originally made as amended,[68] and can no more be contradicted by parol than any other lawful record.[69] But amendment cannot be employed to alter or review what has been done judicially, but only as to ministerial acts.[70]

(III) *RECORD AND FILING.* Recording a location may be necessary to complete the lay-out,[71] which record should show clearly the facts,[72] and should be made within the time designated by statute,[73] although it has been held that

valid, in the absence of any finding that the third commissioner did not meet and deliberate with the others.

60. Todd *v.* Todd, 3 Hun (N. Y.) 298, 5 Thomps. & C. 531. See also State *v.* James, 4 Wis. 408, holding that one supervisor cannot sign the name of another without his immediate assent and direction.

61. Brown *v.* Ellis, 26 Iowa 85 (although no time was fixed for complying with condition); Patridge *v.* Ballard, 2 Me. 50.

62. *In re* Brown, 51 N. H. 367; Dudley *v.* Cilley, 5 N. H. 558; Webb *v.* Albertson, 4 Barb. (N. Y.) 51.

63. Braintree *v.* Norfolk, 8 Cush. (Mass.) 546.

64. Engler *v.* Knoblaugh, 131 Mo. App. 481, 110 S. W. 16, holding that the order should include in the damages awarded to the owner the expense of erecting such fence.

65. Rich. *v.* Gow, 19 Ill. App. 81.

66. Linblom *v.* Ramsey, 75 Ill. 246.

67. Lowndes County Com'rs' Ct. *v.* Hearne, 59 Ala. 371; Brown *v.* Robertson, 123 Ill. 631, 15 N. E. 30; Du Page County *v.* Martin, 39 Ill. App. 298; *In re* Gardner, 41 Mo. App. 589. See also *In re* East Fallowfield Road, 2 Lanc. L. Rev. (Pa.) 160, amendment by filing affidavit of service of notice. But see *In re* Brown, 51 N. H. 367.

68. Du Page County *v.* Martin, 39 Ill. App. 298.

69. Du Page County *v.* Martin, 39 Ill. App. 298.

70. Hallock *v.* Woolsey, 23 Wend. (N. Y.) 328 [*following* Woolsey *v.* Tompkins, 23 Wend. (N. Y.) 324].

71. *Illinois.*— Highway Com'rs *v.* People, 61 Ill. App. 634; Breese *v.* Poole, 16 Ill. App. 551.

Maine.— Todd *v.* Rome, 2 Me. 55.

Minnesota.— Teick *v.* Carver County, 11 Minn. 292, in both counties where road lies.

Ohio.— King *v.* Kenny, 4 Ohio 79.

Tennessee.— Whitesides *v.* Earles, (Ch. App. 1901) 61 S. W. 1038.

United States.— Burns *v.* Multnomah R. Co., 15 Fed. 177, 8 Sawy. 543; U. S. *v.* Emery, 25 Fed. Cas. No. 15,052, 4 Cranch C. C. 270.

Canada.— *Ex p.* Weade, 8 N. Brunsw. 307.

See 25 Cent. Dig. tit. "Highways," § 162.

But see Ford *v.* Whitaker, 1 Nott & M. (S. C.) 5.

Effect of loss of report.— The mere fact that, twelve years after a highway which has, to all appearances, been duly established, the report of the commissioners cannot be found among the papers in the county clerk's office, affords no ground for disputing the legal existence of the highway. State *v.* O'Laughlin, 29 Kan. 20. Where the original report is lost a copy may be used for filing. Frame *v.* Boyd, 35 N. J. L. 457. But see *In re* Howell's Mills State Road, 6 Whart. (Pa.) 352.

72. Orono *v.* Penobscot County, 30 Me. 302; Sumner *v.* Peebles, 5 Wash. 471, 32 Pac. 221, 1000; Basterach *v.* Atkinson, 7 N. Brunsw. 439.

73. Fenwick Hall Co. *v.* Old Saybrook, 69 Conn. 32, 36 Atl. 1068 (immediate recording held not necessary); Wright *v.* Middlefork Highway Com'rs, 145 Ill. 48, 33 N. E. 876.

Filing held ineffective as made too late see Highway Com'rs *v.* People, 61 Ill. App. 634 (after three years); Martin *v.* Stillwell, 50 N. J. L. 530, 14 Atl. 563; Wayne *v.* Caldwell, 1 S. D. 483, 47 N. W. 547, 36 Am. St. Rep. 750; Morris *v.* Edwards, 132 Wis. 91, 112 N. W. 248; Dolphin *v.* Pedley, 27 Wis. 469.

however, are to the contrary,[86] and it is held that so long as the order remains unexecuted the board has power to change it;[87] and that where a board of county commissioners rejects a report of viewers appointed by it to lay out and locate a public road such board may at the same session reconsider its action by which the report was rejected.[88]

(VI) *OPERATION AND EFFECT* — (A) *Conclusiveness.* Where the proper tribunal has acted on a lay-out of a road as to matters within its jurisdiction its decision is conclusive[89] and *res judicata*[90] in other proceedings until vacated or declared void by some legal process or proceeding, only, however, as to matters within its jurisdiction,[91] directly in issue,[92] and actually adjudicated,[93] as a result of proceedings conducted according to the statutes authorizing them.[94]

(B) *Presumption of Regularity.* The action of an inferior tribunal having jurisdiction is presumed to be regular.[95] This is especially true after there has

Oregon.— Roe *v.* Union County, 19 Oreg. 315, 24 Pac. 235.

Pennsylvania.— *In re* Brown Tp. Road, 42 Leg. Int. 406.

See 25 Cent. Dig. tit. "Highways," § 163.

86. Thorpe *v.* Worcester County, 9 Gray (Mass.) 57; New Marlborough *v.* Berkshire County, 9 Metc. (Mass.) 423; *In re* Bucks County Road, 3 Whart. (Pa.) 105, holding that the court may quash an order issued by its clerk in recess.

87. Burkett *v.* San Joaquin County, 18 Cal. 702.

If commissioners of highways regard the damages assessed as too high they may revoke all proceedings had by a written order to that effect. People *v.* Highway Com'rs, 88 Ill. 141. See also Cutler *v.* Sours, 80 Ill. App. 618.

88. Higgins *v.* Curtis, 39 Kan. 283, 18 Pac. 207.

89. *Illinois.*— Farrelly *v.* Kane, 172 Ill. 415, 50 N. E. 118 (as to location); Gordon *v.* Wabash County Road Dist. No. 3 Highway Com'rs, 169 Ill. 510, 48 N. E. 451 (as to damages sustained).

Indiana.— Monroe County *v.* Conner, 155 Ind. 484, 58 N. E. 828 (as to regularity of election for building roads); Suits *v.* Murdock, 63 Ind. 73.

Missouri.— Searcy *v.* Clay County, 176 Mo. 493, 75 S. W. 657 (holding that a surveyor's error cannot be shown); Seafield *v.* Bohne, 169 Mo. 537, 69 S. W. 1051; State *v.* Schenkel, 129 Mo. App. 224, 108 S. W. 635.

New York.— Matter of Fenn, 128 N. Y. App. Div. 10, 112 N. Y. Suppl. 431, as to public necessity.

Oregon.— French-Glenn Live Stock Co. *v.* Harney County, 36 Oreg. 138, 58 Pac. 35.

Washington.— State *v.* Adams County Super. Ct., 29 Wash. 1, 69 Pac. 366.

See 25 Cent. Dig. tit. "Highways," § 166.

But see *In re* Strafford, 14 N. H. 30.

90. *Connecticut.*—Webb *v.* Rocky-Hill, 21 Conn. 468.

Delaware.— Wilson *v.* Cochran, 4 Harr. 88.

Iowa.— Hupert *v.* Anderson, 35 Iowa 578.

Maine.— Woodman *v.* Somerset County, 25 Me. 300.

Massachusetts.—Craigie *v.* Mellen, 6 Mass. 7.

New Hampshire.— Winship *v.* Enfield, 42 N. H. 197.

Pennsylvania.— Millcreek Tp. *v.* Reed, 29 Pa. St. 195.

The pleadings must set up the judgment as *res judicata.* Kinzer *v.* Brown, 170 Ind. 81, 83 N. E. 618.

91. People *v.* Allen, 37 N. Y. App. Div. 248, 55 N. Y. Suppl. 1057 [*affirmed* in 162 N. Y. 615, 57 N. E. 1122]; Grady *v.* Dundon, 30 Oreg. 333, 47 Pac. 915; Galveston, etc., R. Co. *v.* Baudat, 18 Tex. Civ. App. 595, 45 S. W. 939.

92. Speir *v.* Utrecht, 121 N. Y. 420, 24 N. E. 692.

93. Speir *v.* Utrecht, 121 N. Y. 420, 24 N. E. 692.

94. Jones *v.* Zink, 65 Mo. App. 409.

95. *Arkansas.*— Brumley *v.* State, 83 Ark. 236, 103 S. W. 615.

California.— Siskiyou County *v.* Gamlich, 110 Cal. 94, 42 Pac. 468; Los Angeles County *v.* San Jose Land, etc., Co., 96 Cal. 93, 30 Pac. 969, by statute.

Illinois.— Hankins *v.* Calloway, 88 Ill. 155; Morgan *v.* Green, 17 Ill. 395; Dumoss *v.* Francis, 15 Ill. 543; Willow Branch, etc., Highway Com'rs *v.* People, 69 Ill. App. 326.

Indiana.— Todd *v.* Crail, 167 Ind. 48, 77 N. E. 402; Heagy *v.* Black, 90 Ind. 534; Crossley *v.* O'Brien, 24 Ind. 325, 87 Am. Dec. 329.

Iowa.— Quinn *v.* Baage, 138 Iowa 426, 114 N. W. 205 (especially after lapse of time); Davenport Mut. Sav. Fund, etc., Assoc. *v.* Schmidt, 15 Iowa 213.

Kansas.— Willis *v.* Sproule, 13 Kan. 257.

Montana.— Carron *v.* Clark, 14 Mont. 301, 36 Pac. 178.

New Hampshire.— Proctor *v.* Andover, 42 N. H. 348.

New Jersey.— Conover *v.* Bird, 56 N. J. L. 228, 28 Atl. 428.

New York.— People *v.* Heddon, 32 Hun 299; Fowler *v.* Mott, 19 Barb. 204; Wildrick *v.* Hager, 10 N. Y. St. 764; Colden *v.* Thurbur, 2 Johns. 424.

Oregon.— French-Glenn Live Stock Co. *v.* Harney County, 36 Oreg. 138, 58 Pac. 35; Thompson *v.* Multnomah County, 2 Oreg. 34.

Texas.— Sneed *v.* Falls County, (Civ. App. 1897) 42 S. W. 121, holding that the face of the record of the commissioners' court need not affirmatively show a compliance with all the requirements.

Questions relating to appeals in highway proceedings are discussed elsewhere in this article.[14]

(II) *WAIVER AND ESTOPPEL* — (A) *In General.* Objections to a lay-out of a road may be waived [15] by failure to make objections,[16] or delay in making them,[17] or by consenting to the irregularity.[18]

(B) *Applying For and Accepting Damages:* Application for [19] and acceptance

to location if referred to in petition and report.

Texas.— Howe *v.* Rose, 35 Tex. Civ. App. 328, 80 S. W. 1019, proposal to remit all damages if road located differently from report of jury treated as an objection.

See 25 Cent. Dig. tit. "Highways," § 173.

14. See *infra*, II, C, 5, k, (I).

15. Campau *v.* Le Blanc, 127 Mich. 179, 86 N. W. 535, 8 Detroit Leg. N. 273 (appeal to township board waives previous irregularities of highway commissioner); Nye *v.* Clark, 55 Mich. 599, 22 N. W. 57 (by petitioning and fencing); State *v.* Richmond, 26 N. H. 232; Woodworth *v.* Spirit Mound Tp., 10 S. D. 504, 74 N. W. 443 (only by parties interested, however).

A general appearance operates as a waiver of service and jurisdiction of the person. Hanson *v.* Cloud County, (Kan. App. 1898) 55 Pac. 468; Hurst *v.* Martinsburg, 80 Minn. 40, 82 N. W. 1099 (one appearing cannot object that other owners were not served with notice); Issenhuth *v.* Baum, 11 S. D. 223, 76 N. W. 928. See, however, McKee Highway Com'rs *v.* Smith, 217 Ill. 250, 75 N. E. 396, no waiver by general appearance after motion to dismiss was overruled. *Compare In re* Patten, 16 N. H. 277.

Acquiescence in the lay-out may work an estoppel to object thereto. Freetown *v.* Bristol County, 9 Pick. (Mass.) 46 (by inaction during expenditure); State *v.* Boscawen, 32 N. H. 331 (for twenty years); *In re* Woolsey, 95 N. Y. 135; Roller *v.* Kirby, 1 Ohio Dec. (Reprint) 76, 1 West. L. J. 550; McMurtrie *v.* Stewart, 21 Pa. St. 322 (seven years' use); Felch *v.* Gilman, 22 Vt. 38; State *v.* Wertzel, 62 Wis. 184, 22 N. W. 150.

A grantee of one estopped is himself barred. Miller *v.* Schenck, 78 Iowa 372, 43 N. W. 225; Gurnsey *v.* Edwards, 26 N. H. 224.

A town may be estopped as an individual would be. Ives *v.* East Haven, 48 Conn. 272; Freetown *v.* Bristol County, 9 Pick. (Mass.) 46; State *v.* Boscawen, 32 N. H. 331. See Damp *v.* Dane, 29 Wis. 419.

16. Humboldt County *v.* Dinsmore, 75 Cal. 604, 17 Pac. 710 (by appearing without contest); Stronsky *v.* Hickman, 116 Iowa 651, 88 N. W. 825 (by failure to object after notice); Seafield *v.* Bohne, 169 Mo. 537, 69 S. W. 1051 (by failure to file exceptions); Huntress *v.* Effingham, 17 N. H. 584.

Estoppel held not to arise see Roehrborn *v.* Schmidt, 16 Wis. 519, by presence and silence.

17. Nobleboro *v.* Lincoln County, 68 Me. 548 (after judgment); Carpenter's Petition, 67 N. H. 574, 32 Atl. 773; *In re* Kennett, 24 N. H. 139; People *v.* Mills, 109 N. Y. 69, 15 N. E. 886 (not first on appeal); Marble *v.* Whitney, 28 N. Y. 297; Vondron *v.* Cranberry Tp., 8 Ohio S. & C. Pl. Dec. 227, 6 Ohio N. P. 534 (by failure to object to location at proceedings before commissioners). See *In re* Patten, 16 N. H. 277.

Objection must be made before reference. White *v.* Landaff, 35 N. H. 128; Stevens *v.* Goffstown, 21 N. H. 454.

Estoppel held not to arise see Underwood *v.* Bailey, 56 N. H. 187; Damp *v.* Dane, 29 Wis. 419, by failure to object before justice who could not inquire into regularity of proceedings.

18. Miller *v.* Schenck, 78 Iowa 372, 43 N. W. 225 (one who had dedicated land for street is estopped); Keeler *v.* Lauer, 73 Kan. 388, 85 Pac. 541; Young *v.* Milan, 73 N. H. 552, 64 Atl. 16 (expressions of satisfaction); Patterson *v.* Hill County, 43 Tex. Civ. App. 546, 95 S. W. 39 (by agreement to donate land); McCown *v.* Hill, (Tex. Civ. App. 1903) 73 S. W. 850 (by consent to route as reported). See, however, Pagel *v.* Fergus County, 17 Mont. 586, 44 Pac. 86 (consent to private road does not admit public road); Scott *v.* State, 1 Sneed (Tenn.) 629 (no estoppel by activity in having road laid out and subsequently buying land).

Petitioning for a road is no waiver of irregularities in the lay-out (Chase *v.* Cochran, 102 Me. 431, 67 Atl. 320; La Barre *v.* Bent, 154 Mich. 520, 118 N. W. 6, petitioner for highway, worked on it, and was paid therefor; Hoy *v.* Hubbell, 125 N. Y. App. Div. 60, 109 N. Y. Suppl. 301. See Clarke *v.* Mayo, 4 Call (Va.) 374), unless joined with a release of damages (Trickey *v.* Schlader, 52 Ill. 78; Warfield *v.* Hohman, 128 Ill. App. 243); but a petition to change a road may estop petitioner from objecting to the road as laid out (Kelley *v.* State, 46 Tex. Cr. 23, 80 S. W. 382).

Consent of legislature to laying out highway over state lands see EMINENT DOMAIN, 15 Cyc. 611.

Necessity of consent of landowner in exceptional cases see EMINENT DOMAIN, 15 Cyc. 602 *et seq.*

19. *Kansas.*—Ogden *v.* Stokes, 25 Kan. 517.

Massachusetts.— Pitkin *v.* Springfield, 112 Mass. 509.

Nebraska.— Hoye *v.* Diehls, 78 Nebr. 77, 110 N. W. 714 (indefinite description); Davis *v.* Boone County, 28 Nebr. 837, 45 N. W. 249.

New York.— Lansing *v.* Caswell, 4 Paige 519.

Pennsylvania.— See *In re* Appleby Manor Road, 1 Grant 443.

Texas.— Allen *v.* Parker County, 23 Tex. Civ. App. 536, 57 S. W. 703, where irregularities not fatal to jurisdiction and plaintiff claimed damages.

See 25 Cent. Dig. tit. "Highways," § 175.

missioners whose decisions have been reversed;[33] but although in some jurisdictions the right of appeal is held to belong to every resident taxpayer in the town, who, as such, is liable to assessment for highway labor,[34] the weight of authority is to the effect that one is not aggrieved so as to entitle him to appeal unless he is interested in or affected by the proceedings in some manner differently from the public, citizens, and taxpayers generally,[35] and some courts specifically confine the right to persons whose lands have been or will be taken.[36]

(3) Decisions Reviewable. Except where the right to appeal from interlocutory orders is given by statute,[37] only a final determination of the proceedings may be reviewed on appeal or writ of error.[38] A judgment or order is final, within the meaning of this rule, when it makes a complete disposition of the cause or proceeding;[39] and, according to the weight of authority, it is only a final order

meaning of a statute giving the right of appeal to every person who considers himself aggrieved by the decision. People *v.* May, 27 Barb. (N. Y.) 238.

A landowner may waive his appeal from the decision of commissioners laying out a street, by going before the jury for assessing damages, and giving evidence to increase his damages. Lansing *v.* Caswell, 4 Paige (N. Y.) 519. Likewise a person who knowingly accepts the damages awarded him by the county commissioners' court is not afterward entitled to appeal from such award. Karnes County *v.* Nichols, (Tex. Civ. App. 1899) 54 S. W. 656.

33. Lowndes County Com'rs' Ct. *v.* Bowie, 34 Ala. 461; Lafollette *v.* Road Com'r, 105 Tenn. 536, 58 S. W. 1065. But see *In re* Ripley Selectmen, 39 Me. 350.

34. People *v.* Cortelyou, 36 Barb. (N. Y.) 164; Smith *v.* Harkins, 39 N. C. 486.

Under the Wisconsin statute it is not necessary that the appellants be owners of land affected by the highway, or that they have any special interest therein, provided they consider themselves aggrieved. State *v.* Wheeler. 97 Wis. 96, 72 N. W. 225.

35. *Delaware.*— *In re* Long Point Road, 5 Harr. 152.

Iowa.— McCune *v.* Swafford, 5 Iowa 552.

Kentucky.— Com. *v.* Dudley, 5 T. B. Mon. 21; Taylor *v.* Brown, 3 Bibb 78; Barr *v.* Stevens, 1 Bibb 292.

Massachusetts.— Chandler *v.* Railroad Com'rs, 141 Mass. 208, 5 N. E. 509.

New Hampshire.— Bennett *v.* Tuftonborough, 72 N. H. 63, 54 Atl. 700.

Tennessee.— Goldman *v.* Grainger County Justices, 3 Head 107.

See 25 Cent. Dig. tit. "Highways," § 178.

And see Moore *v.* Hancock, 11 Ala. 245, holding that no individual has the right to intervene and put questions on the record by bills of exception, under a statute giving the privilege of bills of exceptions only to parties to a suit and in the trial of a cause.

A person owning land within one mile of the proposed road, which real estate would be affected by the construction of the road, has been held to have such an actual and substantial interest as to entitle him to appeal. Fleming *v.* Hight, 95 Ind. 78.

36. Butler Grove Highway Com'rs *v.* Barnes, 195 Ill. 43, 52 N. E. 775; Taylor *v.* Normal Highway Com'rs, 88 Ill. 526; Vacoune *v.* Police Jury, 1 Mart. N. S. (La.) 596; Foster *v.* Dunklin, 44 Mo. 216; Overbeck *v.* Galloway, 10 Mo. 364. *Compare* Oswego *v.* Kellogg, 99 Ill. 590.

37. Warner *v.* Doran, 30 Iowa 521; Jeter *v.* Board, 27 Gratt. (Va.) 910 [*distinguishing* Trevilian *v.* Louisa R. Co., 3 Gratt. (Va.) 326]. *Compare* Newell *v.* Perkins, 39 Iowa 244.

38. *Illinois.*— Ravatte *v.* Race, 152 Ill. 672, 38 N. E. 933; Roosa *v.* Henderson County, 59 Ill. 446.

Indiana.— Kelley *v.* Augsperger, 171 Ind. 155, 85 N. E. 1004; Kirsch *v.* Braun, 153 Ind. 247, 53 N. E. 1082; Wilson *v.* McClain, 131 Ind. 335, 30 N. E. 1093; Anderson *v.* Claman, 123 Ind. 471, 24 N. E. 175. Tomlinson *v.* Peters, 120 Ind. 237, 21 N. E. 910; Neptune *v.* Taylor, 108 Ind. 459, 8 N. E. 566.

Kentucky.— Helm *v.* Short, 7 Bush 623.

Maine.— Moore's Appeal, 68 Me. 405.

Missouri.— Platte County Court *v.* McFarland, 12 Mo. 166. But see Bennett *v.* Woody, 137 Mo. 377, 38 S. W. 972, holding that Rev. St. (1899) § 7801, contemplates appeals as well from the judgment of the county court assessing the damages, as from the final judgment ordering the road to be established and opened.

Nebraska.—Jones *v.* Daul, 5 Nebr. (Unoff.) 236, 97 N. W. 1029, holding that where the county board merely ascertains the amount of the damages to be assessed on a given tract, but declines to determine whether the claimant is the owner of the land or entitled to the damages, its order is not appealable.

Ohio.— Anderson *v.* McKinney, 24 Ohio St. 467.

Tennessee.— Evans *v.* Shields, 3 Head 70.

See 25 Cent. Dig. tit. "Highways," § 179.

39. Kelley *v.* Augsperger, 171 Ind. 155, 85 N. E. 1004.

Conditional order.—An order establishing the road on condition that the assessed damages be paid by the petitioners is final and appealable, although conditional. McNichols *v.* Wilson, 42 Iowa 385; Dwiggins *v.* Denver, 24 Ohio St. 629.

A judgment of an intermediate court disposing of an appeal thereto is final within the meaning of the rule. Hall *v.* McDonald, 171 Ind. 9, 85 N. E. 707; Helm *v.* Short, 7 Bush (Ky.) 623.

questions are.[45] The joint decision of commissioners of different counties is not appealable in some jurisdictions on account of a lack of statutory provision therefor.[46]

(B) *To What Tribunal Appeal May Be Taken.* An appeal in highway proceedings can be taken only to a court or judge having jurisdiction thereof,[47] and where the jurisdiction of different courts is dependent upon the amount of damages, the amount claimed and not that allowed by the highway board is determining.[48] As the right of the public in highways is a perpetual easement,[49] a proceeding to establish a highway involves a freehold within the meaning of statutes conferring appellate jurisdiction of such questions on certain courts.[50]

missing an application to vacate a decision of commissioners in proceedings to lay out a highway, without a hearing on the merits, on the erroneous determination that application was not made in time, is appealable. Matter of Glenside Woolen Mills, 92 Hun 188, 36 N. Y. Suppl. 593. It has also been held that an appeal lies from a void order of the supreme court on certiorari to review the proceedings and determination of highway commissioners (People *v.* Ferris, 36 N. Y. 218 [*reversing* 41 Barb. 121]), and that where the special term, on motion, has corrected the judgment of the general term, by allowing costs against appellant who brought the appeal from the commissioners of highways, and whose lands were taken for the road, and disallowed costs as against the county judge and referees, the general term will not review the decision of the special term, since the question was one resting in the discretion of the judge at special term (People *v.* Robinson, 25 How. Pr. 345).

45. Wells *v.* York County, 79 Me. 522, 11 Atl. 417; Goodwin *v.* Hallowell, 12 Me. 271; *In re* Cornplanter Tp. Road, 26 Pa. Super. Ct. 20 (holding that a decision of the court of quarter sessions on questions of fact is irreviewable on appeal); *In re* Hector Tp. Road, 19 Pa. Super. Ct. 120.

In Indiana the only remedy for an aggrieved party, when the commissioners' court acts without authority of law in setting aside its final order establishing a highway after it has been made and recorded, is by appeal (Badger *v.* Merry, 139 Ind. 631, 39 N. E. 309); and it also lies where the board of commissioners dismisses the petition unless the petitioners open and maintain the road at their own expense (Crossley *v.* O'Brien, 24 Ind. 325, 87 Am. Dec. 329), but not from an order sustaining a demurrer to an answer to a petition for a highway, as no such pleadings as an answer and demurrer are proper in such case (Logan *v.* Kiser, 25 Ind. 393).

Matters of law, such as the sufficiency of a verdict, are the subject of appeal under the Massachusetts statutes. Lanesborough *v.* Berkshire County, 22 Pick. (Mass.) 278.

The validity and the regularity of the proceedings, as well as the question of damages, may be reviewed under the Minnesota statutes. Pairier *v.* Itasca County, 68 Minn. 297, 71 N. W. 382.

46. Freeman *v.* Franklin County, etc., 74 Me. 326; *In re* Banks, 29 Me. 288; People *v.* Nelson, 26 How. Pr. (N. Y.) 346.

There is statutory provision in New York for the appointment of commissioners by the supreme court on the disagreement of the highway commissioners of two or more towns of different counties and for an appeal from the decision of the commissioners so appointed. Matter of Barrett, 7 N. Y. App. Div. 482, 40 N. Y. Suppl. 266.

47. People *v.* Van Alstyne, 3 Abb. Dec. (N. Y.) 575, 3 Keyes 35; Northington *v.* Taylor County, (Tex. Civ. App. 1901) 62 S. W. 936 (holding that an appeal from the commissioners' court in proceedings under Sayles Annot. Civ. St. art. 4674, requiring the establishment of first-class roads from county-seat to county-seat, should be taken to the district court, and not to the county court); State *v.* Goldstucker, 40 Wis. 124. And see Bennett *v.* Bryan, 1 Ky. L. Rep. 274.

A change of venue may be granted, as appeals from the order of the board of commissioners establishing or relocating a highway are on the same footing with ordinary civil actions. Schmied *v.* Keeney, 72 Ind. 309.

Deputy town clerk sitting on appellate board.—Where a town clerk is incapacitated to sit as a member of the township board on an appeal to it from the highway commissioner in laying out a public highway, the deputy clerk is not authorized to sit as a member of the board, as the deputy acts for his principal and cannot perform duties which his principal is incapacitated to perform. Dubois *v.* Riley Tp. Bd., 126 Mich. 587, 85 N. W. 1067.

48. Gorman *v.* St. Mary, 20 Minn. 392; Dell Rapids *v.* Irving, 9 S. D. 222, 68 N. W. 313.

A constitutional provision that justices shall not have jurisdiction where the amount in controversy exceeds one hundred dollars, or the title to real estate is involved, is not violated by a statute providing for appeal to a jury, summoned by a justice of the peace, as the appeal is really to the jury. State *v.* Rapp, 39 Minn. 65, 38 N. W. 926.

49. See *supra*, I, note 4.

50. Chaplin *v.* Wheatland Tp. Highway Com'rs, 126 Ill. 264, 18 N. E. 765; Lee County Highway Com'rs *v.* Chicago, etc., R. Co., 34 Ill. App. 32; Goudy *v.* Lake View, 31 Ill. App. 652.

In Canada highway proceedings are held not to involve title to lands or to present

lishment of the highway is a proper and necessary party is a question decided differently in different jurisdictions, it being held in some that it is,[60] and in others that it is not.[61]

(E) *Proceedings For Transfer.* The proceedings necessary to transfer a highway proceeding from the highway board to a court are prescribed and regulated entirely by statute, and when there are specific provisions relating to highway proceedings, they control over statutes relating to appeals generally.[62] An appeal or error proceeding is premature when instituted before the final termination of the proceedings before the board.[63] When a disposition of the proceedings has been made, the appeal must be taken within the time limited by statute;[64] and before a transfer of the proceedings is effected there must be a compliance with statutory requirements relating to the petition or application for appeal,[65] the

60. Talladega County Road, etc., Com'rs *v.* Thompson, 15 Ala. 134; Chase County *v.* Carter, 24 Kan. 511; Cannon *v.* McAdams, 7 Heisk. (Tenn.) 376; Evans *v.* Shields, 3 Head (Tenn.) 70.

61. Schmied *v.* Keeney, 72 Ind. 309; Jamieson *v.* Cass County, 56 Ind. 466; Wright *v.* Wells, 27 Ind. 65; Barr *v.* Stevens, 1 Bibb (Ky.) 292.

The rule in Indiana is relaxed when the board does not sit as a court, but simply calls into action the authority created by law to make a reassessment for the protection and reimbursement of the county. Goodwin *v.* Warren County, 146 Ind. 164, 44 N. E. 1110.

62. Baugher *v.* Rudd, 53 Ark. 417, 14 S. W. 623; Kimble *v.* Leisher, 5 Ky. L. Rep. 466.

A statute which takes effect before an appeal is taken, and which does not except pending cases from its operation, regulates the time and mode of taking such appeal. Webster *v.* Androscoggin County, 64 Me. 434.

Where the mode of appealing is not prescribed by statute, the statute regulating appeals from justices' courts have been followed in some jurisdictions (Blair *v.* Coakley, 136 N. C. 405, 48 S. E. 804. See also Peoria County *v.* Harvey, 18 Ill. 364), and in others a mode previously in use has been adopted (Twombly *v.* Madbury, 27 N. H. 433).

63. Sangamon County *v.* Brown, 13 Ill. 207; Irwin's Appeal, 7 Pa. Super. Ct. 354.

Under the North Carolina statutes, an appeal is not premature when taken before the order opening the road is executed (McDowell *v.* Western North Carolina Insane Asylum, 101 N. C. 656, 8 S. E. 118; Warlick *v.* Lowman, 101 N. C. 548, 8 S. E. 120), and an appeal from an order of the county commissioners establishing a public road, and directing a jury to be summoned to lay it out and assess damages, may be taken as well after the confirmation of the report of the jury as before (Lambe *v.* Love, 109 N. C. 305, 13 S. E. 773).

64. *Indiana.*— Robson *v.* Richey, 159 Ind. 660, 65 N. E. 1032.

Missouri.— Sidwell *v.* Jett, 213 Mo. 601, 112 S. W. 56.

North Carolina.— Blair *v.* Coakley, 136 N. C. 495, 48 S. E. 804.

Oregon.— Miller *v.* Union County, 48 Oreg. 266, 86 Pac. 3 [*followed* in Pierce *v.* Union County, 48 Oreg. 622, 86 Pac. 5].

Pennsylvania.— *In re* Crescent Tp. Road, 18 Pa. Super. Ct. 160, limiting the rule to questions which are not jurisdictional in their nature.

See 25 Cent. Dig. tit. "Highways," § 190.

Under the Maine statute an appeal may be taken after the decision has been placed on file (Gray *v.* Cumberland County, 83 Me. 429, 22 Atl. 376), and before the first day of the next term of the supreme judicial court (Appleton *v.* Piscataquis County, 80 Me. 284, 14 Atl. 284). Under a prior statute, an appeal could not be taken until after the decision had been entered of record. *In re* Russell, 51 Me. 384.

The time of a final order, and not that of a prior conditional one, is the starting point of the period of limitation. Wilson *v.* Whitsell, 24 Ind. 306.

Evasion of statute.—A person affected with notice of the proceedings from the beginning, who has allowed the time for taking an appeal to expire, cannot accomplish the same object by moving the court to strike off the order of confirmation, and then appealing from the refusal of the court to grant his motion. Pittsburg, etc., R. Co.'s Appeal, 130 Pa. St. 190, 18 Atl. 600; *In re* Winter Ave., 23 Pa. Super. Ct. 353; *In re* North Franklin Tp. Road, 8 Pa. Super. Ct. 358.

Where the statute does not expressly limit the time, the intervention of a term of court before the appeal is entered does not render it irregular and void. Shelburn *v.* Eldridge, 10 Vt. 123.

Where all the required steps are taken within the time allowed, it is immaterial which is taken first. Restad *v.* Scambler, 33 Minn. 515, 24 N. W. 197. And see Libbey *v.* McIntosh, 60 Iowa 329, 14 N. W. 354, holding that the filing of the transcript before service of the notice of appeal is a mere irregularity which does not affect the jurisdiction.

The fact that judgment has been entered on the award of viewers does not render too late an appeal taken within the prescribed time after the filing of the award. Brown *v.* Beaver Borough, 2 Pa. Dist. 318, 12 Pa. Co. Ct. 313.

65. Whittaker *v.* Gutheridge, 52 Ill. App. 460, holding that a petition for an appeal

(4) Scope of Review, Trial De Novo, and Presumptions. Appellate jurisdiction in highway proceedings is confined to the subject-matter of the original petition,[84] and to the issues framed in the board or court where the proceedings were first instituted, even though there is a trial *de novo* on appeal;[85] and the appellate court will not take cognizance of or consider matters not embraced in the record,[86] which can be made up and matter incorporated therein only in the manner prescribed by the statute and practice of the particular jurisdiction;[87] and matters not stated therein will be presumed not to have been done,[88] an exception existing as to steps not jurisdictional in their nature and which are not absolutely required to be in the record.[89] Where no evidence is introduced in the appellate tribunal, the review proceeds on questions of law and jurisdiction much in the same manner

165 Ill. 17, 45 N. E. 1000 [*affirming* 61 Ill. App. 381].

84. *In re* Patten, 16 N. H. 277. And see Russell *v.* Leatherwood, 114 N. C. 683, 19 S. E. 643.

85. Kinzer *v.* Brown, 170 Ind. 81, 83 N. E. 618; Fulton *v.* Cummings, 132 Ind. 453, 30 N. E. 949; Indianapolis, etc., R. Co. *v.* Hood, 130 Ind. 594, 30 N. E. 705; Denny *v.* Bush, 95 Ind. 315; Green *v.* Elliott, 86 Ind. 53; Schmied *v.* Keeney, 72 Ind. 309; Crossley *v.* O'Brien, 24 Ind. 325, 87 Am. Dec. 329; Daggy *v.* Coats, 19 Ind. 259; Raab *v.* Roberts, 30 Ind. App. 6, 64 N. E. 618, 65 N. E. 191 (holding that on a trial *de novo* the facts controverted by the remonstrance or answer are the facts in issue); Greene County Justices *v.* Graham, 6 Baxt. (Tenn.) 77. But see Cross *v.* Lafourche Interior Police Jury, 7 Rob. (La.) 121.

Where the right of appeal is limited by statute to the issue of damages, the determination of the commissioner's court is conclusive as to all other matters. Huggins *v.* Hurt, 23 Tex. Civ. App. 404, 56 S. W. 944. Likewise, on appeal from a decision on a petition to set aside the proceedings establishing the highway, the court cannot entertain a motion to amend the original petition establishing the highway as a motion in the original cause. Ashcraft *v.* Lee, 75 N. C. 157.

Opening of issues after trial.— The refusal of an intermediate court to which an appeal has been taken to open the issues and permit a motion to be filed after one trial of the appeal has been had, and after the case has been sent to another county for retrial, and a large amount of costs has been accumulated, is a proper exercise of discretion, and not reviewable. Fifer *v.* Ritter, 159 Ind. 8, 64 N. E. 463.

Evidence foreign to the issue involved should be excluded. Gayle *v.* Jackson County Com'rs Ct., 155 Ala. 204, 46 So. 261.

The issues should be properly worded so as to take into consideration the public convenience, where they are submitted to the jury on a trial *de novo*. King *v.* Blackwell, 96 N. C. 322, 1 S. E. 485.

Only that part of the road against which objections are urged need be viewed and taken into consideration. Sonora Highway Com'rs *v.* Carthage, 27 Ill. 140.

86. Wood *v.* Campbell, 14 B. Mon. (Ky.) 422; *In re* Gardner, 41 Mo. App. 589; *In re* Lower Macungie Tp. Road, 26 Pa. St. 221; *In re* Herrick Tp., etc., Road, 16 Pa. Super. Ct. 579.

The appellate jurisdiction of county commissioners must be shown by the record in order to entitle their acts to any validity. Guilford *v.* Piscataquis County, 40 Me. 296. And see Eden *v.* Hancock County, 84 Me. 52, 24 Atl. 461.

The judgment of the lower court will not be disturbed where the record does not show the grounds upon which it was based (Cox *v.* Lindley, 80 Ind. 327; McCain *v.* Putman, 36 S. W. 552, 18 Ky. L. Rep. 376), or where there is no separation of law and facts in the record (Harding *v.* Putman, 21 S. W. 100, 14 Ky. L. Rep. 677; Welch *v.* Ward, 6 Ky. L. Rep. 584). Where the objection urged against the sufficiency of the description in the petition for a road view is based on allegations of fact outside of the record, the decision of the lower court overruling it will not be reversed unless manifest error has been committed. *In re* Cornplanter Tp. Road, 26 Pa. Super. Ct. 20.

Identity of two petitions.— The action of county commissioners in establishing a public road after dismissal of another like petition will not be reviewed on appeal, where the record does not show that the petitions are identical, and that the evidence, proof, and necessity for the road were the same in both cases. Warlich *v.* Lowman, 111 N. C. 532, 16 S. E. 336.

87. Scotten *v.* Divilbiss, 60 Ind. 37; Burntrager *v.* McDonald, 34 Ind. 277 (holding that a ruling of the circuit court can be presented to the supreme court only by a bill of exceptions); Purviance *v.* Drover, 20 Ind. 238; Brabham *v.* Custer County, 3 Nebr. (Unoff.) 801, 92 N. W. 989.

88. North Henderson Highway Com'rs *v.* People, 2 Ill. App. 24; Wilson *v.* Wheeler, 125 Ind. 173, 25 N. E. 190; Wabaunsee County *v.* Muhlenbacker, 18 Kan. 129; *In re* Greensburg Road, 1 Am. L. Reg. (Pa.) 124.

89. Baker *v.* Windham, 25 Conn. 597; *In re* James, 43 Hun (N. Y.) 67; Miller *v.* Hamilton County, 9 Ohio Dec. (Reprint) 312, 12 Cinc. L. Bul. 152; *In re* App's Tavern Road, 17 Serg. & R. (Pa.) 388; Baltimore Turnpike Road Case, 5 Binn. (Pa.) 481.

That the public good requires the road to be opened need not be entered on the record as an express finding. Brabham *v.* Custer County, (Nebr. 1902) 92 N. W. 989.

as on a writ of error;[90] but, under the statutes of some jurisdictions, there is a trial *de novo* on appeal,[91] and where such a trial is had, the court disregards irregularities in the original proceedings and proceeds to try the matter anew on the merits.[92] The usual presumptions in favor of the correctness and regularity of the proceed-

90. Murphy *v.* Blandford, 11 S. W. 715, 11 Ky. L. Rep. 125; People *v.* Milton Highway Com'rs, 37 N. Y. 360; People *v.* Cline, 23 Barb. (N. Y.) 197; *In re* Cornplanter Tp. Road, 26 Pa. Super. Ct. 20; *In re* Manheim Tp. Road, 12 Pa. Super. Ct. 279; Beard *v.* Campbell County Justices, 3 Head (Tenn.) 97. And see People *v.* Dutchess County Judges, 23 Wend. (N. Y.) 360.

An appeal from an order overruling a motion to quash the proceedings is in the nature of certiorari, and brings up the record for the consideration of the superior court. *In re* Sewickley Tp. Road, 23 Pa. Super. Ct. 170.

An appeal from a judgment on exceptions to the report of a jury ordered to lay out a road between certain termini embraces only such exceptions, and does not include the merits of the petition, as it is not regular on the hearing of such exceptions, for the court to consider the propriety of such order. Anders *v.* Anders, 49 N. C. 243.

91. *Indiana.*— Fifer *v.* Ritter, 159 Ind. 8, 64 N. E. 463; Black *v.* Thomson, 107 Ind. 162, 7 N. E. 184; Schmied *v.* Keeney, 72 Ind. 309; Bowers *v.* Snyder, 66 Ind. 340; Scraper *v.* Pipes, 59 Ind. 158; Moore *v.* Smock, 6 Ind. 392; Malone *v.* Hardesty, Smith 53.

New York.— Rector *v.* Clark, 78 N. Y. 21; People *v.* Goodwin, 5 N. Y. 568; People *v.* Albright, 14 Abb. Pr. 305, 23 How. Pr. 306.

Pennsylvania.— Hibberd's Appeal, 6 Kulp 497, appeal from award of jury to court of quarter sessions.

Rhode Island.— Hazard *v.* Middletown, 12 R. I. 227.

Tennessee.— Green County Justices *v.* Graham, 6 Baxt. 77.

See 25 Cent. Dig. tit. "Highways," § 199.

In Kentucky this is now the practice. Louisville, etc., R. Co. *v.* Gerard, 130 Ky. 18, 112 S. W. 915. Under earlier statutes the right to a trial *de novo* did not exist. Rawlings *v.* Biggs, 85 Ky. 251, 3 S. W. 147, 8 Ky. L. Rep. 919; Smith *v.* McMeekin, 79 Ky. 24, 1 Ky. L. Rep. 259; Helm *v.* Short, 7 Bush 623; Morris *v.* Salle, 19 S. W. 527, 14 Ky. L. Rep. 117.

In Missouri the practice is now as stated in the text. Mayes *v.* Palmer, 206 Mo. 293, 103 S. W. 1140. Formerly such a trial was not authorized. Nickerson *v.* Lynch, 135 Mo. 471, 37 S. W. 128; St. Louis County *v.* Lind, 42 Mo. 348.

Qualified right to trial de novo.— Under some statutes there is a trial *de novo* on all questions presented by the notice of appeal (Williams *v.* Turner Tp., 15 S. D. 182, 87 N. W. 968), and under others, the appeal brings before the court the propriety of the amount of damages, and all other matters referred to in the application for appeal (Gorman *v.* St. Mary, 20 Minn. 392). Under the Illinois statutes, which restrict the power and authority of supervisors on appeal to call a jury to assess damages to cases where the state of the proceedings require it, that course may be taken only when it has not already been taken. People *v.* Highway Com'rs, 188 Ill. 150, 58 N. E. 989.

92. Kelley *v.* Augsperger, 171 Ind. 155, 85 N. E. 1004; Hughes *v.* Beggs, 114 Ind. 427, 16 N. E. 817; Fleming *v.* Hight, 95 Ind. 78; Breitweiser *v.* Fuhrman, 88 Ind. 28 (holding that it is error to refuse to allow a party to show that the county board unlawfully prevented him from filing a remonstrance); Brown *v.* McCord, 20 Ind. 270; Louisville, etc., R. Co. *v.* Gerard, 130 Ky. 18, 112 S. W. 915 (holding that it is necessary to prove jurisdictional facts in the appellate court, when they are put in issue by exceptions); Bennett *v.* Hall, 184 Mo. 407, 83 S. W. 439; Lafollette *v.* Road Com'r, 105 Tenn. 536, 58 S. W. 1065.

Dilatory or technical objections are out of place on such a trial and need not be entertained. People *v.* Smith, 15 Ill. 326. Thus a motion to set aside the proceedings of the lower board is useless, as the trial on appeal is *de novo*. Dillman *v.* Crooks, 91 Ind. 158. Likewise the court may properly refuse to allow appellant to file a plea in abatement alleging that less than six persons signing the petition resided in the neighborhood, since he has a right to contest the jurisdiction without filing any plea. Irwin *v.* Armuth, 129 Ind. 340, 28 N. E. 702.

The reports of viewers are of no value on such a trial and cannot be attacked for irregularity (Clift *v.* Brown, 95 Ind. 53); nor are they competent evidence, as they simply embody conclusions as to matters which are to be tried anew (Freck *v.* Christian, 55 Ind. 320; Coyner *v.* Boyd, 55 Ind. 166. And see Washington Ice Co. *v.* Lay, 103 Ind. 48, 2 N. E. 222, holding that the petition need not be offered in evidence. *Compare* Daggy *v.* Coats, 19 Ind. 259, holding that the necessary papers of record in the cause are operative in the appellate court to make a *prima facie* case, at least for the party in whose favor they are). However, it is not error for the court to permit the petitioners to read to the jury the report of viewers, with a plat of the lands reported benefited attached as an exhibit, under instructions that the contents of these papers are not evidence of the fact therein contained, but may be used to apply to other evidence. Fulton *v.* Cummings, 132 Ind. 453, 30 N. E. 949.

It is the province of the jury in such a trial to pass upon the credibility and weight of evidence; and its conclusion, when approved by the trial court, will not be disturbed on appeal. Raab *v.* Roberts, 30 Ind. App. 6, 64 N. E. 618, 65 N. E. 191.

holding hearings at the proper time and place,[3] a valid decision may be arrived at by any two of the three referees,[4] and, upon making their report, the proceeding is then before the court for affirmance, modification, or reversal.[5]

(6) DETERMINATION AND DISPOSITION OF CAUSE; DISMISSAL. The reviewing court will affirm or reverse the decision of the lower court or board in accordance with its views as to whether or not material error was committed,[6] or it may affirm the proceedings in part and reverse them in part;[7] and while it has no power to validate proceedings taken without jurisdiction,[8] it is not compelled to reverse the proceedings for every technical and harmless error, but may itself correct, or allow to be corrected, the mistake,[9] or remand the record to the lower court for correction.[10] The appellate court possesses power either to make a final dispo-

Time to object.—An objection that a committee appointed to determine an appeal were not sworn before fixing upon the time and place for the hearing comes too late if made, in the first instance, after their report. Raymond *v.* Cumberland County, 63 Me. 110.

3. People *v.* Strevell, 27 Hun (N. Y.) 218, holding that the referees may meet to consider the matter outside of the town in which the highway is located.

Where an adjournment without day is had, the powers of the referees are exhausted. Rogers *v.* Runyan, 9 How. Pr. (N. Y.) 248.

After the hearing has been closed, the only power then left to the referees is to decide, including the incidental power of adjourning from time to time for this purpose, and to prepare and sign, and cause to be filed, the evidence of their decision; they have no power to entertain a motion of third persons to open the cause for a further hearing, and for the reception of evidence impeaching the original testimony. People *v.* Ferris, 41 Barb. (N. Y.) 121, 18 Abb. Pr. 64, 27 How. Pr. 193 [*reversed* on other grounds in 36 N. Y. 218, 1 Transcr. App. 19, 34 How. Pr. 189].

4. Action *v.* York County, 77 Me. 128; People *v.* Burton, 65 N. Y. 452; People *v.* Sherman, 15 Hun (N. Y.) 575.

Their decision is not vitiated by the fact that appellant executed an undertaking to the town pledging private aid to the enterprise, where it appeared that such decision was not procured or induced by such undertaking. State *v.* Geneva Town Bd., 107 Wis. 1, 82 N. W. 550.

5. Peirce *v.* Portsmouth, 58 N. H. 311.

An error of the commissioners or referees does not extend back to the prior procedings, but may be fully redressed by setting aside the report. leaving the appeal to be proceeded with as if no hearing had been had and report made. Underwood *v.* Bailey, 58 N. H. 59.

The report must be made within the time limited by statute, and the court has no authority to accept a report made after such time, although the delay in making it was in accordance with an express written agreement between the parties, indorsed on the back of the warrant at the time of the view and hearing. Belfast's Appeal, 53 Me. 431.

6. Hawkins *v.* Robinson, 5 J. J. Marsh. (Ky.) 8; Peirce *v.* Portsmouth, 58 N. H. 311; Matter of Tappan Highway, 83 Hun (N. Y.) 613, 31 N. Y. Suppl. 625; People *v.* Hildreth, 1 Silv. Sup. (N. Y.) 358, 5 N. Y. Suppl. 308 [*affirmed* in 126 N. Y. 360, 27 N. E. 558] (holding that, when it appears that the general route was followed, it would be improper for an appellate court, without any knowledge of the obstacles in the proposed road, to interfere with the conclusion of the commissioners and referees appointed by the county court); *In re* Quemahoning Tp. Road,, 27 Pa. Super. Ct. 150 (holding that the omission to name the township in the petition, order of view, and report is not cause for reversal, where the termini are so precisely described in the report as to leave no room for doubt as to the location of the road).

Causes arising subsequent to the action of the board are not grounds of reversal, the only causes which the appellate court can recognize being those existing at the time the action was taken. Donnell *v.* York County, 87 Me. 223, 32 Atl. 884.

Under the Maine statutes the committee appointed by the supreme court on appeal reports whether the decision of the county commissioners should be affirmed or reversed (Cole *v.* Cumberland County, 78 Me. 532, 7 Atl. 397), and the only power of the court is to accept or reject the report of the committee (*In re* Brunswick, 37 Me. 446).

Findings.—Where the trial on appeal is *de novo* the verdict of the jury or decision of the court must embrace a finding of all the facts which the board would have been required to find to entitle the petitioners to the highway (Scraper *v.* Pipes, 59 Ind. 158), but in a special finding it is not necessary to state in detail the preliminary steps taken before the board of commissioners, if indeed it is proper to state them at all (Lowe *v.* Brannan, 105 Ind. 247, 4 N. E. 580).

7. Bryant *v.* Penobscot County, 79 Me. 128, 8 Atl. 460; Anthony *v.* Berkshire County, 14 Pick. (Mass.) 189; People *v.* Baker, 19 Barb. (N. Y.) 240. *Contra*, Sherburne Highway Com'rs *v.* Chenango Judges, 25 Wend. (N. Y.) 453; State *v.* Whitingham, 7 Vt. 390; Royalton *v.* Fox, 5 Vt. 458.

8. Cumberland Valley R. Co. *v.* Martin, 100 Md. 165, 59 Atl. 714.

9. Gordon *v.* Wabash County Highway Com'rs, 169 Ill. 510, 48 N. E. 451; Carpenter *v.* Windsor Tp., etc., Highway Com'rs, 64 Mich. 476, 31 N. W. 460; Anderson *v.* Myrtle Tp. Bd., 75 Mo. 57.

10. Sidener *v.* Esser, 22 Ind. 201 [*followed*

action.[25] It will not lie where the proceedings conform in all respects to the requirements of law,[26] or where there exists the right of appeal,[27] or other adequate remedy.[28] Neither is it available to question the public necessity for the road or the proper exercise of the discretion vested in the board;[29] and in nearly all cases the general rule that certiorari is not a writ of right but is a writ issuable in the discretion of the court to prevent substantial injustice[30] is applicable.[31] However, to prevent substantial injustice, the writ will issue,

Town way.—According to the practice in Maine and Massachusetts, certiorari cannot issue to a town to remove its proceedings in the case of a private or town way. Harlow *v.* Pike, 3 Me. 438; Todd *v.* Rome, 2 Me. 55; Robbins *v.* Lexington, 8 Cush. (Mass.) 292.

When a bill of exceptions is allowed on a petition for a highway, the remedy on such bill of exceptions is by writ of certiorari. *In re* Landaff, 34 N. H. 163.

25. Kinderhook Highway Com'rs *v.* Claw, 15 Johns. (N. Y.) 537; Lawton *v.* Cambridge Highway Com'rs, 2 Cai. (N. Y.) 179.

In Michigan, the decision of the township board, on appeal from the determination of a commissioner of highways, will be reviewed by certiorari only in case of peculiar and exceptional circumstances. Soller *v.* Brown Tp. Bd., 67 Mich. 422, 34 N. W. 888; Burt *v.* Sumpter Highway Com'rs, 32 Mich. 190.

26. Hightower *v.* Jones, 85 Ga. 697, 11 S. E. 872; Behrens *v.* Melrose Tp. Highway Com'rs, 169 Ill. 558, 48 N. E. 578.

27. *Illinois.*—Hegenbaumer *v.* Heckenkamp, 202 Ill. 621, 67 N. E. 389; Wright *v.* Carrollton Highway Com'rs, 150 Ill. 138, 36 N. E. 980.

Maine.—Hodgdon *v.* Lincoln County, 68 Me. 226.

Maryland.—Gaither *v.* Watkins, 66 Md. 576, 8 Atl. 464.

Michigan.—Nightingale *v.* Simmons, 66 Mich. 528, 33 N. W. 414; Flint, etc., R. Co. *v.* Norton, 64 Mich. 248, 31 N. W. 134.

New York.—People *v.* Onondaga County Ct., 152 N. Y. 214, 46 N. E. 325 [*affirming* 4 N. Y. App. Div. 542, 38 N. Y. Suppl. 920]; Matter of Taylor, 8 N. Y. App. Div. 395, 40 N. Y. Suppl. 839; People *v.* Thayer, 88 Hun 136, 34 N. Y. Suppl. 592.

See 25 Cent. Dig. tit. "Highways," § 204.

Under the former New York statutes, the right to appeal did not exist in some cases, and in such instances there was a right to certiorari. People *v.* Mosier, 50 Hun 64, 8 N. Y. Suppl. 621.

Where the proceedings are void for want of jurisdiction, the fact that parties interested had the right to appeal does not deprive them of their right to a writ of certiorari. Schuchman *v.* Jefferson County Highway Com'rs, 52 Ill. App. 497. Thus parties who have not been given notice of the proceedings lose nothing by their failure to appeal, but may seek their remedy by certiorari. Names *v.* Olive Tp., etc., Highway Com'rs, 30 Mich. 490.

Where an appeal has been refused, a writ of certiorari will be awarded to bring up the cause. Shields *v.* Greene County Justices, 2 Coldw. (Tenn.) 60.

28. Nobleboro *v.* Lincoln County, 68 Me. 548 (writ of error to correct error not apparent on face of record); *In re* Tucker, 27 N. H. 405; Devine *v.* Olney, 68 N. J. L. 284, 53 Atl. 466 (application for appointment of freeholders to review assessment); People *v.* McDonald, 4 Hun (N. Y.) 187 [*affirmed* in 69 N. Y. 362]. But see Walker *v.* Winkler, 60 N. J. L. 105, 37 Atl. 445, holding that a certiorari will not be dismissed because the prosecutor, before suing out the writ, applied to the court of common pleas for the appointment of freeholders, under the statute, to review the action of the surveyors in laying out the road.

29. Tiedt *v.* Carstensen, 61 Iowa 334, 16 N. W. 214; Thorpe *v.* Worcester County, 9 Gray (Mass.) 57; Kingman *v.* Plymouth County, 6 Cush. (Mass.) 306; Hampton *v.* Poland, 50 N. J. L. 367, 13 Atl. 174; State *v.* Pierson, 37 N. J. L. 363; Fretz's Appeal, 15 Pa. St. 397. *Contra,* People *v.* Ireland, 75 Hun (N. Y.) 600, 27 N. Y. Suppl. 582.

30. See CERTIORARI, 6 Cyc. 748.

31. White *v.* Lincoln County, 70 Me. 317; Howland *v.* Penobscot County, 49 Me. 143; North Berwick *v.* York County, 25 Me. 69; *In re* Vassalborough, 19 Me. 338; Granville *v.* Hampden County, 97 Mass. 193; Grand Trunk R. Co. *v.* Berlin, 68 N. H. 168, 36 Atl. 554; *In re* Landaff, 34 N. H. 163; Hancock *v.* Worcester, 62 Vt. 106, 18 Atl. 1041. And see Com. *v.* Hall, 8 Pick. (Mass.) 440; *In re* Appleby Manor Road, 1 Grant (Pa.) 443.

The writ has been issued where it appeared on the record that surveyors were appointed in less than one year after a former decision (*In re* Highway, 3 N. J. L. 1038); that a member of the court of sessions was an interested party (State *v.* Delesdernier, 11 Me. 473); that the proceedings were closed earlier than the time allowed by law (*In re* Windham, 32 Me. 452), or recorded later than the time prescribed (Cornville *v.* Somerset County, 33 Me. 237); or that the road was not completely and intelligibly described (Portland, etc., R. Co. *v.* York County, 65 Me. 292; Lewiston *v.* Lincoln County, 30 Me. 19).

The writ has been refused or quashed where the only ground therefor was an immaterial one of form (Monterey *v.* Berkshire County, 7 Cush. (Mass.) 394; *Ex p.* Miller, 4 Mass. 565), such as an omission to state the name of one person whose land is taken, or to describe his land as of a person unknown (North Reading *v.* Middlesex County, 7 Gray (Mass.) 109). It has also been held that it is not a ground for certiorari that the court, in the appointment

of statute, being that the county or town is not liable, but that the party who invokes the action of the officials is.[66] Statutes requiring the giving of cost bonds in highway proceedings are generally given a liberal construction, and irregularities in regard to the contents, sureties, approval, or filing are rarely held to be incurable or fatal to jurisdiction.[67]

(II) *OF PROCEEDINGS FOR REVIEW.* The right of an appellate court to make any award of costs in highway proceedings has been denied;[68] but on the other hand, it has been held that it should at least dispose of the costs made in its own court,[69] and the statutes of some states confer upon it a discretion as to the terms of the award,[70] while in other states the rule giving costs to the prevailing party is applicable.[71] A party seeking a review of the proceedings by either the original

agent's account at an adjourned sitting of the commissioners, and not necessarily at a regular term. Sumner *v.* Oxford County, 37 Me. 112.

Payment and collection.—Under the Minnesota statute, the county is not liable for payment of commissioners' services in opening a road, until their work is finished and the road opened (Thorn *v.* Washington County, 14 Minn. 233); and under a statute providing that the fees of the commissioners appointed to open a state road through three counties named shall be paid out of the county treasuries of the three counties "in proportion, as near as may be, to the extent of said road situated in each of said counties," one of such commissioners cannot, in an action against one of the counties, and upon proof that a certain number of days' service was performed by him in that county, recover the sum due for such services, since payment by the counties according to the terms of the act might impose a different measure of liability upon each county from that of paying for all the work upon the portion of the road lying in that county (Steele *v.* Randolph County, 63 Ill. 460). Under the New York statutes a petitioner is not remitted to a presentation of his claim to the supervisors, but on confirming a commissioners' report in proceedings to lay out a highway, the county court has authority, under Code Civ. Proc. § 3240, to allow the petitioner's costs and disbursements in excess of the fifty dollars provided by Highway Law, § 152. *In re* Peterson, 94 N. Y. App. Div. 143, 87 N. Y. Suppl. 1014.

Reimbursement may be had by petitioners who have expended money in procuring the establishment of the highway of the remaining petitioners, unless the petition has been materially altered without their consent. Jewett *v.* Cornforth, 3 Me. 107; Jewett *v.* Hodgdon, 3 Me. 103; Burnham *v.* Steele, 8 N. H. 182.

66. Smith *v.* Belknap County, 71 N. H. 203, 51 Atl. 628. *Compare* Onderdonk *v.* Plainfield, 42 N. J. L. 480.

67. Hopkins *v.* Contra Costa County, 106 Cal. 566, 39 Pac. 933; Hill *v.* Ventura County, 95 Cal. 239, 30 Pac. 385; Humboldt County *v.* Dinsmore, 75 Cal. 604, 17 Pac. 710; State *v.* Barlow, 61 Iowa 572, 16 N. W. 733; Eble *v.* State, 77 Kan. 179, 93 Pac. 803, 127 Am. St. Rep. 412 (holding that one petitioner may be a surety on the bond of another petitioner); Casey *v.* Kilgore, 14 Kan. 478; Miller *v.* Hamilton County, 9 Ohio Dec. (Reprint) 312, 12 Cinc. L. Bul. 152.

A bond is not required under the Oregon statutes (Douglas County *v.* Clark, 15 Oreg. 3, 13 Pac. 511), and in Massachusetts the fact that a town, in applying to the county commissioners to lay out a highway, gave no recognizance for costs, is not a ground for quashing the commissioners' proceedings upon the application of one over whose lands the way was located (Blake *v.* Norfolk County, 114 Mass. 583). A remonstrant who appears in his own name to defend his own rights does not come within a statute providing that any member of the community defending a suit brought against the community shall give bond. Shelton *v.* Derby, 27 Conn. 414.

68. People *v.* Spring Wells Tp. Bd., 12 Mich. 434; Butman *v.* Fowler, 17 Ohio 101.

Where the error might have been remedied in the lower court by amendment on motion, costs will be refused in the higher court. Mount Olive Tp. *v.* Hunt, 51 N. J. L. 274, 17 Atl. 291; People *v.* Ferris, 36 N. Y. 218 [*reversing* 41 Barb. 121].

Where the proper parties are not before the court, it will make no award of costs. Evans *v.* Shields, 3 Head (Tenn.) 70.

69. Ball *v.* Humphrey, 4 Greene (Iowa) 204.

Payment cannot be required until the appeal has been determined and the costs have been adjudged. Scott *v.* Lasell, 71 Iowa 180, 32 N. W. 322.

70. People *v.* Schodack Highway Com'rs, 27 How. Pr. (N. Y.) 158; People *v.* Flake, 14 How. Pr. (N. Y.) 527. *Compare* People *v.* Heath, 20 How. Pr. (N. Y.) 304.

In the absence of any statute governing the matter, the appellate court must exercise its discretion. *Ex p.* Williams, 4 Yerg. (Tenn.) 579.

A joint liability for the fees of referees attaches where several appeals are heard at one and the same hearing. Disosway *v.* Winant, 1 Abb. Dec. (N. Y.) 508, 3 Keyes 412, 2 Transcr. App. 192, 33 How. Pr. 460 [*reversing* 34 Barb. 578, 1 Abb. Pr. 216].

71. Sangamon County *v.* Brown, 13 Ill. 207 (holding that the obtaining of a material increase of damages on an appeal is a successful prosecution of the appeal which subjects the county to liability for costs); State

board or tribunal or a higher court is chargeable with the costs of the steps which he takes to obtain such review upon the dismissal of his exceptions, either of his own motion or by the court; [72] and where the cause is dismissed by the appellate court for want of jurisdiction in the lower board or court, the applicant for the road is liable for all the costs of the proceedings, including those of appeal.[73]

m. Operation and Effect of Establishment — (I) *IN GENERAL.* When all the steps required by statute have been regularly taken, a road is established and is, in contemplation of law, open, notwithstanding the fact that it is not actually open,[74] or that the time for an aggrieved party to apply for a discontinuance has not expired,[75] and when so established, it remains such until vacated by the public authorities or abandoned.[76] The public has a perpetual easement, which is a freehold, in its highways,[77] as the valid establishment of a public highway deprives an owner of land over which it passes of his freehold therein,[78] although he still retains certain prescriptive rights, such as easements which are not inconsistent with the easement of the highway.[79]

(II) *CHARACTER, LOCATION, AND EXTENT OF ROAD.*[80] The character of a road is usually determined by the terms of the statute and order under and by

v. Flaherty, 46 Minn. 128, 48 N. W. 686; Harris *v.* Coltraine, 10 N. C. 312; Tripp *v.* Carbondale, 8 Luz. Leg. Reg. (Pa.) 1.

Partial affirmance.—Where, on the trial of a highway appeal, there is a finding establishing such highway, but allowing damages therefor to a remonstrant, the costs accruing from the trial of the former issue should be assessed against such remonstrant, and that accruing upon the latter against the petitioners. Jamieson *v.* Cass County, 56 Ind. 466. Under a statute making the referees' fees a county charge when the highway commissioners' decision is "reversed" on appeal, the word "reversed" applies to a case of reversal in part, as well as to an entire reversal. People *v.* Orange County, 20 Hun (N. Y.) 196 [*affirmed* in 85 N. Y. 641].

Liability of petitioner.— In Maine the district court on appeal has no authority to award costs either for or against the original petitioners (*In re* Jordan, 32 Me. 472), while Iowa Code (1873), § 963, provides that if an appeal has been taken by claimant, the petitioner for the highway or the county must pay the costs occasioned by the appeals (Hanrahan *v.* Fox, 47 Iowa 102).

As the commissioners have no personal interest in the matter, an award of costs should not be made against them personally (Russell Com'rs' Ct. *v.* Tarver, 25 Ala. 480; Alexander *v.* Rubensam, 12 Ill. App. 120), except where they have made themselves parties to the appeal or certiorari (Russell Com'rs' Ct. *v.* Tarver, *supra*; Sonora Highway Com'rs *v.* Carthage, 27 Ill. 140).

72. Smith *v.* Brasher, 67 Mo. App. 556; *In re* Stowe Tp. Road, 20 Pa. Super. Ct. 404.

73. Dyer *v.* Steuben County, 84 Ind. 542; Wilhite *v.* Wolfe, 90 Mo. App. 18.

74. Ferris *v.* Ward, 9 Ill. 499; Harrow *v.* State, 1 Greene (Iowa) 439.

Under the Minnesota statutes, a county road does not in all cases become a public highway open to public use, immediately upon the order of the county commissioners granting the prayer of the petition. Thus, where the road is over inclosed lands, it is essential that the road be opened by the supervisors of the town. State *v.* Leslie, 30 Minn. 533, 16 N. W. 408.

When contingent on act of landowner.— Where a street has been laid out and confirmed, subject to the right of the owner of the land to have compensation before it is opened, it becomes a public highway when opened as such by the owner of the land, and may lawfully be used as such, although a turnpike road and toll gate are thereby avoided. Greensburg, etc., Turnpike Road Co. *v.* Breidenthal, 1 Phila. (Pa.) 170.

75. Cragie *v.* Mellen, 6 Mass. 7.

Likewise, under a statute providing that if the court approve the report allowing a road it shall direct the breadth of the road, and at the next court the whole proceedings shall be entered on record, and thenceforth the road shall be deemed to be a lawful road, the road becomes a public highway on the report being confirmed and the exceptions dismissed, without waiting for the expiration of the succeeding term of court. Hibberd *v.* Delaware County, 1 Pa. Super. Ct. 204.

76. Champlain *v.* Morgan, 20 Ill. 181. See *infra*, II, D, 2, e; II, D, 3.

77. People *v.* Magruder, 237 Ill. 340, 86 N. E. 615; Perry *v.* Bozarth, 198 Ill. 328, 64 N. E. 1076; Farrelly *v.* Kane, 172 Ill. 415, 50 N. E. 118; Waggeman *v.* North Peoria, 160 Ill. 277, 43 N. E. 347; Brusby Mound *v.* McClintock, 146 Ill. 643, 35 N. E. 159.

A patent for public lands is subject to the easement of a highway under an act of congress granting a right of way for highways over public lands not reserved for public use. Bequette *v.* Patterson, 104 Cal. 282, 37 Pac. 917; McRose *v.* Bottyer, 81 Cal. 122, 22 Pac. 393. And see PUBLIC LANDS, 32 Cyc. 866.

78. Aden *v.* Road Dist. No. 3, 97 Ill. App. 347.

79. Augusta *v.* Moulton, 75 Me. 284.

80. **Of highway acquired by user** see *supra*, II, B, 6.

Of highway established by dedication see DEDICATION, 13 Cyc. 488.

dence,[1] the use of a way by the public and the limits thereof being considered a public fact concerning which any one with knowledge may speak.[2] Any or all of the records of the proceedings establishing the way or certified copies thereof, including the notes and maps of the surveyors and viewers, are admissible,[3] especially under statutes requiring a record to be made,[4] or under statutes making them or a certified copy thereof competent evidence;[5] and under the presumption of regularity which attaches to the proceedings of the board,[6] the record, to be admissible, need not be explicit as to all the preliminary steps, provided it shows jurisdiction and the final order;[7] but the records are not admissible when so incomplete or manifestly irregular as to be misleading and untrue,[8] or when made by one without author-

Compare Shepherd *v.* Turner, 129 Cal. 530, 62 Pac. 106, holding that while it is competent to prove the use made of the road, it is not competent to prove such user by the declaration of third persons or by reputation.

1. *Georgia.*— Penick *v.* Morgan County, 131 Ga. 385, 62 S. E. 300, holding admissible evidence of acts of control and dominion over road by public authorities.

Illinois.— Ferris *v.* Ward, 9 Ill. 499; Nealy *v.* Brown, 6 Ill. 10; Eyman *v.* People, 6 Ill. 4.

New York.— Chapman *v.* Gates, 46 Barb. 313.

Pennsylvania.— Morrow *v.* Com., 48 Pa. St. 305.

Tennessee.— Mankin *v.* State, 2 Swan 206.

See 25 Cent. Dig. tit. "Highways," § 228.

The actual location of the road may be proved by parol testimony as to its opening and use. Louk *v.* Woods, 15 Ill. 256; Arnold *v.* Flattery, 5 Ohio 271.

To prove that a road is not a public highway, testimony of the county supervisor who has charge of all the highways and public road of the county is admissible. Miles *v.* Postal Tel. Cable Co., 55 S. C. 403, 33 S. E. 493.

2. Brown *v.* Jefferson County, 16 Iowa 339.

3. Penick *v.* Morgan County, 131 Ga. 385, 62 S. E. 300; Louk *v.* Woods, 15 Ill. 256; Roehrborn *v.* Schmidt, 16 Wis. 519; Reg. *v.* McGowan, 17 N. Brunsw. 191. And see Atty.-Gen. *v.* Antrobus, [1905] 2 Ch. 188, 69 J. P. 141, 3 Loc. Gov. 1071, 92 L. T. Rep. N. S. 790, 21 T. L. R. 471.

The original survey and minutes of the commissioners in the laying out of a road are admissible in evidence, instead of authenticated copies (King *v.* Kenny, 4 Ohio 79); and when the original records have been destroyed by fire, secondary evidence of their contents is competent (Wildrick *v.* Hager, 10 N. Y. St. 764).

A report found on the files of the town, but not otherwise recorded, is sufficient evidence of the laying out of a highway. Hardy *v.* Houston, 2 N. H. 309.

An act of the legislature recognizing the road as a highway, together with proof that a person under whom plaintiff claims title was cognizant of the application to the legislature for the passage of the act, and subsequently acted under it as commissioner, is admissible in evidence. Tyson *v.* Baltimore County, 28 Md. 510.

4. Jonestown Road Case, 1 Serg. & R. (Pa.) 487 (certified copy); Randall *v.* Rovelstad, 105 Wis. 410, 81 N. W. 819.

The neglect to have filed and recorded the proper records, as required by law, does not raise a presumption that the authorities proceeded contrary to statute in establishing the road, or render inadmissible evidence that the necessary acts were in fact done. Carron *v.* Clark, 14 Mont. 301, 36 Pac. 178.

5. Waterman *v.* Raymond, 34 Ill. 42; Epler *v.* Niman, 5 Ind. 459, transcript of proceedings.

6. See *supra*, II, C, 5, n, (II), (A).

7. *Illinois.*— Dumoss *v.* Francis, 15 Ill. 543.

Iowa.— State *v.* Lane, 26 Iowa 223.

Missouri.— State *v.* Gilbert, 73 Mo. 20.

New York.— Sage *v.* Barnes, 9 Johns. 365.

Ohio.— McClelland *v.* Miller, 28 Ohio St. 488; Beebe *v.* Scheidt, 13 Ohio St. 406; Arnold *v.* Flattery, 5 Ohio 271.

See 25 Cent. Dig. tit. "Highways," § 231.

Compare Williams *v.* Holmes, 2 Wis. 129, holding that before a petition for laying out a road is admissible in evidence, it must be affirmatively shown that there were six freeholders, petitioners.

Omission of provisions as to compensation or damages does not affect the admissibility of the records. Howard *v.* State, 47 Ark. 431, 2 S. W. 331; Thompson *v.* Major, 58 N. H. 242. But see Dunning *v.* Matthews, 16 Ill. 308.

8. Watrous *v.* Southworth, 5 Conn. 305; State *v.* Snyder, 25 Iowa 208 (holding the record in question objectionable for uncertainty in not stating the termini of the road); State *v.* Berry, 21 Me. 169 (holding that the records of a town which are not admissible to prove the existence of a legal town way cannot be admitted to show the limits or outside lines of the road); Young *v.* Garland, 18 Me. 409.

Jurisdiction must be shown in order to render the records admissible. Mankin *v.* State, 2 Swan (Tenn.) 206.

Where certification is required, failure to obtain it is fatal to the admissibility of the records. Blodget *v.* Royalton, 14 Vt. 288.

Slight discrepancies, or clerical mistakes, which may be readily corrected by reference to other papers of the record, are of no moment in passing on the admissibility of the evidence (Humboldt County *v.* Dinsmore, 75 Cal. 604, 17 Pac. 710; State *v.* Prine, 25 Iowa 231); but where selectmen, in laying out a highway, referred for a particular de-

ity.[9] Such records are at least *prima facie* evidence of the facts which they recite,[10] and are not subject to direct contradiction by parol evidence,[11] except as to jurisdictional facts,[12] although evidence *aliunde* may be received to explain and supply defects therein,[13] or to identify the subject-matter.[14] The writings or parol testimony offered must be relevant and purport to be evidence of the matters intended to be proved.[15]

(c) *Weight and Sufficiency.* In considering evidence as to the legal or actual existence and limits of a highway, care should be taken against giving any one item conclusive effect,[16] and of giving any independent weight to evidence which

scription to a plan recorded in the registry of deeds, in proving the limits of such highway, the records thus referred to should be produced as a part of the description (Hall *v.* Manchester, 39 N. H. 295).

Although inadmissible to prove a laying out, on account of irregularity, the records may nevertheless be admitted as evidence to show the commencement of the way, in order to rebut a presumption of a dedication (Avery *v.* Stewart, 1 Cush. (Mass.) 496), or to show a prescriptive right (Wright *v.* Fanning, (Tex. Civ. App. 1905) 86 S. W. 786).

9. Gray *v.* Waterman, 40 Ill. 522.

The certificate of a person not acting judicially but only as commissioner to see the work executed is but *prima facie* evidence of the facts recited therein, and may be contradicted by parol. Davis *v.* Concordia Police Jury, 19 La. 533.

The appointment of a person who has made a report must be established, before such report may be admitted in evidence. Fowler *v.* Savage, 3 Conn. 90.

A report embodying matters not within the jurisdiction of the persons making it is no evidence of such matters. Schuylkill County's Appeal, 38 Pa. St. 459.

10. Waterman *v.* Raymond, 34 Ill. 42; Lowe *v.* Aroma, 21 Ill. App. 598 (holding that Rev. St. c. 121, § 52, making the town clerk's record *prima facie* evidence of the regularity of proceedings in relation to highways, applies where the road was established before, as well as after, its enactment); Shaffer *v.* Weech, 34 Kan. 595, 9 Pac. 202 (map and field notes of surveyor); Willis *v.* Sproule, 13 Kan. 257; Roehrborn *v.* Schmidt, 16 Wis. 519.

11. *Louisiana.*— Innis *v.* Kemper, 3 Mart. N. S. 119.

Maine.— Blaisdell *v.* Briggs, 23 Me. 123.

Michigan.— Moore *v.* People, 2 Dougl. 420

Missouri.— Butler *v.* Barr, 18 Mo. 357.

New Hampshire.— State *v.* Rye, 35 N. H. 368; Dudley *v.* Butler, 10 N. H. 281.

North Carolina.— Cline *v.* Lemon, 4 N. C. 323.

Ohio.— Beebe *v.* Scheidt, 13 Ohio St. 406.

See 25 Cent. Dig. tit. "Highways," § 232.

The records of one county are not subject to impeachment in a collateral way by the records of another county. Bradbury *v.* Benton, 69 Me. 194.

12. People *v.* Seward, 27 Barb. (N. Y.) 94 [*affirmed* in 30 N. Y. 470]; Anderson *v.* Hamilton County, 12 Ohio St. 635.

13. Ackerson *v.* Van Vleck, 72 Iowa 57, 33 N. W. 362; Keyes *v.* Tait, 19 Iowa 123; Oliphant *v.* Atchison County, 18 Kan. 386; Smith *v.* Cumberland County, 42 Me. 395; Austin *v.* Allen, 6 Wis. 134, holding that, in proving that the signers of the petition were freeholders, resort to documentary evidence is not necessary. *Compare* Butterfield *v.* Pollock, 45 Iowa 257 (holding that in determining the sufficiency of a notice, extrinsic evidence is inadmissible to explain it); Stewart *v.* Wallis, 30 Barb. (N. Y.) 344.

Evidence of user in aid of defective record see *supra*, II, C, 5, i, (VI), (B).

14. Penick *v.* Morgan County, 131 Ga. 385, 62 S. E. 300, where testimony to show that the road referred to in the minutes was the road testified about was held to have been properly received.

15. Shepherd *v.* Turner, 129 Cal. 530, 62 Pac. 106 (holding that as the refusal to vacate a highway does not tend to make the premises a highway, an order making such refusal is inadmissible); Wooster *v.* Butler, 13 Conn. 309; Lincoln *v.* Com., 164 Mass. 1, 41 N. E. 112; State *v.* Alstead, 18 N. H. 59 (holding that the testimony of one that he has acted as a road surveyor, and in execution of his warrant caused a road to be repaired, is not evidence of such road having been established as a public highway, when there is no evidence that it was within his district, and his warrant has not been produced or accounted for).

The condition of a road is not evidence as to whether or not it is a highway. Zimmerman *v.* State, 4 Ind. App. 583, 31 N. E. 550.

Identification of the records and the entries therein by showing when the book or record came into existence, in whose custody it is, and when the entries therein were made is a condition precedent to its admissibility. Shepherd *v.* Turner, 129 Cal. 530, 62 Pac. 106; Penick *v.* Morgan County, 131 Ga. 385, 62 S. E. 300.

Facts showing a sufficient identification see Hall *v.* Manchester, 40 N. H. 410.

Verdicts and judgments between other parties are not admissible to show the establishment of a highway, except in the case of highways claimed by prescription and user. Fowler *v.* Savage, 3 Conn. 90.

16. Beach *v.* Meriden, 46 Conn. 502.

A plan filed by a town in compliance with a statutory requirement, showing a number of roads, some of which were admitted to be county roads, and showing also brooks and other things not called for by the act, is not conclusive evidence that a way delineated

is of no worth unless accompanied by other evidence.[17] Thus, surveys, reports, and other preliminary proceedings are insufficient to establish the existence of the highway without proof of an actual opening to public use;[18] and in general the rules and standards prevailing in other civil actions[19] are applicable in passing on the weight and sufficiency of evidence relating to the existence of a highway.[20]

D. Alteration, Vacation, and Abandonment — 1. ALTERATION[21] — a. In General — (I) *WHAT CONSTITUTES ALTERATION.* An alteration of a highway, as the expression is used, generally refers to a change in the course thereof,[22] and therefore necessarily involves to some extent the establishment of a new highway, and the vacation of the part of the old highway for which the substitution is made.[23] But the term has been extended to include a widening or narrowing,[24] and the

thereon is a county road. Butchers' Slaughtering, etc., Assoc. *v.* Boston, 139 Mass. 290, 30 N. E. 94. Likewise a plat returned by county commissioners of the location of a public road is not conclusive evidence of its actual location. Hiner *v.* People, 34 Ill. 297.

Order to remove fence.— An order of the town supervisor requiring an occupant of land to remove a fence on the ground that it encroaches upon a public highway is not conclusive evidence of the legal existence of such highway. Soule *v.* State, 19 Wis. 593.

17. Brantly *v.* Huff, 62 Ga. 532.

18. Ottawa *v.* Yentzer, 160 Ill. 509, 43 N. E. 601. And see O'Connell *v.* Chicago Terminal Transfer R. Co., 184 Ill. 308, 56 N. E. 355.

Subsequent surveys leave the proof of the existence of the road precisely as it was before. Gentleman *v.* Soule, 32 Ill. 271, 83 Am. Dec. 264.

19. See EVIDENCE, 17 Cyc. 753.

20. See Neff *v.* Smith, 91 Iowa 87, 58 N. W. 1072; State *v.* Horn, 34 Kan. 556, 9 Pac. 208 (holding that where the record of the county board recites that two of the viewers acted and made a report, but the report itself shows otherwise, the report is the better evidence and must prevail); Warner *v.* Holyoke, 112 Mass. 362; Bellevue *v.* Hunter, 105 Minn. 343, 117 N. W. 445; Arndt *v.* Thomas, 90 Minn. 355, 96 N. W. 1125; Postal *v.* Martin, 4 Nebr. (Unoff.) 534, 95 N. W. 8; State *v.* Morse, 50 N. H. 9; State *v.* Stites, 13 N. J. L. 172 (holding that a written petition for a highway is more conclusive, as evidence of the route applied for, than the subsequent declarations of the applicants); Tincher *v.* State, 19 Tex. 156; Bare *v.* Williams, 101 Va. 800, 45 S. E. 331; Austin *v.* Allen, 6 Wis. 134 (holding that proof of peaceable possession under claim of title is *prima facie* evidence that the signers of the petition were freeholders).

Evidence sufficient to go to jury see Reed *v.* Harlan, 2 Ohio Dec. (Reprint) 553, 3 West. L. Month. 632.

The sufficiency and effect of the records are for the determination of the court alone. State *v.* Prine, 25 Iowa 231.

A recorded plat is not evidence of the existence of a road, but is only evidence of its precise locality. Naylor *v.* Beeks, 1 Oreg. 216.

Absence of record proof.— Evidence that a road has been used and traveled by the public, and kept in repair by the road overseer of the district in which it is located, is sufficient *prima facie* to establish the existence of such road as a public highway (Madison Tp. *v.* Scott, 9 Kan. App. 871, 61 Pac. 967); and the mere absence of record proof is insufficient to establish the fact that the place in question is not a public highway (State *v.* Robinson, 12 Wash. 491, 41 Pac. 884).

Sufficiency of evidence to support finding of necessity of highway see *supra*, II, C, 1, b, (II), (C), note 90.

21. **At railroad crossing** see RAILROADS, 33 Cyc. 266.

Change of grade of city streets see MUNICIPAL CORPORATIONS, 28 Cyc. 839.

Of city streets see MUNICIPAL CORPORATIONS, 28 Cyc. 838.

22. Gloucester *v.* Essex County, 3 Metc. (Mass.) 375; Buchholz *v.* New York, etc., R. Co., 71 N. Y. App. Div. 452, 75 N. Y. Suppl. 824 [*affirmed* in 177 N. Y. 550, 69 N. E. 1121]; Hutchinson *v.* Chester, 33 Vt. 410; State *v.* Burgeson, 108 Wis. 174, 84 N. W. 241; Harrison *v.* Milwaukee County, 51 Wis. 645, 8 N. W. 731.

"Alter" means to change or modify; to change in form without destroying identity. Heiple *v.* Clackamas County, 20 Oreg. 147, 25 Pac. 291.

A change making a right angle instead of an obtuse angle in an existing highway is an "alteration" thereof. People *v.* Jones, 63 N. Y. 306.

23. People *v.* Jones, 63 N. Y. 306; Buchholz *v.* New York, etc., R. Co., 71 N. Y. App. Div. 452, 75 N. Y. Suppl. 824 [*affirmed* in 177 N. Y. 550, 69 N. E. 1121]; Millcreek Tp. *v.* Reed, 29 Pa. St. 195; *In re* Loyalsock Tp. Road, 26 Pa. Super. Ct. 219; West Penn. Road, 23 Pa. Co. Ct. 477.

A technical alteration is the substitution of one way for another. Bigelow *v.* Worcester, 169 Mass. 390, 48 N. E. 1; Johnson *v.* Wyman, 9 Gray (Mass.) 186.

"Alteration" distinguished from "discontinuance" see Thompson *v.* Crabb, 6 J. J. Marsh. (Ky.) 222.

Operation and effect of alteration see *infra*, II, D, 1, a, (VI).

24. Boston, etc., R. Co. *v.* Middlesex County, 177 Mass. 511, 59 N. E. 115; New England R. Co. *v.* Worcester County R. Com'rs, 171 Mass. 135, 50 N. E. 549; Holmes *v.* Jersey City, 12 N. J. Eq. 299; People *v.*

be presumed that formal proceedings were taken for the alteration of the highway in question.[69]

(B) *Petition and Parties* — (1) PETITION — (a) IN GENERAL. Under the provisions of some early statutes an application to change or alter a public highway could be made by motion, provided notice was given, but the later statutes of practically all the states require such application to be made by written petition, the form and contents of which are usually expressly prescribed.[70] It is not necessary that the statutory form be strictly followed. A substantial compliance is sufficient, expressing with reasonable certainty the action desired.[71] The petition must state specifically the object; and that must appear to be clearly within the purview of the act giving the court jurisdiction, otherwise the proceedings are irregular.[72] It should further describe the existing road,[73] the route of the proposed road,[74] the termini thereof,[75] the character of the alterations pro-

the commissioners other land, with a view to effecting a necessary change in the road, and the road is by order of the commissioners opened on the lands conveyed, and is so used by the public and by the proper authorities, there is a legal change in the location of the highway, notwithstanding the want of statutory proceedings for that purpose.

69. Leigh Urban Dist. Council *v.* King, [1901] 1 K. B. 747, 65 J. P. 243, 70 L. J. K. B. 313, 83 L. T. Rep. N. S. 777, 17 T. L. R. 205.

70. See the statutes of the several states, and cases cited *infra*, this note.

In Kentucky under the provisions of the general statutes an application to open a new road, or to change an old one, could be made by motion, provided the usual notice had been given in writing of the proposed application; but the act of 1894, which is chapter 110 of the Kentucky statutes, made a material change in these proceedings by requiring that such application should be by written petition, signed by at least five landholders of the county, and setting forth a description of the road, etc. Ford *v.* Collins, 108 Ky. 553, 56 S. W. 993, 994, 22 Ky. L. Rep. 251.

71. Harris *v.* Mahaska County, 88 Iowa 219, 55 N. W. 324; Jenkins *v.* Riggs, 100 Md. 427, 59 Atl. 758.

72. Wisner *v.* Barber County, 73 Kan. 324, 85 Pac. 288 (holding that a defective statement of a change prayed for in a highway will not render the petition void, where, notwithstanding the defect, the purpose of the petition can be gathered from the language used); Wilhite *v.* Wolf, 179 Mo. 472, 78 S. W. 793; *In re* Church Road, 5 Watts & S. (Pa.) 200.

73. Cox *v.* East Fork Tp. Highway Com'rs, 194 Ill. 355, 62 N. E. 791; Kelley *v.* Augsperger, 171 Ind. 155, 85 N. E. 1004; Lowe *v.* Brannan, 105 Ind. 247, 4 N. E. 580 (holding that under a petition professing to describe an existing highway, but in fact describing a highway as it will exist if the improvement is made, the court cannot order the straightening of an existing highway not described); Shute *v.* Decker, 51 Ind. 241 (holding that the description of a highway, in a petition for its change, as beginning at the state line in a certain section is too indefinite, where the section lies a mile in extent on the state line; but if the point in the road where the proposed change is to commence is definitely pointed out, and the line of the change designated, it will be sufficient); Scherer *v.* Bailey, 34 Ind. App. 172, 72 N. E. 472 (holding that a petition failing to describe the old road is fatally defective, notwithstanding a description of the proposed change); Raymond *v.* Cumberland County, 63 Me. 112.

74. Kelley *v.* Augsperger, 171 Ind. 155, 85 N. E. 1004; Scherer *v.* Bailey, 34 Ind. App. 172, 72 N. E. 472; *In re* Chartiers Tp. Road, 48 Pa. St. 314; *In re* Nelson's Mill Road, 2 Leg. Op. (Pa.) 54; Neis *v.* Franzen, 18 Wis. 537.

A description which is sufficiently definite to enable a surveyor to locate the highway is all that the law requires. Conaway *v.* Ascherman, 94 Ind. 187; Zeibold *v.* Foster, 118 Mo. 349, 24 S. W. 155.

Township or county.— A petition for the alteration of a highway must state the township (State *v.* Convery, 53 N. J. L. 588, 22 Atl. 345; Parkhurst *v.* Vanderveer, 48 N. J. L. 80, 2 Atl. 771) or county (*In re* Quemahoning Tp. Road, 27 Pa. Super. Ct. 150) in which the proposed road lies. But the omission to name the township in the petition, order of view, and report is not cause for the reversal of an order of confirmation, where the termini are so precisely described in the report as to leave no room for doubt as to the location of the road. *In re* Quemahoning Tp. Road, *supra*.

75. Raymond *v.* Cumberland County, 63 Me. 112; Johns *v.* Marion County, 4 Oreg. 46.

Reasonable certainty is required in defining the termini of the proposed route. *In re* West Penn Road, 23 Pa. Co. Ct. 477.

The caption of a petition may be considered in connection with the petition in determining whether the termini and the names of the township and county are sufficiently stated. *In re* Quemahoning Tp. Road, 27 Pa. Super. Ct. 150.

Description held sufficient see *In re* Lee, 4 Pennew. (Del.) 576, 60 Atl. 862; Hyde Park *v.* Norfolk County, 117 Mass. 416.

Where the petition designates other points on the road besides the termini, the proceedings will be set aside on exceptions. *In re*

posed,[76] and whatever else the statute may require.[77] Unless required by statute,[78] it is not necessary that the petition shall contain any averment as to notice,[79] or as to the length [80] or width [81] of the proposed road, or that it will be of public utility.[82] The petition should describe the petitioners, so as to make it appear that they have an interest in the subject-matter of the legal controversy which the petition initiates,[83] and should state the names of the property-owners over whose lands the proposed road is to be located.[84] A new and separate highway cannot be laid out upon an application to alter an existing highway.[85] Nor does a petition to lay out a road give jurisdiction to alter an already existing road.[86] But there is no objection to asking in the same petition for the vacation of one highway and the establishment of another in lieu thereof,[87] unless such alteration will effect such a radical change in the route of the road as practically to amount to a new road.[88]

(b) AMENDMENT. A petition to alter a highway is subject to amendment in a proper case.[89] But the commissioners have no right to amend a petition signed

Dallas Tp. Road, 8 Kulp (Pa.) 58, holding that the viewers should be left free to exercise their own judgment and discretion for the public good rather than be bound or controlled by that of the petitioners for private purposes. Bnt see *In re* Covington Road, Wilcox (Pa.) 121, holding that in proceedings to vacate and relay part of a road it was not error for the petition to mention other points in the road besides the termini.

76. Raymond *v.* Cumberland County, 63 Me. 112.

77. Intention to vacate part supplied.— Where the statute does not permit the alteration or change of a portion of a highway without at the same time vacating the part rendered unnecessary by reason of the alteration, the intention to vacate such unnecessary part should be specifically mentioned in the application, and set out on the plans and surveys accompanying the same. *In re* Washington Pike, 9 Pa. Dist. 52.

78. Wilson *v.* Berkstresser, 45 Mo. 283 (notice); Leath *v.* Summers, 25 N. C. 108 (necessity and utility).

79. Conaway *v.* Ascherman, 94 Ind. 187.

80. Bowers *v.* Snyder, 88 Ind. 302.

81. Zeibold *v.* Foster, 118 Mo. 349, 24 S. W. 155.

82. Conaway *v.* Ascherman, 94 Ind. 187; Bowers *v.* Snyder, 88 Ind. 302.

To move the discretion of the court, it is proper to recite in the petition the particular defects in the present location of the road (*In re* Ottercreek Tp. Public Road, 104 Pa. St. 261); but this need not be done (*In re* Manheim Tp. Road, 12 Pa. Super. Ct. 279).

83. Conaway *v.* Ascherman. 94 Ind. 187; State *v.* Nelson, 57 Wis. 147, 15 N. W. 14.

Residence.— Under the Pennsylvania act of June 13, 1836, a petition to change an old road need not indicate the residence of the petitioners. *In re* Friendsville, etc., Road, 16 Pa. Co. Ct. 172.

The petition should show that the petitioners are freeholders, and that six of them "reside in the immediate neighborhood of the highway proposed to be located, vacated, or of the change to be made." Conaway *v.* Ascherman, 94 Ind. 187.

84. Conaway *v.* Ascherman, 94 Ind. 187, where the change will vacate an existing way running over the lands of more than one person, and relocate it upon the lands held by two or more different owners. And see Wagner *v.* Mahrt, 32 Wash. 542, 73 Pac. 675.

Consent.— Where the petition does not disclose that consent of the landowner was not had, for the purpose of admitting evidence as to proceedings based upon that petition, it will be presumed that such consent was obtained. Wagner *v.* Mahrt, 32 Wash. 542, 73 Pac. 675.

85. See *supra*, II, D, 1, a, (I).

86. Norton *v.* Truitt, 70 N. J. L. 611, 57 Atl. 130.

87. Anderson *v.* Wood, 80 Ill. 15; Brown *v.* Roberts, 23 Ill. App. 461 [*affirmed* in 123 Ill. 631, 15 N. E. 30]; Harris *v.* Mahaska County, 88 Iowa 219, 55 N. W. 324; Green *v.* Loudenslager, 54 N. J. L. 478, 24 Atl. 367; State *v.* Bergen, 21 N. J. L. 342; Conrad *v.* Lewis County, 10 W. Va. 784. And see *supra*, II, C, 5, e, (IV).

Such a petition is not double because it seeks to have a part of an old highway vacated and a new one established in lieu thereof, as a change of highway implies a departure from the road already established and the opening of a new road. Kelley *v.* Augsperger, 171 Ind. 155, 85 N. E. 1004. The change of a highway necessarily requires the vacation of a portion of the highway and the location of such portion upon a different line, and in this sense a vacation and location are authorized in the same proceeding. Bowers *v.* Snyder, 88 Ind. 302. And see Patton *v.* Creswell, 120 Ind. 147, 21 N. E. 663; State *v.* Burgeson, 108 Wis. 174, 84 N. W. 241.

88. Bacon *v.* Noble, 20 Ohio Cir. Ct. 281, 11 Ohio Cir. Dec. 49.

89. New Marlborough *v.* Berkshire County, 9 Metc. (Mass.) 423 (holding that a petition to county commissioners to alter a town way according to a report of selectmen, which the town is alleged to have unreasonably refused to accept, may be amended, even after a hearing of the parties on the petition, by striking out the alleged unreasonable neglect of the town, and substituting an allegation of the unreasonable neglect of the selectmen to alter

validity of their report,[12] but it will be presumed to have been made in conformity with the statute, where nothing to the contrary appears.[13] The report of the viewers is not conclusive and final,[14] but is subject to the approval of the court.[15] When insufficient,[16] or incorrect in form or detail,[17] the report may be recommitted or referred back for correction.

(G) *Order or Judgment* — (1) IN GENERAL. The order for the alteration of a highway must be for such a way as the one described in the petition.[18] The order should preferably follow the terms of the statute, but if it substantially conforms thereto, it will be sufficient.[19] Such an order is usually required to contain a description of the highway so altered,[20] and the kind of improvement to be

Londongrove Road, 2 Lanc. L. Rev. 160. But the omission to designate the township in which the road is situated is not such an irregularity as will justify reversal, where the petition and order designate the township in which the road begins and ends, and there is no uncertainty as to its location. *In re* Manheim Tp. Road, 12 Pa. Super. Ct. 279. Moreover it must state briefly the improvements through which the old road passes. *In re* West Penn Road, 23 Pa. Co. Ct. 477. It should fix the termini at some fixed and permanent object, and a slight change of termini for the purpose of starting from some fixed object will not invalidate the action of the viewers. *In re* Friendsville Road, 16 Pa. Co. Ct. 172. The act of June 13, 1836, requires that the report of viewers should set forth *inter alia* that they were severally sworn or affirmed. *In re* West Penn Road, *supra*. But there is nothing in the act which requires the oath taken by the viewers to be in writing and attached to the report. *In re* West Penn Road, *supra*. Neither is it necessary to attach to the report the copy of the notice posted, or the proof of said posting. It is sufficient if the report sets forth that the notice of the proposed meeting was duly put up at least ten days before the time of meeting in the vicinity of the place to be viewed. *In re* West Penn Road, *supra*.

The inclusion of matters upon which the viewers are not authorized to pass renders the report irregular and illegal. *In re* Sunbury Borough Church St., 8 Pa. Dist. 457. But where the tribunal appointing the viewers had power to authorize them to do what they actually did, it may subsequently ratify such unauthorized acts. Hark *v.* Gladwell, 49 Wis. 172, 5 N. W. 323

12. Craig *v.* North, 3 Metc. (Ky.) 187; Fowler *v.* Larabee, 59 N. J. L. 259, 35 Atl. 911.

Description of proposed route.— A statute regulating the alteration of public roads requires the utmost attainable certainty in the description to be given by the viewers of the route of the proposed alteration. Craig *v.* North, 3 Metc. (Ky.) 187. But see Robson *v.* Ryler, 14 Tex. Civ. App. 374, 37 S. W. 872, holding that the degree of certainty required in the description of the road is not the highest, but only such as is reasonable. If the description be such as that the places designated will enable persons familiar with the locality to locate the way with reasonable certainty, it will be deemed sufficient.

Mere ambiguity and lack of precision of statement, if, in substance, the order was complied with, is not a sufficient ground to quash the proceedings. *In re* Brecknock Tp. Road, 2 Woodw. (Pa.) 13.

13. Heagy *v.* Black, 90 Ind. 534, holding that if the report be favorable, and silent as to the public utility of the location or change, or if they do not report that the location or change is not of public utility, it should be presumed that they deemed it of public utility.

14. *In re* Penn Tp. Cove Road, 8 Pa. Dist. 391 (holding that the fact that the road as relocated requires a retaining wall, which, as erected, is of doubtful integrity, presents a reason for non-approval of the report of viewers); Robson *v.* Byler, 14 Tex. Civ. App. 374, 37 S. W. 872.

15. *In re* Penn Tp. Cove Road, 8 Pa. Dist. 391.

The report of viewers is not prima facie evidence of the matters therein contained, but is merely intended to aid the court, and may be by it rejected in whole or in part, either on its own knowledge, or after hearing opposing evidence. Bennett *v.* Greenup County, 17 S. W. 167, 13 Ky. L. Rep. 349.

16. Fowler *v.* Larabee, 59 N. J. L. 259, 35 Atl. 911, failure to assess damages.

Clerical errors.— The report of a jury of view laying out a road and vacating an old road, thereby rendering it useless, should state the courses and distances of the road vacated; but such omission is merely a clerical error, and may be corrected by referring the report back. *In re* Londongrove Road, 2 Lanc. L. Rev. (Pa.) 160.

17. Deering *v.* Cumberland County, 87 Me. 151, 32 Atl. 797; *In re* Brecknock Tp. Road, 2 Woodw. (Pa.) 13.

18. Lowe *v.* Brannan, 105 Ind. 247, 4 N. E. 580; People *v.* Springwells Tp. Board, 12 Mich. 434; Robinson *v.* Logan, 31 Ohio St. 466.

19. Cox *v.* East Fork Tp. Highway Com'rs, 194 Ill. 355, 62 N. E. 791; Mitchell *v.* Thornton, 21 Gratt. (Va.) 164.

Surplusage.— If a statement improperly included in an order may be treated as surplusage, the remainder of the order will not be affected. Tolono Highway Com'rs *v.* Bear, 224 Ill. 259, 79 N. E. 581.

20. Levee Dist No. 9 *v.* Farmer, 101 Cal. 178, 35 Pac. 569, 23 L. R. A. 388 (holding that an order of the board of supervisors laying out a new road, and vacating an old

is *prima facie* liable for all the costs, there being nothing to show but that he caused all the costs.[68]

(VI) *OPERATION AND EFFECT.* It has been repeatedly decided that an alteration by competent authority of an existing road or way operates as a discontinuance of such portions of the old road as are not embraced within the limits fixed for the new one,[69] and no special order of discontinuance is necessary.[70] There are, however, certain cases in which alteration will not have this effect, as where the old road is not thereby rendered unnecessary;[71] where there is strictly no alteration, but rather the establishment of a new road;[72] or where there is no record to show that an alteration was intended.[73] In any case the old road continues the public highway until the new is laid out and made practicable.[74] Where a road has

no ground for a writ of certiorari to remove the record of their proceedings in altering the way conformably to such petition.

68. Reader *v.* Smith, 88 Ind. 440.

69. *Georgia.*— Ponder *v.* Shannon, 54 Ga. 187; Nichols *v.* Sutton, 22 Ga. 369.

Illinois.— Cox *v.* East Fork Tp. Highway Com'rs, 194 Ill. 355, 62 N. E. 791.

Indiana.— Kelley *v.* Augsperger, 171 Ind. 155, 85 N. E. 1004.

Iowa.— Stahr *v.* Carter, 116 Iowa 380, 90 N. W. 64.

Maine.— Cyr *v.* Dufour, 68 Me. 492.

Massachusetts.— Com. *v.* Boston, etc., R. Co., 150 Mass. 174, 22 N. E. 913; Hobart *v.* Plymouth County, 100 Mass. 159; Bowley *v.* Walker, 8 Allen 21; Goodwin *v.* Marblehead, 1 Allen 37; Johnson *v.* Wyman, 9 Gray 186; Bliss *v.* Deerfield, 13 Pick. 102; Com. *v.* Cambridge, 7 Mass. 158; Com. *v.* Westborough, 3 Mass. 406.

New York.— People *v.* Jones, 63 N. Y. 306; People *v.* Dolge, 45 Hun 310 [*affirmed* in 110 N. Y. 680, 18 N. E. 483].

Pennsylvania.— Millcreek Tp. *v.* Reed, 29 Pa. St. 195; *In re* Manheim Tp. Road, 12 Pa. Super. Ct. 279; *In re* West Penn Road, 23 Pa. Co. Ct. 477; *In re* Friendville, etc., Road, 16 Pa. Co. Ct. 172.

Vermont.— Closson *v.* Hamblet, 27 Vt. 728.

Virginia.— Bare *v.* Williams, 101 Va. 800, 45 S. E. 331.

West Virginia.— Poling *v.* Ohio River R. Co., 38 W. Va. 645, 18 S. E. 782, 24 L. R. A. 215.

See 25 Cent. Dig. tit. "Highways," § 253.

70. *California.*— Brook *v.* Horton, 68 Cal. 554, 10 Pac. 204.

Iowa.— Rector *v.* Christy, 114 Iowa 471, 87 N. W. 489.

Maryland.— Jenkins *v.* Riggs, 100 Md. 427, 59 Atl. 758.

Massachusetts.— Com. *v.* Boston, etc., R. Co., 150 Mass. 174, 22 N. E. 913; Hobart *v.* Plymouth County, 100 Mass. 159; Bowley *v.* Walker, 8 Allen 21.

Wisconsin.— State *v.* Reesa, 59 Wis. 106, 17 N. W. 873; Hark *v.* Gladwell, 49 Wis. 172, 5 N. W. 323.

See 25 Cent. Dig. tit. "Highways," § 253.

Under W. Va. Code (1868), c. 43, § 32, providing that "when any road is altered, the former road shall be discontinued to the extent of such alteration," no separate order is necessary to effect such discontinuance. Yates *v.* West Grafton, 33 W. Va. 507, 11 S. E. 8.

71. Rector *v.* Christy, 114 Iowa 471, 87 N. W. 489; Bennett *v.* Clemence, 6 Allen (Mass.) 10 (holding that, for the purpose of proving that an existing way has not been discontinued by the substitution of a new way therefor, evidence is competent to prove the existence of a public landing to which the way furnishes a necessary access, or can reasonably be considered as appurtenant); Atty.-Gen. *v.* Morris, etc., R. Co., 19 N. J. Eq. 386 (holding that the vacation of a public highway which crosses another public street or highway, even where for a short distance it runs along the highway so crossed, where the two highways are parts of different routes, will not vacate the part of the road crossed by the highways so vacated).

72. Vedder *v.* Marion County, 28 Oreg. 77, 36 Pac. 535, 41 Pac. 3, holding that the establishment of a new road upon a petition for the establishment of such road, and also for the vacation of an old road, does not operate to vacate the latter, where the new road does not lie within the termini of the old one, and connects with it only at one end.

73. Johnson *v.* Wyman, 9 Gray (Mass.) 186, holding that, in the absence of any record of the laying out of either way, evidence of the construction and subsequent repair of the new way by public authority does not necessarily presuppose the discontinuance of the old one.

74. Lawson *v.* Shreveport Waterworks Co., 111 La. 73, 35 So. 390; Witter *v.* Damitz, 81 Wis. 385, 51 N. W. 575. See also Heagy *v.* Black, 90 Ind. 534; Keystone Bridge Co. *v.* Summers, 13 W. Va. 476.

The neglect of the town authorities to put such new highway in fit condition to be traveled cannot deprive the public of the right to use the old highway. Witter *v.* Damitz, 81 Wis. 385, 51 N. W. 575.

By statute it is sometimes provided that before a public road can be vacated by the opening of a new road in accordance with the statute for changing and vacating, it must appear that the new road is open and in good condition, and an order vacating the old road must have been made. Phelps *v.* Pacific R. Co., 51 Mo. 477. Under such statute an order shutting up the old road before the new one is opened is void, and a subsequent order setting aside the first furnishes no ground for

been discontinued by the effect of an alteration therein, it can be reëstablished only by the proper statutory proceedings,[75] or by the dedication of the owner.[76]

b. Relocation. Under the Massachusetts statute, the county commissioners are authorized to relocate or locate anew any road laid out by the authority of a town, or otherwise, either for the purpose of establishing the boundaries, or of making alterations in the course or width of the same.[77] Under this authority the commissioners may make some departure from the old or existing boundaries,[78] and so much of the old road as is not included within the new lines is thereby discontinued.[79] To relocate is the same thing as to locate anew;[80] and under a petition to relocate the commissioners may widen a road and change its grade, and include within its boundaries new strips of land, and exclude other strips.[81] All the expenses of locating anew may be assessed upon the petitioners, the town, or the county, as the commissioners may order.[82]

2. VACATION[83] **— a. Power to Vacate** — (I) *BY LEGISLATIVE ACT.* Public highways are created by statute either directly or through delegated power, and are under full control of the legislature.[84] While this control is, as regards vacation generally, exercised through the instrumentality of local governmental subdivisions of the state,[85] the legislature may, in the absence of constitutional limitations,[86] discontinue highways by direct legislative act.[87]

complaint. Bridgeport, etc., Turnpike Road's Appeal, 171 Pa. St. 312, 33 Atl. 145.

75. Yates *v.* West Grafton, 33 W. Va. 507, 11 S. E. 8.

76. Yates *v.* West Grafton, 33 W. Va. 507, 11 S. E. 8.

77. Mass. Gen. St. c. 43, § 12. And see Cambridge *v.* Middlesex County, 167 Mass. 137, 44 N. E. 1089; Richards *v.* Bristol County, 120 Mass. 401; Hyde Park *v.* Norfolk County, 117 Mass. 416; Stockwell *v.* Fitchburg, 110 Mass. 305.

The word "relocate," without addition or qualification, means to locate again, and implies a preservation of the identity of the way without material change. Bennett *v.* Wellesley, 189 Mass. 308, 75 N. E. 717.

Distinguished from alteration.— A relocation of the way under Rev. Laws, c. 48, § 12, is a different proceeding in law from an alteration of a way under section 1 or section 65 of the same chapter, although a relocation may sometimes include an alteration in the course or width of the way, and an alteration under section 1 or section 65 may sometimes involve, at least in part, a kind of relocation. Holbrook *v.* Douglas, 200 Mass. 94, 85 N. E. 854. The jurisdiction of the county commissioners to act under one section or the other is determined by the language of the petition, interpreted in its application to the way referred to. Holbrook *v.* Douglas, 200 Mass. 94, 85 N. E. 854; Bennett *v.* Wellesley, 189 Mass. 308, 75 N. E. 717; Watertown *v.* Middlesex County, 176 Mass. 22, 56 N. E. 971.

78. Cambridge *v.* Middlesex County, 167 Mass. 137, 44 N. E. 1089.

The main purpose of locating anew or relocating is to establish the boundary lines of a road which are in doubt or dispute. Bennett *v.* Wellesley, 189 Mass. 308, 75 N. E. 717; Tufts *v.* Somerville, 122 Mass. 273. Relocating is not intended to be used as a method of making important changes in a way. By the express terms of the statute it can only be done when the whole road to be relocated is in a single town. Bennett *v.* Wellesley, *supra.*

79. See *supra,* II, D, 1, a, (VI).

80. Cambridge *v.* Middlesex County, 167 Mass. 137, 44 N. E. 1089; Hyde Park *v.* Norfolk County, 117 Mass. 416.

81. Watertown *v.* Middlesex County, 176 Mass. 22, 56 N. E. 971; Cambridge *v.* Middlesex County, 167 Mass. 137, 44 N. E. 1089; Richards *v.* Bristol County, 120 Mass. 401; Hyde Park *v.* Norfolk County, 117 Mass. 416.

82. Richards *v.* Bristol County, 120 Mass. 401; Hyde Park *v.* Norfolk County, 117 Mass. 416.

83. **Of city streets** see MUNICIPAL CORPORATIONS, 28 Cyc. 840.

Vested rights in highways see CONSTITUTIONAL LAW, 8 Cyc. 905.

84. Chrisman *v.* Brandes, 137 Iowa 433, 112 N. W. 833. And see *supra,* II, C, 1; II, C, 4; II, C, 5, a.

85. See *infra,* II, D, 2, a, (II); II, D, 2, a, (III).

86. See cases cited *infra,* this note.

Under Mich. Const. art. 4, § 23, which prohibits the legislature from discontinuing highways laid out by township authorities, although the right to vacate state roads is unquestioned, an act which declares certain township highways to be state roads, and thus places it in the power of the legislature to vacate them, is void. Davies *v.* Saginaw County, 89 Mich. 295, 50 N. W. 862.

87. State *v.* Marion County, (Ind. 1907) 82 N. E. 482; Hanselman *v.* Born, 71 Kan. 573, 81 Pac. 192; Davies *v.* Saginaw County, 89 Mich. 295, 50 N. W. 862; Yost *v.* Philadelphia, etc., R. Co., 29 Leg. Int. (Pa.) 85.

Highways established by dedication or prescription.— The provision of the Revised Statutes of New Hampshire, c. 53, § 7, that no highway not laid out agreeably to statute law shall be deemed a public highway, unless

continuous thoroughfares extending to other towns.[97] The fact that the vote is conditional has been held not to make the vacation void.[98]

b. What Roads May Be Vacated — (I) *IN GENERAL.* Where statutes confer general authority to vacate public highways, it is immaterial how such highways originated, whether by long usage,[99] dedication,[1] or under authority of a special charter.[2] The application to vacate may be limited to a part of a road,[3] and in such case it is lawful to vacate such part only;[4] but the vacation cannot lawfully be less extensive than the application.[5] In the absence of express statutory authority,[6]

that where the vote of a town was "to rescind all action taken by the selectmen relating" to a proposed highway, and the "action taken by the selectmen" was the laying out of the highway in question, the purpose of the vote was sufficiently stated to be the discontinuance of the highway); Currier *v.* Davis, 68 N. H. 596, 41 Atl. 239 (holding, however, that a highway originating by user cannot be discontinued by a town without the consent of the court); Drew *v.* Cotton, 68 N. H. 22, 42 Atl. 239; Thompson *v.* Major, 58 N. H. 242 (holding that where a highway laid out by a town subsequently became a part of a new town, the latter town could discontinue the same as if laid out by its own selectmen).

In Connecticut a town in town meeting cannot discontinue a highway. Greist *v.* Amrhyn, 80 Conn. 280, 68 Atl. 521.

In New Hampshire the consent of the supreme judicial court to the discontinuance of highways by towns is necessary in all cases, except where the highway was laid out by the selectmen; and the exception does not include highways existing by prescription, it not being made to appear that they were laid out by the selectmen. *In re* Campton, 41 N. H. 197.

A public landing is not a way, and a town has no power to discontinue it. Com. *v.* Tucker, 2 Pick. (Mass.) 44.

Actual shutting up of road is unnecessary to render vacation effectual. Coakley *v.* Boston, etc., R. Co., 159 Mass. 32, 33 N. E. 930.

Alteration.— A statute providing that "a town, at a meeting regularly called for the purpose, may discontinue any town way or private way," does not authorize a town, by a mere vote, to alter one of the boundary lines of a town way, and discontinue that portion of the way which lies outside of the newly located line. Such action can properly be taken only by a tribunal proceeding judicially, after notice thereof to the landowners along the way. Lincoln *v.* Warren, 150 Mass. 309, 23 N. E. 45.

The private interest of the voters does not debar them from voting, or the town from acting. New London *v.* Davis, 73 N. H. 72, 59 Atl. 369.

Time when vote takes effect.— A vote absolute in its terms takes effect from its passage, although the meeting at which it is passed may be adjourned to a subsequent day. Bigelow *v.* Hillman, 37 Me. 52. Whether such a vote can be reconsidered after the rights of third persons have intervened *quære.* Bigelow *v.* Hillman, *supra.*

97. Drew *v.* Cotton, 68 N. H. 22, 42 Atl. 239; Styles *v.* Victoria, 8 Brit. Col. 406.

98. See cases cited *infra*, this note.

For example the general discontinuing power may be exercised to take effect at a time subsequent to the vote, or when another highway shall be laid out and constructed to take the place of the old one. Coakley *v.* Boston, etc., R. Co., 159 Mass. 32, 33 N. E. 930; New London *v.* Davis, 73 N. H. 72, 59 Atl. 369.

Whether the condition is precedent or subsequent depends on the intent of the parties. Sears *v.* Fuller, 137 Mass. 326.

Effect of illegal proviso.— A proviso in the vote of discontinuance empowering abutting owners to use the way as a private way for their especial use does not render the discontinuance void, even if the proviso itself is illegal, as converting a town way into a private way, where the town thereafter ceased to work the road, and posted notice that it was not a public way. Coakley *v.* Boston, etc., R. Co., 159 Mass. 32, 33 N. E. 930.

99. State *v.* Snedeker, 30 N. J. L. 80.

1. State *v.* Snedeker, 30 N. J. L. 80.

2. State *v.* Snedeker, 30 N. J. L. 80.

Where a turnpike road has been abandoned for many years by the company which built it, and has been used by the public as an ordinary highway, and repaired at the public expense, it becomes subject to the laws concerning roads, and the surveyors of the highways have power to vacate it. The power and jurisdiction of the surveyors over such a highway is the same as they have over any other highway, except only as to those holding under the turnpike company, and entitled to their chartered rights. State *v.* Snedeker, 30 N. J. L. 80.

3. Condict *v.* Ramsey, 65 N. J. L. 503, 47 see State *v.* Bassett, 33 N. J. L. 26.

4. State *v.* Bassett, 33 N. J. L. 26.

Any portion of a road which is useless is a road for all the purposes of exercising authority for its discontinuance, and may be discontinued without affecting the residue. People *v.* Nichols, 51 N. Y. 470; *In re* Swanson St., 163 Pa. St. 323, 30 Atl. 207. And see State *v.* Bassett, 33 N. J. L. 26.

In Indiana the statute not only confers the authority in general terms to vacate highways, but expressly provides for the vacation of a highway, "or any part thereof." Hughes *v.* Beggs, 114 Ind. 427, 16 N. E. 817.

5. Condict *v.* Ramsey, 65 N. J. L. 503, 47 Atl. 423.

6. See the statutes of the several states, and cases cited *infra*, this note.

town,[22] or of the officers upon whom the power of discontinuing or vacating highways is conferred.[23]

(II) *PETITION AND PARTIES* — (A) *In General.* In most jurisdictions application for the vacation of a public highway must be made by written petition,[24] signed by the petitioners.[25] While the petition need not follow the exact statutory form,[26] it must contain everything that is required to be set forth therein

Kentucky.— Big Sandy R. Co. *v.* Boyd County, 124 Ky. 345, 101 S. W. 354, 31 Ky. L. Rep. 17.

Maryland.— Cumberland Valley R. Co. *v.* Martin, 100 Md. 165, 59 Atl. 714.

Massachusetts.— Loring *v.* Boston, 12 Gray 209; Harrington *v.* Berkshire County, 22 Pick. 263, 33 Am. Dec. 741.

Minnesota.— Miller *v.* Corinna, 42 Minn. 391, 44 N. W. 127.

Missouri.— State *v.* Wells, 70 Mo. 635 (holding that a county court cannot, without the regular statutory proceeding, discontinue a public road by a mere order to the road overseer); Sheppard *v.* May, 83 Mo. App. 272 (holding that where the law provides for the vacation of public highways on petition to the county court of twelve householders of the township where the road is located, the attempt of the county court to declare a road vacant on suggestion of the overseer is void for want of jurisdiction; hence its order is no justification for the obstruction of such road).

Nebraska.— McNair *v.* State, 26 Nebr. 257, 41 N. W. 1099.

North Carolina.—State *v.* Shuford, 28 N. C. 162.

Ohio.— Silverthorn *v.* Parsons, 8 Ohio Cir. Dec. 349.

See 25 Cent. Dig. tit. "Highways," § 263.

Necessity of bond by petitioners.— That petitioners applying to a county board for the vacation of a highway did not file a bond for the payment of the expenses of the proceedings will not invalidate the same. Sullivan *v.* Robbins, 109 Iowa 235, 80 N. W. 340.

22. Cromwell *v.* Connecticut Brown Stone Quarry Co., 50 Conn. 470.

By contract.— A town has no power to agree, for a valuable consideration, to discontinue a highway. Cromwell *v.* Connecticut Brown Stone Quarry Co., 50 Conn. 470 (holding further that a town cannot enforce a promise of the other party of which its own promise to destroy a public right — as to discontinue a highway — was the consideration); Anderson *v.* Hamilton County, 12 Ohio St. 635 (holding further that evidence of such a contract or arrangement, offered to invalidate the effect of the record establishing the road, is incompetent); Silverthorn *v.* Parsons, 8 Ohio Cir. Dec. 349; State *v.* Castle, 44 Wis. 670.

23. Rice *v.* Chicago, etc., R. Co., 30 Ill. App. 481, holding that commissioners of highways, under the law, have no authority to substitute one road for another by surrendering a public highway to a railroad company in exchange for a new one to be provided by it.

24. *Illinois.*— Rice *v.* Chicago, etc., R. Co, 30 Ill. App. 481.

Iowa.— Lamansky *v.* Williams, 125 Iowa 578, 101 N. W. 445.

Kansas.— Mills *v.* Neosho County, 50 Kan. 635, 32 Pac. 361.

Missouri.— Sheppard *v.* May, 83 Mo. App. 272.

North Carolina.—State *v.* Shuford, 28 N. C. 162.

Oregon.— Fisher *v.* Union County, 43 Oreg. 23, 72 Pac. 797.

Pennsylvania.— *In re* Abington Road, 3 Pa. Dist. 226; *In re* Hamiltonban Tp. Road, 19 Pa. Co. Ct. 648.

See 25 Cent. Dig. tit. "Highways," § 264.

Contra.— Brown *v.* Sagadahoc County, 68 Me. 537.

25. *In re* Abington Road, 3 Pa. Dist. 226; *In re* Hamiltonban Tp. Road, 19 Pa. Co. Ct. 648.

In Nebraska the statutory provision that a petition for the vacation of a public road shall be signed by at least ten electors residing within five miles of the road is jurisdictional. Letherman *v.* Hauser, 77 Nebr. 731, 110 N. W. 745.

In Nevada, St. (1866) 252, § 5, requires the signatures of twenty-four freeholders in counties containing one hundred or more legal voters. State *v.* Washoe County, 12 Nev. 17.

In Pennsylvania, where a road has simply been cut through, but has not been made passable for public travel, it cannot be vacated, except upon the petition of a majority of such original petitioners. *In re* Heath Tp., etc., Road, 21 Pa. Co. Ct. 254; *In re* Huntington Road, 3 Kulp 373. Where it has been opened in part, an application by the original petitioners cannot be sustained; but such application will not be defeated by merely showing that the road has been worked on by the public authorities. It must appear that part of the road has actually been opened for safe and convenient public travel. *In re* Heath Tp., etc., Road, *supra.* A petition not signed by a majority of original petitioners for the road, and not averring that the road was open in part, will be dismissed. *In re* Rapho Tp., etc., Road, 7 Del. Co. 571.

A petition in behalf of the town may, in the absence of any statutory provision on the subject, be signed by the selectmen, or by the agent or attorney of the town, in its name. New London *v.* Davis, 73 N. H. 72, 59 Atl. 369; *In re* Milton, 20 N. H. 261.

Signature induced by fraud.— That one was induced through fraud to sign a petition to the county board for the vacation of a highway is not a ground for declaring void the action of the board. Sullivan *v.* Robbins, 109 Iowa 235, 80 N. W. 340.

26. Devoe *v.* Smeltzer, 86 Iowa 385, 53

diction in the court or tribunal, and does not disclose some prejudicial error in the proceedings, in such cases presumptions of law arise and sustain the judgment or order.[68]

(B) *Conclusiveness and Collateral Attack* — (1) IN GENERAL. In some states it seems that the principle which obtains in suits at common law, that a former judgment is conclusive upon all points directly in issue upon the trial, does not apply strictly to proceedings to procure the discontinuance of highways.[69] But as a rule it is held that an order or judgment discontinuing a public road must be deemed conclusive so long as it remains in force,[70] and the correctness of such a proceeding cannot be attacked collaterally,[71] unless it is void.[72]

(2) BAR TO FURTHER PROCEEDINGS. It is commonly provided by statute that after the final determination of a proceeding to discontinue a highway no further proceedings shall be had in reference to the same highway,[73] until the expiration of a limited time.[74] In the absence of a statute on the subject no general rule can be laid down as to how far a court or board will go in entertaining successive petitions to vacate.[75]

(VIII) *DEFECTS AND OBJECTIONS AND WAIVER THEREOF.*[76] In cases of this character objections to the regularity of the proceedings must be seasonably taken at the hearing or they cannot be made available on appeal.[77]

record and papers relating to the establishment, location, alteration, widening, or vacation of any road, shall be *prima facie* evidence in all cases that all necessary antecedent provisions have been complied with, and that the action of the commissioners or other persons and officers in regard thereto has been regular in all respects, applies only where the papers show jurisdiction on their face. Imhoff *v.* Somerset Highway Com'rs, 89 Ill. App. 66. The presumption raised is not conclusive, but is subject to rebuttal. Schroeder *v.* Klipp, 120 Wis. 245, 97 N. W. 909.

68. Smith *v.* Frenzer, 12 Ohio Cir. Ct. 250, 5 Ohio Cir. Dec. 658.

69. *In re* Strafford, 14 N. H. 30.

70. Bradbury *v.* Walton, 94 Ky. 163, 21 S. W. 869, 14 Ky. L. Rep. 823; Briggs *v.* Bowen, 60 N. Y. 454.

71. Sullivan *v.* Robbins, 109 Iowa 235, 80 N. W. 340; Ellis *v.* Blue Mountain Forest Assoc., 69 N. H. 385, 41 Atl. 856, 42 L. R. A. 570; Briggs *v.* Bowen, 60 N. Y. 454; Haynes *v.* Lassell, 29 Vt. 157.

72. People *v.* Three Judges Suffolk County, 24 Wend. (N. Y.) 249; Hill *v.* Hoffman, (Tenn. Ch. App. 1899) 58 S. W. 929.

73. See cases cited *infra*, this note.

In Iowa, Code (1873), § 927, providing that if a commissioner, after a general examination, "shall not be in favor of establishing a proposed highway, he will so report, and no further proceedings shall be had thereon," is applicable to proceedings to vacate a highway. Devoe *v.* Smeltzer, 86 Iowa 385, 53 N. W. 287; Cook *v.* Trigg, 52 Iowa 709, 3 N. W. 725.

74. See cases cited *infra*, this note.

In New Jersey, Revision, p. 1013, § 100, provides that in case the surveyors shall return that they think the laying out, vacation, or alteration of the road to be necessary, no new application touching said road shall be made under one year after said appointment. Under such a provision surveyors of the highways cannot be appointed to vacate a road while proceedings upon a previous appointment of surveyors to vacate the same road are still pending. State *v.* Adams, 55 N. J. L. 334, 26 Atl. 914 [*reversing* (Sup. 1891) 21 Atl. 938].

Under N. Y. Laws (1847), c. 455, § 9, a refusal of referees to discontinue a road is no bar to new proceedings within four years for that purpose; such a decision is not one for "laying out, altering or discontinuing a road." People *v.* Nichols, 51 N. Y. 470.

75. See cases cited *infra*, this note.

In an early New Hampshire case it is said: "Even if there have been a decision upon the merits of a road petition, it has not been the practice here to apply to it the common law principle, that a former judgment is conclusive upon all points directly in issue upon the trial, and necessarily determined. But perhaps if the merits of a road petition had been repeatedly passed upon and examined, the court might, by analogy to proceedings in suits at law, exercise a legal discretion, and refuse to entertain it." *In re* Strafford, 14 N. H. 30. If a second petition is founded upon the same vote of the town which formed the basis of the former application, the matter will be regarded as *res judicata*, and the petition will be dismissed. *In re* Bath, 22 N. H. 576. Upon a fresh vote, however, the presumption is that a new state of facts has arisen, and the court will take such a course with a petition founded upon such a vote, as though no previous application had been made. *In re* Bath, *supra*.

76. Waiver of notice see *supra*, II, D, 2 d, (III).

77. Williamson *v.* Houser, 169 Ind. 397, 82 N. E. 771 (holding that a landowner who did not appear before the commissioners cannot present an application for damages or a remonstrance that the proposed vacation is not of public utility for the first time in the circuit court on appeal); Millett *v.* Franklin

more the right to appeal should appear affirmatively from the record; otherwise the appeal will be dismissed.[85]

(x) *CERTIORARI.* A proceeding to discontinue a highway is judicial in its nature and therefore reviewable by certiorari.[86] It is the duty of the superior tribunal to inspect the record as it is returned in obedience to the writ,[87] and to determine whether the inferior tribunal had jurisdiction,[88] or whether it exceeded its jurisdiction,[89] or otherwise proceeded in violation of law.[90] Matters within the discretion of the inferior tribunal will not be reviewed.[91] A petition for a writ of certiorari is an application to the judicial discretion of the court,[92] and will not be granted for formal and technical errors only, where no real injustice has been done;[93] nor will it be granted, even where more substantial errors are apparent in the proceedings, upon the application of one whose rights are not affected injuriously by such errors.[94]

vacate are entitled to appeal from the commissioners' decision. Imhoff *v.* Somerset Highway Com'rs, 89 Ill. App. 66. In Kentucky it has been held that the owners of land through which a highway passes has not such an interest in the road as to entitle him to question, by appeal or writ or error, the order of a county court discontinuing such way. Cole *v.* Shannon, 1 J. J. Marsh. (Ky.) 218.

Parties to proceeding.— Under the statutes of some states either party to a petition to discontinue a public highway has a right to appeal. Ashcraft *v.* Lee, 81 N. C. 135; Fisher *v.* Union County, 43 Oreg. 223, 72 Pac. 797.

Party or person aggrieved.— Ind. Rev. St. (1843) pp. 186, 187, provides that if the person aggrieved by the decision, and appealing therefrom, be not a party to the matter or proceeding, the appeal shall not be allowed, unless he makes himself a party by affidavit setting forth explicity the nature of his interest in the subject-matter. Odell *v.* Jenkins, 8 Ind. 522.

Persons aggrieved are sometimes granted the right to appeal. Under such a provision freeholders remonstrating against the discontinuance of a county road may appeal to the circuit court from a judgment of the county court vacating the road, and adjudging costs against them. *In re* Big Hollow Road, 40 Mo. App. 363 [*affirmed* in 111 Mo. 326, 19 S. W. 947].

Person who may feel himself aggrieved.— Minn. Gen. St. (1878) c. 13, § 59, provides that "any person who may feel himself aggrieved" by an order discontinuing a highway may appeal. This is not to be taken literally. A person having no interest which could be affected might imagine himself aggrieved, yet the statute could not have intended to give such a person a right to appeal. The person claiming the right must undoubtedly be in a position to be injuriously affected by the order or determination made; in a position to sustain special injury, disadvantage, or inconvenience not common to himself with the other inhabitants or property-owners of the town. One through whose land a new road is laid out is in such a position; and so is one through, to, or along whose land an old road to be discontinued runs. State *v.* Holman, 40 Minn. 369, 41 N. W. 1073; State *v.* Barton, 36 Minn. 145, 30 N. W. 454; Schuster *v.* Lemond, 27 Minn. 253, 6 N. W. 802.

85. Odell *v.* Jenkins, 8 Ind. 522.

86. People *v.* Shaw, 34 N. Y. App. Div. 61, 54 N. Y. Suppl. 218.

87. Troxell *v.* Dick, 216 Ill. 98, 74 N. E. 694, holding that, when the return is made, the superior tribunal tries the case upon the record alone, and not upon the allegations contained in the petition for the writ, or on facts not contained in the record so returned.

The answer or return to a writ of certiorari to revise an order vacating a highway must show that the board had jurisdiction to make the order which they defend. State *v.* Washoe, County, 12 Nev. 17.

88. Troxell *v.* Dick, 216 Ill. 98, 74 N. E. 694.

89. Troxell *v.* Dick, 216 Ill. 98, 74 N. E. 694; People *v.* Three Judges, Suffolk County, 24 Wend. (N. Y.) 249.

90. Troxell *v.* Dick, 216 Ill. 98, 74 N. E. 694; Sullivan *v.* Robbins, 109 Iowa 235, 80 N. W. 340; Moore *v.* Sandown, 19 N. H. 93.

Defects in proceedings.— If on presentation of a proper petition to vacate a portion of a state road, the board of supervisors acquire jurisdiction to act, and do not in their final determination of the case exceed their jurisdiction, defects in their intermediate proceedings will not invalidate their conclusion or make it subject to review on certiorari. People *v.* Shiawassee County, 38 Mich. 642.

91. See cases cited *infra*, this note.

The expediency of vacating highways is for the board, and their action is not reviewable by certiorari. Chrisman *v.* Brandes, 137 Iowa 433, 112 N. W. 833; Com. *v.* Roxbury, 8 Mass. 457; People *v.* Shiawassee County, 38 Mich. 642.

92. Holden *v.* Berkshire, 7 Metc. (Mass.) 561.

Effect of laches.— The court, in its discretion, will not grant a writ of certiorari to reverse proceedings which have been long acquiesced in by all parties, and especially those principally interested. Holden *v.* Berksire, 7 Metc. (Mass.) 561.

93. Holden *v.* Berkshire, 7 Metc. (Mass.) 561.

94. Holden *v.* Berkshire, 7 Metc. (Mass.)

Nor does a statute providing that all roads that have not been opened or used within a certain time shall be deemed vacated apply so as to vacate a part of the width of a road not actually used.[30]

c. By Failure to Open, Construct, or Repair. In the absence of any statutory provision on the subject, the fact that there has been delay in opening up a highway cannot generally be relied on to defeat the right to the way.[31] Nor will failure to keep a road in repair constitute an abandonment of the road.[32] But statutes exist in most states providing that highways shall be considered vacated unless opened within a certain time after their establishment.[33] These statutes are con-

13 Ohio St. 42; Fox *v.* Hart, 11 Ohio 414. And see *infra*, II, D, 3, d.

30. *Illinois.*— Taylor *v.* Pearce, 179 Ill. 145, 53 N. E. 622.

Kansas.—Webb *v.* Butler County, 52 Kan. 375, 34 Pac. 973; Topeka *v.* Russam, 30 Kan. 550, 2 Pac. 669.

Maine.— Heald *v.* Moore, 79 Me. 271, 9 Atl. 734.

Nebraska.— Krueger *v.* Jenkins, 59 Nebr. 641, 81 N. W. 844.

New Jersey.— South Amboy *v.* New York, etc., R. Co., 66 N. J. L. 623, 50 Atl. 368; Humphreys *v.* Woodstown, 48 N. J. L. 588, 7 Atl. 301.

New York.—Walker *v.* Caywood, 31 N. Y. 51; Mangam *v.* Sing Sing, 26 N. Y. App. Div. 464, 50 N. Y. Suppl. 647 [*affirmed* in 164 N. Y. 560, 58 N E. 1089].

Ohio.— Peck *v.* Clark, 19 Ohio 367; Dodson *v.* Cincinnati, 5 Ohio Dec. (Reprint) 295, 4 Am. L. Rec. 312.

South Dakota.— Baker *v.* Hogaboom, 12 S. D. 405, 81 N. W. 730.

See 25 Cent. Dig. tit. "Highways," § 284.

31. Impson *v.* Sac County, (Iowa 1904) 98 N. W. 118; Davies *v.* Huebner, 45 Iowa 574 (holding that where a highway has been established by the proper legal authority, although never actually opened, mere non-user for a period of ten years will not operate to defeat the right of the public therein, where there has been no adverse use of the land); Bruce *v.* Saline County, 26 Mo. 262 (holding that the lapse of six years after a road is ordered to be opened, before it is really opened, does not authorize a presumption that it has been abandoned).

32. Brumley *v.* State, 82 Ark. 236, 103 S. W. 615; State *v.* Mobley, 1 McMull. (S. C.) 44.

33. See the statutes of the several states, and cases cited *infra*, this note.

The effect of such a statute is to invalidate the laying out of the highway if it is not opened within the prescribed time. Seidschlag *v.* Antioch, 207 Ill. 280, 69 N. E. 949 [*affirming* 109 Ill. App. 291]; Marble *v.* Whitney, 28 N. Y. 297.

What constitutes "opening."—What must be done to constitute an opening of the road within the meaning of the statute is not precisely defined. It may be formally opened by the road overseers along the line of the road, or it may be informally opened by themselves or by others; or it may be opened in fact by the public travel taking possession of it and using it. Wilson *v.* Janes, 29 Kan. 233. The opening of a highway for travel, under such a statute, is accomplished by removing obstructions existing at the time the highway is established, and it is not essential to the opening of a highway that unlawful obstructions subsequently erected thereon should be removed. Wragg *v.* Penn Tp., 94 Ill. 11, 34 Am. Rep. 199. A road is "opened," where the trees on it have been felled and cut up for more than the statutory period, although it is impassable except for those on foot. Baker *v.* Runnels, 12 Me. 235. It cannot be said that a road has been "opened" when nothing has been done to a large portion of it, and the remainder was a road opened and used as such before. State *v.* Cornville, 43 Me. 427. But it is not necessary, in order to prevent the discontinuance of a highway by operation of the statute, that it should be in such a state of repair as not to be subject to indictment. State *v.* Cornville, *supra.* Where a culvert is put in an established highway by the officer having authority to work the same, and the road is traveled more or less until fenced in by plaintiff, the facts are sufficient to show an acceptance of such highway by the public. Devoe *v.* Smeltzer, 86 Iowa 385, 53 N. W. 287. In the following cases the "opening" of the road was held sufficient to take the case out of the statute: Wiley *v.* Brimfield, 59 Ill. 306; Baker *v.* Runnels, 12 Me. 235; Marble *v.* Whitney, 28 N. Y. 297.

When limitation begins to run.— The time when the limitation begins to run is usually to be determined by reference to the particular statute. Under the Ohio statute the seven years' limitation runs from the date of the order granted for the opening. McClelland *v.* Miller, 28 Ohio St. 488. In Kansas, in the case of a county road established by a special act, the provision of Gen. St. (1901) § 6058, that any county road should be vacated if it remains unopened for seven years after the order is made or the authority given for opening the same, refers to the time that the act is passed, and not to the time an order for an opening of the road is made by the county commissioners. Cowley County *v.* Johnson, 76 Kan. 65, 90 Pac. 805. In New York the twenty-third section of the act which was passed March 19, 1813 (2 Rev. Laws 277) enacts, "that if any public highway already laid out, or hereafter to be laid out, shall not be opened and worked within six years after the passing of this act, or from the time of its being so laid out, the same shall cease to be

lature to provide for taking the fee of the land appropriated, and divesting the owners of all proprietary interest therein,[49] yet to accomplish that purpose it is necessary plainly to declare an intention so to do,[50] and an easement only will be taken unless the statute plainly contemplates and provides for the appropriation of a larger interest.[51] A town is also authorized to accept a deed of the fee of lands for highway purposes.[52] Where an abutting owner owns the fee of a highway, a grant or conveyance of the land abutting on such highway carries the fee in the highway to the center thereof,[53] except in so far as title thereto is reserved by the terms of the conveyance.[54] An intention on the part of a grantor to with-

Neal, 7 N. H. 275; Glasby v. Morris, 18 N. J. Eq. 72; Mott v. Eno, 181 N. Y. 346, 74 N. E. 229. In the absence of evidence to the contrary this title is presumed to extend to the center of the way. Newton v. New York, etc., R. Co., 72 Conn. 420, 44 Atl. 813; Benham v. Potter, 52 Conn. 248; Rawls v. Tallahassee Hotel Co., 43 Fla. 288, 31 So. 237; Huffman v. State, 21 Ind. App. 449, 52 N. E. 713, 69 Am. St. Rep. 368; Smith v. Slocomb, 11 Gray (Mass.) 280; Paige v. Schenectady R. Co., 77 N. Y. App. Div. 571, 79 N. Y. Suppl. 266 [*reversing* 38 Misc. 384, 77 N. Y. Suppl. 889]; Adams v Rivers, 11 Barb. (N. Y.) 390; Houston v. Finnigan, (Tex. Civ. App. 1905) 85 S. W. 470; Harrison v. Rutland, [1893] 1 Q. B. 142, 57 J. P. 278, 62 L. J. Q. B. 117, 68 L. T. Rep. N. S. 35, 4 Reports 155, 41 Wkly. Rep. 322; *In re* White, [1898] 1 Ch. 659, 67 L. J. Ch. 430, 78 L. T. Rep. N. S. 550, 46 Wkly. Rep. 479; University College v Oxford, 68 J. P. 471, 20 T. L. R. 637. But this presumption is rebutted where the deed under which the owner holds grants the land to the side of the way only. Smith v. Slocomb, 11 Gray (Mass.) 280.

Dutch law.— The ownership of the fee of roads established during the Dutch occupancy of New York is governed by the Dutch law, which vests it in the public. Mott v. Clayton, 9 N. Y. App. Div. 181, 41 N. Y. Suppl. 87.

A gift of the right of way is not a transfer of the absolute property in the soil. Smith v. Rome, 19 Ga. 89, 63 Am. Dec. 298; Lade v. Shepherd, Str. 1004, 93 Eng. Reprint 997. A grant of a highway, without any other words indicating an intent to enlarge the import of the word, conveys only an easement. Jamaica Pond Aqueduct Corp. v. Chandler, 9 Allen (Mass.) 159.

49. Hawesville v. Hawes, 6 Bush (Ky.) 232; Mott v. Eno, 181 N. Y. 346, 74 N. E. 229; Kings County v. Sea View R. Co., 23 Hun (N. Y.) 180; Raleigh, etc., R. Co. v. Davis, 19 N. C. 451.

Merger of easement in fee.— The easement which the public has in a highway does not merge in the fee of the servient estate, when acquired by the state. People v. Marin County, 103 Cal. 223, 37 Pac. 203, 26 L. R. A. 659.

50. Boston v. Richardson, 13 Allen (Mass.) 146 (holding that evidence that the selectmen had staked out a highway for the town's use is immaterial to show that the town either did or did not own the land under such way); Mott v. Eno, 181 N. Y. 346, 74 N. E. 229; Kings County v. Sea View R. Co., 23 Hun (N. Y.) 180.

51. Kings County v. Sea View R. Co., 23 Hun (N. Y.) 180.

The general rule is that when the language of the statute will bear a construction which will leave the fee in the landowner, that construction will be preferred. Mott v. Eno, 181 N. Y. 346, 74 N. E. 229.

52. Alling v. Burlock, 46 Conn. 504.

Particular deeds construed.—Where land was conveyed by a warranty deed to a town "for the sole use and purpose of a public highway," it was held that the deed conveyed more than an easement, and that so long as the premises continued to be used for a highway the town had a complete title to the fee of the land. Taylor v. Danbury Public Hall Co., 35 Conn. 430. So where owners of land abutting on a road conveyed a strip to the city by a deed reciting that the grantors "grant, release and forever quit claim" so much of their lands as might be necessary for a road of a specified breadth "to and for the sole and only use of a public road forever," it was held that the deed conveyed to the city a fee in the land covered thereby. Mitchell v. Einstein, 105 N. Y. App. Div. 413, 94 N. Y. Suppl. 210 [*reversing* 42 Misc. 358, 86 N. Y. Suppl 759]. Where one grants land for the purpose of a public highway, adding also "the reversion and remainder," his reversionary right vests in his grantee. Vaughn v. Stuzaker, 16 Ind. 338.

53. See BOUNDARIES, 5 Cyc. 906, 907.

54. See cases cited *infra*, this note.

Particular deeds construed.—An exception or reservation of an existing highway passing through the lands conveyed is held to embrace only the easement or right of the public in the highway and does not except the fee. Peck v. Smith, 1 Conn. 103, 6 Am. Dec. 216; Day v. Philbrook, 85 Me. 90, 26 Atl. 999; Kuhn v. Farnsworth, 69 Me. 404; Stetson v. Dow, 16 Gray (Mass.) 372; Capron v. Kingman, 64 N. H. 571, 14 Atl. 868; Leavitt v. Towle, 8 N. H. 96; Myers v. Bell Tel. Co., 83 N. Y. App. Div. 623, 82 N. Y. Suppl. 83; Abraham v. Abbott, 8 Oreg. 53; Kister v. Reeser, 98 Pa. St. 1, 42 Am. Rep. 608. In Munn v. Worrall, 53 N. Y. 44, 13 Am. Rep. 470, it was held that an exception in a deed in the following words· "Saving and excepting from the premises hereby conveyed all, and so much, and such part and parts thereof as has or have been lawfully taken for a public road or roads," was an exception

hold his interest in a road to the middle of it, after parting with all his right and title to the adjoining land, is never to be presumed.[55]

2. On Vacation or Abandonment.[56] From the principles stated in the preceding section it regularly follows that when the highway is discontinued or abandoned the land becomes discharged of this servitude,[57] and the entire and exclusive enjoyment reverts to the proprietor of the soil,[58] except where the fee to the highway has passed to the public.[59] This general rule governs even in cases where a new and different one is substituted for the one abandoned.[60] Where the public easement upon lands has been once extinguished, it cannot be revived except by new dedication or condemnation.[61] Under the statutes of some states the adjoining owners are entitled to reclaim the soil of a vacated road to the center thereof,[62] unless the ground was originally taken in unequal proportions, in which case the

of the land covered by a public highway across the premises, and not simply of the easement therein, and the fee of such land remained in the grantor and passed to a subsequent purchaser from him. The exception is "from the premises," and the decision is based upon the phraseology, without impairing the general doctrine of the above cases. A reservation of the right to open a highway "the whole length of said east line. And if, at any future time, a public highway shall be laid out . . . all the rights of [the grantor], in said reserved highway, shall revert to [the grantee]," reserves the right to dedicate a highway, the fee therein to belong to the grantee. Dunn *v.* Sanford, 51 Conn. 443. Where one dedicated a strip of land in front of his premises to the public as a highway, and expressly excepted it as such in his deed of the land, the grantee cannot assume the ownership of the strip, although it was never actually used as a public highway. Southern Pac. R. Co. *v.* Ferris, 93 Cal. 263, 28 Pac. 828, 18 L. R. A. 510.

55. Ball *v.* Ball, 1 Phila. (Pa.) 36.

56. **Of city street** see Municipal Corporations, 28 Cyc. 846.

57. Blain *v.* Staab, 10 N. M. 743, 65 Pac. 177; Pettibone *v.* Purdy, 7 Vt. 514.

58. *Colorado.*— Olin *v.* Denver, etc., R. Co., 25 Colo. 177, 53 Pac. 454.

Connecticut.—Woodruff *v.* Neal, 28 Conn. 165; Buel *v.* Clark, 1 Root 49.

Maryland.—Williamson *v.* Carnan, 1 Gill & J. 184.

Mississippi.— Hatch *v.* Monroe County, 56 Miss. 26, holding, however, that an order by the county board that a highway be "discontinued as a public road," but "be kept open as a private right of way," does not so surrender the public right as to warrant a landowner in inclosing the road for his private use.

New Mexico.— Blain *v.* Staab, 10 N. M. 743, 65 Pac. 177.

New York.— Mangam *v.* Sing Sing, 11 N. Y. App. Div. 212, 42 N. Y. Suppl. 950; Jackson *v.* Hathaway, 15 Johns. 447, 8 Am. Dec. 263.

Pennsylvania.— Flick's Estate, 6 Kulp 329.

Texas.— Hall *v.* La Salle County, 11 Tex. Civ. App. 379, 32 S. W. 433.

Vermont.— Pettibone *v.* Purdy, 7 Vt. 514.

United States.— Harris *v.* Elliott, 10 Pet. 25, 9 L. ed. 333; Barclay *v.* Howell, 6 Pet. 498, 8 L. ed. 477.

See 25 Cent. Dig. tit. "Highways," § 289.

Easements of this character may cease to exist, like all other burdens upon land, and when they do the land is freed from the encumbrance as completely as though it had never existed, and the owner of the soil has an absolute title to the same. Benham *v.* Potter, 52 Conn. 248.

According to the civil law, a grant of land calling for a public road as a boundary conveyed no title to the soil covered by the road; but the title to the road-bed remained in the sovereignty. Hence, upon the abandonment of the road as a highway, the land covered by it became vacant public domain, subject to entry, and did not belong, as it would at common law, to proprietors whose lands were bounded by the road. Mitchell *v.* Bass, 33 Tex. 259.

Consideration for such reversion.— The acquisition of title to vacated streets by reversion to the abutting lot-owners is supported by the consideration of the enhanced price paid for such lots in consequence of the prospective use of such streets. Olin *v.* Denver, etc., R. Co., 25 Colo. 177, 53 Pac. 454.

59. Lake City *v.* Fulkerson, 122 Iowa 569, 98 N. W. 376.

60. Benham *v.* Potter, 52 Conn. 248; Flick's Estate, 6 Kulp (Pa.) 329.

61. Cooper *v.* Detroit, 42 Mich. 584, 4 N. W. 262.

62. *Kansas.*— Southern Kansas R. Co. *v.* Showalter, 57 Kan. 681, 47 Pac. 831.

Michigan.— Scudder *v.* Detroit, 117 Mich. 77, 75 N. W. 286.

New York.— Mitchell *v.* Einstein, 105 N. Y. App. Div. 413, 94 N. Y. Suppl. 210 [*reversing* 42 Misc. 358, 86 N. Y. Suppl. 759].

Pennsylvania.— *In re* Magnet St., etc., Public Road, 5 Pa. Dist. 771, 19 Pa. Co. Ct. 70.

Wisconsin.— Paine Lumber Co. *v.* Oshkosh, 89 Wis. 449, 61 N. W. 1108.

See 25 Cent. Dig. tit. "Highways," § 289.

Effect on private easements.—While the effect of N. Y. Laws (1867), c. 697, authorizing the closing of the Bloomingdale road, was to extinguish the public easement, it did not operate to extinguish private easements and rights in lands covered by the public highway, but left them as they were. Holloway *v.* Southmayd, 139 N. Y. 390, 34 N. E.

crops,[73] and pasturage upon and above the surface of the soil covered by the highway.[74]

b. For Constructing or Repairing Highway. Upon the laying out of a highway the public acquire not only the right of way, but also the powers and privileges incident to that right,[75] among which is the right to keep the highway in proper repair.[76] To accomplish this purpose the proper officers may do any act in the highway that is necessary or proper to make and keep the way safe and convenient for the public travel.[77] They may raise or lower the surface,[78] dig up the earth,[79] cut down trees,[80] and use the earth, stone, and gravel within the limits of the highway in a reasonable and proper manner.[81]

1023, 101 Am. St. Rep. 97, 65 L. R. A. 949; Suffield *v.* Hathaway, 44 Conn. 521, 26 Am. Rep. 483; Old Town *v.* Dooley, 81 Ill. 255. On the other hand, inasmuch as the law places upon towns the duty of constructing and repairing all necessary highways within their respective limits, it is the corresponding right of the officers representing towns in this behalf to dispose of water flowing from springs upon a public way, by such methods as will in their judgment most economically and completely establish its safety. Suffield *v.* Hathaway, *supra.*

73. Denniston *v.* Clark, 125 Mass. 216; Cole *v.* Drew, 44 Vt. 48, 8 Am. Rep. 363.

74. Parker *v.* Jones, 1 Allen (Mass.) 270; Tucker *v.* Eldred, 6 R. I. 404.

Public have no right of pasturage.— The public have no right in a highway but to pass and repass thereon. They cannot therefore justify turning their cattle thereon for the purpose of grazing. Woodruff *v.* Neal, 28 Conn. 165; Stackpole *v.* Healy, 16 Mass. 33, 8 Am. Dec. 121; Harrison *v.* Brown, 5 Wis. 27. And it seems that the legislature has no authority to enact that cattle may go at large and feed in the highway, without compensation to the owner of the soil over which the highway is laid out. Stackpole *v.* Healy, *supra. Contra*, Hardenburgh *v.* Lockwood, 25 Barb. (N. Y.) 9, holding that the right to allow cattle, horses, or sheep to go at large on highways is one of the easements or servitudes pertaining to the land occupied as a highway; and the owner of land taken for a highway may be presumed to have been compensated for this as well as other easements to which land so taken is subject.

75. See *infra*, III, B.

76. *California.*— Smith *v.* San Luis Obispo, 95 Cal. 463, 30 Pac. 591.

Connecticut.— Benham *v.* Potter, 52 Conn. 248; Woodruff *v.* Neal, 28 Conn. 165; Peck *v.* Smith, 1 Conn. 103, 6 Am. Dec. 216.

Illinois.— Palatine *v.* Kreuger, 121 Ill. 72, 12 N. E. 75.

Iowa.— Overman *v.* May, 35 Iowa 89.

Massachusetts.— Upham *v.* Marsh, 128 Mass. 546; Boston *v.* Richardson, 13 Allen 146.

Vermont.— Cole *v.* Drew, 44 Vt. 49, 8 Am. Rep. 363; Pettibone *v.* Purdy, 7 Vt. 514.

See 25 Cent. Dig. tit. "Highways," §§ 292, 293.

77. Boston *v.* Richardson, 13 Allen (Mass.) 146.

Upon the question of necessity, the judgment and action of these public officers cannot be revised by the jury in any action at law. And if the act be done within the scope of the surveyor's authority, it does not become illegal by reason of the motive which influenced it. Upham *v.* Marsh, 128 Mass. 546.

78. Denniston *v.* Clark, 125 Mass. 216; Boston *v.* Richardson, 13 Allen (Mass.) 146.

79. Boston *v.* Richardson, 13 Allen (Mass.) 146; Adams *v.* Emerson, 6 Pick. (Mass.) 57.

80. *Iowa.*— Deaton *v.* Polk County, 9 Iowa 594.

Massachusetts.— Boston *v.* Richardson, 13 Allen 146.

New Hampshire.— Makepeace *v.* Worden, 1 N. H. 16.

New York.— Niagara Falls Suspension Bridge Co. *v.* Bachman, 4 Lans. 523 [*reversed* on other grounds in 66 N. Y. 261].

Rhode Island.— Tucker *v.* Eldred, 6 R. I. 404.

England.— Turner *v.* Ringwood Highway Bd., L. R. 9 Eq. 418, 21 L. T. Rep. N. S. 745, 18 Wkly. Rep. 424.

See 25 Cent. Dig. tit. "Highways," § 293.

The only right the public acquire in relation to such trees is that of cutting down and removing to a convenient distance, for the use of the owner, such trees as it is necessary to remove in order to the making or repair of the road in a proper and reasonable manner. They acquire no right to use any trees or timber growing on the land for the purpose of building or repairing the road. Baker *v.* Shephard, 24 N. H. 208; Niagara Falls Suspension Bridge Co. *v.* Bachman, 4 Lans. (N. Y.) 523 [*reversed* on other grounds in 66 N. Y. 261]; Tucker *v.* Eldred, 6 R. I. 404. And see Makepeace *v.* Worden, 1 N. H. 16.

81. New Haven *v.* Sargent, 38 Conn. 50, 9 Am. Rep. 360; Overman *v.* May, 35 Iowa 89; Anderson *v.* Van Tassel, 53 N. Y. 631; Jackson *v.* Hathaway, 15 Johns. (N. Y.) 447, 8 Am. Dec. 263; Felch *v.* Gilman, 22 Vt. 38.

Whether the use made of the stone was reasonable and proper is a mixed question of law and fact. Overman *v.* May, 35 Iowa 89.

Split stone.— The ownership of split stone lying upon land taken for a highway is not affected by the location, and the officers of the town have no right to use such stone in constructing the highway. Small *v.* Danville, 51 Me. 359.

B. Rights of Public — 1. To Use Highway For Other Public Purposes.[82] The right of the public in a highway consists in the privilege of passage,[83] and such privileges as are annexed as incidents by usage or custom,[84] as the right to make sewers and drains,[85] lay gas and water pipes,[86] make reservoirs,[87] and many other

Right to remove materials from one point to another.—As to the right of the authorities to take material from within the limits of a highway at one point, not for, or as an incident to, the improvement of the highway at that point, but for use upon that or other highways remote from the owner's land, without making compensation therefor, the authorities are at variance. In Bissell *v.* Collins, 28 Mich. 277, 15 Am. Rep. 217, the officials were held authorized to take gravel from below grade on one street, and haul it out to improve another, filling with less valuable material the excavation thus made. In line with this case are Bundy *v.* Catto, 61 Ill. App. 209; Upham *v.* Marsh, 128 Mass. 546; Denniston *v.* Clark, 125 Mass. 216, 222; Adams *v.* Emerson, 6 Pick. (Mass.) 57; Baxter *v.* Winooski Turnpike Co., 22 Vt. 114, 52 Am. Dec. 84; Huston *v.* Ft. Atkinson, 56 Wis. 350, 14 N. W. 444. In Denniston *v.* Clark, *supra*, it is said that highway officials are authorized "for the purpose of repairing the same highway, turnpike or railroad, to take earth, gravel or stones from one part and deposit them on another," and that all the highways within one municipal jurisdiction are, for such purposes, to be regarded as one. New Haven *v.* Sargent, 38 Conn. 50, 9 Am. Rep. 360, decides only that the city is entitled to use, to grade one street, soil which must necessarily be removed in grading another street. In Robert *v.* Sadler, 104 N. Y. 229, 10 N. E. 428, 58 Am. Rep. 498, the court of appeals, after reviewing some of these cases, with others from New York, declined to accede to the Michigan doctrine, and declared that the municipality could not remove, for use in other places, the gravel, etc., from within the boundaries of the highway, where this removal was not necessary to, or intended for, the establishment of the proper grade on that part of the highway. To the same effect are Anderson *v.* Bement, 13 Ind. App. 248, 41 N. E. 547; Ladd *v.* French, 3 Silv. Sup. (N. Y.) 1, 6 N. Y. Suppl. 56. In Niagara Falls Suspension Bridge Co. *v.* Bachman, 4 Lans. (N. Y.) 523 [*reversed* on other grounds in 66 N. Y. 261], it was said that gravel might be removed to other parts of the road, but it is apparent that this was gravel necessary to be removed in order to get the highway to its grade. In Turner *v.* Rising Sun, etc., Co., 71 Ind. 547, it is decided that, although, by a lawful appropriation, a public highway had become the property of the turnpike company, for the purpose of maintaining and constructing its road thereon, with a statutory provision authorizing it to take from the land so occupied stone, gravel, etc., for the road's construction, yet, under the law, it could not open a gravel pit in the highway, and haul out the gravel generally upon its road, without compensating the landowner therefor.

82. **City streets** see Municipal Corporations, 28 Cyc. 853.

Highways by dedication see Dedication, 13 Cyc. 493, 494.

Purpose of use and modes of travel see *infra*, VII, A.

83. *Indiana.*— Huffman *v.* State, 21 Ind. App. 449, 52 N. E. 713, 69 Am. St. Rep. 368.

Maine.—Burr *v.* Stevens, 90 Me. 500, 38 Atl. 547; Stinson *v.* Gardiner, 42 Me. 248, 66 Am. Dec. 281.

New Hampshire.— Winchester *v.* Capron, 63 N. H. 605, 4 Atl. 795, 56 Am. Rep. 554.

New Jersey.— State *v.* Laverack, 34 N. J. L. 201.

New York.— Kelsey *v.* King, 1 Transcr. App. 133, 33 How. Pr. 39.

England.— Hickman *v.* Maisey, [1901] 1 Q. B. 752, 69 L. J. Q. B. 511, 82 L. T. Rep. N. S. 321, 16 L. T. Rep. N. S. 274, 48 Wkly. Rep. 385; Harrison *v.* Rutland, [1893] 1 Q. B. 142, 62 L. J. Q. B. 117, 57 J. P. 278, 68 L. T. Rep. N. S. 35, 4 Reports 155, 41 Wkly. Rep. 322.

See 25 Cent. Dig. tit. "Highways." § 298.

84. Palatine *v.* Kreuger, 121 Ill. 72, 12 N. E. 75; Old Town *v.* Dooley, 81 Ill. 255; Overman *v.* May, 35 Iowa 89; State *v.* Laverack, 34 N. J. L. 201; Holloway *v.* Southmayd, 139 N. Y. 390, 34 N. E. 1047, 1052; Jackson *v.* Hathaway, 15 Johns. (N. Y.) 447, 8 Am. Dec. 263.

Right of repair see *supra*, III, A, 3, b.

No distinction between streets and highways.—As to the rights of the public in highways held under valid dedications and acceptances, and the power of the legislature over the same, there is no distinction between streets of incorporated cities and towns and country roads. Hardman *v.* Cabot, 60 W. Va. 664, 55 S. E. 756, 7 L. R. A. N. S. 506.

The user of a highway by touts for the purpose of watching the trials of race-horses on adjoining downs was held to be an unreasonable user, and such as to render them liable in an action of trespass to the owner of the soil. Hickman *v.* Maisey, [1900] 1 Q. B. 752, 69 L. J. Q. B. 511, 82 L. T. Rep. N. S. 321, 16 T. L. R. 274, 48 Wkly. Rep. 385.

85. Boston *v.* Richardson, 13 Allen (Mass.) 146; State *v.* Laverack, 34 N. J. L. 201; West *v.* Bancroft, 32 Vt. 367.

86. State *v.* Laverack, 34 N. J. L. 201; West *v.* Bancroft, 32 Vt. 367.

87. West *v.* Bancroft, 32 Vt. 367, holding that the proper public authorities of a town have a right to place in a highway a reservoir for the purpose of retaining water to sprinkle the highway with, and the owner of the fee of the land where such reservoir is placed cannot maintain an action against such authorities for so doing.

nuisance.[15] So trover lies for cutting timber within the limits of a highway,[16] or for taking earth or stone not necessary to the construction or repair thereof.[17] No action lies for obstructing a highway until it is opened.[18]

IV. HIGHWAY DISTRICTS AND OFFICERS.

A. Districts — 1. NATURE. Road districts are involuntary political subdivisions of the state created by general laws to aid in the administration of government.[19]

Pleading.—A complaint for impeding plaintiff's ingress and egress to his lots, by obstructing the highway on which they abut, need not aver he had the right of ingress and egress, such right being presumed. Yates *v.* Big Sandy R. Co., 89 S. W. 108, 28 Ky. L. Rep. 206. A complaint alleging that defendant placed an embankment four feet high in the highway in front of and parallel with plaintiff's lots, thereby impeding his ingress and egress, shows apparent injury. Yates *v.* Big Sandy R. Co., *supra.*

Who may sue.— One may sue for damages to lots by obstruction of a highway, although the legal title is held by another as trustee for him. Yates *v.* Big Sandy R. Co., 89 S. W. 108, 28 Ky. L. Rep. 206.

Damages.— In ascertaining the damages an abutting owner sustains by reason of an obstruction or encroachment on the highway, the rule is to prove the value of his property with the obstruction or encroachment, and its value with the same removed, and the difference is the measure of the loss. Ackerman *v.* True, 175 N. Y. 353, 67 N. E. 629 [*reversing* 71 N. Y. App. Div. 143, 75 N. Y. Suppl. 695], holding that the fact that plaintiff can sell his property for more than he could before the alleged encroachment does not render a dismissal of the complaint on the merits proper, where his property is worth about fifteen thousand dollars less with the encroachment than without it. In an action to recover damages for an obstruction of an abutting lot-owner's rights in a highway, where the character of the injury is permanent, and the complaint recognizes the right of defendant to continue in the use of the property wrongfully appropriated, and to acquire, as a result of the suit, the title thereto, the damages should be assessed on the basis of the permanent depreciation in value of the property injured (Indiana, etc., R. Co. *v.* Eberle, 110 Ind. 542, 11 N. E. 467, 59 Am. Rep. 225; Wallace *v.* Kansas City, etc., R. Co., 47 Mo. App. 491, holding that an embankment of stone and earth in a street in front of a lot obstructing ingress and egress thereto is a permanent structure, and damages for such injury are original and may at once be estimated and compensated); but where the action is in trespass, to recover for a past injury, without recognizing the legality of the obstruction, or defendant's right to continue it as a result of the suit, only such damages can be recovered as accrued up to the time of the commencement of the action (Indiana, etc., R. Co. *v.* Eberle, *supra*). Incidental damages in common with the rest of the public are not the subject of recovery. Dantzer *v.* Indianapolis Union R. Co., 141 Ind. 604, 39 N. E. 223, 50 Am. St. Rep. 343, 34 L. R. A. 769; Indiana, etc., R. Co. *v.* Eberle, *supra.* Thus for merely incidental damages as result from the careful construction and prudent operation of a railroad on the land of another, even though it be in a public street, the adjacent proprietor cannot recover. Pittsburgh, etc., R. Co. *v.* Noftsger, 148 Ind. 101, 47 N. E. 332. So an obstruction or discontinuance of the highway at another place, although it may indirectly affect the value of his property by requiring a longer and more circuitous route to reach it, is not an injury or tort for which the landowner can recover damages. Newton *v.* New York, etc., R. Co., 72 Conn. 420, 44 Atl. 813; Jacksonville, etc., R. Co. *v.* Thompson, 34 Fla. 346, 16 So. 282, 26 L. R. A. 410. The mere fact of interference with his right of access will entitle an abutting owner to at least nominal damages. Bannon *v.* Murphy, 38 S. W. 889, 18 Ky. L. Rep. 989. Damages arising from both a temporary and a permanent nuisance may be recovered in the same action. Wallace *v.* Kansas City, etc., R. Co., 47 Mo. App. 491.

15. Hargro *v.* Hodgdon, 89 Cal. 623, 26 Pac. 1106; Coburn *v.* Ames, 52 Cal. 385, 28 Am. Rep. 634; Green *v.* Asher, 11 S. W. 286, 10 Ky. L. Rep. 1006; Smith *v.* Putnam, 62 N. H. 369; Ackerman *v.* True, 175 N. Y. 353, 67 N. E. 629 [*reversing* 71 N. Y. App. Div. 143, 75 N. Y. Suppl. 695].

Abatement by owner.— Every proprietor of land adjoining a highway has a right to reasonable access to its traveled part; and any fence or other obstruction which so annoys or encumbers it as essentially to interfere with this right is a nuisance, and may be removed by such proprietor. Hubbard *v.* Deming, 21 Conn. 356. So where one stops in the road and uses loud and indecent language, he thereby becomes a trespasser, and the owner of the soil has the right to abate the nuisance. State *v.* Davis, 80 N. C. 351, 30 Am. Rep. 86.

Pleading.—Where a complaint to abate a nuisance does not explicitly state that plaintiff has sustained an injury different in kind from the general public, it is insufficient on special demurrer; but when such injury appears by inference it is proper to overrule a motion for judgment on the pleadings at the commencement of the trial. Hargo *v.* Hodgdon, 89 Cal. 623, 26 Pac. 1106.

16. Sanderson *v.* Haverstick, 8 Pa. St. 294.

17. Phillips *v.* Bowers, 7 Gray (Mass.) 21.

18. Southerland *v.* Jackson, 30 Me. 462, 50 Am. Dec. 633.

19. Farmer *v.* Myles, 106 La. 333, 30 So. 858.

B. Officers — 1. Appointment, Election, and Qualification — a. In General. The election [26] or the appointment [27] of highway officers must be made according to statute by the proper authorities,[28] and must be of someone of a class eligible,[29]

under Mass. Gen. St. c. 44, § 6, the surveyors may nevertheless act together, or by a majority of the whole board. McCormick *v.* Boston, 120 Mass. 499. And see Callender *v.* Marsh, 1 Pick. (Mass.) 418. The neglect or refusal of a township committee to assign a road to an overseer, or appropriate money to work it, does not authorize any one to close or obstruct it, or absolve the overseer from his duty enjoined by law to open, clear out, and work the public roads. Morgan *v.* Monmouth Plank Road Co., 26 N. J. L. 99. And see Ward *v.* Folly, 5 N. J. L. 482, holding that the overseer is justified in repairing a road, although not assigned to him in writing by the township committee. While it is the duty of the committee to assign to the overseers in writing their several limits and divisions of the highways, yet if the committee neglects to do so, the overseers are to observe and conform themselves to such assignment as may have at any time theretofore been made. Morgan *v.* Monmouth Plank Road Co., *supra*

26. *Connecticut.*— Pinney *v.* Brown, 60 Conn. 164, 22 Atl. 430, appointment void where not properly warned in town meeting; appointment must be of first selectman for time being as provided by town meeting.

Massachusetts.— Walker *v.* West Boylston, 128 Mass. 550 (at special meeting at which act providing for road commissioners is accepted); Benjamin *v.* Wheeler, 15 Gray 486 (where selectmen were chosen surveyors by town vote).

Michigan.— Davies *v.* Saginaw County, 89 Mich. 295, 50 N. W. 862, a statute creating road districts with road officers is void where the constitution provides for annual elections of town officers.

New Hampshire.— Brewster *v.* Hyde, 7 N. H. 206, where warrant for town meeting was issued without authority.

New Jersey.—Winans *v.* Crane, 36 N. J. L. 394 (statute authorizing town committee to fill vacancies entitles them to elect in case of tie vote); Green *v.* Kleinhans, 14 N. J. L. 473 (at annual town meeting).

See 25 Cent. Dig. tit. "Highways," § 304.

27. *Alabama.*— Thompson *v.* State, 21 Ala. 48, appointment of overseer by probate court while another is in office is voidable.

Delaware.— State *v.* Rothwell, 5 Harr. 312, in writing.

Idaho.— Meservey *v.* Gulliford, 14 Ida. 133, 93 Pac. 780, order of appointment need not recite vacancy.

Kentucky.— Poole *v.* Slayton, 128 Ky. 514, 108 S. W. 903, 33 Ky. L. Rep. 373.

Michigan.— Wayne County Road Com'rs *v.* Wayne County, 148 Mich. 255, 111 N. W. 901 (holding that Act No. 146, Pub. Acts (1905), in so far as it provides in section 6 for the appointment of county road commissioners for Wayne county by the county clerk and the mayor of Detroit, conflicts with the theory of local self-government guaranteed by the constitution, and cannot be sustained); People *v.* Springwells Tp. Bd., 25 Mich. 153 (state commissioners cannot become town officers by acquiescence).

Missouri.— State *v.* Gasconade County Ct., 25 Mo. App. 446, appointed by court only where taxpayers fail to act.

New Jersey.— See Poinier *v.* State, 44 N. J. L. 433, as to statute validating appointment made under an unconstitutional law.

New York.— People *v.* Richmond County, 20 N. Y. 252 (holding that where two persons are appointed to fill vacancies in the office of commissioners of highways, without designating the class to which they shall respectively belong, the one first named in the appointment is to be regarded as appointed to the first class, or that highest in numerical order); Matter of Kerr, 57 Misc. 324, 108 N. Y. Suppl. 591 (holding that where the concurrence of four members of a town board is essential to an appointment of a highway commissioner, no valid appointment is made by a concurrence of four members of whom the appointee is one).

Tennessee.— State *v.* Maloney, (1901) 65 S. W. 871, appointment of officer to board newly created until the next election is an appointment to fill a vacancy within the constitution.

Virginia.— See Painter *v.* St. Clair, 98 Va. 85, 34 S. E. 989, supervisor is a member of the road commission by virtue of his office.

See 25 Cent. Dig. tit. "Highways," § 304.

28. People *v.* Carver, 5 Colo. App. 156, 38 Pac. 332 (by county commissioners in office at the time); Wayne County Road Com'rs *v.* Wayne County, 148 Mich. 255, 111 N. W. 901; People *v.* Havemeyer, 3 Hun (N. Y.) 97 (creation of board of state engineers is valid); Matter of Kerr, 57 Misc. (N. Y.) 324, 108 N. Y. Suppl. 591 (appointee himself cannot make one of the necessary number of board to appoint); Ice *v.* Marion County Ct., 40 W. Va. 118, 20 S. E. 809 (by county court). See, however, Read *v.* Com., 3 Bibb (Ky.) 484, holding that the right of the court to appoint officer cannot be attacked on his trial for delinquency.

29. Allison *v.* State, 60 Ala. 54 (of minor is voidable); Boyd County *v.* Arthur, 118 Ky. 932, 82 S. W. 613, 26 Ky. L. Rep. 906 (cannot order that magistrates be supervisors); Pulaski County *v.* Sears, 117 Ky. 249, 78 S. W. 123, 25 Ky. L. Rep. 1381; Daviess County *v.* Goodwin, 116 Ky. 891, 77 S. W. 185, 25 Ky. L. Rep. 1081 (county judge not eligible to be supervisor of roads).

Residence in the district may be necessary. Spann *v.* State, 14 Ala. 588; People *v.* Markiewicz, 225 Ill. 563, 80 N. E. 256 [*affirming* 126 Ill. App. 203] (as legal voter and resident); People *v.* Whipple, 187 Ill. 547, 58 N. E. 468 [*affirming* 87 Ill. App. 145].

or malicious[62] ministerial acts,[63] or those of his servants,[64] or for his unauthorized acts[65] of trespass.[66] Highway officers are not liable while acting within their authority,[67] or while acting in good faith within their general powers in excess of their special authority,[68] or for errors of judgment,[69] their duty being

206; Sells *v.* Dermody, 114 Iowa 344, 86 N. W. 325 (holding that the fact that a person elected a road supervisor is subject to a penalty for refusing to accept the office does not relieve such officer from individual liability for negligence in failing to perform ministerial duties in keeping the roads in repair); Gould *v.* Schermer, 101 Iowa 582, 70 N. W. 697 (chargeable with ordinary negligence and not merely "gross" negligence); Moynihan *v.* Todd, 188 Mass. 301, 74 N. E. 367, 108 Am. St. Rep. 473. *Contra*, Young *v.* Road Com'rs, 2 Nott & M. (S. C.) 537.

However, in an action against highway commissioners to recover damages resulting from acts done in their official capacity, plaintiff cannot recover against one of the defendants for an act done in his personal capacity, and not directed or assented to by the board. Illinois Agricultural Co. *v.* Cranston, 21 Ill. App. 174. And a road supervisor, liable under Iowa Code, § 1557, for all damages resulting from a defect in a highway which is allowed to remain after a reasonable time for repairing the same after the receipt of a written notice thereof, is not personally liable for failure to repair a defect in a highway where notice thereof has not been given to him. Sells *v.* Dermody, 114 Iowa 344, 86 N. W. 325.

62. *Iowa.*— Wilding *v.* Hough, 37 Iowa 446, malice in tearing down house being provable by showing that road was not improved.

Missouri.— Cook *v.* Hecht, 64 Mo. App. 273.

Nebraska.— Denver *v.* Myers, 63 Nebr. 107, 88 N. W. 191, fraudulent overpayments.

New Hampshire.— Makepeace *v.* Worden, 1 N. H. 16, converting wood for private use.

New Jersey.— Winter *v.* Peterson, 24 N. J. L. 524, 61 Am. Dec. 678.

New York.— Beardslee *v.* Dolge, 143 N. Y. 160, 38 N. E. 205, 42 Am. St. 707 (for false statements in return of proceedings, although intentions were honest); Rector *v.* Clark, 78 N. Y. 21 [*reversing* 12 Hun 189] (for failure to notify and false return).

Ohio.— Brick *v.* Green, Wright 86, refusal to certify to work done.

See 25 Cent. Dig. tit. "Highways," § 313.

63. Tearney *v.* Smith, 86 Ill. 391 (ministerial act of construction of highway); McCord *v.* High, 24 Iowa 336; Clark *v.* Miller, 54 N. Y. 528 [*affirming* 42 Barb. 255, 47 Barb. 38], although refusal to act is based on a *bona fide* opinion that the statute is unconstitutional).

64. Ely *v.* Parsons, 55 Conn. 83, 10 Atl. 499, for unnecessary cutting by laborer acting under general directions. *Contra*, Huey *v.* Richardson, 2 Harr. (Del.) 206, for mistake of competent surveyor.

65. *Louisiana.*— Michel *v.* Terrebonne Police Jury, 9 La. Ann. 67; Michel *v.* West Baton Rouge Police Jury, 3 La. Ann. 123; Morgan *v.* Pointe Coupe Police Jury, 11 La. 157.

Maine.— Field *v.* Towle, 34 Me. 405.

Nebraska.— Denver *v.* Myers, 63 Nebr. 107, 88 N. W. 191, overpayments.

New Hampshire.— Waldron *v.* Berry, 51 N. H. 136; Brown *v.* Rundlett, 15 N. H. 360.

New York.— Mather *v.* Crawford, 36 Barb. 564.

North Carolina.— Hitch *v.* Edgecombe County, 132 N. C. 573, 44 S. E. 30.

Pennsylvania.—Eisenhart *v.* Hykes, 4 Lanc. L. Rev. 98.

66. Beyer *v.* Tanner, 29 Ill. 135 (even if they are misled as to the correct line of a road); Pinkerton *v.* Randolph, 200 Mass. 24, 85 N. E. 892 (cutting trees from street in front of plaintiff's property; selectmen and agents joint trespassers); Ross *v.* Malcom, 40 Pa. St. 284; Webster *v.* White, 8 S. D. 479, 66 N. W. 1145. But see Brown *v.* Bridges, 31 Iowa 138 (officers not liable for minute trespasses); Foot *v.* Stiles, 57 N. Y. 399 (holding that the omission of one elected to the office of commissioner of highways to execute and file an official bond as required by statute does not render his official acts void in such a sense as to make him liable as trespasser therefor).

67. Spitznogle *v.* Ward, 64 Ind. 30; Sage *v.* Laurain, 19 Mich. 137; McConnell *v.* Dewey, 5 Nebr. 385 (unless action given by statute); Driggs *v.* Phillips, 103 N. Y. 77, 8 N. E. 514; Finucan *v.* Ramsden, 95 N. Y. App. Div. 626, 88 N. Y. Suppl. 430.

68. Mann *v.* Richardson, 66 Ill. 481, holding that when public agents acting within the scope of their general powers in good faith contract with parties having full knowledge of the extent of their authority, or who have equal means of knowledge with themselves, they do not become individually liable unless the intent to incur personal responsibility is clearly expressed, although it is found that through ignorance of the law they may have exceeded their authority. See Parks *v.* Ross, 11 How. (U. S.) 362, 13 L. ed. 730.

69. *Illinois.*—Neville *v.* Viner, 115 Ill. App. 364; Summers *v.* People, 109 Ill. App. 430.

Iowa.— Nolan *v.* Reed, 139 Iowa 68, 117 N. W. 25.

Maine.— Wilson *v.* Simmons, 89 Me. 242, 36 Atl. 380. But see Frost *v.* Portland, 11 Me. 271.

Massachusetts.— Benjamin *v.* Wheeler, 8 Gray 409; Callender *v.* Marsh, 1 Pick. 418.

New Hampshire.— Waldron *v.* Berry, 51 N. H. 136; Rowe *v.* Addison, 34 N. H. 306.

New York.— Freeman *v.* Cornwall, 10 Johns. 470.

See 25 Cent. Dig. tit. "Highways," § 313.

authority;[75] nor is the municipality liable when the board or officer upon whom the duty of road work is imposed by statute acts as a public officer carrying into effect a public law for the public good and not as agent of the particular municipality in which he is working,[76] unless a statute expressly or impliedly so provides.[77]

7. Actions and Proceedings — a. Civil. Actions by or against highway officers should join the parties interested,[78] by their official names,[79] and should be brought in the county where the cause of action arose.[80] The officer may set up any competent evidence in defense bearing on the question.[81] The local statutes

143 Mass. 582, 10 N. E. 481. But see District of Columbia *v.* Robinson, 14 App. Cas. (D. C.) 512 [*affirmed* in 180 U. S. 92, 21 S. Ct. 283, 45 L. ed. 440].

75. Goddard *v.* Harpswell, 88 Me. 228, 33 Atl. 980 (selectmen); Wheeler *v.* Essex Public Road Bd., 39 N. J. L. 291; Niland *v.* Bowron, 193 N. Y. 180, 85 N. E. 1012 [*affirming* 113 N. Y. App. Div. 661, 99 N. Y. Suppl. 914]; Atcheson *v.* Portage La Prairie, 10 Manitoba 39.

76. *California.*— Crowell *v.* Sonoma Co., 25 Cal. 313.

Indiana.— Jackson County *v.* Branaman, 169 Ind. 80, 82 N. E. 65; Pittsburgh, etc., R. Co. *v.* Iddings, 28 Ind. App. 504, 62 N. E. 112; Union Civil Tp. *v.* Berryman, 3 Ind. App. 344, 28 N. E. 774.

Kentucky.— Hutchison *v.* Pulaski County Ct., 11 S. W. 607, 11 Ky. L. Rep. 117.

Maine.— Emerson *v.* Washington County, 9 Me. 98.

Maryland.— Anne Arundel County *v.* Duvall, 54 Md. 350, 39 Am. Rep. 393.

Massachusetts.— MacManus *v.* Weston, 164 Mass. 263, 41 N. E. 301, 31 L. R. A. 174; Pratt *v.* Weymouth, 147 Mass. 245, 17 N. E. 538, 9 Am. St. Rep. 691; Clark *v.* Easton, 146 Mass. 43, 14 N. E. 795; Barney *v.* Lowell, 98 Mass. 570; Walcott *v.* Swampscott, 1 Allen 101; White *v.* Phillipston, 10 Metc. 108.

Missouri.— Swineford *v.* Franklin County, 73 Mo. 279 [*affirming* 6 Mo. App. 39, and *following* Reardon *v.* St. Louis County, 36 Mo. 555, holding that a county court in repairing a county road acts for the state and not for the county].

New Hampshire.— O'Brien *v.* Derry, 73 N. H. 198, 60 Atl. 843; Hall *v.* Concord, 71 N. H. 367, 52 Atl. 864, 58 L. R. A. 455; Hardy *v.* Keene, 52 N. H. 370; Ball *v.* Winchester, 32 N. H. 435.

New York.— Winchell *v.* Camillus, 190 N. Y. 536, 83 N. E. 1134 [*affirming* 109 N. Y. App. Div. 341, 95 N. Y. Suppl. 688]; People *v.* Esopus, 74 N. Y. 310; Robinson *v.* Fowler, 80 Hun 101, 30 N. Y. Suppl. 25; Lyth *v.* Evans, 33 Misc. 221, 68 N. Y. Suppl. 356.

Rhode Island.— Smart *v.* Johnston, 17 R. I. 778, 24 Atl. 830.

Wisconsin.— Dodge *v.* Ashland County, 88 Wis. 577, 60 N. W. 830.

See 25 Cent. Dig. tit. "Highways," § 315.

77. Clapper *v.* Waterford, 131 N. Y. 382, 30 N. E. 240; Winchell *v.* Camillus, 109 N. Y. App. Div. 341, 95 N. Y. Suppl. 688 [*affirmed* in 190 N. Y. 536, 83 N. E. 1134]. See also Swineford *v.* Franklin County, 73 Mo. 279.

78. *Illinois.*— Blanchard *v.* La Salle, 99 Ill. 278, by town against treasurer of highway commissioners, remedy on bond being cumulative.

Indiana.— White River Tp. *v.* Cottom, 11 Ind. 216, by township treasurer.

Iowa.— Wells *v.* Stombock, 59 Iowa 376, 13 N. W. 339, by township clerk on supervisor's bond.

Mississippi.— Attala *v.* Niles, 58 Miss. 48, supervisors allowed to defend when overseer did not.

New York.— Babcock *v.* Gifford, 29 Hun 186 (against one commissioner for acts of negligence imputable to all); Gailor *v.* Herrick, 42 Barb. 79 (supervisor who had no right to certain fund cannot sue on bond of commissioner for neglect to deliver it); People *v.* Highland, 8 N. Y. St. 531 (highway commissioner may prosecute overseer).

Texas.— Thornton *v.* Springer, 5 Tex. 587, individual cannot sue overseer for penalty under statute.

Vermont.— Newbury *v.* Johnson, Brayt. 24, by town in case for damages paid to individual injured on unrepaired road.

On change in the personnel of a board those who are its members at the time suit is brought are the proper parties. Armstrong *v.* Landers, 1 Pennew. (Del.) 449, 42 Atl. 617; Hitchman *v.* Baxter, 5 N. Y. Civ. Proc. 226 (successor in office not substituted where statute provides that execution be collected out of the officer's property); Miller *v.* Ford, 4 Rich. (S. C.) 376, 55 Am. Dec. 687 (not members when contract made).

79. Sheaff *v.* People, 87 Ill. 189, 29 Am. Rep. 49 (commissioners of highways are a quasi-corporation, and need not be named individually in an action against them); Rutland Highway Com'rs *v.* Dayton Highway Com'rs, 60 Ill. 58; Lange *v.* Soffell, 33 Ill. App. 624; St. Bartholomew's Parish Road Com'rs *v.* Murray, 1 Rich. (S. C.) 335 (may object only by plea in abatement that they should have sued individually); St. Peter's Parish Road Com'rs *v.* McPherson, 1 Speers (S. C.) 218 (can sue in names of members for the time being). See O'Fallon *v.* Ohio, etc., R. Co., 45 Ill. App. 572 (a suit against a railroad company to recover the cost of constructing and maintaining proper approaches to its crossing is properly brought by the highway commissioners in the name of the town); St. Peter's Parish Road Com'rs *v.* Guerard, 1 Speers (S. C.) 215 (fact that names of commissioners are not set out is not a ground for attacking decree).

80. People *v.* Hayes, 7 How. Pr. (N. Y.) 248.

81. Yealy *v.* Fink, 43 Pa. St. 212, 82 Am. Dec. 556, that townspeople did not want

commonly determine the liability for costs in actions brought by or against highway officers.[82]

b. Penal or Criminal — (I) *IN GENERAL.* Statutes often impose liabilities for penalties,[83] and commonly provide for indictment of road officers,[84] for misfeasance or neglect of their duties in regard to road work and repairs. Under such statutes road officers cannot be prosecuted for misuse of their discretion,[85] and it is a good defense that the work was rendered impossible by facts not attributable to the officer's fault.[86]

(II) *INDICTMENT.* The indictment of a highway officer for a criminal offense should contain plain averments of the offense charged,[87] stating the

bridge. See Jewett *v.* Sweet, 178 Ill. 96, 52 N. E. 962 [*affirming* 77 Ill. App. 641] (commissioners cannot set up rights of adjacent owners); Rex *v.* Norfolk, [1901] 2 K. B. 268, 65 J. P. 454, 70 L. J. K. B. 575, 84 L. T. Rep. N. S. 822, 17 T. L. R. 437, 49 Wkly. Rep. 543 (power of county council to defend an action brought against surveyor or against individuals).

82. See the statutes of the several states. And see People *v.* Madison County, 125 Ill. 334, 17 N. E. 802 [*affirming* 23 Ill. App. 386] (liable as commissioners and not individually); Lyons *v.* People, 38 Ill. 347.

Costs held not recoverable against supervisors see Bettis *v.* Nicholson, 1 Stew. (Ala.) 349; Bittle *v.* Hay, 5 Ohio 269; Carter *v.* Hawley, Wright (Ohio) 74.

Liability of town for costs.— Town held liable see Sebrell *v.* Fall Creek Tp., 27 Ind. 86; McCoy *v.* McClarty, 53 Misc. (N. Y.) 69, 104 N. Y. Suppl. 80. Town held not liable see Gardner *v.* Chambersburgh, 19 Ill. 99.

83. See the statutes of the several states. And see Hizer *v.* Rockford, 86 Ill. 325 (penalty imposed on overseer for neglect to obey order of commissioners); Salt Creek *v.* Mason County Highway Com'rs, 25 Ill. App. 187; Bentley *v.* Phelps, 27 Barb. (N. Y.) 524; State *v.* Chappell, 2 Hill (S. C.) 391.

A statute as to guide-boards does not apply to roads by dedication or use. State *v.* Siegel, 54 Wis. 86, 11 N. W. 435.

Acts held not to subject the officer to the penalty see Moll *v.* Pickaway, 14 Ill. App. 343 (removing plank put down by individual); Com. *v.* House, 4 Pa. L. J. 327 (refusing to open road pending petition for review); U. S. *v.* Custis, 25 Fed. Cas. No. 14,909, 1 Cranch C. C. 417 (overseer not notified of his appointment).

The neglect of a town to erect and maintain guide-posts at all intersections of highways within its limits is one entire offense, and a separate penalty does not accrue for each intersection of roads at which the town has neglected to erect guide-posts. Clark *v.* Lisbon, 19 N. H. 286.

84. See the statutes of the several states. And see the following cases:

Alabama.— Williams *v.* State, 45 Ala. 55.

Illinois.— Lequat *v.* People, 11 Ill. 330. But see Zorger *v.* People, 25 Ill. 193.

Indiana.— State *v.* Hogg, 5 Ind. 515, for failing to repair.

Kentucky.—Com. *v.* Thompson, 4 Bibb 230; Read *v.* Com., 3 Bibb 484.

Michigan.— Hatch *v.* Calhoun Cir. Judge, 127 Mich. 174, 86 N. W. 518.

Mississippi.— State *v.* Adams County, Walk. 368.

New York.— People *v.* Adsit, 2 Hill 619.

North Carolina.— State *v.* Long, 81 N. C. 563. See also State *v.* Britt, 118 N. C. 1255, 24 S. E. 216.

Pennsylvania.— Edge *v.* Com., 7 Pa. St. 275, although supervisors are also liable to civil action for neglect of duty as overseers of the poor.

Virginia.— Com. *v.* Piper, 9 Leigh 657.

See 25 Cent. Dig. tit. "Highways," § 320.

Number of offenses.— However long a road may have been out of repair before indictment, it is but one offense; but if, after conviction, it still continues out of repair, the commissioner may again be indicted. State *v.* Chappell, 2 Hill (S. C.) 391.

Where a court directs a road wider than the law requires, a presentment may be sustained against the surveyor for not keeping it in repair to the legal width. Com. *v.* Caldwell, Litt. Sel. Cas. (Ky.) 168.

Failure to maintain guide-posts when required by law is punishable under the statutes. Lequat *v.* People, 11 Ill. 330; State *v.* Nicholson, 6 N. C. 135. But see State *v.* Smith, 25 Tex. Suppl. 64.

85. Eyman *v.* People, 6 Ill. 4; Shanks *v.* Pearson, 66 Kan. 168, 71 Pac. 252; Com. *v.* Thompson, 126 Pa. St. 614, 17 Atl. 754.

86. Mendham Tp. *v.* Losey, 2 N. J. L. 347 (where township had not furnished money for repair); State *v.* Small, 33 N. C. 571 (bad weather); State *v.* Broyles, 1 Bailey (S. C.) 134 (defense by one commissioner of roads for not repairing his division of a road that it was ordered discontinued by the whole board); Howell *v.* State, 29 Tex. App. 592, 16 S. W. 533 (road abandoned and overseer could not determine its location); Parker *v.* State, 29 Tex. App. 372, 16 S. W. 186 (that inhabitants refused to work or pay and work too expensive); Moore *v.* State, 27 Tex. App. 439, 11 S. W. 457 (impossible to make road passable if overseer had worked all his hands full time).

That defendants opened the road on a different location is no defense. Com. *v.* Johnson, 134 Pa. St. 635, 19 Atl. 803.

87. McCullough *v.* State, 63 Ala. 75 ("failed to discharge his duties as such overseer" held sufficient); State *v.* Brown, 8 Blackf. (Ind.) 69 (road so obstructed by trees as to be nearly impassable).

V. CONSTRUCTION, IMPROVEMENT, AND REPAIR.

A. Statutory Regulation. The construction, improvement, and repair of highways is regulated largely by statutes,[1] the general rules relating to statutes[2] being applicable,[3] as to constitutionality[4] and construction,[5] which must be reasonable.[6] Statutes relating to construction and repair have in some instances been construed as directory rather than mandatory.[7]

B. Mode, Plan, and Sufficiency[8] — **1. IN GENERAL.** The method or plan of work is in the discretion of the road officers,[9] within the restrictions of

(whether road in as good condition as other roads in community held irrelevant); Ward *v.* State, (Ala. 1905) 39 So. 923; Tate *v.* State, 5 Blackf. (Ind.) 73 (that defendant could not keep road in repair through default of county commissioners); Com. *v.* Cassatt, 3 Montg. Co. Rep. (Pa.) 19; Sennett *v.* State, 17 Tex. 308 (must prove failure of other overseers to set up milestones as alleged which prevented him from setting up his); Sigler *v.* State, 17 Tex. 304. See also Com. *v.* Johnson, 134 Pa. St. 635, 19 Atl. 803.

1. See the statutes of the several states. And see cases cited *infra*, note 3.

2. See STATUTES, 36 Cyc. 929.

3. *Kansas.*— State *v.* Shawnee County, 28 Kan. 431.

Massachusetts.— Scituate *v.* Weymouth, 108 Mass. 128.

Minnesota.— Thorn *v.* Washington County, 14 Minn. 233.

Washington.— Lewis County *v.* Hays, 1 Wash. Terr. 100.

Wisconsin.— State *v.* Hogue, 71 Wis. 384, 36 N. W. 860.

See 25 Cent. Dig. tit. "Highways," § 324.

4. State *v.* Marion County, 170 Ind. 595, 85 N. E. 513; People *v.* Springwells Tp. Bd., 25 Mich. 153; Jensen *v.* Polk County, 47 Wis. 298, 2 N. W. 320, holding that an act which provides for the laying out and opening of a state road, and imposes the cost of the road upon the towns and counties through which it is to pass, is not in conflict with Const. art. 8, § 10, forbidding the state to carry on works of internal improvement.

Action under unconstitutional statute.—A contemplated road improvement, voted under an unconstitutional statute, is not made lawful by the fact that a majority of those voting on the subject voted in favor of it. Hixson *v.* Burson, 54 Ohio St. 470, 43 N. E. 1000.

5. *Georgia.*— Howell *v.* Chattooga County, 118 Ga. 635, 45 S. E. 241.

Indiana.— Findling *v.* Foster, 170 Ind. 325, 84 N. E. 529, 81 N. E. 480. See also State *v.* Marion County, 170 Ind. 595, 85 N. E. 513.

Maryland.— Fout *v.* Frederick County, 105 Md. 545, 66 Atl. 487.

Mississippi.— Madison County *v.* Stewart. 74 Miss. 160, 20 So. 857, special act not repealed by general statute.

New Jersey.— Oakes *v.* Glen Ridge, 60 N. J. L. 130, 36 Atl. 708.

New York.— McGuinness *v.* Westchester, 66 Hun 356, 21 N. Y. Suppl. 290, holding that appointment of commissioners of improvements under certain act does not abridge the powers of highway commissioners.

Ohio.— State *v.* Hamilton County, 9 Ohio Dec. (Reprint) 243, 11 Cinc. L. Bul. 274. See also State *v.* Craig, 22 Ohio Cir. Ct. 135, 12 Ohio Cir. Dec. 189.

Texas.— Plowman *v.* Dallas County, (Civ. App. 1905) 88 S. W. 252.

See 25 Cent. Dig. tit. "Highways," § 324.

A codification may repeal by implication prior special acts. Findling *v.* Foster, 170 Ind. 325, 81 N. E. 480, 84 N. E. 529.

6. Smith *v.* Helmer, 7 Barb. (N. Y.) 416, road leading "from" H construed to include portion in H.

7. See Fresno County *v.* Fowler Switch Canal Co., 68 Cal. 359, 9 Pac. 309; Clark Civil Tp. *v.* Brookshire, 114 Ind. 437, 16 N. E. 132.

8. **Construction, improvement, and repair of city streets** see MUNICIPAL CORPORATIONS, 28 Cyc. 946.

9. Dennis *v.* Osborn, 75 Kan. 557, 89 Pac. 925 (error in judgment held no ground for injunction); Cunningham *v.* Frankfort, 104 Me. 208, 70 Atl. 441; Steele *v.* Glen Park, 193 N. Y. 341, 86 N. E. 26 [*affirming* 119 N. Y. App. Div. 918, 105 N. Y. Suppl. 1144]; Smith *v.* Grayson County, 18 Tex. Civ. App. 153, 44 S. W. 921.

Whether the result fulfils the requirement of the statute must be ultimately passed upon by the court and jury when the question arises. Cunningham *v.* Frankfort, 104 Me. 208, 70 Atl. 441.

Only one system can be in force in a county at a time. Wright *v.* Sheppard, 5 Ga. App. 298, 63 S. E. 48.

The order of construction cannot be attacked collaterally except on the ground of fraud. Le Moyne *v.* Washington County, 213 Pa. St. 123, 62 Atl. 516.

The side-path commissioners of a county have authority to take up a curbstone and relocate it so as to make room for a side-path along the sidewalk. O'Donnell *v.* Preston, 74 N. Y. App. Div. 86, 77 N. Y. Suppl. 305.

Under authority "to grade hills" in laying out a way, the commissioners may fill the valleys. Acton *v.* York County, 77 Me. 128.

A change of the line of road may be authorized in improvement (Knox County *v.* Kennedy, 92 Tenn. 1, 20 S. W. 311), or in altering or straightening an existing road

law,[10] and subject to the rights of abutting owners.[11] They may direct how much of the road shall be improved [12] and provide for railroad rights of way.[13] Their duties extend to remedying defects and obstructions caused by snow.[14]

2. Taking Material From Abutters. Statutes sometimes authorize road officers to take materials from the land of abutters, due compensation being provided.[15] The officer is the sole judge of the necessity of the taking,[16] and so long as he does not wilfully annoy the owners of property a court of equity will not restrain him; [17] but the officer cannot pass over cultivated or improved land for this purpose; [18] nor can an overseer take for public use timber prepared for the owner's own use; [19] and purchase of material at a specified price is not authorized under a statute allowing the overseer to take.[20] In the absence of statute no authority to take from abutters exists.[21]

3. Removal of Fences, Buildings, and Other Property. Road officers are commonly required by statute to give a reasonable time on laying out or altering a road for the removal of timber, fences, buildings, or other property,[22] after notice

(Crow v. Judy, 139 Ind. 562, 38 N. E. 415; McClure v. Franklin County, 124 Ind. 154, 24 N. E. 741; Gipson v. Heath, 98 Ind. 100).

10. *Indiana.*— Weaver v. Templin, 113 Ind. 298, 14 N. E. 600.

Kansas.— Barker v. Wyandotte County, 45 Kan. 681, 26 Pac. 585.

Maine.— Acton v. York, 77 Me. 128.

Nebraska.— Hitchcock v. Zink, 80 Nebr. 29, 113 N. W. 795, 127 Am. St. Rep. 743, 13 L. R. A. 1110.

New Jersey.— State v. Passaic, 46 N. J. L. 124.

New York.— People v. Waterford, etc., Turnpike Co., 3 Abb. Dec. 580, 2 Keyes 327.

See 25 Cent. Dig. tit. "Highways," § 323 *et seq.*

Building a new bridge is not repairing highway. State v. White, 16 R. I. 591, 18 Atl. 179, 1038.

11. Tatnall v. Shallcross, 4 Del. Ch. 634.

12. *Illinois.*— Trotter v. Barrett, 164 Ill. 262, 45 N. E. 149; Waugh v. Leech, 28 Ill. 488.

Maine.— Brown v. Skowhegan, 82 Me. 273, 19 Atl. 399, holding that they need not work the entire width of street or connect the traveled portion with abutters.

Massachusetts.— Metcalf v. Boston, 158 Mass. 284, 33 N. E. 586; Com. v. Boston, etc., R. Corp., 12 Cush. 254.

Vermont.— Hutchinson v. Chester, 33 Vt. 410.

England.— Sandgate Urban Dist. Council v. Kent, 79 L. T. Rep. N. S. 425, 15 T. L. R. 59 [*reversing* 61 J. P. 517, 13 T. L. R. 476].

See 25 Cent. Dig. tit. "Highways," § 335.

13. *In re* Sterrett Tp. Road, 114 Pa. St. 627, 7 Atl. 765; Williamsport, etc., R. Co. v. Supervisors, 4 Pa. Co. Ct. 588.

14. Loker v. Brookline, 13 Pick. (Mass.) 343; Brohm v. Somerville Tp., 11 Ont. L. Rep. 588, 7 Ont. Wkly. Rep. 721.

15. See the statutes of the several states. And see the following cases:

Indiana.— Warren County v. Mankey, 29 Ind. App. 55, 63 N. E. 864.

Kansas.— Barrett v. Nelson, 29 Kan. 594.

Maine.— Wellman v. Dickey, 78 Me. 29, 2 Atl. 133; Keene v. Chapman, 25 Me. 126.

Massachusetts.— Hatch v. Hawkes, 126 Mass. 177, holding that any earth, gravel, or stone suitable may be removed by ordinary excavation.

North Carolina.— Collins v. Creecy, 53 N. C. 333, holding that the officer may cut poles on any land adjoining his section and is not confined to land immediately adjoining the spot where the work is done.

Ohio.— Burrows v. Cosler, 33 Ohio St. 567.

Oregon.— Kendall v. Post, 8 Oreg. 141.

South Carolina.— State v. Huffman, 2 Rich. 617; State v. Dawson, Riley 103, timber.

Texas.— N. A. Matthews Lumber Co. v. Van Zandt County, (Civ. App. 1903) 77 S. W. 960.

Wisconsin.— Jackson v. Rankin, 67 Wis. 285, 30 N. W. 301; Goodman v. Bradley, 2 Wis. 257.

See 25 Cent. Dig. tit. "Highways," § 336.

Trespass quare clausum does not lie under these circumstances, the remedy which must be pursued for compensation being that specified in the statute. Keene v. Chapman, 25 Me. 126.

16. Kendall v. Post, 8 Oreg. 141.

For obstructing the officer indictment will sometimes lie. State v. Huffman, 2 Rich. (S. C.) 617.

17. Kendall v. Post, 8 Oreg. 141.

18. Barrett v. Nelson, 29 Kan. 594; Wellman v. Dickey, 78 Me. 29, 2 Atl. 133; Jackson v. Rankin, 67 Wis. 285, 30 N. W. 301.

19. Goodman v. Bradley, 2 Wis. 257.

20. N. A. Matthews Lumber Co. v. Van Zandt County, (Tex. Civ. App. 1903) 77 S. W. 960.

21. Reynolds v. Speers, 1 Stew. (Ala.) 34. See also Ward v. Folly, 5 N. J. L. 485; Scott v. Towyn Rural District Council, 5 Loc. Gov. 1050.

A town is not liable for material unlawfully taken and used in the construction of a town road by the proper officers without any directions or interference on its part. Goddard v. Harpswell, 84 Me. 499, 24 Atl. 958, 30 Am. St. Rep. 373.

22. White v. Foxborough, 151 Mass. 28, 23 N. E. 652 [*distinguishing* Murray v. Norfolk County, 149 Mass. 328, 21 N. E. 757]; Com.

to the landowner or occupant,[23] which notice, under some statutes, must not specify a period which will expire in the winter months.[24] If the owners neglect to remove the property within the time specified it is the duty of the officer to do so,[25] but in removing without notice the officer is a trespasser.[26] Failure to give the notice does not, however, affect the validity of the lay-out.[27] County commissioners have no authority to allow a portion of a building to remain.[28]

4. Guide-Posts. Statutes sometimes require the erection of guide-posts,[29] or guide-boards on trees.[30]

C. Roads Affected — 1. In General. Such highways must be repaired, and only such may be repaired, as have a legal existence, either by having been formally opened[31] and accepted,[32] or created by prescription,[33] or by alterations of

v. Noxon, 121 Mass. 42; Dwight *v.* Springfield, 6 Gray (Mass.) 442.

23. *Illinois.*— Linblom *v.* Ramsey, 75 Ill. 246; Taylor *v.* Marcy, 25 Ill. 518.

Indiana.— Conley *v.* Grove, 124 Ind. 208, 24 N. E. 731; Rutherford *v.* Davis, 95 Ind. 245; Porter *v.* Stout, 73 Ind. 3.

Massachusetts.—White *v.* Foxborough, 151 Mass. 28, 23 N. E. 652.

New York.— Case *v.* Thompson, 6 Wend. 634; Kelley *v.* Horton, 2 Cow. 424.

Wisconsin.— Morris *v.* Edwards, 132 Wis. 91, 112 N. W. 248; Kellar *v.* Earl, 98 Wis. 488, 74 N. W. 364.

See 25 Cent. Dig. tit. "Highways," § 337.

Where part of a highway previously opened but not used is cleared, notice is not necessary. Baker *v.* Hogaboom, 12 S. D. 405, 81 N. W. 730.

24. Conley *v.* Grove, 124 Ind. 208, 24 N. E. 731; Kellar *v.* Earl, 98 Wis. 488, 74 N. W. 364.

25. Brock *v.* Hishen, 40 Wis. 674, holding also that the officer's delay to so remove does not render a new notice necessary.

26. Taylor *v.* Marcy, 25 Ill. 518.

27. Robinson *v.* Winch, 66 Vt. 110, 28 Atl. 884.

28. Colburn *v.* Kittridge, 131 Mass. 470.

A vote of a town that landowners might allow fences to remain one year after lay-out is ineffective. Mann *v.* Marston, 12 Me. 32.

29. Anderson *v.* New Canaan, 66 Conn. 54, 33 Atl. 593; State *v.* Swanville, 100 Me. 402, 61 Atl. 833.

30. See Sharon *v.* Smith, 180 Mass. 539, 62 N. E. 981.

31. *Connecticut.*—Anderson *v.* New Canaan, 70 Conn. 99, 38 Atl. 944.

Indiana.— State *v.* Marion County, 170 Ind. 595, 85 N. E. 513.

Iowa.— State *v.* Stoke, 80 Iowa 68, 45 N. W. 542.

Kansas.— Barker *v.* Wyandotte County, 45 Kan. 681, 698, 26 Pac. 585, 591.

Maine.— Coombs *v.* Franklin County, 71 Me. 239.

Mississippi.— Tegarden *v.* McBean, 33 Miss. 283.

New Hampshire.— Smith *v.* Northumberland, 36 N. H. 38.

New Jersey.— Vantilburgh *v.* Shann, 24 N. J. L. 740.

Ohio.— De Forest *v.* Wheeler, 5 Ohio St. 286.

Wisconsin.—Beyer *v.* Crandon, 98 Wis. 306, 73 N. W. 771.

England.—Reg. *v.* Worthing, etc., Turnpike Road, 2 C. L. R. 1678, 3 E. & B. 989, 23 L. J. M. C. 187, 2 Wkly. Rep. 478, 77 E. C. L. 989; Rex *v.* Llandilo Dist. Road Com'rs, 2 T. R. 232, 100 Eng. Reprint 126.

See 25 Cent. Dig. tit. "Highways," § 326.

Town held bound to repair see Paulsen *v.* Wilton, 78 Conn. 58, 61 Atl. 61 (although title to some of the highway is not in the town); Bradbury *v.* Benton, 69 Me. 194 (where the road was used by the public merely a year after its location); Proctor *v.* Andover, 42 N. H. 348 (although the road was laid out for the accommodation of an individual and subject to gates and bars); Naylor *v.* Beeks, 1 Oreg. 216; Pittsburgh, etc., R. Co. *v.* Com., 104 Pa. St. 583; Newlin Tp. *v.* Davis, 77 Pa. St. 317; Baker *v.* Hogaboom, 12 S. D. 405, 81 N. W. 730; Powers *v.* Woodstock, 38 Vt. 44; State *v.* Shrewsbury, 15 Vt. 283; Warren *v.* Bunnell, 11 Vt. 600.

Town held not bound to repair see Barker *v.* Wyandotte County, 45 Kan. 681, 26 Pac. 585, 45 Kan. 698, 26 Pac. 591 (strip laid out as a street but never used or traveled as a road); Lowell *v.* Moscow, 12 Me. 300; State *v.* Kent County, 83 Md. 377, 35 Atl. 62, 33 L. R. A. 291; Clark *v.* Waltham, 128 Mass. 567; McKeller *v.* Monitor Tp., 78 Mich. 485, 44 N. W. 412 (where bridge not used as a highway for ten years); State *v.* Rye, 35 N. H. 368; Young *v.* Wheelock, 18 Vt. 493.

Where a town has notice that a highway was opened for public use it will be liable. Drury *v.* Worcester, 21 Pick. (Mass.) 44; Stark *v.* Lancaster, 57 N. H. 88.

A sidewalk must be maintained as a road. Manchester *v.* Hartford, 30 Conn. 118.

32. Hayden *v.* Attleborough, 7 Gray (Mass.) 338; Jordan *v.* Otis, 37 Barb. (N. Y.) 50 (holding that repair of a road by a pathmaster does not constitute an acceptance of it); Whitney *v.* Essex, 42 Vt. 520; Barton *v.* Montpelier, 30 Vt. 650; Blodget *v.* Royalton, 14 Vt. 288. See also Hyde *v.* Jamaica, 27 Vt. 443; Page *v.* Weathersfield, 13 Vt. 424.

33. *Maine.*— Chadwick *v.* McCausland, 47 Me. 342; Rowell *v.* Montville, 4 Me. 270 (holding, however, that no use less than twenty years will impose upon the town the obligation); Todd *v.* Rome, 2 Me. 55.

into a new town,[46] or by the fact that a county or town road had been previously laid out over a part of the same route.[47]

D. Upon Whom Duty to Do Road Work Rests — 1. Municipality and Municipal Officers — a. In General. The care and maintenance of highways is vested directly in towns under some statutes,[48] in counties under others.[49] The power and duty to improve and repair lies on the officer designated by statute,[50] such as commissioners of highways,[51] county commissioners,[52] overseers,[53] police juries,[54] surveyors of highways,[55] or township trustees,[56] who must do the work within a reasonable time,[57] in the manner prescribed,[58] after the statutory

N. E. 288; State *v.* Craig, 22 Ohio Cir. Ct. 135, 12 Ohio Cir. Dec. 189.

46. *In re* Page, 37 Me. 553.

47. *In re* Page, 37 Me. 553; Sanger *v.* Kennebec County, 25 Me. 291.

48. *Connecticut.*— Munson *v.* Derby, 37 Conn. 298, 9 Am. Rep. 332.

Iowa.— Nolan *v.* Reed, 139 Iowa 68, 117 N. W. 25; Theulen *v.* Viola Tp., 139 Iowa 61, 117 N. W. 26.

Maine.— State *v.* Boardman, 93 Me. 73, 44 Atl. 118, 46 L. R. A. 750; Rogers *v.* Newport, 62 Me. 101; Emerson *v.* Washington County, 9 Me. 98.

Minnesota.— Hutchinson Tp. *v.* Filk, 44 Minn. 536, 47 N. W. 255; Woodruff *v.* Glendale, 23 Minn. 537, holding that under the statutes the care and maintenance of highways are vested in the towns in their corporate capacity, the supervisors being merely their officers and agents.

Nebraska.— Goes *v.* Gage County, 67 Nebr. 616, 93 N. W. 923.

New Jersey.— Kinmonth *v.* Wall Tp. Committee, 73 N. J. L. 440, 63 Atl. 861.

New York.— People *v.* Vandewater, 176 N. Y. 500, 68 N. E. 876 [*reversing* 83 N. Y. App. Div. 54, 82 N. Y. Suppl. 627]; Matter of Gilroy, 43 N. Y. App. Div. 359, 60 N. Y. Suppl. 200 [*affirmed* in 164 N. Y. 576, 58 N. E. 1087]. But see Rhines *v.* Royalton, 11 N. Y. St. 231.

Pennsylvania.— Chartiers Tp. *v.* Langdon, 114 Pa. St. 541, 7 Atl. 84; Chartiers *v.* Nester, 4 Pa. Cas. 110, 7 Atl. 162; Lower Merion Tp. *v.* Postal Tel. Cable Co., 25 Pa. Super. Ct. 306.

South Carolina.— Shoolbred *v.* Charleston, 2 Bay 63.

Vermont.— Wardsboro *v.* Jamaica, 59 Vt. 514, 9 Atl. 11.

Canada.— Lalonge *v.* St. Vincent de Paul, 27 Quebec Super. Ct. 218.

See 25 Cent. Dig. tit. "Highways," § 323.

49. *Maryland.*— Garrett County *v.* Blackburn, 105 Md. 226, 66 Atl. 31.

Massachusetts.— Springfield *v.* Hampden County, 10 Pick. 59.

South Carolina.— Shoolbred *v.* Charleston, 2 Bay 63.

England.— Derby *v.* Urban Dist., [1896] A. C. 315, 60 J. P. 676, 65 L. J. Q. B. 419, 74 L. T. Rep. N. S. 395, for paved foot-paths.

Canada.— St. Jean *v.* St. Jacques-le-Mineur, 14 Quebec K. B. 343.

See 25 Cent. Dig. tit. "Highways," § 323.

50. *California.*— Ludy *v.* Colusa County, (1895) 41 Pac. 300.

Idaho.— Genesee *v.* Latah County, 4 Ida. 141, 36 Pac. 701.

Indiana.— State *v.* Marion County, (1907) 82 N. E. 482; Driftwood Valley Turnpike Co. *v.* Bartholomew County, 72 Ind. 226.

Kansas.— Hanselman *v.* Born, 71 Kan. 573, 81 Pac. 192 (duty to open roads on section lines); Keiper *v.* Hawk, 7 Kan. App. 271, 53 Pac. 837 (under direction of township trustee).

Kentucky.— Beckham *v.* Slayden, 107 S. W. 324, 32 Ky. L. Rep. 944, 1348.

Louisiana.— Barrow *v.* Hepler, 34 La. Ann. 362.

Massachusetts.— Harvey *v.* Easton, 189 Mass. 505, 75 N. E. 948; New Haven, etc., Co. *v.* Hampshire County, 173 Mass. 12, 52 N. E. 1076; Austin *v.* Carter, 1 Mass. 231.

Michigan.— Peninsular Sav. Bank *v.* Ward, 118 Mich. 87, 76 N. W. 161, 79 N. W. 911.

New York.— Bruner *v.* Lewis, 4 N. Y. Suppl. 403; Rhines *v.* Royalton, 11 N. Y. St. 231.

North Carolina.— Wynn *v.* Beardsley, 126 N. C. 116, 35 S. E. 237.

Ohio.— State *v.* Craig, 22 Ohio Cir. Ct. 135, 12 Ohio Cir. Dec. 189.

Pennsylvania.— *In re* Wilkes-Barre Tp., 8 Kulp 516.

Canada.— Longueuil *v.* Montreal, 16 Quebec Super. Ct. 351.

See 25 Cent. Dig. tit. "Highways," § 323.

51. Bruner *v.* Lewis, 4 N. Y. Suppl. 403; Rhines *v.* Royalton, 11 N. Y. St. 231.

52. State *v.* Craig, 22 Ohio Cir. Ct. 135, 12 Ohio Cir. Dec. 189.

53. Ludy *v.* Colusa County, (Cal. 1895) 41 Pac. 300; Genesee *v.* Latah County, 4 Ida. 141, 36 Pac. 701.

54. Barrow *v.* Hepler, 34 La. Ann. 362.

55. Austin *v.* Carter, 1 Mass. 231; Wynn *v.* Beardsley, 126 N. C. 116, 35 S. E. 237.

56. Keiper *v.* Hawk, 7 Kan. App. 271, 53 Pac. 837.

57. Atwood *v.* Partree, 56 Conn. 80, 14 Atl. 85; Boxford *v.* Essex County, 7 Pick. (Mass.) 337, holding that over three years' delay is unreasonable.

58. *Connecticut.*— Goodspeed's Appeal, 75 Conn. 271, 53 Atl. 728; Wolcott *v.* Pond, 19 Conn. 597.

Massachusetts.— Loker *v.* Brookline, 13 Pick. 343.

New York.— Peckham *v.* Henderson, 27 Barb. 207.

Pennsylvania.— Com. *v.* Reiter, 78 Pa. St. 161.

preliminaries as may have been prescribed by the statutes of their particular states.[59]

b. As Dependent Upon Availability of Funds. The duty to repair and consequent liability for failure has in many cases been held to be dependent upon availability of funds for the work.[60] On the other hand it has been held that the duty to repair is absolute,[61] and that a statute providing therefor is peremptory, and that the question of ability is not open in an action for a defective highway;[62] and this rule applies where a portion of the expense is to be borne by the state,[63] or where, under the statute, if the town is poor a proceeding is provided for casting the expense of the road upon the county;[64] nor can liability be avoided where the means of raising sufficient funds were at hand, as by additional assessment,[65] by borrowing,[66] or by making the repairs upon the credit of the town as authorized by statute;[67] nor where the amount needed to repair was small and could be taken from funds due for repairs already made,[68] or transferred from a fund not exhausted by the building of another road;[69] nor will a town be relieved where failure of funds in the hands of road officers is due to the fault of another town officer,[70] or where the defect has existed during a time within which funds could have been had.[71] Similarly, that there are no funds on hand to meet the cost of opening a road is no answer for failure to open the road, when it is not shown that the officers had exhausted the power of taxation,[72] or when town funds were available,[73] or if, as is sometimes provided, the road committee has power to call out the inhabitants to do the work.[74] Nor have supervisors the right to refuse to open a road merely because funds in their hands are necessary for other purposes,[75] or because sufficient funds are not on hand at any one time to make all necessary improvements.[76] But a township committee

Vermont.— Patchin *v.* Doolittle, 3 Vt. 457; Patchen *v.* Morrison, 3 Vt. 590.

See 25 Cent. Dig. tit. "Highways," § 323.

59. Chiles *v.* State, 45 Ark. 143; People *v.* Studwell, 179 N. Y. 520, 71 N. E. 1137 [*affirming* 91 N. Y. App. Div. 469, 86 N. Y. Suppl. 967]; People *v.* Early, 106 N. Y. App. Div. 269, 94 N. Y. Suppl. 640; State *v.* Hamilton County, 39 Ohio St. 58.

60. *Illinois.*— Carney *v.* Marseilles, 136 Ill. 401, 26 N. E. 491, 29 Am. St. Rep. 328 (repair of bridges); Hall *v.* Rogers, 57 Ill. 307; Klein *v.* People, 31 Ill. App. 302.

Kansas.— Walnut Tp. *v.* Heth, 9 Kan. App. 498, 59 Pac. 289.

Maine.— Studly *v.* Geyer, 72 Me. 286.

New Hampshire.— Patterson *v.* Colebrook, 29 N. H. 94.

New Jersey.— Warner *v.* Reading, 46 N. J. L. 519.

New York.— Flynn *v.* Hurd, 118 N. Y. 19, 22 N. E. 1109; Monk *v.* New Utrecht, 104 N. Y. 552, 11 N. E. 268; Garlinghouse *v.* Jacobs, 29 N. Y. 297.

Texas.— Parker *v.* State, 29 Tex. App. 372, 16 S. W. 186.

Wisconsin.— State *v.* Wood County, 72 Wis. 629, 40 N. W. 381.

See 25 Cent. Dig. tit. "Highways," § 325.

The highway should be closed and warnings given to the public if the highway is unsafe and funds unavailable. Carney *v.* Marseilles, 136 Ill. 401, 26 N. E. 491, 29 Am. St. Rep. 328.

61. Stockwell *v.* Dummerston, 45 Vt. 443; Burns *v.* Elba, 32 Wis. 605.

A distinction is made in Pennsylvania between liability of a town for non-repair and for original construction, and a town may not be liable for failure to construct under circumstances which would render it liable for failure to repair. Perry Tp. *v.* John, 79 Pa. St. 412.

62. Winship *v.* Enfield, 42 N. H. 197.

63. La Monte *v.* Somerset County, (N. J. Sup. 1896) 35 Atl. 1.

64. Glaub *v.* Goshen Tp., 7 Kulp (Pa.) 292.

65. Weed *v.* Ballston Spa, 76 N. Y. 329. See also Scott Tp. *v.* Montgomery, 95 Pa. St. 444.

66. Ivory *v.* Deepark, 116 N. Y. 476, 22 N. E. 1080.

67. Whitlock *v.* Brighton, 2 N. Y. App. Div. 21, 37 N. Y. Suppl. 333 [*affirmed* in 154 N. Y. 781, 49 N. E. 1106].

68. Rhines *v.* Royalton, 15 N. Y. Suppl. 944.

69. Queens County *v.* Phipps, 28 N. Y. App. Div. 521, 51 N. Y. Suppl. 203.

70. Clapper *v.* Waterford, 62 Hun (N. Y.) 170, 16 N. Y. Suppl. 640 [*reversed* on other grounds in 131 N. Y. 382, 30 N. E. 240].

71. Whitlock *v.* Brighton, 2 N. Y. App. Div. 21, 37 N. Y. Suppl. 333 [*affirmed* in 154 N. Y. 781, 49 N. E. 1106].

72. *In re* Lower Merion Tp. Road, 8 Pa. Dist. 561, 22 Pa. Co. Ct. 297, 15 Montg. Co. Rep. 79.

73. Com. *v.* Reiter, 78 Pa. St. 161.

74. Kinmonth *v.* Wall Tp. Committee, 73 N. J. L. 440, 63 Atl. 861.

75. *In re* Roaring Brook Tp. Road, 28 Wkly. Notes Cas. (Pa.) 141.

76. Welch *v.* State, 164 Ind. 104, 72 N. E. 1043.

malicious[99] or corrupt[1] action, or for acting without authority[2] in constructing or maintaining drains, but not for damage caused by drainage established by them within their authority.[3]

3. **Abatement of Drainage Nuisance.** If drainage upon adjacent land is in the nature of a nuisance the landowner may have a right to cure the trouble himself by peaceable abatement,[4] as by filling a ditch,[5] or opening one,[6] or filling his land to bar surface water from the highway.[7]

4. **Enjoining Wrongful Drainage.** Injunction may be allowed to protect individual landowners from irreparable injury from wrongful drainage,[8] only, however, where the work is clearly improper,[9] and not to prevent flowing which is the natural consequence of the building of the road;[10] and it is held that courts ought not to control by injunction the action of road commissioners in deciding on the necessity of a change of drainage and the mode of doing it.[11] Where the facts are in dispute an injunction will not be granted until they are established by a jury.[12]

F. Expenses[13] — 1. **Apportionment.** The statutes of the several states provide that the expense of road work shall be apportioned among the districts, towns, or counties benefited, the manner of apportionment differing widely under the different statutes.[14] A town not in the district in which the road exists may

99. Warfel *v.* Cochran, 34 Pa. St. 381.

1. McOsker *v.* Burrell, 55 Ind. 425.

2. Daum *v.* Cooper, 103 Ill. App. 4 [*affirmed* in 200 Ill. 538, 65 N. E. 1071] (changing system without consent); Plummer *v.* Sturtevant, 32 Me. 325; Conrad *v.* Smith, 32 Mich. 429.

3. Conwell *v.* Emrie, 4 Ind. 209; Eagle Tp. Highway Com'rs *v.* Ely, 54 Mich. 173, 19 N. W. 940 (holding that injury by rendering land more difficult of access is *damnum absque injuria*); Nussbaum *v.* Bell County, 97 Tex. 86, 76 S. W. 430. See also Eldorado Tp. Highway Com'rs *v.* Foster, 134 Ill. App. 520; Packard *v.* Voltz, 94 Iowa 277, 62 N. W. 757, 58 Am. St. Rep. 396.

Successors of negligent commissioners are not liable for their predecessors' acts. Gould *v.* Booth, 66 N. Y. 62.

4. Thompson *v.* Allen, 7 Lans. (N. Y.) 459.

5. Schofield *v.* Cooper, 126 Iowa 334, 102 N. W. 110; Thompson *v.* Allen, 7 Lans. (N. Y.) 459.

6. Groton *v.* Haines, 36 N. H. 388.

7. Murphy *v.* Kelley, 68 Me. 521; Bangor *v.* Lansil, 51 Me. 521.

8. *Illinois.*— Eldorado Tp. Highway Com'rs *v.* Foster, 134 Ill. App. 520; Hotz *v.* Hoyt, 34 Ill. App. 488, so holding, although plaintiff had improperly fenced as his own a portion of the public highway.

Indiana.— Cauble *v.* Hultz, 118 Ind. 13, 20 N. E. 515, so holding where the supervisor was acting without authority and irreparable injury would result.

Michigan.— Smith *v.* Eaton Tp., 138 Mich. 511, 101 N. W. 661 (although the officials intended to carry water along in a public sewer); Conrad *v.* Smith, 32 Mich. 429 (where no need was shown for the ditch).

Nebraska.— Fokenga *v.* Churchill, 2 Nebr. (Unoff.) 304, 96 N. W. 143.

New Jersey.— Slack *v.* Lawrence Tp., (Ch. 1890) 19 Atl. 663.

Pennsylvania.—Woodroffe *v.* Hagerty, 35 Pa. Super. Ct. 576.

Vermont.—Whipple *v.* Fair Haven, 63 Vt. 221, 21 Atl. 533.

See 25 Cent. Dig. tit. "Highways," § 377.

Damages may be allowed upon granting the injunction. Whipple *v.* Fair Haven, 63 Vt. 221, 21 Atl. 533.

9. Hotz *v.* Hoyt, 135 Ill. 388, 25 N. E. 753.

10. Kiley *v.* Bond, 114 Mich. 447, 72 N. W. 253; Churchill *v.* Beethe, 48 Nebr. 87, 66 N. W. 992, 35 L. R. A. 442.

11. Warfel *v.* Cochran, 34 Pa. St. 381.

12. Woodroffe *v.* Hagerty, 35 Pa. Super. Ct. 576.

13. **Fund created by sale of liquor licenses used to repair roads** see Intoxicating Liquors, 23 Cyc. 152 note 40.

Payment as prerequisite to municipal improvements see Municipal Corporations, 28 Cyc. 1088.

14. See the statutes of the different states. And see the following cases:

Illinois.— Elmira Highway Com'rs *v.* Osceola Highway Com'rs, 74 Ill. App. 185.

Indiana.— Sim *v.* Hurst, 44 Ind. 579.

Massachusetts.— Provincetown *v.* Truro, 135 Mass. 263 (holding that a rule of apportionment under a special act to share the expense of a bridge does not cover a highway constructed later); *In re* Ipswich, 24 Pick. 343; Parsons *v.* Goshen, 11 Pick. 396.

New Hampshire.— O'Neil *v.* Walpole, 74 N. H. 197, 66 Atl. 119; Campton *v.* Plymouth, 64 N. H. 304, 8 Atl. 824; Whittredge *v.* Concord, 36 N. H. 530; *In re* Reed, 13 N. H. 381; Peirce *v.* Somersworth, 10 N. H. 369.

New Jersey.— Newark *v.* Essex County, 40 N. J. L. 595 (holding that apportionment covers principal and interest until debt paid); State *v.* Cannon, 33 N. J. L. 218; *In re* Newark Plank Road, etc., 63 N. J. Eq. 710, 53 Atl. 5 (apportionment by ascertaining the proportion of through traffic to the total use of the road).

New York.— Matter of Newburg's Business Men's Assoc., 54 Misc. 13, 103 N. Y. Suppl. 843.

under some statutes be forced to contribute toward it, particularly if greatly benefited,[15] even though not adjoining.[16] The statutes specify by whom the apportionment is to be made, and in order to be valid the apportionment must be made by the officers or court specified,[17] in the manner and upon the proceedings specified in the statute.[18] The apportionment can be attacked only by parties interested in a direct proceeding for that purpose.[19]

2. **Liability of Municipality to Laborer or Materialman.** The municipality is responsible to one who furnishes labor or material for road work on authority,[20] and for road machinery purchased by road officers within their authority;[21] but persons who improve roads without authority may not recover,[22] although in some cases authority may be presumed.[23] Assignments to road officers of claims

Ohio.— Lake County *v.* Ashtabula, 24 Ohio St. 393.

Pennsylvania.— Mahanoy Tp. *v.* Comry, 103 Pa. St. 362.

Vermont.— Sheldon *v.* State, 59 Vt. 36, 7 Atl. 901; Platt *v.* Milton, 58 Vt. 608, 5 Atl. 558 (holding that benefit to town and not merely its business interests must be shown); Weybridge *v.* Addison, 57 Vt. 569; Fairfax *v.* Fletcher, 47 Vt. 326 (allowing no contribution where portion of a road in the town was not of value to it); Londonderry *v.* Peru, 45 Vt. 424.

Wisconsin.— Neis *v.* Franzen, 18 Wis. 537.

See 25 Cent. Dig. tit. "Highways," § 357.

15. Langley *v.* Barnstead, 63 N. H. 246; Hodgson *v.* New Hampton, 56 N. H. 332 (holding that county commissioners may assign expense to town in adjoining county); People *v.* Queens County, 112 N. Y. 585, 20 N. E. 549; Wardsboro *v.* Jamaica, 59 Vt. 514, 9 Atl. 11; Jamaica *v.* Wardsboro, 47 Vt. 451; State *v.* Woodbury, 27 Vt. 731 (although towns not in the same county). But see *In re* Sanborn, 33 N. H. 71; Parker *v.* East Montpelier, 59 Vt. 632, 10 Atl. 463.

16. Langley *v.* Barnstead, 63 N. H. 246; People *v.* Queens County, 112 N. Y. 585, 20 N. E. 549.

17. *In re* Ipswich, 24 Pick. (Mass.) 343; Springfield *v.* Hampden County, 10 Pick. (Mass.) 59; Caines *v.* Hudson County Ave. Com'rs, 37 N. J. L. 12; *In re* Newark Plank Road, etc., 63 N. J. Eq. 710, 53 Atl. 5; People *v.* Queens County, 48 Hun (N. Y.) 324, 1 N. Y. Suppl. 382 [*affirmed* in 112 N. Y. 585, 20 N. E. 549]; Londonderry *v.* Peru, 45 Vt. 424; Jamaica *v.* Wardsboro, 45 Vt. 416.

Mandamus does not lie to compel the county commissioners to order a part of the expense incurred by a town in making a highway to be repaid out of the county treasury. *In re* Ipswich, 24 Pick. (Mass.) 343; Springfield *v.* Hampden County, 10 Pick. (Mass.) 59.

18. *Indiana.*— State *v.* Marion County, (1907) 82 N. E. 482.

Maine.—Howe *v.* Aroostook County, 46 Me. 332, holding also that the record must show at whose expense the road was laid out.

New Hampshire.— O'Neil *v.* Walpole, 74 N. H. 197, 66 Atl. 119; Rye *v.* Rockingham County, 68 N. H. 268, 34 Atl. 743; Whittredge *v.* Concord, 36 N. H. 530.

New Jersey.— Marlboro Tp. *v.* Van Derveer, 47 N. J. L. 259.

New York.— *In re* Newburg's Business Men's Assoc., 54 Misc. 11, 103 N. Y. Suppl. 847.

See 25 Cent. Dig. tit. "Highways," § 357.

19. Bronnenburg *v.* O'Bryant, 139 Ind. 17, 38 N. E. 416; Pierson *v.* Newark, 44 N. J. L. 424; Seanor *v.* Whatcom County, 13 Wash. 48, 42 Pac. 552.

20. Blackford County *v.* Shrader, 36 Ind. 87; Center Tp. *v.* Davis, 24 Ind. App. 603, 57 N. E. 283 (where township directed road supervisor to employ labor); Bryant *v.* Westbrook, 86 Me. 450, 29 Atl. 1109; Morrell *v.* Dixfield, 30 Me. 157; Whately *v.* Franklin County, 1 Metc. (Mass.) 336; Dull *v.* Ridgway, 9 Pa. St. 272.

Work outside the jurisdiction cannot be authorized. Sault Ste. Marie Highway Com'rs *v.* Van Dusan, 40 Mich. 429.

Fees of an attorney hired by petitioner to advise the board are not part of the expenses. Overmeyer *v.* Cass County, 43 Ind. App. 403, 86 N. E. 77.

21. *Iowa.*— Harrison County *v.* Ogden, 133 Iowa 9, 110 N. W. 32.

Michigan.— Pape *v.* Benton Tp., 140 Mich. 165, 103 N. W. 591, payment enforced by mandamus to compel tax levy and not by action for purchase-price.

New York.— People *v.* Montgomery, 48 N. Y. App. Div. 550, 62 N. Y. Suppl. 993. But see Acme Road Machinery Co. *v.* Bridgewater, 185 N. Y. 1, 77 N. E. 879.

Pennsylvania.— F. C. Austin Mfg. Co. *v.* Ayr, 31 Pa. Super. Ct. 356; Climax Road Mach. Co. *v.* Allegheny Tp., 10 Pa. Super. Ct. 437.

Wisconsin.— Western Wheeled Scraper Co. *v.* Chippewa County, 102 Wis. 614, 78 N. W. 764.

22. Bain *v.* Knox County Ct., 13 Ky. L. Rep. 784; Branch *v.* Pointe Coupee Police Jury, 26 La. Ann. 150; Anderson *v.* Hamilton Tp., 25 Pa. St. 75; Bryant *v.* Spring Brook Tp., 5 Luz. Leg. Reg. (Pa.) 203; Bill *v.* Woodbury, 54 Vt. 251; Lamphire *v.* Windsor, 27 Vt. 544; Pratt *v.* Swanton, 15 Vt. 147. But see Police Jury *v.* Hampton, 5 Mart. N. S. (La.) 389.

A road overseer is not an agent of the county to bind it for the price of supplies. N. A. Matthews Lumber Co. *v.* Van Zandt, (Tex. Civ. App. 1903) 77 S. W. 960.

23. Harris *v.* Carson, 40 Ill. App. 147.

3. **Performance and Payment.** Payment should be made only on fulfilment of the contract according to its terms,[50] and on acceptance of the work,[51] in accordance with the decision of the engineer, or architect, or other officer named in the contract.[52]

4. **Contractor's Bonds.**[53] Under many statutes authorizing contracts for road work contractors are required to give bonds,[54] which must follow the statute,[55] although mere informalities in the bond or in its execution will not necessarily avoid the bond.[56]

5. **Actions.** The manner of enforcement of payment for road work depends on local law [57] which governs the parties,[58] pleadings,[59] evidence,[60] and defenses.[61] The public officials should enforce the contracts as made,[62] or avoid them when

App. 550 (paving contract construed not to include part of road between railway tracks); State *v.* Cuyahoga County, 9 Ohio S. & C. Pl. Dec. 76, 6 Ohio N. P. 405 ("earth" includes material costing about the same as earth to remove); Elma *v.* Carney, 9 Wash. 466, 37 Pac. 707 (contract for grading or paving includes only the way between the sidewalks).

50. *Connecticut.*— Jones *v.* Marlborough, 70 Conn. 583, 40 Atl. 460, holding that the contractor cannot recover in *quantum meruit* where he has not complied with contract.

Indiana.— Jackson County *v.* Branaman, 169 Ind. 80, 82 N. E. 65; Laporte County *v.* Wolff, (1904) 72 N. E. 860.

Massachusetts.— Reed *v.* Scituate, 5 Allen 120.

Michigan.— Olds *v.* State Land Office Com'r, 134 Mich. 442, 86 N. W. 956, 96 N. W. 508.

New York.— Brown *v.* New York, 72 N. Y. App. Div. 420, 76 N. Y. Suppl. 26.

Washington.— State *v.* Van Wyck, 20 Wash. 39, 54 Pac. 768.

See 25 Cent. Dig. tit. "Highways," § 349.

An extra sum allowed for work included in the contract is void. State *v.* Cuyahoga County, 9 Ohio S. & C. Pl. Dec. 76, 6 Ohio N. P. 405. See also Olds *v.* State Land Office Com'r, 134 Mich. 442, 86 N. W. 956, 96 N. W. 508.

51. Jones *v.* Marlborough, 70 Conn. 583, 40 Atl. 460.

Mere use of a road is not evidence of its acceptance. Reed *v.* Scituate, 5 Allen (Mass.) 120; Wrought Iron Bridge Co. *v.* Jasper Tp., 68 Mich. 441, 36 N. W. 213; Davis *v.* Barrington, 30 N. H. 517.

52. Mercer Bd. of Internal Imp. *v.* Dougherty, 3 B. Mon. (Ky.) 446; Curley *v.* Hudson County, 66 N. J. L. 401, 49 Atl. 471. See also Ripley County *v.* Hill, 115 Ind. 316, 16 N. E. 156.

The architect's certificate is not conclusive. Campbell County *v.* Youtsey, 12 S. W. 305, 11 Ky. L. Rep. 529; Grass *v.* Haynes, 15 La. Ann. 181.

53. **Liability on bonds** generally see Bonds, 5 Cyc. 721.

54. See the statutes of the several states. And see Hart *v.* State, 120 Ind. 83, 21 N. E. 654, 24 N. E. 151; Faurote *v.* State, 110 Ind. 463, 11 N. E. 472, 111 Ind. 73, 11 N. E. 476, 119 Ind. 600, 21 N. E. 663; State *v.* Sullivan, 74 Ind. 121; Swindle *v.* State, 15 Ind. App. 415, 44 N. E. 60; Brookfield *v.* Reed, 152 Mass. 568, 26 N. E. 138; *In re* Bern Tp., etc., Road, (Pa. 1889) 17 Atl. 205.

Obligors are liable only according to the terms of the bond, and liability cannot be extended. Moss *v.* Rowlett, 112 Ky. 121, 65 S. W. 153, 358, 23 Ky. L. Rep. 1411.

55. Hart *v.* State, 120 Ind. 83, 21 N. E. 654, 24 N. E. 151; Faurote *v.* State, 119 Ind. 600, 21 N. E. 663; Lane *v.* State, 14 Ind. App. 573, 43 N. E. 244.

56. Byrne *v.* Luning Co., (Cal. 1894) 38 Pac. 454 (bond dated one day earlier than contract); Larned *v.* Maloney, 19 Ind. App. 199, 49 N. E. 278 (bond dated two days late).

57. See Lexington *v.* Middlesex County, 165 Mass. 296, 43 N. E. 110; Hull *v.* Berkshire, 9 Pick. (Mass.) 553; Hill *v.* Sunderland, 7 Vt. 215; Bromley Rural Dist. Council *v.* Chittenden, 70 J. P. 409, 4 Loc. Gov. 967; Paré *v.* Deschamps, 7 Quebec Pr. 4.

Mandamus will lie on the relation of a highway supervisor to compel the township trustee to pay out of moneys in his hands applicable thereto an order given by such supervisor to a laborer for work lawfully done on a highway. Potts *v.* State, 75 Ind. 336; Lanesborough *v.* Berkshire County, 6 Metc. (Mass.) 329.

Summary rights to seize and sell the property of landowners liable for road work exist in Louisiana. Pointe Coupée Police Jury *v.* Gardiner, 2 Rob. (La.) 139; Morgan *v.* Pointe Coupée Police Jury, 11 La. 157.

58. Little *v.* Hamilton County, 7 Ind. App. 118, 34 N. E. 499; *In re* Wilkes-Barre Tp., 8 Kulp (Pa.) 516, against township. See also Travis *v.* Ward, 2 Wash. 30, 25 Pac. 908.

59. Clark Civil Tp. *v.* Brookshire, 114 Ind. 437, 16 N. E. 132; Bell *v.* Pavey, 7 Ind. App. 19, 33 N. E. 1011.

60. Barren County Ct. *v.* Kinslow, 9 Ky. L. Rep. 108 (holding the certificate of the surveyor conclusive as to amount and necessity of use of carriage); Grass *v.* Haynes, 15 La. Ann. 181 (holding that evidence must show that the law was fully complied with); McCormick *v.* Boston, 120 Mass. 499 (holding that the questions of the authority to make and ratify contract are for the jury); Snow *v.* Ware, 13 Metc. (Mass.) 42.

61. McDermott *v.* Laporte Tp., 2 Pa. Cas. 105, 3 Atl. 437.

62. Corker *v.* Elmore County, 10 Ida. 255,

peculiar to the particular property;[31] and compensation for the value of the land taken cannot be reduced by offsetting special benefits which should only be applied against incidental injuries to the remaining land.[32]

on other grounds in 167 U. S. 548, 17 S. Ct. 966, 42 L. ed. 270].

Illinois.— Gordon *v.* Wabash County Highway Com'rs, 169 Ill. 510, 48 N. E. 451; Deitrick *v.* Bishop Tp. Highway Com'rs, 6 Ill. App. 70. But see Carpenter *v.* Jennings, 77 Ill. 250.

Indiana.— Sterling *v.* Frick, 171 Ind. 710, 86 N. E. 65, 87 N. E. 237; Renard *v.* Grande, 29 Ind. App. 579, 64 N. E. 644.

Kansas.— Pottawatomie County *v.* O'Sullivan, 17 Kan. 58.

Massachusetts.—Cross *v.* Plymouth County, 125 Mass. 557; Hilbourne *v.* Suffolk County, 120 Mass. 393, 21 Am. Rep. 522; Wood *v.* Hudson, 114 Mass. 513; Green *v.* Fall River, 113 Mass. 262; Meacham *v.* Fitchburg R. Co., 4 Cush. 291; Com. *v.* Justices of Sess. Middlesex County, 9 Mass. 388; Com. *v.* Justices Norfolk County Ct. of Sess., 5 Mass. 435; Com. *v.* Coombs, 2 Mass. 489.

Minnesota.— State *v.* Leslie, 30 Minn. 533, 16 N. W. 408.

New Jersey.— Mangles *v.* Hudson County, 55 N. J. L. 88, 25 Atl. 322, 17 L. R. A. 785.

New York.— *In re* Borup, 182 N. Y. 222, 74 N. E. 838, 108 Am. St. Rep. 796 [*affirming* 102 N. Y. App. Div. 262, 92 N. Y. Suppl. 624]; Eldridge *v.* Binghamton, 120 N. Y. 309, 24 N. E. 462.

North Carolina.— Asheville *v.* Johnston, 71 N. C. 398.

Ohio.— Symonds *v.* Cincinnati, 14 Ohio 147, 45 Am. Dec. 529.

Pennsylvania.— Root's Case, 77 Pa. St. 276; Watson *v.* Pittsburgh, etc., R. Co., 37 Pa. St. 469; Perrysville, etc., Plank-Road Co. *v.* Rea, 20 Pa. St. 97; Schuylkill Nav. Co. *v.* Thoburn, 7 Serg. & R. 411.

Rhode Island.— Allaire *v.* Woonsocket, 25 R. I. 414, 56 Atl. 262.

United States.— Bauman *v.* Ross, 167 U. S. 548, 17 S. Ct. 966, 42 L. ed. 270.

See 25 Cent. Dig. tit. "Highways," § 371.

Benefits shared with estates from which no land has been taken can be set off. Hilbourne *v.* Suffolk County, 120 Mass. 393, 21 Am. Rep. 522.

Different tracts used together may be considered as one piece for the purpose of estimating benefits. Tehama County *v.* Bryan, 68 Cal. 57, 8 Pac. 673; Chicago, etc., R. Co. *v.* Dresel, 110 Ill. 89; Speck *v.* Kenoyer, 164 Ind. 431, 73 N. E. 896 (all land in one body used for a common purpose, although part cut off by an intervening road); Reisner *v.* Atchison Union Depot, etc., Co., 27 Kan. 382; Port Huron, etc., R. Co. *v.* Voorheis, 50 Mich. 506, 15 N. W. 882; Hannibal Bridge Co. *v.* Schaubacher, 57 Mo. 582. But see Natchez, etc., R. Co. *v.* Currie, 62 Miss. 506.

That no damages result may be the effect of offsetting benefits and does not render the taking unconstitutional as a taking without compensation (Trinity College *v.* Hartford, 32 Conn. 452; Rassier *v.* Grimmer, 130 Ind. 219, 28 N. E. 866, 29 N. E. 918; Trosper *v.* Saline County, 27 Kan. 391; Comm. *v.* Justices of Sess. Middlesex County, 9 Mass. 388; Bennett *v.* Hall, 184 Mo. 407, 83 S. W. 439; Lingo *v.* Burford, (Mo. 1892) 18 S. W. 1081), for while the owner of the property taken is entitled to a full compensation for the damage he sustains thereby, if the taking of his property for the public improvement is a benefit rather than an injury to him, he certainly has no equitable claim to damages (Livingston *v.* New York, 8 Wend. (N. Y.) 85, 22 Am. Dec. 622 [*explained* in Bauman *v.* Ross, 167 U. S. 548, 17 S. Ct. 966, 42 L. ed. 270]).

Set-off of benefits against damages for municipal improvements see MUNICIPAL CORPORATIONS, 28 Cyc. 1079.

Although owners may be assessed again.— It is no objection to the statute that the owners of lands assessed for benefits under one proceeding will be left liable to be assessed anew under future proceedings for establishing other highways in other subdivisions. Bauman *v.* Ross, 167 U. S. 548, 17 S. Ct. 966, 42 L. ed. 270.

31. *Indiana.*— Pichon *v.* Martin, 35 Ind. App. 167, 73 N. E. 1009.

Massachusetts.—White *v.* Foxborough, 151 Mass. 28, 23 N. E. 652; Parks *v.* Hampden County, 120 Mass. 395; Upham *v.* Worcester, 113 Mass. 97; Farwell *v.* Cambridge, 11 Gray 413; Dwight *v.* Hampden County, 11 Cush. 201.

Missouri.— Newby *v.* Platte County, 25 Mo. 258; Galbraith *v.* Prentice, 109 Mo. App. 498, 84 S. W. 997.

New Jersey.— Mangles *v.* Hudson County, 55 N. J. L. 88, 25 Atl. 322, 17 L. R. A. 785.

Oregon.— Masters *v.* Portland, 24 Oreg. 161, 33 Pac. 540.

Rhode Island.— Tingley *v.* Providence, 8 R. I. 493.

See 25 Cent. Dig. tit. "Highways," § 371.

But that others on the same highway are benefited is not a reason for not deducting such benefits. Trinity College *v.* Hartford, 32 Conn. 452; Brokaw *v.* Highway Com'rs, 99 Ill. App. 415; Abbott *v.* Cottage City, 143 Mass. 521, 10 N. E. 325, 58 Am. Rep. 143; Howard *v.* Providence, 6 R. I. 514.

Benefits from possible increase of business should not be taken into account. Old Colony, etc., R. Co. *v.* Plymouth County, 14 Gray (Mass.) 155; State *v.* Shardlow, 43 Minn. 524, 46 N. W. 74; Watterson *v.* Allegheny Valley R. Co., 74 Pa. St. 208; Dullea *v.* Taylor, 35 U. C. Q. B. 395.

32. *Georgia.*— Augusta *v.* Marks, 50 Ga. 612.

Illinois.— Shawneetown *v.* Mason, 82 Ill. 337, 25 Am. Rep. 321.

Maryland.— Shipley *v.* Baltimore, etc., R. Co., 34 Md. 336.

Nebraska.— Fremont, etc., R. Co. *v.* Whalen, 11 Nebr. 585, 10 N. W. 491.

Texas.— Dulaney *v.* Nolan County, 85 Tex.

5. **Actions or Proceedings to Recover — a. Jurisdiction and Venue.** The jurisdiction and venue of proceedings for damages depend on local statutes.[33]

b. Form of Action. Damages may be enforced by action [34] or other proceeding, such as mandamus,[35] or a special statutory proceeding established for the purpose, generally in the nature of a petition for a jury to assess damages,[36] the award being sometimes enforceable by warrant of distress.[37] The statutory proceeding is held to be exclusive of other remedies.[38]

c. Parties. Whatever the form of proceeding, seasonable notice thereof must be given to all interested,[39] and they must be joined in the proceeding.[40]

d. Application, Complaint, or Petition. The petition or other pleading must

225, 20 S. W. 70; Paris *v.* Mason, 37 Tex. 447.

Virginia.— Mitchell *v.* Thornton, 21 Gratt. 164.

Wisconsin.— Washburn *v.* Milwaukee, etc., R. Co., 59 Wis. 364, 18 N. W. 328.

See 25 Cent. Dig. tit. "Highways," § 371.

33. See the statutes of the several states. And see Walker *v.* West Boylston, 128 Mass. 550; Bean *v.* Warner, 38 N. H. 247; *Ex p.* Parlee, 25 N. Brunsw. 51.

Transfer on creation of new county.— Where a new county was created pending proceedings for an increase of damages for the location of a highway, and included the highway location, the court should transfer the proceedings to the new county. Waterhouse *v.* Cumberland County, 44 Me. 368.

34. *Michigan.*— Lull *v.* Curry, 10 Mich. 397.

Mississippi.— Copiah County *v.* Lusk, 77 Miss. 136, 24 So. 972.

New Hampshire.— Fiske *v.* Chesterfield, 14 N. H. 240.

Texas.— Holt *v.* Rockwell County, 27 Tex. Civ. App. 365, 65 S. W. 389 (holding that on rejecting award landowner may bring suit without first presenting a claim); Cunningham *v.* San Saba County, 1 Tex. Civ. App. 480, 20 S. W. 941.

Vermont.— Felch *v.* Gilman, 22 Vt. 38.

35. Montgomery Tp. Highway Com'rs *v.* Snyder, 15 Ill. App. 645 (holding that the petition for mandamus to compel commissioners of highways to issue order for payment must show funds on hand); Miller *v.* Bridgewater Tp., 24 N. J. L. 54; *In re* Pringle St., 167 Pa. St. 646, 31 Atl. 948; Brodhead *v.* Lower Saucon Tp., 2 Lehigh Val. L. Rep. (Pa.) 381. But see Boone County *v.* State, 38 Ind. 193.

36. Gordon *v.* Road Dist. No. 3 Highway Com'rs, 169 Ill. 510, 48 N. E. 451; Taylor *v.* Marcy, 25 Ill. 518; Sangamon *v.* Brown, 13 Ill. 207; Highway Com'rs *v.* Jackson, 61 Ill. App. 381 [*affirmed* in 165 Ill. 17, 45 N. E. 1000]; Turner *v.* Wright, 13 Ill. App. 191; Lisbon *v.* Merrill, 12 Me. 210; Golding *v.* North Attleborough, 172 Mass. 223, 51 N. E. 1076; Keith *v.* Brockton, 147 Mass. 618, 18 N. E. 585; Childs *v.* Franklin County, 128 Mass. 97; Higginson *v.* Nahant, 11 Allen (Mass.) 530; Monagle *v.* Bristol County, 8 Cush. (Mass.) 360; Eaton *v.* Framington, 6 Cush. (Mass.) 245; *In re* Lewistown Road, 8 Pa. St. 109; *In re* West Whiteland Road, 4 Pa. Co. Ct. 511.

37. Onset St. R. Co. *v.* Plymouth County, 154 Mass. 395, 28 N. E. 286 (separate distress warrants, although separate lot owners joined in one petition); Gedney *v.* Tewsbury, 3 Mass. 307 (not debt on award but warrant of distress on order of payment).

38. Golding *v.* North Attleborough, 172 Mass. 223, 51 N. E. 1076; Gedney *v.* Tewksbury, 3 Mass. 307. But see Fiske *v.* Chesterfield, 14 N. H. 240.

39. *Maryland.*— George's Creek Coal, etc., Co. *v.* New Central Coal Co., 40 Md. 425.

Massachusetts.— Brown *v.* Lowell, 8 Metc. 172; *In re* Central Turnpike Corp., 7 Pick. 13 (notice to those interested to show cause why a jury should not be impaneled); Barre Turnpike Corp. *v.* Appleton, 2 Pick. 430.

Nebraska.— Pawnee County *v.* Storm, 34 Nebr. 735, 52 N. W. 696, holding actual and not mere notice by advertisement necessary.

New York.— Matter of New York El. R. Co., 70 N. Y. 327; *In re* Feeney, 20 Misc. 272, 45 N. Y. Suppl. 830.

Pennsylvania.— Zack *v.* Pennsylvania R. Co., 25 Pa. St. 394.

Vermont.— Thetford *v.* Kilburn, 36 Vt. 179, notice to town.

See 25 Cent. Dig. tit. "Highways," § 366.

But see Crane *v.* Camp, 12 Conn. 464 (holding that no previous notice to landowners of the appointment of freeholders to assess damages is necessary); Morgan *v.* Oliver, 98 Tex. 218, 82 S. W. 1028 [*reversing* (Civ. App. 1904) 80 S. W. 111].

40. *Connecticut.*— Cullen *v.* New York, etc., R. Co., 66 Conn. 211, 33 Atl. 910, abutter.

Indiana.— Rudisill *v.* State, 40 Ind. 485.

Maine.— Lisbon *v.* Merrill, 12 Me. 210.

Massachusetts.—Dana *v.* Boston, 170 Mass. 593, 49 N. E. 1013; Onset St. R. Co. *v.* Plymouth County, 154 Mass. 395, 28 N. E. 286; Dwight *v.* Hampden County, 7 Cush. 533; Kent *v.* Essex County, 10 Pick. 521.

Nebraska.— Hogsett *v.* Harlan County, 4 Nebr. (Unoff.) 310, 97 N. W. 316.

New Hampshire.— Jewell *v.* Holderness, 41 N. H. 161.

New Jersey.— Hopewell Tp. *v.* Welling, 24 N. J. L. 127.

Pennsylvania.— *In re* Pringle St., 7 Kulp 346.

South Dakota.— Lawrence County *v.* Deadwood, etc., Toll-Road Co., 11 S. D. 74, 75 N. W. 817.

See 25 Cent. Dig. tit. "Highways," § 366.

set out the facts on which the claim for damages is based,[41] strict technical accuracy not, however, being necessary,[42] and failure to object to the sufficiency waives the objection.[43] Amendments are allowed liberally.[44]

e. Limitations. Damages must be claimed within the period fixed by law[45] after lay-out[46] and entry.[47]

f. Assessment of Damages by Commissioners or Jurors. The person entitled to damages for the construction or repair of a highway usually has the right to have the damages assessed by a jury,[48] or under some statutes by commissioners,[49] duly

41. Layman *v.* Hughes, 152 Ind. 484, 51 N. E. 1058.

Lack of written application for a jury is fatal to the jurisdiction. State *v.* Varnum, 81 Wis. 503, 51 N. W. 958.

42. Offutt *v.* Montgomery County, 94 Md. 115, 50 Atl. 419; Sawyer *v.* Keene, 47 N. H. 173, holding the petition sufficient if it can be fully understood.

Petitions held sufficient see Livermore *v.* Norfolk County, 186 Mass. 133, 71 N. E. 305 (statement of alteration of highway in words "widened, straightened and relocated"); Allen *v.* Gardner, 147 Mass. 452, 18 N. E. 222 (although inaccurate); Mill Creek Road Com'rs *v.* Fickinger, 51 Pa. St. 48.

An immaterial variance between summons and complaint is not fatal. Mills Creek Road Com'rs *v.* Fickinger, 51 Pa. St. 48.

43. Lake Erie, etc., R. Co. *v.* Spidel, 19 Ind. App. 8, 48 N. E. 1042.

44. Winchester *v.* Middlesex County, 114 Mass. 481; Sawyer *v.* Keene, 47 N. H. 173.

45. *Illinois.*— Taylor *v.* Marcy, 25 Ill. 518.

Massachusetts.— Everett *v.* Fall River, 189 Mass. 513, 75 N. E. 946 (within one year from date of entry); Keith *v.* Brockton, 147 Mass. 618, 18 N. E. 585; Childs *v.* Franklin County, 128 Mass. 97; Monagle *v.* Bristol County, 8 Cush. 360; Eaton *v.* Framingham, 6 Cush. 245.

Ohio.— Viers' Petition, Tapp. 88.

Pennsylvania.—*In re* Lewiston Road, 8 Pa. St. 109 (within one year from time road opened in front of each lot); *in re* Sharpless St., 1 Chest. Co. Rep. 147 ("may" construed as "must"); *In re* Pringle St., 7 Kulp 346.

Texas.— Cunningham *v.* San Saba County, 1 Tex. Civ. App. 480, 20 S. W. 941, two years from time work began.

Wisconsin.— Tomlinson *v.* Wallace, 16 Wis. 224, ten years' delay fatal.

See 25 Cent. Dig. tit. "Highways," § 365.

Objections to proceedings from length of time elapsed cannot be taken by a petition to set aside the jury's verdict. Wood *v.* Quincy, 11 Cush. (Mass.) 487.

Against those who are under disability such as exempts them from its provisions the statute does not run. Cunningham *v.* San Saba County, 1 Tex. Civ. App. 480, 20 S. W. 941.

46. People *v.* Scio, 3 Mich. 121.

47. Everett *v.* Fall River, 189 Mass. 513, 75 N. E. 946; La Croix *v.* Medway, 12 Metc. (Mass.) 123.

48. *Connecticut.*—Avery *v.* Groton, 36 Conn. 304.

Indiana.— Heath *v.* Sheetz, 164 Ind. 665, 74 N. E. 505.

Massachusetts.— Gilman *v.* Haverhill, 128 Mass. 36; Fowler *v.* Middlesex County, 6 Allen 92; Dwight *v.* Springfield, 6 Gray 442; West Newbury *v.* Chase, 5 Gray 421; Hadley *v.* Middlesex County, 11 Cush. 394; Worcester County *v.* Leicester, 16 Pick. 39; Merrill *v.* Berkshire, 11 Pick. 269; Com. *v.* Justices of Sess. Middlesex County, 9 Mass. 388; Com. *v.* Justices Norfolk County Ct. of Sess., 5 Mass. 435. See also Flagg *v.* Worcester, 8 Cush. 69.

Missouri.— Thurlow *v.* Ross, 144 Mo. 234, 45 S. W. 1125.

New Hampshire.— Baker *v.* Holderness, 26 N. H. 110.

Ohio.— Lamb *v.* Lane, 4 Ohio St. 167.

Pennsylvania.— *In re* West Whiteland Road, 4 Pa. Co. Ct. 511.

Texas.— Galveston, etc., R. Co. *v.* Baudat, 18 Tex. Civ. App. 595, 45 S. W. 939.

Canada.— *Ex p.* Hebert, 8 N. Brunsw. 108.

See 25 Cent. Dig. tit. "Highways," § 367.

But there is no constitutional right to a jury trial. Hymes *v.* Aydelott, 26 Ind. 431; Bauman *v.* Ross, 167 U. S. 548, 17 S. Ct. 966, 42 L. ed. 270.

The jury's verdict is commonly conclusive (Hook *v.* Chicago, etc., R. Co., 133 Mo. 313, 34 S. W. 549; Foster *v.* Dunklin, 44 Mo. 216; People *v.* Kings County, 16 Wend. (N. Y.) 520; *In re* Brandywine Ave., 2 Chest. Co. Rep. (Pa.) 314; *In re* Verree Road, 1 Leg. Gaz. (Pa.) 18. But see People *v.* Kings County, 7 Wend. (N. Y.) 530), only, however, when acting within its jurisdiction (Clark *v.* Saybrook, 21 Conn. 313), and not if the damages it awards are excessive (Com. *v.* Justices Norfolk County Ct. of Sess., 5 Mass. 435).

On disagreement of the jury another jury may be summoned. Hicks *v.* Foster, 32 Ga. 414; Mendon *v.* Worcester County, 10 Pick. (Mass.) 235.

The verdict may be affirmed as to one owner and rejected as to another. Lanesborough *v.* Berkshire County, 22 Pick. (Mass.) 278; Anthony *v.* Berkshire County, 14 Pick. (Mass.) 189.

Selectmen are presumed to be authorized to apply to reduce damages. La Croix *v.* Medway, 12 Metc. (Mass.) 123.

49. Sangamon County *v.* Brown, 13 Ill. 207; Sangamon County Highway Com'rs *v.* Deboe. 43 Ill. App. 25; Baker *v.* Holderness, 26 N. H. 110 (court reference to road commissioners); Dalton *v.* North Hampton, 19 N. H. 362; Matter of Pugh, 22 Misc. 43, 49 N. Y. Suppl. 398 [*reversed* on other grounds

as well as those existing by dedication[81] or by recognition, user, or prescription.[82]

D. Authorized Obstructions; Prescription. Obstructions in a highway may be authorized by act of legislature,[83] or by the municipality in which the road lies,[84] the obstruction being, however, strictly confined to the authority granted.[85] No right to maintain an encroachment upon or obstruction in a highway by an individual can be gained by lapse of time,[86] unless by statute,[87]

has a legal existence. Draper *v.* Mackey, 35 Ark. 497; Galbraith *v.* Littiech, 73 Ill. 209; Clifford *v.* Eagle, 35 Ill. 444; Town *v.* Blackberry, 29 Ill. 137; State *v.* Hedeen, 47 Kan. 402, 28 Pac. 203; Chapman *v.* Gates, 54 N. Y. 132; Ward *v.* State, 42 Tex. Cr. 435, 60 S. W. 757. But a road not legally laid out may be obstructed. Roberts *v.* Cottrellville Highway Com'rs, 25 Mich. 23 (absence of petition by landowners); Christy *v.* Newton, 60 Barb. (N. Y.) 332.

81. Dunn *v.* Gunn, 149 Ala. 583, 42 So. 686; Reg. *v.* Petrie, 3 C. L. R. 829, 6 Cox C. C. 512, 4 E. & B. 737, 1 Jur. N. S. 752, 24 L. J. Q. B. 167, 3 Wkly. Rep. 243, 82 E. C. L. 737. See also Roberts *v.* Cottrellville Highway Com'rs, 25 Mich. 23; Mercer *v.* Woodgate, L. R. 5 Q. B. 26, 39 L. J. M. C. 21, 21 L. T. Rep. N. S. 458, 18 Wkly. Rep. 116.

Where the street dedicated has never been used or opened there is no right to remove an obstruction. Pavonia Land Assoc. *v.* Temfer, (N. J. Ch. 1887) 7 Atl. 423; Roller *v.* Kirby, 1 Ohio Dec. (Reprint) 76, 1 West. L. J. 550.

82. *Alabama.*— Dunn *v.* Gunn, 149 Ala. 583, 42 So. 686.

Iowa.— State *v.* McGee, 40 Iowa 595.

Kentucky.— Smith *v.* Illinois Cent. R. Co., 105 S. W. 96, 31 Ky. L. Rep. 1323.

Michigan.— Krueger *v.* Le Blanc, 62 Mich. 70, 28 N. W. 757. See also Roberts *v.* Cottrellville Highway Com'rs, 25 Mich. 23, under the statute of 1861, p. 153.

New York.— Chapman *v.* Gates, 54 N. Y. 132 [*affirming* 46 Barb. 313]; West Union *v.* Richey, 64 N. Y. App. Div. 156, 71 N. Y. Suppl. 871; People *v.* Hunting, 39 Hun 452. See Doughty *v.* Brill, 1 Abb. Dec. 524, 3 Keyes 612, 3 Transcr. App. 326 [*affirming* 36 Barb. 488].

Ohio.— Arnold *v.* Flattery, 5 Ohio 271.

See 25 Cent. Dig. tit. "Highways," § 421.

83. *Maine.*— State *v.* Webb's River Imp. Co., 97 Me. 559, 55 Atl. 495, right to maintain dams.

New York.— Scofield *v.* Poughkeepsie, 122 N. Y. App. Div. 868, 107 N. Y. Suppl. 767, telephone pole erected under license.

Ohio.— Bingham *v.* Doane, 9 Ohio 165.

Pennsylvania.— Pittsburgh, etc., Bridge Co. *v.* Com., 4 Pa. Cas. 153, 8 Atl. 217. See also Mellick *v.* Pennsylvania R. Co., 203 Pa. St. 457, 53 Atl. 340 [*reversing* 17 Pa. Super. Ct. 12]; Com. *v.* Ruddle, 142 Pa. St. 144, 21 Atl. 814.

Rhode Island.— Sullivan *v.* Webster, 16 R. I. 33, 11 Atl. 771.

See 25 Cent. Dig. tit. "Highways," § 420.

Right of railroad to use highways see RAILROADS, 34 Cyc. 191 *et seq.*

84. Leavenworth *v.* Douglass, 59 Kan. 416, 53 Pac. 123. But see Atty.-Gen. *v.* Barker, 83 L. T. Rep. N. S. 245, 16 T. L. R. 502.

85. Bingham *v.* Doane, 9 Ohio 165; Pittsburgh, etc., Bridge Co. *v.* Com., 4 Pa. Cas. 153, 8 Atl. 217.

A license to place a gate across a road does not empower the licensee to keep the gate locked, with the key in his own possession, which is equivalent to stopping up the road. Com. *v.* Carr, 143 Mass. 84, 9 N. E. 28.

86. *Connecticut.*— Blakeslee *v.* Tyler, 55 Conn. 387, 11 Atl. 291.

Indiana.— State *v.* Phipps, 4 Ind. 515; Terre Haute, etc., R. Co. *v.* Zehner, 15 Ind. App. 273, 42 N. E. 756.

Iowa.— Quinn *v.* Monona County, 140 Iowa 105, 117 N. W. 1100; Quinn *v.* Baage, 138 Iowa 426, 114 N. W. 205.

Kansas.— Eble *v.* State, 77 Kan. 179, 93 Pac. 803, 127 Am. St. Rep. 412.

Maine.—Charlotte *v.* Pembroke Iron Works, 82 Me. 391, 19 Atl. 902, 8 L. R. A. 828.

Massachusetts.— New Salem *v.* Eagle Mill Co., 138 Mass. 8; Morton *v.* Moore, 15 Gray 573.

Missouri.— Wright *v.* Doniphan, 169 Mo. 601, 70 S. W. 146.

New Jersey.— State *v.* Pierson, 37 N. J. L. 222; State *v.* Pierson, 37 N. J. L. 216; Tainter *v.* Morristown, 19 N. J. Eq. 46; Cross *v.* Morristown, 18 N. J. Eq. 305.

New York.— Slattery *v.* McCaw, 44 Misc. 426, 90 N. Y. Suppl. 52 (encroachments); Wildrick *v.* Hager, 10 N. Y. St. 764 [*affirmed* in 119 N. Y. 657, 23 N. E. 1150].

Pennsylvania.— Philadelphia's Appeal, 78 Pa. St. 33; Pittsburgh, etc., Bridge Co. *v.* Com., 4 Pa. Cas. 153, 8 Atl. 217.

Rhode Island.— Foley *v.* Ray, 27 R. I. 127, 61 Atl. 50.

Wisconsin.— State *v.* Wertzel, 62 Wis. 184, 22 N. W. 150.

See 25 Cent. Dig. tit. "Highways," § 422.

87. *Maine.*— Farnsworth *v.* Rockland, 83 Me. 508, 22 Atl. 394.

Massachusetts.— Winslow *v.* Nason, 113 Mass. 411; Com. *v.* Blaisdell, 107 Mass. 234. See also Morton *v.* Moore, 15 Gray 573.

Michigan.— Gregory *v.* Knight, 50 Mich. 61, 14 N. W. 700.

Missouri.— See State *v.* Warner, 51 Mo. App. 174.

New Jersey.— See Tainter *v.* Morristown, 19 N. J. Eq. 46.

New York.— Peckham *v.* Henderson, 27 Barb. 207.

North Carolina.— State *v.* Marble, 26 N. C. 318.

See 25 Cent. Dig. tit. "Highways," § 422.

Compare Henline *v.* People, 81 Ill. 269.

and a statute under which an individual may acquire such a right will be strictly construed.[88]

E. Persons Liable — 1. In General. Any one who causes or permits an obstruction to be placed on the highway is liable therefor.[89] Thus the owner is liable where a contractor abandons a contract to move a building and leaves it in the road,[90] and a landowner is similarly liable for the acts of his licensee.[91] Corporations are liable in like manner as natural persons,[92] and a municipality may itself be liable.[93]

2. Necessity of Notice to Charge Defendant. In some jurisdictions notice to defendant is necessary before liability for obstructions.[94] Thus notice has been held to be necessary before action,[95] indictment,[96] or summary removal.[97] But the requirement is limited to the cases covered by the statute, and thus under the particular circumstances notice has been held unnecessary[98] before summary removal,[99] indictment,[1] or suit to remove,[2] or before an action for a penalty.[3]

F. Remedies[4] — 1. Action for Damages — a. By Private Person — (I) *Right; Procedure.* A private person can bring action for the unlawful obstruction of a public way only if he has sustained special damage thereby, different not merely in degree, but in kind, from that suffered by the community at large.[5] Such actions are governed by the ordinary rules of law and

Evidence that shade trees have been suffered to stand more than twenty years where they were planted, in a public way, raises the presumption that they were planted under lawful authority. Bliss *v.* Ball, 99 Mass. 597.

88. Farnsworth *v.* Rockland, 83 Me. 508, 22 Atl. 394.

89. Dunn *v.* Gunn, 149 Ala. 583, 42 So. 686; Langsdale *v.* Bonton, 12 Ind. 467; Weathered *v.* Bray, 7 Ind. 706; Holliston *v.* New York Cent., etc., R. Co., 195 Mass. 299, 81 N. E. 204; Rockport *v.* Rockport Granite Co., 177 Mass. 246, 58 N. E. 1017, 51 L. R. A. 779; Wartman *v.* Philadelphia, 33 Pa. St. 202; Pennsylvania R. Co. *v.* Kelly, 31 Pa. St. 372; Com. *v.* Milliman, 13 Serg. & R. (Pa.) 403. But see New Basin Canal, etc., Bd. of Control *v.* H. Weston Lumber Co., 109 La. 925, 33 So. 923.

It is the duty of a person who has made an excavation in a highway to restore the road to a safe condition. Elzig *v.* Bales, 135 Iowa 208, 112 N. W. 540.

That the highway is obstructed by others at other places is no defense. Littiech *v.* Mitchell, 73 Ill. 603; Robinson *v.* State, (Tex. Cr. App. 1898) 44 S. W. 509.

That defendant has opened a new road is no defense to obstruction of a public highway. State *v.* Harden, 11 S. C. 360.

90. Caldwell *v.* Pre-emption, 74 Ill. App. 32.

91. Rockport *v.* Rockport Granite Co., 177 Mass. 246, 58 N. E. 1017, 51 L. R. A. 779.

92. Holliston *v.* New York Cent., etc., R. Co., 195 Mass. 299, 81 N. E. 204; Rockport *v.* Rockport Granite Co., 177 Mass. 246, 58 N. E. 1017, 51 L. R. A. 779; Wartman *v.* Philadelphia, 33 Pa. St. 202; Pennsylvania R. Co. *v.* Kelly, 31 Pa. St. 372.

93. Lamb *v.* Pike Tp., 215 Pa. St. 516, 64 Atl. 671; Hughes *v.* Fond du Lac, 73 Wis. 380, 41 N. W. 407. But see Miner *v.* Hopkinton, 73 N. H. 232, 60 Atl. 433.

94. Carver *v.* Com., 12 Bush (Ky.) 264; Hurst *v.* Cassiday, 5 Ky. L. Rep. 771; Le Blanc *v.* Kruger, 75 Mich. 561, 42 N. W. 980; Cooper *v.* Bean, 5 Lans. (N. Y.) 318; Spicer *v.* Slade, 9 Johns. (N. Y.) 359; State *v.* Egerer, 55 Wis. 527, 13 N. W. 461. See Cronenwaite *v.* Hoffman, 88 Mich. 617, 50 N. W. 656.

95. People *v.* Smith, 42 Mich. 138, 3 N. W. 302; Dodge *v.* Stacy, 39 Vt. 558; Wyman *v.* State, 13 Wis. 663, where obstruction was not wilful.

96. Sweeney *v.* People, 28 Ill. 208; State *v.* Robinson, 52 Iowa 228, 2 N. W. 1104; State *v.* Ratliff, 32 Iowa 189; Com. *v.* Noxon, 121 Mass. 42.

97. Cook *v.* Gaylord, 91 Iowa 219, 59 N. W. 30, fences interfering with foot travel outside of cut in road.

98. Carver *v.* Com., 12 Bush (Ky.) 264 (to remove fence erected by owner); Hunter *v.* Jones, 13 Minn. 307; Wyman *v.* State, 13 Wis. 663.

99. Ely *v.* Parsons, 55 Conn. 83, 10 Atl. 499; Davis *v.* Pickerell, 139 Iowa 186, 117 N. W. 276 (fences connected with cattleway across highway); Cool *v.* Commet, 13 Me. 250; Hunter *v.* Jones, 13 Minn. 307.

1. Kelly *v.* Com., 11 Serg. & R. (Pa.) 345.

2. Epler *v.* Niman, 5 Ind. 459.

3. Corning *v.* Head, 86 Hun (N. Y.) 12, 33 N. Y. Suppl. 360.

4. **Action for abatement of obstruction in city streets** see Municipal Corporations, 28 Cyc. 899.

Ejectment for encroachments on city streets see Municipal Corporations, 28 Cyc. 896.

5. *California.*— San José Ranch Co. *v.* Brooks, 74 Cal. 463, 16 Pac. 250; Lewiston Turnpike Co. *v.* Shasta, etc., Wagon Road Co., 41 Cal. 562; Blanc *v.* Klumpke, 29 Cal. 156.

Connecticut.— Clark *v.* Saybrook, 21 Conn. 313.

Delaware.— Johnson *v.* Stayton, 5 Harr. 362.

Indiana.— Sohn *v.* Cambern, 106 Ind. 302, 6 N. E. 813; Powell *v.* Bunger, 91 Ind. 64.

against encroachments on or obstructions in a public road,[37] when, and only when, he is specially injured thereby,[38] and it is necessary to preserve his rights[39] from

has not been determined at law); Irwin *v.* Dixion, 9 How. (U. S.) 10, 13 L. ed. 25.

37. *Alabama.*— Jones *v.* Bright, 140 Ala. 268, 37 So. 79.

California.— Gardner *v.* Stroever, 89 Cal. 26, 26 Pac. 618.

Missouri.— Peterson *v.* Beha, 161 Mo. 513, 62 S. W. 462, although error in lay-out.

Oregon.— Van Buskirk *v.* Bond, 52 Oreg. 234, 96 Pac. 1103.

Virginia.— Terry *v.* McClung, 104 Va. 599, 52 S. E. 355.

See 25 Cent. Dig. tit. "Highways," § 435.

38. *Alabama.*— Jones *v.* Bright, 140 Ala. 268, 37 So. 79; Cabbell *v.* Williams, 127 Ala. 320, 28 So. 405.

California.— Helm *v.* McClure, 107 Cal. 199, 40 Pac. 437; Gardner *v.* Stroever, 89 Cal. 26, 26 Pac. 618.

Georgia.— Coast Line R. Co. *v.* Cohen, 50 Ga. 451.

Illinois.— Nelson *v.* Randolph, 222 Ill. 531, 78 N. E. 914.

Indiana.— Strunk *v.* Pritchett, 27 Ind. App. 582, 61 N. E. 973.

Iowa.— Kelley *v.* Briggs, 58 Iowa 332, 12 N. W. 299; Hougham *v.* Harvey, 33 Iowa 203; Ewell *v.* Greenwood, 26 Iowa 377.

Kansas.— Hayden *v.* Stewart, 71 Kan. 11, 80 Pac. 43; Dyche *v.* Weichselbaum, 9 Kan. App. 360, 58 Pac. 126.

Kentucky.— Bohne *v.* Blankenship, 77 S. W. 919, 25 Ky. L. Rep. 1645.

Louisiana.— Allard *v.* Lobau, 2 Mart. N. S. 317 (although defendant be also indictable); New Orleans *v.* Gravier, 11 Mart. 620.

Maryland.— Gore *v.* Brubaker, 55 Md. 87; Baltimore, etc., R. Co. *v.* Strauss, 37 Md. 237.

Michigan.— Nye *v.* Clark, 55 Mich. 599, 22 N. W. 57.

Minnesota.— Wilder *v.* De Cou, 26 Minn. 10, 1 N. W. 48.

Nebraska.— Letherman *v.* Hauser, 77 Nebr. 731, 110 N. W. 745; Eldridge *v.* Collins, 75 Nebr. 65, 105 N. W. 1085.

New York.— De Witt *v.* Van Schoyk, 110 N. Y. 7, 17 N. E. 425, 6 Am. St. Rep. 342 [*affirming* 35 Hun 103]; Eldert *v.* Long Island Electric R. Co., 28 N. Y. App. Div. 451, 51 N. Y. Suppl. 186 [*affirmed* in 165 N. Y. 651, 59 N. E. 1122]; Purroy *v.* Schuyler, 15 N. Y. St. 337.

Ohio.— McQuigg *v.* Cullins, 56 Ohio St. 649, 47 N. E. 595; Cincinnati Methodist Protestant Church *v.* Laws, 13 Ohio Cir. Ct. 147, 6 Ohio Cir. Dec. 178; Mondle *v.* Toledo Plow Co., 9 Ohio S. & C. Pl. Dec. 281, 6 Ohio N. P. 294.

Oregon.— Luhrs *v.* Sturtevant, 10 Oreg. 170.

Pennsylvania.— Lehigh Coal, etc., Co. *v.* Inter-County St. R. Co., 167 Pa. St. 75, 31 Atl. 471; Wickham *v.* Twaddell, 25 Pa. Super. Ct. 188; Yost *v.* Philadelphia, etc., R. Co., 29 Leg. Int. 85; Smith *v.* Union Switch & Signal Co., 31 Pittsb. Leg. J. 21.

South Carolina.— Gray *v.* Charleston, etc., R. Co., 81 S. C. 370, 62 S. E. 442, holding that there must be a direct and special damage different in kind from that sustained by the public.

Tennessee.— Burkitt *v.* Battle, (Ch. App. 1900) 59 S. W. 429; Hill *v.* Hoffman, (Ch. App. 1899) 58 S. W. 929; Raht *v.* Southern Ry. Co., (Ch. App. 1897) 50 S. W. 72.

Texas.— Evans *v.* Scott, (Civ. App. 1906) 97 S. W. 116; Parsons *v.* Hunt, (Civ. App. 1904) 81 S. W. 120 [*reversed* on other grounds in 98 Tex. 420, 84 S. W. 644].

Virginia.— Terry *v.* McClung, 104 Va. 599, 52 S. E. 355.

West Virginia.— Bent *v.* Trimboli, 61 W. Va. 509, 56 S. E. 881; Wees *v.* Coal, etc., R. Co., 54 W. Va. 421, 46 S. E. 166; Clifton *v.* Weston, 54 W. Va. 250, 46 S. E. 360; Keystone Bridge Co. *v.* Summers, 13 W. Va. 476.

Wisconsin.— Pettibone *v.* Hamilton, 40 Wis. 402.

United States.— Mackall *v.* Ratchford, 82 Fed. 41.

See 25 Cent. Dig. tit. "Highways," § 435.

Injunction refused for failure to show special damage see Wellborn *v.* Davies, 40 Ark. 83; Aram *v.* Schallenberger, 41 Cal. 449 (although access hindered); Clark *v.* Donaldson, 104 Ill. 639 (only an inconvenience shown); Richeson *v.* Richeson, 8 Ill. App. 204; McCowan *v.* Whitesides, 31 Ind. 235; Bell *v.* Edwards, 37 La. Ann. 475; Robinson *v.* Brown, 182 Mass. 266, 65 N. E. 377; Hartshorn *v.* South Reading, 3 Allen (Mass.) 501; Currier *v.* Davis, 68 N. H. 596, 41 Atl. 239; Grey *v.* Greenville, etc., R. Co., 59 N. J. Eq. 372, 46 Atl. 638; West Jersey R. Co. *v.* Camden, etc., R. Co., 52 N. J. Eq. 31, 29 Atl. 423; Perkins *v.* Morristown, etc., Turnpike Co., 48 N. J. Eq. 499, 22 Atl. 180; Halsey *v.* Rapid Transit St. R. Co., 47 N. J. Eq. 380, 2 Atl. 859; Van Wegenen *v.* Cooney, 45 N. J. Eq. 24, 16 Atl. 689; Wakeman *v.* Wilbur, 4 N. Y. Suppl. 938 [*reversed* on other grounds in 147 N. Y. 657, 42 N. E. 341]; Van Buskirk *v.* Bond, 52 Oreg. 234, 96 Pac. 1103; Philadelphia, etc., R. Co. *v.* Philadelphia, etc., Pass. R. Co., 6 Pa. Dist. 487; Wees *v.* Coal, etc., R. Co., 54 W. Va. 421, 46 S. E. 166.

A difference not only in degree but in kind of damage from that suffered by the public must appear. Bigley *v.* Nunan, 53 Cal. 403; Jacksonville, etc., R. Co. *v.* Thompson, 34 Fla. 346, 16 So. 282, 26 L. R. A. 410; Dantzer *v.* Indianapolis Union R. Co., 141 Ind. 604, 39 N. E. 223, 50 Am. St. Rep. 343, 34 L. R. A. 769 (different from damage suffered by those who have property rights in the vicinity); Matlock *v.* Hawkins, 92 Ind. 225; Crook *v.* Pitcher, 61 Md. 510; Houck *v.* Wachter, 34 Md. 265, 6 Am. Rep. 332; Fort *v.* Groves, 29 Md. 188.

39. Stone *v.* Peckham, 12 R. I. 27 (dam not removed when injury to plaintiff can be re-

irreparable injury[40] in a plain case,[41] having due regard to the public interest,[42] and where plaintiff is not himself estopped.[43] Such suits are governed by the usual rules as to parties,[44] pleading,[45] evidence,[46] defenses,[47] trial,[48] and judgment.[49]

3. **Mandamus Against Public Officer to Compel Removal.** Removal of obstructions or encroachments in a highway may be compelled by mandamus against the officers whose duty it is to remove them,[50] on petition setting out the necessary

lieved by altering it); Fielden *v.* Cox, 22 T. L. R. 411.

40. *California.*— Gardner *v.* Stroever, 81 Cal. 148, 22 Pac. 483, 6 L. R. A. 90.

Missouri.— Bailey *v.* Culver, 84 Mo. 531, holding that injunction will be refused unless irreparable damage will take place.

New Jersey.— Halsey *v.* Rapid Transit St. R. Co., 47 N. J. Eq. 380, 20 Atl. 859.

Oregon.— Van Buskirk *v.* Bond, 52 Oreg. 234, 96 Pac. 1103.

Pennsylvania.— Neill *v.* Gallagher, 1 Wkly. Notes Cas. 99.

South Carolina.— Northrop Simpson, 69 S. C. 551, 48 S. E. 613.

See 25 Cent. Dig. tit. "Highways," § 435.

One who has erected costly buildings may enjoin the obstruction of the highway, constituting his only means of ingress and egress to the buildings, before he has suffered actual damage from the obstruction. Ross *v.* Thompson, 78 Ind. 90.

The fact that no actual damages can be proved, so that in an action at law the jury could award nominal damages only, often furnishes the very best reason why a court of equity should interfere in cases where the nuisance is a continuous one. Newell *v.* Sass, 142 Ill. 104, 31 N. E. 176. See also Clowes *v.* Staffordshire Potteries Water-Works Co., L. R. 8 Ch. 125, 42 L. J. Ch. 107, 27 L. T. Rep. N. S. 521.

41. Green *v.* Oakes, 17 Ill. 249; Hill *v.* Hoffman, (Tenn. Ch. App. 1899) 58 S. W. 929.

Where the existence of the highway is in issue an injunction will be refused. Van Buskirk *v.* Bond, 52 Oreg. 234, 96 Pac. 1103.

42. Wees *v.* Coal, etc., R. Co., 54 W. Va. 421, 46 S. E. 166, injunction refused where public benefit outweighs private inconvenience.

43. Richeson *v.* Richeson, 8 Ill. App. 204 (estoppel three years' delay unaccounted for); Brutsche *v.* Bowers, 122 Iowa 226, 97 N. W. 1076 (plaintiff himself an obstructer); Williams *v.* Poole, 103 S. W. 336, 31 Ky. L. Rep. 757.

44. Hill *v.* Hoffman, (Tenn. Ch. App. 1899) 58 S. W. 929, holding that omission of abutting owner is immaterial.

45. *Alabama.*— Cabbell *v.* Williams, 127 Ala. 320, 28 So. 405.

Indiana.— Strunk *v.* Pritchett, 27 Ind. App. 582, 61 N. E. 973.

Iowa.— Brutsche *v.* Bowers, 122 Iowa 226, 97 N. W. 1076.

Kentucky.— Newcome *v.* Crews, 98 Ky. 339, 32 S. W. 947, 17 Ky. L. Rep. 899, holding that an answer founded on prescription must allege actual possession.

New York.— Jones *v.* Doherty, 163 N. Y. 558, 57 N. E. 1113.

Ohio.— Ett *v.* Snyder, 5 Ohio Dec. (Reprint) 523, 6 Am. L. Rec. 415, bill must state that obstruction unlawful.

Tennessee.— Hill *v.* Hoffman, (Ch. App. 1899) 58 S. W. 929.

See 25 Cent. Dig. tit. "Highways," § 435.

46. *Arkansas.*— Halliday *v.* Smith, 67 Ark. 310, 54 S. W. 970.

Indiana.— Martin *v.* Marks, 154 Ind. 549, 57 N. E. 249.

Kentucky.— Evans *v.* Cook, 111 S. W. 326, 33 Ky. L. Rep. 788.

Missouri.— Carlin *v.* Wolff, 154 Mo. 539, 51 S. W. 679, 55 S. W. 441, injunction refused on vague, uncertain, and contradictory evidence.

Texas.— Evans *v.* Scott, 37 Tex. Civ. App. 373, 83 S. W. 874.

See 25 Cent. Dig. tit. "Highways," § 435.

47. Allen *v.* Hopson, 119 Ky. 215, 83 S. W. 575, 26 Ky. L. Rep. 1148 (holding that a denial of relief in special statutory proceeding is no bar to another proceeding); Grace *v.* Walker, 95 Tex. 39, 64 S. W. 930, 65 S. W. 482 [*modifying* (Civ. App. 1901) 61 S. W. 1103] (holding that persons not interested in land over which a highway was constructed cannot interpose the defense that the consent of the owners had not been obtained for the highway, in an action for the obstruction thereof). See also Lawrence *v.* Ewert, 21 S. D. 580, 114 N. W. 709, holding that injunction lies, although defendants are liable criminally.

48. Evans *v.* Scott, (Tex. Civ. App. 1906) 97 S. W. 116 (questions of dedication and prescription for the jury); Evans *v.* Scott, 37 Tex. Civ. App. 373, 83 S. W. 874 (instruction presenting issue not raised by pleadings, error).

49. Peterson *v.* Beha, 161 Mo. 513, 62 S. W. 462.

The judgment must be definite in description (Peterson *v.* Beha, 161 Mo. 513, 62 S. W. 462), but need not recite in what part of road the line between certain sections came (Wilson *v.* Hull, 7 Utah 90, 24 Pac. 799).

50. Peck *v.* Los Angeles County, 90 Cal. 384, 27 Pac. 301 (road overseer); Cook *v.* Gaylord, 91 Iowa 219, 59 N. W. 30; Patterson *v.* Vail, 43 Iowa 142.

Mandamus refused see State *v.* Thompson, 6 N. J. L. J. 214.

It is a good defense that the officer had already served notice to remove (Cook *v.* Gaylord, 91 Iowa 219, 59 N. W. 30), or that the road commissioner believes after investigation that no unlawful encroachment exists (White *v.* Leonidas Tp. Highway Com'rs, 95 Mich. 288, 54 N. W. 875).

Although indictment lies for the officer's neglect, yet mandamus may issue. Brokaw *v.* Bloomington Tp. Highway Com'rs, 130 Ill. 482, 22 N. E. 596, 6 L. R. A. 161. But see

facts.[51] It will be granted only in a clear case and not where the rights of the parties are in dispute.[52]

4. ACTION AGAINST OBSTRUCTER TO COMPEL REMOVAL [53] — **a. In General.** Proceedings at law can commonly be brought to obtain an order for the removal or abatement of an obstruction,[54] with proper parties,[55] upon sufficient pleadings,[56] and on proper evidence.[57]

b. Order and Notice. The order or notice to remove obstructions should be issued by the proper court,[58] and served on the party interested,[59] and must be in the form required by statute,[60] containing a specific description of the encroachment,[61] allowing a proper length of time for removal,[62] and ordering the removal to be made at the proper time.[63]

c. Appeal or Certiorari. The decision as to removal may be reviewed by appeal,[64] or by certiorari.[65]

5. SUMMARY PROCEEDINGS FOR REMOVAL. Proceedings are often provided for

Hale Highway Com'rs *v.* People, 73 Ill. 203; Yorktown Highway Com'rs *v.* People, 66 Ill. 339, both holding *contra*, under an earlier statute.

51. Peck *v.* Los Angeles County, 90 Cal. 384, 27 Pac. 301.

52. Yorktown Highway Com'rs *v.* People, 66 Ill. 339; Hunt *v.* Highway Com'rs, 43 Ill. App. 279.

53. **Removal of obstructions from city streets** see MUNICIPAL CORPORATIONS, 28 Cyc. 896.

54. *California.*— People *v.* McCue, 150 Cal. 195, 88 Pac. 899 (under statute); Smith *v.* Glenn, (1900) 62 Pac. 180; People *v.* Blake, (1884) 3 Pac. 102.

Idaho.— Meservey *v.* Gulliford, 14 Ida. 133, 93 Pac. 780.

Kentucky.— Allen *v.* Hopson, 119 Ky. 215, 83 S. W. 575, 26 Ky. L. Rep. 1148; Witt *v.* Hughes, 66 S. W. 281, 23 Ky. L. Rep. 1836, gate removed.

Maine.— Rockland *v.* Rockland Water Co., 86 Me. 55, 29 Atl. 935.

New York.— Howard *v.* Robbins, 1 Lans. 63.

South Carolina.— Smith *v.* Gilreath, 69 S. C. 353, 48 S. E. 262.

55. Hall *v.* Kauffman, 106 Cal. 451, 39 Pac. 756 (in name of road commissioner); San Benito County *v.* Whitesides, 51 Cal. 416 (in name of road overseer); Grandville *v.* Jenison, 84 Mich. 54, 47 N. W. 600; North Manheim Tp. *v.* Reading, etc., R. Co., 10 Pa. Cas. 261, 14 Atl. 137.

56. Meservey *v.* Gulliford, 14 Ida. 133, 93 Pac. 780; Sloan *v.* Rebman, 66 Iowa 81, 23 N. W. 274.

57. Whaley *v.* Wilson, 120 Ala. 502, 24 So. 855; Eaton *v.* People, 30 Colo. 345, 70 Pac. 426; Savannah, etc., R. Co. *v.* Gill, 118 Ga. 737, 45 S. E. 623. See also Shepherd *v.* Turner, 129 Cal. 530, 62 Pac. 106.

58. Churchill *v.* Com., 13 B. Mon. (Ky.) 333.

59. Krueger *v.* Le Blanc, 62 Mich. 70, 28 N. W. 757; State *v.* Egerer, 55 Wis. 527, 13 N. W. 461.

60. Witt *v.* Hughes, 66 S. W. 281, 23 Ky. L. Rep. 1836; James *v.* Sammis, 132 N. Y. 239, 30 N. E. 502; Olendorf *v.* Sullivan, 13 N. Y. Suppl. 6.

Proper proceedings must be shown on the face of the order. Phillips *v.* Schumacher, 10 Hun (N. Y.) 405 (notice to all commissioners to attend); Fitch *v.* Kirkland Highway Com'rs, 22 Wend. (N. Y.) 132; Spicer *v.* Slade, 9 Johns. (N. Y.) 359.

Failure to comply with the provisions of the statute as to notice does not make the road officer a trespasser. Hathaway *v.* Jenks, 67 Hun (N. Y.) 289, 22 N. Y. Suppl. 421.

61. Ferris *v.* Ward, 9 Ill. 499; Krueger *v.* Le Blanc, 62 Mich. 70, 28 N. W. 757; Vantilburgh *v.* Shann, 24 N. J. L. 740; Hathaway *v.* Jenks, 67 Hun (N. Y.) 289, 22 N. Y. Suppl. 421; Mott *v.* Rush Highway Com'rs, 2 Hill (N. Y.) 472.

Notice held defective in not stating the legal width of the highway (see Cook *v.* Covil, 18 Hun (N. Y.) 288; Mott *v.* Rush Highway Com'rs, 2 Hill (N. Y.) 472; Spicer *v.* Slade, 9 Johns. (N. Y.) 359), or the extent and location of the encroachment (see Le Blanc *v.* Kruger, 75 Mich. 561, 42 N. W. 980; Sardinia *v.* Butler, 149 N. Y. 505, 44 N. E. 179 [*reversing* 78 Hun 527, 29 N. Y. Suppl. 481]).

62. Cook *v.* Gaylord, 91 Iowa 219, 59 N. W. 30; Blackburn *v.* Powers, 40 Iowa 681; Smithtown *v.* Ely, 75 N. Y. App. Div. 309, 11 N. Y. Annot. Cas. 459, 78 N. Y. Suppl. 178 [*affirmed* in 173 N. Y. 624, 70 N. E. 1110]; Spicer *v.* Slade, 9 Johns. (N. Y.) 359.

63. State *v.* Egerer, 55 Wis. 527, 13 N. W. 461.

64. Hall *v.* Kauffman, 106 Cal. 451, 39 Pac. 756; Jameson *v.* Hoppock, 46 N. J. L. 516; Miller *v.* Rose, 21 W. Va. 291. See also Sandy *v.* Lindsay, 6 Ky. L. Rep. 737; Wildrick *v.* Hager, 10 N. Y. St. 764 [*affirmed* in 119 N. Y. 657, 23 N. E. 1150].

65. Roberts *v.* Cottrellville Highway Com'rs, 25 Mich. 23; Newbold *v.* Taylor, 46 N. J. L. 133; Gulick *v.* Groendyke, 38 N. J. L. 114; Warford *v.* Smith, 25 N. J. L. 212; People *v.* East Hampton Highway Com'rs, 30 N. Y. 72. See also Low *v.* Rogers, 8 Johns. (N. Y.) 321.

Certiorari refused see People *v.* East Hampton Highway Com'rs, 30 N. Y. 72; Pearsall *v.* North Hempstead Highway Com'rs, 17 Wend. (N. Y.) 15; Pugsley *v.* Anderson, 3 Wend. (N. Y.) 468.

ing,[87] on a highway legally laid out,[88] but not generally on a highway by user,[89] although under some statutes roads by prescription are held to be included.[90]

b. Recovery; Procedure. The jurisdiction of the court is governed by local law,[91] and in many states it is conferred upon justices of the peace.[92] The usual rules of local practice in like cases govern [93] as to parties,[94] pleading,[95] evidence,[96]

Smith, 52 Wis. 134, 8 N. W. 870; State *v.* Preston, 34 Wis. 675 (obstruction created in good faith).

87. Menard County Road Dist. No. 1 *v.* Beebe, 231 Ill. 147, 83 N. E. 131 [*affirming* 134 Ill. App. 583]; Seidschlag *v.* Antioch, 207 Ill. 280, 69 N. E. 949 [*affirming* 109 Ill. App. 291]; Fleet *v.* Youngs, 7 Wend. (N. Y.) 291.

88. *Illinois.*— Ohio, etc., R. Co. *v.* People, 39 Ill. App. 473.

Indiana.— Davis *v.* Nicholson, 81 Ind. 183.

Mississippi.— Illinois Cent. R. Co. *v.* State, 71 Miss. 253, 14 So. 459.

Missouri.— Wright *v.* Doniphan, 169 Mo. 601, 70 S. W. 146.

New York.— Fowler *v.* Lansing, 9 Johns. 349.

Ohio.— Bisher *v.* Richards, 9 Ohio St. 495.

Pennsylvania.— Clark *v.* Com., 33 Pa. St. 112; Calder *v.* Chapman, 8 Pa. St. 522; Com. *v.* Alexander, 2 Chest. Co. Rep. 267.

Tennessee.— Blackmore *v.* Penn, 4 Sneed 447.

Virginia.— Bailey *v.* Com., 78 Va. 19.

Wisconsin.— Racine *v.* Chicago, etc., R. Co., 92 Wis. 118, 65 N. W. 857; State *v.* Paine Lumber Co., 84 Wis. 205, 54 N. W. 503.

See 25 Cent. Dig. tit. "Highways," § 438.

That the road was traveled for a greater width than laid out does not subject any person to a penalty for obstructing the extra width. Harding *v.* Hale, 61 Ill. 192.

89. Freshour *v.* Hihn, 99 Cal. 443, 34 Pac. 87; Parker *v.* People, 22 Mich. 93; Doughty *v.* Brill, 1 Abb. Dec. (N. Y.) 524, 3 Keyes 612, 3 Transcr. App. 326 [*affirming* 36 Barb. 488]; State *v.* Leaver, 62 Wis. 387, 22 N. W. 576; State *v.* Wertzel, 62 Wis. 184, 22 N. W. 150; State *v.* Babcock, 42 Wis. 138.

90. Scott *v.* New Boston, 26 Ill. App. 108; Littel *v.* Denn, 34 N. Y. 452; Devenpeck *v.* Lambert, 44 Barb. (N. Y.) 596; Fowler *v.* Mott, 19 Barb. (N. Y.) 204; Baylis *v.* Rooe, 1 Silv. Sup. (N. Y.) 356, 5 N. Y. Suppl. 279.

91. **See the statutes of the several states. And see** Brushy Mound *v.* McClintock, 146 Ill. 643, 35 N. E. 159; Tully *v.* Northfield, 6 Ill. App. 356; Parker *v.* Van Houten, 7 Wend. (N. Y.) 145; Woodward *v.* South Carolina, etc., R. Co., 47 S. C. 233, 25 S. E. 146; State *v.* Egerer, 55 Wis. 527, 13 N. W. 461.

92. *Illinois.*— Chatham *v.* Mason, 53 Ill. 411; Crosby *v.* Gipps, 19 Ill. 309 (for obstructing but not for continuing); Ferris *v.* Ward, 9 Ill. 499.

Indiana.— Aldrich *v.* Hawkins, 6 Blackf. 125.

Kentucky.— Cincinnati, etc., R. Co. *v.* Baughman, 116 Ky. 479, 76 S. W. 351, 25 Ky. L. Rep. 705.

Massachusetts.— Hall *v.* Kent, 11 Gray 467.

Mississippi.— Hairston *v.* Francher, 7 Sm. & M. 249, only after judgment of board of police.

New York.— Chapman *v.* Swan, 65 Barb. 210.

See 25 Cent. Dig. tit. "Highways," § 439.

If a question of title is raised the justice has no jurisdiction. State *v.* Huck, 29 Wis. 202; State *v.* Doane, 14 Wis. 483.

93. Fleet *v.* Youngs, 7 Wend. (N. Y.) 291; Justice *v.* Com., 2 Va. Cas. 171.

94. Samuell *v.* Sherman, 170 Ill. 265, 48 N. E. 576; Allen *v.* Hiles, 67 N. J. L. 135, 50 Atl. 440.

95. Sierra County *v.* Butler, 136 Cal. 547, 69 Pac. 418 (penalty not recovered in an action for an injunction); Lovington Tp. *v.* Adkins, 232 Ill. 510, 83 N. E. 1043 (place must be clearly stated); State *v.* Childs, 109 Wis. 233, 85 N. W. 374 (formal complaint unnecessary).

Variance see Hill *v.* Stonecreek Tp. Road Dist. No. 6, 10 Ohio St. 621, holding that an allegation of obstructing a road by erecting a fence across it is not proved by evidence of erecting a fence away from the road causing water to flow on it and obstruct it.

96. **Evidence held admissible see** Lovington Tp. *v.* Adkins, 232 Ill. 510, 83 N. E. 1043 (plat of surveyor); Bethel *v.* Pruett, 215 Ill. 162, 74 N. E. 111 (statements of road officers); Seidschlag *v.* Antioch, 207 Ill. 280, 69 N. E. 949 [*affirming* 109 Ill. App. 291]; Parkey *v.* Galloway, 147 Mich. 693, 111 N. W. 348; West Union *v.* Richey, 64 N. Y. App. Div. 156, 71 N. Y. Suppl. 871; Meeker *v.* Com., 42 Pa. St. 283.

Evidence held inadmissible see Lovington Tp. *v.* Adkins, 232 Ill. 510, 83 N. E. 1043 (order laying out road not of the statutory width); Kyle *v.* Logan, 87 Ill. 64 (survey made *post litem motam*); State *v.* Babcock, 42 Wis. 138.

Sufficiency of evidence.— Evidence held sufficient see Lowe *v.* Aroma, 21 Ill. App. 598; State *v.* Dehn, 126 Wis. 168, 105 N. W. 795. Evidence held insufficient see Dickerman *v.* Marion, 122 Ill. App. 154.

The burden of proof is upon plaintiff. Bethel *v.* Pruett, 215 Ill. 162, 74 N. E. 111; Kane *v.* Farrelly, 192 Ill. 521, 61 N. E. 648; Havana *v.* Biggs, 58 Ill. 483; Grube *v.* Nichols, 36 Ill. 92 (as to continuance of obstruction); Lewiston *v.* Proctor, 27 Ill. 414 (as to existence of road between points named); Chicago, etc., R. Co. *v.* People, 44 Ill. App. 632; Tully *v.* Northfield, 6 Ill. App. 356 (not only as to the placing of the obstruction but that it was on a public highway).

trial,[97] defenses,[98] and appeal.[99] The amount of the penalty is estimated in accordance with the statute,[1] and is sometimes required by the statute to be paid into the road fund.[2] Where the statutory penalty is for obstructing a road, treated as a continuing offense, limitations run only as to matters occurring before the statutory period.[3]

8. CRIMINAL PROSECUTION[4] — **a. In General.** In most jurisdictions it is a criminal offense to obstruct a public highway,[5] and this is so both at common

A preponderance is sufficient; proof beyond a reasonable doubt is unnecessary. Lewiston *v.* Proctor, 27 Ill. 414.

97. Seidschlag *v.* Antioch, 207 Ill. 280, 69 N. E. 949, holding that it is a question for the jury whether the place was a highway.

Instructions: Correct see Bethel *v.* Pruett, 215 Ill. 162, 74 N. E. 111. Erroneous see Whitley Tp. *v.* Linville, 174 Ill. 579, 51 N. E. 832; Wheatfield *v.* Grundmann, 164 Ill. 250, 45 N. E. 164; Louisville, etc., R. Co. *v.* Whitley County Ct., 49 S. W. 332, 20 Ky. L. Rep. 1367, on hypothesis not supported by evidence.

98. Hines *v.* Darling, 99 Mich. 47, 57 N. W. 1081 (no defense that ditch obstructed was not properly laid); Little *v.* Denn, 34 How. Pr. (N. Y.) 68; Bisher *v.* Richards, 9 Ohio St. 495; Com. *v.* Lucas, 23 Pa. Co. Ct. 277.

99. *Illinois.*— Partridge *v.* Snyder, 78 Ill. 519.

Missouri.— Pearce *v.* Myers, 3 Mo. 31.

New York.— Cooper *v.* Bean, 5 Lans. 318.

Ohio.— Bittle *v.* Hay, 5 Ohio 269.

Pennsylvania.— Com. *v.* Keane, 21 Pa. Co. Ct. 327.

Wisconsin.— State *v.* Duff, 83 Wis. 291, 53 N. W. 446; State *v.* Hayden, 32 Wis. 663.

See 25 Cent. Dig. tit. "Highways," § 443.

1. See the statutes of the several states. And see the following cases:

Illinois.— Menard County Road Dist. No. 1 *v.* Beebe, 231 Ill. 147, 83 N. E. 131 [*affirming* 134 Ill. App. 583]; Ferris *v.* Ward, 9 Ill. 499. See also Meacham *v.* Lacey, 133 Ill. App. 208.

Indiana.— Martin *v.* Marks, 154 Ind. 549, 57 N. E. 249.

Kentucky.— Big Sandy R. Co. *v.* Floyd County, 125 Ky. 345, 101 S. W. 354, 31 Ky. L. Rep. 17.

Massachusetts.— Andover *v.* Sutton, 12 Metc. 182.

Michigan.— Shepard *v.* Gates, 50 Mich. 495, 15 N. W. 878, treble damages for wilful wrong.

New Hampshire.— Monroe *v.* Connecticut River Lumber Co., 68 N. H. 89, 39 Atl. 1019, additional expense of maintaining new road included.

New York.— Fleet *v.* Youngs, 7 Wend. 291.

Ohio.— Lawrence R. Co. *v.* Mahoning County, 35 Ohio St. 1, cost of removing obstructions.

Texas.— Fuller *v.* State, 41 Tex. 140, repeal by statute prescribing a different penalty.

See 25 Cent. Dig. tit. "Highways," § 442.

2. See Bailey *v.* Dale, 71 Cal. 34, 11 Pac. 804.

3. Bufford *v.* Hinson, 3 Head (Tenn.) 573; Londonderry *v.* Arnold, 30 Vt. 401. But see Wallingford *v.* Hall, 64 Conn. 426, 30 Atl. 47.

4. Criminal prosecution for obstructing city streets see MUNICIPAL CORPORATIONS, 28 Cyc. 906.

5. *Alabama.*— Georgia Cent. R. Co. *v.* State, 145 Ala. 99, 40 So. 991.

Connecticut.— State *v.* Gorham, 11 Conn. 233, stone wall.

Delaware.— State *v.* Southard, 6 Pennew. 247, 66 Atl. 372, fence.

Illinois.— Henline *v.* People, 81 Ill. 269 (new offense to replace gates removed by commissioners); Wiley *v.* Brimfield, 59 Ill. 306.

Maryland.— Schall *v.* Nusbaum, 56 Md. 512; State *v.* Price, 21 Md. 448.

Massachusetts.— Com. *v.* Wilkinson, 16 Pick. 175, 26 Am. Dec. 654; Com. *v.* Boston, etc., R. Corp., 12 Cush. (Mass.) 254.

Minnesota.— Hutchinson *v.* Filk, 44 Minn. 536, 47 N. W. 255.

Missouri.— State *v.* Campbell, 80 Mo. App. 110.

New Hampshire.— Bryant *v.* Tamworth, 68 N. H. 483, 39 Atl. 431.

New Jersey.— Raritan Tp. *v.* Port Reading R. Co., 49 N. J. Eq. 11, 23 Atl. 127; Atty.-Gen. *v.* Heishon, 18 N. J. Eq. 410.

New York.— Harrower *v.* Ritson, 37 Barb. 301. But see People *v.* Crounse, 51 Hun 489, 4 N. Y. Suppl. 266, 7 N. Y. Cr. 11.

North Carolina.— State *v.* Brown, 109 N. C. 802, 13 S. E. 940, 942; State *v.* Yarrell, 34 N. C. 130. But see State *v.* Pollock, 26 N. C. 303.

Pennsylvania.— Com. *v.* Croushore, 145 Pa. St. 157, 22 Atl. 807; Biddle *v.* Ash, 2 Ashm. 211; Barker *v.* Com., 19 Pa. St. 412 (collecting crowd); Com. *v.* Milliman, 13 Serg. & R. 403 (constables conducting sales); Com. *v.* Spratt, 14 Phila. 365

England.— Hind *v.* Evans, 70 J. P. 548, 4 Loc. Gov. 1152.

See 25 Cent. Dig. tit. "Highways," § 444 *et seq.*

But see Pettinger *v.* People, 20 Mich. 336.

That mandamus is a remedy for obstruction of a highway does not bar an indictment therefor. State *v.* Baltimore, etc., R. Co., 120 Ind. 298, 22 N. E. 307.

Offense held not to have been committed see People *v.* Young, 72 Ill. 411; Wiley *v.* Brimfield, 59 Ill. 306; People *v.* Jackson, 7 Mich. 432, 74 Am. Dec. 729, where obstruction does not affect rights of public but only of individuals.

A landlord is not criminally liable for the act of his tenant. Com. *v.* Switzer, 134 Pa. St. 383, 19 Atl. 681.

by user[11] or dedication,[12] but not where the road,[13] or the portion obstructed,[14] has been abandoned. The usual defenses may be made.[15]

b. Jurisdiction. The jurisdiction of the offense depends on local statute,[16] and is commonly given to justices of the peace.[17]

c. Indictment.[18] The indictment should charge all the elements of the crime,[19]

11. *Indiana.*— Hays *v.* State, 8 Ind. 425.

Missouri.— State *v.* Proctor, 90 Mo. 334, 2 S. W. 472; State *v.* Transue, 131 Mo. App. 323, 111 S. W. 523; State *v.* Baldridge, 53 Mo. App. 415; State *v.* Bradley, 31 Mo. App. 308.

Pennsylvania.— Com. *v.* Slagel, 33 Pa. Super. Ct. 514; Com. *v.* Christie, 13 Pa. Co. Ct. 149.

South Carolina.— State *v.* Washington, 80 S. C. 376, 61 S. E. 896; State *v.* Sartor, 2 Strobh. 60.

Texas.— Lensing *v.* State, (Cr. App. 1898) 45 S. W. 572.

Canada.— Reg. *v.* Buchanan, 5 N. Brunsw. 674.

See 25 Cent. Dig. tit. "Highways," § 445.

But see State *v.* Snyder, 25 Iowa 208 (holding that an indictment charging obstruction of a county road is not met by proof of a "highway" by use); Com. *v.* Low, 3 Pick. (Mass.) 408.

Statute not retrospective.—A statute providing that highways not laid out according to statute shall not be deemed highways is not retroactive as to a highway theretofore lawfully existing; hence prosecution on an indictment then pending as to a nuisance in such highway is not barred by such enactment. State *v.* Atherton, 16 N. H. 203.

12. *Illinois.*— Salter *v.* People, 92 Ill. App. 481.

Kentucky.— Evans *v.* Cook, 111 S. W. 326, 33 Ky. L. Rep. 788; Hughes *v.* Holbrook, 108 S. W. 225, 32 Ky. L. Rep. 1210.

Missouri.— State *v.* Transue, 131 Mo. App. 323, 111 S. W. 523; Power *v.* Dean, 112 Mo. App. 288, 86 S. W. 1100.

Vermont.— State *v.* Wilkinson, 2 Vt. 480, 21 Am. Dec. 560.

England.— Reg. *v.* Londonderry Justices, [1902] 2 Ir. 266.

See 25 Cent. Dig. tit. "Highways," § 445.

13. Com. *v.* Belding, 13 Metc. (Mass.) 10; Shelby *v.* State, 10 Humphr. (Tenn.) 165, nonuser for three years. But see State *v.* Shuford, 28 N. C. 162, holding that there is liability where discontinuance was void.

14. Hamilton *v.* State, 106 Ind. 361, 7 N. E. 9.

15. State *v.* Webb's River Imp. Co., 97 Me. 559, 55 Atl. 495; Com. *v.* Belding, 13 Metc. (Mass.) 10; *Ex p.* Morrison, 6 N. Brunsw. 203.

16. See the statutes of the several states. And see the following cases:

Connecticut.— State *v.* Hyde, 11 Conn. 541; State *v.* Knapp, 6 Conn. 415, 16 Am. Dec. 68.

Kentucky.— Com. *v.* Illinois Cent. R. Co., 104 Ky. 366, 47 S. W. 258, 20 Ky. L. Rep. 606 (circuit court); Evans *v.* Cook, 111 S. W. 326, 33 Ky. L. Rep. 788 (county judge).

Minnesota.— State *v.* Sweeney, 33 Minn. 23, 21 N. W. 847; State *v.* Cotton, 29 Minn. 187, 12 N. W. 529 (district court where title to real estate involved); State *v.* Galvin, 27 Minn. 16, 6 N. W. 380.

Missouri.— State *v.* Bradley, 31 Mo. App. 308.

New Hampshire.— State *v.* Lord, 16 N. H. 357.

South Carolina.— State *v.* Wolfe, 61 S. C. 25, 39 S. E. 179, court of session and magistrate court.

Virginia.— Justice *v.* Com., 2 Va. Cas. 171, superior court.

See 25 Cent. Dig. tit. "Highways," § 447.

17. *Illinois.*— Dolton *v.* Dolton, 201 Ill. 155, 66 N. E. 323, where determination of ownership was incidental only.

Indiana.— Miller *v.* State, 72 Ind. 421.

Louisiana.— West Baton Rouge *v.* Robertson, 8 La. Ann. 69.

Minnesota.— State *v.* Sweeney, 33 Minn. 23, 21 N. W. 847; State *v.* Cotton, 29 Minn. 187, 12 N. W. 529.

Canada.— Reg. *v.* Buchanan, 5 N. Brunsw. 674, although title to land comes in question.

See 25 Cent. Dig. tit. "Highways," § 447.

18. **Indictment against private corporation for obstructing a public highway** see CORPORATIONS, 10 Cyc. 1227.

19. Gregory *v.* Com., 2 Dana (Ky.) 417 (must aver that defendant was the owner); State *v.* Webb's River Imp. Co., 97 Me. 559, 55 Atl. 495; State *v.* Craig, 79 Mo. App. 412; State *v.* Dry Fork R. Co., 50 W. Va. 235, 40 S. E. 447.

Indictments held sufficient see Georgia Cent. R. Co. *v.* State, 145 Ala. 99, 40 So. 991 (although not alleging want of consent by commissioners); Alexander *v.* State, 117 Ala. 220, 23 So. 48; Palatka, etc., R. Co. *v.* State, 23 Fla. 546, 3 So. 158, 11 Am. St. Rep. 395; Com. *v.* American Tel., etc., Co., 84 S. W. 519, 27 Ky. L. Rep. 29; Com. *v.* King, 13 Metc. (Mass.) 115 (indictment good at common law, although statutory remedy provided in addition); State *v.* McCray, 74 Mo. 303; State *v.* Spurgeon, 102 Mo. App. 34, 74 S. W. 453; State *v.* Lucas, 124 N. C. 804, 32 S. E. 553; Richardson *v.* State, 46 Tex. Cr. 83, 79 S. W. 536.

Indictments held insufficient see Com. *v.* Walters, 6 Dana (Ky.) 290 (not alleging that defendant the owner of the land); Com. *v.* Collier, 75 S. W. 236, 25 Ky. L. Rep. 312 (not sufficiently alleging that defendant directed water causing obstruction); Gilbert *v.* State, 78 Nebr. 636, 111 N. W. 377, 78 Nebr. 637, 112 N. W. 293 (omitting allegation that road or track was in common use).

Matters of defense or mitigation need not be alleged. Thus an indictment for obstructing a public road need not allege the materiality of the obstruction, or that the road had been laid off by the proper authorities as a

and beyond a reasonable doubt,[28] showing the existence of a highway by legal lay-out,[29] dedication,[30] or user.[31] The usual rule against variance applies.[32]

(II) *INTENT; WILFULNESS.* The general rule of criminal law that a criminal intent is a necessary element has been held to apply to the crime of obstructing a highway,[33] although a majority of cases hold the intent of the obstructer immaterial.[34] But in some states the statutes specifically require that wilfulness be proved,[35] and under such a statute there can be no legal conviction where

S. C. 425, 54 S. E. 608; Isham *v.* State, 49 Tex. Cr. 324, 92 S. W. 808; Richardson *v.* State, 47 Tex. Cr. 592, 85 S. W. 282; Torno *v.* State, (Tex. Cr. App. 1903) 75 S. W. 500; Hatfield *v.* State, (Tex. Cr. App. 1902) 67 S. W. 110; Dodson *v.* State, (Tex. Cr. App. 1899) 49 S. W. 78; State *v.* Horlacher, 16 Wash. 325, 47 Pac. 748.

28. See cases cited *infra*, this note.

Evidence held sufficient see Brumley *v.* State, 83 Ark. 236, 103 S. W. 615; Johns *v.* State, 104 Ind. 557, 4 N. E. 153; Hays *v.* State, 8 Ind. 425; Clift *v.* State, 6 Ind. App. 199, 33 N. E. 211; Zimmerman *v.* State, 4 Ind. App. 583, 31 N. E. 550; Com. *v.* Carr, 143 Mass. 84, 9 N. E. 28; State *v.* Lord, 16 N. H. 357; Com. *v.* New Bethlehem Borough, 15 Pa. Super. Ct. 158; State *v.* Kendall, 54 S. C. 192, 32 S. E. 300; State *v.* Sartor, 2 Strobh. (S. C.) 60.

Evidence held insufficient see People *v.* Young, 72 Ill. 411; Houston *v.* People, 63 Ill. 185; State *v.* Weimer, 64 Iowa 243, 20 N. W. 171; State *v.* Campbell, 80 Mo. App. 110; People *v.* Livingston, 27 Hun (N. Y.) 105, 63 How. Pr. 242; Farrier *v.* State, 54 Tex. Cr. 536, 113 S. W. 763; Isham *v.* State, 49 Tex. Cr. 324, 92 S. W. 808; McMillan *v.* State, (Tex. Cr. App. 1903) 77 S. W. 790; Hatfield *v.* State, (Tex. Cr. App. 1902) 67 S. W. 110; Watson *v.* State, 25 Tex. App. 651, 8 S. W. 817; Baker *v.* State, 21 Tex. App. 264, 17 S. W. 144; State *v.* Horlacher, 16 Wash. 325, 47 Pac. 748; U. S. *v.* Tucker, 28 Fed. Cas. No. 16,543*a*, Hayw. & H. 269.

Words alone are not an obstruction. Chaffin *v.* State, (Tex. Cr. App. 1893) 24 S. W. 411, threatening language used to road overseer causing him to desist removing fence.

29. *Iowa.*— State *v.* Glass, 42 Iowa 56, holding that where establishment was on condition it must appear that the condition was performed.

Michigan.— Moore *v.* People, 2 Dougl. 420.

Missouri.— State *v.* Ramsey, 76 Mo. 398; State *v.* Cunningham, 61 Mo. App. 188; State *v.* Parsons, 53 Mo. App. 135; State *v.* Scott, 27 Mo. App. 541.

North Carolina.— State *v.* Stewart, 91 N. C. 566.

Pennsylvania.— Com. *v.* Oliphant, Add. 345.

Virginia.— Bailey *v.* Com., 78 Va. 19.

See 25 Cent. Dig. tit. "Highways," § 451.

30. State *v.* Eisele, 37 Minn. 256, 33 N. W. 785. See also State *v.* Dubuque, etc., R. Co., 88 Iowa 508, 55 N. W. 727.

31. *Arkansas.*— Howard *v.* State, 47 Ark. 431, 2 S. W. 331.

Kentucky.— Com. *v.* Abney, 4 T. B. Mon. 477.

Massachusetts.—Com. *v.* Coupe, 128 Mass. 63.

Missouri.— State *v.* Ramsey, 76 Mo. 398; State *v.* Davis, 27 Mo. App. 624; State *v.* Bishop, 22 Mo. App. 435.

New Jersey.— State *v.* New Jersey Cent. R. Co., 32 N. J. L. 220.

Texas.— McWhorter *v.* State, 43 Tex. 666; Hall *v.* State, 13 Tex. App. 269; Michel *v.* State, 12 Tex. App. 108. But see Meuly *v.* State, 3 Tex. App. 382.

See 25 Cent. Dig. tit. "Highways," § 451 *et seq.*

32. *Illinois.*— Lowe *v.* People, 28 Ill. 518; Martin *v.* People, 23 Ill. 395.

Kentucky.— Illinois Cent. R. Co. *v.* Com., 104 Ky. 362, 47 S. W. 255, 20 Ky. L. Rep. 748, 990, near a town and within the town.

North Carolina.—State *v.* Purify, 86 N. C. 681, "public highway and private cartway."

Ohio.— State *v.* Carman, Tapp. 162.

South Carolina.—State *v.* Graham, 15 Rich. 310.

Texas.— Woody *v.* State, (Cr. App. 1902) 69 S. W. 155.

See 25 Cent. Dig. tit. "Highways," § 452.

Variance held not to exist see Palatka, etc., R. Co. *v.* State, 23 Fla. 546, 3 So. 158, 11 Am. St. Rep. 395; State *v.* Teeters, 97 Iowa 458, 66 N. W. 754 (under indictment averring obstruction of highway, conviction for obstruction of highway by dedication or prescription); State *v.* Beeman, 35 Me. 242; State *v.* Transue, 131 Mo. App. 323, 111 S. W. 523.

Immaterial variance see State *v.* Southard, 6 Pennew. (Del.) 247, 66 Atl. 372; State *v.* Weese, 67 Mo. App. 466; State *v.* Pullen, 43 Mo. App. 620; State *v.* Rhodes, 35 Mo. App. 360; Skinner *v.* State, (Tex. Cr. App. 1901) 65 S. W. 1073.

33. Freeman *v.* State, 6 Port. (Ala.) 372; Lensing *v.* State, (Tex. Cr. App. 1898) 45 S. W. 572.

34. *Arkansas.*— McKibbin *v.* State, 40 Ark. 480.

Indiana.— State *v.* Baltimore, etc., R. Co., 120 Ind. 298, 22 N. E. 307; Nichols *v.* State, 89 Ind. 298; State *v.* Phipps, 4 Ind. 515.

Iowa.— State *v.* Gould, 40 Iowa 372.

Pennsylvania.— Com. *v.* Dicken, 145 Pa. St. 453, 22 Atl. 1043.

West Virginia.—State *v.* Chesapeake, etc., R. Co., 24 W. Va. 809.

Wisconsin.— State *v.* Dehn, 126 Wis. 168, 105 N. W. 795.

See 25 Cent. Dig. tit. "Highways," § 446.

35. See the statutes of the several states. And see the following cases:

Alabama.— Prim *v.* State, 36 Ala. 244.

Florida.— Savannah, etc., R. Co. *v.* State, 23 Fla. 579, 3 So. 204.

appeals are allowed in this class of prosecutions, the practice therein being governed by the local law.[45]

f. Punishment. The punishment for obstructing a highway is prescribed by local law.[46]

VII. USE OF HIGHWAY, AND LAW OF THE ROAD.[47]

A. Right and Mode of Use — 1. In General. A public highway is open for use by the entire public,[48] or any part thereof,[49] simply for passage,[50] in any

S. W. 382; Skinner *v.* State, (Cr. App. 1901) 65 S. W. 1073.

England.— Rex *v.* North-Eastern R. Co., 19 Cox C. C. 682, 70 L. J. K. B. 548, 84 L. T. Rep. N. S. 502, 49 Wkly. Rep. 524.

See 25 Cent. Dig. tit. "Highways," § 453.

Instructions held improper see State *v.* Gould, 40 Iowa 372; State *v.* Craig, 79 Mo. App. 412 ("practically" maintained fence at given point misleading); State *v.* Cardwell, 44 N. C. 245; Isham *v.* State, 49 Tex. Cr. 324, 92 S. W. 808; Torno *v.* State, (Tex. Cr. App. 1903) 75 S. W. 500; Pierce *v.* State, (Tex. Cr. App. 1893) 22 S. W. 587.

The court should define "wilful," when requested. Lensing *v.* State, (Tex. Cr. App. 1898) 45 S. W. 572; Sneed *v.* State, 28 Tex. App. 56, 11 S. W. 834.

Instructions must be considered as a whole to determine their correctness and sufficiency. State *v.* Craig, 79 Mo. App. 412; State *v.* Tyler, 54 S. C. 294, 32 S. E. 422.

45. Sanders *v.* State, 18 Ark. 198; Com. *v.* Feriel, 75 S. W. 231, 25 Ky. L. Rep. 314 (only where fine is more than fifty dollars); Conner *v.* State, 21 Tex. App. 176, 17 S. W. 157 (where the record does not show that defendant disobeyed the order).

Appeal refused see Chapin *v.* State, 24 Conn. 236 (although title to land in question); Gregory *v.* Com., 2 Dana (Ky.) 417.

46. *Connecticut.*— State *v.* Smith, 7 Conn. 428.

Illinois.— See Gilbert *v.* People, 121 Ill. App. 423.

Indiana.— State *v.* Southern Indiana Gas Co., 169 Ind. 124, 81 N. E. 1149; Hoch *v.* State, 20 Ind. App. 64, 50 N. E. 93, twenty-five dollars held not excessive.

Kentucky.— Com. *v.* Enders, 8 Ky. L. Rep. 522, fine and imprisonment.

New York.— Syracuse, etc., Plank Road Co. *v.* People, 66 Barb. 25, common-law punishment.

Pennsylvania.— Taggart *v.* Com., 21 Pa. St. 527, fine and abatement of nuisance.

South Carolina.— State *v.* Floyd, 39 S. C. 23, 17 S. E. 505.

See 25 Cent. Dig. tit. "Highways," § 454. And see *supra*, V, I, 2.

47. **Use of city street generally** see Municipal Corporations, 28 Cyc. 907 *et seq.*

Use of city street by municipality for purpose other than highway see Municipal Corporations, 28 Cyc. 853.

Grants of right to use city streets see Municipal Corporations, 28 Cyc. 866.

Temporary use of city streets by abutters see Municipal Corporations, 28 Cyc. 864.

48. *Connecticut.*— Goodwin *v.* Avery, 26 Conn. 585, 68 Am. Dec. 410, right of hackman assigned to place in funeral procession.

Louisiana.— Barbin *v.* Police Jury, 15 La. Ann. 544, even strangers and foreigners.

Maine.— See Wight *v.* Phillips, 36 Me. 551, invitee before road opened.

Mississippi.— Covington County *v.* Collins, 92 Miss. 330, 45 So. 854, 131 Am. St. Rep. 527, 14 L. R. A. 1087.

New York.— Galen *v.* Clyde Plank Road Co., 27 Barb. 543. See People *v.* Moore, 50 Hun 356, 3 N. Y. Suppl. 159, holding that one who builds a village upon his land, reserving the title to the thoroughfares, over which the public officers exercise no authority, cannot prevent tradesmen from entering it for the purpose of delivering their wares, in order to compel the inhabitants to deal with those nominated by him.

Ohio.— Ferris *v.* Bramble, 5 Ohio St. 109.

See 25 Cent. Dig. tit. "Highways," § 456 *et seq.*

Contest for position.— Where two parties, each without any better right than the other, strive to occupy the same place in the public highway, he is in the wrong who first uses force. Goodwin *v.* Avery, 26 Conn. 585, 68 Am. Dec. 410. Thus where plaintiff's cab occupied a position in the line at a cab stand which defendant was entitled to, defendant had no right to take forcible possession of the position by backing his cab against plaintiff's horse, to its injury. Curley *v.* Electric Vehicle Co., 68 N. Y. App. Div. 18, 74 N. Y. Suppl. 35. But see Bundy *v.* Carter, 21 Nova Scotia 296.

49. Dunham *v.* Rackliff, 71 Me. 345; Foster *v.* Goddard, 40 Me. 64; Palmer *v.* Barker, 11 Me. 338; Brooks *v.* Hart, 14 N. H. 307; Reg. *v.* Pratt, L. R. 3 Q. B. 64, 37 L. J. M. C. 23, 16 Wkly. Rep. 146, riding on foot-paths beside roads. But see Compton *v.* Revere, 179 Mass. 413, 60 N. E. 931, holding that the fact that some wagons passed over the highway was insufficient to show that it was open for public travel.

Use of sidewalk by bicyclists and others on city streets see Municipal Corporations, 28 Cyc. 911.

50. Gurnsey *v.* Northern California Power Co., 7 Cal. App. 534, 94 Pac. 858 (holding that a county board can only control road to facilitate travel); Smith *v.* Leavenworth, 15 Kan. 81; State *v.* Buckner, 61 N. C. 558, 98 Am. Dec. 83.

In Louisiana the right of passage over a highway is, under Civ. Code, art. 727, a discontinuous servitude, which, under article 766, can be established only by title, immemorial

proper regulations[58] concerning registration and license;[59] and travelers by automobile have equal rights and liabilities with other forms of travel.[60]

b. Traction Engines and Other Heavy Equipment.[61] Traction engines or other heavy vehicles may be used on highways under proper regulations,[62] such as a requirement that the engine be accompanied by a flagman to warn travel.[63] The use must be reasonable,[64] and not to the inconvenience of other means of travel or to the damage of the road.[65]

c. Bicycles.[66] A bicycle is a vehicle which has a right to use the highway

Michigan.—Wright *v.* Crane, 142 Mich. 508, 106 N. W. 71.

New York.—Nason *v.* West, 31 Misc. 583, 65 N. Y. Suppl. 651.

But not automobile races. Atty.-Gen. *v.* Blackpool, 71 J. P. 478.

58. *California.*—*In re* Berry, 147 Cal. 523, 82 Pac. 44, 109 Am. St. Rep. 160, prohibiting use on country roads at night.

Missouri.—State *v.* Swagerty, 203 Mo. 517, 102 S. W. 483, 10 L. R. A. N. S. 601; Hall *v.* Compton, 130 Mo. App. 675, 108 S. W. 1122.

New Jersey.—State *v.* Unwin, 75 N. J. L. 500, 68 Atl. 110 [*affirming* 73 N. J. L. 529, 64 Atl. 163].

Pennsylvania.—Radnor Tp. *v.* Bell, 27 Pa. Super. Ct. 1.

England.—Musgrave *v.* Kennison, 20 Cox C. C. 874, 69 J. P. 341, 3 Loc. Gov. 932, 92 L. T. Rep. N. S. 865, 21 T. L. R. 600; Troughton *v.* Manning, 20 Cox C. C. 861, 69 J. P. 207, 3 Loc. Gov. 548, 92 L. T. Rep. N. S. 855, 21 T. L. R. 408, 53 Wkly. Rep. 493, prohibition against reckless driving in statute held to mean reckless as to public and not as to passengers.

See 25 Cent. Dig. tit. "Highways," § 457 *et seq.*

59. State *v.* Unwin, 75 N. J. L. 500, 68 Atl. 110 [*affirming* 73 N. J. L. 529, 64 Atl. 163].

60. *Delaware.*—Simeone *v.* Lindsay, 6 Pennew. 224, 65 Atl. 778.

Indiana.—Indiana Springs Co. *v.* Brown, 165 Ind. 465, 74 N. E. 615, 1 L. R. A. N. S. 238.

Iowa.—House *v.* Cramer, 134 Iowa 374, 112 N. W. 3, 10 L. R. A. N. S. 655, by statute.

Kentucky.—Shinkle *v.* McCullough, 116 Ky. 960, 77 S. W. 196, 25 Ky. L. Rep. 1143, 105 Am. St. Rep. 249.

Maine.—Towle *v.* Morse, 103 Me. 250, 68 Atl. 1044.

Massachusetts.—Hennessey *v.* Taylor, 189 Mass. 583, 76 N. E. 224, 3 L. R. A. N. S. 345.

Michigan.—Wright *v.* Crane, 142 Mich. 508, 106 N. W. 71.

Missouri.—Hall *v.* Compton, 130 Mo. App. 675, 108 S. W. 1122; McFern *v.* Gardner, 121 Mo. App. 1, 97 S. W. 972.

New York.—Lorenz *v.* Tisdale, 127 N. Y. App. Div. 433, 111 N. Y. Suppl. 173; Thies *v.* Thomas, 77 N. Y. Suppl. 276.

61. Weight of loads on city streets see MUNICIPAL CORPORATIONS, 28 Cyc. 911.

62. State *v.* Kowolski, 96 Iowa 346, 65 N. W. 306.

63. State *v.* Kowolski, 96 Iowa 346, 65 N. W. 306, holding a flagman necessary even where horses are going in the same direction as the engine.

Such a statute does not apply to machines not in operation (Keeley *v.* Shanley, 140 Pa. St. 213, 21 Atl. 305), or where horses are standing (Cudd *v.* Larson, 117 Wis. 103, 93 N. W. 810).

Where the whistle on a steam roller is operated with no flagman ahead the operator is guilty of negligence. Buchanan *v.* Cranford Co., 112 N. Y. App. Div. 278, 98 N. Y. Suppl. 378.

64. Miller *v.* Addison, 96 Md. 731, 54 Atl. 967; Macomber *v.* Nichols, 34 Mich. 212, 22 Am. Rep. 522, holding further that reasonableness is a question of fact for the determination of the jury.

65. Covington County *v.* Collins, 92 Miss. 330, 45 So. 854, 131 Am. St. Rep. 527, 14 L. R. A. N. S. 1087; Com. *v.* Allen, 148 Pa. St. 358, 23 Atl. 1115, 33 Am. St. Rep. 830, 16 L. R. A. 148 (holding that to run a traction engine, drawing unusually large loads, back and forth several times a day over an ordinary country highway, to the inconvenience and danger of all other travelers and the damage of the road and bridges, which were constructed for ordinary and probable use, constitutes a public nuisance); Reg. *v.* Chittenden, 15 Cox C. C. 725, 49 J. P. 503; Jeffery *v.* St. Pancras Vestry, 63 L. J. Q. B. 618, 10 Reports 554 (steam roller). See also Macomber *v.* Nichols, 34 Mich. 212, 22 Am. Rep. 522, holding that the question cannot depend on whether the engine was calculated to frighten horses of ordinary gentleness.

Expenses of extraordinary traffic consisting of the damages wrought by traction engines may be considered. Chichester *v.* Foster, [1906] 1 K. B. 167, 70 J. P. 73, 75 L. J. K. B. 33, 4 Loc. Gov. 205, 93 L. T. Rep. N. S. 750, 22 T. L. R. 18, 54 Wkly. Rep. 199; Atty.-Gen. *v.* Scott, [1905] 2 K. B. 160, 69 J. P. 109, 74 L. J. K. B. 803, 3 Loc. Gov. 272, 93 L. T. Rep. N. S. 249, 21 T. L. R. 211 [*affirming* [1904] 1 K. B. 404, 68 J. P. 137, 73 L. J. K. B. 196, 2 Loc. Gov. 461, 89 L. T. Rep. N. S. 726]; London County *v.* Wood, [1897] 2 Q. B. 482, 18 Cox C. C. 637, 61 J. P. 567, 66 L. J. Q. B. 712, 77 L. T. Rep. N. S. 312, 13 T. L. R. 558, 46 Wkly. Rep. 143; Reigate Rural Dist. *v.* Sutton District Water Co., 71 J. P. 405, 5 Loc. Gov. 917; High Wycombe Rural Dist. *v.* Palmer, 69 J. P. 167; Hemsworth Rural Dist. *v.* Micklethwaite, 68 J. P. 345, 2 Loc. Gov. 1084; Wycombe Rural Dist. *v.* Smith, 67 J. P. 75; Pethick *v.* Dorset County, 62 J. P. 579, 14 T. L. R. 548; Driscoll *v.* Poplar Bd. of Works, 62 J. P. 40, 14 T. L. R. 99.

66. Use of bicycles on sidewalk on city streets see MUNICIPAL CORPORATIONS, 28 Cyc. 911.

equally with other vehicles,[67] subject to legislative or municipal regulation.[68] Bicyclists should use due care to avoid pedestrians,[69] but are not liable merely for fright of horses caused without the bicyclist's negligence.[70]

3. Stopping and Standing.[71] Travelers may within reason stop temporarily on the highway; [72] but not unreasonably, or to such an extent as to interfere with other travelers or to prevent the free use of the road.[73]

B. Law of the Road — 1. To What Roads Applicable. The law of the road extends to all public highways however created,[74] and may also be applicable to roads not public highways.[75]

67. *Illinois.*— North Chicago St. R. Co. *v.* Cossar, 203 Ill. 608, 68 N. E. 88.

Indiana.— Holland *v.* Bartch, 120 Ind. 46, 22 N. E. 83, 16 Am. St. Rep. 307.

Minnesota.— Thompson *v.* Dodge, 58 Minn. 555, 60 N. W. 545, 49 Am. St. Rep. 533, 28 L. R. A. 608.

Pennsylvania.— Lacy *v.* Winn, 4 Pa. Dist. 409; Lacey *v.* Winn, 3 Pa. Dist. 811.

Rhode Island.— State *v.* Collins, 16 R. I. 371, 17 Atl. 131, 3 L. R. A. 394.

England.—Hatton *v.* Treeby, [1897] 2 Q. B. 452, 18 Cox C. C. 633, 61 J. P. 586, 66 L. J. Q. B. 729, 77 L. T. Rep. N. S. 309, 13 T. L. R. 556, 46 Wkly. Rep. 6.

68. Twilley *v.* Perkins, 77 Md. 252, 26 Atl. 286, 39 Am. St. Rep. 408, 19 L. R. A. 632 (excluded from bridge for fear of frightening horses); State *v.* Bradford, 78 Minn. 387, 81 N. W. 202, 47 L. R. A. 144; State *v.* Yopp, 97 N. C. 477, 2 S. E. 458, 2 Am. St. Rep. 305; Radnor Tp. *v.* Bell, 27 Pa. Super. Ct. 1 (speed regulated).

But a bicycle is not a carriage within the meaning of a statute relating to carriages (Richardson *v.* Danvers, 176 Mass. 413, 57 N. E. 688, 79 Am. St. Rep. 320, 50 L. R. A. 127), nor need a bicycle avoid an ordinary team under a law that light vehicles must give way to heavily laden wagons (Foote *v.* American Product Co., 195 Pa. St. 190, 45 Atl. 934, 78 Am. St. Rep. 806, 49 L. R. A. 764. See also Taylor *v.* Union Traction Co., 184 Pa. St. 465, 40 Atl. 159, 47 L. R. A. 289).

69. North Chicago St. R. Co. *v.* Cossar, 203 Ill. 608, 68 N. E. 88.

70. Thompson *v.* Dodge, 58 Minn. 555, 60 N. W. 545, 49 Am. St. Rep. 533, 28 L. R. A. 608; Haines *v.* Moore, 10 N. J. L. J. 122.

71. Automobile standing on road see Motor Vehicles, 28 Cyc. 30.

Stopping or standing on city, town, or village streets see Municipal Corporations, 28 Cyc. 910.

72. *Iowa.*— Duffy *v.* Dubuque, 63 Iowa 171, 18 N. W. 900, 50 Am. Rep. 743.

Louisiana.— Mahan *v.* Everett, 50 La. Ann. 1162, 23 So. 883.

Maryland.— Murray *v.* McShane, 52 Md. 217, 36 Am. Rep. 367.

Massachusetts.— Smethurst *v.* Barton Square Independent Cong. Church, 148 Mass. 261, 19 N. E. 387, 12 Am. St. Rep. 550, 2 L. R. A. 695; Britton *v.* Cummington, 107 Mass. 347, holding that a person journeying on a highway does not necessarily forfeit his rights as a traveler by temporarily leaving his horse and wagon in charge of a boy of twelve.

New York.— Nead *v.* Roscoe Lumber Co., 54 N. Y. App. Div. 621, 66 N. Y. Suppl. 419, to water horses.

Ohio.— Clark *v.* Fry, 8 Ohio St. 358, 72 Am. Dec. 590.

Pennsylvania.— Lacy *v.* Winn, 4 Pa. Dist. 409, 3 Pa. Dist. 811, bicycle left temporarily beside street.

England.— Goodman *v.* Taylor, 5 C. & P. 410, 24 E. C. L. 630; Rex *v.* Russell, 6 East 427, 2 Smith K. B. 424, 8 Rev. Rep. 506, 102 Eng. Reprint 1350.

See 25 Cent. Dig. tit. "Highways," § 467.

One may turn to the left to stop at his own home. Peltier *v.* Bradley, etc., Co., 67 Conn. 42, 34 Atl. 712, 32 L. R. A. 651; Palmer *v.* Barker, 11 Me. 338; Young *v.* Cowden, 98 Tenn. 577, 40 S. W. 1088 (notwithstanding statute requiring turning to right on stopping). But see Heffernan *v.* Barber, 36 N. Y. App. Div. 163, 55 N. Y. Suppl. 418, holding that the driver must turn to the right, although the stop is near by.

A sudden stop may be negligent. Maas *v.* Fauser, 36 Misc. (N. Y.) 813, 74 N. Y. Suppl. 861.

Whether leaving a team across a street is negligent is a question for the jury. Nesbit *v.* Crosby, 74 Conn. 554, 51 Atl. 550.

Whether defendant was negligent in rolling hogsheads down skids from a truck to the sidewalk without using danger signals or stationing any one to warn pedestrians is a question for the jury. Blaustein *v.* Guindon, 146 N. Y. 368, 41 N. E. 88 [*affirming* 83 Hun 5, 31 N. Y. Suppl. 559].

73. Turner *v.* Holtzman, 54 Md. 148, 39 Am. Rep. 361; Lippincott *v.* Lasher, 44 N. J. Eq. 120, 14 Atl. 103; Atty.-Gen. *v.* Brighton, etc., Co-operative Supply Assoc., [1900] 1 Ch. 276, 69 L. J. Ch. 204, 81 L. T. Rep. N. S. 762, 16 T. L. R. 144, 48 Wkly. Rep. 314 (holding as to stopping of teams on street to unload that if this use prevents the use of the highway to the extent allowed by law it must be stopped); Rex *v.* Jones, 3 Campb. 230, 13 Rev. Rep. 797; Rex *v.* Cross, 3 Campb. 224, 13 Rev. Rep. 794; Martin *v.* London County Council, 80 L. T. Rep. N. S. 866, 15 T. L. R. 431.

74. See cases cited *infra*, note 75 *et seq.*

75. Jaquith *v.* Richardson, 8 Metc. (Mass.) 213; Com. *v.* Gammons, 23 Pick. (Mass.) 201.

The rule extends to all places appropriated either de jure or de facto, to the purpose of passing with carriages, etc., whether they are

e. Pedestrians — (I) *In General.* The law of the road does not apply to pedestrians, who may pass on either side of vehicles,[5] may walk on any part of the road,[6] and need not cross at a regular crossing.[7] Persons driving vehicles are bound to use due care to avoid pedestrians,[8] who, however, have no right of way,[9] and who cannot recover when negligent.[10]

(II) *Crossing Road.* A pedestrian need not cross at a regular crossing,[11] and wherever he crosses he may recover for injuries sustained if he has not been guilty of contributory negligence,[12] although he does not stop, look, and listen,[13]

773, 68 N. Y. Suppl. 840; Foote v. American Product Co., 195 Pa. St. 190, 45 Atl. 934, 78 Am. St. Rep. 806, 49 L. R. A. 764.

5. Yore v. Mueller Coal, etc., Co., 147 Mo. 679, 49 S. W. 855; Savage v. Gerstner, 36 N. Y. App. Div. 220, 55 N. Y. Suppl. 306; Lloyd v. Ogleby, 5 C. B. N. S. 667, 94 E. C. L. 667; Cotterill v. Starkey, 8 C. & P. 691, 34 E. C. L. 965. See also Schaffer v. Baker Transfer Co., 29 N. Y. App. Div. 459, 51 N. Y. Suppl. 1092, where a truck was on the left side of the road, and plaintiff was held not necessarily negligent, as he had a right to expect it to be on the right side.

But a pedestrian should not compel a vehicle to leave the beaten track. Beach v. Parmeter, 23 Pa. St. 196.

6. McManus v. Woolverton, 19 N. Y. Suppl. 545 [*affirmed* in 138 N. Y. 648, 34 N. E. 513], in the center.

7. See *infra*, note 11.

8. *California.*— Sykes v. Lawlor, 49 Cal. 236.

Delaware.—Simeone v. Lindsay, 6 Pennew. 224, 65 Atl. 778.

Missouri.— Lee v. Jones, 181 Mo. 291, 79 S. W. 927, 103 Am. St. Rep. 596; Vaughn v. Scade, 30 Mo. 600 (in crowded street); O'Hara v. Globe Iron, etc., Co., 66 Mo. App. 53.

New York.— Seaman v. Mott, 127 N. Y. App. Div. 18, 110 N. Y. Suppl. 1040; Schaffer v. Baker Transfer Co., 29 N. Y. App. Div. 459, 51 N. Y. Suppl. 1092; Murphy v. Weidmann Cooperage, 1 N. Y. App. Div. 283, 37 N. Y. Suppl. 151; McManus v. Woolverton, 19 N. Y. Suppl. 545 [*affirmed* in 138 N. Y. 648, 34 N. E. 513], holding that extra care must be used in fog.

Pennsylvania.— Streitfeld v. Shoemaker, 185 Pa. St. 265, 39 Atl. 967; Kleinert v. Rees, 6 Pa. Super. Ct. 594.

Rhode Island.— Nelson v. Braman, 22 R. I. 283, 47 Atl. 696; Bennett v. Lovell, 12 R. I. 166, 34 Am. Rep. 628.

Vermont.— Thompson v. National Express Co., 66 Vt. 358, 29 Atl. 311.

United States.— Garside v. New York Transp. Co., 146 Fed. 588.

Persons approaching from rear or sides.— It is not the duty of the driver of a wagon to look out for persons who may approach the wagon from the rear or the sides, and warn them of the danger of falling under the wheels. Rice v. Buffalo Steel House Co., 17 N. Y. App. Div. 462, 45 N. Y. Suppl. 277.

Driver held not negligent see McNamara v. Beck, 21 Ind. App. 483, 52 N. E. 707 (two-year-old child not seen by driver); Young v. Omnibus Co. Gen., 180 Pa. St. 75, 36 Atl. 403 (where plaintiff skating fell against horses whose driver was looking the other way).

9. Belton v. Baxter, 54 N. Y. 245, 13 Am. Rep. 578, 14 Abb. Pr. N. S. 404; Barker v. Savage, 45 N. Y. 191, 6 Am. Rep. 66; Seaman v. Mott, 127 N. Y. App. Div. 18, 110 N. Y. Suppl. 1040; Savage v. Gerstner, 36 N. Y. App. Div. 220, 55 N. Y. Suppl. 306; Reens v. Mail, etc., Pub. Co., 10 Misc. (N. Y.) 122, 30 N. Y. Suppl. 913 [*affirmed* in 150 N. Y. 582, 44 N. E. 1128].

10. Simeone v. Lindsay, 6 Pennew. (Del.) 224, 65 Atl. 778; Moebus v. Herrmann, 108 N. Y. 349, 15 N. E. 415, 2 Am. St. Rep. 440 (holding, however, that a pedestrian need not necessarily look both ways before crossing street); Kleinert v. Rees, 6 Pa. Super. Ct. 594. See also Quirk v. St. Louis United El. Co., 126 Mo. 279, 28 S. W. 1080.

Heedlessly standing in the street is negligence. Evans v. Adams Express Co., 122 Ind. 362, 23 N. E. 1039, 7 L. R. A. 678; Joslin v. Le Baron, 44 Mich. 160, 6 N. W. 214; Stiles v. Geesey, 71 Pa. St. 439.

11. Simons v. Gaynor, 89 Ind. 165; Moebus v. Herrmann, 108 N. Y. 349, 15 N. E. 415, 2 Am. St. Rep. 440; Denver v. Sherret, 88 Fed. 226, 31 C. C. A. 499.

12. Crowley v. Strouse, (Cal. 1893) 33 Pac. 456 (so holding, although plaintiff failed to use the best course); Carland v. Young, 119 Mass. 150; Fales v. Dearborn, 1 Pick. (Mass.) 345; Belton v. Baxter, 58 N. Y. 411 (holding also that it is a question for the jury whether plaintiff should have known of the relative speed of two vehicles approaching); Williams v. Richards, 3 C. & K. 81.

A pedestrian crossing need not anticipate recklessness of vehicles. Stringer v. Frost, 116 Ind. 477, 19 N. E. 331, 9 Am. St. Rep. 875, 2 L. R. A. 614; O'Reilly v. Utah, etc., Stage Co., 87 Hun (N. Y.) 406, 34 N. Y. Suppl. 358.

The high degree of diligence required at a railroad crossing is not required of a person about to cross a public street, to avoid contact with vehicles. Eaton v. Cripps, 94 Iowa 176, 62 N. W. 687.

Plaintiff held negligent see Belton v. Baxter, 54 N. Y. 245, 13 Am. Rep. 578, 14 Abb. Pr. N. S. 404, miscalculation where plaintiff's chances were close.

13. Orr v. Garabold, 85 Ga. 373, 11 S. E. 778; Shea v. Reems, 36 La. Ann. 966; Purtell v. Jordan, 156 Mass. 573, 31 N. E. 652 (plaintiff passing from behind team); Shapleigh v. Wyman, 134 Mass. 118; Bowser v. Wellington, 126 Mass. 391; Moebus v. Herrmann, 108 N. Y. 349, 15 N. E. 415, 2 Am. St. Rep. 440; Barker v. Savage, 45 N. Y.

where he is run down and injured by a team recklessly driven by defendant or his servant.[14]

f. Vehicles Having the Right of Way. Certain vehicles have by law the right of way in the streets,[15] such as fire apparatus,[16] ambulances,[17] and mail wagons.[18]

C. Care and Negligence in Use of Road [19] — **1. In General.** The nature and degree of care to be exercised in the use of highways depends entirely on the circumstances of each particular case,[20] and the duty of care is in general mutual.[21] There is no liability for the effects of an unavoidable accident,[22] and plaintiff can recover when,[23] and only when,[24] defendant's wrongful act or negligence is the

191, 6 Am. Rep. 66; Reens *v.* Mail, etc., Pub. Co., 10 Misc. (N. Y.) 122, 30 N. Y. Suppl. 913 [*affirmed* in 150 N. Y. 582, 44 N. E. 1128]; Chisholm *v.* Knickerbocker Ice Co., 1 N. Y. Suppl. 743 (not watching to see which side a wagon went of a street car).

Wagon passing road corner.— One crossing a street at a corner is not bound to guard against a wagon which may be passing around the corner. Dater *v.* Fletcher, 14 Misc. (N. Y.) 288, 35 N. Y. Suppl. 686; Rottenberg *v.* Segelke, 6 Misc. (N. Y.) 3, 25 N. Y. Suppl. 997 [*affirmed* in 148 N. Y. 734, 42 N. E. 725]; Harris *v.* Commercial Ice Co., 153 Pa. St. 278, 25 Atl. 1133.

14. Orr *v.* Garabold, 85 Ga. 373, 11 S. E. 778; Simons *v.* Gaynor, 89 Ind. 165; Moebus *v.* Herrmann, 108 N. Y. 349, 15 N. E. 415, 2 Am. St. Rep. 440; Van Houten *v.* Fleischman, 1 Misc. (N. Y.) 130, 20 N. Y. Suppl. 643 [*affirmed* in 142 N. Y. 624, 37 N. E. 565]; Cotton *v.* Wood, 8 C. B. N. S. 568, 7 Jur. N. S. 168, 29 L. J. C. P. 333, 98 E. C. L. 568.

15. See Kansas City *v.* McDonald, 60 Kan. 481, 57 Pac. 123, 45 L. R. A. 429.

16. Farley *v.* New York, 152 N. Y. 222, 46 N. E. 506, 57 Am. St. Rep. 511, holding that a statute limiting speed does not apply to the fire department. But see Morse *v.* Sweenie, 15 Ill. App. 486, holding that even the fire department has no right to drive immoderately.

17. Smith *v.* American S. P. C. A., 7 Misc. (N. Y.) 158, 27 N. Y. Suppl. 315.

18. Bolton *v.* Colder, 1 Watts (Pa.) 360. See also Post-Office, 31 Cyc. 1000 *et seq.*

19. **Negligence in operation of automobile** see Motor Vehicles, 28 Cyc. 37.

20. *Alabama.*— Carter *v.* Chambers, 79 Ala. 223.

Colorado.—Adams Express Co. *v.* Aldridge, 20 Colo. App. 74, 77 Pac. 6, holding that travelers must so use highway as not necessarily to injure others traveling thereon.

Maine.— Towle *v.* Morse, 103 Me. 250, 68 Atl. 1044, mutual rights between driver of horse and automobile.

Missouri.— Quirk *v.* St. Louis United El. Co., 126 Mo. 279, 28 S. W. 1080.

New York.— Nead *v.* Roscoe Lumber Co., 54 N. Y. App. Div. 621, 66 N. Y. Suppl. 419.

See 25 Cent. Dig. tit. "Highways," § 459 *et seq.*

A bicyclist is bound to exercise what is under the circumstances due care (Cook *v.* Fogarty, 103 Iowa 500, 72 N. W. 677, 39 L. R. A. 488), the question of his negligence being for the jury (Peltier *v.* Bradley, 67 Conn. 42, 34 Atl. 712, 32 L. R. A. 651; Shortsleeve *v.* Stebbins, 77 N. Y. App. Div. 588, 79 N. Y. Suppl. 40, frightening horse; Hershinger *v.* Pennsylvania R. Co., 25 Pa. Super. Ct. 147, driver suddenly turning). No negligence found in bicyclist see Lee *v.* Jones, 181 Mo. 291, 79 S. W. 927, 103 Am. St. Rep. 596; Pick *v.* Thurston, 25 R. I. 36, 54 Atl. 600.

Whether leading a horse in the street is negligent is a question for the jury. Grinnell *v.* Taylor, 85 Hun (N. Y.) 85, 32 N. Y. Suppl. 684 [*affirmed* in 155 N. Y. 653, 49 N. E. 1097].

21. Fletcher *v.* Dixon, 107 Md. 420, 68 Atl. 875; Baker *v.* Fehr, 97 Pa. St. 70.

A traveler upon a public highway has a right to assume within reasonable limits that others using it will exercise reasonable care. Indianapolis St. R. Co. *v.* Hoffman, 40 Ind. App. 508, 82 N. E. 543.

22. Newcomb *v.* Van Zile, 34 Hun (N. Y.) 275 (vehicle sliding down hill); Center *v.* Finney, 17 Barb. (N. Y.) 94 (when defendant not negligent); Miller *v.* Cohen, 173 Pa. St. 488, 34 Atl. 219.

23. *Massachusetts.*— Turner *v.* Page, 186 Mass. 600, 72 N. E. 329 (endeavor of third person to stop horses); McDonald *v.* Snelling, 14 Allen 290, 92 Am. Dec. 768.

Minnesota.— Griggs *v.* Fleckenstein, 14 Minn. 81, 100 Am. Dec. 199, where defendant's team ran away and caused horses of A to run away and injure plaintiff, and defendant was held liable.

New York.— Engelbach *v.* Ibert, 10 Misc. 535, 31 N. Y. Suppl. 438.

Texas.— Houston Transfer Co. *v.* Renard, (Civ. App. 1904) 79 S. W. 838.

Canada.— Bundy *v.* Carter, 21 Nova Scotia 296, where defendant's wrongful displacing of plaintiff in a line of vehicles was held the proximate cause of injuries occurring in plaintiff's struggle to recover his place.

See 25 Cent. Dig. tit. "Highways," § 459 *et seq.*

24. *Illinois.*— North Chicago St. R. Co. *v.* Cossar, 203 Ill. 608, 68 N. E. 88.

Maine.— Smith *v.* French, 83 Me. 108, 21 Atl. 739, 23 Am. St. Rep. 761, holding an owner of cattle not liable for actions of another in driving them out of his field.

Missouri.— Haller *v.* St. Louis, 176 Mo. 606, 75 S. W. 613, where failure to have a flagman was held not the proximate cause of fright of horse at steam roller.

New York.— Berman *v.* Schultz, 84 N. Y. Suppl. 292, boys starting automobile — owner not liable.

3. Frightening Horses. A person frightening horses on a highway is not liable for injury resulting therefrom if he has been guilty of no wrong or negligence;[37] but an action lies for negligently frightening horses and so causing damage,[38] as by automobiles.[39] But persons making use of horses as the means of travel or traffic on the highways have no rights therein superior to those who make use of the ways in other permissible modes; improved methods of locomotion are admissible, and cannot be excluded from existing public roads if not inconsistent with the present methods,[40] and thus automobile noises are not of themselves evidence of negligence,[41] although the operator must take care so to operate his machine as not to frighten horses,[42] and must stop on signal,[43] and even without signal on seeing the fright of horses.[44]

4. Runaways; Horses Left Unhitched in the Road.[45] A person is liable where his horses run away on account of his lack of due care,[46] considering the character

37. Myers *v.* Lape, 101 Ill. App. 182 (horse frightened at pony of small size and unusual color); Pigott *v.* Lilly, 55 Mich. 150, 20 N. W. 879 (shouting directions in endeavor to prevent accident); Heist *v.* Jacoby, 71 Nebr. 395, 98 N. W. 1058; Keeley *v.* Shanley, 140 Pa. St. 213, 21 Atl. 305; Piollet *v.* Simmers, 106 Pa. St. 95, 51 Am. Rep. 496 (whitewashing barrel left beside road); *In re* Upper Mahanoy Tp. Road, 2 Chest. Co. Rep. (Pa.) 375 (from steam locomotive).

38. *Indiana.*— Howe *v.* Young, 16 Ind. 312, by reckless and noisy driving.

Iowa.— Schmid *v.* Humphrey, 48 Iowa 652, 30 Am. Rep. 414, by dogs barking.

Kentucky.—Thomas *v.* Royster, 98 Ky. 206, 32 S. W. 613, 17 Ky. L. Rep. 783, driving by in a gallop.

Maine.— Lynn *v.* Hooper, 93 Me. 46, 44 Atl. 127, 47 L. R. A. 752 (hay cap on side of highway); Jewett *v.* Gage, 55 Me. 538, 92 Am. Dec. 615 (hog loose in road).

Michigan.—Barnes *v.* Brown, 95 Mich. 576, 55 N. W. 439, rope dragging.

Minnesota.— Jones *v.* Snow, 56 Minn. 214, 57 N. W. 478, wagon covered with flags.

Missouri.— Haller *v.* St. Louis, 176 Mo. 606, 75 S. W. 613; Forney *v.* Geldmacher, 75 Mo. 113, 42 Am. Rep. 388 (turning hose on horses); Atkinson *v.* Illinois Milk Co., 44 Mo. App. 153 (driving rapidly up with decorated horse to horse standing).

New York.— Buchanan *v.* Cranford Co., 112 N. Y. App. Div. 278, 98 N. Y. Suppl. 378, whistle on steam roller.

See 25 Cent. Dig. tit. "Highways," § 469.

One transporting unusual articles in a highway should give suitable warning of that fact. McCann *v.* Consolidated Traction Co., 59 N. J. L. 481, 36 Atl. 888, 38 L. R. A. 236; Bennett *v.* Lovell, 12 R. I. 166, 34 Am. Rep. 628.

39. Mason *v.* West, 61 N. Y. App. Div. 40, 70 N. Y. Suppl. 478.

Contributory negligence.— One riding in a carriage who saw that the horses were frightened at an approaching automobile was not guilty of contributory negligence in remaining in the carriage. McIntyre *v.* Orner, 166 Ind. 57, 76 N. E. 750, 117 Am. St. Rep. 359, 4 L. R. A. N. S. 1130.

40. Macomber *v.* Nichols, 34 Mich. 212, 22 Am. Rep. 522.

41. House *v.* Cramer, 134 Iowa 374, 112 N. W. 3, 10 L. R. A. N. S. 655 (engine running while operator leaves car temporarily); Hall *v.* Compton, 130 Mo. App. 675, 108 S. W. 1122; O'Donnell *v.* O'Neill, 130 Mo. App. 360, 109 S. W. 815 (where operator backed machine away and stopped as soon as the horse showed fright); Davis *v.* Maxwell, 108 N. Y. App. Div. 128, 96 N. Y. Suppl. 45 (where horse displayed no sign of fright till automobile got opposite).

42. McIntyre *v.* Orner, 166 Ind. 57, 76 N. E. 750, 117 Am. St. Rep. 359, 4 L. R. A. N. S. 1130; Indiana Springs Co. *v.* Brown, 165 Ind. 465, 74 N. E. 615, 1 L. R. A. N. S. 238; Brinkman *v.* Pacholke, 41 Ind. App. 662, 84 N. E. 762; House *v.* Cramer, 134 Iowa 374, 112 N. W. 3, 10 L. R. A. N. S. 655.

43. *Illinois.*— Ward *v.* Meredith, 220 Ill. 66, 77 N. E. 118 [*affirming* 122 Ill. App. 159].

Indiana.— State *v.* Goodwin, 169 Ind. 265, 82 N. E. 459, statutory signal to stop may be given by any occupant.

Maine.— Towle *v.* Morse, 103 Me. 250, 68 Atl. 1044.

Minnesota.— Mahoney *v.* Maxfield, 102 Minn. 377, 113 N. W. 904, 14 L. R. A. N. S. 251, holding, however, that the automobile driver need not necessarily stop engine.

New York.— Murphy *v.* Wait, 102 N. Y. App. Div. 121, 92 N. Y. Suppl. 253.

See 25 Cent. Dig. tit. "Highways," § 469.

But see Hall *v.* Compton, 130 Mo. App. 675, 108 S. W. 1122, where horse unexpectedly became frightened when stopping machine would have been of no help.

44. Walkup *v.* Beebe, 139 Iowa 395, 116 N. W. 321; Strand *v.* Grinnell Automobile Garage Co., 136 Iowa 68, 113 N. W. 488.

45. **Leaving motor vehicle unattended** see Motor Vehicles, 28 Cyc. 30.

46. Ford *v.* Whiteman, 2 Pennew. (Del.) 355, 45 Atl. 543 (rapid and careless driving); Bigelow *v.* Reed, 51 Me. 325 (although falling of icicles frightened horses); Hall *v.* Huber, 61 Mo. App. 384 (where team is vicious); West *v.* Woodruff, 112 N. Y. App. Div. 133, 97 N. Y. Suppl. 1054; Lynch *v.* Brooklyn City R. Co., 1 Silv. Sup. (N. Y.) 361, 5 N. Y. Suppl. 311 [*affirmed* in 123 N. Y. 657, 25 N. E. 955].

driver is inadmissible;[77] but declarations are admissible if part of *res gestæ*,[78] and the law of the road is admissible,[79] and may be judicially noticed.[80]

c. Trial — (I) *QUESTIONS FOR COURT AND FOR JURY.*[81] Conflicting evidence is for the jury as to questions of fact.[82]

(II) *INSTRUCTIONS.*[83] The court should instruct the jury as to the general principles of law applicable,[84] as to the burden of proof,[85] as to the rights of the parties,[86] as to contributory negligence,[87] and the negligence of defendant,[88] and

Mills, 22 R. I. 211, 47 Atl. 215 (habits of horse); Elwes *v.* Hopkins, [1906] 2 K. B. 1, 21 Cox C. C. 133, 70 J. P. 262, 75 L. J. K. B. 450, 4 Loc. Gov. 615, 94 L. T. Rep. N. S. 547 (evidence of other traffic on road); Plancq *v.* Marks, 21 Cox C. C. 157, 70 J. P. 216, 4 Loc. Gov. 503, 94 L. T. Rep. N. S. 577, 22 T. L. R. 432 (stop-watch as to speed of automobile).

Evidence held incompetent see Belleveau *v.* S. C. Lowe Supply Co., 200 Mass. 237, 86 N. E. 301 (violation of law immaterial unless it contributed to the accident); Hill *v.* Snyder, 44 Mich. 318, 6 N. W. 674 (as to plaintiff's habits of running horses or being intoxicated where it was not claimed that he was intoxicated or running horses at the time); Whissler *v.* Walsh, 165 Pa. St. 352, 30 Atl. 981 (holding that where a driver failed to use care to relieve his horse, who was entangled in a harness whereby he ran away, the disposition of the horse was immaterial on the question of negligence); Bolton *v.* Colder, 1 Watts (Pa.) 360 (custom for leading carriage to incline to right).

77. Dunham *v.* Rackliff, 71 Me. 345; Maguire *v.* Middlesex R. Co., 115 Mass. 239; Tenney *v.* Tuttle, 1 Allen (Mass.) 185; Boick *v.* Bissell, 80 Mich. 260, 45 N. W. 55; O'Neil *v.* Dry Dock, etc., R. Co., 59 N. Y. Super. Ct. 123, 15 N. Y. Suppl. 84 [*affirmed* in 129 N. Y. 125, 29 N. E. 84, 26 Am. St. Rep. 512]; Jacobs *v.* Duke, 1 E. D. Smith (N. Y.) 271.

78. Walkup *v.* Beebe, 139 Iowa 395, 116 N. W. 321 (that another called to defendant to stop his automobile to help plaintiff); Adams *v.* Swift, 172 Mass. 521, 52 N. E. 1068.

Admissions by acts see Adams *v.* Swift, 172 Mass. 521, 52 N. E. 1068.

79. Nadeau *v.* Sawyer, 73 N. H. 70, 59 Atl. 369 (reading statute to jury); Foote *v.* American Product Co., 195 Pa. St. 190, 45 Atl. 934, 78 Am. St. Rep. 806, 49 L. R. A. 764.

80. Turley *v.* Thomas, 8 C. & P. 103, 34 E. C. L. 633.

81. In action for injury by motor vehicle see MOTOR VEHICLES, 28 Cyc. 48.

82. *Illinois.*— Schweinfurth *v.* Dover, 91 Ill. App. 319, identity.

Iowa.— Needy *v.* Littlejohn, 137 Iowa 704, 115 N. W. 483, proximate cause.

Michigan.— Burt *v.* Staffeld, 121 Mich. 390, 80 N. W. 236, negligence of one coasting.

Missouri.— De Maet *v.* Fidelity Storage, etc., Co., 121 Mo. App. 92, 96 S. W. 1045.

Nebraska.— Weber *v.* Lockman, 66 Nebr. 469, 92 N. W. 591, 60 L. R. A. 313.

New York.— Dehmann *v.* Beck, 61 N. Y. App. Div. 505, 70 N. Y. Suppl. 29.

Washington.— Lynch *v.* Kineth, 36 Wash. 368, 78 Pac. 923, 104 Am. St. Rep. 958, character of runaway horses.

See 25 Cent. Dig. tit. "Highways," § 473.

83. In action for injury by motor vehicle see MOTOR VEHICLES, 28 Cyc. 49.

84. Matson *v.* Maupin, 75 Ala. 312; Bennett *v.* Hazen, 66 Mich. 657, 33 N. W. 876; Jennings *v.* Schwab, 64 Mo. App. 13; Lyons *v.* Avis, 5 N. Y. App. Div. 193, 38 N. Y. Suppl. 1104 (duty of care); Moody *v.* Osgood, 60 Barb. (N. Y.) 644 [*affirmed* in 54 N. Y. 488]; Keck *v.* Sandford, 2 Misc. (N. Y.) 484, 22 N. Y. Suppl. 78 (should instruct that fast driving is not of itself evidence of negligence); Newman *v.* Ernst, 10 N. Y. Suppl. 310.

The province of the jury must not be invaded. Christy *v.* Elliott, 216 Ill. 31, 74 N. E. 1035, 108 Am. St. Rep. 196, 1 L. R. A. N. S. 215; Wolf *v.* Hemrich Bros. Brewing Co., 28 Wash. 187, 68 Pac. 440.

85. Brettman *v.* Braun, 37 Ill. App. 17; Smith *v.* Conway, 121 Mass. 216.

86. *Connecticut.*— Plumb *v.* Maher, 76 Conn. 706, 56 Atl. 494.

Illinois.— Ward *v.* Meredith, 220 Ill. 66, 77 N. E. 118 [*affirming* 122 Ill. App. 159]; Christy *v.* Elliott, 216 Ill. 31, 74 N. E. 1035, 108 Am. St. Rep. 196, 1 L. R. A. N. S. 215.

Indiana.— F. W. Cook Brewing Co. *v.* Ball, 22 Ind. App. 656, 52 N. E. 1002, holding that "persons" in charge includes vehicles.

Iowa.— Walkup *v.* Beebe, 139 Iowa 395, 116 N. W. 321 (rights to run automobile); Cook *v.* Fogarty, 103 Iowa 500, 72 N. W. 677, 39 L. R. A. 488; State *v.* Kowolski, 96 Iowa 346, 65 N. W. 306.

Maryland.— Fletcher *v.* Dixon, 107 Md. 420, 68 Atl. 875.

Massachusetts.—Murley *v.* Roche, 130 Mass. 330, plaintiff sitting on sidewalk.

See 25 Cent. Dig. tit. "Highways," § 474.

87. Wells *v.* Gunn, 33 Colo. 217, 79 Pac. 1029; Christy *v.* Elliott, 216 Ill. 31, 74 N. E. 1035, 108 Am. St. Rep. 196, 1 L. R. A. N. S. 215; North Chicago St. R. Co. *v.* Cossar, 203 Ill. 608, 68 N. E. 88; Buxton *v.* Ainsworth, 153 Mich. 315, 116 N. W. 1094; Wright *v.* Fleischmann, 90 N. Y. App. Div. 547, 91 N. Y. Suppl. 116 [*modifying* 41 Misc. 533, 85 N. Y. Suppl. 62]; Cohn *v.* Palmer, 78 N. Y. App. Div. 506, 79 N. Y. Suppl. 762.

88. *Illinois.*—Ward *v.* Meredith, 220 Ill. 66, 77 N. E. 118 [*affirming* 122 Ill. App. 159] (duty of automobilist to stop on frightening horse); Christy *v.* Elliott, 216 Ill. 31, 74

a misdemeanor,[4] and criminal liability for racing,[5] reckless driving,[6] or heavy hauling[7] is often imposed. The complaint should plainly set forth the crime charged,[8] its time,[9] and its place[10] in the public highway.

E. Injuries From Defects or Obstructions — 1. CARE AND DUTY AS TO CONDITION OF ROAD[11] **— a. In General.** Municipalities must use, and are liable to any one injured by their failure to use, at least ordinary diligence[12] at all

4. *Iowa.*— State *v.* Kowolski, 96 Iowa 346, 65 N. W. 306.

Minnesota.— State *v.* Bradford, 78 Minn. 387, 81 N. W. 202, 47 L. R. A. 144, driving team or vehicle on bicycle path.

Pennsylvania.— Com. *v.* Allen, 148 Pa. St. 358, 23 Atl. 1115, 33 Am. St. Rep. 830, 16 L. R. A. 148.

Tennessee.— State *v.* Battery, 6 Baxt. 545, running horse.

England.— Hind *v.* Evans, 70 J. P. 458, 4 Loc. Gov. 1152, leaving horse on road.

Canada.— Reg. *v.* Yates, 6 Can. Cr. Cas. 282, students obstructing sidewalk by marching four abreast.

See 25 Cent. Dig. tit. "Highways," § 476.

But see Posey Tp. *v.* Senour, 42 Ind. App. 580, 86 N. E. 440.

Defacing signboards is a crime by statute, although the boards are erected by an individual. Pullum *v.* State, 88 Ala. 190, 7 So. 148.

Misuse by motor vehicle see MOTOR VEHICLES, 28 Cyc. 49.

Violations of ordinances as to use of city streets see MUNICIPAL CORPORATIONS, 28 Cyc. 915.

5. Redman *v.* State, 33 Ala. 428; State *v.* New, 165 Ind. 571, 76 N. E. 400 [*reversing* 36 Ind. App. 521, 76 N. E. 181]; Watson *v.* State, 3 Ind. 123 (holding that the prosecution need not prove that a bet was made, or the distance or judges appointed); State *v.* Ness, 1 Ind. 64; Goldsmith *v.* State, 1 Head (Tenn.) 154; State *v.* Fidler, 7 Humphr. (Tenn.) 502; Reg. *v.* Swindall, 2 C. & K. 230, 2 Cox C. C. 141, 61 E. C. L. 230.

Permitting one's horse to race and riding in a race are two separate offenses. State *v.* New, 165 Ind. 571, 76 N. E. 400 [*reversing* 36 Ind. App. 521, 76 N. E. 181]; State *v.* Ness, 1 Ind. 64.

Indictments for racing held good see Robb *v.* State, 52 Ind. 218; State *v.* Wagster, 75 Mo. 107 (holding also that an indictment for running a horse-race on a public road will be supported by proof that defendant procured another to ride his horse in the race); Goldsmith *v.* State, 1 Head (Tenn.) 154; State *v.* Catchings, 43 Tex. 654.

6. *Illinois.*— Belk *v.* People, 125 Ill. 584, 17 N. E. 744.

Massachusetts.— Com. *v.* Sherman, 191 Mass. 439, 78 N. E. 98, holding that the fact that the owner was in tonneau of automobile was *prima facie* evidence that he was guilty.

Pennsylvania.— Kennedy *v.* Way, Brightly 186.

Rhode Island.— State *v.* McCabe, (1908) 69 Atl. 1064; State *v.* Smith, 29 R. I. 245, 69 Atl. 1061, "common traveling pace" construed.

Wisconsin.— McCummins *v.* State, 132 Wis. 236, 112 N. W. 25.

See 25 Cent. Dig. tit. "Highways," §§ 476, 477.

7. Kennamer *v.* State, 150 Ala. 74, 43 So. 482; Hamilton *v.* State, 22 Ind. App. 479, 52 N. E. 419. But see Com. *v.* Conley, 10 Ky. L. Rep. 875, hauling logs held not an offense.

8. Kennamer *v.* State, 150 Ala. 74, 43 So. 482; State *v.* New, 165 Ind. 571, 76 N. E. 400 [*reversing* 36 Ind. App. 521, 76 N. E. 181]; State *v.* Messenger, 63 Ohio St. 398, 59 N. E. 105 (should allege weight of load and size of tires); McCummins *v.* State, 132 Wis. 236, 112 N. W. 25.

Charging both failing to stop and failing to keep man in front of locomotive is not duplicitous. State *v.* Kowolski, 96 Iowa 346, 65 N. W. 306.

A criminal intent may be unnecessary under a statute forbidding heavy hauling. Hamilton *v.* State, 22 Ind. App. 479, 52 N. E. 419.

9. State *v.* New, 165 Ind. 571, 76 N. E. 400 [*reversing* 36 Ind. App. 521, 76 N. E. 181].

10. State *v.* New, 165 Ind. 571, 76 N. E. 400 [*reversing* 36 Ind. App. 521, 76 N. E. 181]; Watson *v.* State, 3 Ind. 123; State *v.* Burgett, Smith (Ind.) 340 (holding, however, that the termini of the road may be omitted); State *v.* Fleetwood, 16 Mo. 448.

11. **As to city streets** see MUNICIPAL CORPORATIONS, 28 Cyc. 1358 *et seq.*

12. *Connecticut.*— Biesiegel *v.* Seymour, 58 Conn. 43, 19 Atl. 372.

Indiana.— State *v.* Kamman, 151 Ind. 407, 51 N. E. 483; Porter County *v.* Dombke, 94 Ind. 72.

Maine.— Cunningham *v.* Frankfort, 104 Me. 208, 70 Atl. 441; Moriarty *v.* Lewiston, 98 Me. 482, 57 Atl. 790.

New York.— Lane *v.* Hancock, 142 N. Y. 510, 37 N. E. 473 [*reversing* 67 Hun 623, 22 N. Y. Suppl. 470]; Scofield *v.* Poughkeepsie, 122 N. Y. App. Div. 868, 107 N. Y. Suppl. 767; Farman *v.* Ellington, 46 Hun 41 [*affirmed* in 124 N. Y. 662, 27 N. E. 413].

Pennsylvania.— Fry *v.* Perkiomen Tp., 1 Montg. Co. Rep. 25, holding that more care is required where water is likely to accumulate.

Vermont.— Batty *v.* Duxbury, 24 Vt. 155.

Wisconsin.— Parish *v.* Eden, 62 Wis. 272, 22 N. W. 399, holding that the overseer must see that his orders are obeyed.

See 25 Cent. Dig. tit. "Highways," § 478 *et seq.*

Ordinary care is not enough if the road remained defective. Cunningham *v.* Clay Tp., 69 Kan. 373, 76 Pac. 907; George *v.* Haver-

times[13] to keep the road reasonably safe[14] in view of the probable traffic,[15] but only for ordinary travel in the usual vehicles.[16]

b. Roads and Portions Thereof to Which Duty Extends — (I) *IN GENERAL.* A municipality or public board charged with the duty of maintaining public roads is liable for injuries received on and only on a regular public highway,[17] from the time it is regularly opened for travel,[18] and not for injuries received on a road not public,[19] or one abandoned,[20] unless the road is apparently still open,[21] or for an injury occurring beyond the highway lines,[22] although the line of the highway is not marked.[23] Moreover, the law commonly holds a municipality only to a duty to keep in repair the traveled portion of its roads,[24] if reasonably

hill, 110 Mass. 506; Horton *v.* Ipswich, 12 Cush. (Mass.) 488; Prindle *v.* Fletcher, 39 Vt. 255.

In removing an obstruction placed in a highway by an individual a town is bound to exercise a higher degree of care than in removing equally dangerous objects which are incident to the nature of the soil or to the construction of the road, since a traveler has reason to expect that the highway will have some natural obstructions. Morse *v.* Richmond, 41 Vt. 435, 98 Am. Dec. 600.

13. Farman *v.* Ellington, 46 Hun (N. Y.) 41 [*affirmed* in 124 N. Y. 662, 27 N. E. 413] (holding two days' delay after washout negligent); Glaub *v.* Goshen Tp., 7 Kulp (Pa.) 292 (by night and in storm); Spear *v.* Lowell, 47 Vt. 692; Clark *v.* Corinth, 41 Vt. 449.

Where immediate attempt to repair would be fruitless, as in the case of a thaw of snow, it is sufficient if repairs are made as soon as practicable. Spear *v.* Lowell, 47 Vt. 692.

Sunday work may be necessary. Flagg *v.* Millbury, 4 Cush. (Mass.) 243; Alexander *v.* Oshkosh, 33 Wis. 277.

14. Moriarty *v.* Lewiston, 98 Me. 482, 57 Atl. 790; Church *v.* Cherryfield, 33 Me. 460; Lamb *v.* Pike Tp., 215 Pa. St. 516, 64 Atl. 671; Ackley *v.* Bradford Tp., 32 Pa. Super. Ct. 487; Archibald *v.* Lincoln County, 50 Wash. 55, 96 Pac. 831.

15. Church *v.* Cherryfield, 33 Me. 460; Brader *v.* Lehman Tp., 34 Pa. Super. Ct. 125, mountain roads.

16. Johnson *v.* Highland, 124 Wis. 597, 102 N. W. 1085. See also Doherty *v.* Ayer, 197 Mass. 241, 83 N. E. 677, 125 Am. St. Rep. 355, 14 L. R. A. N. S. 816, holding an automobile not a carriage under a statute requiring highways to be kept safe for carriages.

Merely because not fit for bicycles does not render a road defective (Rust *v.* Essex, 182 Mass. 313, 65 N. E. 397), but defects which make a road insufficient for other vehicles give a bicyclist a right to recover (Hendry *v.* North Hampton, 72 N. H. 351, 56 Atl. 922, 101 Am. St. Rep. 68, 64 L. R. A. 70).

17. *Maine.*— Todd *v.* Rome, 2 Me. 55.

Massachusetts.— Kellogg *v.* Northampton, 8 Gray 504; Hayden *v.* Attleborough, 7 Gray 338; Stedman *v.* Southbridge, 17 Pick. 162; Jones *v.* Andover, 6 Pick. 59.

New Jersey.— Carter *v.* Rahway, 55 N. J. L. 177, 178, 26 Atl. 96.

North Dakota.— Coulter *v.* Great Northern R. Co., 5 N. D. 568, 67 N. W. 1046.

Vermont.— Loveland *v.* Berlin, 27 Vt. 713 (pent road); Hyde *v.* Jamaica, 27 Vt. 443 (when opened under statute or dedication accepted).

Wisconsin.— Donohue *v.* Warren, 95 Wis. 367, 70 N. W. 305.

Canada.— Kennedy *v.* Portage la Prairie, 12 Manitoba 634; Holland *v.* York Tp., 7 Ont. L. Rep. 533, 3 Ont. Wkly. Rep. 287; Lalongé *v.* St. Vincent de Paul Parish, 27 Quebec Super. Ct. 218 (road used by permission of owners); Duchene *v.* Beauport, 23 Quebec Super. Ct. 80 (winter road).

See 25 Cent. Dig. tit. "Highways," § 479.

Rule applied to city streets see MUNICIPAL CORPORATIONS, 28 Cyc. 1346.

Ways held public with the operation of the rule see Paulsen *v.* Wilton, 78 Conn. 58, 61 Atl. 61 (vote of town directing repair); Green *v.* Canaan, 29 Conn. 157; Bliss *v.* Deerfield, 13 Pick. (Mass.) 102 (road paid for by order of the commissioners and traveled); Whitney *v.* Essex, 42 Vt. 520; Blodget *v.* Royalton, 14 Vt. 288 (conviction of town for not repairing).

18. Drury *v.* Worcester, 21 Pick. (Mass.) 44; Bliss *v.* Deerfield, 13 Pick. (Mass.) 102; Hunter *v.* Weston, 111 Mo. 176, 19 S. W. 1098, 17 L. R. A. 633; Madill *v.* Caledon Tp., 3 Ont. L. Rep. 555, 1 Ont. Wkly. Rep. 299 [*affirming* 3 Ont. L. Rep. 66], although town had not assumed control.

19. *New Hampshire.*—Watson *v.* Grand Trunk R. Co., 68 N. H. 170, 36 Atl. 555, where lay-out quashed.

Pennsylvania.— Kaseman *v.* Sunbury, 197 Pa. St. 162, 46 Atl. 1032, railroad embankment in street.

Texas.— Worthington *v.* Wade, 82 Tex. 26, 17 S. W. 520.

Vermont.— Blodget *v.* Royalton, 14 Vt. 288.

Wisconsin.— Bogie *v.* Waupun, 75 Wis. 1, 43 N. W. 667, 6 L. R. A. 59, temporary road across fields.

See 25 Cent. Dig. tit. "Highways," § 479.

20. Bills *v.* Kaukauna, 94 Wis. 310, 68 N. W. 992.

21. Bills *v.* Kaukauna, 94 Wis. 310, 68 N. W. 992.

Revocation of the right to use a road without notice of such revocation does not constitute a defense to an action for injuries caused by an obstruction placed thereon. Dunn *v.* Gunn, 149 Ala. 583, 42 So. 686.

22. Doyle *v.* Vinalhaven, 66 Me. 348.

23. Doyle *v.* Vinalhaven, 66 Me. 348; Spaulding *v.* Groton, 68 N. H. 77, 44 Atl. 88.

24. *Maine.*— Dickey *v.* Maine Tel. Co., 46 Me. 483. But see Savage *v.* Bangor, 40 Me.

straight[25] and wide enough[26] for passing,[27] but must take care of the whole of this.[28] Towns are commonly liable for a defective sidewalk.[29]

(II) *ROADS UNDER REPAIR.*[30] A duty rests upon the municipality to care for travelers while a highway is undergoing repair,[31] as by a barrier[32] or fencing,[33] mere warning being held insufficient.[34] But reasonable obstructions for repair work are not defects upon which liability can be predicated,[35] nor will defects in a temporary road cause liability.[36]

c. Defects and Obstructions Causing Injury — (I) *GENERAL NATURE; ENUMERATION.* A defect or obstruction in a roadway subjecting the municipality to liability is in general any object in, upon, or near the traveled path, which would necessarily obstruct or hinder one in the use of the road for the purpose of traveling, or which from its nature and position would be likely to produce that result by impeding, embarrassing, or opposing passage along the road,[37] as by a

176, 63 Am. Dec. 658 (holding that where the traveled part is obstructed with snow a town is liable for injuries on a way broken out at the side); Bryant *v.* Biddeford, 39 Me. 193 (holding that there may be localities where it is the duty of the town to make the road safe for travel over the whole width laid out).

Massachusetts.—Doherty *v.* Ayer, 197 Mass. 241, 83 N. E. 677, 125 Am. St. Rep. 355, 14 L. R. A. N. S. 816; Moran *v.* Palmer, 162 Mass. 196, 38 N. E. 442; Howard *v.* North Bridgewater, 16 Pick. 189.

New Hampshire.— Saltmarsh *v.* Bow, 56 N. H. 428.

New York.— Newell *v.* Stony Point, 59 N. Y. App. Div. 237, 69 N. Y. Suppl. 583.

Wisconsin.— Hammacher *v.* New Berlin, 124 Wis. 249, 102 N. W. 489; Hebbe *v.* Maple Creek, 121 Wis. 668, 99 N. W. 442; Wheeler *v.* Westport, 30 Wis. 392.

25. Wheeler *v.* Westport, 30 Wis. 392, holding a town liable for line of boulders beside way.

The narrowness and crookedness of a highway duly located does not render a town liable for injury resulting therefrom, as it is only for defects in construction that the town is liable. Smith *v.* Wakefield, 105 Mass. 473.

26. Seeley *v.* Litchfield, 49 Conn. 134, 44 Am. Rep. 213; Perkins *v.* Fayette, 68 Me. 152, 28 Am. Rep. 84. See also Smith *v.* Kanawha County Court, 33 W. Va. 713, 11 S. E. 1, 8 L. R. A. 82, holding that there is no liability where horses are frightened by calves, although the road is only half the statutory width.

27. Mochler *v.* Shaftsbury, 46 Vt. 580, 14 Am. Rep. 634; Hull *v.* Richmond, 12 Fed. Cas. No. 6,861, 2 Woodb. & M. 337.

28. Potter *v.* Castleton, 53 Vt. 435; Bagley *v.* Ludlow, 41 Vt. 425; Matthews *v.* Baraboo, 39 Wis. 674, so holding, although the road is wide enough for three or four teams abreast.

29. Gould *v.* Boston, 120 Mass. 300; Birngruber *v.* Eastchester, 54 N. Y. App. Div. 80, 66 N. Y. Suppl. 278: Hammacher *v.* New Berlin, 124 Wis. 249, 102 N. W. 489. But see Dupuy *v.* Union Tp., 46 N. J. L. 269; Siegler *v.* Mellinger, 203 Pa. St. 256, 52 Atl. 175, 93 Am. St. Rep. 767, holding a side-path five or six feet above the road not negligence.

30. **Injury through repair of city street** see MUNICIPAL CORPORATIONS, 28 Cyc. 1401.

31. *Maine.*—Jacobs *v.* Bangor, 16 Me. 187, 33 Am. Dec. 652.

New York.— Buffalo *v.* Holloway, 7 N. Y. 493, 57 Am. Dec. 550; Snowden *v.* Somerset, 52 N. Y. App. Div. 84, 64 N. Y. Suppl. 1088; Tompert *v.* Hastings Pavement Co., 35 N. Y. App. Div. 578, 55 N. Y. Suppl. 177.

Vermont.— Bates *v.* Sharon, 45 Vt. 474; Batty *v.* Duxbury, 24 Vt. 155; Kelsey *v.* Glover, 15 Vt. 708.

Wisconsin.—Bills *v.* Kaukana, 94 Wis. 310, 68 N. W. 992.

England.—Hurst *v.* Taylor, 14 Q. B. D. 918, 49 J. P. 359, 54 L. J. Q. B. 310, 33 Wkly. Rep. 582.

See 25 Cent. Dig. tit. "Highways," § 483 *et seq.*

32. Snowden *v.* Somerset, 52 N. Y. App. Div. 84, 64 N. Y. Suppl. 1088.

33. Hurst *v.* Taylor, 14 Q. B. D. 918, 49 J. P. 359, 54 L. J. Q. B. 310, 33 Wkly. Rep. 582.

34. Tompert *v.* Hastings Pavement Co., 35 N. Y. App. Div. 578, 55 N. Y. Suppl. 177.

35. Farrell *v.* Oldtown, 69 Me. 72; Morton *v.* Frankfort, 55 Me. 46. See also Mills *v.* Philadelphia, 187 Pa. St. 287, 40 Atl. 821, holding that where a light left burning went out no liability existed.

36. Nicodemo *v.* Southborough, 173 Mass. 455, 53 N. E. 887; Brewer *v.* Sullivan County, 199 Pa. St. 594, 49 Atl. 259.

37. *Connecticut.*— Hewison *v.* New Haven, 34 Conn. 136, 142, 91 Am. Dec. 718.

Kansas.— Reading Tp. *v.* Telfer, 57 Kan. 798, 48 Pac. 134, 57 Am. St. Rep. 355.

Massachusetts.— Cook *v.* Charlestown, 13 Allen 190 note; Hixon *v.* Lowell, 13 Gray 59.

New York.— Whitney *v.* Ticonderoga, 53 Hun 214, 6 N. Y. Suppl. 844 [*affirmed* in 127 N. Y. 40, 27 N. E. 403].

Pennsylvania.— Com. *v.* Erie, etc., R. Co., 27 Pa. St. 339, 67 Am. Dec. 471.

Wisconsin.— Chase *v.* Oshkosh, 81 Wis. 313, 51 N. W. 560, 29 Am. St. Rep. 898, 15 L. R. A. 553.

See 25 Cent. Dig. tit. "Highways," § 483.

The term "defective highways" as used in a statute imposing upon towns liability for damage by reason of defective highways is used in reference to their condition for pub-

ditch across[38] or unguarded beside [39] the way, a hole in the roadway[40] or so near the traveled way that travelers are likely to fall into it in avoiding another obstruction,[41] an uneven surface,[42] projections across the highway,[43] or railroad crossings; [44] objects falling upon the road,[45] except where liability is predicated upon peculiar local statutes not covering such cases,[46] structures in the highway,[47] posts,[48] trees,[49] fences,[50] piles of material,[51] or other objects upon the

lic travel upon them which their designation as highway imports and in view of the purpose for which they are established and maintained (Whitney *v.* Ticonderoga, 127 N. Y. 40, 27 N. E. 403), and such a statute as to defects applies only to defects interfering with travel and not to failure to keep a sluiceway clear, causing water to set back on land of an abutter (Winchell *v.* Camillus, 190 N. Y. 536, 83 N. E. 1134 [*affirming* 109 N. Y. App. Div. 341, 95 N. Y. Suppl. 688].

The obstruction need not wholly stop travel to render the town liable, it is sufficient if travel be impeded. Chase *v.* Oshkosh, 81 Wis. 313, 51 N. W. 560, 29 Am. St. Rep. 898, 15 L. R. A. 553.

38. Nicol *v.* Beaumont, 53 L. J. Ch. 853, 50 L. T. Rep. N. S. 112.

39. Whyler *v.* Bingham Rural Dist., [1901] 1 K. B. 45, 64 J. P. 771, 70 L. J. K. B. 207, 83 L. T. Rep. N. S. 652, 17 T. L. R. 23. But see Brown *v.* Skowhegan, 82 Me. 273, 19 Atl. 399, disallowing recovery where the person injured never became a traveler but was approaching the traveled part.

40. Gale *v.* Dover, 68 N. H. 403, 44 Atl. 535 (defective cover to opening); Schaeffer *v.* Jackson Tp., 150 Pa. St. 145, 24 Atl. 629, 30 Am. St. Rep. 792, 18 L. R. A. 100; Wertz *v* Girardville Borough, 30 Pa. Super. Ct. 260; Bathurst *v.* Macpherson, 4 App. Cas. 256, 48 L. J. P. C. 61. But see Grant *v.* Enfield, 11 N. Y. App. Div. 358, 42 N. Y. Suppl. 107, holding that a depression several inches deep is not a defect.

41. Wakeham *v.* St. Clair Tp., 91 Mich. 15, 51 N. W. 696.

42. Rust *v.* Essex, 182 Mass. 313, 65 N. E. 397 (stone projecting six inches in country road); Pratt *v.* Cohasset, 177 Mass. 488, 59 N. E. 79 (drop of about a foot from graveled part of road to road not so covered); Elliot *v.* Concord, 27 N. H. 104 (embankment); Osterhout *v.* Bethlehem, 55 N. Y. App. Div. 198, 66 N. Y. Suppl. 845 (hole or rut ten inches deep); Lamb *v.* Pike Tp., 215 Pa. St. 516, 64 Atl. 671 (gas pipe projecting).

Unevenness not causing see Brader *v.* Lehman Tp., 34 Pa. Super. Ct. 125 (level flat stone in mountain road); Messenger *v.* Bridgetown, 33 Nova Scotia 291 (projecting surface on filling up excavation).

43. Beecher *v.* People, 38 Mich. 289, 31 Am. Rep. 316 (roof over alley twelve feet high); Hardy *v.* Keene, 52 N. H. 370 (derrick ropes); Hume *v.* New York, 74 N. Y. 264; Embler *v.* Wallkill, 57 Hun (N. Y.) 384, 10 N. Y. Suppl. 797 [*affirmed* in 132 N. Y. 222, 30 N. E. 404] (branches of tree hanging low); Champlin *v.* Penn Yan, 34 Hun (N. Y.) 33 [*affirmed* in 102 N. Y. 680].

Objects overhanging city streets see MUNICIPAL CORPORATIONS, 28 Cyc. 1378.

44. Dixon *v.* Butler Tp., 4 Pa. Dist. 754, 17 Pa. Co. Ct. 114. See also RAILROADS, 33 Cyc. 920 *et seq.*

45. Grove *v.* Ft. Wayne, 45 Ind. 429, 15 Am. Rep. 262; West *v.* Lynn, 110 Mass. 514; Ferguson *v.* Southwold Tp., 27 Ont. 66.

46. See Pratt *v.* Weymouth, 147 Mass. 245, 17 N. E. 538, 9 Am. St. Rep. 691; West *v.* Lynn, 110 Mass. 514; Wakefield *v.* Newport, 62 N. H. 624; Oak Harbor *v.* Kallagher, 52 Ohio St. 183, 39 N. E. 144; Taylor *v.* Peckham, 8 R. I. 349, 91 Am. Dec. 235, 5 Am. Rep. 578; Watkins *v.* County Ct., 30 W. Va. 657, 5 S. E. 654.

Awnings may become defects in the highway when they are not mere incidents or attachments of the building but adapted to the sidewalk and a part of its construction and arrangement for use as such. Day *v.* Milford, 5 Allen (Mass.) 98; Pedrick *v.* Bailey, 12 Gray (Mass.) 161; Drake *v.* Lowell, 13 Metc. (Mass.) 292.

47. Elzig *v.* Bales, 135 Iowa 208, 112 N. W. 540; Hill *v.* Hoffman, (Tenn. Ch. App. 1899) 58 S. W. 929; State *v.* Leaver, 62 Wis. 387, 22 N. W. 576 (a barn occupying nearly one half the width of the highway in a populous village, although travel on the highway could pass it); Rex *v.* Gregory, 5 B. & Ad. 555, 3 L. J. M. C. 25, 2 N. & M. 478, 27 E. C. L. 236; Reg. *v.* Lepine, 15 L. T. Rep. N. S. 158, 15 Wkly. Rep. 45.

48. Coggswell *v.* Lexington, 4 Cush. (Mass.) 307 (near line of highway); Yeaw *v.* Williams, 15 R. I. 20, 23 Atl. 33. But see Macomber *v.* Taunton, 100 Mass. 255; Young *v.* Yarmouth, 9 Gray (Mass.) 386.

49. Patterson *v.* Vail, 43 Iowa 142; Tilton *v.* Wenham, 172 Mass. 407, 52 N. E. 514. But see Washburn *v.* Easton, 172 Mass. 525, 52 N. E. 1070 (holding otherwise as to shade trees not in dangerous position); Bullen *v.* Wakely, 18 Cox C. C. 692, 62 J. P. 166, 77 L. T. Rep. N. S. 689.

50. Smith *v.* Putnam, 62 N. H. 369; Hill *v.* Hoffman, (Tenn. Ch. App. 1899) 58 S. W. 929; Cornelison *v.* State, (Tex. Cr. App. 1899) 49 S. W. 384; Reg *v.* Burrell, 10 Cox C. C. 462, 16 L. T. Rep. N. S. 572, 15 Wkly. Rep. 879.

51. Ring *v.* Cohoes, 77 N. Y. 83, 33 Am. Rep. 574; Schaeffer *v.* Jackson Tp., 150 Pa. St. 145, 24 Atl. 629, 30 Am. St. Rep. 792, 18 L. R. A. 100; Reg. *v.* Longton Gas Co., 8 Cox C. C. 317, 2 E. & E. 651, 6 Jur. N. S. 601, 29 L. J. M. C. 118, 2 L. T. Rep. N. S. 14, 8 Wkly. Rep. 293, 105 E. C. L. 651; Dixon *v.* Chester, 70 J. P. 380, 4 L. G. R. 1127, 22 T. L. R. 501; Preston *v.* Fullwood

(II) *DEFECTS CAUSED BY THE ELEMENTS; SNOW AND ICE.*[63] The municipality will be liable, although the defect is caused by the elements, if it should have known of the condition,[64] as where a way is defective from the presence upon it of snow and ice in large quantities negligently permitted to remain by the municipal authorities [65] after the lapse of sufficient time to clear the way;[66] but a municipality is not ordinarily liable for injuries resulting from mere slipperiness from ice.[67]

(III) *OBSTRUCTIONS CALCULATED TO FRIGHTEN HORSES.*[68] Objects calculated to frighten horses in or near the road constitute defects in the road rendering the municipality liable for injuries caused thereby,[69] although not

63. **Ice and snow in city streets** see MUNICIPAL CORPORATIONS, 28 Cyc. 1372.

64. Tripp *v.* Lyman, 37 Me. 250; Blood *v.* Hubbardston, 121 Mass. 233 (danger from defect increased through elements); Hedricks *v.* Schuylkill Tp., 16 Pa. Super. Ct. 508 (mire). But see Brendlinger *v.* New Hanover Tp., 148 Pa. St. 93, 23 Atl. 1105.

65. *Connecticut.*— Congdon *v.* Norwich, 37 Conn. 414.

Maine.— Rogers *v.* Newport, 62 Me. 101 (town held liable, although wood placed on the road by individuals caused a snowdrift); Savage *v.* Bangor, 40 Me. 176, 63 Am. Dec. 658 (holding that a passageway must be kept clear even after a heavy storm).

Massachusetts.— Rooney *v.* Randolph, 128 Mass. 580.

New Hampshire.— Dutton *v.* Weare, 17 N. H. 34, 43 Am. Dec. 590. But see Drew *v.* Bow, 74 N. H. 147, 65 Atl. 831, holding a gutter not a sluiceway, within a statute imposing liability for injury from defective sluiceway.

New York.— Schrank *v.* Rochester R. Co., 83 Hun 290, 31 N. Y. Suppl. 922, snow piled up by snow-plow.

See 25 Cent. Dig. tit. "Highways," § 483.

But statutes sometimes provide that no actionable defect exists unless something beside the snow and ice contributed to cause it. See the statutes of the several states. And see Miner *v.* Hopkinton, 73 N. H. 232, 60 Atl. 433; McCloskey *v.* Moies, 19 R. I. 297, 33 Atl. 225 (ice on water collected in defective depression); Barton *v.* Montpelier, 30 Vt. 650.

66. Hayes *v.* Cambridge, 136 Mass. 402; Kleng *v.* Buffalo, 156 N. Y. 700, 51 N. E. 1091. See also Dorn *v.* Oyster Bay, 84 Hun (N. Y.) 510, 32 N. Y. Suppl. 341 [*affirmed* in 158 N. Y. 731, 53 N. E. 1124].

67. *Maine.*— Smyth *v.* Bangor, 72 Me. 249.

Massachusetts.— Stone *v.* Hubbardston, 100 Mass. 49.

New York.— Kinney *v.* Troy, 108 N. Y. 567, 15 N. E. 728.

Ohio.— Chase *v.* Cleveland, 44 Ohio St. 505, 9 N. E. 225, 58 Am. Rep. 843.

Pennsylvania.— Mauch Chunk *v.* Kline, 100 Pa. St. 119, 45 Am. Rep. 364.

Canada.— Ringland *v.* Toronto, 23 U. C. C. P. 93.

See 25 Cent. Dig. tit. "Highways," § 483.

68. **Frightening animals in city streets** see MUNICIPAL CORPORATIONS, 28 Cyc. 1380.

Lack of railings see VII, E, 1, d, (III).

Liability for accidents caused by objects outside the traveled portion of the highway see *supra*, VII, E, 1, b, (I).

69. *Connecticut.*— Clinton *v.* Howard, 42 Conn. 294 (pile of stones); Ayer *v.* Norwich, 39 Conn. 376, 12 Am. Dec. 396; Dimock *v.* Suffield, 30 Conn. 129. But see Lee *v.* Barkhampstead, 46 Conn. 213, holding that a moving train is not a structure rendering the town liable.

Illinois.— Galt *v.* Woliver, 103 Ill. App. 71, machine.

Maine.— York *v.* Athens, 99 Me. 82, 58 Atl. 418, pile of rocks.

Minnesota.— Nye *v.* Dibley, 88 Minn. 465, 93 N. W. 524, pile of material.

New York.— Mullen *v.* Glens Falls, 11 N. Y. App. Div. 275, 42 N. Y. Suppl. 113 (steam roller); Wilson *v.* Spafford, 10 N. Y. Suppl. 649 (holding the rule applicable if the object would naturally frighten horses, although not necessarily so). See Burns *v.* Farmington, 31 N. Y. App. Div. 364, 52 N. Y. Suppl. 229.

Pennsylvania.— Baker *v.* North East Borough, 151 Pa. St. 234, 24 Atl. 1079 (water-pipe from which water escaped with hissing sound); Curry *v.* Luzerne Borough, 24 Pa. Super. Ct. 514 (holding that it is not necessary for borough authorities or supervisors to examine the highways and determine what is likely to frighten horses, as well as where they are likely to be frightened; but it is necessary for such officers to provide at all points a reasonably safe highway, even when a horse is frightened).

Rhode Island.— Bennett *v.* Fifield, 13 R. I. 139, 43 Am. Rep. 17.

Vermont.— Morse *v.* Richmond, 41 Vt. 435, 98 Am. Dec. 600.

Canada.— Kelly *v.* Whitchurch Tp., 12 Ont. L. Rep. 83, 7 Ont. Wkly. Rep. 279 [*affirming* 11 Ont. L. Rep. 155, 6 Ont. Wkly. Rep. 839], piles of lumber.

Objects not rendering municipality liable see Farrell *v.* Oldtown, 69 Me. 72 (granite blocks); Nichols *v.* Athens, 66 Me. 402 (common riding wagon); Cushing *v.* Bedford, 125 Mass. 526 (bright red trough); Cook *v.* Montague, 115 Mass. 571 (stone pile in grass beside road); Bemis *v.* Arlington, 114 Mass. 507; Kingsbury *v.* Dedham, 13 Allen (Mass.) 186, 90 Am. Dec. 191; Keith *v.* Easton, 2 Allen (Mass.) 552 (vehicle used as daguerreotype saloon); Hebbard *v.* Berlin, 66 N. H.

sary,[83] unless the facts are such that only one conclusion can be drawn by reasonable minds.[84] A lack of railing commonly gives no right of action to the owner of a horse running away or beyond the control of the driver,[85] unless the statute providing for railings clearly contemplates protection even against the fright of horses.[86]

e. Necessity of Notice of Defect to Charge Municipality.[87] A municipality is liable for injuries only when it has had notice of a defect, either actual[88] or

980 (stone outside limits of highway); Doherty *v.* Ayer, 197 Mass. 241, 83 N. E. 677, 125 Am. St. Rep. 355, 14 L. R. A. N. S. 816 (to guard against sand beside highway); Hudson *v.* Marlborough, 154 Mass. 218, 28 N. E. 147 (accident twenty-five feet from roadway); Barnes *v.* Chicopee, 138 Mass. 67, 52 Am. Rep. 259 (thirty-four feet from traveled part); Puffer *v.* Orange, 122 Mass. 389, 23 Am. Rep. 368 (where no dangerous place near enough to be reached without straying); Marshall *v.* Ipswich, 110 Mass. 522 (round pile of brick); Murphy *v.* Gloucester, 105 Mass. 470 (to prevent travelers driving on to dock twenty-five feet distant).

Michigan.— Kuhn *v.* Walker Tp., 97 Mich. 306, 56 N. W. 556, driving strange hired horse unnecessarily within three feet of the embankment.

New Hampshire.— Miner *v.* Hopkinton, 73 N. H. 232, 60 Atl. 433, a cut is not a dangerous embankment and railing.

New York.— Monk *v.* New Utrecht, 104 N. Y. 552, 11 N. E. 268 (mere error of judgment; certain slope an error in the plan); Patchen *v.* Walton, 17 N. Y. App. Div. 158, 45 N. Y. Suppl. 145; Glasier *v.* Hebron, 82 Hun 311, 31 N. Y. Suppl. 236 (where highway seventeen feet wide and level); Stacy *v.* Phelps, 47 Hun 54 (where absence of warning of trench would not have prevented accident).

Pennsylvania.— Heister *v.* Fawn Tp., 189 Pa. St. 253, 42 Atl. 121, cow scaring horse over unguarded embankment.

Rhode Island.— Waterhouse *v.* Calef, 21 R. I. 470, 44 Atl. 591 (boulders guarding embankment); Chapman *v.* Cook, 10 R. I. 304, 14 Am. Rep. 686 (to mark deviation of private way).

Wisconsin.— Hammacher *v.* New Berlin, 124 Wis. 249, 102 N. W. 489.

United States.— Schimberg *v.* Cutler, 142 Fed. 701, 74 C. C. A. 33.

Where the accident is rare and unexpected defendant ought not to be charged for failure to guard against it. Hubbell *v.* Yonkers, 104 N. Y. 434, 10 N. E. 858, 58 Am. Rep. 522; Glazier *v.* Hebron, 62 Hun (N. Y.) 137, 16 N. Y. Suppl. 503 [*reversed* on other grounds in 131 N. Y. 447, 30 N. E. 239] (no liability, although accident was rare and unforeseen); Beardslee *v.* Columbia Tp., 5 Lack. Leg. N. (Pa.) 290. As to absence of similar accidents see *infra*, VII, E, 4, f, (II).

83. Harris *v.* Great Barrington, 169 Mass. 271, 47 N. E. 881; Babson *v.* Rockport, 101 Mass. 93 (horse backing over embankment); Malloy *v.* Walker Tp., 77 Mich. 448, 43 N. W. 1012, 6 L. R. A. 695; Seeton *v.* Dunbarton, 72 N. H. 269, 56 Atl. 197; Roblee *v.* Indian Lake, 11 N. Y. App. Div. 435, 42 N. Y. Suppl. 326; Wood *v.* Gilboa, 76 Hun (N. Y.) 175, 27 N. Y. Suppl. 586 [*affirmed* in 146 N. Y. 383]; Glazier *v.* Hebron, 62 Hun (N. Y.) 137, 16 N. Y. Suppl. 503 [*reversed* on other grounds in 131 N. Y. 447, 30 N. E. 239]; Maxim *v.* Champion, 50 Hun (N. Y.) 88, 4 N. Y. Suppl. 515 [*affirmed* in 119 N. Y. 626, 23 N. E. 1144] (although the same conditions had existed for sixty-eight years with no accident); Hyatt *v.* Rondout, 44 Barb. (N. Y.) 385 [*affirmed* in 41 N. Y. 619].

84. Seeton *v.* Dunbarton, 72 N. H. 269, 56 Atl. 197.

85. Kingsley *v.* Bloomingdale Tp., 109 Mich. 340, 67 N. W. 333; Glasier *v.* Hebron, 131 N. Y. 447, 30 N. E. 239 [*reversing* 62 Hun 137, 16 N. Y. Suppl. 503]; Waller *v.* Hebron, 5 N. Y. App. Div. 577, 39 N. Y. Suppl. 381; Lane *v.* Wheeler, 35 Hun (N. Y.) 606; Dignan *v.* Spokane County, 43 Wash. 419, 86 Pac. 649. But see Hinckley *v.* Somerset, 145 Mass. 326, 14 N. E. 166 (holding otherwise where loss of control was only momentary and could have been regained if wall had been of sufficient height); Russell *v.* Westmoreland County, 26 Pa. Super. Ct. 425.

The backing of a buggy over an embankment which constituted an approach to a bridge and which was unguarded was not, as a matter of law, such an accident as could not reasonably have been apprehended or expected to occur. Wallace *v.* New Albion, 192 N. Y. 544, 84 N. E. 1122 [*affirming* 121 N. Y. App. Div. 66, 105 N. Y. Suppl. 524].

86. Upton *v.* Windham, 75 Conn. 288, 53 Atl. 660, 96 Am. Rep. 197.

87. **Evidence of notice of defect in city street** see MUNICIPAL CORPORATIONS, 28 Cyc. 1486.

Notice of defect or obstruction in city street see MUNICIPAL CORPORATIONS, 28 Cyc. 1384.

88. *Indiana.*— Rosedale *v.* Ferguson, 3 Ind. App. 596, 30 N. E. 156.

Maine.— Pease *v.* Parsonsfield, 92 Me. 345, 42 Atl. 502.

Massachusetts.— Doherty *v.* Waltham, 4 Gray 596, notice of removal of barrier placed by town.

New Hampshire.— Chamberlain *v.* Enfield, 43 N. H. 356; Johnson *v.* Haverhill, 35 N. H. 74.

Pennsylvania.— North Manheim Tp. *v.* Arnold, 119 Pa. St. 380, 13 Atl. 444, 4 Am. St. Rep. 650.

Rhode Island.— Seamons *v.* Fitts, 20 R. I. 443, 40 Atl. 3; McCloskey *v.* Moies, 19 R. I. 297, 33 Atl. 225, ice and snow.

Wisconsin.— Boltz *v.* Sullivan, 101 Wis. 608, 77 N. W. 870; Bloor *v.* Delafield, 69 Wis. 273, 34 N. W. 115.

Liability held not to exist for want of notice see Young *v.* Macomb, 11 N. Y. App. Div. 480, 42 N. Y. Suppl. 351 (bridge); Otto Tp.

constructive,[89] as where the condition of the road was notorious for a considerable period.[90] The notice need not be to the town in its corporate capacity,[91] but may be to the road officer,[92] and need not be in writing.[93] Notice should be of the

v. Wolf, 106 Pa. St. 608 (gas pipe broken); Brader *v.* Lehman Tp., 34 Pa. Super. Ct. 125; Allen *v.* East Buffalo Tp., 22 Pa. Co. Ct. 346 (ditch not properly filled); Carroll *v.* Allen, 20 R. I. 541, 40 Atl. 419 (soft spot in road).

89. *Maine.*— Savage *v.* Bangor, 40 Me. 176, 63 Am. Dec. 658, thaw where road obstructed with snow.

Massachusetts.— Tilton *v.* Wenham, 172 Mass. 407, 52 N. E. 514; Reed *v.* Northfield, 13 Pick. 94, 23 Am. Dec. 662.

New Hampshire.— Howe *v.* Plainfield, 41 N. H. 135; Johnson *v.* Haverhill, 35 N. H. 74.

Pennsylvania.— Meachem *v.* Corapolis Borough, 31 Pa. Super. Ct. 150; Rech *v.* Borough, 10 North. Co. Rep. 230.

Rhode Island.— Seamons *v.* Fitts, 21 R. I. 236, 42 Atl. 863.

Vermont.— Brown *v.* Swanton, 69 Vt. 53, 37 Atl. 280 (water flowing over road); Clark *v.* Corinth, 41 Vt. 449; Prindle *v.* Fletcher, 39 Vt. 255.

Wisconsin.— Boltz *v.* Sullivan, 101 Wis. 608, 77 N. W. 870; Wiltse *v.* Tilden, 77 Wis. 152, 46 N. W. 234; McCabe *v.* Hammond, 34 Wis. 590; Ward *v.* Jefferson, 24 Wis. 342.

Canada.— Couch *v.* Louise, 16 Manitoba 656 (barbed wire fence across road for three months); Hogg *v.* Brooke, 7 Ont. L. Rep. 273, 2 Ont. Wkly. Rep. 139, 3 Ont. Wkly. Rep. 120.

See 25 Cent. Dig. tit. "Highways," § 487 *et seq.*

But "actual notice" in a statute is not satisfied by evidence of gross inattention. Littlefield *v.* Webster, 90 Me. 213, 38 Atl. 141.

No notice is inferred as the result of heavy rain the previous night. Riley *v.* Eastchester, 18 N. Y. App. Div. 94, 45 N. Y. Suppl. 448.

The sufficiency of notice is a question for the jury. Bunker *v.* Gouldsboro, 81 Me. 188, 16 Atl. 543; Bradbury *v.* Falmouth, 18 Me. 64; Springer *v.* Bowdoinham, 7 Me. 442; Thompson *v.* Bolton, 197 Mass. 311, 83 N. E. 1089 (where defect had existed two years); McCarthy *v.* Dedham, 188 Mass. 204, 74 N. E. 319; Kortendick *v.* Waterford, 135 Wis. 77, 115 N. W. 331; Kennedy *v.* Lincoln, 122 Wis. 301, 99 N. W. 1038.

Notice held sufficiently shown see Howard *v.* Mendon, 117 Mass. 585 (knowledge of town that barriers placed had been constantly taken and left down); Shaw *v.* Potsdam, 11 N. Y. App. Div. 508, 42 N. Y. Suppl. 779 (declarations by commissioner); Brown *v.* Swanton, 69 Vt. 53, 37 Atl. 280 (evidence of plaintiff that while acting as selectman, about a year before the accident, he was told that the sluice was not sufficient to carry off water in spring); Redepenning *v.* Rock, 136 Wis. 372, 117 N. W. 805.

Notice held not sufficiently shown see Valley Tp. *v.* Stiles, 77 Kan. 557, 95 Pac. 572; Hinckley *v.* Somerset, 145 Mass. 326, 14 N. E. 166, conversations between persons not officers of the town.

90. *Indiana.*— Porter County *v.* Dombke, 94 Ind. 72.

Maine.— Colley *v.* Westbrook, 57 Me. 181, 2 Am. Rep. 20; Holt *v.* Penobscot, 56 Me. 15, 96 Am. Dec. 429.

Michigan.— Malloy *v.* Walker Tp., 77 Mich. 448, 43 N. W. 1012, 6 L. R. A. 695, where town officers frequently passed over the road.

New York.— Burns *v.* Farmington, 31 N. Y. App. Div. 364, 52 N. Y. Suppl. 229; Rankert *v.* Junius, 25 N. Y. App. Div. 470, 49 N. Y. Suppl. 850 (open ditch); Pettingill *v.* Olean, 20 N. Y. Suppl. 367.

Pennsylvania.— Brader *v.* Lehman, 34 Pa. Super. Ct. 125.

Wisconsin.— Schuenke *v.* Pine River, 84 Wis. 669, 54 N. W. 1007.

Canada.— Kennedy *v.* Portage la Prairie, 12 Manitoba 634.

See 25 Cent. Dig. tit. "Highways," § 487 *et seq.*

But see Hari *v.* Ohio Tp., 62 Kan. 315, 62 Pac. 1010.

91. French *v.* Brunswick, 21 Me. 29, 38 Am. Dec. 250.

In Maine notice may be to some of the inhabitants. Mason *v.* Ellsworth, 32 Me. 271 (notice to two inhabitants, although not among the principal men); Tuell *v.* Paris, 23 Me. 556; French *v.* Brunswick, 21 Me. 29, 38 Am. Dec. 250; Springer *v.* Bowdoinham, 7 Me. 442. But see Ham *v.* Wales, 58 Me. 222, holding that there is no duty on the inhabitant who receives notice to remove the obstruction.

92. *Kansas.*— Madison Tp. *v.* Scott, 9 Kan. App. 871, 61 Pac. 967.

Maine.— Barnes *v.* Rumford, 96 Me. 315, 52 Atl. 844 (where notice was given to an officer of a previous year); Bunker *v.* Gouldsboro, 81 Me. 188, 16 Atl. 543 (although another is acting surveyor).

New Hampshire.—Hardy *v.* Keene, 52 N. H. 370, so holding, although highway surveyor was not the agent of the town but was a public officer.

Pennsylvania.— Platz *v.* McKean Tp., 178 Pa. St. 601, 36 Atl. 136.

Rhode Island.— Seamons *v.* Fitts, 21 R. I. 236, 42 Atl. 863, 20 R. I. 443, 40 Atl. 3.

Wisconsin.— Goldsworthy *v.* Linden, 75 Wis. 24, 43 N. W. 656.

United States.— Eastman *v.* Clackamas County, 32 Fed. 24, 12 Sawy. 613.

See 25 Cent. Dig. tit. "Highways," § 489.

Notice to one commissioner of a board of town commissioners of highways of a defect is insufficient to charge the board with notice. Malloy *v.* Pelham, 4 N. Y. St. 828.

Although the defect is out of the surveyor's jurisdiction, if he does not so inform the citizen, the town may be held bound thereby. Rogers *v.* Shirley, 74 Me. 144.

93. Erie Tp. *v.* Beamer, 71 Kan. 182, 79 Pac. 1070.

particular defect which caused the accident,[94] and should be notice not only that the defect existed but that it might become dangerous,[95] and that the object complained of is unnecessarily in the highway.[96] Notice is immaterial where the defect was caused by the town's servant,[97] or where the town could not have prevented the accident if notified.[98]

2. RIGHTS AND DUTIES OF PERSON INJURED — a. Who Can Recover[99] — (I) *TRAVELER* — (A) *In General.* A traveler on the highway may recover for injuries from defects or obstructions therein,[1] although he stops temporarily.[2] But one who is not in any sense a traveler cannot usually recover for defects.[3]

(B) *Outside of Traveled Path.*[4] Municipalities are held to have fully performed their duty when they have constructed highways of reasonable width and smoothness, and if a traveler chooses, without reasonable cause, to travel outside such way, he assumes the risk,[5] and thus ordinarily there is no liability

94. McFarland *v.* Emporia Tp., 59 Kan. 568, 53 Pac. 864 (that fence insufficient); Littlefield *v.* Webster, 90 Me. 213, 38 Atl. 141 (holding that notice of another defect or of a cause likely to produce a defect is insufficient); Hurley *v.* Bowdoinham, 88 Me. 293, 34 Atl. 72; Pendleton *v.* Northport, 80 Me. 598, 16 Atl. 253 (holding that notice to municipal officers that a culvert was not of sufficient size readily to vent the water, seeking its way through it in time of a freshet, is not notice of a defect in the way produced by an overflow of the water at such a time); Osterhout *v.* Bethlehem, 55 N. Y. App. Div. 198, 66 N. Y. Suppl. 845.

95. Cunningham *v.* Clay Tp., 69 Kan. 373, 76 Pac. 907.

Diligence after notice.— The fact that defendant town had no reason to expect that the stoppage of the water in a highway would render the road unsafe did not relieve it from liability for failure to exercise diligence after the defect had been developed. Brown *v.* Swanton, 69 Vt. 53, 37 Atl. 280.

Notice of the actual condition is sufficient, although town officers may think it is not a defect. Hinckley *v.* Somerset, 145 Mass. 326, 14 N. E. 166.

96. Bartlett *v.* Kittery, 68 Me. 358.

97. Holmes *v.* Paris, 75 Me. 559; Pratt *v.* Cohasset, 177 Mass. 488, 59 N. E. 79; Hager *v.* Wharton Tp., 200 Pa. St. 281, 49 Atl. 757. See also Brooks *v.* Somerville, 106 Mass. 271.

98. Chamberlain *v.* Enfield, 43 N. H. 356.

99. Persons entitled to redress for injury in city street see MUNICIPAL CORPORATIONS, 28 Cyc. 1414.

1. Dumas *v.* Hampton, 58 N. H. 134 (span turned loose and driven along road); Elliott *v.* Lisbon, 57 N. H. 27; Howrigan *v.* Bakersfield, 79 Vt. 249, 64 Atl. 1130; Sykes *v.* Pawlet, 43 Vt. 446, 5 Am. Rep. 595.

The purpose of the travel is immaterial. Schatz *v.* Pfeil, 56 Wis. 429, 14 N. W. 628; Hammond *v.* Mukwa, 40 Wis. 35.

"Team" in a statute may include horses or cattle in droves driven along the highway. Elliott *v.* Lisbon, 57 N. H. 27.

A blind mare walking unattended on a highway is a traveler only if her owner was not negligent in letting her out. Howrigan *v.* Bakersfield, 79 Vt. 249, 64 Atl. 1130.

It is a question for the jury whether one was traveling on a highway (Sleeper *v.* Worcester, etc., R. Co., 58 N. H. 520; Cummings *v.* Center Harbor, 57 N. H. 17; Hardy *v.* Keene, 52 N. H. 370), unless no evidence exists on which to find that plaintiff was not a traveler (Norris *v.* Haverhill, 65 N. H. 89, 18 Atl. 85).

2. *Iowa.*— Duffy *v.* Dubuque, 63 Iowa 171, 18 N. W. 900, 50 Am. Rep. 743, drinking water.

Maryland.— Murray *v.* McShane, 52 Md. 217, 36 Am. Rep. 367.

Massachusetts.— Smethurst *v.* Barton Square Independent Cong. Church, 148 Mass. 261, 19 N. E. 387, 12 Am. St. Rep. 550, 2 L. R. A. 695 (unloading wagon); Britton *v.* Cummington, 107 Mass. 347 (to pick berries); Babson *v.* Rockport, 101 Mass. 93 (to fill up hole in roadway). But see Richards *v.* Enfield, 13 Gray 344, holding that a traveler upon a highway who stops and ties his horse outside of the limits of the highway using due care cannot, if the horse gets loose and runs upon the highway, and suffers an injury from a defect therein, maintain an action against the town.

New Hampshire.— Varney *v.* Manchester, 58 N. H. 430, 40 Am. Rep. 592 (to see procession pass); Hardy *v.* Keene, 52 N. H. 370 (stopping to watch work).

Wisconsin.— Busse *v.* Rogers, 120 Wis. 443, 98 N. W. 219, 64 L. R. A. 183, turning aside to play for brief time.

3. Lyons *v.* Brookline, 119 Mass. 491 (child sitting on sidewalk); Blodgett *v.* Boston, 8 Allen (Mass.) 237; Fay *v.* Kent, 55 Vt. 557 (boy entering sand put beside road).

Children playing on the highway have been held entitled to recover in some cases (Chicago *v.* Keefe, 114 Ill. 222, 2 N. E. 267, 55 Am. Rep. 860; McGuire *v.* Spence, 91 N. Y. 303, 43 Am. Rep. 668), and not entitled in others (Stinson *v.* Gardiner, 42 Me. 248, 66 Am. Dec. 281; Tighe *v.* Lowell, 119 Mass. 472).

Plaintiff held not a traveler see Brown *v.* Skowhegan, 82 Me. 273, 19 Atl. 399 (crossing ditch approaching road); McCarthy *v.* Portland, 67 Me. 167, 24 Am. Rep. 23 (horse-racing); Leslie *v.* Lewiston, 62 Me. 468.

4. Negligence in leaving the traveled way on city streets see MUNICIPAL CORPORATIONS, 28 Cyc. 1430.

5. Orr *v.* Oldtown, 99 Me. 190, 58 Atl. 914.

upon the municipality for accidents outside the traveled path;[6] but the circumstances may be such that even in such a case the municipality may be held, if the injury is not proximately due to the negligence of the traveler.[7]

(II) *LAWBREAKERS.*[8] A person injured may recover, although he was at the time violating the law by driving on the wrong side of the road,[9] or by driving on Sunday.[10] Under some statutes if the load is heavier than permitted by law the town is not liable.[11]

(III) *PERSONS BOUND TO REPAIR.* Persons bound to repair a road cannot recover for injuries from defects which they should have remedied,[12] but anything less than a duty to repair will not bar plaintiff.[13]

b. Contributory Negligence[14] — (I) *IN GENERAL.* A person using a highway must show such care as a prudent person would use,[15] measured in view of the

6. *Maine.*— Tasker *v.* Farmingdale, 88 Me. 103, 33 Atl. 785; Tasker *v.* Farmingdale, 85 Me. 523, 27 Atl. 464; Hall *v.* Unity, 57 Me. 529, way to watering trough.

Massachusetts.— Dickinson *v.* Boston, 188 Mass. 595, 75 N. E. 68, 1 L. R. A. 664; Carey *v.* Hubbardston, 172 Mass. 106, 51 N. E. 521; Harwood *v.* Oakham, 152 Mass. 421, 25 N. E. 625; Little *v.* Brockton, 123 Mass. 511; Shepardson *v.* Colerain, 13 Metc. 55; Tisdale *v.* Norton, 8 Metc. 388.

New York.— Cleveland *v.* Pittsford, 72 Hun 552, 25 N. Y. Suppl. 630 [*affirmed* in 146 N. Y. 384, 42 N. E. 543].

Vermont.—Whitney *v.* Essex, 38 Vt. 270.

Wisconsin.— Stricker *v.* Reedsburg, 101 Wis. 457, 77 N. W. 897; Welsh *v.* Argyle, 89 Wis. 649, 62 N. W. 517; Cartright *v.* Belmont, 58 Wis. 370, 17 N. W. 237.

See 25 Cent. Dig. tit. "Highways," § 503.

It is a question for the jury whether a side-track appeared to have been traveled to a considerable extent as a part of the public highway and was reasonably accessible. Hebbe *v.* Maple Creek, 121 Wis. 668, 99 N. W. 442.

7. Wakeham *v.* St. Clair Tp., 91 Mich. 15, 51 N. W. 696 (where there was no visible sign to indicate that any portion of road-bed was unsafe); Glidden *v.* Reading, 38 Vt. 52, 88 Am. Dec. 639 (blind man leaving road to avoid approaching team); Coppins *v.* Jefferson, 126 Wis. 578, 105 N. W. 1078 (where only slight deviation would cause wheels to strike obstruction); Boltz *v.* Sullivan, 101 Wis. 608, 77 N. W. 870 (accidental deviation); Wheeler *v.* Westport, 30 Wis. 392 (walking outside traveled track but near to it); Kelly *v.* Whitchurch Tp., 12 Ont. L. Rep. 83, 7 Ont. Wkly. Rep. 279 [*affirming* 11 Ont. L. Rep. 155, 6 Ont. Wkly. Rep. 839] (horse shying and swerving); Hogg *v.* Brooke, 7 Ont. L. Rep. 273, 2 Ont. Wkly. Rep. 139, 3 Ont. Wkly. Rep. 120.

8. **Injury sustained in city street while violating law** see MUNICIPAL CORPORATIONS, 28 Cyc. 1417.

9. *Connecticut.*— O'Neil *v.* East Windsor, 63 Conn. 150, 27 Atl. 237.

Massachusetts.— Damon *v.* Scituate, 119 Mass. 66, 20 Am. Rep. 315.

Missouri.— Beckerle *v.* Weiman, 12 Mo. App. 354.

New Hampshire.— Gale *v.* Lisbon, 52 N. H. 174.

Pennsylvania.— Grier *v.* Sampson, 27 Pa. St. 183.

A bicyclist riding on path not a sidewalk may recover. Schell *v.* German Flatts, 123 N. Y. App. Div. 197, 108 N. Y. Suppl. 219 [*affirming* 54 Misc. 445, 104 N. Y. Suppl. 116].

10. Platz *v.* Cohoes, 89 N. Y. 219, 42 Am. Rep. 286; Sutton *v.* Wauwatosa, 29 Wis. 21, 9 Am. Rep. 534; Armstrong *v.* Toler, 11 Wheat. (U. S.) 258, 6 L. ed. 468. *Contra*, Hinckley *v.* Penobscot, 42 Me. 89; Davis *v.* Somerville, 128 Mass. 594, 35 Am. Rep. 399; Johnson *v.* Irasburgh, 47 Vt. 28, 19 Am. Rep. 111. And see SUNDAY.

11. Howe *v.* Castleton, 25 Vt. 162.

12. Todd *v.* Rowley, 8 Allen (Mass.) 51. But see Wood *v.* Waterville, 4 Mass. 422.

13. Barstow *v.* Augusta, 17 Me. 199; Reed *v.* Northfield, 13 Pick. (Mass.) 94, 23 Am. Dec. 662 (inhabitant who knew of the defect and gave no notice); Doan *v.* Willow Springs, 101 Wis. 112, 76 N. W. 1104 (mere authority to fix bad places).

14. **Negligence contributing to injury in city street** see MUNICIPAL CORPORATIONS, 28 Cyc. 1418, 1493.

15. *Delaware.*— Ford *v.* Whiteman, 2 Pennew. 355, 45 Atl. 543.

Indiana.— Chicago, etc., R. Co. *v.* Leachman, 161 Ind. 512, 69 N. E. 253.

Kansas.— Missouri, etc., Tel. Co. *v.* Vandervort, 71 Kan. 101, 79 Pac. 1068; Cunningham *v.* Clay Tp., 69 Kan. 373, 76 Pac. 907.

Maine.— Farrar *v.* Greene, 32 Me. 574; Jacobs *v.* Bangor, 16 Me. 187, 33 Am. Dec. 652, road being repaired.

Maryland.— Harford County *v.* Hamilton, 60 Md. 340, 45 Am. Rep. 739.

Massachusetts.—Hill *v.* Seekonk, 119 Mass. 85; Thompson *v.* Bridgewater, 7 Pick. 188, holding, however, that a traveler need not look far ahead to guard against obstructions which ought not to exist.

New Hampshire.— Tucker *v.* Henniker, 41 N. H. 317.

New York.— Griffin *v.* New York, 9 N. Y. 456, 61 Am. Dec. 700; Harlow *v.* Humiston, 6 Cow. 189.

Wisconsin.— Groundwater *v.* Washington, 92 Wis. 56, 65 N. W. 871 (holding it misleading to charge that driver was justified in driving over place unless it was rashness to do so); Duthie *v.* Washburn, 87 Wis. 231, 58

is visible and patent;[19] but plaintiff may recover where his own fault did not contribute to the injury,[20] although he may himself have been in some degree

avoid car); Gleason *v.* Bremen, 50 Me. 222; Farrar *v.* Greene, 32 Me. 574.

Maryland.— Knight *v.* Baltimore, 97 Md. 647, 55 Atl. 388, did not look to see hole.

Massachusetts.— Damon *v.* Scituate, 119 Mass. 66, 20 Am. Rep. 315 (plaintiff attempting to pass another when injured); Smith *v.* Smith, 2 Pick. 621, 13 Am. Dec. 464.

Michigan.— Tracey *v.* South Haven Tp., 132 Mich. 492, 93 N. W. 1065; Smith *v.* Walker Tp., 117 Mich. 14, 75 N. W. 141, urging horses through deep water.

Minnesota.— Skjeggerud *v.* Minneapolis, etc., Ry. Co., 38 Minn. 56, 35 N. W. 572.

New Hampshire.— Guertin *v.* Hudson, 71 N. H. 505, 53 Atl. 736; Sprague *v.* Bristol, 63 N. H. 430; Chamberlin *v.* Ossipee, 60 N. H. 212; Aldrich *v.* Monroe, 60 N. H. 118 (where plaintiff failed to chain wheels descending a steep hill); Lavery *v.* Manchester, 58 N. H. 444 (falling into a cellar which plaintiff maintained as a nuisance).

New York.—Clapper *v.* Waterford, 62 Hun 170, 16 N. Y. Suppl. 640; Lieberman *v.* Stanley, 88 N. Y. Suppl. 360.

Pennsylvania.— Conrad *v.* Upper Augusta Tp., 200 Pa. St. 337, 49 Atl. 770; Winner *v.* Oakland Tp., 158 Pa. St. 405, 27 Atl. 1110, 1111; Bechtel *v.* Mahanoy City Borough, 30 Pa. Super. Ct. 135 (driving through narrow passage where safer way was at hand); Morford *v.* Sharpsville Borough, 28 Pa. Super. Ct. 544 (driving horse over embankment where there was no guard-rail); Jejorek *v.* Nanticoke, 9 Kulp 501.

South Carolina.— Duncan *v.* Greenville County, 73 S. C. 254, 53 S. E. 367.

Vermont.— Bovee *v.* Danville, 53 Vt. 183; Clark *v.* Corinth, 41 Vt. 449.

Washington.— Baldwin *v.* Lincoln County, 29 Wash. 509, 69 Pac. 1081, instruction refused that person may use defective highway when necessity demands.

Wisconsin.— Schrunk *v.* St. Joseph, 120 Wis. 223, 97 N. W. 946 (driving over narrow fill covered with water); Krause *v.* Merrill, 115 Wis. 526, 92 N. W. 231; Seaver *v.* Union, 113 Wis. 322, 89 N. W. 163; Carpenter *v.* Rolling, 107 Wis. 559, 83 N. W. 953 (drunkenness); Doan *v.* Willow Springs, 101 Wis. 112, 76 N. W. 1104; Hawes *v.* Fox Lake, 33 Wis. 438.

See 25 Cent. Dig. tit. "Highways," § 498.

Evidence that plaintiff was commonly careful and skilful is incompetent on the question of plaintiff's negligence (McDonald *v.* Savoy, 110 Mass. 49), as is also evidence as to the habits of plaintiff (Langworthy *v.* Green Tp., 88 Mich. 207, 50 N. W. 130), or plaintiff's anxiety to reach home (Harris *v.* Clinton Tp., 64 Mich. 447, 31 N. W. 425, 8 Am. St. Rep. 842), or that plaintiff was habitually reckless (Brennan *v.* Friendship, 67 Wis. 233, 29 N. W. 902).

Evidence of plaintiff's due care held sufficient see Rusch *v.* Davenport, 6 Iowa 443 (inference from circumstances that plaintiff was not negligent); Foster *v.* Dixfield, 18 Me. 380; Carville *v.* Westford, 163 Mass. 544, 40 N. E. 893 (attempt to pull wagon back in road); Snow *v.* Provincetown, 120 Mass. 580.

The negligence of a driver of a vehicle may be imputed to the passengers and so prevent their recovery for a defect in the road. Bartram *v.* Sharon, 71 Conn. 686, 43 Atl. 143, 71 Am. St. Rep. 225, 46 L. R. A. 144; Petrich *v.* Union, 117 Wis. 46, 93 N. W. 819, negligence of husband driving imputed to wife injured by defect. *Compare* Plant *v.* Normanby Tp., 10 Ont. L. Rep. 16, 6 Ont. Wkly. Rep. 31. See, generally, NEGLIGENCE, 29 Cyc. 547 *et seq.*

19. *Connecticut.*— Fox *v.* Glastenbury, 29 Conn. 204, causeway under water.

Massachusetts.— Horton *v.* Ipswich, 12 Cush. 488, snow.

Michigan.— Wakeham *v.* St. Clair Tp., 91 Mich. 15, 51 N. W. 696, driving into open mudhole.

New York.— Sutphen *v.* North Hempstead, 80 Hun 409, 30 N. Y. Suppl. 128, riding bicycle on edge of gutter.

South Carolina.— Magill *v.* Lancaster County, 39 S. C. 27, 17 S. E. 507; Laney *v.* Chesterfield Co., 29 S. C. 140, 7 S. E. 56.

West Virginia.—Phillips *v.* Ritchie County Ct., 31 W. Va. 477, 7 S. E. 427, dangerous landslide.

Wisconsin.— Hopkins *v.* Rush River, 70 Wis. 10, 34 N. W. 909, 35 N. W. 939, flooded ford.

See 25 Cent. Dig. tit. "Highways," § 502.

But although a defect or obstruction may be visible, yet if plaintiff did not in fact see it and was not guilty of negligence in not seeing it he may still recover (Embler *v.* Wallkill, 132 N. Y. 222, 30 N. E. 404, plaintiff swept off load of hay by overhanging limb of tree; Rumrill *v.* Delafield, 82 Wis. 184, 52 N. W. 261, in dark), as for instance in the case of a dangling telegraph or telephone wire (Hayes *v.* Hyde Park, 153 Mass. 514, 27 N. E. 522, 12 L. R. A. 249; Sheldon *v.* Western Union Tel. Co., 51 Hun (N. Y.) 591, 4 N. Y. Suppl. 526 [*affirmed* in 121 N. Y. 697, 24 N. E. 1099].) And see, generally, TELEGRAPHS AND TELEPHONES.

20. *Georgia.*— Branan *v.* May, 17 Ga. 136.

Indiana.— Chicago, etc., R. Co. *v.* Leachman, 161 Ind. 512, 69 N. E. 253.

Maryland.— Charles County *v.* Mandanyohl, 93 Md. 150, 48 Atl. 1058, so holding, although plaintiff might have avoided known defects by going through field.

New Hampshire.— Farnum *v.* Concord, 2 N. H. 392.

New Jersey.—Morhart *v.* North Jersey St. R. Co., 64 N. J. L. 236, 45 Atl. 812, bicyclist riding bent over his wheel.

New York.— Clark *v.* Kirwan, 4 E. D. Smith 21.

Pennsylvania.— Bitting *v.* Maxatawny Tp., 180 Pa. St. 357, 36 Atl. 855; Sprowls *v.* Morris Tp., 179 Pa. St. 219, 36 Atl. 242;

(III) *COUNTY.* Counties are considered as quasi-corporations rather than corporate entities and are therefore not generally, in the absence of statute, liable even for defects in roads under their control;[61] but in many states statutes imposing liability exist, and under such statutes the county may be held.[62]

(IV) *ROAD DISTRICTS.* In the absence of statute road districts are not responsible for injuries caused by defects in roads under their control.[63]

(V) *TOWN.* Towns, being mere quasi-corporations or political subdivisions of the state, are generally not liable to action for defects in their highways, in the absence of statute,[64] particularly where no duty to repair rests on

Springer, 5 Tex. 587. But see Hayes *v.* Porter, 22 Me. 371.

Whether penalty imposed on public officer is exclusive of civil liability see ACTIONS, 1 Cyc. 679.

61. *Arkansas.*—Granger *v.* Pulaski County, 26 Ark. 37.

California.— Barnett *v.* Contra Costa County, 67 Cal. 77, 7 Pac. 177.

Illinois.— Guinnip *v.* Carter, 58 Ill. 296; White *v.* Bond County, 58 Ill. 297, 11 Am. Rep. 65.

Indiana.— Cones *v.* Benton County, 137 Ind. 404, 37 N. E. 272; Abbett *v.* Johnson County, 114 Ind. 61, 16 N. E. 127; Shrum *v.* Washington County, 13 Ind. App. 585, 41 N. E. 349.

Iowa.—Wilson *v.* Wapello County, 129 Iowa 77, 105 N. W. 363.

Kentucky.— Sinkhorn *v.* Lexington, etc., Turnpike Co., 112 Ky. 205, 65 S. W. 356, 23 Ky. L. Rep. 1479.

Massachusetts.—Bliss *v.* Deerfield, 13 Pick. 102.

Nebraska.— Goes *v.* Gage County, 67 Nebr. 616, 93 N. W. 923.

Ohio.— Grimwood *v.* Summit County, 23 Ohio St. 600.

Oregon.— Schroeder *v.* Multnomah County, 45 Oreg. 92, 76 Pac. 772.

Washington.— Clark *v.* Lincoln County, 1 Wash. 518, 20 Pac. 576.

England.— Russell *v.* Devon, 2 T. R. 667, 1 Rev. Rep. 585, 100 Eng. Reprint 359.

See 25 Cent. Dig. tit. "Highways," § 504.

62. See the statutes of the several states. And see Morgan County *v.* Penick, 131 Ga. 385, 62 S. E. 300; Calvert County *v.* Gibson, 36 Md. 229; Anne Arundel County *v.* Duckett, 20 Md. 468, 83 Am. Dec. 557.

Liability as affected by contract.— The lessor of the road having surrendered entire control to the county as lessee is not liable for the county's negligent failure to repair the road, and therefore the undertaking of the county to save the lessor harmless from any suits that might be brought against the lessor by reason of failure to repair the road does not render the county liable. Sinkhorn *v.* Lexington, etc., Turnpike Co., 112 Ky. 205, 65 S. W. 356, 23 Ky. L. Rep. 1479.

63. White *v.* Road Dist. No. 1, 9 Iowa 202; Eikenberry *v.* Bazaar Tp., 22 Kan. 556, 31 Am. Rep. 198.

64. *California.*— Barnett *v.* Contra Costa County, 67 Cal. 77, 7 Pac. 177.

Connecticut.— Beardsley *v.* Hartford, 50 Conn. 529, 47 Am. Rep. 677.

Illinois.— Bussell *v.* Steuben, 57 Ill. 35; Waltham *v.* Kemper, 55 Ill. 346, 8 Am. Rep. 652.

Kansas.— Quincy Tp. *v.* Sheehan, 48 Kan. 620, 29 Pac. 1084; Eikenberry *v.* Bazaar Tp., 22 Kan. 556, 31 Am. Rep. 198.

Maine.— Frazer *v.* Lewiston, 76 Me. 531.

Massachusetts.— Nicodemo *v.* Southborough, 173 Mass. 455, 53 N. E. 887; Fowler *v.* Gardner, 169 Mass. 505, 48 N. E. 619; Brailey *v.* Southborough, 6 Cush. 141; Mower *v.* Leicester, 9 Mass. 247, 6 Am. Dec. 63. See also Hill *v.* Boston, 122 Mass. 344, 23 Am. Rep. 332.

Michigan.—Doak *v.* Saginaw Tp., 119 Mich. 680, 78 N. W. 883; Niles Tp. Highway Com'rs *v.* Martin, 4 Mich. 557, 69 Am. Dec. 333.

Minnesota.—Weltsch *v.* Stark, 65 Minn. 5, 67 N. W. 648; Altnow *v.* Sibley, 30 Minn. 186, 14 N. W. 877, 44 Am. Rep. 191.

Nebraska.—Wilson *v.* Ulysses Tp., 72 Nebr. 807, 101 N. W. 986.

New Hampshire.— Sargent *v.* Gilford, 66 N. H. 543, 27 Atl. 306. But see Wheeler *v.* Troy, 20 N. H. 77.

New Jersey.— Von Vane *v.* Centre Tp., 67 N. J. L. 587, 52 Atl. 359.

Oklahoma.— James *v.* Wellston Tp., 18 Okla. 56, 90 Pac. 100, 13 L. R. A. N. S. 1219.

United States.— See Barnes *v.* District of Columbia, 91 U. S. 540, 23 L. ed. 440.

See 25 Cent. Dig. tit. "Highways," § 505.

The custom of the inhabitants of towns to join and break paths through the snow in highways, if ancient, general, and reasonable, excuses the selectmen from action in ordinary cases. Seeley *v.* Litchfield, 49 Conn. 134, 44 Am. Rep. 213. See also Barnett *v.* Contra Costa County, 67 Cal. 77, 7 Pac. 177.

Lack of funds as affecting liability on city streets see MUNICIPAL CORPORATIONS, 28 Cyc. 1343.

Misfeasance distinguished from nonfeasance.— In England it has been held that a local board, being the highway authority of the district, is not liable for damages caused to a person in consequence of the highway being out of repair where such non-repair is a mere nonfeasance. Sydney *v.* Bourke, [1895] A. C. 433, 59 J. P. 659, 64 L. J. P. C. 140, 72 L. T. Rep. N. S. 605, 11 Reports 482; Pictou *v.* Geldert, [1893] A. C. 524, 63 L. J. P. C. 37, 69 L. T. Rep. N. S. 510, 1 Reports 447, 42 Wkly. Rep. 114; Cowley *v.* Newmarket Local Bd., [1892] A. C. 345, 56 J. P. 805, 62 L. J. Q. B. 65, 67 L. T. Rep. N. S. 486, 1 Reports 45; Maguire *v.* Liverpool, [1905]

actual[7] or constructive,[8] showing that plaintiff was not in fault,[9] and specifying his injuries[10] and the damages claimed.[11] The declaration may be amended to better state the same cause of action,[12] and after verdict will be presumed sufficient.[13] The declaration may be good, although differing somewhat from the statutory notice.[14]

(II) *PLEA OR ANSWER.* As in other actions, the plea or answer must clearly state facts sufficient to constitute a good legal defense.[15] The town may deny the existence of the road as a public highway,[16] even though it has repaired

not allege establishment in the mode authorized by statute.

7. Smiley *v.* Merrill Plantation, 84 Me. 322, 24 Atl. 872 (holding, however, that the complaint need not allege the place of delivery); Low *v.* Windham, 75 Me. 113; Berry *v.* Wauwatosa, 87 Wis. 401, 58 N. W. 751 (holding that an admission in an answer that some notice was served is not an admission that the notice required was duly served); Paulson *v.* Pelican, 79 Wis. 445, 48 N. W. 715; Susenguth *v.* Rantoul, 48 Wis. 334, 4 N. W. 328. *Contra*, Kent *v.* Lincoln, 32 Vt. 591, holding that notice, being no part of the cause of action, need not be alleged.

A general allegation that the required notice was given is sufficient. Cairncross *v.* Pewaukee, 78 Wis. 66, 47 N. W. 13, 10 L. R. A. 473.

8. Reusch *v.* Licking Rolling Mill Co., 118 Ky. 369, 80 S. W. 1168, 26 Ky. L. Rep. 249; Moody *v.* Shelby Tp., 110 Mich. 396, 68 N. W. 259 [*following* Storrs *v.* Grand Rapids, 110 Mich. 483, 68 N. W. 258], that defendant by reasonable care might have known and thereafter had sufficient time to repair. See also Thornton *v.* Springer, 5 Tex. 587, petition defective as not alleging that the road was out of repair for twenty days, and that the overseer had been notified of his appointment. *Compare* Dean *v.* Sharon, 72 Conn. 667, 45 Atl. 963, holding that knowledge is presumed and need not be alleged.

9. *Connecticut.*— Clinton *v.* Howard, 42 Conn. 294.

Georgia.— Penick *v.* Morgan County, 131 Ga. 385, 62 S. E. 300; Kent *v.* Southern Bell Tel., etc., 120 Ga. 980, 48 S. E. 399.

Indiana.— Mt. Vernon *v.* Dusouchett, 2 Ind. 586, 54 Am. Dec. 467.

Massachusetts.— Raymond *v.* Lowell, 6 Cush. 524, 53 Am. Dec. 57; May *v.* Princeton, 11 Metc. 442.

South Carolina.— Walker *v.* Chester County, 40 S. C. 342, 18 S. E. 936.

See 25 Cent. Dig. tit. "Highways," § 522.

No express denial of contributory negligence is required in some jurisdictions. See Reading Tp. *v.* Telfer, 57 Kan. 798, 48 Pac. 134, 57 Am. St. Rep. 355; Corey *v.* Bath, 35 N. H. 530. And see, generally, NEGLIGENCE, 29 Cyc. 575 *et seq.*

10. Corey *v.* Bath, 35 N. H. 530.

11. See cases cited *infra*, this note.

Double damages.— In actions on the case, under Mass. St. (1786) c. 81, § 7, to recover double damages for defects in highways or bridges, it is not necessary to allege that plaintiff is entitled to double damages. Worster *v.* Proprietors Canal Bridge, 16 Pick. (Mass.) 541; Clark *v.* Worthington, 12 Pick. (Mass.) 571.

12. Chapman *v.* Nobleboro, 76 Me. 427; Davis *v.* Hill, 41 N. H. 329; Elson *v.* Waterford, 138 Fed. 1004 [*affirmed* in 149 Fed. 91].

13. Barker *v.* Koozier, 80 Ill. 205 (omission to state that defendant refused to turn); Raymond *v.* Lowell, 6 Cush. (Mass.) 524, 53 Am. Dec. 57; Corey *v.* Bath, 35 N. H. 530.

14. Breen *v.* Cornwall, 73 Conn. 309, 47 Atl. 322 (holding that it may allege cause more specifically in complaint than in notice); Wadleigh *v.* Mt. Vernon, 75 Me. 79; Young *v.* Douglas, 157 Mass. 383, 32 N. E. 354; Spooner *v.* Freetown, 139 Mass. 235, 29 N. E. 662. See also Farlow *v.* Camp Point, 186 Ill. 256, 57 N. E. 781.

15. Dunn *v.* Gunn, 149 Ala. 583, 42 So. 686 (holding insufficient an answer that it was not obvious to defendant that the ditch would be dangerous, as not denying defendant's knowledge that the road was traveled); Wickham *v.* Twaddell, 25 Pa. Super. Ct. 188 (holding insufficient an answer that travel did not need the obstructed space); Carpenter *v.* Rolling, 107 Wis. 559, 83 N. W. 953 (holding that a denial of legal lay-out is not a denial putting the existence of the road in issue); Cuthbert *v.* Appleton, 24 Wis. 383 (holding that a denial that a highway was "in a dangerous condition to travelers exercising ordinary care and diligence" was not a sufficient denial that it was out of repair).

But the purpose for which the material was placed on the highway need not be pleaded. Carlon *v.* Greenfield, 130 Wis. 342, 110 N. W. 208.

16. Todd *v.* Rome, 2 Me. 55; Jones *v.* Andover, 9 Pick. (Mass.) 146; Wentworth *v.* Rochester, 63 N. H. 244; Wooley *v.* Rochester, 60 N. H. 467; Tilton *v.* Pittsfield, 58 N. H. 327; Eames *v.* Northumberland, 44 N. H. 67; Hall *v.* Manchester, 39 N. H. 295.

Mere irregularities in the lay-out cannot be set up. Norris *v.* Haverhill, 65 N. H. 89, 18 Atl. 85 (as for instance that a petition on which the lay-out was made was insufficient in form); Randall *v.* Conway, 63 N. H. 513, 3 Atl. 635 (that the return was made late); Horne *v.* Rochester, 62 N. H. 347; Haywood *v.* Charlestown, 43 N. H. 61; Proctor *v.* Andover, 42 N. H. 348 (that lay-out was wider than petition prayed for).

If the inhabitants of a town, in making a road, deviate from the true location, they are estopped to deny their liability to maintain it as constructed, in an action against them for injury occasioned by want of repair.

not too remote to lack probative force. Evidence of similar accidents at the same place where plaintiff was injured has been variously held to be admissible[41] and inadmissible.[42] Evidence of subsequent repairs is commonly inadmissible,[43] except under special circumstances,[44] as is also as a general rule evidence of the custom and practice in the neighborhood as to the care of roads,[45] although

Indiana.— Porter County *v.* Dombke, 94 Ind. 72.

Kansas.— Cunningham *v.* Clay Tp., 69 Kan. 373, 76 Pac. 907, similar stones in other places to show stone in question not unusual in appearance.

Maine.— Verrill *v.* Minot, 31 Me. 299.

Massachusetts.— Ghenn *v.* Provincetown, 105 Mass. 313.

Wisconsin.— Conrad *v.* Ellington, 104 Wis. 367, 80 N. W. 456.

See 25 Cent. Dig. tit. "Highways," § 531.

Rule applied to action for injury in city street see MUNICIPAL CORPORATIONS, 28 Cyc. 1489.

Condition at other places held immaterial under the particular circumstances see Whitley Tp. *v.* Linville, 174 Ill. 579, 51 N. E. 832 (width in other places held immaterial); Tripp *v.* Lyman, 37 Me. 250; Stoddard *v.* Winchester, 157 Mass. 567, 32 N. E. 948; Schoonmaker *v.* Wilbraham, 110 Mass. 134; Burt *v.* Utah Light, etc., Co., 26 Utah 157, 72 Pac. 497; Coats *v.* Canaan, 51 Vt. 131.

41. Bailey *v.* Trumbull, 31 Conn. 581 (accident fifteen or twenty feet away); Cook *v.* New Durham, 64 N. H. 419, 13 Atl. 650; Griffin *v.* Auburn, 58 N. H. 121; Kent *v.* Lincoln, 32 Vt. 591.

That other horses were frightened is evidence of the dangerous character of the road. Galt *v.* Woliver, 103 Ill. App. 71; Crocker *v.* McGregor, 76 Me. 282, 49 Am. Rep. 611; Nye *v.* Dibley, 88 Minn. 465, 93 N. W. 524; Golden *v.* Chicago, etc., R. Co., 84 Mo. App. 59; Seeton *v.* Dunbarton, 72 N. H. 269, 56 Atl. 197; Darling *v.* Westmoreland, 52 N. H. 401, 13 Am. Rep. 55; Wilson *v.* Spafford, 10 N. Y. Suppl. 649.

Rule applied in action for injury in city street see MUNICIPAL CORPORATIONS, 28 Cyc. 1490.

The absence of such accidents is also held to be admissible. Gould *v.* Hutchins, 73 N. H. 69, 58 Atl. 1046; Embler *v.* Wallkill, 132 N. Y. 222, 30 N. E. 404; Glasier *v.* Hebron, 131 N. Y. 447, 30 N. E. 239, 597 [*reversing* 62 Hun 137, 16 N. Y. Suppl. 503]; Waller *v.* Hebron, 5 N. Y. App. Div. 577, 39 N. Y. Suppl. 381; Maxim *v.* Champion, 50 Hun (N. Y.) 88, 4 N. Y. Suppl. 515 [*affirmed* in 119 N. Y. 626, 23 N. E. 1144]; Stone *v.* Pendleton, 21 R. I. 332, 43 Atl. 643; Garske *v.* Ridgeville, 123 Wis. 503, 102 N. W. 22. *Contra*, Lutton *v.* Vernon, 62 Conn. 1, 23 Atl. 1020, 27 Atl. 589 (in the absence of evidence that the experience of other persons was similar to decedent's); Taylor *v.* Monroe, 43 Conn. 36 (where accident was peculiar); Branch *v.* Libbey, 78 Me. 321, 5 Atl. 71, 57 Am. Rep. 810; Schoonmaker *v.* Wilbraham, 110 Mass. 134; Kidder *v.* Dunstable, 11 Gray (Mass.) 342; Aldrich *v.* Pelham, 1 Gray (Mass.) 510; Langworthy *v.* Green Tp., 88 Mich. 207, 50 N. W. 130.

42. Cunningham *v.* Clay Tp., 69 Kan. 373, 76 Pac. 907; Bremner *v.* Newcastle, 83 Me. 415, 22 Atl. 382, 23 Am. St. Rep. 782; Blair *v.* Pelham, 118 Mass. 420; Merrill *v.* Bradford, 110 Mass. 505; Collins *v.* Dorchester, 6 Cush. (Mass.) 396; Phillips *v.* Willow, 70 Wis. 6, 34 N. W. 731, 5 Am. St. Rep. 114.

43. *Indiana.*—Wabash County *v.* Pearson, 129 Ind. 456, 28 N. E. 1120.

Massachusetts.— Spooner *v.* Freetown, 139 Mass. 235, 29 N. E. 662, so holding in the absence of evidence that the town voted for the repairs or ratified them.

Michigan.— Langworthy *v.* Green Tp., 88 Mich. 207, 50 N. W. 130.

New Hampshire.— Seeton *v.* Dunbarton, 72 N. H. 269, 56 Atl. 197; Dow *v.* Weare, 68 N. H. 345, 44 Atl. 489, such evidence given and stricken out.

New York.— Clapper *v.* Waterford, 131 N. Y. 382, 30 N. E. 240 [*reversing* 62 Hun 170, 16 N. Y. Suppl. 640] (commenting on the danger of such evidence); Getty *v.* Hamlin, 127 N. Y. 636, 27 N. E. 399 [*reversing* 8 N. Y. Suppl. 190]. But see Stone *v.* Poland, 58 Hun 21, 11 N. Y. Suppl. 498 [*distinguishing* Corcoran *v.* Peekskill, 108 N. Y. 151, 15 N. E. 309]; Getty *v.* Hamlin, 46 Hun 1.

Utah.— Burt *v.* Utah Light, etc., Co., 26 Utah 157, 72 Pac. 497.

Wisconsin.— Redepenning *v.* Rock, 136 Wis. 372, 117 N. W. 805; Jennings *v.* Albion, 90 Wis. 22, 62 N. W. 926.

See 25 Cent. Dig. tit. "Highways," § 532.

44. Morrell *v.* Peck, 88 N. Y. 398 (to show control and funds in the hands of defendant); Redepenning *v.* Rock, 136 Wis. 372, 117 N. W. 805 (to contradict claim of town that misled by notice; and to refute defendant's claim that the road was too wet to be repaired). See also Carlon *v.* Greenfield, 130 Wis. 342, 110 N. W. 208.

45. *Connecticut.*— Tiesler *v.* Norwich, 73 Conn. 199, 47 Atl. 161, custom to maintain carriage blocks.

Massachusetts.— Hinckley *v.* Barnstable, 109 Mass. 126 (usage to leave drains uncovered); Judd *v.* Fargo, 107 Mass. 264 (that neighbors were accustomed to obstruct highway with sleds as he did); Kidder *v.* Dunstable, 11 Gray 342.

Michigan.— Malloy *v.* Walker Tp., 77 Mich. 448, 43 N. W. 1012, 6 L. R. A. 695.

New Hampshire.— Rowell *v.* Hollis, 62 N. H. 129; Littleton *v.* Richardson, 32 N. H. 59.

Wisconsin.—Kenworthy *v.* Ironton, 41 Wis. 647, custom to construct highway on hillsides.

See 25 Cent. Dig. tit. "Highways," § 527 *et seq.*

all material questions,[63] as the burden of proof,[64] contributory negligence,[65] defendant's duty and liability,[66] and proximate cause,[67] the necessity and sufficiency of railings or barriers,[68] and whether objects were calculated

under the statute, is one of law arising upon the facts proved. Brooks *v.* Hart, 14 N. H. 307.

Matters not in evidence should not be included in the instructions. Bunker *v.* Gouldsboro, 81 Me. 188, 16 Atl. 543; Handy *v.* Meridian Tp., 114 Mich. 454, 72 N. W. 251; Monk *v.* New Utrecht, 104 N. Y. 552, 11 N. E. 268; Pettingill *v.* Olean, 20 N. Y. Suppl. 367.

63. Wells *v.* Gallagher, 144 Ala. 363, 39 So. 747, 113 Am. St. Rep. 50, 3 L. R. A. N. S. 759; McClure *v.* Feldmann, 184 Mo. 710, 84 S. W. 16; Brown *v.* Mt. Holly, 69 Vt. 364, 38 Atl. 69; Jenewein *v.* Irving, 122 Wis. 228, 99 N. W. 346, 903; Schrunk *v.* St. Joseph, 120 Wis. 223, 97 N. W. 946.

64. McGuinness *v.* Westchester, 66 Hun (N. Y.) 356, 21 N. Y. Suppl. 290; Welling *v.* Judge, 40 Barb. (N. Y.) 193; Schillinger *v.* Verona, 88 Wis. 317, 60 N. W. 272.

65. *Connecticut.*—Williams *v.* Clinton, 28 Conn. 264.

Maine.— Garmon *v.* Bangor, 38 Me. 443.

Maryland.— Alleghany County *v.* Broadwaters, 69 Md. 533, 16 Atl. 223.

New Hampshire.— Hendry *v.* North Hampton, 72 N. H. 351, 56 Atl. 922, 101 Am. St. Rep. 681, 64 L. R. A. 70; Guertin *v.* Hudson, 71 N. H. 505, 53 Atl. 736.

Pennsylvania.— Long *v.* Milford Tp., 137 Pa. St. 122, 20 Atl. 425; Chartiers Tp. *v.* Phillips, 122 Pa. St. 601, 16 Atl. 26; Millcreek Tp. *v.* Perry, 8 Pa. Cas. 474, 12 Atl. 149.

Vermont.— Walker *v.* Westfield, 39 Vt. 246; Rice *v.* Montpelier, 19 Vt. 470.

Wisconsin.— Kenworthy *v.* Ironton, 41 Wis. 647; Dreher *v.* Fitchburg, 22 Wis. 675, 99 Am. Dec. 91.

The burden of proof as to contributory negligence should be explained to the jury. Welling *v.* Judge, 40 Barb. (N. Y.) 193.

Instructions held erroneous see Calvert County *v.* Gibson, 36 Md. 229 (in not submitting to jury plaintiff's knowledge of two roads); Templeton *v.* Warriorsmark Tp., 200 Pa. St. 165, 49 Atl. 950 (suggesting that plaintiff may have been negligent in joining sleighing party over public highway); Collins *v.* Leafey, 124 Pa. St. 203, 16 Atl. 765 (instruction that is the duty of everyone to occupy the highway with such care that no injury can happen to another, where the legal standard of negligence was not defined); Reynolds *v.* Burlington, 52 Vt. 300; Petrich *v.* Union, 117 Wis. 46, 93 N. W. 819.

66. *Connecticut.*— Masters *v.* Warren, 27 Conn. 293.

Kansas.— Cunningham *v.* Clay Tp., 69 Kan. 373, 76 Pac. 907.

Kentucky.— Floyd *v.* Henderson, etc., Gravel Road Co., 56 S. W. 6, 21 Ky. L. Rep. 1718.

Maryland.— Garrett County *v.* Blackburn, 105 Md. 226, 66 Atl. 31.

Massachusetts.— Moran *v.* Palmer, 162 Mass. 196, 38 N. E. 442; Lowe *v.* Clinton, 136 Mass. 24; Taylor *v.* Woburn, 130 Mass. 494; Lyman *v.* Amherst, 107 Mass. 339 (holding that if the judge requires the jury to find that the want of a sufficient railing along the bank was the sole cause of the injury, in order to return a verdict for plaintiff, defendants have no ground of exceptions to his refusal of rulings as to whether the highway was defective from the nature of its material at the place where the horse slipped); Stevens *v.* Boxford, 10 Allen 25, 37 Am. Dec. 616; Kellogg *v.* Northampton, 4 Gray 65; Collins *v.* Dorchester, 6 Cush. 396.

Michigan.— Whoram *v.* Argentine Tp., 112 Mich. 20, 70 N. W. 341.

New York.— Young *v.* Macomb, 11 N. Y. App. Div. 480, 42 N. Y. Suppl. 351.

Rhode Island.— Stone *v.* Pendleton, 21 R. I. 332, 43 Atl. 643.

Vermont.— Rice *v.* Montpelier, 19 Vt. 470; Blodget *v.* Royalton, 14 Vt. 288.

Washington.— Gallagher *v.* Buckley, 31 Wash. 380, 72 Pac. 79.

Wisconsin.— Fehrman *v.* Pine River, 118 Wis. 150, 95 N. W. 105; Vass *v.* Waukesha, 90 Wis. 337, 63 N. W. 280; Goldsworthy *v.* Linden, 75 Wis. 24, 43 N. W. 656; Kenworthy *v.* Ironton, 41 Wis. 647.

See 25 Cent. Dig. tit. "Highways," § 540.

Instructions held erroneous see Lewman *v.* Andrews, 129 Ala. 170, 29 So. 692 (that there was no evidence that there was a public road where plaintiff fell into ditch); Tiesler *v.* Norwich, 73 Conn. 199, 47 Atl. 161 (that carriage block was not an obstruction); Kennedy *v.* Cecil County, 69 Md. 65, 14 Atl. 524 (that no liability attached unless mules frightened by defect); Golden *v.* Chicago, etc., R. Co., 84 Mo. App. 59 ("necessary" effect to frighten horses); Duthie *v.* Washburn, 87 Wis. 231, 58 N. W. 380 (tending to confuse the jury); Draper *v.* Ironton, 42 Wis. 696.

67. Kennedy *v.* Cecil County, 69 Md. 65, 14 Atl. 524; Langworthy *v.* Green, 95 Mich. 93, 54 N. W. 697; Beall *v.* Athens Tp., 81 Mich. 536, 45 N. W. 1014; Fulsome *v.* Concord, 46 Vt. 135.

Whether negligence was the proximate cause of the accident should be brought to the jury's consideration. Kennedy *v.* Cecil County, 69 Md. 65, 14 Atl. 524; Walker *v.* Westfield, 39 Vt. 246.

68. *Kansas.*—Wetmore Tp. *v.* Chamberlain, 64 Kan. 327, 67 Pac. 845, removable barriers.

Massachusetts.— Howard *v.* Mendon, 117 Mass. 585; Lyman *v.* Amherst, 107 Mass. 339, weight falling on railing.

Michigan.— Ross *v.* Ionia Tp., 104 Mich. 320, 62 N. W. 401.

New Hampshire.— Seeton *v.* Dunbarton, 72 N. H. 269, 56 Atl. 197.

damages being allowed only in exceptional cases,[80] and mental suffering being compensated only when accompanied by actual injury.[81] Damages are confined to damages stated in the notice [82] and consequences directly resulting.[83]

i. Appeal and Error.[84] The right of appeal in actions for injuries resulting from defects or obstructions depends on local practice,[85] and is only open on points made in the lower court,[86] and not as to facts found by the jury,[87] or where no substantial error was committed.[88]

VIII. ROAD TAXES.

A. In General — 1. STATUTORY REGULATION — a. In General. The imposition of road taxes is a matter of statutory regulation,[89] being within the constitutional power of the legislature,[90] which must observe the constitutional limits,[91]

ness (Hunt *v.* Winfield, 36 Wis. 154, 17 Am. Rep. 482).

Items held not recoverable see Chidsey *v.* Canton, 17 Conn. 475 (consequential damages, loss of service, expense of nursing); Dubuque Wood, etc., Assoc. *v.* Dubuque, 30 Iowa 176 (loss of goods which plaintiff could not move over the roads); McLaughlin *v.* Bangor, 58 Me. 398 (loss of use of coach held not "damage in his property," within the meaning of the declaration); Brown *v.* Watson, 47 Me. 161, 74 Am. Dec. 482 (being compelled to take circuitous route); Sargent *v.* Hampden, 38 Me. 581 (interest); Weeks *v.* Shirley, 33 Me. 271 (loss of time and expenses held not included under "damage in one's property"); Reed *v.* Belfast, 20 Me. 246 (loss of services of minor son); Smith *v.* Dedham, 8 Cush. (Mass.) 522 (damage from loss of access to highway); Harwood *v.* Lowell, 4 Cush. (Mass.) 310 (mere consequential damages); Lavery *v.* Manchester, 58 N. H. 444 (for injuries caused by falling into cellar which plaintiff maintained as a nuisance); Griffin *v.* Sanbornton, 44 N. H. 246 (damage from obstruction suffered in common with general public); Page *v.* Sumpter, 53 Wis. 652, 11 N. W. 60 (use of mare between injury and her death, including plaintiff's services in taking care of her).

Damages are for the jury and an instruction should not be based on the assumption that injuries will be permanent. Colby *v.* Wiscasset, 61 Me. 304.

New action for incurable injuries discovered after settlement of previous action dismissed see Chartrand *v.* Montreal, 17 Quebec Super. Ct. 143.

Insurance received need not be deducted. Harding *v.* Townshend, 43 Vt. 536, 5 Am. Rep. 304.

80. Burr *v.* Plymouth, 48 Conn. 460; Wilson *v.* Granby, 47 Conn. 59, 36 Am. Rep. 51 (holding damages compensatory merely except for gross negligence, when expenses of suit may be included); Woodman *v.* Nottingham, 49 N. H. 387, 6 Am. Rep. 526); Hull *v.* Richmond, 12 Fed. Cas. No. 6,861, 2 Woodb. & M. 337 (not aggravated where road had been in same condition many years without complaint).

81. Canning *v.* Williamstown, 1 Cush. (Mass.) 451.

82. Boyd *v.* Readsboro, 55 Vt. 163.

83. Noble *v.* Portsmouth, 67 N. H. 183, 30 Atl. 419; Robin *v.* Bartlett, 64 N. H. 426, 13 Atl. 645.

84. **In action for injury in city street** see MUNICIPAL CORPORATIONS, 28 Cyc. 1530.

85. See Strout *v.* Durham, 23 Me. 483.

86. Griffin *v.* Johnson, 84 Ga. 279, 10 S. E. 719; Talbot *v.* Taunton, 140 Mass. 552, 5 N. E. 616.

87. Upton *v.* Windham, 75 Conn. 288, 53 Atl. 660, 96 Am. St. Rep. 197; O'Neil *v.* East Windsor, 63 Conn. 150, 27 Atl. 237; Lee *v.* Barkhampsted, 46 Conn. 213; Burrell Tp. *v.* Uncapher, 117 Pa. St. 353, 11 Atl. 619, 2 Am. St. Rep. 664; Swift *v.* Newbury, 36 Vt. 355; Chappell *v.* Oregon, 36 Wis. 145.

88. Little *v.* Iron River, 102 Wis. 250, 78 N. W. 416.

89. See the statutes of the several states. And see cases cited *infra*, note 90 *et seq.*

Municipal authority to tax for street improvement see MUNICIPAL CORPORATIONS, 28 Cyc. 1669.

90. *California.*— Miller *v.* Kern County, 137 Cal. 516, 70 Pac. 549.

Colorado.— Fairplay *v.* Park County, 29 Colo. 57, 67 Pac. 152.

Illinois.— Butz *v.* Kerr, 123 Ill. 659, 14 N. E. 671.

Indiana.— Gilson *v.* Rush County, 128 Ind. 65, 27 N. E. 235, 11 L. R. A. 835.

North Carolina.— Holton *v.* Mecklenburg County, 93 N. C. 430, although tax is paid in labor in one district and in another in money.

Pennsylvania.— *In re* Middletown Road, 15 Pa. Super. Ct. 167.

Vermont.— Highgate *v.* State, 59 Vt. 39, 7 Atl. 898.

Virginia.— Washington County *v.* Saltville Land Co., 99 Va. 640, 39 S. E. 704.

Wisconsin.— Jensen *v.* Polk County, 47 Wis. 298, 2 N. W. 320.

See 25 Cent. Dig. tit. "Highways," § 380.

Rates may differ in different counties. Haney *v.* Bartown County, 91 Ga. 770, 18 S. E. 28.

91. *California.*— People *v.* Seymour, 16 Cal. 332, 76 Am. Dec. 521.

Idaho.— Humbird Lumber Co. *v.* Kootenai County, 10 Ida. 490, 79 Pac. 396.

Nebraska.— Dixon County *v.* Chicago, etc., R. Co., 1 Nebr. (Unoff.) 240, 95 N. W. 340.

New York.— People *v.* Flagg, 46 N. Y. 401.

A tax or license on vehicles using a public highway is enforced in some jurisdictions.[19]

d. Amount. The amount of highway taxes is commonly limited by general law,[20] and any tax assessed exceeding that authority is void;[21] but a further levy is sometimes provided for on occasion,[22] and upon specified proceedings.[23]

3. Persons and Property Taxed — a. Property. Subject to the restriction that property is liable only as described in the tax proceeding,[24] and except as

of such road. Elliott *v.* Berry, 41 Ohio St. 110.

In Michigan roads in contemplation are proper subjects of taxation, although not laid out. Michigan Land, etc., Co. *v.* L'Anse Tp., 63 Mich. 700, 30 N. W. 331; Sawyer-Goodman Co. *v.* Crystal Falls Tp., 56 Mich. 597, 23 N. W. 334.

19. Tomlinson *v.* Indianapolis, 144 Ind. 142, 43 N. E. 9, 36 L. R. A. 413; Armitage *v.* Crawford County, 24 Pa. Co. Ct. 207, on bicycles for construction of side path.

20. See the statutes of the several states. And see the following cases:

Illinois.— People *v.* Cairo, etc., R. Co., 231 Ill. 438, 83 N. E. 116; Chicago, etc., R. Co. *v.* People, 214 Ill. 302, 73 N. E. 312; Chicago, etc., R. Co. *v.* People, 200 Ill. 237, 65 N. E. 701; Mee *v.* Paddack, 83 Ill. 494.

Michigan.— Peninsular Sav. Bank *v.* Ward, 118 Mich. 87, 76 N. W. 161, 79 N. W. 911; Longyear *v.* Auditor-Gen., 72 Mich. 415, 40 N. W. 738; Mills *v.* Richland Tp., 72 Mich. 100, 40 N. W. 183.

New Jersey.— Norcross *v.* Veal, 51 N. J. L. 87, 16 Atl. 159; Paterson Ave., etc., Road Com'rs *v.* Hudson County, 45 N. J. L. 173; State *v.* Cannon, 33 N. J. L. 218.

North Dakota.— Beggs *v.* Paine, 15 N. D. 436, 109 N. W. 322.

Pennsylvania.— Elsbree *v.* Keller, 35 Pa. Super. Ct. 497; Com. *v.* Crane, 5 Pa. Co. Ct. 421.

South Carolina.— State *v.* Odom, 1 Speers 263.

Wisconsin.— Mueller *v.* Cavour, 107 Wis. 599, 83 N. W. 944; Bigelow *v.* Washburn, 98 Wis. 553, 74 N. W. 362 (computed on assessed valuation for the previous year); Sage *v.* Fifield, 68 Wis. 546, 32 N. W. 629.

United States.— C. N. Nelson Lumber Co. *v.* Loraine, 24 Fed. 456.

Limitation held not to apply see State *v.* Wirt County Ct., 63 W. Va. 230, 59 S. E. 884, 981.

21. Wright *v.* Wabash, etc., R. Co., 120 Ill. 541, 12 N. E. 240; State *v.* Fulmore, (Tex. Civ. App. 1902) 71 S. W. 418; C. N. Nelson Lumber Co. *v.* Loraine, 24 Fed. 456.

22. People *v.* Peoria, etc., R. Co., 232 Ill. 540, 83 N. E. 1054 (only to amount necessary); Cleveland, etc., R. Co. *v.* People, 223 Ill. 17, 79 N. E. 17 (on certificate of highway commissioners); People *v.* Bloomington Tp. Highway Com'rs, 118 Ill. 239, 8 N. E. 684 (in discretion of board); Mee *v.* Paddock, 83 Ill. 494; Longyear *v.* Auditor-Gen., 72 Mich. 415, 40 N. W. 738 (for extraordinary expenses). But see People *v.* Atchison, etc., R. Co., 201 Ill. 365, 66 N. E. 232.

In Illinois an additional levy on a contingency is provided for on a certificate that such contingency exists (People *v.* Cincinnati, etc., R. Co., 213 Ill. 503, 72 N. E. 1119; Cleveland, etc., R. Co. *v.* People, 205 Ill. 582, 69 N. E. 89, only amount certified may be authorized; Chicago, etc., R. Co. *v.* People, 200 Ill. 237, 65 N. E. 701; Chicago, etc., R. Co. *v.* People, 200 Ill. 141, 65 N. E. 705), describing the contingency (St. Louis, etc., R. Co. *v.* People, 224 Ill. 155, 79 N. E. 664; Cleveland, etc., R. Co. *v.* People, 205 Ill. 582, 69 N. E. 89), which certificate is subject to amendment (Cleveland, etc., R. Co. *v.* People, *supra*; Chicago, etc., R. Co. *v.* People, 200 Ill. 141, 65 N. E. 705). No proper contingency was set out in the following cases: People *v.* Belleville, etc., R. Co., 232 Ill. 454, 83 N. E. 950; People *v.* Kankakee, etc., R. Co., 231 Ill. 490, 83 N. E. 117 (needed "to build two bridges"); People *v.* Chicago, etc., R. Co., 231 Ill. 454, 83 N. E. 213; People *v.* Cairo, etc., R. Co., 231 Ill. 438, 83 N. E. 116 (existing contingencies not stated); People *v.* Toledo, etc., R. Co., 231 Ill. 390, 83 N. E. 186; People *v.* Cincinnati, etc., R. Co., 231 Ill. 363, 83 N. E. 119; People *v.* Toledo, etc., R. Co., 231 Ill. 125, 83 N. E. 118; People *v.* Kankakee, etc., R. Co., 231 Ill. 109, 83 N. E. 115; Toledo, etc., R. Co. *v.* People, 226 Ill. 557, 80 N. E. 1059; Chicago, etc., R. Co. *v.* People, 225 Ill. 519, 80 N. E. 336; Litchfield, etc., R. Co. *v.* People, 225 Ill. 301, 80 N. E. 335. A consent to an additional levy may be valid (Cleveland, etc., R. Co. *v.* People, 205 Ill. 582, 69 N. E. 89, consent of town auditors held valid, although not specifying amounts applicable to each improvement); but not if not sufficiently specific (Chicago, etc., R. Co. *v.* People, 206 Ill. 296, 69 N. E. 93), or where only two out of five members intended to comply with the law (Cleveland, etc., R. Co. *v.* People, *supra*).

The invalidity of the additional levy leaves the first levy standing. Cincinnati, etc., R. Co. *v.* People, 207 Ill. 566, 69 N. E. 938.

23. Miller *v.* Kern County, 137 Cal. 516, 70 Pac. 549; Comstock *v.* Yolo County, 71 Cal. 599, 12 Pac. 728; Cincinnati, etc., R. Co. *v.* People, 205 Ill. 538, 69 N. E. 40; Sage *v.* Stevens, 72 Mich. 638, 40 N. W. 919 (on certificate of clerk that tax voted); Michigan Land, etc., Co. *v.* L'Anse Tp., 63 Mich. 700, 30 N. W. 331; Jefferson Iron Co. *v.* Hart, 18 Tex. Civ. App. 525, 45 S. W. 321.

24. Nehasane Park Assoc. *v.* Lloyd, 167 N. Y. 431, 60 N. E. 741; Westgate *v.* Spalding, 8 Pa. Dist. 490, on bicycles for construction of side paths.

A slight misdescription is immaterial. Lloyd *v.* Thomson, 60 N. Y. Suppl. 72.

to criminal liability,[39] on proper complaint,[40] warrant,[41] indictment,[42] and evidence.[43]

5. Collection of Taxes Not Worked Out. In those jurisdictions in which the working out of taxes is allowed taxpayers must commonly be given an opportunity to work out their taxes;[44] and when they fail to do the work the taxes may be collected in money by the supervisors or collector of taxes,[45] on demand,[46] and notice of time and place for payment.[47]

STREET USE. A term used to define a judicial limitation upon the general power of the state to devote the highways to uses for the best interests of the public.[1]

STREET WALKING. Parading in the streets by lewd women, to the encouragement or advertisement of their means of livelihood;[2] the offense of a common prostitute offering herself for sale upon the streets at unusual or unreasonable hours, endeavoring to induce men to follow her for the purpose of prostitution.[3] (See Common Night-Walkers, 8 Cyc. 390; and, generally, Prostitution, 32 Cyc. 731.)

STREET WORK. Work upon a street — work in repairing or making a street.[4]

STRESS. Pressure; strain.[5]

STRESS OF WEATHER. Constraint imposed by continued bad weather.[6]

STRETCHING. See Boundaries, 5 Cyc. 868 note 4.

STRICT. Exacting; rigorous; severe;[7] strenuously enjoined and maintained;

to be unconstitutional did not render the case appealable.

39. Waters *v.* State, 117 Ala. 189, 23 So. 28; State *v.* Joyce, 121 N. C. 610, 28 S. E. 366.

Officers acting without authority are liable for maliciously imprisoning another on the ground that he was a road defaulter. Varner *v.* Thompson, 3 Ga. App. 415, 60 S. E. 216.

That after receiving warning defendant worked in another district is a good defense. James *v.* State, 41 Ark. 451.

40. Brown *v.* State, 63 Ala. 97; State *v.* Tracy, 82 Minn. 317, 84 N. W. 1015, holding that the complaint must negative exceptions to act and state for what year assessment was made.

41. State *v.* Yoder, 132 N. C. 1111, 44 S. E. 689; State *v.* Telfair, 130 N. C. 645, 40 S. E. 976 (warrant amended); State *v.* Neal, 109 N. C. 859, 13 S. E. 784 (must negative payment of money in discharge); State *v.* Baker, 108 N. C. 799, 13 S. E. 214 (facts necessary); Glover *v.* Simmons, 4 McCord (S. C.) 67 (must specify amount of fines).

A justice of the peace cannot issue the warrant. State *v.* Sikes, 44 La. Ann. 949, 11 So. 588.

42. State *v.* Snyder, 41 Ark. 226 (holding that it need not show how notice given); State *v.* Covington, 125 N. C. 641, 34 S. E. 272 (need not allege wilfulness); State *v.* Pool, 106 N. C. 698, 10 S. E. 1033 (must state that offense was committed in defendant's territory or that he was notified to attend, and describe the road); State *v.* Smith, 98 N. C. 747, 4 S. E. 517 (must allege liability to work "as a hand"); Bennett *v.* State, 26 Tex. App. 671, 14 S. W. 336 (must allege liability).

43. Waters *v.* State, 117 Ala. 189, 23 So. 28, evidence held competent that defendant was notified by the overseers to work two different roads at about the same time.

44. Miller *v.* Gorman, 38 Pa. St. 309 (injunction against premature collection); Coxe *v.* Sweeney, 10 Pa. Co. Ct. 289; Delaware, etc., R. Co. *v.* O'Hara, 1 Lanc. L. Rev. (Pa.) 147.

45. Barnard *v.* Argyle, 16 Me. 276; Magill *v.* Hellyer, 2 Pa. Dist. 644; Magill's Case, 13 Pa. Co. Ct. 257. See also Dalton Parish Overseers of Poor *v.* North Eastern R. Co., [1900] A. C. 345, 64 J. P. 612, 69 L. J. Q. B. 650, 82 L. T. Rep. N. S. 693, 16 T. L. R. 419; Dent *v.* Labelle, 27 Quebec Super. Ct. 171.

46. Chinese Tax Cases, 14 Fed. 338, 8 Sawy. 384.

47. Dearing *v.* Heard, 15 Me. 247.

1. Sauer *v.* New York, 40 Misc. (N. Y.) 585, 586, 83 N. Y. Suppl. 27.

2. Callaway *v.* Mims, 5 Ga. App. 9, 16, 62 S. E. 654.

3. Pinkerton *v.* Verberg, 78 Mich. 573, 577, 44 N. W. 579, 18 Am. St. Rep. 473, 7 L. R. A. 507.

4. Mill Valley *v.* House, 142 Cal. 698, 700, 76 Pac. 658; Electric Light, etc., Co. *v.* San Bernardino, 100 Cal. 348, 351, 34 Pac. 819; Tanner *v.* Auburn, 37 Wash. 38, 40, 79 Pac. 494, in all of which cases the following language occurs: "'Street work' is a phrase of common usage, and has a well-defined signification."

5. Webster Dict. [*quoted* in Huntington, etc., Transp. Co. *v.* Western Assur. Co., 61 W. Va. 324, 326, 57 S. E. 140].

6. Huntington, etc., Transp. Co. *v.* Western Assur. Co., 61 W. Va. 324, 326, 57 S. E. 140.

7. Century Dict. [*quoted* in Bowman *v.* Little, 101 Md. 273, 299, 61 Atl. 223, 657, 1084].

of Judgment In Rem, see JUDGMENTS, 23 Cyc. 1407; Lis Pendens as Dependent on Jurisdiction of, see LIS PENDENS, 25 Cyc. 1461; Necessity of Justice's Court Record Showing Jurisdiction of, see JUSTICES OF THE PEACE, 24 Cyc. 634; Objection to Jurisdiction of, see APPEAL AND ERROR, 2 Cyc. 680; Validity of Judgment as Dependent on Jurisdiction of, see JUDGMENTS, 23 Cyc. 683; Want of Jurisdiction as Affecting Operation in Other States of Judgments of State Courts, see JUDGMENTS, 23 Cyc. 1563. Of Allegations — In Indictment or Information, see INDICTMENTS AND INFORMATIONS, 22 Cyc. 301; In Pleading in General, see PLEADING, 31 Cyc. 47. Of Alteration, see ALTERATIONS OF INSTRUMENTS, 2 Cyc. 193. Of Arbitration, see ARBITRATION AND AWARD, 3 Cyc. 589. Of Assignment, see ASSIGNMENTS, 4 Cyc. 12. Of Award of Arbitrators, see ARBITRATION AND AWARD, 3 Cyc. 674. Of Bailment, see BAILMENTS, 5 Cyc. 166. Of Chattel Mortgage, see CHATTEL MORTGAGES, 6 Cyc. 1037. Of Compromise, see COMPROMISE AND SETTLEMENT, 8 Cyc. 504. Of Contract — In General, see CONTRACTS, 9 Cyc. 273; Construction and Operation of Contract as to, see CONTRACTS, 9 Cyc. 577; INDEMNITY, 22 Cyc. 84; Of Sale, see SALES, 34 Cyc. 44; VENDOR AND PURCHASER; Sufficiency of Description to Authorize Specific Performance, see SPECIFIC PERFORMANCE, 36 Cyc. 591. Of Counterfeit, see COUNTERFEITING, 11 Cyc. 303. Of Covenant, see COVENANTS, 11 Cyc. 1058. Of Deed, see DEEDS, 13 Cyc. 528. Of Discovery, see DISCOVERY, 14 Cyc. 306. Of Easement, see EASEMENTS, 14 Cyc. 1139. Of Employment to Constitute Relation of Attorney and Client, see ATTORNEY AND CLIENT, 4 Cyc. 928. Of Exceptions, see APPEAL AND ERROR, 2 Cyc. 714. Of Gambling Contract see GAMING, 20 Cyc. 924. Of Gift, see GIFTS, 20 Cyc. 1211, 1237. Of Inspection, see INSPECTION, 22 Cyc. 1365. Of Insurance Policy, see ACCIDENT INSURANCE, 1 Cyc. 238; FIDELITY INSURANCE, 19 Cyc. 516; FIRE INSURANCE, 19 Cyc. 591; LIFE INSURANCE, 25 Cyc. 703; LIVE-STOCK INSURANCE, 25 Cyc. 1516; MARINE INSURANCE, 26 Cyc. 586; PLATE-GLASS INSURANCE, 30 Cyc. 1642. Of Judgment, Construction of Judgments as to, see JUDGMENTS, 23 Cyc. 1104. Of Lease, see LANDLORD AND TENANT, 24 Cyc. 879. Of Lien — In General, see LIENS, 25 Cyc. 669; Of Attorney, see ATTORNEY AND CLIENT, 4 Cyc. 1012. Of Mechanic's Lien, see MECHANICS' LIENS, 27 Cyc. 17. Of Mortgage, see MORTGAGES, 27 Cyc. 1034. Of Partnership, see PARTNERSHIP, 30 Cyc. 354. Of Pledge, see PLEDGES, 31 Cyc. 793. Of Reference, see REFERENCES, 34 Cyc. 777. Of Release, see RELEASE, 34 Cyc. 1090. Of Set-Off or Counter-Claim, see RECOUPMENT, SET-OFF, AND COUNTER-CLAIM, 34 Cyc. 665. Of Statute, see STATUTES, 36 Cyc. 929, and Cross-References. Of Stipulation, see STIPULATIONS. Of Submission of Controversy, see SUBMISSION OF CONTROVERSY. Of Treaty, see TREATIES. Of Trust, see TRUSTS. Of Will, see WILLS.)

SUBJECT OF ACTION. The thing or subject-matter to which the litigation pertains;[76] the ultimate or primary title, right, or interest which a plaintiff seeks to enforce or protect;[77] the facts constituting plaintiff's cause of action;[78] the thing, the wrongful act for which damages are sought, the contract which is broken, the act which is sought to be restrained, the property of which recovery is asked.[79] (See CASE, 6 Cyc. 679; CAUSE, 6 Cyc. 704; CAUSE OF ACTION, 6 Cyc. 705; SUBJECT-MATTER, *ante*, p. 342.)

76. Revere F. Ins. Co. *v.* Chamberlain, 56 Iowa 508, 511, 8 N. W. 338, 9 N. W. 386; Lapham *v.* Osborne, 20 Nev. 168, 172, 18 Pac. 881.

77. McCormick Harvesting Mach. Co. *v.* Hill, 104 Mo. App. 544, 559, 79 S. W. 745, where it is said that it does not signify merely the wrong to be redressed in the particular case.

78. Rothschild *v.* Whitman, 132 N. Y. 472, 476, 30 N. E. 858; Sugden *v.* Magnolia Metal Co., 58 N. Y. App. Div. 236, 240, 68 N. Y. Suppl. 809; Hall *v.* Werney, 18 N. Y. App. Div. 565, 567, 46 N. Y. Suppl. 33; Lehmair *v.* Griswold, 40 N. Y. Super. Ct. 100, 101.

79. Lassiter *v.* Norfolk, etc., R. Co., 136 N. C. 89, 91, 48 S. E. 642.

"The subject of an action is either property (as illustrated by a real action), or a violated right." Glen, etc., Mfg. Co. *v.* Hall, 61 N. Y. 226, 236, 19 Am. Rep. 278.

It is what was formerly understood as "the subject-matter of the action." Box *v.* Chicago, etc., R. Co., 107 Iowa 660, 666, 78 N. W. 694; Baltimore, etc., R. Co. *v.* Hollen-

Corporation, and Subscribing to or Purchasing Corporate Stock to Popular Vote, see COUNTIES, 11 Cyc. 522; MUNICIPAL CORPORATIONS, 28 Cyc. 1558; Alteration of County to Popular Vote, see COUNTIES, 11 Cyc. 351; Alteration of Municipality to Inhabitants or Owners, see MUNICIPAL CORPORATIONS, 28 Cyc. 209; Amendment of Constitution, see CONSTITUTIONAL LAW, 8 Cyc. 723; Construction of Public Buildings, see COUNTIES, 11 Cyc. 461; Creating New School-Districts to Popular Vote, see SCHOOLS AND SCHOOL-DISTRICTS, 35 Cyc. 839; Expenditure by City to Popular Vote, see MUNICIPAL CORPORATIONS, 28 Cyc. 1548; Grant of License to Use Street to Vote, see MUNICIPAL CORPORATIONS, 28 Cyc. 879; Issue of County Bonds to Popular Vote, see COUNTIES, 11 Cyc. 556; Issue of Municipal Bonds to Popular Vote, see MUNICIPAL CORPORATIONS, 28 Cyc. 1588; Issue of School Bonds to Popular Vote, see SCHOOLS AND SCHOOL-DISTRICTS, 35 Cyc. 990; Levying Taxes by County to Popular Vote, see COUNTIES, 11 Cyc. 580; Levying Taxes by Municipality to Popular Vote, see MUNICIPAL CORPORATIONS, 28 Cyc. 1662; Local Option to Popular Vote, see INTOXICATING LIQUORS, 23 Cyc. 95; Public Improvements to Particular Officer or Board, see MUNICIPAL CORPORATIONS, 28 Cyc. 984; Public Improvements to Popular Vote, see MUNICIPAL CORPORATIONS, 28 Cyc. 957. Of Special Interrogatories, see TRIAL. Of Special Question to Voters, see ELECTIONS, 15 Cyc. 318. To Arbitration — In General, see ARBITRATION AND AWARD, 3 Cyc. 588; Contracts of Municipality, see MUNICIPAL CORPORATIONS, 28 Cyc. 641; Powers of Agents as to, see PRINCIPAL AND AGENT, 31 Cyc. 1392; Powers of Attorney as to, see ATTORNEY AND CLIENT, 4 Cyc. 938; Question of Boundaries, see BOUNDARIES, 5 Cyc. 944. To Competition For Contract For Public Improvement, see MUNICIPAL CORPORATIONS, 28 Cyc. 1025. To Jury — Of Issues in Suits in Equity, see EQUITY, 16 Cyc. 413; Right to, see JURIES, 24 Cyc. 100.)

relief sought could not be given in an action, such as is sought to be submitted.[20] The controversy must be real,[21] and not a merely colorable dispute suggested in order to have the law in the case ascertained,[22] nor a mere abstract question presented to get the advice of the court, the decision of which will not terminate the controversy between the parties,[23] and by which only a preliminary question will

for the possession of a fund, in the hands of the sheriff, raised under different executions against the same defendant, does not constitute such a case as may, under the code of procedure, be submitted to a judge, without a suit between the adverse claimants, because no action could be brought, the parties having no claim one against the other, although they both may have claims against the sheriff who is not a party to the controversy).

Where an action could not be brought within a certain period no controversy can be submitted within that time. Hobart College *v.* Fitzhugh, 27 N. Y. 130.

Unless determinable in an action as distinguished from a special proceeding the controversy cannot be submitted. Woodruff *v.* People, 193 N. Y. 560, 86 N. E. 562, holding that a controversy cannot be submitted where, if the questions are answered in plaintiff's favor, judgment is to be entered directing defendant highway commissioners to lay out a highway petitioned for by plaintiff, such relief being properly granted through mandamus, and where, if the questions are answered in defendant's favor, a judgment is to be entered affirming defendant's order denying plaintiff's petition — relief properly awarded on certiorari.

20. People *v.* Mutual Endowment, etc., Assoc., 92 N. Y. 622, holding that where, in a controversy sought to be submitted, under Code Civ. Proc. § 1279, between the state and a corporation, the only relief to which the former is entitled, if any, is to restrain the corporation from exercising franchises unlawfully, the proceeding should be dismissed, as that relief may not be given therein.

Where the right to salary depended upon the right to a public office, and the right to public office could only be tried in an action in the name of the people, the submission of a controversy by a city as to which of the two defendants was entitled to the office of health physician, in order that it might pay him the salary, could not be had. Buffalo *v.* Mackay, 15 Hun (N. Y.) 204.

21. Kelley *v.* Hogan, 69 N. Y. App. Div. 251, 74 N. Y. Suppl. 682; Williams *v.* Rochester, 2 Lans. (N. Y.) 169; Bloomfield *v.* Ketcham, 5 N. Y. Civ. Proc. 407; Van Sickle *v.* Van Sickle, 8 How. Pr. (N. Y.) 265; Berks County *v.* Jones, 21 Pa. St. 413; Forney *v.* Huntingdon, 6 Pa. Super. Ct. 397; Mudey *v.* Schuylkill County, 2 Leg. Rec. (Pa.) 178; Dunn *v.* Meixell, 1 Lehigh Val. L. Rep. (Pa.) 168.

Where the same attorney prepared the statement and briefs of both parties, a decision of the general term in a controversy submitted on an agreed statement under Code Civ. Proc. § 1279, which provides for such submission, in good faith, of a real controversy, for the purpose of determining the rights of the parties, will be set aside, as not of the independent character contemplated by the code. Wood *v.* Nesbitt, 19 N. Y. Suppl. 423.

There must be an actual dispute between real parties. Witz *v.* Dale, 129 Ind. 120, 27 N. E. 498. The parties must be adversely interested. Champlin, Petitioner, 17 R. I. 512, 23 Atl. 25, holding that Pub. Laws (1876), c. 563, § 16, which provides that any persons interested in any question of the construction of any statute may concur in stating such question to the supreme court, and court of common pleas, in the form of a special case for the opinion of said court, etc., does not authorize the rendition of an opinion as to the construction and constitutionality of a statute upon the petition of persons who are not parties to a case involving adversary claims for decision.

Controversy held to be real within the meaning of the statute see Com. *v.* Cleveland, etc., R. Co., 29 Pa. St. 370; Greene, Petitioner, 17 R. I. 509, 23 Atl. 29.

22. Berks County *v.* Jones, 21 Pa. St. 413; Forney *v.* Huntingdon, 6 Pa. Super. Ct. 397; James *v.* Fennicle, 21 Pa. Co. Ct. 91 (holding that the court will not consider an agreed case which is not based upon a real case, but is simply intended to secure the opinion of the court as a guide to executors in the distribution of an estate); Mudey *v.* Schuylkill County, 2 Leg. Rec. (Pa.) 178; Dunn *v.* Meixell, 1 Lehigh Val. L. Rep. (Pa.) 168.

23. Capen *v.* Washington Ins. Co., 12 Cush. (Mass.) 517 (holding that the court will not give an opinion upon a statement of facts which presents merely a speculative or abstract question, the decision of which either way will not terminate the controversy between the parties; but the agreed statement will be discharged); Woodruff *v.* People, 193 N. Y. 560, 86 N. E. 562; People *v.* Mutual Endowment, etc., Assoc., 92 N. Y. 622 (holding that to give the court cognizance of a case submitted, the facts stated must show that there was, at the time the submission was made, a controversy or question of difference between the parties on the point presented for decision, and that a judgment can be rendered thereon, for the court may not pass upon a mere abstract question); Troy Waste Mfg. Co. *v.* Harrison, 73 Hun (N. Y.) 528, 26 N. Y. Suppl. 109; James *v.* Fennicle, 21 Pa. Co. Ct. 91; Pittsburgh *v.* Allegheny, 1 Pittsb. (Pa.) 97.

The remedy is not intended to enable parties to use the court as advisory in their cases, but is intended as a convenient form of submission of a controversy upon an agreed state of facts for the judgment of the court

SUBROGATION

By Sir Henri Elzear Taschereau, of Ottawa

Member of the Judicial Committee of the Privy Council of Great Britain; and formerly Chief Justice of the Supreme Court of Canada

CROSS-REFERENCES

For Matters Relating to:
Contribution, see CONTRIBUTION, 9 Cyc. 792.
Control of Execution:
By Co-Defendant, see EXECUTIONS, 17 Cyc. 1388.
By Officer Paying the Judgment Debt, see EXECUTIONS, 17 Cyc. 1389.
By Third Person Paying the Judgment Debt, see EXECUTIONS, 17 Cyc. 1388.
Effect of Payment of Judgment by Joint Party or Third Person, see JUDGMENTS, 23 Cyc. 1470.
Equitable Jurisdiction Over Matters of Account Through Subrogation, see ACCOUNTS AND ACCOUNTING, 1 Cyc. 417.
Equity, see EQUITY, 16 Cyc. 1.
Execution, see EXECUTIONS, 17 Cyc. 878.
Principal and Surety, see PRINCIPAL AND SURETY, 32 Cyc. 1.
Subrogation as a Method of Marshaling Assets, see MARSHALING ASSETS, 26 Cyc. 938.
Subrogation in Creditors' Suits, see CREDITORS' SUITS, 12 Cyc. 45.
Subrogation of Particular Classes of Persons:
Directors of Corporation:
With Respect to Statutory Liability, see CORPORATIONS, 10 Cyc. 897.
With Respect to Ultra Vires Debts, see CORPORATIONS, 10 Cyc. 1149.
Fidelity Insurer to Rights of Employer of Dishonest Employee, see FIDELITY INSURANCE, 19 Cyc. 526.
Fire Insurer to Rights of Insured, see FIRE INSURANCE, 19 Cyc. 893.
Fraudulent Grantee of Creditor to Rights of Creditor Whom He Has Paid, see FRAUDULENT CONVEYANCES, 20 Cyc. 626.
Life Insurer to Rights Against One Causing Death, see LIFE INSURANCE, 25 Cyc. 903.
Marine Insurer to Rights of the Insured in Regard to the Loss, see MARINE INSURANCE, 26 Cyc. 710, 713.
Materialman to Lien of Contractor, see MECHANICS' LIENS, 27 Cyc. 91.
Subcontractor to Lien of Contractor, see MECHANICS' LIENS, 27 Cyc. 91.
Trustee in Bankruptcy to Rights of Creditor, see BANKRUPTCY, 5 Cyc. 369.
Workman to Lien of Contractor, see MECHANICS' LIENS, 27 Cyc. 91.

I. DEFINITION AND NATURE.

A. In General. Subrogation is the substitution of another person in the place of a creditor, so that the person in whose favor it is exercised succeeds to the rights of the creditor in relation to the debt.[1] The doctrine is one of equity and

1. Liles *v.* Rogers, 113 N. C. 197, 199, 18 S. E. 104, 37 Am. St. Rep. 627; Sheldon Subr. § 1. To the same effect see Brown *v.* Rouse, 125 Cal. 645, 650, 58 Pac. 267; Johnson *v.* Barrett, 117 Ind. 551, 554, 19 N. E. 199, 10 Am. St. Rep. 83; Boston Safe Deposit, etc., Co. *v.* Thomas, 59 Kan. 470, 475, 53 Pac. 472; Staples *v.* Fox, 45 Miss. 667, 680 [*quoting* Dixon Subr.]; Colt *v.* Sears Commercial Co., 20 R. I. 64, 71, 37 Atl. 311.

Other definitions are: "A substitution, ordinarily the substitution of another person in the place of one creditor, so that the person in whose favor it is exercised succeeds to the rights of the creditor in relation to the debt. More broadly, it is the substitution of one person in the place of another, whether as creditor, or as the possessor of any other rightful claim. The substitute is put in all respects in the place of the party to whose rights he is subrogated." Sheldon Subr. 1, 2 [*quoted* in Townsend *v.* Cleveland

stance upon which they can base their claims can obtain the equitable right to be

Mo. 437, 21 S. W. 796, 35 Am. St. Rep. 761; Bunn v. Lindsay, 95 Mo. 250, 7 S. W. 473, 6 Am. St. Rep. 48; Norton v. Highleyman, 88 Mo. 621; Brown v. Merchants' Bank, 66 Mo. App. 427; Dunn v. Missouri Pac. R. Co., 45 Mo. App. 29.

Nebraska.— Aultman v. Bishop, 53 Nebr. 545, 74 N. W. 55; Seieroe v. Homan, 50 Nebr. 601, 70 N. W. 244; Rice v. Winters, 45 Nebr. 517, 63 N. W. 830; South Omaha Nat. Bank v. Wright, 45 Nebr. 23, 63 N. W. 126; Washburn v. Osgood, 38 Nebr. 804, 57 N. W. 529.

New Hampshire.—Contoocook Fire Precinct v. Hopkinton, 71 N. H. 574, 53 Atl. 797; Woodbury v. Butler, 67 N. H. 545, 38 Atl. 379.

New Jersey.— Fay v. Fay, 43 N. J. Eq. 438, 11 Atl. 122; Tradesmen's Bldg., etc., Assoc. v. Thompson, 32 N. J. Eq. 133; Coe v. New Jersey Midland R. Co., 31 N. J. Eq. 105; Shinn v. Budd, 14 N. J. Eq. 234 (holding that the principle of subrogation has been rigidly restrained within these limits); Wilson v. Brown, 13 N. J. Eq. 277.

New York.— Koehler v. Hughes, 148 N. Y. 507, 42 N. E. 1051; Pease v. Egan, 131 N. Y. 262, 30 N. E. 102; Arnold v. Green, 116 N. Y. 566, 23 N. E. 1; Clute v. Emmerich, 99 N. Y. 342, 2 N. E. 6; Acer v. Hotchkiss, 97 N. Y. 395; Gans v. Thieme, 93 N. Y. 225; Wilkes v. Harper, 1 N. Y. 586; Finegan v. New York, 4 N. Y. App. Div. 15, 38 N. Y. Suppl. 358 (holding that a purchaser at a tax-sale, who is a mere volunteer, and pays his money on a bid and receives certificates, does not thereby become entitled to be subrogated to the right to receive the taxes from the owner of the premises); Walther v. Wetmore, 1 E. D. Smith 7; Matter of Plopper, 15 Misc. 202, 37 N. Y. Suppl. 33; Miller v. Moreau, 10 N. Y. St. 711.

North Carolina.— Howerton v. Sprague, 64 N. C. 451.

Ohio.— Miller v. Stark, 61 Ohio St. 413, 56 N. E. 11.

Pennsylvania.— Campbell v. Foster Home Assoc., 163 Pa. St. 609, 30 Atl. 222, 43 Am. St. Rep. 818, 26 L. R. A. 117; *In re* Clippinger, 162 Pa. St. 627, 29 Atl. 705; Breneman's Appeal, 121 Pa. St. 641, 15 Atl. 650; Miller's Appeal, 119 Pa. St. 620, 13 Atl. 504; Williamson's Appeal, 94 Pa. St. 231; Webster's Appeal, 80 Pa. St. 409; *In re* Wallace 59 Pa. St. 401; Mosier's Appeal, 56 Pa. St. 76, 93 Am. Dec. 783; Hoover v. Epler, 52 Pa. St. 522; McCleary's Appeal, 9 Pa. Cas. 271, 12 Atl. 158; Thompson v. Griggs, 31 Pa. Super. Ct. 608; Flick v. Weller, 2 Kulp 258; Titzel v. Smeigh, 2 Leg. Chron. 271. But see Brice's Appeal, 95 Pa. St. 145, holding that a stranger to an obligation, who pays a part or the whole of the debt, becomes, in absence of any evidence to the contrary, a purchaser of the debt and the accompanying security, to the extent of his payment.

Rhode Island.— *In re* Martin, 25 R. I. 1, 54 Atl. 589.

South Carolina.—Gadsden v. Brown, Speers Eq. 37.

South Dakota.—Pollock v. Wright, 15 S. D. 134, 87 N. W. 584; Ipswich Bank v. Brock, 13 S. D. 409, 83 N. W. 436.

Tennessee.— Motley v. Harris, 1 Lea 577.

Texas.— Willis v. Chowning, 90 Tex. 617, 40 S. W. 395; Faires v. Cockerell, 88 Tex. 428, 31 S. W. 190, 639, 28 L. R. A. 528; Darrow v. Summerhill, 24 Tex. Civ. App. 208, 58 S. W. 158; M. T. Jones Lumber Co. v. Villegas, 8 Tex. Civ. App. 669, 28 S. W. 558; Tarver v. Land Mortg. Bank, 7 Tex. Civ. App. 425, 27 S. W. 40.

Vermont.—Royalton Nat. Bank v. Cushing, 53 Vt. 321.

Virginia.— Burton v. Mill, 78 Va. 468.

Washington.— Murray v. Meade, 5 Wash. 693, 32 Pac. 780. See Washington L. & T. Co. v. Ritz, 37 Wash. 642, 80 Pac. 174.

West Virginia.—Blair v. Mounts, 41 W. Va. 706, 24 S. E. 620; Bates v. Swiger, 40 W. Va. 420, 21 S. E. 874; Crumlish v. Central Imp. Co., 38 W. Va. 390, 18 S. E. 456, 45 Am. St. Rep. 872, 23 L. R. A. 120; McNeil v. Miller, 29 W. Va. 480, 2 S. E. 335.

Wisconsin.— Watson v. Wilcox, 39 Wis. 643, 20 Am. Rep. 63.

United States.—Underwood v. Metropolitan Nat. Bank, 144 U. S. 669, 12 S. Ct. 784, 36 L. ed. 586; Ætna L. Ins. Co. v. Middleport, 124 U. S. 534, 8 S. Ct. 625, 31 L. ed. 537; Beardsley v. Lampasas, 127 Fed. 819, 62 C. C. A. 126; O'Brien v. Wheelock, 78 Fed. 673; Mercantile Trust Co. v. Hart, 76 Fed. 673, 22 C. C. A. 473, 35 L. R. A. 352; Lawrence v. U. S., 71 Fed. 228; Cotton v. Dacey, 61 Fed. 481; Matthews v. Fidelity Title, etc. Co., 52 Fed. 687; Cornell Steamboat Co. v. The Jersey City, 43 Fed. 166; Lewis v. Chittick, 25 Fed. 176.

A famous and often quoted exposition of the doctrine.— Chancellor Johnson, in Gadsden v. Brown, Speers Eq. (S. C.) 37, 41, says: "The doctrine of subrogation is a pure unmixed equity, having its foundation in the principles of natural justice, and from its very nature, never could have been intended for the relief of those who were in a condition in which they were at liberty to elect whether they would or would not be bound, and as far as I have been enabled to learn its history, it never has been so applied. If one with the perfect knowledge of the facts, will part with his money, or bind himself by his contract, in a sufficient consideration, any rule of law which would restore him his money or absolve him from his contract, would subvert the rules of such order. It has been directed in its application exclusively to the relief of those that were already bound, who could not but choose to abide the penalty. . . . . But I have seen no case, and none has been referred to in the argument, in which a stranger, who was in a condition to make terms for himself, and demand any security he might require, has been protected by the principle." Quoting the above in

obtain satisfaction of his claim through subrogation to the rights of his debtor against a third party, the utmost good faith on his own part will not entitle him to prevail, if it appears that his debtor has been guilty of such fraud as to defeat his rights against said third party.[90] Furthermore, subrogation, being purely an equitable right, is limited only by equitable considerations, and it is not therefore available or enforceable where there are subsisting and countervailing equities,[91] and the equities being equal the law will prevail.[92] Subrogation cannot take place by effect of law beyond the amount actually disbursed,[93] under legal necessity.[94] In conventional subrogation the extent of the right is measured by the agreement for subrogation,[95] and by the rights of the one granting the right.[96]

B. Benefit of Mortgage Security — 1. In General. A person who, under such circumstances that he is entitled to subrogation, pays a debt of another secured by mortgage is subrogated to the rights under the mortgage and can enforce the same for his own benefit,[97] and is subrogated to the priority of the mortgage

for the benefit of creditors, the fact that the assignee discharged the debt secured by the pledge with funds of the estate did not entitle him to subrogation to the rights of the pledgee against the stock. Woodside *v.* Grafflin, 91 Md. 422, 46 Atl. 968.

90. Green *v.* Turner, 80 Fed. 41.

91. *Alabama.*— Sawyers *v.* Baker, 77 Ala. 461.

Connecticut.— Orvis *v.* Newell, 17 Conn. 97.

Delaware.— Miller *v.* Stout, 5 Del. Ch. 259.

Kentucky.— Dunlap *v.* O'Bannon, 5 B. Mon. 393.

Missouri.—Wolff *v.* Walter, 56 Mo. 292.

New York.— Union Trust Co. *v.* Monticello, etc., R. Co., 63 N. Y. 311, 20 Am. Rep. 541.

Pennsylvania.— Budd *v.* Oliver, 148 Pa. St. 194, 23 Atl. 1105; McCurdy *v.* Conner, 1 Walk. 155, holding that bail for stay of execution is not entitled to subrogation against a terretenant or creditors.

Virginia.— Exchange Bldg., etc., Co. *v.* Bayless, 91 Va. 134, 21 S. E. 279.

United States.— Gunby *v.* Armstrong, 133 Fed. 417, 66 C. C. A. 627.

92. Ritter *v.* Cost, 99 Ind. 80; Edmunds *v.* Venable, 1 Patt. & H. (Va.) 121.

93. Mallory *v.* Dauber, 83 Ky. 239; Shropshire *v.* His Creditors, 15 La. Ann. 705; Bailey *v.* Warner, 28 Vt. 87 (holding that a party who pays, by agreement, money due on a mortgage, will be subrogated to the rights of the mortgagee only so far as to save him harmless).

If a mortgagor's vendee, before foreclosure, is not a party to a foreclosure decree, a purchaser of all the land thereunder is entitled to be substituted to the mortgagee's rights only to the amount which he paid and they received for the parcel at the sale. Martin *v.* Kelly, 59 Miss. 652.

Where a sale under a power is void for irregularity, the purchaser, or those claiming under him, although subrogated to the rights of the mortgage, can only enforce the mortgage to the extent of the amount paid at the illegal sale under the power. Givens *v.* Carroll, 40 S. C. 413, 18 S. E. 1030, 42 Am. St. Rep. 889.

94. Walker *v.* Municipality No. 1, 5 La. Ann. 10. And see *supra*, III, B.

95. Raleigh Nat. Bank *v.* Moore, 94 N. C. 734; Academy of Music Co. *v.* Davidson. 85 Wis. 129, 55 N. W. 172; Huntington *v.* The Advance, 72 Fed. 793, 19 C. C. A. 194. See Patterson *v.* Clark, 96 Ga. 494, 23 S. E. 496.

The legal subrogation is as extensive as express subrogation. Cox *v.* Baldwin, 1 La. 401.

96. Surghnor *v.* Beauchamp, 24 La. Ann. 471.

97. Kinnah *v.* Kinnah, 184 Ill. 284, 56 N. E. 376; Smith *v.* Dinsmore, 119 Ill. 656, 4 N. E. 648; Jacques *v.* Fackney, 64 Ill. 87; McGuffey *v.* McClain, 130 Ind. 327, 30 N. E. 296; Foley *v.* Gibson, 15 S. W. 780, 12 Ky. L. Rep. 885; Chouler *v.* Smith, 3 Desauss. Eq. (S. C.) 12.

A wife is entitled to be subrogated to the rights of trust creditors of her husband, whose debts against their property she has paid. Roach *v.* Hacker, 2 Lea (Tenn.) 633.

Where a note secured by a chattel mortgage is indorsed to a bank, and a third person, under an agreement with the maker, takes up the note by paying to the bank the amount due thereon, the note not being canceled, such person is subrogated to the rights of the bank in the chattel mortgage. Ploeger *v.* Johnson, (Tex. Civ. App. 1894) 26 S. W. 432.

The ordinary creditor paying the debt of the mortgage creditor is subrogated of right to the mortgage, under Rev. Civ. Code, art. 2160, 2161, providing that a creditor who pays another creditor whose claim is preferable by reason of his privileges shall be subrogated. Hall *v.* Hawley, 49 La. Ann. 1046, 22 So. 205; Ziegler *v.* Creditors, 49 La. Ann. 144, 21 So. 666.

A finding that most of a certain fund went to pay a mortgage is not sufficiently definite to authorize a decree reviving a mortgage for the benefit of the owner of the fund. Bourne *v.* Bourne, 69 Vt. 251, 37 Atl. 1049.

If one of two joint makers of a note secured by a mortgage paid the same before maturity, the payment of the debt acted as an equitable assignment to him of the mortgage, and he was subrogated to the rights of the original creditor, as against his co-maker, for the latter's share of the debt. Truss *v.* Miller, 116 Ala. 494, 22 So. 863.

statutory and code provisions exist prescribing the mode of enforcing the right in particular cases and allow its enforcement at law,[28] and relief may be had at law where the equity and law procedure are blended;[29] and it is held in a very recent case that, although when the right of subrogation is in question the remedy is in equity, when the right itself is conceded, and there remains to be enforced only the right of realizing the value of the subject-matter, such right may be within the cognizance of a court of law.[30] The right of a surety to subrogation need not be determined in the suit between the creditor and the principal;[31] and one who has paid a judgment as surety before the question of his suretyship has been determined may have that relation established by applying to the court that rendered the original judgment, and become thus subrogated to the rights of the judgment creditor.[32]

B. Limitations and Laches — 1. LIMITATION. The right of subrogation, like other rights of action, is barred by failure to take steps to enforce it within the time prescribed by the statute of limitations;[33] and thus where a surety who

New Hampshire.— Edgerly *v.* Emerson, 23 N. H. 555, 55 Am. Dec. 207.

New York.— Dunlop *v.* James, 174 N. Y. 411, 67 N. E. 60; Boyd *v.* Finnegan, 3 Daly, 222.

United States.— Wilkinson *v.* Babbitt, 29 Fed. Cas. No. 17,668, 4 Dill. 207.

England.— Coles *v.* Bulman, 6 C. B. 184, 12 Jur. 586, 17 L. J. C. P. 302, 60 E. C. L. 184.

In Georgia, Code, §§ 2176, 2177, **made** subrogation a legal as well as an equitable right. Hull *v.* Myers, 90 Ga. 674, 16 S. E. 653. See Ezzard *v.* Bell, 100 Ga. 150, 28 S. E. 28.

28. See cases cited *infra*, this note.

In Maryland a surety on a bond, who has paid it, cannot recover by suit in the name of the obligee against himself and his coöbligor, but must proceed under Code, art. 5, § 9, authorizing him to demand an assignment of the bond, "and by virtue of such assignment, to maintain an action in his own name against the principal debtor." Martindale *v.* Brock, 41 Md. 571.

In North Carolina under the code the right of a surety who has paid the debt of his principal to be substituted to all the rights, liens, and securities which the creditor held can only be asserted by a civil action, commenced by the service of a summons (Calvert *v.* Peebles, 82 N. C. 334); but the rule was formerly otherwise (Allen *v.* Wood, 38 N. C. 386).

In Pennsylvania, under the act of May 19, 1887 (Pamphl. Laws 132) where a scire facias has been issued by a surety claiming subrogation on a judgment paid by him for the original debtor the surety has the right to have the question of subrogation tried out on the scire facias he has issued, instead of on a motion summarily to set aside the execution. Thompson *v.* Reash, 15 Pa. Super. Ct. 102; Hutcheson *v.* Reash, 15 Pa. Super. Ct. 96.

In Montana subrogation — an equitable defense — may be pleaded to a legal cause of action. Potter *v.* Lohse, 31 Mont. 91, 77 Pac. 419.

29. Toronto Bank *v.* Hunter, 4 Bosw. (N. Y.) 646, 20 How. Pr. 292 (holding that in an action against the accommodation acceptor by a non-resident holder of the bill, the drawers having become insolvent, defendant may, under the code, which authorizes the court to give equitable, as well as legal, relief in the same action, file an answer, in the nature of a cross bill in equity, demanding subrogation on payment of an amount due plaintiffs); Moore *v.* Watson, 20 R. I. 495, 40 Atl. 345.

A surety may apply to the court by motion to compel the assignment of a judgment against him and his principal on his offer to pay the judgment. Tyler *v.* Hildreth, 77 Hun (N. Y.) 580, 28 N. Y. Suppl. 1042.

30. Polhemus *v.* Prudential Realty Corp., 74 N. J. L. 570, 67 Atl. 303.

31. Grant *v.* Ludlow, 8 Ohio St. 1.

Under Nebr. Code Civ. Proc. § 511, if an issue has been presented and a finding made that one of defendants in a suit is the principal and the other a surety, the relation need not be relitigated in an action for subrogation. Nelson *v.* Webster, 72 Nebr. 332, 100 N. W. 411, 117 Am. St. Rep. 799, 68 L. R. A. 513.

But in proceedings to foreclose a mortgage the guarantor of the mortgage note is entitled, even before payment of the note, to have provision made for his subrogation to the rights of the mortgagors. Manning *v.* Ferguson, 103 Iowa 561, 72 N. W. 762.

32. Todd *v.* Oglebay, 158 Ind. 595, 64 N. E. 32.

33. Kreider *v.* Isenbice, 123 Ind. 10, 23 N. E. 786; Ball *v.* Miller, 17 How. Pr. (N. Y.) 300; Bledsoe *v.* Nixon, 68 N. C. 521. But see Caldwell *v.* Palmer, 6 Lea (Tenn.) 652, holding that neither the statute of limitations nor lapse of time will affect the right of a purchaser at a judicial sale, declared to be void at the instance of the heir of the former owner, to be subrogated to the rights of those creditors whose debts were paid by the purchase-money, and to have the amount of such proceeds received by the heir refunded.

Where one of four joint and several obligors pays the note, he is subrogated to the rights of the payee, and his cause of action for contribution is founded on the written instrument, and therefore the two-year statute of limitations does not apply to his claim.

payment by the surety.[35] A surety, upon payment of the debt, has a right of action for indemnity from his principal, and as this right arises under an implied contract, it would be barred, in most states, sooner than the right of action which the creditor had on the written instrument or judgment. For this reason, where the surety is subrogated to the rights of the creditor on a written contract, or has taken an assignment thereof, he will possess rights superior to those which he had on his implied contract for indemnity.[36]

2. Laches. The right of subrogation is one of equity merely, and due diligence must be exercised in ascertaining it. Laches in taking advantage of the right will forfeit it;[37] and subrogation is not allowed in favor of one who has permitted

St. 552, 91 Am. Dec. 110], holding that an action by one of several cosureties paying a joint judgment against them for subrogation to the rights of the creditor is limited to six years, under Code, § 14, as an action on an implied promise, and not merely for equitable relief.

An application by a cosurety on a bond, as co-defendant, who paid the same, to be subrogated to the rights of plaintiff as against the principal debtor and defendant, must be made within six years from the date of payment (Com. *v.* Marshall, 2 Woodw. (Pa.) 117), and the same period applies in Ohio to a cosurety who has paid a judgment (Neilson *v.* Fry, 16 Ohio St. 552, 91 Am. Dec. 110).

35. See Limitations of Actions, 25 Cyc. 1113.

36. *Alabama.*— Giddens *v.* Williamson, 65 Ala. 439. See Hughes *v.* Howell, 152 Ala. 295, 44 So. 410.

Georgia.— Hull *v.* Myers, 90 Ga. 674, 16 S. E. 653.

Indian Territory.— Sparks *v.* Childers, 2 Indian Terr. 187, 47 S. W. 316.

Mississippi.— Partee *v.* Mathews, 53 Miss. 140.

South Carolina.— Smith *v.* Swain, 7 Rich. Eq. 112.

Texas.— Sublett *v.* McKinney, 19 Tex. 438.

Virginia.— Cromer *v.* Cromer, 29 Gratt. 280.

See 44 Cent. Dig. tit. "Subrogation," § 112.

A surety subrogated to a judgment cannot maintain an action against his principal after the expiration of the time limited for bringing an action thereon by the creditor (Cathcart *v.* Bryant, 28 Wash. 31, 68 Pac. 171); and a surety on a judgment, who pays the judgment, must take steps to enforce his right of subrogation within the period prescribed as a limitation to the enforcement of simple contracts, for this merely equitable right will not be enforced at the expense of a legal one (Hutcheson *v.* Reash, 15 Pa. Super. Ct. 96).

If the surety enforces contribution through the claim of the creditor, his right is not barred until the statute would have run as to the creditor (Northwestern Nat. Bank *v.* Great Falls Opera-House Co., 23 Mont. 1, 57 Pac. 440, holding that under Code Civ. Proc. § 1242, providing that a surety paying a judgment shall be entitled to its benefit to enforce contribution, his right is not barred so long as the judgment is alive), and although a judgment creditor held no securities for his debt, a surety of the judgment debtor having satisfied the judgment, there was an equitable assignment to him, and he might maintain an action against his cosurety after the running of limitations against the statutory actions for contribution, and within the period within which the judgment creditor might have asserted his rights against the principal (Burrus *v.* Cook, 117 Mo. App. 385, 93 S. W. 888).

A surety on a note, who pays the same, and thereby becomes subrogated to the rights of the holder of the note, may pursue upon the note itself, in equity, the same course, within the same limitation period, that the creditor could have pursued at law, had he remained the owner of the note, regardless of the fact that limitations have run against the surety's action at law to recover the money paid out by him on the principal's account. Ferd Heim Brewing Co. *v.* Jordan, 110 Mo. App. 286, 85 S. W. 927.

In South Dakota under Comp. Laws, § 4856, providing that an action for relief for which no period of limitation is provided must be commenced within ten years after the cause of action shall have accrued, an equity suit, by persons voluntarily paying off a mortgage, to be subrogated to the rights of the mortgagee, will be deemed barred within that period after payment. Pollock *v.* Wright, 15 S. D. 134, 87 N. W. 584.

37. *Arkansas.*—Dyer *v.* Jacoway, 76 Ark. 171, 88 S. W. 901 (holding that creditors cannot, because of laches, procure subrogation to the rights of sureties in an indemnity mortgage by a proceeding brought thirty years after the execution of a release by the sureties); Boone County Bank *v.* Byrum, 68 Ark. 71, 56 S. W. 532.

Indiana.— Smith *v.* Harbin, 124 Ind. 434, 24 N. E. 1051.

Kansas.— Hargis *v.* Robinson, 63 Kan. 686, 66 Pac. 988 (holding that equity does not encourage or reward negligence, and subrogation, which is founded on principles of equity and benevolence, is never enforced in favor of one who has been negligent in asserting an equity and to the prejudice of innocent parties who have acquired intervening rights); Hofman *v.* Demple, 52 Kan. 756, 35 Pac. 803.

Maryland.— Noble *v.* Turner, 69 Md. 519, 16 Atl. 124.

Nebraska.— Ocobock *v.* Baker, 52 Nebr. 447, 72 N. W. 582, 66 Am. St. Rep. 519.

Pennsylvania.— *In re* Searight, 163 Pa. St. 222, 29 Atl. 973; Gring's Appeal, 89 Pa. St. 336; Douglass' Appeal, 48 Pa. St. 223;

parties.[46] Creditors to whose rights a party seeks to be subrogated are necessary parties to an action to obtain such subrogation;[47] and plaintiff cannot be subrogated to the rights of a defendant under a contract with a third person in an action to which such third person is not made a party.[48] But a judgment creditor, against whom no decree is prayed, is not a necessary party to a suit in which plaintiff seeks to be subrogated to satisfied judgment liens.[49] It has been held

46. *Arkansas.*— Dyer *v.* Jacoway, 76 Ark. 171, 88 S. W. 901 (holding that creditors cannot obtain subrogation to a deceased surety's right in an indemnity mortgage by a proceeding against the other sureties, to which none of the heirs or legal representatives of the deceased surety are parties); Bond *v.* Montgomery, 56 Ark. 563, 20 S. W. 525, 35 Am. St. Rep. 119.

Georgia.— Wilkins *v.* Gibson, 113 Ga. 31, 38 S. E. 374, 84 Am. St. Rep. 204, holding that a creditor who is the holder of a junior encumbrance, but who claims to have been subrogated to the rights of the senior encumbrancer, as against the rights of an intervening encumbrancer, in setting up the right of subrogation must make the senior encumbrancer a party to the proceeding, or allege a sufficient reason for not doing so, and must also make such allegations and ask for such relief as the senior encumbrancer should make and ask for if he were proceeding in his own right.

Indiana.— Rush *v.* State, 20 Ind. 432.

Kentucky.— Guill *v.* Corinth Deposit Bank, 68 S. W. 870, 24 Ky. L. Rep. 482.

New Jersey.— Schneider *v.* Schmidt, (Ch. 1908) 70 Atl. 688. And see Boice *v.* Conover, 69 N. J. Eq. 580, 61 Atl. 159, holding that where one was subrogated to a judgment lien, all persons interested in the judgment were entitled to be heard.

North Carolina.— Brinson *v.* Thomas, 55 N. C. 414.

South Dakota.— Muller *v.* Flavin, 13 S. D. 595, 83 N. W. 687.

See 44 Cent. Dig. tit. "Subrogation," § 113.

But see Connecticut Mut. L. Ins. Co. *v.* Cornwell, 72 Hun (N. Y.) 199, 25 N. Y. Suppl. 348.

The right to subrogation under a prior mortgage can be litigated only in a proceeding to foreclose said mortgage, in which the junior lien-holders are made parties. Farm, etc., Co. *v.* Meloy, 11 S. D. 7, 75 N. W. 207.

Non-joinder of insolvent debtor immaterial. — In a suit to subrogate a surety who has paid certain debts, to the rights and liens of the creditors against the property of one of the principal debtors, the failure to join the other principal debtor is immaterial, where he is insolvent, and his property is brought into court, and his non-joinder does not affect any rights defendant may have against him. Cauthorn *v.* Berry, 69 Mo. App. 404.

In an action by a creditor partner to be subrogated to a mortgage given by a debtor partner to secure a firm creditor on payment by the creditor partner of a firm debt, the debtor partner is not a necessary party. Schuyler *v.* Booth, 37 Misc. (N. Y.) 35, 74 N. Y. Suppl. 733 [*affirmed* in 76 N. Y. App. Div. 619, 79 N. Y. Suppl. 1146].

Where a bill seeks subrogation to a lien on land, and there are other persons holding liens on the land in conflict with such claims of subrogation, they must be made parties to the bill. Gall *v.* Gall, 50 W. Va. 523, 40 S. E. 380.

An administrator is a proper party defendant to a bill claiming subrogation to a vendor's lien on land of an intestate. Allen *v.* Caylor, 120 Ala. 251, 24 So. 512, 74 Am. St. Rep. 31.

47. Harris *v.* Watson, 56 Ark. 574, 20 S. W. 529; Aultman *v.* Bishop, 53 Nebr. 545, 74 N. W. 55 (holding that the party to whom the debt of another has been paid, the payment of which furnishes the basis of the claim for subrogation, is a proper and necessary party to the action for subrogation); Schilb *v.* Moon, 50 W. Va. 47, 40 S. E. 329 (holding that the judgment creditor in a judgment on a negotiable note must be a party to a suit in equity by a subsequent indorser to enforce substitution to the lien of the judgment against the land of the prior indorser); Hoffman *v.* Shields, 4 W. Va. 490 (holding that it is necessary in a bill to enforce a judgment lien by a surety, where such surety has paid the judgment, that the original judgment creditors whose judgment he has paid be made parties). But see Towe *v.* Newbold, 57 N. C. 212, where the court seems to hold by implication that where a surety has paid money he is entitled to an assignment of all the securities that the creditor held, and to substitution, and the creditor need not be a party.

But where a surety pays a judgment rendered in favor of the state against him and his principal, he may maintain a suit to enforce the lien thereof for his benefit, without making the state a party to the suit. Pickens *v.* Wood, 57 W. Va. 480, 50 S. E. 818.

Where an original creditor has satisfied his claim by a formal instrument sufficient for that purpose, he is not a necessary party to a suit for subrogation to his rights. Boevink *v.* Christiaanse, 69 Nebr. 256, 95 N. W. 652.

48. Citizens' St. R. Co. *v.* Robbins, 144 Ind. 671, 42 N. E. 916, 43 N. E. 649.

49. Fridenburg *v.* Wilson, 20 Fla. 359; McNairy *v.* Eastland, 10 Yerg. (Tenn.) 310.

Similarly in an action for conversion by the mortgagor of a chattel against a purchaser from the mortgagee, who has therefore become subrogated to the rights of such mortgagee by operation of law, the mortgagee is not a necessary party to give defendant complete protection against plaintiff. Potter *v.* Lohse, 31 Mont. 91, 77 Pac. 419.

Conversely in a suit by a judgment creditor, who had purchased his debtor's land

pleaded,[53] **and the** subrogee who, on paying the debt, is entitled to be subrogated to the rights of plaintiff, must ask for such relief in his answer;[54] and plaintiff cannot be subrogated to the rights of a defendant under a contract with a third person in an action in which the terms of the contract are not alleged.[55] But it is held that, although a party does not specifically claim the right of subrogation, equity will grant the relief, where it is justified by the facts alleged and established,[56] under the prayer for general relief.[57] The petition need not anticipate defenses,[58] and the sufficiency of the complaint must be judged from the pleading as a whole.[59] Proof must conform to the pleadings.[60]

F. Evidence. The rules of evidence in civil actions and proceedings generally[61] apply to proceedings to enforce subrogation,[62] the burden of proof being upon claimant to establish his right by clear evidence.[63] It is held, however, that where a stranger to an obligation pays a part of the whole of the debt, there is a presumption that the transaction was a purchase of the debt and accompanying security to the extent of the payment.[64]

rights of the mortgagee, the complaint should allege that the purchaser bought with the belief that he was obtaining the legal title, and should set forth the amount of the price. Griffin *v.* Griffin, 70 S. C. 220, 49 S. E. 561.

Every intendment is to be made against the pleader in an action for subrogation as in other actions. Fidelity, etc., Co. *v.* Jordan, 134 N. C. 236, 46 S. E. 496.

Complaint not demurrable as disclosing no lack of an adequate remedy at law see Home Inv. Co. *v.* Clarson, 15 S. D. 513, 90 N. W. 153.

In an action by a creditor partner to be subrogated to a mortgage given by a debtor partner to secure a firm creditor, on payment by the creditor partner of a firm debt, complaint held to show sufficiently an equitable right to subrogation on payment of the debt, see Schuyler *v.* Booth, 37 Misc. (N. Y.) 35, 74 N. Y. Suppl. 733 [*affirmed* in 76 N. Y. App. Div. 619, 79 N. Y. Suppl. 1146].

53. Crebbin *v.* Moseley, (Tex. Civ. App. 1903) 74 S. W. 815; Strnad *v.* Strnad, 29 Tex. Civ. App. 124, 68 S. W. 69.

In trespass to try title by heirs against one purchasing land at a void administrator's sale to recover the land, if the purchaser wishes to assert an equity of subrogation to the amount of his purchase-money, he must plead it. Wilkin *v.* Owens, (Tex. 1908) 114 S. W. 104, 115 S. W. 1174, 117 S. W. 425 [*reversing* on other grounds (Civ. App. 1908) 110 S. W. 552].

54. Barton *v.* Moore, 45 Minn. 98, 47 N. W. 460. But see Boone County Bank *v.* Byrum, 68 Ark. 71, 56 S. W. 532; Hawpe *v.* Bumgardner, 103 Va. 91, 48 S. E. 554, holding that where a creditor's bill alleges a state of facts entitling plaintiff to be subrogated in equity under the prayer for general relief to the rights of a judgment creditor whose debt he had paid as defendant's surety, the failure to ask specifically for such relief is not ground for dismissing the bill on demurrer.

A junior mortgagee who has the right of subrogation for all prior mortgages paid off by him for the purpose of protecting his lien, when made a defendant in chancery proceedings, should ask for the enforcement of such right in his answer. Ball *v.* Callahan, 95 Ill. App. 615 [*affirmed* in 197 Ill. 318, 64 N. E. 295].

Answer sufficiently raising the issue of subrogation see Sternback *v.* Friedman, 23 Misc. (N. Y.) 173, 50 N. Y. Suppl. 1025 [*modified* in 34 N. Y. App. Div. 534, 54 N. Y. Suppl. 608].

In an action to quiet title, where defendants rely on rights derived from the purchase of a mortgage, and an assignment, and deny any payment thereof, and the court finds that the mortgage has been paid, defendants have no claim for subrogation. Miller *v.* Stevenson, 58 Nebr. 305, 78 N. W. 626.

55. Citizens' St. R. Co. *v.* Robbins, 144 Ind. 671, 42 N. E. 916, 43 N. E. 649.

Allegation of insolvency of judgment debtor unnecessary.—A complaint by one who has paid a judgment, seeking subrogation to the lien thereof as against one having subsequent lien, need not allege insolvency of the judgment debtor, since the right to subrogation depends on the circumstances attending the payment of the judgment, and not on the debtor's insolvency. Spaulding *v.* Harvey, 129 Ind. 106, 28 N. E. 323, 28 Am. St. Rep. 176, 13 L. R. A. 619.

56. Bankers' Loan, etc., Co. *v.* Hornish, 94 Va. 608, 27 S. E. 459.

57. Berry *v.* Bullock, 81 Miss 463, 33 So. 410.

58. Richards *v.* Yoder, 10 Nebr. 429, 6 N. W. 629.

59. Bunting *v.* Gilmore, 124 Ind. 113, 24 N. E. 583, holding that the fact that the complaint contains no allegation that the land described in defendant's mortgage is the same as that contained in the mortgage under which complainant redeemed does not affect its sufficiency when that fact appears from all the averments.

60. Weil *v.* Enterprise Ginnery, etc., Co., 42 La. Ann. 492, 7 So. 622; Davis *v.* Evans, 102 Mo. 164, 14 S. W. 875; Weimer *v.* Talbot, 56 W. Va. 257, 49 S. E. 372.

61. See EVIDENCE, 16 Cyc. 821.

62. Thompson *v.* Humphrey, 83 N. C. 416.

63. Weaver *v.* Norwood, 59 Miss. 665.

64. Neilson *v.* Frey, 16 Ohio St. 552, 91

payment of the debts of the testator may have it out of other property of the testator by subrogation to the debts of creditors, and may enforce contribution by other members of the same class,[72] and the same rule applies to heirs who have paid or whose property has been taken to pay debts of the intestate;[73] and where some of the heirs, after division of the realty, discharge a debt, which is a common liability upon the realty, by agreement with the rest, or pay more than their proportionate share, they are subrogated to the creditors' rights to proceed against the lands of the others.[74] But where heirs of an estate, supposing it to be solvent, pay off mortgages on lands, and, on learning afterward that the estate is insolvent, claim to be subrogated to the rights of the mortgages, if the intent to be subrogated did not exist at the time of payment of the mortgages, the claim cannot be maintained.[75] Where a wife paid a balance due on a mortgage of land in which she had a life-interest, executed by the husband and wife for his debt, her devisees

Where a widow elected to take a legacy bequeathed to her in lieu of dower, and a portion of the amount necessary to satisfy the legacy was used for the payment of testator's debts, she was entitled to be subrogated to the rights of creditors against testator's real estate for the recovery of the amount so taken. Overton *v.* Lea, 108 Tenn. 505, 68 S. W. 250.

If a widow, before the appointment of an administrator, incurs the expense of erecting a suitable monument over the grave of her husband, she is entitled to be subrogated to the rights of the dealer who erected the monument, and may recover therefor against the administrator. Pease *v.* Christman, 158 Ind. 642, 64 N. E. 90.

72. Rhoods' Estate, 3 Rawle (Pa.) 420; Hope *v.* Wilkinson, 82 Tenn. 21, 52 Am. Rep. 149; Foster *v.* Crenshaw, 3 Munf. (Va.) 514; Gallagher *v.* Redmond, 64 Tex. 622.

Cestuis que trustent under a will, whose income is taken to pay debts of the estate, are entitled to be subrogated to the rights of the creditor. Amory *v.* Lowell, 1 Allen (Mass.) 504.

If there be no devise of real estate, if the creditors exhaust the personal estate, then as against the heir at law the legatees may stand in the place of the creditors and come upon the real estate which has descended. Alexander *v.* Miller, 7 Heisk. (Tenn.) 65.

Where legatees pay off and discharge a judgment against the executors of the estate, which constituted a lien on the estate, they are substituted to the rights of the judgment creditor. Place *v.* Oldham, 10 B. Mon. (Ky.) 400; Mitchell *v.* Mitchell, 8 Humphr. (Tenn.) 359.

A devisee whose devise has been sold to pay the debts of the estate, the personal estate being insufficient to pay the debts, is entitled to reimbursement by way of subrogation out of the assets subsequently received and discovered by the executors, the personal estate being the primary fund for the payment of debts, and being charged with the debts. Couch *v.* Delaplaine, 2 N. Y. 397. And where a devisee of land, which by the direction of the devisor was levied on during his life under an execution against himself, after his death bought the land at the execution sale to relieve it of the encumbrance, he is entitled to be subrogated to the rights of the creditor, and to have the amount which he advanced paid out of the personal estate or out of the residuum; but it would not be so if it not only had been levied on but sold during the life of the testator. Redmond *v.* Borroughs, 63 N. C. 242.

73. *Alabama.*— Winston *v.* McAlpine, 65 Ala. 377.

Kentucky.— Place *v.* Oldhams, 10 B. Mon. 400 (holding that heirs against whom a judgment has been recovered in conjunction with the administrator, and who paid the judgment, may in equity be substituted to the rights which the judgment creditor had to file his bill against the administrator to have a discovery of assets and be reimbursed in case there has been a maladministration of assets); Taylor *v.* Taylor, 8 B. Mon. 419, 48 Am. Dec. 400.

Mississippi.— McPike *v.* Wells, 54 Miss. 136.

New Hampshire.— Jenness *v.* Robinson, 10 N. H. 215, holding that where some of the heirs, who hold a mortgage upon the real estate of an intestate to secure a debt due from him, in order to prevent a sale of the land, give a bond for the payment of the debts, and thereby discharge the mortgage as a security for the entire debt, they are entitled to hold the land against the other heirs, respectively, as if the mortgage subsisted until they contributed their several shares toward redemption.

Pennsylvania.— Guier *v.* Kelley, 2 Binn. 294.

South Carolina.— Lyles *v.* Lyles, 1 Hill Eq. 76.

See 44 Cent. Dig. tit. "Subrogation," § 7.

Where the tenant by the curtesy conveys in fee with warranty lands belonging to his children in which he has only a life-estate, and then dies intestate, leaving a widow and children surviving him who are entitled to his personal estate, the children on confirming the title of the purchaser are entitled to be substituted as creditors of the estate of their father for the amount for which the personal representatives of the intestate are liable on the covenant of warranty. House *v.* House, 10 Paige (N. Y.) 158.

74. Winston *v.* McAlpine, 65 Ala. 377.

75. Belcher *v.* Wickersham, 9 Baxt. (Tenn.) 111.

reimbursed his proportion of the demand;[3] but it is held that to entitle a joint debtor on a judgment to subrogation to the rights of the judgment creditors upon a purchase by him of the judgment, it must appear that it was his intention, in making the purchase, to acquire these rights.[4]

4. Partners. A partner who on the dissolution of the partnership pays partnership debts is subrogated to the creditor's rights in the joint property to obtain contribution,[5] and where partners agree that one shall pay a firm debt, the other becomes a surety for him, and, upon making a payment, is subrogated to the rights of the creditor against his copartner;[6] and thus if upon dissolution one partner assumes to pay firm debts, he becomes the principal as between the partners and the other members merely sureties, although as to the creditor they are both principals;[7] and where one partner after going out of the firm under covenant by his partners that they will pay the firm debts and indemnify him against them pays debts he becomes their surety, and is entitled to come in as a creditor and be subrogated to the rights of the creditors whom he has paid.[8] The retiring partner, occupying the position of surety as to a firm debt assumed by his former copartners, who continue the business as a new firm, has the right, upon his being compelled to pay such debt, to a surrender to him by the creditors

who are liable as co-promisors, have no rights of subrogation against each other.

3. Morris *v.* Evans, 2 B. Mon. (Ky.) 84, 36 Am. Dec. 591.

4. Huggins *v.* White, 7 Tex. Civ. App. 563, 27 S. W. 1066.

5. *Illinois.*— Downs *v.* Jackson, 33 Ill. 464, 85 Am. Dec. 289.

Louisiana.—Rowlett *v.* Grieve, 8 Mart. 483, 13 Am. Dec. 296.

New York.— Schuyler *v.* Booth, 76 N. Y. App. Div. 619, 79 N. Y. Suppl. 1146 [*affirming* 37 Misc. 35, 74 N. Y. Suppl. 733], holding that where a partnership has been dissolved and an accounting shows one of the partners to be the creditor of the other, and such creditor partner pays an outstanding firm debt, he will be subrogated to the rights of the creditor whose debt he has paid in mortgages which the debtor partner gave him to secure the firm debt.

South Carolina.— Eakin *v.* Knox, 6 S. C. 14.

Virginia.— Sands *v.* Durham, 99 Va. 263, 38 S. E. 145, 86 Am. St. Rep. 884, 54 L. R. A. 614, 98 Va. 392, 36 S. E. 472, holding that where a partnership has been dissolved, the social assets exhausted in the payment of partnership debts, and a settlement of the partnership accounts made, from which it appears that one partner was in advance to the firm, and with his individual means has paid judgment against it, he is entitled to be subrogated to the rights of the judgment creditors whose judgments he has discharged, and to subject the land owned by his copartner at the time of the docketing of the judgments to their satisfaction.

See 44 Cent. Dig. tit. "Subrogation," § 10.

6. Field *v.* Hamilton, 45 Vt. 35.

7. Conwell *v.* McCowan, 81 Ill. 285 (holding that where, on dissolution of partnership, one partner assumes the payment of a partnership note, and executes a mortgage to the payee of the note to secure its payment, and to indemnify his copartner against the payment thereof, such copartner will be entitled to be subrogated to the rights of the mortgagee to the extent of any payment he may have to make on such partnership note); *In re* McGee, 1 Pearson (Pa.) 42 (holding that when, on the dissolution of the firm, one of the partners assumes a particular debt, he is bound to pay it, and, if another partner discharges it, he is entitled to be subrogated to the claims of the creditor against the one who assumed it); Royalton Nat. Bank *v.* Cushing, 53 Vt. 321 (holding that when upon the dissolution or reconstruction of a firm, one or more of the partners promises to pay the partnership debts in consideration of receiving or retaining the assets, this will place the rest in the position of sureties); Ætna Ins. Co. *v.* Wires, 28 Vt. 93 (holding that where, upon the dissolution of a copartnership, one partner assumes a liability, he does it *prima facie* upon sufficient consideration, leaving his copartners liable only as sureties, and they may take measures to have the claim assigned and collected from the partner liable). And see Tibbetts *v.* Magruder, 9 Dana (Ky.) 79.

The rule applies where one partner is bankrupt.— Thus where a creditor of a partnership, which has been dissolved and the debts thereof assumed by one of the partners, thereby constituting him the principal debtor and the other partner surety, has proved the debt in bankruptcy against the principal debtor, the surety may have himself subrogated to the creditor's rights on paying the balance due on the debt. Schmitt *v.* Greenberg, 58 Misc. (N. Y.) 570, 109 N. Y. Suppl. 881.

8. Olson *v.* Morrison, 29 Mich. 395; Burnside *v.* Fetzner, 63 Mo. 107; Merrill *v.* Green, 55 N. Y. 270; Gilfillan *v.* Dewoody, 157 Pa. St. 601, 27 Atl. 782; Scott's Appeal, 88 Pa. St. 173. But see Griffin *v.* Orman, 9 Fla. 22, holding that where a continuing partner agreed with the retiring partners to pay the firm debts and gave his bond and security to that effect, but no arrangement was made with the creditors, they did not take the continuing partner as principal and the retiring partners as sureties, and the latter, on pay-

rights of the owner in a mortgage given him as security.[31] An indorser of a note, after its maturity, who joins with the maker in giving a bond for the debt, is entitled, upon a tender of the debt, to an assignment of the bond; [32] and although by statute the indorser of a note is not liable thereon until the holder has exhausted his remedies against the maker, yet if the indorser waives that privilege and pays the amount due, he becomes subrogated to the rights of the holder, since such a payment cannot be considered as a voluntary one.[33] Thus where the money of an indorser of a note upon which judgment is obtained is used to satisfy the judgment, the indorser has a right to be subrogated to plaintiff's rights and to keep the judgment alive.[34] No entry on the judgment of such payment is required, in order that the indorser may have the right of subrogation; and an entry of satisfaction, made by plaintiff without the authority of the indorser, will not defeat the latter's right to enforce the judgment in his own favor against the land of the principal debtor; [35] and one who indorses a note to pay a judgment with the express understanding that the judgment shall be assigned is subrogated to the rights of the judgment creditor.[36] Conversely, where the makers and indorsers of negotiable paper are insolvent, the holders thereof may, upon the principle of subrogation, avail themselves of the right of such indorsers arising under a chattel mortgage

and collateral as means of indemnity to him, and he is subrogated to the rights of the maker, if he pays the note, and is entitled to receive the collateral in the same condition in which it stood in the maker's hands, and to all remedies thereon available to the latter; and this right does not depend on contract, but rests on principles of justice and equity. Mankey *v.* Willoughby, 21 App. Cas. 314.

31. Millaudon *v.* Colla, 15 La. 213; Baldwin *v.* Thompson, 6 La. 474; Suares *v.* His Creditors, 3 La. 341; Nichol *v.* De Ende, 3 Mart. N. S. (La.) 310; Kingman *v.* Cornell-Tebbetts Mach., etc., Co., 150 Mo. 282, 51 S. W. 727 (holding that, where the payee of a note secured by a trust deed has compelled the indorser thereof to pay the note, he becomes subrogated to the payee's rights under the deed); Ætna Ins. Co. *v.* Thompson, 68 N. H. 20, 40 Atl. 396, 73 Am. St. Rep. 552 (holding that where sureties on a note secured by mortgage pay the same, they are subrogated to the rights of the mortgagee to the proceeds of an insurance policy on the property); Malone Third Nat. Bank *v.* Shields, 55 Hun (N. Y.) 274, 8 N. Y. Suppl. 298.

Similarly the indorser of a draft is, upon payment thereof by him, entitled to be subrogated to the security in the hands of the accepter. Stevenson *v.* Austin, 3 Metc. (Mass.) 474.

32. Merriken *v.* Goodwin, 2 Del. Ch. 236.

33. Telford *v.* Garrels, 132 Ill. 550, 24 N. E. 573 [*affirming* 31 Ill. App. 441].

But where an administrator renews a note due from the estate giving security thereon, the administrator having no power to impose a direct liability upon the estate he represents by executing a note or other security for money in his representative character (see EXECUTORS AND ADMINISTRATORS, 18 Cyc. 252), the parties to the renewal note are liable individually, and upon payment thereof by the surety he is not entitled to subrogation to the creditor's right against the estate, but only to subject the interest of the administrator to the amount paid as his indorser (Brown *v.* Lang, 4 Ala. 50).

34. Dorsey's Succession, 7 La. Ann. 34; Shaw *v.* McClellan, 1 Pa. L. J. Rep. 384 (holding that the indorser has a right to judgment against the maker of a note, and to the benefit of the recognizance for stay entered on it); Abrams *v.* Ingram, 1 Phila. (Pa.) 398.) And see Johnson *v.* Webster, 81 Iowa 581, 47 N. W. 769.

The judgment passes, however, with all its privileges and infirmities and the surety is subrogated to the rights of the creditor but no more. Partee *v.* Mathews, 53 Miss. 140.

The indorser of a note, given by a creditor to prevent a sale of his debtor's effects under a judgment in favor of a creditor with a prior lien, who paid the latter, and to whom the judgment was afterward assigned, was substituted for the judgment creditor. Cottrell's Appeal, 23 Pa. St. 294.

In Nebraska it is held that an indorser must, in order to have the benefit of the judgment, make and prove his defense of suretyship in the original action and have the judgment against himself and his principal assigned to him. Potvin *v.* Meyers, 27 Nebr. 749, 44 N. W. 25.

Where separate judgments are recovered by the same plaintiff against the maker and indorser of a note, the indorser, upon the payment of the judgment against himself, is entitled to be substituted in equity to the judgment against the maker (Lyon *v.* Bolling, 9 Ala. 463, 44 Am. Dec. 444); and where one judgment was obtained against the maker and another against the indorser, and upon the latter judgment suit was brought in another state, and a judgment recovered, which the indorser paid, he was entitled to be subrogated to the lien of the judgment against the maker of the note (Old Dominion Bank *v.* Allen, 76 Va. 200).

35. Tates *v.* Mead, 68 Miss. 787, 10 So. 75.

36. Treadway *v.* Pharis, 18 S. W. 225, 13 Ky. L. Rep. 787.

given them by the makers to secure them against loss because of their liability as indorsers;[37] and similarly, a surety on a note, on payment by him, is entitled to be subrogated to all the rights and securities of the payee or holder, for the purpose of obtaining reimbursement;[38] and if the note has been reduced to judgment, he may pay the amount due, take an assignment, and become subrogated to the rights of the judgment creditors, and sell and assign his interest, before having any adjudication of his suretyship.[39] It is not necessary that the payment should have been made in money. Anything which the creditor is willing to accept in satisfaction of the debt is sufficient.[40] But the right to subrogation of a surety on a note is confined to the rights and securities of the contract for which he was surety, and do not extend to rights against one as to whom he was a stranger.[41]

E. Sureties or Guarantors — 1. General Rule Stated. A surety who has paid the debt of the principal is at once subrogated to all the rights, remedies, securities, liens, and equities of the creditor, for the purpose of obtaining his reimbursement from the principal debtor.[42] This subrogation to the remedies

37. Harmony Nat. Bank's Appeal, 101 Pa. St. 428 (holding that where a mortgage is given by the maker of a note to secure the indorser, and both become insolvent, the holder of the note is entitled to the benefit of the security; but he can have no higher rights than could the indorser); National Shoe, etc., Bank *v.* Small, 7 Fed. 837. But see Seward *v.* Huntington, 94 N. Y. 104 [*reversing* 26 Hun 217].

Where two persons exchange notes, each note is the proper debt of the maker, and each maker is a purchaser for value of the note received, and thus the relation of principal and surety does not exist, and no promise of either to indemnify the other can be implied, and no rights of subrogation are created. Stickney *v.* Mohler, 19 Md. 490; Coburn *v.* Baker, 6 Duer (N.Y.) 532; Smith's Appeal, 125 Pa. St. 404, 17 Atl. 344; Battin *v.* Meyer, 5 Phila. (Pa.) 73 [*modified* in Taylor's Appeal, 45 Pa. St. 71].

38. Cummings *v.* Little, 45 Me. 183; Myres *v.* Yaple, 60 Mich. 339, 27 N. W. 536 (holding that a surety in a note for the purchase of a chattel by paying the note is subrogated to the rights of the payee); Carpenter *v.* Minter, 72 Tex. 370, 12 S. W. 180. And see Schoonover *v.* Allen, 40 Ark. 132.

A surety on a sealed note, paying it, is entitled to be subrogated to the rights of the holder. Smith *v.* Swain, 7 Rich. Eq. (S. C.) 112.

The guarantor of a note for accommodation is subrogated to the rights of the holder to whom he has made payment against the maker. Babcock *v.* Blanchard, 86 Ill. 165.

A surety in a note for two principal promisors, one deceased, having paid it, may recover the amount paid from the surviving principal promisor. Riddle *v.* Bowman, 27 N. H. 236.

Where a third person assumes payment of a note, and the surety for the maker is compelled thereafter to pay the note, he is entitled to be subrogated to the right of action which the maker would have against the third person. Rodenbarger *v.* Bramblett, 78 Ind. 213.

An action on a promissory note from ostensible partners, accepted by one unacquainted with the existence of a dormant partner, may be brought against all the partners, and where a surety pays the note he is entitled to the usual remedies of sureties, and may be subrogated to the remedy on the contract, or he may have his action for money paid for the use of the partnership. Hill *v.* Voorhies, 22 Pa. St. 68.

39. Frank *v.* Traylor, 130 Ind. 145, 29 N. E. 486, 16 L. R. A. 115; Manford *v.* Firth, 68 Ind. 83, holding that where a surety on a note satisfied the judgment upon it, rendered against him and the maker, and had it assigned to him on the record, he should be subrogated to all the rights of the judgment creditor in and to the judgment, previous to and subsisting at the time of it.

40. Humphreys *v.* Vertner, Freem. (Miss.) 251.

41. Flannery *v.* Utley, 3 S. W. 412, 5 S. W. 776, 8 Ky. L. Rep. 776, 9 Ky. L. Rep. 581.

42. *Alabama.*—Fawcetts *v.* Kimmey, 33 Ala. 261; Houston *v.* Huntsville Branch Bank, 25 Ala. 250; Brown *v.* Lang, 4 Ala. 50; Foster *v.* Athenæum, 3 Ala. 302; Cullum *v.* Emanuel, 1 Ala. 23, 34 Am. Dec. 757.

Arkansas.—Talbot *v.* Wilkins, 31 Ark. 411.

Connecticut.— Stamford Bank *v.* Benedict, 15 Conn. 437; Belcher *v.* Hartford Bank, 15 Conn. 381.

Delaware.— McDowell *v.* Wilmington, etc., Bank, 1 Harr. 369; Miller *v.* Stout, 5 Del. Ch. 259.

Georgia.— Worthy *v.* Battle, 125 Ga. 415, 54 S. E. 667; Ezzard *v.* Bell, 100 Ga. 150, 28 S. E. 28; Davis *v.* Smith, 5 Ga. 274, 47 Am. Dec. 279; Lumpkin *v.* Mills, 4 Ga. 343.

Illinois.— Lochenmeyer *v.* Fogarty, 112 Ill. 572; Moore *v.* Topliff, 107 Ill. 241; Conwell *v.* McCowan, 53 Ill. 363; Billings *v.* Sprague, 49 Ill. 509; Foss *v.* Chicago, 34 Ill. 488; Peirce *v.* Garrett, 65 Ill. App. 682.

Indiana.— Opp *v.* Ward, 125 Ind. 241, 243, 24 N. E. 974, 21 Am. St. Rep. 220; Peirce *v.* Higgins, 101 Ind. 178; Gipson *v.* Ogden, 100 Ind. 20; Pence *v.* Armstrong, 95 Ind. 191;

gated to all defenses which his principal had;[3] and is entitled to be substituted in the place of the creditors as to all means and remedies which the creditors possess to enforce payment of the debt secured from the principal debtors,[4] and the doctrine is sufficiently broad to entitle a surety who has paid the debt of his principal to be subrogated to the remedies and rights which the creditor had, not only against the principal, but against others,[5] and as against his cosureties, in the same manner as against the principal debtor.[6] The surety's right of subrogation extends to mortgages [7] and other liens [8] held by the creditor, and to funds [9]

City Trust, etc., Co., 114 Fed. 529, 52 C. C. A. 313.

3. Morehouse *v.* Brooklyn Heights R. Co., 185 N. Y. 520, 78 N. E. 179.

4. *Alabama.*— Saint *v.* Ledyard, 14 Ala. 244.

Arkansas.—Talbot *v.* Wilkins, 31 Ark. 411.

Indiana.— Rush *v.* State, 20 Ind. 432; Nunemacher *v.* Ingle, 20 Ind. 135; Hubbard *v.* Security Trust Co., 38 Ind. App. 156, 78 N. E. 79.

Iowa.— Skiff *v.* Cross, 21 Iowa 459.

Maryland.— Stehle *v.* United Surety Co., 107 Md. 470, 68 Atl. 600; Merryman *v.* State, 5 Harr. & J. 423.

Missouri.— Sweet *v.* Jeffries, 48 Mo. 279.

New York.— Kolb *v.* Nat. Surety Co., 176 N. Y. 233, 68 N. E. 247; State Bank *v.* Fletcher, 5 Wend. 85; Boughton *v.* Orleans Bank, 2 Barb. Ch. 458; Hayes *v.* Ward, 4 Johns. Ch. 123.

North Carolina.—Tatum *v.* Tatum, 36 N. C. 113.

Where land was sold for partition, the title to be retained as security for the price, for which the purchaser gave his bond, with surety, and became insolvent, the surety who had discharged the bond was entitled to a resale of the land for reimbursement. Arnold *v.* Hicks, 38 N. C. 17; Bittick *v.* Wilkins, 7 Heisk. (Tenn.) 307; *Ex p.* Rushforth, 10 Ves. Jr. 409, 8 Rev. Rep. 10, 32 Eng. Reprint 903; *Ex p.* Turner, 3 Ves. Jr. 243, 3 Rev. Rep. 90, 30 Eng. Reprint 991.

Surety of administrator.— As the creditors and distributees of an intestate have an equity, as against the administrator, that the assets shall be applied exclusively for the purposes of the administration, the surety of an administrator, who has been compelled to answer to the creditors and distributees, or either, for the default of the administrator resulting from his misapplication of his assets, is entitled to be subrogated to this equity, and have it enforced for his indemnity against one who has knowingly contributed to the default by taking from the administrator the assets *mala fide* or without value. Rhame *v.* Lewis, 13 Rich. Eq. (S. C.) 269. Similarly where an administrator sold the land of the estate, but failed to collect the purchase-money, and his sureties, who had been compelled to pay a debt against the estate, brought suit to have his deed to the land set aside as fraudulent, they were entitled to be subrogated to the rights of the creditors, and their claim enforced against the land by an order of the probate court for its sale. Wernecke *v.* Kenyon, 66 Mo. 275.

Where the sureties of a receiver paid the amount due by him in his settlement, they are subrogated to the rights of the beneficiaries to whom they paid the money to follow the trust funds into the hands of one who, with notice, accepted it in payment of the receiver's individual debt (Clark *v.* Harrisonville First Nat. Bank, 57 Mo. App. 277), and where the creditors, or the obligee in a bond given by a receiver for the faithful performance of his duties, on a breach of trust by the receiver, participated in by the bank in which he deposited the funds, of which he had charge, brought suit and recovered judgment against the receiver and the surety on his bond, and the surety paid the judgment, such surety is subrogated to the rights of the creditors to enforce the liability incurred by the bank on account of its participation in the breach of trust by the fiduciary (American Nat. Bank *v.* Fidelity, etc., Co., 129 Ga. 126, 58 S. E. 867).

The sureties of a deputy sheriff, who paid the amount of his defalcation resulting from his failure to account to the state and county for taxes collected by him, are subrogated to the rights of the sheriff, or the state and county, and are entitled to pursue a fund impressed with a trust in favor of the state and county. Hill *v.* Fleming, 128 Ky. 201, 107 S. W. 764, 32 Ky. L. Rep. 1065.

Subrogation to right to collect tax.— If, under the code of Virginia of 1860, a sheriff settles in full with the auditor, and pays all the state taxes not returned delinquent, he cannot thereafter, by distraint, or in any other manner, make out of any taxpayer not returned delinquent the amount so advanced for him by the sheriff, as he cannot be subrogated to the state's rights or remedy for such tax. Hinchman *v.* Morris, 29 W. Va. 673, 2 S. E. 863.

A surety compelled to pay a debt to the state has in general whatever rights the state had to enforce its rights. Dias *v.* Bouchaud, 10 Paige (N. Y.) 445; U. S. *v.* Hunter, 26 Fed. Cas. No. 15,426, 5 Mason 62; Reg. *v.* Robinson, H. & N. 275 note.

5. National Surety Co. *v.* State Sav. Bank, 156 Fed. 21, 84 C. C. A. 187, 14 L. R. A. N. S. 155.

6. Pond *v.* Dougherty, 6 Cal. App. 686, 92 Pac. 1035.

7. See *infra*, VII, E, 3, a, (III).

8. Williams *v.* Jones, Bunb. 275.

9. St. Peter's Catholic Church *v.* Vannote, 66 N. J. Eq. 78, 56 Atl. 1037; Gastonia *v.* McEntee-Peterson Engineering Co., 131 N. C. 359, 42 S. E. 857.

Fund in court.— Where the interest of the principal in a fund in court was assigned to

for a surety to preserve the lien of the judgment against his principal in his own favor is, upon payment by him of the same, to have the judgment assigned to a trustee for his use, for if he permitted the judgment to be satisfied without any assignment, the remedy of subrogation is lost,[37] yet where justice requires, the judgment will be kept alive in equity for the benefit of a surety who has paid the demand;[38] and in equity a surety paying a judgment recovered against himself and his principal is entitled to be subrogated to all the rights of the original creditor, and to have the judgment assigned to himself or a third person for his benefit,[39]

ton *v.* Field, 16 Ark. 216; Drefahl *v.* Tuttle, 42 Iowa 177; Bones *v.* Aiken, 35 Iowa 534; Dunlap *v.* O'Bannon, 5 B. Mon. (Ky.) 393 (holding that a surety in a judgment has a right in equity, on paying the judgment, to be substituted to the equity of the judgment creditor for the assignee of the receipt given an attorney as collector of the judgment); Sotheren *v.* Reed, 4 Harr. & J. (Md.) 307.

37. Peebles *v.* Gay, 115 N. C. 38, 40, 41, 20 S. E. 173, 44 Am. St. Rep. 429; Liles *v.* Rogers, 113 N. C. 197, 18 S. E. 104, 37 Am. St. Rep. 627; Tiddy *v.* Harris, 101 N. C. 589, 8 S. E. 227; Sherwood *v.* Collier, 14 N. C. 380, 24 Am. Dec. 264; Hodges *v.* Armstrong, 14 N. C. 253.

38. Cottrell's Appeal, 23 Pa. St. 294.

Where the principal alone appeals after a judgment against him and the surety, and the surety is obliged to pay the debt, he is entitled to have a judgment of affirmance against his principal assigned to him, and to recover against the sureties on his principal's supersedeas bond. Mitchell *v.* De Witt, 25 Tex. Suppl. 180, 78 Am. Dec. 561.

Where sureties received a void mortgage from their principal to indemnify them, which mortgage, from defect of execution, was not valid as to creditors, they were subrogated to the rights of a judgment creditor of the principal, who had levied on the property. Miller *v.* Pendleton, 4 Hen. & M. (Va.) 436.

39. *Alabama.*— Bragg *v.* Patterson, 85 Ala. 233, 4 So. 716; Turner *v.* Teague, 73 Ala. 554.

Arkansas.—Wilks *v.* Vaughan, 73 Ark. 174, 83 S. W. 913.

Delaware.— Miller *v.* Stout, 5 Del. Ch. 259.

Georgia.— Davenport *v.* Hardeman, 5 Ga. 580; Lumpkin *v.* Mills, 4 Ga. 343.

Illinois.— Chandler *v.* Higgins, 109 Ill. 602.

Indiana.— See Davis *v.* Schlemmer, 150 Ind. 472, 50 N. E. 373.

Iowa.—Anglo-American Land, etc., Co. *v.* Bush, 84 Iowa 272, 50 N. W. 1063; Searing *v.* Berry, 58 Iowa 20, 11 N. W. 708.

Kansas.— Harris *v.* Frank, 29 Kan. 200.

Kentucky.— Morris *v.* Evans, 2 B. Mon. 84, 36 Am. Dec. 591; Wilson *v.* Wilson, 50 S. W. 260, 20 Ky. L. Rep. 1071.

Louisiana.— Sprigg *v.* Beaman, 6 La. 59.

Maine.— Norton *v.* Soule, 2 Me. 341.

Maryland.— Crisfield *v.* State, 55 Md. 192; Creager *v.* Brengle, 5 Harr. & J. 234, 9 Am. Dec. 516.

Missouri.—Benne *v.* Schnecko, 100 Mo. 250, 13 S. W. 82.

New York.— Townsend *v.* Whitney, 75 N. Y. 425 [*affirming* 15 Hun 93]; Smith *v.* National Surety Co., 46 N. Y. App. Div. 633, 62 N. Y. Suppl. 1105; Townsend *v.* Whitney, 15 Hun 93 [*affirmed* in 75 N. Y. 425]; Goodyear *v.* Watson, 14 Barb. 481; Alden *v.* Clark, 11 How. Pr. 209.

North Carolina.— Person *v.* Perry, 70 N. C. 697; Hanner *v.* Douglass, 57 N. C. 262. But see Sherwood *v.* Collier, 14 N. C. 380, 24 Am. Dec. 264.

Ohio.— Hill *v.* King, 48 Ohio St. 75, 26 N. E. 988.

Pennsylvania.— Jennings *v.* Hare, 104 Pa. St. 489; Duffield *v.* Cooper, 87 Pa. St. 443 (holding that if the surety pays a judgment against the principal and himself, he succeeds to the rights of the creditor and is entitled to collect the judgment, and it is not necessary that he must be subrogated under Act April 22, 1856, § 9, as that act applies to judgment liens on real estate, and is intended to adjust and protect the equities of persons holding such liens, and is not designed to prescribe remedies between principal and surety); *In re* Hess, 69 Pa. St. 272; Schnitzel's Appeal, 49 Pa. St. 23 (holding that if, after a judgment entered jointly against two, one of whom is named on the record as surety, a third person intervenes solely at the request of the principal, and becomes bail for stay of execution, taking indemnity from him therefor, and at the expiration of the stay the surety is compelled to pay the judgment, he is entitled to subrogation, as against the bail, to obtain reimbursement); Cottrell's Appeal, 23 Pa. St. 294; Yard *v.* Patton, 13 St. 278; Gearhart *v.* Jordan, 11 Pa. St. 325; Lloyd *v.* Barr, 11 Pa. St. 41; Moore *v.* Bray, 10 Pa. St. 519; Morris *v.* Oakford, 9 Pa. St. 498; Lathrop's Appeal, 1 Pa. St. 512; Foster *v.* Fox, 4 Watts & S. 92; Pott *v.* Nathans, 1 Watts & S. 155, 37 Am. Dec. 456; Burson *v.* Kincaid, 3 Penr. & W. 57; Burns *v.* Huntington Bank, 1 Penr. & W. 395; Buchanan's Estate, 2 Chest. Co. Rep. 74.

South Carolina.— McIntosh *v.* Wright, Rich. Eq. Cas. 385; Lenoir *v.* Winn, 4 Desauss. Eq. 65, 6 Am. Dec. 597.

Tennessee.— Floyd *v.* Goodwin, 8 Yerg. 484, 29 Am. Dec. 130.

Texas.— Sublett *v.* McKinney, 19 Tex. 438.

Vermont.— Bellows *v.* Allen, 23 Vt. 169.

Virginia.— Flood *v.* Hutter, (1898) 32 S. E. 64; Eidson *v.* Huff, 29 Gratt. 338.

West Virginia.— Hawker *v.* Moore, 40 W. Va. 49, 20 S. E. 848.

England.— Parsons *v.* Briddock, 2 Vern. Ch. 608, 23 Eng. Reprint 997.

See 44 Cent. Dig. tit. "Subrogation," § 83.

A surety on an appeal-bond, who pays the judgment, becomes subrogated to all the rights of the creditor. Rodes *v.* Crockett, 2

it against his principal's estate,[41] particularly where the surety pays the amount thereof, with the understanding that the judgment shall remain in force and be assigned to him, and procures the assignment thereof,[42] and in the assignment of a judgment the legal and express subrogation are of equal extent, and all the creditor's rights pass to a surety making payment.[43] This right of the surety is not defeated by the fact that he paid the judgment in ignorance of such right and without stipulating therefor,[44] for an actual assignment to the paying surety is not necessary to enable him to collect the judgment against his principal, the surety succeeding to the rights of the creditor by mere operation of law;[45] and although a surety who has paid part of a judgment against the principal, which has been in fact satisfied by the principal himself, is barred by limitation from recovering the amount paid, he may still have his right of subrogation to the security of the judgment;[46] and a surety who has paid a judgment against the principal has preference over a subsequent judgment creditor of the principal.[47] But while it is true that a surety may be subrogated to the rights of the creditor, in reference to any collateral security which the creditor may hold, and that he may be subrogated to the creditor in the judgment for the purpose of keeping it alive and enforcing it for his own benefit against his co-defendants, yet this doctrine, being one of mere equity and benevolence, will not be enforced at the expense of a legal right;[48] and a surety whose claims against his principal for money paid on a judgment against them has been defeated at law cannot be substituted for plaintiff in the original judgment;[49] and where a surety, on paying a judgment against his principal, has noted on the record that it was paid by him and "fully satisfied," he cannot assert the judgment lien, as against a *bona fide* purchaser of the debtor's land;[50] and a surety who pays the debt must, as a condition of compelling an assignment by the creditor of a judgment obtained by him against the principal, pay the costs incurred by the creditor in obtaining the judgment.[51] Furthermore, a surety having the means of payment put into his hands by the debtor thereby becomes the principal debtor, and, having reconveyed the property to the debtor, it is not competent for him, in order to avoid the effect of this, to allege that the conveyance to him was fraudulent, and to seek to be subrogated to the rights of the judgment.[52] A surety's rights are limited to a judgment on the debt for which he was surety,[53] and a surety bound only for part of the principal's indebtedness cannot be subrogated to security taken by the creditor for another part of the same debt and at another time.[54] In some states this equitable right of the surety to be subrogated to a judgment is incorporated into statutes which declare the paying surety's rights to the benefit

lien has expired by limitation of time before he has instituted a proceeding to keep it in force.

Expired lien.— The lien which a creditor acquires by a levy of his execution on personal property is, if not enforced by sale thereof, only temporary, and expires with the authority to sell under the execution, and therefore a surety of the debtor, who afterward pays the debt, has no right to be subrogated to the lien of the execution on the property. Carr *v.* Glasscock, 3 Gratt. (Va.) 343.

A subsequent transaction of the debtor with a third person cannot impair the equitable right of a surety to substitution to the lien of a creditor's judgment. Johnson *v.* Young, 20 W. Va. 614.

41. Kinard *v.* Baird, 20 S. C. 377.

42. Neal *v.* Nash, 23 Ohio St. 483; Utah Nat. Bank *v.* Forbes, 18 Utah 225, 55 Pac. 61.

43. Sprigg *v.* Beaman, 6 La. 59.

44. Dempsey *v.* Bush, 18 Ohio St. 376.

45. Duffield *v.* Cooper, 87 Pa. St. 443.

46. Kinard *v.* Baird, 20 S. C. 377.

47. Fleming *v.* Beaver, 2 Rawle (Pa.) 128, 19 Am. Dec. 629.

48. Junker *v.* Rush, 136 Ill. 179, 26 N. E. 499, 11 L. R. A. 183; Schmitt *v.* Henneberry, 48 Ill. App. 322; Rittenhouse *v.* Levering, 6 Watts & S. (Pa.) 190; Fink *v.* Mahaffy, 8 Watts (Pa.) 384.

49. Fink *v.* Mahaffy, 8 Watts (Pa.) 384 [*approved* in Rittenhouse *v.* Levering, 6 Watts & S. (Pa.) 190].

50. Taylor *v.* Alliance Trust Co., 71 Miss. 694, 15 So. 121.

51. McKenna *v.* Corcoran, 70 N. J. Eq. 627, 61 Atl. 1026.

52. Monroe *v.* Wallace, 2 Penr. & W. (Pa.) 173.

53. Wagner *v.* Elliott, 95 Pa. St. 487.

54. Crump *v.* McMurtry, 8 Mo. 408 (holding that the doctrine of substitution is not applicable to a case where a creditor having a security for his debt, but fearing that it will prove insufficient, obtains additional se-

sequent to the creation of the obligation,[60] in the absence of proof of a contrary intent;[61] and a surety upon a mortgage debt need not pay off a subsequent mort-

geon, 65 Ill. 11; Jacques v. Fackney, 64 Ill. 87.

Indiana.— Whiteman v. Harriman, 85 Ind. 49; Jones v. Tincher, 15 Ind. 308, 77 Am. Dec. 92.

Iowa.— Murray v. Catlett, 4 Greene 108.

Kentucky.— Storms v. Storms, 3 Bush 77; Morris v. McRoberts, 4 Ky. L. Rep. 825.

Mississippi.— Dickson v. Sledge, (1905) 38 So. 673.

Missouri.— Hackett v. Watts, 138 Mo. 502, 40 S. W. 113; Grady v. O'Reilly, 116 Mo. 346, 22 S. W. 798; Taylor v. Tarr, 84 Mo. 420; Brown v. Kirk, 20 Mo. App. 524.

New Jersey.— Tiffany v. Crawford, 14 N. J. Eq. 278.

New York.— Lewis v. Palmer, 28 N. Y. 271; McLean v. Towle, 3 Sandf. Ch. 117, a famous case.

North Dakota.— Thurston v. Osborne-McMilan El. Co., 13 N. D. 508, 101 N. W. 892, holding that payment by a surety on a note secured by a chattel mortgage given by the principal vests the ownership of the note and mortgage in him, so that he could recover the value of the mortgaged property to the extent of his lien from one who had converted it.

Pennsylvania.—Gossin v. Brown, 11 Pa. St. 527.

South Carolina.— Muller v. Wadlington, 5 Rich. 342; State Bank v. Rose, 1 Strobh. Eq. 257; Lowndes v. Chisholm, 2 McCord Eq. 455, 16 Am. Dec. 667.

Tennessee.— Motley v. Harris, 1 Lea 577; Scanland v. Settle, Meigs 169.

Texas.— James v. Jacques, 26 Tex. 320, 82 Am. Dec. 613, holding, however, that while a surety upon a note secured by deed of trust, who pays off the note of the creditor, becomes substituted to all the creditor's rights under the deed of trust, and is entitled to enforce the lien on the property for his reimbursement, he cannot do so in such manner as to affect the owner of the equity of redemption.

Vermont.—McDaniels v. Flower Brook Mfg. Co., 22 Vt. 274.

Virginia.— Miller v. Pendleton, 4 Hen. & M. 436.

England.— *In re* Kirkwood, L. R. 1 Ir. 108; Parteriche v. Powlet, 2 Atk. 384, 26 Eng. Reprint 632; Drew v. Lockett, 32 Beav. 499, 9 Jur. N. S. 786, 8 L. T. Rep. N. S. 782, 11 Wkly. Rep. 843, 55 Eng. Reprint 196; Goddard v. White, 2 Giffard 449, 6 Jur. N. S. 1364, 3 L. T. Rep. N. S. 313, 66 Eng. Reprint 188; Copis v. Middleton, 2 L. J. Ch. O. S. 82, Turn. & R. 224, 12 Eng. Ch. 224, 37 Eng. Reprint 1083. See also Forbes v. Jackson, 19 Ch. D. 615, 51 L. J. Ch. 690, 30 Wkly. Rep. 652.

Canada.— Garrett v. Johnstone, 13 Grant Ch. (U. C.) 36.

See 44 Cent. Dig. tit. "Subrogation," § 77.

But bail for stay of execution is not entitled to subrogation to the rights of the mortgagee against the terretenant or creditors, because but for his intervention the debt might be paid by the debtor or out of his property. McCurdy v. Conner, 1 Walk. (Pa.) 155.

Guarantors of a mortgage, compelled to pay a deficiency thereon, are entitled to be subrogated to all the securities which are held by the mortgagee as collateral, and so are entitled to a subsequent mortgage obtained by the mortgagee as additional security. Havens v. Willis, 100 N. Y. 482, 3 N. E. 313.

A surety who gave a separate mortgage on conveying a part of his lands in satisfaction of the debt is entitled to be subrogated to the mortgagee's claim on the mortgage of the principal debtor. Loomer v. Wheelwright, 3 Sandf. Ch. (N. Y.) 135.

Rule applied to statutory mortgage.— Under a statute which gives an administrator or executor a mortgage on lands purchased at a sale of the property of decedent, a surety upon a note given to an administrator will be subrogated to the rights of the administrator in his statutory mortgage, to satisfy the amount he has paid as surety. Stanwood v. Clampitt, 23 Miss. 372.

Sureties on an appeal-bond in mortgage foreclosure proceedings, who, after having been compelled to pay the decree against their principal, take an assignment of the mortgage debt and decree of foreclosure, may maintain a bill to set aside a modification of the decree entered on a supplemental bill to which they are not made parties. Allen v. Powell, 108 Ill. 584.

The reason is held to be that the debt, and not the pledgee, is protected by the pledge, and any person liable for the payment of the debt, into whose hands it came, until payment by the original debtor, was entitled to the security, and however it may be modified or into whose hands it may come until the debt is paid the fund or pledge accompanies it and remains for its redemption. Belcher v. Hartford Bank, 15 Conn. 381.

On payment by a surety in an injunction bond of a debt whose collection was enjoined, secured by a deed of trust, he will be substituted in equity to the lien under the trust deed. Billings v. Sprague, 49 Ill. 509.

Where a wife, as surety for her husband, joined him in a mortgage which stated that "the debt is a joint and several one," in an action praying leave to pay the debt and be subrogated to the rights of the mortgagee, she may show that she was simply surety, although she could not do so to defeat the mortgage. Snook v. Munday, 96 Md. 514, 54 Atl. 77.

60. Scott v. Featherston, 5 La. Ann. 306.

61. McArthur v. Martin, 23 Minn. 74, holding that where a surety redeems from a mortgage of his principal, in the absence of proof to the contrary it will be presumed that the act was done with the intent that would be most for the interest of the surety; that

interest;[28] nor can he base a claim for subrogation upon a payment intended as a gift and made without intent for subrogation;[29] and a surety cannot be substituted for the creditor in relation to another security for another part of the debt where the effect would be to deprive the creditor of one of his resources, and thereby cause a partial loss of the debt.[30] It has been held that a surety who has been fully compensated according to his contract for assuming the debt of another is not entitled to subrogation to the rights of the creditor.[31]

6. **Waiver of Loss of Right.** The surety may permit security taken for the debt to be returned to the debtor, thus extinguishing his rights in them;[32] and generally it is a question of intention, with the presumption that the surety intends to keep the debt alive and claim the right of subrogation, but if it clearly appears that the intention was to satisfy and extinguish the debt or demand not only as to the creditor but as between the surety and the principal debtor, the right of subrogation is waived.[33] The taking of additional security by the surety does not of itself affect his right to subrogation to securities of the creditor;[34] and a surety does not lose his right to be subrogated to a lien upon the principal's real estate from the fact that he received a mortgage from the principal to secure him, and afterward released a part of it, without notice of any interest or equity of defendants, who were purchasers from the principal,[35] unless superior equities in third persons have intervened.[36] But accepting an independent security, which is not cumulative merely, and the enforcement of which is not consistent, and cannot be concurrent with the enforcement of the right of subrogation, displaces and defeats the latter right;[37] and a surety who has paid the judgment against himself and his principal, and who has been defeated in an action to recover of the principal the amount paid, cannot be substituted to the rights of plaintiff in the original action.[38]

7. **Sureties For Particular Classes of Persons — a. Sheriffs and Other Officers.** Sureties of a sheriff who have been compelled to pay a judgment, because of the sheriff's failure to return an execution, are subrogated to the right of the sheriff to recover the amount from plaintiff and his attorneys, who subse-

well, 12 Gill & J. (Md.) 36), is entitled to subrogation only to the extent of the actual value of the depreciated medium at the time of payment.

Right to statutory penalty against sheriff. — A defendant in an execution, surety for the other defendants therein, who pays the amount thereof to plaintiff after the sheriff has failed to return it for thirty days after the return-day, has no right to the thirty per cent damages which the law imposes, for the benefit of such plaintiff, on the sheriff for such failure. Sanders *v.* Commonwealth Bank, 2 Metc. (Ky.) 327.

Where the sureties have allowed a set-off to part of the creditors' demand, their right of subrogation is not limited to the amount of the judgment against them for the balance, but extends to the whole amount of the creditor's claim. Keokuk *v.* Love, 31 Iowa 119.

28. Miles *v.* Bacon, 4 J. J. Marsh. (Ky.) 457; Eaton *v.* Lambert, 1 Nebr. 339. And see Comer *v.* Mackey, 73 Hun (N. Y.) 236, 25 N. Y. Suppl. 1023 [*affirmed* in 147 N. Y. 574, 42 N. E. 29].

29. Scott *v.* Scott, 83 Vt. 251, 2 S. E. 431.

Injunction to limit surety's recovery.— Where a surety has paid a judgment against his principal and takes an assignment of it, an injunction against his enforcing the judgment, except as to the portion of the debt due from his cosureties, will be granted. McDaniels *v.* Lee, 37 Mo. 204.

30. Crump *v.* McMurtry, 8 Mo. 408. See Vance *v.* Monroe, 4 Gratt. (Va.) 52.

31. Culbertson *v.* Salinger, 131 Iowa 307, 108 N. W. 454.

32. Tyus *v.* De Jarnette, 26 Ala. 280; Cooper *v.* Jenkins, 32 Beav. 337, 1 New Rep. 383, 55 Eng. Reprint 132.

33. Watts *v.* Eufaula Nat. Bank, 76 Ala. 474; Houston *v.* Huntsville Branch Bank, 25 Ala. 250. See Croft *v.* Moore, 9 Watts (Pa.) 451.

34. Ballew *v.* Roler, 124 Ind. 557, 24 N. E. 976, 9 L. R. A. 481.

35. Crawford *v.* Richeson, 101 Ill. 351.

Where three of several sureties settled with the creditor by giving a new bond, in which their principal did not appear, and one of them paid it, he was entitled in equity to recover from his principal; the second bond extinguishing liability on the first only as to the creditor, and the surety being subrogated to the rights of the creditor under the first bond. Dodd *v.* Wilson, 4 Del. Ch. 108, 399.

36. Henley *v.* Stemmons, 4 B. Mon. (Ky.) 131.

37. Watts *v.* Eufaula Nat. Bank, 76 Ala. 474; Cornwell's Appeal, 7 Watts & S. (Pa.) 305; Cooper *v.* Jenkins, 32 Beav. 337, 1 New Rep. 383, 55 Eng. Reprint 132.

38. Fink *v.* Mahaffy, 8 Watts (Pa.) 384.

proceedings against the principal has no right of subrogation against the original surety for the debt; but the latter is entitled to be subrogated to the creditor's right against him;[65] and where the interposition of the second surety has been the means of involving the first in ultimate liability to pay, the equity of the first surety preponderates and gives him precedent right to the assignment of collaterals.[66] Indemnity given to a surety is extinguished by the release of the surety and does not pass to a subsequent surety.[67]

g. Sureties on Judicial Bonds. The bail on a replevin bond is upon payment of the bond entitled to subrogation to the rights of the creditor.[68] Similarly the surety of a joint debtor in a forthcoming bond becomes, on forfeiture thereof, surety for the debt, and, when he has discharged it he is entitled to be substituted to all the rights of the creditor against the original debtor subsisting at the time he became bound for the debt;[69] and where, on a judgment against the subsequent indorser, the liability of the prior indorser is fixed, security of the subsequent indorser in a forthcoming bond is entitled to be substituted to the rights of the principal to the extent of that liability;[70] but as the equitable lien of a creditor on securities given by the principal to the surety to indemnify the latter is derived through the sureties and is thus discharged by any act which discharges the sureties from liability, subsequent sureties on a replevin bond, deriving their right of subrogation through the creditor, lose the right of subrogation to the securities by any act which discharges the original sureties.[71] Where a judgment is affirmed on appeal the sureties on an error or appeal-bond, being liable, may at any time pay the judgment,[72] and upon doing so they become subrogated to all the rights of the judgment creditor at the time of payment,[73] and their equity is superior to

65. Hammock *v.* Baker, 3 Bush (Ky.) 208; Daniel *v.* Joyner, 38 N. C. 513; Dent *v.* Wait, 9 W. Va. 41, holding that if the principal debtor brings in a second surety in such a way as to discharge the first one, and the second surety afterward pays the debt, he cannot come upon the surety who has been discharged, upon the ground of subrogation, although he may upon the principal.

The reason is that the new surety, by joining the principal in a bond by which he obtains time in the collection of the debt, changed the terms upon which the original surety was bound and prejudiced his rights. Moore *v.* Lassiter, 16 Lea (Tenn.) 630.

A supplemental surety is entitled to be subrogated to any rights which the creditor has against the surety. Bender *v.* George, 92 Pa. St. 36. Thus sureties on a bond can recover from bail given on arrest of the principal (Parsons *v.* Briddock, 2 Vern. Ch. 608, 23 Eng. Reprint 997); but a surety is not subrogated to rights against a supplemental surety (March *v.* Barnet, 121 Cal. 419, 53 Pac. 933, 66 Am. St. Rep. 44, holding that sureties on a bond for the release of attachment against the property of the principal given after a judgment against the principal and an indorser of a note are not entitled to subrogation against such indorser).

66. Pott *v.* Nathans, 1 Watts & S. (Pa.) 155, 37 Am. Dec. 456; Burns *v.* Huntington Bank, 1 Penr. & W. (Pa.) 395; Mitchell *v.* De Witt, 25 Tex. Suppl. 180, 78 Am. Dec. 561; Parsons *v.* Briddock, 2 Vern. Ch. 608, 23 Eng. Reprint 997.

67. Hunter *v.* Richardson, 1 Duv. (Ky.) 247.

68. Kane *v.* State, 78 Ind. 103, holding that where the bail on a replevin bond has been compelled to pay fines assessed against a liquor seller for violation of the bond, he is entitled to be subrogated to the rights of the state on such bond against the principal.

Thus a person who becomes replevin bail upon a judgment rendered upon a note secured by a mortgage, and who is compelled to pay the same, is entitled to be subrogated to the mortgagee or any holder of the mortgage. Pence *v.* Armstrong, 95 Ind. 191.

Where a surety on a delivery bond for property levied on was required to pay the amount of the judgment, he is subrogated to all the rights of the original creditor as against the property or its proceeds. Hubbard *v.* Security Trust Co., 38 Ind. App. 156, 78 N. E. 79.

69. Leake *v.* Ferguson, 2 Gratt. (Va.) 419; Robinson *v.* Sherman, 2 Gratt. (Va.) 178, 44 Am. Dec. 381.

70. Conaway *v.* Odbert, 2 W. Va. 25.

71. Havens *v.* Foudry, 4 Metc. (Ky.) 247.

72. Black *v.* Epperson, 40 Tex. 162.

73. Foster *v.* Whitaker, 12 Ga. 57 (holding that when plaintiff recovers specifically in trover certain property and the value of its use during conversion from an insolvent defendant whose surety on appeal is obliged to pay the value of the use, such surety, being subrogated to the rights of plaintiff, can collect the value of the use from the person who by contract with defendant had such use during the conversion); State Bank *v.* Kahn, 49 Misc. (N. Y.) 500, 98 N. Y. Suppl. 858; Smith *v.* National Surety Co., 28 Misc. (N. Y.) 628, 59 N. Y. Suppl. 789 [*affirmed* in 46 N. Y. App. Div. 633, 62 N. Y. Suppl. 1105] (hold-

in his possession to his reimbursement,[8] and he is entitled to have the decedent's land sold, and to be repaid out of the proceeds of the sale if no fraud is shown [9] and his equity is superior to that of legatees,[10] devisees,[11] or heirs.[12] A personal representative who pays a debt, or makes an advance to creditors, legatees, or distributees, will, to the extent of the assets for which he is liable, be subrogated to all the rights of such creditors, legatees, or distributees, including priority and dignity of claim; [13] and the right of the executor will extend to one for whom

If an administrator pendente lite has paid debts of the estate and costs of litigation exceeding the amount of the personal estate, he is entitled to be subrogated to the rights of the creditors against the lands of the estate, and may subject the lands in the hands of the heirs, and the lands in the hands of the devisee, if necessary, to his reimbursement. Woolley *v.* Pemberton, 41 N. J. Eq. 394, 5 Atl. 139.

Where an administrator advances money to complete the purchase of, or pay a lien on, the trust estate, he is entitled to stand in the place of the creditor, whose claim he has paid. Robb's Appeal, 41 Pa. St. 45.

Subrogation to right of distributee against third person.— Where a husband has received property from his wife's father as advancements on her share of the property, and after the father's death the administrator, in a suit by the wife, is compelled to pay her her full share of the estate, such administrator is subrogated to her rights against her husband. Stayner *v.* Bower, 42 Ohio St. 314.

An administrator who pays a debt guaranteed by his intestate becomes subrogated to the rights of the creditor in the collateral security. Lee *v.* Butler, 167 Mass. 426, 46 N. E. 52, 57 Am. St. Rep. 466.

Where an administrator charges himself in his account with the debt of a debtor to the estate, he is subrogated to the rights of the estate against the debtor. Parker *v.* Smith, (Tex. 1889) 11 S. W. 909.

8. Milam *v.* Ragland, 19 Ala. 85; Livingston *v.* Newkirk, 3 Johns. Ch. (N. Y.) 312.

9. Crowley *v.* Mellon, 52 Ark. 1, 11 S. W. 876; Denton *v.* Tyson, 118 N. C. 542, 24 S. E. 116; Pea *v.* Waggoner, 5 Hayw. (Tenn.) 242; Gaw *v.* Huffman, 12 Gratt. (Va.) 628; Kinney *v.* Harvey, 2 Leigh (Va.) 70, 21 Am. Dec. 597.

Subrogation to mortgage discharged.— If the executrix, the widow of the deceased, pays a mortgage out of her individual funds, she is entitled to be subrogated to the mortgage lien (Jefferson *v.* Edrington, 53 Ark. 545, 14 S. W. 99, 903, holding, however, that where a widow, who was also executrix of her husband's estate, paid off one mortgage on his lands out of her individual means, and another out of the funds of the estate, but on her final accounting as executrix she was credited with having paid both out of her individual means, she must release all claims against the estate based on the showing in her final account as to the payment of the two mortgages out of her individual means; Pinneo *v.* Goodspeed, 22 Ill. App. 59 [*affirmed* in 120 Ill. 524, 12 N. E. 196]); without proof of specific intent at the time of payment to keep the mortgage alive (Jefferson *v.* Edrington, *supra*). Similarly, an administrator who sells land subject to a mortgage, and afterward pays off the mortgage out of the general assets of the estate, will have a clear equity against the purchaser, and be entitled to reimbursement out of the land (Greenwell *v.* Heritage, 71 Mo. 459 [*following* Welton *v.* Hull, 50 Mo. 296]); and administrators, having redeemed the decedent's lands from mortgage, are subrogated to the right of the mortgagees to collect so much of the mortgage debt as is equal to the widow's share of the amount paid to redeem, by causing the interest assigned to her as dower to be sold for the purpose of foreclosing the mortgage to that extent, without an assignment or act of transfer of the mortgages, since they hold such right for the benefit of the creditors, as quasi-assignees for the purpose of contribution (Salinger *v.* Black, 68 Ark. 449, 60 S. W. 229).

Where an administrator purchases for his own benefit a portion of the trust property, and pays off a mortgage thereon, the court, upon setting aside the sale, will allow the administrator to stand in the place of the mortgagee as to the amount so paid. Woodruff *v.* Cook, 2 Edw. (N. Y.) 259.

Where land is charged with the payment of debts by will, and the executrix advances the money and pays the debts, she should be substituted to the rights of the creditors whose demands she had paid, and authorized to sell for her own benefit. Ducker *v.* Stubblefield, 9 B. Mon. (Ky.) 577.

10. Pendergass *v.* Pendergass, 26 S. C. 19, 1 S. E. 45.

11. Gaw *v.* Huffman, 12 Gratt. (Va.) 628, holding that if, after exhausting testator's personal estate, there still remains a balance due the executor on account of debts paid by him, which would be binding on the heirs, the executor is entitled to stand in the place of the creditors, and charge the balance to testator's real estate, which is liable in the hands of the devisees in proportion to the value at the time of his death of the estate devised to each devisee.

12. Collinson *v.* Owens, 6 Gill & J. (Md.) 4. See McCullough *v.* Wise, 57 Ala. 623.

13. Bennett *v.* Chandler, 199 Ill. 97, 64 N. E. 1052 [*modifying* 101 Ill. App. 409].

An executor, who has made advances to legatees from his own funds, is entitled to be subrogated to their rights, but can be credited only with a *pro rata* share of the assets available for distribution at the time of the accounting. Tickel *v.* Quinn, 1 Dem. Surr. (N. Y.) 425.

son in good faith assumes and pays an encumbrance on land, to which he has no title, but believes in good faith that he is the owner, he becomes the equitable owner of the encumbrance, and the same constitutes a lien on the land;[30] and one who at the time of paying the mortgage debt erroneously believes himself the owner of the property, while in fact the record shows him entitled to but a life-estate, is nevertheless entitled to subrogation against the remainder-man to the extent to which such remainder-man was bound to pay the mortgage to protect his estate;[31] but a person is not entitled to subrogation for purposes of contribution on payment of a mortgage secured in part on his own land, and in part on that of another, unless he has paid the entire mortgage debt,[32] and the owner of mortgaged property is not entitled to be subrogated to the rights of a mortgagee because of other liens against the property subsequent to the mortgage.[33] One who, not being a mere volunteer, pays the purchase-price of land instead of the purchaser is subrogated to the vendor's lien;[34] but only as to the lien on the land purchased, not that covering other land;[35] and a purchaser under a judgment against the

weiler *v.* Hart, 10 N. Y. App. Div. 156, 41 N. Y. Suppl. 862 [*affirmed* in 159 N. Y. 543, 54 N. E. 1093]. But see Blydenburgh *v.* Seabury, 104 N. Y. App. Div. 141, 93 N. Y. Suppl. 330, holding that the mere possibility that a person making a payment on a real estate mortgage might become the owner of the premises, as an heir of the holder of the title, did not give her such an interest in the mortgaged property as to entitle her to subrogation to the rights of the holder of the mortgage as to such payment.

Where a person having a future interest in property on which there is a judgment lien, for the purpose of protecting such interest, pays the judgment debt, he becomes an equitable assignee of the judgment, and may keep alive and enforce the lien, so far as necessary, for his own benefit. Sutton *v.* Sutton, 26 S. C. 33, 1 S. E. 19.

30. Simpson *v.* Ennis, 114 Ga. 202, 39 S. E. 853; Bayard *v.* McGraw, 1 Ill. App. 134 [*affirmed* in 96 Ill. 146]; Taylor *v.* Roniger, 147 Mich. 99, 110 N. W. 503; Gooch *v.* Botts, 110 Mo. 419, 20 S. W. 192. See Roberts *v.* Best, 172 Mo. 67, 72 S. W. 657; Murphy *v.* Smith, (Tex. Civ. App. 1899) 50 S. W. 1040.

But the origin or source of the payer's title must be shown in order that it may appear that he justifiably believed he had title. Wadsworth *v.* Blake, 43 Minn. 509, 45 N. W. 1131, holding that upon these facts alone appearing, where one claiming title to land voluntarily discharges a mortgage thereon given by his grantor, and a third party is subsequently adjudged to be the owner in fee, the former is not entitled to have the amount so paid adjudged a charge upon the land.

31. Wilder *v.* Wilder, 75 Vt. 178, 53 Atl. 1072.

32. Springer *v.* Foster, 27 Ind. App. 15, 60 N. E. 720.

33. Pulitzer *v.* National L. Assoc., 24 Misc. (N. Y.) 18, 53 N. Y. Suppl. 94.

34. *Iowa.*— Dillow *v.* Warfel, 71 Iowa 106, 32 N. W. 104.

Kentucky.—Woodland Cemetery Co. *v.* Ellison, 80 S. W. 169, 25 Ky. L. Rep. 2069.

Missouri.— Lewis *v.* Chapman, 59 Mo. 371.

Texas.— Ford *v.* Ford, 22 Tex. Civ. App. 453, 54 S. W. 773.

Virginia.— Fulkerson *v.* Taylor, 100 Va. 426, 41 S. E. 863.

See 44 Cent. Dig. tit. "Subrogation," § 88.

One who has paid off an encumbrance upon land, which the grantee assumed and agreed to pay as part of the purchase-money, is entitled to the benefit of a vendor's lien against the land to the amount so paid. Williams *v.* Crow, 84 Mo. 298.

A purchaser under a decree, obtained without appearance of defendant, on an attachment upon land as the property of defendant, in which he has only an equity, without designating it to be such, who has paid off the vendor's lien, will be subrogated to the vendor's rights. Lane *v.* Marshall, 1 Heisk. (Tenn.) 30.

Where purchase-money notes and the land are transferred by the vendor to a third person, and a lien retained for payment, the transfer subrogates such person to all the rights of the vendor against the original vendee. Polk *v.* Kyser, 21 Tex. Civ. App. 676, 53 S. W. 87 [*citing* Hamblen *v.* Folts, 70 Tex. 132, 7 S. W. 834].

Where an owner of land finds it bound by a lien for the purchase-money due by his grantor, and, to protect himself, pays off the lien, he is entitled to be subrogated to the rights of the holder of the lien. Fulkerson *v.* Taylor, 100 Va. 426, 41 S. E. 863.

Where two purchasers of land give their joint note for part of the price, the vendor retaining his lien, and one of them pays the note, he does not discharge the lien, but becomes subrogated thereto, and can enforce it against a third person, who has purchased, subject to the vendor's lien, the interest of the co-purchaser after a partition. Dowdy *v.* Blake, 50 Ark. 205, 6 S. W. 897, 7 Am. St. Rep. 88. But where no lien was retained for property sold to persons who gave their joint note for the price, one of the makers, by paying the note, cannot obtain any relief against the property on the ground of subrogation, since he merely stands in the vendor's shoes. Harris *v.* Elliott, 45 W. Va. 245, 32 S. E. 176.

35. Larson *v.* Oisefos, 118 Wis. 368, 95 N. W. 399.

rate specified in such mortgages, in a suit for the foreclosure thereof;[80] but, although the owner of a first mortgage, or his assignee, will be protected to the extent of such mortgage, in case he becomes the owner of the equity of redemption, as against any subsequent encumbrance existing at the time he becomes such owner, and may foreclose such subsequent encumbrance, or require the holder thereof to redeem, this right will not be extended so as to permit such first mortgagee, after he has purchased the equity of redemption, or his grantee, to give a mortgage which shall take precedence, by way of subrogation, of the encumbrance existing at the time he became the owner of the equity of redemption;[81] and one who has contracted to purchase land and has redeemed the same from an existing lien is not deemed the legal owner of the land for the purpose of subrogation where such contract has not been fully carried out;[82] and where an equity of redemption in mortgaged property is sold under execution for a debt other than the debt secured by the mortgage, the sale vests the estate sold in the purchaser subject to the payment of the mortgage debt.[83] But the purchaser cannot hold the entire interest in the land, having paid only the value of the equity of redemption, and if the mortgage debt is satisfied from other property the original holder of the equity of redemption will be subrogated to the rights of the mortgagee to enable him to indemnify himself out of the mortgaged premises;[84] and if the purchaser of the equity of redemption by words in the conveyance assumes the mortgage, upon a foreclosure bringing an amount less than the debt, the mortgagee is entitled to be subrogated to the rights of the mortgagor, and the purchaser will be compelled to pay the balance.[85] It seems that where the purchaser of land at an execution sale accepts money tendered for redemption by a person not entitled to redeem, the person paying the money will be subrogated to the purchaser's right to the deed.[86]

4. Purchasers at Execution, Foreclosure, Judicial, and Other Sales — a. In General. A purchaser at an execution or judicial sale is subrogated to the rights of the creditor;[87] and upon paying off encumbrances is entitled to be subrogated to

109; Walker *v.* King, 45 Vt. 525; McNeil *v.* Miller, 29 W. Va. 480, 2 S. E. 335. But see Schreyer *v.* Saunders, 39 N. Y. App. Div. 8, 56 N. Y. Suppl. 921, 38 N. Y. App. Div. 627, 56 N. Y. Suppl. 1116.

Estoppel to assert prior mortgage against purchaser of equity of redemption see Bunting *v.* Gilmore, 124 Ind. 113, 24 N. E. 583.

Where a widow sues for dower in land sold by the administrator of her husband, out of the proceeds of which sale a judgment on a mortgage by husband and wife was satisfied, the purchaser cannot be subrogated to the rights of the mortgagee. Sweaney *v.* Mallory, 62 Mo. 485; Jones *v.* Bragg, 33 Mo. 337, 84 Am. Dec. 49 [*distinguishing* Valle *v.* Fleming, 29 Mo. 152, 77 Am. Dec. 557]. And see Cox *v.* Garst, 105 Ill. 342. But on the other hand it has been held that where the proceeds of decedent's lands, sold by order of court, were applied to the payment of a mortgage made by him and his widow, the purchaser was subrogated to the rights of the mortgagee as against the widow's claim to dower. House *v.* Fowle, 22 Oreg. 303, 29 Pac. 890.

80. Braden *v.* Graves, 85 Ind. 92.

81. Dugan *v.* Lyman, (N. J. Ch. 1892) 23 Atl. 657.

The payment of a purchase-money mortgage by a firm on lands standing in the individual names of the partners does not subrogate it to the vendor's lien. Ratcliff *v.* Mason, (Ky. 1890) 14 S. W. 960.

82. Landis *v.* Wolf, 119 Ill. App. 11, holding that where one who has contracted to purchase land redeems the same from an existing lien, he is not, for the purpose of subrogation, to be deemed the legal owner thereof merely because there has been offered to him a deed of such land which he did not, and was not bound to, accept.

83. Funk *v.* McReynolds, 33 Ill. 481.

84. Funk *v.* McReynolds, 33 Ill. 481.

85. Davis *v.* Hulett, 58 Vt. 90, 4 Atl. 139. But see Weeks *v.* Garvey, 56 N. Y. Super. Ct. 557, 4 N. Y. Suppl. 890.

86. *In re* Eleventh Ave., 81 N. Y. 436.

87. *Indiana.*— Hines *v.* Dresher, 93 Ind. 551; Whitehead *v.* Cummins, 2 Ind. 58.

Kentucky.— Case *v.* Woolley, 6 Dana 17, 32 Am. Dec. 54.

Missouri.— See Duke *v.* Brandt, 51 Mo. 221.

North Carolina.— Conner *v.* Gwin, 2 N. C. 121.

Pennsylvania.— McGuire *v.* Warren, Wilcox 193.

Texas.— Willson *v.* Phillips, 27 Tex. 543.

See 44 Cent. Dig. tit. "Subrogation," § 41.

The purchaser at a road tax-sale is entitled to be subrogated to the rights of the county, and to have a lien upon the real estate for all taxes paid by him, with interest from the dates of such payments. Bois *v.* Merriam, 5 Fed. 439.

In Alabama it is held that a purchaser of

purchaser.[1] But the right extends only to a purchaser in good faith.[2] Furthermore if there was no subsisting lien to be discharged by the purchaser at the sale made under a decree of foreclosure there is no room for subrogation, as the purchaser could not occupy a better position than plaintiff in the void decree.[3]

(II) *EXECUTORS' OR ADMINISTRATORS' SALES.* On a void sale by an executor or administrator the purchaser in good faith, without notice, may be substituted to the rights of the creditors whose debts were paid by his money;[4] even though the administrator was guilty of a misdemeanor in attempting to sell,[5] and the same rule is held to apply to a purchaser at a sale by one assuming, without authority, to act as executor,[6] and although a foreign administrator who has not complied with the statute requiring such administrators to record their letters and give a bond has no authority to exercise a power of sale contained in

caveat emptor applicable in such case. Willson *v.* Brown, 82 Ind. 471.

One who buys in land at a judicial sale under partition proceedings by the purchaser's heirs, although the deed given him is without warranty, acquires all the rights of the heirs at the time of sale. Givens *v.* Carroll, 40 S. C. 413, 18 S. E. 1030, 42 Am. St. Rep. 889.

Effect of conveyance to third party.—Where the mortgagee or a stranger to the record purchases the mortgaged premises at a void sale under foreclosure proceedings, and then conveys by warranty deed said premises to a third party, the latter becomes subrogated in equity to the rights of the mortgagee in said mortgaged premises, as well as the mortgage debt thereon, to the extent of his purchase, and may demand a valid foreclosure of said mortgage for his protection. Jordan *v.* Sayre, 29 Fla. 100, 10 So. 823.

1. Jordan *v.* Sayre, 29 Fla. 100, 10 So. 823; Bruschke *v.* Wright, 166 Ill. 183, 46 N. E. 813, 57 Am. St. Rep. 125; Rogers *v.* Benton, 39 Minn. 39, 38 N. W. 765, 12 Am. St. Rep. 613; Finlayson *v.* Peterson, 11 N. D. 45, 89 N. W. 855, holding also that where the one subrogated takes possession by express consent of the mortgagor after default, he cannot be ejected until his debt and just claims for taxes are paid.

2. King *v.* Huni, 118 Ky. 450, 81 S. W. 254, 25 Ky. L. Rep. 2266, 85 S. W. 723, 27 Ky. L. Rep. 528. But see McLaughlin *v.* Daniel, 8 Dana (Ky.) 182, holding that the right of a purchaser of property sold under execution to be substituted to the place of the creditor, when the property is recovered from him or his vendee by virtue of superior title, is not affected by his knowing at the time of his purchase that the property so belonged to a stranger and was not subject to the execution.

A purchaser at a void guardian's sale who fraudulently prevented competition of bidding will not be subrogated to the rights of encumbrancers whose claims he has paid off in part payment of the purchase-price. Devine *v.* Harkness, 117 Ill. 145, 7 N. E. 52.

3. Meher *v.* Cole, 50 Ark. 361, 7 S. W. 451, 7 Am. St. Rep. 101.

4. *Arkansas.*— Harris *v.* Watson, 56 Ark. 574, 20 S. W. 529; Bond *v.* Montgomery, 56 Ark. 563, 20 S. W. 525, 35 Am. St. Rep. 119.

Illinois.— Kinney *v.* Knoebel, 51 Ill. 112.

Indiana.— Jones *v.* French, 92 Ind. 138, holding that a purchaser in good faith of land from an administrator, where the purchase-money paid by him is applied to the payment of the intestate's debts, will, if the sale be set aside, be entitled to a lien on the land for the amount of money paid, even though there may have been sufficient personal property to pay the debts, and although no additional bond was filed by the administrator, and although another tract of land was sold for a sufficient sum to pay the debts.

Mississippi.— Pool *v.* Ellis, 64 Miss. 555, 1 So. 725; Short *v.* Porter, 44 Miss. 533.

Missouri.— Valle *v.* Fleming, 29 Mo. 152, 77 Am. Dec. 557, holding that where land is purchased in good faith at an administrator's sale, which is void because the requirements of the statute are not pursued, and the purchase-money is applied in extinguishment of a mortgage to which such land was subject, the purchaser will be subrogated to the rights of the mortgagee to the extent of the purchase-money applied in the extinguishment of the mortgage, and the owner will not be entitled to recover possession until he repays such purchase-money.

Nebraska.— Veeder *v.* McKinley-Lanning L. & T. Co., 61 Nebr. 892, 86 N. W. 982.

New Jersey.— Merselis *v.* Vreeland, 8 N. J. Eq. 575.

North Carolina.— Lanier *v.* Heilig, 149 N. C. 384, 63 S. E. 69; Perry *v.* Adams, 98 N. C. 167, 3 S. E. 729, 2 Am. St. Rep. 326; Springs *v.* Harvan, 56 N. C. 96; Scott *v.* Dunn, 21 N. C. 425, 30 Am. Dec. 174.

South Carolina.— Hunter *v.* Hunter, 63 S. C. 78, 41 S. E. 33, 90 Am. St. Rep. 663.

Tennessee.— Caldwell *v.* Palmer, 6 Lea 652; Bennett *v.* Coldwell, 8 Baxt. 483.

Virginia.— Hudgin *v.* Hudgin, 6 Gratt. 320, 52 Am. Dec. 124.

Wisconsin.— Blodgett *v.* Hitt, 29 Wis. 169.

See 44 Cent. Dig. tit. "Subrogation," § 43.

But see Beall *v.* Price, 13 Ohio 368, 42 Am. Dec. 204, holding that where a purchaser at a void administrator's sale sells to another with warranty, the latter cannot, upon the death and insolvency of his vendor, be substituted for him in his claim against the estate of the decedent for advances made.

5. Bond *v.* Montgomery, 56 Ark. 563, 20 S. W. 525, 35 Am. St. Rep. 119.

6. Waggener *v.* Lyles, 29 Ark. 47.

the widow of the vendee.[19] *A fortiori* a third person who pays the purchase-money on behalf of the purchaser to the vendor, upon an express agreement between the three that he shall have a lien for it upon the land, will be held in equity to succeed to the vendor's lien,[20] although the agreement be in parol;[21] but not where the intention of the parties was to clear the title of the liens.[22] Similarly, if payment of the vendor's lien is made under such circumstances as would operate as a fraud if the vendee should be permitted to insist that the security for the debt was discharged by the payment, he will be subrogated to the lien.[23] But a person advancing money to a purchaser of land, which is used in completing his payment of the purchase-money, who at the time takes a deed of trust on the premises to secure himself, there being no privity or arrangement between him and the vendor that he shall succeed to the lien of the vendor, will not be entitled to be subrogated to the rights of the vendor, so as to hold the entire premises against a second purchaser from the first of a part of the land, who was in possession under his contract before the execution of the trust deed.[24]

4. Maritime Liens. A creditor to whom a ship has been hypothecated for advances made before it was built, without an agreement that upon the payment the lien should be continued in his favor, or an assignment of the debt, does not become subrogated to the privilege of materialmen by reason of having paid the orders drawn by the builder in favor of the materialmen;[25] and while a surety on a bond given to release a vessel from attachment in admiralty who has been compelled to pay the whole amount decreed against his principal is entitled to be subrogated to the rights of the libellants against the principal, he has no lien

vendor's lien notes, is entitled to be subrogated to the rights of the holders of the notes); Western Mortg., etc., Co. *v.* Ganzer, 63 Fed. 647, 11 C. C. A. 371. And where a person loans money on a homestead, such loan being invalid, but, before paying over the money, he has part of it applied to discharge a vendor's lien on the land, he is entitled to subrogation to all the rights of the vendor (Texas Land, etc., Co. *v.* Blalock, 76 Tex. 85, 13 S. W. 12); and he does not waive this lien by taking a mortgage upon the land to further secure himself, unless such was the intention of the parties (Harrod *v.* Johnson, 5 Ky. L. Rep. 247); and it has been held that where a vendor's lien note, secured on the maker's homestead, having been indorsed by the payee to a third party, plaintiff, at the instance of the maker and payee, paid the note when due, and in lieu thereof took another note for a like amount, secured on the same premises, plaintiff, although he had notice that the property was a homestead, would be subrogated to the rights of the indorsee, so that he could enforce the note against the homestead if such indorsee was a *bona fide* purchaser for value (Denecamp *v.* Townsend, (Tex. Civ. App. 1895) 33 S. W. 254). Similarly a person who discharged a vendor's lien against a homestead by paying the vendor's lien notes at the maker's request, which request contemplated that the person paying such notes should hold the lien, was entitled to be subrogated thereto (Mergele *v.* Felix, 45 Tex. Civ. App. 55, 99 S. W. 709); and where notes were secured by a deed of trust covering land, part of which was the homestead of the grantor in the deed, and which was encumbered by vendor's liens which the beneficiary in the trust deed paid off with a part of the money secured by the trust deed, the beneficiary was entitled to be subrogated to the rights of the holders of such liens, even though at the time subrogation was asked the notes secured by the trust deed were barred by limitations (Flynt *v.* Taylor, 100 Tex. 60, 93 S. W. 423).

19. Fisher *v.* Johnson, 5 Ind. 492.

20. Mitchell *v.* Butt, 45 Ga. 162; Gunn *v.* Orndorff, 67 S. W. 372, 68 S. W. 461, 23 Ky. L. Rep. 2369; Johnson *v.* Portwood, 89 Tex. 235, 34 S. W. 596, 787.

21. Allen *v.* Caylor, 120 Ala. 251, 24 So. 512, 74 Am. St. Rep. 31.

22. Blake *v.* Pine Mountain Iron, etc., Co., 76 Fed. 624, 22 C. C. A. 430.

23. Hart *v.* Davidson, 84 Tex. 112, 19 S. W. 454.

24. Small *v.* Stagg, 95 Ill. 39. But see Ruse *v.* Bromberg, 88 Ala. 619, 7 So. 384, holding that, although at law an absolute deed intended to operate merely as a mortgage is absolutely void as to the existing creditors of the grantor, yet in equity, where no actual fraud is proven, the grantee, who assumed the payment of the grantor's unpaid purchase-money notes, will be permitted to hold his deed as a means of reimbursement from freeing the land from the purchase-money lien.

A trustee who advances money to his cestui que trust, with which to extinguish a vendor's lien on the trust property, and who takes an imperfect mortgage and bonds as security, is not entitled to be subrogated to the vendor's lien. Norris *v.* Woods, 89 Va. 873, 17 S. E. 552.

25. The Hull of a New Ship, 12 Fed. Cas. No. 6,859, 2 Ware 203; Stalker *v.* The Henry Kneeland, 22 Fed. Cas. No. 13,282.

SUBSCRIPTIONS

By Edwin H. Woodruff
Professor of Law, Cornell University College of Law *

* Author of "Cases on Quasi-Contracts"; "Cases on Domestic Relations"; "Cases on Insurance"; Introduction to the Study of Law." Joint author of "Cases on Contracts."

CROSS-REFERENCES

For Matters Relating to:
- Constitutionality of Statute Validating Subscription, see CONSTITUTIONAL LAW, 8 Cyc. 1024.
- Over Subscription to Bank Stock, see BANKS AND BANKING, 5 Cyc. 436.
- Parol Evidence, see EVIDENCE, 17 Cyc. 612.
- Power of Corporation to Take Subscription, see CORPORATIONS, 10 Cyc. 1130.
- Seal, see SEALS, 35 Cyc. 1165 *et seq.*
- Signature, see SIGNATURES, 36 Cyc. 442.
- Subscription by:
  - County in Aid of Railroad, see COUNTIES, 11 Cyc. 529.
  - Private Person in Aid of Railroad, see RAILROADS, 33 Cyc. 88.
- Subscription Made on Sundays, see SUNDAY.
- Subscription of:
  - Party to:
    - Deed, see DEEDS, 13 Cyc. 554.
    - Mortgage, see MORTGAGES, 27 Cyc. 1105.
  - Witness to Deposition, see DEPOSITIONS, 13 Cyc. 939.
  - Written Instruments in General, see SIGNATURES, 36 Cyc. 442.
- Subscription to:
  - Return of Deposition, see DEPOSITIONS, 13 Cyc. 956.
  - Stock of:
    - Building and Loan Association, see BUILDING AND LOAN SOCIETIES, 6 Cyc. 124.
    - Corporation, see CORPORATIONS, 10 Cyc. 380.
    - Joint Stock Company, see JOINT STOCK COMPANIES, 23 Cyc. 468.
    - Railroad, see RAILROADS, 33 Cyc. 54.

I. DEFINITION AND NATURE.

A subscription contract is a legal obligation to make a payment in money or its equivalent in furtherance of a charitable, business, or other undertaking.[1]

1. **Other definitions.**— A subscription is "the act by which a person makes an agreement over his signature in writing, to furnish a sum of money for a particular pur-

The offer from which the obligation proceeds generally assumes the form of an express written promise [2] to pay money for a stated purpose and becomes binding when accepted,[3] and founded upon a consideration [4] or when the offerer is estopped to deny the validity of the promise.[5] The promise need not be to pay money, but may be to give a note,[6] to convey land,[7] or to furnish labor and material.[8]

II. FORM, EXECUTION, AND DELIVERY.

A. In General. The subscription may be made either by the promisor or his agent.[9]

B. Date and Signature. The paper is not invalid if undated.[10] The signature of the promisor need not be his personal name. Such words as he adopts for his signature will serve for that purpose.[11] The subscription paper need not be signed by the payee.[12]

C. Designation of Payee. It is not necessary that the payee should be named in the subscription paper; it is sufficient if there is an acceptance by the party intended; [13] and this is so even if the payee was not in existence at the time the subscription was made.[14] But there can be no recovery by a payee who was not contemplated.[15]

pose; as, a subscription to a charitable institution, a subscription for a book, for a newspaper, and the like." Bouvier L. Dict. To subscribe is "to agree in writing to furnish a sum of money, or its equivalent, for a designated purpose; as to assist a charitable or religious object, or to take stock in a corporation." Anderson L. Dict.

2. **Agreement to subscribe.**—An instrument by which defendant "agrees to subscribe" is construed to be a present subscription. Strong *v.* Eldridge, 8 Wash. 595, 36 Pac. 696.

Written contract.—A subscription paper to a church fund, containing an unqualified promise to pay, was read to the congregation, and the parties desiring to subscribe announced the amount, and the name and amount were placed on the list by those acting for the church, with the consent of said subscribers; it was held that defendant's subscription so obtained constituted a contract in writing, actions on which are governed by the ten-year statute of limitations. Ft. Madison First M. E. Church *v.* Donnell, 95 Iowa 494, 64 N. W. 412.

3. See *infra*, III.

4. See *infra*, IV.

5. See *infra*, V.

6. Chicago University *v.* Emmert, 108 Iowa 500, 79 N. W. 285.

7. North Ecclesiastical Soc. *v.* Matson, 36 Conn. 26; Harrisburg Bd. of Trade *v.* Eby, 1 Dauph. Co. Rep. (Pa.) 99.

8. State University *v.* Buell, 2 Vt. 48.

9. Rawlings *v.* Young Men's Christian Assoc., 48 Nebr. 216, 66 N. W. 1124.

10. Allen *v.* Clinton County, 101 Ind. 553.

11. Where a subscriber signed only his surname with the addition of the word "family," he bound himself by such adopted signature as though he had signed his full name. Hodges *v.* Nalty, 113 Wis. 567, 89 N. W. 535.

12. Turner *v.* Baker, 30 Ark. 186.

13. *Georgia.*— Wilson *v.* Savannah First Presb. Church, 56 Ga. 554.

Illinois.— Merchants' Bldg. Imp. Co. *v.* Chicago Exch. Bldg. Co., 210 Ill. 26, 71 N. E. 22, 102 Am. St. Rep. 145 [*affirming* 106 Ill. App. 17]; Hall *v.* Virginia, 91 Ill. 535; Friedline *v.* Carthage College, 23 Ill. App. 494.

Indiana.— Bingham *v.* Marion County, 55 Ind. 113.

Kansas.—Fulton *v.* Sterling Land, etc., Co., 47 Kan. 621, 28 Pac. 720.

Michigan.— Detroit First Universalist Church *v.* Pungs, 126 Mich. 670, 86 N. W. 235; Allen *v.* Duffie, 43 Mich. 1, 4 N. W. 427, 38 Am. Rep. 159; Comstock *v.* Howd, 15 Mich. 237.

Missouri.— Swain *v.* Hill, 30 Mo. App. 436.

Texas.— Darnell *v.* Lyon, 85 Tex. 455, 22 S. W. 304, 960.

Vermont.— Shelburne M. E. Soc. *v.* Lake, 51 Vt. 353.

See 45 Cent. Dig. tit. "Subscriptions," § 2.

Illustration.— In Hall *v.* Virginia, 91 Ill. 535, where the subscription was made for the purpose of building a house in a certain town, to be donated to the county, and no payee was named, it was held that the town which advanced money for the purpose, on the faith of the subscription, became the payee.

14. Merchants' Bldg. Imp. Co. *v.* Chicago Exch. Bldg. Co., 210 Ill. 26, 71 N. E. 22, 102 Am. St. Rep. 145; Willard *v.* Rockhill Centre M. E. Church, 66 Ill. 55; Miller *v.* Ballard, 46 Ill. 377; Johnston *v.* Ewing Female University, 35 Ill. 518; Griswold *v.* Peoria University, 26 Ill. 41, 79 Am. Dec. 361; Sherwin *v.* Fletcher, 168 Mass. 413, 47 N. E. 197; Thompson *v.* Page, 1 Metc. (Mass.) 565; New Lindell Hotel Co. *v.* Smith, 13 Mo. App. 7; Westfield Reformed Protestant Dutch Church *v.* Brown, 4 Abb. Dec. (N. Y.) 31, 24 How. Pr. 76 [*affirming* 29 Barb. 335, 17 How. Pr. 287].

Illustration.— One making a subscription to a corporation not in being at the time is liable for the payment of such subscription when the corporation is formed. New Lindell Hotel Co. *v.* Smith, 13 Mo. App. 7.

15. Warwick Turnpike Road Co. *v.* Hutchinson, 56 S. W. 806, 22 Ky. L. Rep. 201; Wheeler *v.* Floral Mill, etc., Co., 9 Nev. 254;

paper.[42] A subscription invalid at the time for want of consideration may be made valid and binding by a consideration arising subsequently between the subscriber and the beneficiary.[43]

F. Benefit to the Promisor. It has been held occasionally that the object being meritorious, and beneficial to the promisor, this benefit to him, although it is to be enjoyed by him in common with other persons, or even with the public generally, furnishes a consideration for the promise.[44]

G. Statutory Duty of the Promisee to Disburse the Fund. In a few cases the promise has been supported partly or wholly upon the theory that if the beneficiary has been authorized, by its own charter or by other legislation, to receive money and appropriate it to the purpose of the subscription, then such legislation together with the promise of the subscriber creates a legal obligation to pay the subscription,[45] the court saying either that the legal duty imposed upon the beneficiary to expend the fund constitutes a consideration,[46] or expressly placing the right to recover under these circumstances upon the ground of public policy.[47]

H. Moral Obligation. While in most instances there is undoubtedly a

act, or incurs the expense, or submits to the inconvenience, this request and performance on the behalf of the institution, is a sufficient consideration to support the promise." For further discussion of implied request see also Barnes *v.* Perine, 12 N. Y. 18.

42. Lasar *v.* Johnson, 125 Cal. 549, 58 Pac. 161; Roberts *v.* Cobb, 103 N. Y. 600, 9 N. E. 500; Barnes *v.* Perine, 12 N. Y. 18.

43. Albany Presb. Church *v.* Cooper, 112 N. Y. 517, 20 N. E. 352, 8 Am. St. Rep. 767, 3 L. R. A. 468.

44. Detroit First Universalist Church *v.* Pungs, 126 Mich. 670, 86 N. W. 235; Comstock *v.* Howd, 15 Mich. 237; Underwood *v.* Waldron, 12 Mich. 73; Pitt *v.* Gentle, 49 Mo. 74; Thomas *v.* Grace, 15 U. C. C. P. 462; Hammond *v.* Small, 16 U. C. Q. B. 371.

Benefit to the promisor.— In Pitt *v.* Gentle, 49 Mo. 74, 77, defendant was sued upon a subscription made to aid in rebuilding a mill, and the court said: "In the West, mills of this kind are essential to enable families to carry on an important branch of domestic industry; and besides, they form *nuclei* of settlements and enhance the value of property where they are located. The defendant, as well as his neighbors, was personally interested in having this one rebuilt, and may be supposed to have been moved in making his subscription by considerations of private interest as well as of benevolence. I have, then, no hesitation in holding that the defendant and the public had sufficient interest in the undertaking to authorize the plaintiffs to trust to his promise to aid." And in Comstock *v.* Howd, 15 Mich. 237, 244, the court says: "We see no difficulty upon the question of a consideration. The object was a meritorious one, for which people generally are willing to expend money, and which, therefore, 'must be regarded as worth money when it is promised: Underwood *v.* Waldron, 12 Mich. 73, 90."

45. Kentucky Female Orphan School *v.* Fleming, 10 Bush (Ky.) 234; Collier *v.* Baptist Education Soc., 8 B. Mon. (Ky.) 68; Irwin *v.* Lombard University, 56 Ohio St. 9, 46 N. E. 63, 60 Am. St. Rep. 727, 36 L. R. A. 239; Ohio Wesleyan Female College *v.* Higgins, 16 Ohio St. 20; Canal Fund Com'rs *v.* Perry, 5 Ohio 56.

46. In Kentucky Female Orphan School *v.* Fleming, 10 Bush (Ky.) 234, 238, where the action was brought upon a subscription note the court said: "The note was no doubt given for a donation intended to be made to appellants, which by section 2 of their charter (Sess. Acts 1846–47, p. 216) they were authorized to receive. The law made it their duty to apply the fund to carrying out the charitable and benevolent purpose of the institution and the donor. This obligation furnished consideration enough to uphold the promise to pay. (Collier *v.* Baptist Education Soc., 8 B. Mon. (Ky.) 68)."

47. **Public policy.**— In Irwin *v.* Lombard University, 56 Ohio St. 9, 21, 46 N. E. 63, 60 Am. St. Rep. 727, 36 L. R. A. 239, the court in stating the grounds of public policy which underlie the right to recover, says: "Institutions of this character are incorporated by public authority for defined purposes. Money recovered by them on promises of this character, cannot be used for the personal and private ends of an individual, but must be used for the purposes defined. To this use the university is restricted not only by the law of its being but as well by the obligations arising from its acceptance of the promise. A promise to give money to one to be used by him according to his inclination and for his personal ends is prompted only by motive. But a promise to pay money to such an institution to be used for such defined and public purposes rests upon consideration. The general course of decisions is favorable to the binding obligation of such promises. They have been influenced, not only by such reasons as those already stated, but in some cases, at least by state policy as indicated by constitutional and statutory provisions. The policy of this state, as so indicated, is promotive of education, religion and philanthropy. In addition to the declarations of the constitution upon the subject, the policy of the state is indicated by numerous legislative enactments providing for the incor-

the expenses of an improvement for which the subscription was taken is decreased by changes in the plan of improvement originally adopted.[81]

B. Substantial Performance. Recovery is allowed, however, where there has been a substantial, although not literal, performance of the conditions.[82] By substantial performance it is understood that although the conditions of the subscription be deviated from in trifling particulars, such deviation does not materially detract from the benefit the subscriber would derive from literal performance, but leaves the subscriber sub-ta[illegible] [illegible]efit he expected.[83]

C. Performance of Collateral Ag[illegible] [illegible]he performance of a collateral and contemporaneous promise is [illegible] [illegible]ion precedent to recovery on the subscription.[illegible]

D. Time of Perform[illegible] [illegible]
of performance, when pres[illegible]
of the contract, and a non-[illegible]
subscriber,[85] although perfor[illegible]

mittee. Mefford v. Sell, 3 Nebr. (Unof[illegible] 566, 92 N. W. 148. Seating capacity of the[illegible] ter. Gerner v. Church, 43 Nebr. 600, [illegible] N. W. 51. Establishing hospital ward. Co[illegible] tage Hospital v. Merrill, 92 Iowa 649, [illegible] N. W. 490. Establishing milk station. Nor[illegible] western Creamery Co. v. Lanning, 83 [illegible] 19, 85 N. W. 823. Establishing[illegible] Northwestern Conference v. M[illegible] 375; Foxcroft Academy v. [illegible] Personnel of church membe[illegible] wegian Lutheran Con[illegible] 151, 96 N. W[illegible]

lated.[86] There are, however, decisions in which this rule is limited or denied.[87] If no time for performance is prescribed then performance must be within a reasonable time, and what is a reasonable time is a question for the jury.[88]

E. Change of Plan or [illegible]rpose.[89] Any material change in the plan or purpose for which the subscri[illegible]tion was made cannot be effected without the consent of the subscriber.[90] [illegible]e is thereby released unless there has been a waiver,[91] or unless he has estoppe[illegible] himself to deny his consent to the change.[92]

S. W. 54, 97 Am. St. Rep. [illegible] 342.

United States.— Cincinnati [illegible]

Be[illegible]

Subsequent formation of corporation.— [illegible] is [illegible] the purpose [illegible] subscrip- [illegible] carried [illegible]ently formed corp[illegible] of which defendant [illegible] to become a member, [illegible] from liability upon his subscrip- [illegible] Osborn v. Bartlett, 72 Me. 120; [illegible] N. H. 538, 3 Atl. 429.

[illegible]eturn to original plan.— In Anderson v. [illegible] Kentucky College, 10 Ky. L. Rep. 725, [illegible] subscriber was to pay when fifteen thousand [illegible]llars [illegible] subscribed. Afterward the [illegible]an was changed so as to limit the amount [illegible] be raised to ten thousand dollars but fif- [illegible] thousand dollars was in fact subscribed. [illegible]bscriber was still held liable.

[illegible] **verdict.**— In Wrought Iron [illegible] Greene, 53 Iowa 562, 5 N. W. [illegible] that where the petition in [illegible] defendant's subscription [illegible] of a bridge fails to [illegible] to the sub-

reements. T
not a condit

e. According to the weight of authority the ti
bed by the subscription contract, is of the essence
mpliance with this requirement is a defense to the
nance was completed shortly after the time stipu-

.)
ea-
62
t-
31
th-
Minn.
school.
yers, 36 Ind.
Favor, 4 Me. 382.
rship. Leland Nor-
g. v. Larson, 121 Iowa
706. Personnel of payees. Wayne, etc., Collegiate Inst. v. Blackmar, 48 N. Y. 663. Suffering financial loss. Kentucky Live Stock Breeders' Assoc. v. Miller, 119 Ky. 393, 84 S. W. 301, 27 Ky. L. Rep. 39. Approval of minister by ministerial association. Somers v. Miner, 9 Conn. 458. Furnishing a guaranty. Porter v. Raymond, 53 N. H. 519. Carrying on work of university. Lincoln University v. Hepley, 28 Ill. App. 629. Refraining from pursuing a debtor. Felt v. Davis, 48 Vt. 506. Building railroad into town. Hanna v. Mosher, (Okla. 1908) 98 Pac. 358. Raising funds from other sources. St. Paul's Episcopal Church v. Fields, 81 Conn. 670, 72 Atl. 145.

81. Giles v. Crosby, 5 Bosw. (N. Y.) 389.

82. *Illinois.*— Merchants' Bldg. Imp. Co. v. Chicago Exch. Bldg. Co., 210 Ill. 26, 71 N. E. 22, 102 Am. St. Rep. 145; Hall v. Virginia City, 91 Ill. 535; Illiopolis M. E. Church v. Garvey, 53 Ill. 401, 5 Am. Rep. 51.

Indiana.—Sult v. Warren School Tp., 8 Ind. App. 655, 36 N. E. 291.

Indian Territory.— Doherty v. Arkansas, etc., R. Co., 5 Indian Terr. 537, 82 S. W. 899 [*reversed* on other grounds in 142 Fed. 104, 73 C. C. A. 328].

Massachusetts.— Atty.-Gen. v. Greenfield Library Assoc., 135 Mass. 563; Ives v. Sterling, 6 Metc. 310; Torrey v. Milbury, 21 Pick. 64.

Missouri.—Missouri Pac. R. Co. v. Tygard, 84 Mo. 263, 54 Am. Rep. 97; St. Louis, etc., R. Co. v. Houck, 120 Mo. App. 634, 97 S. W. 963.

New York.— Wayne, etc., Collegiate Inst. v. Greenwood, 40 Barb. 72 [*reversed* on other grounds in 41 N. Y. 620].

Washington.— Hunt v. Upton, 44 Wash. 124, 87 Pac. 56.

See 45 Cent. Dig. tit "Subscriptions," § 14.

Substantial compliance illustrated.— The condition of a subscription for a building that it shall be donated to the county is substantially complied with by leasing the building to the county without rent for ninety-nine years. Hall v. Virginia City, 91 Ill. 535. And where a contract required plaintiff to construct a certain railroad in consideration of defendants' subscription, and it became necessary for plaintiff to organize a corporation to construct such road in order to condemn a right of way, in which corporation plaintiff held a majority of the stock, the construction of the road by the corporation constituted a sufficient compliance with the contract. Hunt v. Upton, 44 Wash. 124, 87 Pac. 56.

83. St. Louis, etc., R. Co. v. Houck, 120 Mo. App. 634, 97 S. W. 963.

84. Merchants' Bldg. Imp. Co. v. Chicago Exch. Bldg. Co., 210 Ill. 26, 71 N. E. 22, 102 Am. St. Rep. 145; Howell v. Methodist Episcopal Church, 61 Ill. App. 121.

85. *Alabama.*— Thornton v. Sheffield, etc., R. Co., 84 Ala. 109, 4 So. 197, 5 Am. St. Rep. 337.

Connecticut.— St. Paul's Episcopal Church v. Fields, 81 Conn. 670, 72 Atl. 145.

Florida.— Persinger v. Bevill, 31 Fla. 364, 12 So. 366.

Iowa.— Burlington, etc., R. Co. v. Bœstler, 15 Iowa 555.

Kansas.— Memphis, etc., R. Co. v. Thompson, 24 Kan. 170.

Michigan.— Jordan v. Newton, 116 Mich. 674, 75 N. W. 130; Port Huron, etc., R. Co. v. Richards, 90 Mich. 577, 51 N. W. 680.

Minnesota.— Bohn Mfg. Co. v. Lewis, 45 Minn. 164, 47 N. W. 652.

Ohio.—Johnson v. College Hill Narrow Gauge R. Co., 7 Ohio Dec. (Reprint) 466, 3 Cinc. L. Bul. 410.

Oklahoma.— Cooper v. Ft. Smith, etc., R. Co., (1909) 99 Pac. 785; Powers v. Rude, 14 Okla. 381, 79 Pac. 89.

Oregon.— Coos Bay, etc., R., etc., Co. v. Nosher, 30 Oreg. 547, 48 Pac. 361.

Texas.— Garrison v. Cooke, 96 Tex. 228, 72

etc., R. Co. *v.* ...sley, 51 Fed. 738, 2 C. C. A. 480, 19 L. R. A. 796.

See 45 Cent. Dig. tit "Subscriptions," § 16.

Reason for rule.— Such agreement is *stricti juris*, and the obligation of the promisor is akin to that of a guarantor who receive no personal benefit from the performance of the act for which he agrees to become responsible, at least none to which he would not have been entitled if the promise had not been made. Cincinnati, etc., R. Co. *v.* Bensley, 51 Fed. 738, 2 C. C. A. 480, 19 L. R. A. 796.

86. Memphis, etc., R. Co. *v.* Thompson, 24 Kan. 170.

87. Homan *v.* Steele, 18 Nebr. 652, 26 N. W. 472; Seley *v.* Texas, etc., R. Co., 2 Tex. App. Civ. Cas. § 87.

88. *Iowa.*— Paddock *v.* Bartlett, 68 Iowa 16, 25 N. W. 906.

Massachusetts.— Carter *v.* Carter, 14 Pick. 424.

Michigan.— Waters *v.* Union Trust Co., 129 Mich. 640, 89 N. W. 687.

Oklahoma.— Powers *v.* Rude, 14 Okla. 381, 79 Pac. 89.

Wisconsin.— Hodges *v.* O'Brien, 113 Wis. 97, 88 N. W. 901.

See 45 Cent. Dig. tit "Subscriptions," § 16.

89. See also *supra*, XII, A.

90. *Indiana.*— Rothenberger *v.* Glick, 22 Ind. App. 288, 52 N. E. 811.

Indian Territory.— Doherty *v.* Arkansas, etc., R. Co., 5 Indian Terr. 537, 82 S. W. 899 [*reversed* on other grounds in 142 Fed. 104, 73 C. C. A. 328].

Maine.— Fryeburg Parsonage Fund *v.* Ripley, 6 Me. 442.

Massachusetts.— Worcester Medical Inst. *v.* Bigelow, 6 Gray 498.

Minnesota.— Brimhall *v.* Van Campen, 8 Minn. 13, 82 Am. Dec. 118.

Mississippi.— Pratt *v.* Canton Cotton Co., 51 Miss. 470.

New Hampshire.— Troy Cong. Soc. *v.* Goddard, 7 N. H. 430.

New York.— Giles *v.* Crosby, 5 Bosw. 389.

Wisconsin.— La Fayette County Monument Corp. *v.* Ryland, 80 Wis. 29, 49 N. W. 157.

Change of location.—Where subscriptions to public improvements are made with reference to their location, any material subsequent change of location without the consent of a subscriber releases him from his subscription. Pratt *v.* Canton Cotton Co., 51 Miss. 470.

tions, the f... out by a s... subscribers, ... does not c... relieve him... tion. Carr ... *v.* Crosby, ...

W... a ... d... p... to... teen ... The s...

Directing ... Bridge Co. *v.* ... 770, it was held ... an action to recover ... to a fund for the erection ... aver compliance with a provision ... scription requiring the bridge to be of a certain character, and the defect is not assailed by demurrer or other pleading, it is error to direct a verdict for defendant on the ground that such condition has not been established.

91. *Kansas.*— Schuler *v.* Myton, 48 Kan. 282, 29 Pac. 163.

Massachusetts.— Mirick *v.* French, 2 Gray 420; Bryant *v.* Goodnow, 5 Pick. 228.

Michigan.— First Universalist Church *v.* Pungs, 126 Mich. 670, 86 N. W. 235.

Mississippi.— Chicago Bldg., etc., Co. *v.* Higginbotham, (1901) 29 So. 79.

Montana.— Kane *v.* Downing, 14 Mont. 343, 36 Pac. 355.

New York.— Hutchins *v.* Smith, 46 Barb. 235; Reformed Protestant Dutch Church *v.* Brown, 29 Barb. 335, 17 How. Pr. 287 [*affirmed* in 4 Abb. Dec. 31].

Ohio.— Doane *v.* Pickaway, Wright 752.

See 45 Cent. Dig. tit "Subscriptions," § 17.

What constitutes waiver.— Part payment of a subscription and a promise to pay the balance, the subscriber not then knowing that a condition of his subscription had not been complied with, was held not a waiver of the condition. Albany First Presb. Church *v.* Cooper, 45 Hun (N. Y.) 453, 10 N. Y. St. 142 [*affirmed* in 112 N. Y. 517, 20 N. E. 352, 8 Am. St. Rep. 767, 3 L. R. A. 468]; Felt *v.* Davis, 48 Vt. 506. See also upon what constitutes waiver Holbrook *v.* Wilson, 4 Bosw. (N. Y.) 64; Catt *v.* Olivier, 98 Va. 580, 36 S. E. 980.

92. *Ex p.* Booker, 18 Ark. 338; Petty *v.* Church of Christ, 95 Ind. 278; McCleary *v.*

SUBSTANTIAL RIGHT. As used in reference to the right of a party to an action to appeal from an order affecting a substantial right, an essential legal right, not merely a technical one;[17] something to which, upon proved or conceded facts, a party may lay claim as matter of law — which a court may not legally refuse, and to which it can be seen that the party is entitled, within the well settled rules of law;[18] some legal right to which the party who appeals claims to be entitled;[19] a legal right; one which is protected by law.[20] (Substantial Right: Law Depriving Accused of as Ex Post Facto, see CONSTITUTIONAL LAW, 8 Cyc. 1031.)

SUBSTANTIA PRIOR ET DIGNIOR EST ACCIDENTE. A maxim meaning "The substance is prior and of more worth than the accident."[21]

portant particulars." Adams *v.* Edwards, 1 Fed. Cas. No. 53, 1 Fish. Pat. Cas. 1.

In reference to a prescribed form, the term is often used in the sense of comprehending all of the form given that is necessary or essential. Lineberger *v.* Tidwell, 104 N. C. 506, 513, 10 S. E. 758.

Distinguished from "tenor" see Edgerton *v.* State, (Tex. Cr. App. 1902) 70 S. W. 90, 91.

Used in connection with other words.— "Substantially as and for the purpose set forth" see Campbell Printing-Press, etc., Co. *v.* Marden, 64 Fed. 782, 786. "Substantially as described" see Westinghouse *v.* Boyden Power-Brake Co., 170 U. S. 537, 558, 18 S. Ct. 707, 42 L. ed. 1136; Brown *v.* Guild, 23 Wall. (U. S.) 181, 218, 23 L. ed. 161; Seymour *v.* Osborne, 11 Wall. (U. S.) 516, 547, 20 L. ed. 33 [*reversing* 21 Fed. Cas. No. 12,687, 6 Fish. Pat. Cas. 115, 2 Off. Gaz. 675, 9 Phila. (Pa.) 380]; Lowrie *v.* H. A. Meldrum Co., 124 Fed. 761, 764; Paul Boynton Co. *v.* Morris Chute Co., 87 Fed. 225, 227, 30 C. C. A. 617. "Substantially as set forth" see Boyden Power-Brake Co. *v.* Westinghouse Air-Brake Co., 70 Fed. 816, 826, 17 C. C. A. 430; Westinghouse *v.* New York Air-Brake Co., 59 Fed. 581, 596. "Substantially as specified" see Lake Shore, etc., R. Co. *v.* National Car-Brake Shoe Co., 110 U. S. 229, 235, 4 S. Ct. 33, 28 L. ed. 129; O. H. Jewell Filter Co. *v.* Jackson, 140 Fed. 340, 344, 72 C. C. A. 304; Lee *v.* Pillsbury, 49 Fed. 747, 749. "Substantially a true copy" see Thomas *v.* State, 103 Ind. 419, 426, 2 N. E. 808. "Substantially commenced" see Atty.-Gen. *v.* Bournemouth, [1902] 2 Ch. 714, 725, 71 L. J. Ch. 730, 87 L. T. Rep. N. S. 252, 18 T. L. R. 661, 51 Wkly. Rep. 129. "Substantially disputed" see Frost *v.* Craig, 16 Daly (N. Y.) 107, 109, 9 N. Y. Suppl. 528. "Substantially of local or of private interest" see Atty.-Gen. *v.* Manitoba License Holders Assoc., [1902] A. C. 73, 79, 71 L. J. P. C. 28, 85 L. T. Rep. N. S. 591, 18 T. L. R. 94, 50 Wkly. Rep. 431. "Substantially true" see Jeffrey *v.* U. O. G. C., 97 Me. 176, 179, 53 Atl. 1102.

17. Clarke *v.* Nebraska Nat. Bank, 49 Nebr. 800, 802, 69 N. W. 104.

18. People *v.* New York Cent. R. Co., 29 N. Y. 418, 430; Howell *v.* Mills, 53 N. Y. 322, 329.

19. Cook *v.* Dickenson, 5 Sandf. (N. Y.) 663, 664.

20. Armstrong *v.* Herancourt Brewing Co., 53 Ohio St. 467, 480, 42 N. E. 425. See also North *v.* Smith, 73 Ohio St. 247, 249, 76 N. E. 619; Hare *v.* Sears, 17 Ohio S. & C. Pl. Dec. 590, 592.

Includes all positive, material, and absolute rights, as distinguished from those of a merely formal or essential nature. Security Bank *v.* Commonwealth Nat. Bank, 48 How. Pr. (N. Y.) 135, 137.

Is not confined to an absolute legal right, but includes matters which are discretionary. Martin *v.* Windsor Hotel Co., 70 N. Y. 101, 102. But see Howell *v.* Mills, 53 N. Y. 322, 329.

Orders affecting substantial rights: Order determining question of existence of partnership and whether certain property was partnership property. Putnam *v.* Putnam, 2 Ariz. 259, 261, 14 Pac. 356. Order directing a guardian to pay over the amount of a judgment against him as garnishee in a suit against his ward. Coffin *v.* Eisiminger, 75 Iowa 30, 31, 39 N. W. 124. Order directing an attorney to pay money collected into court. Baldwin *v.* Foss, 14 Nebr. 455, 456, 16 N. W. 480. Order directing election for directors of corporation. *In re* Fleming, 16 Wis. 70, 75. Order directing sale of premises instead of partition amongst the owners. Vesper *v.* Farnsworth, 40 Wis. 357, 360. Order discharging a person having property of a judgment debtor, or who is indebted to him, from process for contempt or refusing to answer question properly put upon examination in supplementary proceedings. Ballston Spa Bank *v.* Milwaukee Mar. Bank, 18 Wis. 490, 492. Order refusing to set aside a judgment by default in a foreclosure suit and to let in a meritorious defense not presented in time because of excusable neglect. Johnson *v.* Eldred, 13 Wis. 482, 484. Order sustaining a demurrer to a petition for the removal of an assignee in a voluntary assignment. Burtt *v.* Barnes, 87 Wis. 519, 522, 58 N. W. 790. See APPEAL AND ERROR, 2 Cyc. 591.

Orders not affecting substantial rights: Order refusing to dissolve a temporary injunction. Putnam *v.* Putnam, 2 Ariz. 259, 261, 14 Pac. 356. Order forming order refusing to open default judgment. Keller *v.* Feldman, 2 Misc. (N. Y.) 179, 180, 21 N. Y. Suppl. 581. See APPEAL AND ERROR, 2 Cyc. 591 *et seq.*

21. Morgan Leg. Max. [*citing* Halkerstone Leg. Max.].

13 Cyc. 885. Of Copy — Of Deposition Lost After Return, see DEPOSITIONS, 13 Cyc. 978; Of Lost or Destroyed Record on Appeal, see APPEAL AND ERROR, 2 Cyc. 1076; Of Lost Pleading on Trial De Novo on Appeal From Justice, see JUSTICES OF THE PEACE, 24 Cyc. 730; On Loss or Destruction of Indictment, see INDICTMENTS AND INFORMATIONS, 22 Cyc. 221. Of Count in Declaration, see ASSUMPSIT, ACTION OF, 4 Cyc. 346. Of Devisee or Legatee, see WILLS. Of Different Lease or Other Contract Between Landlord and Tenant, see LANDLORD AND TENANT, 24 Cyc. 913. Of Driver by Hirer of Animal, see ANIMALS, 2 Cyc. 313. Of Equivalents or Elements — In General as Infringement of Patents, see PATENTS, 30 Cyc. 979; As Involving Invention, see PATENTS, 30 Cyc. 855. Of Indemnitor as Party in Action Against Sheriff or Constable, see SHERIFFS AND CONSTABLES, 35 Cyc. 1804. Of Materials — As Infringement of Patents, see PATENTS, 30 Cyc. 978 note 16; As Involving Invention, see PATENTS, 30 Cyc. 856; Or Mechanical Equivalents as Involving Novelty, see PATENTS, 30 Cyc. 830 note 26. Of Mortgage, Effect as to Priorities, see MORTGAGES, 27 Cyc. 1222. Of New — Agreement, Effect as Accord and Satisfaction, see ACCORD AND SATISFACTION, 1 Cyc. 311; Bond, Discharge of Bail in Civil Actions by, see BAIL, 5 Cyc. 36; Bond, Effect on Judgment Collateral to Old Bond, see JUDGMENTS, 23 Cyc. 1498 note 86; Case on Appeal as Amendment, see APPEAL AND ERROR, 3 Cyc. 64 note 95; Creditor or Debtor, see NOVATION, 29 Cyc. 1131; Mortgage After Sale of Equity or Assumption of Mortgagor, Effect as to Grantees, see MORTGAGES, 27 Cyc. 1337 note 55; Mortgage For Mortgage Prior to Mechanic's Lien, Effect on Priorities, see MECHANICS' LIENS, 27 Cyc. 240; Obligation Between Same Parties, see NOVATION, 29 Cyc. 1137; Parties to Contract of Employment, see MASTER AND SERVANT, 26 Cyc. 1024; Securities by Foreign Corporations, see FOREIGN CORPORATIONS, 19 Cyc. 1216 note 53. Of One Note For Another as Payment of Debt, see COMMERCIAL PAPER, 7 Cyc. 1011. Of Other — Bond, Effect as Payment, see BONDS, 5 Cyc. 805; Person, by Curator on Refusing Appointment, see ABSENTEES, 1 Cyc. 204; Property, to That Described in Mortgage, see CHATTEL MORTGAGES, 6 Cyc. 1035; MORTGAGES, 27 Cyc. 1142; Securities, Effect on Lien of Mortgage, see MORTGAGES, 27 Cyc. 1413. Of Parties — In General, see PLEADING, 31 Cyc. 484; Appeal From Order on Motion For, see APPEAL AND ERROR, 2 Cyc. 603; As Subject of Mandamus, see MANDAMUS, 26 Cyc. 204; Effect on Liability of Sureties on Appeal-Bonds, see APPEAL AND ERROR, 2 Cyc. 941 note 34; In Action By and Against Consolidated Corporation, see CORPORATIONS, 10 Cyc. 310; In Action By and Against Executor or Administrator, see EXECUTORS AND ADMINISTRATORS, 18 Cyc. 968, 969; In Action By and Against Guardian and Ward, see GUARDIAN AND WARD, 21 Cyc. 206; In Action By and Against Religious Society, see RELIGIOUS SOCIETIES, 34 Cyc. 1195 note 6; In Action For Partition, see PARTITION, 30 Cyc. 229; In Action of Ejectment, see ABATEMENT AND REVIVAL, 1 Cyc. 90 note 38; EJECTMENT, 15 Cyc. 87; In Action to Set Aside Fraudulent Conveyance, see FRAUDULENT CONVEYANCES, 20 Cyc. 718 note 43; In Appellate Court, see APPEAL AND ERROR, 2 Cyc. 773, 782; In Condemnation Proceedings, see EMINENT DOMAIN, 15 Cyc. 839; In Equity, see EQUITY, 16 Cyc. 200; In Justice's Court, see JUSTICES OF THE PEACE, 24 Cyc. 514; In Mandamus Proceedings, see MANDAMUS, 26 Cyc. 418; In Probate Proceedings, see WILLS; In Proceedings to Foreclose Mortgage by Action, see MORTGAGES, 27 Cyc. 1583; In Replevin Proceedings, see REPLEVIN, 34 Cyc. 1427; In Suit For Injunction, see INJUNCTIONS, 22 Cyc. 916; In Suit to Enforce Mechanic's Lien, see MECHANICS' LIENS, 27 Cyc. 359; Liability For Costs, see COSTS, 11 Cyc. 94; Necessity For, on Death of Party Pending Appeal, see APPEAL AND ERROR, 2 Cyc. 774; On Change in Incumbency of Public Office, see ABATEMENT AND REVIVAL, 1 Cyc. 121; On Change of Executor or Administrator, see ABATEMENT AND REVIVAL, 1 Cyc. 120; On Change of Guardian, see ABATEMENT AND REVIVAL, 1 Cyc. 120; On Change of Receiver, see ABATEMENT AND REVIVAL, 1 Cyc. 121; On Change of Trustee, see ABATEMENT AND REVIVAL, 1 Cyc. 121; On Death of Original Party, see ABATEMENT AND REVIVAL, 1 Cyc. 100; Procedure For in Appellate Court After Death of Party, see APPEAL AND ERROR,

ment.[29] Thus the record must show jurisdiction of the court,[30] opportunity to be heard after notice[31] duly apprising defendant of the facts or of the charges against him,[32] the statute authorizing the proceeding,[33] a regular trial,[34] and the evidence.[35] However, it has been held that on appeal the same presumptions as to jurisdictional facts are indulged in as in the case of actions upon summons and complaint.[36]

IV. ENUMERATION OF SUMMARY PROCEEDINGS.

Among the more important summary proceedings are proceedings against clerks of court for breach of duty,[37] against sheriffs and constables for misconduct in office,[38] and against an attorney for wrongs done in a professional capacity;[39] proceedings for a forcible entry,[40] or for judgment on motion;[41] proceedings to abate nuisances generally,[42] and specifically a liquor nuisance;[43] to collect bills and notes[44] and taxes,[45] specifically municipal[46] and school[47] taxes; to enforce contribution by sureties against their cosureties,[48] a crop lien,[49] a bid at a judgment sale,[50] and liability on bonds, such as appeal,[51] county official,[52] distress,[53] executors' and administrators',[54] forthcoming,[55] garnishment,[56] guardians',[57] prison limits,[58] replevin,[59] and general official[60] bonds, to enforce forfeited recognizances,[61] homestead rights,[62] liens,[63] payment of costs,[64] and the right of exemption;[65] to

Illinois.— Chicago *v.* Rock Island R. Co., 20 Ill. 286.

Indiana.— Batson *v.* Lasselle, 1 Blackf. 119.

Mississippi.— Hyman *v.* Seaman, 33 Miss. 185.

New York.— Buttling *v.* Hatton, 33 N. Y. App. Div. 551, 53 N. Y. Suppl. 1009.

Tennessee.—Crockett *v.* Parkison, 3 Coldw. 219; Hamilton *v.* Burum, 3 Yerg. 355.

West Virginia.— Mayer *v.* Adams, 27 W. Va. 244.

Illustrations of insufficient record see Elizabeth *v.* Central R. Co., 66 N. J. L. 568, 49 Atl. 682; Jersey City *v.* Neihaus, 66 N. J. L. 554, 49 Atl. 444.

Everything necessary to sustain a lawful summary conviction must appear upon the face of the record. Philadelphia *v.* Campbell, 11 Phila. (Pa.) 163.

29. Barton *v.* McKinney, 3 Stew. & P. (Ala.) 274.

30. Jersey City *v.* Neihaus, 66 N. J. L. 554, 49 Atl. 444; Jones *v.* Wilkes-Barre, 2 Kulp (Pa.) 68; Philadelphia *v.* Roney, 2 Phila. (Pa.) 43.

31. Gallitzin Borough *v.* Gains, 15 Pa. Co. Ct. 337, 7 Kulp 479; Lancaster *v.* Baer, 5 Lanc. Bar (Pa.) Dec. 6, 1873.

32. Elizabeth *v.* Central R. Co., 66 N. J. L. 568, 49 Atl. 682; Boothe *v.* Georgetown, 3 Fed. Cas. No. 1,651, 2 Cranch C. C. 356.

33. Com. *v.* Hill, 3 Pa. Dist. 216, 12 Pa. Co. Ct. 559.

34. Elizabeth *v.* Central R. Co., 66 N. J. L. 568, 49 Atl. 682; Keeler *v.* Milledge, 24 N. J. L. 142; Gallitzin Borough *v.* Gains, 15 Pa. Co. Ct. 337, 7 Kulp 479; Com. *v.* Cane, 2 Pars. Eq. Cas. (Pa.) 265; Jones *v.* Wilkes-Barre, 2 Kulp (Pa.) 68; Lancaster *v.* Baer, 5 Lanc. Bar (Pa.) Dec. 6, 1873; Philadelphia *v.* Cohen, 13 Wkly. Notes Cas. (Pa.) 468.

35. Lancaster *v.* Baer, 5 Lanc. Bar (Pa.) Dec. 6, 1873.

Evidence in extenso must be set forth upon the record. Com. *v.* Cane, 2 Pars. Eq. Cas. (Pa.) 265.

36. Shouse *v.* Lawrence, 51 Ala. 559.

37. See CLERKS OF COURT, 7 Cyc. 255.

38. See SHERIFFS AND CONSTABLES, 35 Cyc. 1858, 1895.

39. See ATTORNEY AND CLIENT, 4 Cyc. 975, 997.

40. See FORCIBLE ENTRY AND DETAINER, 19 Cyc. 1118.

41. See JUDGMENTS, 23 Cyc. 768, 1119, 1225.

42. See MUNICIPAL CORPORATIONS, 28 Cyc. 756; NUISANCES, 29 Cyc. 1214.

The abatement of a nuisance by the municipal authorities, after investigation and determination that a nuisance exists, on their order, by a police officer, is a summary proceeding. Western, etc., R. Co. *v.* Atlanta, 113 Ga. 537, 38 S. E. 996, 54 L. R. A. 294.

43. See INTOXICATING LIQUORS, 23 Cyc. 302.

44. See COMMERCIAL PAPER, 8 Cyc. 20.

45. See TAXES.

46. See MUNICIPAL CORPORATIONS, 28 Cyc 1711, 1715 note 99.

47. See SCHOOLS AND SCHOOL-DISTRICTS, 35 Cyc. 1032.

48. See PRINCIPAL AND SURETY, 32 Cyc. 296.

49. See AGRICULTURE, 2 Cyc. 68.

50. See JUDICIAL SALES, 24 Cyc. 52.

51. See APPEAL AND ERROR, 2 Cyc. 961.

52. See COUNTIES, 11 Cyc. 455.

53. See LANDLORD AND TENANT, 24 Cyc. 1324.

54. See EXECUTORS AND ADMINISTRATORS, 18 Cyc. 1279.

55. See EXECUTIONS, 17 Cyc. 1134.

56. See GARNISHMENT, 20 Cyc. 1157.

57. See GUARDIAN AND WARD, 21 Cyc. 240.

58. See EXECUTIONS, 17 Cyc. 1536.

59. See REPLEVIN, 34 Cyc. 1588.

60. See OFFICERS, 29 Cyc. 1463.

61. See RECOGNIZANCES, 34 Cyc. 558 text and note 27.

62. See HOMESTEADS, 21 Cyc. 633.

63. See LIENS, 25 Cyc. 683.

64. See COSTS, 11 Cyc. 105.

65. See EXEMPTIONS, 18 Cyc. 1487.

SUNDAY

EDITED BY N. W. HOYLES, B. A., K. C., LL.D.
Principal of The Law School, Osgoode Hall, Toronto, Canada

labor performed on Sunday is not *ipso facto* illegal.[56] It is immaterial that the work or labor performed by defendant on Sunday is not at his usual place of business, provided it is work of his ordinary calling.[57]

2. **Barbering.** Barbering is laboring within the meaning of general statutes prohibiting labor [58] or "worldly employment" on Sunday,[59] and is not generally considered a work of necessity.[60] However, it is not unlawful under a statute prohibiting the opening of any place of business for the purpose of trade or sale of goods, wares, and merchandise,[61] nor does it constitute a nuisance.[62] The mere keeping open of a barber shop, without performing any labor therein, does not violate a general law against Sabbath breaking.[63]

C. Business or Occupation [64] — 1. **In General.** At common law all business other than judicial proceedings [65] could be lawfully transacted on Sunday.[66] However, the carrying on of one's usual business or occupation on Sunday is

a club in separately selling two bottles of beer on Sunday did not constitute labor.

Under Ill. Cr. Code, c. 38, § 261, no offense is committed unless the labor is of such a character as to disturb the peace and good order of society. McCurdy *v.* Alaska, etc., Commercial Co., 102 Ill. App. 120; Foll *v.* People, 66 Ill. App. 405; Johnson *v.* People, 42 Ill. App. 594.

56. Sun Printing, etc., Assoc. *v.* Tribune Assoc., 44 N. Y. Super. Ct. 136. See also Cleary *v.* State, 56 Ark. 124, 19 S. W. 313.

57. McCain *v.* State, 2 Ga. App. 389, 58 S. E. 550.

58. State *v.* Nesbit, 8 Kan. App. 104, 54 Pac. 326; State *v.* Granneman, 132 Mo. 326, 33 S. W. 784; State *v.* Schatt, 128 Mo. App. 622, 107 S. W. 10; Reg. *v.* Taylor, 19 Can. L. J. N. S. 362.

The fact that the shaving is done in a club-house does not render it any the less the work of the ordinary calling of the barber, for the work is the same as that performed on week days, although the scene of performance is different. McCain *v.* State, 2 Ga. App. 389, 58 S. E. 550.

Hairdresser not within Englaish act.— Palmer *v.* Snow, [1900] 1 Q. B. 725, 64 J. P. 342, 69 L. J. Q. B. 356, 82 L. T. Rep. N. S. 199, 16 T. L. R. 168, 48 Wkly. Rep. 351 [*distinguishing* Phillips *v.* Innes, 4 Cl. & F. 234, 7 Eng. Reprint 90, on the ground that the Scottish act upon which that decision turned was in much more general terms]. construing 29 Car. II, c. 7, § 1.

59. Com. *v.* Waldman, 140 Pa. St. 89, 21 Atl. 248, 11 L. R. A. 563 [*affirming* 8 Pa. Co. Ct. 449]; Paizer *v.* Com., 4 Kulp (Pa.) 286; Com. *v.* Jacobus, 1 Leg. Gaz. (Pa.) 491; Stout's Case, 2 Leg. Rec. (Pa.) 311.

60. *Arkansas.*— State *v.* Frederick, 45 Ark. 347, 55 Am. Rep. 555.

Georgia.— McCain *v.* State, 2 Ga. App. 389, 58 S. E. 550.

Missouri.—State *v.* Kuehner, (App. 1908) 110 S. W. 605; State *v.* Schatt, 128 Mo. App. 622, 107 S. W. 10; State *v.* Wellott, 54 Mo. App. 310.

Ohio.— State *v.* Schuler, 10 Ohio Dec. (Reprint) 806, 23 Cinc. L. Bul. 450. *Contra*, Spaith *v.* State, 10 Ohio Dec. (Reprint) 639, 22 Cinc. L. Bul. 323.

Pennsylvania.— Com. *v.* Waldman, 140 Pa. St. 89, 21 Atl. 248, 11 L. R. A. 563 [*affirming* 8 Pa. Co. Ct. 449].

Texas.— *Ex p.* Kennedy, 42 Tex. Cr. 148, 58 S. W. 129, 51 L. R. A. 270.

Utah.— State *v.* Sopher, 25 Utah 318, 71 Pac. 482, 95 Am. St. Rep. 845, 60 L. R. A. 468.

England.— Phillips *v.* Innes, 4 Cl. & F. 234, 7 Eng. Reprint 90, interpreting the Scottish act.

Canada.— Reg. *v.* Taylor, 19 Can. L. J N. S. 362.

See 45 Cent. Dig. tit. "Sunday," § 6.

In Indiana, it is a question for the jury to determine, under proper instructions from the court, whether the shaving of a customer by a barber is a work of necessity. Ungericht *v.* State, 119 Ind. 379, 21 N. E. 1082, 12 Am. St. Rep. 419.

Accommodation to customers.— In Com. *v.* Williams, 1 Pearson (Pa.) 61, it was held that the fact that the persons shaved were sick on the preceding Saturday and that defendant shaved them on Sunday as a matter of accommodation, without compensation, was immaterial and constituted no defense.

Shaving of injured person.— In Stone *v.* Graves, 145 Mass. 353, 13 N. E. 906, the court refused to rule as a matter of law that the work of shaving an aged and infirm person whose shoulder has been injured so that he could not well shave himself in his own house on Sunday was not a work of necessity.

61. State *v.* Krech, 10 Wash. 166, 38 Pac. 1001.

62. State *v.* Lorry, 7 Baxt. (Tenn.) 95, 32 Am. Rep. 555.

63. State *v.* Frederick, 45 Ark. 347, 55 Am. Rep. 555.

64 **Avocation defined** see Avocation, 4 Cyc. 1075.

65. See *infra*, X, A.

66. Heisen *v.* Smith, 138 Cal. 216, 71 Pac. 180, 94 Am. St. Rep. 39 [*quoting* 2 Bouvier L. Dict. 1067]; Ward *v.* Ward, 75 Minn. 269, 77 N. W. 965; Eden Musee American Co. *v.* Bingham, 58 Misc. (N. Y.) 644, 108 N. Y. Suppl. 200 [*reversed* on other grounds in 125 N. Y. App. Div. 780, 110 N. Y. Suppl. 210]; Merritt *v.* Earle, 31 Barb. (N. Y.) 38 [*affirmed* in 29 N. Y. 115, 86 Am. Dec. 292]; Boynton *v.* Page, 13 Wend. (N. Y.) 425.

generally specifically prohibited by statutes, varying somewhat in their phraseology.[67] The evil aimed at is the engaging in one's usual business or accustomed pursuit, works of necessity and charity excepted, and when this exists, the law is violated.[68] It has been held that a single act in the exercise of one's usual avocation amounts to a violation of the law;[69] but every act done does not constitute a separate offense, as the offense consists in the exercise of an employment or business.[70] Of course it is necessary, in order to sustain a conviction, to show that the act or acts done come within the terms of the statute;[71] while, on the other

Sunday contracts not prohibited at common law see *infra*, V, A.

Exercising the trade of a butcher or baker on a Sunday was no offense at common law. Crepps *v.* Durden, Cowp. 640, 98 Eng. Reprint 1283; Rex *v.* Brotherton, Str. 702, 93 Eng. Reprint 794.

67. See the statutes of the several states.

In Ohio the buying and selling of merchandise on the Sabbath has been held to be within the prohibition of the statute against common labor. Cincinnati *v.* Rice, 15 Ohio 225.

The Pennsylvania acts for licensing inns and taverns have not repealed the act of April 22, 1794, forbidding ordinary employment on Sunday, as to innkeepers. Omit *v.* Com., 21 Pa. St. 426.

68. Mueller *v.* State, 76 Ind. 310, 40 Am. Rep. 245; State *v.* Congers, 14 Ind. 396; Voglesong *v.* State, 9 Ind. 112; Ross *v.* State, 9 Ind. App. 35, 36 N. E. 167; Bennett *v.* Brooks, 91 Mass. 118; Peate *v.* Dicken, 1 C. M. & R. 422, 3 Dowl. P. C. 171, 4 L. J. Exch. 28, 5 Tyrw. 116; Scarfe *v.* Morgan, 1 H. & H. 292, 2 Jur. 569, 7 L. J. Exch. 324, 4 M. & W. 270; Drury *v.* Defontaine, 1 Taunt. 131.

Execution of contracts and other written instruments on Sunday see *infra*, V, F.

A person engaged in several occupations violates the Sabbath law when he pursues any one of them on Sunday. Reed *v.* State, 119 Ga. 562, 46 S. E. 837.

An engagement to marry, made on Sunday, is not such "worldly employment or business" as is prohibited by the act of April 22, 1794. Fleischman *v.* Rosenblatt, 20 Pa. Co. Ct. 512.

Disturbance of others.— The New Hampshire statute prohibits no acts to be done on Sunday except such as are done to the disturbance of others (Clough *v.* Shepherd, 31 N. H. 490); a disturbance, within the meaning of this statute, has been defined to be any business which withdraws the attention of others from the appropriate duties of the Sabbath and turns it to other things, regardless of whether the other persons present do or do not object to its performance (Varney *v.* French, 19 N. H. 233). "It is a matter of law, that, whether any one besides the plaintiff and the defendant was present or not, the sale was business of the plaintiff's secular calling, done 'to the disturbance of others.'" Thompson *v.* Williams, 58 N. H. 248, 249. In State *v.* Ryan, 80 Conn. 582, 69 Atl. 536, it was held that defendant could not complain of an instruction that he was guilty, if his acts were done under such circumstances as to actually disturb the public peace and quiet.

Slot machines.— S. C. Cr. Code (1902), § 501, forbidding the sale, or exposing for sale, of goods on Sunday, applies to slot machines automatically vending wares. Cain *v.* Daly, 74 S. C. 480, 55 S. E. 110.

Complying with another's demand.—A lock-keeper, employed upon a canal which is a public highway, is not guilty of Sabbath-breaking, for opening a lock to admit the passage of a boat upon the demand of the person having her in charge. Murray *v.* Com., 24 Pa. St. 270.

Principal and agent — both liable.— Splane *v.* Com., 9 Pa. Cas. 201, 12 Atl. 431; Com. *v.* Ryan, 15 Pa. Co. Ct. 223; Seaman *v.* Com., 11 Wkly. Notes Cas. (Pa.) 14; Hall *v.* State, 41 Tex. Cr. 423, 55 S. W. 173.

69. Voglesong *v.* State, 9 Ind. 112.

Casual sales, privately made, do not constitute a violation of a statute prohibiting public selling or exposing for sale. Ward *v.* Ward, 75 Minn. 269, 77 N. W. 965; Boynton *v.* Page, 13 Wend. (N. Y.) 425. Neither is a casual purchase, for consumption, an employment or business within the meaning of the Pennsylvania statute. Com. *v.* Hoover, 25 Pa. Super. Ct. 133.

70. Scandrett *v.* State, 124 Ga. 141, 52 S. E. 160; Friedeborn *v.* Com., 113 Pa. St. 242, 6 Atl. 160, 57 Am. Rep. 464; State *v.* James, 81 S. C. 197, 62 S. E. 214, 128 Am. St. Rep. 902, 18 L. R. A. 617; Crepps *v.* Durden, Cowp. 640, 98 Eng. Reprint 1283.

71. State *v.* Binswanger, 122 Mo. App. 78, 98 S. W. 103; Hanks *v.* State, 50 Tex. Cr. 577, 99 S. W. 1011; Watson *v.* State, 46 Tex. Cr. 138, 79 S. W. 31; Todd *v.* State, 30 Tex. App. 667, 18 S. W. 642; Reg. *v.* Silvester, 10 Jur. N. S. 360, 33 L. J. M. C. 79; Reg. *v.* Howarth, 33 U. C. Q. B. 537.

Alcohol is embraced in any one of the terms "goods, wares, or merchandise," the sale of which by retail on Sunday is prohibited by Gantt's digest, section 1618. Bridges *v.* State, 37 Ark. 224.

Fruit is merchandise and the keeper of a fruit stand is a shop-keeper within the meaning of a statute prohibiting a merchant, shopkeeper, or other person from disposing of wares and merchandise on Sunday. Gulfport *v.* Stratakos, 90 Miss. 489, 43 So. 812.

Consumption on premises.—Whether the purchaser consumed the goods on the premises is immaterial in determining whether

hand, if defendant seeks to justify his acts, they must be brought within the exception of the statute.[72]

2. Keeping Open Place of Business For Purpose of Traffic — a. In General. The statutes of many jurisdictions make it unlawful to keep open a place of business on Sunday for the purpose of traffic. Statutes which, in terms, prohibit the keeping open merely have been construed to mean that the prohibition is against the keeping open for purposes of traffic.[73] This "keeping open" for the purpose of doing business with the public indiscriminately is an offense in itself, separate and distinct from that of performing labor on the Sabbath,[74] and exceptions as to necessity and charity applying to the latter do not apply to the former.[75]

b. Elements of Offense. A sale is not necessary to constitute the offense,[76] and evidence showing a sale does not conclusively establish a keeping open for the purpose of traffic.[77] The offense is complete when there exists a readiness on the part of the proprietor to carry on his usual business in his store,[78] and the public is afforded access thereto, even though part or all of the doors and entrances are closed.[79] In general the word "shop" is not the legal equivalent of the word

there was a sale on Sunday. New Castle v. Cummings, 36 Pa. Super. Ct. 443.

Driving cattle.— In Triggs v. Lester, L. R. 1 Q. B. 259, 13 L. T. Rep. N. S. 701, 14 Wkly. Rep. 279, it was held that the "driving or conducting" cattle intended in a statute prohibiting such on Sunday is the ordinary driving, when the cattle themselves are driven, and does not include their conveyance in a van driven with horses.

72. Com. v. Goldsmith, 176 Mass. 104, 57 N. E. 212; State v. Jacques, 69 N. H. 220, 40 Atl. 398; Quinlan v. Conlin, 13 Misc. (N. Y.) 568, 34 N. Y. Suppl. 952.

Collection of camp-meeting fee.— The collection of a compulsory admission fee at the entrance gate to camp-meeting grounds on Sunday is worldly employment or business, prohibited by the act of April 22, 1794, as it does not stand on the same plane as subscriptions solicited or collected during a religious meeting. Com. v. Weidner, 4 Pa. Co. Ct. 437.

Mistake.— The letting of a carriage for hire on Sunday, from a belief that it was to be used in a case of necessity or charity, when in fact it was not so used, is not an offense. Myers v. State, 1 Conn. 502.

Piloting canal-boat.— It is a violation of the Pennsylvania act of April 22, 1794, to pilot a canal-boat laden with coal upon a part of the Schuylkill navigation on the Lord's day, in discharge of the party's ordinary occupation, even though the locks are required to be kept open for lawful travel. Scully v. Com., 35 Pa. St. 511.

73. Jebeles v. State, 131 Ala. 41, 31 So. 377; Snider v. State, 59 Ala. 64.

74. *Re* Lambert, 7 Brit. Col. 396.

75. Com. v. Perry, (Mass. 1887) 11 N. E. 537; Com. v. Dale, 144 Mass. 363, 11 N. E. 534; Com. v. Osgood, 144 Mass. 362, 11 N. E. 536; Com. v. Starr, 144 Mass. 359, 11 N. E. 533; Com. v. Dextra, 143 Mass. 28, 8 N. E. 756; Com. v. Nagle, 117 Mass. 142. See, however, Mueller v. State, 76 Ind. 310, 40 Am. Rep. 245, where it was held that the keeping of a tobacco store open for business, without any pretense of necessity, except to sell in the ordinary way, constituted an infraction of the statute directed against any one being found "at common labor, or engaged in his usual avocation."

76. Jebeles v. State, 131 Ala. 41, 31 So. 377; Griffith v. State, 48 Tex. Cr. 575, 89 S. W. 832. *Compare* Snider v. State, 59 Ala. 64; Smith v. State, 50 Ala. 159.

77. Dixon v. State, 76 Ala. 89.

78. Jebeles v. State, 131 Ala. 41, 31 So. 377; Wright v. Forsyth, 116 Ga. 799, 43 S. E. 46 (holding that a barber who entered his shop for the purpose of shining his own shoes was not guilty of keeping open his shop); Lynch v. People, 16 Mich. 472; State v. Crabtree, 27 Mo. 232.

A barber by shaving customers on Sunday does not necessarily "keep open." *Re* Lambert, 7 Brit. Col. 396.

79. *Arkansas.*— Seelig v. State, 43 Ark. 96.

Connecticut.— State v. Miller, 68 Conn. 373, 36 Atl. 795.

Massachusetts.— Com. v. Harrison, 11 Gray 308; Com. v. Lynch, 8 Gray 384.

Missouri.— State v. Crabtree, 27 Mo. 232.

Texas.— Whitcomb v. State, 30 Tex. App. 269, 17 S. W. 258.

See 45 Cent. Dig. tit. "Sunday," § 7.

Keeping "wide open" unnecessary.— Thus, in Com. v. Kirshen, 194 Mass. 151, 152, 80 N. E. 2, the court, per Morton, J., said: "A shop, warehouse or workhouse may be kept open so as to come within the prohibition of the statute without being kept 'wide open,' or kept open in the same manner and for the same purposes in which and for which it is kept open for business on week days."

Delivery of goods only.— In Goldstein v. Vaughan, [1897] 1 Q. B. 549, 61 J. P. 277, 66 L. J. Q. B. 380, 76 L. T. Rep. N. S. 262, 46 Wkly. Rep. 399, it was held that a workshop was not open for traffic when all that was done was that customers with whom the business arrangements had been previously made brought or fetched away their things on Sunday.

Admission limited to club members.—A social club, to which none but members are admitted, which supplies its members with

2. **Base-Ball Playing.**[15] It is not illegal *per se* to play base-ball on Sunday.[16] However, where it is played in such a manner as to interrupt the repose and religious liberty of the community,[17] or when the game is public and an admission is charged directly or indirectly,[18] it becomes unlawful under statutes prohibiting sporting or public sport, but does not, under statutes prohibiting games.[19] In at least one jurisdiction there is an express statutory prohibition against playing base-ball on Sunday where a fee is charged.[20]

3. **Theatrical Performances.** Theatrical entertainments and performances on Sunday cause agitation and disturbance contrary to law,[21] and are generally expressly prohibited by statute or ordinance. These statutes and ordinances have been held to forbid all performances in theaters or other places of public amusement and entertainment on Sunday,[22] and to cover moving picture shows or exhibitions,[23] but not dancing other than for the purpose of an exhibition or performance.[24] The manager of the theater or opera-house may be found guilty

15. **Base-ball** defined see 5 Cyc. 621.

16. Ontario Field Club *v.* McAdoo, 56 Misc. (N. Y.) 285, 107 N. Y. Suppl. 295.

17. People *v.* Dennin, 35 Hun (N. Y.) 327; People *v.* Hesterberg, 43 Misc. (N. Y.) 510, 89 N. Y. Suppl. 498; People *v.* De Mott, 38 Misc. (N. Y.) 171, 77 N. Y. Suppl. 249. See also Capital City Athletic Assoc. *v* Greenbush Police Com'rs, 9 Misc. (N. Y.) 189, 29 N. Y. Suppl. 804.

18. Seay *v.* Shrader, 69 Nebr. 245, 95 N. W. 690 [*following* State *v.* O'Rourk, 35 Nebr. 614, 53 N. W. 591, 17 L. R. A. 830]; *In re* Rupp, 33 N. Y. App. Div. 468, 53 N. Y. Suppl. 927; People *v.* Demerest, 56 Misc. (N. Y.) 287, 107 N. Y. Suppl. 549; Ontario Field Club *v.* McAdoo, 56 Misc. (N. Y.) 285, 107 N. Y. Suppl. 295; Brighton Athletic Club *v.* McAdoo, 47 Misc. (N. Y.) 432, 94 N. Y. Suppl. 391; People *v.* Poole, 44 Misc. (N. Y.) 118, 89 N. Y. Suppl. 773. *Compare* Paulding *v.* Lane, 55 Misc. (N. Y.) 37, 104 N. Y. Suppl. 1051, where it is held that base-ball playing on Sunday, to which the public are invited. is a violation of law, whether an admission fee is charged or not.

Indirect charging of admission fee.— In determining whether the game is played for gain, the court will look behind the device by which the money is obtained. People *v.* Demerest, 56 Misc. (N. Y.) 287, 107 N. Y. Suppl. 549; Ontario Field Club *v.* McAdoo, 56 Misc. (N. Y.) 285, 107 N. Y. Suppl. 295.

19. *Ex p.* Neet, 157 Mo. 527, 57 S. W. 1025, 80 Am. St. Rep. 638, holding that, although the contra case of State *v.* Williams, 35 Mo. App. 541, was not expressly overruled or disapproved in St. Louis Agricultural, etc., Assoc. *v.* Delano, 108 Mo. 217, 18 S. W. 1101, it must be regarded as overruled.

20. State *v.* Hogreiver, 152 Ind. 652, 53 N. E. 921, 45 L. R. A. 504.

21. Neuendorff *v.* Duryea, 6 Daly (N. Y.) 276.

A place of public worship, where nothing dramatic is introduced, and where the discourses are intended to be instructive and "to make science the handmaid of religion," is not a place "used for public entertainment or amusement," within 21 Geo. III, c. 49, § 1, although the worship conducted therein is not according to any established or usual form. Baxter *v.* Langley, L. R. 4 C. P. 21, 38 L. J. M. C. 1, 19 L. T. Rep. N. S. 321, 17 Wkly. Rep. 254.

Aquarium is place of entertainment within English statute. Terry *v.* Brighton Aquarium Co., L. R. 10 Q. B. 306, 44 L. J. M. C. 173, 32 L. T. Rep. N. S. 458; Warner *v.* Brighton Aquarium Co., L. R. 10 Exch. 291, 44 L. J. M. C. 175 note.

22. New York *v.* Eden Musee American Co., 102 N. Y. 593, 8 N. E. 40; Matter of Hammerstein, 57 Misc. (N. Y.) 52, 108 N. Y. Suppl. 197.

An exhibition of paintings, statuary, wax figures, and passive works of art does not come within the prohibition of public "shows." Eden Musee American Co. *v.* Bingham, 58 Misc. (N. Y.) 644, 108 N. Y. Suppl. 200 [*reversed* on other grounds in 125 N. Y. App. Div. 780, 110 N. Y. Suppl. 210].

Entertainment of religious society is excepted from Massachusetts statute. Com. *v.* Alexander, 185 Mass. 551, 70 N. E. 1017.

23. Moore *v.* Owen, 58 Misc. (N. Y.) 332, 109 N. Y. Suppl. 585; United Vaudeville Co. *v.* Zeller, 58 Misc. (N. Y.) 16, 108 N. Y. Suppl. 789; Gale *v.* Bingham, 110 N. Y. Suppl. 12; Economopoulos *v.* Bingham, 109 N. Y. Suppl. 728. *Contra,* People *v.* Hemleb, 127 N. Y. App. Div. 356, 111 N. Y. Suppl. 690; People *v.* Lynch, 108 N. Y. Suppl. 209; Keith, etc., Amusement Co. *v.* Bingham, 108 N. Y. Suppl. 205 [*reversed* on other grounds in 125 N. Y. App. Div. 791, 110 N. Y. Suppl. 219].

Character of picture as justification.— The exhibition of pictures illustrating lectures delivered at the same time on the story of Joseph and his brethren and also an illustrated lecture on the lumber industry in California do not constitute "public sport, exercise, or show," within the intention of N. Y. Pen. Code, § 265; People *v.* Finn, 57 Misc. (N. Y.) 659, 110 N. Y. Suppl. 22. And in People *v.* Flynn, 108 N. Y. Suppl. 208, pictures shown by means of a slot machine device and certain musical selections communicated through the ears of a person who has inserted a coin in the machine were held to be not unlawful.

24. Matter of Allen, 34 Misc. (N. Y.) 698, 70 N. Y. Suppl. 1017. See also Suesskind *v.*

employment or business on that day,[23] and other statutes more comprehensive in their terms.[24]

C. Contracts Made in Another State. As the enforcement of a contract executed on Sunday is not contrary to public policy or good morals, the general rule that a contract valid where made is valid everywhere [25] obtains, and the contract will be enforced in a state other than the one in which it was made, where it is not shown that it violates the statutes of the state where made.[26] When it is shown to violate the statutes of the state where made, it will not be enforced by the courts of other states,[27] or by the courts of the state where delivered, although final acceptance was made in another state.[28] Likewise, as the Sunday laws of a state have no extraterritorial force, the courts of one state will enforce a contract made on Sunday within its borders, but which contemplates performance in another state, where the performance is not shown to violate the law of such other state.[29]

D. Nature of Contract — 1. Executed and Executory. In some cases the validity of a Sunday contract has been made to turn upon the question whether it was executory or executed, it being held void if executory,[30] and valid if executed.[31] On the other hand, there is authority for the proposition that the fact that the contract is executory or executed is not to be considered in determining its validity.[32]

2. Contracts Not Within Ordinary Calling of Parties. Under the statutes of some jurisdictions, a contract made on Sunday outside of the ordinary calling of the parties is valid.[33]

23. Hussey *v.* Roquemore, 27 Ala. 281; Gookin *v.* Richardson, 11 Ala. 889, 46 Am. Dec. 232; Newbury *v.* Luke, 68 N. J. L. 189, 52 Atl. 625; Reeves *v.* Butcher, 31 N. J. L. 224; Riddle *v.* Keller, 61 N. J. Eq. 513, 48 Atl. 818; Gennert *v.* Wuestner, 53 N. J. Eq. 302, 31 Atl. 609; Nibert *v.* Baghurst, 47 N. J. Eq. 201, 20 Atl. 252; Rush *v.* Rush, (N. J. Ch. 1889) 18 Atl. 221; Morgan *v.* Richards, 1 Browne (Pa.) 171.

24. *Iowa.*— P. J. Bowlin Liquor Co. *v.* Brandenburg, 130 Iowa 220, 106 N. W. 497.

Michigan.— Saginaw, etc., R. Co. *v.* Chappell, 56 Mich. 190, 22 N. W. 278; Brazee *v.* Bryant, 50 Mich. 136, 15 N. W. 49; Winfield *v.* Dodge, 45 Mich. 355, 7 N. W. 906, 40 Am. Rep. 476; Tucker *v.* Mowrey, 12 Mich. 378; Adams *v.* Hamell, 2 Dougl. 73, 43 Am. Dec. 455.

Oklahoma.— Helm *v.* Briley, 17 Okla. 314, 87 Pac. 595.

Pennsylvania.— Berrill *v.* Smith, 2 Miles 402.

Vermont.— Sumner *v.* Jones, 24 Vt. 317.

Wisconsin.— King *v.* Graef, 136 Wis. 548, 117 N. W. 1058, 128 Am. St. Rep. 1101, 20 L. R. A. N. S 86; Hill *v.* Sherwood, 3 Wis. 343.

See 45 Cent. Dig. tit. "Sunday," § 30 *et seq.*

25. See Contracts, 9 Cyc. 672.

26. *Michigan.*— Steere *v.* Trebilcock, 108 Mich. 464, 66 N. W. 342; O'Rourke *v.* O'Rourke, 43 Mich. 58, 4 N. W. 531.

Mississippi.—McKee *v.* Jones, 67 Miss. 405, 7 So. 348.

Rhode Island.— Brown *v.* Browning, 15 R. I. 422, 7 Atl. 403, 2 Am. St. Rep. 908.

Vermont.— Adams *v.* Gay, 19 Vt. 358.

United States.— Swann *v.* Swann, 21 Fed. 299.

See 45 Cent. Dig. tit. "Sunday," § 31.

Contra.— Hill *v.* Wilker, 41 Ga. 449, 5 Am. Rep. 540.

27. Hazard *v.* Day, 14 Allen (Mass.) 487, 92 Am. Dec. 790; Northrup *v.* Foot, 14 Wend. (N. Y.) 248.

28. International Textbook Co. *v.* Ohl, 150 Mich. 131, 111 N. W. 768, 121 Am. St. Rep. 612, 13 L. R. A. N. S. 1157.

29. Said *v.* Stromberg, 55 Mo. App. 438.

Performance in third state.— Where the contract contemplates performance in a state other than the one where made and the one in which the action is brought, the Sunday statutes of that state govern. Brown *v.* Gates, 120 Wis. 349, 97 N. W. 221, 98 N. W. 205.

30. Spahn *v.* Willman, 1 Pennew. (Del.) 125, 39 Atl. 787; Chestnut *v.* Harbaugh, 78 Pa. St. 473; Thomas *v.* Hatch, 53 Wis. 296, 10 N. W. 393.

31. Chestnut *v.* Harbaugh, 78 Pa. St. 473; Shuman *v.* Shuman, 27 Pa. St. 90; Scarfe *v.* Morgan, 1 H. & H. 292, 2 Jur. 569, 7 L. J. Exch. 324, 4 M. & W. 270. See also Schneider *v.* Sansom, 62 Tex. 201, 50 Am. Rep. 521; De Forth *v.* Wisconsin, etc., R. Co., 52 Wis. 320, 9 N. W. 17, 38 Am. Rep. 737; Troewert *v.* Decker, 51 Wis. 46, 8 N. W. 26, 37 Am. Rep. 808.

A judgment confessed on an instrument which was completed or delivered on Sunday is an executed contract, and will not be opened on that ground. Chambers *v.* Brew, 18 Pa. Co. Ct. 399; Lee *v.* Drake, 10 Pa. Co. Ct. 276.

32. Tucker *v.* Mowrey, 12 Mich. 378.

33. *Georgia.*— Dorough *v.* Equitable Mortg. Co., 118 Ga. 178, 45 S. E. 22; Hayden *v.* Mitchell, 103 Ga. 431, 30 S. E. 287 (marriage settlement); Sanders *v.* Johnson, 29 Ga. 526.

d. Loaning Money. The loaning of money on the Sabbath has been held to come within the prohibition of statutes directed against the transaction of secular business on that day.[41]

e. Creation of Agency. Likewise agencies created on Sunday have been held to be void as constituting secular business.[42]

f. Extension of Time. A parol agreement extending the time of payment of a mortgage debt, entered into on Sunday, has been held to be void.[43]

g. Partnership Agreement. An agreement for the formation of a partnership *in præsenti* is void when made on Sunday.[44]

h. Sale or Exchange of Property. A sale or exchange of property on Sunday is quite generally held to be in violation of the Sunday statutes and void.[45] It is not void under statutes prohibiting merely the keeping open of a place of business,[46] the performance of labor,[47] or the exposure of property for sale, where the sale is privately made.[48] Of course if the contract has been really consummated on a previous day it is valid;[49] and if part is valid and part invalid, and the contract is severable, the invalid part will not invalidate the rest.[50] A sale on Sunday is valid as to an innocent second purchaser.[51]

E. Negotiation on Sunday. The mere carrying on of negotiations on Sunday will not invalidate a contract completed on a secular day. The final consummation of the contract on Sunday is necessary to bring it within the prohibition of the Sunday statutes.[52]

Janvrin, 200 Mass. 514, 86 N. E. 785; Stebbins *v.* Peck, 8 Gray (Mass.) 553.

An application to purchase public school land is not void because filed on Sunday. Stephens *v.* Porter, 29 Tex. Civ. App. 556, 69 S. W. 423.

41. Tamplin *v.* Still, 77 Ala. 374; Finn *v.* Donahue, 35 Conn. 216; Meader *v.* White, 66 Me. 90, 22 Am. Rep. 551; Jacobson *v.* Bentzler, 127 Wis. 566, 107 N. W. 7, 115 Am. St. Rep. 1052, 4 L. R. A. N. S. 1151; Troewert *v.* Decker, 51 Wis. 46, 8 N. W. 26, 37 Am. Rep. 808.

42. Davis *v.* Barger, 57 Ind. 54; Clough *v.* Davis, 9 N. H. 500.

43. Rush *v.* Rush, (N. J. Ch. 1889) 18 Atl. 221.

44. Durant *v.* Rhener, 26 Minn. 362, 4 N. W. 610.

45. *Alabama.*— Wadsworth *v.* Dunnam, 117 Ala. 661, 23 So. 699; Dodson *v.* Harris, 10 Ala. 566; O'Donnell *v.* Sweeney, 5 Ala. 467, 39 Am. Dec. 336.

Iowa.— Pike *v.* King, 16 Iowa 49.

Massachusetts.— Ladd *v.* Rogers, 11 Allen 209.

Michigan.—Adams *v.* Hamell, 2 Dougl. 73, 43 Am. Dec. 455.

Minnesota.— Finley *v.* Quirk, 9 Minn. 194, 86 Am. Dec. 93.

New Hampshire.— Smith *v.* Foster, 41 N. H. 215.

New Jersey.— Neibert *v.* Baghurst, (Ch. 1892) 25 Atl. 474.

Pennsylvania.— Foreman *v.* Ahl, 55 Pa. St. 325.

Vermont.— Lyon *v.* Strong, 6 Vt. 219.

Wisconsin.—Williams *v.* Lane, 87 Wis. 152, 58 N. W. 77.

Canada.— Lai *v.* Stall, 6 U. C. Q. B. 506.

See 45 Cent. Dig. tit. "Sunday," § 34.

Delivery on Sunday of goods sold on Saturday constitutes a violation of an ordinance prohibiting the sale of merchandise on Sunday, as a delivery is essential to the consummation of the sale. McDowell *v.* Murfreesboro, 103 Tenn. 726, 54 S. W. 976.

Waiver of delivery.— Where, under the statutes of a state, parties cannot make a valid contract on Sunday, they cannot agree on Sunday to waive the delivery of the property attempted to be sold. Calhoun *v.* Phillips, 87 Ga. 482, 13 S. E. 593.

46. Moore *v.* Murdock, 26 Cal. 514.

47. Birks *v.* French, 21 Kan. 238. *Contra*, Banks *v.* Werts, 13 Ind. 203. The case of Sellers *v.* Dugan, 18 Ohio 489, which held that a sale of corn on Sunday was void, was overruled in Bloom *v.* Richards, 2 Ohio St. 387, which case involved the validity of a contract made on Sunday for the sale of lands.

48. Eberle *v.* Mehrbach, 55 N. Y. 682; Batsford *v.* Every, 44 Barb. (N. Y.) 618; Miller *v.* Roessler, 4 E. D. Smith (N. Y.) 234; Boynton *v.* Page, 13 Wend. (N. Y.) 425.

49. Riley *v.* Du Bois, 14 Ill. App. 236; Peake *v.* Conlan, 43 Iowa 297; Beaumont *v.* Brengeri, 5 C. B. 301, 57 E. C. L. 301.

Bill of sale.— The fact that a bill of sale was executed on Sunday, in pursuance of the terms of a sale made on Friday, did not invalidate such sale. Foster *v.* Wooten, 67 Miss. 540, 7 So. 501. And in one jurisdiction it has been held that the fact that a bill of sale was executed on Sunday does not affect its validity. Fitzgerald *v.* Andrews, 15 Nebr. 52, 17 N. W. 370 [*following* Horacek *v.* Keebler, 5 Nebr. 355].

50. Rosenblatt *v.* Townsley, 73 Mo. 536; Foreman *v.* Ahl, 55 Pa. St. 325.

51. Horton *v.* Buffinton, 105 Mass. 399.

52. *Connecticut.*— Tyler *v.* Waddingham, 58 Conn. 375, 20 Atl. 335, 8 L. R. A. 657.

Delaware.— Terry *v.* Platt, 1 Pennew. 185, 40 Atl. 243.

3. **Assignments.** The annexation of a schedule on Sunday to an assignment made on a prior secular day does not invalidate it.[61] Neither is an assignment invalidated by its partial execution on Sunday.[62] A third person, not a party to the contract of assignment, cannot dispute its validity on the ground that it was made on Sunday.[63]

4. **Bills and Notes.** Under the statutes of most jurisdictions, a promissory note executed on Sunday is void as between the parties.[64] The indorsement of a promissory note on Sunday, by an accommodation surety or otherwise, is also void,[65] except where it does not appear on the face of the indorsement that it was made on Sunday and the note is sought to be enforced by a *bona fide* holder without notice.[66] Likewise the indorsement of a bill of exchange on Sunday renders it void in the hands of one not a *bona fide* holder,[67] but the mere drawing of the bill on Sunday does not invalidate it, in the absence of evidence showing its acceptance on that day.[68] Where the note is merely signed on Sunday but not delivered until some other day, it is valid.[69] And where it is dated on Sunday, but in fact was made and delivered on a week day, it is valid.[70] The fact that the

Sup. 1905) 61 Atl. 12; Norton *v.* Powell, 11 L. J. C. P. 202, 4 M. & G. 42, 43 E. C. L. 31.

Unauthorized acceptance.— A contract of guaranty, signed by one of the parties to it on Sunday, and delivered on that day to an agent of the other party, having no authority to accept a delivery, the assent and signature of the other party not being given until a week day, is not void. Gibbs, etc., Mfg. Co. *v.* Brucker, 111 U. S. 597, 4 S. Ct. 572. 28 L. ed. 534.

61. Clap *v.* Smith, 16 Pick. (Mass.) 247.

62. Farwell *v.* Webster, 71 Wis. 485, 37 N. W. 437, holding that where one of two partners executes an assignment on Sunday, but the other partner executes and delivers it on a secular day, the instrument is not invalid.

63. Tennent-Stribling Shoe Co. *v.* Roper, 94 Fed. 739, 36 C. C. A. 455.

Assignments in trust on Sunday valid.— Donovan *v.* McCarty, 155 Mass. 543, 30 N. E. 221; Faxon *v.* Folvey, 110 Mass. 392.

64. *Alabama.*— Dodson *v.* Harris, 10 Ala. 566; Shippey *v.* Eastwood, 9 Ala. 198; O'Donnell *v.* Sweeney, 5 Ala. 467, 39 Am. Dec. 336.

Arkansas.— Edwards *v.* Probst, 38 Ark. 661; Tucker *v.* West, 29 Ark. 386.

Connecticut.—Wight *v.* Geer, 1 Root 474.

Georgia.— Morgan *v.* Bailey, 59 Ga. 683; Hill *v.* Wilker, 41 Ga. 449, 5 Am. Rep. 540. *Compare* Sanders *v.* Johnson, 29 Ga. 526.

Indiana.— Bosley *v.* McAllister, 13 Ind. 565; Reynolds *v.* Stevenson, 4 Ind. 619.

Iowa.— Collins *v.* Collins, 139 Iowa 703, 117 N. W. 1089, 18 L. R. A. N. S. 1176 (voidable only); Clough *v.* Goggins, 40 Iowa 325; Sayre *v.* Wheeler, 32 Iowa 559.

Maine.— Pope *v.* Linn, 50 Me. 83; Cumberland Bank *v.* Mayberry, 48 Me. 198; Towle *v.* Larrabee, 26 Me. 464.

Massachusetts.— Stevens *v.* Wood, 127 Mass. 123. *Contra,* Geer *v.* Putnam, 10 Mass. 312.

Michigan.—Adams *v.* Hamell, 2 Dougl. 73, 43 Am. Dec. 455.

Minnesota.— Finney *v.* Callendar, 8 Minn. 41; Brimhall *v.* Van Campen, 8 Minn. 13, 82 Am. Dec. 118. *Contra,* as to the casual execution and delivery of a promissory note. Holden *v.* O'Brien, 86 Minn. 297, 90 N. W. 531.

Mississippi.— Miller *v.* Lynch, 38 Miss. 344.

New Hampshire.— State Capital Bank *v.* Thompson, 42 N. H. 369; Varney *v.* French, 19 N. H. 233; Allen *v.* Deming, 14 N. H. 133, 40 Am. Dec. 179.

Oklahoma.— Helm *v.* Briley, 17 Okla. 314, 87 Pac. 595.

Pennsylvania.— Kepner *v.* Keefer, 6 Watts 231, 31 Am. Dec. 460; Linden *v.* Hicks, 2 Luz. Leg. Reg. 101.

Vermont.— Goss *v.* Whitney, 27 Vt. 272; Lovejoy *v.* Whipple, 18 Vt. 379, 46 Am. Dec. 157.

Wisconsin.— Hill *v.* Sherwood, 3 Wis. 343.

Canada.— Houliston *v.* Parsons, 9 U. C. Q. B. 681.

See 45 Cent. Dig. tit. "Sunday," § 38.

Contra.— Ray *v.* Catlett, 12 B. Mon. (Ky.) 532; Kaufman *v.* Hamm, 30 Mo. 387; Glover *v.* Cheatham, 19 Mo. App. 656; More *v.* Clymer. 12 Mo. App. 11 (Illinois statute construed); Main *v.* Johnson, 7 Wash. 321, 35 Pac. 67; Barrett *v.* Aplington, 2 Fed. Cas. No. 1,045.

When payable in another state.— A note executed and delivered in Michigan on Sunday in payment of goods sold and delivered there, although payable in Ohio, where the vendors live, is void under the Michigan statute. Arbuckle *v.* Reaume, 96 Mich. 243, 55 N. W. 808.

65. Ball *v.* Powers, 62 Ga. 757 [*approved* in Harrison *v.* Powers, 76 Ga. 218]; Bar Harbor First Nat. Bank *v.* Kingsley, 84 Me. 111, 24 Atl. 794; Benson *v.* Drake, 55 Me. 555.

66. Heise *v.* Bumpass, 40 Ark. 545; Trieber *v.* Commercial Bank, 31 Ark. 128; Greathead *v.* Walton, 40 Conn. 226; Parker *v.* Pitts, 73 Ind. 597, 38 Am. Rep. 155; Gilbert *v.* Vachon, 69 Ind. 372.

67. Saltmarsh *v.* Tuthill, 13 Ala. 390.

68. Begbie *v.* Levi, 1 Cromp. & J. 180, 9 L. J. Exch. O. S. 51, 1 Tyrw. 130.

69. See Commercial Paper, 7 Cyc. 686 note 74.

70. Stacy *v.* Kemp, 97 Mass. 166: Beman

the Lord's day will be recognized by the courts.[26] Although the contract also contemplates the doing of other acts on secular days, the illegality taints the whole contract and renders it void.[27] Although performance on Sunday of a valid contract will not be treated as a nullity,[28] it will not be given an independently affirmative effect beyond mere performance.[29]

VI. ACTIONS ON SUNDAY CONTRACTS AND TRANSACTIONS.

A. Right of Action — 1. EXISTENCE OF RIGHT — a. In General. It is frequently declared by the courts that no action can be maintained in a court of law or equity for the enforcement of, or relief from, Sunday contracts and transactions.[30] However, it has been held that an instrument executed on Sunday may be canceled in equity.[31] The courts will neither enforce such void contracts,[32] nor will they entertain actions to recover back the property sold or the consideration paid.[33] Thus one cannot recover for services performed on Sun-

Thus a contract contemplating that one of the parties shall take a train on Sunday to proceed to the place where he is to perform his services does not necessarily call for services on Sunday and will not be so interpreted. Goddard *v.* Morrissey, 172 Mass. 594, 53 N. E. 207.

The making of a payment on Sunday, which payment was not returned, will not invalidate the contract. Lamore *v.* Frisbie, 42 Mich. 186, 3 N. W. 910.

26. Carson *v.* Calhoun, 101 Me. 456, 64 Atl. 838.

27. Handy *v.* St. Paul Globe Pub. Co., 41 Minn. 188, 42 N. W. 872, 16 Am. St. Rep. 695, 4 L. R. A. 466; Hallen *v.* Thompson, 48 Misc. (N. Y.) 642, 96 N. Y. Suppl. 142. *Compare* Merritt *v.* Earle, 29 N. Y. 115, 86 Am. Dec. 292 [*affirming* 31 Barb. 38]. *Contra*, La Crandall *v.* Ledbetter, 159 Fed. 702, 86 C. C. A. 570.

28. Gordon *v.* Levine, 197 Mass. 263, 83 N. E. 861, 125 Am. St. Rep. 361, 15 L. R. A. N. S. 243.

29. Horn *v.* Dorchester Mut. F. Ins. Co., 199 Mass. 534, 85 N. E. 853.

30. *Alabama.*— Dodson *v.* Harris, 10 Ala. 566; O'Donnell *v.* Sweeney, 5 Ala. 467, 39 Am. Dec. 336.

Georgia.— Ellis *v.* Hammond, 57 Ga. 179.

Iowa.— Pike *v.* King, 16 Iowa 49.

Maine.— Morton *v.* Gloster, 46 Me. 520.

Massachusetts.— Gordon *v.* Levine, 197 Mass. 263, 83 N. E. 861, 125 Am. St. Rep. 361, 15 L. R. A. N. S. 243; Myers *v.* Meinrath, 101 Mass. 366, 3 Am. Rep. 368.

Mississippi.— Foster *v.* Wooten, 67 Miss. 540, 7 So. 501.

Pennsylvania.— Lee *v.* Drake, 10 Pa. Co. Ct. 276.

Tennessee.— Berry *v.* Planters' Bank, 3 Tenn. Ch. 69.

Vermont.—Adams *v.* Gay, 19 Vt. 358.

Wisconsin.— Jacobson *v.* Bentzler, 127 Wis. 566, 107 N. W. 7, 115 Am. St. Rep. 1052, 4 L. R. A. N. S. 1151; Pearson *v.* Kelly, 122 Wis. 660, 100 N. W. 1064.

See 45 Cent. Dig. tit. "Sunday," § 50.

Contra.— It has been held in Michigan that if one party to a Sunday contract performs his part of it on secular days and the other accepts what is done he must pay for what he receives. Bollin *v.* Hooper, 127 Mich. 287, 86 N. W. 795.

"**The ground** upon which courts have refused to maintain actions in contracts made in contravention of statutes for the observance of the Lord's day is the elementary principle that one who has himself participated in a violation of law cannot be permitted to assert in a court of justice any right founded upon or growing out of the illegal transaction." Gibbs, etc., Mfg. Co. *v.* Brucker, 111 U. S. 597, 601, 4 S. Ct. 572, 28 L. ed. 534.

A judgment entered on a judgment note bearing a Sunday date will not be stricken off because of its execution on Sunday. Hodgson *v.* Nesbit, 25 Pa. Co. Ct. 78. But equity will enjoin the collection of an unjust judgment obtained without defendant's knowledge after an agreement for settlement and discontinuance with plaintiff, although such agreement is void by reason of being made on Sunday. Blakesley *v.* Johnson, 13 Wis. 530.

Injunction.— The fact that plaintiff affixed his signature on Sunday to a petition for the issue of bonds to aid in the construction of a railroad will not prevent him from obtaining an injunction against the issue of the bonds on the ground that the required number of signatures were not affixed on any secular day. De Forth *v.* Wisconsin, etc., R. Co., 52 Wis. 320, 9 N. W. 17, 38 Am. Rep. 737.

31. Smith *v.* Pearson, 24 Ala. 355.

32. *Kentucky.*—Slade *v.* Arnold, 14 B. Mon. 287.

Missouri.— Bernard *v.* Lupping, 32 Mo. 341.

New Hampshire.—Allen *v.* Deming, 14 N. H. 133, 40 Am. Dec. 179.

New Jersey.— Crocket *v.* Vanderveer, 3 N. J. L. 856.

Ohio.— Fountain Square Theater Co. *v.* Evans, 4 Ohio S. & C. Pl. Dec. 151, 3 Ohio N. P. 245.

Pennsylvania.— Linden *v.* Hicks, 2 Luz. Leg. Reg. 101.

Wisconsin.— Pearson *v.* Kelly, 122 Wis. 660, 100 N. W. 1064.

See 45 Cent. Dig. tit. "Sunday," § 50.

33. See *supra*, V, I, 1, b.

the charge is for playing in a game on Sunday where an admission fee is charged, evidence of the payment of a fee to see the game by one or more persons is competent proof that a fee was charged, although other persons saw the game for nothing.[71]

4. Proof and Variance. The state is not limited in its proof to the particular day named in the indictment, but may show a violation of the law on any Sunday preceding the finding of the indictment and within the statute of limitations.[72] The proof need not be as broad as that charged in the indictment, provided a distinct violation of the law is shown.[73] Affirmative testimony as to the commission of the act charged controls over negative testimony as to defendant's general habits on Sunday.[74] Where a principal is sought to be made criminally liable for the act of his agent, either knowledge on his part must be shown [75] or such a habitual recurrence of the act that his assent is implied.[76] In general the proof must correspond with the allegations of the indictment,[77] and a conviction is not warranted when the evidence is so doubtful or conflicting as to raise a reasonable doubt concerning the guilt of defendant.[78] On the other hand, a conviction must be sustained where the evidence clearly shows a commission of the act prohibited by statute.[79]

D. Trial [80] — **1. Province of Court and Jury.**[81] It is for the jury to determine, under proper instructions from the court, whether defendant performed an act which brought him within the statute,[82] and whether the act was under the circum-

71. Heigert *v.* State, 37 Ind. App. 398, 75 N. E. 850.

72. *Arkansas.*— Marre *v.* State, 36 Ark. 222.

Connecticut.— State *v.* Brunker, 46 Conn. 327.

Georgia.— Seale *v.* State, 121 Ga. 741, 49 S. E. 740; Jackson *v.* State, 88 Ga. 787, 15 S. E. 905.

Massachusetts.— Com. *v.* Harrison, 11 Gray 308; Com. *v.* Newton, 8 Pick. 234.

North Carolina.— State *v.* Seaboard Air Line R. Co., 149 N. C. 508, 62 S. E. 1088.

West Virginia.— State *v.* Baltimore, etc., R. Co., 15 W. Va. 362, 36 Am. Rep. 803.

See 45 Cent. Dig. tit. "Sunday," § 70.

73. Com. *v.* Josselyn, 97 Mass. 411.

74. Elsner *v.* State, 30 Tex. 524.

75. Wetzler *v.* State, 18 Ind. 35.

76. State *v.* Baltimore, etc., R. Co., 15 W. Va. 362, 36 Am. Rep. 803.

77. McNealy *v.* State, 94 Ga. 592, 21 S. E. 581.

A verdict without any evidence to support it must be set aside as contrary to law. Westfall *v.* State, 4 Ga. App. 834, 62 S. E. 558.

78. Mayer *v.* State, 33 Ind. 203; Crawford *v.* State, (Tex. Cr. App. 1905) 89 S. W. 1079; Todd *v.* State, 30 Tex. App. 667, 18 S. W. 642; Reg. *v.* Howarth, 33 U. C. Q. B. 537.

Violation of bond.—Where one bought whisky on Saturday and it was delivered to him on Sunday, the fact that the seller violated a stipulation of his bond in selling to the purchaser in question would not authorize a conviction for violating the Sunday law. Crawford *v.* State, (Tex. Cr. App. 1905) 89 S. W. 1079.

Opening for ventilation.—A conviction for exposing and selling goods on Sunday is not sustained by evidence that nothing was sold on that day and that the door was open merely for the purpose of ventilation. City Council *v.* Talck, 3 Rich. (S. C.) 299.

79. Bennett *v.* State, 13 Ark. 694 (retailing); Seale *v.* State, 126 Ga. 644, 55 S. E. 472 (running freight train); Scandrett *v.* State, 124 Ga. 141, 52 S. E. 160 (selling); Gunn *v.* State, 89 Ga. 341, 15 S. E. 458; Savage *v.* State, (Tex. Cr. App. 1906) 93 S. W. 114 (selling); Armstrong *v.* State, 47 Tex. Cr. 510, 84 S. W. 827 (keeping open); Caskey *v.* State, (Tex. Cr. App. 1901) 62 S. W. 753 (keeping open). See also State *v.* Crabtree, 27 Mo. 232.

80. **Right to trial by jury** see Juries, 24 Cyc. 144 note 62.

Trial generally see Criminal Law, 12 Cyc. 504 *et seq.*

81. **Province of court and jury generally** see Criminal Law, 12 Cyc. 587.

82. Manning *v.* State, 6 Ga. App. 240, 64 S. E. 710; Heigert *v.* State, 37 Ind. App. 398, 75 N. E. 850 (holding that in a prosecution for playing baseball on Sunday, in a game where a fee was charged, the question whether an admission fee was charged, within the meaning of the statute, was properly submitted to the jury); State *v.* Atlantic Coast Line R. Co., 149 N. C. 470, 62 S. E. 755.

The purpose for which a person keeps open store on Sunday is necessarily a question of fact and intent to be found by the jury under proper instructions. Snider *v.* State, 59 Ala. 64.

Where the evidence strictly conforms to the charge that the common labor was that of operating a barber shop, then whether that conduct amounts to common labor is a matter of law for the magistrate to decide. *In re* Caldwell, 82 Nebr. 544, 118 N. W. 133.

show the calling of defendant or the specific act of worldly employment which he performed on the Sabbath.[96] However, it is sufficient if the form prescribed by statute is followed,[97] or if the description of the work appear in any part of the record.[98] Technical niceties are not required.[99] The evidence should be returned with, or made a part of, the record;[1] and when it appears from the evidence returned, but not made a part of the record, that the act done was one of necessity, the conviction will be reversed.[2]

E. Review.[3] Certiorari is the proper remedy to bring up a conviction obtained without jurisdiction.[4] On application for such a writ, new evidence cannot be taken to bolster up the lack of evidence of jurisdiction before the magistrate.[5] However, questions of fact within the magistrate's jurisdiction will not be reviewed on certiorari. Defendant's remedy, if any, is by appeal.[6] Habeas corpus is not a proper remedy for attacking the validity of the judgment of the trial court.[7]

X. JUDICIAL PROCEEDINGS AND OTHER OFFICIAL ACTS.

A. General Rule. It is universally recognized that, at common law, Sunday is *dies non juridicus*.[8] The prohibition of the common law extends only to judicial acts, and not to acts performed in a cause which were ministerial in their

96. Com. *v.* Antrim, 9 Pa. Dist. 374, 23 Pa. Co. Ct. 48, 15 Montg. Co. Rep. 212; Noftsker *v.* Com., 8 Pa. Dist. 572, 22 Pa. Co. Ct. 559; Sackville *v.* Com., 24 Pa. Co. Ct. 565; Com. *v.* Fuller, 4 Pa. Co. Ct. 429; Com. *v.* Kemery, 2 Leg. Chron. (Pa.) 321; Hespeler *v.* Shaw, 16 U. C. Q. B. 104.

Thus a record of a summary conviction, setting out that defendant pursued his worldly employment as a ticket agent of a certain railroad and sold tickets on a Sunday named, is defective in not stating what kind of tickets were sold, to whom sold, and for what purpose they were to be used. Com. *v.* Fuller, 4 Pa. Co. Ct. 429.

97. Com. *v.* Wolf, 3 Serg. & R. (Pa.) 48.

98. Johnston *v.* Com., 22 Pa. St. 102; Com. *v.* Johnston, 2 Am. L. Reg. (Pa.) 517.

99. Com. *v.* Jacobus, 1 Leg. Gaz. (Pa.) 491.

Surplusage.—When the judgment specifically states that the offense was committed on a certain Sunday, the additional designation of it as the "seventh" day may be disregarded as surplusage. New Castle *v.* Cummings, 36 Pa. Super. Ct. 443.

1. Com. *v.* Fuller, 4 Pa. Co. Ct. 429; Com. *v.* Patton, 4 Pa. Co. Ct. 135.

2. Com. *v.* Fields, 4 Pa. Co. Ct. 434.

3. **Appeal and error generally see** CRIMINAL LAW, 12 Cyc. 792.

4. Rex *v.* Canadian Pac. R. Co., 12 Can. Cr. Cas. 549; Hespeler *v.* Shaw, 16 U. C. Q. B. 104.

5. Rex *v.* Canadian Pac. R. Co., 12 Can. Cr. Cas. 549.

6. Reg. *v.* Urquhart, 4 Can. Cr. Cas. 256; Hespeler *v.* Shaw, 16 U. C. Q. B. 104.

In Pennsylvania the court of quarter sessions, and not the court of common pleas, has jurisdiction of an appeal. Com. *v.* Rosenthal, 3 Pa. Co. Ct. 26.

In British Columbia the judgment of the county court judge reviewing a conviction before a magistrate is final, and no appeal lies from his decision. *Re* Lambert, 7 Brit. Col. 396, construing the Provincial Summary Convictions Act.

Jury trial on appeal.— On appeal from a summary conviction to the quarter sessions, 13 & 14 Vict. c. 54, authorizes a trial by jury. Hespeler *v.* Shaw, 16 U. C. Q. B. 104.

Appeal as waiver of defects.— In New Castle *v.* Cummings, 36 Pa. Super. Ct. 443, it was held that, as defendant had appealed from the judgment of the mayor and gone to trial in the court of quarter sessions, he must be deemed to have waived any defects in the information which were not substantial and jurisdictional.

7. *In re* Caldwell, 82 Nebr. 544, 118 N. W. 133, holding that the judgment of guilty carried with it of necessity the judgment of the magistrate that the complaint charged defendant with unlawfully engaging in common labor on Sunday, and that he was not within any of the exceptions of the statute.

8. *Alabama.*— Matthews *v.* Ansley, 31 Ala. 20; Nabors *v.* State, 6 Ala. 200; Haynes *v.* Sledge, 2 Port. 530, 27 Am. Dec. 665.

Arkansas.— Tucker *v.* West, 29 Ark. 386.

California.— Sacramento County Reclamation Dist. No. 535 *v.* Hamilton, 112 Cal. 603, 44 Pac. 1074.

Georgia.— Sawyer *v.* Cargile, 72 Ga. 290; Neal *v.* Crew, 12 Ga. 93.

Illinois.— Scammon *v.* Chicago, 40 Ill. 146; Johnston *v.* People, 31 Ill. 469; Baxter *v.* People, 8 Ill. 368.

Indiana.— Qualter *v.* State, 120 Ind. 92, 22 N. E. 100; Cory *v.* Silcox, 5 Ind. 370; Chapman *v.* State, 5 Blackf. 111.

Iowa.— Davis *v.* Fish, 1 Greene 406, 48 Am. Dec. 387.

Kansas.— Parsons *v.* Lindsay, 41 Kan. 336, 21 Pac. 227, 13 Am. St. Rep. 290, 3 L. R. A. 658.

Kentucky.— Meece *v.* Com., 78 Ky. 586.

Maine.— State *v.* Conwell, 96 Me. 172, 51 Atl. 873, 90 Am. St. Rep. 333.

Massachusetts.— Johnson *v.* Day, 17 Pick. 106; Pearce *v.* Atwood, 13 Mass. 324.

good, although it has been dated on Sunday.[26] A notice of the examination of a witness is good, although given on Sunday.[27] On the other hand, it has been held that the service on Sunday of notice of a motion [28] or of plea filed [29] is irregular and void; as is also a notice to take a deposition on Sunday.[30]

c. **Publication.** The weight of authority supports the proposition that the publication, in whole or in part, of a summons or other legal notice in a newspaper published on Sunday is invalid.[31] A notice required to be published each day for a week need not be published on Sunday.[32]

d. **Process or Notice Returnable on Sunday.** As courts do not sit on Sunday, a process or notice returnable on that day is void and no proceedings may be had thereon.[33]

2. **Criminal.** Both at common law and under statute warrants may issue and arrests be made on Sunday.[34] In those jurisdictions where the service of a warrant of arrest on the Sabbath is forbidden by statute,[35] exception is made in the cases of treason, felony, and breach of the peace.[36] Even under these

26. Taylor *v.* Thomas, 2 N. J. Eq. 106.

27. State *v.* Ryan, 113 Iowa 536, 85 N. W. 812.

28. Field *v.* Park, 20 Johns. (N. Y.) 140.

29. Roberts *v.* Monkhouse, 8 East 547, 9 Rev. Rep. 497, 103 Eng. Reprint 453.

30. Sloan *v.* Williford, 25 N. C. 307.

31. *Colorado.*— Schwed *v.* Hartwitz, 23 Colo. 187, 47 Pac. 295, 58 Am. St. Rep. 221.

Georgia.— Sawyer *v.* Cargile, 72 Ga. 290.

Illinois.— Scammon *v.* Chicago, 40 Ill. 146.

Indiana.— Shaw *v.* Williams, 87 Ind. 158, 44 Am. Rep. 756.

Kentucky.— Ormsby *v.* Louisville, 79 Ky. 197, 2 Ky. L. Rep. 66; Brannin *v.* Louisville, 2 Ky. L. Rep. 384.

South Dakota.— McLaughlin *v.* Wheeler, 2 S. D. 379, 50 N. W. 834.

See 45 Cent. Dig. tit. "Sunday," § 77.

Contra.— Heisen *v.* Smith, 138 Cal. 216, 71 Pac. 180, 94 Am. St. Rep. 39; Savings, etc., Soc. *v.* Thompson, 32 Cal. 347 (holding that a part publication in a Sunday newspaper did not vitiate the service); Nixon *v.* Burlington, 141 Iowa 316, 115 N. W. 239; Schenck *v.* Schenck, 52 La. Ann. 2102, 28 So. 302; Hastings *v.* Columbus, 42 Ohio St. 585 (holding that, under the Ohio statute, a summons may be served on Sunday, and that the publication of an ordinance is of a similar nature).

The burden of showing that the publication comes within the terms of the Sunday statute is on defendant. Harrison *v.* Wallis, 44 Misc. (N. Y.) 492, 90 N. Y. Suppl. 44.

32. Matter of Excelsior F. Ins. Co., 16 Abb. Pr. (N. Y.) 8 [*reversed* on other grounds in 38 Barb. 297, 16 Abb. Pr. 11].

33. McRee *v.* McRee, 34 Ala. 165; Peck *v.* Cavell, 16 Mich. 9; Arctic F. Ins. Co. *v.* Hicks, 7 Abb. Pr. (N. Y.) 204; Boyd *v.* Vanderkemp, 1 Barb. Ch. (N. Y.) 273; Gould *v.* Spencer, 5 Paige (N. Y.) 541; Swann *v.* Broome, 3 Burr. 1595, 97 Eng. Reprint 999. holding that a defendant cannot be misled by a notice to appear on Sunday, as the notice must necessarily relate to Monday, when the court does sit. See also Loveridge *v.* Plaistow, 2 H. Bl. 29.

The proceeding to effect a statutory foreclosure of a mortgage is not a judicial proceeding and hence it is not invalidated by the fact that the day appointed in the published notice is Sunday. Sayles *v.* Smith, 12 Wend. (N. Y.) 57, 27 Am. Dec. 117.

Intervention of Sunday in computation of time which must elapse before summons in justice's court is returnable see Justices of the Peace, 24 Cyc. 519 note 96.

34. *Alabama.*— Parish *v.* State, 130 Ala. 92, 30 So. 474.

Connecticut.—Ward *v.* Green, 11 Conn. 455.

Georgia.— Weldon *v.* Colquitt, 62 Ga. 449, 35 Am. Rep. 128.

Kentucky.— Watts *v.* Com., 5 Bush 309; Rice *v.* Com., 3 Bush 14.

Maine.— State *v.* Conwell, 96 Me. 172, 51 Atl. 873, 90 Am. St. Rep. 333 (search warrant); Keith *v.* Tuttle, 28 Me. 326.

Massachusetts.—Wright *v.* Dressel, 140 Mass. 147, 3 N. E. 6 (search warrant); Pearce *v.* Atwood, 13 Mass. 324 (holding, however, that an arrest for violation of the Sabbath laws could not lawfully be made on Sunday).

Canada.— *Re* McGillivray, 13 Can. Cr. Cas. 113, 41 Nova Scotia 321; Reg. *v.* Cavelier, 11 Manitoba 333.

See 45 Cent. Dig. tit. "Sunday," § 79.

35. Wood *v.* Brooklyn, 14 Barb. (N. Y.) 425; Wilson *v.* Tucker, 1 Salk. 78, 91 Eng. Reprint 74; Matter of Eggington, 2 C. L. R. 385, 2 E. & B. 717, 18 Jur. 224, 23 L. J. M. C. 41, 2 Wkly. Rep. 10, 76, 75 E. C. L. 717.

Where a prisoner is regularly discharged on Saturday, he cannot be lawfully arrested in another suit on Sunday. Atkinson *v.* Jameson, 5 T. R. 25, 101 Eng. Reprint 14.

36. *Ex p.* Carroll, 9 Ohio Dec. (Reprint) 261, 12 Cinc. L. Bul. 9; Com. *v.* De Puyter, 16 Pa. Co. St. 589; Corbett *v.* Sullivan, 54 Vt. 619.

English statute construed.— In Rawlins *v.* Ellis, 10 Jur. 1039, 16 L. J. Exch. 5, 16 M. & W. 172, it was held that 29 Car. II, c. 7, § 6, authorizes the arrest on a Sunday of all persons who have been guilty of an indictable offense.

SUPERNUMERARY. A term used during the period of the Revolution, to designate an officer who was thrown out and became unattached by the breaking up or consolidation of his regiment.[33]

SUPERPHOSPHATE. A fertilizer prepared by treating ground bones, bone black, or phosphoric with sulphuric acid, whereby a portion of the insoluble phosphoric acid is rendered soluble in water.[34]

SUPERSEDE. To set aside; to annul.[35] (See SUPERSEDEAS, *post*, p. 596.)

constitutes "superior force," which no prudent administrator of the affairs of a corporation could resist, so that the bank was neither responsible for such proceedings nor for a loss occasioned thereby. McLemore *v.* Louisiana State Bank, 91 U. S. 27, 29, 23 L. ed. 196.

33. Williams *v.* U. S., 137 U. S. 113, 127, 11 S. Ct. 43, 34 L. ed. 590.

"**He is just as much an officer** as any other: but his battalion or corps has been reduced or disbanded, or so arranged in some way, as to leave him, for the present, no command; and the state, to save the expence of full pay and subsistence, discharges him from actual service." Com. *v.* Lilly, 1 Leigh (Va.) 525, 529.

34. Webster Dict. [*quoted* in Goodman *v.* Beard, 93 S. W. 666, 667, 29 Ky. L. Rep. 544].

35. New River Mineral Co. *v.* Seeley, 117 Fed. 981, 982, where it is said: "An order which sets aside or annuls a decree dissolving an injunction must *ipso facto* reinstate the injunction."

"**In a military sense** 'to be superseded' means to have one put in the place, which, by the ordinary course of military promotion, belongs to another." *Ex p.* Hall, 1 Pick. (Mass.) 261, 262.

For Matters Relating to — (*continued*)
Stay of — (*continued*)
Proceedings Pending Appeal — (*continued*)
In Summary Proceedings by Landlord For Possession, see LANDLORD AND TENANT, 24 Cyc. 1455.
Proceedings Pending Review, see REVIEW, 34 Cyc. 1715 notes 65, 66.
Supersedeas as Subject of Relief by Mandamus, see MANDAMUS, 26 Cyc. 216.

I. DEFINITION.

A supersedeas is in practice a writ containing a command to stay a proceeding at law.[1] Originally it was a writ directed to an officer, commanding him to desist from enforcing the execution of another writ which he was about to execute, or which might come in his hands.[2] In modern times the term is often used synonymously with a "stay of proceedings;"[3] and by an extension of the term it has come to be used as a designation of the effect of any proceeding or act in a cause, which, of its own force, causes a suspension or stay of proceedings.[4]

II. NATURE AND SCOPE OF REMEDY.

A. Nature of Remedy. A proceeding by supersedeas is not a proceeding at common law in the strict sense of that term.[5] It is said to be a substitute for the writ of audita querela;[6] and the same rule which governs the one, regulates the other, with but slight exceptions.[7] The writ and the proceeding on which it is founded are regarded as in the nature of a bill in equity,[8] where the matter of discharge set forth in the petition does not appear in the record.[9] While a supersedeas is in one sense a continuation of the original suit,[10] yet in another sense it is the commencement of a new suit, and it is generally so regarded.[11]

B. Scope of Remedy. The primary and principal object of the remedy by the writ of supersedeas is to prevent the abuse of the process of the court.[12] In a proceeding for a supersedeas, that which forms the ground for relief must either

1. Bouvier L. Dict.

Other definitions are: "A writ ordering the suspension or superseding of another writ previously issued." Black L. Dict.

"A writ issued for the purpose of relieving a party from the operation of another writ, which has been or may be issued against him." Burrill L. Dict.

The term signifies, in general, the command to stay some ordinary proceeding at law, on good cause shown, which ought otherwise to proceed. Perteet *v.* People, 70 Ill. 171, 177 [*citing* Jacob L. Dict.]

2. Dulin *v.* Pacific Wood, etc., Co., 98 Cal. 304, 306, 33 Pac. 123; Tyler *v.* Presley, 72 Cal. 290, 291, 13 Pac. 856 [*citing* Abbott L. Dict.; Burrill L. Dict.]; Black L. Dict.; Bouvier L. Dict.

3. Dulin *v.* Pacific Wood, etc., Co., 98 Cal. 304, 306, 33 Pac. 123; Bouvier L. Dict. See APPEAL AND ERROR, 2 Cyc. 885 *et seq.*

4. Dulin *v.* Pacific Wood, etc., Co., 98 Cal. 304, 306, 33 Pac. 123; Black L. Dict.; Bouvier L. Dict.

5. Mobile Branch Bank *v.* Coleman, 20 Ala. 140.

6. Thompson *v.* Lassiter, 86 Ala. 536, 6 So. 33; Payne *v.* Thompson, 48 Ala. 535; Pearsall *v.* McCartney, 28 Ala. 110; Bruce *v.* Barnes, 20 Ala. 219; Mobile Branch Bank *v.* Coleman, 20 Ala. 140; Dunlap *v.* Clements, 18 Ala. 778; Edwards *v.* Lewis, 16 Ala. 813; Rutland *v.* Pippin, 7 Ala. 469; Lockhart *v.* McElroy, 4 Ala. 572; Marsh *v.* Haywood, 6 Humphr. (Tenn.) 210.

Audita querela see AUDITA QUERELA, 4 Cyc. 1058.

In Alabama the writ of audita querela has gone into disuse, and the proceeding by petition and supersedeas has been substituted for it. Dunlap *v.* Clements, 18 Ala. 778; Lockhart *v.* McElroy, 4 Ala. 572.

7. Mobile Branch Bank *v.* Coleman, 20 Ala. 140.

8. Thompson *v.* Lassiter, 86 Ala. 536, 6 So. 33; Mobile Branch Bank *v.* Coleman, 20 Ala. 140.

A proceeding by supersedeas is preferable to a bill in equity, as it saves the right of trial by jury and is more speedy and less expensive. Dunlap *v.* Clements, 18 Ala. 778.

9. Jesse French Piano, etc., Co. *v.* Bradley, 143 Ala. 530, 39 So. 47; Mobile Branch Bank *v.* Coleman, 20 Ala. 140.

10. Nadenbousch *v.* Sharer, 2 W. Va. 285.

11. Pearsall *v.* McCartney, 28 Ala. 110; Edwards *v.* Lewis, 16 Ala. 813; Shearer *v.* Boyd, 10 Ala. 279; Nadenbousch *v.* Sharer, 2 W. Va. 285.

12. Jesse French Piano, etc., Co. *v.* Bradley, 143 Ala. 530, 39 So. 47; Mobile Branch Bank *v.* Coleman, 20 Ala. 140; Lockhart *v.* McElroy, 4 Ala. 572.

supersede the orders and decrees of inferior courts does not authorize the supreme court to supervise the discretion of a chancellor in the exercise of a conceded power for the protection of property *pendente lite*.[25] That court can simply suspend or supersede, for the time being, the execution of such orders and decrees as are of a nature to be actively and affirmatively enforced,[26] and are *in fieri*;[27] but have no power, in this mode, to reverse the action of the inferior court, or to set aside, or annul, or supersede orders or decrees, which are merely of a negative or prohibitory character,[28] or such as have been executed.[29] Nor has the supreme court, in a proceeding of this character, the power to supersede the fiat of a chancellor awarding extraordinary process.[30]

IV. JURISDICTION AND AUTHORITY TO GRANT SUPERSEDEAS.[31]

A court has authority, under its general powers, to supersede its own executions in a proper case, especially when it has general jurisdiction of the subject.[32] The subject is, however, usually regulated by statute.[33] Thus in some states the judges of the circuit court may issue the writ of supersedeas in vacation, returnable to the court in term-time.[34] But a circuit court judge has no power or jurisdiction to grant an order for supersedeas to the judgments or decrees of the supreme

25. Roberson *v.* Roberson, 3 Lea (Tenn.) 50; Bramley *v.* Tyree, 1 Lea (Tenn.) 531; Baird *v.* Cumberland, etc., Turnpike Co., 1 Lea (Tenn.) 394.

Appointment of receiver.—Where the court has the discretionary power to appoint a receiver, the order making the appointment cannot be reversed by the supreme court on writ of supersedeas. Troughber *v.* Akin, 109 Tenn. 451, 73 S. W. 118; Enochs *v.* Wilson, 11 Lea (Tenn.) 228; Roberson *v.* Roberson, 3 Lea (Tenn.) 50; Bramley *v.* Tyree, 1 Lea (Tenn.) 531; Baird *v.* Cumberland, etc., Turnpike Co., 1 Lea (Tenn.) 394. Matters of mere form, not going to the jurisdiction of the chancellor to appoint the receiver, cannot in general be considered when collaterally presented. Troughber *v.* Akin, *supra*. But if the court had not the power to appoint a receiver, the supreme court may supersede the appointment. Roberson *v.* Roberson, *supra*; Baird *v.* Cumberland, etc., Turnpike Co., 1 Lea (Tenn.) 394; Richmond *v.* Yates, 3 Baxt. (Tenn.) 204; Cone *v.* Paute, 12 Heisk. (Tenn.) 506.

26. Blake *v.* Dodge, 8 Lea (Tenn.) 465; Roberson *v.* Roberson, 3 Lea (Tenn.) 50; Baird *v.* Cumberland, etc., Turnpike Co., 1 Lea (Tenn.) 394; Redmond *v.* Redmond, 9 Baxt. (Tenn.) 561; McMinnville, etc., R. Co. *v.* Huggins, 7 Coldw. (Tenn.) 217.

27. Redmond *v.* Redmond, 9 Baxt. (Tenn.) 561.

28. Redmond *v.* Redmond, 9 Baxt. (Tenn.) 561; McMinnville, etc., R. Co. *v.* Huggins, 7 Coldw. (Tenn.) 217.

An injunction is a prohibitory writ, and its office is to restrain, and not to compel, performance. It does not authorize any act to be done; and there can be no proceeding under it capable of being stayed by a supersedeas. Baird *v.* Cumberland, etc., Turnpike Co., 1 Lea (Tenn.) 394; Park *v.* Meek, 1 Lea (Tenn.) 78; Redmond *v.* Redmond, 9 Baxt. (Tenn.) 561; McMinnville, etc., R. Co. *v.* Huggins, 7 Coldw. (Tenn.) 217; Mabry *v.* Ross, 1 Heisk. (Tenn.) 769.

Other illustrations.—Under the authority given to the supreme court by Tenn. Code, §§ 3833, 3934, 4512, 4513, authorizing the court to supersede interlocutory orders and decrees, that court cannot supersede the decree of a chancellor refusing to dismiss a bill upon motion; nor a decree refusing to quash attachments and discharge levies, such orders being of a mere negative or prohibitory character. Redmond *v.* Redmond, 9 Baxt. (Tenn.) 561.

29. Redmond *v.* Redmond, 9 Baxt. (Tenn.) 561.

30. Woods *v.* Batey, 15 Lea (Tenn.) 733; Baird *v.* Cumberland, etc., Turnpike Co., 1 Lea (Tenn.) 394; Redmond *v.* Redmond, 9 Baxt. (Tenn.) 561.

The appointment of a receiver is ordinarily in the nature of extraordinary process. Baird *v.* Cumberland, etc., Turnpike Co., 1 Lea (Tenn.) 394.

31. To allow stay pending appeal see APPEAL AND ERROR, 2 Cyc. 891 *et seq.*

32. Payne *v.* Thompson, 48 Ala. 535; Lockhart *v.* McElroy, 4 Ala. 572.

33. In Alabama the practice is regulated by statute. Aiken Dig. 208, § 38.

34. *Ex p.* Pearl Roller Mill Co., 154 Ala. 232, 45 So. 423.

In Alabama there is an act declaring that "the Judges of the Circuit Courts respectively shall have power and authority in vacation to supersede any execution when it shall satisfactorily appear to them that the same shall have improperly issued from the clerk's office of any of the Circuit Courts." Lockhart *v.* McElroy, 4 Ala. 572.

In New York, an application, under 2 Rev. St. p. 556, §§ 36, 37, for an order of supersedeas, may be made to a judge of the first district, although the action is triable elsewhere. Wells *v.* Jones, 2 Abb. Pr. 20; Sturgess *v.* Weed, 13 How. Pr. 130.

ipal Corporations, see MUNICIPAL CORPORATIONS, 28 Cyc. 281. Of Prisons, see PRISONS, 32 Cyc. 318. Of Private Schools, see SCHOOLS AND SCHOOL-DISTRICTS, 35 Cyc. 814. Of Public Schools, see SCHOOLS AND SCHOOL-DISTRICTS, 35 Cyc. 817 *et seq.* Of Public Water-Supply, see WATERS. Of Railroads, see RAILROADS, 33 Cyc. 44, 45. Of Receivers, see RECEIVERS, 34 Cyc. 246. Of Referees, see REFERENCES, 34 Cyc. 829. Of Religious Societies, see RELIGIOUS SOCIETIES, 34 Cyc. 1182. Of Telegraph or Telephone Companies, see TELEGRAPHS AND TELEPHONES. Of Trustees, see TRUSTS. Of Warehouses, see WAREHOUSEMEN. Of Wharves, see WHARVES. Of Work, see MASTER AND SERVANT, 26 Cyc. 1292, 1549, 1565.)

SUPERVISOR. One who supervises; an OVERSEER, *q. v.*; an INSPECTOR, *q. v.*; a SUPERINTENDENT,[10] *q. v.* (Supervisor: Of County — In General, see COUNTIES, 11 Cyc. 380; Appointment of Drainage Commissioners by, see DRAINS, 14 Cyc. 1037. Of Election, see ELECTIONS, 15 Cyc. 310. Of Highways, see STREETS AND HIGHWAYS, *ante*, p. 212. Of Roads, Obstructing or Interfering With Performance of Duties of, see OBSTRUCTING JUSTICE, 29 Cyc. 1331 note 40. Of the Poor, see PAUPERS, 30 Cyc. 1068. Of Town, see TOWNS.)

SUPERVISORY CONTROL. A phrase commonly used to designate the jurisdiction of a higher court over an inferior one, and especially when referring to the actions of the latter in probate matters.[11]

SUPER VISUM CORPORIS. Literally "Upon view of the body."[12] (See CORONERS, 9 Cyc. 988.)

SUPPLEMENT. As a noun, a supplying by addition of what is wanting;[13] that which supplies a deficiency; that which fills up, completes or makes an addition to something already organized, arranged or set apart; a part added to or a continuation of;[14] that which supplies a deficiency, or meets a want; a STORE, *q. v.*; a SUPPLY, *q. v.*; that which fills up or completes something already organized, arranged or set apart specifically, something added to a book or paper to make good its deficiencies or correct its errors.[15] As a verb, to fill up or supply by addition; to add to.[16]

SUPPLEMENTAL. Something added to supply defects in the thing to which it is added, or in aid of which it is made;[17] something additional; something added to supply what is wanting;[18] that which supplies a deficiency or meets a want.[19] (Supplemental: Abstract of Record, see APPEAL AND ERROR, 3 Cyc. 89. Affidavit For Attachment, see ATTACHMENT, 4 Cyc. 521 note 76. Answer or Affidavit of

10. Century Dict.; Webster Dict. [both *quoted* in New York L. Ins. Co. *v.* Rhodes, 4 Ga. App. 25, 30, 60 S. E. 828].

Used to indicate an agent of an insurance company, the term embraces general agency, carrying with it authority to bind the company. New York L. Ins. Co. *v.* Rhodes. 4 Ga. App. 25, 30, 60 S. E. 828.

"The word . . . when applied to county officers, has a legal signification. The duties of the officer are various and manifold; sometimes judicial, and at others, legislative and executive. From the necessity of the case, it would be impossible to reconcile them to any particular head, and, therefore, in matters relating to the police and fiscal regulations of counties, they are allowed to perform such duties as may be enjoined upon them by law, without any nice examination into the exact character of the powers conferred." People *v.* El Dorado County, 8 Cal. 58, 62; State *v.* Armsby County, 7 Nev. 392, 397.

11. *In re* McIntyre, 1 Alaska 73, 79. See also *In re* Weston, 28 Mont. 207, 217, 72 Pac. 512.

12. Black L. Dict. See also Moran *v.* Territory, 14 Okla. 544, 551, 78 Pac. 111; Reg. *v.* Hammond, 1 Can. Cr. Cas. 373, 395.

13. Rahway Sav. Inst. *v.* Rahway, 53 N. J. L. 48, 51, 20 Atl. 756, where such is said to be the ordinary meaning of the term.

14. Webster Dict. [*quoted* in State *v.* Wyandot County, 16 Ohio Cir. Ct. 218, 221, 9 Ohio Cir. Dec. 90], where it is said: "It is used sometimes as a synonym of appendix." See also McCleary *v.* Babcock, 169 Ind. 228, 233, 82 N. E. 453.

15. Webster Dict. [*quoted* in Lancaster Intelligencer *v.* Lancaster County, 9 Pa. Dist. 392, 394].

16. Webster Dict. [*quoted* in Lancaster Intelligencer *v.* Lancaster County, 9 Pa. Dist. 392, 394].

17. Rapalje & L. L. Dict. [*quoted* in Lancaster Intelligencer *v.* Lancaster County, 9 Pa. Dist. 392, 394].

18. Webster Dict. [*quoted* in McCleary *v.* Babcock, 169 Ind. 228, 233, 82 N. E. 453].

19. Webster Dict. [*quoted* in Loomis *v.* Runge, 66 Fed. 856, 859, 14 C. C. A. 148, where an act of the legislature was construed as supplemental rather than mandatory].

SUPPLY or **SUPPLIES.**[23] As a noun, that which is or can be supplied; available aggregate of things needed or demanded; an amount sufficient for a given use or purpose;[24] anything yielded or afforded to meet a want;[25] an amount sufficient for a given use or purpose;[26] such stores of food, etc., as are kept on hand for daily use;[27] necessaries collected and held for distribution and use;[28] that which is supplied; sufficiency of things for use or want; a quantity of something furnished or on hand;[29] the act of furnishing with what is wanted;[30] that which supplies a want; sufficiency of things for use or want; especially the food, and the like, which meets the daily necessities of an army or other large body of men.[31] As a verb, to make provision for; to provide; to serve instead of; to take the place of.[32] (Supply or Supplies: Agricultural Lien For, see AGRICULTURE, 2 Cyc. 56. Allowance to Sheriff or Constable For Office, see SHERIFFS AND CONSTABLES, 35 Cyc. 1587. Exemption of, see EXEMPTIONS, 18 Cyc. 1423. Extra Wages to Seamen as Compensation For Insufficiency of, see SEAMEN, 35 Cyc. 1213. For Prison, Purchase of, see PRISONS, 32 Cyc. 328. Furnished by Husband For Wife's Business, see HUSBAND AND WIFE, 21 Cyc. 1439 note 40. Of Electric Power or Light, see ELECTRICITY, 15 Cyc. 468. Of Gas, see GAS, 20 Cyc. 1160. Of Water, see MUNICIPAL CORPORATIONS, 28 Cyc. 636; WATERS. Power of — Clerk of Court to Purchase, see CLERKS OF COURTS, 7 Cyc. 224; Municipality to Levy Tax For, see

23. **Derived from** *sub*, meaning under, *plere*, to fill. *In re* Hazle Tp., 6 Kulp (Pa.) 491, 493.

As a noun it is generally used in the plural. *In re* Hazle Tp., 6 Kulp (Pa.) 491, 493.

24. Strickland *v.* Stiles, 107 Ga. 308, 310, 33 S. E. 85; Standard Dict. [*quoted* in Fuller *v.* Schrenk, 58 N. Y. App. Div. 222, 227, 68 N. Y. Suppl. 781].

As used in reference to a city, in its broad etymological sense, the term embraces anything which is furnished to a city or its inhabitants; but as used in the Greater New York Charter, requiring competitive bids for supplies, it has no application to contracts for furnishing water to the inhabitants of New York. Gleason *v.* Dalton, 28 N. Y. App. Div. 555, 557, 51 N. Y. Suppl. 337.

In reference to a plantation the term has been said to indicate all those things required and used by the planter in the production and preparation of the crops for consumption or for sale. Wright *v.* Walton, 56 Miss. 1, 6.

25. Farmers' L. & T. Co. *v.* New York, 4 Bosw. (N. Y.) 80, 89.

26. Waymart Water Co. *v.* Waymart, 4 Pa. Super. Ct. 211, 220, where such is said to be the primary meaning of the term.

27. Conner *v.* Littlefield, 79 Tex. 76, 77, 15 S. W. 217 [*citing* Webster Dict.].

28. Boston Blower Co. *v.* Carman Lumber Co., 94 Va. 94, 99, 26 S. E. 390.

29. Imperial Dict. [*quoted* in Fuller *v.* Schrenk, 58 N. Y. App. Div. 222, 228, 68 N. Y. Suppl. 781].

30. Webster Dict. [*quoted* in *In re* Hazle Tp., 6 Kulp (Pa.) 491, 493].

31. Webster Dict. [*quoted* in People *v.* Pullman's Palace Car Co., 175 Ill. 125, 155, 51 N. E. 664, 64 L. R. A. 366].

As applied to a vessel, in its ordinary acceptation, a term understood to mean those articles which a boat may find it necessary to purchase for consumption and use on the voyage. Gibbons *v.* The Fanny Barker, 40 Mo. 253, 255.

Has been held to include: Board furnished by a landlord to his tenant. Jones *v.* Eubanks, 86 Ga. 616, 619, 12 S. E. 1065. Money furnished by a landlord and used by a tenant in making and gathering his crop. Strickland *v.* Stiles, 107 Ga. 308, 310, 33 S. E. 85. Mules sold by a landlord to a tenant for the cultivation of his crop. Trimble *v.* Durham, 70 Miss. 295, 297, 12 So. 207. See also Robertson *v.* Ward, 12 Sm. & M. (Miss.) 490, 491. Pencils, paper, rubber bands, blanks, ink, and articles of that description, required and constantly used by county officers, as used in a statute regulating the making of contracts for supplies for county officers. Dewell *v.* Hughes County, 8 S. D. 452, 454, 66 N. W. 1079. Powder or dynamite used in the construction of a railroad, or fuses to set off the powder, shovels and carts and the like, under a statute giving a lien to persons furnishing supplies for the construction of a railroad. Carson *v.* Shelton, 128 Ky. 248, 250, 107 S. W. 793, 32 Ky. L. Rep. 1083, 15 L. R. A. N. S. 509. Wines and liquors, under an authority granted a sleeping car company to sell supplies to persons traveling on its cars. People *v.* Pullman's Palace Car Co., 175 Ill. 125, 155, 51 N. E. 664, 64 L. R. A. 366.

Does not include: A kiln for drying lumber under a statute giving a lien for "supplies necessary" furnished to certain class of corporations. Boston Blower Co. *v.* Carman Lumber Co., 94 Va. 94, 99, 26 S. E. 390. A pier hired by a city for the purpose of casting away offal, under a city charter providing that supplies furnished the city, involving the expenditure of more than a named amount, must be by contract founded on sealed bids, etc. Farmers' L. & T. Co. *v.* New York, 4 Bosw. (N. Y.) 80, 89. Sawed logs. Connor *v.* Littlefield, 79 Tex. 76, 77, 15 S. W. 217.

32. Century Dict. [*quoted* in Reading *v.* Shepp, 2 Pa. Dist. 137, 140, where in construing a statute the court held that the word was used in the sense of taking the place of the former].

Primary sense.— In a city ordinance **grant-**

beyond what is prescribed or wanted in law; the residue of an estate after the debts and legacies are paid;[62] that which is left from a fund which has been appropriated for a particular purpose; the remainder of a thing; the overplus; the RESIDUE,[63] *q. v.* (Surplus: Agreement to Account For as Making Deed Mortgage, see MORTGAGES, 27 Cyc. 1004. Of County Funds Raised For Special Purpose, Appropriation to General Purposes, see COUNTIES, 11 Cyc. 583. Of Insurance Company — Distribution of, see INSURANCE, 22 Cyc. 1402; Liability to Taxation, see TAXATION; Mode of Assessment For Taxation, see TAXATION. Of Judicial Sale as Property Subject to Judgment Lien, see JUDGMENTS, 23 Cyc. 1371 note 20. Of Tax-Sale, see TAXATION. On Dissolution of Bank, see BANKS AND BANKING, 5 Cyc. 573. On Enforcement of Pledge, see PLEDGES, 31 Cyc. 864. On Foreclosure of Mortgage — In General, see CHATTEL MORTGAGES, 7 Cyc. 116; MORTGAGES, 27 Cyc. 1497, 1767; Lien of Attachment on, see ATTACHMENTS, 4 Cyc. 627 note 56. On Sale of Property — By Executor or Administrator Under Order of Court, see EXECUTORS AND ADMINISTRATORS, 18 Cyc. 841; In Attachment Proceedings, see ATTACHMENT, 4 Cyc. 718; In Distress Proceedings, see LANDLORD AND TENANT, 24 Cyc. 1323; Subject to Dower, see DOWER, 14 Cyc. 900; To Enforce Vendor's Lien, see VENDOR AND PURCHASER; Under Execution, see EXECUTIONS, 17 Cyc. 1359; Under Mechanic's Lien, see MECHANICS' LIENS, 27 Cyc. 451; Upon Setting Aside Fraudulent Conveyance, see FRAUDULENT CONVEYANCES, 20 Cyc. 827. On Sale of Railroads Under Foreclosure of Liens or Mortgages, see RAILROADS, 33 Cyc. 606. On Tax-Sale, see TAXATION. Reservation of — Effect on Assignment For Benefit of Creditors, see ASSIGNMENTS FOR BENEFIT OF CREDITORS, 4 Cyc. 184; Effect on Conveyance, see FRAUDULENT CONVEYANCES, 20 Cyc. 561, 568; To Debtor in Insolvency Proceedings, see INSOLVENCY, 22 Cyc. 1355. Right of — Creditor of Tenant to After Satisfaction of Landlord's Lien, see LANDLORD AND TENANT, 24 Cyc. 1264; Owner to on Sale of Land For Taxes, see INTERNAL REVENUE, 22 Cyc. 1610; TAXATION. When Capital Stock of Corporation Deemed to Include, see CORPORATIONS, 10 Cyc. 365.)

explained by extrinsic evidence. Western Union R. Co. *v.* Smith, 75 Ill. 496, 502.

62. State *v.* Parker, 35 N. J. L. 575, 577.

"Surplus personalty" left by decedent, as meaning what is left after payment of funeral expenses, charges of administration and debts see Towery *v.* McGaw, 56 S. W. 727, 728, 982, 22 Ky. L. Rep. 155. See also Coates' Appeal, 2 Pa. St. 129, 137.

In a will directing the payment of certain legacies out of the residue of testator's estate and providing that "if, after the payment of these legacies, there should remain any surplus undisposed of, I give and bequeath the same unto my sons," etc., the term includes real estate. Lamb *v.* Lamb, 131 N. Y. 227, 236, 30 N. E. 133. But see Allen *v.* Allen, 18 How. (U. S.) 385, 391, 15 L. ed. 396, where the term was held not to include real estate.

63. Bouvier L. Dict. [*quoted* in State *v.* Butler County, 77 Kan. 527, 536, 94 Pac. 1004]. See also McConnell *v.* Allen, 120 N. Y. App. Div. 548, 551, 105 N. Y. Suppl. 16.

In the nomenclature of bankers the term does not include "undivided profits." Leather Manufacturers' Nat. Bank *v.* Treat, 128 Fed. 262, 263, 62 C. C. A. 644.

In a war revenue act providing for payment of certain sums by bankers according to the amount of their capital stock and providing "in estimating capital surplus shall be included," the term is used in its natural and ordinary sense, as including any overplus of assets over liabilities and not in the restricted sense in which it is used in national banking legislation. Leather Manufacturers' Nat. Bank *v.* Treat, 116 Fed. 774, 775.

Distinguished from "capital stock" see Bank of Commerce *v.* Tennessee, 161 U. S. 134, 147, 16 S. Ct. 456, 40 L. ed. 645.

Meaning among insurance companies.— Expert evidence was held admissible to show that the meaning of the term, in this connection, is a sum of money or assets which has been accumulated over and above all debts and liabilities of any and all kinds whatsoever. Fry *v.* Providence Sav. L. Assur. Soc., (Tenn. Ch. App. 1896) 38 S. W. 116, 126. In a provision in an insurance policy entitling insured to participate in the distribution of the "surplus" of the company issuing it, the term is used to designate the amount of funds in the hands of the company after deducting its liabilities as ascertained by certain rules adopted by the insurance department for determining the value of each risk. Greeff *v.* Equitable L. Assur. Soc., 160 N. Y. 19, 34, 54 N. E. 712, 73 Am. St. Rep. 659, 46 L. R. A. 288.

"Surplus assets," in a statute fixing the rights of shareholders in the distribution of such assets on the winding up of a company, are held to mean that which remains after all the outside liabilities of the company have been satisfied. *In re* Crichton's Oil Co., [1902] 2 Ch. 86, 93, 71 L. J. Ch. 531, 86 L. T. Rep. N. S. 787, 18 T. L. R. 556.

ment by Landlord For Improvements, see LANDLORD AND TENANT, 24 Cyc. 1105; Dispensing With Notice of Reëntry, see LANDLORD AND TENANT, 24 Cyc. 1392; Effect of Agreement For Increase or Reduction of Rent as, see LANDLORD AND TENANT, 24 Cyc. 1167; Effect of Taking New Lease on First Lease, see LANDLORD AND TENANT, 24 Cyc. 1025; Effect on Liability For Rent, see LANDLORD AND TENANT, 24 Cyc. 1162; Plea of in Action For Rent, see LANDLORD AND TENANT, 24 Cyc. 1214; Termination of Tenancy by, see LANDLORD AND TENANT, 24 Cyc. 1366, 1382, 1385, 1390. Of Levy of Execution Affecting Satisfaction of Judgment, see JUDGMENTS, 23 Cyc. 1490. Of Life-Estate as Termination Thereof, see ESTATES, 16 Cyc. 645. Of Mining Lease, see MINES AND MINERALS, 27 Cyc. 703. Of Municipal Warrant or Certificate of Indebtedness For Reissue, Funding, or Redemption, see MUNICIPAL CORPORATIONS, 28 Cyc. 1571. Of Negotiable Instrument — As Consideration For New Obligation, see COMMERCIAL PAPER, 7 Cyc. 697; As Discharge, see COMMERCIAL PAPER, 7 Cyc. 1048; On Execution of New Instrument, Necessity For, see COMMERCIAL PAPER, 7 Cyc. 1014; On Payment, see COMMERCIAL PAPER, 7 Cyc. 1017. Of Oil, Gas, or Salt Lease, see MINES AND MINERALS, 27 Cyc. 739. Of Original Patent on Reissue, see PATENTS, 30 Cyc. 926. Of Police Power by Municipality, see MUNICIPAL CORPORATIONS, 28 Cyc. 694. Of Policy of Fire Insurance — In General, see FIRE INSURANCE, 19 Cyc. 649; As Defense to Action on Premium Notes, see FIRE INSURANCE, 19 Cyc. 616; Right of Insured, see FIRE INSURANCE, 19 Cyc. 609 note 74. Of Policy of Life Insurance — In General, see LIFE INSURANCE, 25 Cyc. 783; Affecting Rights of Beneficiary Under Surrendered Policy, see LIFE INSURANCE, 25 Cyc. 892; As Fraud on Creditors, see FRAUDULENT CONVEYANCES, 20 Cyc. 361; Value on, Right of Pledgee or Assignee of Policy to Take at, see LIFE INSURANCE, 25 Cyc. 776. Of Possession — After Appeal in Action of Unlawful Detainer Affecting Amount in Controversy, see APPEAL AND ERROR, 2 Cyc. 580 note 44; By Adverse Claimant, Effect on Running of Statute, see ADVERSE POSSESSION, 1 Cyc. 1013; By Bailee as Waiver of Lien, see BAILMENTS, 5 Cyc. 196; By Covenantee to Holder of Paramount Legal Title as Constructive Eviction, see COVENANTS, 11 Cyc. 1127; Loss of Title Acquired by Adverse Possession by, see ADVERSE POSSESSION, 1 Cyc. 1139; Of Premises on Which Chattels Are Located as Delivery of Chattels, see SALES, 35 Cyc. 193; Of Public Lands, Inference From Failure to List For Taxation, see PUBLIC LANDS, 32 Cyc. 1098. Of Powers of Municipal Government Generally, see MUNICIPAL CORPORATIONS, 28 Cyc. 276. Of Power to Exempt From Taxation, see TAXATION. Of Power to Tax, see TAXATION. Of Preference as Condition of Allowance of Claim in Bankruptcy, see BANKRUPTCY, 5 Cyc. 330, 331. Of Principal by Bail in Civil Actions — In General, see BAIL, 5 Cyc. 44; As Affecting Right to Bail, see BAIL, 5 Cyc. 11; Plea of in Action on Bond, see BAIL, 5 Cyc. 59. Of Principal by Bail in Criminal Prosecution — In General, see BAIL, 5 Cyc. 126; As Affecting Right to Bail, see BAIL, 5 Cyc. 75; As Ground For Relief From Forfeiture, see BAIL, 5 Cyc. 134. Of Property — Assessed For Abatement of Nuisance by Municipality, see MUNICIPAL CORPORATIONS, 28 Cyc. 758; Assessed For Public Improvements, see MUNICIPAL CORPORATIONS, 28 Cyc. 1209; By Debtor as Ground For Discharge From Execution Against the Person, see EXECUTIONS, 17 Cyc. 1526, 1529; Held Under Forthcoming or Delivery Bond in Attachment, as Discharge of Obligors on Bond, see ATTACHMENT, 4 Cyc. 694; In Replevin, Power of Court to Compel, see REPLEVIN, 34 Cyc. 1517; Liabilities of Sheriffs and Constables For, see SHERIFFS AND CONSTABLES, 35 Cyc. 1673. Of Security — As Condition Precedent to Action on Debt or Liability Secured by Pledge, see PLEDGES, 31 Cyc. 868; As Consideration For Mortgage, see MORTGAGES, 27 Cyc. 1053, 1192; As Discharge of Negotiable Instrument, see COMMERCIAL PAPER, 7 Cyc. 1046; As Discharge of Surety, see PRINCIPAL AND SURETY, 32 Cyc. 216; For Mechanic's Lien, see MECHANICS' LIENS, 27 Cyc. 276. Subject to Statute of Frauds, see FRAUDS, STATUTE OF, 20 Cyc. 218. See also RELINQUISHMENT, 34 Cyc. 1199.)

SURREPTIO. A civil law term meaning "surprise," that is, where one man

these may be selected.[49] The only sure rule seems to be that which demands construction according to intent.[50]

(II) *TIME OF DEATH OF TESTATOR.* Where the death of the testator has been taken as the period of survivorship, various reasons have been given,[51] such as a general rule of construction subject to express intent;[52] or to preserve the estate

the application of that rule would lead to this determination in two sets of events. If a testator gives a sum of money or the residue of his estate to be paid or distributed among a number of persons, and refers to the contingency of any one or more of them dying, and then gives the estate or the money to the survivor, in that simple form of gift, where the gift is to take effect immediately on the death of the testator, the period of distribution is the period of death; and accordingly the event of the death upon which that contingency is to take place is necessarily to be referred to the interval of time between the date of the will and the death of the testator. . . . Then, by parity of reasoning, or rather as a necessary consequence of the same principle, if a testator gives a life estate in a sum of money or in the residue of his estate, and at the expiration of that life estate directs the money to be paid or the residue to be divided among a number of objects, and then refers to the possibility of some one or more of those persons dying, without specifying the time, and directs, in that event, the payment to be made or the distribution to be made among the survivors, it is understood and regarded by the law that he means the contingency to extend over the whole period of time that must elapse before the payment is made or the distribution takes place. The result, therefore, is, that in the event of such a gift the survivors are to be ascertained in like manner by a reference to the period of payment or of distribution, namely, the expiration of the life estate").

Period of distribution see *infra*, p. 635.

49. Drakeford *v.* Drakeford, 33 Beav. 43, 46, 9 L. T. Rep. N. S. 10, 11 Wkly. Rep. 977, 55 Eng. Reprint 282 [*distinguished* in Howard *v.* Collins, L. R. 5 Eq. 349, 351], holding that the rule "is this: that, in cases of survivorship, the class is to be ascertained at the period of distribution, if no other time is expressed by the testator" and that, where a fund was bequeathed for life to the widow, then for life to the testator's brother, at whose death the principal was to be divided between his surviving children and another, and the widow outlived the brother, so that her death became the period of distribution, the survivorship was referred to a different period, namely, the death of the brother. *Compare* Macklin *v.* Daniel, 18 Ont. 434, 436 (where the time of distribution and of survivorship was held to be the time when the estate should have been put in order for the payment of legacies and was not postponed to their payment).

Time of exercising power.—Where a testator appointed two brothers executors and trustees and provided that in the event of death or inability or refusal to act of either trustee then his surviving brothers and sisters or a majority of them should appoint a new trustee, "surviving" related to the time of making such appointment. Saunders *v.* Bradley, 6 Ont. L. Rep. 250, 253, 2 Ont. Wkly. Rep. 697 [*affirmed* in 6 Ont. Wkly. Rep. 436].

50. Martin *v.* Kirby, 11 Gratt. (Va.) 67, 70, where it is said: "It may admit of very grave question whether this is a subject upon which anything like a fixed rule of construction can be established. The question, and the only legitimate enquiry, is, what is the intention of the testator?"

Construction subject to intent see *supra*, p. 630, text and notes 42, 43, 44; *infra*, this page, text and note 52, p. 634, text and note 53, p. 635, text and note 62.

51. See *infra*, text and notes 52–60.

For example see Moore *v.* Lyons, 25 Wend. (N. Y.) 119, 143, 150, 155, where in construing a devise to one for life "and from and after her death" to her daughters, by name, "or 'to the survivors or survivor of them,' their or her heirs and assigns forever," in one opinion [p. 143] it was said that "words of survivorship in a will should, in all cases where there is no special intent manifest to the contrary, be taken to refer to the death of the testator;" in another [p. 150], "the weight of authority, both here and in England . . . unquestionably is in favor of applying the terms of survivorship, upon the devise of a remainder, to the death of the testator, instead of the time of the termination of the particular estate, where it is necessary to give effect to the probable intention of the testator in providing for the issue of the objects of his bounty, upon the death of their parents before the time appointed for the remainder to vest in possession; and especially where the devise is to the individuals by name and not to them as a class;" in another [p. 155], "the words, 'the survivor or survivors' in a context similar to that of the present will, have acquired a technical meaning differing from that sense in which they would otherwise be taken, and referring the survivorship to the testator's own death." *Compare* Brown *v.* Bigg, 7 Ves. Jr. 279, 286 note 61, 32 Eng. Reprint 114, where it is said that a statement in the opinion as follows: "The general leaning of the Court is against construing the words of survivorship to relate to the death of the testator; if any other period can be fixed upon: the testator generally supposing, the legatee will survive him," was retracted by the master of the rolls in his judgment.

52. Eberts *v.* Eberts, 42 Mich. 404, 406, 4 N. W. 172; Embury *v.* Sheldon, 68 N. Y. 227, 235 [*distinguished* in Buel *v.* Southwick, 70 N. Y. 581, 588; Converse *v.* Kellogg, 7

survivorship is not confined to a death before that of the testator.[65] A single provision for survivorship may relate to successive periods, of distribution, consisting in deaths of members of the class one after another.[66]

(IV) *TIME OF ANY OF SEVERAL DEATHS.* Where there is a gift over, in case of the death of any of a number of persons, to the survivor or survivors, there may be successive survivorships at successive deaths,[67] as in case of a gift or gifts to several, with a gift over, to survivors, of the part of any of them who shall die without having issue, the survivorship there being referred to the time of the death of any one of them,[68] such being the natural sense of the words so used.[69]

c. Letting in Issue. Words of survivorship are sometimes held to include issue of deceased members of the class specified, and this result is reached by

surviving at another period. Howard *v.* Collins, L. R. 5 Eq. 349, 351.

Where the devise is not immediate the more reasonable construction selects the period of distribution. *In re* Gregson, 2 De G. J. & S. 428, 439, 10 Jur. N. S. 1138, 34 L. J. Ch. 41, 11 L. T. Rep. N. S. 460, 5 New Rep. 99, 13 Wkly. Rep. 193, 67 Eng. Ch. 334, 46 Eng. Reprint 441.

Substituted class included in the survivorship see Atkinson *v.* Bartrum, 28 Beav. 219, 220, 9 Wkly. Rep. 885, 54 Eng. Reprint 349, holding that, in a bequest in remainder, to be divided equally between the testator's surviving brothers and sisters or their children, the word "'surviving' must govern the whole sentence, and that the brothers and sisters would take if they survived the tenants for life, but, if not, the nephews and nieces who survived the tenants for life alone take" — the word to be treated as covering both the brothers and sisters and their children.

"Should none of my children survive me" as the condition of a gift over, and following a direction to trustees to divide the estate among all testator's children, and pay to each upon coming of age, his share, taking into consideration the amount necessary for education, may, in view of the carelessness of the will and a motive for such intention, be held to create a right of survivorship among the children at the time of each payment. *Re* Sandison, 6 Northwest Terr. 313, 318.

In default of a second male heir.— In a devise to testator's son for life and "at his decease to the second male heir of him and his present wife, and his heirs male for ever; and in default of a second male heir to their eldest surviving female heir or child," the survivorship is of the son and his said wife, not of the testator. *Re* Brown, 5 Ont. L. Rep. 386, 387, 2 Ont. Wkly. Rep. 101.

65. *In re* Cramer, 170 N. Y. 271, 277, 63 N. E. 279 [*affirming* 59 N. Y. App. Div. 541, 69 N. Y. Suppl. 299]; Nellis *v.* Nellis, 99 N. Y. 505, 512, 3 N. E. 59; Keating *v.* Reynolds, 1 Bay (S. C.) 80, 87, where it is said of the word "survivor" that it "carries with it the idea of the longest liver".

66. See *infra*, this page, B, 1, c, (IV).

67. Clifton *v.* Crawford, 27 Ont. App. 315, 318.

68. Marshall *v.* Safe Deposit, etc., Co., 101 Md. 1, 8, 60 Atl. 476; Anderson *v.* Brown, 84 Md. 261, 270, 35 Atl. 937; Lawrence *v.* Phillips, 186 Mass. 320, 322, 71 N. E. 541; *In re* Wilcox, 64 N. J. Eq. 322, 324, 54 Atl. 296; Ashhurst *v.* Potter, 53 N. J. Eq. 608, 610, 611, 32 Atl. 698; Mead *v.* Maben, 131 N. Y. 255, 259, 261, 30 N. E. 98 [*reversing* 60 Hun 268, 14 N. Y. Suppl. 732]; Buel *v.* Southwick, 70 N. Y. 581, 586; *In re* Robson, [1899] W. N. 260, 261; McDonnell *v.* McDonnell, 24 Ont. 468; Forsyth *v.* Galt, 21 U. C. C. P. 408, 425 [*affirmed* in 22 U. C. C. P. 115]; Ray *v.* Gould, 15 U. C. Q. B. 131, 137. *Compare* *infra*, p. 642, as to case of last survivor on failure of issue.

Likewise where the gift was to children named, in trust for their children, and should any of those named die without children, then to the surviving heirs. Malseed's Estate, 15 Wkly. Notes Cas. (Pa.) 368, invoking the rule which favors the vesting of estates.

Rule referring to time of distribution invoked see Ashhurst *v.* Potter, 53 N. J. Eq. 608, 610, 611, 32 Atl. 698; *In re* Mortimer, 54 L. J. Ch. 414, 415, 52 L. T. Rep. N. S. 383, 33 Wkly. Rep. 441.

Not to postpone vesting.— Marshall *v.* Safe Deposit, etc., Co., 101 Md. 1, 8, 60 Atl. 476, where the only alternative period was the end of a twenty years' trust, upon which the principal was to be divided, and it was held that the earlier period, namely, the death of any member of the class, although within the twenty years, should be preferred.

As the period of the contingency upon which survivors are to take see Den *v.* Sayre, 3 N. J. L. 183, 190; *In re* Wilcox, 64 N. J. Eq. 322, 324, 54 Atl. 296.

Death of any under a certain age without issue see Bouverie *v.* Bouverie, 11 Jur. 661, 662, 16 L. J. Ch. 411, 2 Phil. 349, 22 Eng. Ch. 349, 41 Eng. Reprint 977 [*distinguished* in Vorley *v.* Richardson, 8 De G. M. & G. 126, 129, 2 Jur. N. S. 362, 25 L. J. Ch. 335, 4 Wkly. Rep. 397, 57 Eng. Ch. 99, 44 Eng. Reprint 337]; Shergold *v.* Boone, 13 Ves. Jr. 370, 375, 9 Rev. Rep. 195, 33 Eng. Reprint 332; Ryan *v.* Cooley, 15 Ont. App. 379, 386 [*modifying* 14 Ont. 13, 18]; Cook *v.* Noble, 5 Ont. 43, 46.

Death without issue before majority of youngest see Scott *v.* Duncan, 29 Grant Ch. (U. C.) 496, 497.

69. King *v.* Frost, 15 App. Cas. 548, 554, 63 L. T. Rep. N. S. 422 (where it is said: "The obvious meaning of the words 'survivors and survivor' in that clause is — such of the sons as may be living at the time of the death on which the disposition of the property is altered"); *In re* Benn, 29 Ch. D. 839, 844, 53 L. T. Rep. N. S. 240, 34 Wkly. Rep. 6

various means,[70] sometimes by applying the words literally to the whole surviving stock of beneficiaries,[71] by construing the word "survivor" or its equivalent as "other" [72] or "surviving *stirps*," [73] or as relating to the death of the testator,[74] while, in some cases, the courts have not committed themselves to any strict construction of the words, but found the intention in the context.[75] But the

(where it is said: "Here the natural meaning of 'surviving' is living at the death of the child, the estate devised to whom for life is given over on his death"); Leeming *v.* Sherratt, 2 Hare 14, 25, 16 Jur. 663, 11 L. J. Ch. 423, 24 Eng. Ch. 14, 67 Eng. Reprint 6; Beckwith *v.* Beckwith, 46 L. J. Ch. 97, 99, 36 L. T. Rep. N. S. 128, 25 Wkly. Rep. 282; Ranelagh *v.* Ranelagh, 2 Myl. & K. 441, 448, 7 Eng. Ch. 441, 39 Eng. Reprint 1012 (where "survivors" is said to be "used in its plain and obvious sense as meaning such of the four individuals named as shall be living when any of them shall happen to die").

70. See *infra*, text and notes 71–78.

Effect of statutes see Rivenett *v.* Bourquin, 53 Mich. 10, 12, 18 N. W. 537 (holding that a provision that if any child die before testatrix, the survivors or their legal representatives shall take, is not such an unequivocal exclusion of issue of a predeceased child as to prevail against How. St. 5, 812, providing against the lapse of legacies when the legatee leaves issue surviving the testator "unless a different disposition shall be made or directed by the will"); *In re* Bentz, 221 Pa. St. 380, 384, 70 Atl. 788, holding that the "surviving issue" substituted for a deceased legatee by St. May 6, 1844 (Pub. Laws 564), so as to prevent a lapse of the bequest by reason of prior death of legatee, living issue includes the children not named in the will, although their brothers and sisters are named). See also Thorington *v.* Hall, 111 Ala. 323, 324, 331, 21 So. 335, 56 Am. St. Rep. 54, holding that a power of appointment, in favor of three named children of the testator, was restricted to the particular children named, and therefore, in the absence of any showing upon the record that the three named included all the testator's children, was not within the application of Code, § 1862, providing: "When a disposition under an appointment or power is directed to be made to the children of any person, without restricting it to any particular children, it may be exercised in favor of the grandchildren or other descendants of that person," the court declining, however, to decide what would have been the effect of the statute had such showing been made. The opinion contains no allusion to any possible effect of the word "survivors" to enlarge the scope of the power.

Agreement against divestiture see Thorington *v.* Hall, 111 Ala. 323, 330, 21 So. 335, 56 Am. St. Rep. 54, holding that a remainder to three and the survivors or survivor of them, upon death, intestate, or remarriage, of the life-tenant, subject to her power of appointment, by will, among the three exclusively, was vested in them, subject to divestiture only in favor of members of the class of three, that, therefore, an agreement between them against divestiture, letting in heirs of members deceased within the life-tenancy, was valid.

71. Dooling *v.* Hobb, 5 Harr. (Del.) 405, 407; Harris *v.* Berry, 7 Bush (Ky.) 113, 115; Kemp *v.* Bradford, 61 Md. 330, 333; Naglee's Appeal, 33 Pa. St. 89, 91 [*sustained* at least as to the rights of the parties in *In re* Devine, 199 Pa. St. 250, 256, 48 Atl. 1072 (*criticizing* Dodson *v.* Ball, 60 Pa. St. 492, 495, 100 Am. Dec. 586, where it is said that Guthrie's Appeal, 37 Pa. St. 9, 22, strongly denied some of the positions of Naglee's Appeal, *supra*)]; *In re* Cary, 81 Vt. 112, 118, 69 Atl. 736.

Flexible in meaning.—"'Survivors,' as written, is a flexible term, not necessarily meaning the testator's surviving children only, but, when molded by the context and spirit of the will, may consistently with the literal import comprehend all his surviving descendants who were intended to be beneficiaries." Harris *v.* Berry, 7 Bush (Ky.) 113, 115.

72. See *infra*, p. 640, text and note 79.

"Others who had . . . not died childless" suggested as construction of "survivors" on death without issue see Birney *v.* Richardson, 5 Dana (Ky.) 424, 429 [*distinguished* in Bayless *v.* Prescott, 79 Ky. 252, 255, 2 Ky. L. Rep. 262, and *cited* with approval in Harris *v.* Berry, 7 Bush (Ky.) 113, 115].

73. Lucena *v.* Lucena, 7 Ch. D. 255, 261, 47 L. J. Ch. 203, 37 L. T. Rep. N. S. 420, 26 Wkly. Rep. 254; Wake *v.* Varah, 2 Ch. D. 348, 358, 45 L. J. Ch. 533, 34 L. T. Rep. N. S. 437, 24 Wkly. Rep. 621.

74. See *supra*, p. 634, text and note 53.

75. Birney *v.* Richardson, 5 Dana (Ky.) 424, 429, 431 [*distinguished* and *criticized* in Bayless *v.* Prescott, 79 Ky. 252, 255, 2 Ky. L. Rep. 262: and *cited* with approval in Harris *v.* Berry, 7 Bush (Ky.) 113, 115]: Hendricks *v.* Hendricks, 177 N. Y. 402, 407, 69 N. E. 736 [*reversing* 78 N. Y. App. Div. 212, 79 N. Y. Suppl. 516]; Lewis' Appeal, 18 Pa. St. 318, 325; Buckley *v.* Reed, 15 Pa. St. 83, 86 (holding that a direction to divide a remainder, at the death of the widow, amongst testator's "surviving children, or 'the heirs,'" amounts to a direction for division "among such of the children as should then survive and the legal representatives of those then dead," adding, "when too it is realized that some of the legatees were daughters, who might marry and bear children, the legal propriety of the reading becomes more and more obvious. If essential to subserve such a possible interest, the operation of the word 'survivor' would be restrained to the period of the testator's death"); Park's Estate, 21 Wkly. Notes Cas. (Pa.) 227, 228; Malseed's Estate, 15 Wkly. Notes Cas. (Pa.) 368; Shepard *v.* Shepard, 60 Vt. 109, 119, 120, 14 Atl. 536; Waite *v.* Littlewood, L. R. 8 Ch. 70 73, 42 L. J. Ch. 216, 28 L. T. Rep. N. S. 123,

among those standing in the same degree of relationship to the testator or to a distribution not in accordance with the general scheme of the will in its entirety;[81] or, as it has been said in one case, to take in persons not living who should be born before the period of distribution.[82] This construction depends always upon the intention of the testator as learned from the will;[83] bnt it has been said to be a

Rep. 196, 32 Eng. Reprint 252. See also *In re* Arnold, L. R. 10 Eq. 252, 258, 39 L. J. Ch. 875, 23 L. T. Rep. N. S. 337, 18 Wkly Rep. 912, where, after advocating the construction "other" to effectuate the intention, "other surviving children" was construed "other children" and the word surviving rejected.

81. *In re* Fox, 222 Pa. St. 108, 113, 70 Atl 954 *Compare Re* Usticke, 35 Beav. 338, 340, 14 Wkly. Rep. 447, 55 Eng. Reprint 926 [*criticized* in *In re* Arnold, L. R. 10 Eq. 252, 258, 39 L. J. Ch. 875, 23 L T. Rep. N. S. 337, 18 Wkly. Rep. 912], where the opinion was expressed that the tendency of all modern authorities is to hold that the word "survivor" must have its ordinary plain meaning; and it is said, further, that those cases "in which there is a gift over, if the whole class die without issue, are quite distinct, for there would be an intestacy, unless the words were construed 'others or other'").

82. See Davidson *v.* Dallas, 14 Ves. Jr. 576, 578, 9 Rev. Rep. 350, 33 Eng. Reprint 642 [*cited* in Leeming *v.* Sherratt, 2 Hare 14, 24, 16 Jur. 663, 11 L. J. Ch. 423, 24 Eng. Ch. 14, 67 Eng. Reprint 6].

83. See Duryea *v.* Duryea, 85 Ill. 41, 49, construing the word in its ordinary sense, where it is said: "The authorities seem to hold there is no rule fairly deducible from the cases on this subject, that will justify the reading of 'survivor' as equivalent to 'other,' except it is to be done whenever, from the context or other provisions of the will, it is rendered certain such must have been the intention of the testator"); Gorham *v.* Betts, 86 Ky. 164, 168, 5 S. W. 465, 9 Ky. L. Rep. 607 (where it is said of the word "survivors:" "The controversy has been whether the word should have its literal and natural meaning, or whether it should *prima facie* be construed as equivalent to the word 'others' in the absence of circumstances or something in the context showing that it was used in a strictly literal sense. There is a line of older cases, as in Wilmot *v.* Wilmot, 8 Vesey Jr. 10, 6 Rev. Rep. 196, 32 Eng. Reprint 252, holding to the latter view. Some eminent judges have also held that the words were convertible terms; but where the word 'survivor' has been given the force of 'other,' thus letting in the issue of a deceased member of a class by inheritance from the parent, it has been usually done, as was the case in Harris, &c. *v.* Berry, &c., 7 Bush, 114, to avoid some consequence which it was quite certain the testator did not intend. It was necessary in order to effect an intention appearing upon the entire will. The later cases, however, hold that the word 'survivor,' when unexplained by the context, is to be given its natural meaning, and interpreted according to its literal import. As this rule may often defeat the unexpressed intention of the testator, courts readily listen to any argument drawn from the context or other provisions of the will, showing that 'survivor' was used by him as synonymous with 'other;' but unless this appear, it may now be regarded as the settled rule that its literal meaning is to be given to it"); Anderson *v.* Brown, 84 Md. 261, 269, 35 Atl. 937 (where it is said: "All the cases to which we have been referred or examined in which 'survivor' has been construed as the equivalent of 'other' appear to have been so decided because there was something in the will to make it clear that the testator intended the issue of predeceased children to take, or that some other clearly expressed intention would otherwise be rendered inoperative"); *In re* Benn, 29 Ch. D. 839, 844, 53 L. T. Rep. N. S. 240, 34 Wkly. Rep. 6; *In re* Johnson, 53 L. J. Ch. 1116, 1117 (where it is said: "The question whether the word 'survivor' is to be read as 'other' has been the subject of innumerable cases; but there is one never-failing guide to all the authorities, namely, that it is the duty of the Court to ascertain what the meaning of the testator is, and if it can satisfy itself that the word ought to be read as 'other' it is right to substitute the one word for the other"); Beckwith *v.* Beckwith, 46 L. J. Ch. 97, 99, 36 L. T. Rep. N. S. 128, 25 Wkly. Rep. 282 (holding that "survivors" is not to be construed "others" *ex vi termini*).

Illustrated see Ashhurst *v.* Potter, 53 N. J. Eq. 608, 611, 32 Atl. 698, where it is said: "A testator, for example, after a life estate given to 'one' of his children, might well, in a gift over to his 'surviving children,' intend his '"other" children,' and they would be properly designated as the children 'other' than the life tenant," distinguishing the case at bar on the ground that there the previous estate was not that of one of the brothers and sisters of whom those surviving were to take, wherefore the construction "other" would impute to the testator the intention to substitute an inappropriate word.

Construction as "other" refused where the language of the will was precise and showed that the survivors were to take as tenants for life for their separate use, a provision wholly inconsistent with any intention that the children of a deceased member of the class should stand in his place as their parent. Winterton *v.* Crawfurd, 1 Russ. & M. 407, 411, 5 Eng. Ch. 407, 39 Eng. Reprint 157 [*cited* with approval in Taaffe *v.* Conmee, 10 H. L. Cas. 64, 77, 8 Jur. N. S. 919, 6 L. T. Rep. N. S. 666, 11 Eng. Reprint 749].

Seldom adopted unless interchangeable see Ashhurst *v.* Potter, 53 N. J. Eq. 608, 611, 32 Atl. 698 (where it is said: "But these

benefit of survivorship the last survivor on his own death without issue, the construction " others " has been both rejected [91] **and accepted.**[92]

f. Definite Failure of Issue. Survivorship, based upon death without issue, **has been held to restrict the failure of issue to a definite one** [93] **— since the persons described as survivors are not likely to live until a general failure occurs** [94] **— but only as evidence of intention,**[95] **and there are cases otherwise decided.**[96]

146, 149, 12 Can. L. T. Occ. Notes 274 (rejecting the construction "other").

91. King *v.* Frost, 15 App. Cas. 548, 553, 63 L. T. Rep. N. S. 422.

92. Askew *v.* Askew, 57 L. J. Ch. 629, 633, 58 L. T. Rep. N. S. 472, 36 Wkly. Rep. 620.

93. Moody *v.* Walker, 3 Ark. 147, 200: Richardson *v.* Noyes, 2 Mass. 56, 62, 69, 3 Am. Dec. 24; Den *v.* Allaire, 20 N. J. L. 6, 11; Den *v.* Combs, 18 N. J. L. 27, 33 (where the words "without issue" were supplied, not expressed); Waldron *v.* Gianini, 6 Hill (N. Y.) 601, 606; Lion *v.* Burtiss, 20 Johns. (N. Y.) 483, 487; Anderson *v.* Jackson, 16 Johns. (N. Y.) 382, 436, 437, 8 Am. Dec. 330 [*explained* and *distinguished* in Wilkes *v.* Lion, 2 Cow. (N. Y.) 333, 392]; Moffat *v.* Strong, 10 Johns. (N. Y.) 12, 16; Pond *v.* Bergh, 10 Paige (N. Y.) 140, 151; Vedder *v.* Everston, 3 Paige (N. Y.) 281, 290, 293; Johnson *v.* Currin, 10 Pa. St. 498, 503; Abbott *v.* Essex County, 18 How. (U. S.) 202, 216, 15 L. ed. 352; Ranelagh *v.* Ranelagh, 2 Myl. & K. 441, 448, 7 Eng. Ch. 441, 39 Eng. Reprint 1012; Nicholls *v.* Skinner, Prec. Ch. 528, 529, 24 Eng. Reprint 236; Hughes *v.* Sayer, 1 P. Wms. 534, 535, 24 Eng. Reprint 504 (holding that the limitation over to survivors prevented the word "children" from being construed "issue" in the indefinite sense). See also Fosdick *v.* Cornell, 1 Johns. (N. Y.) 440, 452, 3 Am. Dec. 340 [*followed* as authority for the rule in Jackson *v.* Staats, 11 Johns. 337, 348, 6 Am. Dec. 376; Jackson *v.* Blanshan, 3 Johns. 292, 297, 3 Am. Dec. 485] (where the devise over to survivors, after failure of issue, was held a strong indication that the failure intended was definite); Roe *v.* Jeffery, 7 T. R. 589, 596, 101 Eng. Reprint 1147 (where such a provision was construed as intending a definite failure of issue, no direct allusion, however, being made to the force of the words of survivorship); Gould *v.* Stokes, 26 Grant Ch. (U. C.) 122, 124. *Compare* Lewis *v.* Claiborne, 5 Yerg. (Tenn.) 369, 373, 26 Am. Dec. 270 (holding that, where entails are abolished, a limitation to survivors of a class, in case of any dying without issue, applies in the construction of "dying without issue" in case of realty, as it always does in case of personalty, to a dying without issue previous to death of the first taker instead of an indefinite failure of issue); Gray *v.* Richford, 2 Can. Sup. Ct. 431, 434, 450 (where the language "die without leaving any issue . . . or the children of such issue surviving him," was held, upon much consideration of authorities, to import a definite failure of issue).

94. Johnson *v.* Currin, 10 Pa. St. 498, 503 (where it is said: "No sane man could intend to limit an estate over to persons in being upon an indefinite failure of issue of the first taker; that is, upon a failure that would happen after all those who are called survivors, and their children's children, would be in their graves"); Nicholl *v.* Skinner, Prec. Ch. 528, 529, 24 Eng. Reprint 236; Hughes *v.* Sayer, 1 P. Wms. 534, 535, 24 Eng. Reprint 504.

95. Bedford's Appeal, 40 Pa. St. 18, 23 (where the fact that the word "children" was used instead of "issue" seems to have been the main ground of decision, but it was said: "It has often been held that a limitation over by will to survivors or persons in being, after the death of the first taker without issue, raises a strong presumption that the testator did not contemplate an indefinite failure of issue"); Abbott *v.* Essex County, 18 How. (U. S.) 202, 216, 15 L. ed. 352 (where it is said: "It is true that cases may be found which decide that the term 'survivor' does not of itself necessarily import a definite failure of issue, and no doubt there are many cases where it would be necessary to disregard the obvious import of this term, in order to carry out the general intent of a testator, otherwise apparent; but a large number of English, and nearly all the American, cases acknowledge the force of this term as evidence of the testator's intending a definite contingency").

If a personal benefit to survivors is intended see Greenwood *v.* Verdon, 1 Kay & J. 74, 83, 89, 24 L. J. Ch. 65, 3 Wkly. Rep. 124, 69 Eng. Reprint 375 [*explained* in Little *v.* Billings, 27 Grant Ch. (U. C.) 353, 358]; Forsyth *v.* Galt, 21 U. C. C. P. 408, 420 [*affirmed* in 22 U. C. C. P. 115]. See also Massey *v.* Hudson, 2 Meriv. 130, 132, 16 Rev. Rep. 158, 35 Eng. Reprint 889, where, however, it was held that the presumption of such intent was destroyed by the words "executors, administrators, or assigns" in the gift to "survivor."

96. Hollett *v.* Pope, 3 Harr. (Del.) 542, 545 (holding that a legacy to three, and, in case one of them dies without issue, then to the remaining two or the survivor of them, refers to a general failure of issue); Caulk *v.* Caulk, 3 Pennew. (Del.) 528, 539, 544, 52 Atl. 340 [*repudiating* the doctrine of Anderson *v.* Jackson, 16 Johns. 382, 8 Am. Dec. 330, and *adopting*, as recognized in Delaware, the dissenting opinion therein of Chancellor Kent]; Smith's Appeal, 23 Pa. St. 9, 10 [*distinguished* in Bedford's Appeal, 40 Pa. St. 18, 23 (but only on the ground that the provision in default of issue created an entail)]; Little *v.* Billings, 27 Grant Ch. (U. C.) 353, 357 [*cited* with approval in Crawford *v.* Broddy, 25 Ont. 635, 637 (*reversed* on other grounds in 22 Ont. App. 307)].

that is temporary, stop of a man's right.[27] From office, a deprivation of office for the time;[28] exclusively an interruption in the exercise of the officer's duties, of his authority.[29] Of an employee, a temporary interruption or cessation of labor.[30] Of payment, a term which contains the idea of the failure to pay from inability to do so.[31] Of a right in an estate, a partial extinguishment thereof, or an extin-

Mere suspension of the execution of a contract is not an abandonment, and such suspension under a clause of a state contract, itself providing that if the execution of the contract shall be suspended by the state at any time for any cause no claim for prospective profits of work not done shall be made or allowed, but the contractors shall complete the work when the state shall order it resumed, would not be a breach, but the termination of a contract by the state is a breach when there is no provision therefor. Baker *v.* State, 77 N. Y. App. Div. 528, 531, 78 N. Y. Suppl. 922.

Suspension of partnership distinguished from "dissolution" see Williston *v.* Camp, 9 Mont. 88, 96, 22 Pac. 501, holding that an assignment for creditors of the firm might be said correctly to have "suspended" its business without saying that it dissolved the partnership.

Suspension of rent.— "It would avoid dispute to provide that the rent shall 'cease and be suspended' or shall 'be suspended and cease to be payable'" during eviction. See 3 Stroud Jud. Dict. 2001.

27. See 3 Stroud L. Dict. 2002 [*quoting* and *explaining* Cowell L. Dict.].

28. *Ex p.* Diggs, 52 Ala. 381, 383.

Distinguished from removal see State *v.* Richmond, 29 La. Ann. 705, 706; Stack *v.* O'Hara, 98 Pa. St. 213, 232; Poe *v.* State, 72 Tex. 625, 629, 10 S. W. 737. *Compare* Nolen *v.* State, 118 Ala. 154, 159, 24 So. 251.

Permanent "suspension" equal to removal. — A "suspension" which is to continue perpetually unless the person suspended be restored to office by a joint resolution of the general assembly is in legal contemplation a removal, and St. (1886–1887) p. 1, undertaking to authorize the governor so to "suspend" tax assessors, is void as a violation of the constitution, since that prescribes the only mode by which a tax assessor can be removed. Nolen *v.* State, 118 Ala. 154, 159, 24 So. 251. *Compare,* however, Poe *v.* State, 72 Tex. 625, 629, 10 S. W. 737, where it is said: "While the suspension is by the terms of the law only a temporary deprivation of the office, it in every case may be what it in effect was in this, a permanent deprivation of the office. Still, a suspension is in no proper sense the same thing as a removal. We are not at liberty by construction or otherwise to hold that the provisions of the Constitution with regard to removals apply equally to suspensions from office."

As applied to a priest of the Roman catholic church, "suspension is a judicial act based on something which calls for such sentence" and a "sentence of suspension follows a trial for an offense, from which the priest may appeal." Suspension is not to be confounded with "removal" which is "the exercise of episcopal authority according to the bishop's judgment. It may be without supposition of wrong, and it leaves the priest . . . without employment." Stack *v.* O'Hara, 98 Pa. St. 213, 232.

A statute prescribing suspension from office as the consequence of some act or event is penal, and is therefore not to be enlarged in its scope by construction, and cannot be retroactive. *Ex p.* Diggs, 52 Ala. 381, 383, in regard to the effect of St. No. 155, March 2, 1875, providing for the suspension of a county solicitor against whom an indictment is pending.

29. State *v.* Richmond, 29 La. Ann. 705, 706.

30. Lethbridge *v.* New York, 59 N. Y. Super. Ct. 486, 487, 15 N. Y. Suppl. 562, the opinion at special term, there affirmed.

Distinguished from removal see Lethbridge *v.* New York, 59 N. Y. Super. Ct. 486, 487, 15 N. Y. Suppl. 562.

May be discharge.— See McNamara *v.* New York, 152 N. Y. 228, 233, 46 N. E. 507 (where it is said: "Suspension without pay because there is no work is a practical discharge"); Wardlaw *v.* New York, 137 N. Y. 194, 197, 33 N. E. 140 [*quoted* in McNamara *v.* New York, *supra*] (holding that if the plaintiff "understood . . . that his services were no longer required . . . and that compensation was no longer to be paid to him . . . and that such was the purpose of this notice from the commissioner and both parties acted accordingly, then the . . . notice operated to terminate the employment, though it was called a suspension instead of a dismissal").

31. See *In re* Wolf, 30 Fed. Cas. No. 17,923, 4 Sawy. 168, 169, 17 Nat. Bankr. Reg. 423, where, in holding that the fact that a note payable "one day after date" remained due forty days did not constitute such a suspension of payment as to amount to an act of bankruptcy, it was said: "Suspension of payment means something more than a failure of the maker of such paper as this to seek the holder and pay him. Business men understand very well what the term means; there is the idea in it of a failure to pay from an inability to do so."

Need not be permanent to come within the meaning of the words of the Bankr. Act (1883), § 4, subs. 1, clause h, "if the debtor gives notice to any of his creditors that he has suspended, or that he is about to suspend, payment of his debts." Crook *v.* Morley, [1891] A. C. 316, 319, 61 L. J. Q. B. 97, 65 L. T. Rep. N. S. 389.

By trader.— A suspension of payment within the meaning of Bankrupt Law Consolidation Act (12 & 13 Vict. c. 106, § 225) takes place where a trader who is unable to meet his engagements with his creditors and is desirous of laying the state of affairs before them enters into such an arrangement as an assignment for creditors, and a plea

to put an oath; to administer an oath to a person;[58] to use profane language.[59] (Swear: In General, see BLASPHEMY, 5 Cyc. 710; PROFANITY, 32 Cyc. 578; OATHS AND AFFIRMATIONS, 29 Cyc. 1296. As Administering Oath — Swearing Coroner's Jury, see CORONERS, 9 Cyc. 988; Swearing Grand Jury, Showing as to in Indictment or Information, see INDICTMENTS AND INFORMATIONS, 22 Cyc. 235 text and note 31, 236 text and notes 32, 37, 237 text and notes 38–42; Swearing Juror as Affecting Right to Challenge, see JURIES, 24 Cyc. 363; Swearing Witnesses, Record by Clerk, see CLERKS OF COURTS, 7 Cyc. 222 note 37. As Disorderly Conduct, see DISORDERLY CONDUCT, 14 Cyc. 469, 470. As Taking Oath — In General, see OATHS AND AFFIRMATIONS, 29 Cyc. 1296; "Swear and Depose," Not Sufficient For Allegation of Oath in Indictment For Perjury, see PERJURY, 30 Cyc. 1432 note 51; Swearing Falsely, as Crime Not Amounting to Perjury, see PERJURY, 30 Cyc. 1400; Swearing Falsely, as Crime of Perjury, see PERJURY, 30 Cyc. 1395; Swearing Falsely, as Subject of Libel or Slander, see LIBEL AND SLANDER, 25 Cyc. 284, 441; Swearing to Affidavit, see AFFIDAVITS, 2 Cyc. 16; Swearing to Complaint, see SWORN COMPLAINT, and Cross-References Thereunder, *post*, p. 659; Swearing to False Report of Corporation, see CORPORATIONS, 10 Cyc. 875. Evidence of in Prosecution For Disorderly Conduct, see DISORDERLY CONDUCT, 14 Cyc. 476 note 59.)

SWEARING. See SWEAR, and Cross-References Thereunder.

SWEATING. A term which, as used to describe a cause of damage to a cargo of grain, means moisture dropped upon the cargo from condensation, which arises if there is moisture which evaporates and then condenses in the hold.[60]

SWEATING SYSTEM. An expression, obviously figurative, which involves a system oppressive to the workman, whereby an unconscionable or unjust profit is wrung from the sweat of his brow by paying insufficient wages for his work.[61]

SWEEPAGE. A form of herbage, apparently that taken by mowing.[62] (See also HERBAGE, 21 Cyc. 433.)

SWEEPINGS. See DRAFF, 14 Cyc. 1017.

Declaring.'" Stroud Jud. Dict. [*citing* St. 13 & 14 Vict. c. 21, § 4; Interpr. Act (1889), § 3].

Judicial administration not implied.—"Any utterance or an affirmation, with an appeal to God, is to swear an oath, no matter how or before whom the utterance is made. That is its common import." The word "swore" "does not technically and necessarily imply a judicial administration of an oath." U. S. *v.* Howard, 132 Fed. 325, 340.

"Sworn to" in the verification of a plea and referring to the plea "must be taken to mean, that the testator declared on oath, the facts it set forth were true." Powers *v.* Bryant, 7 Port. (Ala.) 9, 15.

58. Black L. Dict.

"Sworn" is equivalent to "sworn to" in a magistrate's certificate to an oath. Com. *v.* Bennett, 7 Allen (Mass.) 533, 534.

"Duly sworn" or "sworn according to law" is defined by Rev. St. c. 1, § 23, rule 21, as applied to any officer who is required to take and subscribe the oath prescribed in the constitution, as meaning "that such officer had taken and subscribed the same, as well as made oath faithfully and impartially to perform the duties of the office to which he had been elected or appointed" and, when applied to any person other than such officer, "that such person had taken an oath faithfully and impartially to perform the duties assigned to him in the case specified." Bennett *v.* Treat, 41 Me. 226, 227.

"Swearing the peace" at common law see State *v.* Sargent, 74 Minn. 242, 244, 76 N. W. 1129.

59. Black L. Dict.

60. See The Pearlmoor, [1904] P. 286, 9 Aspin. 540, 73 L. J. P. D. & Adm. 50, 54, 90 L. T. Rep. N. S. 319, 20 T. L. R. 199, so construing the term when used in bills of lading to describe a cause of damage for which the owners of the vessel disclaimed responsibility, holding that the term did not include damage by heating of the grain itself, nor from contact with the iron work of the ship and the accumulation of water together. See also La Motte *v.* Angel, 1 Hawaii 237, 244; Adrian *v.* Live Yankee, 1 Fed. Cas. No. 88.

61. Collard *v.* Marshall, [1892] 1 Ch. 571, 576, 61 L. J. Ch. 268, 66 L. T. Rep. N. S. 248, 40 Wkly. Rep. 473.

"There is generally a middleman taking advantage of the circumstances in which the workman is placed, and grinding down for his own profit the wages of those employed below the fair rate." Collard *v.* Marshall, [1892] 1 Ch. 571, 576, 61 L. J. Ch. 268, 66 L. T. Rep. N. S. 248, 40 Wkly. Rep. 473.

Not constituted by employing more boys than a labor union thinks right see Collard *v.* Marshall, [1892] 1 Ch. 571, 577, 61 L. J. Ch. 268, 66 L. T. Rep. N. S. 248, 40 Wkly. Rep. 473.

62. See 2 Stroud Jud. Dict. 868, *sub. verb.* "Herbage" [*citing* Elphinstone, Norton & C. Interpr. Deeds 586].

cheat or dishonest person.[71] (Swindler: As a Libelous Word Actionable *per se*, see LIBEL AND SLANDER, 25 Cyc. 261 text and note 68. In Slander Not Actionable *per se*, see LIBEL AND SLANDER, 25 Cyc. 267 text and note 16. See also SWINDLE, *ante*, p. 656; SWINDLING.)

SWINDLING. A word which has no legal and technical meaning, and commonly implies that there has been recourse to petty and mean artifices for obtaining money, which may or may not be strictly illegal;[72] cheating and defrauding grossly with deliberate artifice.[73] As defined by Texas statutes,[74] the acquisition of any personal or movable property, money, or instrument of writing conveying or securing a valuable right, by means of some false or deceitful pretense or device, or fraudulent representation, with intent to appropriate the same to the use of the party so acquiring, or destroying or impairing the rights of the party justly entitled to the same.[75] (Swindling: Imputation of as Libel, see LIBEL AND SLANDER, 25 Cyc. 282. Necessity of Injury Resulting to Constitute Offense, see FALSE PRETENSES, 19 Cyc. 411 note 48. Requisites of Pretense, see FALSE PRETENSES, 19 Cyc. 394 note 47. Statutory Offense, see FALSE PRETENSES, 19 Cyc. 392. See also CHEAT, 7 Cyc. 123; COMMON-LAW CHEAT, 8 Cyc. 389.)

SWINE. The original generic term for animals of the kind described by the word hog or shoat.[76] (Swine: In General, see ANIMALS, 2 Cyc. 288. Description

71. Savile *v.* Jardine, 2 H. Bl. 531, 532 [*cited* as to the meaning of "cheat" in Stevenson *v.* Hayden, 2 Mass. 406, 408; Weil *v.* Altenhofen, 26 Wis. 708, 710].

72. Cunningham *v.* Baker, 104 Ala. 160, 171, 16 So. 68, 53 Am. St. Rep. 27, adding: "The disappointed and vexed creditor not infrequently will apply the term swindler to a delinquent debtor, and an absconding debtor is not infrequently spoken of as having swindled his creditors."

Applicable to fraudulent sale to prevent creditors from attaching the property sold. Odiorne *v.* Bacon, 6 Cush. (Mass.) 185, 191.

That the term imports a crime is denied (Hall *v.* Rogers, 2 Blackf. (Ind.) 429, 430; Chase *v.* Whitlock, 3 Hill (N. Y.) 139, 140), but there are *dicta* to the contrary (Forrest *v.* Hansen, 9 Fed. Cas. No. 4,943, 1 Cranch C. C. 63, where it is said: "To charge a man with swindling, seems, therefore, to be substantially to charge him with an offence for which he may be liable to a prosecution at common law"; J'Anson *v.* Stewart, 1 T. R. 748, 752, 99 Eng. Reprint 1357 [*cited* in Forest *v.* Hansen, *supra*], where it is said of a defendant in libel: "When he took upon himself to justify generally the charge of swindling, he must be prepared with the facts which constitute the charge." and "If the plaintiff had been a common swindler, the defendant ought to have indicted him; but he has no right to libel him in this way").

"Implies a high degree of moral depravity . . . its essence is fraud." Forrest *v.* Hansen, 9 Fed. Cas. No. 4,943, 1 Cranch C. C. 63.

73. Wyatt *v.* Ayres, 2 Port. (Ala.) 157, 161.

74. Tex. Cr. Code 773*a*; Tex. Pen. Code (1895), art. 943; Tex. Pen. Code, art. 790.

75. Cline *v.* State, 43 Tex. 494, 497; La Moyne *v.* State, 53 Tex. Cr. 221, 228, 111 S. W. 950, 953; Cummings *v.* State, 36 Tex. Cr. 152, 153, 36 S. W. 266; Blum *v.* State, 20 Tex. App. 578, 591, 54 Am. Rep. 530; May *v.* State, 15 Tex. App. 430, 436; Stringer *v.* State, 13 Tex. App. 520, 522.

Essentials.—"(1) The intent to defraud; (2) an actual act of fraud committed; (3) false pretenses; and (4) the fraud must be committed or accomplished by means of the false pretenses made use of for the purpose,—that is, they must be the cause which induced the owner to part with his property. An essential element . . . is that the party injured must have relied upon, believed as true, and been deceived by, the fraudulent representations or devices of the party accused." Thorpe *v.* State, 40 Tex. Cr. 346, 347, 50 S. W. 383 [*quoting* and *adopting* the charge of the court below]. Intent is an essential element. Stringer *v.* State, 13 Tex. App. 520, 522. False representations must be the inducement. De Young *v.* State, (Tex. Cr. App. 1897) 41 S. W. 598, 599; Blum *v.* State, 20 Tex. App. 578, 594, 54 Am. Rep. 530; Buckalew *v.* State, 11 Tex. App. 352, 356. A mistaken opinion originally that the person defrauded will not take the place of a false pretense. Blum *v.* State, *supra*.

Not essential are benefit to the person guilty or injury to the person intended to be defrauded if the wilful design to receive benefit or cause injury is evident, under Tex. Pen. Code (1879), art. 944, subd. 4. La Moyne *v.* State, 53 Tex. Cr. 221, 228, 111 S. W. 950.

As distinguished from theft swindling must result in parting with title or property in the subject-matter. Cline *v.* State, 43 Tex. 494, 497, 498; Bink *v.* State, 50 Tex. Cr. 450, 452, 98 S. W. 249; Taylor *v.* State, 32 Tex. Cr. 110, 112, 22 S. W. 148; Curtis *v.* State, 31 Tex. Cr. 39, 40, 19 S. W. 604; Frank *v.* State, 30 Tex. App. 381, 382, 17 S. W. 936; Pitts *v.* State, 5 Tex. App. 122, 124. In swindling either of the two intents to appropriate or to deprive the owner may be sufficient, while in theft they must combine. May *v.* State, 15 Tex. App. 430, 437.

76. State *v.* Godet, 29 N. C. 210, 211.

TAVERN-KEEPER. One who obtains a license to keep a tavern and for whom it is kept; [90] a person who makes it his business to entertain travelers and passengers, and provide lodging and necessaries for them and their horses and attendants; [91] a person a part of whose business at least it is to sell intoxicating liquors; [92] a person who makes it a business to keep a house of entertainment for travelers; [93] a person who receives and entertains as guests those who choose to visit his house; [94] synonymous with "innkeepers." [95]

TAX. To assess, fix, or determine judicially.[96] (See TAXATION, *post*, p. 706.)

TAXABLE COSTS. Full indemnity for the expenses of a party who is successful in a suit between party and party whether at law or in equity; [97] such costs as a party is entitled to have taxed by law.[98] (See, generally, COSTS, 11 Cyc. 1.)

TAXABLE INHABITANT. One who is, or who may lawfully be, taxed; one who possesses all the qualifications necessary to authorize the proper taxing authorities to assess him with the tax.[99] (See TAXATION, *post*, p. 767.)

TAXABLE PROPERTY. See TAXATION, *post*, p. 767.

TAXABLE VALUE. See TAXATION, *post*, p. 1009 *et seq.*

90. Com. *v.* Burns, 4 J. J. Marsh. (Ky.) 177, 181, where it is said that this is true, although another person as his agent may actually keep it.

91. Com. *v.* Shortridge, 3 J. J. Marsh. (Ky.) 638, 640; St. Louis *v.* Siegrist, 46 Mo. 593, 595.

92. Territory *v.* Gutierrez, 12 N. M. 254, 290, 78 Pac. 139; Jensen *v.* State, 60 Wis. 577, 582, 19 N. W. 374.

93. Curtis *v.* State, 5 Ohio 324, where this is said to be true, although no liquor is kept.

94. People *v.* Jones, 54 Barb. (N. Y.) 311, 316, 1 Cow. Cr. 381.

95. Bonner *v.* Welborn, 7 Ga. 296, 306; Crown Point *v.* Warner, 3 Hill (N. Y.) 150, 156.

Does not include one who keeps a mere boarding house or lodging house, or even one who keeps a house for lodging strangers for the season (Southwood *v.* Myers, 3 Bush (Ky.) 681, 685), nor would it include one who merely keeps a restaurant where meals are furnished (People *v.* Jones, 54 Barb. (N. Y.) 311, 316, 1 Cow. Cr. 381).

To constitute an inn-keeper, a tavern-keeper, or hotel-keeper, the party so designated must receive and entertain as guests those who choose to visit his house; and a restaurant where meals are furnished is not an inn or tavern. People *v.* Jones, 54 Barb. (N. Y.) 311, 317, 1 Cow. Cr. 381.

96. Webster Dict. [*quoted* in Hewlett *v.* Nutt, 79 N. C. 263, 265]. See also Beebe *v.* Wells, 37 Kan. 472, 473, 15 Pac. 565.

97. Rowland *v.* Maddock, 183 Mass. 360, 365, 67 N. E. 347.

"Taxable," as applied to costs, having the same effect as "necessary" see Wilson *v.* Lange, 84 N. Y. Suppl. 519, 520.

98. Wright *v.* Smith, 19 Vt. 110, 112. See also Nicholls *v.* Rensselaer County Mut. Ins. Co., 22 Wend. (N. Y.) 125, 128.

Where an action was brought against several defendants on contract, and after defendants had answered separately, plaintiff was allowed to change into an action of tort on payment of the "taxable costs" the term was held to include separate costs to each defendant. George *v.* Reed, 104 Mass. 366, 367.

99. *In re* Annexation of Chester Tp., 174 Pa. St. 177, 180, 34 Atl. 457.

Construed in statute as meaning legal voters who are taxable see Elkins *v.* Deshler, 25 N. J. L. 177, 180.

CROSS-REFERENCES

For Matters Relating to:

Acquisition of Tax Title by Cotenant, see TENANCY IN COMMON.
Appeal in Cases Relating to Taxes or Revenue, see APPEAL AND ERROR, 2 Cyc. 550, 578.
Conclusiveness of Judgment in Tax Proceedings, see JUDGMENTS, 23 Cyc. 1346.
Customs Duties, see CUSTOMS DUTIES, 12 Cyc. 1104.
Delegation to Judiciary of Powers in Regard to Taxation, see CONSTITUTIONAL LAW, 8 Cyc. 836.
Disqualification by Interest as Taxpayer:
Of Judge, see JUDGES, 23 Cyc. 578.
Of Juror, see JURIES, 24 Cyc. 271, 272.
Of Justice of the Peace, see JUSTICES OF THE PEACE, 24 Cyc. 490.
Internal Revenue, see INTERNAL REVENUE, 22 Cyc. 1592.

revenue,[17] to be used for public or governmental purposes,[18] and not as payment for some special privilege granted or service rendered.[19] Taxes and taxation are therefore distinguishable from various other contributions, charges, or burdens paid or imposed for particular purposes or under particular powers or functions of the government.[20] Whether a particular contribution, charge, or burden is to

of military service in the state militia is not a "tax" in the sense of the constitution, the practice of commuting for military service being analogous to that of commuting for highway labor. People *v.* Chenango, 8 N. Y. 317, 325.

17. Mays *v.* Cincinnati, 1 Ohio St. 268, 273; Com. *v.* Conglomerate Min. Co., 5 Dauph. Co. Rep. (Pa.) 66, 68; State *v.* Winnebago Lake, etc., Plank Road Co., 11 Wis. 35, 40.

Fees of public officers, unless for purposes of general revenue, not taxes see *infra*, I, A, 2, e.

License-fees, unless for purposes of general revenue, not taxes see *infra*, I, A, 2, c.

Export stamps.—A requirement that articles intended for exportation shall be stamped, in order to prevent fraud and secure the carrying out of the declared intent of the law, is not laying a tax or duty on such articles, although a small charge is made for the stamp. Pace *v.* Burgess, 92 U. S. 372, 23 L. ed. 657. But if the stamp were required as a source of revenue to the government, it would amount to a tax. Almy *v.* California, 24 How. (U. S.) 169, 16 L. ed. 644.

18. *Maine.*—Allen *v.* Jay, 60 Me. 124, 127, 11 Am. Rep. 185; Opinion of Justices, 58 Me. 590, 591.

Massachusetts.— Mead *v.* Acton, 139 Mass. 341, 344, 1 N. E. 413.

Michigan.— People *v.* Salem Tp. Bd., 20 Mich. 452, 474, 4 Am. Rep. 400.

Missouri.— State *v.* Switzler, 143 Mo. 287, 314, 45 S. W. 245, 65 Am. St. Rep. 653, 40 L. R. A. 280.

New Jersey.— Elizabethtown Water Co. *v.* Wade, 59 N. J. L. 78, 83, 35 Atl. 4.

New York.— Heerwagen *v.* Crosstown St. R. Co., 90 N. Y. App. Div. 275, 286, 86 N. Y. Suppl. 218, where the court said: "The crucial attributes of a tax are that it is a toll upon property without the consent of the owner, and the money secured is to be applied towards governmental expenses of the body politic for whose benefit the imposition is to be made."

North Dakota.— Yeatman *v.* King, 2 N. D. 421, 425, 51 N. W. 721, 33 Am. St. Rep. 797.

Pennsylvania.— Philadelphia Disabled Firemen's Relief Assoc. *v.* Wood, 39 Pa. St. 73, 82; Sharpless *v.* Philadelphia, 21 Pa. St. 147, 169, 59 Am. Dec. 759.

South Carolina.— Feldman *v.* Charleston, 23 S. C. 57, 62, 55 Am. Rep. 6.

United States.— Morgan's Steamship Co. *v.* Louisiana Bd. of Health, 118 U. S. 455, 461, 6 S. Ct. 1114, 30 L. ed. 237.

Necessity for public purpose see *infra*, I, D, 1.

What constitutes public purpose.— While taxation must be for a public purpose this does not necessarily mean that it must be exclusively in support of the government. Davidson *v.* Ramsey County, 18 Minn. 482. See also *infra*, I, D, 2.

19. Wagner *v.* Rock Island, 146 Ill. 139, 34 N. E. 545, 21 L. R. A. 519; Manistee River Imp. Co. *v.* Sands, 53 Mich. 593, 19 N. W. 199; St. Louis Brewing Assoc. *v.* St. Louis, 140 Mo. 419, 37 S. W. 525, 41 S. W. 911; Morgan's Steamship Co. *v.* Louisiana Bd. of Health, 118 U. S. 455, 6 S. Ct. 1114, 30 L. ed. 237; Hamilton *v.* Dillin, 11 Fed. Cas. No. 5,979.

Taxes do not include water rates paid by private consumers for water actually used to a municipality which owns and operates a waterworks system (Wagner *v.* Rock Island, 146 Ill. 139, 34 N. E. 545, 21 L. R. A. 519; Preston *v.* Detroit Water Com'rs, 117 Mich. 589, 76 N. W. 92; Jones *v.* Detroit Water Com'rs, 34 Mich. 273; St. Louis Brewing Assoc. *v.* St. Louis, 140 Mo. 419, 37 S. W. 525, 41 S. W. 911; Silkman *v.* Yonkers Water Com'rs, 152 N. Y. 327, 46 N. E. 612, 37 L. R. A. 827 [*affirming* 71 Hun 37, 24 N. Y. Suppl. 806]; Alter *v.* Cincinnati, 56 Ohio St. 47, 46 N. E. 69, 35 L. R. A. 737); tolls for the actual use of passage over land or water highways (Manistee River Imp. Co. *v.* Sands, 53 Mich. 593, 19 N. W. 199 [*affirmed* in 123 U. S. 288, 8 S. Ct. 113, 31 L. ed. 149]); wharfage charges (Keokuk Northern Line Packet Co. *v.* Keokuk, 95 U. S. 80, 24 L. ed. 377); fees of public officers (see *infra*, I, A, 2, e); or a bonus required to be paid for the renewal of the charter of a corporation (Baltimore *v.* Baltimore, etc., R. Co., 6 Gill (Md.) 288, 48 Am. Dec. 531).

20. People *v.* Brooklyn, 4 N. Y. 419, 55 Am. Dec. 266; State *v.* Winnebago Lake, etc., Plank Road Co., 11 Wis. 35; *In re* Meador, 16 Fed. Cas. No. 9,375, 1 Abb. 317; Cooley Taxation (3d ed.) 5. See also cases cited *supra*, notes 14, 16, 17; and *infra*, this note; and, generally, *infra*, II, A, 2, b, c, d, e, f.

Duty distinguished from tax see U. S. *v.* Fifty-Nine Demijohns Aquadiente, etc., 39 Fed. 401, 402.

Excise distinguished from tax see Oliver *v.* Washington Mills, 11 Allen (Mass.) 268, 274; and INTERNAL REVENUE, 22 Cyc. 1598 note 4.

"**Forfeitures, fines and penalties** are in no true sense taxes levied." Allis *v.* Jefferson County, 34 Ark. 307, 310.

Judgments distinguished from taxes see Peirce *v.* Boston, 3 Metc. (Mass.) 520, 521.

Subsidies distinguished from taxes see Black L. Dict. *sub verb* "Tax."

Tolls distinguished from taxes see Manistee River Imp. Co. *v.* Sands, 53 Mich. 593, 596, 19 N. W. 199; St. Louis *v.* Western Union Tel. Co., 148 U. S. 92, 97, 13 S. Ct. 485, 37

nations according to that upon which the tax is laid or the purpose for which it is imposed.[56]

4. **Taxation and Representation.** Taxation without representation, or without the consent in some form of those who are to be taxed, is vicious in principle and contrary to the fundamental principles of good government;[57] but the principle of representation applies to political communities, as such, and not to individuals, and is satisfied by their adequate representation in the legislative body which votes the tax.[58] Hence this principle does not prevent any state from taxing the property of persons who have not the right to vote, such as infants, married women, and non-residents.[59]

B. Origin, Nature, and Extent of Taxing Power — 1. In General. The power of taxation rests upon necessity, and is an essential and inherent attribute of sovereignty, belonging as a matter of right to every independent state or government,[60] and it is as extensive as the range of subjects over which the power of that government extends.[61] As to such subjects and in the absence of consti-

497, 501; Black L. Dict. [*quoted* in Pingree *v.* Auditor-Gen., 120 Mich. 95, 99, 78 N. W. 1025, 44 L. R. A. 679].

"A tax of so much per centum on the invoiced or appraised money value of the goods subject to the tax." Perry Princ. Pol. Econ. 557 [*quoted* in Pingree *v.* Auditor-Gen., 120 Mich. 95, 98, 78 N. W. 1025, 44 L. R. A. 679].

"'*Ad valorem*' means a quotient part of the existing value of property, not an adjustment of burdens to each individual man, in view of his particular gains or damages." Little Rock *v.* Board of Improvements, 42 Ark. 152, 162.

Specific and ad valorem taxes distinguished see Union Trust Co. *v.* Wayne Prob. Judge, 125 Mich. 487, 84 N. W. 1101; Pingree *v.* Auditor-Gen., 120 Mich. 95, 78 N. W. 1025, 44 L. R. A. 679; Bailey *v.* Fuqua, 24 Miss. 497.

These terms are ordinarily used in relation to tariff taxes, but there is nothing in the distinction itself to so limit the application. Pingree *v.* Auditor-Gen., 120 Mich. 95, 98, 78 N. W. 1025, 44 L. R. A. 679 [*quoting* Perry Princ. Pol. Econ. 557].

56. See Levi *v.* Louisville, 97 Ky. 394, 30 S. W. 973, 16 Ky. L. Rep. 872, 28 L. R. A. 480.

Particular taxes defined see *supra*, I, A, 1.

In addition to the general system of property taxation "taxation may be based on income, on licenses, and on franchises, and a head or poll tax." Levi *v.* Louisville, 97 Ky. 394, 401, 30 S. W. 973, 16 Ky. L. Rep. 872, 28 L. R. A. 480.

Capitation or poll tax see *infra*, II, F, 3; III, A, 6, c.

Excise tax see *infra*, II, F, 1; III, A, 6, a.

Income tax see *infra*, II, F, 2; III, A, 6, b.

Legacy and inheritance taxes see *infra*, XVI.

Tax on transfers of corporate stock see *infra*, XVII.

57. Gage *v.* Graham, 57 Ill. 144; Harward *v.* St. Clair, etc., Levee, etc., Co., 51 Ill. 130; Keasy *v.* Bricker, 60 Pa. St. 9.

58. *Connecticut.*— State *v.* Williams, 68 Conn. 131, 35 Atl. 24, 421, 48 L. R. A. 465.

Kentucky.— Clark *v.* Leathers, 5 S. W. 576, 9 Ky. L. Rep. 558.

Maine.— Opinion of Justices, 18 Me. 458.

New York.— People *v.* Brooklyn, 4 N. Y. 419, 55 Am. Dec. 266.

North Carolina.— Moore *v.* Fayetteville, 80 N. C. 154, 30 Am. Rep. 75; Lockhart *v.* Harrington, 8 N. C. 408.

Virginia.— *In re* Case of the County Levy, 5 Call 139.

Wisconsin.— Chicago, etc., R. Co. *v.* State, 128 Wis. 553, 108 N. W. 557.

See 45 Cent. Dig. tit. "Taxation," § 4.

Taxation in District of Columbia.—As bearing on the question of taxation without representation, it is to be noted that the power of taxation of persons and property in the District of Columbia, where there is no direct representation of the people, is vested in congress generally and without limit. See Loughborough *v.* Blake, 5 Wheat. (U. S.) 317, 5 L. ed. 98.

59. Smith *v.* Macon, 20 Ark. 17; Wheeler *v.* Wall, 6 Allen (Mass.) 558; Moore *v.* Fayetteville, 80 N. C. 154, 30 Am. Rep. 75; Thomas *v.* Gay, 169 U. S. 264, 18 S. Ct. 340, 42 L. ed. 740.

60. *California.*— People *v.* Coleman, 4 Cal. 46, 60 Am. Dec. 581.

Illinois.— Porter *v.* Rockford, etc., R. Co., 76 Ill. 561.

Indiana.— Hanna *v.* Allen County, 8 Blackf. 352.

Maine.— Camden *v.* Camden Village, 77 Me. 530, 1 Atl. 689.

New Jersey.— New Jersey R., etc., Co. *v.* Collectors, 26 N. J. L. 519.

New York.— People *v.* Pitt, 169 N. Y. 521, 62 N. E. 662, 58 L. R. A. 372.

Ohio.— Debolt *v.* Ohio L. Ins., etc., Co., 1 Ohio St. 563.

Pennsylvania.— Commonwealth Bank *v.* Com., 19 Pa. St. 144.

Utah.— Union Refrigerator Transit Co. *v.* Lynch, 18 Utah 378, 55 Pac. 639, 48 L. R. A. 790.

Wisconsin.— State *v.* Thorne, 112 Wis. 81, 87 N. W. 797, 55 L. R. A. 956.

United States.— McCulloch *v.* Maryland, 4 Wheat. 316, 428, 4 L. ed. 579; Duer *v.* Small, 7 Fed. Cas. No. 4,116, 4 Blackf. 263, 17 How. Pr. (N. Y.) 201.

See 45 Cent. Dig. tit. "Taxation," § 2.

61. *California.*— People *v.* Coleman, 4 Cal. 46, 60 Am. Dec. 581.

to the essential characteristics of a tax,[72] as the taxing power cannot be used for the imposition of burdens which are not taxes.[73]

2. **Power of United States.** For the purposes of the general government, congress has power to lay and collect taxes, subject to the limitations imposed by the federal constitution.[74] That instrument provides that congress shall have power "to lay and collect Taxes, Duties, Imposts and Excises, to pay the Debts and provide for the common Defence and general Welfare of the United States;" [75] but it is the generally accepted interpretation that this clause is to be read as if it declared that "Congress shall have power to lay and collect taxes, etc., in order to pay the debts and provide for the common defense and general welfare of the United States," [76] the second clause of the provision constituting a qualification of the first and limiting the power of taxation to the objects specified.[77] So also congress has no authority to tax the state governments or the means, agencies, or instrumentalities by which they are carried on,[78] nor to interfere with state taxes either in amount, assessment, collection, or means of payment.[79]

3. **Power of States.** Subject to the general rules above stated,[80] under which a state cannot tax the property of the United States,[81] or its governmental agencies,[82] and except in so far as it is limited or restrained by the provisions of the constitutions, national and state, the taxing power of a state is general and absolute, and extends to all persons, property, and business within its jurisdiction or reach; [83] and the liability of the same person or property to taxation by

The reason why such property is not taxed is that it would render necessary other taxation for the payment of the taxes so laid so that the public would be taxing itself to raise money to pay over to itself. Public School Trustees *v.* Trenton, 30 N. J. Eq. 667; Norfolk *v.* Perry, 108 Va. 28, 61 S. E. 866, 128 Am. St. Rep. 940. A further reason which has been assigned is that such taxation might result in a sale of the property, thereby destroying its public character. Camden *v.* Camden Village Corp., 77 Me. 530, 1 Atl. 689.

Property of states see *infra*, III, C, 3.

Property of municipal corporations see *infra*, III, C, 4.

72. McClelland *v.* State, 138 Ind. 321, 37 N. E. 1089; Citizens Sav., etc., Assoc. *v.* Topeka, 20 Wall. (U. S.) 655, 22 L. ed. 455.

Nature of taxes see *supra*, I, A, 2, a.

73. Sharpless *v.* Philadelphia, 21 Pa. St. 147, 169, 59 Am. Dec. 759 (where the court said: "Taxation is a mode of raising revenue for public purposes. When it is prostituted to objects in no way connected with the public interests or welfare, it ceases to be taxation, and becomes plunder);" Citizens Sav., etc., Assoc. *v.* Topeka, 20 Wall. (U. S.) 655, 664, 22 L. ed. 455 (holding that to employ the power of taxation in aid of private individuals or private enterprises is not taxation and "is none the less a robbery because it is done under the forms of law and is called taxation").

"**The term 'taxation'** imports the raising of money for public use, and excludes the raising of it for private uses." Mead *v.* Acton, 139 Mass. 341, 344, 1 N. E. 413.

Assessments for improvements are, however, imposed under the general power of taxation, although distinguishable from ordinary taxes. See *supra*, I, A, 2, d.

74. License Tax Cases, 5 Wall. (U. S.) 462, 18 L. ed. 497; South Carolina *v.* U. S., 39 Ct. Cl. 257 [*affirmed* in 199 U. S. 437, 26 S. Ct. 110, 50 L. ed. 261].

75. U. S. Const. art. 1, § 8. See also Union Bank *v.* Hill, 3 Coldw. (Tenn.) 325; Van Brocklin *v.* Anderson, 117 U. S. 151, 6 S. Ct. 670, 29 L. ed. 845; and, generally, Customs Duties, 12 Cyc. 1108; Internal Revenue, 22 Cyc. 1600.

76. Black Const. L. (3d ed.) 207; 1 Story Const. §§ 907-921.

77. 1 Story Const. §§ 907, 908.

78. Union Bank *v.* Hill, 3 Coldw. (Tenn.) 325 (no authority to tax state courts); U. S. *v.* Baltimore, etc., R. Co., 17 Wall. (U. S.) 322, 21 L. ed. 597; Buffington *v.* Day, 11 Wall. (U. S.) 113, 20 L. ed. 122 (no authority to tax salaries of judicial officers of a state); Black Const. L. (3d ed.) 450. And see *infra*, III, D, 1.

79. Whitcaker *v.* Haley, 2 Oreg. 128.

80. See *supra*, I, B, 1.

81. Van Brocklin *v.* Tennessee, 117 U. S. 151, 6 S. Ct. 670, 29 L. ed. 845 [*reversing* 15 Lea (Tenn.) 33]. See also *infra*, III, C, 2.

82. McCullough *v.* Maryland, 4 Wheat. (U. S.) 316, 4 L. ed. 579. See also *infra*, III, D, 2.

83. *California.*— State Bank *v.* San Francisco, 142 Cal. 276, 75 Pac. 832, 100 Am. St. Rep. 130, 64 L. R. A. 918.

Idaho.— Stein *v.* Morrison, 9 Ida. 426, 75 Pac. 246.

Illinois.— Harder's Fire-Proof Storage, etc., Co. *v.* Chicago, 235 Ill. 58, 85 N. E. 245; Greenleaf *v.* Morgan County, 184 Ill. 226, 56 N. E. 295, 75 Am. St. Rep. 168; State Treasurer *v.* Wright, 28 Ill. 509.

Iowa.— Judy *v.* Beckwith, 137 Iowa 24, 114 N. W. 565, 15 L. R. A. N. S. 142.

Kentucky.— Johnson *v.* Bradley-Watkins Tie Co., 120 Ky. 136, 85 S. W. 726, 27 Ky. L. Rep. 540.

save in pursuance of a positive law, nor in any other manner than in accordance with its provisions.[35]

2. Delegation of Taxing Power. It is not competent for the legislature to delegate its power of taxation, wholly or in part, to either of the other departments of government, or to any individual, private corporation, officer, board, or commission.[36] An exception exists in the case of the municipal corporations of the state, to which the legislature may lawfully delegate the power of taxation so far as necessary for their own purposes and in respect to property within their jurisdiction,[37] provided the purpose is a public one.[38] But even in this case the power must be expressly and distinctly granted,[39] and must be exercised in strict conformity to the terms of the grant;[40] and the municipality cannot delegate to an administrative officer or board the authority to determine when, to what extent, or for what purposes taxes shall be laid.[41]

35. Stanley *v.* Little Pittsburg Min. Co., 6 Colo. 415; Barlow *v.* Sumter County, 47 Ga. 639; Queens County Water Co. *v.* Monroe, 83 N. Y. App. Div. 105, 82 N. Y. Suppl. 610; Zanesville *v.* Richards, 5 Ohio St. 589.

36. *Arkansas.*— Pulaski County *v.* Irvin, 4 Ark. 473.

California.— Bixler *v.* Sacramento County, 59 Cal. 698; Smith *v.* Farrelly, 52 Cal. 77; Houghton *v.* Austin, 47 Cal. 646; Hardenburgh *v.* Kidd, 10 Cal. 402.

Illinois.— Porter *v.* Rockford, etc., R. Co., 76 Ill. 561; Wabash River Leveeing Directors *v.* Houston, 71 Ill. 318; Gage *v.* Graham, 57 Ill. 144.

Kansas.— Hovey *v.* Wyandotte County, 56 Kan. 577, 44 Pac. 17; Wyandotte County *v.* Abbott, 52 Kan. 148, 34 Pac. 416.

Kentucky.— James *v.* U. S. Fidelity, etc., Co., 133 Ky. 299, 117 S. W. 406; Cypress Pond Draining Co. *v.* Hooper, 2 Metc. 350.

Louisiana.— Flower *v.* Legras, 24 La. Ann. 204.

New Jersey.—Van Cleve *v.* Passaic Valley Sewerage Com'rs, 71 N. J. L. 574, 60 Atl. 214, 108 Am. St. Rep. 754; Bernards Tp. *v.* Allen, 61 N. J. L. 228, 39 Atl. 716.

Ohio.— See Dexter *v.* Raine, 10 Ohio Dec. (Reprint) 25, 18 Cinc. L. Bul. 61.

Pennsylvania.— Keeler *v.* Westgate, 10 Pa. Dist. 240.

Tennessee.— Reelfoot Lake Levee Dist. *v.* Dawson, 97 Tenn. 151, 36 S. W. 1041, 34 L. R. A. 725.

Texas.— Norris *v.* Waco, 57 Tex. 635.

United States. — Meriwether *v.* Garrett, 102 U. S. 472, 26 L. ed. 197; Parks *v.* Wyandotte County, 61 Fed. 436.

See 45 Cent. Dig. tit. "Taxation," § 60.

Mode of determining valuation.—The right to exercise a judgment or discretion as to the method that shall be employed in arriving at the valuation of property sought to be taxed is vested in the legislature and this power cannot be delegated. James *v.* U. S. Fidelity, etc., Co., 133 Ky. 299, 117 S. W. 406.

37. *Alabama.*—Baldwin *v.* Montgomery, 53 Ala. 437.

Arkansas.— Carson *v.* St. Francis Levee Dist., 59 Ark. 513, 27 S. W. 590.

Florida.— Moseley *v.* Tift, 4 Fla. 402.

Indiana.— Marion School City *v.* Forrest, 168 Ind. 94, 78 N. E. 187; Logansport *v.* Seybold, 59 Ind. 225.

Iowa.— State *v.* Des Moines, 103 Iowa 76, 72 N. W. 639, 64 Am. St. Rep. 157, 39 L. R. A. 285.

Kentucky.—Short *v.* Bartlett, 114 Ky. 143, 70 S. W. 283, 24 Ky. L. Rep. 932.

Louisiana.— Slack *v.* Ray, 26 La. Ann. 674.

Maryland.— Alexander *v.* Baltimore, 5 Gill 383, 46 Am. Dec. 630.

Michigan.— People *v.* Hurlbut, 24 Mich. 44, 9 Am. Rep. 103.

Missouri.—St. Louis *v.* Laughlin, 49 Mo. 559.

New Hampshire.— State *v.* Noyes, 30 N. H. 279.

New Jersey.—Van Cleve *v.* Passaic Valley Sewerage Com'rs, 71 N. J. L. 574, 60 Atl. 214, 108 Am. St. Rep. 754.

North Carolina.— Caldwell *v.* Burke County Justices, 57 N. C. 323.

Pennsylvania.— Philadelphia *v.* Philadelphia Traction Co., 206 Pa. St. 35, 55 Atl. 762; Jermyn *v.* Fowler, 186 Pa. St. 595, 40 Atl. 972; Butler's Appeal, 73 Pa. St. 448.

Texas.—Kinney *v.* Zimpleman, 36 Tex. 554.

Virginia.— Gilkeson *v.* Frederick Justices, 13 Gratt. 577; Bull *v.* Read, 13 Gratt. 78.

See also Municipal Corporations, 28 Cyc. 1659.

38. Atty.-Gen. *v.* Eau Claire, 37 Wis. 400, 438, where the court said: "In legislative grants of the power to municipal corporations, the public use must appear. . . . The legislature can delegate the power to tax to municipal corporations for public purposes only; and the validity of the delegation rests on the public purpose." See also *supra*, I, D, 1; and, generally, Municipal Corporations, 28 Cyc. 1660, 1663.

39. State *v.* Braxton County Ct., 60 W. Va. 339, 55 S. E. 382; Felton *v.* Hamilton County, 97 Fed. 823, 38 C. C. A. 432; Winnipeg Protestant School Dist. *v.* Canadian Pac. R. Co., 2 Manitoba 163.

40. Hinson *v.* Lott, 40 Ala. 123; Com. *v.* Citizens' Nat. Bank, 117 Ky. 946, 80 S. W. 158, 25 Ky. L. Rep. 2100; Judge *v.* Campbell County Ct. *v.* Taylor, 8 Bush (Ky.) 206; Maurin *v.* Smith, 25 La. Ann. 445; Montgomery County *v.* Tallant, 96 Va. 723, 32 S. E. 479; Virginia, etc., R. Co. *v.* Washington County, 30 Gratt. (Va.) 471.

41. St. Louis *v.* Clemens, 52 Mo. 133; State *v.* Koster, 38 N. J. L. 308; Davis *v.* Read, 65 N. Y. 566; Thompson *v.* Schermerhorn, 6 N. Y. 92, 55 Am. Dec. 385.

for conflict with provisions of the federal or state constitution,[49] or where the proceedings under it, which it is attempted to cure, were void *ab initio*, as for fraud, want of jurisdiction or authority, or other fatal defect.[50]

II. CONSTITUTIONAL REQUIREMENTS AND RESTRICTIONS.

A. In General — 1. NATURE AND EFFECT OF PROVISIONS. Limitations upon the taxing power both of the United States and of the several states are found in the federal constitution;[51] and the general principle of the separation of the three departments of government forbids such an exercise of the power of taxation as would infringe upon the constitutional rights of the courts or of the executive.[52] There are also in the different state constitutions various provisions relating expressly to taxation,[53] such as the provisions requiring equality and uniformity in taxation,[54] or taxation according to value,[55] or imposing restrictions as to its purpose,[56] or as to its rate or amount.[57] The principle of home rule is also now generally established by constitutional provisions, its application to matters of taxation being found in the declaration that the legislature may levy taxes only for state purposes, those for the uses of municipal corporations being left entirely within the control of the latter under the general authorization of the legislature.[58] The power of taxation being essential to government, and being usually confided

49. Hawkins *v.* Mangum, 78 Miss. 97, 28 So. 872; Dean *v.* Borchsenius, 30 Wis. 236 (holding that a tax wrong in substance and in principle, and inherently unjust and vicious, cannot be legalized or made valid as a whole, or without correction by subsequent legislative enactment); First Nat. Bank *v.* Covington, 103 Fed. 523; Exchange Bank Tax Cases, 21 Fed. 99 [*affirmed* in 122 U. S. 154, 7 S. Ct. 1244, 30 L. ed. 1088]. *Compare* People *v.* Williams, 3 Thomps. & C. (N. Y.) 338.

50. People *v.* McCreery, 34 Cal. 432; Turner *v.* Pewee Valley, 100 Ky. 288, 38 S. W. 143, 688, 18 Ky. L. Rep. 755; Slaughter *v.* Louisville, 89 Ky. 112, 8 S. W. 917, 12 Ky. L. Rep. 61; Hagner *v.* Hall, 10 N. Y. App. Div. 581, 42 N. Y. Suppl. 63 [*affirmed* in 159 N. Y. 552, 54 N. E. 1092]; Selpho *v.* Brooklyn, 9 N. Y. St. 700; Evans *v.* Fall River County, 9 S. D. 130, 68 N. W. 195. But see Francklyn *v.* Long Island City, 32 Hun (N. Y.) 451 [*affirmed* in 102 N. Y. 692]; Collins *v.* Long Island City, 9 N. Y. Suppl. 866 [*affirmed* in 132 N. Y. 321, 30 N. E. 835]; Kettelle *v.* Warwick, etc., Water Co., 23 R. I. 114, 49 Atl. 492.

51. **Application to taxation of general constitutional provisions** relating to: Due process of law see CONSTITUTIONAL LAW, 8 Cyc. 1115, 1130. Equal protection of the laws see CONSTITUTIONAL LAW, 8 Cyc. 1071. Impairing obligation of contracts see CONSTITUTIONAL LAW, 8 Cyc. 936, 940, 944, 975. Privileges and immunities of citizens secured to them by constitutional provision see CONSTITUTIONAL LAW, 8 Cyc. 1047.

The fifth and seventh amendments to the constitution of the United States are designed as restrictions upon legislation by the federal government, and not upon state governments in respect to their own citizens, and therefore do not affect the validity of a state law imposing a tax on the gross earnings of a railway company. North Missouri R. Co. *v.* Maguire, 49 Mo. 490, 8 Am. Rep. 141.

Taxation of commerce see COMMERCE, 7 Cyc. 470.

52. See Black Const. L. (3d ed.) 83 *et seq.*; Cooley Taxation 41.

Taxation of property in custodia legis.—A statute providing that real estate held by a state officer in his official or judicial capacity, in trust for the benefit of some person, shall be subject to taxation, and the taxes levied thereon shall be a lien enforced as are other taxes, is not an unconstitutional invasion of the functions of the court of chancery in the administration of estates, since the law is at least valid in so far as it makes such taxes a lien on the land, which lien the chancery court can enforce by appropriate proceedings. Chancellor *v.* Elizabeth, 65 N. J. L. 479, 47 Atl. 454.

53. See the constitutions of the several states.

54. See *infra*, II, B.

55. See *infra*, II, D.

56. See *infra*, II, A, 3.

57. See *infra*, II, E.

58. See the following cases:

California.— Fatjo *v.* Pfister, 117 Cal. 83, 48 Pac. 1012.

Illinois.— Chicago *v.* Wolf, 221 Ill. 130, 77 N. E. 414; Dunnovan *v.* Green, 57 Ill. 63.

Kentucky.— Paducah St. R. Co. *v.* McCracken County, 105 Ky. 472, 49 S. W. 178, 20 Ky. L. Rep. 1294; South Covington, etc., R. Co. *v.* Bellevue, 105 Ky. 283, 49 S. W. 23, 20 Ky. L. Rep. 1184, 57 L. R. A. 50.

Louisiana.— State *v.* Police Jury, 47 La. Ann. 1244, 17 So. 792.

Missouri.— State *v.* St. Louis, 216 Mo. 47, 115 S. W. 534; State *v.* Ashbrook, 154 Mo. 375, 55 S. W. 627, 77 Am. St. Rep. 765, 48 L. R. A. 265.

Montana.— Hauser *v.* Miller, 37 Mont. 22, 94 Pac. 197.

New York.— People *v.* State Tax Com'rs, 174 N. Y. 417, 67 N. E. 69; People *v.* Romer, 48 Misc. 436, 95 N. Y. Suppl. 518 [*affirmed* in 110 N. Y. App. Div. 816, 97 N. Y. Suppl. 550].

in the largest measure to the legislative discretion, constitutional limitations upon its exercise will not be inferred or implied, but must be distinctly and positively expressed.[59] On the other hand, such constitutional provisions as are designed for the protection of taxpayers, or such as impose penalties or forfeitures upon them, will be strictly construed.[60] In the absence of constitutional restrictions the power of the legislature in regard to taxation is practically absolute and unlimited,[61] so long as it is exercised for public purposes,[62] and taxes may be imposed which are not equal, uniform, or according to value;[63] and while such taxation may be unwise, inequitable, or oppressive, it cannot merely upon this ground be declared unconstitutional,[64] the proper remedy being by appeal to the legislature and not to the courts.[65]

2. Statement of Object of Tax. The constitutions of several states provide that every law imposing a tax shall state distinctly the object of the same, to which only it shall be applied.[66] It is held, however, that this applies only to the ordinary and general taxes for state purposes, and such as are imposed generally on all the taxable property in the state, and not to local taxes for local purposes,[67]

Texas.— Missouri, etc., R. Co. *v.* Shannon, 100 Tex. 379, 100 S. W. 138, 10 L. R. A. N. S. 681.

59. *Alabama.*— Southern R. Co. *v.* St. Clair County, 124 Ala. 491, 27 So. 23; Capital City Water Co. *v.* Montgomery County, 117 Ala. 303, 23 So. 970.

Kentucky.— South Covington, etc., R. Co. *v.* Bellevue, 105 Ky. 283, 49 S. W. 23, 20 Ky. L. Rep. 1184, 57 L. R. A. 50.

Michigan.—Walcott *v.* People, 17 Mich. 68.

Minnesota.— See State *v.* Winona, etc., R. Co., 21 Minn. 315.

New Jersey.— State *v.* Parker, 32 N. J. L. 426.

Virginia.— Eyre *v.* Jacob, 14 Gratt. 422, 73 Am. Dec. 367.

Wisconsin.— State *v.* Thorne, 112 Wis. 81, 87 N. W. 797, 55 L. R. A. 95.

United States.— Lane County *v.* Oregon, 7 Wall. 71, 19 L. ed. 101.

60. King *v.* Hatfield, 130 Fed. 564; Denike *v.* Rourke, 7 Fed. Cas. No. 3,787, 3 Biss. 39.

61. See *supra*, I, B.

62. See *supra*, I, D.

63. *Connecticut.*— State *v.* Travelers' Ins. Co., 73 Conn. 255, 47 Atl. 299, 57 L. R. A. 481.

Mississippi.— Smith *v.* Aberdeen Corp., 25 Miss. 458.

Nebraska.— Burlington, etc., R. Co. *v.* Lancaster County, 4 Nebr. 293.

New York.— Genet *v.* Brooklyn, 99 N. Y. 296, 1 N. E. 777; People *v.* Brooklyn, 4 N. Y. 419, 55 Am. Dec. 266.

Pennsylvania.—Weber *v.* Reinhard, 73 Pa. St. 370, 13 Am. Rep. 747.

64. State *v.* Travelers' Ins. Co., 73 Conn. 255, 47 Atl. 299, 57 L. R. A. 481; People *v.* Brooklyn, 4 N. Y. 419, 55 Am. Dec. 266; Weber *v.* Reinhard, 73 Pa. St. 370, 13 Am. Rep. 747.

65. Genet *v.* Brooklyn, 99 N. Y. 296, 1 N. E. 777.

66. See the constitutions of the several states; and the following cases:

Michigan.—Trowbridge *v.* Detroit, 99 Mich. 443, 58 N. W. 368.

Missouri.— State *v.* Henderson, 160 Mo. 190, 60 S. W. 1093.

New York.— People *v.* Kings County, 52 N. Y. 556.

Ohio.— *In re* Oil Well, 18 Ohio Cir. Ct. 885, 9 Ohio Cir. Dec. 860; State *v.* Fangbouer, 14 Ohio Cir. Ct. 104, 12 Ohio Cir. Dec. 801.

South Carolina.— Southern R. Co. *v.* Kay, 62 S. C. 28, 39 S. E. 785.

Virginia.— Com. *v.* Brown, 91 Va. 762, 21 S. E. 357, 28 L. R. A. 110.

Washington.— Mason *v.* Purdy, 11 Wash. 591, 40 Pac. 130.

See 45 Cent. Dig. tit. "Taxation," § 66.

Stating the tax.— A law which merely directs a tax to be levied for certain purposes, leaving it to the commissioners named in the act to determine the amount to be raised, does not "state the tax" within the meaning of the constitution. Hanlon *v.* Westchester, 57 Barb. (N. Y.) 383, 8 Abb. Pr. N. S. 261.

Amendatory or supplemental legislation.— The constitutional provision applies to a tax statute, although it is merely an amendment of a former law. People *v.* Moring, 47 Barb. (N. Y.) 642 [*affirmed* in 3 Abb. Dec. 539, 3 Keyes 374, 4 Transcr. App. 522]. But see Com. *v.* Brown, 91 Va. 762, 21 S. E. 357, 28 L. R. A. 110, where it is said that a law which merely continues an old tax is not affected by the constitutional requirement, provided the act which originally imposed the tax sufficiently stated its object.

Reference to another statute.— In some states the constitution also provides that it shall not be sufficient for a tax law to refer to any other statute to fix the tax or its object. But this is not violated by a reference to another law merely for the purpose of designating the machinery to be employed in assessing and collecting the tax. Trowbridge *v.* Detroit, 99 Mich. 443, 58 N. W. 368.

Object of the tax stated by the constitution.— A statute is not invalid for failure to state the object of the tax which it levies where the constitution itself directs how that particular tax shall be appropriated. Walcott *v.* People, 17 Mich. 68.

67. Guthrie County *v.* Conrad, 133 Iowa 171, 110 N. W. 454; Guest *v.* Brooklyn, 8

or to special taxes on peculiar kinds of property or such as are in the nature of license or occupation fees;[68] nor does the provision apply to laws which merely provide or regulate the machinery for assessing and collecting the tax.[69] An exact enumeration of all the items of expenditure to which the revenue of the state may be applied is neither practicable nor required by such a constitutional provision; it is sufficient if the tax law states in general terms that the taxes are to be applied to "the ordinary and current expenses of the state," or to its "general fund," without greater detail.[70]

3. **Restrictions as to Purposes of Taxation.** In the absence of specific constitutional restrictions, the legislature of a state is vested with the authority to determine the objects and purposes for which the taxing power shall be exercised,[71] subject only to the condition that such purposes shall be public,[72] and lawful.[73] It is, however, commonly provided that taxes shall be imposed by the legislative authority only for state purposes,[74] and that the legislature shall not levy taxes on the inhabitants or property of municipal corporations for local or corporate purposes.[75]

B. Equality and Uniformity — 1. In General — a. Constitutional Provisions.[76] The constitutions of many of the states contain the requirement that taxation shall be equal and uniform, that all property in the state shall be taxed in proportion to its value, that all taxes shall be uniform upon the same class of subjects within the territorial limits of the authority levying the tax, or that the legislature shall provide for an equal and uniform rate of assessment and taxation;[77] and in the face of such provisions a tax law which violates the prescribed

Hun (N. Y.) 97 [*affirmed* in 69 N. Y. 506]; *In re* Ford, 6 Lans. (N. Y.) 92; Sun Mut. Ins. Co. *v.* New York, 5 Sandf. (N. Y.) 10 [*affirmed* in 8 N. Y. 241]; Southern R. Co. *v.* Kay, 62 S. C. 28, 39 S. E. 785.

68. Jones *v.* Chamberlain, 109 N. Y. 100, 16 N. E. 72 (tax for bounties); *In re* McPherson, 104 N. Y. 306, 10 N. E. 685, 58 Am. Rep. 502 (succession tax on legacies to non-relatives); New York Exempt Firemen's Benev. Fund *v.* Roome, 93 N. Y. 313, 45 Am. Rep. 217; People *v.* Moring, 3 Abb. Dec. (N. Y.) 539, 3 Keyes 374, 4 Transcr. App. 522; Com. *v.* Brown, 91 Va. 762, 21 S. E. 357, 28 L. R. A. 110.

69. Trowbridge *v.* Detroit, 99 Mich. 443, 58 N. W. 368; Clark *v.* Sheldon, 106 N. Y. 104, 12 N. E. 341; People *v.* Ulster County, 36 Hun (N. Y.) 491; Michigan R. Tax Cases, 138 Fed. 223 [*affirmed* in 201 U. S. 245, 26 S. Ct. 459, 50 L. ed. 744].

70. Westinghausen *v.* People, 44 Mich. 265, 6 N. W. 641; People *v.* Home Ins. Co., 92 N. Y. 328; People *v.* Orange County, 17 N. Y. 235; Matter of Atty.-Gen., 58 Hun (N. Y.) 218, 12 N. Y. Suppl. 754; People *v.* National F. Ins. Co., 27 Hun (N. Y.) 188; People *v.* Orange County, 27 Barb. (N. Y.) 575 [*affirmed* in 17 N. Y. 245]; Mason *v.* Purdy, 11 Wash. 591, 40 Pac. 130.

71. People *v.* Pacheco, 27 Cal. 175; People *v.* Burr, 13 Cal. 343.

72. Public purpose as essential to validity of tax law see *supra*, I, D, 1.

There are express constitutional requirements in some jurisdictions that taxation shall be for public purposes only (State *v.* St. Louis, 216 Mo. 47, 115 S. W. 534: State *v.* Switzler. 143 Mo. 287, 45 S. W. 245, 65 Am. St. Rep. 653, 40 L. R. A. 280; Hauser *v.* Miller, 37 Mont. 22, 94 Pac. 197); but this is a general requirement growing out of the essential character of a tax and applies regardless of any express constitutional restriction (see *supra*, I, D, 1).

73. Marion Tp. Bd. *v.* Education *v.* State, 51 Ohio St. 531, 38 N. E. 614, 46 Am. St. Rep. 588, 25 L. R. A. 770; Debolt *v.* Ohio L. Ins., etc., Co., 1 Ohio St. 563.

74. *In re* Taxation of Min. Claims, 9 Colo. 635, 21 Pac. 476; Gooding *v.* Proffitt, 11 Ida. 380, 83 Pac. 230; Fisher *v.* Steele, 39 La. Ann. 447, 1 So. 882; State *v.* St. Louis, 216 Mo. 47, 115 S. W. 534.

Bounties for destruction of wild animals.— A statute providing a bounty for the destruction of certain wild animals is not in violation of a constitutional prohibition against the levying of taxes or the imposition of burdens on the people except to raise sufficient revenue "for the economical administration of the government." Dimmit County *v.* Frazier, (Tex. Civ. App. 1894) 27 S. W. 829.

75. People *v.* School Trustees, 78 Ill. 136; State *v.* St. Louis, 216 Mo. 47, 115 S. W. 534; *Ex p.* Loving, 178 Mo. 194, 77 S. W. 508; Hauser *v.* Miller, 37 Mont. 22, 94 Pac. 197; State *v.* Wheeler, 33 Nebr. 563, 50 N. W. 770. See also *supra*, II, A, 1.

76. Application of the 14th amendment of the federal constitution in regard to "the equal protection of the laws" see Constitutional Law, 8 Cyc. 1071.

77. See the constitutions of the several states; and the following cases:

Colorado.— Leonard *v.* Reed, 46 Colo. 307, 104 Pac. 410, 13 Am. St. Rep. 77.

Florida.— Hayes *v.* Walker, 54 Fla. 163, 44 So. 747.

Georgia.— Penick *v.* Foster, 129 Ga. 217, 58 S. E. 773, 12 L. R. A. N. S. 1159.

and the necessities of practical administration will permit.[18] Hence the courts will not pronounce a statute invalid on this ground unless it appears that it was framed on a plan or principle not calculated to produce equality and uniformity, or that its administration will result in such flagrant injustice as to evidence an entire disregard of the constitutional requirement.[19]

e. Fraud or Defects in Execution of Tax Law. The constitutional requirement of equality and uniformity has regard to the laws which may be passed for the imposition of taxes, and not to their practical working or execution;[20] and hence a law properly framed cannot be declared invalid because injustice or inequality results from the error or misconduct of the officers charged with its administration,[21] or because it is practically possible, under the terms of the statute, to escape taxation on some kinds of property by manipulation or evasion.[22] But misconduct on the part of taxing officers resulting in an assessment which is contrary to the constitutional principles of equality and uniformity may invalidate the particular assessment so made,[23] or at least entitle those discriminated against to relief against the assessment to the extent to which it is improper.[24]

18. *California.*— People *v.* Whyler, 41 Cal. 351.

Illinois.— Crozer *v.* People, 206 Ill. 464, 69 N. E. 489.

Kansas.— McIntyre *v.* Williamson, 8 Kan. App. 711, 54 Pac. 928.

Massachusetts.— Cheshire *v.* Berkshire County Com'rs, 118 Mass. 386; Com. *v.* People's Five Cents Savings Bank, 5 Allen 428.

Minnesota.— Comer *v.* Folsom, 13 Minn. 219.

Nevada.—Virginia *v.* Chollar-Potosi Gold, etc., Min. Co., 2 Nev. 86.

New Hampshire.— Wyatt *v.* State Bd. of Equalization, 74 N. H. 552, 70 Atl. 387.

Oregon.— Yamhill County *v.* Foster, 53 Oreg. 124, 99 Pac. 286; Crawford *v.* Linn County, 11 Oreg. 482, 5 Pac. 738.

Pennsylvania.—Weber *v.* Reinhard, 73 Pa. St. 370, 13 Am. Rep. 747; Grim *v.* Weissenberg School Dist., 57 Pa. St. 433, 98 Am. Dec. 237; Kirby *v.* Shaw, 19 Pa. St. 258.

Vermont.—Allen *v.* Drew, 44 Vt. 174.

Washington.—State *v.* Parmenter, 50 Wash. 164, 96 Pac. 1047, 19 L. R. A. N. S. 707; Tekoa *v.* Reilly, 47 Wash. 202, 91 Pac. 769, 13 L. R. A. N. S. 901.

19. *Arkansas.*— Patterson *v.* Temple, 27 Ark. 202.

Connecticut.— Hopkins' Appeal, 77 Conn. 644, 60 Atl. 657. See also State *v.* Travelers' Ins. Co., 73 Conn. 255, 47 Atl. 299, 57 L. R. A. 481.

Kansas.— McIntyre *v.* Williamson, 8 Kan. App. 711, 54 Pac. 928.

Kentucky.— Slack *v.* Maysville, etc., R. Co., 13 B. Mon. 1.

Massachusetts.— White *v.* Gove, 183 Mass. 333, 67 N. E. 359; Com. *v.* People's Five Cents Savings Bank, 5 Allen 428.

Minnesota.— State *v.* Hennepin County Dist. Ct., 33 Minn. 235, 22 N. W. 625.

Nevada.— Virginia *v.* Chollar-Potosi Gold, etc., Min. Co., 2 Nev. 86.

New York.— Genet *v.* Brooklyn, 99 N. Y. 296, 1 N. E. 777.

Wisconsin.— Dean *v.* Gleason, 16 Wis. 1.

United States.— Chamberlain *v.* Walter, 60 Fed. 788; Dundee Mort., etc., Co. *v.* Multnomah County School Dist. No. 1, 19 Fed. 359.

20. Spencer *v.* People, 68 Ill. 510; Kirkpatrick *v.* New Brunswick, 40 N. J. Eq. 46; Apperson *v.* Memphis, 1 Fed. Cas. No. 497, 2 Flipp. 363.

21. Missouri, etc., Trust Co. *v.* Smart, 51 La. Ann. 416, 25 So. 443; State *v.* Maxwell, 27 La. Ann. 722; Missouri, etc., R. Co. *v.* Shannon, 100 Tex. 379, 100 S. W. 138, 10 L. R. A. N. S. 681; Dundee Mortg., etc., Co. *v.* School Dist. No. 1, 21 Fed. 151. See also Illinois Cent. R. Co. *v.* Com., 128 Ky. 268, 108 S. W. 245, 32 Ky. L. Rep. 1112, 110 S. W. 265, 33 Ky. L. Rep. 326.

A tax may be rendered illegal for lack of uniformity either in consequence of the law providing for it or the misconduct of those charged with its administration, but so long as this is not a result of the law the law cannot be held invalid on this ground and the remedy, if any, must be confined to the illegal proceedings under it. Dundee Mortg., etc., Co. *v.* School Dist. No. 1, 21 Fed. 151.

22. State *v.* Savage, 65 Nebr. 714, 91 N. W. 716; Christian Moerlein Brewing Co. *v.* Hagerty, 8 Ohio Cir. Ct. 330, 4 Ohio Cir. Dec. 276; Mercantile Nat. Bank *v.* New York, 28 Fed. 776.

23. James *v.* American Surety Co., 133 Ky. 313, 117 S. W. 411; McTwiggan *v.* Hunter, 18 R. I. 776, 30 Atl. 962 (holding that where the assessors of taxes wilfully and intentionally omit property which should be assessed for taxation, the entire assessment is rendered illegal); Marsh *v.* Clark County, 42 Wis. 502 (holding that violations or evasions of duty imposed by law to secure a just and uniform rule of assessment, whether occurring by mistake in law or fraud in fact, which go to impair the general equality and uniformity of the assessment, and thereby to defeat the uniform rule of taxation, vitiate the whole assessment as the foundation of a valid tax).

Unintentional omissions in assessing property for taxation, due merely to an error of judgment or inadvertence, will not affect the validity of the tax. Chicago, etc., R. Co. *v.* State, 128 Wis. 553, 108 N. W. 557.

24. Lively *v.* Missouri, etc., R. Co., 102 Tex. 545, 120 S. W. 852 (holding that where

equally available to all taxpayers possessing property of the exempted class;[30] it being held that the requirement of equality and uniformity does not mean that all property must be taxed so as to prevent the granting of any exemptions, but merely that such property as is made subject to taxation shall be taxed equally and uniformly,[31] although in some cases the provisions are so worded or coupled with other provisions as to show an intention to prevent the granting of any exemptions.[32] The right to grant exemptions is, however, exclusively a legislative power, and does not belong to municipal corporations unless specifically accorded to them by statute.[33]

(II) *CORPORATE PROPERTY.* An exemption from taxation granted to a corporation is generally considered to be no less violative of the constitutional rule than one accorded to a private person,[34] particularly where the provision is so worded as to show an intention to prevent the granting of any exemptions,[35]

regard to certain classes of property therein specified. Christley *v.* Butler County, 37 Pa. Super. Ct. 32.

30. *Alabama.*— Daughdrill *v.* Alabama L. Ins., etc., Co., 31 Ala. 91, where the exemption was sustained as having been granted in consideration of advantages accruing to the public.

Iowa.— Leicht *v.* Burlington, 73 Iowa 29, 34 N. W. 494.

Kansas.—Ottawa County *v.* Nelson, 19 Kan. 234, 27 Am. Rep. 101.

Louisiana.— New Orleans *v.* Kennard, 34 La. Ann. 851; New Orleans *v.* Fourchy, 30 La. Ann. 910; New Orleans *v.* Davidson, 30 La. Ann. 554; Lynch *v.* Alexandria, 9 La. Ann. 498.

Maryland.— Simpson *v.* Hopkins, 82 Md. 478, 33 Atl. 714.

Michigan.— People *v.* Auditor-Gen., 7 Mich. 84.

Mississippi.— Adams *v.* Tombigbee Mills, 78 Miss. 676, 29 So. 470.

New York.— People *v.* Miller, 84 N. Y. App. Div. 168, 82 N. Y. Suppl. 621.

Oklahoma.— Pryor *v.* Bryan, 11 Okla. 357, 66 Pac. 348.

Texas.— Missouri, etc., R. Co. *v.* Shannon, 100 Tex. 379, 100 S. W. 138, 10 L. R. A. N. S. 681; Raymond *v.* Kibbe, 43 Tex. Civ. App. 209, 95 S. W. 727.

Vermont.— Colton *v.* Montpelier, 71 Vt. 413, 45 Atl. 1039.

Virginia.—Williamson *v.* Massey, 33 Gratt. 237.

Washington.— Columbia, etc., R. Co. *v.* Chilberg, 6 Wash. 612, 34 Pac. 163.

Wisconsin.—Wisconsin Cent. R. Co. *v.* Taylor County, 52 Wis. 37, 8 N. W. 833.

United States.— Peacock *v.* Pratt, 121 Fed. 772, 58 C. C. A. 48; Williams *v.* Rees, 2 Fed. 882, 9 Biss. 405.

See 45 Cent. Dig. tit. "Taxation," § 310.

Credits.— Credits are in effect the mere legal right to demand the delivery of money or other property in the future, and until such transfer of possession is made the property is taxed wherever it may be so that the total actual property of the state may be once taxed without taxing credits. State *v.* Parmenter, 50 Wash. 164, 96 Pac. 1047, 19 L. R. A. N. S. 707.

Public property.— The word "property" as used in a constitution providing that taxation shall be uniform on all property subject to be taxed within the limits of the authority levying the tax does not require the taxing of public property or any of the lawful instrumentalities of government. Penick *v.* Foster, 129 Ga. 217, 58 S. E. 773, 12 L. R. A. N. S. 1159. See also People *v.* McCreery, 34 Cal. 432.

31. New Orleans *v.* Commercial Bank, 10 La. Ann. 735; Williamson *v.* Massey, 33 Gratt. (Va.) 237; Columbia, etc., R. Co. *v.* Chilberg, 6 Wash. 612, 34 Pac. 163; Wisconsin Cent. R. Co. *v.* Taylor County, 52 Wis. 37, 8 N. W. 833. See also cases cited *supra*, notes 15, 30.

Partial exemption.—A right to exempt as a whole will not authorize a partial exemption conditional upon the property paying an arbitrary percentage, where the constitution requires that taxes shall be proportional. *In re* Opinion of Justices, 195 Mass. 607, 84 N. E. 499.

32. People *v.* McCreery, 34 Cal. 432; Chattanooga *v.* Nashville, etc., R. Co., 7 Lea (Tenn.) 561; Chesapeake, etc., R. Co. *v.* Miller, 19 W. Va. 408. See also cases cited *supra*, note 29.

33. State *v.* Hannibal, etc., R. Co., 75 Mo. 208; State *v.* Gracey, 11 Nev. 223. See also, generally, MUNICIPAL CORPORATIONS, 28 Cyc. 1686.

34. *Alabama.*— Sumter County *v.* Gainesville Nat. Bank, 62 Ala. 464, 34 Am. Rep. 30; Mobile *v.* Stonewall Ins. Co., 53 Ala. 570.

California.— Crosby *v.* Lyon, 37 Cal. 242.

Iowa.— Davenport *v.* Chicago, etc., R. Co., 38 Iowa 633.

Kentucky.— German Nat. Ins. Co. *v.* Louisville, 54 S. W. 732, 21 Ky. L. Rep. 1179.

Nebraska.— State *v.* Poynter, 59 Nebr. 417, 81 N. W. 431.

New Jersey.— State *v.* Richards, 52 N. J. L. 156, 18 Atl. 582.

Oregon.— Hogg *v.* Mackay, 23 Oreg. 339, 31 Pac. 779, 37 Am. St. Rep. 682, 19 L. R. A. 77.

Tennessee.— Chattanooga *v.* Nashville, etc., R. Co., 7 Lea 561.

West Virginia.— Chesapeake, etc., R. Co. *v.* Miller, 19 W. Va. 408.

See 45 Cent. Dig. tit. "Taxation," § 311.

35. Chattanooga *v.* Nashville, etc., R. Co.,

a specific direction, uniformity does not mean universality, but only that the tax shall be uniform on those kinds or classes of property selected to bear its burden, and it may be imposed on realty alone or on personalty alone.[44]

(II) *BETWEEN RESIDENTS AND NON-RESIDENTS.* The federal constitution secures to the citizens of each state all the privileges and immunities of citizens in the several states; and this prevents a state from taxing the property of non-residents, found within its borders, at a higher rate than is imposed on its own citizens, or exacting from them higher license or privilege taxes.[45] The same result is also held to follow from the constitutional provisions requiring the taxation of all property at an equal and uniform rate.[46]

(III) *BETWEEN CORPORATIONS.* Unless restrained by some constitutional provision for the equal taxation of all property within the state, applicable as well to corporations as to individuals,[47] it is competent for the legislature to divide

ation as of the first day of May in each year and that real property may be assessed at any time between that date and the last Monday of June. Wisconsin Cent. R. Co. *v.* Lincoln County, 57 Wis. 137, 15 N. W. 121.

44. *Dakota.*— Farris *v.* Vannier, 6 Dak. 186, 42 N. W. 31, 3 L. R. A. 713.

Louisiana.— Oubre *v.* Donaldsonville, 33 La. Ann. 386.

New Jersey.— Chancellor *v.* Elizabeth, 65 N. J. L. 479, 47 Atl. 454.

Pennsylvania.— Com. *v.* Mammoth Vein Coal, etc., Co., 3 Dauph. Co. Rep. 220.

United States.— Louisiana *v.* Pilsbury, 105 U. S. 278, 26 L. ed. 1090 [*reversing* 31 La. Ann. 1].

In dividing a county or township the legislature may relieve the personal property of the detached territory from liability for the previous debts of the county or township while continuing the liability of real property. Ottawa County *v.* Nelson, 19 Kan. 234, 27 Am. Rep. 101.

45. *Alabama.*—Wiley *v.* Parmer, 14 Ala. 627.

Arkansas.— Scott *v.* Watkins, 22 Ark. 556.

Colorado.— Smith *v.* Farr, 46 Colo. 364, 104 Pac. 401; Leonard *v.* Reed, 46 Colo. 307, 104 Pac. 410, 133 Am. St. Rep. 77.

Kentucky.— Rash *v.* Halloway, 82 Ky. 674; Daniel *v.* Richmond, 78 Ky. 542.

Louisiana.— McGuire *v.* Parker, 32 La. Ann. 832.

Massachusetts.— Oliver *v.* Washington Mills, 11 Allen 268.

Missouri.— State *v.* North, 27 Mo. 464; Crow *v.* State, 14 Mo. 237.

New Hampshire.— State *v.* Lancaster, 63 N. H. 267.

United States.— Ward *v.* Maryland, 12 Wall. 418, 20 L. ed. 449; Crandall *v.* Nevada, 6 Wall. 35, 18 L. ed. 744, 745; Corfield *v.* Coryell, 6 Fed. Cas. No. 3,230, 4 Wash. 371.

46. *Arkansas.*— Redd *v.* St. Francis County, 17 Ark. 416.

Colorado.— Leonard *v.* Reed, 46 Colo. 307, 104 Pac. 410, 133 Am. St. Rep. 77.

Georgia.— Mutual Reserve Fund L. Assoc. *v.* Augusta, 109 Ga. 73, 35 S. E. 71. *Compare* Jones *v.* Columbus, 25 Ga. 610.

Indiana.— See Buck *v.* Beach, 164 Ind. 37, 71 N. E. 963, 108 Am. St. Rep. 272.

Kansas.— *In re* Page, 60 Kan. 842, 58 Pac. 478, 47 L. R. A. 68; Marion, etc., R. Co. *v.* Champlin, 37 Kan. 682, 16 Pac. 222.

Louisiana.— Amat's Succession, 18 La. Ann. 403.

Massachusetts.— See Provident Sav. Inst. *v.* Boston, 101 Mass. 575, 3 Am. Rep. 407.

Nebraska.— State *v.* Poynter, 59 Nebr. 417, 81 N. W. 431.

South Carolina.— State *v.* Charleston, 2 Speers 719.

Tennessee.— Nashville *v.* Althorp, 5 Coldw. 554.

Canada.— Hudson Bay Co. *v.* Atty.-Gen., Manitoba t. Wood 209, holding that a tax of a certain sum per acre on lands belonging to residents and of five times as much on lands of non-residents is invalid, as violating the fundamental principle of equality in taxation.

See 45 Cent. Dig. tit. "Taxation," § 73.

Tax for grazing cattle.— A state tax on cattle driven into the state for grazing purposes during a portion of the year is invalid if it is imposed on the property of non-residents alone or at a higher rate than on the cattle of resident owners. Kiowa County Com'rs *v.* Dunn, 21 Colo. 185, 40 Pac. 357; Graham *v.* Chautauqua County, 31 Kan. 473, 2 Pac. 549; Farris *v.* Henderson, 1 Okla. 384, 33 Pac. 380; Reser *v.* Umatilla County, 48 Oreg. 326, 86 Pac. 595. See also Kelley *v.* Rhoades, 7 Wyo. 237, 51 Pac. 593, 75 Am. St. Rep. 904, 39 L. R. A. 594.

Discrimination as to time of making assessment.— A statute regulating the assessment and taxation of logs belonging to non-residents is not unconstitutional in providing for an assessment in April, while logs belonging to residents are assessed in May. Nelson Lumber Co. *v.* Loraine, 22 Fed. 54.

47. Georgia State Bldg., etc., Assoc. *v.* Savannah, 109 Ga. 63, 35 S. E. 67; Hawkeye Ins. Co. *v.* French, 109 Iowa 585, 80 N. W. 660; Cumberland Tel., etc., Co. *v.* Hopkins, 121 Ky. 850, 90 S. W. 594, 28 Ky. L. Rep. 846; Detroit *v.* Mackinaw Transp. Co., 140 Mich. 174, 103 N. W. 557; Teagan Transp. Co. *v.* Detroit Bd. of Assessors, 139 Mich. 1, 102 N. W. 273.

Tax imposed on all corporations.— A franchise or other tax which applies to all corporations subject to the power of the state, without discrimination, is valid and constitutional. Paducah St. R. Co. *v.* McCracken

equal distribution of the tax upon all the property subject to it, there is no constitutional objection to providing for the valuation of different kinds of property by different boards or officers,[56] or at different times,[57] or according to a different mode of procedure.[58]

New York.— People *v.* Fraser, 145 N. Y. 593, 40 N. E. 165.

Washington.—Andrews *v.* King County, 1 Wash. 46, 23 Pac. 409, 22 Am. St. Rep. 136.

Wyoming.— Frontier Land, etc., Co. *v.* Baldwin, 3 Wyo. 764, 31 Pac. 403.

United States.— Cummings *v.* Merchants' Nat. Bank, 101 U. S. 153, 25 L. ed. 903; Taylor *v.* Louisville, etc., R. Co., 88 Fed. 350, 31 C. C. A. 537; Railroad, etc., Cos. *v.* Tennessee Bd. of Equalizers, 85 Fed. 302; Shreveport First Nat. Bank *v.* Lindsay, 45 Fed. 619 [*reversed* on other grounds in 156 U. S. 485, 15 S. Ct. 472, 39 L. ed. 505]. *Compare* Bell's Gap R. Co. *v.* Com., 134 U. S. 232, 10 S. Ct. 533, 33 L. ed. 892.

Classification.— Where there is a proper ground for the classification of different kinds of property (see *infra*, II, B, 2), it is not a violation of the requirement of equality and uniformity that different classes are assessed at different rates in proportion to their values if all property of each class is assessed uniformly in proportion to its value (Smith *v.* Kelly, 24 Oreg. 464, 33 Pac. 642).

Tax on income or receipts of corporations. — A tax upon a corporation may be proportioned to its income or earnings, as well as to the value of its franchises or the property possessed. Kneeland *v.* Milwaukee, 15 Wis. 454; Milwaukee, etc., R. Co. *v.* Waukesha County, 9 Wis. 431 note; Minot *v.* Philadelphia, etc., R. Co., 18 Wall. (U. S.) 206, 21 L. ed. 888. But see State *v.* U. S., etc., Express Co., 60 N. H. 219.

Tax on rents reserved.— A statute taxing rents reserved in leases, which are to be assessed at a principal sum, the interest on which at the legal rate would produce a sum equal to such annual rents, is not invalid as fixing the valuation of a particular kind of property, instead of leaving it to be determined as in the case of other property. Livingston *v.* Hollenbeck, 4 Barb. (N. Y.) 9; Loring *v.* State, 16 Ohio 590.

Property unlawfully omitted.— There is no constitutional objection to a statute providing for the taxation of property which was unlawfully omitted from assessment, or for its reassessment where there was a gross undervaluation. State *v.* Weyerhauser, 68 Minn. 353, 71 N. W. 265.

Income not property.— A constitutional provision that "taxes shall be *ad valorem* only and uniform on all species of property taxed" does not require that the gross earnings of merchants and the interest on bonds and notes shall be taxed at the same rate as real estate; for income is not "property" in this sense. Waring *v.* Savannah, 60 Ga. 93.

Right to object to assessment.— A corporation whose franchise has been assessed at its fair cash value by the board of assessors cannot complain of the inequality caused by the fact that other officers have, in violation of the constitution and statutes, assessed property at less than its fair cash value. Louisville R. Co. *v.* Com., 105 Ky. 710, 49 S. W. 486, 20 Ky. L. Rep. 1509.

56. *Arkansas.*— Wells *v.* Crawford County, 63 Ark. 576, 40 S. W. 710, 37 L. R. A. 371.

Illinois.— People *v.* Cook County, 176 Ill. 576, 52 N. E. 334. See also Burton Stock Car Co. *v.* Traeger, 187 Ill. 9, 58 N. E. 418.

Indiana.— Whitney *v.* Ragsdale, 33 Ind. 107, 5 Am. Rep. 185.

Kentucky.— Com. *v.* Taylor, 101 Ky. 325, 41 S. W. 11, 19 Ky. L. Rep. 552.

Maryland.— State *v.* Baltimore, 105 Md. 1, 65 Atl. 369.

Nevada.— Sawyer *v.* Dooley, 21 Nev. 390, 32 Pac. 437.

New Jersey.— Bergen, etc., R. Co. *v.* State Bd. of Assessors, 74 N. J. L. 742, 67 Atl. 668; State Bd. of Assessors *v.* Central R. Co., 48 N. J. L. 146, 4 Atl. 578.

United States.— Cummings *v.* Merchants' Nat. Bank, 101 U. S. 153, 25 L. ed. 903.

Property of individuals and of corporations see *infra*, II, B, 4, b.

Necessity of equalization.— Under a constitutional provision requiring uniformity in taxation, it is the duty of a state, where different kinds of property are assessed by different boards or officers, to provide for equalization between them. Railroad, etc., Cos. *v.* Tennessee Bd. of Equalizers, 85 Fed. 302. And see Missouri, etc., R. Co. *v.* Geary County, 9 Kan. App. 350, 58 Pac. 121.

57. *Illinois.*— McVeagh *v.* Chicago, 49 Ill. 318.

Kentucky.— Worten *v.* Paducah, 123 Ky. 44, 93 S. W. 617, 29 Ky. L. Rep. 450.

Oklahoma.— Gay *v.* Thomas, 5 Okla. 1, 46 Pac. 578.

Washington.— Wright *v.* Stinson, 16 Wash. 368, 47 Pac. 761.

Wisconsin.— Wisconsin Cent. R. Co. *v.* Lincoln County, 57 Wis. 137, 15 N. W. 121.

58. *Georgia.*— McLendon *v.* La Grange, 107 Ga. 356, 33 S. E. 405.

Kansas.— Ottawa County *v.* Nelson, 19 Kan. 234, 27 Am. Rep. 101. And see Geary County *v.* Missouri, etc., R. Co., 62 Kan. 168, 61 Pac. 693.

Kentucky.— Com. *v.* Taylor, 101 Ky. 325, 41 S. W. 11, 19 Ky. L. Rep. 552.

New Jersey.— Bergen, etc., R. Co. *v.* State Bd. of Assessors, 74 N. J. L. 742, 67 Atl. 668.

Oklahoma.— Boyd *v.* Wiggins, 7 Okla. 85, 54 Pac. 411.

Texas.— Missouri, etc., R. Co. *v.* Shannon, 100 Tex. 379, 100 S. W. 138, 10 L. R. A. N. S. 681.

Virginia.— Com. *v.* Brown, 91 Va. 762, 21 S. E. 357, 28 L. R. A. 110.

Washington.— Nathan *v.* Spokane County, 35 Wash. 26, 76 Pac. 521, 102 Am. St. Rep. 888, 65 L. R. A. 336.

Wisconsin.— Chicago, etc., R. Co. *v.* State, 128 Wis. 553, 108 N. W. 557.

or by allowing a discount for prompt payment to one class of taxpayers and not to another.[66]

(B) *Imposition of Penalty.*[67] A statute imposing a penalty for delinquency in the payment of taxes, or for failure or refusal to return property for assessment, is not invalid on the ground of inequality or unjust discrimination;[68] but a penalty cannot be imposed for any default or omission which is wholly that of the public officers and not of the taxpayer.[69]

h. Fixing Situs of Property For Purpose of Taxation. The legislature may, without violating the constitutional provisions in regard to equality and uniformity of taxation, fix the *situs* of personal property for purposes of taxation,[70] and give it a *situs* other than the domicile of the owner,[71] it being sufficient if the property where it is taxed is taxed equally and uniformly with other property in the same taxing locality,[72] but real property must be taxed where it is actually situated.[73]

66. Louisville, etc., R. Co. *v.* Louisville, 29 S. W. 865, 16 Ky. L. Rep. 796.

67. As violation of provision requiring taxation according to value see *infra*, II, D, 4.

68. *California.*— Biddle *v.* Oaks, 59 Cal. 94.

Kansas.— Missouri, etc., R. Co. *v.* Miami County Com'rs, 67 Kan. 434, 73 Pac. 103; Missouri, etc., R. Co. *v.* Labette County, 9 Kan. App. 545, 59 Pac. 383.

Nevada.—Virginia *v.* Chollar-Potosi Gold, etc., Min. Co., 2 Nev. 86.

Pennsylvania.— Fox's Appeal, 112 Pa. St. 337, 4 Atl. 149.

South Carolina.— *Ex p.* Lynch, 16 S. C. 32.

Tennessee.— Myers *v.* Park, 8 Heisk. 550.

Vermont.— Bartlett *v.* Wilson, 59 Vt. 23, 8 Atl. 321.

Washington.— State *v.* Whittlesey, 17 Wash. 447, 50 Pac. 119.

United States.— Doll *v.* Evans, 7 Fed. Cas. No. 3,969, 9 Phila. (Pa) 364.

See 45 Cent. Dig. tit. "Taxation," §§ 84, 121.

But see Scammon *v.* Chicago, 44 Ill. 269.

Where property has been omitted from the assessment of a particular year or years and has thereby escaped taxation, it is not a violation of the constitutional provision as to equality and uniformity to assess such property in a subsequent year for the back taxes which should have been paid. Biddle *v.* Oakes. 59 Cal. 94; Galusha *v.* Wendt, 114 Iowa 597, 87 N. W. 512; Redwood County *v.* Winona, etc., Land Co., 40 Minn. 512, 41 N. W. 465, 42 N. W. 473 [*affirmed* in 159 U. S. 526, 16 S. Ct. 83, 40 L. ed. 247].

A provision that taxes shall bear interest after the date on which they are payable does not violate the constitutional requirement as to equality and uniformity. Galveston, etc., R. Co. *v.* Galveston, 96 Tex. 520, 74 S. W. 537.

69. Redwood County *v.* Winona, etc., Land Co., 40 Minn. 512, 41 N. W. 465, 42 N. W. 475 [*affirmed* in 159 U. S. 526, 16 S. Ct. 83, 40 L. ed. 247], holding that where it is the duty of the taxing officers to assess land and there is no duty on the part of the owner to list them for taxation, and lands are omitted from an assessment by such officers, it is competent to reassess them in a subsequent year for the back taxes, but that no penalty can be imposed, as by the addition of interest, for the non-payment of such taxes, the owner not having been in default.

70. *Illinois.*— Mendota First Nat. Bank *v.* Smith, 65 Ill. 44.

Kansas.—Ottawa County *v.* Nelson, 19 Kan. 234, 27 Am. Rep. 101.

New Jersey.— Vanatta *v.* Runyon, 41 N. J. L. 98.

Oregon.— Crawford *v.* Linn County, 11 Oreg. 482, 5 Pac. 738.

United States.— Dundee Mortg. Trust Inv. Co. *v.* Parrish, 24 Fed. 197.

See 45 Cent. Dig. tit. "Taxation," § 83.

Mortgages.— The rule stated in the text applies to a statute authorizing mortgages to be taxed in the county where they are recorded, without reference to the residence of the owner (Crawford *v.* Linn County, 11 Oreg. 482, 5 Pac. 738; Dundee Mortg. Trust Inv. Co. *v.* Parrish, 24 Fed. 197), and to a statute requiring mortgages to be taxed in the town or city where the premises are situated (Vanatta *v.* Runyon, 41 N. J. L. 98).

Corporate property.—A statute making personal property of a domestic corporation subject to taxation in the state, although actually out of the state, does not contravene the constitutional requirement of uniformity. Com. *v.* Union Refrigerator Transit Co., 181 Ky. 131, 80 S. W. 490, 26 Ky. L. Rep. 23, 81 S. W. 268, 26 Ky. L. Rep. 397.

Shares of stock.—A statute making shares of national bank stock taxable at the place where the bank is situated without regard to the residence of the owners is not unconstitutional. Mendota First Nat. Bank *v.* Smith, 65 Ill. 44. *Contra*, Union Nat. Bank *v.* Chicago, 24 Fed. Cas. No. 14,374, 3 Biss. 82.

Railroad property.— The scope of the power of the legislature to fix the *situs* of railroad property for taxation has regard to the nature of such property as personalty. Chicago. etc., R. Co. *v.* State, 128 Wis. 553, 108 N. W. 557.

71. Mendota First Nat. Bank *v.* Smith, 65 Ill. 44; Crawford *v.* Linn County, 11 Oreg. 482, 5 Pac. 738. See also cases cited *supra*, note 70.

72. See Vanatta *v.* Runyon, 41 N. J. L. 98.

73. Com. *v.* Wyoming County, 22 Pa. Co. Ct. 418.

3. Different Localities — a. In General. While all state taxes must be uniform throughout the state,[85] and all local taxes uniform throughout the particular subdivision of the state by which they are levied,[86] this does not mean that taxes for the same purpose must be imposed in different territorial subdivisions at the same time,[87] or that one subdivision cannot be taxed for a particular local purpose unless the other subdivisions are also taxed;[88] nor does it prevent the creation of different taxing districts within the state,[89] and so there may be different rates of local taxation in such different subdivisions, provided there is uniformity within each particular county, municipality, or taxing district;[90] but to render taxation uniform each taxing district should confine itself to the objects of taxation within its limits.[91]

b. Taxing One Locality For Benefit of Another. The constitutional requirement of uniformity in taxation forbids the imposition of a tax on one municipality or part of the state for the purpose of benefiting or raising money for another.[92]

being based on legitimate distinctions and the burden being equal within the class. Gaar *v.* Shannon, (Tex. Civ. App. 1908) 115 S. W. 361.

85. *Indiana.*— Henderson *v.* London, etc., Ins. Co., 135 Ind. 23, 34 N. E. 565, 41 Am. St. Rep. 410, 20 L. R. A. 827.

Kentucky.— Hager *v.* Walker, 128 Ky. 1, 107 S. W. 254, 32 Ky. L. Rep. 748, 129 Am. St. Rep. 238, 15 L. R. A. N. S. 195.

Maine.— *In re* Opinion of Justices, 97 Me. 595, 55 Atl. 827.

Mississippi.— Murray *v.* Lehman, 61 Miss. 283.

Ohio.— Warring *v.* Hazlewood, 3 Ohio Dec. (Reprint) 315.

Oregon.— Yamhill County *v.* Foster, 53 Oreg. 124, 99 Pac. 286.

Pennsylvania.— *In re* Hannick, 4 C. Pl. 38; *In re* Collector's Bond, 4 Lanc. L. Rev. 40.

Tennessee.— State *v.* Butler, 11 Lea 410.

United States.— Dundee Mortg., etc., Inv. Co. *v.* School-Dist. No. 1, 21 Fed. 151.

See 45 Cent. Dig. tit. "Taxation," § 96. And see *supra*, II, B, 1, c.

86. Jackson County *v.* State. 155 Ind. 604, 58 N. E. 1037; Hager *v.* Walker, 128 Ky. 1, 107 S. W. 254, 32 Ky. L. Rep. 748, 129 Am. St. Rep. 238, 15 L. R. A. N. S. 195; Yamhill County *v.* Foster, 53 Oreg. 124, 99 Pac. 286.

87. Pine Grove Tp. *v.* Talcott, 19 Wall. (U. S.) 666, 22 L. ed. 227 [*affirming* 23 Fed. Cas. No. 13,735, 1 Flipp. 120].

88. Plaquemines Parish Police Jury *v.* Packard, 28 La. Ann. 199; Murph *v.* Landrum, 76 S. C. 21, 56 S. E. 850.

Local taxes for local purposes generally see *supra*, II, B, 1, b, (V).

89. Miller *v.* Wicomico County, 107 Md. 438, 69 Atl. 118; Talcott *v.* Pine Grove Tp., 23 Fed. Cas. No. 13.735, 1 Flipp. 120 [*affirmed* in 19 Wall. (U. S.) 666, 22 L. ed. 227]. See also *supra*, II, B, 1, b, (V).

Each county in the state is a separate taxing district and has public and corporate purposes to be accomplished by means of taxation limited alone to citizens or property within its territory. Murph *v.* Landrum, 76 S. C. 21, 56 S. E. 850.

90. *Georgia.*— Georgia Midland. etc., R. Co. *v.* State, 89 Ga. 597. 15 S. E. 301; Columbus Southern R. Co. *v.* Wright, 89 Ga. 574, 15 S. E. 293.

Kansas.— Baker *v.* Atchison County, 67 Kan. 527, 73 Pac. 70; Francis *v.* Atchison, etc., R. Co., 19 Kan. 303.

Kentucky.— Hager *v.* Walker, 128 Ky. 1, 107 S. W. 254. 32 Ky. L. Rep. 748, 129 Am. St. Rep. 238, 15 L. R. A. N. S. 195.

Louisiana.—Plaquemines Parish Police Jury *v.* Packard, 28 La. Ann. 199.

Maryland.— Miller *v.* Wicomico County, 107 Md. 438, 69 Atl. 118; Daly *v.* Morgan, 69 Md. 460, 16 Atl. 287, 1 L. R. A. 757.

Massachusetts.— Hodgdon *v.* Haverhill, 193 Mass. 406, 79 N. E. 830.

Missouri.— State *v.* Chicago, etc., R. Co., 195 Mo. 228, 93 S. W. 784, 113 Am. St. Rep. 661.

Nebraska.— Pleuler *v.* State, 11 Nebr. 547, 10 N. W. 481.

New York.— People *v.* Moore, 11 N. Y. St. 859.

Oregon.— East Portland *v.* Multnomah County, 6 Oreg. 62.

Virginia.— Gilkeson *v.* Frederick County Justices, 13 Gratt. 577.

Wisconsin.— Battles *v.* Doll, 113 Wis. 357, 89 N. W. 187.

United States.— Pine Grove Tp. *v.* Talcott, 19 Wall. 666, 22 L. ed. 227. See also Foster *v.* Pryor, 189 U. S. 325, 23 S. Ct. 549, 47 L. ed. 835.

See 45 Cent. Dig. tit. "Taxation," § 96.

But see Pump *v.* Lucas County, 69 Ohio St. 448, 69 N. E. 666.

Each city, county, or taxing district may have its own rate of taxation and the requirement of equality and uniformity as to local taxation is fully met if the tax is uniform throughout each particular taxing district. Miller *v.* Wicomico County, 107 Md. 438, 69 Atl. 118.

91. Berlin Mills Co. *v.* Wentworth, 60 N. H. 156.

92. *Arkansas.*— Hutchinson *v.* Ozark Land Co., 57 Ark. 554, 22 S. W. 173, 38 Am. St. Rep. 258.

California.— People *v.* Townsend, 56 Cal. 633.

Maryland.— Prince George's County *v.* Laurel, 70 Md. 443, 17 Atl. 388, 3 L. R. A. 528.

4. TAXATION OF INDIVIDUALS AND CORPORATIONS — a. **Discrimination in General.** For the purposes of a general tax on property there cannot lawfully be any discrimination between that owned by individuals and that owned by corporations, but all must be taxed at the same equal rate.[1] But this rule is not violated by imposing a special franchise tax on corporations,[2] or by laying special duties upon them in the exercise of the police power, when their operations affect the general public.[3]

b. As to Mode of Assessment or Valuation. The constitutional requirement of equality and uniformity is not violated by a statute which provides a special mode of assessing or appraising the property of corporations, when this is rendered necessary by the nature or distribution of the property, and when the plan devised is inherently fair and just;[4] and on this principle, it is competent to commit the assessment of corporate property to special boards or officers.[5] But a system

include rural lands it is not unconstitutional to tax such lands at the same rate as other lands within the municipality. See also New Orleans *v.* Cazelar, 27 La. Ann. 156.

1. *Alabama.*— Mobile *v.* Stonewall Ins. Co., 53 Ala. 570.

Iowa.— Davenport *v.* Chicago, etc., R. Co., 38 Iowa 633.

Kansas.—Atchison, etc., R. Co. *v.* Howe, 32 Kan. 737, 5 Pac. 397.

Kentucky.—Vanceburg, etc., Turnpike Road Co. *v.* Maysville, etc., R. Co., 117 Ky. 275, 77 S. W. 1118, 25 Ky. L. Rep. 1404.

Maryland.— State *v.* Cumberland, etc., R. Co., 40 Md. 22.

Minnesota.— State *v.* Canda Cattle Car Co., 85 Minn. 457, 89 N. W. 66.

New Jersey.— Central R. Co. *v.* State Bd. of Assessors, 48 N. J. L. 1, 2 Atl. 789, 57 Am. Rep. 516.

Texas.— Lively *v.* Missouri, etc., R. Co., 102 Tex. 545, 120 S. W. 852.

Virginia.— Shenandoah Val. R. Co. *v.* Clarke County, 78 Va. 269.

West Virginia.— Franklin Ins. Co. *v.* State, 5 W. Va. 349.

Wisconsin.— Chicago, etc., R. Co. *v.* State, 128 Wis. 553, 108 N. W. 557. But see State *v.* Hastings, 12 Wis. 47.

See 45 Cent. Dig. tit. "Taxation," §§ 100, 101.

But see Fox *v.* Com'rs, 1 Pa. Co. Ct. 197; Michigan Cent. R. Co. *v.* Powers, 201 U. S. 245, 26 S. Ct. 459, 50 L. ed. 744 [*affirming* 138 Fed. 223] (holding that nothing in the federal constitution prevents a state from singling out railroad and other corporate property and taxing it for state purposes in a manner and at a rate different from that applicable to other property); Peacock *v.* Pratt, 121 Fed. 772, 58 C. C. A. 48; and, generally, *supra*, II, B, 2.

2. Southern R. Co. *v.* Coulter, 113 Ky. 657, 68 S. W. 873, 24 Ky. L. Rep. 203; Com. *v.* Lowell Gas Light Co., 12 Allen (Mass.) 75; Adams Express Co. *v.* Kentucky, 166 U. S. 171, 17 S. Ct. 527, 41 L. ed. 960.

3. Cincinnati, etc., R. Co. *v.* Sullivan, 32 Ohio St. 152, sustaining the validity of an ordinance which required a railroad company to light its road within the city limits and provided that on default the lighting might be done by the city at the expense of the company and an assessment levied to pay for the same.

4. *Arkansas.*— St. Louis, etc., R. Co. *v.* Worthen, 52 Ark. 529, 13 S. W. 254, 7 L. R. A. 374.

Georgia.— Columbus Southern R. Co. *v.* Wright, 89 Ga. 574, 15 S. E. 293.

Indiana.— Louisville, etc., R. Co. *v.* State, 25 Ind. 177, 87 Am. Dec. 358.

Iowa.— United States Express Co. *v.* Ellyson, 28 Iowa 370.

Nebraska.— Chicago, etc., R. Co. *v.* Richardson County, 72 Nebr. 482, 100 N. W. 950.

New Hampshire.— Wyatt *v.* State Bd. of Equalization, 74 N. H. 552, 70 Atl. 387.

New Jersey.— Bergen, etc., R. Co. *v.* State Bd. of Assessors, 74 N. J. L. 742, 67 Atl. 668.

North Carolina.—Atlantic, etc., R. Co. *v.* New Bern, 147 N. C. 165, 60 S. E. 925.

Washington.— Eureka Dist. Gold Min. Co. *v.* Ferry County, 28 Wash. 250, 68 Pac. 727.

Wisconsin.— Chicago, etc., R. Co. *v.* State, 128 Wis. 553, 108 N. W. 557.

United States.— Michigan Cent. R. Co. *v.* Powers, 201 U. S. 245, 26 S. Ct. 459, 50 L. ed. 744 [*affirming* 138 Fed. 223]; State Railroad Tax Cases, 92 U. S. 575, 23 L. ed. 663; Chamberlain *v.* Walter, 60 Fed. 788.

See 45 Cent. Dig. tit. "Taxation," §§ 102, 103.

Difference in time of assessment.— It is competent for the legislature to provide that railroad property shall be assessed annually, while ordinary real estate is assessed but once in two years (St. Louis, etc., R. Co. *v.* Worthen, 52 Ark. 529, 13 S. W. 254, 7 L. R. A. 374); or in five years (Chamberlain *v.* Walter, 60 Fed. 788).

Methods of valuing railroad property.— Method held valid see Wyatt *v.* State Bd. of Equalization, 74 N. H. 552, 70 Atl. 387; Michigan Cent. R. Co. *v.* Powers, 201 U. S. 245, 26 S. Ct. 459, 50 L. ed. 744 [*affirming* 138 Fed. 223]; State Railroad Tax Cases, 92 U. S. 575, 23 L. ed. 663. Method held invalid see Chattanooga *v.* Nashville, etc., R. Co., 7 Lea (Tenn.) 561.

The New Jersey statutes providing for the taxation of railroad and canal property are not unconstitutional. United New Jersey R., etc., Co. *v.* Baird, 75 N. J. L. 788, 69 Atl. 472; United New Jersey R., etc., Co. *v.* Parker, 75 N. J. L. 771, 69 Atl. 239 [*modifying* 75 N. J. L. 120, 67 Atl. 672, 686]; Bergen, etc., R. Co. *v.* State Bd. of Assessors, 74 N. J. L. 742, 67 Atl. 668.

5. *Arkansas.*— St. Louis, etc., R. Co. *v.*

is not to be evaded by taxing the same thing under different names.[10] It is not, however, every duplication of taxation which is objectionable on this ground,[11] and the terms "double" and "duplicate" have sometimes been used to designate respectively that which is objectionable or prohibited and that which is not.[12] Double taxation in the objectionable or prohibited sense exists only where the same property is taxed twice when it ought to be taxed but once,[13] and to constitute such double taxation the second tax must be imposed upon the same property,[14] by the same state or government,[15] during the same taxing

Kentucky.— Cumberland Tel., etc., Co. *v* Hopkins, 121 Ky. 850, 90 S. W. 594, 28 Ky. L. Rep. 846.

Maryland.— Monticello Distilling Co. *v*. Baltimore, 90 Md. 416, 45 Atl. 210.

Massachusetts.— Williams *v*. Brookline, 194 Mass. 44, 79 N. E. 779; Richards *v*. Dagget, 4 Mass. 534.

New Hampshire.— Nashua Sav. Bank *v*. Nashua, 46 N. H. 389.

Oregon.— Ellis *v*. Frazier, 38 Oreg. 462, 63 Pac. 642, 53 L. R. A. 454.

Pennsylvania.— See Com. *v*. Preston Coal Co., 2 Dauph. Co. Rep. 263.

West Virginia.— State *v*. Allen, 65 W. Va. 335, 64 S. E. 140.

United States.— San Francisco *v*. Mackey, 21 Fed. 539.

Double taxation on the same land under the same title is not permissible (State *v*. Allen, 65 W. Va. 335, 64 S. E. 140); but where there are adverse claimants to the same land it is not double taxation to require each claimant to list his claim and pay taxes upon it (Eastern Kentucky Coal Lands Corp. *v*. Com., 127 Ky. 667, 106 S. W. 260, 32 Ky. L. Rep. 129, 108 S. W. 1138, 33 Ky. L. Rep. 49).

Tax on raw material and on finished products.— It would be a case of duplicate taxation if the same article were taxed in the hands of the same person first as raw material and again, in the same year, as a finished product; but this objection does not apply to a statute which separates the raw material from the product and imposes the tax on either class only once. See Christian Moerlein Brewing Co. *v*. Hagerty, 8 Ohio Cir. Ct. 330, 4 Ohio Cir. Dec. 276.

Taxation of chattels real.— A statute providing for the taxation of chattels real as personalty is not unconstitutional as imposing double taxation. Harvey Coal, etc., Co. *v*. Dillon, 59 W. Va. 605, 63 S. E. 928, 6 L. R. A. N. S. 628.

Tax on property and on administration of same in probate court.—Where the executors of a decedent's estate had paid all the taxes due on the real and personal property of the estate for the year in which they applied for letters testamentary, a demand by the clerk of the probate court for the payment of an additional docket fee, proportioned to the size of the estate, imposed by statute, could not be enforced, as it would constitute double taxation. Cook County *v*. Fairbank, 222 Ill. 578, 78 N. E. 895.

10. State *v*. Louisiana, etc., R. Co., 196 Mo. 523, 94 S. W. 279. See also Panola County *v*. Carrier, 92 Miss. 148, 45 So. 426.

Double taxation should be avoided not only in not taxing the same property twice in the same year for the same purpose but also in not taxing the same thing twice whatever its form. Com. *v*. Walsh, 133 Ky. 103, 106 S. W. 240, 32 Ky. L. Rep. 460, 117 S. W. 398.

Omitted property.— A person should not be separately assessed on a particular article of personal property as omitted property when it is shown that he has been assessed for and paid the taxes upon a greater valuation of personal property than he actually owned. Com. *v*. Harris, (Ky. 1909) 118 S. W. 294.

Bridge and railroad property.— Where a bridge belonging to a railroad is taxed as a part of the railroad and the taxes paid, it cannot be again taxed as a bridge. State *v*. Louisiana, etc., R. Co., 196 Mo. 523, 94 S. W. 279.

11. San Francisco *v*. Fry, 63 Cal. 470; Judy *v*. Beckwith, 137 Iowa 24, 114 N. W. 565, 15 L. R. A. N. S. 142.

Tax on loans and debts.— The lender of money is not subjected to double taxation by reason of a statutory provision requiring the payment of taxes on money loaned by him and on solvent debts due him over his own indebtedness. People *v*. McCreery, 34 Cal. 432. And see Kingsley *v*. Merrill, 122 Wis. 185, 99 N. W. 1044, 67 L. R. A. 200.

Assets of insolvent bank.— Notes and solvent credits of an insolvent state bank passing to an assignee before the day for listing property for taxation may be taxed to the assignee, and the fact that the creditors of the bank have their interests in the assets of the bank assessed to them individually as an indebtedness properly collectable does not constitute double taxation. Gerard *v*. Duncan, 84 Miss. 731, 36 So. 1034, 66 L. R. A. 461.

12. Judy *v*. Beckwith, 137 Iowa 24, 114 N. W. 565, 15 L. R. A. N. S. 142.

13. Stumpf *v*. Storz, 156 Mich. 228, 120 N. W. 618, 132 Am. St. Rep. 521, 23 L. R. A. N. S. 152.

14. Montgomery County Bd. of Revenue *v*. Montgomery Gaslight Co., 64 Ala. 269; Eastern Kentucky Coal Lands Corp. *v*. Com., 127 Ky. 667, 106 S. W. 260, 32 Ky. L. Rep. 129, 108 S. W. 1138, 33 Ky. L. Rep. 49.

15. Chesebrough *v*. San Francisco, 153 Cal. 559, 96 Pac. 288; San Francisco *v*. Fry, 63 Cal. 470; Judy *v*. Beckwith, 137 Iowa 24, 114 N. W. 565, 15 L. R. A. N. S. 142; State *v*. Nelson, 107 Minn. 319, 119 N. W. 1058; Bradley *v*. Bauder, 36 Ohio St. 28, 38 Am. Rep. 547.

public purposes,[5] and are in some cases expressly authorized, either generally or within certain limits, by constitutional provisions.[6] Not being laid upon property, they are not within the constitutional requirements as to equality and uniformity or as to taxation by value,[7] unless the principle of uniformity is violated by an arbitrary exemption of a certain class of persons from the tax.[8]

III. LIABILITY OF PERSONS AND PROPERTY.

A. Private Persons and Property — 1. LIABILITY TO TAXATION — a. Statutory Provisions — (I) *IN GENERAL.* The determination of the property or objects to be affected by a tax, as well as the rate or amount, belongs to the legislature, and except in the rare cases where the constitution itself prescribes a specific tax, the foundation for all lawful state taxation must be laid by a valid act of the legislature.[9] Like any other statute, a law imposing taxation may be repealed either by a particular declaration of the legislature to that effect or by the enactment of a wholly new statute covering the whole ground of taxation and inconsistent with the continuance in force of any earlier laws.[10] But the repeal of a tax law will not prevent the collection of taxes which had already been duly assessed or levied under it and so become a charge on the property.[11]

5. *Colorado.*— People *v.* Ames, 24 Colo. 422, 51 Pac. 426.
Illinois.— Sawyer *v.* Alton, 4 Ill. 127.
Minnesota.— Faribault *v.* Misener, 20 Minn. 396.
Tennessee.— Kuntz *v.* Davidson County, 6 Lea 65.
Washington.— Thurston County *v.* Tenino Stone Quarries, 44 Wash. 351, 87 Pac. 634, 9 L. R. A. N. S. 306.
United States.— Morgan *v.* Rowan, 17 Fed. Cas. No. 9,807, 2 Cranch C. C. 148.
Aliens may be required to pay a poll tax in the absence of any constitutional restriction, and a constitutional provision that "all male citizens" over a certain age "shall be liable to a poll tax" does not prevent the legislature from imposing a poll tax on inhabitants of the state who are not citizens of the state. Kuntz *v.* Davidson County, 6 Lea (Tenn.) 65.

6. See Southern R. Co. *v.* Mecklenburg County, 148 N. C. 220, 61 S. E. 690; Kuntz *v.* Davidson County, 6 Lea (Tenn.) 65; Solon *v.* State, 54 Tex. Cr. 261, 114 S. W. 349; Proffit *v.* Anderson, (Va. 1894) 20 S. E. 887.

7. Sawyer *v.* Alton, 4 Ill. 127; Ottawa County *v.* Nelson, 19 Kan. 234, 27 Am. Rep. 101; East Portland *v.* Multnomah County, 6 Oreg. 62; Thurston County *v.* Tenino Stone Quarries, 44 Wash. 351, 87 Pac. 634, 9 L. R. A. N. S. 306. *Compare* Nance *v.* Howard, 1 Ill. 242; Kansas City *v.* Whipple, 136 Mo. 475, 38 S. W. 295, 58 Am. St. Rep. 657, 35 L. R. A. 747.

8. State *v.* Ide, 35 Wash. 576, 77 Pac. 961, 102 Am. St. Rep. 914, 67 L. R. A. 280. See also Kansas City *v.* Whipple, 136 Mo. 475, 38 S. W. 295, 57 Am. St. Rep. 657, 35 L. R. A. 747.
But the legislature is not prohibited from exempting certain classes of persons from the payment of poll taxes if the classification is made upon a reasonable and proper basis. Bluitt *v.* State, 56 Tex. Cr. 525, 121 S. W. 168; Solon *v.* State, 54 Tex. Cr. 261, 114 S. W. 349; Tekoa *v.* Reilly, 47 Wash. 202, 91 Pac. 769, 13 L. R. A. N. S. 901.

9. Neary *v.* Philadelphia, etc., R. Co., 7 Houst. (Del.) 419, 9 Atl. 405; Webster *v.* People, 98 Ill. 343; Virginia, etc., R. Co. *v.* Washington County, 30 Gratt. (Va.) 471.
Requisites of tax statute.— A taxing act is fatally defective if the legislature does not designate the property out of which the tax is to be made and prescribe a mode of enforcing it. State *v.* Chamberlin, 37 N. J. L. 388. And see People *v.* State Tax Com'rs, 174 N. Y. 417, 67 N. E. 69, 105 Am. St. Rep. 674, 63 L. R. A. N. S. 884.
Contract to refund.— The illegality of a contract by a city to refund to an individual the amount of taxes assessed against him does not render the taxation of other property invalid. State *v.* Thayer, 69 Minn. 170, 71 N. W. 931.

10. *California.*— Crosby *v.* Patch, 18 Cal. 438.
Indiana.— State *v.* Brugh, 5 Ind. App. 592, 32 N. E. 869.
Kentucky.— Callahan *v.* Singer Mfg. Co., 92 S. W. 581, 29 Ky. L. Rep. 123; Bevins *v.* Com., 86 S. W. 544, 27 Ky. L. Rep. 735.
Louisiana.— Wintz *v.* Girardey, 31 La. Ann. 381.
New York.— Cone *v.* Lauer, 131 N. Y. App. Div. 193, 115 N. Y. Suppl. 644. holding that the general tax law of 1896 repealed by implication the special acts relating to taxation in Suffolk county.
Pennsylvania.— Philadelphia *v.* Kingsley, 5 Pa. Co. Ct. 75; Price *v.* Hunter, 21 Wkly. Notes Cas. 306.
Virginia.— Fox *v.* Com., 16 Gratt. 1.
Wyoming.— Frontier Land, etc., Co. *v.* Baldwin, 3 Wyo. 764, 31 Pac. 403.
United States.— Union Pac. R. Co. *v.* Ryan, 113 U. S. 516, 5 S. Ct. 601, 28 L. ed. 1098.
See 45 Cent. Dig. tit. "Taxation," § 134.

11. *Alabama.*— Hooper *v.* State, 141 Ala. 111, 37 So. 662; State *v.* Sloss, 83 Ala. 93, 3 So. 745.

retrospectively without being unconstitutional,[15] such a statute will not be so construed unless in accordance with its plain meaning,[16] and repealing statutes will not be construed as operating retrospectively so as to remit taxes already assessed and payable under the earlier statute.[17]

b. Persons Liable — (I) *In General.* Except in so far as it may be restricted by the constitution or subject to specific exemptions, the legislative power to tax is coextensive with its general control over the inhabitants of the state and their property; and every person who subjects himself or his property to the jurisdiction of the state comes within that power.[18] The liability to personal taxation is governed not by one's citizenship but by his residence.[19]

(II) *Persons Under Disabilities.* The liability for the payment of taxes on property is not ordinarily affected by the fact that the owner is a person under disability,[20] as in the case of property, either real or personal,[21] belonging to infants,[22] insane persons,[23] or married women.[24]

c. Time When Liability Attaches. As between the state and the taxpayer, the latter is liable for the taxes on such taxable property as he owned on the day fixed by law for the completion of the assessment, or, according to the statute, on the day fixed for the filing of taxpayers' lists or schedules, his liability attaching as of that date.[25] Consequently in the absence of statute no liability for taxes

8 B. & S. 83, 36 L. J. Q. B. 81, 15 L. T. Rep. N. S. 466, 15 Wkly. Rep. 345.

Circumstances to aid construction.— A statute imposing taxes is not to be interpreted by its language alone, but in connection with other tax statutes prior and contemporaneous, and in the light of contemporaneous and subsequent practical understanding of it by taxing officers and the public. East Livermore *v.* Livermore Falls Trust, etc., Co., 103 Me. 418, 69 Atl. 306, 15 L. R. A. N. S. 952.

15. See Constitutional Law, 8 Cyc, 1022.

16. *Kentucky.*— Bierley *v.* Quick Run, etc., R. Co., 29 S. W. 874, 17 Ky. L. Rep. 36.

Louisiana.— New Orleans *v.* Rhenish Westphalian Lloyds, 31 La. Ann. 781.

New York.— People *v.* Spring Valley Hydraulic Gold Co., 92 N. Y. 383.

South Carolina.— State *v.* Burger, 1 McMull. 410.

United States.— Locke *v.* New Orleans, 4 Wall. 172, 18 L. ed. 334.

Construction against retrospective operation of statutes generally see Constitutional Law, 8 Cyc. 1022; Statutes, 36 Cyc. 1205.

17. State *v.* Certain Lands, 40 Ark. 35; Oakland *v.* Whipple, 44 Cal. 303.

18. Monticello Distilling Co. *v.* Baltimore, 90 Md. 416, 45 Atl. 210; Central Petroleum Co. *v.* Com., 25 Leg. Int. (Pa.) 316.

Women.— The personal estate of an unmarried woman is liable to taxation, although she is not allowed to vote. Wheeler *v.* Wall, 6 Allen (Mass.) 558.

A surgeon of the United States army stationed at a particular place and residing there in the performance of his duties is bound to pay taxes assessed on his household furniture. Finley *v.* Philadelphia, 32 Pa. St. 381.

Confiscated property.— The assessment of taxes against the adjudicatee of confiscated property, during his tenure thereof, is legal and valid. Brent *v.* New Orleans, 41 La. Ann. 1098, 6 So. 793.

19. Pendleton *v.* Com., 110 Va. 229, 65 S. E. 536.

Property of non-residents see *infra*, III, A, 4.

20. De Hatre *v.* Edmonds, 200 Mo. 246, 98 S. W. 744.

21. Payson *v.* Tufts, 13 Mass. 493.

22. Louisville *v.* Sherley, 80 Ky. 71; Payson *v.* Tufts, 13 Mass. 493; West Chester School Dist. *v.* Darlington, 38 Pa. St. 157; Bellefonte *v.* Spring Tp., 10 Pittsb. Leg. J. (Pa.) 450.

To whom taxable when held by a guardian see *infra*, III, A, 3, h.

23. De Hatre *v.* Edmonds, 200 Mo. 246, 98 S. W. 744. See also People *v.* Tax Com'rs, 100 N. Y. 215, 3 N. E. 85 [*reversing* 36 Hun 359]; Mason *v.* Thurber, 1 R. I. 481. But see Hunt *v.* Lee, 10 Vt. 297, holding that under a proper construction of the Vermont statutes an idiot under guardianship is not liable to be assessed and taxed for money on hand or money due, the question whether such assessment might be made against the guardian not being presented for decision.

To whom taxable when held by a committee see *infra*, III, A, 3, h.

24. De Hatre *v.* Edmonds, 200 Mo. 246, 98 S. W. 744. See also Collins *v.* Pease, 146 Mo. 135, 47 S. W. 925.

25. *Kansas.*— Long *v.* Culp, 14 Kan. 412.

Missouri.— State *v.* Snyder, 139 Mo. 549, 41 S. W. 216.

New Jersey.— State *v.* Jersey City, 44 N. J. L. 156; State *v.* Hardin, 34 N. J. L. 79.

New York.— People *v.* Chenango County, 11 N. Y. 563.

United States.— People *v.* New York Tax Com'rs, 104 U. S. 466, 26 L. ed. 632.

In Arkansas it is held that the statute requiring landowners to list their lands for taxation on or before the first day of January of each year is merely directory and does not exempt lands purchased from the state after the first day of January from taxation until

particular property to be assessed in his name, or returns it to the assessor as his, is estopped to deny his liability for the taxes upon it;[44] and the same rule has been applied as to the amount of the tax, where he has acquiesced in its valuation at a certain sum.[45] Where the taxpayer has submitted to the payment of the tax, it is not ordinarily open to other persons, such as his creditors, to object to it.[46]

2. **Nature of Property — a. In General.** All property within the jurisdiction of the state is subject to its taxing power, except where specifically exempted;[47]

the *de facto* possession of Alexandria county, and the political department of her government had uniformly asserted, and her judicial department expressly affirmed, her title thereto, and congress had more than once recognized the transfer as a settled fact, a resident of that county, suing to recover taxes paid under protest upon his property there situate, was estopped to raise the question of the validity of the retrocession. Phillips *v.* Payne, 92 U. S. 130, 23 L. ed. 649.

44. *Alabama.*— Rodgers *v.* Gaines, 73 Ala. 218.

California.— People *v.* Stockton, etc., R. Co., 49 Cal. 414.

Connecticut.— Ives *v.* North Canaan, 33 Conn. 402; Goddard *v.* Seymour, 30 Conn. 394.

Idaho.—Inland Lumber, etc., Co. *v.* Thompson, 11 Ida. 508, 83 Pac. 933, 114 Am. St. Rep. 274.

Illinois.— Dennison *v.* Williamson County, 153 Ill. 516, 39 N. E. 118.

Iowa.— Slimmer *v.* Chickasaw County, 140 Iowa 448, 118 N. W. 779.

Kentucky.— Chesapeake, etc., R. Co. *v.* Com., 129 Ky. 318, 108 S. W. 248, 32 Ky. L. Rep. 1119, 111 S. W. 334, 33 Ky. L. Rep. 882; Illinois Cent. R. Co. *v.* Com., 128 Ky. 268, 108 S. W. 245, 32 Ky. L. Rep. 1112, 110 S. W. 265, 33 Ky. L. Rep. 326; Southern R. Co. *v.* Coulter, 113 Ky. 657, 68 S. W. 873, 24 Ky. L. Rep. 203.

Mississippi.— Fox *v.* Pearl River Lumber Co., 80 Miss. 1, 31 So. 583.

Wisconsin.—Hamacker *v.* Commercial Bank, 95 Wis. 359, 70 N. W. 295.

See 45 Cent. Dig. tit. "Taxation," § 144.

The same rules apply to corporations with regard to property given in for taxation by their proper officers or agents. People *v.* Stockton, etc., R. Co., 49 Cal. 414; Illinois Cent. R. Co. *v.* Com., 128 Ky. 268, 108 S. W. 245, 32 Ky. L. Rep. 1112, 110 S. W. 265, 33 Ky. L. Rep. 326.

A receiver of a bank is estopped to resist the payment of a tax based upon a property statement made to the assessor by the cashier of the bank prior to its insolvency. Hamacker *v.* Commercial Bank, 95 Wis. 359, 70 N. W. 295.

But a guardian in a proceeding to recover taxes charged against him as guardian is not estopped from making the defense that by reason of the death of the ward, and administration granted on the estate before the property was listed, he was without authority to list the same for taxation. Sommers *v.* Boyd, 48 Ohio St. 648, 29 N. E. 497.

45. Phelps Mortg. Co. *v.* Oskaloosa Bd. of Equalization, 84 Iowa 610, 51 N. W. 50. *Compare* Hale *v.* Jefferson County, 39 Mont. 137, 101 Pac. 973.

Commutation of taxes.—Where the charter of a railroad company conditions the exercise of its corporate privileges upon the payment to the state of a certain percentage of its earnings, by way of a tax, and the company actually proceeds to operate its road, there is an implied acceptance of the condition and an agreement to pay the stated tax which rests on contract and cannot be evaded or denied. State *v.* Chicago, etc., R. Co., 128 Wis. 449, 108 N. W. 594.

46. *In re* Pennsylvania Bank Assignees' Account, 39 Pa. St. 103. In this case a tax was properly laid on bank dividends actually declared, and it was held that creditors of the bank could not dispute it collaterally, although the bank was insolvent at the time and the dividend was a fraud on stock-holders and creditors.

47. *Illinois.*— People *v.* Ravenswood Hospital, 238 Ill. 137, 87 N. E. 305.

Kentucky.— Wolfe County *v.* Beckett, 127 Ky. 252, 105 S. W. 447, 32 Ky. L. Rep. 167, 17 L. R. A. N. S. 688.

Massachusetts.— *In re* Opinion of Justices, 195 Mass. 607, 84 N. E. 499.

Missouri.— State *v.* Mission Free School, 162 Mo. 332, 62 S. W. 998.

Pennsylvania.— Northampton County *v.* Glendon Iron Co., 1 Lehigh Val. L. Rep. 81.

Texas.— Hall *v.* Miller, 102 Tex. 289, 115 S. W. 1168 [*affirming* (Civ. App. 1908) 110 S. W. 165].

Subject to constitutional limitations everything to which the legislative power extends may be taxed, whether person or property, tangible or intangible, franchise, privilege, occupation, or right. Wolfe County *v.* Beckett, 127 Ky. 252, 105 S. W. 447, 32 Ky. L. Rep. 167, 17 L. R. A. N. S. 688.

Scope of term "property."— In a constitutional provision for levying a tax by valuation, so that every person shall contribute in proportion to the value of his property, the word "property" is a generic term and includes all property of whatever description, whether tangible or intangible. State *v.* Savage, 65 Nebr. 714, 91 N. W. 716.

Commodities imported from abroad.— An imported article in the importer's possession, in the original package, continues to be a part of the foreign commerce of the country and is not part of the property in the state subject to taxation; but when the article has passed into the hands of a purchaser, it is no longer an import and is subject to taxa-

incidents to and a part of the abutting property and are not subject to a separate assessment for taxation,[76] but to be assessed as real property with and as a part of the riparian lands.[77] It is also held that water power for mill purposes is not a distinct subject of taxation which can be taxed independently of the land,[78] or of the mills which it drives;[79] but that a water power or mill privilege on or appurtenant to certain lands, although unimproved or unused,[80] may be considered and included as an element increasing the valuation of the land.[81] Where water power in actual use is created by a dam or reservoir in one taxing district and applied to mills situated in another district, the practice varies in different jurisdictions[82] as to whether the water power should be considered as appurtenant to and taxed in connection with the land where the dam is situated,[83] or whether the dam and land on which it is situated should be taxed at a reasonable valuation independently of the water power created thereby,[84] and the water power be taxed where it is applied in connection with and is increasing the value of the mills.[85] A right in one person to flow by means of a dam, which he does not own, the lands of another is a mere easement, and not an estate subject to separate taxation;[86] but where one person acquires title to the waters of a pond and a permanent dam and sluiceway connected therewith on the land of another, he acquires an interest taxable as real estate.[87] It has been held that a ditch for conveying water for mining purposes has no separate independent value subject to taxation;[88] but that a ditch for transporting logs has a value separate and distinct from the lands through which it runs and may be separately assessed,[89]

76. State *v.* St. Paul, etc., R. Co., 81 Minn. 422, 84 N. W. 302; State *v.* Minneapolis Mill Co., 26 Minn. 229, 2 N. W. 839. See also State *v.* Jersey City, 25 N. J. L. 525.

Where a license is given to the owner of land lying on a navigable stream to wharf out below high water mark, so far as the grant extends the property is vested in the grantee and is subject to taxation. Bentley *v.* Sippel, 25 N. J. L. 530.

Land lying between a levee and the river, although submerged at the high stage of the river, is the property of the riparian owner subject to public uses, and when used by the riparian owner for purposes of revenue or otherwise is subject to taxation. Mathis *v.* Board of Assessors, 46 La. Ann. 1570, 16 So. 454.

77. State *v.* Minneapolis Mill Co., 26 Minn. 229, 2 N. W. 839.

78. Union Water Co. *v.* Auburn, 90 Me. 60, 37 Atl. 331, 60 Am. St. Rep. 240, 37 L. R. A. 651; Boston Mfg. Co. *v.* Newton, 22 Pick. (Mass.) 22.

79. Lowell *v.* Middlesex County Com'rs, 6 Allen (Mass.) 131.

80. Saco Water Power Co. *v.* Buxton, 98 Me. 295, 56 Atl. 914.

81. Penobscot Chemical Fibre Co. *v.* Bradley, 99 Me. 263, 59 Atl. 83; Saco Water Power Co. *v.* Buxton, 98 Me. 295, 56 Atl. 914; Lowell *v.* Middlesex County, 152 Mass. 372, 25 N. E. 469, 9 L. R. A. 356; Winnipiscogee Lake Cotton, etc., Mfg. Co. *v.* Gilford, 64 N. H. 337, 10 Atl. 849. See also Quinebaug Reservoir Co. *v.* Union, 73 Conn. 294, 47 Atl. 328.

82. See Union Water Co. *v.* Auburn, 90 Me. 60, 37 Atl. 331, 60 Am. St. Rep. 240, 37 L. R. A. 651; and cases cited *infra*, notes 83–85.

83. Amoskeag Mfg. Co. *v.* Concord, 66 N. H. 562, 34 Atl. 241, 32 L. R. A. 621; Winnipiseogee Lake Cotton, etc., Mfg. Co. *v.* Gilford, 64 N. H. 337, 10 Atl. 849; Cocheco Mfg. Co. *v.* Strafford, 51 N. H. 455.

84. Union Water Co. *v.* Auburn, 90 Me. 60, 37 Atl. 331, 60 Am. St. Rep. 240, 37 L. R. A. 651.

While the water power as such is not to be included this does not mean that the capacity of the property for valuable use is to be excluded, and therefore a dam and the land which it covers with water are liable to be taxed, although independently of their use in connection with mills, the dam and the land so overflowed are only of nominal value. Pingree *v.* Berkshire County, 102 Mass. 76.

85. Union Water Co. *v.* Auburn, 90 Me. 60, 37 Atl. 331, 60 Am. St. Rep. 240, 37 L. R. A. 651; Boston Mfg. Co. *v.* Newton, 22 Pick. (Mass.) 22. See also East Granby *v.* Hartford Electric Light Co., 76 Conn. 169, 56 Atl. 514; Fall River *v.* Bristol County, 125 Mass. 567.

Power used in another state.— The Connecticut statute providing that where water power originating in one town is used in another it shall be listed for taxation where used, applies only to towns within the state, and does not prevent the taxation of water power originating in that state and used in another state. Quinebaug Reservoir Co. *v.* Union, 73 Conn. 294, 47 Atl. 328.

86. Fall River *v.* Bristol County, 125 Mass. 567.

87. Flax Pond Water Co. *v.* Lynn, 147 Mass. 31, 16 N. E. 742.

88. Hale *v.* Jefferson County, 39 Mont. 137, 101 Pac. 973.

89. Sullivan *v.* State, 117 Ala. 214, 23 So. 678.

c. Personal Property — (I) *IN GENERAL.* Personal property of all kinds, unless exempt, is subject to taxation,[12] whether it be tangible or intangible;[13] but in order to be taxable it must come within the descriptive terms or application of the statute imposing the tax,[14] or within the statutory definitions of personal

75 N. Y. App. Div. 131, 77 N. Y. Suppl. 382 [*affirmed* in 175 N. Y. 511, 67 N. E. 1088].

12. *Georgia.*— Joiner *v.* Adams, 114 Ga. 389, 40 S. E 281.

Iowa.— Leon Loan, etc., Co. *v.* Leon Bd. of Equalization, 86 Iowa 127, 53 N. W. 94, 41 Am. St. Rep 486, 17 L. R. A. 199.

Louisiana.— Griggsry Constr. Co. *v.* Freeman, 108 La. 435, 32 So. 399, 58 L. R. A. 349.

Minnesota.— State *v.* Western Union Tel. Co., 96 Minn. 13, 104 N. W. 567.

United States.—Adams Express Co. *v.* Ohio State Auditor, 166 U. S. 185, 17 S. Ct. 607, 41 L. ed. 965.

See 45 Cent. Dig. tit. "Taxation," § 152 *et seq.*

Abstract books have been held to be personal property and taxable as such notwithstanding their manuscript character, and the fact that they are valuable only for the information which they contain, which must be obtained by consultation or extracts therefrom (Leon Loan, etc., Co. *v.* Leon Bd. of Equalization, 86 Iowa 127, 53 N. W. 94, 91 Am. St. Rep. 486, 17 L. R A. 199. *Contra,* Loomis *v.* Jackson, 130 Mich. 594, 90 N. W. 328; Perry *v* Big Rapids, 67 Mich. 146, 34 N. W. 530, 11 Am. St. Rep. 570); even where they are written largely in abbreviations and cipher peculiar to the set requiring an expert to use them (Booth, etc., Abstract Co. *v.* Phelps, 8 Wash. 549, 36 Pac. 489, 40 Am. St. Rep. 921, 23 L. R. A. 864).

Tools and commissary store goods kept by a corporation as a part of or in connection with an outfit for doing construction work are subject to taxation. Griggsry Constr. Co. *v.* Freeman, 108 La. 435, 32 So. 399, 58 L. R. A. 349.

Fertilizer owned and held by a person at the time personal property is required to be listed and assessed is subject to taxation, although it is the intention of the owner to apply it to his land which is also to be taxed. Joiner *v.* Adams, 114 Ga. 389, 40 S. E. 281.

Spirituous liquors of all kinds, although their manufacture and sale are regulated by law under the exercise of the police power, are valuable personal property and taxable as such (Louisville *v.* Louisville Pub Warehouse Co., 107 Ky. 184, 53 S. W. 291, 21 Ky. L. Rep. 867; Carstairs *v.* Cochren, 95 Md. 488, 52 Atl. 601; Fowble *v.* Kemp, 92 Md. 630, 48 Atl. 379; Monticello Distillery Co. *v.* Baltimore, 90 Md. 416, 45 Atl. 210; Dunbar *v.* Boston, 101 Mass. 317); and a dealer in spirituous liquors, in listing the amount of his purchases for taxation, is not entitled to deduct the amount of the United States internal revenue tax paid thereon (Lehman *v.* Grantham, 78 N. C. 115).

13. State *v.* Western Union Tel. Co., 96 Minn. 13, 104 N. W. 567; State *v.* Savage, 65 Nebr. 714, 91 N. W. 716; People *v.* Roberts, 159 N. Y. 70, 53 N. E. 685, 45 L. R. A. 126 [*reversing* 35 N. Y. App. Div. 624, 54 N. Y. Suppl. 1112]; Adams Express Co. *v.* Ohio State Auditor, 166 U. S. 185, 17 S. Ct. 604, 41 L. ed. 965.

It is not material in what this intangible property consists, whether privileges, corporate franchises, contracts, or obligations, it being sufficient that it is property which, although intangible, exists and has value. To ignore this intangible property or to hold that it is not subject to taxation at its accepted value would be to eliminate from the reach of the taxing power a large portion of the wealth of the country. Adams Express Co. *v.* Ohio State Auditor, 166 U. S. 185, 17 S. Ct. 604, 41 L. ed. 965.

14. Municipality No. 3 *v.* Johnson, 6 La. Ann. 20; Rising Sun St. Lighting Co. *v.* Boston, 181 Mass. 211, 63 N. E. 408.

Property leased for profit.—A statute requiring "personal property . . . leased for profit" to be assessed for taxation does not apply to lamps and lanterns owned and controlled by a company and used by it in the performance of a lighting contract with a city but not leased to the city. Rising Sun St. Lighting Co. *v.* Boston, 181 Mass. 211, 63 N. E. 408.

Household furniture.— Within the application of a statute providing for the taxation of "all household furniture" all the furnishings in a boarding-house or hotel which is the keeper's home where he eats, sleeps, and lives, except the bar furniture, bottles, wines, etc., are subject to taxation without regard to what part is used for domestic and what for business purposes, but in order to be so taxable it must appear that the keeper makes his home in such boarding-house or hotel. McWilliams *v.* Gable, 3 Pa. Co. Ct. 467.

Logs on water.—A river is a "body of water" within the application of a statute requiring timber, logs, and lumber lying "in or upon any body of water" in the state outside of boundary or limits of any town therein to be taxed in the town nearest and opposite such property. Berlin Mills Co. *v.* Wentworth's Location, 60 N. H. 156.

Good-will.— In Indiana it has been held that the good-will of a newspaper conducted by an individual or partnership is not as such property subject to taxation within the application of the Indiana statute (Hart *v.* Green, 159 Ind. 182, 64 N. E. 661, 95 Am. St. Rep. 280, 58 L. R. A. 949); but in New York it has been held that the good-will of a corporation acquired and built up in that state and having a market value there where its business is conducted is subject to taxation as "capital employed by it within this state" and is not exempt merely because it is intangible (People *v.* Roberts, 159 N. Y.

during the fiscal year or on a valuation computed by equalizing the average values for successive shorter periods.[23]

(IV) *MONEY.*[24] Money is not only the standard of value, but is also taxable personal property of the owner,[25] provided he has it in his possession at the time of the assessment or it is held for him by a person from whom he is entitled to receive it on demand.[26]

(V) *CREDITS, INVESTMENTS, AND SECURITIES* — (A) *In General.* Loans and investments of money and debts due to the taxpayer are assessable for taxation as his personal property, if within the terms of the statute, whether represented by accounts receivable, pecuniary interests under contracts, promissory notes, bonds, mortgages, or otherwise.[27] To be thus taxable it is not necessary

and selling the lumber is engaged in a "trading or mercantile business" within the application of the statute.

Iowa.— Iowa Pipe, etc., Co.'s Appeal, 101 Iowa 170, 70 N. W. 115, holding that a company engaged in the manufacture and sale of sewer pipe and drain tile, made from water salt and clay, is a "manufacturer," within the application of the code, section 816.

Massachusetts.—Hittinger *v.* Westford, 135 Mass. 258, holding that within the application of the Massachusetts statute a storehouse for ice is not a "store," and that the cutting of ice upon a pond and storing it in a building is not a "manufacture."

New Hampshire.— Russell *v.* Mason, 69 N. H. 359, 41 Atl. 287, holding that the owners of land who cut timber thereon and saw it into lumber for the purpose of selling it are not "tradesmen" within the application of a statute making the stock in trade of merchants, mechanics, and tradesmen taxable at its average value for the year.

Pennsylvania.— Campbell *v.* Campbell, 26 Leg. Int. 261 (holding that a manufacturer who has no store or warehouse apart from his manufactory is not subject to taxation under the act of 1846); Hay *v.* Harding, 5 Phila. 234 (holding that "shoddy" is a manufacture within the application of the revenue law of 1862).

Tennessee.—American Steel, etc., Co. *v.* Speed, 110 Tenn. 524, 75 S. W. 1037, 100 Am. St. Rep. 814, holding that the term "merchant," as used in the Tennessee statute of 1901, includes a foreign corporation having an agent in that state to whom it ships goods to be kept in stock and used to fill contracts of sale made by the company's salesmen or orders filed by purchasers with the agent.

Wisconsin.— Sanford *v.* Spencer, 62 Wis. 230, 22 N. W. 465, holding that lumber cut for sale is "merchants' goods" within the application of the statute.

See 45 Cent. Dig. tit. "Taxation," § 157.

Internal revenue stamps are not property within the application of the tax laws and, although kept in quantities by a dealer for the purpose of sale, are not taxable as "stock in trade." Palfrey *v.* Boston, 101 Mass. 329, 3 Am. Rep. 364.

Sewing machines delivered under a contract in the form of a lease providing for the payment of certain monthly rentals until a certain sum is paid, with the option of returning the machine or purchasing it for the sum of one cent, remain the property of the sewing machine company and are taxable as a part of its "stock in trade." Singer Mfg. Co. *v.* Essex County, 139 Mass. 266, 1 N. E. 419.

23. Iowa Pipe, etc., Co.'s Appeal, 101 Iowa 170, 70 N. W. 115; Myers *v.* Baltimore County, 83 Md. 385, 35 Atl. 144, 55 Am. St. Rep. 349, 24 L. R. A. 309. See also Russell *v.* Mason, 69 N. H. 359, 41 Atl. 287.

24. **Bank deposits** see *infra*, III, B, 2, a, (VI).

25. St. John *v.* Mobile, 21 Ala. 224; Critchfield *v.* Nance County, 77 Nebr. 807, 110 N. W. 538; State *v.* Thomas, 16 Utah 86, 50 Pac. 615 (holding, however, that money cannot be assessed for more than its legal value); People *v.* New York Tax Com'rs, 104 U. S. 466, 26 L. ed. 632 (holding that property which is in fact money on the day of the assessment cannot escape taxation on the ground that it was employed in the purchase of goods for exportation).

26. Arnold *v.* Middletown, 41 Conn. 206; Com. *v.* Clarkson, 1 Rawle (Pa.) 291.

27. *Alabama.*— Alabama Gold L. Ins. Co. *v.* Lott, 54 Ala. 499.

California.— Savings, etc., Soc. *v.* San Francisco, 146 Cal. 673, 80 Pac. 1086; Security Sav. Bank *v.* San Francisco, 132 Cal. 599, 64 Pac. 898; San Francisco *v.* La Societe Francaise D'Epargnes, etc., 131 Cal. 612, 63 Pac. 1016; Savings, etc., Soc. *v.* Austin, 46 Cal. 416. But see Mendocino Bank *v.* Chalfant, 51 Cal. 471; People *v.* Hibernia Sav., etc., Soc., 51 Cal. 243, 21 Am. Rep. 704.

Illinois.— Griffin *v.* La Salle County, 184 Ill. 275, 56 N. E. 397; Jacksonville *v.* McConnel, 12 Ill. 138.

Kentucky.— Johnson *v.* Com., 7 Dana 338.

Louisiana.— Standard Mar. Ins. Co. *v.* Bd. of Assessors, 123 La. 717, 49 So. 483, outstanding accounts taxable as credits.

Maryland.— Buchanan *v.* Talbot County, 47 Md. 286.

Michigan.— Port Huron *v.* Wright, 150 Mich. 279, 114 N. W. 76; Marquette *v.* Michigan Iron, etc., Co., 132 Mich. 130, 92 N. W. 934.

Mississippi.—Adams *v.* Clarke, 80 Miss. 134, 31 So. 216.

Nebraska.— Lancaster County *v.* McDonald, 73 Nebr. 453, 103 N. W. 78; Jones *v.* Seward County, 10 Nebr. 154, 4 N. W. 946.

is immaterial what form the transaction may assume, and an absolute deed of land or any other form of conveyance which was actually intended by the parties as security for a loan is taxable as a mortgage.[43] Neither is it material that the amount of the mortgage debt is greater than the value of the premises;[44] or, on the other hand, that the mortgagor is insolvent and payment depends on the sale of the land.[45] But of course a mortgage which has been actually satisfied or canceled and discharged of record is no longer taxable,[46] nor is it taxable after it has merged in the fee by the mortgagee's purchase of the land.[47] In some jurisdictions a tax on mortgages is imposed in the form of a registration or recording tax,[48] or privilege tax.[49]

d. Annuities. In some states annuities are taxable whether created by will, settlement, or otherwise;[50] but in others, where an annuity is charged upon land, it is not taxable in addition to the land itself.[51]

e. Licenses, Membership Rights, and Franchises. A license may be regarded as property and as such subject to taxation,[52] and franchises of all kinds are property subject to taxation;[53] but membership rights in various associations, although a source of profit, are ordinarily regarded as being in the nature of a personal privilege and not subject to taxation as property.[54] So it has been held that a

41 So. 947 (privilege tax); Drummond *v.* Smith, 118 N. Y. Suppl. 718 (recording tax); and cases cited *infra*, notes 48, 49.

43. Thomas *v.* Holmes County, 67 Miss. 754, 7 So. 552; Patrick *v.* Littell, 36 Ohio St. 79, 38 Am. Rep. 552.

44. Appleby *v.* East Brunswick Tp., 44 N. J. L. 153.

45. State *v.* Jones, 24 Minn. 251.

46. McCoppin *v.* McCartney, 60 Cal. 367; Earles *v.* Ramsay, 61 N. J. L. 194, 38 Atl. 812; Ross *v.* Portland, 42 Oreg. 134, 70 Pac. 373.

47. Frick *v.* Overholt, 3 Pa. Co. Ct. 538.

48. Mutual Ben. L. Ins. Co. *v.* Martin County, 104 Minn. 179, 116 N. W. 572; People *v.* Dimond, 121 N. Y. App. Div. 559, 106 N. Y. Suppl. 277; People *v.* Gass, 120 N. Y. App. Div. 147, 104 N. Y. Suppl. 885 [*affirmed* in 190 N. Y. 565, 83 N. E. 1129]; White *v.* Walsh, 62 Misc. (N. Y.) 423, 114 N. Y. Suppl. 1015.

In New York the mortgage tax law of 1905 imposed a certain tax on mortgages and exempted mortgages on which such tax had been paid from local taxation. People *v.* Keefe, 119 N. Y. App. Div. 713, 104 N. Y. Suppl. 154 [*affirmed* in 190 N. Y. 555, 83 N. E. 1130]. This statute was superseded by the act of 1906 substituting a recording tax on mortgages recorded after July 1, 1906. People *v.* Dimond, 121 N. Y. App. Div. 559, 106 N. Y. Suppl. 277; White *v.* Walsh, 62 Misc. (N. Y.) 423, 114 N. Y. Suppl. 1015. The statute exempts mortgages so recorded from other taxation (see People *v.* Dimond, *supra*; Drummond *v.* Smith, 118 N. Y. Suppl. 718); but prior mortgages are subject to general taxation (People *v.* Dimond, *supra*); or at least are subject to such taxation where they have not been recorded and the recording tax paid (Drummond *v.* Smith, *supra*).

Transactions subject to recording tax.—An agreement for the extension or renewal of an existing mortgage is in effect a mortgage and subject to the Minnesota registry tax. Mutual Ben. L. Ins. Co. *v.* Martin County, 104 Minn. 179, 116 N. W. 572. A mortgage of a leasehold interest in land is entitled to record and subject to the New York recording tax. People *v.* Gass, 120 N. Y. App. Div. 147, 104 N. Y. Suppl. 885 [*affirmed* in 190 N. Y. 565, 83 N. E. 1129]. The New York statute also provides that executory contracts for the sale of real property under which the vendee has or is entitled to possession shall be deemed mortgages. White *v.* Walsh, 62 Misc. (N. Y.) 423, 114 N. Y. Suppl. 1015, holding that an instrument leasing property for a term of years and containing provisions for a purchase thereof by the lessee on certain contingencies is an executory contract of sale within the application of the statute.

49. Barnes *v.* Moragne, 145 Ala. 313, 41 So. 947, construing the act of 1903 imposing a privilege tax on recorded mortgages and making such tax a substitute for *ad valorem* taxes thereon.

50. Wetmore *v.* State, 18 Ohio 77; Chisholm *v.* Shields, 21 Ohio Cir. Ct. 231, 11 Ohio Cir. Dec. 361.

51. Berks County *v.* Jones, 21 Pa. St. 413. And see Richey *v.* Shute, 43 N. J. L. 414.

52. Drysdale *v.* Pradat, 45 Miss. 445; Coulson *v.* Harris, 43 Miss. 728.

License fees and taxes see, generally, LICENSES, 25 Cyc. 593.

53. California Bank *v.* San Francisco, 142 Cal. 276, 75 Pac. 832, 100 Am. St. Rep. 130, 64 L. R. A. 918 (holding that a corporate franchise is property and taxable as such); Maestri *v.* New Orleans Bd. of Assessors, 110 La. 517, 34 So. 658 (holding that an exclusive privilege of erecting and maintaining a public market in a city for a term of years is a franchise and is property subject to taxation); Coulson *v.* Harris, 43 Miss. 728 (holding that a license to retail spirituous liquors under the Mississippi statutes of 1857 and 1865, is a franchise, and that such franchise is property subject to taxation).

Corporate franchise see *infra*, III, B, 1, f.

54. San Francisco *v.* Anderson, 103 Cal.

or has been discharged;[5] and under some statutes the executor or administrator is personally and individually liable for the payment of taxes so assessed against him in his representative capacity,[6] so that his own property may be taken to enforce the payment thereof;[7] and such liability is not relieved by a subsequent distribution of the estate.[8] As real estate upon the death of the owner ordinarily

New York.— *In re* Babcock, 115 N. Y. 450, 22 N. E. 263; People *v.* Wells, 94 N. Y. App. Div. 463, 87 N. Y. Suppl. 745, 88 N. Y. Suppl. 1113 [*affirmed* in 179 N. Y. 566, 71 N. E. 1136]; Bowe *v.* McNab, 11 N. Y. App. Div. 386, 42 N. Y. Suppl. 938; McMahon *v.* Beekman, 65 How. Pr. 427.

Ohio.— Sommers *v.* Boyd, 48 Ohio St. 648, 29 N. E. 497; *In re* Robb, 5 Ohio S. & C. Pl. Dec. 227, 5 Ohio N. P. 52.

Oregon.— Johnson *v.* Oregon City, 2 Oreg. 327.

See 45 Cent. Dig. tit. "Taxation," § 174.

Assessment to executor before probate.— A will vests in the executors named therein a legal control over the estate, which will justify an assessment of the personal property of the estate against them before the will is admitted to probate or letters testamentary are granted. People *v.* Barker, 150 N. Y. 52, 44 N. E. 785 [*affirming* 35 N. Y. Suppl. 953].

Ancillary administrator.— Money or property held by an ancillary administrator is subject to taxation in the state granting his letters, especially where taxes are not paid on it at the principal place of administration. Dorris *v.* Miller, 105 Iowa 564, 75 N. W. 482.

Credits of estates.— Where by the terms of a will the administrator was to keep the estate intact until the youngest child became of age, and in the meanwhile he loaned money to the heirs taking their notes therefor, it was held that such loans could not be considered as advances since no advances were authorized, but that the notes represented debts to the estate and were taxable as credits. *In re* Seaman, 135 Iowa 543, 113 N. W. 354.

Where administration is granted on the estate of a deceased ward the assets vest immediately in the administrator whose title by relation dates back to the time of the decease and therefore he and not the former guardian is the proper person to list the personal estate for taxation. Sommers *v.* Boyd, 48 Ohio St. 648, 29 N. E. 497.

Where a mortgage has been specifically devised to a person and the executors have no title thereto or to the money secured thereby, it is not to be assessed for taxation to them. Gray *v.* Leggett, 40 N. J. L. 308.

5. Augusta *v.* Kimball, 91 Me. 605, 40 Atl. 666, 41 L. R. A. 475; Carleton *v.* Ashburnham, 102 Mass. 348; Nelson *v.* Becker, 63 Minn. 61, 65 N. W. 119; People *v.* New York Tax Com'rs, 17 Hun (N. Y.) 293.

Legacy not delivered.— Where the statute requires the whole of an undistributed estate to be assessed to the executors, a legatee cannot be assessed for a legacy not yet due and still in the executor's hands. Barstow *v.* Big Rapids, 56 Mich. 35, 22 N. W. 103; Herrick *v.* Big Rapids, 53 Mich. 554, 19 N. W. 182.

Form of settlement.— Property should not be taxed to an administrator after there has been a settlement and distribution of the estate by amicable arrangement among all the parties interested and of which the assessors have notice, although there has been no formal settlement and decree in the probate court. Carleton *v.* Ashburnham, 102 Mass. 348.

6. New York *v.* Goss, 124 N. Y. App. Div. 680, 109 N. Y. Suppl. 151; Williams *v.* Holden, 4 Wend. (N. Y.) 223; Dennison *v.* Henry, 17 U. C. Q. B. 276. See also Dresden *v.* Bridge, 90 Me. 489, 38 Atl. 545, holding, however, that the executor or administrator, as the case may be, is not personally liable unless the assessment was made against him notwithstanding it was made after the death of the decedent.

Not personally liable for prior taxes.— An executor or administrator is not personally liable for the payment of a tax assessed against and due from decedent in his lifetime, and in an action to recover such taxes the judgment should be against the personal representative in his representative capacity. Eno *v.* Cornish, Kirby (Conn.) 296. And where an assessment is made for back taxes on omitted property for years during the lifetime of the decedent in which the property was not assessed, the executor or administrator is not personally liable for the payment of the tax, as his personal liability arises from the statutory duty of listing property in his hands for taxation, and the statutory lien on such property to secure reimbursement for the taxes paid by him, and the statute does not require him to make lists of property which the decedent has omitted to make in his lifetime. Scott *v.* People, 210 Ill. 594, 71 N. E. 582. So also the executor of a trustee who comes into possession of the trust estate but who holds it merely as a kind of bailee to preserve it intact and delivers it over to other trustees when appointed is not personally liable for the payment of taxes previously assessed upon the trust estate. State *v.* Mississippi Valley Trust Co., 209 Mo. 472, 108 S. W. 97.

7. Williams *v.* Holden, 4 Wend. (N. Y.) 223 (holding that individual property of an executor or administrator may be taken for a tax imposed upon him in his representative capacity where no property of the testator or intestate can be found); Dennison *v.* Henry, 17 U. C. Q. B. 276.

8. New York *v.* Goss, 124 N. Y. App. Div. 680, 109 N. Y. Suppl. 151.

A representative acts in his own wrong if he fails to appropriate property of the estate to the payment of a tax which should be paid out of the estate and makes a settlement or otherwise parts with the property without

(II) *CREDITS AND SECURITIES HELD BY NON-RESIDENT AGENT OR TRUSTEE.* Property in the nature of loans, investments, and securities, held and controlled by a non-resident, is not taxable, although he holds it as agent or trustee for a resident citizen, to whom the income or profits are payable,[78] unless a statute expressly makes such property taxable to the principal or beneficiary, which is the case in some states.[79]

c. Property of Decedents' Estates.[80] While ordinarily the domicile of a decedent determines the *situs* for purposes of taxation of his personal property which is of an intangible character or not permanently located elsewhere, and also the place of administering his estate,[81] the general rule is that after administration has been granted the title to such property vests in the personal representative, and that its *situs* for taxation is at the domicile of the executor or administrator,[82] notwithstanding the decedent at the time of his death was a resident of another state,[83] or the distributees are residents of another state,[84] or the will was executed in another state.[85] The domicile of a personal representative, however, for purposes of such taxation, is his official domicile, which is the place of his appointment,[86] and although the legal title to the estate is vested in

State *v.* New Orleans Bd. of Assessors, 47 La. Ann. 1544, 18 So. 519; State *v.* Fidelity, etc., Co., 35 Tex. Civ. App. 214, 80 S. W. 544; State Tax, etc., Bonds Case, 15 Wall. (U. S.) 300, 21 L. ed. 179.

78. *Kansas.*— Fisher *v.* Rush County, 19 Kan. 414, holding that a resident of Kansas who conveyed land situated in Iowa, taking in payment certain notes secured by a mortgage on the land and which are made payable in Iowa and left there for collection, is not subject to taxation on such notes in the state of Kansas. See also Wilcox *v.* Ellis, 14 Kan. 588, 19 Am. Rep. 107.

Massachusetts.— Dorr *v.* Boston, 6 Gray 131.

New York.— People *v.* Smith, 88 N. Y. 576; People *v.* Gardner, 51 Barb. 352.

Oregon.— Poppleton *v.* Yamhill County, 18 Oreg. 377, 23 Pac. 253, 7 L. R. A. 449.

Rhode Island.— Anthony *v.* Caswell, 15 R. I. 159, 1 Atl. 290.

See 45 Cent. Dig. tit. "Taxation," § 198.

But see Bullock *v.* Guilford, 59 Vt. 516, 9 Atl. 360.

This is the converse of the rule previously stated, in regard to the taxability of credits and securities belonging to a non-resident but held and controlled by a local or resident agent. See *supra*, III, A, 4, d, (II).

79. Hunt *v.* Perry, 165 Mass. 287, 43 N. E. 103; Lee *v.* Dawson, 8 Ohio Cir. Ct. 365, 4 Ohio Cir. Dec. 442; Conner *v.* Wilson, 6 Ohio Dec. (Reprint) 941, 9 Am. L. Rec. 1; Selden *v.* Brooke, 104 Va. 832, 52 S. E. 632.

Application of the New York statute in the case of property held by trustees some of whom are residents and others non-residents see People *v.* Feitner, 168 N. Y. 360, 61 N. E. 280 [*reversing* 63 N. Y. App. Div. 174, 71 N. Y. Suppl. 261]; People *v.* Barker, 135 N. Y. 656, 32 N. E. 252; People *v.* Coleman, 119 N. Y. 137, 23 N. E. 488, 7 L. R. A. 407 [*reversing* 53 Hun 482, 6 N. Y. Suppl. 285].

80. **Place of taxation** as between different taxing districts in the same state see *infra*, V, D, 3.

81. Bonaparte *v.* State, 63 Md. 465. See also People *v.* New York Tax, etc., Com'rs, 38 Hun (N. Y.) 536.

82. *Kentucky.*— Baldwin *v.* Shine, 84 Ky. 502, 2 S. W. 164, 8 Ky. L. Rep. 496.

Missouri.— State *v.* St. Louis County Ct., 47 Mo. 594.

New Jersey.— State *v.* Jones, 39 N. J. L. 650; State *v.* Holmdel Tp., 39 N. J. L. 79.

New York.— People *v.* Gaus, 169 N. Y. 19, 61 N. E. 987.

Ohio.— Tafel *v.* Lewis, 75 Ohio St. 182, 78 N. E. 1003; Brown *v.* Noble, 42 Ohio St. 405. See also Hawk *v.* Bonn, 6 Ohio Cir. Ct. 452, 3 Ohio Cir. Dec. 535.

Oregon.— Johnson *v.* Oregon City, 2 Oreg. 327.

Pennsylvania.— See Lewis *v.* Chester County, 60 Pa. St. 325.

Virginia.— Com. *v.* Williams, 102 Va. 778, 47 S. E. 867.

United States.— Dallinger *v.* Rapallo, 15 Fed. 434, 14 Fed. 32.

See 45 Cent. Dig. tit. "Taxation," § 199.

83. Baldwin *v.* Shine, 84 Ky. 502, 2 S. W. 164, 8 Ky. L. Rep. 496; Tafel *v.* Lewis, 75 Ohio St. 182, 78 N. E. 1003. See also cases cited *supra*, note 82.

Ancillary administration.— Bonds of a Missouri corporation in the hands of an ancillary administrator appointed in that state are taxable in Missouri as having an actual *situs* there, although the owner died domiciled in another state and the bonds were transferred to Missouri merely for the purpose of ancillary administration. State *v.* St. Louis County Ct., 47 Mo. 594.

84. Baldwin *v.* Shine, 84 Ky. 502, 2 S. W. 164, 8 Ky. L. Rep. 496; Tafel *v.* Lewis, 75 Ohio St. 182, 78 N. E. 1003.

85. Tafel *v.* Lewis, 75 Ohio St. 182, 78 N. E. 1003, where the will was both executed and probated in a foreign country but the executor derived his authority by appointment of the probate court in the state of his residence.

86. Gallup *v.* Schmidt, 154 Ind. 196, 56 N. E. 443; Com. *v.* Peebles, 134 Ky. 121, 119

him it does not follow him wherever he may have a residence in his individual capacity, as it would the original owner;[87] so that if a representative appointed in one state resides in another state where no administration was taken out, such residence does not give intangible property or tangible property not removed by him to the latter state a *situs* for taxation in such state,[88] although personal property actually removed to and held by him in the latter state or funds taken and invested there may be taxed there.[89]

d. Shipping.[90] Ordinarily the legal *situs* of sea-going vessels for the purpose of taxation is the port where they are registered under the laws of the United States as their home port, and this is not lost by mere absence and employment elsewhere, nor affected by the residence of their owners.[91] But this rule as to the *situs* of vessels is not absolute or conclusive;[92] and while a vessel registered and having its home port in one state is not subject to taxation in another state where it may happen to be merely temporarily and transiently as an incident to the commerce in which it is engaged,[93] a vessel which is employed exclusively or for an indefinite length of time in one state may be taxed in that state, although it is registered in another state,[94] and the owner is a non-resident.[95] It has also been held that the *situs* of vessels plying between ports of different states and engaged in the coastwise trade depends either upon the actual domicile of the owner or the permanent *situs* of the property entirely regardless of the place of enrolment,[96] and that, although a vessel may be registered or enrolled in a different

S. W. 774, 23 L. R. A. N. S. 1130; Hawk *v.* Bonn, 6 Ohio Cir. Ct. 452, 3 Ohio Cir. Dec. 535. See also Bonaparte *v.* State, 63 Md. 465.

87. Com. *v.* Peebles, 134 Ky. 121, 119 S. W. 774, 23 L. R. A. N. S. 1130.

88. Com. *v.* Peebles, 134 Ky. 121, 119 S. W. 774, 23 L. R. A. 1130; Hawk *v.* Bonn, 6 Ohio Cir. Ct. 452, 3 Ohio Cir. Dec. 535; Lewis *v.* Chester County, 60 Pa. St. 325.

89. Lewis *v.* Chester County, 60 Pa. St. 325. See also Hawk *v.* Bonn, 6 Ohio Cir. Ct. 452, 3 Ohio Cir. Dec. 535.

90. Liability to taxation generally see *supra*, III, A, 2, c, (II).

Place of taxation as between different taxing districts in the same state see *infra*, V, C, 2, g.

91. *California.*— San Francisco *v.* Talbot, 63 Cal. 485. See also California Shipping Co. *v.* San Francisco, 150 Cal. 145, 88 Pac. 704; Olson *v.* San Francisco, 148 Cal. 80, 82 Pac. 850, 113 Am. St. Rep. 191, 2 L. R. A. N. S. 197.

Florida.— Johnson *v.* De Bary-Baya Merchants' Line, 37 Fla. 499, 19 So. 640, 37 L. R. A. 518.

Illinois.— Irvin *v.* New Orleans, etc., R. Co., 94 Ill. 105, 34 Am. Rep. 208; Wilkey *v.* Pekin, 19 Ill. 160.

Indiana.— New Albany *v.* Meekin, 3 Ind. 481, 56 Am. Dec. 522.

Michigan.— Roberts *v.* Charlevoix Tp., 60 Mich. 197, 26 N. W. 878.

New Jersey.— New York, etc., R. Co. *v.* Haight, 30 N. J. L. 428.

New York.— People *v.* New York Tax, etc., Com'rs, 58 N. Y. 242; People *v.* New York Tax Com'rs, 23 N. Y. 224.

United States.— Hays *v.* Pacific Mail Steamship Co., 17 How. 596, 15 L. ed. 254; Yost *v.* Lake Erie Transp. Co., 112 Fed. 746, 50 C. C. A. 511. *Compare* St. Louis *v.* Wiggins Ferry Co., 11 Wall. 423, 20 L. ed. 192.

Canada.— Halifax *v.* Kenny, 3 Can. Sup. Ct. 497.

See 45 Cent. Dig. tit. "Taxation," §§ 13, 200.

92. National Dredging Co. *v.* State, 99 Ala. 462, 12 So. 720; Johnson *v.* De Bary-Baya Merchants' Line, 37 Fla. 499, 19 So. 640, 37 L. R. A. 518; Old Dominion Steamship Co. *v.* Com., 102 Va. 576, 46 S. E. 783, 102 Am. St. Rep. 855 [*affirmed* in 198 U. S. 299, 25 S. Ct. 686, 49 L. ed. 1059]; Norfolk, etc., R. Co. *v.* State Bd. of Public Works, 97 Va. 23, 32 S. E. 779; North Western Lumber Co. *v.* Chehalis County, 25 Wash. 95, 64 Pac. 909.

93. San Francisco *v.* Talbot, 63 Cal. 485; Johnson *v.* De Bary-Baya Merchants' Line, 37 Fla. 499, 19 So. 640, 37 L. R. A. 518; State *v.* Haight, 30 N. J. L. 428; Hays *v.* Pacific Mail Steamship Co., 17 How. (U. S.) 596, 15 L. ed. 254. See also cases cited *supra*, note 91.

94. National Dredging Co. *v.* State, 99 Ala. 462, 12 So. 720; Old Dominion Steamship Co. *v.* Com., 102 Va. 576, 46 S. E. 783, 102 Am. St. Rep. 855 [*affirmed* in 198 U. S. 299, 25 S. Ct. 686, 49 L. ed. 1059]; North Western Lumber Co. *v.* Chehalis County, 25 Wash. 95, 64 Pac. 909.

95. National Dredging Co. *v.* State, 99 Ala. 462, 12 So. 720; Old Dominion Steamship Co. *v.* Com., 102 Va. 576, 46 S. E. 783, 102 Am. St. Rep. 855 [*affirmed* in 198 U. S. 299, 25 S. Ct. 686, 49 L. ed. 1059].

96. Ayer, etc., Tie Co. *v.* Kentucky, 202 U. S. 409, 26 S. Ct. 679, 50 L. ed. 1082 [*reversing* 117 Ky. 161, 77 S. W. 686, 79 S. W. 290, 25 Ky. L. Rep. 1068, 2061, 85 S. W. 1096, 27 Ky. L. Rep. 585]. See also American Mail Steamship Co. *v.* Crowell, 76 N. J. L. 54, 68 Atl. 752.

to collect the tax.[15] It is also necessary that the receipts in respect to which the person is sought to be taxed should be plainly within the terms, such as "income" or "profits," employed in the statute;[16] and under some laws of this kind it is held that "income" means net income, not gross receipts.[17] The income of the preceding year may be and commonly is taken as the basis of the assessment.[18]

c. Persons Subject to Poll Tax.[19] Statutes requiring male inhabitants of a state to pay poll taxes are not restricted to such inhabitants as are citizens,[20] but apply to resident aliens.[21] They do not, however, apply to persons residing only temporarily in the state for a part of the year and domiciled in another state,[22] or to persons residing on lands purchased by or ceded to the United States for navy yards, forts, or arsenals, and over which the government of the United States has sole and exclusive jurisdiction.[23] The question as to what particular inhabitants or classes of inhabitants are or are not by reason of age or other circumstances or conditions required to pay poll taxes depends upon the provisions of the statutes.[24]

275; Lining *v.* Charleston, 1 McCord (S. C.) 345; Plumer *v.* Com., 3 Gratt. (Va.) 645; Langston *v.* Glasson, [1891] 1 Q. B. 567, 55 J. P. 567, 60 L. J. Q. B. 356, 65 L. T. Rep. N. S. 159, 39 Wkly. Rep. 476; Bowers *v.* Harding, [1891] 1 Q. B. 560, 55 J. P. 376, 60 L. J. Q. B. 474, 64 L. T. Rep. N. S. 201, 39 Wkly. Rep. 558; Robson *v.* Virginia, 4 Northwest Terr. (Can.) 80. See also Goodwin *v.* Ottawa, 12 Ont. L. Rep. 236.

Salaries of ministers and teachers.— Statutes relating to income taxes have been held not to apply to the salaries of ministers (Com. *v.* Cuyler, 5 Watts & S. (Pa.) 275; Plumer *v.* Com., 3 Gratt. (Va.) 645. But see Miller *v.* Kirkpatrick, 29 Pa. St. 226), or of teachers in the public schools (Com. *v.* Cuyler, *supra*).

15. Marr *v.* Vienna, 10 Can. L. J. 275; Matter of Ashworth, 7 Can. L. J. 47.

16. New Orleans *v.* Hart, 14 La. Ann. 803 (holding that the word "income," as used in the act of 1856, means money received in compensation for labor or services, such as wages, commissions, brokerage, etc., and not the fruits of capital invested in merchandise, stocks, etc.); Wilcox *v.* Middlesex County, 103 Mass. 544; Pearson *v.* Chace, 10 R. I. 455 (annual income distinguished from annuity); Nizam's State R. Co. *v.* Wyatt, 24 Q. B. D. 548, 59 L. J. Q. B. 430, 62 L. T. Rep. N. S. 765 (government annual subvention to a railway company); Turner *v.* Cuxon, 22 Q. B. D. 150, 53 J. P. 148, 58 L. J. Q. B. 131, 60 L. T. Rep. N. S. 332, 37 Wkly. Rep. 254 (pension to a curate renewable at option of authorities).

17. See Millar *v.* Douglass, 42 Tex. 288; Lawless *v.* Sullivan, 6 App. Cas. 373, 50 L. J. P. C. 33, 44 L. T. Rep. N. S. 897, 29 Wkly. Rep. 917; Matter of Yarwood, 7 Can. L. J. 47; *In re* Hamilton Bank, 12 Brit. Col. 207; *Re* Biddle Cope, 5 Brit. Col. 37. *Compare* Lott *v.* Hubbard, 44 Ala. 593, holding that where income is taxable, a taxpayer cannot relieve himself from liability for such tax on the ground that he applied the income to the reduction of his indebtedness on a purchase of real estate on which he had paid full taxes.

18. Glasgow *v.* Rowse, 43 Mo. 479; Drexel *v.* Com., 46 Pa. St. 31; Lamontaigne *v.* Macleod, 5 Northwest Terr. (Can.) 199.

19. **Constitutional validity of poll taxes** see *supra*, II, F, 3.

20. Kuntz *v.* Davidson County, 6 Lea (Tenn.) 65.

21. Opinion of Justices, 7 Mass. 523 (holding that the terms "inhabitants" and "residents" as regards poll taxes apply to resident aliens); Kuntz *v.* Davidson County, 6 Lea (Tenn.) 65 (holding that a statute requiring every male "inhabitant" of the state to pay a poll tax applies to a resident alien, although he has never applied for naturalization papers).

22. State *v.* Ross, 23 N. J. L. 517.

Road tax.— A statute requiring persons "residing" in a road district to be listed annually and required to perform a certain amount of labor or to pay in lieu thereof a certain tax does not apply to persons temporarily in a road district engaged in the construction of a railroad but without any intention of remaining longer than such work requires. On Yuen Hai Co. *v.* Ross, 14 Fed. 338, 8 Sawy. 384.

23. Opinion of Justices, 1 Metc. (Mass.) 580, holding that persons residing on such lands where there is no reservation of jurisdiction to the state except the right to serve civil and criminal process on such lands are not subject to the payment of poll taxes.

24. See the statutes of the several states. And see Boston, etc., Glass Co. *v.* Boston, 4 Metc. (Mass.) 181; Faribault *v.* Misener, 20 Minn. 396; White *v.* Kershaw Dist. Tax Collector, 3 Rich. (S. C.) 136.

Minors.— Under a statute requiring male inhabitants over sixteen years of age to pay poll taxes, and providing that a minor having no parent, master, or guardian shall be personally taxed for his poll, and that the poll tax of every other person under guardianship shall be assessed to his guardian, the poll tax of minors in the employ of a manufacturing corporation and receiving salaries cannot be assessed to the corporation. Boston, etc., Glass Co. *v.* Boston, 4 Metc. (Mass.) 181.

is any distribution made or ordered to be made to stock-holders out of the earnings or profits of the company,[98] including a stock dividend;[99] but not including a mere numerical increase in the number of shares of stock of the corporation not representing any distribution of earnings or profits,[1] or a distribution or return to shareholders of the capital stock or any part of it or the property represented by it or of the assets of the company as distinguished from earnings.[2] Taking the word "dividend" in this sense, it has been held not to be material, for the purposes of the tax law, where or how it was earned,[3] or when it was earned,[4] or if actually declared whether it was earned or not.[5] If the tax is laid upon dividends exceeding a certain percentage of the capital stock, this will be taken as meaning

of a dividend declared by a corporation before the date fixed for the assessment of property for taxation, but payable at a future date, does not constitute part of the surplus fund of the corporation, taxable to it, but is a debt which the corporation is entitled to have deducted from its taxable assets. People *v.* Barker, 86 Hun (N. Y.) 131, 33 N. Y. Suppl. 388.

98. Com. *v.* Western Land, etc., Co., 156 Pa. St. 455, 26 Atl. 1034; Com. *v.* Pittsburg, etc., R. Co., 74 Pa. St. 83.

Profits applied to betterments are not "dividends earned," within the meaning of that phrase in a tax statute. State *v.* Comptroller, 54 N. J. L. 135, 23 Atl. 122.

Distribution among members of limited partnership.— Under the Pennsylvania statute relating to limited partnerships, which gives to such associations most of the characteristics of a corporation, they are to be taxed on their capital stock, the tax being measured by any distribution or division of profits which corresponds to dividends in a corporation. See Com. *v.* Sanderson, etc., Imp. Co., 3 Dauph. Co. Rep. (Pa.) 116.

Scrip certificates are not properly dividends and are generally taxable to the corporation rather than to the stock-holders. See Adams *v.* Shields, 7 Ohio S. & C. Pl. Dec. 193, 5 Ohio N. P. 190.

99. State *v.* Farmers' Bank, 11 Ohio 94; Allegheny *v.* Pittsburgh, etc., R. Co., 179 Pa. St. 414, 36 Atl. 161; Lehigh Crane Iron Co. *v.* Com., 55 Pa. St. 448; Com. *v.* Cleveland, etc., R. Co., 29 Pa. St. 370; Com. *v.* Western Union Tel. Co., 2 Dauph. Co. Rep. (Pa.) 30.

1. Com. *v.* Erie, etc., R. Co., 74 Pa. St. 94; Com. *v.* Pittsburg, etc., R. Co., 74 Pa. St. 83; Com. *v.* Western Union Tel. Co., 2 Dauph. Co. Rep. (Pa.) 30.

There is no presumption that an increase of stock authorized by law is a stock dividend so as to be taxable, but whether the increase is real or only a pretense is a question of fact for the jury. Com. *v.* Erie, etc., R. Co., 74 Pa. St. 94.

Consolidation of corporations.— Where a consolidation of three corporations is effected by one of them absorbing the others and increasing its capital stock by more than double and dividing the increased stock among the shareholders in all three of the corporations, such distribution cannot be considered a stock dividend. Allegheny *v.* Federal St., etc., Pass. R. Co., 179 Pa. St. 424, 36 Atl. 320.

2. People *v.* Roberts, 41 N. Y. App. Div. 21, 58 N. Y. Suppl. 254; Credit Mobilier of America *v.* Com., 67 Pa. St. 233. And see Com. *v.* Central Transp. Co., 145 Pa. St. 89, 22 Atl. 209, in which case it appeared that the par value of the shares of stock of a corporation was reduced, and the difference between the old and new par was paid to the stock-holders in cash, and it was held that this was not a dividend but a reduction of the capital stock. On the other hand, in Com. *v.* Western Land, etc., Co., 156 Pa. St. 455, 26 Atl. 1034, where an enormous distribution to stock-holders was made, nearly equal to the capital stock, it was held to be a dividend and taxable, and a division of the capital or assets of the company, because it was shown that after this payment the market value of the stock did not sink below par.

3. People *v.* Roberts, 155 N. Y. 408, 50 N. E. 53, 41 L. R. A. 228, holding that it is immaterial that the dividends were earned outside the state and that the company made no profit on its business within the state.

4. State *v.* Franklin Bank, 10 Ohio 91. *Contra*, Com. *v.* Brush Electric Light Co., 145 Pa. St. 147, 22 Atl. 844.

Profits before enactment of law.— It has been held that the state is entitled to the tax on all dividends declared after the enactment of the statute, whether the profits accrued before or after the law went into effect. State *v.* Franklin Bank, 10 Ohio 91. But see People *v.* Albany Ins. Co., 92 N. Y. 458; Com. *v.* Wyoming Valley Canal Co., 50 Pa. St. 410; Com. *v.* Pennsylvania Ins. Co., 13 Pa. St. 165.

Under the Pennsylvania statute providing for a tax on corporations according to dividends where they have "made or declared" during any year dividends amounting to six per cent or more on the par value of their capital stock, and in other cases for taxation according to the actual appraised value, a corporation is not to be taxed according to dividends where its earnings during the year are less than six per cent and it declares a dividend of over six per cent made up in part of accumulated earnings of previous years in none of which did the earnings amount to six per cent and during which it had been taxed according to the actual value of its stock. Com. *v.* Brush Electric Light Co., 145 Pa. St. 147, 22 Atl. 844.

5. Columbia Conduit Co. *v.* Com., 90 Pa. St. 307; Com. *v.* Pittsburg, etc., R. Co., 74 Pa. St. 83.

be taxed to the depositors.[51] The opinion has also been advanced that the money of a depositor may be taxed to him, and the deposits of the bank, including his, also be taxed to the bank;[52] although this has been held, particularly in the case of savings banks, to be objectionable as double taxation.[53] Still another doctrine is that while the bank may be taxed on the amount of its deposits, it is rather to be regarded as a franchise tax than as a tax on property.[54] The courts of New York maintain the rule that, for the purpose of ascertaining the amount of taxable property of a savings bank, the amount of its deposits should be deducted from its gross assets, as being a liability.[55]

(VII) *LOANS AND INVESTMENTS.* Under the general laws for the taxation of intangible personal property, or under laws relating specially to banking institutions, these corporations are held to be taxable on notes, mortgages, stocks, bonds, and other securities and evidences of indebtedness representing their loans, discounts, and investments.[56] In several states, however, it is held that savings

Ohio.— Patton *v.* Commercial Bank, 10 Ohio S. & C. Pl. Dec. 321, 7 Ohio N. P. 401.

Pennsylvania.— Philadelphia Sav. Fund Soc. *v.* Yard, 9 Pa. St. 359.

Vermont.— Montpelier Sav. Bank, etc., Co. *v.* Montpelier, 73 Vt. 364, 50 Atl. 1117.

See 45 Cent. Dig. tit. "Taxation," § 236.

Deposits invested in realty.— Under the law of Maryland, deposits in a savings bank which it has invested in real estate, on which real estate it pays taxes, are not taxable to the bank. State *v.* Central Sav. Bank, 67 Md. 290, 10 Atl. 290, 11 Atl. 357.

51. *Iowa.*— Branch *v.* Marengo, 43 Iowa 600.

Kentucky.— Com. *v.* Commerce Bank, 118 Ky. 547, 81 S. W. 679, 26 Ky. L. Rep. 407; Owensboro Deposit Bank *v.* Daviess County, 102 Ky. 174, 39 S. W. 1030, 44 L. R. A. 825.

Nebraska.— Critchfield *v.* Nance County, 77 Nebr. 807, 110 N. W. 538.

New Hampshire.— *In re* Perry, 16 N. H. 44.

Rhode Island.— Providence Sav. Inst. *v.* Gardiner, 4 R. I. 484.

Texas.— Campbell *v.* Riviere, (Civ. App. 1893) 22 S. W. 993; Campbell *v.* Wiggins, 2 Tex. Civ. App. 1, 20 S. W. 730.

See 45 Cent. Dig. tit. "Taxation," § 236.

Depositor indebted to bank.— While a bank may credit a customer's deposit on his overdue paper held by the bank, the money belongs to the customer, and is subject to his checks until the bank exercises this right; and, until this is actually done, the money is taxable in the depositor's hands as if he owed nothing to the bank. Com. *v.* Wathen, 126 Ky. 573, 104 S. W. 364, 31 Ky. L. Rep. 980.

General or special deposits.— The Nebraska statute requiring every person to list all his moneys for taxation, and providing that the word "money" shall include "money deposited in bank," is not restricted to special deposits but includes general deposits. Critchfield *v.* Nance County, 77 Nebr. 807, 110 N. W. 538.

A time deposit in a private banking institution is taxable to the depositor as a credit. Hall *v.* Greenwood County, 22 Kan. 37.

52. Yuba County *v.* Adams, 7 Cal. 35; New London Sav. Bank *v.* New London, 20 Conn. 111; Columbus Exch. Bank *v.* Hines, 3 Ohio St. 1.

53. See *supra*, II, C, 1.

54. Coite *v.* Hartford Sav. Soc., 32 Conn. 173; Jones *v.* Winthrop Sav. Bank, 66 Me. 242; Com. *v.* Lancaster Sav. Bank, 123 Mass. 493; Com. *v.* People's Five Cents Sav. Bank, 5 Allen (Mass.) 428; Provident Sav. Inst. *v.* Massachusetts, 6 Wall. (U. S.) 611, 18 L. ed. 907; Connecticut Sav. Soc. *v.* Coite, 6 Wall. (U. S.) 594, 18 L. ed. 897. *Contra*, Wyatt *v.* State Bd. of Equalization, 74 N. H. 552, 70 Atl. 387; Bartlett *v.* Carter, 59 N. H. 105.

55. People *v.* Barker, 154 N. Y. 128, 47 N. E. 973; Matter of Haight, 32 N. Y. App. Div. 496, 53 N. Y. Suppl. 226; People *v.* Barker, 19 N. Y. App. Div. 64, 45 N. Y. Suppl. 811 [*reversed* on other grounds in 154 N. Y. 122, 47 N. E. 1103]; People *v.* Beers, 67 How. Pr. (N. Y.) 219.

56. *Illinois.*— Republic Bank *v.* Hamilton, 21 Ill. 53.

Kentucky.— German Bank *v.* Louisville, 108 Ky. 377, 56 S. W. 504, 22 Ky. L. Rep. 9.

Michigan.— Latham *v.* Detroit Bd. of Assessors, 91 Mich. 509, 52 N. W. 15.

Mississippi.— U. S. Bank *v.* State, 12 Sm. & M. 456.

New York.— People *v.* Coleman, 135 N. Y. 231, 31 N. E. 1022 [*affirming* 18 N. Y. Suppl. 675].

Ohio.— Stark County Bank *v.* McGregor, 6 Ohio St. 45, holding that under the tax law of 1852, all the assets of a bank, including specie and balances in other banks, must, if employed in any way whereby the bank obtains or reserves interest, profit, or a consideration, be averaged for taxation; but specie unemployed, not on hand for sale, and from which the bank derives no profit, need not be returned to the assessor, nor balances due from other banks on which no interest, profit, or consideration is reserved or received.

Pennsylvania.— Pennsylvania Ins. Co. *v.* Loughlin, 139 Pa. St. 612, 21 Atl. 163; Philadelphia Sav. Fund Soc. *v.* Yard, 9 Pa. St. 359; Com. *v.* McKean County, 24 Pa. Co. Ct. 33. *Compare* Hunter's Appeal, 3 Pa. Cas. 1, 10 Atl. 429.

Washington.— Pacific Nat. Bank *v.* Pierce County, 20 Wash. 675, 56 Pac. 936.

or on its furniture or other personal property,[64] nor on its mortgages or other loans or investments;[65] and a state statute laying a tax on the presidents of all banks must be held invalid so far as it purports to affect the presidents of the national banks.[66]

(II) *CAPITAL STOCK.* The capital stock of a national bank, considered as the property of the bank and as distinct from the interests of its stock-holders, as represented by their shares of stock, is not subject to any taxation by the states or by their authority, whether in the form of a franchise tax or a tax on the property itself;[67] the only way such stock can be reached being by an assessment of the shares of the different stock-holders.[68]

(III) *REAL ESTATE.* Under the express provision of the act of congress

Rep. 1656; Schuster *v.* Louisville, 89 S. W. 689, 28 Ky. L. Rep. 588; Louisville Third Nat. Bank *v.* Stone, 174 U. S. 432, 19 S. Ct. 759, 43 L. ed. 1035; Owensboro Nat. Bank *v.* Owensboro, 173 U. S. 664, 19 S. Ct. 537, 43 L. ed. 850; Louisville First Nat. Bank *v.* Stone, 88 Fed. 409.

64. *Arizona.*— Arizona Nat. Bank *v.* Long, 6 Ariz. 311, 57 Pac. 639.

California. — San Francisco First Nat. Bank *v.* San Francisco, 129 Cal. 96, 61 Pac. 778; People *v.* Mills Nat. Bank, 123 Cal. 53, 55 Pac. 685, 69 Am. St. Rep. 32, 45 L. R. A. 747.

Iowa.— Oskaloosa Nat. State Bank *v.* Young, 25 Iowa 311.

Kentucky.— See Paducah City Nat. Bank *v.* Paducah, (1888) 9 S. W. 218.

Montana.— Billings First Nat. Bank *v.* Province, 20 Mont. 374, 51 Pac. 821.

Nevada. — State *v.* Nevada First Nat. Bank, 4 Nev. 348.

United States.— Owensboro Nat. Bank *v.* Owensboro, 173 U. S. 664, 19 S. Ct. 537, 43 L. ed. 850; San Francisco *v.* Crocker-Woolworth Nat. Bank, 92 Fed. 273; Covington City Nat. Bank *v.* Covington, 21 Fed. 484.

65. Winnemucca First Nat. Bank *v.* Kreig, 21 Nev. 404, 32 Pac. 641.

66. Linton *v.* Childs, 105 Ga. 567, 32 S. E. 617.

67. *Georgia.*— Macon *v.* Macon First Nat. Bank, 59 Ga. 648.

Idaho.— Weiser Nat. Bank *v.* Jeffreys, 14 Ida. 659, 95 Pac. 23.

Iowa.— Judy *v.* National State Bank, 133 Iowa 252, 110 N. W. 605.

Kansas.— Leoti First Nat. Bank *v.* Fisher, 45 Kan. 726, 26 Pac. 482. See also Pollard *v.* Newton First Nat. Bank, 47 Kan. 406, 28 Pac. 202.

Kentucky.— Owen County Ct. *v.* Farmers' Nat. Bank, 59 S. W. 7, 22 Ky. L. Rep. 916.

Michigan.— Smith *v.* Tecumseh First Nat. Bank, 17 Mich. 479.

New Jersey.— State *v.* Newark, 39 N. J. L. 380.

Ohio.— Miller *v.* Cincinnati First Nat. Bank, 46 Ohio St. 424, 21 N. E. 860.

Texas.— Lampasas First Nat. Bank *v.* Lampasas, 33 Tex. Civ. App. 530, 78 S. W. 42.

Utah.— Salt Lake City Nat. Bank *v.* Golding, 2 Utah 1.

United States.— Owensboro Nat. Bank *v.* Owensboro, 173 U. S. 664, 19 S. Ct. 537, 43 L. ed. 850; Bradley *v.* Illinois, 4 Wall. 459, 18 L. ed. 433; Bank of Commerce *v.* New York, 2 Black 620, 17 L. ed. 451; Brown *v.* French, 80 Fed. 166; Collins *v.* Chicago, 6 Fed. Cas. No. 3,011, 4 Biss. 472; Omaha First Nat. Bank *v.* Douglas County, 9 Fed. Cas. No. 4,809, 3 Dill. 298.

See 45 Cent. Dig. tit. "Taxation," §§ 24, 231.

Tax on surplus earnings.— In New Hampshire it has been held that a statute providing for the taxation of stock-holders on the par value of their shares and taxation of the bank on its surplus in excess of the surplus required to be kept on hand by the act of congress is not in conflict with the federal statutes, it being held that such surplus represents a voluntary accumulation of undivided profits, and that to tax the shares of the shareholders at their par value and the surplus to the bank, and the payment of such taxes by the bank out of its profits, decreasing to that extent the profits subject to division among the stock-holders, is in effect the same as taxing the stock-holders alone upon the market value of their shares. Peterborough First Nat. Bank *v.* Peterborough, 56 N. H. 38, 32 Am. Rep. 416.

Waiver or estoppel.— It has been held that where a national bank voluntarily returns its capital stock for taxation, and states, in its answer in an action to recover the taxes thereon as increased on equalization, that it is willing to pay the tax as returned, it may be held liable for the taxes on the value of its stock as returned, although an assessment thereof would be unauthorized, but will not be held liable for any amount due to the increase of valuation. Lampasas First Nat. Bank *v.* Lampasas, 33 Tex. Civ. App. 530, 78 S. W. 42. But an assessment upon the capital stock of a national bank is not merely irregular but void, and the bank is not estopped to recover taxes paid under protest under such an assessment by the fact that its cashier through mistake listed such capital for taxation or by the fact that it did not apply to the board of equalization for relief against the assessment, such board having no jurisdiction in regard to property over which the taxing authority has no jurisdiction. Weiser Nat. Bank *v.* Jeffreys, 14 Ida. 659, 95 Pac. 23.

68. Miller *v.* Cincinnati First Nat. Bank, 46 Ohio St. 424, 21 N. E. 860; Collins *v.* Chicago, 6 Fed. Cas. No. 3,011, 4 Biss. 472. See also cases cited *supra*, note 67.

Taxation of shares of stock-holders see *infra*, III, B, 2, b, (IV).

(B) *Meaning of "Moneyed Capital."* The term "moneyed capital," as used in the act of congress above referred to, means capital employed in the form of money and not in any other form which capital may assume and so employed in business as to yield a profit from its use as money.[96] Hence capital invested and employed in railroads, public service corporations, insurance, mining, manufacturing, and other such forms of business is not within the meaning of the statute.[97] It is restricted to capital employed in substantially the same way as the capital of the national banks, that is, in making loans and discounts,[98] and in fact there is a strong tendency to limit the phrase to banking operations pure and simple,[99] excluding on the one hand the operations of trust companies and of savings banks;[1] and on the other hand the operations of private individuals in loaning money on mortgages or other securities,[2] and to interpret the phrase "moneyed capital" as meaning no more than those forms of capital which come into actual competition with the capital of the national banks in the same kind of operations.[3]

(C) *What Constitutes Illegal Discrimination.* The act of congress is designed to prevent the taxation of national bank stock at a higher rate than is imposed on other moneyed capital; if the burden imposed is no greater, there is no legal ground of complaint.[4] The act does not require that the mode or manner of taxing such stock shall correspond in all respects to that adopted in taxing other moneyed capital,[5] and a different system may be adopted with reference to such

96. Richmond First Nat. Bank *v.* Turner, 154 Ind. 456, 57 N. E. 110; Talbott *v.* Silver Bow County, 139 U. S. 438, 11 S. Ct. 594, 35 L. ed. 210; Puget Sound Nat. Bank *v.* King County, 57 Fed. 433; Exchange Nat. Bank *v.* Miller, 19 Fed. 372.

97. Consolidated Nat. Bank *v.* Pima County, 5 Ariz. 142, 48 Pac. 291; Silver Bow County *v.* Davis, 6 Mont. 306, 12 Pac. 688; McMahon *v.* Palmer, 102 N. Y. 176, 6 N. E. 400, 55 Am. Rep. 796; Aberdeen First Nat. Bank *v.* Chehalis County, 166 U. S. 440, 17 S. Ct. 629, 41 L. ed. 1069; Talbott *v.* Silver Bow County, 139 U. S. 438, 11 S. Ct. 594, 35 L. ed. 210; Redemption Nat. Bank *v.* Boston, 125 U. S. 60, 8 S. Ct. 772, 31 L. ed. 689; Mercantile Nat. Bank *v.* New York, 121 U. S. 138, 7 S. Ct. 826, 30 L. ed. 895.

98. Talbott *v.* Silver Bow County, 139 U. S. 438, 11 S. Ct. 594, 35 L. ed. 210; Mercantile Nat. Bank *v.* New York, 121 U. S. 138, 7 S. Ct. 826, 30 L. ed. 895; Mercantile Nat. Bank *v.* Shields, 59 Fed. 952.

99. Ankeny *v.* Blakley, 44 Oreg. 78, 74 Pac. 485; Palmer *v.* McMahon, 133 U. S. 660, 10 S. Ct. 324, 33 L. ed. 772; Mercantile Nat. Bank *v.* New York, 121 U. S. 138, 7 S. Ct. 826, 30 L. ed. 895; Hepburn *v.* Carlisle School Directors, 23 Wall. (U. S.) 480, 23 L. ed. 112.

1. Jenkins *v.* Neff, 163 N. Y. 320, 57 N. E. 408 [*affirming* 47 N. Y. App. Div. 394, 62 N. Y. Suppl. 321 (*affirming* 29 Misc. 59, 60 N. Y. Suppl. 582), and *affirmed* in Jenkins *v.* Neff, 186 U. S. 230, 22 S. Ct. 905, 46 L. ed. 1140]; Redemption Nat. Bank *v.* Boston, 125 U. S. 60, 8 S. Ct. 772, 31 L. ed. 689; Mercantile Nat. Bank *v.* New York, 121 U. S. 138, 7 S. Ct. 826, 30 L. ed. 895.

2. Aberdeen First Nat. Bank *v.* Chehalis County, 6 Wash. 64, 32 Pac. 1051. But see Com. *v.* Girard Nat. Bank, 6 Phila. (Pa.) 431; Primm *v.* Fort, 23 Tex. Civ. App. 605, 57 S. W. 86, 972; Toledo First Nat. Bank *v.* Lucas County, 25 Fed. 749.

3. Mechanics' Nat. Bank *v.* Baker, 65 N. J. L. 549, 48 Atl. 582; Primm *v.* Fort, 23 Tex. Civ. App. 605, 57 S. W. 86, 972; Washington Nat. Bank *v.* King County, 9 Wash. 607, 38 Pac. 219; Commercial Nat. Bank *v.* Chambers, 182 U. S. 556, 21 S. Ct. 863, 45 L. ed. 1227; Wellington First Nat. Bank *v.* Chapman, 173 U. S. 205, 19 S. Ct. 407, 43 L. ed. 669; Aberdeen First Nat. Bank *v.* Chehalis County, 166 U. S. 440, 17 S. Ct. 629, 41 L. ed. 1069; Baltimore Nat. Bank *v.* Baltimore, 100 Fed. 24, 40 C. C. A. 254.

4. *California.*— Miller *v.* Heilbron, 58 Cal. 133.

New York.— People *v.* Neff, 29 Misc. 59, 60 N. Y. Suppl. 582.

Oregon.— Ankeny *v.* Blakley, 44 Oreg. 78, 74 Pac. 485.

Texas.— Engelke *v.* Schlenker, 75 Tex. 559, 12 S. W. 999.

United States.— Davenport Nat. Bank *v.* Davenport Bd. of Equalization, 123 U. S. 83, 8 S. Ct. 73, 31 L. ed. 94; Nevada Nat. Bank *v.* Dodge, 119 Fed. 57, 56 C. C. A. 145; Baltimore Nat. Bank *v.* Baltimore, 100 Fed. 24, 40 C. C. A. 254; Mercantile Nat. Bank *v.* New York, 28 Fed. 776.

See 45 Cent. Dig. tit. "Taxation," § 30.

Surplus as affecting value of shares.— A tax law providing for the assessment of shares in the hands of their holders, on the basis of their actual value, does not unjustly discriminate against national banks, on the ground that state banks can divide up all their surplus, while national banks are required to keep on hand an accumulated portion of their surplus. People *v.* New York Tax, etc., Com'rs, 67 N. Y. 516 [*affirmed* in 94 U. S. 415, 24 L. ed. 164].

5. National Sav. Bank *v.* Burlington, 119 Iowa 696, 94 N. W. 234; Whitbeck *v.* Mer-

property, provided there is no injustice, inequality, or intentional discrimination.[6] But the valuation is a part of the rate; and there is an illegal discrimination if the stock of national banks is appraised for taxation at a higher proportion of its actual or market value than the stock of state banks or similar institutions,[7] provided this is done systematically and intentionally by the assessors and in pursuance of a rule hostile to the national banks.[8] If the holders of other forms of moneyed capital are allowed to deduct their debts, and be taxed only on the remainder, a similar deduction must be allowed to owners of national bank shares, or the law is to that extent invalid,[9] at least if the privilege is shown to be extended

cantile Nat. Bank. 127 U. S. 193, 8 S. Ct. 1121, 32 L. ed. 118; Davenport Nat. Bank *v.* Davenport Bd. of Equalization, 123 U. S. 83, 8 S. Ct. 73, 31 L. ed. 94; Richards *v.* Rock Rapids, 31 Fed. 505. And see Primghar State Bank *v.* Rerick, 96 Iowa 238, 64 N. W. 801.

Statute creating penalties.— A retroactive provision of a statute, relating solely to national banks, by which they are charged with a liability for taxes for past years on their capital stock, whether held within or without the state, and subjected to a penalty in addition for delinquency, is an illegal discrimination against them. Covington *v.* Covington First Nat. Bank, 198 U. S. 100, 25 S. Ct. 562, 49 L. ed. 963.

Separate assessment rolls.— The use of separate assessment rolls cannot be made a means of discriminating against shares of stock in the national banks. People *v.* Coleman, 44 Hun (N. Y.) 47.

6. People *v.* Feitner, 191 N. Y. 88, 83 N. E. 592; Davenport Nat. Bank *v.* Davenport Bd. of Equalization, 123 U. S. 83, 8 S. Ct. 73, 31 L. ed. 94. See also cases cited *infra*, note 9 *et seq.*

"**All that has ever been held to be necessary** is, that the system of state taxation of its own citizens, of its own banks, and of its own corporations shall not work a discrimination unfavorable to the holders of the shares of the national banks." Davenport Nat. Bank *v.* Davenport Bd. of Equalization, 123 U. S. 83, 85, 8 S. Ct. 73, 31 L. ed. 94.

Effect in isolated cases.— The fact that a special system of taxation of national banks may not be as favorable as the general system of taxation in an isolated case does not render the system unlawful as discriminating against those institutions so long as there is no intentional discrimination and no inequality in the effect upon their stockholders generally. People *v.* Feitner, 191 N. Y. 88, 83 N. E. 592.

7. Estherville First Nat. Bank *v.* Estherville, 136 Iowa 203, 112 N. W. 829; Schuster *v.* Louisville, 89 S. W. 689, 28 Ky. L. Rep. 588; Williams *v.* Weaver, 75 N. Y. 30; San Francisco Nat. Bank *v.* Dodge, 197 U. S. 70, 25 S. Ct. 384, 49 L. ed. 669; Stanley *v.* Albany County, 121 U. S. 535, 7 S. Ct. 1234, 30 L. ed. 1000; Cummings *v.* Merchants' Nat. Bank, 101 U. S. 153, 25 L. ed. 903; Pelton *v.* Commercial Nat. Bank, 101 U. S. 143, 25 L. ed. 901; New York *v.* Weaver, 100 U. S. 539, 25 L. ed. 705; Hepburn *v.* Carlisle School Directors, 23 Wall. (U. S.) 480, 23 L. ed. 112; First Nat. Bank *v.* Lindsay, 45 Fed. 619 [*reversed* on other grounds in 156 U. S. 485, 15 S. Ct. 472, 39 L. ed. 505]; Toledo First Nat. Bank *v.* Lucas County, 25 Fed. 749; Covington City Nat. Bank *v.* Covington, 21 Fed. 484; Exchange Nat. Bank *v.* Miller, 19 Fed. 372; Albany City Nat. Bank *v.* Maher, 6 Fed. 417, 19 Blatchf. 175; St. Louis Nat. Bank *v.* Papin, 21 Fed. Cas. No. 12,239, 4 Dill. 29.

But there is no discrimination under a statute providing that bank shares shall be assessed "at their value" and other personal property at its "true value in cash," the expressions meaning the same thing, and the former provision not contemplating the book value but the actual value of the shares. Ankeny *v.* Blakley, 44 Oreg. 78, 74 Pac. 485.

8. Albuquerque First Nat. Bank *v.* Albright, 208 U. S. 548, 28 S. Ct. 349, 52 L. ed. 614 [*affirming* 13 N. M. 514, 86 Pac. 548]; Williams *v.* Albany County, 122 U. S. 154, 7 S. Ct. 1244, 30 L. ed. 1088; Pelton *v.* Commercial Nat. Bank, 101 U. S. 143, 25 L. ed. 901; New York *v.* Weaver, 100 U. S. 539, 25 L. ed. 705; First Nat. Bank *v.* Lindsay, 45 Fed. 619; Stanley *v.* Albany County, 15 Fed. 483, 21 Blatchf. 249; Chicago First Nat. Bank *v.* Farwell, 7 Fed. 518, 10 Biss. 270.

9. *Alabama.*— Maguire *v.* Mobile County Bd. of Revenue, etc., Com'rs, 71 Ala. 401; Pollard *v.* State, 65 Ala. 628.

California.— McHenry *v.* Downer, 116 Cal. 20, 47 Pac. 779, 45 L. R. A. 737; Miller *v.* Heilbron, 58 Cal. 133.

New Hampshire.— Peavey *v.* Greenfield, 64 N. H. 284, 9 Atl. 722.

North Carolina.— McAden *v.* Mecklenburg County, 97 N. C. 355, 2 S. E. 670.

Washington.— Newport *v.* Mudgett, 18 Wash. 271, 51 Pac. 466.

United States.— Whitbeck *v.* Mercantile Nat. Bank, 127 U. S. 193, 8 S. Ct. 1121, 32 L. ed. 118; Stanley *v.* Albany County, 121 U. S. 535, 7 S. Ct. 1234, 30 L. ed. 1000; Evansville Nat. Bank *v.* Britton, 105 U. S. 322, 26 L. ed. 1053; New York *v.* Weaver, 100 U. S. 539, 25 L. ed. 705; Charleston Nat. Bank *v.* Melton, 171 Fed. 743; Mercantile Nat. Bank *v.* Shields, 59 Fed. 952; Richards *v.* Rock Rapids, 31 Fed. 505; Evansville Nat. Bank *v.* Britton, 8 Fed. 867, 10 Biss. 503; Albany Nat. Exch. Bank *v.* Hills, 5 Fed. 248, 18 Blatchf. 478; City Nat. Bank *v.* Paducah, 5 Fed. Cas. No. 2,743, 2 Flipp. 61.

See 45 Cent. Dig. tit. "Taxation," § 30.

Stock-holder with no debts.— Although a state statute may be in conflict with the act

capital so invested, which is the property of the bank, but upon the shares of stock which are the property of the stock-holders.[17]

c. Insurance Companies — (I) *IN GENERAL.* In some jurisdictions insurance companies are subject to a privilege tax,[18] in others to a general tax on their property[19] and credits.[20] Any corporation which engages in a business which is essentially that of insurance, in any form, will be liable to be taxed as an insurance company, although its name may not indicate its business;[21] and conversely, if an insurance company engages in any other form of business, such as that of an annuity, security, or trust company, it becomes subject to taxation like other companies employed in those forms of business.[22] The laws for the taxation of insurance companies may apply to mutual companies,[23] although some of the statutes do not apply to such companies.[24]

(II) *CAPITAL AND STOCK.* Insurance companies, like other corporations, may be taxed upon their capital.[25] A tax laid on the capital stock of an insurance company is sometimes regarded as a franchise tax,[26] or privilege tax;[27] but if

Lander, 184 U. S. 111, 22 S. Ct. 394, 46 L. ed. 456 [*affirming* 62 Ohio St. 266, 56 N. E. 1036]; Garnett First Nat. Bank *v.* Ayers, 160 U. S. 660, 16 S. Ct. 412, 40 L. ed. 573; People *v.* New York Tax, etc., Com'rs, 4 Wall. (U. S.) 244, 18 L. ed. 344; Charleston Nat. Bank *v.* Melton, 171 Fed. 743; Hager *v.* American Nat. Bank, 159 Fed. 396, 86 C. C. A. 334; Exchange Nat. Bank *v.* Miller, 19 Fed. 372. But see Whitney Sav. Bank *v.* Parker, 41 Fed. 402.

In Kentucky it has been held that if state banks are allowed to deduct the amount of capital invested in United States bonds a similar deduction must be allowed in the valuation of shares of national bank stock (Marion Nat. Bank *v.* Burton, 121 Ky. 876, 90 S. W. 944, 28 Ky. L. Rep. 864, 10 L. R. A. N. S. 947); but that if other banks are not allowed to deduct the value of assets invested in government bonds, no such deduction can be claimed in the valuation of shares in national banks, as this would be a discrimination in their favor as against state banks and trust companies (Hager *v.* Citizens' Nat. Bank, 127 Ky. 192, 105 S. W. 403, 914, 32 Ky. L. Rep. 95).

17. Cleveland Trust Co. *v.* Lander, 184 U. S. 111, 22 S. Ct. 394, 46 L. ed. 456. See also cases cited *supra*, note 16.

18. See Ætna L. Ins. Co. *v.* Coulter, 74 S. W. 1050, 25 Ky. L. Rep. 193; Detroit F. & M. Ins. Co. *v.* Hartz, 132 Mich. 518, 94 N. W. 7; Northwestern Mut. L. Ins. Co. *v.* Lewis, etc., County, 28 Mont. 484, 72 Pac. 982, 98 Am. St. Rep. 572; Wilmington Underwriters' Ins. Co. *v.* Stedman, 130 N. C. 221, 41 S. E. 279.

Tax on premiums as privilege tax see *infra*, III, D, 2, c, (IV).

19. German Nat. Ins. Co. *v.* Louisville, 54 S. W. 732, 21 Ky. L. Rep. 1179; Ohio Farmers' Ins. Co. *v.* Hard, 10 Ohio S. & C. Pl. Dec. 469, 8 Ohio N. P. 36.

Reinsurances, as to which suits are pending between an insurance company and the reinsurer, are proper subjects of taxation against the company. Home Ins. Co. *v.* Board of Assessors, 48 La. Ann. 451, 19 So. 280.

Deduction of debts.— Under a statute providing that in making up the amount of credits which any person is required to list, he shall be entitled to deduct from the gross amount of such credits the amount of all *bona fide* debts owing by him, an insurance company is not entitled to deduct from its credits losses by fires or policy cancellations which may thereafter occur, although they do in fact occur before the taxes become delinquent. Home F. Ins. Co. *v.* Lynch, 19 Utah 189, 56 Pac. 681.

20. State *v.* Board of Assessors, 47 La. Ann. 1498, 18 So. 462, holding that uncollected premiums are taxable as credits.

21. People *v.* Wemple, 58 Hun (N. Y.) 248, 12 N. Y. Suppl. 271 [*affirmed* in 126 N. Y. 623, 27 N. E. 410].

22. Fidelity, etc., Co. *v.* Coulter, 74 S. W. 1053, 25 Ky. L. Rep. 200; Ætna L. Ins. Co. *v.* Coulter, 74 S. W. 1050, 25 Ky. L. Rep. 193; Nelson *v.* St. Paul Title Ins., etc., Co., 64 Minn. 101, 66 N. W. 206.

23. New Orleans *v.* State Mut. Ins. Co., 18 La. Ann. 675; Lee Mut. F. Ins. Co. *v.* State, 60 Miss. 395; Ohio Farmers' Ins. Co. *v.* Hard, 10 Ohio S. & C. Pl. Dec. 469, 8 Ohio N. P. 36; Fire Ins. Co. *v.* County, 9 Pa. St. 413.

24. See Murray *v.* Berkshire L. Ins. Co., 104 Mass. 586; Worcester Mut. F. Ins. Co. *v.* Worcester, 7 Cush. (Mass.) 600; International, etc., Ins. Co. *v.* Haight, 35 N. J. L. 279.

25. New Orleans *v.* Union Ins. Co., 18 La. Ann. 416; Buffalo Mut. Ins. Co. *v.* Erie County, 4 N. Y. 442.

Corporations generally see *supra*, III, B, 1, g.

Unpaid subscriptions.— Unpaid notes given to joint stock insurance companies for unpaid subscriptions to their capital stock are taxable to them as "credits" at their true value in money. Farmers' Ins. Co. *v.* La Rue, 22 Ohio St. 630.

26. See Manufacturers' Ins. Co. *v.* Loud, 99 Mass. 146, 96 Am. Dec. 715; Com. *v.* Berkshire L. Ins. Co., 98 Mass. 25; and, generally, *supra*, III, B, 1, f, g.

27. Holly Springs Sav., etc., Co. *v.* Marshal County, 52 Miss. 281, 24 Am. Rep. 668.

and this of course includes the right of way.[60] But the method now most in vogue is to provide that the road as a whole, including everything necessary to its operation as such, shall be assessed by a state board, the total valuation being then apportioned among the various municipalities through which the line passes, while to the local authorities is confided the duty of assessing such real property of the road within their limits as is outside the needs and uses of the company for its operation as a railroad, but held or used for separate or auxiliary purposes.[61]

stock-holders. Davenport *v.* Mississippi, etc., R. Co., 12 Iowa 539; State *v.* Hannibal, etc., R. Co., 37 Mo. 265.

In Virginia the acts of 1879–1880 authorize county supervisors to levy a tax on the real estate of railroad companies whose roads pass through their counties, but the assessment is to be based upon the assessment made by the state upon the same property for state purposes. Shenandoah Valley R. Co. *v.* Clarke County, 78 Va. 269.

60. St. Louis, etc., R. Co. *v.* Miller County, 67 Ark. 498, 55 S. W. 926; *Re* Midland R. Co., 19 Can. L. J. 330; Niagara Falls Park, etc., R. Co. *v.* Niagara, 31 Ont. 29. See also Adams *v.* Kansas City, etc., R. Co., 74 Miss. 331, 21 So. 11.

Right to use highway crossing.— The right of a domestic railroad corporation to use a highway crossing is a special franchise subject to taxation. New York, etc., R. Co. *v.* Roll, 32 Misc. (N. Y.) 321, 66 N. Y. Suppl. 748.

61. See the statutes of the several states; and the following cases:

Arkansas.— St. Louis R. Co. *v.* Worthen, 52 Ark. 529, 13 S. W. 254, 7 L. R. A. 374.

Connecticut.— Osborn *v.* Hartford, etc., R. Co., 40 Conn. 498, holding that wharves and docks, such as to accommodate the business of the road when most pressing, although not in use all the time, are so far necessary to the operation of the road as not to be subject to local taxation.

Illinois.— Illinois Cent. R. Co. *v.* Cavins, 238 Ill. 380, 87 N. E. 371. See also Chicago, etc., R. Co. *v.* People, 195 Ill. 184, 62 N. E. 869.

Indiana.— Jeffersonville *v.* Louisville, etc., Bridge Co., 169 Ind. 645, 83 N. E. 337, holding that a company incorporated as a bridge company which owns not only an interstate bridge and its approaches, together with a railroad track across the bridge, but also a terminal railroad having its own rolling-stock, and furnishing terminal facilities and facilities for the interchange of traffic between other railroads is assessable by the state board of tax commissioners as a corporation owning a railroad and not by the township assessor as a bridge company.

Iowa.— Herter *v.* Chicago, etc., R. Co., 114 Iowa 330, 86 N. W. 266, holding that grain elevators, owned by a railroad company and situated on its lands, used exclusively for taking in or storing grain for shipment over such road, are not subject to local taxation.

Kansas.— Union Pac. R. Co. *v.* Wyandotte County, 69 Kan. 572, 77 Pac. 274.

Michigan.— Detroit *v.* Detroit, etc., R. Co., 149 Mich. 530, 113 N. W. 365 (holding that a railroad constructed and used as a steam railroad and owned by a company organized under the general railroad law is assessable by the state board of assessors and not subject to local taxation, although the road is laid along the streets of a city and was originally built by a company not organized under the general railroad law); Auditor-Gen. *v.* Flint, etc., R. Co., 114 Mich. 682, 72 N. W. 992 (sidings and spur tracks used in originating and shipping freight).

Missouri.— State *v.* Wiggins Ferry Co., 208 Mo. 622, 106 S. W. 1005 (holding that under the Missouri statutes a railroad need not be owned or operated by a railroad company or be of any particular length, and that where a ferry company operated a number of tracks over which cars were drawn to and from the ferry, the tracks being also used for storage, for loading and unloading, and for regular traffic and switching purposes, the tracks constituted a railroad and were subject to assessment by the state board of equalization and not by the city assessor); State *v.* Chicago, etc., R. Co., 162 Mo. 391, 63 S. W. 495; State *v.* Severance, 55 Mo. 378.

Nebraska.— State *v.* Savage, 65 Nebr. 714, 91 N. W. 716; Adams County *v.* Kansas City, etc., R. Co., 71 Nebr. 245, 99 N. W. 245; Burlington, etc., R. Co. *v.* Lancaster County, 15 Nebr. 251, 18 N. W. 71.

New Jersey.— United New Jersey R., etc., Co. *v.* Parker, 75 N. J. L. 771, 69 Atl. 239 [*modifying* 75 N. J. L. 120, 67 Atl. 672 (Sup. 1907) 67 Atl. 686]; *In re* New Jersey Cent. R. Co., 71 N. J. L. 475, 58 Atl. 1089; National Docks R. Co. *v.* State Bd. of Assessors, 64 N. J. L. 486, 45 Atl. 783; United New Jersey R., etc., Co. *v.* Jersey City, 55 N. J. L. 129, 26 Atl. 135. See also New York Bay R. Co. *v.* Newark, 76 N. J. L. 832, 71 Atl. 276 [*reversing* 75 N. J. L. 389, 67 Atl. 1049]; United New Jersey R., etc., Co. *v.* Newark, 76 N. J. L. 830, 71 Atl. 275 [*reversing* 75 N. J. L. 385, 67 Atl. 1075].

New York.— See People *v.* Clapp, 152 N. Y. 490, 46 N. E. 842, 39 L. R. A. 237.

North Carolina.— Atlantic, etc., R. Co. *v.* New Berne, 147 N. C. 165, 60 S. E. 925, holding that under Revisal (1905), § 5290, authorizing the corporation commission to assess the right of way and superstructures thereon, the word "superstructures" covers all buildings situated on the right of way.

South Dakota.— St. Paul, etc., R. Co. *v.* Howard, 23 S. D. 34, 119 N. W. 1032.

Utah.— Rio Grande Western R. Co. *v.* Salt Lake Inv. Co., 35 Utah 528, 101 Pac. 586.

Virginia.— See Virginia, etc., R. Co. *v.* Washington County, 30 Gratt. 471.

on foot,[64] and where it is so assessed as an integral part of the road it should be assessed by the state board and not by the local authorities;[65] but it may be separately taxed if separately owned,[66] and in such cases may be assessed by the local authorities.[67]

(III) *ROLLING-STOCK AND EQUIPMENT.* The locomotives, cars, and other rolling-stock of a railroad are generally regarded and treated as personalty for the purpose of taxation.[68] In this character they are capable of having a *situs* of their own, and hence they are taxable to a company using them within the state, although they are owned by a foreign corporation.[69] On the other hand, the taxing power of the state is not necessarily restricted to such engines and cars as remain constantly within the state, but may extend to those which, in performing their regular journeys, pass through and out of the state,[70] but rolling-stock employed exclusively without the state is not taxable, although owned by a domestic corporation.[71]

(IV) *CAPITAL AND STOCK.* As in the case of other corporations,[72] the capital or capital stock of a railroad company is distinct from the shares of stock belonging to the shareholders,[73] and may be taxed to the corporation itself;[74] and under some statutes such companies are taxable upon their capital or capital stock,[75] the tax

Louisiana, etc., R. Co., 215 Mo. 479, 114 S. W. 956.

64. People *v.* Atchison, etc., R. Co., 225 Ill. 593, 80 N. E. 272; Campbell County Bd. of Equalization *v.* Louisville, etc., R. Co., 109 S. W. 303, 33 Ky. L. Rep. 78; State *v.* Hannibal, etc., R. Co., 97 Mo. 348, 10 S. W. 436 [*distinguishing* State *v.* Hannibal, etc., R. Co., 89 Mo. 98, 14 S. W. 511], holding that under Rev. St. (1879) § 6901, a railroad bridge owned by a railroad company and constituting a part of the track is taxable only as a part of the road and not as a separate structure, notwithstanding it is used in part as a toll bridge for the passage of teams, wagons, and the like.

65. People *v.* Atchison, etc., R. Co., 225 Ill. 593, 80 N. E. 272; Anderson *v.* Chicago, etc., R. Co., 117 Ill. 26, 7 N. E. 129; Campbell County Bd. of Equalization *v.* Louisville, etc., R. Co., 109 S. W. 303, 33 Ky. L. Rep. 78; Chicago, etc., R. Co. *v.* Richardson County, 61 Nebr. 519, 85 N. W. 532 [*overruling* Cass County *v.* Chicago, etc., R. Co., 25 Nebr. 348, 41 N. W. 246, 2 L. R. A. 188].

66. St. Louis, etc., R. Co. *v.* Williams, 53 Ark. 58, 13 S. W. 796; Chicago, etc., R. Co. *v.* People, 153 Ill. 409, 38 N. E. 1075, 29 L. R. A. 69; State *v.* Mississippi River Bridge Co., 109 Mo. 253, 19 S. W. 421.

67. St. Louis, etc., R. Co. *v.* Williams, 53 Ark. 58, 13 S. W. 796; Chicago, etc., R. Co. *v.* People, 153 Ill. 409, 38 N. E. 1075, 29 L. R. A. 69.

68. Midland R. Co. *v.* State, 11 Ind. App. 433, 38 N. E. 57; State Treasurer *v.* Somerville, etc., R. Co., 28 N. J. L. 21; Toronto R. Co. *v.* Toronto, 6 Ont. L. Rep. 187, 2 Ont. Wkly. Rep. 579.

69. Denver, etc., R. Co. *v.* Church, 17 Colo. 1, 28 Pac. 468, 31 Am. St. Rep. 252; Kennedy *v.* St. Louis, etc., R. Co., 62 Ill. 395; Reinhart *v.* McDonald, 76 Fed. 403.

70. Hall *v.* American Refrigerator Transit Co., 24 Colo. 291, 51 Pac. 421, 65 Am. St. Rep. 223, 56 L. R. A. 89; Denver, etc., R. Co *v.* Church, 17 Colo. 1, 28 Pac. 468, 31 Am. St. Rep. 252; Pullman's Palace Car Co. *v.* Com., 107 Pa. St. 156 [*affirmed* in 141 U. S. 18, 11 S. Ct. 876, 35 L. ed. 613]; Com. *v.* Pullman's Palace Car Co., 4 Dauph. Co. Rep. (Pa.) 309.

71. People *v.* Knight, 173 N. Y. 255, 65 N. E. 1102; People *v.* Campbell, 88 Hun (N. Y.) 544, 34 N. Y. Suppl. 801.

72. See *supra*, III, B, 1, g.

73. Porter *v.* Rockford, etc., R. Co., 76 Ill. 561; South Nashville St. R. Co. *v.* Morrow, 87 Tenn. 406, 11 S. W. 348, 2 L. R. A. 853; Minot *v.* Philadelphia, etc., R. Co., 18 Wall. (U. S.) 206, 21 L. ed. 888.

74. Porter *v.* Rockford, etc., R. Co., 76 Ill. 561.

75. *Connecticut.*— Nichols *v.* New Haven, etc., Co., 42 Conn. 103.

Illinois.— Porter *v.* Rockford, etc., R. Co., 76 Ill. 561.

Indiana.— Michigan Cent. R. Co. *v.* Porter, 17 Ind. 380.

Pennsylvania.— Com. *v.* Ontario, etc., R. Co., 188 Pa. St. 205, 41 Atl. 607.

United States.—Minot *v.* Philadelphia, etc., R. Co., 18 Wall. 206, 21 L. ed. 888.

Charter provisions.— Under a charter provision requiring a certain tax on "capital stock paid in," stock is to be included which was not paid for in money but issued by the company and used instead of money in acquiring the rights of the original purchasers of the road and treated and considered by the company as so much stock paid in and entitling the holders thereof to all the rights and privileges of other stock-holders. People *v.* Michigan Southern, etc., R. Co., 4 Mich. 398. Under a charter provision limiting the rate of taxation upon the "stock" of a railroad company, the limitation applies only to the capital stock actually paid in, and if the value of the property of the company is greater than the capital stock paid in the excess is not stock and is subject to taxation at the ordinary rate at which the property of individuals is assessed. Goldsmith *v.* Rome R. Co., 62 Ga. 473.

being in some cases regarded as a franchise tax,[76] and in others as a property tax,[77] based not upon the par value but upon the actual value of the stock,[78] or including all the property of the corporation,[79] together with the value of its franchises,[80] or the fair cash value of the capital stock, including the franchise, over and above the assessed value of the tangible property.[81] It has also been held that as the shares of stock are distinct from the capital of the corporation the stock-holders may be taxed on their shares notwithstanding the corporation is also taxed upon its capital or property.[82] Ordinarily, however, the shares of stock-holders are not taxed where the corporation itself is taxed on its capital or property,[83] but are taxable to the shareholders where the corporation is not so taxed.[84]

(v) *EARNINGS OR RECEIPTS.* A tax laid upon railroad companies in proportion to their income or gross receipts is generally considered as a franchise or privilege tax.[85] Such taxes have been fully sustained by the courts; [86] and this is also true of taxes laid on gross or net receipts over and above a certain fixed sum

76. See Pratt *v.* Boston St. Com'rs, 139 Mass. 559, 2 N. E. 675; Minot *v.* Philadelphia, etc., R. Co., 18 Wall. (U. S.) 206, 21 L. ed. 888.

Under the New York statutes imposing a franchise tax on capital employed within the state a railroad company is not subject to such taxes on that part of its capital invested in cars permanently engaged outside of the state or invested in stock of foreign corporations. People *v.* Campbell, 88 Hun (N. Y.) 544, 34 N. Y. Suppl. 801.

77. Nichols *v.* New Haven, etc., Co., 42 Conn. 103; Com. *v.* Delaware, etc., R. Co., 165 Pa. St. 44, 30 Atl. 522, 523; Pullman's Palace Car Co. *v.* Com., 107 Pa. St. 156.

78. Nichols *v.* New Haven, etc., Co., 42 Conn. 103.

79. Michigan Cent. R. Co. *v.* Porter, 17 Ind. 380; Floyd County *v.* New Albany, etc., R. Co., 11 Ind. 570; Com. *v.* Ontario, etc., R. Co., 188 Pa. St. 205, 41 Atl. 607; Com. *v.* Delaware, etc., R. Co., 165 Pa. St. 44, 30 Atl. 522, 523.

80. Com. *v.* Ontario, etc., R. Co., 188 Pa. St. 205, 41 Atl. 607; Com. *v.* Delaware, etc., R. Co., 165 Pa. St. 44, 30 Atl. 522, 523.

81. Porter *v.* Rockford, etc., R. Co., 76 Ill. 561.

82. South Nashville St. R. Co. *v.* Morrow, 87 Tenn. 406, 11 S. W. 348, 2 L. R. A. 853. See also *supra*, II, C, 5, c; III, B, 1, j.

83. Michigan Cent. R. Co. *v.* Porter, 17 Ind. 380; Com. *v.* Chesapeake, etc., R. Co., 116 Ky. 951, 77 S. W. 186, 25 Ky. L. Rep. 1126. See also *supra*, III, B, 1, j.

84. Georgia R., etc., Co. *v.* Wright, 124 Ga. 596, 53 S. E. 251 [*reversed* on other grounds in 207 U. S. 127, 28 S. Ct. 47, 52 L. ed. 134]; Com. *v.* Chesapeake, etc., R. Co., 116 Ky. 951, 77 S. W. 186, 25 Ky. L. Rep. 1126; Pratt *v.* Boston St. Com'rs, 139 Mass. 559, 2 N. E. 675; Wright *v.* Louisville, etc., R. Co., 195 U. S. 219, 25 S. Ct. 16, 49 L. ed. 167 [*reversing* 117 Fed. 1007, 54 C. C. A. 672].

85. *In re* Railroad Taxation, 102 Me. 527, 66 Atl. 726; State *v.* Maine Cent. R. Co., 74 Me. 376; State *v.* Philadelphia, etc., R. Co., 45 Md. 361, 24 Am. Rep. 511; Philadelphia Contributionship *v.* Com., 98 Pa. St. 48.

Contra, Galveston, etc., R. Co. *v.* Davidson, (Tex. Civ. App. 1906) 93 S. W. 436.

86. *Iowa.*— Dubuque *v.* Chicago, etc., R. Co., 47 Iowa 196.

Maine.— *In re* Railroad Taxation, 102 Me. 527, 66 Atl. 726.

Maryland.— State *v.* Philadelphia, etc., R. Co., 45 Md. 361, 24 Am. Rep. 511.

Michigan.— Pere Marquette R. Co. *v.* Ludington, 133 Mich. 397, 95 N. W. 417; Fort St. Union Depot Co. *v.* Railroad Com'r, 118 Mich. 340, 76 N. W. 631.

Minnesota.—State *v.* District Ct., 54 Minn. 34, 55 N. W. 816.

South Carolina.— State *v.* Hood, 15 Rich. 117.

Texas.— State *v.* Missouri, etc., R. Co., (1907) 100 S. W. 146.

United States.— U. S. *v.* Marquette, etc., R. Co., 17 Fed. 719.

See 45 Cent. Dig. tit. "Taxation," § 257.

Tolls and transportation charges.— The sums received by one railroad company from another as compensation for the use of its tracks are within the meaning of a statute taxing the gross receipts of railroads "for tolls and transportation." Com. *v.* New York, etc., R. Co., 145 Pa. St. 38, 22 Atl. 212; New York, etc., R. Co. *v.* Com., 158 U. S. 431, 15 S. Ct. 896, 39 L. ed. 1043. But not within a statute taxing receipts "from passengers and freight." Com. *v.* New York, etc., R. Co., 145 Pa. St. 200, 22 Atl. 806.

Union depot companies.— Where the several railroad companies which use the terminal facilities of a union depot, and which own all the stock of the union depot company, pay the state tax on their gross earnings, the depot company itself is not liable to such tax. State *v.* St. Paul Union Depot Co., 42 Minn. 142, 43 N. W. 840, 6 L. R. A. 234.

Receipts from carriage of mails.— A railroad company is not liable to assessment on gross earnings derived from carrying the United States mails, where such earnings include moneys received from carriage of interstate and foreign mails, and it is impossible to determine what proportion of mail originated and terminated within the state. People *v.* Morgan, 168 N. Y. 1, 60 N. E. 1041.

or percentage, the contingency that the minimum earnings may not be exceeded being a point for the consideration of the legislature, not of the courts.[87] In some states also the tax is on the value of the railroad as a whole, but is determined by capitalizing its net earnings at a fixed rate or at the current rates of interest.[88]

(VI) *DIVIDENDS.* Where a railroad is taxed on the dividends declared on its capital stock, this means the amount of capital actually paid in and not the nominal capital.[89] The law may be applicable to a stock dividend,[90] but not to a sale of stock below its par value resorted to as a means of raising money,[91] or a mere increase in the number of shares of stock not representing any distribution of profits.[92]

(VII) *BONDED AND OTHER DEBT.* In some states railroad corporations are required to pay a tax on their outstanding bonded or other debt, or on the interest paid to creditors, which, however, unless the bonds are made "tax free," is in reality a charge on the creditor rather than on the corporation.[93] For this reason the company cannot be taxed on bonds held by non-resident owners,[94] although if it accumulates and sets apart a fund to pay the interest on its foreign-held bonds, such fund, before distribution, is taxable as its own property.[95]

(VIII) *PROPERTY MORTGAGED OR LEASED.* It is generally held that in the assessment and valuation of a railroad as a whole, for the purpose of taxation, there should be included any lines which it is operating under lease as a part of its system.[96] But a contrary rule prevails in some states, and particularly where the tax laws are explicit in requiring the assessment of property to its owner.[97]

87. Fort St. Union Depot Co. *v.* Railroad Com'r, 118 Mich. 340, 76 N. W. 631; McGavisk *v.* State, 34 N. J. L. 509.

88. State *v.* Virginia, etc., R. Co., 23 Nev. 283, 46 Pac. 723, 35 L. R. A. 759. But *compare* Board for Assessment of Railroad Co.'s Property *v.* Alabama Cent. R. Co., 59 Ala. 551.

89. Citizens' Pass. R. Co. *v.* Philadelphia, 49 Pa. St. 251.

Taxation of corporate dividends generally see *supra*, III, B, 1, k.

90. Com. *v.* Cleveland, etc., R. Co., 29 Pa. St. 370. See also *supra*, III, B, 1, k.

91. Com. *v.* Erie, etc., R. Co., 10 Phila. (Pa.) 465.

92. Com. *v.* Pittsburg, etc., R. Co., 74 Pa. St. 83.

93. Boston, etc., R. Co. *v.* State, 62 N. H. 648; Sawyer *v.* Nashua, 59 N. H. 404; Com. *v.* Philadelphia, etc., R. Co., 150 Pa. St. 312, 24 Atl. 612; Maltby *v.* Reading, etc., R. Co., 52 Pa. St. 140; U. S. *v.* Balitmore, etc., R. Co., 17 Wall. (U. S.) 322, 21 L. ed. 597; Northern Cent. R. Co. *v.* Jackson, 7 Wall. (U. S.) 262, 19 L. ed. 88; Haight *v.* Pittsburg, etc., R. Co., 6 Wall. (U. S.) 15, 18 L. ed. 818.

Taxation of corporate bonds in general see *supra*, III, B, 1, l.

Double taxation.— The holder of railroad bonds may be required to pay a tax on them notwithstanding the company is taxed on its stock and its "funded and floating debt," and this is declared to be "in lieu of all other taxes on railroad property and franchises." Bridgeport *v.* Bishop, 33 Conn. 187.

94. State Tax, etc., Bonds Case, 15 Wall. (U. S.) 300, 21 L. ed. 179. And see *supra*, III, A, 4, d, (I).

95. U. S. *v.* Erie R. Co., 106 U. S. 327, 1 S. Ct. 223, 27 L. ed. 151; Michigan Cent. R. Co. *v.* Slack, 100 U. S. 595, 25 L. ed. 647.

96. *Illinois.*—Huck *v.* Chicago, etc., R. Co., 86 Ill. 352.

Kentucky.— Com. *v.* Ingalls, 121 Ky. 194, 89 S. W. 156, 28 Ky. L. Rep. 164; Jefferson County *v.* Kentucky Bd. of Valuation, etc., 117 Ky. 531, 78 S. W. 443, 25 Ky. L. Rep. 1637; Com. *v.* Kinniconick, etc., R. Co., 104 S. W. 290, 31 Ky. L. Rep. 859.

Minnesota.— State *v.* Northern Pac. R. Co., 32 Minn. 294, 20 N. W. 234.

New Hampshire.— Atlantic, etc., R. Co. *v.* State, 60 N. H. 133.

United States.— Indianapolis, etc., R. Co. *v.* Vance, 96 U. S. 450, 24 L. ed. 752. See also Marye *v.* Baltimore, etc., R. Co., 127 U. S. 117, 8 S. Ct. 1037, 32 L. ed. 94.

See 45 Cent. Dig. tit. "Taxation," § 261.

Leased line outside the state.— A railroad company is not subject to taxation in Pennsylvania on so much of its capital stock as is represented by the value of a leasehold interest in a railroad wholly beyond the borders of the state. Com. *v.* Delaware, etc., R. Co., 1 Dauph. Co. Rep. (Pa.) 153.

Privilege for joint use.— A railroad company which has the privilege of using a car hoist and third rail jointly with their owner, to whose land they are affixed, is not liable for taxes imposed on them. Irvin *v.* New Orleans, etc., R. Co., 94 Ill. 105, 34 Am. Rep. 208.

97. *Connecticut.*— State *v.* Housatonic R. Co., 48 Conn. 44.

Mississippi.— Yazoo, etc., R. Co. *v.* Adams, 76 Miss. 543, 25 So. 366.

Missouri.— State *v.* St. Louis County, 84 Mo. 234.

New Mexico.—Valencia County *v.* Atchison,

(VII) *TELEGRAPH AND TELEPHONE COMPANIES.* A telegraph or telephone company,[40] if employed in transmitting messages between points in two or more states, is within the provision of the federal constitution as to interstate commerce, and hence cannot be taxed by a state on messages so transmitted or on its receipts therefrom;[41] but each state may tax so much of the company's property as lies within its own borders, and this may be determined either on the mileage basis or as a proportional part of the value of its entire system or of its whole capital.[42] The local authorities may also impose a license-fee on interstate telegraph companies, which may be a fixed sum or graduated according to the number of poles, instruments, or messages sent, provided it is reasonably proportioned to the expense involved in the inspection and other regulation and control of such companies, and is not primarily a means of raising revenue.[43] Subject to these restrictions, and to such exemptions as the state may choose to grant,[44] or the substitution of special kinds of taxes for general taxes,[45] the prop-

taxation of turnpike companies do not authorize a division of a turnpike road-bed into sections corresponding to the different taxing districts through which it passes and their assessment in each as so much real estate. Bergen County Turnpike Co. *v.* Haas, 61 N. J. L. 174, 39 Atl. 654.

40. A railroad company which operates a telegraph system, but only for its own purposes and in connection with the running of its trains, is not taxable as a "telegraph company." Adams *v.* Louisville, etc., R. Co., (Miss. 1893) 13 So. 932. But if a railroad company having no separate franchise or authority to carry on a general telegraph business assumes such a franchise and carries on the business, it is estopped to deny the existence of the franchise and is subject to taxation under a statute providing for the taxation of franchises of telegraph companies. Minneapolis, etc., R. Co. *v.* Oppegard, (N. D. 1908) 118 N. W. 830.

41. Western Union Tel. Co. *v.* Seay, 132 U. S. 472, 10 S. Ct. 161, 33 L. ed. 409 [*reversing* 80 Ala. 273, 60 Am. Rep. 99]; Ratterman *v.* Western Union Tel. Co., 127 U. S. 411, 8 S. Ct. 1127, 32 L. ed. 229; Western Union Tel. Co. *v.* Pendleton, 122 U. S. 347, 7 S. Ct. 1126, 30 L. ed. 1187; Western Union Tel. Co. *v.* Texas, 105 U. S. 460, 26 L. ed. 1067. See also COMMERCE, 7 Cyc. 450, 482.

Interprovincial lines in Canada see Great North Western Tel. Co. *v.* Fortier, 12 Quebec K. B. 405.

42. *Alabama.*— Southern Express Co. *v.* Mobile, 49 Ala. 404.

Maine.— State *v.* Western Union Tel. Co., 73 Me. 518.

Missouri.— State *v.* Western Union Tel. Co., 165 Mo. 502, 65 S. W. 775.

New York.— People *v.* Gold, etc., Tel. Co., 98 N. Y. 67.

Pennsylvania.— Com. *v.* Western Union Tel. Co., 2 Dauph. Co. Rep. 40.

United States.—Western Union Tel. Co. *v.* Taggart, 163 U. S. 1, 16 S. Ct. 1054, 41 L. ed. 49; Postal Tel. Cable Co. *v.* Adams, 155 U. S. 688, 15 S. Ct. 268, 39 L. ed. 311; Massachusetts *v.* Western Union Tel. Co., 141 U. S. 40, 11 S. Ct. 889, 35 L. ed. 628; Western Union Tel. Co. *v.* Atty.-Gen., 125 U. S. 530, 8 S. Ct. 961, 31 L. ed. 790.

Tax on dividends.—Where telegraph companies are taxed according to their dividends, if one telegraph company leases its lines to another company, which agrees to pay an amount equal to ten per cent on the par value of all the shares except those owned by the lessee, the lessor company is liable to be taxed according to a dividend of ten per cent on the whole of its capital. Atlantic, etc., Tel. Co. *v.* Com., 66 Pa. St. 57.

43. *Maryland.*— Postal Tel. Cable Co. *v.* Baltimore, 79 Md. 502, 29 Atl. 819, 24 L. R. A. 161.

Nebraska.—Western Union Tel. Co. *v.* Fremont, 39 Nebr. 692, 58 N. W. 415, 26 L. R. A. 698.

New York.— Philadelphia *v.* Postal Tel. Co., 67 Hun 21, 21 N. Y. Suppl. 556.

Pennsylvania.— Taylor *v.* Postal Tel. Cable Co., 202 Pa. St. 583, 52 Atl. 128; New Hope Borough *v.* Postal Tel. Cable Co., 202 Pa. St. 532, 52 Atl. 127; Chester *v.* Philadelphia, etc., Tel. Co., 148 Pa. St. 120, 23 Atl. 1070; Allentown *v.* Western Union Tel. Co., 148 Pa. St. 117, 23 Atl. 1070, 33 Am. St. Rep. 820.

Virginia.— See Postal Tel. Cable Co. *v.* Richmond, 99 Va. 102, 37 Atl. 789, 86 Am. St. Rep. 877.

United States.— Atlantic, etc., Tel. Co. *v.* Philadelphia, 190 U. S. 160, 23 S. Ct. 817, 47 L. ed. 995 [*reversing* 102 Fed. 254, 42 C. C. A. 325]; Western Union Tel. Co. *v.* New Hope, 187 U. S. 419, 23 S. Ct. 204, 47 L. ed. 240; Postal Tel. Co. *v.* Charleston, 153 U. S. 692, 14 S. Ct. 1094, 38 L. ed. 871; St. Louis *v.* Western Union Tel. Co., 148 U. S. 92, 13 S. Ct. 990, 37 L. ed. 810; Sunset Tel., etc., Co. *v.* Medford, 115 Fed. 202; Philadelphia *v.* Western Union Tel. Co., 89 Fed. 454, 32 C. C. A. 246.

License fees and taxes generally see COMMERCE, 7 Cyc. 451; LICENSES, 25 Cyc. 620.

44. See Atty.-Gen. *v.* Detroit, 113 Mich. 388, 71 N. W. 632, exemption of telephone companies from local taxation.

45. Portland *v.* New England Tel., etc., Co., 103 Me. 240, 68 Atl. 1040 (substitution of excise tax); State *v.* Northwestern Tel. Exch. Co., 84 Minn. 459, 87 N. W. 1131 (substitution of gross earnings tax).

Application of statutes.— The Minnesota

or consumers,[54] or constructed in a public highway under an ordinance subject to revocation.[55]

(IX) *GAS COMPANIES.* A corporation of this sort is taxable, according to the laws of the particular state, on its franchises,[56] on its easement of occupying the public streets,[57] on its capital and surplus or undivided profits,[58] and on its physical property;[59] and as to the latter it is generally held that gas pipes and mains laid under the streets are assessable as real estate.[60] In Pennsylvania a gas company is regarded as a "public corporation" in such sense as to be exempt from taxation for local purposes, under the laws of that state, on such of its property as is necessary for conducting its business,[61] although in some other states a contrary view prevails.[62]

(X) *MINING COMPANIES.*[63] Mining companies, unless exempt, are subject to taxation upon their property,[64] or according to the different statutes are taxable

Newport Tax Assessors, 19 R. I. 632, 36 Atl. 426, 36 L. R. A. 266. But see Herkimer County Light, etc., Co. *v.* Johnson, 37 N. Y. App. Div. 257, 55 N. Y. Suppl. 924.

54. People *v.* Feitner, 99 N. Y. App. Div. 274, 90 N. Y. Suppl. 904 [*affirmed* in 181 N. Y. 549, 74 N. E. 1124].

55. Newport Illuminating Co. *v.* Newport Tax Assessors, 19 R. I. 632, 36 Atl. 426, 36 L. R. A. 266.

56. Patterson, etc., Gas, etc., Co. *v.* State Bd. of Assessors, 69 N. J. L. 116, 54 Atl. 246; People *v.* Wells, 42 Misc. (N. Y.) 606, 87 N. Y. Suppl. 595; People *v.* Olean Assessors, 15 N. Y. St. 461.

57. Baltimore Consol. Gas Co. *v.* Baltimore, 101 Md. 541, 61 Atl. 532, 109 Am. St. Rep. 584, 1 L. R. A. N. S. 263.

58. New Orleans City Gas Light Co. *v.* Bd. of Assessors, 31 La. Ann. 475; People *v.* Brooklyn City Bd. of Assessors, 76 N. Y. 202. See also Com. *v.* Lowell Gas Light Co., 12 Allen (Mass.) 75, tax on market value of capital stock in excess of value of real estate and machinery.

59. Newport Light Co. *v.* Newport, 20 S. W. 434, 14 Ky. L. Rep. 464; Com. *v.* Lowell Gas Light Co., 12 Allen (Mass.) 75; Memphis Gaslight Co. *v.* State, 6 Coldw. (Tenn.) 310, 98 Am. Dec. 452.

As manufacturing establishment.—Under a statute providing for the taxation of "manufacturing establishments" the pipes used to convey gas from the place of manufacture to the company's customers, although laid through and under the public streets of a city, are the property of the company and taxable as a part of the establishment, but pipes owned by the city or private persons into which the company delivered gas for consumption would not be included. Memphis Gaslight Co. *v.* State, 6 Coldw. (Tenn.) 310, 98 Am. Dec. 452.

The payment of a license-tax does not exempt a gas company from *ad valorem* taxation. Newport Light Co. *v.* Newport, 20 S. W. 434, 14 Ky. L. Rep. 464.

Advance deposits.—An advance payment required of customers on account of gas to be used and as a guaranty for the return of the meter, etc., is a mere pledge so long as no unpaid obligation accrues against the customer and is not taxable to the company, but to the extent of any default it becomes a payment thereon and taxable to the company. Parsons Natural Gas Co. *v.* Rockhold, 79 Kan. 661, 100 Pac. 639.

60. Capital City Gas-Light Co. *v.* Charter Oak Ins. Co., 51 Iowa 31, 50 N. W. 579; Herkimer County Light, etc., Co. *v.* Johnson, 37 N. Y. App. Div. 257, 55 N. Y. Suppl. 924; Providence Gas Co. *v.* Thurber, 2 R. I. 15, 55 Am. Dec. 621; Consumers' Gas Co. *v.* Toronto, 27 Can. Sup. Ct. 453; *In re* Gas Company, 7 Can. L. J. 104. *Contra*, People *v.* Brooklyn Bd. of Assessors, 39 N. Y. 81; Memphis Gaslight Co. *v.* State, 6 Coldw. (Tenn.) 310, 98 Am. Dec. 452, holding that gas pipes laid in a street for distributing gas to consumers are taxable as personal property but not as realty.

Gas pipes and meters as machinery see Com. *v.* Lowell Gas Light Co., 12 Allen (Mass.) 75.

61. St. Mary's Gas Co. *v.* Elk County, 191 Pa. St. 458, 43 Atl. 321; Schuylkill County *v.* Citizens' Gas Co., 148 Pa. St. 162, 23 Atl. 1055; Pittsburgh's Appeal, 123 Pa. St. 374, 16 Atl. 621; Coatesville Gas Co. *v.* Chester County, 97 Pa. St. 476; St. Mary's Gas Co. *v.* Elk County, 15 Pa. Co. Ct. 411; Abbott *v.* Chester Gas Co., 1 Chest. Co. Rep. (Pa.) 158; Northampton County *v.* Easton Gas Co., 1 Chest. Co. Rep. (Pa.) 157.

Dwelling-houses erected for the accommodation of workmen are merely conveniences and not necessary for the company's proper work and are therefore subject to taxation. West Chester Gas Co. *v.* Chester County, 30 Pa. St. 232.

Validity of borough ordinance imposing license-tax on pipes of gas company see Kittanning Borough *v.* Kittanning Consol. Natural Gas Co., 26 Pa. Super. Ct. 355.

62. Newport Light Co. *v.* Newport, 20 S. W. 434, 14 Ky. L. Rep. 464; Com. *v.* Lowell Gas Light Co., 12 Allen (Mass.) 75.

63. Taxation of mines, mining claims, and minerals generally see *supra*, III, A, 2, b, (II).

64. Hart *v.* Plum, 14 Cal. 148 (holding that an exemption from taxation of mining claims does not include the flumes or machinery necessary to work them); People *v.* Henderson, 12 Colo. 369, 21 Pac. 144; Hope Min. Co. *v.* Kennon, 3 Mont. 35 (holding that

1866 acquire any immunity from state taxation, but is subject to taxation in the same manner as other foreign corporations.[91]

(II) *CARRYING ON BUSINESS WITHIN STATE.*[92] Where the state taxes such foreign corporations as "carry on business" within its limits, it is held that an isolated or occasional sale or other business transaction does not bring a company within this description.[93] Nor does the maintenance of an office within the taxing state, which is kept merely as a convenient place for interviewing customers, or where directors' meetings are held, transfer books kept, and dividends declared,[94] nor the maintenance of an office merely for the purpose of soliciting business,[95] or an agency for the exhibition of samples and the taking of orders, when such orders must be sent to the home office to be filled and accounts settled there,[96] or the consignment of goods of a foreign corporation to a resident commission merchant for sale constitute doing business within the application of the statute;[97] and it is to be observed that if the statute requires both the carrying on of business and the employing of capital within the state, it is possible for a corporation to carry on business without employing capital within the meaning of the statute.[98] But it is not essential that the whole business of a corporation should be done within the state, it being sufficient if a substantial part of its regular business is so carried on;[99] and a foreign corporation is within the taxing law when it maintains a branch office within the state, or a sales agency, to which its goods are consigned, from whence they are sold, and where the proceeds are collected and a bank account kept.[1] A railroad corporation is considered as doing business in any state where a portion of its line is built and operated.[2] But

91. Atty.-Gen. *v.* Western Union Tel. Co., 141 U. S. 40, 11 S. Ct. 889, 35 L. ed. 628; Western Union Tel. Co. *v.* Wright, 158 Fed. 1004.

92. **What constitutes carrying on business** generally see FOREIGN CORPORATIONS, 19 Cyc. 1267.

93. Missouri Coal, etc., Co. *v.* Ladd, 160 Mo. 435, 61 S. W. 191; People *v.* Horn Silver Min. Co., 105 N. Y. 76, 11 N. E. 155; Kilgore *v.* Smith, 122 Pa. St. 48, 15 Atl. 698; Com. *v.* Standard Oil Co., 101 Pa. St. 119; Cooper Mfg. Co. *v.* Ferguson, 113 U. S. 727, 5 S. Ct. 739, 28 L. ed. 1137.

94. People *v.* Horn Silver Min. Co., 105 N. Y. 76, 11 N. E. 155; People *v.* Feitner, 77 N. Y. App. Div. 189, 78 N. Y. Suppl. 1017.

95. People *v.* Roberts, 30 N. Y. App. Div. 150, 51 N. Y. Suppl. 866; People *v.* Roberts, 22 N. Y. App. Div. 282, 47 N. Y. Suppl. 949.

96. People *v.* Roberts, 27 N. Y. App. Div. 455, 50 N. Y. Suppl. 355; People *v.* Roberts, 25 N. Y. App. Div. 13, 48 N. Y. Suppl. 1028; People *v.* Roberts, 22 N. Y. App. Div. 282, 47 N. Y. Suppl. 949; People *v.* Wells, 42 Misc. (N. Y.) 86, 85 N. Y. Suppl. 533 [*affirmed* in 93 N. Y. App. Div. 613, 87 N. Y. Suppl. 1144].

97. People *v.* Roberts, 25 N. Y. App. Div. 13, 48 N. Y. Suppl. 1028.

98. People *v.* Roberts, 154 N. Y. 1, 47 N. E. 974 [*reversing* 90 Hun 474, 35 N. Y. Suppl. 968]. See also *infra*, III, B, 3, e, (II).

99. People *v.* Horn Silver Min. Co., 105 N. Y. 76, 11 N. E. 155 [*affirming* 38 Hun 276].

1. Armour Packing Co. *v.* Clark, 124 Ga. 369, 52 S. E. 145; People *v.* Wells, 183 N. Y. 264, 76 N. E. 24; People *v.* Feitner, 167 N. Y. 622, 60 N. E. 1118; People *v.* Roberts, 158 N. Y. 162, 52 N. E. 1102; People *v.* Wemple, 131 N. Y. 64, 29 N. E. 1002, 27 Am. St. Rep. 542; People *v.* Horn Silver Min. Co., 105 N. Y. 76, 11 N. E. 155; People *v.* Glynn, 125 N. Y. App. Div. 328, 109 N. Y. Suppl. 868; People *v.* Feitner, 49 N. Y. App. Div. 108, 62 N. Y. Suppl. 1107; People *v.* Barker, 23 N. Y. App. Div. 530, 48 N. Y. Suppl. 558 [*affirmed* in 155 N. Y. 665, 49 N. E. 1102]; People *v.* Roberts, 91 Hun (N. Y.) 158, 36 N. Y. Suppl. 368 [*affirmed* in 149 N. Y. 608, 44 N. E. 1127 (*affirmed* in 171 U. S. 658, 19 S. Ct. 70, 43 L. ed. 323)]; People *v.* Campbell, 80 Hun (N. Y.) 466, 30 N. Y. Suppl. 472 [*affirmed* in 145 N. Y. 587, 40 N. E. 239]; People *v.* Wemple, 61 Hun (N. Y.) 83, 15 N. Y. Suppl. 446 [*affirmed* in 131 N. Y. 64, 29 N. E. 1002, 27 Am. St. Rep. 542]; People *v.* New York Tax, etc., Com'rs, 39 Misc. (N. Y.) 282, 79 N. Y. Suppl. 485; People *v.* Feitner, 31 Misc. (N. Y.) 553, 65 N. Y. Suppl. 518; Singer Mfg. Co. *v.* Adams, 165 Fed. 877, 91 C. C. A. 461; Southern Cotton Oil Co. *v.* Wemple, 44 Fed. 24. But see People *v.* Wells, 98 N. Y. App. Div. 82, 90 N. Y. Suppl. 313 [*affirmed* in 182 N. Y. 553, 75 N. E. 1132]; People *v.* Barker, 5 N. Y. App. Div. 246, 39 N. Y. Suppl. 151 [*affirmed* in 149 N. Y. 623, 44 N. E. 1128].

A foreign banking corporation having its principal office in the state, and branch offices and agencies in other cities managed from the main office, is doing business within the state, within the meaning of the tax law. People *v.* Raymond, 188 N. Y. 551, 80 N. E. 1117 [*affirming* 117 N. Y. App. Div. 62, 102 N. Y. Suppl. 85].

2. Com. *v.* New York, etc., R. Co., 129 Pa. St. 463, 18 Atl. 412, 15 Am. St. Rep. 724; Erie R. Co. *v.* Pennsylvania, 21 Wall. (U. S.) 492, 22 L. ed. 595.

held for a private beneficiary is taxable.[12] Also the credits of a foreign corporation, such as accounts receivable, promissory notes, etc., are taxable when they arise out of corporate business transacted within the state.[13] So also its bonds or other obligations may be taxed when held by residents of the state.[14]

e. Capital and Stock — (I) *IN GENERAL.* Although a license or privilege tax on foreign corporations may be graduated according to the amount of their capital stock,[15] and although so much of the capital of a corporation as is employed in a given state may be there taxed,[16] yet no state can impose taxes on the capital stock, as a whole, of any corporations except those which are organized under its own laws.[17]

(II) *CAPITAL EMPLOYED WITHIN STATE.* It is within the power of a state to tax so much of the capital of a foreign corporation as is invested or employed within the taxing state, and this rule is adopted in several jurisdictions.[18] For the purpose of such a statute, the amount of capital employed in the state is measured by the total value of the property within the state owned by the corporation,[19] and used by it in the transaction of its ordinary business,[20] as distinguished from a mere independent investment,[21] with a proper allowance or

v. Union Tank Line Co., 94 Minn. 320, 102 N. W. 721; Baltimore, etc., R. Co. *v.* Allen, 22 Fed. 376; and, generally, *supra*, III, B, 2, d, (III).

Sleeping cars.— See Carlisle *v.* Pullman Palace Car Co., 8 Colo. 320, 7 Pac. 164, 54 Am. Rep. 553; Covington *v.* Pullman Co., 121 Ky. 218, 89 S. W. 116, 28 Ky. L. Rep. 199; Orleans Bd. of Assessors *v.* Pullman Palace Car Co., 60 Fed. 37, 8 C. C. A. 490. And see *supra*, III, A, 5, e.

Ferry-boats plying between states.— See St. Louis *v.* Wiggins Ferry Co., 40 Mo. 580.

As to taxation of property in transit through the state see *supra*, III, A, 5, e.

12. Baltimore City Appeal Tax Ct. *v.* Gill, 50 Md. 377; People *v.* Albany, 40 N. Y. 154.

Taxation of property held in trust generally see *supra*, III, A, 3, h.

13. *Georgia.*— Armour Packing Co. *v.* Savannah, 115 Ga. 140, 41 S. E. 237.

Louisiana.— Monongahela River Consol. Coal, etc., Co. *v.* Bd. of Assessors, 115 La. 564, 39 So. 601, 112 Am. St. Rep. 275, 2 L. R. A. N. S. 637. *Compare* Barber Asphalt Pav. Co. *v.* New Orleans, 41 La. Ann. 1015, 6 So. 794.

Minnesota.— State *v.* Northern Pac. R. Co., 95 Minn. 43, 103 N. W. 731.

New York.— People *v.* Wells, 184 N. Y. 275, 77 N. E. 19, 121 Am. St. Rep. 840, 12 L. R. A. N. S. 905.

Ohio.— Hubbard *v.* Brush, 61 Ohio St. 252, 55 N. E. 829.

Texas.— Jesse French Piano, etc., Co. *v.* Dallas, (Civ. App. 1901) 61 S. W. 942.

But credits which do not originate within the state or arise out of business transacted there are not taxable. Union Tank Line Co.'s Appeal, 204 Ill. 347, 68 N. E. 504, 98 Am. St. Rep. 221; London, etc., Bank *v.* Block, 136 Fed. 138, 69 C. C. A. 136.

Money deposited in bank.— Where moneys realized in the course of a business carried on by a foreign corporation through a local agent are deposited daily in one of the banks of the state for transmission, the average daily balance is taxable in the state. New England Mut. L. Ins. Co. *v.* Bd. of Assessors, 121 La. 1068, 47 So. 27, 26 L. R. A. N. S. 1120.

14. Georgia Cent. R. Co. *v.* Wright, 124 Ga. 630, 53 S. E. 207; Baltimore City Appeal Tax Ct. *v.* Patterson, 50 Md. 354; Com. *v.* New York, etc., Co., 145 Pa. St. 57, 22 Atl. 212, 236; Pittsburg, etc., R. Co. *v.* Com., 66 Pa. St. 73, 5 Am. Rep. 344.

15. Atty.-Gen. *v.* Bay State Min. Co., 99 Mass. 148, 96 Am. Dec. 717; People *v.* Horne Silver Min. Co., 105 N. Y. 76, 11 N. E. 155 [*affirming* 38 Hun 276]; People *v.* Wemple, 61 Hun (N. Y.) 83, 15 N. Y. Suppl. 446 [*affirmed* in 131 N. Y. 64, 29 N. E. 1002, 7 Am. St. Rep. 542]. See also *supra*, III, B, 3, c.

16. See Com. *v.* Standard Oil Co., 101 Pa. St. 119; and *infra*, III, B, 3, e, (II).

17. Western Union Tel. Co. *v.* Lieb, 76 Ill. 172; Riley *v.* Western Union Tel. Co., 47 Ind. 511; Michigan Cent. R. Co. *v.* Porter, 17 Ind. 380; Foster-Cherry Commission Co. *v.* Caskey, 66 Kan. 600, 72 Pac. 268; Com. *v.* Standard Oil Co., 101 Pa. St. 119.

18. Metropolitan L. Ins. Co. *v.* Orleans Bd. of Assessors, 115 La. 698, 39 So. 846, 116 Am. St. Rep. 179; Blackstone Mfg. Co. *v.* Blackstone, 13 Gray (Mass.) 488; Matter of Tiffany, 80 Hun (N. Y.) 486, 30 N. Y. Suppl. 494. See also COMMERCE, 7 Cyc. 478.

19. State *v.* Western Union Tel. Co., 165 Mo. 502, 65 S. W. 775; People *v.* Wemple, 133 N. Y. 323, 31 N. E. 238; International L. Assur. Soc. *v.* Tax Com'rs, 28 Barb. (N. Y.) 318, 17 How. Pr. 206; People *v.* Roberts, 25 N. Y. App. Div. 16, 49 N. Y. Suppl. 10 [*affirmed* in 156 N. Y. 688, 50 N. E. 1120]; Beaufort County *v.* Old Dominion Steamship Co., 128 N. C. 558, 39 S. E. 18.

20. People *v.* Wemple, 150 N. Y. 46, 44 N. E. 787; People *v.* Wemple, 133 N. Y. 323, 31 N. E. 238.

21. People *v.* Wemple, 150 N. Y. 46, 44 N. E. 787 [*affirming* 78 Hun 63, 29 N. Y. Suppl. 92], holding that money invested in real estate by a foreign corporation as an

poration cannot be said to "employ capital" in a state where it merely maintains an agency in charge of a salaried agent and owns no property but an inconsiderable amount of office furniture.[34] It is held, however, that bonds deposited with a state officer by a foreign insurance or guaranty company, as required by law as a condition to its doing business within the state, are taxable as capital employed in the state.[35]

f. Earnings or Receipts.[36] A tax on the gross earnings or receipts within the state of a foreign corporation is a proper and legitimate exercise of the taxing power,[37] as it is in reality a tax on the privilege of doing business within the state measured by the volume of business transacted;[38] but the legislature must provide

34. People *v.* Roberts, 154 N. Y. 1, 47 N. E. 974 [*reversing* 90 Hun 474, 35 N. Y. Suppl. 968]; People *v.* Campbell, 139 N. Y. 68, 34 N. E. 753; People *v.* Miller, 90 N. Y. App. Div. 545, 85 N. Y. Suppl. 849; People *v.* Roberts, 8 N. Y. App. Div. 201, 40 N. Y. Suppl. 417 [*affirmed* in 151 N. Y. 619, 45 N. E. 1134].

35. People *v.* Home Ins. Co., 29 Cal. 533; International L. Assur. Soc. *v.* Tax Com'rs. 28 Barb. (N. Y.) 318; State *v.* Maryland Fidelity, etc., Co., 35 Tex. Civ. App. 214, 80 S. W. 544; Scottish Union, etc., Ins. Co. *v.* Bowland, 196 U. S. 611, 25 S. Ct. 345, 49 L. ed. 619; Western Assur. Co. *v.* Halliday, 126 Fed. 257, 61 C. C. A. 271 [*affirmed* in 110 Fed. 259].

But on the repeal of a statute requiring such a deposit the securities deposited become subject to withdrawal and, although remaining on deposit, are not subject to taxation as money invested in business within the state. People *v.* New England Mut. L. Ins. Co., 26 N. Y. 303.

36. **Corporate earnings or receipts** generally see *supra*, III, B, 1, i.

Gross receipts from interstate business see COMMERCE, 7 Cyc. 477, 479, 481, 483.

37. *Illinois.*— Raymond *v.* Hartford F. Ins. Co., 196 Ill. 329, 63 N. E. 745.

Kansas.— McNall *v.* Metropolitan L. Ins. Co., 65 Kan. 694, 70 Pac. 604.

Kentucky.— Southern Bldg., etc., Assoc. *v.* Norman, 98 Ky. 294, 32 S. W. 952, 17 Ky. L. Rep. 887, 56 Am. St. Rep. 367, 31 L. R. A. 41.

Michigan.— Fargo *v.* Auditor-Gen., 57 Mich. 598, 24 N. W. 538.

Ohio.— State *v.* Hahn, 50 Ohio St. 714, 35 N. E. 1052; Western Union Tel. Co. *v.* Mayer, 28 Ohio St. 521.

Pennsylvania.— Com. *v.* Delaware, etc., Canal Co., 4 Dauph. Co. Rep. 154 [*affirmed* in (1888) 17 Atl. 175, 1 L. R. A. 232].

South Carolina.— Southern Express Co. *v.* Hood, 15 Rich. 66, 94 Am. Dec. 141.

United States.— British Foreign Mar. Ins. Co. *v.* Board of Assessors, 42 Fed. 90.

Canada.— Phœnix Ins. Co. *v.* Kingston Corp., 7 Ont. 343.

See 45 Cent. Dig. tit. "Taxation," § 291.

What receipts included.—A statute imposing a tax upon the gross receipts of express companies applies only to the gross receipts which a foreign express company doing business in a state has received within the state for itself, and does not include collections belonging to other express and railroad companies or amounts due to other connecting companies and received to their use. Southern Express Co. *v.* Hood, 15 Rich. (S. C.) 66, 94 Am. Dec. 141. The Ohio statute requiring foreign insurance companies to pay a tax of a certain percentage on their gross premiums relates in terms to premiums "received by it in the state" and therefore the company is not required to pay such per cent on the business done within the state or on premiums received from the state but only on the amount of premiums received "in" the state. New York Mut. L. Ins. Co. *v.* State, 79 Ohio St. 305, 87 N. E. 259.

Under the Massachusetts statute the provisions of section 24, imposing an excise tax of one fourth of one per cent on the net value of policies held by residents, and section 28, providing that if the state, where a foreign insurance company was incorporated, imposes a tax on the premiums received by Massachusetts companies doing business therein, such foreign corporation shall pay a similar tax at the highest rate so imposed in the other state, are not cumulative, and no tax should be assessed under section 28 unless the amount would be greater than the tax assessed according to section 24, and if a tax is assessed under section 28, no tax should be assessed under section 24. Metropolitan L. Ins. Co. *v.* Com., 198 Mass. 466, 84 N. E. 863.

Under the Texas statute of 1907 a lower rate of tax on gross receipts of foreign insurance companies is allowed in case the company complies with the provisions of the statute requiring the investment of a deposit of seventy-five per cent of the reserve apportioned to the policies written on the lives of citizens of that state. See Kansas City L. Ins. Co. *v.* Love, 101 Tex. 531, 109 S. W. 863.

38. Southern Bldg., etc., Assoc. *v.* Norman, 98 Ky. 294, 32 S. W. 952, 17 Ky. L. Rep. 887, 56 Am. St. Rep. 367, 31 L. R. A. 41; Western Union Tel. Co. *v.* Mayer, 28 Ohio St. 521. See also cases cited *supra*, note 37.

Invalid as a property tax.—S. C. St. (1897). Code (1892), § 1809, imposing a tax on the gross receipts of foreign corporations which is imposed in addition to certain license-taxes, and requires such receipts to be entered "with the other items now included in the taxable property" of the company, does not impose a privilege tax but a tax on property, and as it is levied not upon property within the jurisdiction of the state at the time of the assessment but upon money which has passed

taxes on its capital or property in the foreign state or not;[43] but if all of its property is situated and taxed to the corporation in the same state where the stock-holders reside, the same rules should be applied as in the case of domestic corporations similarly taxed, and the stock-holders relieved from taxation on their shares.[44]

C. Public Property — 1. GENERAL PRINCIPLES. The United States has no authority to tax the property of a state,[45] nor a state to extract revenue from the property of the federal government,[46] and from the nature of the case neither government will lay taxes upon its own property.[47] Hence as a general rule all public property is exempt from taxation, either by express exemption or by necessary implication,[48] including not only the property of the state itself, but also the public property of its political subdivisions, such as counties and municipal corporations.[49] While in the absence of constitutional prohibition the state may include in its scheme of taxation such property of its own or of its municipal subdivisions,[50] the presumption is always against an intention to do so, and such property is impliedly exempt unless an intention to include it is clearly mani-

Ohio.— Lee *v.* Sturges, 46 Ohio St. 153, 19 N. E. 560, 2 L. R. A. 556.

Shares of stock-holders generally see *supra*, III, B, 1, j.

43. *Indiana.*— Hasely *v.* Ensley, 40 Ind. App. 598, 82 N. E. 809.

Iowa.— Judy *v.* Beckwith, 137 Iowa 24, 114 N. W. 565, 15 L. R. A. N. S. 142.

Kentucky.— Com. *v.* Peebles, 134 Ky. 121, 119 S. W. 774, 23 L. R. A. N. S. 1130.

Missouri.—Ogden *v.* St. Joseph, 90 Mo. 522, 3 S. W. 25.

Ohio.— Lee *v.* Sturges, 46 Ohio St. 153, 19 N. E. 560, 2 L. R. A. 556.

Pennsylvania.— McKeen *v.* Northampton County, 49 Pa. St. 519, 88 Am. Dec. 515.

Rhode Island.— Dyer *v.* Osborne, 11 R. I. 321, 23 Am. Rep. 460.

Under the New Jersey statutes the shares of stock in foreign corporations are not taxable where the corporation has within twelve months paid taxes on its property in its own state. Trenton *v.* Standard F. Ins. Co., 77 N. J. L. 757, 73 Atl. 606 [*affirming* 76 N. J. L. 79, 68 Atl. 1111]; State *v.* Ramsey, 54 N. J. L. 546, 24 Atl. 445.

44. Com. *v.* Ledman, 127 Ky. 603, 106 S. W. 247, 32 Ky. L. Rep. 452; Stroh *v.* Detroit, 131 Mich. 109, 90 N. W. 1029; Hubbard *v.* Brush, 61 Ohio St. 252, 55 N. E. 829 [*affirming* 18 Ohio Cir. Ct. 884, 9 Ohio Cir. Dec. 859]. See also McLeod *v.* Sandall, 26 N. Brunsw. 526.

If only a part of the property is situated in the state and taxed to the corporation, it has been held that the rule does not apply and that the stock-holders are subject to taxation on their shares. Lee *v.* Sturges, 46 Ohio St. 153, 19 N. E. 560, 2 L. R. A. 556. But under the Kentucky statute if a foreign corporation pays taxes upon its franchises and property within the state, the stock-holders are not subject to taxation on their shares, although only a part of the property of the corporation is situated and taxed within the state. Com. *v.* Walsh, 133 Ky. 103, 106 S. W. 240, 32 Ky. L. Rep. 460, 117 S. W. 398.

45. See *infra*, III, C, 3, a.

46. See *infra*, III, C, 2, a.

47. Camden *v.* Camden Village Corp., 77 Me. 530, 1 Atl. 689; Worcester County *v.* Worcester, 116 Mass. 193, 17 Am. Rep. 159; Public School Trustees *v.* Trenton, 30 N. J. Eq. 667.

The reason of the rule is not based upon constitutional prohibition, but upon the fact that the state would merely be taxing itself to raise money to pay over to itself (Public School Trustees *v.* Trenton, 30 N. J. Eq. 667), or, as stated in one case, "would be merely taking money out of one pocket and putting it into another" (People *v.* Doe, 36 Cal. 220), so that there would be no gain in revenue, but on the contrary a loss to the extent of the cost of assessing and collecting the tax (see Biscoe *v.* Coulter, 18 Ark. 423).

48. *California.*— People *v.* Doe, 36 Cal. 220.

Connecticut.—West Hartford *v.* Hartford Water Com'rs, 44 Conn. 360.

Illinois.— People *v.* Salomon, 51 Ill. 37.

Kansas.— Blue Jacket *v.* Johnson County, 3 Kan. 299.

Kentucky.— Louisville *v.* Com., 1 Duv. 295, 85 Am. Dec. 624.

Louisiana.—Alexandria *v.* O'Shee, 51 La. Ann. 719, 25 So. 382; Tulane Education Fund *v.* New Orleans Bd. of Assessors, 38 La. Ann. 292.

New Hampshire.— Franklin St. Soc. *v.* Manchester, 60 N. H. 342.

New Jersey.— Public Schools *v.* Trenton, 30 N. J. Eq. 667.

Texas.— Traylor *v.* State, 19 Tex. Civ. App. 86, 46 S. W. 81.

See 45 Cent. Dig. tit. "Taxation," § 295.

A private alley-way is not exempt from taxation in the character of public property. Hill *v.* Williams, 104 Md. 595, 65 Atl. 413.

49. People *v.* Doe, 36 Cal. 220; Camden *v.* Camden Village Corp., 77 Me. 530, 1 Atl. 689; Worcester County *v.* Worcester, 116 Mass. 193, 17 Am. Rep. 159; Public Schools *v.* Trenton, 30 N. J. Eq. 667.

Property of municipal corporations see *infra*, III, C, 4.

Property of state see *infra*, III, C, 3.

50. Louisville *v.* Com., 1 Duv. (Ky.) 295, 85 Am. Dec. 624; Public Schools *v.* Trenton, 30 N. J. Eq. 667. See also *infra*, III, C, 3, a; III, C, 4, a.

where the tax is laid, not upon the capital or the property of the corporation, but upon its franchises.[58] And a stock-holder in a bank or other corporation of which the capital is invested in United States securities is not a holder of such securities, and therefore he is taxable in respect to his stock, as distinguished from taxing the institution on its capital without regard to the fact of such investment.[59]

4. Franchises, Patents, and Other Rights Granted by United States. The states have no power to impose any taxes on franchises granted to corporations by the laws of the United States.[60] So also the exclusive rights or privileges

New York.— People *v.* Barker, 154 N. Y. 128, 47 N. E. 973; People *v.* Norton, 53 N. Y. App. Div. 557, 65 N. Y. Suppl. 992; International L. Assur. Soc. *v.* Tax Com'rs, 28 Barb. 318, 17 How. Pr. 206 [*affirmed* in 31 N. Y. 32].

Pennsylvania.—Com. *v.* Provident Life, etc., Co., 9 Pa. Dist. 479.

Utah.— Salt Lake City Nat. Bank *v.* Golding, 2 Utah 1.

West Virginia.— Martinsburg Old Nat. Bank *v.* State, 58 W. Va. 559, 52 S. E. 494, 3 L. R. A. N. S. 584.

United States.— Home Sav. Bank *v.* Des Moines, 205 U. S. 503, 27 S. Ct. 571, 51 L. ed. 901; Louisville First Nat. Bank *v.* Kentucky, 9 Wall. 353, 19 L. ed. 701; New York *v.* New York Tax Com'rs, 2 Wall. 200, 17 L. ed. 793; New York Commerce Bank *v.* New York, 2 Black 620, 17 L. ed. 451.

See 45 Cent. Dig. tit. "Taxation," §§ 20, 26.

The undivided profits of a national bank, beyond the amount required by law to be kept as a surplus fund, are taxable, although invested in government bonds. Concord First Nat. Bank *v.* Concord, 59 N. H. 75.

58. People *v.* Home Ins. Co., 92 N. Y. 328; Monroe County Sav. Bank *v.* Rochester, 37 N. Y. 365; Home Ins. Co. *v.* New York, 134 U. S. 594, 10 S. Ct. 593, 33 L. ed. 1025; Home Ins. Co. *v.* New York, 119 U. S. 129, 8 S. Ct. 1385, 30 L. ed. 350; Hamilton Mfg. Co. *v.* Massachusetts, 6 Wall. (U. S.) 632, 18 L. ed. 904; Provident Sav. Inst. *v.* Massachusetts, 6 Wall. (U. S.) 611, 18 L. ed. 907; Connecticut Sav. Soc. *v.* Coite, 6 Wall. (U. S.) 594, 18 L. ed. 897 [*affirming* 32 Conn. 173]. See also People *v.* Morgan, 178 N. Y. 433, 70 N. E. 967, 67 L. R. A. 960 [*reversing* 86 N. Y. App. Div. 577, 83 N. Y. Suppl. 998].

59. *Alabama.*— McIver *v.* Robinson, 53 Ala. 456.

Illinois.— People *v.* Bradley, 39 Ill. 130.

Iowa.— Independence First Nat. Bank *v.* Independence, 123 Iowa 482, 99 N. W. 142; National State Bank *v.* Burlington, 119 Iowa 696, 94 N. W. 234. See also Security Sav. Bank *v.* Carroll, 128 Iowa 230, 103 N. W. 379.

Louisiana.— Shreveport First Nat. Bank *v.* Board of Reviewers 41 La. Ann. 181, 5 So. 408.

Missouri.— St. Louis Bldg., etc., Assoc. *v.* Lightner, 47 Mo. 393.

New Jersey.— Jewell *v.* Hart, 31 N. J. L. 434; Fox *v.* Haight, 31 N. J. L. 399.

New York.— Utica *v.* Churchill, 33 N. Y. 161; People *v.* Barton, 44 Barb. 148.

Ohio.— Frazer *v.* Siebern, 16 Ohio St. 614; Cleveland Trust Co. *v.* Lander, 19 Ohio Cir. Ct. 271, 10 Ohio Cir. Dec. 452.

Texas.— Harrison *v.* Vines, 46 Tex. 15; Adair *v.* Robinson, 6 Tex. Civ. App. 275, 25 S. W. 734.

United States.— Cleveland Trust Co. *v.* Lander, 184 U. S. 111, 22 S. Ct. 394, 46 L. ed. 456; New York *v.* New York Tax Com'rs, 4 Wall. 244, 18 L. ed. 344; Van Allen *v.* Assessors, 3 Wall. 573, 18 L. ed. 229; People's Sav. Bank *v.* Layman, 134 Fed. 635; Exchange Nat. Bank *v.* Miller, 19 Fed. 372; Chicago First Nat. Bank *v.* Farwell, 7 Fed. 518, 10 Biss. 270.

See 45 Cent. Dig. tit. "Taxation," § 28.

Although the assessment is against the corporation where required by statute instead of against the stock-holders individually, if the tax is in fact upon the shares of stock as distinguished from the capital of the corporation, no deduction is allowable on account of capital invested in United States bonds. German American Sav. Bank *v.* Burlington, 118 Iowa 84, 91 N. W. 829.

Valuation of shares of stock-holders see *infra*, VI, D, 5, h.

60. Western Union Tel. Co. *v.* Visalia, 149 Cal. 744, 87 Pac. 1023; San Francisco *v.* Western Union Tel. Co., 96 Cal. 140, 31 Pac. 10, 17 L. R. A. 301; San Benito County *v.* Southern Pac. R. Co., 77 Cal. 518, 19 Pac. 827; Western Union Tel. Co. *v.* Lakin, 53 Wash. 326, 101 Pac. 1094; California *v.* Central Pac. R. Co., 127 U. S. 1, 8 S. Ct. 1073, 32 L. ed. 150. See also Atlantic, etc., R. Co. *v.* Lesueur, 2 Ariz. 428, 19 Pac. 157.

But a ratification or confirmation by congress of a franchise granted by a local legislature has only the same effect as a prior authorization and does not make such franchise one granted by congress. Honolulu Rapid Transit, etc., Co. *v.* Wilder, 211 U. S. 137, 29 S. Ct. 44, 53 L. ed. 121 [*affirming* 18 Hawaii 666], franchise granted by Hawaiian government between July 7, 1898, and Sept. 28, 1899, ratified and confirmed by acts of congress of 1900.

Franchise of railroad company.—A railroad company is not subject to state taxation on a franchise granted by the United States (California *v.* Central Pac. R. Co., 127 U. S. 1, 8 S. Ct. 1073, 32 L. ed. 150); but when a railroad chartered by a state and having a state franchise to operate its road, afterward receives a franchise from the federal government, the state franchise is not merged in the federal franchise so as to prevent the state taxation of the state franchise and the physical property of the road (People *v.* Central

that it may be lost by non-user, that is, by acquiescence in actual taxation, and if this continues for a long period of years, it will raise a presumption of surrender.[88] Ordinarily an exemption from taxation is a mere personal privilege,[89] although it may be either a personal privilege or a privilege annexed to particular property.[90] The purpose of granting exemptions from taxation is ordinarily found in motives of public policy, such as the encouragement of manufacturing and other industries,[91] or the support of educational, charitable, or religious institutions;[92] but it is sometimes a proper and even necessary measure to avoid double taxation of particular persons or property,[93] although an exemption of this character is not properly speaking an exemption, but rather a mere regulation as to the mode of assessment.[94]

B. Grant or Creation — 1. Power to Exempt in General. Unless restrained by constitutional provisions, the legislature of a state has full power to exempt any persons or corporations or classes of property from taxation, according to its views of public policy or expediency.[95] But no such power or authority belongs inherently to the municipal corporations of the state;[96] and still less can a mere

88. New Jersey *v.* Wright, 117 U. S. 648, 6 S. Ct. 907, 29 L. ed. 1021.

89. Com. *v.* Owensboro, etc., R. Co., 81 Ky. 572; State *v.* Great Northern R. Co., 106 Minn. 303, 119 N. W. 202; Wilson *v.* Gaines, 9 Baxt. (Tenn.) 546 [*affirmed* in 103 U. S. 417, 26 L. ed. 401]. See also *infra*, IV, C, 5, a.

90. Grand Canyon R. Co. *v.* Treat, (Ariz. 1908) 95 Pac. 187; State *v.* Great Northern R. Co., 106 Minn. 303, 119 N. W. 202; Morris Canal, etc., Co. *v.* State Bd. of Assessors, 76 N. J. L. 627, 71 Atl. 328.

The distinction between exemptions which are personal privileges and those which are annexed to particular property is important as affecting the assignability or transfer of the exemption. State *v.* Great Northern R. Co., 106 Minn. 303, 119 N. W. 202; Morris Canal, etc., Co. *v.* State Bd. of Assessors, 76 N. J. L. 627, 71 Atl. 328. See also *infra*, IV, C, 5.

A commuted system of taxation in lieu of property taxation is a personal privilege. State *v.* Great Northern R. Co., 106 Minn. 303, 119 N. W. 202.

91. Grand Canyon R. Co. *v.* Treat, (Ariz. 1908) 95 Pac. 187; Palmes *v.* Louisville, etc., R. Co., 19 Fla. 231. See also *infra*, IV, D, 3, g, k.

92. Anniston City Land Co. *v.* State, 160 Ala. 253, 48 So. 659; Matlack *v.* Jones, 2 Disn. (Ohio) 2. See also *infra*, IV, E.

93. McIver *v.* Robinson, 53 Ala. 456; *In re* Opinion of Justices, 195 Mass. 607, 84 N. E. 499; Com. *v.* People's Five Cent Sav. Bank, 5 Allen (Mass.) 428; Trenton *v.* Standard F. Ins. Co., 77 N. J. L. 757, 73 Atl. 606 [*affirming* 76 N. J. L. 79, 68 Atl. 1111]; Jersey City Gaslight Co. *v.* Jersey City, 46 N. J. L. 194.

94. Jersey City Gaslight Co. *v.* Jersey City, 46 N. J. L. 194; Carroll *v.* Alsup, 107 Tenn. 257, 64 S. W. 193.

95. *Arizona.*— Bennett *v.* Nichols, 9 Ariz. 138, 80 Pac. 392.

Louisiana.— St. Ann's Asylum *v.* Parker, 109 La. 592, 33 So. 613.

Maryland.— William Wilkens Co. *v.* Baltimore, 103 Md. 293, 63 Atl. 562; State *v.* Baltimore, etc., R. Co., 48 Md. 49.

Massachusetts.— Day *v.* Lawrence, 167 Mass. 371, 45 N. E. 751.

Michigan.— Chippewa County *v.* Auditor-Gen., 65 Mich. 408, 32 N. W. 651.

Minnesota.— Nobles County *v.* Hamline University, 46 Minn. 316, 48 N. W. 1119; St. Paul, etc., R. Co. *v.* Parcher, 14 Minn. 297.

Mississippi.— Adams *v.* Winona Cotton Mills, 92 Miss. 743, 46 So. 401.

Missouri.— Scotland County *v.* Missouri, etc., R. Co., 65 Mo. 123; Sloan *v.* Pacific R. Co., 61 Mo. 24, 21 Am. Rep. 397; St. Louis *v.* Boatmen's Ins., etc., Co., 47 Mo. 150.

Montana.— Northern Pac. R. Co. *v.* Carland, 5 Mont. 146, 3 Pac. 134.

New Jersey.— Little *v.* Bowers, 48 N. J. L. 370, 5 Atl. 178.

New York.— Matter of Rochester Trust, etc., Co., 42 Misc. 581, 87 N. Y. Suppl. 628.

Oklahoma.— Pryor *v.* Bryan, 11 Okla. 357, 66 Pac. 348.

Oregon.— Wallace *v.* Josephine County Bd. of Equalization, 47 Oreg. 584, 86 Pac. 365.

Pennsylvania.— Butler's Appeal, 73 Pa. St. 448.

Tennessee.— Knoxville, etc., R. Co. *v.* Hicks, 9 Baxt. 442.

Texas.— State *v.* Colorado Bridge Co., (Civ. App. 1903) 75 S. W. 818.

Wisconsin.— State *v.* Winnebago Lake, etc., Plank Road Co., 11 Wis. 35.

United States.— Minot *v.* Philadelphia, etc., R. Co., 18 Wall. 206, 21 L. ed. 888; Jefferson Branch Bank *v.* Skelley, 1 Black 436, 17 L. ed. 173; Piqua Branch Ohio Bank *v.* Knoop, 16 How. 369, 14 L. ed. 977; Louisville, etc., R. Co. *v.* Gaines, 3 Fed. 266, 2 Flipp. 621; Wells *v.* Central Vermont R. Co., 29 Fed. Cas. No. 17,390, 14 Blatchf. 426.

See 45 Cent. Dig. tit. "Taxation," § 307.

The taxing power of a territory includes the power to grant exemptions from taxation. Bennett *v.* Nichols, 9 Ariz. 138, 80 Pac. 392; Pryor *v.* Bryan, 11 Okla. 357, 66 Pac. 348.

96. *Georgia.*—Augusta Factory *v.* Augusta, 83 Ga. 734, 10 S. E. 359.

and where it exists it should be carefully scrutinized and not permitted to extend either in scope or duration beyond what the terms of the concession clearly require,[45] or so as to create an absolute and irrevocable exemption unless the language of the statute clearly so requires.[46] But this rule of strict construction will not be applied where the statute itself prescribes the rules for its own interpretation and requires the construction to be liberal,[47] nor will it be applied to a law com-

288, 48 Am. Dec. 531; Gordon v. Baltimore, 5 Gill 231.

Massachusetts.— Portland Bank v. Apthorp, 12 Mass. 252.

Michigan.—Atty.-Gen. v. Detroit, 113 Mich. 388, 71 N. W. 632; East Saginaw Mfg. Co. v. East Saginaw, 19 Mich. 259, 2 Am. Rep. 82.

Minnesota.— State v. Great Northern R. Co., 106 Minn. 303, 119 N. W. 202.

Missouri.— State v. Casey, 210 Mo. 235, 109 S. W. 1; Pacific R. Co. v. Cass County, 53 Mo. 17; North Missouri R. Co. v. Maguire, 49 Mo. 490, 8 Am. Rep. 141; State v. Dulle, 48 Mo. 282; St. Louis v. Boatmen's Ins., etc., Co., 47 Mo. 150; Trenton v. Humel, 134 Mo. App. 595, 114 S. W. 1131.

New Hampshire.— Brewster v. Hough, 10 N. H. 138.

New Jersey.— Little v. Bowers, 48 N. J. L. 370, 5 Atl. 178; Freese v. Woodruff, 37 N. J. L. 139; State v. Newark Collectors, 26 N. J. L. 519; State v. Minton, 23 N. J. L. 529.

New York.— Rochester v. Rochester R. Co., 182 N. Y. 99, 74 N. E. 953, 70 L. R. A. 773; *In re* Prime, 136 N. Y. 347, 32 N. E. 1091, 18 L. R. A. 713; People v. Long Island City, 76 N. Y. 20; People v. Roper, 35 N Y. 629; Matter of Rochester Trust, etc., Co., 42 Misc. 581, 87 N. Y. Suppl. 628.

Pennsylvania.— Jones, etc., Mfg. Co. v. Com., 69 Pa. St. 137; Commonwealth Bank v. Com., 19 Pa. St. 144.

Tennessee.—Nashville, etc., R. Co. v. Hodges, 7 Lea 663.

Utah.— Parker v. Quinn, 23 Utah 332, 64 Pac. 961; Judge v. Spencer, 15 Utah 242, 48 Pac. 1097.

Vermont.— Herrick v. Randolph, 13 Vt. 525.

Washington.— Puget Sound Agricultural Co. v. Pierce County, 1 Wash. Ter. 159.

Wisconsin.— Douglas County Agricultural Soc. v. Douglas County, 104 Wis. 429, 80 N. W. 740; Weston v. Shawano County, 44 Wis. 242.

United States.— Mobile, etc., R. Co. v. Tennessee, 153 U. S. 486, 14 S. Ct. 968, 38 L. ed. 793; New Orleans City, etc., R. Co. v. New Orleans, 143 U. S. 192, 12 S. Ct. 406, 36 L. ed. 121; Chicago, etc., R. Co. v. Missouri, 120 U. S. 569; 7 S. Ct. 693, 30 L. ed. 732; Vicksburg, etc., R. Co. v. Dennis, 116 U. S. 665, 6 S. Ct. 625, 29 L. ed. 770; Southwestern R. Co. v. Wright, 116 U. S. 231, 6 S. Ct. 375, 29 L. ed. 626; Hoge v. Richmond, etc., R. Co., 99 U. S. 348, 25 L. ed. 303; Erie R. Co. v. Pennsylvania, 21 Wall. 492, 22 L. ed. 595; North Missouri R. Co. v. Maguire, 20 Wall. 46, 22 L. ed. 287; Minot v. Philadelphia, etc., R. Co., 18 Wall. 206, 21 L. ed. 888; Tomlinson v. Branch, 15 Wall. 460, 21 L. ed. 189; Tomlinson v. Jessup, 15 Wall. 454, 21 L. ed. 204; Wilmington, etc., R. Co. v. Reid, 13 Wall. 264, 20 L. ed. 568; Savings Soc. v. Coite, 6 Wall. 594, 18 L. ed. 897; Gilman v. Sheboygan, 2 Black 510, 17 L. ed. 305; Jefferson Branch Bank v. Skelley, 1 Black 436, 17 L. ed. 173; Ohio L. Ins., etc., Co. v. Debolt, 16 How. 416, 14 L. ed. 997; Philadelphia, etc., R. Co. v. Maryland, 10 How. 376, 13 L. ed. 461; Charles River Bridge v. Warren Bridge, 11 Pet. 420, 9 L. ed. 773, 938; Providence Bank v. Billings, 4 Pet. 514, 7 L. ed. 939; Davenport Nat. Bank v. Mittelbuscher, 15 Fed. 225, 4 McCrary 361.

Canada.— Canadian Pac. R. Co. v. Winnipeg, 30 Can. S. Ct. 558; Beauvais v. Montreal, 14 Quebec Super. Ct. 385; Limoilou v. Seminary of Quebec, 7 Quebec Q. B. 44.

See 45 Cent. Dig. tit. "Taxation," § 322.

Illustrations and applications of rule.— Statutory exemptions from taxation will not be extended by judicial construction to property other than that expressly designated. Thurston County v. House of Providence Sisters of Charity, 14 Wash. 264, 44 Pac. 252. A law exempting those persons from the payment of a poll tax who have lost a hand or foot does not exempt one who has lost part of his fingers or whose foot is useless. Bigham v. Clubb, 42 Tex. Civ. App. 312, 95 S. W. 675. The fact that in an act amending the charter of a railroad corporation special provision is made for ascertaining the taxes to become due by the corporation to the state, nothing being said about the manner of ascertaining other taxes, is not of itself enough to work an exemption of the property of the corporation from all taxation not levied for state purposes. Silence in regard to such other taxes cannot be construed as a waiver of the right of the state to levy them. There must be something said affirmatively, and which is explicit enough to show clearly that the legislature intended to relieve the corporation from this part of the burden borne by other real and personal property, before such an act shall amount to a contract not to levy them. Bailey v. Magwire, 22 Wall. (U. S.) 215, 22 L. ed. 850.

45. Morris Canal, etc., Co. v. State Bd. of Assessors, 76 N. J. L. 627, 71 Atl. 328; Yazoo, etc., R. Co. v. Thomas, 132 U. S. 174, 10 S. Ct. 68, 33 L. ed. 302; Walters v. Western. etc., R. Co., 68 Fed. 1002. See also cases cited *supra*, notes 43, 44.

46. State v. Great Northern R. Co., 106 Minn. 303, 119 N. W. 202; Little v. Bowers, 46 N. J. L. 300 [*affirmed* in 48 N. J. L. 370, 5 Atl. 178]; Probasco v. Moundsville, 11 W. Va. 501. See also *infra*, IV, C, 9, a.

47. People v. Chicago Theological Sem-

from assessments,[55] but not from local assessments for public improvements,[56] unless the language of the grant very clearly includes burdens of this sort.[57] So

Co. *v.* Jersey City, 41 N. J. L. 471; Camden, etc., R. Co. *v.* Appeal Com'rs, 18 N. J. L. 71.

New York.— People *v.* Brooklyn Bd. of Assessors, 141 N. Y. 476, 36 N. E. 508; Johnson Home *v.* Seneca Falls, 37 N. Y. App. Div. 147, 55 N. Y. Suppl. 803; Mutual Ins. Co. *v.* Poughkeepsie, 51 Hun 595, 4 N. Y. Suppl. 93. But see People *v.* Davenport, 91 N. Y. 574, construing a particular exemption as relating only to state taxation, notwithstanding the exempting clause of the statute applied in terms to "assessment or taxation."

North Carolina.— Richmond, etc., R. Co. *v.* Orange County, 74 N. C. 506.

Ohio.— State *v.* State Auditor, 15 Ohio St. 482.

Pennsylvania.— Finney *v.* Mercer County, 1 Serg. & R. 62.

South Carolina.—State Bank *v.* Charleston, 3 Rich. 342. See also Martin *v.* Charleston, 13 Rich. Eq. 50.

Texas.— International, etc., R. Co. *v.* Anderson County, 59 Tex. 654.

United States.—Yazoo, etc., R. Co. *v.* Yazoo, etc., Levee Com'rs, 37 Fed. 24 [*affirmed* in 132 U. S. 190, 10 S. Ct. 74. 33 L. ed. 308].

See 45 Cent. Dig. tit. "Taxation," § 324.

55. Louisiana, etc., R. Co. *v.* Shaw, 121 La. 997, 46 So. 994 (special tax voted in aid of railroad); Louisiana, etc., R. Co. *v.* State Bd. of Appraisers, 120 La. 471, 45 So. 394 (special taxes levied in aid of public schools). See also New Jersey R., etc., Co. *v.* Newark, 27 N. J. L. 185. But see Hendrie *v.* Kalthoff, 48 Mich. 306, 12 N. W. 191, holding that the exemption of a street railroad company from general taxation will not relieve it from the payment of a dog tax.

56. *Arkansas.*— Ft. Smith Paving Dist. No. 5 *v.* Sisters of Mercy, 86 Ark. 109, 109 S. W. 1165, assessment not included, although exemption is from "state, county, municipal and special" taxation.

California.— San Diego *v.* Linda Vista Irr. Dist., 108 Cal. 189, 41 Pac. 291, 35 L. R. A. 33.

Connecticut.—Bridgeport *v.* New York, etc., R. Co., 36 Conn. 255, 4 Am. Rep. 63.

Illinois.— Adams County *v.* Quincy, 130 Ill. 566, 22 N. E. 624, 6 L. R. A. 155; Illinois Cent. R. Co. *v.* Decatur, 126 Ill. 92, 18 N. E. 315, 1 L. R. A. 613 (assessment not include, although exemption is from "all taxation of every kind"); Chicago *v.* Baptist Theological Union, 115 Ill. 245, 2 N. E. 254; Illinois, etc., Canal *v.* Chicago, 12 Ill. 403 (assessment not included, although exemption is from "taxation of every description").

Indiana.— Ft. Wayne First Presb. Church *v.* Ft. Wayne, 36 Ind. 338, 10 Am. Rep. 35.

Kentucky.— Kilgus *v.* Good Shepherd Orphanage, 94 Ky. 439, 444, 22 S. W. 750, 15 Ky. L. Rep. 318; Zable *v.* Louisville Baptist Orphans' Home, 92 Ky. 89, 17 S. W. 212, 13 Ky. L. Rep. 385, 13 L. R. A. 668 (assessment not included, although exemption is from "all taxation by State or local laws for any purpose whatever"); Louisville *v.* McNaughten, 44 S. W. 380, 19 Ky. L. Rep. 1695.

Maryland.—Baltimore *v.* Proprietors Green Mt. Cemetery, 7 Md. 517.

Massachusetts.— Boston Asylum, etc. *v.* Boston St. Com'rs, 180 Mass. 485, 62 N. E. 961; Worcester Agricultural Soc. *v.* Worcester, 116 Mass. 189; Boston Seamen's Friend Soc. *v.* Boston, 116 Mass. 181, 17 Am. Rep. 153.

Michigan.— Lake Shore, etc., R. Co. *v.* Grand Rapids, 102 Mich. 374, 60 N. W. 767, 29 L. R. A. 195; Lefevre *v.* Detroit, 2 Mich. 586.

Missouri.— Sheehan *v.* Good Samaritan Hospital, 50 Mo. 155, 11 Am. Rep. 412.

New Jersey.— Paterson *v.* Society for Establishing Useful Manufactures, 24 N. J. L. 385.

New York.— Roosevelt Hospital *v.* New York, 84 N. Y. 108; *In re* New York, 11 Johns. 77.

Ohio.— Lima *v.* Lima Cemetery Assoc., 42 Ohio St. 128, 51 Am. Rep. 809; Gilmour *v.* Pelton, 5 Ohio Dec. (Reprint) 447, 6 Am. L. Rec. 26.

Pennsylvania.— *In re* Broad St., 165 Pa. St. 475, 30 Atl. 1007; Northern Liberties *v.* St. John's Church, 13 Pa. St. 104; Philadelphia *v.* Franklin Cemetery, 2 Pa. Super. Ct. 569. But see Erie *v.* First Universalist Church, 105 Pa. St. 278; Olive Cemetery Co. *v.* Philadelphia, 93 Pa. St. 129, 39 Am. Rep. 732.

Rhode Island.— *In re* College St., 8 R. I. 474.

South Dakota.— Winona, etc., R. Co. *v.* Watertown, 1 S. D. 46, 44 N. W. 1072.

Wisconsin.— Yates *v.* Milwaukee, 92 Wis. 352, 66 N. W. 248.

United States.— Illinois Cent. R. Co. *v.* Decatur, 147 U. S. 190, 13 S. Ct. 293, 37 L. ed. 132.

See also MUNICIPAL CORPORATIONS, 28 Cyc. 1131.

57. *District of Columbia.*— District of Columbia *v.* Sisters of Visitation, 15 App. Cas. 300, "any and all taxes or assessments."

Massachusetts.— Harvard College *v.* Boston, 104 Mass. 470, "all civil impositions, taxes and rates."

Minnesota.— State *v.* St. Paul, 36 Minn. 529, 32 N. W. 781 ("all public taxes and assessments"); First Div. St. Paul, etc., R. Co. *v.* St. Paul, 21 Minn. 526 ("all taxes and assessments whatever"). See also St. Paul *v.* St. Paul, etc., R. Co., 23 Minn. 469.

New Jersey.— Hudson County Catholic Protectory *v.* Kearney Tp. Committee, 56 N. J. L. 385, 28 Atl. 1043 ("any tax or assessment"); State *v.* Newark, 36 N. J. L. 478, 13 Am. Rep. 464 [*reversing* 35 N. J. L. 157, 10 Am. Rep. 223] ("taxes or assessments").

Rhode Island.— Swan Point Cemetery *v.* Tripp, 14 R. I. 199, "all taxes and assessments."

Wisconsin.— Milwaukee Electric R., etc.,

4. **Acquisition of Property by Exempt Person or Corporation.** A general grant of exemption from taxation may extend to all property subsequently acquired by the exempt person or corporation, whether previously taxable or not, if such is the manifest intent of the statute;[62] but generally if a railroad or other corporation acquires the property or franchises of a similar corporation, it cannot extend its own exemption from taxation to cover the property so acquired, if that was previously taxable.[63] And even where an institution, such as a church or school, enjoys an exemption from taxes on all the property which it may acquire and hold, still it must assume the payment of taxes assessed for the current fiscal year on any property which it purchases or acquires otherwise.[64]

5. **Transfer of Exemption — a. In General.** Exemption from taxation granted by the legislature to an individual or a corporation is not a franchise, nor is it an estate or interest inherent in or running with the particular property exempted; but it is a mere privilege personal to the grantee; and unless there is express statutory authority therefor, the exemption will not pass to a successor of the corporation or to a person taking the property by sale, assignment, or other transfer.[65] So in construing grants of exemption they will be construed as per-

used synonymously and the company is exempt from payment of all taxes and not merely from paying a license-tax. Bowling Green *v.* Kentucky Masonic Mut. L. Ins. Co., 5 Ky. L. Rep. 697.

62. Northwestern University *v.* Hanberg, 237 Ill. 185, 86 N. E. 734; Proprietors Rural Cemetery *v.* Worcester County, 152 Mass. 408, 25 N. E. 618, 10 L. R. A. 365; Southern R. Co. *v.* Jackson, 38 Miss. 334; Franklin Needle Co. *v.* Franklin, 65 N. H. 177, 18 Atl. 318.

63. State *v.* Baltimore, etc., R. Co., 48 Md. 49; Lake Shore, etc., R. Co. *v.* Grand Rapids, 102 Mich. 374, 60 N. W. 767, 29 L. R. A. 195; State *v.* Northern Pac. R. Co., 32 Minn. 294, 20 N. W. 234; Southwestern R. Co. *v.* Wright, 116 U. S. 231, 6 S. Ct. 375, 29 L. ed. 626; Burlington, etc., R. Co. *v.* Putnam County, 4 Fed. Cas. No. 2,169, 5 Dill. 289. But see Southern R. Co. *v.* Jackson, 38 Miss. 334.

64. McHenry Baptist Church *v.* McNeal, 86 Miss. 22, 38 So. 195; People *v.* Wells, 179 N. Y. 524, 71 N. E. 1136 [*affirming* 92 N. Y. App. Div. 622, 87 N. Y. Suppl. 1143]; Ætna Ins. Co. *v.* New York, 153 N. Y. 331, 47 N. E. 593; Colored Orphans Benefit Assoc. *v.* New York, 104 N. Y. 581, 12 N. E. 279; St. Francis Sisters of Poor *v.* New York, 51 Hun (N. Y.) 355, 3 N. Y. Suppl. 433 [*affirmed* in 112 N. Y. 677, 20 N. E. 411]; People *v.* Sawyer, 27 N. Y. Suppl. 202; Humphreys *v.* Little Sisters of Poor, 7 Ohio Dec. (Reprint) 194, 1 Cinc. L. Bul. 286; Philadelphia *v.* Pennsylvania Co. for Instruction of Blind, 214 Pa. St. 138, 63 Atl. 420; Philadelphia *v.* Barber, 160 Pa. St. 123, 28 Atl. 644. See also St. James Church *v.* New York, 41 Hun (N. Y.) 309; Church of St. Monica *v.* New York, 55 N. Y. Super. Ct. 160. But see Hennepin County *v.* St. Paul, etc., R. Co., 33 Minn. 534, 24 N. W. 196.

65. *Arkansas.*— Arkansas Midland R. Co. *v.* Berry, 44 Ark. 17; Memphis, etc., R. Co. *v.* Berry, 41 Ark. 436.

Connecticut.— New Haven *v.* Sheffield, 30 Conn. 160.

District of Columbia.— Alexandria Canal R., etc., Co. *v.* District of Columbia, 1 Mackey 217.

Florida.— Bloxham *v.* Florida Cent. R. Co., 35 Fla. 625, 17 So. 902.

Iowa.— Long *v.* Olson, 115 Iowa 388, 88 N. W. 933.

Kentucky.— Com. *v.* Nashville, etc., R. Co., 93 Ky. 430, 20 S. W. 383; Com. *v.* Masonic Temple Co., 87 Ky. 349, 8 S. W. 699; Com. *v.* Owensboro, etc., R. Co., 81 Ky. 572; Evansville, etc., R. Co. *v.* Com., 9 Bush 438.

Maryland.—Baltimore, etc., R. Co. *v.* Ocean City, 89 Md. 89, 42 Atl. 922.

Minnesota.— State *v.* Great Northern R. Co., 106 Minn. 303, 119 N. W. 202; State *v.* Chicago, etc., R. Co., 106 Minn. 290, 119 N. W. 211. But see Stevens County *v.* St. Paul, etc., R. Co., 36 Minn. 467, 31 N. W. 942.

Missouri.— State *v.* Chicago, etc., R. Co., 89 Mo. 523, 14 S. W. 522; Lionberger *v.* Rowse, 43 Mo. 67.

New Jersey.— Morris Canal, etc., Co. *v.* State Assessors, 76 N. J. L. 627, 71 Atl. 328.

New York.— Rochester *v.* Rochester R. Co., 182 N. Y. 99, 74 N. E. 953 [*reversing* 98 N. Y. App. Div. 521, 91 N. Y. Suppl. 87].

Tennessee.— State *v.* Mercantile Bank, 95 Tenn. 212, 31 S. W. 989; Nashville, etc., Turnpike Co. *v.* White, 92 Tenn. 370, 22 S. W. 75; Memphis *v.* Phœnix F. & M. Ins. Co., 91 Tenn. 566, 19 S. W. 1044; State *v.* Butler, 15 Lea 104; State *v.* Whitworth, 8 Lea 594; Wilson *v.* Gaines, 9 Baxt. 546; State *v.* Hicks, 9 Yerg. 486, 30 Am. Dec. 423; Wilson *v.* Gaines, 3 Tenn. Ch. 597.

Virginia.—Lake Drummond Canal, etc., Co. *v.* Com., 103 Va. 337, 49 S. E. 506, 68 L. R. A. 92.

United States.— Rochester R. Co. *v.* Rochester, 205 U. S. 236, 7 S. Ct. 469, 51 L. ed. 784; Home Ins. Co. *v.* Tennessee, 161 U. S. 200, 16 S. Ct. 476, 40 L. ed. 670; Phœnix F. & M. Ins. Co. *v.* Tennessee, 161 U. S. 174, 16 S. Ct. 471, 40 L. ed. 660; Mercantile Bank *v.* Tennessee, 161 U. S. 161, 16 S. Ct. 461, 40 L. ed. 656; Picard *v.* East Tennessee R. Co., 130 U. S. 637, 9 S. Ct. 640, 32 L. ed. 1051; Chicago, etc., R. Co. *v.* Missouri, 122 U. S.

formed the basis of the grant [90] or of any of the conditions upon which its continuance depends,[91] by the death of the original grantee,[92] or the diversion of the property to other uses than those in consideration of which it was exempted,[93] and also by a surrender or release of the exemption, either express or implied from acquiescence in the assessment of taxes and their payment without protest.[94]

b. Earning of Specified Income or Dividend. Where exemption from taxation is granted to a corporation until it shall earn net income at a certain rate or declare a dividend, upon the happening of this event the exemption expires and the property becomes liable to taxation; [95] and it is not necessary that there should be any legislative act or resolution declaring the happening of the condition.[96]

9. Revocable and Irrevocable Exemptions — a. In General. It is in the power of a state legislature, unless restrained by some constitutional provision, to exempt property of an individual or corporation from future taxation, in whole or in part, or during a certain period, and such a grant, if plainly expressed and distinctly contractual in its nature and founded upon a consideration, constitutes a binding and irrevocable obligation on the part of the state.[97] But on the other

ation to a person in whose hands it is not exempt, it is not subject to taxation for the current year. Clearwater Timber Co. *v.* Nez Perce County, 155 Fed. 633.

90. See Myers *v.* Akins, 8 Ohio Cir. Ct. 228, 4 Ohio Cir. Dec. 425; Hand *v.* Savannah, etc., R. Co., 12 S. C. 314.

91. Morris Canal, etc., Co. *v.* State Bd. of Assessors, 76 N. J. L. 627, 71 Atl. 328.

92. Kelsey *v.* Badger, 7 Watts (Pa.) 516, holding that donation lands are exempt from taxation only during the life of the soldier who is the original grantee, and that the exemption does not extend to his devisee or heir at law.

93. Electric Traction Co. *v.* New Orleans, 45 La. Ann. 1475, 14 So. 231; Holthaus *v.* Adams County, 74 Nebr. 861, 105 N. W. 632. See also *infra*, IV, E, 2, e, (VII); IV, E, 3, d, (IV).

Use of property for charitable purposes.— Under the charter of a corporation exempting its property and income from taxation "so long as it shall be entirely devoted to Masonic and charitable purposes," a city, seeking to tax the property for a particular year, must show that it was not then used for such purposes. Newport *v.* Masonic Temple Assoc., 103 Ky. 592, 45 S. W. 881, 46 S. W. 697, 20 Ky. L. Rep. 266.

94. State *v.* Wright, 41 N. J. L. 478; New Jersey *v.* Wright, 117 U. S. 648, 6 S. Ct. 907, 29 L. ed. 1021. See also Hand *v.* Savannah, etc., R. Co., 17 S. C. 219.

95. *Arkansas.*— St. Louis, etc., R. Co. *v.* Loftin, 30 Ark. 693.

Connecticut.— State *v.* Norwich, etc., R. Co., 30 Conn. 290.

North Carolina.— Richmond, etc., R. Co. *v.* Brogden, 74 N. C. 707.

West Virginia.— Baltimore, etc., R. Co. *v.* Marshall County, 3 W. Va. 319.

United States.— Parmley *v.* St. Louis, etc., R. Co., 18 Fed. Cas. No. 10,768, 3 Dill. 25.

See 45 Cent. Dig. tit. "Taxation," § 336.

Effect of increase of capital.—Where a railroad company is exempted from taxation until its tolls are sufficient to pay a dividend of six per cent on its capital stock, and subsequently the amount of its capital stock is increased by legislative authority, the company is not liable to taxation until its tolls are sufficient to pay a dividend of six per cent upon the total amount of capital stock as increased. State *v.* Norwich, etc., R. Co., 30 Conn. 290.

96. Baltimore, etc., R. Co. *v.* Marshall County, 3 W. Va. 319.

97. *Arizona.*— Bennett *v.* Nichols, 9 Ariz. 138, 80 Pac. 392.

Connecticut.— Osborne *v.* Humphrey, 7 Conn. 335.

Georgia.— State *v.* Western, etc., R. Co., 66 Ga. 563.

Kentucky.— Hodgenville, etc., R. Co. *v.* Com., 34 S. W. 1075, 17 Ky. L. Rep. 1410; Com. *v.* Louisville, etc., R. Co., 31 S. W. 464, 17 Ky. L. Rep. 405.

Missouri.— Mechanics' Bank *v.* Kansas City, 73 Mo. 555.

New Hampshire.— *In re* Opinion of Ct., 58 N. H. 623.

Ohio.— Cincinnati Commercial Bank *v.* Bowman, 1 Handy 246.

Pennsylvania.— Coney *v.* Owen, 6 Watts 435. But see Mott *v.* Pennsylvania R. Co., 30 Pa. St. 9, 72 Am. Dec. 664, holding that the legislature has no power to grant an irrevocable exemption from taxation which will be binding upon future legislatures.

Tennessee.—Knoxville, etc., R. Co. *v.* Hicks, 9 Baxt. 442.

Texas.— International, etc., R. Co. *v.* State, 75 Tex. 356, 12 S. W. 685.

Wisconsin.— Weston *v.* Shawano County, 44 Wis. 242.

United States.— Northwestern University *v.* People, 99 U. S. 309, 25 L. ed. 387 [*reversing* 80 Ill. 333, 22 Am. Rep. 187]; Jefferson Branch Bank *v.* Skelley, 1 Black 436, 17 L. ed. 173; Louisville, etc., R. Co. *v.* Gaines, 3 Fed. 266, 2 Flipp. 621.

Canada.— Alexander *v.* Huntsville, 24 Ont. 665. See also Henderson *v.* Stisted Tp., 17 Ont. 673.

See 45 Cent. Dig. tit. "Taxation," § 338.

Exemptions in corporate charters see *infra*, IV, C, 9, b.

Constitutional prohibition.— Where the state has adopted a constitution which pro-

where the exemption is contained in a corporate charter it may lack the elements of a binding contract and constitute a mere gratuity subject to repeal.[3]

c. Reservation of Right to Alter or Amend. If the legislature, in creating a corporation, reserves to itself the right to alter or amend the charter, or if a similar reservation is embodied in the general statute under which corporations are organized, this constitutes a part of the contract itself, and consequently a subsequent revocation or repeal of an exemption from taxation enjoyed by the corporation is not a violation of the obligation of the contract, but is within the rightful power of the legislature.[4] And the same is true, in the absence of such a

Louisiana.— Municipality No. 1 *v.* Louisiana State Bank, 5 La. Ann. 394.

Maine.— State *v.* Knox, etc., R. Co., 78 Me. 92, 2 Atl. 846; State *v.* Dexter, etc., R. Co., 69 Me 44

Maryland.— Baltimore City Appeal Tax Ct. *v.* Baltimore Cemetery Co., 50 Md. 432; Baltimore *v.* Baltimore, etc., R. Co., 6 Gill 288, 48 Am. Dec. 531.

Minnesota.—State *v.* Sioux City, etc., R. Co., 82 Minn. 158, 84 N. W. 794.

Mississippi.— Mobile, etc., R. Co. *v.* Moseley, 52 Miss. 127; O'Donnell *v.* Bailey, 24 Miss. 386.

Missouri.— State *v.* Westminster College, 175 Mo. 52, 74 S. W. 990; State *v.* Mission Free School, 162 Mo. 332, 62 S. W. 998; St. Vincent's College *v.* Schaefer, 104 Mo. 261, 16 S. W. 395; State *v.* Hannibal, etc., R. Co., 101 Mo. 136, 13 S. W. 505; Mechanics' Bank *v.* Kansas City, 73 Mo. 555; Scotland County *v.* Missouri, etc., R. Co., 65 Mo. 123.

New Jersey.— Cooper Hospital *v.* Camden, 68 N. J. L. 691, 54 Atl. 419; State *v.* Railroad Taxation Com'r, 37 N. J. L. 240; Douglass *v.* State, 34 N. J. L. 485; State *v.* Berry, 17 N. J. L. 80.

New York.— Raquette Falls Land Co. *v.* Hoyt, 109 N. Y. App. Div. 119, 95 N. Y. Suppl. 1029 [*affirmed* in 187 N. Y. 550, 80 N. E. 1119]; People *v.* Dohling, 6 N. Y. App. Div. 86, 39 N. Y. Suppl. 765.

North Carolina.— See Raleigh, etc., R. Co. *v.* Reid, 64 N. C. 155.

Ohio.— Matheny *v.* Golden, 5 Ohio St. 361; Cincinnati Commercial Bank *v.* Bowman, 1 Handy 246, 12 Ohio Dec. (Reprint) 125.

Pennsylvania.—Wagner Free Inst. *v.* Philadelphia, 132 Pa. St. 612, 19 Atl. 297, 19 Am. St. Rep. 613; Iron City Bank *v.* Pittsburgh, 37 Pa. St. 340; Mattis *v.* Ruth, 1 Lack. Leg. N. 311. See also Com. *v.* Pottsville Water Co., 94 Pa. St. 516; Erie R. Co. *v.* Com., 3 Brewst. 368.

Rhode Island.— Brown University *v.* Granger, 19 R. I. 704, 36 Atl. 720, 36 L. R. A. 847.

South Carolina.— State *v.* Charleston, 5 Rich. 561.

Tennessee.— Knoxville, etc., R. Co. *v.* Hicks, 9 Baxt. 442; Union Bank *v.* State, 9 Yerg. 490.

Vermont.— See Herrick *v.* Randolph, 13 Vt. 525.

United States.— Gulf, etc., R. Co. *v.* Hewes, 183 U. S. 66, 22 S. Ct. 26, 46 L. ed. 86; Central R., etc., Co. *v.* Wright, 164 U. S. 327, 17 S. Ct. 80, 41 L. ed. 454; St. Anna's Asylum *v.* New Orleans, 105 U. S. 362, 26 L. ed. 1128; Northwestern University *v.* People, 99 U. S. 309, 25 L. ed. 387; Erie R. Co. *v.* Pennsylvania, 21 Wall. 492, 22 L. ed. 595; Pacific R. Co. *v.* Maguire, 20 Wall. 36, 22 L. ed. 282; Minot *v.* Philadelphia, etc., R. Co., 18 Wall. 206, 21 L. ed. 888; Humphrey *v.* Pegues, 16 Wall. 244, 21 L. ed. 326; Wilmington, etc., R. Co. *v.* Reid, 13 Wall. 264, 20 L. ed. 568; Jefferson Branch Bank *v.* Skelley, 1 Black 436, 17 L. ed. 173; Ohio L. Ins., etc., Co. *v.* Debolt, 16 How. 416, 14 L. ed. 997; Gordon *v.* Appeal Tax Ct., 3 How. 133, 11 L. ed. 529; Georgia R., etc., Co. *v.* Wright, 132 Fed. 912; Louisiana Citizens' Bank *v.* Orleans Parish Assessors, 54 Fed. 73; Tennessee *v.* Bank of Commerce, 53 Fed. 735; Yazoo, etc., R. Co. *v.* Levee Com'rs, 37 Fed. 24.

See 45 Cent. Dig. tit. "Taxation," § 399.

Grant of exemption subsequent to charter.—An exemption from taxation conferred upon a corporation subsequent to its creation, and not in the nature of an amendment to its charter, nor based on any new consideration, may be repealed. St. Louis, etc., R. Co. *v.* Loftin, 30 Ark. 693; Grand Lodge F. & A. M. *v.* New Orleans, 44 La. Ann. 659, 11 So. 148.

No exemption from municipal taxation of the business of a street railway company results from provisions in its agreement with the municipality preserving its easements for railway purposes in land to be conveyed by it to the city, and granting it the right to construct and operate its railway through certain streets, subject to the control and regulation of the city officers. Savannah, etc., R. Co. *v.* Savannah, 198 U. S. 392, 25 S. Ct. 690, 49 L. ed. 1097. And see New York *v.* State Bd. of Tax Com'rs, 199 U. S. 53, 25 S. Ct. 715, 50 L. ed. 85.

3. Hanover Tp. *v.* Newark Camp Meeting Assoc., 76 N. J. L. 65, 68 Atl. 753 [*affirmed* in 76 N. J. L. 827, 71 Atl. 1134]; Cooper Hospital *v.* Camden, 68 N. J. L. 691, 54 Atl. 419.

Each case depends on its own facts. In every case there is present the element of an agreement evinced by the acceptance of the charter, and the question necessarily is whether there is such a consideration as will make the agreement a binding contract. Hanover Tp. *v.* Newark Camp Meeting Assoc., 76 N. J. L. 65, 68 Atl. 753 [*affirmed* in 76 N. J. L. 827, 71 Atl. 1134].

Necessity for consideration generally see *infra*, IV, C, 9, d.

4. *Georgia.*— Macon, etc., R. Co. *v.* Goldsmith, 62 Ga. 463. But see Western, etc., R. Co. *v.* State, 54 Ga. 428.

specifically exempted by law are subject to pay taxes.[57] In some jurisdictions, however, statutes have from time to time been enacted exempting either entirely or to a limited extent certain classes of persons,[58] such as ministers of the gospel,[59] soldiers,[60] or volunteer firemen.[61] But an exemption of this kind which is personal in its nature does not extend to the family of the person exempt,[62] or pass to one who inherits or acquires the property of such person.[63]

3. Corporations and Their Property — a. In General.[64] In pursuance of the rule of strict construction of statutes granting exemptions,[65] an exemption accorded to a corporation or to corporations of a particular class will be carefully limited to the terms of the grant;[66] and, although a general exemption of a corporation's property will cover all the property necessary to the exercise of its franchise or the accomplishment of the purposes of its incorporation,[67] it is not so as to property

57. Smith *v.* Macon, 20 Ark. 17 (lands of infants and married women are subject to taxation); Gilliland *v.* Citadel Square Baptist Church, 33 S. C. 164, 11 S. E. 684 (land not exempt because owner's name is unknown); Westville *v.* Munro, 32 Nova Scotia 511 (widow's exemption).

58. See the statutes of the several states; and the cases cited *infra,* notes 59–61.

Exemption of Indians.— See Farrington *v.* Wilson, 29 Wis. 383; *In re* New York Indians, 5 Wall. (U. S.) 761, 18 L. ed. 708.

Negroes.—An early Connecticut statute exempted from taxation the property of "persons of color." Johnson *v.* Norwich, 29 Conn. 407. See also Copp *v.* Norwich, 24 Conn. 28, holding that the exemption did not apply in the case of property conveyed by one white person to another in trust for the support of a negro.

The act for the relief of certain persons in the American bottom and granting certain exemptions from taxation applied only to residents whose farms or improvements were submerged or whose crops were damaged or destroyed by the overflow of the Mississippi river and not to owners of town lots in such territory. Wettig *v.* Bowman, 47 Ill. 17.

59. Baldwin *v.* McClinch, 1 Me. 102; Gridley *v.* Clark, 2 Pick. (Mass.) 403; Ruggles *v.* Kimball, 12 Mass. 337; Kidder *v.* French, Smith (N. H.) 155; People *v.* Peterson, 31 Hun (N. Y.) 421; Prosser *v.* Secor, 5 Barb. (N. Y.) 607.

To be entitled to the exemption the minister should be a settled minister over some particular society entitled to his services (Ruggles *v.* Kimball, 12 Mass. 337; Kidder *v.* French, Smith (N. H.) 155), although it is not necessary that the society should be under any legal obligation to pay him any fixed salary (Baldwin *v.* McClinch, 1 Me. 102); and it has also been held that one who has been a minister but has withdrawn from the active duties of his calling on account of age and infirmity is entitled to the exemption if he has not taken up any other occupation (People *v.* Peterson, 31 Hun (N. Y.) 421).

60. White *v.* Marion, 139 Iowa 479, 117 N. W. 254; People *v.* Brooklyn Assessors, 18 Hun (N. Y.) 386 [*affirmed* in 84 N. Y. 610]; Crawford *v.* Burrell Tp., 53 Pa. St. 219. See also Chauvenet *v.* Anne Arundel County, 3 Md. 259, property of officers residing within the grounds of the naval academy at Annapolis.

Valuation of property.— Under the Iowa statute giving soldiers an exemption of eight hundred dollars unless the soldier or his wife owns property of the actual value of five thousand dollars, such property for the purpose of determining the right to the exemption should be taken at its actual and not at its assessed value, and in valuing his property all property owned by him should be included, whether it is subject to taxation or exempt, and the value of a life-estate should also be included. White *v.* Marion, 139 Iowa 479, 117 N. W. 254.

But an exemption from sale under execution, or by virtue of any deed of trust or mortgage, or judgment or decree of any court, does not constitute an exemption from taxation or prevent a sale of the property for non-payment of taxes. Slane *v.* McCarroll, 40 Iowa 61.

61. See People *v.* Cahill, 181 N. Y. 403, 74 N. E. 422 [*affirming* 102 N. Y. App. Div. 620, 92 N. Y. Suppl. 1141], holding, however, that the statutes exempting volunteer firemen of the municipality of Watertown from taxation to the amount of five hundred dollars were intended to apply only to municipal and not to state and county taxes.

62. Crawford *v.* Burrell Tp., 53 Pa. St. 219, holding that a soldier's exemption is a personal privilege and does not extend to his wife.

63. Platt *v.* Rice, 10 Watts (Pa.) 352.

Transfer of exemption generally see *supra,* IV, C, 5.

64. **Liability to taxation** generally see *supra,* III, B.

65. See *supra,* IV, C, 2, a.

66. New Orleans *v.* New Orleans Canal, etc., Co., 32 La. Ann. 104; Singer Mfg. Co. *v.* Heppenheimer, 58 N. J. L. 633, 34 Atl. 1061, 32 L. R. A. 643; Union Canal Co. *v.* Dauphin County, 3 Brewst. (Pa.) 124; Gordon *v.* Appeal Tax Ct., 3 How. (U. S.) 133, 11 L. ed. 529.

A charter provision exempting the stock of a corporation from taxation implies that nothing but the stock shall be exempt and does not exempt the corporation from the payment of a license-tax. New Orleans *v.* New Orleans Canal, etc., Co., 32 La. Ann. 104.

67. Anne Arundel County *v.* Annapolis,

from taxation on their shares,[81] but it does not also exempt the corporation from taxation on its capital stock,[82] or on its surplus and undivided profits,[83] or from the payment of an occupation or privilege tax.[84] In order to avoid what is sometimes regarded as double taxation,[85] the statutes frequently provide expressly for the taxation of corporations upon their capital or property and the exemption of the shareholders from taxation on their shares of stock, or *vice versa*;[86] but, strictly speaking, this is rather a mere regulation as to the mode of taxing substantially the same property than an exemption from taxation.[87] It is ordinarily held that an exemption of the capital or capital stock of a corporation includes the property represented thereby, or such as is essential to the carrying on of the corporate purposes of the corporation;[88] but this is not necessarily the case, the question being dependent upon the intention of the legislature.[89] It has been held that a charter provision exempting the stock of a corporation will not exempt the corporation from paying a license-tax.[90]

c. Consolidation of Exempt Corporations. Where a consolidation of two corporations takes place, one of which enjoyed an immunity from taxation, its property continues to be exempt in the hands of the consolidated company, if there is nothing in the statutes to prevent;[91] and conversely, all that part of the property which belonged to the non-exempt corporation continues liable to taxation as before.[92] But where the effect of the consolidation is to dissolve each of

81. Union, etc., Bank *v.* Memphis, 101 Tenn. 154, 46 S. W. 557; State *v.* Hernando Ins. Co., 97 Tenn. 85, 36 S. W. 721; Shelby County *v.* Union, etc., Bank, 161 U. S. 149, 16 S. Ct. 558, 40 L. ed. 650; Bank of Commerce *v.* Tennessee, 161 U. S. 134, 16 S. Ct. 456, 40 L. ed. 645; Farrington *v.* Tennessee, 95 U. S. 679, 24 L. ed. 558 [*reversing* 8 Baxt. (Tenn.) 539].

82. Union, etc., Bank *v.* Memphis, 101 Tenn. 154, 46 S. W. 557; State *v.* Hernando Ins. Co., 97 Tenn. 85, 36 S. W. 721 [*overruling* Memphis *v.* Union, etc., Bank, 91 Tenn. 546, 19 S. W. 758]; Shelby County *v.* Union, etc., Bank, 161 U. S. 149, 16 S. Ct. 558, 40 L. ed. 650; Union, etc., Bank *v.* Memphis, 111 Fed. 561, 49 C. C. A. 455 [*reversed* on other grounds in 189 U. S. 71, 23 S. Ct. 604, 47 L. ed. 712].

83. Shelby County *v.* Union, etc., Bank, 161 U. S. 149, 16 S. Ct. 558, 40 L. ed. 650; Bank of Commerce *v.* Tennessee, 161 U. S. 134, 16 S. Ct. 456, 40 L. ed. 645.

84. Union, etc., Bank *v.* Memphis, 101 Tenn. 154, 46 S. W. 557.

85. See McIver *v.* Robinson, 53 Ala. 456; Jersey City Gaslight Co. *v.* Jersey City, 46 N. J. L. 194; and, generally, *supra*, II, C, 5, c.

86. See McIver *v.* Robinson, 53 Ala. 456; Jersey City Gaslight Co. *v.* Jersey City, 46 N. J. L. 194; Carroll *v.* Alsup, 107 Tenn. 257, 64 S. W. 193; and, generally, *supra*, III, B, 1, g, j.

The stock-holder's exemption cannot be claimed in a case where the corporation itself is not taxed, as in the case of national banks. McIver *v.* Robinson, 53 Ala. 456.

87. Jersey City Gaslight Co. *v.* Jersey City, 46 N. J. L. 194; Carroll *v.* Alsup, 107 Tenn. 257, 64 S. W. 193.

88. *Connecticut.*— New Haven *v.* City Bank, 31 Conn. 106.

Georgia.— Rome R. Co. *v.* Rome, 14 Ga. 275.

Indiana.— Connersville *v.* State Bank, 16 Ind. 105.

Maryland.— Anne Arundel County Com'rs *v.* Annapolis, etc., R. Co., 47 Md. 592 [*affirmed* in 103 U. S. 1, 26 L. ed. 359]; Baltimore *v.* Baltimore, etc., R. Co., 6 Gill 288, 48 Am. Dec. 531.

Missouri.— Scotland County *v.* Missouri, etc., R. Co., 65 Mo. 123.

But see New Orleans Second Municipality *v.* Commercial Bank, 5 Rob. (La.) 151, holding that a provision in the charter of a bank exempting "the capital" of the bank from taxation does not exempt real or personal property of the bank, nothing being exempt except the capital paid in by the stockholders.

89. Central R., etc., Co. *v.* Wright, 164 U. S. 327, 17 S. Ct. 80, 41 L. ed. 454.

90. New Orleans *v.* New Orleans Canal, etc., Co., 32 La. Ann. 104. But see Grand Gulf, etc., R. Co. *v.* Buck, 53 Miss. 246, holding that a charter provision exempting "the capital stock" of a corporation "and all other property" belonging to it prohibits the legislature from imposing a privilege tax.

91. *Kentucky.*— Louisville, etc., R. Co. *v.* Com., 89 Ky. 531, 12 S. W. 1064, 11 Ky. L. Rep. 734.

Mississippi.— Louisville, etc., R. Co. *v.* Taylor, 68 Miss. 361, 8 So. 675.

New Jersey.— Camden, etc., R., etc., Co. *v.* Woodruff, 36 N. J. L. 94.

Texas.— Campbell *v.* Wiggins, 2 Tex. Civ. App. 1, 20 S. W. 730.

United States.— Tennessee *v.* Whitworth, 117 U. S. 139, 6 S. Ct. 649, 29 L. ed. 833; Branch *v.* Charleston, 92 U. S. 677, 23 L. ed. 750; Tomlinson *v.* Branch, 15 Wall. 460, 21 L. ed. 189.

See 45 Cent. Dig. tit. "Taxation," § 365.

Contra.— Arkansas' Midland R. Co. *v.* Berry, 44 Ark. 17; St. Louis, etc., R. Co. *v.* Berry, 41 Ark. 509.

92. State *v.* Philadelphia, etc., R. Co., 45

(II) *Branch Lines.* An exemption from taxation granted generally to a railroad does not ordinarily extend to a branch line which it constructs under authority given by the charter or a subsequent statute,[16] especially if the branch is substantially an independent road, having different stock-holders and a separate treasury.[17]

(III) *Right of Way and Other Realty.* Under the terms ordinarily used in the statutes, an exemption from taxation granted to a railway will include its road-bed and right of way,[18] and the land used for its termini,[19] and generally also any real estate which is necessary to the proper operation of the road and is actually in use for such purposes.[20] But a contract by the state to exempt railroad lands from taxation will not be permitted to extend in scope beyond what the terms of the concession clearly require; [21] and an exemption cannot be claimed in respect to any lands held and owned by the company which are not needed for railroad purposes and are not actually devoted to such uses,[22] except perhaps

taxation as property reasonably necessary for the running of trains and transaction of railroad business, where such line is used for commercial purposes for compensation. Minneapolis, etc., R. Co. *v.* Oppegard, (N. D. 1908) 118 N. W. 830.

16. Baltimore, etc., R. Co. *v.* District of Columbia, 3 MacArthur (D. C.) 122; Wilmington, etc., R. Co. *v.* Alsbrook, 110 N. C. 137, 14 S. E. 652 [*affirmed* in 146 U. S. 279, 13 S. Ct. 72, 36 L. ed. 972]; Southwestern R. Co. *v.* Wright, 116 U. S. 231, 6 S. Ct. 375, 29 L. ed. 626 [*affirming* 68 Ga. 311]. See also Wright *v.* Southwestern R. Co., 64 Ga. 783. But see Atlantic, etc., R. Co. *v.* Allen, 15 Fla. 637.

17. State *v.* Chicago, etc., R. Co., 89 Mo. 523, 14 S. W. 522; Chicago, etc., R. Co. *v.* Missouri, 122 U. S. 561, 7 S. Ct. 1300, 30 L. ed. 1135; *In re* Canadian Pac. R. Co., 5 Northwest. Terr. 192.

18. *Arizona.*— Atlantic, etc., R. Co. *v.* Yavapai County, (1889) 21 Pac. 768; Atlantic, etc., R. Co. *v.* Lesueur, 2 Ariz. 428, 19 Pac. 157, 1 L. R. A. 244.

Massachusetts.— Charlestown *v.* Middlesex County, 1 Allen 199; Worcester *v.* Western R. Corp., 4 Metc. 564.

Montana.— Northern Pac. R. Co. *v.* Carland, 5 Mont. 146, 3 Pac. 134.

New Jersey.— State *v.* Wetherill, 41 N. J. L. 147; State *v.* Middle Tp. Collector, 38 N. J. L. 270.

New Mexico.— U. S. Trust Co. *v.* Territory, 10 N. M. 416, 62 Pac. 987.

North Carolina.— Richmond, etc., R. Co. *v.* Alamance County, 84 N. C. 504.

United States.— New Mexico *v.* U. S. Trust Co., 174 U. S. 545, 19 S. Ct. 784, 43 L. ed. 1079.

Canada.— Great Western R. Co. *v.* Rouse, 15 U. C. Q. B. 168.

See 45 Cent. Dig. tit. "Taxation," § 373.

19. State *v.* Fuller, 40 N. J. L. 328; State *v.* Camden, 38 N. J. L. 299. See also *In re* United New Jersey R., etc., Co., 75 N. J. L. 334, 68 Atl. 167.

20. *Michigan.*— Grand Rapids, etc., R. Co. *v.* Grand Rapids, 137 Mich. 587, 100 N. W. 1012; Dix *v.* Flint, etc., R. Co., 119 Mich. 682, 78 N. W. 889.

New Jersey.— New Jersey Junction R. Co. *v.* Jersey City, 63 N. J. L. 120, 43 Atl. 577; State *v.* Woodruff, 36 N. J. L. 94.

Texas.— Anderson County *v.* Kennedy, 58 Tex. 616.

Wisconsin.— State *v.* Willcuts, 140 Wis. 448, 122 N. W. 1048; Merrill R., etc., Co. *v.* Merrill, 119 Wis. 249, 96 N. W. 686; Wisconsin Cent. R. Co. *v.* Lincoln County, 57 Wis. 137, 15 N. W. 121.

United States.— McHenry *v.* Alford, 168 U. S. 651, 18 S. Ct. 242, 42 L. ed. 614.

A stone quarry owned by a railroad company and which supplies the stone and gravel for ballasting the company's tracks is exempt from taxation whether the quarry work is done by the railroad company or by a lessee. People *v.* Illinois Cent. R. Co., 231 Ill. 151, 83 N. E. 132.

Gravel land purchased to provide materials for the repair of the railroad are exempt from taxation, and the exemption also includes a branch line from the gravel pits to the main line. State *v.* Hancock, 35 N. J. L. 537 [*reversing* 33 N. J. L. 315].

21. Tucker *v.* Ferguson, 22 Wall. (U. S.) 527, 22 L. ed. 805. And see Vermont Cent. R. Co. *v.* Burlington, 28 Vt. 193; Chesapeake, etc., R. Co. *v.* Virginia, 94 U. S. 718, 24 L. ed. 310.

22. *Delaware.*— Philadelphia, etc., R. Co. *v.* Neary, 5 Del. Ch. 600, 8 Atl. 363.

Georgia.— Wright *v.* Southwestern R. Co., 64 Ga. 783; Bibb County Ordinary *v.* Central R., etc., Co., 40 Ga. 646.

Michigan.— Grand Rapids, etc., R. Co. *v.* Grand Rapids, 137 Mich. 587, 100 N. W. 1012.

Mississippi.— Lewis *v.* Vicksburg, etc., R. Co., 67 Miss. 82, 6 So. 773.

New Jersey.— State *v.* Middle Tp. Collector, 38 N. J. L. 270; Camden, etc., Transp. Co. *v.* Woodruff, 36 N. J. L. 94; New Jersey R., etc., Co. *v.* Newark Collectors, 25 N. J. L. 315. See Pennsylvania R. Co. *v.* Leggett, 41 N. J. L. 319, as to distinction between needful and actual use of land for railroad purposes and indispensable uses.

North Carolina.— Richmond, etc., R. Co. *v.* Alamance County, 76 N. C. 212.

North Dakota.— Fargo, etc., R. Co. *v.* Brewer, 3 N. D. 34, 53 N. W. 177.

United States.— Ford *v.* Delta, etc., Land Co., 43 Fed. 181.

freight and passenger stations,[33] engine and car houses,[34] work shops and repair shops,[35] office buildings,[36] bridges,[37] wharves, piers, and docks.[38] The exemption may also include a grain elevator, provided it is necessary for use in receiving and transferring grain shipped over the company's road, although not where the company uses it for business of a general warehouseman.[39] As to railroad hotels, the rule is that such a structure may be exempt, as property "necessary" to the operation of the road, if it is needed for the safety and convenience of the traveling public and is used exclusively for persons arriving and departing on the company's trains, but not where it is conducted for the accommodation of the general public or is maintained as a place of summer resort.[40]

(VI) *ROLLING-STOCK AND EQUIPMENT.* The cars, engines, and other rolling-stock of a railroad company have been repeatedly held to be within the terms of a general exemption of its property.[41] On the other hand, it has been

33. *Massachusetts.*— Worcester *v.* Western R. Corp., 4 Metc. 564. See also Norwich, etc., R. Co. *v.* Worcester County, 151 Mass. 69, 23 N. E. 721.

Mississippi.— See Vicksburg, etc., R. Co. *v.* Lewis, 68 Miss. 29, 10 So. 32.

Montana.— Northern Pac. R. Co. *v.* Carland, 5 Mont. 146, 3 Pac. 134.

North Carolina.— Richmond, etc., R. Co. *v.* Alamance, 84 N. C. 504.

Pennsylvania.— Northampton County *v.* Lehigh Coal, etc., Co., 75 Pa. St. 461.

Virginia.— Richmond *v.* Richmond, etc., R. Co., 21 Gratt. 604.

Wisconsin.— Milwaukee, etc., R. Co. *v.* Milwaukee, 34 Wis. 271.

See 45 Cent. Dig. tit. "Taxation," § 374.

34. Worcester *v.* Western R. Corp., 4 Metc. (Mass.) 564; Vicksburg, etc., R. Co. *v.* Bradley, 66 Miss. 518, 6 So. 321. But see Boston, etc., R. Co. *v.* Cambridge, 8 Cush. (Mass.) 237, where more land was used for such purposes than the company was authorized to appropriate.

35. Northern Pac. R. Co. *v.* Carland, 5 Mont. 146, 3 Pac. 134; Richmond, etc., R. Co. *v.* Alamance, 84 N. C. 504; North Carolina R. Co. *v.* Alamance, 77 N. C. 4. See also Allegheny Valley R. Co. *v.* Verona School Dist., 29 Pittsb. Leg. J. N. S. (Pa.) 314, holding that where a railroad company's shops were used both for repairs on rolling-stock and also for the building of new stock, such shops were exempt from taxation only in the proportion that the repair business bore to the whole work.

36. Richmond, etc., R. Co. *v.* Alamance, 84 N. C. 504; Pennsylvania R. Co.'s Appeal, 3 Pa. Co. Ct. 162.

37. Central R. Co. *v.* Mutchler, 41 N. J. L. 96; Central Vermont R. Co. *v.* St. Johns, 14 Can. Sup. Ct. 288 [*affirmed* in 14 App. Cas. 590].

38. State *v.* Baltimore, etc., R. Co., 48 Md. 49; Chicago, etc., R. Co. *v.* Bayfield County, 87 Wis. 188, 58 N. W. 245. But see St. Louis County *v.* St. Paul, etc., R. Co., 45 Minn. 510, 48 N. W. 334, holding that a wharf owned by a railroad company but leased to a tenant to be used in selling and shipping coal is not exempt, although the lease binds the tenant to ship a certain quantity of coal over the lines of the railroad.

39. *Illinois.*— Illinois Cent. R. Co. *v.* People, 119 Ill. 137, 6 N. E. 451; *In re* Swigert, 119 Ill. 83, 6 N. E. 469.

Maryland.— State *v.* Baltimore, etc., R. Co., 48 Md. 49.

Michigan.— Detroit Union R. Depot, etc., Co. *v.* Detroit, 88 Mich. 347, 50 N. W. 302.

New Jersey.— *In re* Erie R. Co., 65 N. J. L. 608, 48 Atl. 601; Pennsylvania R. Co. *v.* Jersey City, 49 N. J. L. 540, 9 Atl. 782, 60 Am. Rep. 648.

Tennessee.— State *v.* Nashville, etc., R. Co., 86 Tenn. 438, 6 S. W. 880.

Wisconsin.— Chicago, etc., R. Co. *v.* Douglas County, 122 Wis. 273, 99 N. W. 1030; Chicago, etc., R. Co. *v.* Bayfield County, 87 Wis. 188, 58 N. W. 245; Milwaukee, etc., R. Co. *v.* Milwaukee, 34 Wis. 271.

See 45 Cent. Dig. tit. "Taxation," § 374.

40. State *v.* Baltimore, etc., R. Co., 48 Md. 49; Hennepin County *v.* St. Paul, etc., R. Co., 42 Minn. 238, 44 N. W. 63; Day *v.* Joiner, 6 Baxt. (Tenn.) 441 (but ticket offices in a hotel building owned by a railroad may be exempt, although the hotel itself is conducted as a source of profit to the company, and therefore is not exempt); Chicago, etc., R. Co. *v.* Crawford County, 48 Wis. 666, 5 N. W. 3; Milwaukee, etc., R. Co. *v.* Crawford County, 29 Wis. 116. See also *In re* United New Jersey R., etc., Co., 75 N. J. L. 334, 68 Atl. 167.

41. Mobile, etc., R. Co. *v.* Moseley, 52 Miss. 127.

Rolling-stock used on another road.— Rolling-stock owned by one railroad company whose property is exempt from taxation is not exempt where it is wholly employed in operating another road, although the company owning the rolling-stock is a stockholder in such road. Raleigh, etc., R. Co. *v.* Wake County, 87 N. C. 414.

Machinery, tools, and implements used in the manufacture and repair of cars and engines are exempt from taxation. Richmond, etc., R. Co. *v.* Alamance, 84 N. C. 504.

Horses and stables being indispensable to the operation of a horse-car passenger railway are exempt from taxation. Northampton County *v.* Easton, etc., Pass. R. Co., 8 Pa. Co. Ct. 442. See also People's Pass. R. Co. *v.* Taylor, 22 Pa. Super. Ct. 156. But see

meaning of such terms.[70] And a corporation which owns patents, and licenses other companies, in which it is a stock-holder, to use them in manufacturing, is not a manufacturing corporation within the exemption laws.[71]

(III) *CORPORATIONS FOR MANUFACTURE OF PARTICULAR COMMODITIES.* In quite a number of the states, instead of according an exemption from taxation to manufacturing corporations generally, this privilege is accorded to manufacturing companies engaged in particular lines of business, such as companies which are engaged in manufacturing furniture and other articles of wood,[72] paper and

63 N. Y. Suppl. 76. Mixing paints by a process which results in a new commodity of value, recognized by a distinctive name, different from any of its ingredients, and produced by the use of capital, labor, and machinery. People *v.* Roberts, 51 N. Y. App. Div. 77, 64 N. Y. Suppl. 494. Making artificial ice by frigorific process. People *v.* Knickerbocker Ice Co., 99 N. Y. 181, 1 N. E. 669. But *compare* Greenville Ice, etc., Co. *v.* Greenville, 69 Miss. 86, 10 So. 574. Working fire clay into brick, tiles, and other articles. Com. *v.* Savage Fire Brick Co., 157 Pa. St. 512, 27 Atl. 374. Steam flouring mill. Carlin *v.* Western Assur. Co., 57 Md. 515, 40 Am. Rep. 440. Building locomotive engines. Norris *v.* Com., 27 Pa. St. 494.

70. See the cases cited *infra*, this note.

Cutting and storing natural ice.— Hittinger *v.* Westford, 135 Mass. 258; People *v.* Knickerbocker Ice Co., 99 N. Y. 181, 1 N. E. 669. *Compare* Atty.-Gen. *v.* Lorman, 59 Mich. 157, 26 N. W. 311, 60 Am. Rep. 287.

Generating electric light, heat, and power.— Frederick Electric Light, etc., Co. *v.* Frederick City, 84 Md. 599, 36 Atl. 362, 36 L. R. A. 130; Williams *v.* Park, 72 N. H. 305, 56 Atl. 463, 64 L. R. A. 33; Electric Storage Battery Co. *v.* State Bd. of Assessors, 61 N. J. L. 289, 41 Atl. 1117; Com. *v.* Edison Electric Light, etc., Co., 170 Pa. St. 231, 32 Atl. 419; Com. *v.* Brush Electric Light Co., 145 Pa. St. 147, 22 Atl. 844; Com. *v.* Northern Electric Light, etc., Co., 145 Pa. St. 105, 22 Atl. 839, 14 L. R. A. 107; Com. *v.* Edison Electric Light, etc., Co., 1 Dauph. Co. Rep. (Pa.) 127. *Contra*, People *v.* Wemple, 129 N. Y. 543, 29 N. E. 808, 14 L. R. A. 708; People *v.* Campbell, 88 Hun (N. Y.) 527, 34 N. Y. Suppl. 711.

Generating and selling steam heat.— Com. *v.* Arrott Mills Co., 145 Pa. St. 69, 22 Atl. 243.

Laundry.— Com. *v.* Keystone Laundry Co., 203 Pa. St. 289, 52 Atl. 326; Com. *v.* Barnes Bros. Co., 26 Pa. Co. Ct. 423.

Mining and quarrying.—Wellington *v.* Belmont, 164 Mass. 142, 41 N. E. 62; Byers *v.* Franklin Coal Co., 106 Mass. 131; People *v.* Horn Silver Min. Co., 105 N. Y. 76, 11 N. E. 155; Com. *v.* Juniata Coke Co., 157 Pa. St. 507, 27 Atl. 373, 22 L. R. A. 232; Com. *v.* Lackawanna Iron, etc., Co., 129 Pa. St. 346, 18 Atl. 133; Com. *v.* Thomas Iron Co., 12 Pa. Co. Ct. 654; Com. *v.* Coplay Iron Co., 11 Pa. Co. Ct. 295; Com. *v.* East Bangor Consol. Slate Co., 10 Pa. Co. Ct. 363; Horn Silver Min. Co. *v.* New York, 143 U. S. 305, 12 S. Ct. 403, 36 L. ed. 164; *In re* Rollins Gold, etc., Min. Co., 102 Fed. 982. But see Com. *v.* East Bangor Consol. Slate Co., 162 Pa. St. 599, 29 Atl. 706, holding that a corporation owning a quarry from which it takes slate and works it up into sizes and shapes desired may be so far considered a manufacturing company as to be able to claim exemption from taxation on that part of its capital which is engaged in this part of its business.

Slaughtering cattle.— People *v.* Roberts, 155 N. Y. 408, 50 N. E. 53, 41 L. R. A. 228 [*reversing* 20 N. Y. App. Div. 521, 47 N. Y. Suppl. 123]; People *v.* Roberts, 11 N. Y. App. Div. 449, 42 N. Y. Suppl. 317. *Compare* Engle *v.* Sohn, 41 Ohio St. 691, 52 Am. Rep. 103.

Miscellaneous.— Grinding cereals and making cattle fodder. Atlas Feed Products Co. *v.* New Orleans, 113 La. 611, 37 So. 531. Mixing teas and roasting and mixing coffee. People *v.* Roberts, 82 Hun (N. Y.) 352, 31 N. Y. Suppl. 243 [*affirmed* in 145 N. Y. 375, 40 N. E. 7]. Refining bullion into standard silver bars. People *v.* Horn Silver Min. Co., 105 N. Y. 76, 11 N. E. 155. Building and operating dry docks. People *v.* New York Floating Dry-Dock Co., 92 N. Y. 487 [*affirming* 11 Abb. N. Cas. 40, 63 How. Pr. 451]. Buying and selling foreign books. People *v.* Roberts, 90 Hun (N. Y.) 533, 36 N. Y. Suppl. 73. Buying and selling securities of other corporations. Com. *v.* Westinghouse Electric, etc., Co., 151 Pa. St. 265, 24 Atl. 1107, 1111. Building and maintaining an aqueduct. Dudley *v.* Jamaica Pond Aqueduct Co., 100 Mass. 183. Planing mill. Whited *v.* Bledsoe, 49 La. Ann. 325, 21 So. 538. Saw-mill. Jones *v.* Raines, 35 La. Ann. 996. Making soda, vichy, seltzer, and similar drinks. Crescent City, etc., Co. *v.* New Orleans, 48 La. Ann. 768, 19 So. 943. Grain elevator and warehouse company. Mohr *v.* Minnesota El. Co., 40 Minn. 343, 41 N. W. 1074. And hay is not a manufactured article. Frazee *v.* Moffitt, 18 Fed. 584, 20 Blatchf. 267.

71. People *v.* Campbell, 88 Hun (N. Y.) 530, 34 N. Y. Suppl. 713 [*reversed* on other grounds in 148 N. Y. 759, 43 N. E. 177].

72. Globe Lumber Co. *v.* Clement, 110 La. 438, 34 So. 595; Chickasaw Cooperage Co. *v.* Jefferson Parish Police Jury, 48 La. Ann. 523, 19 So. 476; Brooklyn Cooperage Co. *v.* New Orleans, 47 La. Ann. 1314, 17 So. 804; Rosedale Cypress Lumber, etc., Co. *v.* Buslé, 45 La. Ann. 459, 12 So. 484; Carpenter *v.* Brusle, 45 La. Ann. 456, 12 So. 483; Gast *v.* Board of Assessors, 43 La. Ann. 1104, 10 So. 184; Washburn *v.* New Orleans, 43 La. Ann.

taxes are payable on capital invested in the factory or plant,[83] nor on such part of it as is represented by the manufactured products into which it has temporarily passed,[84] nor on patents under which the business is carried on.[85] But the company cannot claim exemption on parts of its capital invested in dwelling-houses for its employees,[86] nor in mortgages or the stocks or bonds of other corporations.[87] If part of the capital is employed in the proper business of manufacturing, and part in some other line or branch of business, not necessarily connected with the main business of the company, although more or less incident to it, this does not render the entire capital subject to taxation, but only that portion of it which is so diverted from manufacturing.[88] Although the capital stock of the corporation is exempt, the shares of stock in the hands of their respective holders may still be liable to be taxed.[89]

l. Miscellaneous Corporations. Various other kinds of corporations have from time to time been favored with exemption from taxation, either on the ground of their performing public services or for the encouragement of beneficial industries.[90] But the principle is common to all that the company can claim exemption only as to so much of its property as is necessary and proper to the actual conduct of its particular business, and not in respect to property which may be devoted to other uses or which is held as a mere convenience or incident to the business.[91]

m. Foreign Corporations.[92] Although foreign corporations are not generally relieved by statute from local taxation, yet in some states an exception is made in favor of corporations engaged in manufacturing industries and carrying on their business within the taxing state.[93] Also it is not unusual to exempt from

83. Anne Arundel County *v.* Baltimore Sugar Refining Co., 99 Md. 481, 58 Atl. 211; Adams *v.* Tombigbee Mills, 78 Miss. 676, 29 So. 470; Com. *v.* Bethlehem Iron Co., 5 Dauph. Co. Rep. (Pa.) 118; Com. *v.* Cambria Iron Co., 5 Dauph. Co. Rep. (Pa.) 101.

The capital stock of a domestic corporation which is exclusively employed in manufacturing within the state is exempt from state taxation, although it is owned or leased by a foreign corporation. Com. *v.* American Cement Co., 203 Pa. St. 298, 52 Atl. 330.

84. Electric Traction Co. *v.* New Orleans, 45 La. Ann. 1475, 14 So. 231.

85. American Mutoscope Co. *v.* State Bd. of Assessors, 70 N. J. L. 172, 56 Atl. 369.

86. Com. *v.* Westinghouse Air Brake Co., 151 Pa. St. 276, 24 Atl. 1111, 1113; Com. *v.* Mahoning Rolling-Mill Co., 129 Pa. St. 360, 18 Atl. 135.

87. Com. *v.* Lackawanna Iron, etc., Co., 129 Pa. St. 346, 18 Atl. 133; Com. *v.* Croft, etc., Co., 26 Pa. Co. Ct. 474; Com. *v.* Jarecki Mfg. Co., 5 Dauph. Co. Rep. (Pa.) 154; Com. *v.* Cambria Iron Co., 5 Dauph. Co. Rep. (Pa.) 101.

88. *In re* Consolidated Electric Storage Co., (N. J. Ch. 1893) 26 Atl. 983; People *v.* Campbell, 144 N. Y. 166, 38 N. E. 990; Com. *v.* East Bangor Consol. Slate Co., 162 Pa. St. 599, 29 Atl. 706; Com. *v.* Juniata Coke Co., 157 Pa. St. 507, 27 Atl. 373, 22 L. R. A. 232; Com. *v.* Savage Fire Brick Co., 157 Pa. St. 512, 27 Atl. 374; Com. *v.* Thackra Mfg. Co., 156 Pa. St. 510, 27 Atl. 13; Com. *v.* Westinghouse Air Brake Co., 151 Pa. St. 276, 24 Atl. 1111, 1113; Com. *v.* Wm. Mann Co., 150 Pa. St. 64, 24 Atl. 601; Com. *v.* Weikel. etc., Spice Co., (Pa. 1892) 24 Atl. 603; Com. *v.* Lackawanna Iron, etc., Co., 129 Pa. St. 346, 18 Atl. 133; Com. *v.* Cambria Iron Co., 5 Dauph. Co. Rep. (Pa.) 101.

89. State *v.* Board of Assessors, 47 La. Ann. 1498, 18 So. 462.

90. See the statutes of the several states. And see Layman *v.* Iowa Tel. Co., 123 Iowa 591, 99 N. W. 205 (commutation of taxes of telephone companies); Detroit Union R. Depot, etc., Co. *v.* Detroit, 88 Mich. 347, 50 N. W. 302 (union depot company to pay annual tax on gross earnings in lieu of other taxes on property); Detroit, etc., Plank-Road Co. *v.* Detroit, 81 Mich. 562, 46 N. W. 12 (turnpike company to pay a specific tax on net profits and exempted from all other taxes on property); Le Roy *v.* East Saginaw City R. Co., 18 Mich. 203, 100 Am. Dec. 162 (commutation of taxes of street railroad company by payment of a specific amount annually in lieu of all other taxes); Ridgway Light, etc., Co. *v.* Elk County, 191 Pa. St. 465, 43 Atl. 323 (a natural gas company is engaged in a business of a public interest and therefore exempt from taxation); Matter of Hamilton, 13 Can. L. J. 18 (gravel roads owned by a corporation exempt as public highways).

91. Louisville *v.* Louisville Bd. of Trade, 90 Ky. 409, 14 S. W. 408, 12 Ky. L. Rep. 397, 9 L. R. A. 629 (building owned by board of trade, but partly rented to third persons not exempt as to part rented); Detroit Union R. Depot, etc., Co. *v.* Detroit, 88 Mich. 347, 50 N. W. 302 (grain elevator owned by union depot company exempt); Detroit, etc., Plank-Road Co. *v.* Detroit, 81 Mich. 562, 46 N. W. 12 (toll collector's residence owned by turnpike company exempt).

92. Liability to taxation see *supra*, III, B, 3.

93. People *v.* Campbell, 145 N. Y. 587, 40 N. E. 239 [*affirming* 80 Hun 466, 30 N. Y. Suppl. 472]; People *v.* Wemple, 133 N. Y.

the operation of the charity is exempt, although it may be used in a manner to yield some return and thereby reduce expenses.[12]

c. Hospitals. A public hospital is a charitable institution, or under some statutes an "almshouse," so as to be exempt from taxation;[13] but not so if it is entirely self-supporting or is conducted for private gain or as an adjunct to a medical college, or is private in the sense that the public have no right of admission to it.[14] But it is none the less a public charity because patients of sufficient pecuniary ability are required to pay for what they receive, if the proceeds are applied exclusively to the purposes of the institution and if indigent patients are treated without charge;[15] because it is not owned by the state or a municipal

Minnesota.— State *v.* St. Barnabas Hospital, 95 Minn. 489, 104 N. W. 551.

Mississippi.— Ridgeley Lodge No. 23 I. O. O. F. *v.* Redus, 78 Miss. 352, 29 So. 163.

New Jersey.— Sisters of Peace *v.* Westervelt, 64 N. J. L. 510, 45 Atl. 788 [*affirmed* in 65 N. J. L. 685, 48 Atl. 789].

New York.— People *v.* Sayles, 32 N. Y. App. Div. 197, 53 N. Y. Suppl. 67; People *v.* Brooklyn Bd. of Assessors, 27 Hun 559.

Ohio.— Humphries *v.* Little Sisters of the Poor, 29 Ohio St. 201.

Oregon.— Hibernian Benev. Soc. *v.* Kelly, 28 Oreg. 173, 42 Pac. 3, 52 Am. St. Rep. 769, 30 L. R. A. 167.

Pennsylvania.—American Sunday School Union *v.* Philadelphia, 161 Pa. St. 307, 29 Atl. 26, 23 L. R. A. 695; Pocono Pines Assembly *v.* Monroe County, 29 Pa. Super. Ct. 36; Pennsylvania Hospital *v.* Delaware County, 15 Pa. Co. Ct. 540; Young Men's Christian Assoc. *v.* Donohugh, 13 Phila. 12.

South Dakota.— State *v.* Lawrence County Bd. of Equalization, 16 S. D. 219, 92 N. W. 16.

Texas.— Morris *v.* Lone Star Chapter No. 6 R. A. M., 68 Tex. 698, 5 S. W. 519; Barbee *v.* Dallas, 26 Tex. Civ. App. 571, 64 S. W. 1018.

Utah.— Parker *v.* Quinn, 23 Utah 332, 64 Pac. 961.

12. Pennsylvania Hospital *v.* Delaware County, 169 Pa. St. 305, 32 Atl. 456; Philadelphia *v.* Pennsylvania Hospital, 154 Pa. St. 9, 25 Atl. 1076; House of Refuge *v.* Smith, 140 Pa. St. 387, 21 Atl. 353. See also *infra*, IV, E, 1, c, d.

13. *Arkansas.*— Hot Springs School Dist. *v.* Female Academy Sisters of Mercy, 84 Ark. 497, 106 S. W. 954.

Illinois.— Proctor Hospital *v.* Peoria County Bd. of Review, 233 Ill. 583, 84 N. E. 618; Cook County Bd. of Review *v.* Chicago Policlinic, 233 Ill. 268, 84 N. E. 220; Chicago German Hospital *v.* Cook County Bd. of Review, 233 Ill. 246, 84 N. E. 215.

Massachusetts.— Massachusetts Soc. for Prevention of Cruelty to Animals *v.* Boston, 142 Mass. 24, 6 N. E. 840.

New York.— People *v.* Reilly, 178 N. Y. 609, 70 N. E. 1107; Matter of Kimberly, 27 N. Y. App. Div. 470, 50 N. Y. Suppl. 586; New York Western Dispensary *v.* New York, 56 N. Y. Super. Ct. 361, 4 N. Y. Suppl. 547; Matter of Curtiss, 7 N. Y. Suppl. 207, 1 Connoly Surr. 471.

United States.— Williamson *v.* New Jersey, 130 U. S. 189, 9 S. Ct. 453, 32 L. ed. 915.

England.— Colchester *v.* Kewney, L. R. 1 Exch. 368, 4 H. & C. 445, 35 L. J. Exch. 204, 14 L. T. Rep. N. S. 888, 14 Wkly. Rep. 994 [*affirmed* in L. R. 2 Exch. 253, 36 L. J. Exch. 172, 16 L. T. Rep. N. S. 463, 15 Wkly. Rep. 930].

Canada.— Matter of Ottawa Sisters of Charity, 7 Can. L. J. 157.

See 45 Cent. Dig. tit. "Taxation," § 390.

An institution for the blind, which does not receive pay from patients under any circumstances, is an "almshouse," and a bequest to it is not liable to the legacy tax. Matter of Underhill, 20 N. Y. Suppl. 134, 2 Connoly Surr. 262.

14. *Kentucky.*— Wathen *v.* Louisville, 85 S. W. 1195, 27 Ky. L. Rep. 635; Gray St. Infirmary *v.* Louisville, 65 S. W. 11, 23 Ky. L. Rep. 1274, 55 L. R. A. 270, both applying the rule stated in the text to an infirmary run as an adjunct to a medical college.

New York.— People *v.* Nowles, 34 Misc. 501, 70 N. Y. Suppl. 277.

North Dakota.— Engstad *v.* Grand Forks County, 10 N. Dak. 54, 84 N. W. 577.

Pennsylvania.— Delaware County *v.* Sisters of St. Francis, 2 Del. Co. 149.

England.— Needham *v.* Bowers, 21 Q. B. D. 436, 59 L. T. Rep. N. S. 404, 37 Wkly. Rep. 125.

In Canada it has been held that a hospital is entitled to exemption as a "public hospital," although it is owned and carried on by and for the benefit of certain physicians, where it is subject to governmental regulation and control and public funds are by statute contributed to its support. Struthers *v.* Sudbury, 27 Ont. App. 217.

Hospital organized for profit.— To be exempt from taxation under the Illinois statutes property must belong to and stand in the name of an institution organized for public charity, and be actually and exclusively used for charitable purposes, and a hospital, if organized as a corporation for profit, cannot claim the exemption, although it is actually conducted as a public hospital. People *v.* Ravenswood Hospital, 238 Ill. 137, 87 N. E. 305.

15. *Arkansas.*— Hot Springs School Dist. *v.* Sisters of Mercy Little Rock Female Academy, 84 Ark. 497, 106 S. W. 954.

Illinois.— Cook County Bd. of Review *v.* Chicago Policlinic, 233 Ill. 268, 84 N. E. 220; German Hospital *v.* Cook County Bd. of Review, 233 Ill. 246, 84 N. E. 215; Cook County Bd. of Review *v.* Provident Hospital, etc., Assoc., 233 Ill. 242, 84 N. E. 216; St

tions,[33] the exemption will extend to educational institutions carried on by private individuals as well as to incorporated institutions.[34] Nor is it essential to constitute an "educational" institution that it should be incorporated exclusively for such purpose or that there should be a regular corps of teachers with regular classes of students,[35] but its objects must have some educational value and it must perform some educational function;[36] and it is always essential to the exemption that the educational work of the institution should be carried on; when it ceases or is abandoned, the property becomes subject to taxation.[37]

b. Public or Charitable Character of Institution. If an exemption from taxation is granted generally to schools or educational institutions, without requiring that they shall be public or charitable institutions, it may be claimed by a private school maintained by an individual or corporation as a business enterprise.[38] In some states, however, it is considered that such an institution is not within the spirit of the exemption laws,[39] and this is clearly the case where the exemption is limited to school property "not used with a view to profit."[40]

general knowledge of kindred subjects, and to that end, of furnishing popular instruction and recreation." Matter of Mergentime, 129 N. Y. App. Div. 367, 113 N. Y. Suppl. 948 [*affirmed* in 195 N. Y. 572, 88 N. E. 1125]. *Compare* Academy of Fine Arts *v.* Philadelphia County, 22 Pa. St. 496, holding that an institution for the study and exhibition of works of art is not an "academy," within the meaning of the statute, although styled an "academy of fine arts." But a young men's christian association is not a "seminary of learning" within the application of an exemption statute. New York Y. M. C. A. *v.* New York, 113 N. Y. 187, 21 N. E. 86 [*reversing* 44 Hun 102].

Chautauqua assembly.— The property of a local "Chautauqua" is not exempt from taxation on the ground of its educational features, where its sessions last but a few days in the year, and its purposes are social as well as educational, and stock-holders in the corporation receive benefit from its earnings in the way of free tickets to its meetings. Bosworth *v.* Kentucky Chautauqua Assembly, 112 Ky. 115, 65 S. W. 602, 23 Ky. L. Rep. 1393.

"College" and "university."— These terms contrasted and explained see Yale University *v.* New Haven, 71 Conn. 316, 42 Atl. 87, 43 L. R. A. 490.

The word "school" in an exemption statute has been held to mean any institution of learning, and is not limited to the lower grades of schools to the exclusion of higher institutions like colleges. Omaha Medical College *v.* Rush, 22 Nebr. 449, 35 N. W. 222. But the term "school-house" as used in the New York statutes applies only to buildings provided for the public common schools. Colored Orphans' Assoc. *v.* New York, 104 N. Y. 581, 12 N. E. 279; Chegaray *v.* New York, 13 N. Y. 220 [*reversing* 2 Duer 521, and *overruling* Chegaray *v.* Jenkins, 5 N. Y. 376].

The term "institutions of learning" as used in the Illinois statute does not include private schools which teach only the rudimentary branches commonly taught in public schools, but if the course of instruction includes the higher branches it is not material that it also includes branches ordinarily taught in the public schools. People *v.* St. Francis Xavier Female Academy, 233 Ill. 26, 84 N. E. 55.

33. See Chegaray *v.* New York, 13 N. Y. 220 [*reversing* 2 Duer 521].

The term "society" in a statute exempting from taxation school-houses owned by religious societies applies only to incorporated societies. St. Monica Church *v.* New York, 119 N. Y. 91, 23 N. E. 294, 7 L. R. A. 70.

34. Jackson *v.* Preston, 93 Miss. 366, 47 So. 547, 21 L. R. A. N. S. 164; Montclair Military Academy *v.* Bowden, 64 N. J. L. 214, 47 Atl. 490.

35. Matter of Mergentime, 129 N. Y. App. Div. 367, 113 N. Y. Suppl. 948 [*affirmed* in 195 N. Y. 572, 88 N. E. 1125].

36. *In re* Vineland Historical, etc., Soc., 66 N. J. Eq. 291, 56 Atl. 1039.

37. Grubb *v.* Weaver, 19 Pa. Co. Ct. 609.

38. *Arkansas.*— Phillips County *v.* Sister Estelle, 42 Ark. 336.

Georgia.— Linton *v.* Lucy Cobb Inst., 117 Ga. 678, 45 S. E. 53.

Indiana.— Indianapolis *v.* Sturdevant, 24 Ind. 391.

Louisiana.— State *v.* Orleans Parish Bd. of Assessors, 52 La. Ann. 223, 26 So. 872.

Michigan.— Detroit Home, etc., School *v.* Detroit, 76 Mich. 521, 43 N. W. 593, 6 L. R. A. 97.

Minnesota.— Ramsey County *v.* Stryker, 52 Minn. 144, 53 N. W. 1133.

Missouri.— State *v.* Johnston, 214 Mo. 656, 113 S. W. 1083, 21 L. R. A. N. S. 171.

New Jersey.— Montclair Military Academy *v.* State Bd. of Assessors, 65 N. J. L. 516, 47 Atl. 558.

Canada.— Wylie *v.* Montreal, 12 Can. Sup. Ct. 384.

See 45 Cent. Dig. tit. "Taxation," § 400.

39. Indianapolis *v.* McLean, 8 Ind. 328; State *v.* Ross, 24 N. J. L. 497; People *v.* Mezger, 181 N. Y. 511, 73 N. E. 1130; Chegaray *v.* New York, 13 N. Y. 220; Chegaray *v.* Jenkins, 3 Sandf. (N. Y.) 409 [*affirmed* in 5 N. Y. 376].

40. Brenau Assoc. *v.* Harbison, 120 Ga. 929, 48 S. E. 363; Montgomery *v.* Wyman, 130 Ill. 17, 22 N. E. 845; *In re* Dille, 119 Iowa 575, 93 N. W. 571.

is not necessary, to meet this requirement, that the particular school should be controlled by the state, but only that it should be open and free to all children of suitable age.[50]

d. Sectarian Schools. If the statute exempts "property used for school purposes," or "educational institutions" generally, it may be considered broad enough to include parochial and other schools maintained by particular churches or sects exclusively for the benefit of their own people, provided they are not conducted for gain.[51] But such sectarian or denominational schools are not "free public schools" or "institutions of purely public charity,"[52] although a religious denominational school which offers educational advantages to all who may apply, not limiting the admission of pupils to children of members of the denomination, although it may give a preference to such children, and which is supported by voluntary contributions and not conducted for profit, may be exempt as a purely public charity.[53]

e. What Property Exempt — (I) *In General.* The question as to what property of an educational institution is exempt depends largely upon the wording of the statute.[54] Under the statutes as generally framed all the property belonging to a school or college and used directly, immediately, and exclusively for its proper purposes is exempt from taxation,[55] including the school or college buildings,[56] the land on which they stand or which is used in connection with them,[57] and the personal property constituting the educational equipment, such as libraries, apparatus, and necessary furniture.[58]

(II) *Nature of Ownership, Occupancy, or Use.* To be entitled to exemption it is ordinarily necessary that the property should be owned by the school or college; it is not enough that it is used for such purposes if owned by a third person.[59] Further, the exemption ordinarily extends only to such prop-

50. Phillips County *v.* Sister Estelle, 42 Ark. 536; Baltimore City Appeal Tax Ct. *v.* St. Peter's Academy, 50 Md. 321; Northampton County *v.* Lafayette College, 128 Pa. St. 132, 18 Atl. 516.

51. Rettew *v.* St. Patrick's Roman Catholic Church, 4 Pennew. (Del.) 593, 58 Atl. 828; Warde *v.* Manchester, 56 N. H. 508, 22 Am. Rep. 504; Hebrew Free School Assoc. *v.* New York, 4 Hun (N. Y.) 446; Church of St. Monica *v.* New York, 55 N. Y. Super. Ct. 160, 13 N. Y. St. 308; Gilmour *v.* Pelton, 5 Ohio Dec. (Reprint) 447, 6 Am. L. Rec. 26.

52. Thiel College *v.* Mercer County, 101 Pa. St. 530; Mullen *v.* Juenet, 6 Pa. Super. Ct. 1; St. Joseph's Church *v.* Providence Tax Assessors, 12 R. I. 19, 34 Am. Rep. 597.

53. Louisville *v.* Nazareth Literary, etc., Inst., 100 Ky. 518, 36 S. W. 994, 19 Ky. L. Rep. 1102; Baltimore City Appeal Tax Ct. *v.* Grand Lodge G. O. H., 50 Md. 421; Hennepin County *v.* Grace, 27 Minn. 503, 8 N. W. 761; White *v.* Smith, 189 Pa. St. 222, 42 Atl. 125, 43 L. R. A. 498 [*reversing* 8 Pa. Super. Ct. 205]; Episcopal Academy *v.* Philadelphia, 150 Pa. St. 565, 25 Atl. 55; Haverford College *v.* Rhoads, 6 Pa. Super. Ct. 71; Ursinus College *v.* Collegeville, 17 Montg. Co. Rep. (Pa.) 61; White *v.* Smith, 27 Pittsb. Leg. J. N. S. 330.

54. County Com'rs *v.* Colorado Seminary, 12 Colo. 497, 21 Pac. 490; Nobles County *v.* Hamline University, 46 Minn. 316, 48 N. W. 1119; Northwestern University *v.* People, 99 U. S. 309, 25 L. ed. 387.

55. *In re* Northwestern University Property Assessment, 206 Ill. 64, 69 N. E. 75; Tulane University *v.* Board of Assessors, 115 La. 1025, 40 So. 445; Harvard College *v.* Kettell, 16 Mass. 204; Academy of Sacred Heart *v.* Irey, 51 Nebr. 755, 71 N. W. 752.

56. Stevens Inst. *v.* Bowes, 78 N. J. L. 205, 73 Atl. 38; Willard *v.* Pike, 59 Vt. 202, 9 Atl. 907.

57. Stevens Inst. *v.* Bowes, 74 N. J. L. 80, 70 Atl. 730; Northampton County *v.* Lehigh University, 13 Pa. Co. Ct. 659; Cassiano *v.* Ursuline Academy, 64 Tex. 673. And see *infra*, IV, E, 2, e, (III).

Although the word "building" is the only one used in specifying the property exempt, this will include the land upon which the building stands and which is essential to its convenient enjoyment. Cassiano *v.* Ursuline Academy, 64 Tex. 673.

58. Baltimore County Appeal Tax Ct. *v.* St. Peter's Academy, 50 Md. 321. But see Kansas City *v.* Kansas City Medical College, 111 Mo. 141, 20 S. W. 35, holding that a statute exempting real property used for school purposes, "with the buildings thereon," does not include office furniture, nor the furniture of a chemical laboratory not fastened to the building.

59. *Indiana.*— Travelers' Ins. Co. *v.* Kent, 151 Ind. 349, 50 N. E. 562, 51 N. E. 723.

Kentucky.— Nazareth Literary, etc., Inst. *v.* Com., 14 B. Mon. 266.

Louisiana.—Armand *v.* Dumas, 28 La. Ann. 403.

Minnesota.— Hennepin County *v.* Bell, 43 Minn. 344, 45 N. W. 615.

New York.— People *v.* Brooklyn Bd. of

in some cases are broad enough to include property yielding a revenue, where such revenue is applied directly and exclusively to the maintenance of the school or college.[75]

(VIII) *TRUST OR ENDOWMENT FUNDS.* In most of the states it is held that the exemption from taxation granted to an institution of learning includes not only its real estate and physical equipment, but also funds donated or bequeathed to it, by way of endowment or in trust for its uses, the income from which is entirely devoted to the maintenance of the institution.[76]

f. Literary and Scientific Societies. In some cases the exemption statutes expressly include the property of literary and scientific institutions or societies,[77]

Kansas.— Stahl *v.* Kansas Educational Assoc., 54 Kan. 542, 38 Pac. 796.

Louisiana.— State *v.* Board of Assessors, 35 La. Ann. 668.

New York.— Pratt Inst. *v.* New York, 99 N. Y. App. Div. 525, 91 N. Y. Suppl. 136 [*affirmed* in 183 N. Y. 151, 75 N. E. 1119].

Oregon.—Willamette Univ. *v.* Knight, 35 Oreg. 33, 56 Pac. 124.

Virginia.— Com. *v.* Hampton Normal, etc., Inst., 106 Va. 614, 56 S. E. 594.

75. *Colorado.*— Colorado Seminary *v.* Arapahoe County, 30 Colo. 507, 71 Pac. 410.

Connecticut.— New Haven *v.* Sheffield Scientific School, 59 Conn. 163, 22 Atl. 156.

Kentucky.— Com. *v.* Hamilton College, 125 Ky. 329, 101 S W. 405, 30 Ky. L. Rep. 1338.

Massachusetts.— Hardy *v.* Waltham, 7 Pick. 108, charter provision.

Missouri.— North St. Louis Gymnastic Soc. *v.* Hudson, 85 Mo. 32.

New Jersey.— Englewood Boys School *v.* Chamberlain, 55 N. J. L. 292, 26 Atl. 913.

Pennsylvania.— Northampton County *v.* Lafayette College, 5 Pa. Co. Ct. 407.

Tennessee.—Vanderbilt Univ. *v.* Cheney, 116 Tenn. 259, 94 S. W. 90; University of the South *v.* Skidmore, 87 Tenn. 155, 9 S. W. 892, charter provision.

United States.—Whitman College *v.* Berryman, 156 Fed. 112, holding that a charter provision of a college providing that its "property, income and proceeds shall not be subject to taxation," includes within the exemption all property of the corporation, whether used directly for college purposes or as a source of income.

Sale of farm products by agricultural college.—A college of agriculture may sell its surplus agricultural products, such as milk, butter, and eggs, without losing its exemption; hence where an agricultural institute maintained a model dairy farm for the purpose of scientific instruction, a large part of the products thereof being consumed within the institute, and the revenue derived from marketing the surplus being devoted to the support of the school as a mere incident, and the state did not show what part of such property constituted a source of revenue as distinguished from that which was devoted solely to educational purposes, it was held that neither the farm nor its products were subject to taxation. Com. *v.* Hampton Normal, etc., Inst., 106 Va. 614, 56 S. E. 594.

76. *Connecticut.*— New Haven *v.* Sheffield Scientific School, 59 Conn. 163, 22 Atl. 156.

Kentucky.— Com. *v.* Gray, 114 Ky. 665, 74 S. W. 702, 25 Ky. L. Rep. 52; Com. *v.* Pollitt, 76 S. W. 412, 25 Ky. L. Rep. 790.

Massachusetts.—Williston Seminary *v.* Hampshire, 147 Mass. 427, 18 N. E. 210.

Missouri.— State *v.* Westminster College, 175 Mo. 52, 74 S. W. 990.

Ohio.— Little *v.* United Presb. Theological Seminary, 72 Ohio St. 417, 74 N. E. 193; Gerke *v.* Purcell, 25 Ohio St. 229. But see State *v.* Cappeller, 8 Ohio Dec. (Reprint) 219, 6 Cinc. L. Bul. 339.

Pennsylvania.— See Wagner Inst.'s Appeal, 116 Pa. St. 555, 11 Atl. 402, as to what constitutes an endowment.

Rhode Island.— Brown Univ. *v.* Granger, 19 R. I. 704, 36 Atl. 720, 36 L. R. A. 847.

See 45 Cent. Dig. tit. "Taxation," § 399.

But see County Com'rs *v.* Colorado Seminary, 12 Colo. 497, 21 Pac. 490 (holding under a particular statute that land donated to an educational institution to be sold and the proceeds devoted to the purposes of the institution is not while remaining unsold and unoccupied exempt from taxation); Nevin *v.* Krollman, 38 N. J. L. 574 (holding that an endowment consisting of land is not within the application of a statute exempting "the endowment or fund" of an educational institution).

77. See Orono *v.* Sigma Alpha Epsilon Soc., 105 Me. 214, 74 Atl. 19; Phi Beta Epsilon Corp. *v.* Boston, 182 Mass. 457, 65 N. E. 824; Wesleyan Academy *v.* Wilbraham, 99 Mass. 599; People *v.* Lawler, 74 N. Y. App. Div. 553, 77 N. Y. Suppl. 840 [*affirmed* in 179 N. Y. 535, 71 N. E. 1136]; People *v.* Feitner, 31 Misc. (N. Y.) 565, 65 N. Y. Suppl. 587; Cincinnati College *v.* State, 19 Ohio 110.

What institutions or societies included.— The exemption statutes relating to literary and scientific institutions do not include college fraternities. Orono *v.* Sigma Alpha Epsilon Soc., 105 Me. 214, 74 Atl. 19; Phi Beta Epsilon Corp. *v.* Boston, 182 Mass. 457, 65 N. E. 824; People *v.* Lawler, 74 N. Y. App. Div. 553, 77 N. Y. Suppl. 840 [*reversing* 36 Misc. 594, 73 N. Y. Suppl. 1082, and *affirmed* in 179 N. Y. 535, 71 N. E. 1136]. And a corporation having for its paramount object the dissemination of theosophical ideas and the procuring of converts thereto is neither a "scientific" nor a "literary" institution. New England Theosophical Corp. *v.* Boston Bd. of Assessors, 172 Mass. 60, 51 N. E. 456, 42 L. R. A. 281. So also a law society is not a charitable or a literary institution.

county, it is usually considered as within the taxing district represented by the county to which it is attached for judicial purposes.[33] The creation and determination of the taxing districts of the state is a matter within the discretion of the legislature, with which the courts will not interfere; [34] and when such a district is once lawfully established, it will retain its character and boundaries until divided or modified in some manner authorized by law.[35]

2. Legislative Power to Fix Situs of Property. The legislature has power to fix the *situs* of personal property for purposes of taxation, placing it either at the owner's domicile or where the property itself is situated,[36] and also to invest executive officers with authority to determine the place for the listing of personal property as between different counties or different places in the same county.[37]

B. Domicile or Residence of Owner — 1. In General. Except where, as just stated, the statute fixes the *situs* of personal property for the purpose of taxation at the place where the property is situated, it is to be assessed to the owner only at the place of his domicile, and cannot legally be assessed anywhere else.[38] And the owner's domicile is commonly fixed for this purpose by the place of his residence on a certain day in the year, prescribed by statute, usually the day on which the returns of personal property are required to be made or on which the assessment is begun.[39]

2. What Constitutes Domicile. Within the meaning of the tax laws the terms "residence," "inhabitancy," and "place of abode" are all ordinarily equivalent to the more exact term "domicile." [40] And a person's domicile is his fixed and

Tax districts in New York.— By statute in this state a tax district is defined as a political subdivision of the state having a board of assessors authorized to assess property therein. A county is not a tax district within the meaning of the statute. People *v.* Columbia County, 182 N. Y. 556, 75 N. E. 1133; Utica *v.* Oneida County, 109 N. Y. App. Div. 189, 95 N. Y. Suppl. 839; People *v.* Schoharie County, 39 Misc. (N. Y.) 162, 79 N. Y. Suppl. 145.

33. Meade County *v.* Hoehn, 12 S. D. 500, 81 N. W. 887; Dupree *v.* Stanley County, 8 S. D. 20, 65 N. W. 426; Llano Cattle Co. *v.* Faught, 69 Tex. 402, 5 S. W. 494. *Compare* Yellowstone County *v.* Northern Pac. R. Co., 10 Mont. 414, 25 Pac. 1058.

34. *Michigan.*— Pioneer Iron Co. *v.* Negaunee, 116 Mich. 430, 74 N. W. 700.

New Jersey.— Street-Lighting Dist. No. 1 *v.* Drummond, 63 N. J. L. 493, 43 Atl. 1061. But see Van Cleve *v.* Passaic Valley Sewerage Com'rs, 71 N. J. L. 574, 60 Atl. 214 (holding that a grant of power of local taxation, to be valid, must conform to the fundamental doctrine that the area over which such power extends shall be coincident with the political district of the state exercising some power of local government over the area selected for taxation); Carter *v.* Wade, 59 N. J. L. 119, 35 Atl. 649.

New York.— Litchfield *v.* Vernon, 41 N. Y. 123.

Ohio.— Hill *v.* Higdon, 5 Ohio St. 243, 67 Am. Dec. 289; Scovill *v.* Cleveland, 1 Ohio St. 126.

Utah.— Kimball *v.* Grantsville City, 19 Utah 368, 57 Pac. 1, 45 L. R. A. 628.

35. Whelan *v.* Cassidy, 64 Nebr. 503, 90 N. W. 229. And see Armstrong *v.* Russellville Dist. Turnpike Co., 29 S. W. 307, 16 Ky. L. Rep. 879; White Pine County *v.* Ash, 5 Nev. 279 (creation of new county); Cumru Tp. *v.* Berks County Poor Directors, 112 Pa. St. 264, 3 Atl. 578.

36. *Georgia.*—Walton County *v.* Morgan County, 120 Ga. 548, 48 S. E. 243.

Iowa.— Layman *v.* Iowa Tel. Co., 123 Iowa 591, 99 N. W. 205.

Massachusetts.— Scollard *v.* American Felt Co., 194 Mass. 127, 80 N. E. 233.

North Carolina.—Winston *v.* Salem, 131 N. C. 404, 42 S. E. 889; Hall *v.* Fayetteville, 115 N. C. 281, 20 S. E. 373.

Texas.— Missouri, etc., R. Co. *v.* Shannon, 100 Tex. 379, 100 S. W. 138, 10 L. R. A. N. S. 681.

Wisconsin.— Chicago, etc., R. Co. *v.* State, 128 Wis. 553, 108 N. W. 557.

And see *supra*, III, A, 4, d, (I); III, A, 5, b, (I).

Purpose of tax as affecting situs of property.— The legislature cannot arbitrarily give property a *situs* for taxation, but the tax burdens must be imposed on the state at large, the county at large, and the smaller taxing districts at large, according as the purpose thereof is purely general or purely local. Chicago, etc., R. Co. *v.* State, 128 Wis. 553, 108 N. W. 557.

37. State *v.* Hynes, 82 Minn. 34, 84 N. W. 636; Clarke *v.* Stearns County, 66 Minn. 304, 69 N. W. 25.

38. Hartland *v.* Church, 47 Me. 169; Preston *v.* Boston, 12 Pick. (Mass.) 7; Matter of Douglas, 48 Hun (N. Y.) 318, 1 N. Y. Suppl. 126; People *v.* O'Donnell, 96 N. Y. Suppl. 297; *In re* Cartright, 6 Can. L. J. 189.

39. See Hunt *v.* McFadgen, 20 Ark. 277; People *v.* Feitner, 40 Misc. (N. Y.) 368, 82 N. Y. Suppl. 258; Philadelphia Nat. Bank *v.* Pottstown Security Co., 14 Montg. Co. Rep. (Pa.) 106.

40. Borland *v.* Boston, 132 Mass. 89, 42

erty to be assessed for taxes there, and other such indications.[45] In the absence of any other sufficient test, it is considered that his domicile is at the place where he spends the greater part of the year,[46] or, according to the statute in New York, at the place where his principal business is transacted.[47]

4. Residence Situated Partly in Two Jurisdictions. Where a dwelling-house is divided by the boundary line between two taxing districts, the owner is taxable in that district in which stands the most necessary part of the house or the living rooms of the family.[48]

5. Change or Abandonment of Domicile — a. In General. A taxpayer may change his domicile by abandoning his present home and removing to another and settling himself there permanently with no intention of returning to the former abode, and so cease to be taxable at the place of his former residence;[49] but a merely simulated removal from one place to another, which is no more than a device to evade or escape taxation, will not have this effect;[50] and his liability for a tax will not be abated by his removal to another place after the day when he is notified to return his list of taxable property or after it is assessed to him.[51] Since, for the purpose of taxation, one must have a residence or domicile somewhere, he cannot abandon a domicile once acquired until he has actually acquired another;[52] and a domicile once established will be presumed to continue where it has been until a change is affirmatively shown.[53]

b. Intent. In determining the question of a change of domicile, the intention of the party with reference to the permanence of his residence in the new place is important. If he means it to be a merely temporary residence, followed by a return to his former home, there is no legal change of domicile; otherwise if he intends to establish himself permanently in the new place and not to return to the former.[54] But a change of domicile cannot legally be effected by intention

there. Milsaps *v.* Jackson, 88 Miss. 504, 42 So. 234.

45. Ellis *v.* People, 199 Ill. 548, 65 N. E. 428; Covington *v.* Wayne, 58 S. W. 776, 22 Ky. L. Rep. 826; Barron *v.* Boston, 187 Mass. 168, 72 N. E. 951; Thayer *v.* Boston, 124 Mass. 132, 26 Am. Rep. 650; People *v.* Crowley, 21 N. Y. App. Div. 304, 47 N. Y. Suppl. 457; People *v.* Barker, 70 Hun (N. Y.) 397, 24 N. Y. Suppl. 63 [*affirmed* in 139 N. Y. 658, 35 N. E. 208].

46. Cabot *v.* Boston, 12 Cush. (Mass.) 52; People *v.* Barker, 17 N. Y. Suppl. 788; Ailman *v.* Griswold, 12 R. I. 339; Greene *v.* Gardner, 6 R. I. 242.

47. See Paddock *v.* Lewis, 179 N. Y. 591, 72 N. E. 1146 [*affirming* 59 N. Y. App. Div. 430, 69 N. Y. Suppl. 1]; Bowe *v.* Jenkins, 69 Hun (N. Y.) 458, 23 N. Y. Suppl. 548; Douglas *v.* New York, 2 Duer (N. Y.) 110; Bartlett *v.* New York, 5 Sandf. (N. Y.) 44; People *v.* Barker, 17 N. Y. Suppl. 789; People *v.* Tax, etc., Com'rs, 3 N. Y. Suppl. 674.

48. Judkins *v.* Reed, 48 Me. 386; Chenery *v.* Waltham, 8 Cush. (Mass.) 327.

49. Kirkland *v.* Whately, 4 Allen (Mass.) 462; People *v.* Moore, 52 Hun (N. Y.) 13, 4 N. Y. Suppl. 778; Wade *v.* Matheson, 4 Lans. (N. Y.) 158 [*affirmed* in 47 N. Y. 658]; Mason *v.* Thurber, 1 R. I. 481; Jones *v.* St. John, 30 Can. Sup. Ct. 122.

An insane person is not precluded from changing his residence on the ground that he is incapable of forming an intention to do so, as the guardian may form such intention and change the residence of his ward. Brookover *v.* Kase, 41 Ind. App. 102, 83 N. E. 524. But if the insane person is not in the custody of his committee but is confined in an asylum the removal of the asylum from one county to another will not change the residence of the insane person, in the absence of any such intention on the part of his committee. New York *v.* Brinckerhoff, 63 Misc. (N. Y.) 445, 118 N. Y. Suppl. 449.

50. Thayer *v.* Boston, 124 Mass. 132, 26 Am. Rep. 650; Draper *v.* Hatfield, 124 Mass. 53.

But one may lawfully and effectively change his domicile notwithstanding his purpose in so doing is to diminish the amount of his taxes. Draper *v.* Hatfield, 124 Mass. 53.

51. State *v.* Brown Tobacco Co., 140 Mo. 218, 41 S. W. 776; Warren *v.* Werner, 14 Wis. 366.

52. Schmoll *v.* Schenck, 40 Ind. App. 581, 82 N. E. 805; Porterfield *v.* Augusta, 67 Me. 556; Borland *v.* Boston, 132 Mass. 89, 42 Am. Rep. 424; Bulkley *v.* Williamstown, 3 Gray (Mass.) 493; Kellogg *v.* Winnebago County, 42 Wis. 97.

53. *In re* Nichols, 54 N. Y. 62; People *v.* O'Rourke, 32 N. Y. App. Div. 66, 52 N. Y. Suppl. 1057; New York *v.* Brinckerhoff, 63 Misc. (N. Y.) 445, 118 N. Y. Suppl. 449; Kirby *v.* Bradford County, 134 Pa. St. 109, 19 Atl. 494.

54. *Indiana.*— Schmoll *v.* Schenck, 40 Ind. App. 581, 82 N. E. 805.

Iowa.— Babcock *v.* Bd. of Equalization, 65 Iowa 110, 21 N. W. 207.

Kentucky.— Lebanon *v.* Biggers, 117 Ky. 430, 78 S. W. 213, 25 Ky. L. Rep. 1528.

Maine.— Stockton *v.* Staples, 66 Me. 197;

b. Land in More Than One Taxing District. In the absence of statutory directions to the contrary, where a single tract of land or farm lies partly within two or more taxing districts, each district is entitled to tax that portion within its own limits, on a proportional valuation;[66] but in order to prevent certain mischiefs incident to the assessment of an entire property in different parcels and by different sets of assessors, this rule has in some jurisdictions been changed by statute,[67] and in several states the statutes now meet this case by providing that the whole lot or farm shall be assessable in that district where the owner or occupant resides or where the dwelling-house or "mansion house" is situated.[68]

A, 2, b, (III)) should be taxed as a part of the land to which it appertains and to which it is incident and at the place where such land is situated (Matter of Hall, 116 N. Y. App. Div. 729, 102 N. Y. Suppl. 5 [*affirmed* in 189 N. Y. 552, 82 N. E. 1127]. But see Helena Water Works Co. *v.* Settles, 37 Mont. 237, 95 Pac. 838).

Mining rights in land.— In Kentucky, prior to the act of March 19, 1894, relating to the taxation of coal, oil, and gas privileges in the lands of another in the county where the lands are situated, such privileges were taxable only in the county where the person owning the privilege resided. Kirk *v.* Western Gas, etc., Co., 37 S. W. 849, 18 Ky. L. Rep. 692.

Standing timber.— Trees bought by a lumber company for the purpose of allowing them to stand for several years before cutting them are taxable in the county where they are situated, irrespective of the company's domicile. Coldiron *v.* Kentucky Lumber Co., 32 S. W. 224, 17 Ky. L. Rep. 598.

Lands rented to tenants.— For special rules in certain states as to taxation of real property leased to tenants see Robson *v.* Du Bose, 79 Ga. 721, 4 S. E. 329; Pease *v.* Whitney, 5 Mass. 380.

Taxation of bridges and notice for purposes of tax see *supra*, III, A, 2, b, (IV).

Lands below high-water mark.—A borough, the boundary of which is high-water mark of a bay, has no power to tax land and piers thereon outside high-water mark. Central R. Co. *v.* Atlantic Highlands, 75 N. J. L. 80, 66 Atl. 936.

66. Robson *v.* Du Bose, 79 Ga. 721, 4 S. E. 329; Barger *v.* Jackson, 9 Ohio 163; Patton *v.* Long, 68 Pa. St. 260.

67. See Bausman *v.* Lancaster County, 50 Pa. St. 208; and cases cited *infra*, note 68.

Construction of statutes.— Since as a general rule land is taxable in the tax district, actual or technical, in which it is situated, any statute creating an exception to the rule must be strictly construed. People *v.* Marens, 62 Misc. (N. Y.) 317, 116 N. Y. Suppl. 189 [*affirmed* in 134 N. Y. App. Div. 170, 118 N. Y. Suppl. 838].

68. See the statutes of the several states; and the following cases:

New Jersey.— Potter *v.* Orange, 62 N. J. L. 192, 40 Atl. 647; State *v.* Pohatcong Tp., (Sup. 1894) 28 Atl. 673; Warren Mfg. Co. *v.* Dalrymple, 56 N. J. L. 449, 28 Atl. 671; Stewart *v.* Flummerfelt, 53 N. J. L. 540, 22 Atl. 119; State *v.* Washer, 51 N. J. L. 122, 16 Atl. 49; Compton *v.* Dally, 47 N. J. L. 84; State *v.* Abbott, 42 N. J. L. 111; State *v.* Britton, 42 N. J. L. 103; State *v.* Warford, 37 N. J. L. 397; State *v.* Jewell, 34 N. J. L. 259; State *v.* Hay, 31 N. J. L. 275; State *v.* Reinhardt, 31 N. J. L. 218; State *v.* Hoffman, 30 N. J. L. 346.

New York.— People *v.* Gray, 185 N. Y. 196, 77 N. E. 1172; Tebo *v.* Brooklyn, 134 N. Y. 341, 31 N. E. 984; People *v.* Wilson, 125 N. Y. 367, 26 N. E. 454; Dorn *v.* Backer, 61 N. Y. 261; People *v.* Gray, 109 N. Y. App. Div. 116, 95 N. Y. Suppl. 825 [*affirmed* in 185 N. Y. 196, 77 N. E. 1172]; People *v.* Howell, 106 N. Y. App. Div. 140, 94 N. Y. Suppl. 488; Gordon *v.* Becker, 71 Hun 282, 24 N. Y. Suppl. 1018; People *v.* Gaylord, 52 Hun 335, 5 N. Y. Suppl. 348; Chamberlain *v.* Sherman, 53 Misc. 474, 103 N. Y. Suppl. 239; Saunders *v.* Springsteen, 4 Wend. 429. See also People *v.* Wilson, 113 N. Y. App. Div. 1, 98 N. Y. Suppl. 1080, holding that a tract of land containing more than thirty thousand acres, somewhat unevenly divided between two towns, the whole tract being mountainous and woody and covered with lakes, and containing a number of buildings, some of which were in each town, and used for residences, hunting lodges, servants' residences, and in the manufacture on a large scale of maple sugar and lumber, is not a "farm or lot" within the meaning of the statute.

North Carolina.— Hairston *v.* Stinson, 35 N. C. 479.

Ohio.— Hughey *v.* Horrel, 2 Ohio 231.

Pennsylvania.— York Haven Water, etc., Co.'s Appeal, 212 Pa. St. 622, 62 Atl. 97; Bausman *v.* Lancaster County, 50 Pa. St. 208; Follett *v.* Butler County, 31 Pa. Super. Ct. 571; Follett *v.* Butler County, 30 Pa. Super. Ct. 21 [*affirmed* in 219 Pa. St. 509, 69 Atl. 76]; Com. *v.* Wheelock, 13 Pa. Super. Ct. 282; *In re* Stahl, 1 Lanc. L. Rev. 329. See also Quigley *v.* Reiff, 39 Pa. Super. Ct. 425.

Division by township and borough lines.— Under the Pennsylvania statutes where lands are situated partly in a township and partly in a borough, the portion lying within the borough is properly assessable there, although the mansion house is in the township. Com. *v.* Wyoming County, 22 Pa. Co. Ct. 418. And conversely where a farm is divided by a township and borough line and the mansion house is in the borough, the land in the township is to be assessed in the township and the land in the borough assessed in the

its business is carried on, and personal property belonging to the firm and employed or invested in its business is to be assessed to the firm as such and at its place of business, irrespective of the residence of the individual partners.[17]

E. Property Temporarily in Taxing District or in Transit.[18] Property which is only temporarily within the limits of a given county or other taxing district, or which is in transit through it, does not constitute a part of its taxable wealth, and therefore cannot be assessed for taxation there.[19]

F. Corporations and Corporate Property — 1. Domicile of Corporation for Purposes of Taxation. A corporation has its domicile, for the purpose of taxation, at the place where its principal business office is located;[20] and if the

17. *Kentucky.*— Louisville *v.* Tatum, 111 Ky. 747, 64 S. W. 836, 23 Ky. L. Rep. 1014.

Massachusetts.— Spinney *v.* Lynn, 172 Mass. 464, 52 N. E. 523; Duxbury *v.* Plymouth County, 172 Mass. 383, 52 N. E. 535; Cloutman *v.* Concord, 163 Mass. 444, 40 N. E. 763; Ricker *v.* American L. & T. Co., 140 Mass. 346, 5 N. E. 284; Barker *v.* Watertown, 137 Mass. 227; Bemis *v.* Boston, 14 Allen 366; Peabody *v.* Essex County, 10 Gray 97.

Michigan.— Williams *v.* Saginaw, 51 Mich. 120, 16 N. W. 260.

Missouri.—Plattsburg School Dist. *v.* Bowman, 178 Mo. 654, 77 S. W. 880.

New Jersey.— Taylor *v.* Love, 43 N. J. L. 142.

Vermont.— Fairbanks *v.* Kittredge, 24 Vt. 9.

See 45 Cent. Dig. tit. "Taxation," § 447.

Different places of business.— Under the Massachusetts statute, partners having places of business in two or more towns shall be taxed in each of such places for the proportion of property employed therein. Duxbury *v.* Plymouth County, 172 Mass. 383, 52 N. E. 535. A place of business within the application of the statute means a place where the business is carried on by the partners under their own control and on their own account. Little *v.* Cambridge, 9 Cush. (Mass.) 298.

18. **Taxation of property temporarily in state or in transit through it** see *supra*, III, A, 5, e.

19. Walton *v.* Westwood, 73 Ill. 125; Hill *v.* Caldwell, 134 Ky. 90, 119 S. W. 749 (cattle temporarily in pasture in a county other than the residence of the owner): Flowerree Cattle Co. *v.* Lewis, etc., County, 33 Mont. 32, 81 Pac. 398; Conley *v.* Chedic, 7 Nev. 336.

Reason of rule.— Personal property which is passing through a county for the purpose of finding a market elsewhere, or is destined for some other county in the state, is not property in the county through which it is passing, for the purpose of taxation. To constitute it property for that purpose in any particular county, it must be in such a situation as to make it a part of the wealth of that county; it must belong in it, or be incorporated with the other property of the county. Conley *v.* Chedic, 7 Nev. 336.

What constitutes transit.— In order that property within a county may be regarded as in transit, so as to be exempt from taxation therein, there must be at least an intention and fixed purpose to remove it within a reasonable time; and an intention to remove it at some future time, depending upon certain contingencies, which may or may not happen, is insufficient. State Trust Co. *v.* Chehalis County, 79 Fed. 282, 24 C. C. A. 584. And see John Hancock Ice Co. *v.* Rose. 67 N. J. L. 86, 50 Atl. 364. Grain purchased by an agent and stored in his warehouse subject to the order of the owner is not in transit so as to exempt the agent from liability for taxes. Walton *v.* Westwood, 73 Ill. 125.

A portable sawmill temporarily in use in a town other than that in which the owner resides or has his place of business is not "situated or employed" in such town within the meaning of the statute for purposes of taxation. Ingraham *v.* Coles, 150 Mass. 155, 23 N. E. 48.

A steam derrick used in the erection of a mill by the owner in a place other than his residence is not subject to taxation in the latter place, the exceptions made by the statute to the rule that personal property shall be taxed at the residence of the owner not including steam derricks. Dresser *v.* Hopkinton, 75 N. H. 138, 71 Atl. 534.

Taxation of itinerant merchants or peddlers see Woodward *v.* Jacobs, 27 Ind. App. 188, 60 N. E. 1015.

Logs in process of manufacture at a mill see Wisconsin Sulphite Fibre Co. *v.* D. K. Jeffris Lumber Co., 132 Wis. 1, 111 N. W. 237.

20. *Arkansas.*— Harris Lumber Co. *v.* Grandstaff, 78 Ark. 187, 95 S. W. 772.

California.— San Joaquin, etc., Canal, etc., Co. *v.* Merced County, 2 Cal. App. 593, 84 Pac. 285.

Connecticut.— Field *v.* Guilford Water Co., 79 Conn. 70, 63 Atl. 723.

Georgia.— Greene County *v.* Wright, 126 Ga. 504, 54 S. E. 951.

Illinois.— Munson *v.* Crawford, 65 Ill. 185.

Maine.— Portland, etc., R. Co. *v.* Saco, 60 Me. 196.

Michigan.— Detroit Transp. Co. *v.* Detroit Bd. of Assessors, 91 Mich. 382, 51 N. W. 978.

Missouri.— Pacific R. Co. *v.* Cass County, 53 Mo. 17.

New Jersey.— Warren Mfg. Co. *v.* Warford, 37 N. J. L. 397; Warren R. Co. *v.* Person, 32 N. J. L. 134; Jersey City, etc., R. Co. *v.* Haight, 30 N. J. L. 443.

New York.— People *v.* Barker, 157 N. Y.

b. Right of Way, Tracks, and Other Realty. In the ordinary distribution of railroad taxation between the state and the municipalities, the former sometimes reserves the right to tax the real property of the road as a whole, or to have it assessed as a whole for state taxes by a state board; [53] but the more usual arrangement is for the state to tax capital stock and franchises, leaving to the local authorities the right to tax the physical property of the road within their respective limits, such as road-bed, tracks, bridges, shops, and other improvements.[54]

c. Rolling-Stock and Equipment Rolling-stock and other such equipment of a railroad is sometimes apportioned among the several counties through which the road passes, for the purpose of local taxation, in proportion to the mileage of the road in each county.[55] But in the absence of a statute authorizing such a distribution, property of this kind is taxable only at the domicile of the corporation, that is, its head office or principal place of business.[56]

6. MISCELLANEOUS CORPORATIONS. Decisions relating to special statutory rules for the taxation of the property of certain particular kinds of corporations are collated in the note hereto.[57]

352; State *v.* Back, 72 Nebr. 402, 100 N. W. 952, 69 L. R. A. 561; Franklin County *v.* Nashville, etc., R. Co., 12 Lea (Tenn.) 521.

53. *Illinois.*—Chicago, etc., R. Co. *v.* Grant, 167 Ill. 489, 47 N. E. 750; Chicago, etc., R. Co. *v.* People, 4 Ill. App. 468.

Kentucky.— Louisville, etc., R. Co. *v.* Warren County Ct., 5 Bush 243.

Missouri.— State *v.* Hannibal, etc., R. Co., 135 Mo. 618, 37 S. W. 532.

Nebraska.— Chicago, etc., R. Co. *v.* Cass County, 72 Nebr. 489, 101 N. W. 11.

Pennsylvania.—Western New York, etc., R. Co. *v.* Venango County, 183 Pa. St. 618, 38 Atl. 1088.

See 45 Cent. Dig. tit. "Taxation," § 462.

54. See the statutes of the several states; and the cases cited *infra*, this note.

The following kinds of railroad property have been held taxable by local authorities: Tracks and railroad bed. Sparks *v.* Macon, 98 Ga. 301, 25 S. E. 459; Sangamon, etc., R. Co. *v.* Morgan County, 14 Ill. 163, 56 Am. Dec. 497; Morgan's L. & T., etc., Co. *v.* Bd. of Reviewers, 41 La. Ann. 1156, 3 So. 507; Camden, etc., R. Co. *v.* Atlantic City, 60 N. J. L. 242, 41 Atl. 1116. Fences along the right of way. Santa Clara County *v.* Southern Pac. R. Co., 118 U. S. 394, 6 S. Ct. 1132, 30 L. ed. 118. Track, road, and bridges. Detroit *v.* Wayne Cir. Judge, 127 Mich. 604, 86 N. W. 1032. Bridge not constructed as part of the road and used for general travel. St. Joseph, etc., R. Co. *v.* Devereux, 41 Fed. 14. Rails, sleepers, and bridges. Providence, etc., R. Co. *v.* Wright, 2 R. I. 459. Machine and repair shops. Oregon Short Line R. Co. *v.* Yeates, 2 Ida. (Hasb.) 397, 17 Pac. 457. Freight yards leased or used for private purposes. State *v.* Hannibal, etc., R. Co., 135 Mo. 618, 37 S. W. 532; Delaware, etc., R. Co. *v.* Newark, 60 N. J. L. 60, 37 Atl. 629. Franchise of a street railway company. Detroit *v.* Wayne Cir. Judge, 127 Mich. 604, 86 N. W. 1032.

55. Cook County *v.* Chicago, etc., R. Co., 35 Ill. 460; Evansville, etc., R. Co. *v.* West, 138 Ind. 697, 37 N. E. 1012; Pittsburgh, etc., R. Co. *v.* Backus, 133 Ind. 625, 33 N. E. 432; Baltimore, etc., R. Co. *v.* Wicomico County, 93 Md. 113, 48 Atl. 853; Richmond, etc., R. Co. *v.* Alamance, 84 N. C. 504.

56. *Iowa.*— Dubuque *v.* Illinois Cent. R. Co., 39 Iowa 56.

Maryland.— Baltimore City Appeal Tax Ct. *v.* Western Maryland R. Co., 50 Md. 274.

Minnesota.— State *v.* Iverson, 97 Minn. 286, 106 N. W. 309.

Missouri.— Pacific R. Co. *v.* Cass County, 53 Mo. 17.

Utah.— Union Refrigerator Transit Co. *v.* Lynch, 18 Utah 378, 55 Pac. 639, 48 L. R. A. 790.

Virginia.— Elizabeth City County *v.* Newport News, 106 Va. 764, 56 S. E. 801.

See 45 Cent. Dig. tit. "Taxation," § 463.

Compare Territory *v.* Yavapai County Delinquent Tax List, 3 Ariz. 117, 21 Pac. 768; Atlantic, etc., R. Co. *v.* Lesueur, 2 Ariz. 428, 19 Pac. 157, 1 L. R. A. 244, holding that for the purpose of taxation the *situs* of rolling-stock of a railway company is wherever such stock is habitually used in the business.

Steamboat owned by railroad.—A county assessor has no authority to assess a steamboat used by a railroad exclusively for the transfer of freight and passengers between terminals, even though it were not assessed by the railroad assessors. Little Rock, etc., R. Co. *v.* Williams, 101 Tenn. 146, 46 S. W. 448.

57. See the cases cited *infra*, this note.

Turnpike companies.— A statute of New Jersey directs that the personal estate of such a company shall be taxed where the treasurer resides, if tolls are collected in several townships or wards. Within the meaning of this statute a plank road company is a turnpike company. Haight *v.* State, 32 N. J. L. 449; Jersey City, etc., Plank Road Co. *v.* Haight, 30 N. J. L. 443.

Toll-bridge companies.— In New York the real property of such companies is to be assessed in the town or ward where it lies, the provision of the statute directing their assessment in the town or ward where the tolls are collected applying only to their

on persons and property subject thereto.[4] It is not a judicial power,[5] but is a legislative function to be exercised only by the state or some inferior political division to which the state has delegated the power;[6] and as a legislative function it cannot be delegated to administrative officers,[7] although the further proceedings, such as in extending, assessing, and collecting the taxes, are administrative.[8]

2. Power and Authority of Legislature — a. In General. The power of a state legislature to levy taxes is general and unlimited, in respect to amount and to the persons or property subject, except in so far as it is restrained by constitutional provisions,[9] or territorially limited by the boundaries of the state,[10] or by the vesting in local authorities of the exclusive right to levy taxes for their proper local purposes.[11] And although the constitutions sometimes limit the power of the legislature in this respect by requiring the levy of a tax to be based on previous estimates of the probable revenue and the estimated expenses of the state,[12] or by requiring tax levies to be periodically made,[13] yet as a general rule the legislature is left to its own judgment and discretion in regard to the manner in which this power shall be exercised.[14]

4. *Alabama.*— Maguire *v.* Mobile County, 71 Ala. 401; Perry County *v.* Selma, etc., R. Co., 58 Ala. 546.

Colorado.— People *v.* Ames, 24 Colo. 422, 51 Pac. 426.

Iowa.— Tallman *v.* Cooke, 43 Iowa 330.

Louisiana.— State *v.* Maginnis, 26 La. Ann. 558.

Wisconsin.— Chicago, etc., R. Co. *v.* State, 128 Wis. 553, 108 N. W. 557.

See 45 Cent. Dig. tit. "Taxation," § 486.

5. Yamhill County *v.* Foster, 53 Oreg. 124, 99 Pac. 286.

6. Reno County School Dist. No. 127 *v.* Reno County School Dist. No. 45, 80 Kan. 641, 103 Pac. 126; Yamhill County *v.* Foster, 53 Oreg. 124, 99 Pac. 286; Chicago, etc., R. Co. *v.* State, 128 Wis. 553, 108 N. W. 557.

7. Chicago, etc., R. Co. *v.* State, 128 Wis. 553, 108 N. W. 557.

8. Chicago, etc., R. Co. *v.* State, 128 Wis. 553, 108 N. W. 557.

9. *Arkansas.*— Van de Griff *v.* Haynie, 28 Ark. 270.

Florida.— Cheney *v.* Jones, 14 Fla. 587.

Illinois.— Bank of Republic *v.* Hamilton County, 21 Ill. 53.

New York.— People *v.* Bleckwenn, 55 Hun 169, 7 N. Y. Suppl. 914 [*affirmed* in 129 N. Y. 637, 29 N. E. 1031].

Vermont.— Wells *v.* Austin, 59 Vt. 157, 10 Atl. 405.

See 45 Cent. Dig. tit. "Taxation," § 470. See also *supra*, I, B, 3.

Constitutional requirements and restrictions see *supra*, II.

10. See *supra*, I, C, 1.

11. People *v.* Houston, 54 Cal. 536. *Compare* Dickson *v.* Burckmyer, 67 S. C. 526, 46 S. E. 343.

12. Stein *v.* Morrison, 9 Ida. 426, 75 Pac. 246; Choat *v.* Phelps, 63 Kan. 762, 66 Pac. 1002. See also Chicago, etc., R. Co. *v.* State, 128 Wis. 553, 108 N. W. 557.

13. State *v.* Bailey, 56 Kan. 81, 42 Pac. 373. *Compare* Davis *v.* Brace, 82 Ill. 542 (as to a standing levy); Chicago, etc., R. Co. *v.* State, 128 Wis. 553, 108 N. W. 557.

14. *Indiana.*—Washington Nat. Bank *v.* Daily, 166 Ind. 631, 77 N. E. 53.

Kansas.— State *v.* Bailey, 56 Kan. 81, 42 Pac. 373, holding that the legislature may levy taxes by requiring a gross sum to be collected from the taxable property of the state, as well as by fixing a rate per cent.

Maryland.—Faust *v.* Twenty-Third German-American Bldg. Assoc., 84 Md. 186, 35 Atl. 890, holding that the legislature may make the levy and assessment of a tax directly, without the intervention of any officer.

Massachusetts.— *In re* Opinion of Justices, 126 Mass. 547, holding that under the state constitution the senate has an equal right with the house of representatives to originate an inquiry into the returns made from the towns, for the purpose of settling a valuation and of concluding on the proportion of ratable property within each town.

New York.— *In re* Flower, 129 N. Y. 643, 29 N. E. 463 [*reversing* 55 Hun 158, 7 N. Y. Suppl. 866]; *In re* Union College, 129 N. Y. 308, 29 N. E. 460 [*reversing* 7 N. Y. Suppl. 866] (both of which hold that the legislature cannot provide for the apportionment of a tax among the persons assessed, without also providing for notice or a hearing on the part of the taxpayer); Gubner *v.* McClellan, 130 N. Y. App. Div. 716, 115 N. Y. Suppl. 755.

North Dakota.— Sykes *v.* Beck, 12 N. D. 242, 96 N. W. 844.

See 45 Cent. Dig. tit. "Taxation," § 471.

Levy of poll or capitation tax.— The assessment of half a poll tax on an individual is illegal. Southampton *v.* Easthampton, 8 Pick. (Mass.) 380. Under a statutory provision (Mass. Rev. St. c. 27), that there shall be assessed upon polls, as nearly as the same can be conveniently done, one-sixth part of the whole sum to be raised, provided the whole poll tax assessed in any one year shall not exceed one dollar and fifty cents upon any individual, one-sixth of the state tax must be assessed on the polls, although if added to the town and county tax it would bring the poll tax on each individual above one dollar and fifty cents. Goodrich *v.* Lunenburg, 9 Gray (Mass.) 38. In assessing taxes for county and township purposes and for city purposes, at the same time, in a city, a separate poll tax must be assessed

b. Apportionment. Where the statute requires certain county authorities to apportion the state and county taxes among the several townships or other minor municipal divisions, according to the value of taxable property therein, it is essential to the validity of the taxes that the apportionment should at least substantially comply with the requirements of the statute,[54] as that it must not unreasonably exceed the amount to be raised by taxation;[55] although the apportionment will not be invalidated by mere clerical errors,[56] unless they have the effect to increase the tax to be borne by certain parcels of land beyond their just proportion.[57] If the county authorities improperly refuse to apportion the taxes they may be compelled to do so by mandamus.[58]

5. **Requisites and Validity of Levy — a. In General.** Although it has been held that no tax can be sustained as valid unless it is levied in accordance with the letter of the statute,[59] as a general rule the forms, methods, and various steps which the statute requires to be performed before the owners of property are properly chargeable with the tax, such as the filing of a petition for a levy,[60] an order for the submission of the question to popular vote,[61] the making of a previous estimate of the necessary or probable expenses of the municipality,[62] and notice to taxpayers of the meeting of the board which is to levy the tax[63] are conditions precedent to the validity of the tax and must be at least substantially followed in all material particulars;[64] and a failure substantially to comply with the stat-

54. *Michigan.*— Hoffman *v.* Lynburn, 104 Mich. 494, 62 N. W. 728; Shelden *v.* Marion Tp., 101 Mich. 256, 59 N. W. 614; Boyce *v.* Auditor-Gen., 90 Mich. 314, 51 N. W. 457; Boyce *v.* Sebring, 66 Mich. 210, 33 N. W. 815, holding that the statute does not require any particular form to be adopted or the word "apportion" to be used in the record, and that the mathematical computation by which is ascertained the amount of state and county tax to be raised by each township need not appear of record, but simply the result reached by such computation.

New Jersey.— Eatontown Tp. *v.* Monmouth County, 51 N. J. L. 100, 15 Atl. 830; Sea Isle City *v.* Cape May County, 50 N. J. L. 50, 12 Atl. 771; Bayonne *v.* Hudson County, 46 N. J. L. 93; Skirm *v.* Cox, 38 N. J. L. 302.

Tennessee.— State *v.* Cincinnati, etc., R. Co., 13 Lea 500.

Washington.—Coolidge *v.* Pierce County, 28 Wash. 95, 68 Pac. 391.

Canada.— *In re* Scott, 13 U. C. Q. B. 346.

See 45 Cent. Dig. tit. "Taxation," § 485.

Signature.— The failure of the chairman of the county board to sign an apportionment and equalization of the county tax, as required by statute, renders such apportionment invalid. Weston *v.* Monroe, 84 Mich. 341, 47 N. W. 446 [*distinguishing* Lacey *v.* Davis, 4 Mich. 140, 66 Am. Dec. 524].

Deduction of debts.— In apportioning the state and school tax among the several townships in a county, the board of assessors must distribute it according to the value of the property after deducting debts, as shown by the duplicates of the assessors of the several townships of the then present year and not of the preceding year. Skirm *v.* Cox, 38 N. J. L. 302.

55. Chicago, etc., R. Co. *v.* Baldridge, 177 Ill. 229, 52 N. E. 263; Alvord *v.* Collin, 20 Pick. (Mass.) 418.

56. Case *v.* Dean, 16 Mich. 12.

57. Case *v.* Dean, 16 Mich. 12.

58. People *v.* Jackson County, 24 Mich. 237. See also Mandamus, 26 Cyc. 334.

59. Hough *v.* North Adams, 196 Mass. 290, 82 N. E. 46.

60. Williams *v.* Lawrence County, 121 Ind. 239, 23 N. E. 76.

61. Peoria, etc., R. Co. *v.* People, 183 Ill. 19, 55 N. E. 714.

62. Waggoner *v.* Maumus, 112 La. 229, 36 So. 332; Wilson *v.* Anderson, 28 La. Ann. 261; St. Louis County *v.* Nettleton, 22 Minn. 356; State *v.* Wise, 12 Nebr. 313, 11 N. W. 329; Oregon R. Co. *v.* Umatilla County, 47 Oreg. 198, 81 Pac. 352.

63. Lahman *v.* Hatch, 124 Cal. 1, 56 Pac. 621; State *v.* Manhattan Silver Min. Co., 4 Nev. 318.

64. *Alabama.*— State Auditor *v.* Jackson County, 65 Ala. 142.

California.— Hewes *v.* Reis, 40 Cal. 255.

Idaho.— Shoup *v.* Willis, 2 Ida. (Hasb.) 120, 6 Pac. 124.

Missouri.— State *v.* Hannibal, etc., R. Co., 101 Mo. 136, 13 S. W. 505.

Oklahoma.— Nelson *v.* Oklahoma City, etc., R. Co., 24 Okla. 617, 104 Pac. 42.

Texas.— Dawson *v.* Ward, 71 Tex. 72, 9 S. W. 106.

Virginia.— Gilkeson *v.* Frederick County Justices, 13 Gratt. 577.

See 45 Cent. Dig. tit. "Taxation," §§ 486–489.

Mode of ordering levy.— Where an order of the board of supervisors showed that the committee on county taxes reported that they had examined the accounts of the county and recommended that a tax of a certain amount for all purposes be levied for the year on all the taxable property of the county, and that upon motion the report was adopted by the board, it is in effect an order for the levy of such a tax. Mix *v.* People, 72 Ill. 241.

Disregard of express directions.— The positive requirements of the statute in regard to

b. Effect of Partial Illegality.[4] If a tax is levied for several purposes, one of which is illegal, or if the rate or amount exceeds the statutory limitation, to any extent whatever, many decisions hold that the entire levy is absolutely void,[5] although according to others the partial invalidity or excess will not affect so much of the levy as is lawful, if it is possible to separate the legal from the illegal.[6]

9. Relevy or Subsequent Levy. A levy of taxes which is illegal or invalid for irregularities may generally be cured by a relevy in proper form;[7] and so where provision should have been made, in a general levy, for special purposes or extra expenses, but this was omitted, the authority of the levying board is not exhausted, but may be exercised by a new levy for such purposes.[8]

10. Judicial Control of Levies.[9] If the boards or officers authorized to levy taxes refuse to perform their duty, a court of competent jurisdiction may compel them to do so.[10] And so an injunction lies to restrain the levy of a tax which is clearly illegal or in excess of their authority, on the application of a party who shows that direct injury will result to himself or his property.[11] But courts have

Conclusiveness of tax rolls in collateral proceedings see *infra*, VI, E, 12, d.

4. **Effect of partial invalidity of tax roll** see *infra*, VI, E, 10.

5. *Maine*.— Huse *v.* Merriam, 2 Me. 375.

Massachusetts.— Libby *v.* Burnham, 15 Mass. 144; Stetson *v.* Kempton, 13 Mass. 272, 7 Am. Dec. 145. But see Colman *v.* Anderson, 10 Mass. 105.

Michigan.— Hewitt *v.* White, 78 Mich. 117, 43 N. W. 1043; Boyce *v.* Sebring, 66 Mich. 210, 33 N. W. 815; Lacey *v.* Davis, 4 Mich. 140, 66 Am. Dec. 524. But see Michigan Land, etc., Co. *v.* Republic Tp., 65 Mich. 628, 32 N. W. 882; Lake Superior Ship Canal, etc., Co. *v.* Thompson Tp., 56 Mich. 493, 23 N. W. 183, both holding that if the tax is properly levied but excessive, it is void only as to the excess.

Texas.— Dean *v.* Lufkin, 54 Tex. 265; San Antonio *v.* Raley, (Civ. App. 1895) 32 S. W. 180.

Vermont.— Johnson *v.* Colburn, 36 Vt. 693.

United States.— Clarke *v.* Strickland, 5 Fed. Cas. No. 2,864, 2 Curt. 439.

See 45 Cent. Dig. tit. "Taxation," § 481. See also *supra*, VI, A, 3, c.

6. *Florida*.— Pensacola *v.* Louisville, etc., R. Co., 21 Fla. 492 [*overruling* Basnett *v.* Jacksonville, 19 Fla. 664].

Illinois.— Mix *v.* People, 72 Ill. 241.

Kansas.— Smith *v.* Leavenworth County, 9 Kan. 296.

Nebraska.— Burlington, etc., R. Co. *v.* Saunders County, 16 Nebr. 123, 19 N. W. 698.

New Hampshire.— Taft *v.* Barrett, 58 N. H. 447.

New Jersey.— Sherman *v.* McClurg, 27 N. J. L. 253.

North Carolina.— Clifton *v.* Wynne, 80 N. C. 145.

Ohio.— Cummings *v.* Fitch, 40 Ohio St. 56.

Tennessee.— Bright *v.* Halloman, 7 Lea 309.

See 45 Cent. Dig. tit. "Taxation," § 481. See also *supra*, VI, A, 3, c.

7. People *v.* Wemple, 53 Hun (N. Y.) 197, 6 N. Y. Suppl. 732 [*affirmed* in 117 N. Y. 77, 22 N. E. 761]; McLean *v.* State, 8 Heisk. (Tenn.) 22.

But an original assessment which is void cannot be cured by a relevy. People *v.* Wemple, 53 Hun (N. Y.) 197, 6 N. Y. Suppl. 732 [*affirmed* in 117 N. Y. 77, 22 N. E. 761].

8. State *v.* Maguire, 52 Mo. 420; People *v.* Schoharie County, 49 Hun (N. Y.) 308, 2 N. Y. Suppl. 142 [*reversed* on other grounds in 121 N. Y. 345, 24 N. E. 830].

9. **Jurisdiction and powers of courts to review assessments in general** see *infra*, VII, C, 1.

10. Wharton *v.* Cass Tp. School Directors, 42 Pa. St. 358; Clay *v.* Hawkins County, 5 Lea (Tenn.) 137; Reg. *v.* Land Tax Com'rs, 16 Q. B. 381, 15 Jur. 190, 20 L. J. Q. B. 211, 71 E. C. L. 381; *In re* Holborn Land Tax Assessment, 5 Exch. 548; *In re* Glatton Land-Tax, 9 L. J. Exch. 211, 6 M. & W. 689.

Mandamus to compel levy in general see Mandamus, 26 Cyc. 320 *et seq.*

Mandamus to compel levy of tax to pay judgment against municipal corporation see Benjamin *v.* East Baton Rouge Parish, 23 La. Ann. 329; State *v.* Ewing, 116 Mo. 129, 22 S. W. 476. See also Mandamus, 26 Cyc. 325 *et seq.*

11. *Georgia*.— Schwartz *v.* National Packing Co., 122 Ga. 533, 50 S. E. 494.

Kansas.— Andrews *v.* Love, 46 Kan. 264, 26 Pac. 746; Challiss *v.* Atchison, 39 Kan. 276, 18 Pac. 195; Wyandotte, etc., Bridge Co. *v.* Wyandotte County, 10 Kan. 326, all of which hold, however, that before an injunction can be granted some step must be taken by the taxing officers toward the levying or collection of the tax.

Maryland.— Webster *v.* Baltimore County, 51 Md. 395.

New York.—Magee *v.* Cutler, 43 Barb. 239.

North Dakota.— Torgrinson *v.* Norwich School Dist. No. 31, 14 N. D. 10, 103 N. W. 414.

Ohio.— Griffith *v.* Crawford County, 1 Ohio Dec. (Reprint) 457, 10 West. L. J. 97.

United States.— Gregg *v.* Sanford, 65 Fed. 151, 12 C. C. A. 525.

See 45 Cent. Dig. tit. "Taxation," § 507.

Compare Norton *v.* Milner, 89 Ind. 197.

Injunction to restrain assessment see *infra*, VII, C, 5.

employed in making the assessment,[36] or a fixed annual or other salary,[37] is a matter of statutory regulation in the different states, as is also the proportion in which the pay of the assessors shall be divided between the state and the municipalities.[38] Whatever it be, this compensation is payable only to the board or assessor actually doing the work,[39] and will include everything pertaining to his duties as assessor for which no extra allowance is specially made,[40] and will cover the pay of deputies or assistants, except where their employment is authorized by statute or by the municipal authorities under whom the assessor works,[41] and an assessor cannot claim to be paid twice for his services merely because his successor in office uses the assessment roll which he made.[42] Special provision is sometimes made for fees for the discovery and listing of omitted or concealed property,[43] but an assessor cannot claim compensation for listing property which is legally exempt from taxation.[44]

3. Duties and Powers of Assessors — a. In General. An assessor of taxes, being a public officer, can act officially only in pursuance of authority conferred

And see Bell *v.* Arkansas County, 44 Ark. 493; Harrison *v.* Com., 83 Ky. 162; Williams *v.* Sharkey County, 74 Miss. 122, 20 So. 860; Hughston *v.* Carroll County, 68 Miss. 660, 10 So 51; Hill *v.* Warren County, (Miss. 1890) 8 So. 257.

36 See the statutes of the several states. And see Daily *v.* Daviess County, 165 Ind. 99, 74 N. E. 977; Whitley County *v.* Garty, 161 Ind 464, 68 N. E. 1012; Moody *v.* Newburyport, 3 Metc. (Mass.) 431: People *v.* Jones, 175 N. Y. 471, 67 N. E. 1088 [*affirming* 68 N. Y. App Div. 396, 74 N. Y. Suppl. 294]; Marquette *v.* Berks County, 3 Pa. Super. Ct. 36; Young *v.* Huntington County, 20 Pa. Co. Ct. 374.

Double compensation.— A statute which provides for a board of review composed of the assessor, auditor, and treasurer of the county, and two freeholders, who shall each receive a *per diem* compensation while acting as members of the board, does not authorize the county assessor, while acting as a member of the board, to draw an additional *per diem for* services performed as assessor. Daily *v.* Daviess County, 165 Ind. 99, 74 N. E. 977.

Mileage.— Assessors are not entitled to mileage in addition to their *per diem* compensation. Taylor *v.* Umatilla County, 6 Oreg. 401; Young *v.* Huntington County, 20 Pa. Co. Ct. 374.

Overpayments to an assessor may be recovered by the proper county authorities. Campbell *v.* Boone County, 41 Ind. App. 710, 83 N. E. 357; Caldwell *v.* Boone County, 41 Ind. App. 40, 83 N. E. 355.

37. Dodge *v.* San Francisco, 135 Cal. 512, 67 Pac. 973.

Power to change salaries.— Where the statute authorizes the county commissioners to "determine" the salaries of the township assessors within certain limits, they may change such a salary from time to time. Allen County *v.* Chapman, 22 Ind. App. 60, 53 N. E. 187.

Salary voted by town.— Under a statute providing that the auditors shall not allow any claim for personal services except where compensation is fixed by law or by vote of the town, a tax lister can recover only such compensation as the town votes him. Barnes *v.* Bakersfield, 57 Vt. 375.

38. State *v.* Holladay, 61 Mo. 524; Wilbarger County *v.* Perkins, 86 Tex. 348, 24 S. W. 794.

39. State *v.* Jumel, 30 La. Ann. 235.

Where it is the duty of the collector, and not the receiver, to make assessments for both state and county purposes, an agreement by an inferior court that the services should be performed by the receiver is void, and he cannot recover thereon. Adams *v.* Dougherty County, 21 Ga. 206.

40. Williams *v.* Chariton County, 85 Mo. 645.

Making militia rolls.— Where the making of a roll of persons liable to militia duty is part of the duty of an assessor of taxes, he cannot claim extra compensation for it. McClung *v.* St. Paul, 14 Minn. 420; State *v.* Ryland, 14 Nev. 46; Dilley *v.* Luzerne County, 8 Pa. Co. Ct. 162.

Reassessment.— Compensation of assessor for making a reassessment ordered by the county board see Crawford County *v.* Huls, 12 Ill. App. 406.

Compensation of assessor for making copies of assessment rolls for cities see Alameda County *v.* Dalton, 9 Cal. App. 26, 98 Pac. 85.

Compensation for each line of the tax roll actually extended by the assessor see Pearsall *v.* Brower, 120 N. Y. App. Div. 584, 105 N. Y. Suppl. 207.

41. Tulare County *v.* May, 118 Cal. 303, 50 Pac. 427; Lynch *v.* Butte County, 102 Cal. 446, 36 Pac. 806; Roberts *v.* People, 9 Colo. 458, 13 Pac. 630; Warner *v.* State Auditors, 128 Mich. 500, 87 N. W. 638; Beaumont *v.* Ramsey County, 32 Minn. 108, 19 N. W. 727.

42. State *v.* Graham, 23 La. Ann. 780.

43. Reed *v.* Cunningham, 121 Iowa 555, 96 N. W. 1119; Harrison *v.* Wilkerson, 80 S. W. 1190, 26 Ky. L. Rep. 260; Hoak *v.* Lancaster County, 29 Pa. Super. Ct. 585.

44. Powers *v.* Osbon, 118 Ky. 810, 82 S. W. 419, 26 Ky. L. Rep. 744; Berry *v.* Missoula County, 6 Mont. 121, 9 Pac. 899.

a list or schedule of the same and return it to the assessors as a basis for their assessment. Some of these statutes are held merely directory, no penalty attaching for a failure to comply.[7] But generally it is provided that some penalty or disadvantage shall be visited on the taxpayer who refuses or neglects to list his property; and the courts have affirmed the constitutionality of statutes providing that, in such case, the assessor shall estimate the value of such person's property according to the best information he can obtain, and that the taxpayer shall have no appeal from the valuation so fixed; [8] or that the assessor, after valuing the property according to his own judgment, shall add a certain percentage to the estimate so reached (even as much as fifty or one hundred per cent) and then proceed to assess the tax on the aggregate; [9] or imposing a specific penalty on the delinquent taxpayer,[10] or even rendering him liable to indictment and punishment.[11]

b. Notice or Demand. Statutes requiring the assessor to demand from the taxpayer a list of his taxable property, or to notify him of his duty to return it, have sometimes been held merely directory; [12] but generally this requirement is held to be mandatory, so that the assessor cannot make a valid assessment or impose any penalties on the delinquent, unless he has first given the proper notice or duly demanded the list.[13] Exceptions are necessarily made where the tax-

7. Merchants' Mut. Ins. Co. *v.* Board of Assessors, 40 La. Ann. 371, 3 So. 891; State *v.* Delevan, 1 Wis. 345.

8. *California.*— Orena *v.* Sherman, 61 Cal. 101.

Georgia.— Georgia, R., etc., Co. *v.* Wright, 124 Ga. 596, 53 S. E. 251.

Louisiana.— State *v.* Louisiana Mut. Ins. Co., 19 La. Ann. 474.

Massachusetts.— Charlestown *v.* Middlesex County, 101 Mass. 87; Otis Co. *v.* Ware, 8 Gray 509; Porter *v.* Norfolk County, 5 Gray 365. And see White *v.* New Bedford, 160 Mass. 217, 35 N. W. 678.

Nevada.— State *v.* Washoe County Bd. of Equalization, 7 Nev. 83.

New Jersey.— State *v.* State Comptroller, 54 N. J. L. 135, 23 Atl. 122; Sharp *v.* Apgar, 31 N. J. L. 358.

Oklahoma.— Pentecost *v.* Stiles, 5 Okla. 500, 49 Pac. 921.

See 45 Cent. Dig. tit. "Taxation," § 550.

Void assessment.—A law which provides that a party failing to list his property shall have no relief if "overtaxed" will not shut him out from his appropriate remedy against a void assessment. Mechanics' Sav. Bank *v.* Granger, 17 R. I. 77, 20 Atl. 202.

An owner who leaves the assessment of his land to the assessor, and fails to object thereto, is liable for the taxes assessed. Moores *v.* Thomas, (Miss. 1909) 48 So. 1025.

9. Boyer *v.* Jones, 14 Ind. 354; Fox's Appeal, 112 Pa. St. 337, 4 Atl. 149; Sanderson *v.* Lackawanna County, 1 Pa. Co. Ct. 342; *Ex p.* Lynch, 16 S. C. 32; Bartlett *v.* Wilson, 59 Vt. 23, 8 Atl. 321; Howes *v.* Bassett, 56 Vt. 141. See also State *v.* Allen, 2 McCord (S. C.) 55. *Contra*, McCormick *v.* Fitch, 14 Minn. 252.

A wilful undervaluation of property returned for taxation is of itself a "false return" within the meaning of a statute providing that in case of a false return the assessor shall find the true amount taxable and add to it a penalty. Ohio Farmers' Ins. Co. *v.* Hard, 59 Ohio St. 248, 52 N. E. 635.

10. See *infra*, VI, C, 3, c; XV, A, 3, b.

11. Caldwell *v.* State, 14 Tex. App. 171. See also *infra*, VI, C, 3, b.

12. Hudson *v.* Miller, 10 Kan. App. 532, 63 Pac. 21; Boothbay *v.* Race, 68 Me. 351; State *v.* Western Union Tel. Co., 4 Nev. 338; Hazzard *v.* O'Bannon, 36 Fed. 854. See also State *v.* Casey, 210 Mo. 235, 109 S. W. 1, holding that an assessor's failure to comply with Rev. St. (1899) § 5575, relative to giving notice, will not invalidate an assessment.

Visit to precinct.— The failure of an assessor or his assistant to make at least one visit to each precinct to receive tax returns will not alone vitiate the assessment. Reid *v.* Southern Dev. Co., 52 Fla. 595, 42 So. 206.

13. *California.*— People *v.* Shippee, 53 Cal. 675.

Kentucky.— Trigg *v.* Glasgow, 2 Bush 594; Jones *v.* Com., 14 B. Mon. 1. But *compare* Louisville, etc., Mail Co. *v.* Barbour, 88 Ky. 73, 9 S. W. 516, 10 Ky. L. Rep. 836.

Michigan.— Turner *v.* Muskegon County Cir. Judge, 95 Mich. 1, 54 N. W. 705.

Rhode Island.— Matteson *v.* Warwick, etc., Water Co., 28 R. I. 570, 68 Atl. 577.

Vermont.— Thomas *v.* Leland, 70 Vt. 223, 39 Atl. 1094.

United States.— Powder River Cattle Co. *v.* Custer County, 45 Fed. 323.

See 45 Cent. Dig. tit. "Taxation," § 551.

Sufficiency of notice or demand.—A personal application on the part of the assessor has been held sufficient. Melvin *v.* Weare, 56 N. H. 436. But on the other hand it has been held that where the statute requires a written or printed notice a mere verbal notice is insufficient (Cape Girardeau *v.* Buehrmann, 148 Mo. 198, 49 S. W. 985), although it is not material that the notice, if otherwise sufficient, is not dated (State *v.* Seahorn, 139 Mo. 582, 39 S. W. 809).

On whom served.— In the case of a partnership, the notice may be served on either partner. State *v.* Owsley, 17 Mont. 94, 42 Pac. 105.

they should accept it as true if they have no ground to doubt its correctness; but if they are not satisfied of its accuracy, they may conduct an investigation as to the extent and value of the person's property, and may increase his assessment on satisfactory proof that the list was not correct,[42] provided he has been given notice and opportunity to be heard.[43] But this cannot be done on mere surmise or where there is no ground in the evidence to fix a valuation different from that sworn to by the owner.[44]

i. Addition of Omitted Property.[45] Items of taxable property omitted from a taxpayer's sworn list may be added by the assessor on discovering their existence and taxability;[46] but this should only be done on notice to the taxpayer and giving him an opportunity to explain the omission or contest the liability of the property to taxation.[47]

3. Proceedings on Failure to Return List or Making False List[48] **— a. Right and Duty of Assessor to Ascertain and Value Property** — (I) *In General.*[49] If the taxpayer neglects or refuses to return the sworn list of his taxable property required of him by statute, or makes a false or insufficient list, it usually is the right and duty of the assessor to proceed to ascertain the nature and extent of that person's taxable property from the best sources of information at his com-

42. *Georgia.*— Georgia R., etc., Co. *v.* Wright, 124 Ga. 596, 53 S. E. 251.

Illinois.— Felsenthal *v.* Johnson, 104 Ill. 21.

Kentucky.— Baldwin *v.* Shine, 84 Ky. 502, 2 S. W. 164, 8 Ky. L. Rep. 496.

Massachusetts.—Lanesborough *v.* Berkshire County, 131 Mass. 124; Hall *v.* Middlesex County, 10 Allen 100; Newburyport *v.* Essex County, 12 Metc. 211.

Michigan.— Bowman *v.* Montcalm Cir. Judge, 129 Mich. 608, 89 N. W. 334.

Missouri.— State *v.* Spencer, 114 Mo. 574, 21 S. W. 837.

Nevada.— State *v.* Central Pac. R. Co., 10 Nev. 47; State *v.* Kruttschnitt. 4 Nev. 178.

New Jersey.—Newton Trust Co. *v.* Atwood, 77 N. J. L 141, 71 Atl. 110.

New York.—People *v.* Halsey, 37 N. Y. 344 [*affirming* 53 Barb. 547, 36 How. Pr. 487].

Oregon.— Oregon, etc., Mortg. Sav. Bank *v.* Jordan, 16 Oreg. 113, 17 Pac. 621.

Vermont.— Fulham *v.* Howe, 60 Vt. 351, 14 Atl. 652.

West Virginia.— Younger *v.* Meadows, 63 W. Va. 275. 59 S. E. 1087.

Wisconsin.—State *v.* Gaylord, 73 Wis. 306, 41 N. W. 518; Lawrence *v.* Janesville, 46 Wis. 364, 1 N. W. 338, 50 N. W. 1102; Matheson *v.* Mazomanie, 20 Wis. 191.

See 45 Cent. Dig. tit. "Taxation," § 562. And see *infra*, VI, C, 6, a, (IV).

43. State *v.* Spencer, 114 Mo. 574, 21 S. W. 837, even though the statute does not require such notice. And see cases cited *supra*, note 42.

44. Gibson *v.* Clark, 131 Iowa 325, 108 N. W. 527; People *v.* Reddy, 43 Barb. (N. Y.) 539.

Where a return of personalty shows valid indebtedness in excess of the value of the personalty, an assessment notwithstanding such return is erroneous. People *v.* Odell, 129 N. Y. App. Div. 475, 114 N. Y. Suppl. 199.

45. **Omissions from tax rolls** see *infra*, VI, E, 9.

46. *Arkansas.*— Kinsworthy *v.* Mitchell, 21 Ark. 145.

California.— Rosasco *v.* Tuolumne County, 143 Cal. 430, 77 Pac. 148; Henne *v.* Los Angeles County, 129 Cal. 297, 61 Pac. 1081.

Indiana.— Gallup *v.* Schmidt, (1899) 54 N. E. 384.

Kansas.— Johnson County *v.* Hewitt, 76 Kan. 816, 93 Pac. 181, 14 L. R. A. N. S. 493, holding that where omitted property is duly valued and the proper amount of taxes thereon charged against the owner, the failure of the county clerk to correct the assessor's return does not vitiate the tax.

Minnesota.— Thompson *v.* Tinkcom, 15 Minn. 295.

Nebraska.— Roe *v.* St. John, 7 Nebr. 139.

Ohio.— Cameron *v.* Cappeller, 41 Ohio St. 533.

Pennsylvania.— Baugh *v.* Elkin, 24 Pa. Co. Ct. 203.

United States.— Askamp *v.* Lewis, 103 Fed. 906.

See 45 Cent. Dig. tit. "Taxation," § 563.

But *compare* Tores *v.* Rowan County Justices, 6 N. C. 167.

Taxpayer's right of appeal from a judgment listing omitted property for taxation see Com. *v.* Adams Express Co., 124 Ky. 85, 98 S. W. 288, 30 Ky. L. Rep. 309.

47. Moors *v.* Boston Street Com'rs, 134 Mass. 431; Ware *v.* Bradbury, 29 Fed. Cas. No. 17,168, 3 Sumn. 186. See also Com. *v.* Adams Express Co., 124 Ky. 85, 98 S. W. 288, 30 Ky. L. Rep. 309. But *compare* Rosasco *v.* Tuolumne, 143 Cal. 430, 77 Pac. 148; Wabash, etc., R. Co. *v.* Johnson, 108 Ill. 11.

48. **Effect of failure to make list or statement of property on right of review** see *infra*, VII, B, 3, c.

Penalties for failure to make list or making false list see *infra*, XV, A, 3, b.

49. **Notice or demand as condition precedent to assessment of property on failure to list** see *supra*. VI, C, 2, b.

where the two parcels are owned by the same person,[81] unless the assessment may be saved by the aid of a statute curing defects and irregularities,[82] or unless the

229, 36 So. 332; Howcott *v.* Fifth Louisiana Levee Dist., 46 La. Ann. 322, 14 So. 848. And see Head *v.* Howcott Land Co., 119 La. 331, 44 So. 117.

Maine.— Barker *v.* Blake, 36 Me. 433.

Maryland.— See Hill *v.* Williams, 104 Md. 595, 65 Atl. 413.

Massachusetts.— Lancy *v.* Boston, 186 Mass. 128, 71 N. E. 302; Jennings *v.* Collins, 99 Mass. 29, 96 Am. Dec. 687; Hayden *v.* Foster, 13 Pick. 492.

Michigan.— Auditor-Gen. *v.* Ayer, 122 Mich. 136, 80 N. W. 997; Cooley *v.* Waterman, 16 Mich. 366.

Minnesota.— Farnham *v.* Jones, 32 Minn. 7, 19 N. W. 83.

Mississippi.— Dunn *v.* Winston, 31 Miss. 135. But see Moores *v.* Thomas, (1909) 48 So. 1025, holding that the provision of the Code (1906), § 4283, that all subdivisions of a section shall be set down, if they belong to different persons, is merely directory, and that an assessment *in solido* of two tracts of land belonging to different individuals does not invalidate the assessment.

Nebraska.— Hart *v.* Murdock, 80 Nebr. 274, 114 N. W. 268; Spiech *v.* Tierney, 56 Nebr. 514, 76 N. W. 1090.

North Dakota.— State Finance Co. *v.* Browdle, 16 N. D. 193, 112 N. W. 76; State Finance Co. *v.* Beck, 15 N. D. 374, 109 N. W. 357; Roberts *v.* Fargo First Nat. Bank, 8 N. D. 504, 79 N. W. 1049.

Ohio.—Douglas *v.* Dangerfield, 10 Ohio 152.

Pennsylvania.— Fisk *v.* Corey, 141 Pa. St. 334, 21 Atl. 594; McLaughlin *v.* Kain, 45 Pa. St. 113.

Virginia.— Douglas Co. *v.* Com., 97 Va. 397, 34 S. E. 52.

Wisconsin.— Neu *v.* Voege, 96 Wis. 489, 71 N. W. 880; Towne *v.* Salentine, 92 Wis. 404, 66 N. W. 395; Siegel *v.* Outagamie County, 26 Wis. 70; Orton *v.* Noonan, 25 Wis. 672; Knox *v.* Huidekoper, 21 Wis. 527; State *v.* Williston, 20 Wis. 228.

See 45 Cent. Dig. tit. "Taxation," §§ 574, 575.

Joint owners.—Where two different persons own distinct parcels of the same lot of land, in severalty, it cannot properly be assessed to them as joint owners. Romig *v.* Lafayette, 33 Ind. 30; Knox *v.* Huidekoper, 21 Wis. 527.

Unknown owners.— The rule stated in the text applies also where the owners of realty are unknown; separate lots or parcels must be separately assessed and taxed. Shimmin *v.* Inman, 26 Me. 228.

Apportionment of taxes.— It is implied in the rule stated in the text that, the joint assessment being void, there can be no apportionment of the tax between the owners jointly assessed for it. But in Michigan this is otherwise by statute. See Kneeland *v.* Hull, 116 Mich. 55, 74 N. W. 300.

Building covering several lots.— Where a building covers several lots belonging to different owners, it is held proper, in New York, to include all the lots in one assessment, instead of assessing a certain amount against the owner of each lot. People *v.* Feitner, 169 N. Y. 604, 62 N. E. 1099 [*affirming* 65 N. Y. App. Div. 318, 73 N. Y. Suppl. 97].

81. *Alabama.*— Walker *v.* Chapman, 22 Ala. 116.

California.— People *v.* Hollister, 47 Cal. 408.

Florida.— McKeown *v.* Collins, 38 Fla. 276, 21 So. 103.

Illinois.— Howe *v.* People, 86 Ill. 288.

Indiana.— Cockrum *v.* West, 122 Ind. 372, 23 N. E. 140. See Parker *v.* Wayne County, 56 Ind. 38.

Iowa.— Martin *v.* Cole, 38 Iowa 141.

Kansas.— See Spalding *v.* Watson, 35 Kan. 39, 10 Pac. 105.

Maine.— Nason *v.* Ricker, 63 Me. 381.

Maryland.— Allegany County *v.* Union Min. Co., 61 Md. 545.

Massachusetts.— Sandwich *v.* Fish, 2 Gray 298; Hayden *v.* Foster, 13 Pick. 492.

Michigan.— Wright *v.* Dunham, 13 Mich. 414.

Nebraska.— Dundy *v.* Richardson County, 8 Nebr. 508, 1 N. W. 565.

Nevada.— Peers *v.* Reed, 23 Nev. 404, 48 Pac. 897; Wright *v.* Cradlebaugh, 3 Nev. 341.

New York.— May *v.* Traphagen, 139 N. Y. 478, 34 N. E. 1064 [*reversing* 19 N. Y. Suppl. 679]; Bennett *v.* Kovarick, 23 Misc. 73, 51 N. Y. Suppl. 752; Litchfield *v.* Brooklyn, 13 Misc. 693, 34 N. Y. Suppl. 1090; French *v.* Whittlesey, 30 N. Y. Suppl. 363.

North Dakota.— Griffin *v.* Denison Land Co., (1908) 119 N. W. 1041.

Pennsylvania.— Fisk *v.* Corey, 141 Pa. St. 334, 21 Atl. 594; Insurance Co. *v.* Yard, 17 Pa. St. 338.

Rhode Island.—Mowry *v.* Slatersville Mills, 20 R. I. 94, 37 Atl. 538; Taylor *v.* Narragansett Pier Co., 19 R. I. 123, 33 Atl. 519; Evans *v.* Newell, 18 R. I. 38, 25 Atl. 347; Young *v.* Joslin, 13 R. I. 675.

Texas.— McCombs *v.* Rockport, 14 Tex. Civ. App. 560, 37 S. W. 988. *Compare* Guerguin *v.* San Antonio, (Civ. App. 1899) 50 S. W. 140.

Wisconsin.— Neu *v.* Voege, 96 Wis. 489, 71 N. W. 880.

United States.— French *v.* Edwards, 13 Wall. 506, 20 L. ed. 702.

Canada.— Reed *v.* Smith, 1 Manitoba 341; Wildman *v.* Tait, 32 Ont. 274; Aston *v.* Innis, 26 Grant Ch. (U. C.) 42.

See 45 Cent. Dig. tit. "Taxation," § 574.

Taxable and non-taxable property.— If two parcels of land are wrongfully assessed together, and one is not taxable, the tax on that, if paid under protest, may be recovered back. St. Mary's Church *v.* Tripp, 14 R. I. 307.

82. *Massachusetts.*— Sargent *v.* Bean, 7 Gray 125.

it has been held that an assessment of real property is invalid if it is made in the name of the deceased owner,[9] or of the estate of the decedent,[10] or if it is assessed to "the heirs" of the deceased without naming them or without a more particular description of them.[11] But on the other hand it has been held that an assessment of real property is valid, where made in the name of the estate of the decedent,[12] before the heirs go into possession;[13] or in the name of the deceased owner,[14] if the heirs do not cause the land to be assessed in their names,[15] or if notice of the decedent's death has not been given to the assessor,[16] or the property is vacant and the owner does not reside in the tax district;[17] or if it is made to the heirs

9. *Alabama.*— Scott *v.* Brown, 106 Ala. 604, 17 So. 731; Jackson *v.* King, 82 Ala. 432, 3 So. 232.

District of Columbia.— Kann *v.* King, 25 App. Cas. 182 [*reversed* on other grounds in 204 U. S. 43, 27 S. Ct. 213, 51 L. ed. 360].

Louisiana.— Boagni *v.* Pacific Imp. Co., 111 La. 1063, 36 So. 129; George *v.* Cole, 109 La. 816, 33 So. 784; Millaudon *v.* Gallagher, 104 La. 713, 29 So. 307; Kohlman *v.* Glaudi, 52 La. Ann. 700, 27 So. 116; Cucullu *v.* Brakenridge Lumber Co., 49 La. Ann. 1445, 22 So. 409; Montgomery *v.* Marydale Land, etc., Co., 46 La. Ann. 403, 15 So. 63; Kearns *v.* Collins, 40 La. Ann. 453, 4 So. 498 (deceased person to whom the property did not belong at the time); Stafford *v.* Twitchell, 33 La. Ann. 520; Fix *v.* Dierker, 30 La. Ann. 175.

Maine.— Morrill *v.* Lovett, 95 Me. 165, 49 Atl. 666, 26 L. R. A. 634.

Massachusetts.— Kerslake *v.* Cummings, 180 Mass. 65, 61 N. E. 760.

New Hampshire.— Burpee *v.* Russell, 64 N. H. 62, 5 Atl. 837.

New Mexico.— Stewart *v.* Bernalillo County, 11 N. M. 517, 70 Pac. 574.

Rhode Island.— Taft *v.* Ballou, 23 R. I. 213, 49 Atl. 895.

See 45 Cent. Dig. tit. "Taxation," §§ 704–706.

Death during fiscal year.—An assessment of property for taxes made in the name of one who was living and the owner of the property at the beginning of the fiscal year will bind his heirs. *In re* Kauffman, 104 Iowa 639, 74 N. W. 8; Clifford *v.* Michiner, 49 La. Ann. 1511, 22 So. 811.

10. *Alabama.*— Jackson *v.* King, 82 Ala. 432, 3 So. 232.

Florida.— L'Engle *v.* Wilson, 21 Fla. 461.

Maine.— Fairfield *v.* Woodman, 76 Me. 549.

Michigan.— Fowler *v.* Campbell, 100 Mich. 398, 59 N. W. 185. But *compare* Dickison *v.* Reynolds, 48 Mich. 158, 12 N. W. 24.

Missouri.— State *v.* Kenrick, 159 Mo. 631, 60 S. W. 1063.

New Mexico.— Territory *v.* Perea, 10 N. M. 362, 62 Pac. 1094.

New York.— Trowbridge *v.* Horan, 78 N. Y. 439; Matter of Chadwick, 59 N. Y. App. Div. 334, 69 N. Y. Suppl. 853; Adams *v.* Monroe County, 18 N. Y. App. Div. 415, 46 N. Y. Suppl. 48 [*affirmed* in 154 N. Y. 619, 49 N. E. 144]; People *v.* Valentine, 5 N. Y. App. Div. 520, 38 N. Y. Suppl. 1087; Matter of Kenworthy, 63 Hun 165, 17 N. Y. Suppl. 655. But *compare* Sanders *v.* Carley, 83 N. Y. App. Div. 193, 83 N. Y. Suppl. 106 [*affirmed* in 178 N. Y. 622, 70 N. E. 1108], holding that an assessment of non-resident lands is not invalid because the owner of the premises is designated as "estate of ——," as such designation may be regarded as surplusage.

North Carolina.— Morrison *v.* McLauchlin, 88 N. C. 251.

Virginia.— Douglas Co. *v.* Com., 97 Va. 397, 34 S. E. 52.

See 45 Cent. Dig. tit. "Taxation," §§ 704–706.

11. *Michigan.*— Fowler *v.* Campbell, 100 Mich. 398, 59 N. W. 185. But *compare* Dickison *v.* Reynolds, 48 Mich. 158, 12 N. W. 24.

Missouri.— Berlien *v.* Bieler, 96 Mo. 491, 9 S. W. 916.

New York.— Sandy Hill *v.* Akin, 77 Hun 537, 28 N. Y. Suppl. 889; Matter of Reid, 52 N. Y. App. Div. 243, 65 N. Y. Suppl. 373. *Compare* Wheeler *v.* Anthony, 10 Wend. 346.

Pennsylvania.— County Com'rs *v.* Hazelhurst, 3 Pa. L. J. Rep. 297.

United States.— Bush *v.* Williams, 4 Fed. Cas. No. 2,225, Brunn. Col. Cas. 234, Cooke (Tenn.) 360.

See 45 Cent. Dig. tit. "Taxation," §§ 704–706.

12. Moale *v.* Baltimore, 61 Md. 224; Coles *v.* Platt, 24 N. J. L. 108, holding that an assessment of taxes to the estate of J. B. C., where the estate is well known and commonly so designated, is not void for uncertainty or lack of form in not naming the persons assessed. See also Endicott *v.* Corson, 50 N. J. L. 381, 13 Atl. 265.

13. Gonzales *v.* Saux, 119 La. 657, 44 So. 332; Surget *v.* Newman, 43 La. Ann. 873, 9 So. 561; Carter *v.* New Orleans, 33 La. Ann. 816. See also New Orleans *v.* Stemple, 175 U. S. 309, 20 S. Ct. 110, 44 L. ed. 174.

14. Grant *v.* Bartholomew, 57 Nebr. 673, 78 N. W. 314; Koth *v.* Pallachucola Club, 79 S. C. 514, 61 S. E. 77; Holroyd *v.* Pumphrey, 18 How. (U. S.) 69, 15 L. ed. 264.

15. Husbands *v.* Polivick, 128 Ky. 652, 96 S. W. 825, 29 Ky. L. Rep. 890.

16. Williams *v.* Chaplain, 112 La. 1075, 36 So. 859.

17. Sewell *v.* Watson, 31 La. Ann. 589, holding that vacant property, the owner of which does not reside in the parish where it is situated, may be validly assessed as the property of its immediately preceding but deceased owner, of whose succession it is a part and in whose name it stood on the public records.

(II) *DETERMINATION OF VALUE.* The legislature may decide the manner in which different forms of property may be valued for taxation.[25] To constitute a valid assessment of property for taxation, the valuation of the property must be made by the proper assessing officer himself,[26] and he cannot delegate this duty to another.[27] In making the estimate the assessor must apply his own knowledge and exercise his own judgment,[28] and he is neither bound nor permitted, unless the statute so directs, to adopt a valuation made by a different assessor or board of assessors or board of review.[29] Unless otherwise specified, his estimate should be based upon and correspond with the fair cash value of the property; [30] and the amount it would bring at a fair private sale is ordinarily a just criterion of this value; [31] but in forming his estimate the assessor should avail himself of all proper sources of information and take into consideration all facts and circumstances

House Bill No. 270, 7 Colo. 635, 21 Pac. 476; Lebanon *v.* Ohio, etc., R. Co., 77 Ill. 539; Hunt *v.* Union Tp., 27 N. J. L. 433.

All available property should be taxed according to its value for the purpose of establishing the proportional ability and duty of individual owners to bear their burdens as citizens. *In re* Opinion of Justices, 195 Mass. 607, 84 N. E. 499.

25. St. Louis Consol. Coal Co. *v.* Miller, 236 Ill. 149, 86 N. E. 205. See also Royal Mfg. Co. *v.* New Jersey Bd. of Equalization, 76 N. J. L. 402, 70 Atl. 978, holding that since Pub. Laws (1906), 210, creating the county board of taxation, there has been no warrant scaling down valuation of taxable property by adopting a uniform percentage of actual value, although such was the general practice for years.

Legislative authority.— The power of the legislature to assess state taxes and to compel their payment directly to the state treasurer, without other official assistance, implies power to determine the value of the property to be assessed, and consequently a power of discrimination in selecting and fixing the taxable values. State *v.* Sterling, 20 Md. 502. And there is no constitutional objection to the legislature making the gross output of producing mines the criterion to govern assessors in determining the valuation. *In re* House Bill No. 270, 7 Colo. 635, 21 Pac. 476.

Mineral lands "improved and under development" see Com. *v.* Pocahontas Coal, etc., Co., 107 Va. 666, 60 S. E. 84.

26. Hyatt *v.* Allen, 54 Cal. 353; Tampa *v.* Mugge, 40 Fla. 326, 24 So. 489; Hoefling *v.* San Antonio, 15 Tex. Civ. App. 257, 38 S. W. 1127. See also State *v.* Cudahy Packing Co., 103 Minn. 419, 115 N. W. 645, 1039, holding that the revenue system contemplates an original assessment by the assessor, its correction by the auditor, and its equalization by various boards.

27. Woodman *v.* Auditor-Gen., 52 Mich. 28, 17 N. W. 227.

28. *Florida.*— King *v.* Gwynn, 14 Fla. 32.

Illinois.— St. Louis, etc., R. Co. *v.* Surrell, 88 Ill. 535.

Iowa.— Burnham *v.* Barber, 70 Iowa 87, 30 N. W. 20.

Michigan.— Crooks *v.* Whitford, 47 Mich. 283, 11 N. W. 159.

Nevada.— State *v.* Central Pac. R. Co., 10 Nev. 47.

New York.— People *v.* McNamara, 18 N. Y. App. Div. 17, 45 N. Y. Suppl. 456.

See 45 Cent. Dig. tit. "Taxation," § 580.

29. Granger *v.* Parsons, 2 Pick. (Mass.) 392; Missouri, etc., R. Co. *v.* Shannon, (Tex. Civ. App. 1906) 97 S. W. 527 [*affirmed* in 100 Tex. 379, 100 S. W. 138, 10 L. R. A. N. S. 681].

Conclusiveness of judgments fixing valuation.— An assessor is not bound to estimate a property at a certain sum because that sum was fixed as its value in a previous year by the judgment either of a court or of a board of review. Legendre *v.* St. Charles Parish Assessor, 108 La. 515, 32 So. 523; People *v.* Zundel, 157 N. Y. 513, 52 N. E. 570.

Statutes requiring adoption of valuation made by other board or assessor see Pitcher *v.* Jackman, 15 Ind. 107; People *v.* Adams, 125 N. Y. 471, 26 N. E. 746 [*affirming* in part and *reversing* in part 10 N. Y. Suppl. 295]; Wilson *v.* Marsh, 34 Vt. 352.

Approval of valuations.— It is competent for an assessor to employ others to make the valuations in the first instance, if he himself examines, revises, and adopts their estimates. Snell *v.* Ft. Dodge, 45 Iowa 564; Jermyn *v.* Fowler, 186 Pa. St. 595, 40 Atl. 972; Dean *v.* Gleason, 16 Wis. 1.

Right of auditor to direct assessor as to valuation of real property see Hamilton County *v.* Albers, 28 Ohio Cir. Ct. 830.

30. Stein *v.* Mobile, 17 Ala. 234; State *v.* Illinois Cent. R. Co., 27 Ill. 64, 79 Am. Dec. 396; State *v.* Savage, 65 Nebr. 714, 91 N. W. 716; State *v.* Osborn, 60 Nebr. 415, 83 N. W. 357; Clark *v.* Middleton, 74 N. H. 188, 66 Atl. 115.

There is a marked distinction between "full and true value" and "full and true cash value," as used in statutes relating to taxation. Richardson *v.* Howard, 23 S. D. 86, 120 N. W. 768.

31. State *v.* Randolph Tp., 25 N. J. L. 427; Brown *v.* Greer, 3 Head (Tenn.) 695. And see Salscheider *v.* Ft. Howard, 45 Wis. 519. But *compare* People *v.* Feitner, 34 Misc. (N. Y.) 299, 69 N. Y. Suppl. 793 [*affirmed* in 63 N. Y. App. Div. 615, 72 N. Y. Suppl. 1124 (*affirmed* in 168 N. Y. 675, 61 N. E. 1132)].

In some states it is required, and in all it is proper even if not necessary, that the improvements should be valued separately from the land, although the two valuations are added together to fix the total assessment.[52]

(III) *PLATTED AND UNPLATTED CITY PROPERTY.* It is provided by law in some states that lands within the limits of a city, but which have not been platted or subdivided into lots, shall not be assessed at a higher rate than suburban or agricultural lands, although this does not require them to be valued with reference to their possible use for purposes of agriculture; but they must be appraised at their actual value.[53]

(IV) *PROPERTY PARTLY EXEMPT.* It is error to assess taxable and exempt property together, but if the whole tax is not greater than what is properly chargeable to the taxable property, the assessment will not be disturbed.[54] Where one portion of a parcel of improved property is subject to taxation and another portion exempt, as where part of a large building is used for charitable, educational, or religious purposes, and the rest for business purposes, and the portions are not physically separable, the proper method of valuation is to estimate the value of the property as a whole, and then deduct the value of the exempt portion.[55]

(V) *INCREASING VALUATION BETWEEN PERIODICAL ASSESSMENTS.* In some states the appraisement of real property for taxation is made only at intervals of several years, the valuation once fixed remaining until the next periodical assessment.[56] The assessors, however, are authorized and directed to increase

App. Div. 944, 111 N. Y. Suppl. 1135 (*affirmed* in 193 N. Y. 614, 86 N. E. 1129)].

Washington.— Eureka Dist. Gold Min. Co. *v.* Ferry County, 28 Wash. 250, 68 Pac. 727.

Canada.— *In re* Vancouver Incorporation Act, 9 Brit. Col. 495.

See 45 Cent. Dig. tit. "Taxation," § 587.

As to improvements erected by a tenant under a mining lease see Gorrell *v.* Murphy, 1 Leg. Gaz. Rep. (Pa.) 195.

The value of buildings that do not belong to the owner of the soil should for assessment be measured by what it would cost to replace them if they were destroyed; and the fact that the ground is favorably situated commercially does not add to their value separately from the soil on which they stand. Tulane Imp. Co. *v.* Board of Assessors, 121 La. 941, 46 So. 928.

52. *California.*— Miller *v.* Kern County, 137 Cal. 516, 70 Pac. 549; People *v.* Culverwell, 44 Cal. 620.

Idaho.— People *v.* Owyhee Lumber Co., 1 Ida. 420; People *v.* Owyhee Min. Co., 1 Ida. 409.

Iowa.— Robertson *v.* Anderson, 57 Iowa 165, 10 N. W. 341.

Maryland.—Allegany County *v.* Union Min. Co., 61 Md. 545.

Massachusetts.— Tremont, etc., Mills *v.* Lowell, 163 Mass. 283, 39 N. E. 1028.

Nebraska.— Dundy *v.* Richardson County, 8 Nebr. 508, 1 N. W. 565.

See 45 Cent. Dig. tit. "Taxation," § 587.

Mills and machinery.— In proceedings to abate an assessment of a manufacturing plant, the machinery is to be treated as a separate class from the land and the buildings thereon, and, although each should properly be valued in connection with the other, yet if the land or the buildings be overvalued, an abatement may be ordered, although the machinery is rightly valued. Hamilton Mfg. Co. *v.* Lowell, 185 Mass. 114, 69 N. E. 1080.

Buildings owned by tenant.— Buildings erected on leased land by a tenant under a lease for ninety-nine years, renewable forever, are to be separately assessed to him at their value. Philadelphia, etc., R. Co. *v.* Baltimore City Appeal Tax Ct., 50 Md. 397.

53. Eschenburg *v.* Lake County, 129 Ind. 398, 28 N. E. 865; South Bend *v.* Cushing, 123 Ind. 290, 24 N. E. 114; Benoist *v.* St. Louis, 15 Mo. 668; Ransom *v.* Potter, 22 Ohio Cir. Ct. 388, 12 Ohio Cir. Dec. 478.

In the absence of such a statute, it is the duty of the assessor of lands within the corporate limits of a city to assess them at their true value, whether they are used for farming purposes or divided into lots for building purposes. Janesville *v.* Markoe, 18 Wis. 350.

54. Morris Canal, etc., Co. *v.* Haight, 35 N. J. L. 178; Roberts *v.* Jersey City, 25 N. J. L. 525.

55. *Maine.*— Auburn *v.* Young Men's Christian Assoc., 86 Me. 244, 29 Atl. 992.

Maryland.—Frederick County *v.* St. Joseph Sisters of Charity, 48 Md. 34.

Massachusetts.— Cambridge *v.* Middlesex County, 114 Mass. 337.

Nebraska.— Rohrbough *v.* Douglas County, 76 Nebr. 679, 107 N. W. 1000.

New York.— Worden *v.* Oneida County, 35 N. Y. App. Div. 206, 54 N. Y. Suppl. 952.

Ohio.— Cleveland Library Assoc. *v.* Pelton, 36 Ohio St. 253.

See 45 Cent. Dig. tit. "Taxation," § 588.

56. State *v.* Atwood Lumber Co., 96 Minn. 392, 105 N. W. 276.

Omitted property.— Where taxable property has been omitted from a triennial assessment, such property may be included in an assessment made in the following year, although there may have been no erections, ad-

at the time of the assessment;[66] but the interest of a remainder-man in a principal fund, which is to take effect in possession after the death of a life annuitant, is to be assessed for its present value, to be ascertained by the tables of mortality.[67]

7. Deduction of Indebtedness[68] — a. In General. In several states a taxpayer is allowed to deduct his *bona fide* indebtedness from the amount of his taxable personal property;[69] and an assessment is void if made without allowing such deduction when properly claimed by a person entitled to it.[70] But generally, where a person owns property in several places, the deduction is to be allowed only at the place of his own domicile, and hence cannot be claimed by non-residents.[71]

b. Deduction From Credits. In the absence of statute there can be no deductions from taxes on credits for debts owing by the taxpayer, and a statute authorizing such deduction should be strictly construed.[72] Within the meaning of such laws, money, whether in hand or in bank, is not a "credit" from which the deduction can be made,[73] neither is money loaned at interest, whether secured by note, bond, mortgage, or otherwise,[74] nor shares of stock in a national or state bank.[75] Where the law requires the taxpayer to file a list or schedule of the debts which

securities just before period for assessment see *supra*, III, A, 1, e.

66. State *v.* Melroy, (N. J. Sup. 1890) 19 Atl. 732; Richey *v.* Shurts, 41 N. J. L. 279; Gano *v.* Apgar, 41 N. J. L. 230; Hill *v.* Hansom, 36 N. J. L. 50; State *v.* Cornell, 31 N. J. L. 374.

Taxability of annuities in general see *supra*, III, A, 2, d.

67. State *v.* Melroy, (N. J. Sup. 1890) 19 Atl. 732; Wills *v.* Lippincott, 50 N. J. L. 349, 13 Atl. 6; Crispin *v.* Vansyckle, 49 N. J. L. 366, 8 Atl. 120; Wyckoff *v.* Jones, 39 N. J. L. 650.

68. **Deductions of indebtedness:** Of corporations generally see *infra*, VI, D, 5, e, (II). Of insurance companies see *infra*, VI, D, 7, b. Of railroad companies see *infra*, VI, D, 8, f.

Deduction of value of property of corporation not taxable see *infra*, VI, D, 5, e, (I).

69. See the statutes of the several states. And see Clark *v.* Belknap, 13 S. W. 212, 11 Ky. L. Rep. 791 (holding that a statutory provision allowing such a deduction is nugatory, where the law is so framed that no deduction can be made from the kinds of property enumerated in it, and it embraces all known kinds of property); Steere *v.* Walling, 7 R. I. 317 (holding that movable machinery is personal property, from the value of which the owner's actual indebtedness may be deducted); *In re* Assessment, etc., of Taxes, 4 S. D. 6, 54 N. W. 818.

Estate of devisee.— In order to determine how much of the estate of a devisee should be assessed for taxation, the amount which such devisee should contribute to the payment of decedent's debts should be ascertained and deducted from the devisee's estate. Schaeffer *v.* Ardery, 241 Ill. 27, 89 N. E. 294.

70. Howell *v.* Richards, 47 N. J. L. 434, 1 Atl. 495; Hughes *v.* Kelley, 69 Vt. 443, 38 Atl. 91.

An assignee for the benefit of creditors is a "trustee" within the meaning of the New Jersey tax law, and as such is taxable for the estate of the assignor in his hands, without deduction for the debts due from the assignor to his creditors. Clark *v.* Grover, 37 N. J. L. 174.

71. Perkins *v.* Bishop, 34 N. J. L. 45; People *v.* Barker, 159 N. Y. 569, 54 N. E. 1093 [*affirming* 35 N. Y. App. Div. 486, 54 N. Y. Suppl. 848]; People *v.* Barker, 145 N. Y. 239, 39 N. E. 1065; People *v.* Barker, 141 N. Y. 118, 35 N. E. 1073, 23 L. R. A. 95. But *compare In re* Assessment, etc., of Taxes, 4 S. D. 6, 54 N. W. 818.

72. Bailies *v.* Des Moines, 127 Iowa 124, 102 N. W. 813.

Deduction of indebtedness from unsecured credits see Willows Bank *v.* Glenn County, 155 Cal. 352, 101 Pac. 13.

73. Morris *v.* Jones, 150 Ill. 542, 37 N. E. 928; Stewart *v.* Duerr, 20 Ohio Cir. Ct. 505, 11 Ohio Cir. Dec. 310; Pullman State Bank *v.* Manring, 18 Wash. 250, 51 Pac. 464. But *compare* Com. *v.* Kentucky Distilleries, etc., Co., 132 Ky. 521, 116 S. W. 766; Clark *v.* Maher, 34 Mont. 391, 87 Pac. 272.

74. *Indiana.*— Clark *v.* Carter, 40 Ind. 190, under the statute of 1869. But under Rev. St. (1881) §§ 6332, 6333, and 6336, it is otherwise. Moore *v.* Hewitt, 147 Ind. 464, 46 N. E. 905.

Kansas.— Lappin *v.* Nemaha County, 6 Kan. 403.

Nebraska.— Lancaster County *v.* McDonald, 73 Nebr. 453, 103 N. W. 78.

Nevada.— Drexler *v.* Tyrrell, 15 Nev. 114; State *v.* State First Nat. Bank, 4 Nev. 348.

Ohio.— Payne *v.* Watterson, 37 Ohio St. 121.

See 45 Cent. Dig. tit. "Taxation," § 596.

But *compare* Taylor *v.* Caribou, 102 Me. 401, 67 Atl. 2.

A note and mortgage taken in exchange for property is not "money loaned and invested," but is a credit from which the holder may deduct the just debts by him owing at the time of making his tax return. Oleson *v.* Cuming County, 81 Nebr. 209, 115 N. W. 783.

75. Chapman *v.* Wellington First Nat. Bank, 56 Ohio St. 310, 47 N. E. 54; Burrows *v.* Smith, 95 Va. 694, 29 S. E. 674. But *compare* Bramel *v.* Manring, 18 Wash. 421, 51 Pac. 1050; Pullman State Bank *v.* Manring, 18 Wash. 250, 51 Pac. 464.

in force which permit such deductions to be made;[86] and when the privilege is duly claimed by the landowner it must be allowed by the assessor.[87]

8. Omissions of Taxable Property — a. Effect in General. In some jurisdictions it is held that the intentional omission of property liable to taxation from the assessment roll invalidates all taxes levied thereon and gives a right of complaint against the entire assessment to any one whose own burdens are unduly increased by such omission;[88] but that if the omission is accidental and unintentional, resulting from the negligence of the assessor or from a want or mistake of judgment on his part, without fraud, it will not vitiate the whole proceeding.[89] But the rule more generally adopted is that the assessment is not invalidated, at least as to a person who is properly taxed, by any such omission, from whatever cause arising, and whether intentional or not.[90]

b. Addition of Omitted Property.[91] After the completion of his assessment

Faddell *v.* New York, 50 Misc. 422, 100 N. Y. Suppl. 581 [*affirmed* in 114 N. Y. App. Div. 911, 100 N. Y. Suppl. 1133]; Matter of Murphy, 9 Misc. (N. Y.) 647, 30 N. Y. Suppl. 511.

Under New Jersey Tax Act (1903), § 10, (Pamphl. Laws (1903), p. 400) no deduction from the assessed value of real property can be made by the assessor on account of any mortgage debt. Hartshorne *v.* Avon-by-the-Sea, 75 N. J. L. 407, 67 Atl. 935. Prior to the enactment of this statute, however, the rule in this state under earlier statutes was otherwise. See Myers *v.* Campbell, 64 N. J. L. 186, 44 Atl. 863; Rosell *v.* Buck, 62 N. J. L. 575, 41 Atl. 968; Myers *v.* Campbell, 59 N. J. L. 378, 35 Atl. 788; Appleby *v.* East Brunswick Tp., 44 N. J. L. 153; State *v.* Silvers, 41 N. J. L. 505; King *v.* Manning, 40 N. J. L. 461; State *v.* Williamson, 33 N. J. L. 77; Pershine *v.* Grey, 29 N. J. L. 380; Woodward *v.* Pearson, 24 N. J. L. 254.

86. See the statutes of the several states. And see Smith *v.* Keagle, (Cal. 1888) 20 Pac. 152; People *v.* San Francisco, 77 Cal. 136, 19 Pac. 257; Chicago, etc., R. Co. *v.* State, 128 Wis. 553, 108 N. W. 557.

In assessing oil and gas privileges under a lease there should be deducted from the value thereof the part represented by the amount of oil reserved to the lessor by the lease, the remainder being taxable against the lessee. Wolfe County *v.* Beckett, 127 Ky. 252, 105 S. W. 447, 32 Ky. L. Rep. 167, 17 L. R. A. N. S. 688.

87. Palomares Land Co. *v.* Los Angeles County, 146 Cal. 530, 80 Pac. 931; Henne *v.* Los Angeles County, 129 Cal. 297, 61 Pac. 1081; Abbott *v.* Frost, 185 Mass. 398, 70 N. E. 478.

88. Auditor-Gen. *v.* Prescott, 94 Mich. 190, 53 N. W. 1058; Coles *v.* Platt, 24 N. J. L. 108; Semple *v.* Langlade County, 75 Wis. 354, 44 N. W. 749; Johnston *v.* Oshkosh, 65 Wis. 473, 27 N. W. 320; Smith *v.* Smith, 19 Wis. 615, 88 Am. Dec. 107; Hershey *v.* Milwaukee County, 16 Wis. 185, 82 Am. Dec. 713; Weeks *v.* Milwaukee, 10 Wis. 242. But *compare* Bond *v.* Kenosha, 17 Wis. 284; Dean *v.* Gleason, 16 Wis. 1, both holding that the omission of railroad property does not affect the assessment.

89. *Massachusetts.* — Williams *v.* Lunenburg School Dist. No. 1, 21 Pick. 75, 32 Am. Dec. 243.

Michigan.— Perkins *v.* Nugent, 45 Mich. 156, 7 N. W. 757.

Minnesota.—Corbet *v.* Rocksbury, 94 Minn. 397, 103 N. W. 11.

Nebraska.— Burlington, etc., R. Co. *v.* Saline County, 12 Nebr. 396, 11 N. W. 854. See also Kittle *v.* Shervin, 11 Nebr. 65, 7 N. W. 861.

New Jersey.— Coles *v.* Platt, 24 N. J. L. 108.

Wisconsin.— Chicago, etc., R. Co. *v.* State, 128 Wis. 553, 108 N. W. 557; Smith *v.* Smith, 19 Wis. 615, 88 Am. Dec. 707; Dean *v.* Gleason, 16 Wis. 1; Weeks *v.* Milwaukee, 10 Wis. 242.

Canada.— Meisner *v.* Meisner, 32 Nova Scotia 320.

See 45 Cent. Dig. tit. "Taxation," § 766.

90. *California.*— People *v.* McCreery, 34 Cal. 432.

Connecticut.— Sanford *v.* Dick, 15 Conn. 447.

Illinois.— Dunham *v.* Chicago, 55 Ill. 357.

Iowa.— Sioux City, etc., R. Co. *v.* Osceola County, 45 Iowa 168.

Maine.— Greenville *v.* Blair, 104 Me. 444, 72 Atl. 177; Longfellow *v.* Quimby, 33 Me. 457.

New Hampshire.— Thompson *v.* Newtown, 21 N. H. 595; Smith *v.* Messer, 17 N. H. 420.

New York.—New York *v.* Tucker, 182 N. Y. 535, 75 N. E. 1128 [*affirming* 91 N. Y. App. Div. 214, 86 N. Y. Suppl. 509]; Van Deventer *v.* Long Island City, 139 N. Y. 133, 34 N. E. 774.

Ohio.— Columbus Exch. Bank *v.* Hines, 3 Ohio St. 1.

Pennsylvania.— Philadelphia Contributionship *v.* Yard, 17 Pa. St. 331.

Rhode Island.— McTwiggan *v.* Hunter, 19 R. I. 265, 33 Atl. 5, 29 L. R. A. 526; Capwell *v.* Hopkins, 10 R. I. 378.

Vermont.— Blodgett *v.* Holbrook, 39 Vt. 336; Spear *v.* Braintree, 24 Vt. 414.

Washington.— Eureka Dist. Gold Min. Co. *v.* Ferry County, 28 Wash. 250, 68 Pac. 727; Puget Sound Agricultural Co. *v.* Pierce County, 1 Wash. Terr. 159.

United States.— Muscatine *v.* Mississippi, etc., R. Co., 17 Fed. Cas. No. 9,971, 1 Dill. 536.

See 45 Cent. Dig. tit. ' Taxation," § 766.

91. Assessment of omitted property by reviewing board or officer see *infra*, VII, B, 5, b.

erty, according to their real value.[46] The legislature may direct the manner of arriving at the value of franchises for taxation by any method reasonably fair in its operation, although it has no power to establish an arbitrary rule having no relation to the ascertainment of the true value.[47] One method of appraising corporate franchises much in vogue is to take the market value of the whole capital stock of the company and deduct from it the value of all its real property and tangible personal property, the remainder being the value of the franchise.[48] But under some statutes the amount of capital stock outstanding,[49] or of that employed within the state, is made the basis for estimating the franchise tax, the latter being calculated as a percentage on such capital, and varying with the amount

valuation of such franchises as so fixed, and, where the board omits to do so, the assessors have no power to determine such value. People *v.* Keno, 61 Misc. 345, 114 N. Y. Suppl. 1094.

Each highway crossing of a railroad company in a town in which it has only one line of railroad is not a special franchise to be valued separately, but all its special privileges therein, constituting parts of and operated as one system, constitute its special franchise for taxation. People *v.* Gourley, 64 Misc. (N. Y.) 605, 118 N. Y. Suppl. 776 [*reversed* on other grounds in 135 N. Y. App. Div. 869, 120 N. Y. Suppl. 200].

But where some of the crossings are wholly in one town, and others wholly in another town, all of which are assessed at a gross valuation by the state board of tax commissioners, the town assessors cannot apportion between them the gross valuation of the franchises as fixed by the board. People *v.* Gourley, 135 N. Y. App. Div. 869, 120 N. Y. Suppl. 200 [*reversing* 64 Misc. 605, 118 N. Y. Suppl. 776].

46. Baltimore Consol. Gas Co. *v.* Baltimore, 101 Md. 541, 61 Atl. 532, 109 Am. St. Rep. 584, 1 L. R. A. N. S. 263; Western Union Tel. Co. *v.* Omaha, 73 Nebr. 527, 103 N. W. 84; Southern Gum Co. *v.* Laylin, 66 Ohio St. 578, 64 N. E. 564; Gulf, etc., R. Co. *v.* Hewes, 183 U. S. 66, 22 S. Ct. 26, 46 L. ed. 86. See also Illinois Cent. R. Co. *v.* Grayson County, 99 S. W. 625, 30 Ky. L. Rep. 780.

47. Western Union Tel. Co. *v.* Omaha, 73 Nebr. 527, 103 N. W. 84.

48. *California.*— Crocker *v.* Scott, 149 Cal. 575, 87 Pac. 102; State Bank *v.* San Francisco, 142 Cal. 276, 75 Pac. 832, 100 Am. St. Rep. 130, 64 L. R. A. 918; Spring Valley Water Works *v.* Schottler, 62 Cal. 69.

Kentucky.— Morrell Refrigerator Car Co. *v.* Com., 128 Ky. 447, 108 S. W. 926, 32 Ky. L. Rep. 1383, 1389 (proportionate part of capital stock of refrigerating car company); Com. *v.* Covington, etc., Bridge Co., 114 Ky. 343, 70 S. W 849, 24 Ky. L. Rep. 1177; Southern R. Co. *v.* Coulter, 113 Ky. 657, 68 S. W. 873, 24 Ky. L. Rep. 203; Louisville Bridge Co. *v.* Louisville, 112 Ky. 347, 65 S. W. 814, 23 Ky. L. Rep. 1655; Louisville R. Co. *v.* Com., 105 Ky. 710, 49 S. W. 486, 20 Ky. L. Rep. 1509 (holding that the fact that the corporation is to exist only for a limited time may be taken into account in valuing the franchise); Paducah St. R. Co. *v.* McCracken County, 105 Ky. 472, 49 S. W. 178, 20 Ky. L. Rep. 1294 (holding that the indebtedness of the corporation and the cost of operating its business are not to be deducted); Henderson Bridge Co. *v.* Com., 99 Ky. 623, 31 S. W. 486, 17 Ky. L. Rep. 389, 29 L. R. A. 73; Com. *v.* Chesapeake, etc., R. Co., 91 S. W. 672, 28 Ky. L. Rep. 1110; Owensboro Waterworks Co. *v.* Owensboro, 74 S. W. 685, 24 Ky. L. Rep. 2530. But under the act of March 15, 1906, the assessing board may consider the two items of gross earnings and net income of a foreign corporation in the state in fixing the valuation of its franchise. James *v.* American Surety Co., 133 Ky. 313, 117 S. W. 411, holding further that such statute is prospective only.

Massachusetts.— Tremont, etc., Mills *v.* Lowell, 178 Mass. 469, 59 N. E. 1007; Firemen's Fire Ins. Co. *v.* Com., 137 Mass. 80; Boston, etc., R. Co. *v.* Com., 100 Mass. 399; Manufacturers' Ins. Co. *v.* Loud, 99 Mass. 146, 96 Am. Dec. 715. See also American Glue Co. *v.* Com., 195 Mass. 528, 81 N. E. 302, 122 Am. St. Rep. 268.

North Carolina.— Jackson *v.* North Carolina Corp. Commission, 130 N. C. 385, 42 S. E. 123.

United States.— Taylor *v.* Secor, 92 U. S. 575, 23 L. ed. 663; Coulter *v.* Weir, 127 Fed. 897, 62 C. C. A. 429 [*modified* in 128 Fed. 1019, 62 C. C. A. 681].

See 45 Cent. Dig. tit. "Taxation," § 625.

Money paid by a corporation for the purpose of effecting an organization or putting the company into legal shape to do business is not a taxable asset in the hands of the company, as the value of the corporation's franchise is not dependent on the amount expended in creating it. Com. *v.* Ledman, 127 Ky. 603, 106 S. W. 247, 32 Ky. L. Rep. 452.

Bonds, notes, accounts, cash, stock in other corporations, and other credits of a telephone corporation are intangible property, and not subject to assessment by the local assessor, but are to be considered by the board of valuation in fixing the franchise tax. Com. *v.* Cumberland Tel., etc., Co., 124 Ky. 535, 99 S. W. 604, 30 Ky. L. Rep. 723.

49. Knickerbocker Imp. Co. *v.* State Bd. of Assessors, 73 N. J. L. 94, 62 Atl. 266 (holding that stock owned by the corporation which issued it should not be considered in determining the amount of the franchise tax); People's Inv. Co. *v.* State Bd. of Assessors, 66 N. J. L. 175, 48 Atl. 579.

(II) *INDEBTEDNESS.* If the right of deducting debts from the assessed value of property is extended to taxpayers generally, or if the statutes make no exception in this particular as to corporations, these bodies as well as natural persons are entitled to the privilege.[63] But just as in the case of individuals, the debt, to be deducted, must be a direct obligation of the company, presently due, and one which it is bound and expects to discharge.[64]

(III) *REAL PROPERTY.* As land is separately assessed and taxed, it is commonly provided that the value of the real estate owned by a corporation shall be deducted from the assessed value of its capital or assets.[65] But if the land is

United States.— Coulter *v.* Weir, 127 Fed. 897, 62 C. C. A. 429.

See 45 Cent. Dig. tit. "Taxation," § 620.

But *compare* Schley *v.* Lee, 106 Md. 390, 67 Atl. 252; Emory *v.* State, 41 Md. 38.

Patent rights may be included in determining the franchise tax required of a corporation on its appraised capital. People *v.* Knight, 174 N. Y. 475, 67 N. E. 65, 63 L. R. A. 87 [*reversing* 67 N. Y. App. Div. 333, 73 N. Y. Suppl. 745]; People *v.* Kelsey, 101 N. Y. App. Div. 325, 91 N. Y. Suppl. 955 [*affirmed* in 181 N. Y. 512, 73 N. E. 1130].

63. State Bd. of Equalization *v.* People, 191 Ill. 528, 61 N. E. 339, 58 L. R. A. 513; Com. *v.* St. Bernard Coal Co., 9 S. W. 709, 10 Ky. L. Rep. 596; Standard L., etc., Ins. Co. *v.* Detroit Bd. of Assessors, 95 Mich. 466, 55 N. W. 112; Detroit Common Council *v.* Detroit Bd. of Assessors, 91 Mich. 78, 51 N. W. 787, 16 L. R. A. 59; People *v.* Barker, 141 N. Y. 196, 36 N. E. 184 [*affirming* 72 Hun 126, 25 N. Y. Suppl. 340]; People *v.* Asten, 100 N. Y. 597, 3 N. E. 788; People *v.* Feitner, 92 N. Y. App. Div. 518, 87 N. Y. Suppl. 304; Heerwagen *v.* Crosstown St. R. Co., 90 N. Y. App. Div. 275, 86 N. Y. Suppl. 218 [*modified* in 179 N. Y. 99, 71 N. E. 729]; People *v.* Pond, 37 N. Y. App. Div. 330, 57 N. Y. Suppl. 490; People *v.* Coleman, 1 N. Y. Suppl. 666. But *compare* State *v.* Sellers, 151 Ala. 557, 44 So. 548 (amount of recorded mortgages not to be deducted); Henderson Bridge Co. *v.* Com., 99 Ky. 623, 31 S. W. 486, 17 Ky. L. Rep. 389, 29 L. R. A. 73 [*affirmed* in 166 U. S. 150, 17 S. Ct. 532, 41 L. ed. 953]; State *v.* Duluth Gas, etc., Co., 76 Minn. 96, 78 N. W. 1032, 57 L. R. A. 63; State *v.* Karr, 64 Nebr. 514, 90 N. W. 298 (franchise tax); Farmers' L. & T. Co. *v.* New York, 7 Hill (N. Y.) 261.

Bonded indebtedness.— In assessing the value of easements in a street belonging to a gas company, the appeal tax court cannot treat the bonded indebtedness of a company as an asset for the purpose of taxation. Baltimore City Consol. Gas Co. *v.* Baltimore, 105 Md. 43, 65 Atl. 628, 121 Am. St. Rep. 553.

In the taxation of trust companies, the amount of the capital and accumulated surplus must be ascertained by deducting from the gross assets at their true value the liabilities and debts of the company. Fidelity Trust Co. *v.* State Bd. of Equalization, 77 N. J. L. 128, 71 Atl. 61.

64. Michigan, etc., R. Co. *v.* Auditor-Gen., 9 Mich. 448 (corporate bonds); Royal Highlanders *v.* State, 77 Nebr. 18, 108 N. W. 183 (outstanding beneficiary certificates of a fraternal benefit association); People *v.* Feitner, 167 N. Y. 622, 60 N. E. 1118 (debts not due); People *v.* Miller, 94 N. Y. App. Div. 564, 88 N. Y. Suppl. 197 [*affirmed* in 180 N. Y. 16, 72 N. E. 525] (preferred stock not a debt); People *v.* Feitner, 61 N. Y. App. Div. 129, 70 N. Y. Suppl. 500 [*affirmed* in 171 N. Y. 641, 63 N. E. 786] (indebtedness as indorser or surety); People *v.* Barker, 86 Hun (N. Y.) 131, 33 N. Y. Suppl. 388 (dividends declared but unpaid); People *v.* Barker, 28 Misc. (N. Y.) 13, 59 N. Y. Suppl. 926 [*affirmed* in 165 N. Y. 305, 59 N. E. 137, 151 (*reversing* 48 N. Y. App. Div. 248, 63 N. Y. Suppl. 167)] (bonds issued in lieu of dividends); People *v.* Barker, 37 N. Y. Suppl. 106 (debentures not actually issued).

65. See the statutes of the several states. And see the following cases:

Louisiana.— Merchants' Mut. Ins. Co. *v.* Board of Assessors, 40 La. Ann. 371, 3 So. 891; Louisiana Oil Co. *v.* Board of Assessors, 34 La. Ann. 618.

Maine.— Wheeler *v.* Waldo County, 88 Me. 174, 33 Atl. 983.

New Jersey.— Fidelity Trust Co. *v.* State Bd. of Equalization, 77 N. J. L. 128, 71 Atl. 61.

New York.— People *v.* Coleman, 115 N. Y. 178, 21 N. E. 1056; People *v.* New York Tax Com'r, 104 N. Y. 240, 10 N. E. 437; People *v.* Asten, 100 N. Y. 597, 3 N. E. 788; People *v.* Brooklyn Bd. of Assessors, 39 N. Y. 81; People *v.* Feitner, 58 N. Y. App. Div. 555, 69 N. Y. Suppl. 27; People *v.* Campbell, 70 Hun 507, 24 N. Y. Suppl. 208; People *v.* Coleman, 44 Hun 410; People *v.* Hilts, 27 Misc. 290, 58 N. Y. Suppl. 434 [*affirmed* in 47 N. Y. App. Div. 629, 62 N. Y. Suppl. 1145]; People *v.* Barker, 16 Misc. 258, 39 N. Y. Suppl. 106 [*affirmed* in 47 N. Y. App. Div. 27, 39 N. Y. Suppl. 776 (*affirmed* in 151 N. Y. 639, 45 N. E. 1133)]; People *v.* New York Tax, etc., Com'rs, 4 N. Y. Suppl. 47; People *v.* Olean, 15 N. Y. St. 461; People *v.* Coleman, 9 N. Y. St. 29.

West Virginia.— State *v.* Graybeal, 60 W. Va. 357, 55 S. E. 398.

See 45 Cent. Dig. tit. "Taxation," § 632.

In Pennsylvania, however, the real estate of quasi-public corporations, unless exempt from such taxation by statute, is taxed by including the value thereof in the assessment of the capital stock. Conoy Tp. *v.* York Haven Electric Power Plant Co., 222 Pa. St. 319, 71 Atl. 207; Com. *v.* Western Union Tel. Co., 2 Dauph. Co. Rep. 40.

d. Assessment of Shares of Stock — (I) *IN GENERAL.* Shares of stock in a banking institution, as distinct from the capital stock, are to be assessed to the individual stock-holders, and this, although the law requires the bank to list and report the stock-holders and the number of their shares.[87] Such stock is ordinarily required to be assessed at its full and true market value, rather than its book value or its nominal price.[88] Whether or not it is of the class of credits or property from which the stock-holder's indebtedness may be deducted, for the purposes of the assessment, depends on the local statute.[89]

(II) *NATIONAL BANK STOCK.* Shares of stock in a national banking association are to be assessed for taxation at their actual market value, not necessarily their par value,[90] the only limitation imposed by congress being that they

v. Barker, 154 N. Y. 128, 47 N. E. 173 (savings bank deposits); *In re* Haight, 32 N. Y. App. Div. 496, 53 N. Y. Suppl. 226; Griffin *v.* Heard, 78 Tex. 607, 14 S. W. 892.

87. *Alabama.*— Sumter County *v.* Gainesville Nat. Bank, 62 Ala. 464, 34 Am. Rep. 30.

Arizona.— Western Inv. Banking Co. *v.* Murray, 6 Ariz. 215, 56 Pac. 728.

Missouri.— State *v.* Merchants' Bank, 160 Mo. 640, 61 S. W. 676; Stanberry *v.* Jordan, 145 Mo. 371, 46 S. W. 1093; State *v.* Catron, 118 Mo. 280, 24 S. W. 439; Springfield *v.* Springfield First Nat. Bank, 87 Mo. 441; Hannibal First Nat. Bank *v.* Meredith, 44 Mo. 500.

Virginia.— State Bank *v.* Richmond, 79 Va. 113.

United States.— Exchange Nat. Bank *v.* Miller, 19 Fed. 372.

See 45 Cent. Dig. tit. "Taxation," § 644. And see *supra*, III, B, 2, a, (IV).

National banks are agents of their stockholders for the purpose of listing their stock for taxation and paying the tax thereon. Blue Hill First Nat. Bank *v.* Webster County, 77 Nebr. 815, 113 N. W. 190, 77 Nebr. 813, 110 N. W. 535.

Surplus fund.— Under a statute authorizing the taxation of the stock of a corporation in the hands of stock-holders, and exempting from taxation so much of the property of the corporation as is represented by the stock taxed in the hands of stock-holders, the surplus fund of a bank is exempt from taxation, as it belongs to the stock-holders and is represented by the stock. Belvidere Bank *v.* Tunis, 23 N. J. L. 546.

Assessment of national bank stock to stock-holder as omitted property see Judy *v.* Pleasant Nat. State Bank, 133 Iowa 252, 110 N. W. 605.

The refusal of the bank officers to furnish a list of shareholders to the assessor does not justify him in making the assessment for such stock against the bank property. Springfield *v.* Springfield First Nat. Bank, 87 Mo. 441.

88. *Indiana.*— State *v.* State Bank, 6 Blackf. 349.

Iowa.— National State Bank *v.* Burlington, 119 Iowa 696, 94 N. W. 234.

Maryland.— Schley *v.* Montgomery County, 106 Md. 407, 67 Atl. 250, holding also that only such deductions should be made therefrom as are reasonable on account of fluctuations and actual conditions.

Mississippi.—Alexander *v.* Thomas, 70 Miss. 517, 12 So. 708.

New Jersey.— Stratton *v.* Collins, 43 N. J. L. 562.

New York.— People *v.* Albany Bd. of Assessors. 2 Hun 583. But *compare* People *v.* Miller, 84 N. Y. App. Div. 168, 82 N. Y. Suppl. 621 [*modified* in 177 N. Y. 461, 69 N. E. 1103].

See 45 Cent. Dig. tit. "Taxation," § 644.

Market value or book value.— The book value of bank stock. that is. the amount which each share would be entitled to receive on a distribution among stock-holders of the entire capital and the surplus above all liabilities, is not necessarily the measure of its value for purposes of taxation; its market value may be higher, taking into consideration the bank's business, franchises, and prospects. Stratton *v.* Collins, 43 N. J. L. 562. And see National Bank of Commerce *v.* New Bedford, 155 Mass. 313. 29 N. E. 532; Ankeny *v.* Blakley, 44 Or. 78, 74 Pac. 485.

Under the present statute in New York, providing a method for the assessment and taxation of shares in banks, when the assessors ascertain the value of shares of bank stock from the total value of the corporate properties, they must include the value of the real estate and cannot deduct it in making the assessment. *In re* Ossining First Nat. Bank. 182 N. Y. 460. 75 N. E. 306. But see People *v.* Tax, etc., Com'rs. 80 N. Y. 573.

Valuation by assessor on owner's failure to state value see Dean *v.* Kopperl. 1 Tex. App. Civ. Cas. § 746.

89. See the statutes of the several states. And see Farmington *v.* Downing, 67 N. H. 141. 30 Atl. 345; Williams *v.* Weaver, 75 N. Y. 30; People *v.* Dolan, 36 N. Y. 59, 1 Transcr. App. 118; Stanley *v.* Albany County, 121 U. S. 535. 7 S. Ct. 1234, 30 L. ed. 1000.

90. *Illinois.*— Illinois Nat. Bank *v.* Kinsella, 201 Ill. 31. 66 N. E. 338.

Iowa.— Estherville First Nat. Bank *v.* Estherville, 136 Iowa 203, 112 N. W. 829.

Massachusetts.— Adams *v.* New Bedford, 155 Mass. 317, 29 N. E. 532; National Bank of Commerce *v.* New Bedford, 155 Mass. 313, 29 N. E. 532.

Nebraska.— Blue Hill First Nat. Bank *v.* Webster County, 77 Nebr. 815, 113 N. W. 190, 77 Nebr. 813. 110 N. W. 535, holding also that where a bank owns real estate of a greater value than that at which it is

b. Valuation of Property. The assessment of railroad property is to be based on its value for the purpose for which it is intended and devoted.[7] The cost of construction or of acquisition, or the cost of replacement, may be considered in fixing this valuation, but it is not in itself a fair measure of value;[8] and it is also proper to consider the aggregate amount of the company's capital stock and bonded debt, as representing its investment and therefore indicating the value of its property.[9] But productiveness rather than cost should be the standard, and hence the question should be, what would the property sell for, as a railroad, at a fair and free sale;[10] and on this question the earning capacity of the road, as evidenced by its net profits, is a very important consideration, although perhaps not absolutely controlling;[11] and so also is the rental value of the road.[12] In this connection also the market value of the company's stock and bonds may properly be taken into account;[13] and in general the assessors should base their valuation upon all the factors which enter into the market value of the property,[14] obtaining

7. State *v.* Illinois Cent. R. Co., 27 Ill. 64, 79 Am. Dec. 396; Louisville, etc., R. Co. *v.* State, 8 Heisk. (Tenn.) 663.

"Property used for railroad and canal purposes," upon the question of its valuation under N. J. Act March 27, 1888, § 3. subd. 2, see Long Dock Co. *v.* State Bd. of Assessors, (N. J. Sup. 1909) 73 Atl. 53.

In New Jersey under Pamphl. Laws (1884), p. 142, as amended by Pamphl. Laws (1888), p. 269, the board of assessors must ascertain the value of: (1) The main stem, (2) other real property, (3) tangible personal property, and (4) the franchise; it being presumed that the road-bed as laid is to be taxed as main stem, whether the railroad company conducts a passenger or freight business, or both. Jersey City *v.* State Bd. of Assessors, 74 N. J. L. 720, 68 Atl. 227 [*reversing* 73 N. J. L. 170, 63 Atl. 23].

Revaluation.—Where all the property of a railroad company has been valued for taxation for certain years, a revaluation for those years cannot be made. Com. *v.* Ledman, 127 Ky. 603, 106 S. W. 247, 32 Ky. L. Rep. 452.

8. *Kentucky.*— Owensboro, etc., R. Co. *v.* Logan County, 11 S. W. 76, 11 Ky. L. Rep. 99.

Louisiana.— Morgan's Louisiana, etc., R., etc., Co. *v.* Iberia Parish Bd. of Reviewers, 41 La. Ann. 1156, 3 So. 507.

New Jersey.— Central R. Co. *v.* State Bd. of Assessors, 49 N. J. L. 1, 7 Atl. 306.

New York.—People *v.* Keator, 36 Hun 592 [*affirming* 67 How. Pr. 277]; People *v.* Haren, 3 N. Y. Suppl. 86.

Oregon.— Oregon, etc., R. Co. *v.* Jackson County, 38 Oreg. 589, 64 Pac. 307, 65 Pac. 369.

Pennsylvania.— Com. *v.* Lake Shore, etc., R. Co., 3 Dauph. Co. Rep. 172.

United States.— Cincinnati Southern R. Co. *v.* Guenther, 19 Fed. 395.

See 45 Cent. Dig. tit. "Taxation," § 653.

9. Porter *v.* Rockford, etc., R. Co., 76 Ill. 561; Chicago, etc., R. Co. *v.* Cole, 75 Ill. 591; Oregon, etc., R. Co. *v.* Jackson County, 38 Oreg. 589. 64 Pac. 307, 65 Pac. 369.

10. State *v.* Illinois Cent. R. Co., 27 Ill. 64, 79 Am. Dec. 396; Morgan's Louisiana, etc., R., etc., Co. *v.* Iberia Parish, 41 La. Ann. 1156, 3 So. 507; Atlantic, etc., R. Co. *v.* State, 60 N. H. 133 (holding that the fact that the road is run at a net loss does not show it to be of no value); People *v.* Pond, 13 Abb. N. Cas. (N. Y.) 1.

11. *Illinois.*— State *v.* Illinois Cent. R. Co., 27 Ill. 64, 79 Am. Dec. 396.

Louisiana.— Morgan's Louisiana, etc., R., etc., Co. *v.* Iberia Parish, 41 La. Ann. 1156, 3 So. 507.

Nebraska.— State *v.* Savage, 65 Nebr. 714, 91 N. W. 716.

Nevada.— State *v.* Nevada Cent. R. Co., 28 Nev. 186, 81 Pac. 99, 113 Am. St. Rep. 834; State *v.* Nevada Cent. R. Co., 26 Nev. 357, 68 Pac. 294, 69 Pac. 1042; State *v.* Virginia, etc., R. Co., 24 Nev. 53, 49 Pac. 945, 50 Pac. 607.

New York.— People *v.* Hicks, 105 N. Y. 198, 11 N. E. 653; People *v.* Hicks, 40 Hun 598; People *v.* Keator, 36 Hun 592 [*affirming* 67 How. Pr. 277]; People *v.* Wilder, 3 N. Y. St. 159; People *v.* Haren, 3 N. Y. Suppl. 86; People *v.* Assessor, 2 N. Y. Suppl. 240.

Oregon.— Oregon, etc., R. Co. *v.* Jackson County, 38 Oreg. 589, 64 Pac. 307, 65 Pac. 369.

United States.— Louisville, etc., R. Co. *v.* Coulter, 131 Fed. 282 [*reversed* on other grounds in 196 U. S. 599, 25 S. Ct. 342, 49 L. ed. 615].

See 45 Cent. Dig. tit. "Taxation," § 653.

12. Clark *v.* Vandalia R. Co., 172 Ind. 409, 86 N. E. 851; Atlantic, etc., R. Co. *v.* State, 60 N. H. 133; People *v.* Feitner, 75 N. Y. App. Div. 527, 78 N. Y. Suppl. 308 [*affirmed* in 174 N. Y. 532, 66 N. E. 1114]; Oregon, etc., R. Co. *v.* Jackson County, 38 Oreg. 589, 64 Pac. 307, 65 Pac. 369.

13. State *v.* Savage, 65 Nebr. 714, 91 N. W. 716; Oregon, etc., R. Co. *v.* Jackson County, 38 Oreg. 589, 64 Pac. 307, 65 Pac. 369; Taylor *v.* Louisville, etc., R. Co., 88 Fed. 350, 31 C. C. A. 537.

14. *Indiana.*— Pittsburgh, etc., R. Co. *v.* Backus, 133 Ind. 625, 33 N. E. 432 (connections with trunk or interstate lines); Indianapolis, etc., R. Co. *v.* Backus, 133 Ind. 609, 33 N. E. 443; Terre Haute, etc., R. Co. *v.* Marion County, Wils. 380.

Mississippi.— Yazoo, etc., R. Co. *v.* Adams, 85 Miss. 772, 38 So. 348, right of the com-

applies only to lands used in connection with the business of the railroad; other real property, owned by the road but not so used, is to be valued in the same manner as the real estate of private individuals.[34] The land and the buildings or improvements on it are to be separately assessed if the statute so directs.[35]

(II) *RAILROAD BRIDGES.* A railroad bridge is assessable as real estate,[36] and its value for purposes of taxation is not measured by its cost, but by its earnings or its value as a part of the railroad system.[37]

(III) *STATE OR LOCAL ASSESSMENT.* The distribution of the right to assess the right of way, road-bed, and other real property of railroad companies, as between the state board and the local authorities, varies greatly in the different states; but the general tendency is to assign to the state officers all that which constitutes a part of the continuous line of railway, and to the local taxing officers all property not used for railroad purposes and also such as is incidental or accessory to the operation of the road.[38]

150]; People *v.* Reid, 64 Hun 553, 19 N. Y. Suppl. 528. But see Albany, etc., R. Co. *v.* Canaan, 16 Barb. 244; Albany, etc., R. Co. *v.* Osborn, 12 Barb. 223.

Oregon.— Oregon, etc., R. Co. *v.* Jackson County, 38 Oreg. 589, 64 Pac. 307, 65 Pac. 369.

Texas.— State *v.* St. Louis Southwestern R. Co., 43 Tex. Civ. App. 533, 96 S. W. 69.

Virginia.— Baltimore, etc., R. Co. *v.* Koontz. 77 Va. 698.

See 45 Cent. Dig. tit. "Taxation," § 661.

But *compare* Huntington *v.* Central Pac. R Co., 12 Fed. Cas. No. 6,911. 2 Sawy. 503.

Depreciation of adjoining property not considered.— In fixing the valuation of real estate of a railroad company within a town for purposes of taxation, the damages the company would be compelled to pay for depreciation of land adjoining that taken, if it were now constructing its road, cannot be included. People *v.* Hilts, 62 N. Y. Suppl. 1145 [*affirmed* in 163 N. Y. 594, 57 N. E. 1122].

Leased road.— Where all the property of a railroad company consists of real estate. and lies in one tax district, and is leased to another corporation, the assessors have no right arbitrarily to fix the value of the lessor's property by considering its rental value, and then tax the difference between the value so fixed and the assessed value of the real estate as "capital and surplus." People *v.* Feitner, 174 N. Y. 532, 66 N. E. 1114.

34. Toledo, etc., R. Co. *v.* Lafayette, 22 Ind. 262. See also Oregon, etc., R. Co. *v.* Jackson County, 38 Oreg. 589, 64 Pac. 307, 65 Pac. 369.

35. State *v.* Hannibal, etc., R. Co., 110 Mo. 265, 19 S. W. 816; New York, etc., R. Co. *v.* Yard, 43 N. J. L. 121; Huntington *v.* Central Pac. R. Co., 12 Fed. Cas. No. 6,911, 2 Sawy. 503.

Railroad built on another's land.— Where a railroad is constructed on land of another, under a parol arrangement with the owner, the works constructed for use for railroad purposes, such as embankments. bridges. culverts. and tracks, are assessable to the railroad company. although the land itself is assessable to the owner. Hoboken R. etc., Co. *v.* State Bd. of Assessors, 62 N. J. L. 561, 41 Atl. 728.

36. People *v.* Atchison, etc., R. Co., 206 Ill. 252, 68 N. E. 1059; Pittsburgh, etc., R. Co. *v.* West Virginia Bd. of Public Works. 172 U. S. 32, 19 S. Ct. 90, 43 L. ed. 354; Keithsburg Bridge Co. *v.* McKay, 42 Fed. 427. See also Cowen *v.* Aldridge, 114 Fed. 44. 51 C. C. A. 670; and *supra*, III, B, 2, d, (II).

Bridge taxable as part of road.—A bridge owned by a railroad company on its line of road is properly returned for taxation as so much mileage of railroad, and cannot be again taxed as a bridge. Schmidt *v.* Galveston, etc., R. Co., (Tex. Civ. App. 1893) 24 S. W. 547.

Toll-bridge.—A railroad bridge owned by a railroad company and constituting a part of its track is taxable only as a part of the road, and not as a separate structure, notwithstanding it is used in part as a toll-bridge for the passage of teams, wagons, and the like. State *v.* Hannibal, etc., R. Co., 97 Mo. 348, 10 S. W. 436. *Compare* State *v.* Hannibal, etc., R. Co., 89 Mo. 98, 14 S. W. 511.

37. Alexandria Canal R., etc., Co. *v.* District of Columbia, 1 Mackey (D. C.) 217; People *v.* Weaver. 67 How. Pr. (N. Y.) 477 [*affirmed* in 34 Hun 321], earnings. See also Chicago, etc., R. Co. *v.* Com., 115 Ky. 278, 72 S. W. 1119, 24 Ky. L. Rep. 2124.

Assessment of railroad bridge by the "mileage rule" as an integral part of the entire roadway see State *v.* Louisiana, etc., R. Co., 215 Mo. 479, 114 S. W. 956.

38. See the statutes of the several states. And see the following cases:

Alabama.— Nashville, etc., R. Co. *v.* State, 129 Ala. 142, 30 So. 619, holding that depots, platforms, stations, and water tanks. owned by a railroad company and situated on its right of way, are to be assessed by the local authorities.

Arkansas.— St. Louis, etc., R. Co. *v.* Miller County, 67 Ark. 498, 55 S. W. 926, holding that all real estate, including structures thereon. other than that denominated "railroad tracks," shall be listed by the local assessors.

Illinois.— Railroad track must be assessed

different parts so as to make one continuous line, may be classed as "railroad track." [44]

(v) *PROPERTY INCLUDED IN "REAL ESTATE."* It is entirely competent for the legislature, for the purposes of taxation, to make that realty which would be personal property at common law, and *vice versa*; [45] and therefore the question whether particular railroad property is assessable as real estate or as personalty depends largely on the provisions of the local statute.[46]

9. **MISCELLANEOUS CORPORATIONS.** The general rules stated above,[47] except in so far as they are changed or modified by special statutory provisions, apply in regard to assessments of taxes against certain classes of corporations which differ from other corporations either in respect to the nature of their business, or in respect to the nature of the property which they hold,[48] such as express companies,[49] turnpike and toll road companies,[50] sleeping car companies,[51] street railroads,[52]

Co. *v.* People, 4 Ill. App. 468; Pfaff *v.* Terre Haute, etc., R. Co., 108 Ind. 144, 9 N. E. 93.

There is no distinction, within the New Jersey act of March 27, 1888, between the principal or main line of a railroad, and a lawfully authorized branch line of railroad, but the property of each must be assessed in part as "main stem," and in part as "other real estate used for railroad purposes," according to the circumstances of the property. Jersey City *v.* State Bd. of Assessors, 75 N. J. L. 571, 69 Atl. 200 [*modifying* 73 N. J. L. 164, 63 Atl. 21].

What constitutes "main stem."—What is the "main stem" of a railroad is a question of fact, depending on the actual use of the line at the time of assessment; but as between a line used mainly for passenger traffic and a line used mainly for freight traffic, the former is the main stem; and as between two lines of track used for freight traffic, the longer line, in the absence of other distinguishing features, is the main stem. Jersey City *v.* State Bd. of Assessors. 73 N. J. L. 164, 63 Atl. 21 [*modified* in 75 N. J. L. 571, 69 Atl. 200].

44. Anderson *v.* Chicago, etc., R. Co., 117 Ill. 26, 7 N. E. 129. And see Baltimore City Appeal Tax Ct. *v.* Western Maryland R. Co., 50 Md. 274. But *compare* Cass County *v.* Chicago, etc., R. Co., 25 Nebr. 348, 41 N. W. 246, 2 L. R. A. 188.

45. Johnson *v.* Roberts, 102 Ill. 655; Central Iowa R. Co. *v.* Wright County, 67 Iowa 199, 25 N. W. 128; Missouri, etc., R. Co. *v.* Labette County, 9 Kan. App. 545, 59 Pac. 383; Steere *v.* Walling, 7 R. I. 317. See also Bangor, etc., R. Co. *v.* Harris, 21 Me. 533; and *supra*, VI, C, 5, a.

46. See the statutes of the several states. And see the following cases:

Indiana.— Louisville, etc., R. Co. *v.* State, 25 Ind. 177, 87 Am. Dec. 358, holding that it is within the power of the legislature to treat rolling machinery of a railroad as real property for purpose of taxation.

Maine.— Portland, etc., R. Co. *v.* Saco, 60 Me. 196, holding that, under the statute, the track of the road and the land on which it is built are not "real estate."

Maryland.— Baltimore City Appeal Tax Ct. *v.* Western Maryland R. Co., 50 Md. 274, holding that where a railroad is built on the bed of a public street, or in a tunnel under the street, the easement may be assessed and taxed as real estate.

Minnesota.— Chicago, etc., R. Co. *v.* Houston County, 38 Minn. 531, 38 N. W. 619, grain elevator as real estate.

New Jersey.— *In re* New York Bay R. Co., 75 N. J. L. 115, 67 Atl. 513.

United States.— New Mexico *v.* United States Trust Co., 174 U. S. 545, 19 S. Ct. 784, 43 L. ed. 1079, improvements as real estate.

See 45 Cent. Dig. tit. "Taxation," § 666.

47. See *supra*, VI, D, 1-5.

48. See the statutes of the several states.

Valuation of property of ferry company incorporated in another state see State *v.* Wiggins Ferry Co., 208 Mo. 622, 106 S. W. 1005.

49. *Indiana.*— State *v.* Adams Express Co., 144 Ind. 549, 42 N. E. 483.

Maine.— State *v.* Boston, etc., Exp. Co., 100 Me. 278, 61 Atl. 697.

Pennsylvania.— Com. *v.* U. S. Exp. Co., 157 Pa. St. 579, 27 Atl. 396.

South Carolina.— Southern Exp. Co. *v.* Hood, 15 Rich. 66, 94 Am. Dec. 141.

United States.— Fargo *v.* Hart, 193 U. S. 490, 24 S. Ct. 498, 48 L. ed. 761; Coulter *v.* Weir, 127 Fed. 897, 62 C. C. A. 429 [*modified* in 128 Fed. 1019, 62 C. C. A. 681].

And see 45 Cent. Dig. tit. "Taxation," § 667.

Liability to taxation see *supra*, III, B, 2, e, (IV).

50. Campbell Turnpike Road Co. *v.* Highland Dist., 130 Ky. 812, 114 S. W. 286; People *v.* Selkirk, 180 N. Y. 401, 73 N. E. 248.

Liability to taxation see *supra*, III, B, 2, e, (VI).

51. Carlile *v.* Pullman Palace Car Co., 8 Colo. 320, 7 Pac. 164, 54 Am. Rep. 553; Com. *v.* Central Transp. Co., 145 Pa. St. 89, 22 Atl. 209; State *v.* Pullman's Palace Car Co., 64 Wis. 89, 23 N. W. 871; Pullman's Palace Car Co. *v.* Bd. of Assessors, 55 Fed. 206; Pullman Southern Car Co. *v.* Nolan, 22 Fed. 276 [*affirmed* in 117 U. S. 34, 51, 6 S. Ct. 635, 643, 29 L. ed. 785, 791].

52. *California.*— San Francisco, etc., R. Co. *v.* Scott, 142 Cal. 222, 75 Pac. 575.

b. Authority and Duty to Make. The making of the assessment list or roll is a duty which can be performed, with proper legal effect, only by the particular board or officer designated by the statute.[70] It is a duty which cannot be delegated, and the roll is invalid if prepared by any third person,[71] unless he be a mere clerk or agent acting under the direction and supervision of the proper officer.[72]

c. Requisites in General. The assessment list must be made in at least substantial conformity with the directions of the statute and contain all the essential particulars which the law requires;[73] and further it must show on its face that it purports to be an official list made by the proper officer acting in his official capacity,[74] and must be certain and specific in designating the persons and property taxable and the amount of taxes charged.[75]

Texas.— See Sullivan *v.* Bitter, 51 Tex. Civ. App. 604, 113 S. W. 193, holding that an assessment of property for taxation includes a list of the property to be taxed in some form and an estimate of the sums which are to guide in apportioning the tax. But *compare* Hernandez *v.* San Antonio, (Civ. App. 1897) 39 S. W. 1022.

Vermont.— Downing *v.* Roberts, 21 Vt. 441.

See 45 Cent. Dig. tit. "Taxation," § 675.

But *compare* Harris *v.* State, 96 Tenn. 496, 34 S. W. 1017.

After the completion of the tax list or assessment roll, the assessor is not required to keep a book containing the original list and assessment of each person's property. People *v.* Stockton, etc., R. Co., 49 Cal. 414.

Unless a legal levy has been made, the extension of an assessment upon a tax roll affords no authority for the collection of the tax. Reno County School Dist. No. 127 *v.* Reno County School Dist. No. 45, 80 Kan. 641, 103 Pac. 126.

70. Alameda County *v.* Dalton, 9 Cal. App. 26, 98 Pac. 85; Middletown *v.* Berlin, 18 Conn. 189. majority of assessors.

Successor in office.— Where a county assessor resigns his office after having duly listed and valued all the taxable property, leaving nothing to be done but to copy the assessment sheets into the list or roll required by statute, the work may lawfully be completed by his successor. Bode *v.* New England Inv. Co., 1 N. D. 121, 45 N. W. 197; Farrington *v.* New England Inv. Co., 1 N. D. 102, 45 N. W. 191.

Authority as to contents of roll.— Under a law requiring the town clerk to prepare the assessment roll, so far as possible, from the assessment of the preceding year, after its revision by the town assessors, he has power to place on the roll an assessment which had been stricken therefrom by the assessors. People *v.* Schoonover, 47 N. Y. App. Div. 278, 62 N. Y. Suppl. 180 [*reversing* 26 Misc. 576, 57 N. Y. Suppl. 498, and *affirmed* in 166 N. Y. 629, 60 N. E. 1118].

71. Paldi *v.* Paldi, 84 Mich. 346, 47 N. W. 510; People *v.* Hagadorn, 104 N. Y. 516, 10 N. E. 891; Ne-ha-sa-ne Park Assoc. *v.* Lloyd. 7 N. Y. App. Div. 359, 40 N. Y. Suppl. 58.

72. Covington *v.* Rockingham, 93 N. C. 134.

73. *Idaho.*— People *v.* Owyhee Min. Co., 1 Ida. 409, as to classification of property.

Illinois.— Dennis *v.* Maynard, 15 Ill. 477.

New York.— People *v.* Adams, 125 N. Y. 471, 26 N. E. 746.

Texas.— Lofton *v.* Miller, (Civ. App. 1909) 118 S. W. 911 (holding that the tax rolls are to be made out from lists made up from information furnished by property-owners); State *v.* Farmer, (Civ. App. 1900) 57 S. W. 84 [*affirmed* in 94 Tex. 232, 59 S. W. 541].

Vermont.— Willard *v.* Pike, 59 Vt. 202, 9 Atl. 907; Clove Spring Iron Works *v.* Cone, 56 Vt. 603; Stearns *v.* Miller, 25 Vt. 20; Doe *v.* Whitlock, 1 Tyler 305.

See 45 Cent. Dig. tit. "Taxation," § 677.

Copying former roll.—An assessment is void which is made by copying the roll of the preceding year. Davidson *v.* Sterrett, 13 Ky. L. Rep. 265; State *v.* Cook, 82 Mo. 185.

Time of making entries.— The failure of the assessor to enter the assessment as soon as made, on the book prescribed for that purpose, does not invalidate the assessment as against the owner of the property. Grundy County *v.* Tennessee Coal, etc., Co., 94 Tenn. 295, 29 S. W. 116.

Partly exempt property.— Property which is by law exempt from taxes except for school and highway purposes should not be stricken from the assessment roll, but should be marked "exempt" so that it may be made the basis of assessment for school and highway taxes. People *v.* Reilly, 41 N. Y. App. Div. 378, 58 N. Y. Suppl. 558.

Designation of year.— Where there has been but one assessment for a certain calendar year, a statement in the assessment book that it is the book of assessments for that year is a proper designation of the year, although the fiscal year includes the first half of the succeeding calendar year. Chapman *v.* Zoberlein, 152 Cal. 216, 92 Pac. 188.

74. House *v.* Stone, 64 Tex. 677; Bartlett *v.* Wilson, 59 Vt. 23, 8 Atl. 321; Smith *v.* Hard, 59 Vt. 13, 8 Atl. 317.

75. Green *v.* Craft, 28 Miss. 70; Stoddard *v.* Lyon, 18 S. D. 207, 99 N. W. 1116. See also Greenleaf *v.* Bartlett, 146 N. C. 495, 60 S. E. 419, 14 L. R. A. N. S. 660.

Hence a description which merely gives the name of the owner and the number of acres, without anything to fix the exact location of the land, is insufficient; [14] **but if such description is accompanied by other descriptive matter by which the particular land may be located and identified it is sufficient.**[15] **So also an assessment of a "lot" or "house and lot" on a designated street or street corner in a city is insufficient,**[16] **although the description may be sufficient if, in addition, the number of the house is stated.**[17] **It has been said that a description which would be sufficient in a conveyance of land between individuals will be sufficient in a tax assessment;** [18] **or, according to other cases, the description is sufficient if it contains such data as will enable a competent surveyor to identify the property with reasonable certainty.**[19] **Some decisions also maintain that parol evi-**

Mississippi.— Cogburn *v.* Hunt, 54 Miss. 675

Missouri.— State *v.* Burrough, 174 Mo. 700, 74 S. W. 610.

New Hampshire.— See Drew *v.* Morrill, 62 N. H. 23, particular description of resident lands not required.

New Jersey.— Newcomb *v.* Franklin Tp., 46 N. J. L. 437.

New York.— *In re* New York Cent., etc., R. Co., 90 N. Y. 342; Tallman *v.* White, 2 N. Y. 66; Clinton *v.* Krull, 125 N. Y. App. Div. 157, 111 N. Y. Suppl. 105; Rochester *v.* Farrar, 44 Misc. 394, 89 N. Y. Suppl. 1035.

North Carolina.— Fulcher *v.* Fulcher, 122 N. C. 101, 29 S. E. 91.

North Dakota.—Griffin *v.* Denison Land Co., (1908) 119 N. W. 1041; State Finance Co. *v.* Mulberger, 16 N. D. 214, 112 N. W. 986, 125 Am. St. Rep. 650; Grand Forks County *v.* Frederick, 16 N. D. 118, 112 N. W. 839, 125 Am. St. Rep. 621 (holding that the description of land in an assessment roll must be so definite as to afford the owner the means of identification of the land as his land, and must also inform intending purchasers what lands are offered for sale; and if it does not answer these requirements, the mere fact that the owner is aware that it is his land that is intended to be assessed, and that he owns no other land in the block, is immaterial and does not validate the assessment); State Finance Co. *v.* Mather, 15 N. D. 386, 109 N. W. 350; Power *v.* Bowdle, 3 N. D. 107, 54 N. W. 404, 44 Am. St. Rep. 511. 21 L. R. A. 328.

Ohio.— Douglas *v.* Dangerfield, 10 Ohio 152; Lafferty *v.* Byers, 5 Ohio 458.

Oregon.— Title Trust Co. *v.* Aylsworth, 40 Oreg. 20, 66 Pac. 276.

Pennsylvania.— Everhart *v.* Nesbitt, 182 Pa. St. 500, 38 Atl. 525; Glass *v.* Gilbert, 58 Pa. St. 266; Lyman *v.* Philadelphia, 56 Pa. St. 488; Philadelphia *v.* Miller, 49 Pa. St. 440; Woodside *v.* Wilson, 32 Pa. St. 52; Dunden *v.* Snodgrass, 18 Pa. St. 151; Dunn *v.* Ralyea, 6 Watts & S. 475.

Rhode Island.— Kettelle *v.* Warwick, etc., Water Co., 23 R. I. 114, 49 Atl. 492; Evans *v.* Newell, 18 R. I. 38, 25 Atl. 347.

Tennessee.— Morristown *v.* King, 11 Lea 669; Peck *v.* East Tennessee Lumber, etc., Co., (Ch. App. 1899) 53 S. W. 1107.

Texas.— State *v.* Farmer, 94 Tex. 232, 59 S. W. 541; Yenda *v.* Wheeler. 9 Tex. 408.

Utah.— Jungk *v.* Snyder, 28 Utah 1, 78 Pac. 168.

West Virginia.— Maxwell *v.* Cunningham, 50 W. Va. 298, 40 S. E. 499.

Canada.— Schultz *v.* Alloway, 10 Manitoba 221; Nanton *v.* Villeneuve, 10 Manitoba 213.

See 45 Cent. Dig. tit. "Taxation," § 720.

The headings of the columns of an assessment roll are a part of the description of the land assessed. State *v.* Vaile, 122 Mo. 33, 26 S. W. 672.

Where a part of a lot becomes exempt from taxation, the remainder is taxable as a distinct parcel. St. Peter's Church *v.* Scott County, 12 Minn. 395.

Effect of curative statute see Com. *v.* Louisville, 47 S. W. 865, 20 Ky. L. Rep. 893.

Form of tract.—A description of land in an assessment as six acres will, in the absence of proof to the contrary, be regarded as six acres in the form of a square. Immegart *v.* Gorgas, 41 Iowa 439.

14. Driggers *v.* Cassady, 71 Ala. 529; Jones *v.* Blanchard, 62 N. H. 651; Ainsworth *v.* Dean, 21 N. H. 400; Holmes *v.* Union County School District No. 15, 11 Oreg. 332, 8 Pac. 287; Tilton *v.* Oregon Cent. Military Road Co., 23 Fed. Cas. No. 14,055, 3 Sawy. 22.

15. Greene *v.* Lunt, 58 Me. 518 (numbers and lots and ranges); Westhampton *v.* Searle, 127 Mass. 502; Clark *v.* Mulford, 43 N. J. L. 550; State *v.* Woodbridge Tp., 42 N. J. L. 401.

16. Jones *v.* Pelham, 84 Ala. 208, 4 So. 22; Kelsey *v.* Abbott, 13 Cal. 609; Whitmore *v.* Learned, 70 Me. 276; Bingham *v.* Smith, 64 Me. 450; Parker *v.* Elizabeth, 39 N. J. L. 689.

17. Roberts *v.* Welsh, 192 Mass. 278, 78 N. E. 408; State *v.* Newark, 36 N. J. L. 288.

18. Dike *v.* Lewis, 4 Den. (N. Y.) 237; Slaughter *v.* Dallas, 101 Tex. 315, 107 S. W. 48 [*modifying* (Tex. Civ. App. 1907) 103 S. W. 218]; Orton *v.* Noonan, 23 Wis. 102; Curtis *v.* Brown County, 22 Wis. 167. But *compare* Jones *v.* Pelham, 84 Ala. 208, 4 So. 22; Buckner *v.* Sugg, 79 Ark. 442, 96 S. W. 184 (where it is said that in taxation proceedings, the description of the land must be such as fully apprises the owner, without recourse to the superior knowledge peculiar to him as owner, that the particular tract of his land is sought to be charged with a tax lien); People *v.* Mahoney, 55 Cal. 286.

19. Otis *v.* People, 196 Ill. 542. 63 N. E.

(XI) *ABBREVIATIONS AND FIGURES.* The description in an assessment list is not invalidated by the use of figures and abbreviations if they are such as are in familiar use and easily understood, and not misleading, and full enough to point out the particular land with certainty,[52] except that the name of the town or district should not be abbreviated.[53]

5. EXTENDING AMOUNT OF TAX. To complete a valid assessment it is necessary that the amount of the tax on each listed item or parcel of property shall be computed and extended on the proper tax book or roll in accordance with the statutory provisions relative thereto, and until this is done no legal liability attaches,[54] except where the omission of this step or defects therein can be brought

Buildings on different parts of tract.— Where a tract of land lies partly within and partly without the limits of a city, both parts being improved, and the improvements on the whole tract are included in the assessment of that part which lies within the city, and there is no means of determining how they should be apportioned, the tax on the improvements is void. Coolidge *v.* Pierce County, 28 Wash. 95, 68 Pac. 391.

Assessment of improvements as personalty. —Where, after the assessment of a tract of land, a valuable mill is erected on it, and it is reported as an additional assessment to the tax collector, an assessment thereon is not void because the collector gave in the mill as personal property. Tunica County *v.* Tate, 78 Miss. 294, 29 So. 74.

52. Baird *v.* Monroe, 150 Cal. 560, 89 Pac. 352; Buck *v.* People. 78 Ill. 560; Olcott *v.* State, 10 Ill. 481; Watkins *v.* Couch, 134 Iowa 1, 111 N. W. 315; Jenkins *v.* McTigue, 22 Fed. 148.

Applications of rule.— The ordinary ditto marks, or the abbreviation "do" for "ditto," are permissible. Bandow *v.* Wolven, 20 S. D. 445, 107 N. W. 204; Hodgdon *v.* Burleigh, 4 Fed. 111. The description may designate the points of the compass by their ordinary abbreviations and their combinations, as "N," "W," or "NW," "SE," and the like. Law *v.* People, 80 Ill. 268; Jefferson County *v.* Johnson, 23 Kan. 717; Sibley *v.* Smith, 2 Mich. 486; Beggs *v.* Paine, 15 N. D. 436. 109 N. W. 322. So also the abbreviation "ex" for except, "a" for acres, and "cor" for corner may be employed in the description. State *v.* Vaile, 122 Mo. 33, 26 S. W. 672. And the abbreviation "excp't rip'n r'g't" has been held sufficiently certain to be used for the words "excepting riparian rights." Newaygo Portland Cement Co. *v.* Sheridan Tp., 137 Mich. 475, 100 N. W. 747.

Fractions may be indicated by their ordinary arithmetical abbreviations; but "NW4" or "W2" is not a sufficient method of writing "the northwest quarter" or "the west half." State Finance Co. *v.* Mulberger, 16 N. D. 214, 112 N. W. 986, 125 Am. St. Rep. 650; State Finance Co. *v.* Trimble, 16 N. D. 199, 112 N. W. 984; Power *v.* Bowdle, 3 N. D. 107, 54 N. W. 404, 44 Am. St. Rep. 511, 21 L. R. A. 328; Power *v.* Larabee, 2 N. D. 141, 49 N. W. 724. But *compare* Riddle *v.* Messer, 84 Ala. 236, 4 So. 185.

The term "east middle" of a given town lot is unintelligible in a tax assessment. State Finance Co. *v.* Mather, 15 N. D. 386, 109 N. W. 350.

53. Wing *v.* Minor, (Miss. 1890) 7 So. 347, holding that an assessment of "lot 7, block 5. O. S." does not authorize a tax-sale of lot 7, block 5, in Ocean Springs.

54. *Alabama.*— State *v.* Sloss, 87 Ala. 119, 6 So. 309.

Arizona.— Territory *v.* Yavapai County, 9 Ariz. 405, 84 Pac. 519.

Colorado.— Boston, etc., Smelting Co. *v.* Elder, 20 Colo. App. 90, 77 Pac. 258.

Florida.— Levy *v.* Ladd, 35 Fla. 391, 17 So. 635.

Illinois.— Cleveland, etc., R. Co. *v.* People, 223 Ill. 17, 79 N. E. 17; Law *v.* People, 87 Ill. 385; Davis *v.* Brace, 82 Ill. 542.

Iowa.— *In re* Seaman, 135 Iowa 543, 113 N. W. 354.

Kansas.— Moon *v.* March, 40 Kan. 58, 19 Pac. 334. But *compare* Walker *v.* Douglass, 2 Kan. App. 706, 43 Pac. 1143.

Michigan.— Seymour *v.* Peters, 67 Mich. 415, 35 N. W. 62.

Minnesota.— McCormick *v.* Fitch, 14 Minn. 252.

Missouri.— State *v.* St. Louis, etc., R. Co., 135 Mo. 77, 36 S. W. 211; State *v.* St. Louis, etc., R. Co., 117 Mo. 1. 22 S. W. 910.

New Hampshire.— Derry Nat. Bank *v.* Griffin, 68 N. H. 183, 34 Atl. 740.

New Jersey.— State *v.* Perkins, 24 N. J. L. 409.

New York.—Wilcox *v.* City, etc., Contract Co., 128 N. Y. App. Div. 227, 112 N. Y. Suppl. 532 [*affirmed* in 198 N. Y. 588, 92 N. E. 1084] (as to proper book); People *v.* Carmichael, 64 Misc. 271, 118 N. Y. Suppl. 354; People *v.* Golding, 55 Misc. 425, 106 N. Y. Suppl. 821 (holding that the failure of the supervisors to extend the taxes after preparation of the assessment roll is a jurisdictional defect).

Oregon.— See Waterhouse *v.* Clatsop County, 50 Oreg. 176, 91 Pac. 1083, holding that the extension of taxes on the assessment roll is a part of the process of collection and not of the assessment, apportionment, or levy.

Pennsylvania.— Greenough *v.* Fulton Coal Co., 74 Pa. St. 486. See also McDermott *v.* Hoffman, 70 Pa. St. 31.

Washington.— Lockwood *v.* Roys, 11 Wash. 697, 40 Pac. 346.

See 45 Cent. Dig. tit. "Taxation," § 736.

A library tax is properly extended as a part of the general tax of the city with

within the terms of a curative statute as a mere irregularity.[55] The same rule applies where the law requires the several amounts of distinct taxes levied on the same assessment to be separately set forth.[56] An error in computing and extending the amount of the tax will vitiate the assessment unless the amount of the excess is so trifling as to be negligible.[57] The duty of making this computation and entry is ordinarily a judicial duty of the proper board or officer and cannot be delegated to a third person,[58] except that it may be made up by one acting under the direction and supervision of the proper board or officer;[59] but the time of performing it is not regarded as very material, provided it is done before any attempt to enforce the tax.[60]

6. **AUTHENTICATION — a. Signature of Assessors.** The statutes ordinarily require the assessment roll to be signed by the assessors, and a compliance with this provision is essential to the validity of further proceedings,[61] although under some statutes the assessor's signature to the oath or certificate attached to the

respect to which it is assessed. Chicago *v.* Cook County, 136 Ill. App. 120.

On what valuation the taxes are to be extended see People *v.* Chicago, etc., R. Co., 223 Ill. 300, 79 N. E. 22 (equalized valuation); *In re* Seaman, 135 Iowa 543, 113 N. W. 354 (actual value).

Correction of errors in the extension see State *v.* Johnson, 135 Wis. 192, 115 N. W. 801; State *v.* Florin, 135 Wis. 192, 115 N. W. 800; State *v.* Krumenauer, 135 Wis. 185, 115 N. W. 798.

Extending back taxes see Mecartney *v.* Morse, 137 Ill. 481, 24 N. E. 576, 26 N. E. 376; Gage *v.* People, (Ill. 1886) 8 N. E. 197; Swinney *v.* Beard, 71 Ill. 27.

55. See the statutes of the several states. And see Cairo, etc., R. Co. *v.* Mathews, 152 Ill. 153, 38 N. E. 623; Cornoy *v.* Wetmore, 92 Iowa 100, 60 N. W. 245; Milwaukee, etc., R. Co. *v.* Kossuth County, 41 Iowa 57; Sully *v.* Kuehl, 30 Iowa 275; Eldridge *v.* Kuehl, 27 Iowa 160; State *v.* Lounsberry, 125 Mo. 157, 28 S. W. 448.

56. Thatcher *v.* People, 79 Ill. 597; Thayer *v.* Stearns, 1 Pick. (Mass.) 482; Case *v.* Dean, 16 Mich. 12. See also Wall *v.* Trumbull, 16 Mich. 228.

57. *Illinois.*— Hammond *v.* Carter, 155 Ill. 579, 40 N. E. 1019; Thatcher *v.* People, 79 Ill. 597.

Massachusetts.— Libby *v.* Burnham, 15 Mass. 144.

Michigan.— Grand Rapids *v.* Welleman, 85 Mich. 234, 48 N. W. 534; Case *v.* Dean, 16 Mich. 12.

New York.— Colman *v.* Shattuck, 2 Hun 497, 5 Thomps. & C. 34 [*affirmed* in 62 N. Y. 348].

Wisconsin.— Kelley *v.* Corson, 8 Wis. 182.

See 45 Cent. Dig. tit. "Taxation, §§ 736, 739.

Estoppel of state.—Where the auditor-general computes, on the basis of reports made to him by a railroad company, the taxes imposed by law on the company's capital and property, but does not pass judgment on the correctness of the reports, the state is not estopped from enforcing payment of the correct amount. Lake Shore, etc., R. Co. *v.* People, 46 Mich. 193, 9 N. W. 249.

58. People *v.* Hagadorn, 104 N. Y. 516, 10 N. E. 891 (board of supervisors); Bellinger *v.* Gray, 51 N. Y. 610. But *compare* Reno County School Dist. No. 127 *v.* Reno County School Dist. No. 45, 80 Kan. 641, 103 Pac. 126, ministerial duty only.

What officer is to extend tax see Chiniquy *v.* People, 78 Ill. 570 (county clerk); Milwaukee, etc., R. Co. *v.* Kossuth County, 41 Iowa 57 (clerk of board of supervisors).

59. People *v.* Wemple, 139 N. Y. 240, 34 N. E. 883 [*reversing* 67 Hun 495, 22 N. Y. Suppl. 497]; Covington *v.* Rockingham, 93 N. C. 134.

60. Harwood *v.* Brownell, 48 Iowa 657; Utica First Nat. Bank *v.* Waters, 7 Fed. 152, 19 Blatchf. 242.

61. *Maine.*— Foxcroft *v.* Nevens, 4 Me. 72.

Michigan.— Lowe *v.* Detroit, 138 Mich. 541, 101 N. W. 810; Darmstaetter *v.* Moloney, 45 Mich. 621, 8 N. W. 574; Sibley *v.* Smith, 2 Mich. 486.

Missouri.— Howard *v.* Heck, 88 Mo. 456, sign and seal the assessor's book.

New Hampshire.— Gordon *v.* Rundlett, 28 N. H. 435 (signature by selectmen); Chase *v.* Sparhawk, 22 N. H. 134. See also Bailey *v.* Ackerman, 54 N. H. 527.

North Carolina.— Kelly *v.* Craig, 27 N. C. 129.

Vermont.— Bartlett *v.* Wilson, 59 Vt. 23, 8 Atl. 321; Smith *v.* Hard, 59 Vt. 13, 8 Atl. 317.

See 45 Cent. Dig. tit. "Taxation," § 745.

But *compare* Boyle *v.* West, 107 La. 347, 31 So. 794; Townsen *v.* Wilson, 9 Pa. St. 270.

Sufficiency of signature.—A tax deed will not be held void because the official title of the assessor was omitted after his signature to the oath as to the correctness of the assessment roll. Shoup *v.* Central Branch Union Pac. R. Co., 24 Kan. 547.

Requirement of seal to assessment roll see Shoup *v.* Central Branch Union Pac. R. Co., 24 Kan. 547; Linton *v.* Wanke, 118 N. Y. Suppl. 965 [*affirmed* in 133 N. Y. App. Div. 922, 117 N. Y. Suppl. 1139].

In an action to collect the taxes, it is probable that the proceedings would not be defeated by the mere failure of the assessor to sign the roll, although this would defeat a tax-sale. See Bath *v.* Whitmore, 79 Me. 182, 9 Atl. 119.

text and subject-matter, and also, if possible, so as to make the assessment effective.[26]

b. Admissibility of Extrinsic Evidence. Parol extrinsic evidence cannot be received to vary or contradict the particulars set forth in an assessment list or roll;[27] and the testimony of the assessors is not admissible to impeach or controvert their own assessments.[28] Parol evidence, however, may be admitted for the purpose of explaining descriptive matter in the assessment list or applying it to its intended object, provided the list itself furnishes an unmistakable clue for the application of such testimony.[29] Where it becomes necessary in any kind of action to determine to whom property was assessed at a given time, or who paid the taxes on it, the assessment list is the best evidence on this issue, and extrinsic evidence cannot be received unless the failure to produce the list is excused by showing its loss or destruction or in some other satisfactory manner.[30]

c. Conclusiveness in General. In the assessment and valuation of property the assessors or other proper officers act judicially, and therefore their determinations as to values and other questions of fact are final and conclusive unless impeached for fraud or want of jurisdiction, and until reversed or set aside by some tribunal having authority to review their action.[31]

26. *Louisiana.*—Webre *v.* Lutcher, 45 La. Ann. 574, 12 So. 834.

Maine.— Saco Water Power Co. *v.* Buxton, 98 Me. 295, 56 Atl. 914.

Nevada.— State *v.* Real Del Monte Gold, etc.. Min. Co., 1 Nev. 523.

Pennsylvania.— Laird *v.* Hiester, 24 Pa. St. 452.

Vermont.—Waterman *v.* Davis. 66 Vt. 83, 28 Atl. 664.

Washington.— Shipley *v.* Gaffner, 48 Wash. 169, 93 Pac. 211, holding that where the place for the name of the owner of property is left blank in the assessment roll, it amounts to a statement that the owner is unknown.

See 45 Cent. Dig. tit. "Taxation," § 783.

An assessment of a waterworks company for "capital invested in merchandise and manufacturing" includes its pipes, hydrants, etc.; but not its corporate franchise to construct waterworks in a city and use the streets therefor, or its "solvent credits," since these are separate kinds of property and should be listed separately. Adams *v.* Vicksburg Waterworks Co., 94 Miss. 601, 47 So. 530; Adams *v.* Bullock, 94 Miss. 27, 47 So. 527, 530.

27. *California.*—Allen *v.* McKay, 139 Cal. 94, 72 Pac. 713. And see People *v.* Stockton, etc., R. Co., 49 Cal. 414; People *v.* San Francisco Sav. Union, 31 Cal. 132.

Louisiana.— Gaither *v.* Green, 40 La. Ann. 362, 4 So. 210.

Maine.— Sweetsir *v.* Chandler. 98 Me. 145, 56 Atl. 584.

Michigan.— Case *v.* Dean, 16 Mich. 12.

Mississippi.— McQueen *v.* Bush, 76 Miss. 283, 24 So. 196; Vicksburg Bank *v.* Adams, 74 Miss. 179, 21 So. 401.

Oregon.—West Portland Park Assoc. *v.* Kelly, 29 Oreg. 412, 45 Pac. 901.

Washington.— Carlisle *v.* Chehalis County, 32 Wash. 284, 73 Pac. 349.

Where an assessment is not complete, and is undergoing direct adjudication in a suit, a misdescription therein may be shown by parol. Vicksburg Bank *v.* Adams, 74 Miss. 179, 21 So. 401.

28. Saco Water Power Co. *v.* Buxton, 98 Me. 295, 56 Atl. 914; Von Storch *v.* Scranton City, 3 Pa. Co. Ct. 567; Tierney *v.* Union Lumbering Co., 47 Wis. 248, 2 N. W. 289; Plumer *v.* Marathon County, 46 Wis. 163, 50 N. W. 416.

29. State *v.* Real Del Monte Gold, etc., Min. Co., 1 Nev. 523; Conklin *v.* El Paso, (Tex. Civ. App. 1897) 44 S. W. 879.

Identifying property assessed.— Parol evidence is not admissible to show what particular lot of land an assessor had in mind in making the assessment roll. Harvey *v.* Meyer, 117 Cal. 60, 48 Pac. 1014.

30. *Alabama.*— Doe *v.* Edmondson, 145 Ala. 557, 40 So. 505.

Connecticut.—Averill *v.* Sanford, 36 Conn. 345; Marlborough *v.* Sisson, 23 Conn. 44.

Georgia.— Livingston *v.* Hudson, 85 Ga. 835, 12 S. E. 17.

Illinois.—Andrews *v.* People, 75 Ill. 605.

Indiana.— Bright *v.* Markle, 17 Ind. 308.

Louisiana.— State *v.* Edgar, 26 La. Ann. 726.

New Hampshire.— Forest *v.* Jackson, 56 N. H. 357; Farrar *v.* Fessenden, 39 N. H. 268; Pittsfield *v.* Barnstead, 38 N. H. 115.

Pennsylvania.— Stark *v.* Shupp, 112 Pa. St. 395, 3 Atl. 864; McCall *v.* Lorimer, 4 Watts 351; Simon *v.* Brown, 3 Yeates 186, 2 Am. Dec. 368.

Vermont.— Sherwin *v.* Bugbee, 17 Vt. 337.

Washington.— Seattle *v.* Parker, 13 Wash. 450, 43 Pac. 369.

See also *supra*, VI, C, 1, e.

But *compare* Holmead *v.* Chesapeake. etc., Canal Co., 12 Fed. Cas. No. 6,626, 1 Hayw. & H. 77.

31. *Arkansas.*—Vance *v.* Austell, 45 Ark. 400.

California.— Modoc County *v.* Churchill, 75 Cal. 172, 16 Pac. 771, as to value.

Illinois.— St. Louis Bridge, etc., Co. *v.* People, 127 Ill. 627, 21 N. E. 348; Illinois, etc., R., etc., Co. *v.* Stookey, 122 Ill. 358, 13 N. E.

all the assessed property within the district affected.[53] The compensation of the officers constituting the board is generally fixed by law.[54]

c. Method of Equalization. In order to effect an equalization it is the duty of the board to ascertain whether the valuation of assessable property in each town or district bears a just relation to that in all the other towns or districts, and if it does not, the board is to increase or diminish the aggregate valuation in any town or district by adding or deducting such a percentage as will in its opinion be necessary to produce such relation.[55] For this purpose the board may take as a standard the particular township or district assessment roll which, in its judgment, most nearly represents a true and just valuation, and make the others conform to it.[56] The increase or diminution ordered should be specified as a percentage, and not as a gross or lump sum,[57] and should be made applicable to all the taxable property of the district affected, and not to a particular class or kind.[58] It is not "equalization," or within the functions of the board to transfer property from the assessment list of one district to that of another,[59] or to make an addition to the valuation in all the districts indiscriminately,[60] although it may lawfully reduce the total of the assessment list of any district below that made by the assessors.[61]

d. Records of Board. The board of equalization must keep a written record of its proceedings if required by statute as an essential to the validity of further proceedings.[62] And the record must contain enough to show clearly what action was taken by the board in regard to the equalization of taxes,[63] and must be signed by the members if the law so directs.[64] But presumptions will be indulged in

53. Black *v.* McGonigle, 103 Mo. 192, 15 S. W. 615; State *v.* Anderson, 38 N. J. L. 82; Kelley *v.* Corson, 11 Wis. 1.

Annual valuations see State *v.* Nichols, 29 Wash. 159, 69 Pac. 771.

Equalizing assessments on new buildings and structures see State *v.* Lewis, 20 Ohio Cir. Ct. 319, 11 Ohio Cir. Dec. 13.

54. See the statutes of the several states. And see Outagamie County *v.* Greenville, 77 Wis. 165, 45 N. W. 1090.

55. *Illinois.*—McKee *v.* Champaign County, 53 Ill. 477; People *v.* Nichols, 49 Ill. 517.

Iowa.— Harney *v.* Mitchell County, 44 Iowa 203.

Michigan.— Goudreau *v.* St. Ignace, 97 Mich. 413, 56 N. W. 772; Chamberlain *v.* St. Ignace, 92 Mich. 332, 52 N. W. 634; Boyce *v.* Sebring, 66 Mich. 210, 33 N. W. 815. See also Auditor-Gen. *v.* Griffin, 140 Mich. 427, 103 N. W. 854.

Nebraska.— Lancaster County *v.* Whedon, 76 Nebr. 753, 108 N. W. 127.

New Jersey.— Sea Isle City *v.* Cape May County, 50 N. J. L. 50, 12 Atl. 771.

New York.— People *v.* Wayne County, 49 Hun 476, 2 N. Y. Suppl. 555.

Utah.— Salt Lake City *v.* Armstrong, 15 Utah 472, 49 Pac. 641.

Wisconsin.— Kelley *v.* Corson, 8 Wis. 182.

Canada.— Simcoe *v.* Norfolk County, 5 Can. L. J. N. S. 181. And see *In re* Simcoe County, 5 Can. L. J. N. S. 294; *In re* Strachan, 41 U. C. Q. B. 175; *In re* Gibson, 20 U. C. Q. B. 111.

See 45 Cent. Dig. tit. "Taxation," § 793.

But under a provision authorizing the county board to increase or diminish individual assessments, the board has no power to raise or diminish the entire assessment roll. Wells *v.* State Bd. of Equalization, 56 Cal. 194.

56. Lee *v.* Mehew, 8 Okla. 136, 56 Pac. 1046; Bardrick *v.* Dillon, 7 Okla. 535, 54 Pac. 785; Webb *v.* Renfrew, 7 Okla. 198, 54 Pac. 448.

57. State *v.* Coe, (N. J. Sup. 1899) 44 Atl. 952. See also Tallmadge *v.* Rensselaer County, 21 Barb. (N. Y.) 611.

58. People *v.* Nichols, 49 Ill. 517 (must include unimproved as well as improved lands); Sinclair *v.* Learned, 51 Mich. 335, 16 N. W. 672 (both realty and personalty); New Jersey Zinc Co. *v.* Sussex County Bd. of Equalization, 70 N. J. L. 186, 56 Atl. 138; West Hoboken Tp. *v.* Anderson, 38 N. J. L. 173. See also Weiser Nat. Bank *v.* Jeffreys, 14 Ida. 659, 95 Pac. 23 (holding that the statutory method of equalization applies to the taxable property in the county, and not to the property over which the taxing power has no jurisdiction); Auditor-Gen. *v.* Longyear, 110 Mich. 223, 68 N. W. 130.

59. McCowen Independent School Dist. *v.* Local Bd. of Review, 131 Iowa 195, 108 N. W. 220.

60. Kimball *v.* Merchants' Sav., etc., Co., 89 Ill. 611. And see McCutchen *v.* Lyon County, 95 Iowa 20, 63 N. W. 455.

61. Tweed *v.* Metcalf, 4 Mich. 579.

62. Perry County *v.* Selma, etc., R. Co., 65 Ala. 391; State Auditor *v.* Jackson County, 65 Ala. 142; Fowler *v.* Russell, 45 Kan. 425, 25 Pac. 871; Auditor-Gen. *v.* Reynolds, 83 Mich. 471, 47 N. W. 442; Silsbee *v.* Stockle, 44 Mich. 561, 7 N. W. 160, 367. But see Tweed *v.* Metcalf, 4 Mich. 579.

63. Paldi *v.* Paldi, 84 Mich. 346, 47 N. W. 510.

64. State Auditor *v.* Jackson County, 65

failure to appear before the board of review, since he voluntarily submits himself to the jurisdiction of the state, for purposes of taxation, by acquiring and holding property therein.[99] But the necessity for pursuing the statutory remedy does not exist where the assessment complained of is void and illegal,[1] as where the assessors acted entirely without jurisdiction,[2] or where the assessment was fraudulently made,[3] or is so incomplete or devoid of proper authentication that there is nothing legally sufficient to lay before the board as a basis for their action.[4]

2. Grounds of Review — a. Defects and Irregularities. Defects, errors, and irregularities, not fundamental in their nature, but occurring in the exercise of lawful jurisdiction, may be corrected by the board of equalization or review, and should not be brought before the courts in the first instance.[5] This rule applies, for instance, where property is assessed in the wrong name,[6] or in the name of a deceased person,[7] or where it is erroneously classified as real instead of personal property or *vice versa*.[8]

See Whatcom County *v.* Fairhaven Land Co., 7 Wash. 101, 34 Pac. 563.

Wisconsin.— Milwaukee *v.* Wakefield, 134 Wis. 462, 113 N. W. 34, 115 N. W. 137; Boorman *v.* Juneau County, 76 Wis. 550, 45 N. W. 675; Lawrence *v.* Janesville, 46 Wis. 364, 1 N. W. 338, 50 N. W. 1102.

Wyoming.— Kelley *v.* Rhoads, 7 Wyo. 237, 51 Pac. 593, 75 Am. St. Rep. 904, 39 L. R. A. 594.

United States.— Beeson *v.* Johns, 124 U. S. 56, 8 S. Ct. 352, 31 L. ed. 360; Stanley *v.* Albany County, 121 U. S. 535, 7 S. Ct. 1234, 30 L. ed. 1000; Ledoux *v.* La Bee, 83 Fed. 761; Dundee Mortg., etc., Co. *v.* Charlton, 32 Fed. 192, 13 Sawy. 25.

See 45 Cent. Dig. tit. "Taxation," §§ 808, 809.

No board of equalization elected.—A taxpayer who filed no complaint about his assessment cannot complain that no board of equalization was elected, where the statute provides that such a board may be chosen, when the taxpayer complains, if none has already been elected. Crecelius *v.* Louisville, 49 S. W. 547, 20 Ky. L. Rep. 1551.

Second application to board not required.—A taxpayer need not make more than one complaint to the board of review before resorting to the courts; that is, he need not go back to the board for the purposes of pointing out an alleged error in its former action, before bringing his appeal. Ingersoll *v.* Des Moines, 46 Iowa 553.

99. Crawford *v.* Polk County, 112 Iowa 118, 83 N. W. 825; Citizens' Sav. Bank *v.* New York, 37 N. Y. App. Div. 560, 56 N. Y. Suppl. 205 [*affirmed* in 166 N. Y. 594, 59 N. E. 1120].

1. *Arkansas.*— Clay County *v.* Brown Lumber Co., 90 Ark. 413, 119 S. W. 251, holding that where an assessment is invalid because of jurisdictional defects, the taxpayer may invoke judicial remedies, and is not confined to those prescribed by the assessment laws.

Iowa.— Dickey *v.* Polk County, 58 Iowa 287, 12 N. W. 290.

Kentucky.— Ryan *v.* Louisville, 133 Ky. 714, 118 S. W. 992, on exempt property.

Nebraska.— Hutchinson *v.* Omaha, 52 Nebr. 345, 72 N. W. 218.

New York.— People *v.* Feitner, 45 Misc. 12, 90 N. Y. Suppl. 826 [*affirmed* in 99 N. Y. App. Div. 274, 90 N. Y. Suppl. 904 (*affirmed* in 181 N. Y. 549, 74 N. E. 1124)].

South Dakota.— Dakota L. & T. Co. *v.* Codington County, 9 S. D. 159, 68 N. W. 314.

See 45 Cent. Dig. tit. "Taxation," §§ 808, 809.

2. Layman *v.* Iowa Tel. Co., 123 Iowa 591, 99 N. W. 205; St. Paul *v.* Merritt, 7 Minn. 258; McLean *v.* Jephson, 123 N. Y. 142, 25 N. E. 409, 9 L. R. A. 493.

3. Citizens' Nat. Bank *v.* Columbia County, 23 Wash. 441, 63 Pac. 209.

4. Vittum *v.* People, 183 Ill. 154, 55 N. E. 689; Smith *v.* McQuiston, 108 Iowa 363, 79 N. W. 130; Topsham *v.* Purinton, 94 Me. 354, 47 Atl. 919; May *v.* Traphagen, 139 N. Y. 478, 34 N. E. 1064.

5. Louisville, etc., R. Co. *v.* Bd. of Public Instruction, 50 Fla. 222, 39 So. 480; State *v.* Southern Land, etc., Co., 45 Fla. 374, 33 So. 999; Tragar *v.* Clayton, McGloin (La.) 228; Auditor-Gen. *v.* Ayer, 122 Mich. 136, 80 N. W. 997; Union Stock Yards Nat. Bank *v.* Thurston County, 65 Nebr. 408, 91 N. W. 286, 92 N. W. 1022. See also *supra*, VII, B, 1, b. But *compare* United New Jersey R., etc., Co. *v.* Parker, 75 N. J. L. 771, 69 Atl. 239 [*modifying* (Sup. 1907) 67 Atl. 686, 75 N. J. L. 120, 67 Atl. 672].

Property no longer in existence.— It is no objection to the assessment of property as of a given date that the property has since then ceased to exist. Shelby County *v.* Mississippi, etc., R. Co., 16 Lea (Tenn.) 401, 1 S. W. 32.

Errors held fundamental.— Where the assessor errs in determining as to the extent or number of new structures on a certain tract of land, the error is fundamental, and does not come within a statute authorizing the correction of clerical errors. Mitchell *v.* Hamilton County, 10 Ohio Dec. (Reprint) 628, 22 Cinc. L. Bul. 292. And this is also true where there was no authority to levy the particular tax. Kennedy *v.* Montgomery County, 98 Tenn. 165, 38 S. W. 1075.

6. Geddes *v.* Cunningham, 104 La. 306, 29 So. 138; Fowler *v.* Springfield, 64 N. H. 108, 5 Atl. 770; Carpenter *v.* Dalton, 58 N. H. 615.

7. Geddes *v.* Cunningham, 104 La. 306, 29 So. 138.

8. Connecticut Valley Lumber Co. *v.* Mon-

payer shall have an opportunity to be heard in opposition to the assessment or valuation of his property before his liability is conclusively fixed.[13] But the denial of this opportunity, or the failure to constitute a board of equalization or review, or of such a board to meet, is a matter which can be complained of only by a party who can show that he himself is prejudiced thereby.[14]

b. Persons Entitled. The right of appeal to the officer or board of equalization or review is ordinarily given to any person "interested" or having property assessed on the roll.[15] If this right is not in terms restricted to taxpayers, the city in which property is located may complain that the assessment is too low.[16] But where shares of corporate stock are assessed directly to the individual shareholders, it has been held that the corporation itself is not a party in interest in such sense as to have a right of appeal.[17] Several taxpayers are not authorized to unite in a petition for review, unless they complain of an error or illegality which affects them all in the same manner.[18]

c. Failure to Return List or Inventory.[19] In some states a taxpayer who neglects or refuses to return a list or schedule of his taxable property, as required

13. Orr *v.* State Bd. of Equalization, 3 Ida. 190, 28 Pac. 416; Hough *v.* Hastings, 18 Ill. 312; State *v.* Baltimore, 105 Md. 1, 65 Atl. 369; Fowble *v.* Kemp, 92 Md. 630, 48 Atl. 379; Monticello Distilling Co. *v.* Baltimore, 90 Md. 416, 45 Atl. 210; Exchange Bank Tax Cases, 21 Fed. 99.

No implied repeal of law giving right of review.— A statute providing a remedy against illegal assessments should not be deemed embraced in a general repeal of all laws relating to assessments, in an act prescribing and regulating the method of assessing taxes. Shear *v.* Columbia County, 14 Fla. 146; Warner Iron Co. *v.* Pace, 89 Tenn. 707, 15 S. W. 1077.

14. Cowell *v.* Doub, 12 Cal. 273; Scott County *v.* Hinds, 50 Minn. 204, 52 N. W. 523.

15. People *v.* Centralia Gas, etc., Co., 238 Ill. 113, 87 N. E. 370 (holding that a company in possession of premises and claiming to be the owner thereof is *prima facie* entitled to object to a tax, although assessed in the name of another company); State *v.* State Tax Collector, 104 La. 468, 29 So. 39; Com. *v.* Delaware Division Canal Co., 123 Pa. St. 594, 16 Atl. 584, 2 L. R. A. 798; Dundee Mortgage, etc., Co. *v.* Charlton, 32 Fed. 192, 13 Sawy. 25.

"A person aggrieved" within the meaning of such a statute means one whose pecuniary interests are or may be adversely affected. Hough *v.* North Adams, 196 Mass. 290, 82 N. E. 46.

Vendor or purchaser of property see *In re* Southern Wood Mfg. Co., 49 La. Ann. 926, 22 So. 39; State *v.* Bd. of Assessors, McGloin (La.) 25; Hamilton *v.* Ames, 74 Mich. 298, 41 N. W. 930 (assignee); State *v.* Lawson, (N. J. Sup. 1900) 45 Atl. 911.

Mortgagor of realty entitled to complain see Detroit *v.* Detroit Bd. of Assessors, 91 Mich. 78, 51 N. W. 787, 16 L. R. A. 59.

One having color of title to land may apply for an abatement of the taxes assessed thereon. Carpenter *v.* Dalton, 58 N. H. 615.

Owner of exempt property.— Where the statute provides a proceeding to obtain relief when an "owner of assessable property" has been unjustly assessed thereon, it will not be construed as affording relief to an owner of property on which taxes could not legally be assessed, but which is nevertheless erroneously assessed. Arapahoe County *v.* Denver Union Water Co., 32 Colo. 382, 76 Pac. 1060.

Agent.— One who is assessed for money in his hands as agent may have the assessment corrected so as to show that the principal is ultimately liable for the tax. Title Guaranty, etc., Co. *v.* Los Angeles County, 3 Cal. App. 619, 86 Pac. 844.

Rule in Canada.— Any elector or ratepayer may complain of the wrongful omission from the assessment roll of the name of a person which should be inserted therein. Matter of Roman Catholic Separate Schools, 18 Ont. 606.

16. St. Louis Bridge Co. *v.* People, 128 Ill. 422, 21 N. E. 428; People *v.* Ontario County, 50 Misc. (N. Y.) 63, 100 N. Y. Suppl. 330 [*affirmed* in 114 N. Y. App. Div. 915, 100 N. Y. Suppl. 1136]. But *compare* Kenilworth *v.* Bd. of Tax Equalization, 78 N. J. L. 302, 72 Atl. 966 [*affirmed* in 78 N. J. L. 439, 74 Atl. 480], holding that where a borough consents to the confirmation of assessments of ratables as made by its assessor before the county board of taxation and such assessment is confirmed, the borough cannot be said to be aggrieved by the action of the county board so as to justify an appeal to the state board.

17. People *v.* Feitner, 71 N. Y. App. Div. 572, 76 N. Y. Suppl. 245; People *v.* Wall St. Bank, 39 Hun (N. Y.) 525; People *v.* Button, 17 N. Y. Suppl. 315. *Contra*, Independence First Nat. Bank *v.* Independence, 123 Iowa 482, 99 N. W. 142; Citizens' Nat. Bank *v.* Columbia County, 23 Wash. 441, 63 Pac. 209.

18. Barrett's Appeal, 73 Conn. 288, 47 Atl. 243; Tampa *v.* Mugge, 40 Fla. 326, 24 So. 489; State *v.* Grow, 74 Nebr. 850, 105 N. W. 898; People *v.* O'Donnel, 113 N. Y. App. Div. 713, 99 N. Y. Suppl. 436 [*affirmed* in 187 N. Y. 536, 80 N. E. 1117].

19. **Proceedings on failure of taxpayer to return list or making false list** see *supra*, VI, C, 3.

tions of the board, although exercising his own judgment and discretion as to details.[60]

c. Change of Valuation or Amount of Tax. In reviewing an individual assessment, the board of equalization is bound neither by the valuation placed on the property by its owner nor by that of the assessor, and does not act as an arbitrator between these two parties, but as an official body charged with the duty of ascertaining the true taxable value of the property, and therefore it may make such changes in the assessment as are necessary to carry its determination into effect.[61] But county boards have no authority to change valuations made by the state board on property committed to the exclusive jurisdiction of the latter;[62] and generally an appeal does not lie from one board of equalization to another, each possessing its own well-defined jurisdiction and authority.[63]

d. Increase of Valuation or Tax. Ordinarily the officer or board of equalization is restricted to correcting assessments alleged to be excessive, and has no authority to increase valuations previously made by the assessor or other proper

60. Hampson *v.* Dysart, 6 Ariz. 98, 53 Pac. 581; Security Sav. Bank, etc. *v.* Los Angeles County, (Cal. 1893) 34 Pac. 437; Farmers', etc., Bank *v.* Los Angeles Bd. of Equalization, 97 Cal. 318, 32 Pac. 312; Murphy *v.* Lincoln County Bd. of Equalization, 7 Ida. 745, 59 Pac. 715; Connor *v.* Waxahachie, (Tex. 1889) 13 S. W. 30; Ferris *v.* Kimble, 75 Tex. 476, 12 S. W. 689.

In case of conflicting instructions, the assessor is bound to follow the directions of the state controller rather than those of the board of equalization. Cook *v.* Galveston, etc., R. Co., 5 Tex. Civ. App. 644, 24 S. W. 544.

61. *Alabama.*— State *v.* Sloss-Sheffield Steel, etc., Co., 162 Ala. 234, 50 So. 366; *Ex p.* Howard-Harrison Iron Co., 130 Ala. 185, 30 So. 400.

Arizona.— Hampson *v.* Dysart, 6 Ariz. 98, 53 Pac. 581.

Connecticut.— Bradley *v.* New Haven, 73 Conn. 646, 48 Atl. 960.

Georgia.— Collier *v.* Morrow, 90 Ga. 148, 15 S. E. 768.

Illinois.— Chicago, etc., R. Co. *v.* Bureau County, 25 Ill. 580.

Michigan.— Ward *v.* Echo Tp., 145 Mich. 56, 108 N. W. 364.

Mississippi.— Tunica County *v.* Tate, 78 Miss. 294, 29 So. 74.

Nebraska.— State *v.* Karr, 64 Nebr. 514, 90 N. W. 298.

Nevada.— State *v.* Meyers, 23 Nev. 274, 46 Pac. 51.

New Jersey.— Woodstown *v.* Salem County Bd. of Assessors, (Sup. 1903) 56 Atl. 124.

New York.— People *v.* Roberts, 27 N. Y. App. Div. 400, 50 N. Y. Suppl. 302 [*affirmed* in 158 N. Y. 666, 52 N. E. 1125]; People *v.* Barker, 22 N. Y. App. Div. 161, 47 N. Y. Suppl. 1020. See also People *v.* Schoonover, 26 Misc. 576, 57 N. Y. Suppl. 498 [*reversed* on other grounds in 47 N. Y. App. Div. 278, 62 N. Y. Suppl. 180 (*affirmed* in 166 N. Y. 629, 60 N. E. 1118)].

Ohio.— Gazlay *v.* Humphreys, 7 Ohio Dec. (Reprint) 102, 1 Cinc. L. Bul. 114.

Oregon.— Shumway *v.* Baker County, 3 Oreg. 246.

Wisconsin.— State *v.* Lawler, 103 Wis. 460, 79 N. W. 777; State *v.* Gaylord, 73 Wis. 306, 41 N. W. 518; Wauwatosa *v.* Gunyon, 25 Wis. 271.

See 45 Cent. Dig. tit. "Taxation," § 837.

Contra.— Houghton *v.* Austin, 47 Cal. 646.

The state board of equalization has power to increase or reduce the valuation of railroad property as well as other property. Braden *v.* Union Trust Co., 25 Kan. 362.

Necessity of valuation by assessor.—A board of equalization cannot place a valuation on property for assessment which has been returned by the assessor without having any value placed on it. Lyman *v.* Howe, 64 Ark. 436, 42 S. W. 830.

Change of valuation between assessment periods.—Annual boards of equalization may change the appraisement in any one year of the decennial periods, but such revaluation must be based upon some change of value or condition. Black *v.* Hagerty, 16 Ohio Cir. Ct. 255, 9 Ohio Cir. Dec. 93. But in equalizing values and correcting errors made by the decennial appraisers a board of review must at all times be guided and controlled by values as they existed at the time of making the decennial appraisement, and not by values as at present existing. National Land, etc., Co. *v.* Davies, 29 Ohio Cir. Ct. 334 [*affirmed* in 76 Ohio St. 407, 81 N. E. 755]. As to apportionment of valuation between owner of surface and owner of coal, when coal is conveyed after the decennial appraisement see Johnson *v.* Lacey, 30 Ohio Cir. Ct. 619.

A resolution of a town meeting reducing an annual military tax is ineffectual. Atwater *v.* O'Reilly, 81 Conn. 367, 71 Atl. 505.

Death of taxpayer as limiting time to make corrections see Williamson's Estate, 153 Pa. St. 508, 26 Atl. 246 [*affirming* 1 Pa. Dist. 159, 11 Pa. Co. Ct. 235].

62. People *v.* Sacramento County, 59 Cal. 321; Pensacola *v.* Louisville, etc., R. Co., 21 Fla. 492; Baltimore, etc., R. Co. *v.* Oregon Tp., 170 Ind. 300, 84 N. E. 529 [*affirming* (Ind. App. 1907) 81 N. E. 105].

63. See McGee *v.* State, 32 Nebr. 149, 49 N. W. 220.

of review, to cover omitted property; this ordinarily will not be valid unless the taxpayer is given notice and an opportunity to apply for a review and correction.[97]

(II) *REQUISITES AND SUFFICIENCY.* It is generally held that personal notice to taxpayers is not necessary where a public statute, of which all persons are bound to take notice, specifies the day and place where the board of equalization shall meet, this being sufficient notice to give the board jurisdiction over any particular assessment.[98] And it has also been held that a published general

Ohio Cir. Ct. 334]; State *v.* Lewis, 25 Ohio Cir. Ct. 227; Euclid Ave. Sav., etc., Co. *v.* Hubbard, 22 Ohio Cir. Ct. 20, 12 Ohio Cir. Dec. 279; Phillips *v.* Hunter, 9 Ohio Cir. Ct. 698, 6 Ohio Cir. Dec. 746. But see Lewis *v.* State, 69 Ohio St. 473, 69 N. E. 980, as to increasing assessments on buildings improved during the year.

Oregon.— Ankeny *v.* Blakley, 44 Oreg. 78, 74 Pac. 485.

Pennsylvania.— Philadelphia Ins. Contributionship *v.* Yard, 17 Pa. St. 331; Larimer *v.* McCall, 4 Watts & S. 133.

South Carolina.— State *v.* Boyd, 35 S. C. 233, 14 S. E. 496.

South Dakota.— Avant *v.* Flynn, 2 S. D. 153, 49 N. W. 15.

Texas.— San Antonio *v.* Hoefling, 90 Tex. 511, 39 S. W. 918; Hoefling *v.* San Antonio, 15 Tex. Civ. App. 257, 38 S. W. 1127; Gage *v.* Nevill, 3 Tex. App. Civ. Cas. § 274.

Washington.— Lewis *v.* Bishop, 19 Wash. 312, 53 Pac. 165.

Wisconsin.— State *v.* Sackett, 117 Wis. 580, 94 N. W. 314. But see State *v.* Wharton, 117 Wis. 558, 94 N. W. 359.

United States.— French *v.* Edwards, 13 Wall. 506, 20 L. ed. 702; Santa Clara County *v.* Southern Pac. R. Co., 18 Fed. 385; Albany City Bank *v.* Maher, 6 Fed. 417, 19 Blatchf. 175; Jessup *v.* Chicago, etc., R. Co., 13 Fed. Cas. No. 7,300. But *compare* State R. Tax Cases, 92 U. S. 575, 23 L. ed. 663.

Canada.— Nicholls *v.* Cumming, 1 Can. Sup. Ct. 395; Tobey *v.* Wilson, 43 U. C. Q. B. 230.

See 45 Cent. Dig. tit. "Taxation," § 854.

But *compare* Bd. of Equalization *v.* Land Owners, 51 Ark. 516, 11 S. W. 822; Pulaski County Bd. of Equalization Cases, 49 Ark. 518, 6 S. W. 1; Satterwhite *v.* State, 142 Ind. 1, 40 N. E. 654, 1087; State *v.* Cudahy Packing Co., 103 Minn. 419, 115 N. W. 645, 1039, holding that the requirement that notice shall be given of the meetings of the city and state boards of equalization is directory, and that a failure to give such notice is no defense to a tax unless it is shown to have resulted prejudicially.

Exceptional cases.— Notice to individual taxpayers is not required before making a change in the entire assessment of a taxing district. Hallo *v.* Helmer, 12 Nebr. 87, 10 N. W. 568; Dundy *v.* Richardson County, 8 Nebr. 508, 1 N. W. 565. Nor is it necessary to give special notice of a transfer of a personal property assessment from one township to another, where the assessment is not increased. Ellis *v.* People, 199 Ill. 548, 65 N. E. 428. Nor is notice necessary where the board of review is to act entirely upon its own knowledge of the property and opinion as to its value, without hearing evidence. Collier *v.* Morrow, 90 Ga. 148, 15 S. E. 768. And so where a statute provides for the construction of a system of sewers in a city, and the levy of assessments therefor according to area, without regard to improvements, the levy of the assessment is a mere mathematical computation, and if full notice is provided for as to all prior proceedings, it is not necessary that the act should provide an opportunity for lot owners to be heard on the assessments after they are levied. Gillette *v.* Denver, 21 Fed. 822.

Failure to give notice.— Where a tax law provides an opportunity for the taxpayer to be heard but notice thereof is not given, and the assessing officer refuses to hear any complaint, the statute is not invalid on that account, but the tax is voidable and the assessment if attacked in due form and in due time will be set aside for the irregularity. People *v.* Feitner, 191 N. Y. 88, 83 N. E. 592 [*reversing* 120 N. Y. App. Div. 838, 105 N. Y. Suppl. 993].

97. *Illinois.*— Carney *v.* People, 210 Ill. 434, 71 N. E. 365.

Maryland.— Myers *v.* Baltimore County, 83 Md. 385, 35 Atl. 144, 55 Am. St. Rep. 349, 34 L. R. A. 309.

New York.— Bennett *v.* Buffalo, 17 N. Y. 383.

Ohio.— Champaign County Bank *v.* Smith, 7 Ohio St. 42.

United States.— Western Ranches *v.* Custer County, 89 Fed. 577.

See 45 Cent. Dig. tit. "Taxation," § 854.

But *compare* Oregon, etc., Mortg. Sav. Bank *v.* Jordan, 16 Oreg. 113, 17 Pac. 621.

98. *Arkansas.*— St. Louis, etc., R. Co. *v.* Worthen, 52 Ark. 529, 13 S. W. 254, 7 L. R. A. 374.

Colorado.— People *v.* Lothrop, 3 Colo. 428.

Idaho.— Inland Lumber, etc., Co. *v.* Thompson, 11 Ida. 508, 83 Pac. 933, 114 Am. St. Rep. 274.

Kansas.— Gillett *v.* Lyon County Treasurer, 30 Kan. 166, 1 Pac. 577.

Maryland.— O'Neal *v.* Virginia, etc., Bridge Co., 18 Md. 1, 79 Am. Dec. 669; Methodist Church *v.* Baltimore, 6 Gill 391, 48 Am. Dec. 540.

Minnesota.— State *v.* Hynes, 82 Minn. 34, 84 N. W. 636.

Missouri.— State *v.* Springer, 134 Mo. 212, 35 S. W. 589; State *v.* New Lindell Hotel Co., 9 Mo. App. 450.

Nebraska.— Hacker *v.* Howe, 72 Nebr. 385, 101 N. W. 255. In this state it was formerly held otherwise. See McGee *v.* State, 32 Nebr. 149, 49 N. W. 220; South Platte Land Co. *v.*

the nature of the change proposed to be made in the assessment.[4] The provisions of the statute must also be followed in regard to the manner of serving or giving the notice.[5]

(III) *PERSONS NOTIFIED.* Where personal notice is required it ordinarily must be served on the owner of the property to be affected,[6] or his agent,[7] or executor or administrator.[8] In case of a corporation service may be had on any officer of the company authorized to accept notice,[9] and need not be made on the individual stock-holders.[10]

(IV) *WAIVER OF NOTICE.* A voluntary appearance of a taxpayer or his agent before the officer or board of equalization or review, for the purpose of obtaining relief against the assessment or contesting a proposed increase of it, is a waiver of notice or of any objections to the form or service of the notice.[11] But not so where the appearance by the taxpayer or his counsel is only for the

4. *California.*— Security Sav. Bank, etc., *v.* Los Angeles County, (1893) 34 Pac. 437; Farmers', etc., Bank *v.* Los Angeles Bd. of Equalization, 97 Cal. 318, 32 Pac. 312.

Indiana.— Reynolds *v.* Bowen, 138 Ind. 434, 36 N. E. 756, 37 N. E. 962; Florer *v.* Sheridan, 137 Ind. 28, 36 N. E. 365, 23 L. R. A. 278.

Maryland.— Alleghany County *v.* New York Min. Co., 76 Md. 549, 25 Atl. 864.

New Jersey.— State *v.* Warford, 32 N. J. L. 207.

New York.— People *v.* Feitner, 191 N. Y. 88, 83 N. E. 592 [*reversing* 120 N. Y. App. Div. 838, 105 N. Y. Suppl. 993], holding that the notice must be such that compliance therewith is possible, and that the taxpayer may object or protest even though he has no grounds for doing either.

Ohio.— Wells *v.* Adair, 11 Ohio Dec. (Reprint) 783, 29 Cinc. L. Bul. 205.

See 45 Cent. Dig. tit. "Taxation," § 855.

But *compare* Poppleton *v.* Yamhill County, 18 Oreg. 377, 23 Pac. 253, 7 L. R. A. 449, holding that the notice given by the board of equalization or county court sitting as such board, to a taxpayer of a proposed increase of his assessment, need not specify the property to be added thereto.

5. *Indiana.*— Eaton *v.* Union County Nat. Bank, 141 Ind. 159, 40 N. E. 693 (holding that verbal notice on the day of hearing is insufficient, under a statute requiring written notice); International Bldg., etc., Assoc. *v.* Marion County, 30 Ind. App. 12, 65 N. E. 297.

Kentucky.— Ward *v.* Wentz, 130 Ky. 705, 113 S. W. 892, by posting in a conspicuous place on the premises.

New Jersey.— State *v.* Drake, 33 N. J. L. 194, service on tenant of property-owner not sufficient.

New York.— Board of Supervisors *v.* Betts, 6 N. Y. Suppl. 934, holding that where the statute requires that the assessors "shall cause notices" of the assessment to be put up, a posting by a person other than the assessor is sufficient.

Ohio.— Hayes *v.* Yost, 24 Ohio Cir. Ct. 18, holding that posting a letter is not equivalent to personal service.

Texas.— Graham *v.* Lasater, (Civ. App. 1894) 26 S. W. 472, holding that a postal card containing the required notice is "written" notice.

United States.— Sturges *v.* Carter, 114 U. S. 511, 5 S. Ct. 1014, 29 L. ed. 240.

See 45 Cent. Dig. tit. "Taxation," § 855.

6. People *v.* Centralia Gas, etc., Co., 238 Ill. 113, 87 N. E. 370 (holding that under the statutory provision requiring notice to the person or corporation to be affected, the owner of the property is such person, and not necessarily the person in whose name it is assessed); State *v.* Drake, 33 N. J. L. 194 (holding that service on a tenant of the owner of the property is not sufficient).

Notice served on one owner of an undivided interest in property will not bind any of the others. Perkins *v.* Zumstein, 4 Ohio Cir. Ct. 371, 2 Ohio Cir. Dec. 601.

Lessee of premises.—A personal covenant in a lease that the lessee will pay the taxes does not, as between the taxing district and the lessee, make the latter the owner or taxpayer within the meaning of the statute entitling him to notice. New Auditorium Pier Co. *v.* Atlantic City Taxing Dist., 74 N. J. L. 303, 65 Atl. 855.

7. State *v.* DeBow, 46 N. J. L. 286.

8. Gallup *v.* Schmidt, 154 Ind. 196, 56 N. E. 443; Reynolds *v.* Bowen, 138 Ind. 434, 36 N. E. 756, 37 N. E. 962; Gamble *v.* Patrick, 22 Okla. 915, 99 Pac. 640.

9. Allison Ranch Min. Co. *v.* Nevada County, 104 Cal. 161, 37 Pac. 875.

10. James Clark Distilling Co. *v.* Cumberland, 95 Md. 468, 52 Atl. 661; Ladd *v.* Gilson, 26 Wash. 79, 66 Pac. 126.

11. *Alabama.*— Tillis *v.* Covington County, 91 Ala. 396, 8 So. 794; Calhoun County *v.* Woodstock Iron Co., 82 Ala. 151, 2 So. 132.

California.— Savings, etc., Soc. *v.* San Francisco, 146 Cal. 673, 80 Pac. 1086; Farmers', etc., Bank *v.* Los Angeles Bd. of Equalization, 97 Cal. 318, 32 Pac. 312; California Domestic Water Co. *v.* Los Angeles County, 10 Cal. App. 185, 101 Pac. 547.

Connecticut.— Sanford's Appeal, 75 Conn. 590, 54 Atl. 739; Quinebaug Reservoir Co. *v.* Union, 73 Conn. 294, 47 Atl. 328.

Illinois.— People *v.* Odin Coal Co., 238 Ill. 279, 87 N. E. 410; American Express Co. *v.* Raymond, 189 Ill. 232, 59 N. E. 528.

Indiana.— Deniston *v.* Terry, 141 Ind. 677, 41 N. E. 143; International Bldg., etc., Assoc.

property should be confined to its value at the time of the assessment complained of, and evidence of its value at some former time is not admissible except as a starting point from which to estimate subsequent appreciation or depreciation.[31] Evidence of the assessed valuation of other property in the same town or district and similarly situated is not generally considered to be admissible,[32] except that it may be admitted for the purpose of showing a rule of the assessors to value all such property at a certain percentage of its actual value and to show whether or not such rule was observed in the case complained of.[33] The members of the board of review are not required to inspect the property in person, but they may send experts to examine it.[34]

(III) *WEIGHT AND SUFFICIENCY.* The affidavit or sworn statement of the taxpayer is evidence to be considered by the board of review, and while it is not conclusive, still if it is not contradicted or impeached by evidence, it must be accepted as correct;[35] and the same is true of schedules or reports filed by corporations.[36] And on the other hand, the assessor's sworn statement is sufficient to sustain the action of the board, taken in accordance with it, if not overborne by testimony.[37] Aside from these considerations, any evidence which has a direct bearing on the question of value may serve as the basis of the board's determination, if uncontradicted.[38] But in case of a conflict in the testimony the ordinary rules of evidence apply, and the decision should be given in accordance with the clear preponderance of testimony.[39]

tor in the probate court is competent evidence of the value of the estate. Erie County *v.* Walker, 10 Ohio Dec. (Reprint) 558, 22 Cinc. L. Bul. 106. So also the inspectors' report made to assist the assessor in his valuation of land is admissible as to its value. T. B. Scott Lumber Co. *v.* Oneida County, 72 Wis. 158, 39 N. W. 343. But on the question of the valuation of property of a railroad company, evidence that it had advanced its freight rates is irrelevant and improper. Chicago, etc., R. Co. *v.* Boone County, 44 Ill. 240.

31. *Alabama.*— State *v.* Bienville Water-Supply Co., 89 Ala. 325, 8 So. 54.

Illinois.— Chicago, etc., R. Co. *v.* Boone County, 44 Ill. 240.

Maine.— Penobscot Chemical Fibre Co. *v.* Bradley, 99 Me. 263, 59 Atl. 83.

Massachusetts.— Lowell *v.* Middlesex County, 152 Mass. 372, 25 N. E. 469, 9 L. R. A. 356.

New Hampshire.— Winnipiseogee Lake Cotton, etc., Mfg. Co. *v.* Laconia, 68 N. H. 248, 35 Atl. 252; Winnipiseogee Lake Cotton, etc., Mfg. Co. *v.* Gilford, 67 N. H. 514, 35 Atl. 945.

See 45 Cent. Dig. tit. "Taxation," § 862.

32. Alabama Mineral Land Co. *v.* Perry County, 95 Ala. 105, 10 So. 550; Chicopee *v.* Hampden County, 16 Gray (Mass.) 38; People *v.* Feitner, 27 Misc. (N. Y.) 371, 58 N. Y. Suppl. 875.

Evidence as to the selling price of other tracts not similarly situated and some of which are in neighboring towns is not admissible. Haven *v.* Essex County, 155 Mass. 467, 29 N. E. 1083.

33. Greenwoods Co. *v.* New Hartford, 65 Conn. 461, 32 Atl. 933; Penobscot Chemical Fibre Co. *v.* Bradley, 99 Me. 263, 59 Atl. 83; Manchester Mills *v.* Manchester, 58 N. H. 38.

34. Nova Ceasarea Harmony Lodge No. 2 *v.* Hagerty, 11 Ohio Dec. (Reprint) 595, 28 Cinc. L. Bul. 67. See also White *v.* Lincoln, 79 Nebr. 153, 112 N. W. 369.

35. Sherman *v.* McClurg, 27 N. J. L. 253; People *v.* Barker, 48 N. Y. 70; People *v.* Feitner, 90 N. Y. App. Div. 9, 85 N. Y. Suppl. 587; People *v.* Holland, 61 Barb. (N. Y.) 273; People *v.* Reddy, 43 Barb. (N. Y.) 539; People *v.* Pulteney Bd. of Assessors, 101 N. Y. Suppl. 176; Adriance *v.* New York, 12 How. Pr. (N. Y.) 224.

Where the board receives a verified statement of the party complaining, and the truth thereof is not disputed, it cannot reject the statement or act otherwise than in accordance therewith, unless the evidence justifies it, since they are acting judicially and are bound by the evidence before them. People *v.* Failing, 130 N. Y. App. Div. 888, 114 N. Y. Suppl. 514; People *v.* Hall, 130 N. Y. App. Div. 360, 114 N. Y. Suppl. 511 [*modifying* 57 Misc. 308, 109 N. Y. Suppl. 402].

36. Kansas Pac. R. Co. *v.* Riley County, 20 Kan. 141; State *v.* Hannibal, etc., R. Co., 101 Mo. 120, 13 S. W. 406; People *v.* Hall, 130 N. Y. App. Div. 360, 114 N. Y. Suppl. 511 [*modifying* 57 Misc. 308, 109 N. Y. Suppl. 402]; People *v.* Feitner, 30 Misc. (N. Y.) 665, 64 N. Y. Suppl. 298.

37. State *v.* Northern Belle Mill, etc., Co., 12 Nev. 89.

38. Gager *v.* Prout, 48 Ohio St. 89, 26 N. E. 1013.

That a corporation declares a dividend is presumptive evidence that its capital is unimpaired; but this may be rebutted. People *v.* Barker, 165 N. Y. 305, 59 N. E. 137, 151.

39. Clement *v.* People, 177 Ill. 144, 52 N. E. 382; Penobscot Chemical Fibre Co. *v.* Bradley, 99 Me. 263, 59 Atl. 83; People *v.* Feitner, 61 N. Y. App. Div. 456, 70 N. Y.

f. Judgment or Decision and Record — (I) *SCOPE AND EXTENT OF RELIEF.* The board of equalization, in granting relief, is generally limited to the scope of the application made to it,[46] although in some jurisdictions it has power to increase an assessment instead of reducing it.[47] If the valuation is found to be merely excessive, it may be set aside as to the excess and affirmed as to the residue;[48] but if the assessment is arbitrary and fraudulent, it should be vacated entirely, and not merely as to the excess.[49] There is generally no authority to award costs to the successful applicant for relief,[50] or to allow him interest on so much of the tax as is adjudged excessive, where the whole has been paid under protest.[51]

(II) *RENDITION AND FORM OF DECISION.* The decision of an officer or board of equalization is usually in the form of a resolution or order, and while it should specify the persons or property affected,[52] it is not to be judged by strict rules, and will not be invalidated by any informality, provided it shows clearly what action was taken by the board.[53] Although the courts will not interfere with the discretion of the board, it may be compelled by mandamus to take up and decide any particular complaint.[54] Formal notice to the taxpayer of the decision of the board is not generally required.[55]

(III) *RECORD OF PROCEEDINGS* — (A) *In General.* If the statute requires the board of equalization to keep a record of its proceedings and enter thereon the action taken in particular cases, it is generally held mandatory, and a disregard of it fatal to the validity of its determinations.[56] The record when made must show affirmatively upon its face the jurisdiction of the officer or board and that he or they acted within the same;[57] but in other respects it will be aided by all reasonable presumptions,[58] and irregularities, informalities, or clerical errors in the record, or in the manner of preparing or keeping it, will not invalidate the

46. State *v.* Ormsby County, 6 Nev. 95.

A revision without making any change in the assessment will not invalidate it. Chicago, etc., R. Co. *v.* Bureau County, 25 Ill. 580.

Apportionment between resident and nonresident trustees see People *v.* Wells, 182 N. Y. 314, 74 N. E. 878.

47. See *supra*, VII, B, 5, d. But see Lowell *v.* Middlesex County, 3 Allen (Mass.) 546.

Addition of penalty see Patton *v.* Commercial Bank, 10 Ohio S. & C. Pl. Dec. 321, 7 Ohio N. P. 401.

48. State *v.* Dickerson, 25 N. J. L. 427.

49. Brennan *v.* Buffalo, 13 N. Y. App. Div. 453, 43 N. Y. Suppl. 597.

50. Penobscot Chemical Fibre Co. *v.* Bradley, 99 Me. 263, 59 Atl. 83; Lowell *v.* Middlesex County, 3 Allen (Mass.) 546.

51. Lowell *v.* Middlesex County, 3 Allen (Mass.) 550.

52. People *v.* Ashbury, 46 Cal. 523.

53. *California.*— La Grange Hydraulic Gold Min. Co. *v.* Carter, 142 Cal. 560, 76 Pac. 241.

Indiana.— Seymour First Nat. Bank *v.* Isaacs, 161 Ind. 278, 68 N. E. 288.

Michigan.— Case *v.* Dean, 16 Mich. 12.

Mississippi.— Mixon *v.* Clevenger, 74 Miss. 67, 20 So. 148; Grayson *v.* Richardson, 65 Miss. 222, 3 So. 579.

Missouri.— State *v.* Baker, 170 Mo. 383, 70 S. W. 872.

Nevada.— State *v.* Washoe County, 14 Nev. 140.

Pennsylvania.— Manor Real Estate, etc., Co. *v.* Cooner, 209 Pa. St. 531, 58 Atl. 918.

See 45 Cent. Dig. tit. "Taxation," § 869.

54. People *v.* Knight, 66 N. Y. App. Div. 150, 72 N. Y. Suppl. 929. And see *infra*, VII, C, 4, a, (I).

55. Com. *v.* New England Slate, etc., Co., 13 Allen (Mass.) 391. But *compare* People *v.* Knight, 66 N. Y. App. Div. 150, 72 N. Y. Suppl. 929.

56. Hillsborough County *v.* Londonderry, 46 N. H. 11; Hayes *v.* Yost, 24 Ohio Cir. Ct. 18; Ratterman *v.* Niehaus, 4 Ohio Cir. Ct. 502, 2 Ohio Cir. Dec. 673; Wise *v.* Kromberg, 7 Ohio Dec. (Reprint) 541, 3 Cinc. L. Bul. 541; Muller *v.* Fratz, 6 Ohio Dec. (Reprint) 811, 8 Am. L. Rec. 310; Hecht *v.* Boughton, 2 Wyo. 385. *Contra*, Hutchinson *v.* Board of Equalization, 66 Iowa 35, 23 N. W. 249; Auditor-Gen. *v.* Buckeye Iron Co., 132 Mich. 454, 93 N. W. 1080.

57. *Arizona.*— Copper Queen Consol. Min. Co. *v.* Cochise County Bd. of Equalization, 7 Ariz. 364, 65 Pac. 149.

Michigan.— Delray Land Co. *v.* Springwells Tp., 149 Mich. 397, 112 N. W. 1132 (record held insufficient for uncertainty); Bialy *v.* Bay City, 139 Mich. 495, 102 N. W. 1033.

Montana.— Montana Ore Purchasing Co. *v.* Maher, 32 Mont. 480, 81 Pac. 13.

New Jersey.—State *v.* Warford, 32 N. J. L. 207; Nixon *v.* Ruple, 30 N. J. L. 58.

Ohio.—Euclid Ave. Sav., etc., Bank *v.* Hubbard, 22 Ohio Cir. Ct. 20, 12 Ohio Cir. Dec. 279.

See 45 Cent. Dig. tit. "Taxation," § 870.

58. Lacey *v.* Davis, 4 Mich. 140, 66 Am. Dec. 524; Godfrey *v.* Douglas County, 28 Oreg. 446, 43 Pac. 171.

proceeding.[63] It must be accepted and obeyed by the officer whose duty it is to make the changes in the assessment roll which are ordered by the board, and he cannot question or review its decisions, but mandamus lies to compel him to perform the simple ministerial duty which the decision of the board imposes on him.[64] It is also binding on the collector of taxes, and conversely it will protect

Washington.— Ladd *v.* Gilson, 26 Wash. 79, 66 Pac. 126; Lewis *v.* Bishop, 19 Wash. 312, 53 Pac. 165; Noyes *v.* King County, 18 Wash. 417, 51 Pac. 1052; Baker *v.* King County, 17 Wash. 622, 50 Pac. 481.

Wisconsin. — See Plumer *v.* Marathon County, 46 Wis. 163, 50 N. W. 416.

United States.— Missouri *v.* Dockery, 191 U. S. 165, 24 S. Ct. 53, 48 L. ed. 133, 63 L. R. A. 571; Stanley *v.* Albany County, 121 U. S. 535, 7 S. Ct. 1234, 30 L. ed. 1000.

See 45 Cent. Dig. tit. "Taxation," § 872.

Liability of property to taxation.— On the question whether particular property is liable to taxation or is exempt by law the decision of the board of equalization is not conclusive. Johnson County *v.* Johnson, 173 Ind. 76, 89 N. E. 590; Horne *v.* Green, 52 Miss. 452; Potter *v.* Ross, 23 N. J. L. 517.

Application of doctrine of res judicata in general.— The rule of *res judicata* in reference to tax assessments rests upon the same basis as in the case of other judgments; and one who relies on the conclusiveness of an assessment must be able to show that all his property was before the board of review when his assessment was settled, for any of it which was not brought to the attention of the board was not in issue before it and of course not adjudicated. Adams *v.* Clarke, 80 Miss. 134, 31 So. 216. For the same reason orders of the board made in proceedings to which a city was not a party are not *res judicata* as to the city. People *v.* Priest, 41 Misc. (N. Y.) 545, 85 N. Y. Suppl. 235. So also the decision of the board as to the assessment of property for the taxes of a given year is not binding on the same board or its successors when the question is as to the assessment of the same property in succeeding years. Lowell *v.* Middlesex County, 152 Mass. 372, 25 N. E. 469, 9 L. R. A. 356; People *v.* Roberts, 155 N. Y. 408, 50 N. E. 53, 41 L R. A. 228.

63. *Illinois.*— Ellis *v.* People, 199 Ill. 548, 65 N. E. 428; Coal Run Coal Co. *v.* Finlen, 124 Ill. 666, 17 N. E. 11; Republic L. Ins. Co. *v.* Pollak, 75 Ill. 292; Spencer *v.* People, 68 Ill. 510.

Indiana.— State *v.* Clinton County, 162 Ind. 580, 68 N. E. 295, 70 N. E. 373, 984; Jones *v.* Rushville Natural Gas Co., 135 Ind. 595, 35 N. E. 390; Pittsburgh, etc., R. Co. *v.* Backus, 133 Ind. 625, 33 N. E. 432; Cleveland, etc., R. Co. *v.* Backus, 133 Ind. 513, 33 N. E. 421, 18 L. R. A. 729. But see Hart *v.* Smith, 159 Ind. 182, 64 N. E. 661, 95 Am. St. Rep. 280, 58 L. R. A. 949.

Kansas.— Torrington *v.* Rickershauser, 41 Kan. 486, 21 Pac. 648. *Compare* Lyon County *v.* Sergeant, 24 Kan. 572.

Kentucky.—Ward *v.* Beale, 91 Ky. 60, 14 S. W. 967, 12 Ky. L. Rep. 671.

Louisiana.— State *v.* Board of Assessors, 30 La. Ann. 261.

Michigan.— Grand Rapids *v.* Welleman, 85 Mich. 234, 48 N. W. 534; Atty.-Gen. *v.* Sanilac County, 42 Mich. 72, 3 N. W. 260; Case *v.* Dean, 16 Mich. 12.

Minnesota.— State *v.* Hynes, 82 Minn. 34, 84 N. W. 636.

Missouri.— State *v.* Western Union Tel. Co., 165 Mo. 502, 65 S. W. 775.

Nebraska.— State *v.* State Bd. of Equalization, 81 Nebr. 139, 115 N. W. 789; State *v.* Grow, 74 Nebr. 850, 105 N. W. 898.

Nevada.— State *v.* Central Pac. R. Co., 21 Nev. 172, 26 Pac. 225, 1109.

New Jersey.—Camden *v.* Mulford, 26 N. J. L. 49.

Oregon.—Rhea *v.* Umatilla County, 2 Oreg. 298.

Tennessee.— Smoky Mt. Land, etc., Co. *v.* Lattimore, 119 Tenn. 620, 105 S. W. 1028, judgment of reassessment.

United States.—Campbellsville Lumber Co. *v.* Hubbart, 112 Fed. 718, 50 C. C. A. 435; McLeod *v.* Receveur, 71 Fed. 455, 18 C. C. A. 188. See also Western Union Tel. Co. *v.* Wright, 166 Fed. 954.

See 45 Cent. Dig. tit. "Taxation," § 872. See also *infra*, VII, C, 1, a.

64. *Arizona.*—Territory *v.* Yavapai County, 9 Ariz. 405, 84 Pac. 519.

Illinois.— People *v.* Opel, 207 Ill. 469, 69 N E. 838.

Indiana.— Seymour First Nat. Bank *v.* Isaacs, 161 Ind. 278, 68 N. E. 288.

Iowa.— Polk County *v.* Sherman, 99 Iowa 60, 68 N. W. 562; Ridley *v.* Doughty, 77 Iowa 226, 42 N. W. 178.

Michigan.— Bialy *v.* Bay City, 139 Mich. 495, 102 N. W. 1033; State Tax Com'rs *v.* Quinn, 125 Mich. 128, 84 N. W. 1.

Nevada.— State *v.* Fish, 4 Nev. 216.

New Jersey.— Englewood *v.* Bergen County Tax Bd. of Equalization, 71 N. J. L. 423, 59 Atl. 15.

Ohio.— State *v.* Lewis, 64 Ohio St. 216, 60 N. E. 198; Sherard *v.* Lindsay, 13 Ohio Cir. Ct. 315, 7 Ohio Cir. Dec. 245.

South Carolina.— State *v.* Covington, 35 S. C. 245, 14 S. E. 499.

Wisconsin.— State *v.* Cornwall, 97 Wis. 565, 73 N. W. 63.

See 45 Cent. Dig. tit. "Taxation," §§ 872, 912.

The opinion of the assessor that the acts of the board of equalization in changing the valuations in the assessment roll were irregular and void will not excuse him from assessing the taxes according to such changed valuations, since the opinion of an officer that the acts of his superior are void does not relieve him from the performance of a statutory duty based on such acts. State Tax Com'rs *v.* Quinn, 125 Mich. 128, 84 N. W.

be so grossly excessive as to raise a presumption of fraud and thereby justify the interference of the court.[78]

b. Assessment of Omitted Property. Whatever revisory jurisdiction over the assessment of taxes may be lodged in the courts, it does not include the power to make an original assessment of omitted property,[79] unless such authority is clearly and expressly given by statute.[80]

2. Appeal From Assessment — a. Jurisdiction and Right of Appeal. Unless specially authorized by statute, no appeal lies from the decision of the assessors or the board of equalization on a particular assessment to the courts of law.[81] In many states, however, such an appeal is provided for by statute in certain cases, and in such cases constitutes the proper remedy of a person aggrieved by the

75 Wis. 354, 44 N. W. 749. *Compare* West *v.* Ballard, 32 Wis. 168.

See 45 Cent. Dig. tit. "Taxation," §§ 884-886. See also *supra*, VII, B, 7, f, (IV), (A).

78. State Bd. of Equalization *v.* People, 191 Ill. 528, 61 N. E. 339, 58 L. R. A. 513; Keokuk, etc., Bridge Co. *v.* People, 176 Ill. 267, 52 N. E. 117; State *v.* London, etc., Mortg. Co., 80 Minn. 277, 83 N. W. 339; Templeton *v.* Pierce County, 25 Wash. 377, 65 Pac. 553.

79. State *v.* Mobile County Revenue, etc., Com'rs, 73 Ala. 65; Judy *v.* Pleasant Nat. State Bank, 133 Iowa 252, 110 N. W. 605; Com. *v.* Pennsylvania Co., 145 Pa. St. 266, 23 Atl. 549. But *compare* Boody *v.* Watson, 64 N. H. 162, 9 Atl. 794.

80. Williamson *v.* Mimms, 49 Ark. 336, 5 S. W. 320; Hopkins *v.* Van Wyck, 80 Md. 7, 30 Atl. 556.

In Kentucky a supplemental means for assessing omitted property, by the county court, is provided for by statute. See Com. *v.* Glover, 132 Ky. 588, 116 S. W. 769; Com. *v.* Paducah, 126 Ky. 77, 102 S. W. 882, 31 Ky. L. Rep. 528; Com. *v.* Lovell, 125 Ky. 491, 101 S. W. 970, 31 Ky. L. Rep. 105; Com. *v.* Collins, 72 S. W. 819, 24 Ky. L. Rep. 2042. See also Louisville, etc., R. Co. *v.* Com., 1 Bush 250. But *compare* Pennington *v.* Woolfolk, 79 Ky. 13. This proceeding is a proceeding on behalf of the commonwealth, and it is the real party in interest, although the revenue agent if successful obtains compensation for his efforts; and it is instituted by the county revenue agent filing a statement, which he need not verify, containing a description and the value of the property proposed to be assessed. Com. *v.* Glover, *supra*; Com. *v.* Chaudet, 125 Ky. 111, 100 S. W. 819, 30 Ky. L. Rep. 1157. Such a proceeding against a trust company as a trustee for a designated beneficiary is against the trustee and no judgment can be rendered against the trust estate, but the judgment is against the trust company which is personally liable. Com. *v.* Churchill, 131 Ky. 251, 115 S. W. 189. And the question whether a *cestui que trust* whose estate is sought to be assessed in such a proceeding against a trustee is a resident of the county in which the proceeding is brought, as alleged in the petition, is not placed in issue by an averment in the answer of want of knowledge or information sufficient to constitute a belief on that subject in the mind of the trustee, since it is his duty to know the residence of the *cestui que trust*. Com. *v.* Lovell, *supra*.

81. *Arizona.*— Cochise County *v.* Copper Queen Consol. Min. Co., 8 Ariz. 221, 71 Pac. 946.

Arkansas.— Clay County *v.* Brown Lumber Co., 90 Ark. 413, 119 S. W. 251, no appeal from decision in matters as to value unless specially provided for.

Idaho.— Humbird Lumber Co. *v.* Morgan, 10 Ida. 327, 77 Pac. 433; Feltham *v.* Washington County, 10 Ida. 182, 77 Pac. 332.

Illinois.— Ohio, etc., R. Co. *v.* Lawrence County, 27 Ill. 50; Worthington *v.* Pike County, 23 Ill. 363.

Kansas.— State Auditor *v.* Atchison, etc., R. Co., 6 Kan. 500, 7 Am. Rep. 575.

Kentucky.— In this state there is no appeal from the decision of the state board of equalization. Paducah St. R. Co. *v.* McCracken County, 105 Ky. 472, 49 S. W. 178, 20 Ky. L. Rep. 1294; Ward *v.* Beale, 91 Ky. 60, 14 S. W. 967, 12 Ky. L. Rep. 671. But an appeal may be taken to the county court from the decision of a board of supervisors. Ward *v.* Beale, *supra*.

Louisiana.— See New Orleans Gas Light Co. *v.* Board of Assessors, 31 La. Ann. 270, holding that no appeal lies from the decision of referees to whom a real estate owner has submitted a complaint for over-assessment.

Michigan.— McDonald *v.* Escanaba, 62 Mich. 555, 29 N. W. 93.

North Carolina.— Murdock *v.* Iredell County, 138 N. C. 124, 50 S. E. 567; Wade *v.* Craven County, 74 N. C. 81.

Oregon.— French *v.* Harney County, 33 Oreg. 418, 54 Pac. 211. *Compare* Rhea *v.* Umatilla County, 2 Oreg. 298.

Washington.— Buchanan *v.* Adams County, 15 Wash. 699, 46 Pac. 643; Knapp *v.* King County, 15 Wash. 541, 46 Pac. 1047; Olympia Water Works *v.* Thurston County Bd. of Equalization, 14 Wash. 268, 44 Pac. 267.

Wisconsin.—West *v.* Ballard, 32 Wis. 168.

See 45 Cent. Dig. tit. "Taxation," §§ 877, 879, 889.

But *compare* Schmuck *v.* Hartman, 222 Pa. St. 190, 70 Atl. 1091, holding that, although no right of appeal from a judgment in favor of a taxpayer against a tax assessment is given by statute, the supreme court, by reason of its general jurisdiction to examine and correct all errors of the lower courts, will

such as certiorari, has been given by statute; [85] and on the other hand, where the statute provides a remedy by appeal a writ of review will not lie.[86] In order to sustain an appeal the record must show that jurisdiction as to the subject-matter appealed from exists,[87] and the party must take such steps as the law directs to obtain and preserve his right of appeal.[88] Where an appeal is thus given from the assessing or reviewing officers to a court of original jurisdiction, the decision of that court is generally final, so that no appeal will lie to a higher court,[89] although under some statutes this also is allowed.[90]

b. Time of Taking Appeal. The statutes granting a right of appeal from tax assessments restrict the time within which such a proceeding for review may be taken, usually prescribing a short period, in order that the collection of the public revenues may not be unduly delayed; [91] and it is generally held that the

953; Keokuk, etc., Bridge Co. *v.* People, 185 Ill. 276, 56 N. E. 1049.

85. Smoky Mountain Land, etc., Co. *v.* Lattimore, 119 Tenn. 620, 105 S. W. 1028; Low *v.* Lincoln County Ct., 27 W. Va. 785.

86. Rogers *v.* Hays, 3 Ida. 597, 32 Pac. 259.

87. Marion *v.* National Loan, etc., Co., 122 Iowa 629, 98 N. W. 488.

A proper record showing the essential facts of jurisdiction is essential, and neither the consent of the parties nor silence on the part of the appellee can take the place of such a record. Peterson *v.* Clarence Bd. of Review, 138 Iowa 717, 116 N. W. 818. But the fact that the records of the county commissioners are irregular does not affect the right of a taxpayer to appeal. *In re* Lehigh, etc., Coal Co.'s Assessment, 225 Pa. St. 272, 74 Atl. 65.

88. Burns *v.* McNally, 90 Iowa 432, 57 N. W. 908.

Necessity for bill of exceptions as provided by statute see State *v.* State Bd. of Equalization, etc., 81 Nebr. 139, 115 N. W. 789.

Presumption that all things required by the statute in order to appeal were done see Singer Mfg. Co. *v.* Denver, 46 Colo. 50, 103 Pac. 294.

Estoppel.—Where a taxpayer makes no return of his property an over-assessment thereof is not open to review by application to the courts. Travelers' Ins. Co. *v.* Bd. of Assessors, 122 La. 129, 47 So. 439, 24 L. R. A. N. S. 388. So in New Jersey the supreme court will not review the action of the state board of equalization in dismissing an appeal, where the action appealed from was consented to by the petitioner. Kenilworth *v.* Bd. of Equalization, 78 N. J. L. 302, 72 Atl. 966 [*affirmed* in 78 N. J. L. 439, 74 Atl. 480].

89. *Colorado.*— Teller County *v.* Pinnacle Gold Min. Co., 36 Colo. 492, 85 Pac. 1005; Pilgrim Consol. Min. Co. *v.* Teller County, 20 Colo. App. 311, 78 Pac. 617. *Compare* Gillett *v.* Logan County, 13 Colo. App. 380, 58 Pac. 335.

Kentucky.— Marion County *v.* Wilson, 105 Ky. 302, 49 S. W. 8, 799, 20 Ky. L. Rep. 1193, 1452.

Maryland.— Gadd *v.* Anne Arundel County, 82 Md. 646, 33 Atl. 433; Wells *v.* Thomas, 72 Md. 26, 19 Atl. 118; Meyer *v.* Steuart, 48 Md. 423.

Ohio.— Street *v.* Francis, 3 Ohio 277.

Pennsylvania.— Kimber *v.* Schuylkill County, 20 Pa. St. 366.

Texas.— Scottish-American Mortg. Co. *v.* Bd. of Equalization, (Civ. App. 1898) 45 S. W. 757.

West Virginia.— Ritchie County Bank *v.* Ritchie County Ct., 65 W. Va. 208, 63 S. E. 1098 (holding that no appeal lies from, or writ of error to, a judgment or order by a circuit court on an appeal from an order of a county court in respect to an erroneous assessment involving only a question of valuation); Bluefield Water Works, etc., Co. *v.* State, 63 W. Va. 480, 60 S. E. 403; McLean *v.* State, 61 W. Va. 537, 56 S. E. 884. But *compare* Charleston, etc., Bridge Co. *v.* Kanawha County Ct., 41 W. Va. 658, 24 S. E. 1002.

90. Com. *v.* Churchill, 131 Ky. 251, 115 S. W. 189; Com. *v.* Lexington Roller Mills Co., 104 S. W. 318, 31 Ky. L. Rep. 924 (appeal to circuit court from county court in a proceeding to assess omitted property); Morgan *v.* Warner, 45 N. Y. App. Div. 424, 60 N. Y. Suppl. 963 [*affirmed* in 162 N. Y. 612, 57 N. E. 1118]; State *v.* South Penn Oil Co., 42 W. Va. 80, 24 S. E. 688 (county court to circuit court). And see State *v.* Baltimore, 105 Md. 1, 65 Atl. 369. But *compare* People *v.* Barker, 152 N. Y. 417, 46 N. E. 875 [*reversing* 6 N. Y. App. Div. 356, 39 N. Y. Suppl. 682 (*affirming* 17 Misc. 497, 41 N. Y. Suppl. 236)].

91. See the statutes of the several states. And see the following cases:

Arkansas.— Clay County *v.* Brown Lumber Co., 90 Ark. 413, 119 S. W. 251, holding that, although complaints against an alleged excessive valuation or assessment of property must be made at the term of court beginning on the first Monday in October next following the session of the board of equalization, the hearing may be continued.

Massachusetts.— Brodbine *v.* Revere, 182 Mass. 598, 66 N. E. 607.

Mississippi.— Simmons *v.* Scott County, 68 Miss. 37, 8 So. 259.

New York.— People *v.* Hadley, 76 N. Y. 337; People *v.* Christie, 14 N. Y. St. 525.

Pennsylvania.— Com. *v.* Crum Lynne Iron, etc., Co., 27 Pa. Super. Ct. 508; *In re* Margwauth, 10 Kulp 336; Pierce *v.* Lackawanna County, 1 Lack. Leg. Rec. 469.

courts have no jurisdiction or authority to entertain an appeal after the time limited by law.[92]

c. **Parties.** A proceeding for the assessment and collection of a tax is between the taxpayer and the state or municipality levying the tax, so that an appeal may be taken either by the person whose property is affected by the assessment complained of [93] or by the state or municipality; [94] and in the former case the county or other municipal corporation is the proper party defendant, and not the board of equalization whose judgment is appealed from.[95]

d. **Pleading and Practice.** On appeals of this kind no special formality is required outside the particular directions of the statute.[96] It is commonly required that notice of the appeal shall be given to the officer or board from whose decision the appeal is taken or to some officer of the municipality concerned,[97] and the appellant may also be required to give an appeal-bond or security for costs, although this is not invariably the case.[98] Some form of complaint or petition to the reviewing court is generally necessary,[99] and also an answer

Tennessee.—Warner Iron Co. *v.* Pace, 89 Tenn. 707, 15 S. W. 1077.

Virginia.— Fulkerson *v.* Bristol Treasurer, 95 Va. 1, 27 S. E. 815.

But *compare* Ingersoll *v.* Des Moines, 46 Iowa 553.

After notice of tax.—Where the statute allows an appeal at any time within nine months after notice of the tax and provides for the giving of such notice to residents but not to persons who are not inhabitants of the state, a non-resident, taxed for personal property, may appeal at any time within nine months after actual notice of the tax. Downing *v.* Farmington, 68 N. H. 187, 38 Atl. 729.

After adjournment of board.—Where an appeal must be taken within twenty days after the adjournment of the board of equalization, the time begins to run from the final adjournment of the board, not from an adjournment in the nature of a recess taken in order to give time for the service of notice on interested parties. Barz *v.* Klemme Bd. of Equalization, 133 Iowa 563, 111 N. W. 41.

92. Rhoads *v.* Philadelphia. 2 Phila. (Pa.) 149; *In re* Nottawasaga Tp., 4 Ont. L. Rep. 1. And see *In re* Allan, 10 Ont. 110; Scott *v* Listowel. 12 Ont. Pr. 77; *In re* Ronald, 9 Ont. Pr. 232. But *compare* State *v.* Meehan, 92 Minn. 283, 100 N. W. 6.

93. White *v.* Portland, 67 Conn. 272, 34 Atl. 1022 (holding that where a tenant by the curtesy appeals from an alleged illegal assessment on the real estate the remainderman is not a proper party); *In re* British Mortg. Loan Co.. 29 Ont. 641.

Appeals by "tax ferrets" and revenue agents see *In re* Woodbury County, 129 Iowa 588, 105 N. W. 1023; Adams *v.* Stonewall Cotton Mills. 89 Miss. 865, 43 So. 65.

Appeal by one taxpayer from action on another's assessment.—Where the board of review reduces the assessment of a certain corporation, on its application, and another taxpayer appeals from this decision to the district court and obtains a judgment raising the assessment, the corporation is entitled to appeal to the supreme court. Van Camp *v.* Custer County, 2 Ida. (Hasb.) 29, 33, 2 Pac. 721.

94. *Ex p.* Howard-Harrison Iron Co., 120 Ala. 185, 30 So. 400; Farmers' L. & T. Co. *v.* Newton, 97 Iowa 502, 66 N. W. 784; Com. *v.* Huffman, 55 S. W. 7, 21 Ky. L. Rep. 1343; Shelby County *v.* Mississippi, etc., R. Co., 16 Lea (Tenn.) 401, 1 S. W. 32.

95. Oregon, etc., Sav. Bank *v.* Catlin, 15 Oreg. 342, 15 Pac. 462; Mackin *v.* Taylor County Ct., 38 W. Va. 338, 18 S. E. 632.

96. Prairie County *v.* Matthews. 46 Ark. 383; Catron *v.* Archuleta County, 18 Colo. 553, 33 Pac. 513 (not affected by laws regulating appeals in general); Schoonover *v.* Petcina, 126 Iowa 261, 100 N. W. 490.

97. Peterson *v.* Clarence Bd. of Review, 138 Iowa 717, 116 N. W. 818; Marion *v.* National Loan, etc., Co., 122 Iowa 629, 98 N. W. 488; German American Sav. Bank *v.* Burlington, 118 Iowa 84, 91 N. W. 829; Richards *v.* Rock Rapids, 72 Iowa 77, 33 N. W. 372; *In re* Downey, 8 Can. L. J. 198; Reg. *v.* Lancashire Justices, 34 L. T. Rep. N. S. 124. But *compare* Delaware, etc., Canal Co. *v.* Walsh, 11 Phila. (Pa.) 587.

Any defects in the service of the notice are cured by the appearance of the person served. Richards *v.* Rock Rapids, 72 Iowa 77, 33 N. W. 372.

98. Tunica County *v.* Tate, 78 Miss. 294, 29 So. 74; Pain *v.* Brantford, 9 Can. L. J. N. S. 261.

No appeal-bond required see Marion *v.* Cedar Rapids, etc., R. Co., 120 Iowa 259, 94 N. W. 501; Ingersoll *v.* Des Moines, 46 Iowa 553; Com. *v.* Reed, 121 Ky. 432, 89 S. W. 294, 28 Ky. L. Rep. 381.

The state cannot be required to give an appeal-bond, and the state tax collector and board of assessors being state functionaries, their appeal is the appeal of the state and no bond is required to perfect it. Merchants' Mut. Ins. Co. *v.* Bd. of Assessors, 40 La. Ann. 371, 3 So. 891; Adams *v.* Kuhn, 72 Miss. 276, 16 So. 598.

99. State *v.* Sloss-Sheffield Steel, etc., Co., 162 Ala. 234, 50 So. 366; Peterson *v.* Clarence Bd. of Review, 138 Iowa 717, 116 N. W. 818; Wahkonsa Inv. Co. *v.* Ft. Dodge, 125 Iowa

duplicate and warrant are in his hands;[50] or in some cases it may be directed to the municipal corporation levying the tax, in its corporate name.[51]

f. Time of Taking Proceedings. Where the statute prescribes a period within which application must be made for a writ of certiorari to review assessments, it is mandatory, and the writ must be refused if the application comes too late;[52] and independently of statute, the laches of the relator will be ground for denying him relief,[53] except in cases where he had no notice of the proceedings, for in that event the statutory limitation does not apply and he is not chargeable with laches if he acts with reasonable promptness after discovering the assessment.[54]

g. Petition. Statutory certiorari to review an action of tax assessors is substantially a new trial of the matters decided by them; the petition is the complaint, and the return the answer, and general rules of pleading are applicable.[55] The petition or application for certiorari to review a tax assessment may state conclusions of fact without supporting evidence;[56] but it must show clearly and directly the grounds of objection to the assessment on which the relator relies,[57] and that he is injured or prejudiced by the assessment as it stands.[58] If it is claimed that the assessment is illegal, the petition must set forth specifically,

N. Y. 275 [*modifying* 18 Hun 4]; People *v.* Board of Assessors, 16 Hun (N. Y.) 407; People *v.* Fredericks. 48 Barb. (N. Y.) 173; People *v.* Reddy, 43 Barb. (N. Y.) 539; People *v.* New York Tax, etc., Com'rs, 43 Barb. (N. Y.) 494.

But local assessors are not entitled to intervene in certiorari proceedings to review the action of the state board of assessors because of the fact that they are criticized in the petition. People *v.* Priest, 181 N. Y. 300, 73 N. E. 1100 [*reversing* 101 N. Y. App. Div. 223, 91 N. Y. Suppl. 772 (*reversing* 41 Misc. 545, 85 N. Y. Suppl. 235)]; People *v.* Priest, 101 N. Y. App. Div. 263, 91 N. Y. Suppl. 1001 [*reversing* 41 Misc. 548, 85 N. Y. Suppl. 237].

A town clerk is not a necessary party to certiorari proceedings to review an assessment by reason of the fact that the assessment roll after it is completed is required to be deposited with him. Matter of Winegard, 78 Hun (N. Y.) 58, 28 N. Y. Suppl. 1039 [*affirming* 5 Misc. 54, 25 N. Y. Suppl. 48].

A supervisor of a town is not a necessary party to such proceeding. People *v.* Smith, 24 Hun (N. Y.) 66 [*affirmed* in 85 N. Y. 628].

50. Reese *v.* Sherrer, 49 N. J. L. 610, 10 Atl. 286; Washington Tp. *v.* Howell, 24 N. J. L. 519.

51. Woodbridge Tp. *v.* State, 43 N. J. L. 262; *In re* Belmont, 40 Misc. (N. Y.) 133, 81 N. Y. Suppl. 280 [*affirmed* in 83 N. Y. App. Div. 643, 82 N. Y. Suppl. 1110]. But *compare* People *v.* Priest, 101 N. Y. App. Div. 263, 91 N. Y. Suppl. 1001 [*reversing* 41 Misc. 548, 85 N. Y. Suppl. 237]; People *v.* Priest, 95 N. Y. App. Div. 44, 88 N. Y. Suppl. 11.

52. Hunt *v.* Warshung, 48 N. J. L. 613, 9 Atl. 199; Warshung *v.* Hunt, 47 N. J. L. 256; People *v.* Feitner, 168 N. Y. 441, 61 N. E. 763; People *v.* Feitner, 71 N. Y. App. Div. 572, 76 N. Y. Suppl. 245; People *v.* Feitner, 41 N. Y. App. Div. 496, 58 N. Y. Suppl. 670; People *v.* Barker, 22 N. Y. App. Div. 161, 47 N. Y. Suppl. 1020; People *v.* Wemple, 60 Hun (N. Y.) 225, 14 N. Y. Suppl. 859; People *v.* Wells, 39 Misc. (N. Y.) 602, 80 N. Y. Suppl. 610; People *v.* Feitner, 30 Misc. (N. Y.) 646, 64 N. Y. Suppl. 269.

53. *District of Columbia.*— Padgett *v.* District of Columbia, 17 App. Cas. 255.

Michigan.— *In re* Lantis, 9 Mich. 324, 80 Am. Dec. 58.

New Jersey.— Union Waxed, etc.. Paper Co. *v.* State Bd. of Assessors, 73 N. J. L. 374, 63 Atl. 1006; Pompton Steel, etc., Co. *v.* Wayne Tp., 65 N. J. L. 487, 47 Atl. 469; State *v.* Camden Bd. of Tax Assessors, 53 N. J. L. 319, 21 Atl. 938; State *v.* Binninger, 42 N. J. L. 528; Jersey City Land, etc., Co. *v.* Love. 42 N. J. L. 355.

New York.— *In re* Lord. 78 N. Y. 109.

Canada.— *Ex p.* Gerow, 9 N. Brunsw. 269.

See 45 Cent. Dig. tit. "Taxation," § 902.

Unconstitutional tax law.— Where objection to an assessment is based on the unconstitutionality of the statute under which it was made, the laches of the relator is no bar to certiorari brought to set it aside, nor cause for its dismissal. State *v.* Jersey City, 45 N. J. L. 256.

54. Wood *v.* District of Columbia, 6 Mackey (D. C.) 142; People *v.* Adams, 125 N. Y. 471, 26 N. E. 746; People *v.* Hicks, 105 N. Y. 198, 11 N. E. 653; People *v.* Port Jervis, 23 Misc. (N. Y.) 317, 52 N. Y. Suppl. 59.

55. People *v.* Stillwell, 190 N. Y. 284, 83 N. E. 56; People *v.* Hall. 57 Misc. (N. Y.) 308, 109 N. Y. Suppl. 402.

56. *In re* Cathedral of Incarnation, 91 N. Y. App. Div. 543, 86 N. Y. Suppl. 900.

57. Flaherty *v.* Atlantic City, 73 N. J. L. 458, 63 Atl. 992; Matter of New York, 117 N. Y. App. Div. 811, 103 N. Y. Suppl. 87; People *v.* Carmichael, 64 Misc. (N. Y.) 271, 118 N. Y. Suppl. 354.

58. People *v.* Wells, 101 N. Y. App. Div. 600, 92 N. Y. Suppl. 5 [*reversed* on the facts in 182 N. Y. 314, 78 N. E. 878]; People *v.* Harkness, 84 Hun (N. Y.) 445, 32 N. Y. Suppl. 344.

of conflict the decision of the court should be in accordance with the preponderance of the proof.[81] The court may order a reference where it finds that there is a question of fact requiring evidence for its determination.[82]

j. Determination and Disposition of Cause. In proceedings of this kind, the court will not generally set aside the entire assessment if, without doing so, it can give proper relief to the particular relator.[83] If it finds error or injustice in his assessment, it may correct and adjust the assessment, reducing it if necessary

600, 92 N. Y. Suppl. 5 [*reversed* on the facts in 182 N. Y. 314, 74 N. E. 878]; People *v.* Wells, 99 N. Y. App. Div. 455, 91 N. Y. Suppl. 283 [*affirmed* in 181 N. Y. 245, 73 N. Y. Suppl. 961]; People *v.* Barker. 48 N. Y. App. Div. 248, 63 N. Y. Suppl. 167 [*reversed* on other grounds in 165 N. Y. 305, 59 N. E. 137, 157]; People *v.* Williams, 90 Hun (N. Y.) 501, 36 N. Y. Suppl. 65; People *v.* Badgley, 67 Hun (N. Y.) 65, 22 N. Y. Suppl. 26 [*reversed* on other grounds in 138 N. Y. 314, 33 N. E. 1076]; People *v.* Mechanicville, 6 Lans. (N. Y.) 105; People *v.* Feitner, 39 Misc. (N. Y.) 467, 80 N. Y. Suppl. 152; People *v.* Haight, 24 Misc. (N. Y.) 425, 53 N. Y. Suppl. 723; People *v.* Zoeller, 15 N. Y. Suppl. 684.

The strict rules of evidence applicable to trials do not prevail in a proceeding to review a tax assessment. People *v.* Ouderkirk, 120 N. Y. App. Div. 650, 105 N. Y. Suppl. 134.

81. As sustaining the rule stated in the text and as determining questions upon the weight and sufficiency of the evidence in particular cases see People *v.* Glynn, 194 N. Y. 387, 87 N. E. 434 [*affirming* 127 N. Y. App. Div. 933, 111 N. Y. Suppl. 1139]; People *v.* Feitner, 107 N. Y. App. Div. 267, 95 N. Y. Suppl. 10; People *v.* Jacobs, 106 N. Y. App. Div. 614, 94 N. Y. Suppl. 483 [*affirmed* in 185 N. Y. 548, 77 N. E. 1195]; People *v.* Wells. 99 N. Y. App. Div. 455, 91 N. Y. Suppl. 283 [*affirmed* in 181 N. Y. 245, 73 N. E. 961]; People *v.* Feitner, 96 N. Y. App. Div. 615, 88 N. Y. Suppl. 779; People *v.* Feitner, 95 N. Y. App. Div. 481, 88 N. Y. Suppl. 774; People *v.* Miller, 84 N. Y. App. Div. 168, 82 N. Y. Suppl. 621 [*modified* on other grounds in 177 N. Y. 461, 69 N. E. 1103]; People *v.* Feitner, 61 N. Y. App. Div. 456, 70 N. Y. Suppl. 545 [*affirmed* in 168 N. Y. 677, 61 N. E. 1133]; People *v.* Feitner, 51 N. Y. App. Div. 178, 64 N. Y. Suppl. 539; People *v.* Feitner, 27 Misc. (N. Y.) 371, 58 N. Y. Suppl. 875 [*reversed* on other grounds in 43 N. Y. App. Div. 198, 59 N. Y. Suppl. 327]; People *v.* Haight, 24 Misc. (N. Y.) 425, 53 N. Y. Suppl. 723; People *v.* Zoeller, 15 N. Y. Suppl. 684; People *v.* Flushing Bd. of Assessors, 6 N. Y. St. 3.

Findings of fact and conclusions of law as in an equitable action are not required. State *v.* Patterson, 138 Wis. 475, 120 N. W. 227.

82. Childs *v.* Howland, 48 N. J. L. 425, 4 Atl. 430; People *v.* Kaufman. 121 N. Y. App. Div. 599, 106 N. Y. Suppl. 305; People *v.* Feitner, 43 N. Y. App. Div. 198, 59 N. Y. Suppl. 327; People *v.* Carmichael, 64 Misc. (N. Y.) 271, 118 N. Y. Suppl. 354; People *v.* Feitner, 39 Misc. (N. Y.) 474, 80 N. Y. Suppl. 138; People *v.* Feitner, 39 Misc. (N. Y.) 467, 80 N. Y. Suppl. 152; People *v.* Feitner, 39 Misc. (N. Y.) 463, 80 N. Y. Suppl. 140 [*reversed* on other grounds in 86 N. Y. App. Div. 46. 83 N. Y. Suppl. 1114 (*affirmed* in 178 N. Y. 577, 70 N. E. 1106)]; People *v.* Platt, 92 N. Y. 349, 36 N. Y. Suppl. 531; People *v.* Coleman, 48 Hun (N. Y.) 602, 1 N. Y. Suppl. 112, 551; People *v.* Zoeller, 15 N. Y. Suppl. 684.

Where a number of certiorari proceedings are brought by distinct sets of relators to review assessments of various parcels of property, and the testimony of experts is necessary, and it will be difficult to bring them together for the purposes of trial in court, the court in the exercise of its discretion may send the proceedings to various referees under orders containing provisions for expediting the proceedings. People *v.* Feitner, 53 Misc. (N. Y.) 334, 104 N. Y. Suppl. 794.

Findings of referee.— Under a statute providing that where the validity of a tax assessment is disputed, it may be submitted to a referee and his report shall constitute part of the proceedings on which the court may determine its validity, the findings of the referee are not conclusive on the court. People *v.* Barker, 28 Misc. (N. Y.) 13, 59 N. Y. Suppl. 926 [*reversed* on other grounds in 48 N. Y. App. Div. 248, 63 N. Y. Suppl. 107 (*reversed* in 165 N. Y. 305, 59 N. E. 137, 151)]. While the tax law (N. Y. Consol. Laws, c. 60, § 290) provides that the testimony in such cases may be taken by a referee and reported with his conclusions, the final determination as to the correctness of the assessing officer's valuation rests with the special term to which he reports and on appeal with the appellate division, and it is not merely the referee's report with the annexed proof which the court has to review but the decision of the special term with all matters upon which it is founded. People *v.* State Tax Com'rs, 196 N. Y. 39, 89 N. E. 581 [*modifying* 128 N. Y. App. Div. 13, 112 N. Y. Suppl. 392], 197 N. Y. 33, 90 N. E. 112.

83. Van Vorst *v.* Kingsland, 23 N. J. L. 85. *Compare* Vreeland *v.* Bergen, 34 N. J. L. 438.

Property partly exempt.—Where an assessment is made of a parcel of realty as a whole, and part of it is found to be exempt from taxation, as being devoted to religious uses, it is proper for the court to set aside so much of the assessment as relates to that portion. Sisters of Peace *v.* Westervelt, 64 N. J. L. 510, 45 Atl. 788.

honestly applied their judgment, in a case not free from doubt, although their decision was wrong.[95]

4. Mandamus to Correct Assessment[96] **— a. Nature and Scope of Remedy —** (I) *Compelling Official Action.* If assessors omit property from their lists which should have been assessed, mandamus lies on the relation either of the proper public officer or of an individual taxpayer to compel them to make an assessment of it, although their judgment as to the amount of the assessment will not be controlled by this writ.[97] Assessors may also be required in this manner to supply defects or correct informalities in the assessment roll,[98] to transfer property from the name of the original owner to the name of a purchaser thereof,[99] or to enter on the roll the changes ordered by the board of equalization.[1] In like manner the writ lies to compel the board of equalization to hear and determine complaints of taxpayers, although of course their judgment must be left free.[2] But even where this writ would otherwise be available, the right to it may be lost by the laches or unreasonable delay of the relator.[3] The writ will not go to the assessors or board after they have completed their work on the assessment roll and it has been placed in the hands of the collector.[4]

(II) *Correcting Errors in Assessment.* Mandamus does not lie to control any administrative officer in the discharge of duties which require the exercise of judgment and discretion on his part, but only to enforce the performance of a plain ministerial duty. Hence the writ will not be granted to enable a taxpayer to obtain a reduction of an assessment which he alleges to be excessive.[5]

(*affirmed* in 179 N. Y. 535, 71 N. E. 1136)]; People *v.* Barker, 25 N. Y. Suppl. 393; People *v.* Zoeller, 15 N. Y. Suppl. 684; People *v.* McComber, 7 N. Y. Suppl. 71; People *v.* Keator, 67 How. Pr. (N. Y.) 277.

95. People *v.* Rushford, 81 N. Y. App. Div. 298, 80 N. Y. Suppl. 891; People *v.* Williams, 90 Hun (N. Y.) 501, 36 N. Y. Suppl. 65; People *v.* Christie, 14 N. Y. St. 525.

96. **Mandamus to compel levy and assessment** generally see Mandamus, 26 Cyc. 320 *et seq.*

97. *California.*— Hyatt *v.* Allen, 54 Cal. 353; People *v.* Shearer, 30 Cal. 645.

Illinois.— State Bd. of Equalization *v.* People, 191 Ill. 528, 61 N. E. 339, 58 L. R. A. 513.

Louisiana.— State *v.* Orleans Parish Bd. of Assessors, 52 La. Ann. 223, 26 So. 872.

Maine.— Knight *v.* Thomas, 93 Me. 494, 45 Atl. 499.

West Virginia.— State *v.* Herrald, 36 W. Va. 721, 15 S. E. 974.

See 45 Cent. Dig. tit. "Taxation," § 911.

Effect of delay.—An application for mandamus to compel the assessors to place omitted property on the roll will be denied when made so late as to deprive the owners of any right to review the assessment. Maurer *v.* Cliff, 94 Mich. 194, 53 N. W. 1055. And see Knight *v.* Thomas, 93 Me. 494, 45 Atl. 499.

98. People *v.* Ontario County, 114 N. Y. App. Div. 915, 100 N. Y. Suppl. 1136 [*affirming* 50 Misc. 63, 100 N. Y. Suppl. 330]; Harris *v.* State, 96 Tenn. 496, 34 S. W. 1017.

Supplying affidavit.—Where assessors omit to incorporate in their affidavit to the assessment roll a clause required by the statute, they will not be compelled by mandamus to add it, if it appears that, with the affidavit so amended, they could not truthfully make oath to it. People *v.* Fowler, 55 N. Y. 252.

99. Dye *v.* State, 73 Ohio St. 231, 76 N. E. 829.

1. People *v.* Strother, 67 Cal. 624, 8 Pac. 383; Union Oil Co. *v.* Campbell, 48 La. Ann. 1350, 20 So. 1007; State *v.* Bd. of Assessors, 30 La. Ann. 261. See also *supra*, VII, B, 7, f, (IV), (A).

2. Loewenthal *v.* People, 192 Ill. 222, 61 N. E. 462; Gunning *v.* People, 76 Ill. App. 574; People *v.* Wells, 110 N. Y. App. Div. 336, 97 N. Y. Suppl. 333; People *v.* Knight, 66 N. Y. App. Div. 150, 72 N. Y. Suppl. 929. See also People *v.* Delaware County, 60 N. Y. 381 [*reversing* 2 Hun 102, 4 Thomps. & C. 336 (*reversing* 47 How. Pr. 24)].

3. People *v.* Olsen, 215 Ill. 620, 74 N. E. 785. And see Knight *v.* Thomas, 93 Me. 494, 45 Atl. 499.

4. Gaither *v.* Green, 40 La. Ann. 362, 4 So. 210; Colonial L. Assur. Co. *v.* New York County, 24 Barb. (N. Y.) 166, 13 How. Pr. 305, 4 Abb. Pr. 84. And see Knight *v.* Thomas, 93 Me. 494, 45 Atl. 499.

5. *Iowa.*— Meyer *v.* Dubuque County, 43 Iowa 592.

Kentucky.— Southern Pac. R. Co. *v.* Com., 134 Ky. 410, 120 S. W. 309.

Maryland.— Baltimore County *v.* Winand, 77 Md. 522, 26 Atl. 1110.

Massachusetts.— Gordon *v.* Sanderson, 165 Mass. 375, 43 N. E. 128; Gibbs *v.* Hampden County, 19 Pick. 298; *In re* Morse, 18 Pick. 443.

Michigan.— Atty.-Gen. *v.* Sanilac County, 42 Mich. 72, 3 N. W. 260.

Nebraska.— State *v.* Savage, 65 Nebr. 714, 91 N. W. 716.

But where the assessors have acted illegally and without jurisdiction, in assessing property which is not taxable or not within their territory, they may be required by mandamus to strike the assessment from the roll.[6] And so they may be required to deduct an unwarranted increase in the assessment, or otherwise to correct it when they have violated their plain statutory duty either in fixing it originally or in changing it contrary to law.[7] The correction of merely clerical or mathematical errors may also be obtained by means of this writ.[8]

b. Existence of Other Remedy. Mandamus is an extraordinary remedy and is not granted where the petitioner has a full and adequate remedy in the ordinary course of law; hence this writ cannot be used as a means of correcting a tax assessment where there is an available and sufficient remedy by appeal or certiorari.[9]

5. INJUNCTION TO RESTRAIN ASSESSMENT — a. In General. Although injunction may be an appropriate remedy to prevent the collection of an illegal tax already assessed,[10] the courts set their faces strongly against the use of this writ to restrain an expected or intended but uncompleted assessment, the functions of assessors being quasi-judicial and the illegality or impropriety of the assessment not being ordinarily a matter of anticipation but a matter for consideration after the assessment is made;[11] nor will an assessment be restrained for mere irregulari-

Nevada.—Hardin *v.* Guthrie, 26 Nev. 246, 66 Pac. 744.

Pennsylvania.— Bedford Borough *v.* Anderson, 45 Pa. St. 388.

Wisconsin.— Brown *v.* Oneida County, 103 Wis. 149, 79 N. W. 216.

Canada.— *In re* Dickson, 10 U. C. Q. B. 395.

See 45 Cent. Dig. tit. "Taxation," §§ 911, 912. See also MANDAMUS, 26 Cyc. 323.

Unconstitutionality of statute.— To correct an alleged error in a tax duplicate on the ground that the statute under which the assessment was made is unconstitutional is not a plain ministerial duty for which mandamus may be granted. *Ex p.* Lynch, 16 S. C. 32.

6. Anne Arundel County *v.* Baltimore Sugar Refining Co., 99 Md. 481, 58 Atl. 211; People *v.* Wilson, 119 N. Y. 515, 23 N. E. 1064; People *v.* New York Tax, etc., Com'rs, 41 Hun (N. Y.) 373; People *v.* Lockport, 46 Barb. (N. Y.) 588, 598; People *v.* Olmsted, 45 Barb. (N. Y.) 644; People *v.* Barton, 44 Barb. (N. Y.) 148; Utica Bank *v.* Utica, 4 Paige (N. Y.) 399, 27 Am. Dec. 72; Smith *v.* King, 14 Oreg. 10, 12 Pac. 8; State *v.* Lafayette County, 3 Wis. 816. See also MANDAMUS, 26 Cyc. 324. But *compare* Steel *v.* Fell, 29 Oreg. 272, 45 Pac. 794.

Where a county trustee erroneously refuses to take jurisdiction and hear a proceeding by a state revenue agent for the reassessment or back assessment of taxes on property, mandamus is the proper remedy to compel him to do so. State *v.* Taylor, 119 Tenn. 229, 104 S. W. 242.

7. State *v.* Dodge County, 20 Nebr. 595, 31 N. W. 117; People *v.* Priest, 180 N. Y. 532, 72 N. E. 1149 [*affirming* 90 N. Y. App. Div. 520, 85 N. Y. Suppl. 481]; People *v.* Olmsted, 45 Barb. (N. Y.) 644; Adriance *v.* New York, 12 How. Pr. (N. Y.) 224; State *v.* Covington, 35 S. C. 245, 14 S. E. 499; State *v.* Boyd, 35 S. C. 233, 14 S. E. 496; State *v.* Cromer, 35 S. C. 213, 14 S. E. 493. And see State *v.* Raine, 47 Ohio St. 447, 25 N. E. 54, holding that mandamus will issue to a county auditor to compel him to correct errors committed by him for several years in transferring to the tax duplicates deductions illegally made by the annual board of equalization, although these corrections present difficulties requiring the exercise of a sound judgment coupled with an extensive knowledge of the law.

8. People *v.* Schoharie County, 39 Misc. (N. Y.) 162, 79 N. Y. Suppl. 145; People *v.* Wilson, 7 N. Y. Suppl. 627 [*affirmed* in 119 N. Y. 515, 23 N. E. 1064].

9. Ridley *v.* Doughty, 77 Iowa 226, 42 N. W. 178; State *v.* Drexel, 75 Nebr. 751, 107 N. W. 110; McGee *v.* State, 32 Nebr. 149, 49 N. W. 220; People *v.* Keefe, 119 N. Y. App. Div. 713, 104 N. Y. Suppl. 154 [*affirmed* in 190 N. Y. 555, 83 N. E. 1130] (holding that certiorari and not mandamus is the proper remedy to review an assessment for taxation made by officers having jurisdiction to make the assessment); People *v.* Wells, 110 N. Y. App. Div. 336, 97 N. Y. Suppl. 333; People *v.* Feitner, 72 N. Y. App. Div. 45, 76 N. Y. Suppl. 219; People *v.* Board of Taxes, etc., 55 N. Y. App. Div. 544, 67 N. Y. Suppl. 241; People *v.* Feitner, 44 N. Y. App. Div. 239, 60 N. Y. Suppl. 614; James *v.* Bucks County, 13 Pa. St. 72.

A remedy by suit to recover taxes paid under protest is not such an adequate remedy as to prevent the issue of mandamus to reduce an assessment of personal property the valuation of which has been wrongfully increased by the county auditor. State *v.* Cromer, 35 S. C. 213, 14 S. E. 493.

10. See *infra*, X, D, 2.

11. *Indiana.*— McConnell *v.* Hampton, 164 Ind. 547, 73 N. E. 1092.

Michigan.—Hiller *v.* Grandy, 13 Mich. 540.

Missouri.— State *v.* Hager, 92 Mo. 511, 4 S. W. 925.

New Mexico.— Albuquerque First Nat. Bank *v.* Albright, 13 N. M. 514, 86 Pac. 548.

where an excessive valuation is fraudulently or wrongfully put upon the property.[39] But under the power now generally given by statute to the courts to correct irregularities and defects in assessments, such radical action will not be taken if it is possible to do equity by canceling the illegal part of an assessment and allowing the remainder to stand, reducing it to a just amount, apportioning the tax among different pieces of property or different owners when it has been erroneously assessed as a whole, or otherwise adjusting the assessment to the legal rights of the complainant.[40] Such an action must be brought within the time limited by the statute, if any.[41] The question of costs, except when regulated by statute, rests in the discretion of the court.[42]

b. Parties. An action to vacate an illegal assessment may be maintained by any one having a direct interest in the property and who may be affected by the taxes in question.[43] Generally the only necessary defendant is the municipal corporation levying the tax, and not administrative officers or any third persons.[44]

c. Pleading and Evidence. The presumption is in favor of the correctness and regularity of the assessment,[45] and the plaintiff must distinctly and specifically allege the errors or grounds of illegality on which he relies and assume the burden of proving them by competent and satisfactory evidence.[46]

defendant being protected by a bond. A. H. Stange Co. *v.* Merrill, 134 Wis. 514, 115 N. W. 115.

39. Wells, etc., Express *v.* Crawford County, 63 Ark. 576, 40 S. W. 710, 37 L. R. A. 371; Milwaukee Iron Co. *v.* Hubbard, 29 Wis. 51.

40. *Alabama.*— Tennessee Coal, etc., Co. *v.* State, 141 Ala. 103, 37 So. 433.

Nebraska.— Lynam *v.* Anderson, 9 Nebr. 367, 2 N. W. 732.

New Jersey.— Blume *v.* Bowes, 65 N. J. L. 470, 47 Atl. 487; Press Printing Co. *v.* Bd. of Assessors, 51 N. J. L. 75, 16 Atl. 173; State *v.* Montclair, etc., R. Co., 43 N. J. L. 524.

New York.— *In re* Auchmuty, 90 N. Y. 685; People *v.* Feitner, 75 N. Y. Suppl. 1086.

South Dakota.— Rochford *v.* Fleming, 10 S. D. 24. 71 N. W. 317.

See 45 Cent. Dig. tit. "Taxation," § 925.

41. Hurt *v.* Bristol, 104 Va. 213, 51 S. E. 223; Wells *v.* Lincoln Dist. Bd. of Education, 20 W. Va. 157; Gilkey *v.* Merrill, 67 Wis. 459, 30 N. W. 733, not before the taxes have been extended. See also *In re* Union College, 129 N. Y. 308, 29 N. E. 460, holding that the statutory requirement that any proceeding to test the validity of any "sale" of land for taxes shall be commenced within one year from the passage of the statute, does not apply to a proceeding to test the validity of an "assessment."

42. State *v.* New Orleans, 105 La. 768, 30 So. 97; Newark Brass Works *v.* State Bd. of Assessors, 63 N. J. L. 500, 43 Atl. 695; People *v.* Pratt, 19 N. Y. Suppl. 565, 22 N. Y. Civ. Proc. 294; Manor Real Estate, etc., Co. *v.* Cooner, 209 Pa. St. 531, 58 Atl. 918.

43. Thomas *v.* Auditor-General, 120 Mich. 535, 79 N. W. 812 (joinder of plaintiffs having a common interest in vacating the assessment); Kent *v.* Exeter, 68 N. H. 469, 44 Atl. 607 (administrator of deceased taxpayer); Spear *v.* Door County, 65 Wis. 298, 27 N. W. 60 (holding that a mortgagor who has covenanted to pay taxes may sue to set aside an illegal tax even after foreclosure and sale); Pier *v.* Fond du Lac County, 53 Wis. 421, 10 N. W. 686 (former owner of land who conveyed it by warranty deed with full covenants, under which a liability might arise if a hostile title were acquired under the tax assessment).

44. *Florida.*— Pensacola *v.* Louisville, etc., R. Co., 21 Fla. 492, holding that neither the city tax collector nor the county tax assessor is a necessary party to a petition to declare an assessment unlawful.

Michigan.— Thomas *v.* Auditor-General, 120 Mich. 535, 79 N. W. 812; Adams *v.* Auditor-General, 43 Mich. 453, 5 N. W. 457.

Missouri.— Newmeyer *v.* Missouri, etc., R. Co., 52 Mo. 81, 14 Am. Rep. 394, state not necessary party.

New York.— *In re* Jones, 18 Hun 327, holding that a purchaser of the property at a tax-sale is not a necessary party to a proceeding to vacate the assessment.

Wisconsin.— Gilman *v.* Sheboygan County, 79 Wis. 26, 48 N. W. 111, holding that it is not necessary to join parties in whose names plaintiff's land was erroneously assessed.

See 45 Cent. Dig. tit. "Taxation," § 927.

45. Wells, etc., Express *v.* Crawford County, 63 Ark. 576, 40 S. W. 710, 37 L. R. A. 371; Moffat *v.* Calvert County, 97 Md. 266, 54 Atl. 960; Henderson *v.* Hughes County, 13 S. D. 576, 83 N. W. 682. And see Johnson Home *v.* Seneca Falls, 37 N. Y. App. Div. 147, 55 N. Y. Suppl. 803.

46. *Florida.*— Tampa *v.* Kaunitz, 39 Fla. 683, 23 So. 416, 63 Am. St. Rep. 202; Pensacola *v.* Bell, 22 Fla. 466.

Illinois.— Buttenuth *v.* St. Louis Bridge Co., 123 Ill. 535, 17 N. E. 439, 5 Am. St. Rep. 545.

Indiana.— Theobald *v.* Clapp, 43 Ind. App. 191, 87 N. E. 100, judgment for plaintiff held not sustained by the findings.

Iowa.— King *v.* Parker, 73 Iowa 757, 34 N. W. 451.

effect must be clearly manifested in the statute, as the lien will neither be created by implication nor enlarged by construction.[3] Nor will a statutory provision of this kind be given a retrospective operation unless plainly required by its terms.[4] Further, the repeal of the statute will divest the liens which it created, unless they are expressly or impliedly preserved.[5]

2. Prerequisites to Attaching of Lien — a. Validity and Sufficiency of Assessment. In order that a tax may attach as a lien upon particular property it is necessary that there shall have been a valid assessment of it, complete in all essentials, and certain and definite in respect to describing the property, the owner, and the amount of the tax.[6]

Kelly, 19 Pa. Co. Ct. 348; Rutt *v.* Burkey, 18 Pa. Co. Ct. 445; Taylor *v.* Bowling, 18 Pa. Co. Ct. 259; United Security L. Ins., etc., Co. *v.* Dougherty, 18 Pa. Co. Ct. 217; Wetzel *v.* Goodyear, 17 Pa. Co. Ct. 110; Ellis *v.* Kies, 1 Dauph. Co. Rep. 195; Chester *v.* Roan, 8 Del. Co. 66; Wolfe *v.* Reily, 8 Kulp 448; Scranton *v.* Scanlon, 7 Lack. Leg. N. 15; Gubert *v.* Aiello, 3 Lack. Leg. N. 294; Philadelphia *v.* Duffy, 4 Phila. 289.

Rhode Island.— Quimby *v.* Wood, 19 R. I. 571, 35 Atl. 149; People's Sav. Bank *v.* Tripp, 13 R. I. 621.

South Carolina.— Barker *v.* Smith, 10 Rich. 226.

South Dakota.— Miller *v.* Anderson, 1 S. D. 539, 47 N. W. 957, 11 L. R. A. 317.

Tennessee.— State *v.* Campbell, (1897) 41 S. W. 937.

Texas.— Jodon *v.* Brenham, 57 Tex. 655.

West Virginia.— Cabin Creek Dist. Bd. of Education *v.* Old Dominion Iron, etc., Mfg. Co., 18 W. Va. 441.

United States.—Haine *v.* Madison Parish, etc., Levee Com'rs, 19 Wall. 655, 22 L. ed. 223; Tompkins *v.* Little Rock, etc., R. Co., 18 Fed. 344, 5 McCrary 597 [*affirmed* in 125 U. S. 109, 8 S. Ct. 762, 31 L. ed. 615]; Georgetown *v.* Smith, 10 Fed. Cas. No. 5,347, 4 Cranch C. C. 91.

See 45 Cent. Dig. tit. "Taxation," §§ 931, 932.

Power of municipal corporations.— Municipal corporations have no authority to make the taxes levied by them liens on real or personal property, unless power to do so has been granted them by charter or statute. Philadelphia *v.* Greble, 38 Pa. St. 339. See MUNICIPAL CORPORATIONS, 28 Cyc. 1704.

3. Creighton *v.* Manson, 27 Cal. 613; Anderson *v.* State, 23 Miss. 459; Miller *v.* Anderson, 1 S. D. 539, 47 N. W. 957, 11 L. R. A. 317. *Compare* Snyder *v.* Mogart, 5 Pa. Dist. 146, 17 Pa. Co. Ct. 1, where a statute was held to create a tax lien by necessary implication.

Statute declaring liability of property.—A statute declaring that all personal property subject to taxation shall be liable to be seized and sold for taxes does not make the taxes a lien thereon. *In re* Citizens' Bank Assignment, 2 Ohio Dec. (Reprint) 230, 2 West. L. Month. 121.

Statute giving priority of payment.— No tax lien is created by a statute which merely gives to taxes a preference or prior right of payment as against all other debts or claims against the owner of the property. Anderson *v.* State, 23 Miss. 459.

Under a contract between the state and a corporation, providing for its incorporation, authorizing it to build a railroad, imposing taxes, and making them a lien on its property, the lien for taxes is similar to a mortgage lien. People *v.* Michigan Cent. R. Co., 145 Mich. 140, 108 N. W. 772.

4. Burnet *v.* Dean, 60 N. J. Eq. 9, 46 Atl. 532.

5. See *infra*, VIII, E, 1.

6. *California.*— People *v.* Pearis, 37 Cal. 259; Moss *v.* Shear, 25 Cal. 38, 85 Am. Dec. 94. But see Couts *v.* Cornell, 147 Cal. 560, 82 Pac. 194, 109 Am. St. Rep. 168.

Florida.— L'Engle *v.* Florida Cent., etc., R. Co., 21 Fla. 353.

Illinois.— Sanford *v.* People, 102 Ill. 374.

Louisiana.— Brusle *v.* Sauve, 20 La. Ann. 560.

New Jersey.— Pfeiffer *v.* Miles, 48 N. J. L. 450, 4 Atl. 429.

New York.— Barlow *v.* Saint Nicholas Bank, 63 N. Y. 399, 20 Am. Rep. 547; Burr *v.* Palmer, 53 N. Y. App. Div. 358, 65 N. Y. Suppl. 1056; Rose *v.* Northrup, 41 Misc. 238, 84 N. Y. Suppl. 52 [*affirmed* in 88 N. Y. App. Div. 621, 85 N. Y. Suppl. 1145]; *In re* Van Beuren, 66 N. Y. Suppl. 267.

Texas.— State *v.* Farmer, 94 Tex. 232, 59 S. W. 541.

Utah.— Gillmor *v.* Dale, 27 Utah 372, 75 Pac. 932.

See 45 Cent. Dig. tit. "Taxation," § 935.

Contra.— Peckham *v.* Milliken, 99 Ind. 352; Chester *v.* Roan, 8 Del. Co. (Pa.) 66, holding that a tax lien on land may be valid, although the tax was assessed to the wrong person.

Sufficiency of description of property to create lien see Watkins *v.* Couch, 134 Iowa 1, 111 N. W. 315.

Assessment against owner of land personally.— Under Tax Law, § 89, providing that unpaid taxes may be assessed against the land itself the next year after that for which they are delinquent, where unpaid taxes were assessed each year against the owner of land personally, they did not constitute a lien on the land, and hence a purchaser on foreclosure of a mortgage was not entitled to compel the referee to pay such taxes out of the proceeds of the sale. Greenfield *v.* Beaver, 30 Misc. 366, 62 N. Y. Suppl. 471.

no such lien exists where the payment was voluntary, in the legal sense, or was made at the request of the owner and for his mere accommodation.[8] Nor can this lien be made effective against a subsequent purchaser from the real owner who had no notice of the circumstances under which the taxes were paid.[9] Although a tax lien may be kept alive for the benefit of a surety paying the taxes, a tax collector, who pays the taxes out of his own funds, cannot be considered a surety, and he has no lien therefor.[10]

(III) *CORPORATION PAYING TAX ON STOCKS OR BONDS* — (A) *In General.* The courts have sustained the validity of the statutes in force in several of the states requiring corporations to pay the taxes assessed upon the shares of their capital stock in the hands of individual stock-holders, or upon their outstanding bonded indebtedness, and directing, or intending, that the corporation shall then deduct and retain the amount of such taxes from dividends payable to its shareholders or from interest on its bonds, as the case may be.[11] It is generally held that such a provision makes the tax a debt due from the corporation, for which

Maryland.— Hebb *v.* Moore, 66 Md. 167, 7 Atl. 255.

Michigan.— Richards *v.* Lewis L. Arms Shingle, etc., Co., 74 Mich. 57, 41 N. W. 860.

Mississippi.— Ingersoll *v.* Jeffords, 55 Miss. 37.

New Jersey.— Farmer *v.* Ward, 75 N. J. Eq. 33, 71 Atl. 401; Manning *v.* Tuthill, 30 N. J. Eq. 29.

New York.— Oliphant *v.* Burns, 146 N. Y. 218, 40 N. E. 980.

Ohio.— Nowler *v.* Coit, 1 Ohio 519, 13 Am. Dec. 640.

Pennsylvania.— Jackson *v.* Pittsburgh, 8 Pa. Dist. 150.

Texas.— Hensel *v.* Kegans, 8 Tex. Civ. App. 583, 28 S. W. 705.

Washington.— Childs *v.* Smith, 51 Wash. 457, 99 Pac. 304, 130 Am. St. Rep. 1107; Spokane *v.* Security Sav. Soc., 46 Wash. 150, 89 Pac. 466; Hemen *v.* Rinehart, 45 Wash. 1, 87 Pac. 953; Ball *v.* Clothier, 34 Wash. 299, 75 Pac. 1099; Rothschild *v.* Rollinger, 32 Wash. 307, 73 Pac. 367; Dunsmuir *v.* Port Angeles Gas, etc., Co., 30 Wash. 586, 71 Pac. 9; Packwood *v.* Briggs, 25 Wash. 530, 65 Pac. 846.

West Virginia.— See Hinchman *v.* Morris, 29 W. Va. 673, 2 S. E. 863.

See 45 Cent. Dig. tit. "Taxation," § 987.

Compare, however, Wood *v.* Gruble, 31 Kan. 69, 1 Pac. 277; Preston *v.* Wright, 81 Me. 306, 17 Atl. 128, 10 Am. St. Rep. 257.

Extent of lien.—Where the land consists of separate lots, and no rights of third persons have intervened, it is error to declare a lien on each lot for the taxes paid on it by another, but the whole amount should be adjudged a lien on the lots collectively. Goodnow *v.* Litchfield, 63 Iowa 275, 19 N. W. 226.

Duration of lien.—Where one, believing that he holds a valid mortgage lien not barred by limitation, pays in good faith delinquent general taxes to protect the lien, so as to procure an equitable lien on the land therefor, he is subrogated to the rights and liens of the county and state, against which limitation does not run; Ballinger Annot. Code & St. § 1740; Pierce Code, § 8678, providing that taxes assessed upon realty shall after levy be a lien thereon until paid. Childs *v.* Smith, 51 Wash. 457, 99 Pac. 304, 130 Am. St. Rep. 1107.

Effect of purchase at tax-sale.—Where a mortgagee without authority purchases the property at a tax-sale, he occupies the same position as if he had paid the taxes before sale, and is therefore only entitled to subrogation to the tax lien. Farmer *v.* Ward, 75 N. J. Eq. 33, 71 Atl. 401. See *infra,* XIV, C, 3.

8. *Connecticut.*—Sperry *v.* Butler, 75 Conn. 369, 53 Atl. 899.

Indiana.— Snoddy *v.* Leavitt, 105 Ind. 357, 5 N. E. 13; Sohn *v.* Wood, 75 Ind. 17.

New Jersey.— Rankin *v.* Coar, 46 N. J. Eq. 566, 22 Atl. 177, 11 L. R. A. 661.

New York.— Koehler *v.* Hughes, 4 Misc. 236, 24 N. Y. Suppl. 760.

Tennessee.— Ferguson *v.* Quinn, 97 Tenn. 46, 36 S. W. 576, 33 L. R. A. 688.

Texas.—Furche *v.* Mayer, (Civ. App. 1895) 29 S. W. 1099.

See 45 Cent. Dig. tit. "Taxation," § 987.

Erroneous belief in lien of judgment or mortgage.— Where a judgment creditor or mortgagee pays taxes on land, believing in good faith, although erroneously, that the judgment or mortgage is still a lien on the land, the payment is not voluntary, and he acquires an equitable lien on the land for the taxes so paid with interest from the several dates of payment. Childs *v.* Smith, 51 Wash. 457, 99 Pac. 304, 130 Am. St. Rep. 1107; Hemen *v.* Rinehart, 45 Wash. 1, 87 Pac. 953; Dunsmuir *v.* Port Angeles Gas, etc., Co., 30 Wash. 586, 71 Pac. 9; Packwood *v.* Briggs, 25 Wash. 530, 65 Pac. 846.

9. Merrill *v.* Tobin, 82 Iowa 520, 48 N. W. 1044; Bowen *v.* Duffie, 66 Iowa 88, 23 N. W. 277.

10. *In re* Wallace, 59 Pa. St. 401.

11. New Orleans *v.* Louisiana Sav. Bank, etc., Co., 31 La. Ann. 826; Donovan *v.* Firemen's Ins. Co., 30 Md. 155; Com. *v.* Lehigh Valley R. Co, 129 Pa. St 429, 18 Atl. 406, 410; Com. *v.* Delaware Div. Canal Co., 123 Pa. St. 594, 16 Atl. 584, 2 L. R. A. 798; Catawissa R. Co.'s Appeal, 78 Pa. St. 59; Maltby *v.* Reading, etc., R. Co., 52 Pa. St. 140; Com. *v.* Wilkesbarre, etc., R. Co., 14 Pa. Co. Ct. 205; Com. *v.* New York, etc., R. Co., 9 Pa. Co. Ct. 305; South Nashville St. R. Co.

Statutes sometimes provide for the apportionment of taxes among the proper subdivisions or parcels of the real estate assessed.[20]

c. Payment From Property in Custody of Law. Where property subject to taxes has been sold under decree of foreclosure or other judicial process and the proceeds brought into court, even if the statute does not expressly direct the payment of the taxes out of the fund, it is entirely proper for the court to do so,[21] and the same is true in regard to property in the possession of a receiver appointed by the court.[22]

20. See Morris, etc., Dredging Co. *v.* Bayonne, 75 N. J. L. 59, 67 Atl. 20, holding that under Gen. Tax Act (1903) (Pub. Laws (1903), p. 414), § 61, the council of the city of Bayonne are required on proper application of any person interested to apportion taxes among the proper subdivisions or parcels of real estate assessed for taxes in said city.

21. Degner *v.* Baltimore, 74 Md. 144, 21 Atl. 697; Georgetown College *v.* Perkins, 74 Md. 72, 21 Atl. 551; Baltimore *v.* Chase, 2 Gill & J. (Md.) 376; Poughkeepsie Sav. Bank *v.* Winn, 56 How. Pr. (N. Y.) 368.

Intervention by state.— The state has a right to intervene in a suit to enforce its lien for taxes on property involved therein, and obtain an order for payment out of proceeds arising from the judicial sale of such property (Huckleby *v.* State, 57 Fla. 433, 48 So. 979); and where the state does intervene in such a case parties wishing to question the legality of the tax must do so by answer (Huckleby *v.* State, *supra*).

Lien not divested by judicial sale see *supra*, VIII, D, 2.

22. *Connecticut.*— Lamkin *v.* Baldwin, etc., Mfg. Co., 72 Conn. 57, 43 Atl. 593, 1042, 44 L. R. A. 786.

Georgia.— Dysart *v.* Brown, 100 Ga. 1, 26 S. E. 767, holding that where it appears that an insolvent corporation, whose assets are in the hands of a receiver, is already two years in default in the payment of its state and county taxes, and that the taxes for a third year will soon become due, it is the duty of the judge by whom the receiver was appointed, upon a proper application by the tax collector, to order the receiver, if no other means are available for the purpose, to sell a sufficiency of the property of the corporation to raise the money with which to pay the overdue taxes; and the fact that all of the income derived by a receiver from carrying on the business of a corporation whose assets are in his hands is requisite to the operation of that business is no legal excuse for such long delay in paying its taxes.

Idaho.— Palmer *v.* Pettingill, 7 Ida. 346, 55 Pac. 653.

Illinois.—Wiswall *v.* Kunz, 173 Ill. 110, 50 N. E. 184, holding that while property held by a receiver should be assessed to the receiver, the fact that it is assessed in the name of the party for whom the receiver holds possession does not affect the validity of the tax: and it is within the power of the court appointing the receiver to allow the amount of the tax, as a claim against the receiver, and order the same paid by the receiver to the tax collector; and that the taxes upon this property in the hands of the receiver, assessed after his appointment, may properly be regarded as part of the costs and expenses of the receivership, and may be ordered paid in full, as other costs and expenses.

Indiana.— See Stoner *v.* Bitters, 151 Ind. 575, 52 N. E. 149.

Kentucky.— Spalding *v.* Com., 88 Ky. 135, 10 S. W. 420, 10 Ky. L. Rep. 714, holding that the proper procedure is for the court appointing a receiver of property of a decedent's estate which is in litigation to direct him to list the property in the county court, and pay the taxes, but it is not improper for the former court to grant leave to institute a suit in the county court against the receiver, to compel him to list the property; and the county court having ordered the receiver to do so, and its order having been appealed to the court appointing him, and there affirmed, the latter court may be considered as having directed the listing.

New Jersey.— *In re* U. S. Car Co., 60 N. J. Eq. 514, 43 Atl. 673 [*reversing* 57 N. J. Eq. 357, 42 Atl. 272].

New York.— Central Trust Co. *v.* New York City, etc., R. Co., 110 N. Y. 250, 18 N. E. 92, 1 L. R. A. 260 [*reversing* 47 Hun 587] (holding that where a railroad corporation was insolvent and all its property was in the hands of a receiver appointed in an action to foreclose a mortgage thereon, the amount of which exceeded the value of all the property, and the receiver as such was operating the road under order of the court, and had in his hands moneys arising from the gross earnings sufficient to pay a tax imposed upon the corporation under and pursuant to the Corporation Act of 1881 (Laws (1881), c. 361), the state was not confined to the proceedings prescribed in said act to collect such tax, but the court, on petition and application of the attorney-general, made in the foreclosure suit, and on notice to the corporation and to the receiver might, in its discretion, make an order directing the receiver to pay the same out of said gross earnings); Matter of Columbian Ins. Co., 3 Abb. Dec. 239, 3 Keyes 123. And see Decker *v.* Gardiner, 124 N. Y. 334, 26 N. E. 814, 11 L. R. A. 480.

Pennsylvania.— Com. *v.* Buffalo, etc., R. Co., 2 Dauph. Co. Rep. 216. And see Philadelphia, etc., R. Co. *v.* Com., 104 Pa. St. 80.

United States.— See *Ex p.* Tyler, 149 U. S. 164, 13 S. Ct. 785, 37 L. ed. 689.

d. To Whom Payment Made.[23] A payment of taxes, in order to be effective in relieving the person and his property from liability, must be made to the officer primarily authorized to receive them,[24] or at least to someone legally delegated to act in his behalf in receiving and receipting for the taxes.[25]

e. Time and Place For Payment. The statutes ordinarily fix the time when taxes shall become due and payable and prescribe the length of time which may elapse before they shall be considered delinquent.[26] After that time, although the citizen still has the right to relieve his property by paying the taxes, they usually carry a penalty or interest, which must be included in the payment.[27] But when land has been sold for delinquent taxes, the owner's right to discharge the tax by payment is lost and he has instead a right of redemption which must be obtained by means of the appropriate procedure.[28] On the other hand, payment of taxes

Excuse for non-payment.— The facts that a receiver had sold the property, which was realty, by the court's order and approval, and the purchaser had taken it subject to taxes, were held a "good and sufficient cause" for non payment within the meaning of Horner Rev. St. Ind. (1897) § 6436, providing that where a receiver neglects to pay taxes on property he may be cited to show cause why such taxes, with penalty, should not be paid. Stoner *v.* Bitters, 151 Ind. 575, 52 N. E. 149.

Certificates issued by a receiver given priority see Union Trust Co. *v.* Illinois Midland Co., 117 U. S. 434, 6 S. Ct. 809, 29 L. ed. 963.

License-fee assessed against insolvent corporation in hands of receiver entitled to priority see *In re* U. S. Car Co., 60 N. J. Eq. 514, 43 Atl. 673 [*reversing* 57 N. J. Eq. 357, 42 Atl. 272].

23. Authority to collect see *infra*, X, A, 4.

24. Sherrick *v.* State, 167 Ind. 345, 79 N. E. 193; Auditor Public Accounts *v.* Western Union Tel. Co., 46 S. W. 704, 20 Ky. L. Rep. 469; Young *v.* King, 3 R. I. 196; Texas, etc., R. Co. *v.* State, 43 Tex. Civ. App. 580, 97 S. W. 142. *Compare* Jones *v.* Dils, 18 W. Va. 759.

25. Randall *v.* Dailey, 66 Wis. 285, 28 N. W. 352, holding that where payment is made to a person authorized by the county treasurer to receive the taxes, the fact that the receipt is signed only by a stamp with a facsimile of the treasurer's signature will not affect the rights of the taxpayer as against a subsequent purchaser of the land at tax-sale. But see Marshall *v.* Baldwin, 11 Phila. (Pa.) 403, holding that proof of payment of taxes to a conveyancer is not proof of payment to a proper person.

26. See the statutes of the several states. And see the following cases:

Maryland.— State *v.* Safe-Deposit, etc., Co., 86 Md. 581, 39 Atl. 523; Condon *v.* Maynard, 71 Md. 601, 18 Atl. 957.

Massachusetts.— Com. *v.* Commonwealth Bank, 22 Pick. 176.

Mississippi.— Carlisle *v.* Yoder, 69 Miss. 384, 12 So. 255.

Nevada.— State *v.* Eureka Consol. Min. Co., 8 Nev. 15.

North Carolina.— State *v.* Bryant, 121 N. C. 560, 28 S. E. 551.

Ohio.— Hoglen *v.* Cohan, 30 Ohio St. 436; McMillan *v.* Robbins, 5 Ohio 28.

Oklahoma.— Norton *v.* Choctaw, etc., R. Co., 16 Okla. 482, 86 Pac. 287.

South Carolina.—Willis *v.* Heighway, 49 S. C. 476, 19 S. E. 135.

Tennessee.— Rucker *v.* Hyde, 118 Tenn. 358, 100 S. W. 739.

Texas.— Lufkin *v.* Galveston, 73 Tex. 340, 11 S. W. 340; Clark *v.* Elmendorf, (Civ. App. 1904) 78 S. W. 538.

United States.— McGunnegle *v.* Rutherford, 16 Fed. Cas. No. 8,815*a*, Hempst. 45, construing early statute of Arkansas.

See 45 Cent. Dig. tit. "Taxation," § 969.

Time for payment of license-tax.— Taxes and fees for business licenses are payable in advance, that is, they must be paid before the license is delivered. State *v.* Spencer, 49 Mo. 342.

Tax collector's business hours.—A collector or receiver of taxes has a right to appoint certain reasonable hours of the business day, during which alone his office will be open for the receipt of taxes. Lancaster *v.* Kray, 21 Lanc. L. Rev. (Pa.) 383.

The registry tax on mortgages, provided by Minn. Gen. Laws (1907), c. 328, must be paid on the filing for record of an agreement for an extension or renewal of the mortgage. Mutual Ben. L. Ins. Co. *v.* Martin County, 104 Minn. 179, 526, 116 N. W. 572, 575.

27. Bracey *v.* Ray, 26 La. Ann. 710 (if a delinquent tax is actually received by the collector without the penalty, a sale cannot afterward be made for the penalty); Connolly's Case, 5 Wkly. Notes Cas. (Pa.) 8 (collector should receive taxes at any time when offered, without regard to the question whether the payment is in time to entitle the taxpayer to vote at a coming election); State *v.* Folk, 45 S. C. 491, 23 S. E. 628 (the fact that the statute makes default in the payment of poll taxes a misdemeanor will not prevent the collector from accepting voluntary payment of delinquent poll taxes with penalties).

Interest and penalties see *infra*, IX, A, 2, e.

28. Coombs *v.* Steere, 8 Ill. App. 147; Squire *v.* McCarthy, 77 Nebr. 431, 112 N. W. 327, 77 Nebr. 429, 109 N. W. 768.

is restricted to cases where the officer is authorized or required by law to furnish official tax statements, and it is held that in the absence of any such authority or requirement the taxpayer who relies on what he is told does so at his own peril.[44] A landowner, it has been held, is not bound as a matter of law to take notice of a new map giving a new description of his lands, and if, relying on the old description and the old map, he attempts to pay his taxes, and supposes he has done so on all his lands, but fails to do so on some of them, which are subsequently sold for taxes without his knowledge, the deed made in pursuance of such sale is void.[45] Where the owner of land goes to the county treasurer's office, in good faith, for the purpose of paying the taxes thereon, and, although using reasonable diligence to ascertain and pay them, fails to do so by reason of being actually misled by the assessment, and the treasurer's advertised list of sales of unseated lands, the land being there designated by a wrong warrant number, a sale of the land for such taxes is void.[46]

2. **Mode and Amount of Payment — a. Mode of Making Payment** — (I) *In General.* As a general rule, the law requires taxes to be paid actually in cash, and all at once, unless where a statute allows their discharge in instalments;[47] but the same result may be accomplished by retention of funds belonging to the taxpayer, by transfer of credits, or anything else which is equivalent to actnal payment.[48] But private arrangements between the taxpayer and the collector are not regarded with favor, and a tax cannot be discharged by the collector merely

v. Anderson, 142 Pa. St. 357, 21 Atl. 976, 21 L. R. A. 751; Freeman *v.* Cornwell, (1888) 15 Atl. 873; Breisch *v.* Coxe, 81 Pa. St. 336; Baird *v.* Cahoon, 5 Watts & S. 540; Trexler *v.* Africa, 27 Pa. Super. Ct. 385, 33 Pa. Super. Ct. 395; Philadelphia *v.* Glanding, 8 Pa. Co. Ct. 367.

Washington.— Taylor *v.* Debritz, 48 Wash. 373, 93 Pac. 528; Bullock *v.* Wallace, 47 Wash. 690, 92 Pac. 675.

Wisconsin.— Nelson *v.* Churchill, 117 Wis. 10, 93 N. W. 799; Edwards *v.* Upham, 93 Wis. 455, 67 N. W. 728; Bray, etc., Land Co. *v.* Newman, 92 Wis. 271, 65 N. W. 494; Gould *v.* Sullivan, 84 Wis. 659, 54 N. W. 1013, 36 Am. St. Rep. 955, 20 L. R. A. 487; Randall *v.* Dailey, 66 Wis. 285, 28 N. W. 352.

See 45 Cent. Dig. tit. "Taxation," §§ 990, 1267.

Unauthorized officer.— The rule has no application where the officer applied to is not the one authorized to receive the tax. Edwards *v.* Upham, 93 Wis. 455, 67 N. W. 728.

44. Elliot *v.* District of Columbia, 3 MacArthur (D. C.) 396; Kahl *v.* Love, 37 N. J. L. 5. But *compare* Rosecrans *v.* District of Columbia, 5 Mackey (D. C.) 120. In Raley *v.* Guinn, 76 Mo. 263, it was held that a tax deed could not be defeated by showing that before advertisement or sale of the land the owner went to the office of the collector to pay the taxes, and was told that there were none against the land, as the publication of the delinquent list, as required by law, gave him correct information on the subject.

45. Richter *v.* Beaumont, 67 Miss. 285, 7 So. 357; Lewis *v.* Monson, 151 U. S. 545, 14 S. Ct. 424, 38 L. ed. 265.

46. Freeman *v.* Cornwell, (Pa. 1888) 15 Atl. 873.

47. Litchfield *v.* Brooklyn, 10 Misc. (N. Y.) 74, 31 N. Y. Suppl. 151. And see Harrington *v.* Dickinson, 155 Mich. 161, 118 N. W. 931; and *infra*, IX, A, 2, d.

Contract for services in payment.—An agreement between a taxpayer of a county or city and such corporation that certain services were to be rendered by him in consideration that his taxes were to be canceled will not avail the taxpayer in an action between him, or his grantee, and the purchaser of real property at tax-sale, notwithstanding he may have performed his part of the contract, it not appearing that the county or city had complied with its contract and paid the taxes. Merriam *v.* Dovey, 25 Nebr. 618, 41 N. W. 550.

48. Thus a county treasurer may withhold so much of an officer's salary as is necessary to pay a tax lien on the latter's property. Beckett *v.* Wishon, 5 Ohio S. & C. Pl. Dec. 257, 5 Ohio N. P. 155. And see Ewing *v.* Robeson, 15 Ind. 26, as to state auditor retaining the interest accruing on state bonds, for the payment of taxes. So where a county treasurer deposits in a bank receipts for taxes due from the bank, receives credit for the amount of such taxes, and afterward draws the money out by check, the transaction amounts to a payment of the taxes. Wasson *v.* Lamb, 120 Ind. 514, 22 N. E. 720, 16 Am. St. Rep. 342, 6 L. R. A. 191. Where a county treasurer deposited the county funds in a bank, and used the bank as a medium for the collection of taxes, by placing tax receipts in its hands and permitting it to collect the amount and credit it to the deposit account, the delivery to the bank of a receipt for the amount of the taxes assessed against the bank, and a credit of the amount of such receipt to the deposit account, constituted, as between the county and the county treasurer, a collection of the tax due from the bank. Brown *v.* Sheldon State Bank, 139 Iowa 83, 117 N. W. 289.

marking it "paid" on his books,[49] although in some states it has been held that he may, if he chooses, account for the tax in his return, and then sue on the promise of the taxpayer to pay him.[50]

(II) *SET-OFF OR COUNTER-CLAIM.* As a tax is not a debt in the ordinary sense, nor the liability for it founded upon contract, it cannot be paid or discharged by setting off or counter-claiming against it a debt due from the municipality to the individual taxpayer,[51] and still less of course a debt due from the collector of taxes in his private capacity.[52]

b. Medium of Payment — (I) *IN GENERAL.* The legislature has power to prescribe the kind of funds in which taxes shall be payable,[53] and may declare that only gold and silver coin shall be receivable for this purpose.[54] But in the absence of such a restriction, taxes may be paid in any lawful current money, although the collector has no authority to accept anything else, unless specially allowed by law.[55]

(II) *STATE AND MUNICIPAL BONDS, WARRANTS, AND OTHER OBLIGATIONS.* State scrip, county warrants or orders, treasurers' certificates, school-district orders, state or municipal bonds or the coupons therefrom, and all other such evidences of indebtedness are not receivable in payment of taxes, unless specifically made so by some constitutional or statutory provision.[56] But where

49. Reutchler *v.* Hucke, 3 Ill. App. 144; Ambler *v.* Clayton, 23 Iowa 173. And see Maxwell *v.* Hunter, 65 Iowa 121, 21 N. W. 481.

Credit on account.— Inasmuch as a tax collector is only authorized to receive cash for taxes, the fact that he is given credit on his account for taxes by a taxpayer does not amount to a payment. Figures *v.* State, (Tex. Civ. App. 1907) 99 S. W. 412.

50. Jacks *v.* Dyer, 31 Ark. 334; Elson *v.* Spraker, 100 Ind. 374; Schaum *v.* Showers, 49 Ind. 285; Pontiac *v.* Axford, 49 Mich. 69, 12 N. W. 914; Shriver *v.* Cowell, 92 Pa. St. 262; McCracken *v.* Elder, 34 Pa. St. 239.

51. *Indiana.*— Scobey *v.* Decatur County, 72 Ind. 551.

Iowa.— Hedge *v.* Des Moines, 141 Iowa 4, 119 N. W. 276.

Kentucky.—Anderson *v.* Mayfield, 93 Ky. 230, 19 S. W. 598, 14 Ky. L. Rep. 370.

Louisiana.— New Orleans *v.* Davidson, 30 La. Ann. 541, 31 Am. Rep. 228.

North Carolina.— Gatling *v.* Carteret County, 92 N. C. 536, 53 Am. Rep. 432: Cobb *v.* Elizabeth City, 75 N. C. 1.

South Carolina.— Trenholm *v.* Charleston, 3 S. C. 347, 16 Am. Rep. 732.

Wisconsin.— Keep *v.* Frazier, 4 Wis. 224.

United States.—Apperson *v.* Memphis, 1 Fed. Cas. No. 497, 2 Flipp. 363.

See 45 Cent. Dig. tit. "Taxation," § 972. And see *supra*, I, A, 2, b.

52. Com. *v.* Mahon, 12 Pa. Super. Ct. 616; Shoemaker *v.* Swiler, 2 Leg. Op. (Pa.) 7; Miller *v.* Wisener, 45 W. Va. 59, 30 S. E. 237.

53. Coit *v.* Claw, 28 Ark. 516; English *v.* Oliver, 28 Ark. 317.

54. Prescott *v.* McNamara, 73 Cal. 236, 14 Pac. 877; State Treasurer *v.* Wright, 28 Ill. 509; Whiteaker *v.* Haley, 2 Oreg. 128.

United States legal tender notes.— The acts of congress making the notes of the United States a legal tender for the payment of debts do not apply to involuntary contributions in the nature of taxes or assessments exacted under state laws, but only to debts in the strict sense of the term; and if a state requires payment of its taxes in coin, these notes are not a legal tender therefor. Whiteaker *v.* Haley, 2 Oreg. 128; Hagar *v.* Reclamation Dist. No. 7, 111 U. S. 701, 4 S. Ct. 663, 28 L. ed. 569; Lane County *v.* Oregon, 7 Wall. (U. S.) 71, 19 L. ed. 101. See Crutcher *v.* Sterling, 1 Ida. 306.

55. *Arkansas.*— Coit *v.* Claw, 28 Ark. 516; Hunt *v.* McFadgen, 20 Ark. 277.

Indiana.— Richards *v.* Stogsdell, 21 Ind. 74.

Louisiana.— Shreveport *v.* Gregg, 28 La. Ann. 836.

Michigan.— Staley *v.* Columbus Tp., 36 Mich. 38.

New York.— McLanahan *v.* Syracuse, 18 Hun 259.

Pennsylvania.— Nutting *v.* Lynn, 18 Pa. Super. Ct. 59, agreement of collector to accept commodities in lieu of cash.

Texas.— Figures *v.* State, (Civ. App. 1907) 99 S. W. 412.

See 45 Cent. Dig. tit. "Taxation," § 973 *et seq.*

56. *Alabama.*— Burke *v.* Armstrong, 52 Ala. 48.

Arkansas.— Hughes *v.* Ross, 38 Ark. 275; Graham *v.* Parham, 32 Ark. 676; Loftin *v.* Watson, 32 Ark. 414; Askew *v.* Columbia County, 32 Ark. 270; Wallis *v.* Smith, 29 Ark. 354; English *v.* Oliver, 28 Ark. 317; Wells *v.* Cole, 27 Ark. 603; Gaines *v.* Rives, 8 Ark. 220.

Colorado.— Morgan *v.* Pueblo, etc., R. Co., 6 Colo. 478.

Florida.— Frier *v.* State, 11 Fla. 300.

Louisiana.— State *v.* Lemarie, 25 La. Ann. 412 (illegal state warrants); Roman *v.* Ory, 12 Rob. 517.

Missouri.— Kansas City, etc., R. Co. *v.* Thornton, 152 Mo. 570, 54 S. W. 445.

release or remit particular taxes altogether or authorize their compromise or settlement on part payment,[11] unless prevented by a constitutional prohibition.[12] But a grant to a person to take the benefit of past due taxes to his own use, like a grant of exemption from future taxation, is to be strictly construed, and the right is not to be taken by implication.[13] It seems that counties, towns, and municipal corporations cannot compromise or release claims for taxes legally assessed, at least if the debtor is able to pay, unless they are authorized by the legislature to do so,[14] and certainly they cannot do so even then if there is a constitutional prohibition.[15] Where a tax has been regularly assessed under a statute and the liability therefor is fully fixed, the repeal of the statute does not have the effect of remitting such tax, unless such an intention on the part of the legislature appears.[16]

11. Demoville *v.* Davidson County, 87 Tenn. 214, 10 S. W. 353 (holding that the act of March 9, 1887, releasing druggists of a certain class from liability for taxes under certain revenue laws, was simply an exercise of the state's power to compromise or release its claims against debtors, and therefore it was no objection to the act that no provision was made for refunding the tax of such druggists of that class as had already paid); McHenry *v.* Alford, 168 U. S. 651, 18 S. Ct. 242, 42 L. ed. 614 (compromise). See also *In re* Kilby Bank, 23 Pick. (Mass.) 93; Auditor-Gen. *v.* O'Connor, 83 Mich. 464, 47 N. W. 443.

Counties.— The legislature has the right to release county as well as state taxes. Demoville *v.* Davidson County, 87 Tenn. 214, 10 S. W. 353.

Construction and application of particular statutes see Files *v.* Pocahontas, etc., R. Co., 48 Ark. 529, 3 S. W. 817; *In re* Kilby Bank, 23 Pick. (Mass.) 93; Auditor-Gen. *v.* O'Connor, 83 Mich. 464, 47 N. W. 443 (statute applicable to taxes reassessed); Demoville *v.* Davidson County, 87 Tenn. 214, 10 S. W. 353 (holding that the act of March 9, 1887, releasing druggists of a certain class from liability for taxes under certain revenue laws, being a release of all liability, extended to the liability incurred to counties as well as to the state).

Compliance with invalid statute. — Where an unconstitutional statute remitting certain taxes assessed against a railroad company was acquiesced in by the local authorities, who refrained from requiring the collector to collect the taxes or to account for them, this did not prevent the assertion of a claim for such taxes in the succeeding year. Perry County *v.* Selma, etc., R. Co., 58 Ala. 546.

12. Illinois Cent. R. Co. *v.* Com., 128 Ky. 268, 108 S. W. 245, 32 Ky. L. Rep. 1112, 110 S. W. 265, 33 Ky. L. Rep. 326 (holding that an agreement between the state board of valuation and assessment and a railroad company to release the latter for taxes for previous years on condition that it pay the taxes for the particular year was void, where the assessments for the previous years had become final, Ky. Const. § 52, providing that the general assembly shall have no power to release or authorize the release, in whole or in part, of indebtedness due to the commonwealth or to any county or municipality); Southern R. Co. *v.* Coulter, 113 Ky. 657, 68 S. W. 873, 24 Ky. L. Rep. 203. And see Citizens' Nat. Bank *v.* Com., 118 Ky. 51, 80 S. W. 479, 81 S. W. 686, 25 Ky. L. Rep. 2254, 26 Ky. L. Rep. 62; Louisville *v.* Louisville, etc., R. Co., 111 Ky. 1, 63 S. W. 14, 23 Ky. L. Rep. 390.

Unliquidated demand.— In Kentucky it is held that the constitutional prohibition against releasing or authorizing the release, in whole or in part, of indebtedness due to the commonwealth or to any county or municipality, does not forbid the compromise of an unliquidated demand for taxes, and that a judgment upon an agreed stipulation of facts will not be disturbed ordinarily, except for fraud or mistake. Com. *v.* Southern Pac. R. Co., 134 Ky. 421, 120 S. W. 313.

13. Files *v.* Pocahontas, etc., R. Co., 48 Ark. 529, 3 S. W. 817. See also Territory *v.* Gaines, 11 Ariz. 270, 93 Pac. 281.

14. State *v.* Fyler, 48 Conn. 145. But see San Antonio *v.* San Antonio St. R. Co., 22 Tex. Civ. App. 148, 54 S. W. 281, sustaining the compromise of a suit for taxes. *Compare* MUNICIPAL CORPORATIONS, 28 Cyc. 1711.

In Arizona, Rev. St. (1901) par. 973, conferring on boards of supervisors power to direct and control the prosecution and defense of all suits to which the county is a party, and to compromise the same and to do and perform all other acts and things which may be necessary to the full discharge of the chief legislative authority of the county government, did not confer on a county's board of supervisors authority to compromise an action for the collection of taxes. Territory *v.* Gaines, 11 Ariz. 270, 93 Pac. 281. A compromise of delinquent taxes, made subsequent to the passage of the act of March 19, 1903 (Laws (1903), p. 168, No. 92), amending Revenue Law, § 91 (Rev. St. (1901) par. 3922), and specifying the conditions under which a board of supervisors may compromise taxes, which compromise is not based on any of the conditions specified, is void. Territory *v.* Gaines, *supra*.

15. Citizens' Nat. Bank *v.* Com., 118 Ky. 51, 80 S. W. 479, 81 S. W. 686, 25 Ky. L. Rep. 2254, 26 Ky. L. Rep. 62; Louisville *v.* Louisville, etc., R. Co., 111 Ky. 1, 63 S. W. 14, 23 Ky. L. Rep. 390. And see MUNICIPAL CORPORATIONS, 28 Cyc. 1711. *Compare* *supra*, this section, note 14.

16. Debolt *v.* Ohio L. Ins., etc., Co., 1 Ohio St. 563. See *supra*, I, F.

there is some constitutional or statutory provision expressly or impliedly giving him such right although the tax is paid without compulsion.[55]

b. What Constitutes Voluntary Payment.[56] A payment is voluntary, in the sense that no action lies to recover back the amount, not only where it is made willingly and without objection;[57] but in all cases where there is no compulsion or duress nor any necessity of making the payment as a means of freeing the person or property from legal restraint or the grasp of legal process.[58] Hence a payment made in pursuance of a bargain or compromise between the taxpayer and the state or municipality is voluntary,[59] and so is a payment of taxes levied under a void statute, since the citizen should know that its invalidity is a complete defense and that he could not be coerced into making payment.[60] So also where there

Suppl. 454 [*affirmed* in 67 N. Y. App. Div. 619, 73 N. Y. Suppl. 1149].

Ohio.— Mays *v.* Cincinnati, 1 Ohio St. 268; Wehmer *v.* Hamilton County Treasurer, 11 Ohio Dec. (Reprint) 190, 25 Cinc. L. Bul. 165; Adams Express Co. *v.* Cincinnati Gas Light Co., 10 Ohio Dec. (Reprint) 389, 21 Cinc. L. Bul. 18.

Oregon.— Johnson *v.* Crook County, 53 Oreg. 329, 100 Pac. 294; Eugene *v.* Lane County, 50 Oreg. 468, 93 Pac. 255.

Pennsylvania.— Taylor *v.* Philadelphia Bd. of Health, 31 Pa. St. 73, 72 Am. Dec. 724; Christ Church Hospital *v.* Philadelphia County, 24 Pa. St. 229; Meylert *v.* Sullivan County, 19 Pa. St. 181; Patterson *v.* Philadelphia, 5 Pa. Co. Ct. 626; Luzerne County *v.* Com., 15 Montg. Co. Rep. 153.

Rhode Island.— Matteson *v.* Warwick, etc., Water Co., 28 R. I. 570, 68 Atl. 577.

Tennessee.— Cincinnati, etc., R. Co. *v.* Hamilton County, 120 Tenn. 1, 113 S. W. 361; Nashville, etc., R. Co. *v.* Marion County, 120 Tenn. 347, 108 S. W. 1058; Union, etc., Bank *v.* Memphis, 107 Tenn. 66, 64 S. W. 13; Dickins *v.* Jones, 6 Yerg. 483, 27 Am. Dec. 488.

Texas.— Gaar *v.* Shannon, (Civ. App. 1909) 115 S. W. 361; Moller *v.* Galveston, 23 Tex. Civ. App. 693, 57 S. W. 1116.

Wyoming.— Moore *v.* Sweetwater County, 2 Wyo. 8.

United States.— Elliott *v.* Swartwout, 10 Pet. 137, 9 L. ed. 373; Kentucky Bank *v.* Stone, 88 Fed. 383 [*affirmed* without opinion in 174 U. S. 799, 19 S. Ct. 881, 43 L. ed. 1187]; Corkle *v.* Maxwell, 7 Fed. Cas. No. 3,231, 3 Blatchf. 413.

Canada.— Street *v.* Lambton County, 12 U. C. C. P. 294; Grantham *v.* Toronto, 3 U. C. Q. B. 212; Bogie *v.* Montreal, 16 Quebec Super. Ct. 593.

See 45 Cent. Dig. tit. "Taxation," § 999.

Compare Riker *v.* Jersey City, 38 N. J. L. 225, 20 Am. Rep. 386, holding that a voluntary payment of taxes may be recovered back where the assessment has been set aside by a judicial decision.

55. Indianapolis *v.* Morris, 25 Ind. App. 409, 58 N. E. 510; Bankers' Life Assoc. *v.* Douglas County, 61 Nebr. 202, 85 N. W. 54; People *v.* Madison County, 51 N. Y. 442. Under Iowa Code, § 1417, requiring the board of supervisors to direct the treasurer to refund to the taxpayer any tax erroneously or illegally exacted or paid, a taxpayer may recover in an action at law taxes erroneously or illegally exacted or paid, although paid voluntarily and without protest. Slimmer *v.* Chickasaw County, 140 Iowa 448, 118 N. W. 779.

56. **Presumption that payment was voluntary** see *infra*, IX, C, 6, g.

57. Falvey *v.* Hennepin County, 76 Minn. 257, 79 N. W. 302; Barney, etc., Mfg. Co. *v.* Montgomery County, 11 Ohio Dec. (Reprint) 790, 29 Cinc. L. Bul. 366.

58. Wills *v.* Austin, 53 Cal. 152; Santa Rosa Bank *v.* Chalfant, 52 Cal. 170; Brazil *v.* Kress, 55 Ind. 14; Edinburg *v.* Hackney, 54 Ind. 83; Lima Tp. *v.* Jenks, 20 Ind. 301; Jenks *v.* Lima Tp., 17 Ind. 326; Feist *v.* New York, 74 N. Y. App. Div. 627, 77 N. Y. Suppl. 517; Drake *v.* Shurtliff, 24 Hun (N. Y.) 422; Union Bank *v.* New York, 51 Barb. (N. Y.) 159 [*reversed* on other grounds in 51 N. Y. 638]. *Compare* Bellinger *v.* Gray, 51 N. Y. 610; Fishkill Landing First Nat. Bank *v.* Shuster, 2 Alb. L. J. 459. And see Williams *v.* Merritt, 152 Mich. 621, 116 N. W. 386; Johnson *v.* Crook County, 53 Oreg. 329, 100 Pac. 294; Nashville, etc., R. Co. *v.* Marion County, 120 Tenn. 347, 108 S. W. 1058; Cincinnati, etc., R. Co. *v.* Hamilton County, 120 Tenn. 1, 113 S. W. 361. A payment of taxes in order to be involuntary, so as to entitle the taxpayer to recover them for illegality, must be made on compulsion to prevent an immediate seizure of the taxpayer's goods or the arrest of his person; mere threats of litigation or apprehension of levy of distress warrants being insufficient. Cincinnati, etc., R. Co. *v.* Hamilton County, *supra*. To make a payment of taxes involuntary, it must appear that the officer authorized to collect the same had in his hands process authorizing the seizure of the person or property of the taxpayer, that such seizure was imminent, and that there were no other legal means of protecting the person or property than by payment; and under such circumstances payment under protest saves the rights of a taxpayer to recover if the taxes are illegal. Nashville, etc., R. Co. *v.* Marion County, *supra*.

59. Palomares Land Co. *v.* Los Angeles County, 146 Cal. 530, 80 Pac. 931; Lee *v.* Templeton, 13 Gray (Mass.) 476; Ostrum *v.* San Antonio, 30 Tex. Civ. App. 462, 71 N. W. 304.

60. Lange *v.* Soffell, 33 Ill. App. 624; Detroit *v.* Martin, 34 Mich. 170, 22 Am. Rep.

b. Requisites and Sufficiency of Protest. If the statute does not require a protest to be in writing, no particular formality in making it is necessary;[82] but if a written protest is required, the statute is not satisfied by an oral objection, even though accompanied by a memorandum written on the tax bill or on the margin of the assessment roll.[83] If in writing, the protest should not be couched in general terms, but should state distinctly and specifically the grounds on which the taxpayer objects to the legality of the tax,[84] except that it need not set forth facts of which the tax collector has notice, or which he is bound to know, officially.[85]

6. Actions or Proceedings For Recovery of Taxes — a. Nature and Form of Remedy. The proper remedy for the recovery of taxes paid is an action at law in the form of assumpsit as for money had and received,[86] unless some other remedy is provided by statute,[87] not a proceeding in equity.[88] Where a taxpayer brings an action under a statute to recover interest on taxes wrongfully exacted, it cannot recover independently thereof.[89]

b. Conditions Precedent. It may or may not be a condition precedent to the maintenance of an action to recover back taxes paid that plaintiff shall first have applied to the board of equalization or review for such relief as it could afford,[90] or that he shall have endeavored to have the assessment vacated or set aside,[91] these matters depending on the local statutes. But in the absence of a statute specifically requiring it, it is not necessary that plaintiff shall have made a formal demand for the restoration of the taxes or exhibited or submitted his claim to the local officers.[92]

Hamilton County, 120 Tenn. 1, 113 S. W. 361.

Texas.— Gaar *v.* Shannon, (Civ. App. 1909) 115 S. W. 361.

Washington.— Montgomery *v.* Cowlitz County, 14 Wash. 230, 44 Pac. 259.

United States.— Oceanic Steamship Co. *v.* Tappan, 18 Fed. Cas. No. 10,405, 16 Blatchf. 296. *Compare,* however, Herold *v.* Kahn, 159 Fed. 608, 86 C. C. A. 598, 163 Fed. 947, 90 C. C. A. 307.

Canada.—Benjamin *v.* Elgin County Corp., 26 U. C. Q. B. 660.

See 45 Cent. Dig. tit. "Taxation," § 1003.

82. Lyon *v.* Guthard, 52 Mich. 271, 17 N. W. 839; Custer County *v.* Chicago, etc., R. Co., 62 Nebr. 657, 87 N. W. 341.

83. Kehe *v.* Blackhawk County, 125 Iowa 549, 101 N. W. 281; Knowles *v.* Boston, 129 Mass. 551; Traverse Beach Assoc. *v.* Elmwood Tp., 142 Mich. 78, 105 N. W. 30; Phœbus *v.* Manhattan Social Club, 105 Va. 144, 52 S. E. 839. *Compare* Borland *v.* Boston, 132 Mass. 89, 42 Am. Rep. 424.

84. Mackay *v.* San Francisco, 128 Cal. 678, 61 Pac. 382; Meek *v.* McClure, 49 Cal. 623; Lingle *v.* Elmwood Tp., 142 Mich. 194, 105 N. W. 604; Whitney *v.* Port Huron, 88 Mich. 268, 50 N. W. 316, 26 Am. St. Rep. 291; Peninsula Iron Co. *v.* Crystal Falls Tp., 60 Mich. 79, 26 N. W. 840; Bankers' L. Assoc. *v.* Douglas County, 61 Nebr. 202, 85 N. W. 54; Davis *v.* Otoe County, 55 Nebr. 677, 76 N. W. 465. *Compare* Rumford Chemical Works *v.* Ray, 19 R. I. 456, 34 Atl. 814.

85. Smith *v.* Farrelly, 52 Cal. 77; Mason *v.* Johnson, 51 Cal. 612; Centennial Eureka Min. Co. *v.* Juab County, 22 Utah 395, 62 Pac. 1024.

86. *Alabama.*— Raisler *v.* Athens, 66 Ala. 194.

Illinois.— Chicago *v.* Klinkert, 94 Ill. App. 524.

Michigan.— Michigan Sanitarium, etc., Assoc. *v.* Battle Creek, 138 Mich. 676, 101 N. W. 855; Daniels *v.* Watertown Tp., 55 Mich. 376, 21 N. W. 350; Grand Rapids *v.* Blakely, 40 Mich. 367, 29 Am. Rep. 539.

Nebraska.—Turner *v.* Althaus, 6 Nebr. 54.

New York.— Guaranty Trust Co. *v.* New York, 108 N. Y. App. Div. 192, 95 N. Y. Suppl. 770; Dale *v.* New York, 71 N. Y. App. Div. 227, 75 N. Y. Suppl. 576, 1123.

See 45 Cent. Dig. tit. "Taxation," § 1006.

87. See *supra,* IX, C, 2.

Special remedy provided by statute see Adams *v.* Monroe County, 154 N. Y. 619, 49 N. E. 144.

Proceedings for refund see *supra,* IX, B, 4.

88. Crawford *v.* Bradford, 23 Fla. 404, 2 So. 782; Kimball *v.* Merchants' Sav., etc., Co., 89 Ill. 611.

89. Home Sav. Bank *v.* Morris, 141 Iowa 560, 120 N. W. 100.

90. See the statutes of the different states. And see the following cases:

Michigan.— Michigan Sav. Bank *v.* Detroit, 107 Mich. 246, 65 N. W. 101.

Montana.— Barrett *v.* Shannon, 19 Mont. 397, 48 Pac. 746.

New York.— Citizens' Sav. Bank *v.* New York, 166 N. Y. 594, 59 N. E. 1120 [*affirming* 37 N. Y. App. Div. 560, 56 N. Y. Suppl. 295].

Tennessee.— Ward *v.* Alsup, 100 Tenn. 619, 46 S. W. 573.

Texas.—Hardesty *v.* Fleming, 57 Tex. 395.

91. See Clarke *v.* Stearns County, 66 Minn. 304, 69 N. W. 25; Jex *v.* New York, 103 N. Y. 536, 9 N. E. 39; Bruecher *v.* Port Chester, 101 N. Y. 240, 4 N. E. 272.

92. *Arkansas.*— State *v.* Thompson, 10 Ark. 61.

belief of ownership, the statute begins to run from the end of the litigation which settles the question of title.[96]

d. Parties Plaintiff. The proper plaintiff in an action of this kind is the person who is ultimately entitled to the money if it shall be recovered.[97] In some states one taxpayer is allowed to bring such a suit in behalf of himself and of all other persons similarly interested; [98] but in such case plaintiff must have a substantial interest in the controversy, and he cannot assume to represent others if his own pecuniary interest is a mere trifle.[99]

e. Defendants. An action for the recovery of illegal taxes paid to a collector or other receiving officer may be maintained against such officer personally if he still has the money in his possession.[1] But after he has paid it over to the proper officers of the county or other municipal corporation his own responsibility is at an end, and the suit should then be brought against the municipality.[2] In the

96. Goodnow *v.* Wells, 78 Iowa 760, 38 N. W. 172; Wood *v.* Curran, 76 Iowa 560, 41 N. W. 214; Goodnow *v.* Oakley, 68 Iowa 25, 25 N. W. 912; Bradley *v.* Cole, 67 Iowa 650, 25 N. W. 849; Goodnow *v.* Litchfield, 63 Iowa 275, 19 N. W. 226; Goodnow *v.* Stryker, 62 Iowa 221, 14 N. W. 345, 17 N. W. 506; Goodnow *v.* Moulton, 51 Iowa 555, 2 N. W. 395.

97. Shoemaker *v.* Grant County, 36 Ind. 175; Schultze *v.* New York, 103 N. Y. 307, 8 N. E. 528; Bristol *v.* Morganton, 125 N. C. 365, 34 S. E. 512; Norfolk, etc., R. Co. *v.* Smyth County, 87 Va. 521, 12 S. E. 1009.

Where a bank has paid taxes on shares of its stock, an action to recover the payment may be maintained in the name of the bank without joining the stock-holders. State Nat. Bank *v.* Memphis, 116 Tenn. 641, 94 S. W. 606, 7 L. R. A. N. S. 663.

Action by consignee.— Where an inhabitant of a town is taxed on his property and the assessors include therein property which he holds as consignee of another person, he cannot maintain an action against the town to recover back the amount of the tax on the property held by him as consignee. Stickney *v.* Bangor, 30 Me. 404.

98. Whaley *v.* Com., 110 Ky. 154, 61 S. W. 35, 23 Ky. L. Rep. 1292; Kilbourne *v.* Allyn, 7 Lans. (N. Y.) 352 [*affirmed* in 59 N. Y. 21, 17 Am. Rep. 291]. *Contra*, Jackson Tp. *v.* Thoman, 51 Ohio St. 285, 37 N. E. 523.

99. Sparks *v.* Robinson, 115 Ky. 453, 74 S. W. 176, 24 Ky. L. Rep. 2336; Hawkins *v.* Nicholas County, 89 S. W. 484, 28 Ky. L. Rep. 479.

1. *Dakota.*— Rushton *v.* Burke, 6 Dak. 478, 43 N. W. 815.

Kansas.— Pawnee County *v.* Atchison, etc., R. Co., 21 Kan. 748.

Kentucky.— Owen County Fiscal Ct. *v.* F. & A. Cox Co., 132 Ky. 738, 117 S. W. 296; Com. *v.* Baske, 124 Ky. 468, 99 S. W. 316, 30 Ky. L. Rep. 400; Com. *v.* Stone, 114 Ky. 511, 71 S. W. 428, 24 Ky. L. Rep. 1297; Whaley *v.* Com., 110 Ky. 154, 61 S. W. 35, 23 Ky. L. Rep. 1292; Blair *v.* Carlisle, etc., Turnpike Co., 4 Bush 157; First Nat. Bank *v.* Christian County, 106 S. W. 831, 32 Ky. L. Rep. 634.

Michigan.— Lyon *v.* Guthard, 52 Mich. 271, 17 N. W. 839.

Ohio.— Hornberger *v.* Case, 9 Ohio Dec. (Reprint) 434, 13 Cinc. L. Bul. 511; Herzberg *v.* Willey, 9 Ohio Dec. (Reprint) 426, 13 Cinc. L. Bul. 334.

Rhode Island.— Lindsay *v.* Allen, 19 R. I. 721, 36 Atl. 840.

Wyoming.— Powder River Cattle Co. *v.* Johnson County, 3 Wyo. 597, 29 Pac. 361, 31 Pac. 278.

See 45 Cent. Dig. tit. "Taxation," § 1011.

2. *California.*— Craig *v.* Boone, 146 Cal. 718, 81 Pac. 22.

Iowa.— Ottumwa Independent Dist. *v.* Taylor, 100 Iowa 617, 69 N. W. 1009.

Kansas.— St. Louis, etc., R. Co. *v.* Labette County, (1901) 66 Pac. 1045.

Kentucky.— Com. *v.* Donnelly, 85 S. W. 720, 27 Ky. L. Rep. 454. *Compare* Com. *v.* Baske, 124 Ky. 468, 99 S. W. 316, 30 Ky. L. Rep. 400.

Minnesota.— Dakota County *v.* Parker, 7 Minn. 267.

Mississippi.— Tuttle *v.* Everett, 51 Miss. 27, 24 Am. Rep. 622.

Missouri.— Loring *v.* St. Louis, 80 Mo. 461; Davis *v.* Bader, 54 Mo. 168; Lewis County *v.* Tate, 10 Mo. 650.

New York.— Chegaray *v.* New York, 2 Duer 521 [*reversed* on other grounds in 13 N. Y. 220]; Robinson *v.* Brooklyn, 9 N. Y. St. 716.

Rhode Island.—See Fish *v.* Higbee, 22 R. I. 223, 47 Atl. 212.

Texas.— Hardesty *v.* Fleming, 57 Tex. 395.

Wisconsin.— Kellogg *v.* Winnebago County, 42 Wis. 97.

Wyoming.— Kelley *v.* Rhoads, 7 Wyo. 237. 51 Pac. 593, 75 Am. St. Rep. 904, 39 L. R. A. 594. See Johnson County *v.* Searight Cattle Co., 3 Wyo. 777, 31 Pac. 268.

See 45 Cent. Dig. tit. "Taxation," § 1011.

Compare Olney *v.* Gaddis, 90 Ill. App. 622; Kimball *v.* Corn Exch. Nat. Bank, 1 Ill. App. 209; Foss *v.* Whitehouse, 94 Me. 491, 48 Atl. 109.

No action against county.— In some jurisdictions no action can be maintained by a taxpayer against a county for taxes wrongfully collected, whether the taxes have been paid out by the county or not, no right of action being given by statute. Owen County Fiscal Ct. *v.* F. & A. Cox Co., 132 Ky. 738. 117 S. W. 296; First Nat. Bank *v.* Christian County, 106 S. W. 831, 32 Ky. L. Rep. 634.

Money paid over to state.— In an action

before suit brought, if that is required by the statute.[9] The plea or answer should meet specifically the allegations of the complaint and raise an issue.[10]

g. Evidence. The presumption is in favor of the validity of tax laws and of the regularity of official action taken under them; and the burden is on plaintiff to prove the illegality of the tax or other grounds on which he particularly relies to establish his right to recover back the amount he has paid in the form of taxes.[11] In particular, he must prove the fact of payment to the officer authorized by law to receive the taxes,[12] and that the payment was not voluntary, but was made

the sheriff, in obedience to a warrant attached to the roll, notified plaintiff of the tax specified, that the exaction was just and due, and unless it was paid, he would "in due time" collect it by sale of the property, but which nowhere alleged that the sheriff was either in the act of selling, or that he threatened immediately to do so, or that plaintiff, believing that the menace would be instantly executed, was by the abrupt urgency ensnared into meeting the payment, or that he had no other expedient of freeing his property. Johnson *v.* Crook County, 53 Oreg. 329, 100 Pac. 294.

9. Custer County *v.* Chicago, etc., R. Co., 62 Nebr. 657, 87 N. W. 341; Richmond, etc., R. Co. *v.* Reidsville, 109 N. C. 494, 13 S. E. 865; Chicago, etc., R. Co. *v.* Langlade, 55 Wis. 116, 12 N. W. 357.

Necessity of demand before suit see *supra*, IX, C, 6, b.

10. Savings, etc., Soc. *v.* San Francisco, 146 Cal. 673, 80 Pac. 1086; Clark *v.* Greene, 23 R. I. 118, 52 Atl. 889.

11. *California.*— Savings, etc., Soc. *v.* San Francisco, 146 Cal. 673, 80 Pac. 1086.

Connecticut.— Where it was not shown that a tax was larger than it would have been had the average amount of goods kept on hand for sale during the year been taken in making the assessment of a trading business, as required by Conn. Gen. St. (1902) § 2342, nor that goods on hand at the date of the assessment was not the average amount kept during the year, the court could not assume that any part of the tax was excessive. Jackson *v.* Union, 82 Conn. 266, 73 Atl. 773.

Georgia.— Douglasville *v.* Johns, 62 Ga. 423.

Maine.— Portland, etc., R. Co. *v.* Saco, 60 Me. 196.

Massachusetts.— All Saints Parish *v.* Brookline, 178 Mass. 404, 59 N. E. 1003, 52 L. R. A. 778. And see Masonic Education, etc., Trust *v.* Boston, 201 Mass. 320, 87 N. E. 602.

Michigan.— Turnbull *v.* Alpena Tp., 74 Mich. 621, 42 N. W. 114. See Ward *v.* Echo Tp., 145 Mich. 56, 108 N. W. 364.

Nebraska.— Davis *v.* Otoe County, 55 Nebr. 677, 76 N. W. 465.

New York.— See Matter of Medina, 52 Misc. 621, 103 N. Y. Suppl. 1018 [*affirmed* in 121 N. Y. App. Div. 929, 106 N. Y. Suppl. 1148].

Ohio.— Hamilton County *v.* Wood, 7 Ohio Dec. (Reprint) 533, 3 Cinc. L. Bul. 841; Perrin *v.* County Com'rs, 6 Ohio Dec. (Reprint) 1085, 10 Am. L. Rec. 311.

Rhode Island.— Warwick, etc., Water Co. *v.* Carr, 24 R. I. 226, 52 Atl. 1030.

Wyoming.— Marks *v.* Uinta County, 11 Wyo. 488, 72 Pac. 894.

See 45 Cent. Dig. tit. "Taxation," § 1013.

Illegality of tax.— A decree of a court adjudging the tax to be void and reciting the presence of both parties by counsel is sufficient proof of such invalidity. Gage *v.* Saginaw, 128 Mich. 682, 84 N. W. 1100, 87 N. W. 1027. But where the ground of objection is that the tax was levied in part for an illegal object, it is not necessary to show that the money was applied to that object. Gillette *v.* Hartford, 31 Conn. 351. And see Cresswell Ranch, etc., Co. *v.* Roberts County, (Tex. Civ. App. 1894) 27 S. W. 737.

Fraudulent or arbitrary overvaluation see Solomon *v.* Oscoda Tp., 77 Mich. 365, 43 N. W. 990; Galveston County *v.* Galveston Gas Co., 72 Tex. 509, 10 S. W. 583; Ostrum *v.* San Antonio, 30 Tex. Civ. App. 462, 71 S. W. 304; Home F. Ins. Co. *v.* Lynch, 19 Utah 189, 56 Pac. 681; Carlisle *v.* Chehalis County, 32 Wash. 284, 73 Pac. 349.

Exemption of property see Stony Wold Sanatorium *v.* Keese, 112 N. Y. App. Div. 738, 98 N. Y. Suppl. 1088.

Non-residence of plaintiff see Bailey *v.* Buell, 59 Barb. (N. Y.) 158 [*reversed* in 50 N. Y. 662].

Time of payment see Lingle *v.* Elmwood Tp., 142 Mich. 194, 105 N. W. 604.

Verified statement of taxpayer as ground of estoppel see Centennial Eureka Min. Co. *v.* Juab County, 22 Utah 395, 62 Pac. 1024.

Condition precedent to power to tax.— If a charitable corporation omits after notice from the assessors to bring in the list and statement of all real and personal estate held by it for charitable purposes required by Mass. Rev. Laws, c. 12, § 41, the corporation under section 5, clause 3, of the same chapter, still is exempt from taxation for that year unless such omission was wilful, and, in an action brought by it against a city to recover a tax paid under protest, the burden of proving that such an omission was wilful is on defendant. Masonic Education, etc., Trust *v.* Boston, 201 Mass. 320, 87 N. E. 602.

Evidence held sufficient see Rice *v.* Muskegon, 150 Mich. 679, 114 N. W. 661.

12. Smith *v.* Readfield, 27 Me. 145; Daniels *v.* Watertown Tp., 55 Mich. 376, 21 N. W. 350.

Election and qualification.— If payment was made to the proper officer plaintiff need not prove that he was legally elected and qualified. Hathaway *v.* Addison, 48 Me. 440.

this shall be accomplished,[22] and from time to time to change the same, in its discretion, there being no such thing as a vested right in the continuance of a mere remedy,[23] subject only to the limitation that the taxpayer shall not be deprived of his property without due process of law,[24] and that, whatever methods of collecting the taxes are ordained, they shall apply uniformly to all persons or property of the same class or kind.[25] The regulation of administrative details in the collection of the taxes levied by counties and other municipal divisions may, to a limited extent, be left to the determination of the local authorities.[26]

b. Constitutional and Statutory Provisions. Constitutional directions as to the collection of taxes must of course be observed and obeyed by the legislature,[27] but otherwise, as above stated, its discretion is practically unlimited.[28] The repeal of a statute providing for the levy and collection of taxes will not operate retrospectively so as to affect unpaid taxes already due or pending proceedings for their collection.[29] And the repealing effect of a new tax law will be confined within narrow limits, so that it will not be held to abrogate laws applicable to particular localities nor the details of previous general laws which are not clearly in conflict with it.[30]

2. APPOINTMENT, QUALIFICATION, AND TENURE OF COLLECTORS — **a. Creation and Abolition of Office.** If the constitution creates the office of tax collector, or names the officer who shall act in that capacity, its provisions cannot be varied in the least degree by the legislature.[31] But otherwise it belongs to the legislature to create this office and to abolish and change it at pleasure, although the effect may be that persons lawfully acting as tax collectors shall be legislated out of their office.[32] Authority may also be given to cities or other municipal corporations to create the office of tax collector, for their own purposes, and to prescribe his duties, but such authorization must be strictly pursued.[33]

b. Eligibility. Whatever may be prescribed by law as the qualifications of a

22. State *v.* Certain Lands, 40 Ark. 35; Lucas *v.* Purdy, 142 Iowa 359, 120 N. W. 1063; State *v.* Milburn, 9 Gill (Md.) 97; State *v.* Illinois, etc., Bridge Co., 73 Mo. 442.

23. *In re* Elizabeth, 49 N. J. L. 488, 10 Atl. 363.

24. Griswold College *v.* Davenport, 65 Iowa 633, 22 N. W. 904; Cincinnati, etc., R. Co. *v.* Kentucky, 115 U. S. 321, 6 S. Ct. 57, 29 L. ed. 414.

25. McComb *v.* Bell, 2 Minn. 295; Com. *v.* Swab, 8 Pa. Co. Ct. 111.

26. Southern R. Co. *v.* Kay, 62 S. C. 28, 39 S. E. 785. And see Pittsburgh, etc., R. Co. *v.* Harden, 137 Ind. 486, 37 N. E. 324, holding that an authority to county commissioners to suspend the collection of taxes against a railroad until the road is sufficiently advanced to justify them in collecting the taxes carries with it authority subsequently to order their collection on compliance by the road with the conditions required by law.

27. See *supra*, II, A.

28. See *supra*, X, A, 1, a.

29. *Arkansas.*— State *v.* Certain Lands, 40 Ark. 35.

California.— Oakland *v.* Whipple, 44 Cal. 303.

Louisiana.— Gaither *v.* Green, 40 La. Ann. 362, 4 So. 210.

Missouri.— State *v.* Rainey, 74 Mo. 229.

Pennsylvania.— Com. *v.* Honey Brook Coal Co., 2 Pearson 365.

Washington.— Washington Nat. Bank *v.* King County, 9 Wash. 607, 38 Pac. 219. See Spokane County *v.* Northern Pac. R. Co., 5 Wash. 89, 31 Pac. 420.

See 45 Cent. Dig. tit. "Taxation," § 1018.

Compare Gorley *v.* Sewell, 77 Ind. 316.

30. *Connecticut.*—Atwater *v.* O'Reilly, 81 Conn. 367, 71 Atl. 505.

Illinois.— Brown *v.* Hogle, 30 Ill. 119.

Pennsylvania.— Evans *v.* Phillipi, 117 Pa. St. 226, 11 Atl. 630, 2 Am. St. Rep. 655; Bitting *v.* Com., 7 Pa. Cas. 545, 12 Atl. 29; Com. *v.* Scheckler, 1 Pa. Co. Ct. 505; Cooper *v.* Newcomer, 6 Lanc. L. Rev. 9; *In re* Election in Upper Leacock Tp., 3 Lanc. L. Rev. 225. *Compare* Com. *v.* Topper, 219 Pa. 221, 68 Atl. 666.

Texas.— Harrington *v.* Galveston County, 1 Tex. App. Civ. Cas. § 792.

Washington.— State *v.* Purdy, 14 Wash. 243, 44 Pac. 857.

Compare State *v.* Milburn, 9 Gill (Md.) 97.

31. Mutual L. Ins. Co. *v.* Martien, 27 Mont. 437, 71 Pac. 470.

32. State *v.* Lavigne, 23 La. Ann. 111. And see People *v.* Crooks, 53 N. Y. 648; Com. *v.* Topper, 219 Pa. St. 221, 68 Atl. 666, holding that Pa. Act, June 25, 1885 (Pamphl. Laws 187), providing for the election of a collector of taxes, supersedes the office of collector of school taxes under the former system, and the new officer is the only person authorized to collect taxes of any kind.

33. People *v.* Bedell, 2 Hill (N. Y.) 196; Hamilton County *v.* Arnold, 65 Ohio St. 479, 63 N. E. 81; State *v.* Strong, (Tenn. Ch.

g. Duration and Tenure of Office. A collector of taxes may generally enter upon the exercise of his office as soon as he has taken the oath and given the bond,[57] and he is entitled to retain his office for the full term for which he was elected or appointed,[58] and ordinarily until his successor is elected or appointed and qualified.[59] But he may resign and withdraw from the office,[60] and, subject to special statutory provisions in that behalf, he may be suspended or removed from office, either by the governor of the state or by the power to which he owes his appointment, if he is guilty of misconduct in office.[61] And the office of tax collector may become vacant where residence within a certain district is essential and the incumbent ceases to be a resident.[62]

h. Deputies and Assistants. Unless it be contrary to the statute, a collector of taxes may appoint deputies or assistants to aid him in discharging the duties of his office.[63] But he must be responsible for their collections,[64] and he may maintain a private action against a deputy for money collected by the latter and not paid over.[65]

3. COMPENSATION OF COLLECTORS — a. Right to Compensation — (I) *IN GENERAL.* A tax collector is entitled to fees or commissions only in the cases and to the extent prescribed by the statute; and if the law makes no provision for his compensation in respect to particular services rendered or the collection of particular taxes, he can claim none.[66] If the sheriff or treasurer of a county is *ex*

57. Falconer *v.* Shores, 37 Ark. 386.

58. Jimeson *v.* Cowperthwaite, 42 N. J. L. 159; People *v.* Hardy, 8 Utah 68, 29 Pac. 1118; Hadley *v.* Chamberlin, 11 Vt. 618.

Extending term of office see Beebe *v.* Robinson, 64 Ala. 171; People *v.* Crooks, 53 N. Y. 648.

Term of appointee by governor to fill vacancy see State *v.* Herring, 208 Mo. 708, 106 S. W. 984.

59. Haley *v.* Petty, 42 Ark. 392; People *v.* Woodruff, 32 N. Y. 355; Briggs *v.* Carr, 27 R. I. 477, 63 Atl. 487.

Delivery of tax books to successor in office see Price *v.* Adamson, 37 Mo. 145; Somers *v.* Burke County, 123 N. C. 582, 31 S. E. 873, 68 Am. St. Rep. 834; Ridgway Tp. *v.* Wheeler, 90 Pa. St. 450.

60. Spaulding *v.* Northumberland, 64 N. H. 153, 6 Atl. 642; Johnston *v.* Wilson, 2 N. H. 202, 9 Am. Dec. 50; Waters *v.* Edmondson, 8 Heisk. (Tenn.) 384.

61. *Alabama.*— Peck *v.* Holcombe, 3 Port. 329.

California.— Woods *v.* Varnum, 85 Cal. 639, 24 Pac. 843.

Florida.— State *v.* Johnson, 30 Fla. 499, 11 So. 855.

Georgia.— State *v.* Frazier, 48 Ga. 137.

Louisiana. — State *v.* Barrow, 29 La. Ann. 243; State *v.* Fisher, 26 La. Ann. 537; State *v.* Yoist, 25 La. Ann. 396.

Pennsylvania.— Com. *v.* Connor, 207 Pa. St. 263, 56 Atl. 443; Mattern *v.* Connor, 17 York Leg. Rec. 77.

See 45 Cent. Dig. tit. "Taxation," § 1038.

Compare Gorman *v.* Boise County, 1 Ida. 553; Hager *v.* Lucas, 120 Ky. 307, 86 S. W. 552, 27 Ky. L. Rep. 710.

62. Com. *v.* Topper, 219 Pa. St. 221, 68 Atl. 666.

63. Whitford *v.* Lynch, 10 Kan. 180; Prater *v.* Strother, 13 S. W. 252, 11 Ky. L. Rep. 831; Parker *v.* Southern Bank, 46 La. Ann. 563, 15 So. 200; Aldrich *v.* Aldrich, 8 Metc. (Mass.) 102. *Compare* Fremont County *v.* Brandon, 6 Ida. 482, 56 Pac. 264.

Bonds of deputy collectors see Post *v.* Sheppard, 4 Gill (Md.) 276; McCormick *v.* Fitch, 14 Minn. 252.

64. Evans *v.* State, 36 Tex. 323; Lee County Justices *v.* Fulkerson, 21 Gratt. (Va.) 182; Corbett *v.* Johnston, 11 U. C. C. P. 317.

65. Ratliff *v.* Ferguson, 86 Ky. 89, 5 S. W. 311, 9 Ky. L. Rep. 376; Box *v.* McKelvey, 8 Heisk. (Tenn.) 861.

66. *Alabama.*— Dunklin *v.* Gafford, 17 Ala. 814.

California.— Butte County *v.* Merrill, 141 Cal. 396, 74 Pac. 1036; People *v.* San Francisco, 28 Cal. 429.

Georgia.—Justices Fulton County Inferior Ct. *v.* Yoakum, 19 Ga. 611.

Idaho.— Gorman *v.* Boise County, 1 Ida. 647.

Illinois.— Mason County *v.* Mason, etc., Special Drain. Dist., 140 Ill. 539, 30 N. E. 676.

Indiana.— Paoli *v.* Charles, 164 Ind. 690, 74 N. E. 508.

Maryland.— Duvall *v.* Perkins, 77 Md. 582, 26 Atl. 1085.

Minnesota.— Chapel *v.* Ramsey County, 71 Minn. 18, 73 N. W. 520.

Nevada.— State *v.* Donnelly, 20 Nev. 214, 19 Pac. 680.

Pennsylvania.— Philadelphia *v.* Moore, 208 Pa. St. 327, 57 Atl. 710; Philadelphia *v.* McMichael, 208 Pa. St. 297, 57 Atl. 705; Kirkendall *v.* Luzerne County, 25 Pa. Super. Ct. 429.

South Dakota.— Centerville *v.* Turner County, 23 S. D. 424, 122 N. W. 350.

Washington.— State *v.* Mudgett, 21 Wash. 99, 57 Pac. 351.

West Virginia.— Hawkins *v.* Bare, 63 W. Va. 431, 60 S. E. 391.

See 45 Cent. Dig. tit. "Taxation," § 1043.

The same rule applies to mileage or travel fees incurred in enforcing the payment of taxes.[74]

(III) *As Between Successive Collectors.* As a rule a collector of taxes, or a sheriff in his capacity as a collector, is not entitled to commissions on taxes collected by his successor in office.[75] But an outgoing sheriff is entitled to the commissions on the amount of taxes he pays to his successor in office, as required by statute.[76] And it has been held under certain circumstances that where the substantial and responsible duties of the collector of back taxes were performed by one collector, while actual payment was made to his successor, the former was entitled to the statutory fees.[77]

b. Amount of Salary or Commissions. The amount receivable by a tax collector as salary, commissions, or fees is ordinarily regulated by statute, and the provisions of the law in this particular will be strictly followed and will be superior to any local ordinance or any private contract between the local authorities and the collector.[78] A statute allowing the tax collector a commission on the "sum

74. Thralls *v.* Sumner County, 24 Kan. 594; Labette County *v.* Franklin, 16 Kan. 450; Joslyn *v.* Tracy, 19 Vt. 569; Henry *v.* Tilson, 17 Vt. 479.

75. Union County *v.* Cowser, 24 Ark. 51, holding that a sheriff is not entitled to commissions except where he collects the taxes, and if he fails to take the tax book, and it is delivered to his successor, he has no claim for commissions on the taxes collected by his successor. See also Graves *v.* Bullen, (Tex. Civ. App. 1909) 115 S. W. 1177, holding that where plaintiff was legally elected collector of a county, he became entitled to the office and the emoluments thereof as soon as he took the oath of office and qualified. In the case last cited defendant, before retiring from the office of tax collector, executed, as paid, the tax receipts of a large number of taxpayers in the county, listed on his official tax roll. The taxes had not been paid or tendered, defendant's purpose being to advance the money and pay the taxes, holding the receipts as a personal claim for the money so advanced against the taxpayers, and thus benefit by the commissions after his term. When plaintiff qualified as tax collector, these receipts had not been removed from the office nor delivered by defendant to the taxpayers, nor the taxes paid either by them or by defendant, who, after retiring from the office, paid the taxes in full. It was held that such transaction was without authority, and that plaintiff was entitled to recover commissions on the taxes so paid.

Collector employed by treasurer.— A person employed or appointed by a county treasurer under Ohio Rev. St. § 2858, as collector of delinquent personal taxes, in making his contract of employment assumed the risk of the death of the treasurer appointing him, and of the loss of income which a revocation of his appointment by the successor of the treasurer would entail, and he was not entitled to commissions on taxes after the termination of his employment by the death of the treasurer appointing him, and revocation of his appointment by the successor, the right to compensation being coexistent with the right to hold the position. Brady *v.* French, 9 Ohio S. & C. Pl. Dec. 202, 6 Ohio N. P. 127.

76. Randolph County *v.* Trogden, 75 N. C. 350.

77. Watson *v.* Schnecko, 13 Mo. App. 208, holding that a collector who performed all preliminary duties as to the collection of back taxes, began a suit to recover them, and conducted it to judgment, was entitled to the commissions provided by the statutes, although he was not in office when the judgment was rendered and when the taxes were collected thereon.

Penalty accruing to officer demanding taxes as fee.— Under a statute to enforce the collection of taxes against banks, etc. (Ohio Act March 14, 1853), providing that if the taxes should remain unpaid until a certain day, the treasurer of the county should "forthwith demand payment of the amount of such taxes, and five per centum penalty thereon, which penalty shall be for the use of the treasurer," it was held that the treasurer making the demand was entitled to such penalty as fees, and might retain it, and might recover it from his successor if collected by the latter. It was said, however, that he was not entitled to the one per cent commission for collection of the taxes, as that accrued, if at all, to the treasurer who actually collected the money. Thomas *v.* Hamilton County Auditor, 6 Ohio St. 113.

78. *Arkansas.*—Wilson *v.* State, 51 Ark. 212, 10 S. W. 491.

California.—Alameda County *v.* Dalton, 148 Cal. 246, 82 Pac. 1050; Yolo County *v.* Colgan, 132 Cal. 265, 64 Pac. 403, 84 Am. St. Rep. 41; Orange County *v.* Harris, 97 Cal. 600, 32 Pac. 594; Swinnerton *v.* Monterey County, 76 Cal. 113, 18 Pac. 135; Faughnan *v.* Tuolumne County, 35 Cal. 133.

Florida.— State *v.* Drew, 16 Fla. 303.

Idaho.—Fremont County *v.* Brandon, 6 Ida. 482, 56 Pac. 264; Wickersham *v.* Elmore County, 4 Ida. 137, 36 Pac. 700; Cunningham *v.* Moody, 3 Ida. 125, 28 Pac. 395; Gorman *v.* Boise County, 1 Ida. 647.

Illinois.— Ryan *v.* People, 117 Ill. 486, 6 N. E. 37; Waukegan *v.* Foote, 91 Ill. App. 588.

the treasury the entire amount collected, and his compensation is then audited, allowed, and paid as other claims against the state or county.[84] And, although he has no lien on the money in his hands, he is a preferred creditor and entitled to prior payment out of the funds raised by his collections.[85]

4. AUTHORITY TO COLLECT[86] — **a. In General.** To constitute full authority for the collection of taxes, the person assuming that function must be the officer designated by statute or ordinance or commission,[87] and he must have been duly elected or appointed,[88] and have qualified for the office,[89] and must be provided with the necessary warrant or other process of authorization.[90] A tax collector

84. *Alabama.*— Shaver *v.* Robinson, 59 Ala. 195.

California.— Donahue *v.* El Dorado County, 49 Cal. 248.

Idaho.— Moscow *v.* Latah County, 5 Ida. 36, 46 Pac. 874; Wickersham *v.* Elmore County, 4 Ida. 137, 36 Pac. 700; Guheen *v.* Curtis, 3 Ida. 443, 31 Pac. 805; Cunningham *v.* Moody, 3 Ida. 125, 28 Pac. 395.

Louisiana.— Scarborough *v.* Stevens, 3 Rob. 147.

Maryland.— Allen *v.* State, 98 Md. 697, 57 Atl. 646; Seidenstricker *v.* State, 2 Gill 374.

Missouri.— State *v.* Smith, 13 Mo. App. 421.

Tennessee.— State *v.* Murphy, 101 Tenn. 515, 47 S. W. 1098; McLean *v.* State, 8 Heisk. 22; Winchester *v.* Slatter, 2 Heisk. 65.

Texas.— Dean *v.* State, 54 Tex. 313. See Bailey *v.* Aransas County, 46 Tex. Civ. App. 547, 102 S. W. 1159.

See 45 Cent. Dig. tit. "Taxation," § 1048.

Commissions on poll taxes.— The requirement of the Alabama constitution that the money derived from the poll tax shall be "exclusively" applied in aid of the school fund does not import that such tax shall not bear the expense of its own collection, but reference is intended to the net amount derived from such tax. Shaver *v.* Robinson, 59 Ala. 195.

Payment by county tax collector to contractor with county.— The fact that the tax collector of a county is not a party to a contract of the county with another person to pay him a certain per cent of all moneys collected by him on delinquen tax rolls does not affect the duty of the tax collector to obey an order of the commissioners' court to make payment to such other person according to such contract. Bailey *v.* Aransas County, 46 Tex. Civ. App. 547, 102 S. W. 1159.

85. Chapman *v.* Smith, 20 Ga. 572; Grimes *v.* Goodell, 3 Nev. 79.

86. **As dependent on time of payment** see *supra*, IX, A, 1, e.

De facto collectors see *supra*, X, 2, f.

87. *California.*— Mitchell *v.* Crosby, 46 Cal. 97.

Georgia.— Smith *v.* Goldsmith, 63 Ga. 736.

Indiana.— Burns Annot. St. (1901) § 7634, providing that the state auditor shall direct and superintend the collection of all moneys due the state, did not authorize such auditor to collect foreign insurance taxes, required to be paid into the "treasury of the state" by Burns Annot. St. (1901) § 7664. Sherrick *v.* State, 167 Ind. 345, 79 N. E. 193. See also Dailey *v.* State, 171 Ind. 646, 87 N. E. 4 [*transferred* from the appellate court, 42 Ind. App. 690, 86 N. E. 498].

Kentucky.— Com. *v.* Louisville Water Co., 132 Ky. 305, 116 S. W. 712; Com. *v.* Wade, 126 Ky. 791, 104 S. W. 965, 31 Ky. L. Rep. 1185.

Maryland.— Allegany County *v.* Union Min. Co., 61 Md. 545.

Nebraska.— Logan County *v.* Carnahan, 66 Nebr. 685, 92 N. W. 984, 95 N. W. 812.

Pennsylvania.— Com. *v.* Topper, 219 Pa. St. 221, 68 Atl. 666; Com. *v.* Connor, 207 Pa. St. 263, 56 Atl. 443.

See 45 Cent. Dig. tit. "Taxation," § 1051.

Authority by municipal ordinance.— A collector of taxes in a town under an ordinance must strictly follow its directions in his proceedings, and when acting under a special authority he must show affirmatively the warrant of his proceeding. Allen *v.* Scott, 13 Ill. 80.

Illegality of prior proceedings.— A collector is not excused from the performance of any duty as such by the illegality of the prior proceedings of the town, unless it prevents him from performing his duty safely. Kellar *v.* Savage, 17 Me. 444.

Organization of new county.— Where territory is detached from a county and organized into a new county, the treasurer of the old county cannot be required to collect from the taxpayers of the new county taxes levied prior to the division. State *v.* Clevenger, 27 Nebr. 422, 43 N. W. 243, 20 Am. St. Rep. 674.

88. Slade *v.* Governor, 14 N. C. 365; Dickey *v.* Alley, 12 N. C. 453; Lenoir *v.* Wellborn, 12 N. C. 451; Pottsville Borough Town Council's Appeal, 1 Mona. (Pa.) 705. And see *supra*, X, A, 2, d.

89. Baker *v.* Webber, 102 Me. 414, 67 Atl. 144. See *supra*, X, A, 2, e.

90. See *infra*, X, A, 4, e. And see Shaw *v.* Orr, 30 Iowa 355 (as to effect of temporary surrender of tax list to the county treasurer); Cadman *v.* Smith, 15 Okla. 633, 85 Pac. 346 (authority to proceed with the collection of taxes is derived from the warrant, not from the provisions of the statute); Texas, etc., R. Co. *v.* State, 43 Tex. Civ. App. 580, 97 S. W. 142.

Certification of levy.— It is the duty of the sheriff or collector of revenue to take notice of the levy of taxes by the fiscal court and to collect and distribute it as by law required, and a special certification of the levy is not

amount actually due from the collector to the public authorities and remaining unpaid.[39] But if the law imposes a penalty upon the collector for his delinquency, either in the form of liquidated damages or in the form of interest at an extraordinary rate, this also is included in the liability of the sureties.[40]

(IV) *TERM OR PERIOD COVERED.* Where a tax collector is elected or appointed for a limited term, the sureties on his bond are responsible only for his official acts within that term, and hence not for collections made after its expiration.[41] But it makes no difference that some of the money was collected before the bond was executed,[42] or that part of the taxes were imposed by a levy made after the giving of the bond, if within the collector's term.[43] Where the collector is continued in office for more than one term, but gives separate bonds with different sureties, the liability of the sureties is to be estimated the same as if a different

tain sum, although there is no specification as to him in the bond. People *v.* Love, 25 Cal. 520. Where the bond stipulates, in regard to the sureties, that "we or either of us will pay" the sum of ten thousand dollars, the fact that a sum of one or two thousand dollars is prefixed to the signatures of the sureties will not alter their joint and several liability as fixed by the terms of the instrument. Baker County *v.* Huntington, 48 Oreg 593, 87 Pac. 1036, 89 Pac. 144.

39. State *v.* Daspit, 30 La. Ann. 1112; Brunswick *v.* Snow, 73 Me. 177, holding that where a collector fails to pay over taxes collected, the measure of the liability of the sureties is the amount actually collected as taxes and interest, and interest thereon from the date of demand, less payments made by the collector, and also deducting the compensation of the collector for collections actually made and paid over.

Interest see Hartford *v.* Franey, 47 Conn. 76; Com. *v.* Carson, 26 Pa. Super. Ct. 437. Under Ballinger & C. Comp. Oreg. § 4595, allowing interest on moneys after the same become due, interest cannot be allowed on a disputed claim until judgment is rendered, whether the dispute is as to the fact of liability or only as to the amount, and therefore, when the sureties on the bond of a sheriff as tax collector controverted their liability for his default, although acknowledging the extent of his defalcation, it was held that interest was not allowable on the demand against them until its liquidation by judgment Baker County *v.* Huntington, 48 Oreg. 593, 87 Pac. 1036, 89 Pac. 144.

Commissions of collector see State *v.* Perkins, 114 La. 301, 38 So. 196.

Credits.—Where, in an action against the sureties of a sheriff on his bond as tax collector for a devastavit in the collection of taxes, it was conceded that he had not previously received credit for certain claims payable out of the levies of prior years, which he in fact paid out of the taxes of 1905 collected by him, his sureties were entitled to credit for such claims as against the amount of the sheriff's liability for that year. Ætna Indem. Co. *v.* Lawrence County, 107 S. W. 339, 32 Ky. L. Rep. 894.

40. *Arkansas.*—Christian *v.* Ashley County, 24 Ark 142.

Illinois.— Tappan *v.* People, 67 Ill. 339.

Louisiana.— State *v.* Breed. 10 La. Ann. 491.

South Carolina.— State *v.* Harrison, Harp. 88. But *compare* State Treasurers *v.* Hilliard, 8 Rich. 412.

Tennessee.— McLean *v.* State, 8 Heisk. 22.

See 45 Cent. Dig. tit. "Taxation," § 1106.

41. *Alabama.*— Brewer *v.* King, 63 Ala. 511.

Illinois.—Walker *v.* People, 95 Ill. App. 637.

Maine.— Trescott *v.* Moan, 50 Me. 347.

Maryland.— Johnson *v.* State, 3 Harr. & M. 223.

Mississi pi.— Montgomery *v.* Governor, 7 How. 68.

Missouri.— Moss *v.* State, 10 Mo. 338, 47 Am. Dec. 116.

New Jersey.— Freehold Tp. *v.* Patterson, 38 N. J. L. 255.

North Carolina.— Prince *v.* McNeill, 77 N. C. 398; Coffield *v.* McNeill, 74 N. C. 535.

Tennessee.— Maddox *v.* Shacklett, (Ch. App. 1895) 36 S. W. 731; State *v.* Orr, 12 Lea 725; Chandler *v.* State, 1 Lea 296; Allison *v.* State, 8 Heisk. 312; McLean *v.* State, 8 Heisk. 22.

See 45 Cent. Dig. tit. "Taxation," § 1107.

Contra.— Com. *v.* Stambaugh, 164 Pa. St. 437, 30 Atl. 293. But *compare* Sullivan County *v.* Middendorf, 7 Pa. Super. Ct. 71.

Collector reëlected but not qualified.— Where a collector gave a bond conditioned that "during his continuance in said office" he would well and truly pay over all money collected, etc., and was reëlected in the following year but failed to qualify, although he continued to perform the duties of the office, it was held that his sureties were liable for the money collected by him in such following year. Lynn *v.* Cumberland, 77 Md. 449, 26 Atl. 1001.

42. Fidelity, etc., Co. *v.* Com., 104 Ky. 579, 47 S. W. 579, 49 S. W. 467; Combs *v.* Breathitt County, 38 S. W. 138, 39 S. W. 33, 18 Ky. L. Rep. 809; Hudson *v.* Miles, 185 Mass. 582, 71 N. E. 63, 102 Am. St. Rep. 370; Harris *v.* State, 55 Miss. 50; Conover *v.* Middletown Tp., 42 N. J. L. 382.

43. Grayham *v.* Washington County Ct., 9 Dana (Ky.) 182; State *v.* Kelley, 43 Tex. 667.

person had been appointed to fill the second term,[44] although some of the decisions hold that if the collector has in his hands, at the beginning of the second term, public money which he has not accounted for, the sureties on the bond for the second term are liable for it.[45]

(v) *Breach of Condition* — (a) *Payment Without Authority.* If the tax collector pays over the money in his hands to any person other than the officer authorized by law to receive it, it is a breach of the condition of his bond; and even if the municipality entitled to the taxes eventually receives the whole of the money, he is still liable in nominal damages.[46]

(b) *Failure to Pay Over Collections.* The collector and his sureties are liable for taxes received by him and which he has failed to pay over at the appointed time;[47] and it is immaterial, so far as respects the liability of the sureties, whether he had a warrant or other lawful authority to make the collection; if the taxes have been voluntarily paid to him, it is his duty to account for them, and failure to do so is a breach of the condition of the bond.[48]

44. Crawford *v.* Carson, 35 Ark. 565; U. S. *v.* Eckford, 1 How. (U. S.) 250, 11 L. ed. 120.

Apportionment of liability among different sets of sureties.— In suits on the bonds of a collector of taxes to recover a deficiency in his accounts, extending over three years, there being no evidence as to precisely when the deficit commenced or in which of the three years it occurred, it was held proper to divide the total deficit among the three bonds in the proportion of the sums collected by the collector on each yearly commitment of taxes into his hands. Phipsburg *v.* Dickinson, 78 Me. 457, 7 Atl. 9.

45. *Arkansas.*— Haley *v.* Petty, 42 Ark. 392.

Connecticut.—Hartford *v.* Franey, 47 Conn. 76.

North Carolina.— Fitts *v.* Hawkins, 9 N. C. 394.

Oregon.— Lake County *v.* Neilon, 44 Oreg. 14, 74 Pac. 212.

Pennsylvania.—Castor's Appeal, 2 Pennyp. 337.

Tennessee.— Miller *v.* Moore, 3 Humphr. 189.

Texas.— Tinsley *v.* Rusk County, 42 Tex. 40.

West Virginia.—Spencer Dist. Bd. of Education *v.* Cain, 28 W. Va. 758.

United States.— Walker County *v.* Fidelity, etc., Co., 107 Fed. 851, 47 C. C. A. 15.

See 45 Cent. Dig. tit. "Taxation," §§ 1107, 1108.

Contra.— Coons *v.* People, 76 Ill. 383; Newman *v.* Metcalfe County Ct., 4 Bush (Ky.) 67; Voisin *v.* Guillet, 4 Rob. (La.) 267; Lewenthall *v.* State, 51 Miss. 645; Frost *v.* Mixsell, 38 N. J. Eq. 586.

46. *Illinois.*— People *v.* Yeazel, 84 Ill. 539.

Louisiana.— School Directors *v.* Delahoussaye, 30 La. Ann. 1097.

Michigan.— People *v.* Bender, 36 Mich. 195.

North Carolina.— Clifton *v.* Wynne, 80 N. C. 145.

West Virginia.—Spencer Dist. Bd. of Education *v.* Cain, 28 W. Va. 758.

47. *California.*— Lawrence *v.* Doolan, 68 Cal. 309, 5 Pac. 484, 9 Pac. 159.

Kentucky.— Pulaski County *v.* Elrod, 66 S. W. 1017, 23 Ky. L. Rep. 2231; Combs *v.* Breathitt County, 46 S. W. 505, 20 Ky. L. Rep. 529.

Mississippi.— Boykin *v.* State, 50 Miss. 375.

New York.— Looney *v.* Hughes, 30 Barb. 605.

North Carolina.— Perry *v.* Campbell, 63 N. C. 257.

Tennessee.— McLean *v.* State, 8 Heisk. 22.

West Virginia.— Bennett *v.* McWhorter, 2 W. Va. 441.

Canada.—Baby *v.* Drew, 5 U. C. Q. B. 556.

See 45 Cent. Dig. tit. "Taxation," § 1111.

Taxes not included in bond.—Where the official duty of the collector is limited to the collection of certain particular taxes, money paid to him in liquidation of other taxes is not within the undertaking of his sureties, and they are not liable for his failure to pay it over. Ward *v.* Stahl, 81 N. Y. 406; Com. *v.* Reinhart, 15 Pa. Co. Ct. 487.

Failure, after redemption, to repay amount of overbid to purchaser.—Under Miss. Annot. Code (1892), §§ 3819, 3820, 3824, providing that on a purchaser paying at a tax-sale a sum in excess of the amount of taxes, when the excess at the time of redemption is in the hands of the tax collector, it shall be refunded to the purchaser, and the collector's bond shall be liable therefor, etc., the liability of a tax collector to repay an overbid at a tax-sale arises when redemption has been effected, and a failure to then pay it a breach of his bond. Indianola Bank *v.* Dodds, 90 Miss. 767, 44 So. 767. Under section 3820, providing that, where the owner of land sold for taxes shall accept the overbid of the purchaser, he shall pay interest, and section 3824, providing that the tax collector, on redemption being effected, shall refund the overbid to the purchaser, a tax collector is not liable for interest on overbids on lands being redeemed; the overbids being on deposit with him to await the contingency of redemption. Indianola Bank *v.* Dodds, *supra*.

48. *Florida.*— State *v.* Rushing, 17 Fla. 226.

(c) *Failure to Collect.* Failure of a tax collector to collect the legal taxes within the time required by law is a breach of the condition of his bond for which his sureties are liable,[49] at least to the extent of such taxes as were lost through his remissness or neglect,[50] although the sureties may show in mitigation of damages, if not in bar of the action, any circumstances which made it impossible for their principal to effect collections or which would be a sufficient legal excuse for his failure to do so.[51] The sureties are also liable for taxes for which the collector has given receipts without making the collection.[52]

(vi) *Application of Payments.*[53] If a tax collector serves for two successive terms and is in default, and makes payments on account of his liability to the municipality which he serves, it is his right to appropriate them to the deficit of either term, and if he does not so appropriate them the municipality may do so, and if neither makes an appropriation, the law will apply the payments to the oldest debt.[54] And if a payment is thus appropriated or applied on the deficit of the first term, and is sufficient to discharge it, the liability of the sureties on the bond given for that term is extinguished; but on the other hand, the sureties on the bond for the second term are liable for the resulting deficiency in the collector's accounts for that term.[55]

Maine.— Johnson *v.* Goodridge, 15 Me. 29.

Maryland.— Lynn *v.* Cumberland, 77 Md. 449, 26 Atl. 1001.

Michigan.— Berrien County Treasurer *v.* Bunbury, 45 Mich. 79, 7 N. W. 704.

Mississippi.—Adams *v.* Saunders, 89 Miss. 784, 42 So. 602.

Pennsylvania.— Com. *v.* Stambaugh, 164 Pa. St. 437, 30 Atl. 293.

Stipulation for sufficient warrant.— If the condition of the bond is that the collector shall collect and pay over all taxes for which he shall have a "sufficient warrant under the hands" of the proper officers, his sureties are not liable for money collected by him without such a warrant or outside of its terms. Foxcroft *v.* Nevens, 4 Me. 72.

Liability on sheriff's bond see Sheriffs and Constables, 35 Cyc. 1940.

49. *Alabama.*— State *v.* Lott, 69 Ala. 147.

California.— People *v.* Smith, 123 Cal. 70, 55 Pac. 765.

Maryland.— State *v.* Dorsey, 3 Gill & J. 75.

Mississippi.— Boykin *v.* State, 50 Miss. 375.

New York.—Fake *v.* Whipple, 39 Barb. 339 [*affirmed* in 39 N. Y. 394, 7 Transcr. App. 115].

Vermont.— Montpelier *v.* Clarke, 67 Vt. 479, 32 Atl. 252.

Virginia.— Ballard *v.* Thomas, 19 Gratt. 14.

See 45 Cent. Dig. tit. "Taxation," § 1112.

50. People *v.* Smith, 123 Cal. 70, 55 Pac. 765; Colerain *v.* Bell, 9 Metc. (Mass.) 499; State *v.* Irby, 1 McMull. (S. C.) 485. Under Ky. St. (1903) § 4147, providing that if the sheriff or collector of revenue without reasonable excuse fails to pay to any person entitled thereto the amount due upon any claim allowed by the fiscal court and payable out of the taxes levied by it, if collected or collectable by him, he and his sureties shall be liable therefor, where a special levy was made by the fiscal court to pay a judgment against a county, and a collector of state and county taxes was appointed and gave bond, and his attention was called to the special tax, but he refused to collect it, but did not pretend that it was not collectable, he and his sureties were liable on his official bond. Com. *v.* Wade, 126 Ky. 791, 104 S. W. 965, 31 Ky. L. Rep. 1185.

51. *Kentucky.*— Lyons *v.* Breckinridge County Ct., 101 Ky. 715, 42 S. W. 748, 19 Ky. L. Rep. 951, complaints of illegality of tax and threats to enjoin collection not sufficient to release sureties.

Maine.— Harpswell *v.* Orr, 69 Me. 393, collector deprived of one of the regular remedies for enforcing collection.

Massachusetts.— Colerain *v.* Bell, 9 Metc. 499, inability of particular persons to pay their taxes.

Mississippi.— Montgomery *v.* Governor, 7 How. 68, death of collector during term.

New York.— Fake *v.* Whipple, 39 N. Y. 394, too short time allowed for collection of taxes.

Pennsylvania.— Com. *v.* Titman, 148 Pa. St. 168, 23 Atl. 1120, no warrant issued to collector.

See 45 Cent. Dig. tit. "Taxation," § 1111.

52. McLean *v.* State, 8 Heisk. (Tenn.) 22. *Compare* Ward *v.* Marion County, 26 Tex. Civ. App. 361, 62 S. W. 557, 63 S. W. 155. It is otherwise if the sureties do not contract for the collection of the taxes, but only for the payment over of taxes collected; for an arrangement between the collector and a taxpayer by which the taxes are credited to the latter without actual payment, or by which his private claim against the collector is offset against the taxes, is not a payment of the taxes. Hartford *v.* Franey, 47 Conn. 76.

53. See also *supra*, IX, A, 4.

54. Readfield *v.* Shaver, 50 Me. 36, 79 Am. Dec. 592. But *compare* Elliott *v.* Allen, 30 S. W. 986, 17 Ky. L. Rep. 318.

55. *Kentucky.*— Helm *v.* Com., 79 Ky. 67.

Louisiana.— State *v.* Powell, 40 La. Ann.

conclusive of all claims and matters of defense which might have been litigated in such proceeding.[67]

(II) *LIEN OF BOND ON PROPERTY OF COLLECTOR AND SURETIES.* The statutory lien of a collector's bond on his property, and in some states on that of his sureties also, is not merely a remedy to enforce his duty of accounting, but is a part of the contract constituted by the giving of the bond, and has much the same effect as a mortgage.[68] It attaches ordinarily at the time of executing the bond, but in some states only from the rendition of a judgment against the collector.[69] The lien binds property acquired after the execution of the bond,[70] and follows the property into the hands of any purchaser, with or without notice.[71] It is entitled to such priority over other liens as the statute may give it,[72] and is not released by an extension of the time for paying over the taxes collected, at least if the sureties consent thereto.[73] This lien can be foreclosed only in equity.[74] In a decree for the sale of land under the lien of such a bond, it is error to allow defendant to redeem within the time fixed for redemption from sale under execution.[75]

(III) *ACTION OR SUIT* — (A) *Right of Action and Conditions Precedent.* A formal demand of payment is not generally a condition precedent to the institution of a suit on a tax collector's bond,[76] although in some states it is necessary that his accounts shall have been audited or adjusted, so that the precise sum may be ascertained for which judgment shall be demanded.[77] Ordinarily the sureties may be joined in the action as defendants;[78] but in some jurisdictions, apparently on the theory that their undertaking is in the nature of a guaranty, they cannot be sued until after the recovery of a judgment against their principal,[79] or even, in some states, until after the exhaustion of remedies against the principal and his property.[80] At common law the proper form of action on a tax collector's

67. State *v.* McBride, 76 Ala. 51; Boyd *v.* Randolph, 91 Ky. 472, 16 S. W. 133, 13 Ky. L. Rep. 53.

68. Knighton *v.* Curry, 62 Ala. 404.

69. See the statutes of the different states. And see Dallas County *v.* Timberlake, 54 Ala. 403; State *v.* Emerson, 3 Houst. (Del.) 85; Lippincott *v.* Barker, 2 Binn. (Pa.) 174, 4 Am. Dec. 433.

70. Baker *v.* Schuessler, 85 Ala. 541, 5 So. 328; Crawford *v.* Richardson, 101 Ill. 351; Pearce *v.* State, 49 La. Ann. 643, 21 So. 737.

71. Irby *v.* Livingston, 81 Ga. 281, 6 S. E. 591; Hook *v.* Richeson, 115 Ill. 431, 5 N. E. 98; Pearce *v.* State, 49 La. Ann. 643, 21 So. 737.

72. Crisfield *v.* Murdock, 127 N. Y. 315, 27 N. E. 1046 [*affirming* 55 Hun 143, 8 N. Y. Suppl. 593] (no priority over unrecorded prior mortgage executed by one of the sureties); Chatfield *v.* Rodger, 75 N. Y. App. Div. 631, 78 N. Y. Suppl. 1113.

73. Crawford *v.* Richeson, 101 Ill. 351.

74. Knighton *v.* Curry, 62 Ala. 404; Chatfield *v.* Rodger, 75 N. Y. App. Div. 631, 78 N. Y. Suppl. 1113.

75. Crisfield *v.* Murdock, 127 N. Y. 315, 27 N. E. 1046.

76. *Louisiana.*— Iberville *v.* Sherburne, 17 La. 342.

Maine.— Scarborough *v.* Parker, 53 Me. 252.

Massachusetts.— Sweetser *v.* Hay, 2 Gray 49.

North Carolina.—McGuire *v.* Williams, 123 N. C. 349, 31 S. E. 627; State *v.* Woodside, 31 N. C. 496; State *v.* McIntosh, 31 N. C. 307.

Vermont.— Houston *v.* Russell, 52 Vt. 110; Middlebury *v.* Nixon, 1 Vt. 232.

See 45 Cent. Dig. tit. "Taxation," § 1123.

Contra.— Com. *v.* McClure, 49 S. W. 789, 20 Ky. L. Rep. 1568; Com. *v.* Williams, 14 Bush (Ky.) 297; Cook *v.* Hays, 9 Gratt. (Va.) 142. *Compare*, however, Lancaster *v.* Arnold, 45 S. W. 82, 20 Ky. L. Rep. 34.

77. Foote *v.* Lake County, 109 Ill. App. 312 [*affirmed* in 206 Ill. 185, 69 N. E. 47]; Com. *v.* McClure, 49 S. W. 789, 20 Ky. L. Rep. 1568; Branch Tp. *v.* Youndt, 23 Pa. St. 182; Com. *v.* Geesey, 1 Pa. Super. Ct. 502. But *compare* Knighton *v.* Curry, 62 Ala. 404; Tappen *v.* People, 67 Ill. 339. And see Maryland Fidelity, etc., Co. *v.* Logan County, 119 Ky. 428, 84 S. W. 341, 27 Ky. L. Rep. 66, holding that a previous settlement of the collector's accounts is not necessary to the maintenance of an action on his bond where he has absconded.

78. See *supra*, X, A, 10, c, (I), (B); *infra*, X, A, 10, c, (III), (C).

79. Goree *v.* State, 22 Ark. 236. But *compare* State *v.* Winfree, 12 La. Ann. 643. And see Post *v.* Sheppard, 4 Gill (Md.) 276.

80. Marks *v.* Butler, 24 Ill. 567; Blanchard *v.* State, 6 La. 290. But *compare* Richmond *v.* Toothaker, 69 Me. 451; Looney *v.* Hughes, 30 Barb. (N. Y.) 605 [*affirmed* in 26 N. Y. 514]. And see Hartland *v.* Hackett, 57 Vt. 92, holding that the two remedies

joined as defendants, but if the bond is joint and several it is not necessary that all should be included in the suit.[5]

(D) *Pleading*. The declaration, petition, or complaint should show the right of plaintiff to maintain the action, which may be predicated on the refusal of the proper officer to institute the proceeding.[6] It should also allege the levy and assessment of the taxes,[7] and the official duty of defendant to collect them, which will include his election or appointment and the delivery to him of the warrant or other process which authorized him to act,[8] and it should aver distinctly the collection by defendant of a certain and definite sum of money,[9] in his capacity as collector of taxes and while he continued in office,[10] and his refusal or failure to pay it over to the proper officer at the proper time.[11] The plea or answer should be responsive to the declaration and should negative its essential allegations.[12] A material variance between the conditions relied on in the declaration and those in the bond may be fatal.[13]

(E) *Evidence*. It is incumbent on plaintiff to prove the execution, approval,

Bond with indefinite obligee.—Where a collector's bond is made payable to "whomsoever it may concern," and he fails to obey the law requiring him to settle annually with the school trustees for school taxes collected by him, and to pay over the amount in his hands, the trustees are the proper parties to sue on the bond, the statute requiring actions to be prosecuted in the name of the "real party in interest." Walton *v.* Jones, 7 Utah 462, 27 Pac. 580.

5. Lott *v.* Mobile County, 79 Ala. 69; Sprigg *v.* State, 54 Md. 469; Adams *v.* Conner, 73 Miss. 425, 19 So. 198; Moore *v.* Foote, 32 Miss. 469; Butler *v.* State, 2 Tex. Unrep. Cas. 535.

6. See Stokes County *v.* Wall, 117 N. C. 377, 23 S. E. 358; Pender County *v.* McPherson, 79 N. C. 524.

School-district as beneficial plaintiff in suit by state.—Where a suit is brought on a tax collector's bond in the name of the state, although for the use of a school-district. the statement should set forth the manner in which the judgment should be entered in order to secure the proper amount to the school-district, but the omission of this particular may be cured by amendment, and if there is no demurrer, the amendment will be considered as having been made, after trial on the merits and judgment. Com. *v.* Gruver, 13 Pa. Super. Ct. 553.

In some of the early decisions it was ruled that a declaration in a suit of this kind was not objectionable for not setting out the condition of the bond and the breaches to be relied on. State *v.* Kizer, 6 Blackf. (Ind.) 44; Wilson *v.* Ridgely, 46 Md. 235.

7. State *v.* Johnson, 6 Blackf. (Ind.) 217; State *v.* Leonard, 6 Blackf. (Ind.) 173; Evans *v.* State, 2 Blackf. (Ind.) 387; Middlebury *v.* Nixon, 1 Vt. 232. *Compare* People *v.* Love, 25 Cal. 520.

8. State *v.* Leonard, 6 Blackf. (Ind.) 173; Evans *v.* State, 2 Blackf. (Ind.) 387; Brown *v.* Com., 6 J. J. Marsh. (Ky.) 635; Whitfield *v.* Wooldridge, 23 Miss. 183.

9. *California.*— People *v.* Love, 25 Cal. 520.

Indiana.— State *v.* Johnson, 6 Blackf. 217; State *v.* Evans, 3 Blackf. 379.

Kentucky.— Com. *v.* Moren, 78 S. W. 432, 25 Ky. L. Rep. 1635.

Mississippi.—Whitfield *v.* Wooldridge, 23 Miss. 183.

New York.— Jansen *v.* Ostrander, 1 Cow. 670; Lathrop *v.* Allen, 19 Johns. 229.

Oregon.— Fargo *v.* Benton County, 1 Oreg. 262.

Pennsylvania.— Com. *v.* Gruver, 13 Pa. Super. Ct. 553.

See 45 Cent. Dig. tit. "Taxation," § 1127.

Penalties and damages.—Where the statute affixes certain penalties to defaults by collectors, the declaration in an action on the collector's bond to recover those penalties must aver as a breach of the bond a neglect to comply with the statutory requirements. Lee *v.* State, 22 Ark. 231. But see State *v.* Lewenthall, 55 Miss. 589.

10. Rany *v.* Governor, 4 Blackf. (Ind.) 2; Morgan County *v.* Lutman, 63 Mo. 210; State *v.* Grimsley, 19 Mo. 171; Rochester *v.* Symonds, 7 Wend. (N. Y.) 392.

11. *Arkansas.*— Goree *v.* State, 22 Ark. 236; Jones *v.* State, 14 Ark. 170.

Missouri.— State *v.* Patton, 42 Mo. 530.

New Jersey.— Newark *v.* Davis, 18 N. J. L. 21.

Texas.— Shaw *v.* State, 43 Tex. 355.

Virginia.—An allegation that the collector had failed to pay the taxes on demand, instead of at the time appointed by law, is not good, but will be cured by verdict. Winslow *v.* Com., 2 Hen. & M. 459.

See 45 Cent. Dig. tit. "Taxation," § 1127.

12. *Kentucky.*— Com. *v.* McClure, 49 S. W. 789, 20 Ky. L. Rep. 1568.

Mississippi.— McNutt *v.* Lancaster, 9 Sm. & M. 570, as to plea that bond is not binding because never approved.

New York.—Williams *v.* Holden, 4 Wend. 223 (regularity of assessment cannot be put in issue by plea); Jansen *v.* Ostrander, 1 Cow. 670 (*nil debet* not a good plea).

Ohio.— Short *v.* Lancaster, 17 Ohio 96.

Wyoming.— Sweetwater County *v.* Young, 3 Wyo. 684, 29 Pac. 1002.

See 45 Cent. Dig. tit. "Taxation," § 1127.

13. State *v.* Wilson, 107 Md. 129, 68 Atl. 609.

recovered belongs to several different municipalities, the judgment should apportion it among them, although failure to do so furnishes no ground of objection to defendant.[24] A judgment against the collector and his sureties may be enforced by proceedings in equity.[25]

11. **Criminal Responsibility of Collectors.** By force of statutes in the different states, a tax collector may be liable to criminal prosecution when he embezzles the public money in his hands or unlawfully refuses to pay it over,[26] or if he unlawfully collects taxes when none are due, or wilfully and unlawfully exacts or demands more than is due.[27] But if he acts under a good and sufficient warrant in proceeding to collect a tax duly levied, he is not criminally liable for his act in exacting payment from a person who was improperly assessed.[28]

B. Property Subject to Process For Collection[29] — 1. **In General.** The personal property of the taxpayer is the primary fund out of which all his taxes are to be made,[30] and for this purpose almost every variety of personal property is subject to compulsory process, provided it is found within the district in which the collector's authority runs,[31] and he is not restricted to those particular articles on which the particular assessment was laid or on which a particular tax lien rests.[32] As a general rule there is no exemption of any class or kind of personalty from distress or seizure for taxes;[33] it is immaterial that the property in question may be by law exempt from levy and sale on ordinary executions,[34] or even that

24. Tappan *v.* People, 67 Ill. 339.

25. Com. *v.* Ford, 29 Gratt. (Va.) 683.

26. See the statutes of the different states. And see Woods *v.* Varnum, 85 Cal. 639, 24 Pac. 843; People *v.* Otto, 70 Cal. 523, 11 Pac 675; State *v.* Dudenhefer, 122 La. 288, 47 So. 614; State *v.* Walton, 62 Me. 106; State *v.* Nicholson, 67 Md. 1, 8 Atl. 817; State *v.* Neilon, 43 Oreg. 168, 73 Pac. 321; Com. *v.* McCullough, 19 Pa. Super. Ct. 412. But *compare* Hellings *v.* Com., 5 Rawle (Pa.) 64, holding that under the early act of 1799 in Pennsylvania, since it pointed out a specific remedy against a collector who embezzled taxes, an indictment would not lie. See, generally, Embezzlement, 15 Cyc. 486.

Defalcation of deputies.— In a prosecution against a sheriff for embezzling money collected as taxes, money collected by his deputies, which was mingled with the money of the sheriff's office and as such presumptively came into his possession, is properly included in the amount alleged to have been converted by the sheriff. State *v.* Neilon, 43 Oreg. 168, 73 Pac. 321.

27. State *v.* Green, 87 Mo. 583; State *v.* Green, 24 Mo. App. 227.

28. Buck *v.* Com., 90 Pa. St. 110.

29. **Property subject to distraint see** *infra*, X, C, 4, c.

30. Cones *v.* Wilson, 14 Ind. 465.

Exhaustion of personalty before selling land for taxes see *infra*, XI, B, 2.

31. Patchin *v.* Ritter, 27 Barb. (N. Y.) 34; Ward *v.* Aylesworth, 9 Wend. (N. Y.) 281; State *v.* Graham, 2 Hill (S. C.) 457; Ross *v.* Holtzman, 20 Fed. Cas. No. 12,075, 3 Cranch C. C. 301.

Promissory notes and mortgages are "goods and chattels" subject to levy under a tax warrant, if the officer can get possession of them without trespass. Blain *v.* Irby, 25 Kan. 499.

Railroad property.— The track or road-bed of a railway cannot be levied on for taxes, but its rolling-stock and other personal property may be, and also its franchise of earning tolls. Hackley *v.* Mack, 60 Mich. 591, 27 N. W. 871; Chicago, etc., R. Co. *v.* Custer County, 69 Nebr. 429, 95 N. W. 859; Randall *v.* Elwell, 52 N. Y. 521, 11 Am. Rep. 747.

Municipal waterworks cannot be sold for taxes, being essential to the public health and comfort, but they may be placed in the hands of a receiver for the collection of the taxes due. Covington *v.* Campbell County, 113 Ky. 612, 68 S. W. 669, 24 Ky. L. Rep. 433.

Stock of a private corporation not subject to levy under a tax warrant except by statute see Barnes *v.* Hall, 55 Vt. 420.

A judgment in favor of a taxpayer not subject to process in absence of a statute see Acme Harvesting Mach Co. *v.* Hinckley, 23 S. D. 509, 122 N. W. 482.

Dispensary.— The property of a dispensary, part of a system of state and local institutions for the sale of liquors, is subject to sale on execution for delinquent taxes due the state. Sheffield *v.* Blakely Dispensary, 111 Ga. 1, 36 S E. 302.

Debts due taxpayer.— Under a statute which authorizes the sale of debts due to a delinquent taxpayer, the collector may sell debts due for daily wages, such debts being taxable. White *v.* Martin, 75 Miss. 646, 23 So. 289, 65 Am. St. Rep. 616.

32. Berwin *v.* Legras, 28 La. Ann. 352. See Oteri *v.* Parker, 42 La. Ann. 374, 7 So. 570.

33. Solomon *v.* Willis, 89 Ala. 596, 7 So. 160; Scales *v.* Alvis, 12 Ala. 617, 46 Am. Dec. 269; Dennis *v.* Maynard, 15 Ill. 477; Reams *v.* McHargue, 111 Ky. 163, 63 S. W. 437, 23 Ky. L. Rep. 540; Com. *v.* Lay, 12 Bush (Ky.) 283, 23 Am. Rep. 718.

34. Gentry *v.* Purcell, 84 Ind. 83; Wilmington *v.* Sprunt, 114 N. C. 310, 19 S. E. 348; McKee *v.* Christman, 103 Pa. St. 431; Oliver

officer is not required to sell the land if he can find personal property sufficient to satisfy the tax,[43] at least if it is on the premises;[44] and indeed it is a statutory requirement in many states that personal property of the delinquent taxpayer shall be exhausted before proceeding to sell his land.[45] But the personal property of a purchaser of land is not liable, unless by statute, for the satisfaction of a tax assessed on the land while it belonged to his vendor.[46]

4. PROPERTY IN HANDS OF RECEIVER. A tax collector cannot seize and sell property in the hands of a receiver, even for the purpose of collecting taxes.[47] The remedy is by application to the court to direct payment by the receiver, or for a sale of property for the purpose, where there are no available funds.[48]

C. Actions and Proceedings For Enforcement and Collection — 1. SUMMARY REMEDIES — a. In General. Summary proceedings are commonly authorized by law and resorted to for the collection of taxes; and they are not governed by the rules applicable to ordinary judicial proceedings, but only by such as the statute prescribes.[49] But a law of this kind is strictly construed and will not be extended by implication, and strict compliance with its provisions is essential to the validity of the proceedings.[50] In addition to the proceedings by distress, attachment, and tax executions, discussed in the succeeding sections, we may here mention, as examples of more or less summary methods of collecting taxes, the authority of a court which has an estate under its control, as in the case of a probate administration or a receivership, to order payment of taxes on a

Spiech *v.* Tierney, 56 Nebr. 574, 76 N. W. 1090; State *v.* Cain, 18 Nebr. 631, 26 N. W. 371. *Compare* Maus *v.* Logansport, etc., R. Co., 27 Ill. 77.

43. *Indiana.*— Ring *v.* Ewing, 47 Ind. 246; Midland R. Co. *v.* State, 11 Ind. App. 433, 38 N. E. 57.

Iowa.— Emerick *v.* Sloan, 18 Iowa 139.

New York.—Van Rensselaer *v.* Cottrell, 7 Barb. 127, 4 How. Pr. 376.

Pennsylvania.— McGregor *v.* Montgomery, 4 Pa. St. 237.

Vermont.— Shaw *v.* Peckett, 25 Vt. 423.

United States.— Semmes *v.* McKnight, 21 Fed. Cas. No. 12,653, 5 Cranch C. C. 539.

See 45 Cent. Dig. tit. "Taxation," § 1156.

Exceptions to rule.—Where lands are assessed as property of a non-resident, although the owner is in fact a resident, the collector cannot seize his personal property but must levy on the land. Lunt *v.* Wormell, 19 Me. 100. So where a farm belonging to a wife was improperly assessed to her husband. Hallock *v.* Rumsey, 22 Hun (N. Y.) 89. And the personal estate of a decedent is not liable for taxes accruing on his real estate after his death. Ross *v.* Holtzman, 20 Fed. Cas. No. 12,075, 3 Cranch C. C. 391.

44. Maus *v.* Logansport, etc., R. Co., 27 Ill. 77; Lake Shore, etc., R. Co. *v.* Roach, 80 N. Y. 339; Hayman *v.* Rothwell, 11 Fed. Cas. No. 6,267, 1 Hayw. & H. 156.

Crops and timber on land are liable to be seized and sold to satisfy a tax assessed on the land. Blodgett *v.* German Sav. Bank, 69 Ind. 153; Morrow *v.* Dows, 28 N. J. Eq. 459.

45. See *infra*, XI, B, 2.

46. Biggins *v.* People, 96 Ill. 381; Everson *v.* Syracuse, 39 Hun (N. Y.) 485; Atlantic, etc., R. Co. *v.* Cleino, 2 Fed. Cas. No. 631, 2 Dill. 175. *Compare* Henry *v.* Horstick, 9 Watts (Pa.) 412; Niver *v.* Perigo, 1 Leg. Gaz. (Pa.) 462.

47. *Georgia.*— Dysart *v.* Brown, 100 Ga. 1, 26 S. E. 767.

Idaho.— Palmer *v.* Pettingill, 6 Ida. 346, 55 Pac. 653.

South Carolina.— Cleveland *v.* McCrary, 46 S. C. 252, 24 S. E. 175.

Tennessee.—Weaver *v.* Duncan, (Ch. App. 1899) 56 S. W. 39.

United States.— *Ex p.* Tyler, 149 U. S. 164, 13 S. Ct. 785, 37 L. ed. 689; Clark *v.* McGhee, 87 Fed. 789, 31 C. C. A. 321. But see Central Trust Co. *v.* Wabash, etc., R. Co., 26 Fed. 11.

And see RECEIVERS, 34 Cyc. 231 *et seq.*

Injunction against enforcement of tax.— A court whose receiver is in charge of a railroad may properly issue an injunction *pendente lite* forbidding the state taxing officers to collect disputed taxes levied against a part of the railroad property. Clark *v.* McGhee, 87 Fed. 789, 31 C. C. A. 321. And on a bill by a receiver to enjoin the enforcement of a tax alleged to be invalid, the power of the federal court to issue a temporary injunction is not affected by the fact that the state law denies any relief against an illegal tax except payment under protest and suit to recover the amount. *Ex p.* Tyler, 149 U. S. 164, 13 S. Ct. 785, 37 L. ed. 689, 149 U. S. 191, 13 S. Ct. 793, 37 L. ed. 698. And see *Ex p.* Chamberlain, 55 Fed. 704.

48. See *supra*, IX, A, 1, c.

Sale of real property see *infra*, XI, D, 1.

49. Oteri *v.* Parker, 42 La. Ann. 374, 7 So. 570 (the seizure of a vessel for taxes is not a proceeding *in rem*, to be governed by the rules of admiralty); Lavergne *v.* New Orleans, 28 La. Ann. 677 (as to notice).

50. *Alabama.*—Rivers *v.* Thompson, 43 Ala. 633.

Georgia.— D'Antignac *v.* Augusta City Council, 31 Ga. 700.

Louisiana.— Police Jury *v.* Bullit, 8 Mart.

common in the revenue laws of the states,[39] and such statutory authorization of suit may be made retroactive,[40] and may apply to taxes on omitted property or to taxes of previous years.[41] As to the form of action, if the suit is brought as at common law, it should be in assumpsit, but if on the statute, either debt or case.[42]

(II) *EXCLUSIVENESS OF STATUTORY REMEDIES.* It is held in some states that where the statute creates and prescribes a particular remedy for the collection of delinquent taxes, it is exclusive, and therefore prohibits the maintenance of an action at law.[43] But exceptions to this rule are sometimes made where

at law may be maintained for the recovery of taxes, although the statute provides a special remedy for their collection, provided this statutory remedy is not in terms made exclusive. Perry County *v.* Selma, etc., R. Co., 58 Ala. 546; Burlington *v.* Burlington, etc., R. Co., 41 Iowa 134; Dubuque *v.* Illinois Cent. R. Co., 39 Iowa 56; State *v.* Southern Steamship Co., 13 La. Ann. 497; Dugan *v.* Baltimore, 1 Gill & J. (Md.) 499; State *v.* Memphis, etc., R. Co., 14 Lea (Tenn.) 56; Cave *v.* Houston, 65 Tex 619; Clegg *v.* Galveston County, 1 Tex. App. Civ. Cas. § 58.

Promise of taxpayer.— Where the taxpayer promises the collector, on a good consideration, to pay the amount of the tax, it seems that an action may be maintained on this promise Burr *v.* Wilcox, 13 Allen (Mass.) 269 But *compare* Brule County *v.* King, 11 S. D. 294, 77 N. W. 107.

39. See the statutes of the different states. And see Territory *v.* Gaines, 11 Ariz. 270, 93 Pac. 281; People *v.* Reis, 76 Cal. 269, 18 Pac. 309; McCrary *v.* Lake City Electric Light Co., 139 Iowa 548, 117 N. W. 964; Boston *v.* Turner, 201 Mass. 190, 87 N. E. 634; Menominee *v.* S. K. Martin Lumber Co., 119 Mich. 201, 77 N. W. 704; Delta, etc., Land Co. *v.* Adams, 93 Miss. 340, 48 So. 190; State *v.* Tittmann, 103 Mo. 553, 15 S. W. 936. A judgment and order for sale of land for taxes, and a forfeiture to the state at the sale, is sufficient to support an action of debt against the owner for the delinquent taxes. People *v.* International Salt Co., 233 Ill. 223, 84 N. E. 278; Sanderson *v.* La Salle, 117 Ill. 171, 7 N. E. 114; Biggins *v.* People, 106 Ill. 270.

Construction of statutes.— Proceedings at law for the collection of taxes, where forfeitures are not involved, should be construed liberally. Mason *v.* Belfast Hotel Co., 89 Me. 384, 36 Atl. 624.

Discretion of officer.— Under Ariz. Rev. L. § 86 (Rev. St. (1901) par. 3917), as amended by the act of March 19, 1903 (Laws (1903), p. 165, No. 92), requiring the county tax collector to sue for the collection of delinquent taxes, it is the duty of such officer to bring such suit, in the exercise of which he has no discretion. Territory *v.* Gaines, 11 Ariz. 270, 93 Pac. 281.

Tax laws of another state.— The courts of Illinois will not enforce the revenue laws of another state, where the demands of that state have been satisfied. Kessler *v.* Kedzie, 106 Ill. App. 1.

40 York *v.* Goodwin, 67 Me. 260; Rochester *v* Rochester R. Co., 109 N. Y. App. Div. 638, 96 N. Y. Suppl. 152 [*modified* on other grounds in 187 N. Y. 216, 79 N. E. 1010]. And see Biggins *v.* People, 106 Ill. 270. *Compare*, however, Delta, etc., Land Co. *v.* Adams, 93 Miss. 340, 48 So. 190, holding that Code (1906), § 4256, making every lawful tax a debt, and providing a new method of collecting it by action, while under the prior law back taxes were not debts, and were collectable, when on realty, by sale of the land, created a new obligation to pay, as well as a new remedy, and could have no retroactive effect, and hence a personal decree could not be rendered for back taxes due before the enactment of the section, although assessed thereafter, as they were not debts.

41. Galusha *v.* Wendt, 114 Iowa 597, 87 N. W. 512; Delta, etc., Land Co. *v.* Adams, 93 Miss. 340, 48 So. 190; Hull *v.* Alexander, 69 Ohio St. 75, 68 N. E. 642; Toledo Bridge Co. *v.* Yost, 22 Ohio Cir. Ct. 376, 12 Ohio Cir. Dec. 448. But an action for taxes on property omitted from taxation for preceding years is statutory, and cannot be maintained unless the statute has been substantially complied with. Judy *v.* Pleasant Nat. State Bank, 133 Iowa 252, 110 N. W. 605.

42. Baltimore *v.* Howard, 6 Harr. & J. (Md.) 383; Gillespie *v.* Sefrin, 1 Chest. Co. Rep. (Pa.) 61; Franklin *v.* Warwick, etc., Water Co., 24 R. I. 224, 52 Atl. 988; Meredith *v.* U. S., 13 Pet. (U. S.) 486, 10 L. ed. 258.

43. *Iowa.*— Plymouth County *v.* Moore, 114 Iowa 700, 87 N. W. 662; Cedar Rapids, etc., R. Co. *v.* Carroll County, 41 Iowa 153.

Kansas.— Stafford County *v.* Stafford First Nat. Bank, 48 Kan. 561, 30 Pac. 22.

Kentucky.— Johnston *v.* Louisville, 11 Bush 527.

Louisiana.— Alexandria *v.* Heyman, 35 La. Ann. 301.

Michigan.— Detroit *v.* Jepp, 52 Mich. 458, 18 N. W. 217.

Missouri.— State *v.* Snyder, 139 Mo. 549, 41 S. W. 216. But *compare* State *v.* Cummings, 151 Mo. 49, 52 S. W. 29.

Ohio.— Mayer *v.* Cincinnati German Bldg. Assoc., 2 Cinc. Super. Ct. 336.

Pennsylvania.— Bouck *v.* Kittanning, 1 Am. L. Reg. 125.

South Dakota.— Hanson County *v.* Gray, 12 S. D. 124, 80 N. W. 175, 76 Am. St. Rep. 591.

Utah.— Crismon *v.* Reich, 2 Utah 111.

Virginia.— Marye *v.* Diggs, 98 Va. 749, 37 S. E. 315, 51 L. R. A. 902.

Canada.— Carson *v.* Veitch, 9 Ont. 706.

See 45 Cent. Dig. tit. "Taxation," § 1189.

(v) *Authority of Particular Officers.* The statutes usually designate the particular state or municipal officer who shall have authority to institute and prosecute suits for the recovery of delinquent taxes; and where this is the case such an action will not lie in the name of any other officer.[52]

(vi) *Joinder and Consolidation.* Taxes levied for different years or other fiscal periods are distinct causes of action, and can be united in one suit only under circumstances which would justify such joinder in the case of other liabilities, or when it is so directed by the statute.[53] The same rule applies to taxes due to different treasuries, as to the state and a county, to a county and a school-district, or to a county and town.[54] So also the taxes due from the same owner on separate parcels of land should be sued for in as many separate suits, but these may be consolidated on motion, and it is generally proper to do so.[55]

(vii) *Persons Liable to Suit.* The suit should be brought against the person who is directly and primarily liable for the payment of the tax,[56] and this is ordinarily the one to whom the property was assessed, although he may have parted with the title in the mean time, no personal liability attaching to the purchaser unless by force of a statute.[57] If death or insolvency intervenes, the action may be against the personal representatives or assignee of the taxpayer.[58]

156; Reed *v.* Creditors, 39 La. Ann. 115, 1 So. 784.

52. See the statutes of the several states. And see the following cases:

Kentucky.— Lucas *v.* Com., 121 Ky. 423, 89 S. W. 292, 28 Ky. L. Rep. 372; Campbell County *v.* Newport, etc., Bridge Co., 112 Ky. 659, 66 S. W. 526, 23 Ky. L. Rep. 2056.

Louisiana.— New Orleans *v.* Jeter, 13 La. Ann. 509.

Maine.— Lord *v.* Parker, 83 Me. 530, 22 Atl. 392.

Michigan.— Auditor-Gen. *v.* Lake George, etc., R. Co., 82 Mich. 426, 46 N. W. 730.

Mississippi.— Yazoo, etc., R. Co. *v.* West, 78 Miss. 789, 29 So. 475; State *v.* Hill, 70 Miss. 106, 11 So. 789.

Nebraska.— Moore *v.* Furnas County Live Stock Co., 78 Nebr. 558, 111 N. W. 464.

Nevada.— State *v.* Central Pac. R. Co., 10 Nev. 87.

New Mexico.— U. S. Trust Co. *v.* Territory, 10 N. M. 416, 62 Pac. 987.

North Carolina.— Worth *v.* Wright, 122 N. C. 335, 29 S. E. 361.

Pennsylvania.— Casey *v.* Wade, 3 Walk. 282; Hayes *v.* Grier, 4 Binn. 80.

Tennessee.— State *v.* Baldwin University, 97 Tenn. 358, 37 S. W. 1; Grundy County *v.* Tennessee Coal, etc., Co., 94 Tenn. 295, 29 S. W. 116.

See 45 Cent. Dig. tit. "Taxation," § 1186.

Authority to compromise.— County officers having authority to sue for taxes due to the county may compromise such a suit and accept payment of less than the entire amount of taxes due. St. Louis, etc., R. Co. *v.* Anthony, 73 Mo. 431. But they cannot compromise a suit instituted by the state. State *v.* Central Pac. R. Co., 9 Nev. 79. See *supra*, X, A, 4, g.

Want of authority of county board.— A statutory requirement that an action by a county treasurer to recover personal taxes shall only be brought by the direction of the county board is waived by filing an answer and proceeding to trial without objection. Moore *v.* Furnas County Live Stock Co., 78 Nebr. 558, 111 N. W. 464.

Presumptions.— It may be presumed, in the absence of evidence to the contrary, that selectmen added the word "selectmen," if necessary, after their signatures to a written authority to the collector of taxes to bring an action for taxes, where such written authority has been destroyed. Greenville *v.* Blair, 104 Me. 444, 72 Atl. 177.

53. State *v.* Yellow Jacket Silver Min. Co., 14 Nev. 220.

54. *Alabama.*— State *v.* Adler, 123 Ala. 87, 26 So. 502.

California.— Los Angeles County *v.* Ballerino, 99 Cal. 593, 32 Pac. 581, 34 Pac. 329.

Illinois.— Dalby *v.* People, 124 Ill. 66, 16 N. E. 224.

Kentucky.— Pfirrman *v.* Clifton Dist., 96 S. W. 810, 29 Ky. L. Rep. 1003.

Maine.— Mason *v.* Belfast Hofel Co., 89 Me. 381, 36 Atl. 622.

55. Whitney *v.* Morton County, 73 Kan. 502, 85 Pac. 530; *In re* Stutsman County, 88 Fed. 337.

56. Dalby *v.* People, 124 Ill. 66, 16 N. E. 224.

57. *Illinois.*— Biggins *v.* People, 96 Ill. 381.

Indiana.— Volger *v.* Sidener, 86 Ind. 545; Blodgett *v.* German Sav. Bank, 69 Ind. 153.

Massachusetts.— Webber Lumber Co. *v.* Shaw, 189 Mass. 366, 75 N. E. 640.

Michigan.— Laketon Tp. *v.* Akeley, 74 Mich. 695, 42 N. W. 165.

New York.— Everson *v.* Syracuse, 29 Hun 485 [*reversed* on other grounds in 100 N. Y. 577].

United States.— Atlantic, etc., R. Co. *v.* Cleino, 2 Fed. Cas. No. 631, 2 Dill. 175.

Effect of foreclosure of mortgage see Webber Lumber Co. *v.* Shaw, 189 Mass. 366, 75 N. E. 640; Sherwin *v.* Boston Five Cents Sav. Bank, 137 Mass. 444; Andrews *v.* Worcester County Mut. F. Ins. Co., 5 Allen (Mass.) 65.

58. Galusha *v.* Wendt, 114 Iowa 597, 87 N. W. 512 (executor or administrator): Scollard *v.* Edwards, 194 Mass. 77, 80 N. E. 4

unless he can show that he was deprived of the hearing to which he was entitled or that he had a perfectly valid excuse for failing to claim it.[88] To make a defense of double taxation available, defendant must show that he has paid one of the taxes.[89]

(IV) *SET-OFF OR COUNTER-CLAIM.* The general rule is that a set-off or counter-claim cannot be interposed in an action for the recovery of delinquent taxes.[90]

(V) *LIMITATION OF ACTIONS.* No statute of limitations runs against the right of the state to collect its taxes, unless expressly made applicable;[91] but in respect to municipalities, and also the state when included within the statute, the ordinary period of limitations applicable to "liabilities founded on statute" or to claims not specially enumerated may be pleaded in defense to a suit for the recovery of taxes,[92] unless there is a statute specifically prescribing the period of limitations for suits of this class, which, in that case, would alone be applicable.[93] The statute begins to run from the date of the assessment of the taxes,[94] or from the time of delinquency, that is, the expiration of the time allowed the property-

88. State *v.* Mechanics', etc., Bank, 23 La. Ann 307; New York *v.* Tucker, 182 N. Y. 535, 75 N. E. 1128.

89. Heath *v.* McCrea, 20 Wash. 342, 55 Pac. 432.

90. Newport, etc., Bridge Co. *v.* Douglass, 12 Bush (Ky.) 673; New Orleans *v.* Davidson, 30 La. Ann. 541, 31 Am. Rep. 228; Camden *v.* Allen, 26 N. J. L. 398. And see *supra*, I, A, 2, b; X, C, 1, e. *Compare*, however, Louisville, etc., R. Co. *v.* Com., 30 S. W. 624, 17 Ky. L. Rep. 136; New Orleans *v.* New Orleans Waterworks Co., 36 La. Ann. 432.

91. Hood *v.* New Orleans, 49 La. Ann. 1461, 22 So. 401; Reed *v.* Creditors, 39 La. Ann. 115, 1 So. 784; Wasteney *v.* Schott, 58 Ohio St. 410, 51 N. E. 34 [*affirming* 13 Ohio Cir. Ct. 339, 7 Ohio Cir. Dec. 222].

92 *California.*— San Francisco *v.* Luning, 73 Cal. 610, 15 Pac. 311.

Iowa.— Brown *v.* Painter, 44 Iowa 368.

Kentucky.— Chesapeake, etc., R. Co. *v.* Com., 129 Ky. 318, 108 S. W. 248, 32 Ky. L. Rep 1119, 111 S. W. 334, 33 Ky. L. Rep. 882; Illinois Cent. R. Co. *v.* Com., 128 Ky. 268, 108 S. W. 245, 32 Ky. L. Rep. 1112, 110 S. W 265, 33 Ky. L. Rep. 326; Com. *v.* Rosenfield, 118 Ky. 374, 80 S. W. 1178, 25 Ky. L. Rep. 2229, 82 S. W. 433, 26 Ky. L. Rep. 726; Citizens' Nat. Bank *v.* Com., 118 Ky. 51, 80 S. W. 479, 25 Ky. L. Rep. 2254, 81 S. W. 686, 26 Ky. L. Rep. 62; Louisville, etc., Ferry Co. *v.* Com., 108 Ky. 717, 57 S. W. 624, 626, 22 Ky. L. Rep. 446, 480.

Louisiana.— Saloy *v.* Woods, 40 La. Ann. 585, 4 So. 209. *Contra*, Miramon *v.* New Orleans, 52 La. Ann. 1623, 28 So. 107.

Missouri.— State *v.* Vogelsang, 183 Mo. 17, 81 S. W. 1087.

Montana.— Custer County *v.* Story, 26 Mont. 517, 69 Pac. 56.

Nevada.— State *v.* Yellow Jacket Silver Min. Co., 14 Nev. 220.

United States.— Bristol *v.* Washington County, 177 U. S. 133, 20 S. Ct. 585, 44 L. ed. 701; San Francisco *v.* Jones, 20 Fed. 188.

See 45 Cent. Dig. tit. "Taxation," § 1202.

Contra.— Perry County *v.* Selma, etc., R. Co., 58 Ala. 546; Hoover *v.* Engles. 63 Nebr. 688, 88 N. W. 869; Hagerman *v.* Territory, 11 N. M. 156, 66 Pac. 526; Wilmington *v.* Cronly, 122 N. C. 383. 388, 30 S. E. 9; Greenlaw *v.* Dallas, 33 Tex. Civ. App. 100, 75 S. W. 812; Abney *v.* State, 20 Tex. Civ. App. 101, 47 S. W. 1043.

93. See the statutes of the different states. And see the following cases:

California — Los Angeles County *v.* Ballerino, 99 Cal. 593, 32 Pac. 581, 34 Pac. 329; San Francisco *v.* Luning, 73 Cal. 610, 15 Pac. 311.

Georgia.— Georgia R., etc., Co. *v.* Wright, 124 Ga. 596, 53 S. E. 251.

Iowa.— Shearer *v.* Citizens' Bank, 129 Iowa 564, 105 N. W. 1025; Bell *v.* Stevens, 116 Iowa 451, 90 N. W. 87.

Kentucky.— Chesapeake, etc., R. Co. *v.* Com., 129 Ky. 318, 108 S. W. 248, 32 Ky. L. Rep. 1119, 111 S. W. 334, 33 Ky. L. Rep. 882; Illinois Cent. R. Co. *v.* Com., 128 Ky. 268, 108 S. W. 245, 32 Ky. L. Rep. 1112, 110 S. W. 265. 33 Ky. L. Rep. 326; Lucas *v.* Com., 121 Ky. 423, 89 S. W. 292, 28 Ky. L. Rep. 372. And see Morgan *v.* Frankfort, 135 Ky. 178, 121 S. W. 1033.

Maryland.— Baldwin *v.* State, 89 Md. 587, 43 Atl. 857.

Michigan.— Sturgis *v.* Flanders, 97 Mich. 546, 56 N. W. 934.

Missouri.— State *v.* Edwards, 162 Mo. 660, 63 S. W. 388.

Tennessee.— Union, etc., Bank *v.* Memphis, 101 Tenn. 154, 46 S. W. 557.

Texas.— Ollivier *v.* Houston, 22 Tex. Civ. App. 55, 54 S. W. 940; Clegg *v.* Galveston County, 1 Tex. App. Civ. Cas. 58. See Hernandez *v.* San Antonio, (Civ. App. 1897) 39 S. W. 1022.

See 45 Cent. Dig. tit. "Taxation," § 1202.

94. Thornburg *v.* Cardell, 123 Iowa 313, 95 N. W. 239, 98 N. W. 791; Citizens' Nat. Bank *v.* Com., 118 Ky. 51, 80 S. W. 479, 25 Ky. L. Rep. 2254, 81 S. W. 686, 26 Ky. L. Rep. 62; Louisville, etc., R. Co. *v.* Com., 1 Bush (Ky.) 250; Louisville *v.* Louisville Courier-Journal Co., 84 S. W. 773, 27 Ky. L.

against them for such agent's compensation, if it appears that the failure to pay was caused by their wilful default or negligence.[5]

(II) *PROCESS AND SERVICE.* The summons or other process in an action of this kind should conform to any directions of the statute.[6] In the case of unknown or non-resident owners of property, it may be served by publication if the law so provides.[7]

f. Pleading — (I) *DECLARATION, COMPLAINT, PETITION, OR BILL* — (A) *Form and Requisites in General.* It is competent for the legislature to prescribe a special form of declaration, complaint, petition, or bill to be used in tax suits, and when this is followed it need contain no more than the statute requires.[8] Otherwise the pleading must conform to the ordinary rules,[9] and if the suit is against a person other than the one to whom the tax was assessed, it must show statutory authority for bringing it and the facts on which it is based.[10]

(B) *Allegations.*[11] The declaration, complaint, petition, or bill should contain allegations showing plaintiff's authority to sue, if he is a public officer empowered to sue in his own name on certain conditions,[12] and facts showing that the matter is within the jurisdiction of the court, as to amount and venue,[13] and it should allege the levy and assessment of the tax,[14] defendant's liability thereto,[15] and compliance with any statutory directions as to proceedings preliminary to the

State *v.* Red River Valley El. Co., 69 Minn. 131, 72 N. W. 60.

5. Miss. Annot. Code (1892), § 4200. This provision does not apply to suits for back taxes which the taxpayer declined to pay, and which could not be otherwise collected because of appeals and contests. Delta, etc., R. Co. *v.* Adams, 93 Miss. 340, 48 So. 190.

6. See the statutes of the different states. And see Lucas *v.* Com., 121 Ky. 423, 89 S. W. 292, 28 Ky. L. Rep. 372 (summons is not void, although not issued within the prescribed number of days after filing of a statement by a revenue officer); Wilson *v.* Benton, 11 Lea (Tenn.) 51 (law does not require that the warrant should show by what authority suit is brought).

7. Com. *v.* Vanderbilt, 118 Ky. 787, 82 S. W. 426, 26 Ky. L. Rep. 716; Wall *v.* Holladay-Klotz Land, etc., Co., 176 Mo. 406, 75 S. W. 385; Turner *v.* Gregory, 151 Mo. 100, 52 S. W. 234; Stoneman *v.* Bilby, 43 Tex. Civ. App. 293, 96 S. W. 50; Williams *v.* Young, 41 Tex. Civ. App. 212, 90 S. W. 940; Peterson *v.* Lara, 46 Wash. 448, 90 Pac. 596.

8. People *v.* Central Pac. R. Co., 83 Cal. 393, 23 Pac. 303; Stockton *v.* Western F. & M. Ins. Co., 73 Cal. 621, 15 Pac. 314; State *v.* Hannibal, etc., R. Co., 101 Mo. 136, 13 S. W. 505; Wade *v.* Kimberley, 5 Ohio Cir. Ct. 33, 3 Ohio Cir. Dec. 18; Cummings *v.* Fitch, 7 Ohio Dec. (Reprint) 36, 1 Cinc. L. Bul. 77.

Surplusage see Gibson *v.* Miller, 28 Ohio Cir. Ct. 421.

9. See People *v.* Central Pac. R. Co., 83 Cal. 393, 23 Pac. 303; Zacharie's Succession, 30 La. Ann. 1260.

10. State *v.* Sloss, 87 Ala. 119, 6 So. 309; *In re* Johnson, 104 Ill. 50.

11. **Bill to enjoin disposal of property and for a personal decree.**—A suit to enjoin a corporation from disposing of the balance of its property until taxes due have been paid. and for a personal decree for the amount of the taxes, is not an attachment in chancery, and the bill need not contain the averments required in such case. Delta, etc., Land Co. *v.* Adams, 93 Miss. 340, 48 So. 190.

12. Charleston *v.* Lawry, 89 Me. 582, 36 Atl. 1103; Orono *v.* Emery, 86 Me. 362, 29 Atl. 1095; Ricker *v.* Brooks, 155 Mass. 400, 29 N. E. 534; Oliver *v.* Colonial Gold Co., 11 Allen (Mass.) 283; Mortenson *v.* West Point Mfg. Co., 12 Nebr. 197, 10 N. W. 714.

13. People *v.* Central Pac. R. Co., 83 Cal. 393, 23 Pac. 303; Ottawa Gas Light, etc., Co. *v.* People, 138 Ill. 336, 27 N. E. 924; Miller *v.* Crawford Independent School Dist., 26 Tex. Civ. App. 495, 63 S. W. 894.

14. *California.*— People *v.* Central Pac. R. Co., 83 Cal. 393, 23 Pac. 303.

Illinois.— Ottawa Gas Light, etc., Co. *v.* People, 138 Ill. 336, 27 N. E. 924.

Indiana.— Vogel *v.* Vogler, 78 Ind. 353; Conwell *v.* Connersville, 8 Ind. 358.

Kentucky.— Louisville *v.* Commonwealth, 3 Metc. 148; Louisville *v.* Louisville Gas Co., 22 S. W. 550, 17 Ky. L. Rep. 177; Kentucky Cent. R. Co. *v.* Com., 17 S. W. 196, 13 Ky. L. Rep. 484; Kentucky Cent. R. Co. *v.* Pendleton County, 2 S. W. 176, 8 Ky. L. Rep. 517.

Massachusetts.— Houghton *v.* Davenport, 23 Pick. 235.

North Dakota.— Swenson *v.* Greenland, 4 N. D. 532, 62 N. W. 603.

Rhode Island.— Franklin *v.* Warwick, etc., Water Co., 24 R. I. 224, 52 Atl. 988.

South Carolina.— State *v.* Cheraw, etc., R. Co., 54 S. C. 564, 32 S. E. 691.

Texas.— Miller *v.* Crawford Independent School Dist., 26 Tex. Civ. App. 495, 62 S. W. 894; Moody *v.* Galveston, 21 Tex. Civ. App. 16, 50 S. W. 481; Maddox *v.* Rockport, (Civ. App. 1898) 38 S. W. 397.

See 45 Cent. Dig. tit. "Taxation," § 1205 *et seq.*

15. Vassalboro *v.* Smart, 70 Me. 303; State *v.* Renshaw, 166 Mo. 682, 66 S. W. 953.

to show the fact and amount of the assessment and defendant's liability thereto,[37] unless it shows on its face that the assessment was erroneously made,[38] and the official delinquent list is presumptive evidence that the tax remains due and unpaid.[39] Other matters in issue must be proved by such evidence as is considered sufficient in ordinary suits at law.[40]

h. Trial, Judgment, and Review — (I) *TRIAL.* With respect to the time of trial and the facts and findings necessary to support a judgment, the directions of the statutes must be carefully observed.[41] Where defendant denies the right to tax his property, all questions bearing upon that right may be inquired into.[42] Questions of fact, such as the place of defendant's residence, or an alleged device to escape taxation, must go to the jury.[43]

(II) *JUDGMENT* — (A) *In General.* The judgment in an action for taxes must be based on a valid assessment,[44] and on pleadings sufficient in law to sustain it,[45] otherwise it may be set aside; but these requirements being fulfilled, it possesses all the ordinary attributes of a judgment,[46] is final and conclusive as to all

supervisor that he made the tax roll, that he delivered it to the county treasurer, and that he obtained it from the latter's office for use upon the trial is sufficient identification to justify its introduction in evidence. And see State *v.* Chicago R. Co., 165 Mo. 597, 65 S. W. 989.

37. *California.*— Modoc County *v.* Churchill, 75 Cal. 172, 16 Pac. 771.

Illinois.— Harding *v.* People, 202 Ill. 122, 66 N. E. 962; Carrington *v.* People, 195 Ill. 484, 63 N. E. 163.

Michigan.— Muskegon *v.* S. K. Martin Lumber Co., 86 Mich. 625, 49 N. W. 489.

Missouri.— State *v.* Vogelsang, 183 Mo. 17, 81 S. W. 1087; State *v.* Phillips, 137 Mo. 259, 38 S. W. 931.

Nevada.— State *v.* Nevada Cent. R. Co., 26 Nev. 357, 68 Pac. 294, 69 Pac. 1042.

Vermont.— Bowman *v.* Downer, 28 Vt. 532.

38. State *v.* Merchants' Bank, 160 Mo. 640, 61 S. W. 676. And see Loeber *v.* Leininger, 175 Ill. 484, 51 N. E. 703.

39. Carney *v.* People, 210 Ill. 434, 71 N. E. 365.

40. *Illinois.*— Twin City Gas Works *v.* People, 156 Ill. 387, 40 N. E. 950.

Kentucky.— Louisville Tank Line *v.* Com., 123 Ky. 81, 93 S. W. 635, 29 Ky. L. Rep. 257; McMakin *v.* Com., 80 S. W. 188, 25 Ky. L. Rep. 2195.

Maryland.— Westminster *v.* Westminster Sav. Bank, 92 Md. 62, 48 Atl. 34.

Mississippi.— Warren County *v.* Craig, (1901) 29 So. 821.

Nevada.— State *v.* Meyers, 23 Nev. 274, 46 Pac. 51.

Wisconsin.— Washburn *v.* Washburn Waterworks Co., 120 Wis. 575, 98 N. W. 539.

41. See the statutes of the different states. And see Brunson *v.* Starbuck, 32 Ind. App. 457, 70 N. E. 163; James Clark Distilling Co. *v.* Cumberland, 95 Md. 468, 52 Atl. 661; State *v.* Evans, 53 Mo. App. 663; Hancock *v.* Merriman, 46 Wis. 159, 49 N. W. 970.

42. Grundy County *v.* Tennessee Coal, etc., Co., 94 Tenn. 295, 29 S. W. 116.

43. Ovid Tp. *v.* Haire, 133 Mich. 353, 94 N. W. 1060; Com. *v.* Erie, etc., R. Co., 74 Pa. St. 94. In assumpsit for taxes, whether defendant's domicile was in the town in which he was taxed, at a certain time, or in a town of another state, was held to be a question for the jury. Smith *v.* Stannard, 81 Vt. 319, 70 Atl. 568.

44. *Alabama.*— State *v.* Sloss, 87 Ala. 119, 6 So. 309.

Maine.— Bucksport *v.* Buck, 89 Me. 320, 36 Atl. 456.

Minnesota.— State *v.* Nelson, 107 Minn. 319, 119 N. W. 1058 (holding that where defendant was the owner of stock in a foreign corporation, but it had never been listed or assessed in any manner for taxation, the court, in a suit to collect personal taxes, could not treat such stock as if it had been listed and a tax assessed thereon); Thompson *v.* Davidson, 15 Minn. 412.

Tennessee.— East Tennessee, etc., R. Co. *v.* Morristown, (Ch. App. 1895) 35 S. W. 771.

United States.— San Bernardino County *v.* Southern Pac. R. Co., 118 U. S. 417, 6 S. Ct. 1144, 30 L. ed. 125.

Mere irregularities not shown to be prejudicial and not rendering an assessment void will not prevent judgment for the full amount of the assessment. Covington, etc., Bridge Co. *v.* Covington, 100 S. W. 269, 30 Ky. L. Rep. 1115; State *v.* Duluth Gas, etc., Co., 76 Minn. 96, 78 N. W. 1032, 57 L. R. A. 63. And see *supra*, X, C, 6, d, (II).

45. People *v.* Hager, 19 Cal. 462; Falls Branch Jellico Land, etc., Co. *v.* Com., 83 S. W. 108, 26 Ky. L. Rep. 1028; Hays *v.* New Orleans, 32 La. Ann. 1307; Bland *v.* Windsor, 187 Mo. 108, 86 S. W. 162.

46. Sebree *v.* Nutter, 87 S. W. 1072, 27 Ky. L. Rep. 1080; First Presb. Church *v.* New Orleans, 30 La. Ann. 259, 31 Am. Rep. 224. *Compare* Mercier's Succession, 42 La. Ann. 1135, 8 So. 732, 11 L. R. A. 817.

Judgment as debt.— A judgment for taxes which is both *in personam* against the taxpayer and *in rem* against his real estate is a "debt" within the meaning of the legal tender act of congress. Rhodes *v.* Farrell, 2 Nev. 60.

Personal liability see Louisville *v.* Robinson, 119 Ky. 908, 85 S. W. 172, 27 Ky. L. Rep. 375; Beatrice *v.* Wright, 72 Nebr. 689, 101 N. W. 1039.

(c) *Costs and Fees.* An unsuccessful defendant in a tax suit is ordinarily chargeable with the fees and expenses of officers in the proceedings to enforce the tax,[56] and generally with the costs of the action, provided a demand for payment of the tax was first made,[57] and in some states provision is also made by law for the payment of attorney's fees.[58] Whether or not the costs can be charged against the state or county, in a case where defendant prevails, depends entirely upon the local statute.[59]

(III) *APPEAL AND ERROR.* Where the law prescribes a particular procedure for reviewing a tax judgment, it is exclusive of other methods of review, such as certiorari, which would ordinarily be available.[60] On appeal, if it appears that the judgment is for a greater amount of taxes than could lawfully be levied, or includes an illegal item, it will be reversed or the illegal charge will be stricken out;[61] and on the other hand, if it omits items which it was the duty of the court to include, an appeal lies on behalf of the state.[62] The judgment will not be reversed for harmless or immaterial error, nor for errors cured by the subsequent course of proceedings.[63] An appeal-bond takes the place of the property assessed and releases the lien of the tax upon it.[64]

7. ATTACHMENT OR ARREST — a. Nature of Remedy and When Available. Payment of taxes cannot be enforced by arrest of the person unless by the authority of an explicit statute;[65] and even when this proceeding is authorized by law, it is

576, 38 Pac. 905; U. S. Trust Co. *v.* Territory, 10 N. M. 416, 62 Pac. 987; Wheeling, etc., R. Co. *v.* Wolfe, 13 Ohio Cir. Ct. 374, 7 Ohio Cir. Dec. 201; McCombs *v.* Rockport, 14 Tex. Civ. App. 560, 37 S. W. 988.

56. Webster *v.* Auditor-Gen., 121 Mich. 668, 80 N. W. 705; Rogers *v.* Marlboro County, 32 S. C. 555, 11 S. E. 383; State *v.* Baldwin University, 97 Tenn. 358, 37 S. W. 1. See State *v.* Eclipse Towboat Co., 26 La. Ann. 716.

57. Eliot *v.* Prime, 98 Me. 48, 56 Atl. 207; Dover *v.* Maine Water Co., 90 Me. 180, 38 Atl. 101; York *v.* Goodwin, 67 Me. 260.

58. *Arkansas.*— Kelley *v.* Laconia Levee Dist., 74 Ark. 202, 85 S. W. 249, 87 S. W. 638.

California.— People *v.* Central Pac. R. Co., 105 Cal. 576, 38 Pac. 905.

Missouri.— State *v.* Edwards, 144 Mo. 467, 46 S. W. 160.

Tennessee.— State *v.* Baldwin University, 97 Tenn. 358, 37 S. W. 1.

United States.— Ketchum *v.* Pacific R. Co., 14 Fed. Cas. No. 7,738, 4 Dill. 41.

59. See the statutes of the different states. And see the following cases:

Idaho.— People *v.* Moore, 1 Ida. 662.

Illinois.— People *v.* Emigh, 100 Ill. 517.

Kansas.— Whitney *v.* Morton County, 73 Kan. 502, 85 Pac. 530.

Louisiana.— Mahan *v.* Sundry Defendants, 22 La. Ann. 583.

Michigan.— Auditor-Gen. *v.* Bolt, 124 Mich. 185, 82 N. W. 845; Auditor-Gen. *v.* Baker, 84 Mich. 113, 47 N. W. 515.

See 45 Cent. Dig. tit. "Taxation," § 1220.

60. State *v.* Ames, 93 Minn. 187, 100 N. W. 889; State *v.* Faribault Waterworks, 65 Minn. 345, 68 N. W. 35; Washington County *v.* German-American Bank, 28 Minn. 360, 10 N. W. 21; State *v.* Jones, 24 Minn. 86. And see State *v.* Merchants' Bank, 160 Mo. 640, 61 S. W. 676.

Parties on appeal see *Ex p.* Washington Nat. Bank, 163 Ind. 476, 72 N. E. 260 (assessor as party to judgment); Thornburg *v.* Cardell, 123 Iowa 313, 95 N. W. 239, 98 N. W. 791 (three counties as joint plaintiffs); Adams *v.* Kuhn, 72 Miss. 276, 16 So. 598.

61. People *v.* Hastings, 26 Cal. 668; Wilmington *v.* McDonald, 133 N. C. 548, 45 S. E. 864.

62. State *v.* California Min. Co., 15 Nev. 234, 259.

63. People *v.* O'Gara Coal Co., 231 Ill. 172, 83 N. E. 140; Carney *v.* People, 210 Ill. 434, 71 N. E. 365; Keokuk, etc., Bridge Co. *v.* People, 176 Ill. 267, 52 N. E. 117; Gallup *v.* Schmidt, 154 Ind. 196, 56 N. E. 443; State *v.* Sadler, 21 Nev. 13, 23 Pac. 799; Buchanan *v.* Cook, 70 Vt. 168, 40 Atl. 102.

64. People *v.* Preston, 1 Ida. 374.

65. Marshall *v.* Wadsworth, 64 N. H. 386, 10 Atl. 685.

Collection of military taxes by imprisonment under Conn. Gen. St. (1902) § 2395, as amended by Pub. Acts (1907), c. 50, see Atwater *v.* O'Reilly, 81 Conn. 367, 71 Atl. 505.

Contempt proceedings.— In New York, a person against whom a tax is assessed on his personal property may be committed as for a contempt on account of his neglect to pay the tax. Matter of McLean, 62 Hun (N. Y.) 1, 16 N. Y. Suppl. 417; McLean *v.* Jephson, 26 Abb. N. Cas. (N. Y.) 40, 13 N. Y. Suppl. 834; McMahon *v.* Redfield, 12 Daly (N. Y.) 1; Matter of Kahn, 19 How. Pr. (N. Y.) 475. And see State *v.* Smith, 31 N. J. L. 216, holding that when a tax brought before the court by certiorari is affirmed, the court may in its discretion enforce the payment thereof by attachment.

Prosecution for obstructing collector.— Statute in California making it a misdemeanor to obstruct or hinder any public officer in the collection of taxes in which the state is interested see *Ex p.* Sam Wah, 91 Cal. 510, 27 Pac. 766.

liable as a trespasser.[76] This is the case where he fails to levy on personal property which is available for the purpose,[77] or where he does not comply with the law requiring him to deposit a certified copy of his warrant with the jailer.[78]

d. Release or Discharge. One imprisoned for non-payment of taxes may obtain his release on giving bond,[79] or on the poor debtor's oath;[80] but he is not entitled as of right to the writ of personal replevin and to be discharged thereon,[81] or to be released simply on his production of sufficient property to pay the tax;[82] nor can he take advantage of an order releasing the collector from his personal liability to the town for the taxes in question.[83]

e. Defenses, Objections, and Review. On appeal from an order committing defendant for failure to pay his tax, or other review of the proceedings, he may show that the collector made no sufficient effort to levy on personal property,[84] or that defendant was not liable to be charged with the tax in question;[85] but he cannot object that the levy or assessment was excessive, at least if he made no effort to have it corrected at the proper time.[86]

8. Criminal Prosecution or Recovery of Fine. It is sometimes, by statute, made a misdemeanor, punishable by fine, for a corporation or association to fail to pay its taxes after they become delinquent.[87]

D. Remedies For Wrongful Enforcement — 1. Limitations of Judicial Authority. For cogent reasons of public policy the courts are slow to interfere with the orderly and speedy collection of the public revenues, and will not interfere with proceedings to enforce the payment of taxes except in the clearest cases and for the most imperative reasons.[88] In some states they are forbidden by statute to issue the writ of injunction to restrain or interfere with the collection

76. Wilcox *v.* Gladwin, 50 Conn. 77; Townsend *v.* Walcutt, 3 Metc. (Mass.) 152; Boardman *v.* Goldsmith, 48 Vt. 403.

77. Snow *v.* Clark, 9 Gray (Mass.) 190; Flint *v.* Whitney, 28 Vt. 680.

78. Gordon *v.* Clifford, 28 N. H. 402; Henry *v.* Tilson, 19 Vt. 447.

79. Athens *v.* Ware, 39 Me. 345; Hoxie *v.* Weston, 19 Me. 322.

80. Skinner *v.* Lyford, 73 Me. 282.

81. Aldrich *v.* Aldrich, 8 Metc. (Mass.) 102.

82. Osgood *v.* Welch, 19 N. H. 105.

83. Hoxie *v.* Weston, 19 Me. 322.

84. Kerr *v.* Atwood, 188 Mass. 506, 74 N. E. 917.

Return as evidence.— Where the return on a tax warrant states that the collector has made diligent search for goods of the taxpayer, without finding any, it is *prima facie* evidence in favor of the collector to show a diligent search. Kerr *v.* Atwood, 188 Mass. 506, 74 N. E. 917. In New York it is conclusive. Matter of McLean, 62 Hun (N. Y.) 1, 16 N. Y. Suppl. 417.

85. Draves *v.* People, 97 Ill. App. 151; McLean *v.* Jephson, 123 N. Y. 142, 25 N. E. 409, 9 L. R. A. 493 [*reversing* 41 Hun 479]; *In re* Nichols, 54 N. Y. 62.

Enlistment in the United States army does not exempt one from a preëxisting liability to taxation on account of his property, or from liability to arrest on warrant for non-payment. Webster *v.* Seymour, 8 Vt. 135.

86. *In re* McLean, 3 N. Y. Suppl. 45.

87. Ky. St. (1903) § 4091, providing that any corporation, company, or association failing to pay its taxes, penalty, and interest, after they become delinquent, "shall be deemed guilty of a misdemeanor, and, on conviction, shall be fined fifty dollars for each day the same remains unpaid, to be recovered by indictment or civil action," etc. The penalty imposed by this section cannot be recovered in a suit issued by the revenue agent under Ky. St. (1903) § 4263, making it the duty of the revenue agent, when directed by the auditor, to institute suits, motions, or proceedings in the name of the commonwealth against any delinquent officer or other person, to recover any money which may be due the commonwealth, as a person charged with having committed a misdemeanor does not owe the commonwealth any money until he has been convicted of such misdemeanor. Louisville Water Co. *v.* Com., 132 Ky. 311, 116 S. W. 711.

88. *Connecticut.*— Dodd *v.* Hartford, 25 Conn. 232.

Georgia.— Scofield *v.* Perkerson, 46 Ga. 350; Cody *v.* Lennard, 45 Ga. 85; Eve *v.* State, 21 Ga. 50.

Illinois.— Felsenthal *v.* Johnson, 104 Ill. 21.

Kansas.— Kansas Pac. R. Co. *v.* Russell, 8 Kan. 558.

New York.— Brass *v.* Rathbone, 8 N. Y. App. Div. 78, 40 N. Y. Suppl. 466 [*affirmed* in 153 N. Y. 435, 47 N. E. 905]; Messeck *v.* Columbia County, 50 Barb. 190; New York L. Ins. Co. *v.* New York, 1 Abb. Pr. 250.

Pennsylvania.— Black *v.* Boyd, 155 Pa. St 163, 26 Atl. 5.

United States.— Nye *v.* Washburn, 125 Fed. 817; Steubenville, etc., R. Co. *v.* Tuscarawass County, 22 Fed. Cas. No. 13,388.

See 45 Cent. Dig. tit. "Taxation," § 1230 *et seq.*

on account of mere errors or irregularities in the proceedings not affecting the substantial justice of the tax,[97] nor on account of technical objections or circumstances of hardship in the particular case which do not undermine the foundations of the complainant's obligation to pay his tax.[98]

(II) *ILLEGALITY OF TAX.* Where a tax is illegal, because levied under an unconstitutional statute, or for an unlawful purpose, or by persons having no authority whatever to make the levy, or assessed on persons or property not subject to taxation, it is the doctrine of many cases that this is sufficient ground to justify a court of equity in enjoining proceedings for its collection,[99] unless pro-

County, 11 N. D. 107, 90 N. W. 260; Fleming *v.* Power, 77 S. C. 528, 58 S. E. 430; Taylor *v.* Secor, 92 U. S. 575, 23 L. ed. 663; Heine *v.* Madison Parish, etc., Levee Com'rs, 19 Wall. (U. S.) 655, 22 L. ed. 223; Dows *v.* Chicago, 11 Wall. (U. S.) 108, 20 L. ed. 65; Parmley *v.* St. Louis, etc., R. Co., 18 Fed. Cas. No. 10,767, 3 Dill. 13. And see *infra*, X, D, 2, b, (II).

97. *Illinois.*— Munson *v.* Minor, 22 Ill. 594.

Indiana.— Ricketts *v.* Spraker, 77 Ind. 371; Jones *v.* Summer, 27 Ind. 510.

Iowa.— Security Sav. Bank *v.* Carroll, 131 Iowa 605, 109 N. W. 212.

Kansas.— Chicago, etc., R. Co. *v.* Grant, 55 Kan. 386, 40 Pac. 654; Dutton *v.* Citizens' Nat. Bank, 53 Kan. 440, 36 Pac. 719; Smith *v.* Leavenworth County, 9 Kan. 296; Seward *v.* Rheiner, 2 Kan. App. 95, 43 Pac. 423.

Missouri.— Dickhaus *v.* Olderheide, 22 Mo. App. 76.

Ohio.— Wagner *v.* Zumstein, 10 Ohio Dec. (Reprint) 515, 21 Cinc. L. Bul. 317.

Oregon.— Yamhill County *v.* Foster, 53 Oreg. 124, 99 Pac. 286.

Wisconsin.— Hixon *v.* Oneida County, 82 Wis. 515, 52 N. W. 445.

United States.— Taylor *v.* Secor, 92 U. S. 575, 23 L. ed. 663; Jackson Lumber Co. *v.* McCrimmon, 164 Fed. 759; Woodman *v.* Latimer, 2 Fed. 842; Woodman *v.* Ely, 2 Fed. 839; Parmley *v.* St. Louis, etc., R. Co., 18 Fed. Cas. No. 10,767, 3 Dill. 13.

See 45 Cent. Dig. tit. "Taxation," § 1230 *et seq.*

98. Wilson *v.* Hamilton County, 68 Ind. 507; Graham *v.* Chautauqua County, 31 Kan. 473, 2 Pac. 549; Burlington, etc., R. Co. *v.* Saunders County, 16 Nebr. 123, 19 N. W. 698.

Taxpayer as creditor of municipality.— Where a person whose property has been assessed for taxation by a city or county is a creditor of the municipality, he cannot have an injunction to restrain the collection of the tax until his debt shall have been paid. Fremont *v.* Mariposa County, 11 Cal. 361; Finnegan *v.* Fernandina, 15 Fla. 379, 21 Am. Rep. 292; Scobey *v.* Decatur County, 72 Ind. 551.

99. *Alabama.*— Montgomery *v.* Sayre, 65 Ala. 564; Mobile *v.* Baldwin, 57 Ala. 61, 29 Am. Rep. 712.

Arkansas.— Little Rock *v.* Barton, 33 Ark. 436; Oliver *v.* Memphis, etc., R. Co., 30 Ark. 128.

Dakota.— Frost *v.* Flick, 1 Dak. 131, 46 N. W. 508.

District of Columbia.— Alexander *v.* Dennison, 2 MacArthur 562.

Florida.— Finnegan *v.* Fernandina, 15 Fla. 379, 21 Am. Rep. 292.

Georgia.— Southwestern R. Co. *v.* Wright, 68 Ga. 311; Georgia Mut. Loan Assoc. *v.* McGowan, 59 Ga. 811; Vanover *v.* Davis, 27 Ga. 354.

Illinois.— Carr *v.* Arnold, 239 Ill. 37, 87 N. E. 870; Hanberg *v.* Western Cold Storage Co., 231 Ill. 32, 82 N. E. 842; Allwood *v.* Cowen, 111 Ill. 481; Lemont *v.* Singer, etc., Stone Co., 98 Ill. 94; Kimball *v.* Merchants', etc., Trust Co., 89 Ill. 611; Swinney *v.* Beard, 71 Ill. 27; Vieley *v.* Thompson, 44 Ill. 9; Ottawa *v.* Walker, 21 Ill. 605, 71 Am. Dec. 121.

Indiana.— State *v.* Clinton County, 162 Ind. 580, 68 N. E. 295, 70 N. E. 373, 984; Yocum *v.* Brazil First Nat. Bank, 144 Ind. 272, 43 N. E. 231; Scott *v.* Knightstown, 84 Ind. 108; Indianapolis, etc., R. Co. *v.* Tipton County, 70 Ind. 385; Riley *v.* Western Union Tel. Co., 47 Ind. 511; Jeffersonville *v.* Paterson, 32 Ind. 140; Toledo, etc., R. Co. *v.* Lafayette, 22 Ind. 262; Cleveland, etc., R. Co. *v.* Ensley, (App. 1909) 89 N. E. 607; Nyce *v.* Schmoll, 40 Ind. App. 555, 82 N. E. 539.

Iowa.— Bednar *v.* Carroll, 138 Iowa 338, 116 N. W. 315; Security Sav. Bank *v.* Carroll, 131 Iowa 605, 109 N. W. 212; Smith *v.* Peterson, 123 Iowa 672, 99 N. W. 552; Williams *v.* Penny, 25 Iowa 436; Olmstead *v.* *v.* Henry County, 24 Iowa 33.

Kansas.— Burnes *v.* Atchison, 2 Kan. 454.

Kentucky.— Gates *v.* Barrett, 79 Ky. 295; Owen County Fiscal Court *v.* F. & A. Cox Co., 132 Ky. 738, 117 S. W. 296; Mt. Sterling Oil, etc., Co. *v.* Ratliff, 127 Ky. 1, 104 S. W. 993, 31 Ky. L. Rep. 1229.

Maryland.— Baltimore *v.* Gail, 106 Md. 684, 68 Atl. 282; Joesting *v.* Baltimore, 97 Md. 589, 55 Atl. 456.

Massachusetts.— Freeland *v.* Hastings, 10 Allen 570.

Mississippi. — Meridian *v.* Bagsdale, 67 Miss. 86, 6 So. 619.

Missouri.— St. Louis, etc., R. Co. *v.* Epperson, 97 Mo. 300, 10 S. W. 478.

Nebraska.— Philadelphia Mortg., etc., Co. *v.* Omaha, 63 Nebr. 280, 88 N. W. 523, 90 N. W. 1005, 93 Am. St. Rep. 442; Union Pac. R. Co. *v.* Cheyenne County, 64 Nebr. 777, 90 N. W. 917; Grand Island, etc., R. Co. *v.* Dawes County, 62 Nebr. 44, 86 N. W. 934; Morris *v.* Merrel, 44 Nebr. 423, 62 N. W. 865.

North Carolina.— Purnell *v.* Page, 133

by forcing payment of the tax or that the party would not be adequately protected by the remedies which the law affords him, such as a review of the assessment on appeal or certiorari, action of trespass, suit to recover back the taxes paid, or the like.[3] And in any case injunction will not issue unless the illegality of the tax is shown very clearly,[4] nor will it be granted if it is admitted or

cago, 24 Fed. Cas. No. 14,374, 3 Biss. 82; Union Pac. R. Co. *v.* Lincoln County, 24 Fed. Cas. No. 14,379, 2 Dill. 279. And see Illinois L. Ins. Co. *v.* Newman, 141 Fed. 449, holding that a federal court of equity is without power to enjoin the collection of a tax levied under the authority of a state on the ground of its illegality alone, although such power is conferred by statute on the courts of the state.

See 45 Cent. Dig. tit. "Taxation," § 1231. And see *infra*, X, D, 2, b.

3. *Alabama.*— Mobile *v.* Baldwin, 57 Ala. 61, 29 Am. Rep. 712; Alabama Gold L. Ins. Co. *v.* Lott, 54 Ala. 499.

California.— Crocker *v.* Scott, 149 Cal. 575, 87 Pac. 102; Robinson *v.* Gaar, 6 Cal. 273; De Witt *v.* Hays, 2 Cal. 463, 56 Am. Dec. 352.

Colorado.— Hallett *v.* Arapahoe County, 40 Colo. 308, 90 Pac. 678; Woodward *v.* Ellsworth, 4 Colo. 580; Price *v.* Kramer, 4 Colo. 546.

Connecticut.— Rowland *v.* Weston First School Dist., 42 Conn. 30; Arnold *v.* Middletown, 39 Conn. 401.

District of Columbia.— Buchanan *v.* MacFarland, 31 App. Cas. 6; Burgdorf *v.* District of Columbia, 7 App. Cas. 405; Washington Market Co. *v.* District of Columbia, 4 Mackey 416; Harkness *v.* District of Columbia, 1 MacArthur 121.

Florida.— H. W. Metcalf Co. *v.* Martin, 54 Fla. 531, 45 So. 463, 127 Am. St. Rep. 149; Baldwin *v.* Tucker, 16 Fla. 258.

Idaho.— Wilkerson *v.* Walters, 1 Ida. 564.

Indiana.— Hendricks *v.* Gilchrist, 76 Ind. 369; Brown *v.* Herron, 59 Ind. 61.

Kansas.— Burnes *v.* Atchison, 2 Kan. 454.

Maryland.— O'Neal *v.* Virginia, etc., Bridge Co., 18 Md. 1, 79 Am. Dec. 669.

Massachusetts.— Loud *v.* Charlestown, 99 Mass. 208; Brewer *v.* Springfield, 97 Mass. 152.

Michigan.— Hagenbuch *v.* Howard, 34 Mich. 1.

Minnesota.— Bradish *v.* Lucken, 38 Minn. 186, 36 N. W. 454; Scribner *v.* Allen, 12 Minn. 148.

Mississippi.— Beck *v.* Allen, 58 Miss. 143.

Missouri.— McPike *v.* Pew, 48 Mo. 525; Steines *v.* Franklin County, 48 Mo. 167, 8 Am. Rep. 87.

Nevada.— Wells *v.* Dayton, 11 Nev. 161.

New Hampshire.— Perley *v.* Dolloff, 60 N. H. 504; Brown *v.* Concord, 56 N. H. 375; Rockingham Ten Cent Sav. Bank *v.* Portsmouth, 52 N. H. 17.

New Jersey.— Lewis *v.* Elizabeth, 25 N. J. Eq. 298; Hoagland *v.* Delaware, 17 N. J. Eq. 106.

New York.— United Lines Tel. Co. *v.* Grant, 137 N. Y. 7, 32 N. E. 1005; Mutual Ben. L. Assur. Co. *v.* New York, 3 Abb. Dec. 344, 3 Keyes 182, 2 Abb. Pr. N. S. 233, 32 How. Pr. 359 [*affirming* 8 Bosw. 683]; Hasbrook *v.* Kingston Bd. of Education, 3 Abb. Dec. 340, 3 Keyes 480, 3 Transcr. App. 106, 5 Abb. Pr. N. S. 399; Sage *v.* Gloversville, 43 N. Y. App. Div. 245, 60 N. Y. Suppl. 791; Rome, etc., R. Co. *v.* Smith, 39 Hun 332 [*affirmed* in 101 N. Y. 684]; Mutual Ben. L. Ins. Co. *v.* New York, 33 Barb. 322, 20 How. Pr. 416 [*affirmed* in 3 Abb. Dec. 344, 3 Keyes 182, 2 Abb. Pr. N. S. 233, 32 How. Pr. 359]; Wilson *v.* New York, 4 E. D. Smith 675, 1 Abb. Pr. 4; Postal Tel. Cable Co. *v.* Grant, 11 N. Y. Suppl. 323; Pacific Mail Steamship Co. *v.* New York, 57 How. Pr. 511.

North Carolina.— Hall *v.* Fayetteville, 115 N. C. 281, 20 S. E. 373.

Pennsylvania.— Manor Real Estate, etc., Co. *v.* Cooner, 209 Pa. St. 531, 58 Atl. 918.

South Carolina.— See Ware Shoals Mfg. Co. *v.* Jones, 78 S. C. 211, 58 S. E. 811.

South Dakota.— Chicago, etc., R. Co. *v.* Rolfson, 23 S. D. 405, 122 N. W. 343.

Texas.— Stephens *v.* Texas, etc., R. Co., 100 Tex. 177, 97 S. W. 309 [*reversing* (Civ. App. 1906) 93 S. W. 436].

Virginia.— Norfolk *v.* Perry Co., 108 Va. 28, 61 S. E. 866, 128 Am. St. Rep. 940.

Wisconsin.— Whittaker *v.* Janesville, 33 Wis. 76; Van Cott *v.* Milwaukee County, 18 Wis. 247. And see Duluth Log Co. *v.* Hawthorne, 139 Wis. 170, 120 N. W. 864.

United States.—Arkansas Bldg., etc., Assoc. *v.* Madden, 175 U. S. 269, 20 S. Ct. 119, 44 L. ed. 159; Taylor *v.* Secor, 92 U. S. 575, 23 L. ed. 663; Dows *v.* Chicago, 11 Wall. 108, 20 L. ed. 65; Linehan R. Transfer Co. *v.* Pendergrass, 70 Fed. 1, 16 C. C. A. 585; Schulenberg-Boeckeler Lumber Co. *v.* Hayward, 20 Fed. 422; Trask *v.* Maguire, 24 Fed. Cas. No. 14,145, 2 Dill. 183 note; Union Pac. R. Co. *v.* Lincoln County, 24 Fed. Cas. No. 14,379, 2 Dill. 279.

See 45 Cent. Dig. tit. "Taxation," §§ 1230, 1238. And see *infra*, X, D, 2, b, (II).

Compare McTwiggan *v.* Hunter, 18 R. I. 776, 30 Atl. 962, holding that when a taxpayer, suing in his own behalf, attacks an assessment for an illegality extending to the whole tax and its assessment on every person taxed, equity will take jurisdiction, although such complaining taxpayer would have an adequate remedy at law.

4. *Illinois.*— Peirce *v.* Carlock, 224 Ill. 608, 79 N. E. 959.

Nebraska.— Rittenhouse *v.* Bigelow, 38 Nebr. 547, 58 N. W. 534.

North Carolina.— Mitchell *v.* Craven County, 74 N. C. 487; Brodnax *v.* Groom, 64 N. C. 244.

Pennsylvania.— Truesdell's Appeal, 58 Pa. St. 148.

atic adoption of a rule or principle of valuation contrary to the constitutional or statutory requirement of equality and uniformity,[18] or where plaintiff's assessment, once legally fixed, was illegally increased without giving him notice or an opportunity to contest it.[19]

(vi) *ASSESSMENT OF PERSONS OR PROPERTY NOT LIABLE.* Equity will enjoin the collection of taxes assessed upon exempt or non-taxable property,[20] and this remedy also is proper where the assessment is made, or the tax sought to be enforced, against one who is not the owner of the property or not liable for the payment of the tax,[21] and where the assessment was illegal because the

Co. *v.* Wolff, 150 Ill. 491, 37 N. E. 930; Kimball *v.* Merchants' Sav., etc., Co., 89 Ill. 611.

Iowa.— Montis *v.* McQuiston, 107 Iowa 651, 78 N. W. 704.

Montana.— Montana Ore Purchasing Co. *v.* Maher, 32 Mont. 480, 81 Pac. 13.

Ohio.— Euclid Ave. Sav., etc. Co. *v.* Hubbard, 22 Ohio Cir. Ct. 20, 12 Ohio Cir. Dec. 279; Cozad *v.* Hubbard, 18 Ohio Cir. Ct. 294, 10 Ohio Cir. Dec. 162.

Oklahoma.—Cranmer *v.* Williamson, 8 Okla. 683, 59 Pac. 249; Caffrey *v.* Overholser, 8 Okla. 202, 57 Pac. 206; Martin *v.* Clay, 8 Okla. 46, 56 Pac. 715; Weber *v.* Dillon, 7 Okla. 568, 54 Pac. 894.

18. *Kansas.*— Chicago, etc., R. Co. *v.* Atchison County, 54 Kan. 781, 39 Pac. 1039; Missouri, etc., R. Co. *v.* Geary County, 9 Kan. App. 350, 58 Pac. 121.

Oregon.— Smith *v.* Kelly, 24 Oreg. 464, 33 Pac. 642.

Pennsylvania.— Kemble *v.* Titusville, 135 Pa. St. 141, 19 Atl. 946.

Washington.—Andrews *v.* King County, 1 Wash. 46, 23 Pac. 409, 22 Am. St. Rep. 136.

Wisconsin.— Spear *v.* Door County, 65 Wis. 298, 27 N. W. 60; Lefferts *v.* Calumet County, 21 Wis. 688.

United States.— Raymond *v.* Chicago Union Traction Co., 207 U. S. 20, 28 S. Ct. 7, 52 L. ed. 78 [*affirming* 114 Fed. 557]; Chicago, etc., R. Co. *v.* Babcock, 204 U. S. 585, 27 S. Ct. 326, 51 L. ed. 636; Stanley *v.* Albany County, 121 U. S. 535, 7 S. Ct. 1234, 30 L. ed. 1000; Cummings *v.* Merchants' Nat. Bank, 101 U. S. 153, 25 L. ed. 903; Pelton *v.* Commercial Nat. Bank, 101 U. S. 143, 25 L. ed. 901; Chicago, etc., R. Co. *v.* Republic County, 67 Fed. 411, 14 C. C. A. 456; Michigan R. Tax Cases, 138 Fed. 223 [*affirmed* in 201 U. S. 245, 26 S. Ct. 459, 50 L. ed. 744]; Louisville, etc., R. Co. *v.* Coulter, 131 Fed. 282; Railroad, etc., Co.'s *v.* Tennessee, 85 Fed. 302; Toledo First Nat. Bank *v.* Lucas County Treasurer, 25 Fed. 749; Dundee Mortg. Trust Inv. Co. *v.* Parrish, 24 Fed. 197; Exchange Nat. Bank *v.* Miller, 19 Fed. 372.

See 45 Cent. Dig. tit. "Taxation," § 1234.

19. *California.*— Lahman *v.* Hatch, 124 Cal. 1, 56 Pac. 621.

Illinois.— Huling *v.* Ehrich, 183 Ill. 315, 55 N. E. 636; McConkey *v.* Smith, 73 Ill. 313; Darling *v.* Gunn, 50 Ill. 424; Cleghorn *v.* Postlewaite, 43 Ill. 428; Glassford *v.* Dorsey, 2 Ill. App. 521.

Indiana.— Seymour First Nat. Bank *v.* Brodhecker, 137 Ind. 693, 37 N. E. 340.

Kansas.— Topeka City R. Co. *v.* Roberts, 45 Kan. 360, 25 Pac. 854; Leavenworth County *v.* Lang, 8 Kan. 284.

Mississippi.—Alabama, etc., R. Co. *v.* Brennan, 69 Miss. 103, 10 So. 451.

United States.— Hills *v.* National Albany Exch. Bank, 12 Fed. 93.

20. *California.*— Robinson *v.* Gaar, 6 Cal. 273.

Colorado.— Colorado Farm, etc., Co. *v.* Beerbohm, 43 Colo. 464, 96 Pac. 443.

Illinois.— Siegfried *v.* Raymond, 190 Ill. 424, 60 N. E. 868; Illinois Cent. R. Co. *v.* Hodges, 113 Ill. 323; Kimball *v.* Merchants' Sav., etc., Co., 89 Ill. 611; Munson *v.* Miller, 66 Ill. 380.

Indiana.— Buck *v.* Miller, 147 Ind. 586, 45 N. E. 647, 47 N. E. 8, 62 Am. St. Rep. 436, 37 L. R. A. 384. *Compare* Telle *v.* Green, 28 Ind. 184.

Iowa.— Bednar *v.* Carroll, 138 Iowa 338, 116 N. W. 315.

Michigan.— Lenawee County Sav. Bank *v.* Adrian, 66 Mich. 273, 33 N. W. 304.

Missouri.— Valle *v.* Ziegler, 84 Mo. 214.

New Jersey.— Morris Canal, etc., Co. *v.* Jersey City, 12 N. J. Eq. 227.

Ohio.— Jones *v.* Davis, 35 Ohio St. 474.

Pennsylvania.— St. Mary's Gas Co. *v.* Elk County, 191 Pa. St. 458, 43 Atl. 321; Arthur *v.* Polk Borough School Dist., 164 Pa. St. 410, 30 Atl. 299.

Virginia.— Staunton *v.* Mary Baldwin Seminary, 99 Va. 653, 39 S. E. 596.

West Virginia.— Crim *v.* Phillipi, 38 W. Va. 122, 18 S. E. 466; Christie *v.* Malden, 23 W. Va. 667.

United States.— U. S. *v.* Rickert, 188 U. S. 432, 23 S. Ct. 478, 47 L. ed. 532; Osborn *v.* U. S. Bank, 9 Wheat. 738, 6 L. ed. 204; McKnight *v.* Dudley, 148 Fed. 204, 78 C. C. A. 162.

Canada.— Canadian Pac. R. Co. *v.* Calgary, 1 Northwest. Terr. 67.

See 45 Cent. Dig. tit. "Taxation," § 1235.

Compare Raleigh, etc., R. Co. *v.* Lewis, 99 N. C. 62, 5 S. E. 82.

21. Searing *v.* Heavysides, 106 Ill. 85; Ream *v.* Stone, 102 Ill. 359; Wangler *v.* Black Hawk County, 56 Iowa 384, 9 N. W. 314; Nicodemus *v.* Hull, 93 Md. 364, 48 Atl. 1049; Texas, etc., R. Co. *v.* Harrison County, 54 Tex. 119. But see Bloxham *v.* Consumers' Electric Light, etc., Co., 36 Fla. 519, 18 So. 444, 51 Am. St. Rep. 44, 29 L. R. A. 507; Broderick *v.* Allamakee County, 104 Iowa 750, 73 N. W. 884.

nor can the power be exercised after the end of the period of time limited by law for that purpose.[23] As to the authority vested in the officer making the sale, it is a naked power not coupled with an interest, and must be exercised in exact conformity with the law; a tax title is *stricti juris*, and its holder must be prepared to show full compliance with the directions of the statute.[24]

2. **Authority of Municipal Corporations.** A municipal corporation has no power or authority to sell land for non-payment of taxes unless this power be granted to it in express terms by statute and unless the power be deducible from a strict construction of the law; a general grant of authority, for example, to "assess and collect taxes" not being sufficient warrant for the sale and conveyance of lands for their non-payment.[25]

3. **Effect of Change of Boundaries.** Where land is assessed for taxes in a county, a subsequent change in the county boundaries, having the effect of transferring the land to another county, will not defeat the lien of the assessment or prevent the tax collector of the former county from enforcing the collection by sale of the land.[26]

4. **Strict Compliance With Statutes Required.** So far as regards provisions of law designed for the protection and security of the citizen, it is essential to the validity of a tax-sale of lands that there shall be a strict compliance with all the directions of the statute, both in relation to the observance of any conditions or prerequisites to the exercise of the power of sale, and to the conduct of the sale itself, as well as to the performance of conditions subsequent to the sale.[27]

N. W. 222; Norris *v.* Hall, 124 Mich. 170, 82 N. W. 832; McNaughton *v.* Martin, 72 Mich. 276, 40 N. W. 326; Hall *v.* Perry, 72 Mich. 202, 40 N. W. 324; Folsom *v.* Whitney, 95 Minn. 322, 104 N. W. 140.

23. White *v.* Portland, 68 Conn. 293, 36 Atl. 46; State *v.* Bellin, 79 Minn. 131, 81 N. W. 763.

24. *California.*— Preston *v.* Hirsch, 5 Cal. App. 485, 90 Pac. 965.

Indiana.— Millikan *v.* Patterson, 91 Ind. 515.

Maryland.— McMahon *v.* Crean, 109 Md. 652, 71 Atl. 995.

New Hampshire.— Cahoon *v.* Coe, 57 N. H. 556.

New York.— Cruger *v.* Dougherty, 43 N. Y. 107; Hubbell *v.* Weldon, Lalor 139.

Tax titles see *infra*, XIV.

25. *Iowa.*— McInerny *v.* Reed, 23 Iowa 410; Ham *v.* Miller, 20 Iowa 450.

Louisiana.— State *v.* New Orleans, 112 La. 408, 36 So. 475.

New York.— Wilcox *v.* Rochester, 54 Hun 72, 7 N. Y. Suppl. 187 [*affirmed* in 129 N. Y. 247, 29 N. E. 99]; Sharp *v.* Johnson, 4 Hill 92, 40 Am. Dec. 259.

Pennsylvania.— Philadelphia *v.* Greble, 38 Pa. St. 339.

Wisconsin.— Knox *v.* Peterson, 21 Wis. 247.

United States.— Beaty *v.* Knowler, 4 Pet. 152, 7 L. ed. 813.

See Municipal Corporations, 28 Cyc. 1717.

26. *California.*— Moss *v.* Shear, 25 Cal. 38, 85 Am. Dec. 94.

Indiana.— Alvis *v.* Whitney, 43 Ind. 83: Morgan County *v.* Hendricks County, 32 Ind. 234.

Iowa.— Ellsworth *v.* Nelson, 81 Iowa 57, 46 N. W. 740; Pitts *v.* Lewis, 81 Iowa 51, 46 N. W. 739; Collins *v.* Storm, 75 Iowa 36, 39 N. W. 161; Hilliard *v.* Griffin, 72 Iowa 331, 33 N. W. 156; Milwaukee, etc., R. Co. *v.* Kossuth County, 41 Iowa 57.

Kansas.— Kansas State Agricultural College *v.* Linscott, 30 Kan. 240, 1 Pac. 81.

Massachusetts.— Harman *v.* New Marlborough, 9 Cush. 525; Waldron *v.* Lee, 5 Pick. 323.

Michigan.—Comins *v.* Harrisville, 45 Mich. 442, 8 N. W. 44.

Mississippi.— Eskridge *v.* McGruder, 45 Miss. 294. And see Deason *v.* Dixon, 54 Miss. 585.

Pennsylvania.— Devor *v.* McClintock, 9 Watts & S. 80; Robinson *v.* Williams, 6 Watts 281.

Wisconsin.— Austin *v.* Holt, 32 Wis. 478.

See 45 Cent. Dig. tit. "Taxation." § 1265.

But *compare* Cotter *v.* Sutherland, 18 U. C. C. P. 357; Doe *v.* Grover, 4 U. C. Q. B. 23. And see Harvey *v.* Douglass, 73 Ark. 221, 83 S. W. 946.

27. *Alabama.*— Oliver *v.* Robinson, 58 Ala. 46; Rivers *v.* Thompson, 43 Ala. 633.

California.— Kelsey *v.* Abbott, 13 Cal. 609; Ferris *v.* Coover, 10 Cal. 589.

District of Columbia.— Kann *v.* King, 25 App. Cas. 182 [*reversed* on other grounds in 204 U. S. 43, 27 S. Ct. 213, 51 L. ed. 360].

Florida.— Starks *v.* Sawyer, 56 Fla. 596, 47 So. 513; Orlando *v.* Equitable Bldg., etc., Assoc., 45 Fla. 507, 33 So. 986; Donald *v.* McKinnon, 17 Fla. 746.

Georgia.— Brooks *v.* Rooney, 11 Ga. 423, 56 Am. Dec. 430.

Illinois.— Williams *v.* Underhill, 58 Ill. 137; Conway *v.* Cable, 37 Ill. 82, 87 Am. Dec. 240.

Indiana.— Millikan *v.* Patterson, 91 Ind. 515.

Iowa.— Abell *v.* Cross, 17 Iowa 171.

But a more liberal rule is applied to those statutory provisions which are intended only for the convenience of officers or to promote system and despatch in the conduct of public business; as to these, a substantial compliance with the statute is sufficient.[28]

5. What Law Governs. So far as concerns the essential elements of the power to sell land for taxes and the conservation of vested rights, such a sale is governed by the law in force at the time of the assessment;[29] but as regards the proceedings relating to the sale itself it is governed by the statute in force when the sale is made,[30] unless there is a saving clause as to pending proceedings.[31] Hence if the existing statute is repealed, the proceedings must be conducted under the new and not the old law;[32] and this is the case where the new statute makes a complete change in the method of collecting taxes or introduces a wholly new system,[33] although the various laws will be so construed, if possible, as to avoid repugnancy or repeal.[34]

Louisiana.— Coucy v. Cummings, 12 La. Ann. 748.

Maine.— French v. Patterson, 61 Me. 203; Payson v. Hall, 30 Me. 319; Flint v. Sawyer. 30 Me. 226; Brown v. Veazie, 25 Me. 359.

Massachusetts.— Harrington v. Worcester, 6 Allen 576; Alvord v. Collin, 20 Pick. 418.

Mississippi.— Minor v. Natchez, 4 Sm. & M. 602, 43 Am. Dec. 488.

Missouri.— Large v. Fisher, 49 Mo. 307; Abbott v. Doling, 49 Mo. 302; Reeds v. Morton, 9 Mo. 878.

New Hampshire.— Cahoon v. Coe, 57 N. H. 556.

New York.— Tallman v. White, 2 N. Y. 66; Bunner v. Eastman, 50 Barb. 639; Hubbell v. Weldon, Lalor 139; Sharpe v. Speir, 4 Hill 76; Jackson v. Shepard, 7 Cow. 88, 17 Am. Dec. 502.

Pennsylvania.— Wister v. Kammerer, 2 Yeates 100.

Tennessee.— Sheafer v. Mitchell, 109 Tenn. 181, 71 S. W. 86; Sampson v. Marr, 7 Baxt. 486; Hamilton v. Burum, 3 Yerg. 355; Michie v. Mullin, 5 Hayw. 90; Bloomstein v. Brien, 3 Tenn. Ch. 55. *Compare* Randolph v. Metcalf, 6 Coldw. 400, holding that the law relating to tax-sales should be liberally construed, and that sales of land for taxes should be held good if there has been a reasonable compliance with the law.

Vermont.— Chandler v. Spear, 22 Vt. 388.

Virginia.— Martin v. Snowden, 18 Gratt. 100; Wilson v. Bell, 7 Leigh 22.

Washington.— Albring v. Petronio, 44 Wash. 132, 87 Pac. 49.

West Virginia.— Webb v. Ritter, 60 W. Va. 193, 54 S. E. 484.

United States.— Ronkendorff v. Taylor, 4 Pet. 349, 7 L. ed. 882; Thatcher v. Powell, 6 Wheat. 119, 5 L. ed. 221; Williams v. Peyton, 4 Wheat. 77, 4 L. ed. 518; Hodgdon v. Burleigh, 4 Fed. 111; Miner v. McLean, 17 Fed. Cas. No. 9,630, 4 McLean 138.

Canada.— Colquhoun v. Driscoll, 10 Manitoba 254; Ryan v. Whelan, 6 Manitoba 565; Cotter v. Sutherland, 18 U. C. C. P. 357.

See 45 Cent. Dig. tit. "Taxation," § 1263 *et seq.*

28. Starks v. Sawyer, 56 Fla. 596, 47 So. 513; Tweed v. Metcalf, 4 Mich. 579; Pierce v. Hall, 41 Barb. (N. Y.) 142; Kane v. Garfield, 60 Vt. 79, 13 Atl. 800; Chandler v. Spear, 22 Vt. 388. And see McMahon v. Crean, 109 Md. 652, 71 Atl. 995; Miller v. Henderson, 50 Wash. 200, 96 Pac. 1052.

Collateral attack see *infra*, XI, N, 3.

29. *Florida.*— Smith v. Philips, 51 Fla. 327, 41 So. 527.

Louisiana.— Schwartz v. Huer, McGloin 81.

Maine.— Brown v. Veazie, 25 Me. 359.

New Hampshire.— Cambridge Proprietors v. Chandler, 6 N. H. 271.

Pennsylvania.— Lambertson v. Hogan, 2 Pa. St. 22.

Sale under execution.— The provisions of the constitution of Illinois concerning the sale of land for taxes have no application to sales on executions obtained after personal suit against delinquent taxpayers; but such suits, and proceedings on executions obtained therein, are governed by the rules and provisions of law applicable to suits generally. Douthett v. Kettle, 104 Ill. 356.

30. *Indiana.*— Stalcup v. Dixon, 136 Ind. 9, 35 N. E. 987.

Louisiana.— Del Castillo v. McConnico, 47 La. Ann. 1473, 17 So. 868; Smith v. New Orleans, 43 La. Ann. 726, 9 So. 773.

Minnesota.— Hage v. St. Paul Land, etc., Co., 107 Minn. 350, 120 N. W. 298; Lawton v. Barker, 105 Minn. 102, 117 N. W. 249.

New York.—Matter of McIntyre, 124 N. Y. App. Div. 66, 108 N. Y. Suppl. 242.

Texas.— Bente v. Sullivan, (Civ. App. 1908) 115 S. W. 350.

And see the cases cited in the following notes.

31. Levy v. Acklen, 2 Tenn. Ch. App. 201.

32. Thomas v. Collins, 58 Mich. 64, 24 N. W. 553; Hage v. St. Paul Land, etc., Co., 107 Minn. 350, 120 N. W. 298; Lawton v. Barker, 105 Minn. 102, 117 N. W. 249; Matter of McIntyre, 124 N. Y. App. Div. 66, 108 N. Y. Suppl. 242.

33. Cromwell v. MacLean, 123 N. Y. 474, 25 N. E. 932; McRee v. McLemore, 8 Heisk. (Tenn.) 440; State v. Whittlesey, 17 Wash. 447, 50 Pac. 119; Treece v. American Assoc., 122 Fed. 598, 58 C. C. A. 266; Bugher v. Prescott, 23 Fed. 20.

34. State v. Leich, 166 Ind. 680, 78 N. E.

mistake or fault of the officer or in consequence of misleading information given by him.[47]

d. Estoppel to Deny Payment. The state is not estopped to enforce the collection of taxes by sale of the land by the fact that, when defendants purchased the land on which they were assessed, there was an erroneous entry on the list in the auditor's office to the effect that the taxes had been paid, nor by the fact that the auditor indorsed on their deed a statement that the taxes were paid.[48]

2. Exhaustion of Personalty — a. Necessity in General. A statute requiring the tax collector to exhaust the personal property of the owner, as a means of collecting the tax, before having recourse to his real estate, is mandatory, and a sale of the land, made without observing this direction, is invalid.[49] But in

47. *Iowa.*— Capital City Gas-Light Co. *v.* Charter Oak Ins. Co., 51 Iowa 31, 50 N. W. 579; Corning Town Co. *v.* Davis, 44 Iowa 622.

Kansas.— Moon *v.* March, 40 Kan. 58, 19 Pac. 334.

Mississippi.— Richter *v.* Beaumont, 67 Miss. 285, 7 So. 357.

Ohio.— Harrison *v.* Owen, 3 Ohio Dec. (Reprint) 55, 2 Wkly. L. Gaz. 315.

Pennsylvania.—Freeman *v.* Cornwell, (1888) 15 Atl. 873.

Washington.— Gleason *v.* Owens, 53 Wash. 483, 102 Pac. 425, 132 Am. St. Rep. 1087.

Wisconsin.— Edwards *v.* Upham, 93 Wis. 455, 67 N. W. 728; Bray, etc., Land Co. *v.* Newman, 92 Wis. 271, 65 N. W. 494.

United States.— Lewis *v.* Monson, 151 U. S. 545, 14 S. Ct. 424, 38 L. ed. 265.

See 45 Cent. Dig. tit. "Taxation," § 1267.

Compare Raley *v.* Guinn, 76 Mo. 263.

Excuses for non-payment of taxes; reliance on official statement or certificate see *supra*, IX, A, 1, g, (II).

48. State *v.* Foster, 104 Minn. 408, 116 N. W. 826; Olmsted County *v.* Barber, 31 Minn. 256, 17 N. W. 473, 944.

49. *Alabama.*— Stoudenmire *v.* Brown, 57 Ala. 481; Doe *v.* Minge, 56 Ala. 121; Scales *v.* Alvis, 12 Ala. 617, 46 Am. Dec. 269.

Indiana.— Michigan Mut. L. Ins. Co. *v.* Kroh, 102 Ind. 515, 2 N. E. 733; Helms *v.* Wagner, 102 Ind. 385, 1 N. E. 730; Volger *v.* Sidener, 86 Ind. 545; Barton *v.* McWhinney, 85 Ind. 481; Morrison *v.* Bank of Commerce, 81 Ind. 335; Sharpe *v.* Dillman, 77 Ind. 280; McWhinney *v.* Brinker, 64 Ind. 360; Abbott *v.* Edgerton, 53 Ind. 196; Ring *v.* Ewing, 47 Ind. 246; Bowen *v.* Donovan, 32 Ind. 379; Catterlin *v.* Douglass, 17 Ind. 213; Cones *v.* Wilson, 14 Ind. 465.

Kentucky.— Leszinsky *v.* Le Grand, 119 Ky. 313, 83 S. W. 1038, 26 Ky. L. Rep. 1235; Julian *v.* Stephens, 11 S. W. 6, 10 Ky. L. Rep. 862; Wheeler *v.* Bramel, 8 S. W. 199, 10 Ky. L. Rep. 301. But see as to effect of present statutes in this state Alexander *v.* Aud, 121 Ky. 105, 88 S. W. 1103, 28 Ky. L. Rep. 69.

Maryland.— Polk *v.* Rose, 25 Md. 153, 89 Am. Dec. 773; Baltimore *v.* Chase, 2 Gill & J. 276.

Nebraska.—Wilhelm *v.* Russell, 8 Nebr. 120; Richardson County *v.* Miles, 7 Nebr. 118; Johnson *v.* Hahn, 4 Nebr. 139.

New York.— Rathbun *v.* Acker, 18 Barb. 393.

Pennsylvania.—Simpson *v.* Meyers, 197 Pa. St. 522, 47 Atl. 868; Kean *v.* Kinnear, 171 Pa. St. 639, 33 Atl. 325; Smith *v.* McGrew, 4 Watts & S. 338; Cox *v.* Grant, 1 Yeates 164; Ulrich *v.* Matika, 30 Pa. Super. Ct. 110; Philadelphia Nat. Bank *v.* Pottstown Security Co., 14 Montg. Co. Rep. 106.

South Carolina.— Johnson *v.* Jones, 72 S. C. 270, 51 S. E. 805. But see Interstate Bldg., etc., Assoc. *v.* Waters, 50 S. C. 459, 27 S. E. 948; Wilson *v.* Cantrell, 40 S. C. 114, 18 S. E. 517.

Tennessee.— Michie *v.* Mullins, 5 Hayw. 90.

Wisconsin.—Allen *v.* Allen, 114 Wis. 615, 91 N. W. 218.

United States.— Hellrigle *v.* Ould, 11 Fed. Cas. No. 6,344, 4 Cranch C. C. 72; Rodbird *v.* Rodbird, 20 Fed. Cas. No. 11,988, 5 Cranch C. C. 125. But see Thompson *v.* Carroll, 22 How. 422, 16 L. ed. 387.

Canada.— Boland *v.* Toronto, 32 Ont. 358; Dobbie *v.* Tully, 10 U. C. C. P. 432; Hamilton *v.* McDonald, 22 U. C. Q. B. 136; Foley *v.* Moodie, 16 U. C. Q. B. 254; Stafford *v.* Williams, 4 U. C. Q. B. 488. But see Stewart *v.* Taggart, 22 U. C. C. P. 284.

See 45 Cent. Dig. tit. "Taxation," § 1268.

Where a tax deed fails to show that the personal property of the delinquent had been exhausted before the sale of his real estate, or that he had no such property, such deed, unless accompanied by proper evidence of that fact, is not admissible as evidence of title. Smith *v.* Kyler, 74 Ind. 575; Ward *v.* Montgomery, 57 Ind. 276.

Sale voidable but not void.— Some of the cases hold that where land is sold without first exhausting the personalty, although the sale is ineffectual to convey title, yet it will transfer to the purchaser the lien of the state and therefore is not absolutely void. St. Clair *v.* McClure, 111 Ind. 467, 12 N. E. 134; State *v.* Casteel, 110 Ind. 174, 11 N. E. 219.

Tax and penalties not released.— The failure of the collector to make the taxes out of available personal property will not save the delinquent owner from the penalty or release him from the tax. Foresman *v.* Chase, 68 Ind. 500.

Who may complain.—Only the taxpayer himself can complain of a sale of his real estate made without first having recourse

where the legal portion of the tax can be clearly and definitely separated from the rest.[63]

b. Statutes Validating Sales For Taxes Partly Illegal. In several of the states laws have been enacted providing that a sale of land for illegal or erroneous taxes shall nevertheless be effectual to pass the title if any portion of the taxes for which the land was sold was legal. The validity of these statutes is sustained, and their effect is that a tax-sale and deed, if otherwise regular, will not be rendered invalid by an error or illegality in the tax, if any part of the taxes for which the land was sold constituted a legal and valid charge upon it.[64]

4. SALE FOR ALL TAXES DUE. Where the statute provides that sales of land for delinquent taxes shall be made for the total amount of the taxes due, including those in arrear for previous years or those assessed under different authorities or for different purposes, a sale for only a portion of the taxes due will not pass title to the purchaser, although he may be entitled to a lien for the taxes paid.[65]

Miss. 33, 3 So. 65, 5 So. 824; Gamble *v.* Witty, 55 Miss. 26; Shattuck *v.* Daniel, 52 Miss. 834; Beard *v.* Green, 51 Miss. 856; Dogan *v.* Griffin, 51 Miss. 782.

Nebraska.— McCann *v.* Merriam, 11 Nebr. 241, 9 N. W. 96. But see the cases cited *infra*, this note.

New Hampshire.— Buttrick *v.* Nashua Iron, etc., Co., 59 N. H. 392.

New York.— People *v.* Wemple, 117 N. Y. 77, 22 N. E. 761; People *v.* Hagadorn, 104 N. Y. 516, 10 N. E. 891; People *v.* Hagadorn, 36 Hun 610 [*affirmed* in 104 N. Y. 516, 10 N. E. 891]. But see New York Protestant Episcopal Public School *v.* Davis, 31 N. Y. 574.

Ohio.— Younglove *v.* Hackman, 43 Ohio St. 69, 1 N. E. 230; Kemper *v.* McClelland, 19 Ohio 308.

Rhode Island.— Young *v.* Joslin, 13 R. I. 675.

Vermont.— Drew *v.* Davis, 10 Vt. 506, 33 Am. Dec. 213.

United States.— Gage *v.* Pumpelly, 115 U. S. 454, 6 S. Ct. 136, 29 L. ed. 449; Hodgdon *v.* Burleigh, 4 Fed. 111; Gresham *v.* Montgomery, 10 Fed. Cas. No. 5,805, 2 Ky. L. Rep. 397.

Canada.—Ridout *v.* Ketchum, 5 U. C. C. P. 50.

See 45 Cent. Dig. tit. "Taxation," § 1277.

Contra.— Bird *v.* Sellers, 113 Mo. 580, 21 S. W. 91; Carman *v.* Harris, 61 Nebr. 635, 85 N. W. 848; Hall *v.* Moore, 3 Nebr. (Unoff.) 574, 92 N. W. 294; Trexler *v.* Africa, 27 Pa. Super. Ct. 385; Cornelius *v.* Dunn, 17 Pa. Co. Ct. 566.

Amount of illegal tax immaterial.— It is immaterial how small may be the illegal element or portion which enters into the aggregate amount of taxes for which the land is sold. Drake *v.* Ogden, 128 Ill. 603, 21 N. E. 511; McLaughlin *v.* Thompson, 55 Ill. 249.

63. Holcomb *v.* Johnson, 43 Wash. 362, 86 Pac. 409.

64. See the statutes of the different states. And see Parker *v.* Cochran, 64 Iowa 757, 21 N. W. 13; Corning Town Co. *v.* Davis, 44 Iowa 622; Genther *v.* Fuller, 36 Iowa 604; Rhodes *v.* Sexton, 33 Iowa 540; Hurley *v.* Powell, 31 Iowa 64; Sully *v.* Kuehl, 30 Iowa 275; Parker *v.* Sexton, 29 Iowa 421; Eldridge *v.* Kuehl, 27 Iowa 160; Southworth *v.* Edmands, 152 Mass. 203, 25 N. E. 106, 9 L. R. A. 118; Hunt *v.* Chapin, 42 Mich. 24, 3 N. W. 873; Upton *v.* Kennedy, 36 Mich. 215.

But a statute providing as to sales of land for taxes that "the courts shall apply the same liberal principles in favor of such titles as in sales by execution" is intended to prevent the mere irregularities which do not avoid execution sales from being held to avoid sales for taxes, and not to cure illegality in the levy or assessment, and does not change the rule that a sale of land for taxes a part of which are levied or assessed illegally is void. Gamble *v.* Witty, 55 Miss. 26.

65. *Iowa.*— Parker *v.* Cochran, 64 Iowa 757, 21 N. W. 13; Crowell *v.* Merrill, 60 Iowa 53, 14 N. W. 81.

Louisiana.— Waddill *v.* Walton, 42 La. Ann. 763, 7 So. 737; Renshaw *v.* Imboden, 31 La. Ann. 661.

Michigan.— Rumsey *v.* Griffin, 138 Mich. 413, 101 N. W. 571; Bending *v.* Auditor-General, 137 Mich. 500, 100 N. W. 777.

Nebraska.— Grant *v.* Bartholomew, 57 Nebr. 673, 78 N. W. 314; McGavock *v.* Pollack, 13 Nebr. 535, 14 N. W. 659; O'Donohue *v.* Hendrix, 13 Nebr. 257, 13 N. W. 281; Tillotson *v.* Small, 13 Nebr. 202, 13 N. W. 201.

North Dakota.— Scott, etc., Mercantile Co. *v.* Nelson County, 14 N. D. 407, 104 N. W. 528.

United States.— Coleman *v.* Peshtigo Lumber Co., 30 Fed. 317.

Statute held directory.— Some of the decisions hold that a statutory provision such as that mentioned in the text is only directory, and not mandatory, and that a failure to obey it is a mere irregularity which does not vitiate the sale. Kessey *v.* Connell, 68 Iowa 430, 27 N. W. 365; Allen *v.* Ramsey County, 98 Minn. 341, 108 N. W. 301.

What taxes included see Crowell *v.* Merrill, 60 Iowa 53, 14 N. W. 81, holding that the statutory provision refers only to state and county taxes, and that a separate sale for delinquent taxes voted in aid of a railroad is properly had.

c. Verification and Certification. Some of the statutes require that the collector's return of delinquent lands shall be attested by him under oath, and under such a statute a tax-sale cannot lawfully be made without an attestation of the list substantially in the form prescribed by the law.[7] And it is also and equally essential that the affidavit shall be sworn to before an officer duly authorized to administer the oath.[8] The same imperative character is to be attributed to a statutory requirement that the delinquent list shall be certified by the clerk of the court or some other officer designated for the purpose;[9] and the certificate must be made at the time required by the statute.[10]

d. Filing and Recording. A statute requiring the delinquent list to be filed or recorded in the office of the county clerk or some other public office is mandatory, and compliance with its provisions is essential to a valid tax-sale of the lands affected, if the record is intended as official evidence of the facts recited in the list, or as notice, or as the foundation for process against the land;[11] but other-

denominate sums of money, since, lands being assessed in dollars and cents, taxes being payable in money, and it being common knowledge that dollars are expressed in the whole numbers and cents and mills decimally, the significance of the figures was clear. Sawyer *v.* Wilson, *supra.* A tax-sale is not void because in the delinquent list the amount due was indicated only by the word "amount," and immediately under it the figures "4 00," without any dollar sign, but with a space between the figure 4 and the two ciphers, as they usually appear when intended to mean dollars. Carter *v.* Osborn, *supra.* See also Chapman *v.* Zoberlein, 152 Cal. 216, 92 Pac. 188; Fox *v.* Wright, 152 Cal. 59, 91 Pac. 1005.

7. *Illinois.*— Weston *v.* People, 84 Ill. 284 (substantial compliance with statute); People *v.* Otis, 74 Ill. 384. *Compare* Chicago, etc., R. Co. *v.* People, 174 Ill. 80, 50 N. E. 1057; Wabash R. Co. *v.* People, 138 Ill. 316, 28 N. E. 57.

Michigan.— Seymour *v.* Peters, 67 Mich. 415, 35 N. W. 62; Upton *v.* Kennedy, 36 Mich. 215.

Ohio.— Stambaugh *v.* Carlin, 35 Ohio St. 209; Skinner *v.* Brown, 17 Ohio St. 33; Ward *v.* Barrows, 2 Ohio St. 241; Hollister *v.* Bennett, 9 Ohio 83; Winder *v.* Sterling, 7 Ohio Pt. II, 190.

Oregon.— Hughes *v.* Linn County, 37 Oreg. 111, 60 Pac. 843.

West Virginia.— Wilkinson *v.* Linkous, 64 W. Va. 205, 61 S. E. 152; Devine *v.* Wilson, 63 W. Va. 409, 60 S. E. 351.

Wisconsin.— Cotzhausen *v.* Kaehler, 42 Wis. 332.

See 45 Cent. Dig. tit. "Taxation," § 1281.

Compare, however, Cook *v.* John Schroeder Lumber Co., 85 Minn. 374, 88 N. W. 971; Bennett *v.* Blatz, 44 Minn. 56, 46 N. W. 319; Mille Lacs County *v.* Morrison, 22 Minn. 178; State *v.* Schooley, 84 Mo. 447.

Not necessary unless required by the statute see Bivens *v.* Henderson, 42 Ind. App. 562, 86 N. E. 426; Hollister *v.* Bennett, 9 Ohio 83.

8. Tabor *v.* People, 84 Ill. 202; Hough *v.* Hastings, 18 Ill. 312; Malony *v.* Mahar, 2 Dougl. (Mich.) 432; Harmon *v.* Stockwell, 9 Ohio 93; Wilkinson *v.* Linkous, 64 W. Va. 205, 61 S. E. 152.

9. *Arkansas.*— Johnson *v.* Elder, 92 Ark. 30, 121 S. W. 1066; Frank Kendall Lumber Co. *v.* Smith, 87 Ark. 360, 112 S. W. 888; Boyd *v.* Gardner, 84 Ark. 567, 106 S. W. 942; Hunt *v.* Gardner, 74 Ark. 583, 86 S. W. 426.

Illinois.— Glos *v.* Cass, 230 Ill. 641, 82 N. E. 827; McCraney *v.* Glos, 222 Ill. 628, 78 N. E. 921; Glos *v.* Dyche, 214 Ill. 417, 73 N. E. 757; Glos *v.* McKerlie, 212 Ill. 632, 72 N. E. 700; Glos *v.* Randolph, 138 Ill. 268, 27 N. E. 941.

Michigan.—Auditor-Gen. *v.* Keweenan Assoc., 107 Mich. 405, 65 N. W. 288.

Nebraska.— Whelen *v.* Stilwell, 4 Nebr. (Unoff.) 24, 93 N. W. 189.

New York.— Kane *v.* Brooklyn, 1 N. Y. Suppl. 306 [*affirmed* in 114 N. Y. 586, 21 N. E. 1053].

United States.— Ontario Land Co. *v.* Wilfong, 162 Fed. 999 [*reversed* on other grounds in 171 Fed. 51, 96 C. C. A. 293].

10. Thus failure to make and record the delinquent list before the day of sale as required by statute invalidates the sale. American Ins. Co. *v.* Dannehower, 89 Ark. 111, 115 S. W. 950; Townsend *v.* Penrose, 84 Ark. 316, 105 S. W. 588; Hunt *v.* Gardner, 74 Ark. 583, 86 S. W. 426. Under Hurd Rev. St. Ill. (1905) c. 120, § 194, providing that the county clerk shall carefully examine the delinquent list on which judgment for taxes has been rendered "on the day advertised for sale," and shall make a certificate "which shall be process on which all real property shall be sold for taxes," a certificate made on any other day than the day advertised for sale is void, and a sale and tax deed based thereon is void; and when the certificate is dated, the date is evidence of the time when the certificate was made. Glos *v.* Cass, 230 Ill. 641, 82 N. E. 827; McCraney *v.* Glos, 222 Ill. 628, 78 N. E. 921; Glos *v.* Dyche, 214 Ill. 417, 73 N. E. 757; Glos *v.* Hanford, 212 Ill. 261, 72 N. E. 439; Glos *v.* Gleason, 209 Ill. 517, 70 N. E. 1045; Kepley *v.* Fouke, 187 Ill. 162, 58 N. E. 303; Kepley *v.* Scully, 185 Ill. 52, 57 N. E. 187.

11. *Arkansas.*— Johnson *v.* Elder, 92 Ark. 30, 121 S. W. 1066; Frank Kendall Lumber

(II) *Requirements as to Newspaper and Designation of Same.* The newspaper in which the delinquent list is to be published must be selected or designated in the manner prescribed by the statute and by the officers to whom authority for that purpose is committed by law,[18] and within the time limited;[19] and if there is no official action of this kind, or if an attempted designation is

at the foot of the record of the delinquent tax list when and in what newspaper the list was published, and for how long, does not require the certificate to state that the newspaper had a *bona fide* circulation in the county for thirty days before the publication. Leigh *v.* Trippe, 91 Ark. 117, 120 S. W. 972. The certificate of a county clerk that a list of lands delinquent for taxes was published in one newspaper for two weeks, weekly, the "first publication being on May 25, the next June 1, and the last, June 8, 1895," and in another paper, "the first publication being May 23, the second May 30, and the last June 6, 1895," shows the length of time notice of the sale was published "before the second Monday in June," within the requirements of the statute. Sawyer *v.* Wilson, 81 Ark. 319, 99 S. W. 389.

California.— Haaren *v.* High, 97 Cal. 445, 32 Pac. 518; Warden *v.* Broome, 9 Cal. App. 172, 98 Pac. 252. Under Cal. Pol. Code, § 3764, requiring the publication of a delinquent list containing the names of the persons and a description of the property and the amount of taxes, penalties, and costs, and section 3765 requiring the collector to publish with the delinquent list a notice that the property will be sold, etc., it was held that where a delinquent list otherwise correct stated that the taxes, penalties, and costs against the property in controversy were nineteen dollars and ninety cents, when the correct amount was nineteen dollars and forty cents, for which the property was in fact sold to the state, the sale was void. Warden *v.* Broome, *supra.*

Illinois.— McCraney *v.* Glos, 222 Ill. 628, 78 N. E. 921; Glos *v.* Hanford, 212 Ill. 261, 72 N. E. 439; McChesney *v.* People, 178 Ill. 542, 53 N. E. 356; Buck *v.* People, 78 Ill. 560; Senichka *v.* Lowe, 74 Ill. 274.

Kansas.— Stout *v.* Coates, 35 Kan. 382, 11 Pac. 151; Douglass *v.* Craig, 4 Kan. App. 99, 46 Pac. 197; Mims *v.* Finney County, 3 Kan. App. 622, 44 Pac. 38.

Minnesota.— Irwin *v.* Pierro, 44 Minn. 490, 47 N. W. 154.

See 45 Cent. Dig. tit. "Taxation," § 1283.

Proof of publication as essential to jurisdiction.— Where the publication of the delinquent list is not direct authority for the sale of the lands, but only the foundation for judicial proceedings *in rem*, culminating in a judgment ordering such sale, it is held that proof of the publication, to be made as the statute directs, is not essential to the jurisdiction of the court, provided the publication was in fact made as the law requires, but the omission of such proof is at most an amendable defect. Mille Lacs County *v.* Morrison, 22 Minn. 178; Raley *v.* Guinn, 76 Mo. 263. But *compare* Holmes *v.* Loughren, 97 Minn. 83, 105 N. W. 558, holding that where the printer's affidavit of publication of a delinquent list was sworn to before a notary public, but no notarial seal was affixed thereto, there was no publication of the delinquent list, and the court had no jurisdiction to enter judgment against a lot contained in it.

Parol proof of publication.— Where the delinquent list and proof of its publication are required to be perpetuated by record, and to be certified by the clerk before the sale, parol evidence is not admissible to supply its omission in a suit to confirm a tax title. Martin *v.* Barbour, 34 Fed. 701.

Presumption as to date.—Although the certificate of the county clerk as to the publication of the delinquent tax, required by Kirby Dig. Ark. § 7086, is not dated, it will be presumed, in the absence of proof to the contrary, that it was entered of record before the date of sale, as is necessary. Cook *v.* Ziff Colored Masonic Lodge, No. 119, 80 Ark. 31, 96 S. W. 618.

Filing and recording certificate.— Under Ill. Revenue Law, § 186 (Hurd Rev. St. (1905) c. 120), requiring the certificate of the publication of a delinquent tax list to be filed as part of the record of the county court, a filing thereof by the county clerk is not a sufficient compliance with the law, although the offices of county clerk and clerk of the county court are filled by the same person, and, notwithstanding Hurd Rev. St. (1905) p. 1946, c. 131, § 1, providing that the words "county clerk" shall be held to include "clerk of the county court," and the words "clerk of the county court" to include "county clerk," unless such construction would be inconsistent with the manifest intent of the legislature or repugnant to the context of the same statute. McCraney *v.* Glos, 222 Ill. 628, 78 N. E. 921.

18. Wren *v.* Nemaha County, 24 Kan. 301; Hall *v.* Ramsey County, 30 Minn. 68, 14 N. W. 263; Troy Press Co. *v.* Mann, 115 N. Y. App. Div. 25, 100 N. Y. Suppl. 516 [*affirmed* in 187 N. Y. 279, 79 N. E. 1006]; State *v.* Purdy, 14 Wash. 343, 44 Pac. 857.

At adjourned meeting.— Under Minn. Gen. St. (1894) § 1581, providing that a newspaper for publication of the delinquent list shall be designated by the county commissioners at their annual meeting in January, the designation is valid if made at an adjourned meeting. Minnesota Debenture Co. *v.* Scott, 106 Minn. 32, 119 N. W. 391.

19. Finnegan *v.* Gronerud, 63 Minn. 53, 65 N. W. 128, 348; Banning *v.* McManus, 51 Minn. 289, 53 N. W. 635; Reimer *v.* Newel, 47 Minn. 237, 49 N. W. 865; Emmons County *v.* Bismarck First Nat. Bank Lands, 9 N. D. 583, 84 N. W. 379.

the other hand, if it is regarded as *in rem*, and especially after the publication of a general citation as above mentioned, the judgment is conclusive upon all persons having any interest.[42]

d. Proceedings and Judgment. The bill, petition, or complaint should describe the land sought to be charged,[43] and set forth the levy and assessment of the tax and the amount due and unpaid.[44] The answer may set up the invalidity of the levy or assessment,[45] or deny the legality of the tax.[46] The assessment list or collector's book is *prima facie* evidence of the liability of the land to the payment of the particular sum shown thereby.[47] The judgment or decree, if for plaintiff or complainant, should describe the land, state the amount of taxes due on each tract, and decree the foreclosure of the lien;[48] and such other or further relief may be granted as the pleadings and evidence will warrant.[49] It is conclusive of the facts essential to the maintenance of the action and of such matters of defense as were or should have been pleaded, including the legality of the tax and levy and the fact of delinquency.[50] The matter of costs and fees in actions of this kind is regulated by the local statute.[51]

3. Proceedings For Judgment — a. Nature and Form of Action. In some states, by constitutional provisions or by statute, real estate cannot be sold for the non-payment of taxes except under the judgment or decree of a court.[52]

Ind. 99, 23 N. E. 683; State *v.* Clymer, 81 Mo. 122.

42. Pritchard *v.* Madren, 24 Kan. 486; Newby *v.* Brownlee, 23 Fed. 320.

43. State *v.* Linney, 192 Mo. 49, 90 S. W. 844; State *v.* Cowgill, 81 Mo. 381.

44. Mix *v.* People, 122 Ill. 641, 14 N. E. 209; Christie *v.* Hartzell, 4 Nebr. (Unoff.) 627, 95 N. W. 637. A bill to enforce a lien on real estate for taxes is defective in failing to allege when the taxes were assessed and the levy made. Miami *v.* Miami Realty, etc., Co., 57 Fla. 366, 49 So. 55. In a tax suit facts must be alleged showing, not only a statutory liability, but complainant's right to recover. Miami *v.* Miami Realty, etc., Co., *supra.* It is the bill of complaint in a tax suit, and not the notice of lien, which must set out the cause of action. Miami *v.* Miami Realty, etc., Co., *supra.*

Lands listed to heirs of deceased owner see Waterbury *v.* O'Loughlin, 79 Conn. 630, 66 Atl. 173.

Amendment.— In a suit to enforce a lien for taxes, a claim of lien for additional taxes for a subsequent year on the same land was properly set up by amended petition, as authorized by Civ. Code Pr. § 694, subs. 3. Frankfort *v.* Herndon, 133 Ky. 583, 118 S. W. 347.

45. Medland *v.* Croft, 1 Nebr. (Unoff.) 419, 95 N. W. 665.

46. Union School Dist. *v.* Bishop, 76 Conn. 695, 58 Atl. 13, 66 L. R. A. 989.

47. Mix *v.* People, 122 Ill. 641, 14 N. E. 209; Mix *v.* People, 116 Ill. 265, 4 N. E. 783; State *v.* Birch, 186 Mo. 205, 85 S. W. 361; Pettibone *v.* Yeiser, 2 Nebr. (Unoff.) 65, 96 N. W. 193.

In Nebraska, in an action to enforce collection of delinquent taxes and assessments on real estate under Comp. St. (1905) c. 77, art. 9, commonly known as the "Scavenger Act," the petition, by express provision of the statute, must be taken as *prima facie* evidence of the legality of the tax and assessment set forth therein and of the several amounts levied on behalf of the state, county, or city, in which the lands are located, and that such taxes are unpaid and delinquent. State *v.* Several Parcels of Land, 78 Nebr. 581, 111 N. W. 367.

48. St. Louis, etc., R. Co. *v.* State, 47 Ark. 323, 1 S. W. 556; Auditor-Gen. *v.* Gurney, 109 Mich. 472, 67 N. W. 525, 1113; State *v.* Kerr, 8 Mo. App. 125.

Separate tracts of land included in same judgment see Mix *v.* People, 116 Ill. 265, 4 N. E. 783; Cave *v.* Houston, 65 Tex. 619; Edmonson *v.* Galveston, 53 Tex. 157; Whatcom County *v.* Fairhaven Land Co., 7 Wash. 101, 34 Pac. 563.

Signature of presiding judge see Raley *v.* Guinn, 76 Mo. 263.

49. Union School Dist. *v.* Bishop, 76 Conn. 695, 58 Atl. 13, 66 L. R. A. 989 (affirmative relief to defendant); Langlois *v.* People, 212 Ill. 75, 72 N. E. 28; Chicago Real Estate L. & T. Co. *v.* People, 104 Ill. App. 290 (appointment of receiver).

50. Doyle *v.* Martin, 55 Ark. 37, 17 S. W. 346; Mix *v.* People, 116 Ill. 265, 4 N. E. 783.

The lien for taxes is not merged in the judgment rendered in a proceeding under the statutes of Indiana, so as to prevent the enforcement of such lien in the ordinary manner for any balance of the taxes unpaid by the proceeds of the tax-sale against the same land when subsequently acquired by the tax debtor from the purchaser at the tax-sale. Beard *v.* Allen, 141 Ind. 243, 39 N. E. 665, 40 N. E. 654.

51. See the statutes of the different states. And see Ward *v.* Alton, 23 Ill. App. 475; Hall *v.* Moore, 3 Nebr. (Unoff.) 574, 92 N. W. 294; Whatcom County *v.* Fairhaven Land Co., 7 Wash. 101, 34 Pac. 563.

52. See the statutes of the different states. And see Webster *v.* Chicago, 62 Ill. 302; Hills *v.* Chicago, 60 Ill. 86; Hinman *v.* Pope, 6 Ill. 131; Bleirdorn *v.* Abel, 6 Iowa 5; Carlin *v.* Cavender, 56 Mo. 286; Strassheim *v.* Jer-

judgments of this kind shall be rendered at a specified term of the court, it is to be taken as mandatory, and a judgment rendered at a different term will be void.[59]

c. Jurisdiction — (I) *IN GENERAL.* Jurisdiction of proceedings of this kind can be entertained only by those courts to which it has been specially committed by law;[60] and as their proceedings are special and statutory and of a more or less summary character, it is necessary that every fact essential to the jurisdiction of the court shall appear on the record.[61]

(II) *JURISDICTION DEPENDING ON DELINQUENCY.* It is held in numerous cases that where the proceeding is by suit to enforce the collection of taxes against real estate, culminating in a judgment, the jurisdiction of the court, as to a particular tract, is not affected by the fact that the taxes upon such tract have previously been paid, this being a matter of defense merely; or at any rate that the judgment, if regular and otherwise valid, and showing jurisdiction on its face cannot be impeached in any collateral proceeding by proof of such prior payment[62]

Repeal of statute.— Minn. Laws (1902), p. 40, c. 2, § 82, repealing the statute of limitations as to the enforcement of taxes, applies to taxes delinquent at the time of its passage, as to which the limitation had not then run. State *v.* Foster, 104 Minn. 408, 116 N. W. 826.

59. Brown *v.* Hogle, 30 Ill. 119; Spurlock *v.* Dougherty, 81 Mo. 171. And see Stilwell *v.* People, 49 Ill. 45; Kinney *v.* Forsythe, 96 Mo. 414, 9 S. W. 918. But *compare* Akers *v.* Burch, 12 Heisk. (Tenn.) 606. And see Douglass *v.* Leavenworth County, 75 Kan. 6, 88 Pac. 557.

Effect of delay in proceedings.— A statute in Minnesota providing that in proceedings to enforce delinquent taxes the answer shall stand for trial at the same or next general or special term of court is held to be merely directory, and hence a delay on the part of the state to bring such a proceeding to trial for over six years does not operate as a discontinuance or entitle defendant to a dismissal. State *v.* Baldwin, 62 Minn. 518, 65 N. W. 80.

60. Covington *v.* Highlands Dist., 113 Ky. 612, 68 S. W. 669, 24 Ky. L. Rep. 433; Wellshear *v.* Kelley, 69 Mo. 343.

61. Territory *v.* Apache County Delinquent Tax List, 3 Ariz. 69, 21 Pac. 888; Chadbourne *v.* Hartz, 93 Minn. 233, 101 N. W. 68; Cordray *v.* Neuhaus, 25 Tex. Civ. App. 247, 61 S. W. 415; M'Clung *v.* Ross, 5 Wheat. (U. S.) 116, 5 L. ed. 46.

In Tennessee, it is stated that the grounds of fact on which the jurisdiction rests are that the land lies in the county, that the sum due for the taxes remains unpaid, and that there was no personal property which could be distrained for the payment. Anderson *v.* Patton, 1 Humphr. 369; Anderson *v.* Williams, 10 Yerg. 234; Hamilton *v.* Burum, 3 Yerg. 355.

In Alabama it is considered that the affidavit which the collector is required to make, as to his inability to find personal property after diligent search, is a jurisdictional fact without which the order of sale is void. Fleming *v.* McGee, 81 Ala. 409, 1 So. 106.

Demand and notice of delinquency.— It has been held essential to the jurisdiction of the court that a proper demand should have been made by the collector on the taxpayer for the amount of the taxes unpaid, and that this must appear on the face of the proceedings. Mayhew *v.* Davis, 16 Fed. Cas. No. 9,347, 4 McLean 213. And in Louisiana it is said that the notice of delinquency required to be given or mailed to the tax debtor is "sacramental," and the failure to give it vitiates all subsequent proceedings. Tensas Delta Land Co. *v.* Sholars, 105 La. 357, 29 So. 908. But see State *v.* St. Paul Trust Co., 76 Minn. 423, 79 N. W. 543.

Exemption of property.— In a proceeding to sell land for non-payment of taxes, the fact that the land is exempt from taxation does not deprive the court of jurisdiction, as that is one of the questions to be decided. Chisago County *v.* St. Paul, etc., R. Co., 27 Minn. 109, 6 N. W. 454.

Illegality of levy as affecting jurisdiction see Emmons County *v.* Bismarck First Nat. Bank's Lands, 9 N. D. 583, 84 N. W. 379.

Appearance for purpose of objecting to jurisdiction see Stearns County *v.* Smith, 25 Minn. 131.

62. *Arkansas.*— Doyle *v.* Martin, 55 Ark. 37, 17 S. W. 346; McCarter *v.* Neil, 50 Ark. 188, 6 S. W. 731; Williamson *v.* Mimms, 49 Ark. 336, 5 S. W. 320; Worthen *v.* Ratcliffe, 42 Ark. 330; Wallace *v.* Brown, 22 Ark. 118, 76 Am. Dec. 421.

California.— Mayo *v.* Foley, 40 Cal. 281.

Iowa.— McGahen *v.* Carr, 6 Iowa 331, 71 Am. Dec. 421; Gaylord *v.* Scarff, 6 Iowa 179.

Minnesota.— Chauncey *v.* Wass, 35 Minn. 1, 25 N. W. 457, 30 N. W. 826; Stewart *v.* Colter, 31 Minn. 385, 18 N. W. 98; Chisago County *v.* St. Paul, etc., R. Co., 27 Minn. 109, 6 N. W. 454.

Missouri.— Hill *v.* Sherwood, 96 Mo. 125, 8 S. W. 781; Jones *v.* Driskill, 94 Mo. 190, 7 S. W. 111; Knoll *v.* Woelken, 13 Mo. App. 275; State *v.* Sargent, 12 Mo. App. 228. But *compare* Huber *v.* Pickler, 94 Mo. 382, 7 S. W. 427.

North Dakota.— Purcell *v.* Farm Land Co., 13 N. D. 327, 100 N. W. 700.

Pennsylvania.— Cadmus *v.* Jackson, 52 Pa. St. 295.

United States.— Thomas *v.* Lawson, 21 How. 331, 16 L. ed. 82; Parker *v.* Overman,

who enters a general appearance and contests the application on the merits thereby waives any defects in the notice.[73]

(II) *NOTICE BY PUBLICATION.* In cases where personal service of process in a suit of this kind cannot be had, the jurisdiction of the court may be founded on a proper service by publication.[74] But this must be based on a proper allegation in the petition or an affidavit or return that defendant is a non-resident or unknown owner,[75] and the citation must be directed to the right person,[76] and by

11 S. W. 573; Milner *v.* Shipley, 94 Mo. 106, 7 S. W. 175.

Tennessee.— *Ex p.* Thacker, 3 Sneed 344.

73. McChesney *v.* People, 178 Ill. 542, 53 N. E. 356; Illinois Cent. R. Co. *v.* People, 170 Ill. 224, 48 N. E. 215; Cairo, etc., R. Co. *v.* Mathews, 152 Ill. 153, 38 N. E. 623; Warren *v.* Cook, 116 Ill. 199, 5 N. E. 538; Mix *v.* People, 106 Ill. 425; People *v.* Dragstran, 100 Ill. 286; English *v.* People, 96 Ill. 566; Hale *v.* People, 87 Ill. 72; People *v.* Sherman, 83 Ill. 165; Tromble *v.* Hoffman, 130 Mich. 676, 90 N. W. 694.

74. *Illinois.*— Glos *v.* Woodard, 202 Ill. 480, 67 N. E. 3; McCauley *v.* People, 87 Ill. 123; Falch *v.* People, 8 Ill. App. 351.

Louisiana.— Bond *v.* Hiestand, 20 La. Ann. 139.

Michigan.— *In re* Wiley, 89 Mich. 58, 50 N. W. 742.

Missouri.— Blodgett *v.* Schaffer, 94 Mo. 562, 7 S. W. 436; Evans *v.* Robberson, 92 Mo. 192, 4 S. W. 941, 1 Am. St. Rep. 701; State *v.* Clarkson, 88 Mo. App. 553.

North Dakota.— Emmons County *v.* Thompson, 9 N. D. 598, 84 N. W. 385.

Texas.— Sellers *v.* Simpson, (Civ. App. 1909) 115 S. W. 888.

The sufficiency of the citation in a suit for taxes against non-resident or unknown owners cannot be inquired into collaterally in trespass to try title against the purchaser at tax-sale. Kenson *v.* Gage, 34 Tex. Civ. App. 547, 79 S. W. 605.

Unknown heirs see Young *v.* Jackson, 50 Tex. Civ. App. 351, 110 S. W. 74. Where a suit to foreclose a tax lien was brought against unknown heirs of a person named and the unknown owners of the land, and the judgment recited that "defendants" were served, and that an attorney appointed filed answer for "defendants," and the foreclosure was in general terms without any mention of any defendants, but "defendants" were given the right to have the property divided and sold in tracts less than the whole survey, the sale to be subject to the right of "defendants" to redeem, the judgment foreclosed the lien as against all the unknown owners made defendants. Sellers *v.* Simpson, (Tex. Civ. App. 1909) 115 S. W. 888.

75. English *v.* Woodman, 40 Kan. 412, 20 Pac. 262; Evarts *v.* Missouri Lumber, etc., Co., 193 Mo. 433, 92 S. W. 372; Warren *v.* Manwarring, 173 Mo. 21, 73 S. W. 447; Coombs *v.* Crabtree, 105 Mo. 292, 16 S. W. 830; State *v.* Clarkson, 88 Mo. App. 553; Brickell *v.* Farrell, 82 Fed. 220. And see Blanton *v.* Nunley, (Tex. Civ. App. 1909) 119 S. W. 881; Wren *v.* Scales, (Tex. Civ. App. 1909) 119 S. W. 879. A judgment foreclosing a tax lien against unknown owners of land rendered upon a citation served by publication is not binding upon persons in actual possession of the land at the time of the filing of the suit and the rendition of the judgment, but not served with citation. Sellers *v.* Simpson, (Tex. Civ. App. 1909) 115 S. W. 888.

Not authorized against resident.— Where the owner of land is an actual resident thereon, service by publication is unauthorized, and a tax judgment and deed obtained therein are properly vacated. Rust *v.* Kennedy, 52 Wash. 472, 100 Pac. 998; Pyatt *v.* Hegquist, 45 Wash. 504, 88 Pac. 933; McManus *v.* Morgan, 38 Wash. 528, 80 Pac. 786.

Sufficiency of affidavit.— Under Sayles Annot. Civ. St. Tex. (1897) art. 5232*o*, providing that, upon affidavit setting out that the owner of land reported sold or returned delinquent for taxes is unknown to the attorney of the state, notice of tax foreclosure suit may be given by publication, an affidavit by the county attorney that the statements are true to the best of his knowledge and belief is sufficient. Young *v.* Jackson, 50 Tex. Civ. App. 351, 110 S. W. 74.

Effect of false return.— The jurisdiction of the court is based on the order of publication and its due publication and proof thereof; and the judgment will be valid, although the order was based on a false return of the officer that the party was a non-resident, when in fact he was a resident; and a sale under the judgment will be good, as against the apparent owner and his grantees, if the purchaser had no notice that he was a resident. Schmidt *v.* Niemeyer, 100 Mo. 207, 13 S. W. 405; Payne *v.* Lott, 90 Mo. 676, 3 S. W. 402. See Martin *v.* Parsons, 49 Cal. 94.

76. Irwin *v.* New Orleans, 28 La. Ann. 670; Earnest *v.* Glaser, 32 Tex. Civ. App. 378, 74 S. W. 605; Bush *v.* Williams, 4 Fed. Cas. No. 2,225, Cooke (Tenn.) 360. The citation served by publication in an action for delinquent state and county taxes may be addressed directly to defendants, and it need not be addessed to any officer or require any officer to make return thereof. Gibbs *v.* Scales, (Tex. Civ. App. 1909) 118 S. W. 188.

Order embracing several properties.— There is no objection to one affidavit and one general order of service of summons by publication being made for several cases in which several lots of land have been assessed to unknown owners by fictitious names. Moss *v.* Mayo, 23 Cal. 421.

of land included, and not in gross against them all.[33] It is error to include taxes not claimed in the petition or complaint,[34] or costs or fees not due or earned at the time of the rendition of the judgment.[35]

(IV) *AMENDMENT AND OPENING OR VACATING.* A tax judgment may be amended in matters of form or for the correction of clerical errors,[36] although not, it seems, where the defect proposed to be amended is such as renders the judgment entirely void.[37] It may be opened or set aside for sufficient cause,[38] on the application of a party in interest,[39] who is not chargeable with laches or unreasonable neglect of his own interests.[40]

(V) *CONCLUSIVENESS AND EFFECT.* A judgment ordering the sale of land for delinquent taxes, when rendered by a court of competent jurisdiction, is binding and conclusive like any other judgment,[41] on the owner of the property and those in privity with him and on other persons joined as defendants,[42] even

willer *v.* Crowe, 32 Minn. 70, 19 N. W. 344; Tidd *v.* Rines, 26 Minn. 201, 2 N. W. 497.

Missouri.— Coombs *v.* Crabtree, 105 Mo. 292, 16 S. W. 830.

Tennessee.— Randolph *v.* Metcalf, 6 Coldw. 400.

United States.—Woods *v.* Freeman, 1 Wall. 398, 17 L. ed. 543.

See 45 Cent. Dig. tit. "Taxation," § 1312.

33. State *v.* Hunter, 98 Mo. 386, 11 S. W. 756; State *v.* Kerr, 8 Mo. App. 125; Borden *v.* Houston, 26 Tex. Civ. App. 29, 62 S. W. 426. But *compare* Jones *v.* Driskill, 94 Mo. 190, 7 S. W. 111. And see Turner *v.* Houston, 21 Tex. Civ. App. 214, 51 S. W. 642.

34. Elsey *v.* Falconer, 56 Ark. 419, 20 S. W. 5.

35. Gage *v.* Goudy, (Ill. 1892) 29 N. E. 896; Gage *v.* Lyons, 138 Ill. 590, 28 N. E. 832; Combs *v.* Goff, 127 Ill. 431, 20 N. E. 9; Gage *v.* Williams, 19 Ill. 563, 9 N. E. 193.

36. Atkins *v.* Hinman, 7 Ill. 437.

37. Kern *v.* Clarke, 59 Minn. 70, 60 N. W. 809.

38. Richcreek *v.* Russell, 34 Ind. App. 217, 72 N. E. 617 (inadvertence, surprise, and excusable neglect); Williams *v.* Kiowa County, 74 Kan. 693, 88 Pac. 70 (tax unlawfully levied); Aitkin County *v.* Morrison, 25 Minn. 295 (land exempt); State *v.* Several Parcels of Land, 75 Nebr. 538, 106 N. W. 663 (motion to open the judgment not grantable as of course after the end of the term).

In Nebraska, where the amount or existence of a tax involved in a scavenger suit for the collection of taxes is not put in issue or determined as a controverted question prior to the entry of a decree, the court retains jurisdiction of the subject-matter for the purpose of correcting mistakes until the confirmation of the sale, under Comp. St. (1903) c. 77, art. 9, §§ 38, 39. State *v.* Several Parcels of Land, 79 Nebr. 668, 113 N. W. 196.

Payment of taxes as condition precedent.— The landowner must pay the taxes, interest, and charges as a condition to the vacation of a defective decree for the sale of the land for taxes. Morgan *v.* Tweddle, 119 Mich. 350, 78 N. W. 121.

39. Swan *v.* Knoxville, 11 Humphr. (Tenn.) 130.

40. Washington County *v.* German-American Bank, 28 Minn. 360, 10 N. W. 21.

41. Mayo *v.* Foley, 40 Cal. 281; Warren *v.* Cook, 116 Ill. 199, 5 N. E. 538; Graceland Cemetery Co. *v.* People, 92 Ill. 619; Job *v.* Tebbetts, 10 Ill. 376; Evarts *v.* Missouri Lumber, etc., Co., 193 Mo. 433, 92 S. W. 372; Wellshear *v.* Kelley, 69 Mo. 343; Chicago Theological Seminary *v.* Gage, 12 Fed. 398, 11 Biss. 289.

In Illinois it was at one time the settled doctrine that a judgment by default in a tax suit was not conclusive on the taxpayer and might be collaterally impeached. Gage *v.* Busse, 114 Ill. 589, 3 N. E. 441; Riverside Co. *v.* Howell, 113 Ill. 256; Gage *v.* Bailey, 102 Ill. 11; Belleville Nail Co. *v.* People, 98 Ill. 399; McLaughlin *v.* Thompson, 55 Ill. 249; Gage *v.* Pumpelly, 115 U. S. 454, 6 S. Ct. 136, 29 L. ed. 449. But this rule was very much narrowed by a statute (1879) which enacted that such a judgment should be conclusive evidence of its regularity and validity in all collateral proceedings, and should estop all parties from raising any objections which existed at or before the rendition of the judgment and could have been presented as a defense thereto, except in cases where the tax had been paid or the land was not liable for the tax. Revenue Laws, § 224. But cases in which the tax is claimed to be illegal or unauthorized fall within the exception. Hammond *v.* People, 169 Ill. 545, 48 N. E. 573; Gage *v.* Goudy, 141 Ill. 215, 30 N. E. 320; Drake *v.* Ogden, 128 Ill. 603, 21 N. E. 511.

Judgment as bar.—A judgment rendered in favor of a delinquent taxpayer on account of informality in the assessment is no bar to an application for judgment against realty for the same taxes the following year. People *v.* Chicago, etc., R. Co., 140 Ill. 210, 29 N. E. 730.

42. Boatmen's Sav. Bank *v.* Grewe, 13 Mo. App. 335.

Parties not joined as defendants.—A judgment in a statutory suit for taxes is strictly against the property, and does not bind the parties further than it may affect their interest in the property itself, yet, unless one having an interest in the land is made a party to the suit, his interest is not affected by the judgment. Walker *v.* Mills, 210 Mo. 684, 109 S. W. 44. Where defendant claims under a tax deed, plaintiff can show that, although he was the owner of the land, he was

In the latter case, and also in the former case provided the necessary facts do appear of record, the judgment is not open to collateral impeachment or attack on account of any errors, irregularities, informalities, or objections which might have been presented in defense to the action,[49] although its invalidity may be shown collaterally where the court was in fact entirely without jurisdiction.[50]

k. Appeal and Review. The statutes generally provide for an appeal from a judgment against land for taxes,[51] by a party to the action having an interest in

ing is taken by intendment in favor of the court's action, but it must appear from the record itself that the facts existed which authorized the court to act, and that it kept within the limits of its lawful authority in so doing. Young *v.* Jackson, 50 Tex. Civ. App. 351, 110 S. W. 74.

49. *Alabama.*— Driggers *v.* Cassady, 71 Ala. 529; Carlisle *v.* Watts, 78 Ala. 486; Gunn *v.* Howell, 27 Ala. 663, 62 Am. Dec. 785.

Arkansas.— Beasley *v.* Equitable Securities Co., 72 Ark. 601, 84 S. W. 224; Burcham *v.* Terry, 55 Ark. 398, 18 S. W. 458, 29 Am. St. Rep. 42; McCarter *v.* Neil, 50 Ark. 188, 6 S. W. 731.

California.— Truman *v.* Robinson, 44 Cal. 623; Reily *v.* Lancaster, 39 Cal. 354; Eitel *v.* Foote, 39 Cal. 439.

Illinois.— Prout *v.* People, 83 Ill. 154; Turner *v.* Jenkins, 79 Ill. 228; Chestnut *v.* Marsh, 12 Ill. 173; Young *v.* Lorain, 11 Ill. 624, 52 Am. Dec. 463. See Brown *v.* Hogle, 30 Ill. 119.

Indiana.— McCann *v.* Jean, 134 Ind. 518, 34 N. E. 316.

Kansas.— McGregor *v.* Morrow, 40 Kan. 730, 21 Pac. 157; English *v.* Woodman, 40 Kan. 412, 20 Pac. 262.

Michigan.— Owens *v.* Auditor-Gen., 147 Mich. 683, 111 N. W. 354; Warren *v.* Auditor-Gen., 131 Mich. 263, 90 N. W. 1063; Wilkin *v.* Keith, 121 Mich. 66, 79 N. W. 887.

Minnesota.— Cook *v.* John Schroeder Lumber Co., 85 Minn. 374, 88 N. W. 971; Minneapolis R. Terminal Co. *v.* Minnesota Debenture Co., 81 Minn. 66, 83 N. W. 485; McNamara *v.* Fink, 71 Minn. 66, 73 N. W. 649; Gribble *v.* Livermore, 64 Minn. 396, 67 N. W. 213; Gilfillan *v.* Hobart, 34 Minn. 67, 24 N. W. 342; Kipp *v.* Collins, 33 Minn. 394, 23 N. W. 554.

Missouri.—Warren *v.* Manwarring, 173 Mo. 21, 73 S. W. 447; Cruzen *v.* Stephens, 123 Mo. 337, 27 S. W. 557, 45 Am. St. Rep. 549; Gibbs *v.* Southern, 116 Mo. 204, 22 S. W. 713; Coombs *v.* Crabtree, 105 Mo. 292, 16 S. W. 830; Schmidt *v.* Niemeyer, 100 Mo. 207, 13 S. W. 405; Allen *v.* Ray, 96 Mo. 542, 10 S. W. 153; Jones *v.* Driskill, 94 Mo. 190, 7 S. W. 111; Allen *v.* McCabe, 93 Mo. 138, 6 S. W. 62; Brown *v.* Walker, 85 Mo. 262; Wellshear *v.* Kelley, 69 Mo. 343; Hogan *v.* Smith, 11 Mo. App. 314. A judgment in a tax suit cannot be set aside in a collateral attack by proof that the taxes for the year specified in the judgment had been paid before the suit was begun. Cooper *v.* Gunter, (Mo. 1908) 114 S. W. 943.

Tennessee.— Neely *v.* Buchanan, (Ch. App. 1899) 54 S. W. 995.

Texas.— Crosby *v.* Bonnowsky, 29 Tex. Civ. App. 455, 69 S. W. 212; Bean *v.* Brownwood, (Civ. App. 1898) 43 S. W. 1036. A judgment on service by publication regular in all respects, and decreeing a lien with foreclosure in favor of the state against all persons claiming any interest in the land, and directing the sale of the land, cannot be collaterally attacked by one failing to show that he was in possession of the land when the suit was filed and citation issued. Gibbs *v.* Scales, (Civ. App. 1909) 118 S. W. 188.

Washington.— Tax-sales being made only after foreclosure, in a proceeding in which the owner is given notice and an opportunity to defend against overcharges, etc., the owner is estopped by the judgment to raise collaterally non-jurisdictional defects, so that the rendition of judgment through mistake for a larger amount of interest than was due would not avoid the sale. Timmerman *v.* McCullagh, 55 Wash. 204, 104 Pac. 212. All presumptions are in favor of the regularity of tax foreclosure proceedings upon a collateral attack upon the sale, and want of jurisdiction must affirmatively appear to invalidate the sale. Timmerman *v.* McCullagh, *supra.*

United States.— Chicago Theological Seminary *v.* Gage, 12 Fed. 398, 11 Biss. 289. See Wilfong *v.* Ontario Land Co., 171 Fed. 51, 96 C. C. A. 293 [*reversing* 162 Fed. 999].

See 45 Cent. Dig. tit. "Taxation," § 1316.

Defendant waiving service of process.— Where, in a statutory suit for taxes, one of the defendants is not served with process, but waives the service, in writing, on the petition instead of the summons attached thereto, the method of waiver is an irregularity only, and does not subject the judgment to collateral attack either by defendants who were served with process or by defendant making waiver. Walker *v.* Mills, 210 Mo. 684, 109 S. W. 44.

50. Mayot *v.* Auditor-Gen., 140 Mich. 593, 104 N. W. 19; Vaughan *v.* Daniels, 98 Mo. 230, 11 S. W. 573. Where the judgment in a tax suit does not show that the court determined that service of proper process had been made on the owners of the land, and the record therein shows a fatally defective notice, the judgment may be collaterally attacked for invalidity of notice. Harris *v.* Hill, (Tex. Civ. App. 1909) 117 S. W. 907.

51. See the statutes of the different states. And see English *v.* People, 96 Ill. 566; Fowler *v.* Pirkins, 77 Ill. 271; State *v.* Lockhart, 89 Minn. 121, 94 N. W. 168; Aurora *v.* Lindsay, 146 Mo. 509, 48 S. W. 642.

2. Personal Notice to Residents. Where the law requires personal notice to be given to the owner of the property, if he is known and a resident, it is mandatory and no valid sale can be made without such notice.[14] Within the meaning of such a provision, the "owner" includes all persons who are interested in the property, as coheirs or joint tenants or tenants in common,[15] and it means the person who owns the property at the time the notice is given, and not a former owner in whose name the land was assessed.[16] The law also intends that reasonably diligent action shall be taken to discover the true owner and make the notice effectual;[17] and thus if the owner is dead, an endeavor must be made to ascertain who are his heirs or representatives, and serve the notice on them, and if they are known or may be discovered, a notice addressed to the "estate" is insufficient.[18] Similar principles apply where the notice is directed to be given to the "occupant" of the premises,[19] or to the person "in actual possession" of the land.[20] Where the statute authorizes this notice to be given by mail, it is sufficient if a proper notice

Missouri.— Nelson *v.* Goebel, 17 Mo. 161; Reeds *v.* Morton, 9 Mo. 878.

New Jersey.— Landis *v.* Sea Isle City, 66 N. J. L. 558, 49 Atl. 685.

New York.— Leland *v.* Bennett, 5 Hill 286; Sharp *v.* Johnson, 4 Hill 92, 40 Am. Dec. 259; Bush *v.* Davison, 16 Wend. 550.

North Carolina.— Hill *v.* Nicholson, 92 N. C. 24; *In re* Macay, 84 N. C. 63. But *compare* Geer *v.* Brown, 126 N. C. 238, 35 S. E. 470.

Ohio.— Hughey *v.* Horel, 2 Ohio 231.

Oregon.— Rafferty *v.* Davis, 54 Oreg. 77, 102 Pac. 305.

Pennsylvania.— Jenks *v.* Wright, 61 Pa. St. 410; Arthurs *v.* Smathers, 38 Pa. St. 40; Thompson *v.* Brackenridge, 14 Serg. & R. 346; Blair *v.* Waggoner, 2 Serg. & R. 472.

Texas.— Bean *v.* Brownwood, 91 Tex. 684, 45 S. W. 897; Edwards *v.* Harnberger, (Civ. App. 1900) 55 S. W. 42. But *compare* Rogers *v.* Moore, 100 Tex. 220, 97 S. W. 685.

Utah.— Olsen *v.* Bagley, 10 Utah 492, 37 Pac. 739.

United States.— Early *v.* Doe, 16 How. 610, 14 L. ed. 1079; Washington *v.* Pratt, 8 Wheat. 681, 5 L. ed. 714; Martin *v.* Barbour, 34 Fed. 701 [*affirmed* in 140 U. S. 634, 11 S. Ct. 944, 35 L. ed. 546]; Marx *v.* Hanthorn, 30 Fed. 579; Moore *v.* Brown, 17 Fed. Cas. No. 9,753, 4 McLean 211.

Canada.— O'Brien *v.* Cogswell, 17 Can. Sup. Ct. 420; Haisley *v.* Somers, 13 Ont. 600; Deverill *v.* Coe, 11 Ont. 222.

See 45 Cent. Dig. tit. "Taxation," § 1334.

Contra.— Noland *v.* Busby, 28 Ind. 154.

Subsequent private sale of lands.—Where the treasurer, as authorized by law, makes a private sale of those lands which have remained unsold for want of bidders at the public sale, the same having been duly advertised, such private sale need not be on notice. Kittle *v.* Shervin, 11 Nebr. 65, 7 N. W. 861.

14. Villey *v.* Jarreau, 33 La. Ann. 291; Crosby *v.* Terry, 41 Tex. Civ. App. 594, 91 S. W. 652; Hollywood *v.* Wellhausen, 28 Tex. Civ. App. 541, 68 S. W. 329. *Compare* Sanders *v.* Earp, 118 N. C. 275, 24 S. E. 8.

Notice held sufficient see McMahon *v.* Crean, 109 Md. 652, 71 Atl. 995.

15. Howze *v.* Dew, 90 Ala. 178, 7 So. 239, 24 Am. St. Rep. 783; *In re* Interstate Land Co., 118 La. 587, 43 So. 173; Thurston *v.* Miller, 10 R. I. 358.

Mortgagee.— In North Carolina it is held that the mortgagee, being the legal owner of the land mortgaged, is the person to whom notice must be given of an intended tax-sale of the property. Hill *v.* Nicholson, 92 N. C. 24; Whitehurst *v.* Gaskill, 69 N. C. 449, 12 Am. Rep. 655.

Owner of timber.—Where the notice served on the record owner was fatally defective, the service of a sufficient notice on one claiming an interest in the timber growing on the land will not make the sale valid. Tucker *v.* Van Winkle, 142 Mich. 210, 105 N. W. 607.

16. Quinlan *v.* Callahan, 81 Ky. 618; *In re* Lafferranderie, 114 La. 6, 37 So. 990; Adolph *v.* Richardson, 52 La. Ann. 1156, 27 So. 665; Lague *v.* Boagni, 32 La. Ann. 912; Hume *v.* Wainscott, 46 Mo. 145; Abbott *v.* Lindenbower, 42 Mo. 162. But *compare* Jones *v.* Landis Tp., 50 N. J. L. 374, 13 Atl. 251. And see Barnard *v.* Hoyt, 63 Ill. 341, holding that where the property is vacant and unoccupied, the notice must be served on the person in whose name the land was assessed, even though he never had or claimed any interest in the premises.

17. Genella *v.* Vincent, 50 La. Ann. 956, 24 So. 690; Hoyle *v.* Southern Athletic Club, 48 La. Ann. 879, 19 So. 937.

18. McGee *v.* Fleming, 82 Ala. 276, 3 So. 1; Carlisle *v.* Watts, 78 Ala. 486; Fennimore *v.* Boatner, 112 La. 1080, 36 So. 860; Genella *v.* Vincent, 50 La. Ann. 956, 24 So. 690; Hoyle *v.* Southern Athletic Club, 48 La. Ann. 879, 19 So. 937.

19. Gage *v.* Bailey, 102 Ill. 11; People *v.* Kelsey, 180 N. Y. 24, 72 N. E. 524 [*reversing* 96 N. Y. App. Div. 148, 89 N. Y. Suppl. 416] (the commission of the forest preserve is an "occupant" within the meaning of such a statute); Leland *v.* Bennett, 5 Hill (N. Y.) 286.

Notice to redeem see *infra*, XII, B, 5, c.

20. Gage *v.* Waterman, 121 Ill. 115, 13 N. E. 543; Foy *v.* Houstman, 128 Iowa 220, 103 N. W. 369.

officer,[42] and that it will be a public sale or sale at public auction.[43] The time within which the owner may redeem from the sale is not usually required to be stated in this notice; but if so, it cannot be omitted.[44]

5. Designation or Description of Property. The notice of tax-sale must describe the lands to be sold with such certainty and particularity that they can be clearly identified, without any reasonable chance of mistake, so that the owner may know that it is his property which is advertised and an intending purchaser may know what lands are to be sold; if the description is insufficient for this purpose, the notice is fatally defective,[45] as is also the case where the description,

42. Salter *v.* Corbett, 80 Kan. 327, 102 Pac. 452; Casner *v.* Gahlman, 60 Kan. 857, 56 Pac. 1131 [*affirming* 6 Kan. App. 295, 51 Pac. 56].

43. Hoffman *v.* Groll, 35 Kan. 652, 12 Pac. 34; Hafey *v.* Bronson, 33 Kan. 598, 7 Pac. 239; Belz *v.* Bird, 31 Kan. 139, 1 Pac. 246.

44. *In re* Tax Sale of Lot No. 172, 42 Md. 196; Becker *v.* Holdridge, 47 How. Pr. (N. Y.) 429; State Finance Co. *v.* Trimble, 16 N. D. 199, 112 N. W. 984.

To whom payment to be made.— The omission to name the person to whom payment of the tax may be made does not affect the validity of the notice or sale. Sanders *v.* Leavey, 38 Barb. (N. Y.) 70.

45. *Alabama.*— Lyon *v.* Hunt, 11 Ala. 295, 46 Am. Dec. 216.

Arkansas.— Boles *v.* McNeil, 66 Ark. 422, 51 S. W. 71; Cooper *v.* Lee, 59 Ark. 460, 27 S. W. 970.

California.— Best *v.* Wohlford, 153 Cal. 17, 94 Pac. 98, description sufficient.

Colorado.— Stough *v.* Reeves, 42 Colo. 432, 95 Pac. 958, holding that the description in a notice of sale for taxes of the property as lots "1 to 24," does not exclude lot 24 by reason of the use of the word "to," as such word is not necessarily a term of exclusion, but one whose meaning is to be ascertained by the reason and sense in which it is used.

Georgia.— Boyd *v.* Wilson, 86 Ga. 379, 12 S. E. 744, 13 S. E. 428, description sufficient.

Indiana.— Brown *v.* Reeves, 31 Ind. App. 517, 68 N. E. 604.

Iowa.— Vaughan *v.* Stone, 55 Iowa 213, 7 N. W. 521; Shawler *v.* Johnson, 52 Iowa 473, 3 N. W. 604. But see Henderson *v.* Oliver, 32 Iowa 512; Burlington, etc., R. Co. *v.* Spearman, 12 Iowa 112.

Kansas.— Knote *v.* Caldwell, 43 Kan. 464, 23 Pac. 625.

Louisiana.— Marin *v.* Sheriff, 30 La. Ann. 293; Thibodaux *v.* Keller, 29 La. Ann. 508; Carmichael *v.* Aikin, 13 La. 205.

Maine.— Millett *v.* Mullen, 95 Me. 400, 49 Atl. 871; Whitmore *v.* Learned, 70 Me. 276; Bingham *v.* Smith, 64 Me. 450; Nason *v.* Ricker, 63 Me. 381; French *v.* Patterson, 61 Me. 203; Griffin *v.* Creppin, 60 Me. 270.

Maryland.— Hill *v.* Williams, 104 Md. 595, 65 Atl. 413; Richardson *v.* Simpson, 82 Md. 155, 33 Atl. 457; Cooper *v.* Holmes, 71 Md. 20, 17 Atl. 711; Guisebert *v.* Etchison, 51 Md. 478. An advertisement of tax-sale is sufficient, although the property be a private alleyway and be termed a lot in the advertisement, its boundaries being properly given, and no one being misled. Hill *v.* Williams, *supra.*

Massachusetts.— Williams *v.* Bowers, 197 Mass. 565, 84 N. E. 317; Farnum *v.* Buffum, 4 Cush. 260.

Michigan.— Tucker *v.* Van Winkle, 142 Mich. 210, 105 N. W. 607; Smith *v.* Auditor-Gen., 138 Mich. 582, 101 N. W. 807; Mann *v.* Carson, 120 Mich. 631, 79 N. W. 941.

Minnesota.— Doherty *v.* Real Estate Title Ins., etc., Co., 85 Minn. 518, 89 N. W. 853; Bidwell *v.* Webb, 10 Minn. 59, 88 Am. Dec. 56.

Missouri.—Stewart *v.* Allison, 150 Mo. 343, 51 S. W. 712; Comfort *v.* Ballingal, 134 Mo. 281, 35 S. W. 609.

Nebraska.— A description of land in a notice of tax-sale is sufficient where the context of the notice shows clearly that land in this state is referred to, and there is but one tract in the state answering the description, although the description would fit another tract situated in another state. Leigh *v.* Green, 64 Nebr. 533, 90 N. W. 255, 101 Am. St. Rep. 592.

New Hampshire.— Langley *v.* Batchelder, 69 N. H. 566, 46 Atl. 1085; Smith *v.* Messer, 17 N. H. 420. And see Drew *v.* Morrill, 62 N. H. 23.

New Jersey.— Hunt *v.* Warshung, 48 N. J. L. 613, 9 Atl. 199.

New York.— People *v.* McGuire, 126 N. Y. 419, 27 N. E. 967; Smith *v.* Buhler, 121 N. Y. 213, 24 N. E. 11 [*affirming* 56 N. Y. Super. Ct. 391, 4 N. Y. Suppl. 632]; Kane *v.* Brooklyn, 114 N. Y. 586, 21 N. E. 1053; White *v.* Wheeler, 51 Hun 573, 4 N. Y. Suppl. 405 [*affirmed* in 123 N. Y. 627, 25 N. E. 952]; People *v.* Golding, 55 Misc. 425, 106 N. Y. Suppl. 821.

North Dakota.— State Finance Co. *v.* Mulberger, 16 N. D. 214, 112 N. W. 986, 125 Am. St. Rep. 650; State Finance Co. *v.* Trimble, 16 N. D. 199, 112 N. W. 984; Blakemore *v.* Cooper, 15 N. D. 5, 106 N. W. 566, 125 Am. St. Rep. 574, 4 L. R. A. N. S. 1074; Lee *v.* Crawford, 10 N. D. 482, 88 N. W. 97; Sweigle *v.* Gates, 9 N. D. 538, 84 N. W. 481.

Ohio.— Lafferty *v.* Byers, 5 Ohio 458. See McGinnis *v.* Willey, Wright 152.

South Dakota.— Bandow *v.* Wolven, 20 S. D. 445, 107 N. W. 204.

Tennessee.— Finley *v.* Gaut, 8 Baxt. 148.

West Virginia.— Barton *v.* Gilchrist, 19 W. Va. 223.

Wisconsin.— Sprague *v.* Coenen, 30 Wis. 209.

United States.— Raymond *v.* Longworth,

equally defective in that case.[51] Where the statute requires a publication of the notice for so many weeks "successively," or once a week for a certain number of weeks, or a certain number of times within a limited number of days or weeks, it must be literally and exactly complied with, at the risk of invalidating the sale.[52] Whether the publication, under a statute of this kind, is required to be continuous up to the date of the sale depends on the wording of the local statute;[53] but if the last publication is made on the day of the sale, it is clear that it must actually be made before the hour fixed for the sale, otherwise it cannot be counted.[54] Two attempts at advertisement, both irregular on account of the time, cannot be coupled together so as to authorize a sale.[55]

7. Posting of Notices. A statute requiring the notices of tax-sales to be posted at certain places, or at public and conspicuous places in the county, is mandatory and failure to obey its directions will invalidate the sale.[56] It is also

until later dates, dates too late to comply with the statute. On motion for an injunction to stay the sale, it was held that the statute was not sufficiently complied with, but that insufficient advertising would not, under the present laws, render the sale void, for which reason the injunction was refused. Wood *v.* Birtle, 4 Manitoba 415.

Publication on Sunday.— The publication is not sufficient if made on Sunday only. Ormsby *v.* Louisville, 79 Ky. 197, 2 Ky. L. Rep. 66. And if the last of the number of days prescribed should be Sunday, the notice should be published on Monday. Alameda Macadamizing Co. *v.* Huff, 57 Cal. 331.

Publication for ten days, Sundays excepted.—Where notice is required to be published for ten days, Sundays excepted, and it is omitted for two days, not Sundays, it is void. Haskell *v.* Bartlett, 34 Cal. 281. It is also defective if it be omitted one week day and published one Sunday. People *v.* McCain, 50 Cal. 210.

51. Person *v.* O'Neal, 32 La. Ann. 228. See Everett *v.* Boyington, 29 Minn. 264, 13 N. W. 45.

52. *Arkansas.*— Pennell *v.* Monroe, 30 Ark. 661.

California.— Carpenter *v.* Shinners, 108 Cal. 359, 41 Pac. 473.

Dakota.—Wambole *v.* Foote, 2 Dak. 1, 2 N. W. 239.

Illinois.— Ricketts *v.* Hyde Park, 85 Ill. 110; Andrews *v.* People, 83 Ill. 529.

Indiana.— Loughridge *v.* Huntington, 56 Ind. 253.

Iowa.— Davis *v.* Magoun, 109 Iowa 308, 80 N. W. 423.

Kansas.— Tidd *v.* Grimes, 66 Kan. 401, 71 Pac. 844.

Louisiana.— Hansen *v.* Mauberret, 52 La. Ann. 1565, 28 So. 167; *In re* New Orleans, 52 La. Ann. 1073, 27 So. 592; Worman *v.* Miller, McGloin 158.

Maine.— Bussey *v.* Leavitt, 12 Me. 378.

Maryland.— Textor *v.* Shipley, 86 Md. 424, 38 Atl. 932.

Minnesota.— Kipp *v.* Collins, 33 Minn. 394, 23 N. W. 554.

Mississippi.— Miller *v.* Delta, etc., Land Co., 74 Miss. 110, 20 So. 875.

New Hampshire.— Mowry *v.* Blandin, 64 N. H. 3, 4 Atl. 882; French *v.* Spalding, 61 N. H. 395; Schoff *v.* Gould, 52 N. H. 512; Cass *v.* Bellows, 31 N. H. 501, 64 Am. Dec. 347.

New York.— Wood *v.* Knapp, 100 N. Y. 109, 2 N. E. 632.

North Carolina.— Matthews *v.* Fry, 141 N. C. 582, 54 S. E. 379.

North Dakota.—Dever *v.* Cornwell, 10 N. D. 123, 86 N. W. 227.

Ohio.— Magruder *v.* Esmay, 35 Ohio St. 221.

Oklahoma.— Cadman *v.* Smith, 15 Okla. 633, 85 Pac. 346.

Oregon.— O'Hara *v.* Parker, 27 Oreg. 156, 39 Pac. 1004.

South Carolina.— Ebaugh *v.* Mullinax, 40 S. C. 244, 18 S. E. 802; Alexander *v.* Messervey, 35 S. C. 409, 14 S. E. 854.

South Dakota.— Bandow *v.* Wolven, 20 S. D. 445, 107 N. W. 204.

Wisconsin.— Chippewa River Land Co. *v.* J. L. Gates Land Co., 118 Wis. 345, 94 N. W. 37, 95 N. W. 954.

United States.— Early *v.* Homans, 16 How. 610, 14 L. ed. 1079; Martin *v.* Barbour, 34 Fed. 701.

Canada.— Gemmel *v.* Sinclair, 1 Manitoba 85; Connor *v.* Douglas, 15 Grant Ch. (U. C.) 456; Kempt *v.* Parkyn, 28 U. C. C. P. 123; McLaughlin *v.* Pyper, 29 U. C. Q. B. 526.

See 45 Cent. Dig. tit. "Taxation," § 1340.

53. See the statutes of the different states. And *compare* Watkins *v.* Inge, 24 Kan. 612, with Delogny *v.* Smith, 3 La. 418.

54. Buckingham *v.* Negrotto, 116 La. 737, 41 So. 54; *In re* Lindner, 113 La. 772, 37 So. 720.

55. Scales *v.* Alvis, 12 Ala. 617, 46 Am. Dec. 269.

56. Baumgardner *v.* Fowler, 82 Md. 631, 34 Atl. 537; Keene *v.* Barnes, 29 Mo. 377; Yenda *v.* Wheeler, 9 Tex. 408; Ramsey *v.* Hommel, 68 Wis. 12, 31 N. W. 271; Iverslie *v.* Spaulding, 32 Wis. 394.

Uninhabited places.— It is not necessary to post a notice of a sale of land for taxes within the limits of the place, if it is uninhabited. Wells *v.* Jackson Iron Mfg. Co., 47 N. H. 235; Wells *v.* Burbank, 17 N. H. 393. So if there is no public place in the locality. Cahoon *v.* Coe, 52 N. H. 518.

Contents of notice.— If the statute requires the posted notice to give the name of the oc-

the discretion of the officer to fix the time of sale,[82] or where the proceedings have been delayed by appeal, injunction, or other process,[83] or where the time for holding tax-sales has been duly extended by competent authority.[84] On similar principles, where the law is such that the sale is to take place after a prescribed publication of notice, it must be held on the very day appointed in the notice or advertisement.[85] Whatever the requirement of the law may be, the day of sale can neither be anticipated nor delayed. If it is held prematurely, that is, on a day earlier than that authorized by law or appointed in the notice, it is invalid,[86] and so if it is held after the expiration of the tax lien or of the warrant or other process of the officer.[87] Nor, as a rule, can a valid tax-sale be made on Sunday or other non-juridical days.[88]

is mandatory and must be strictly complied with. State *v.* Farney, 36 Nebr. 537, 54 N. W. 862. See also Keenan *v.* Slaughter, 49 Tex. Civ. App. 180, 108 S. W. 703.

Presumptions and proof as to time of sale see Taylor *v.* Van Meter, 53 Ark. 204, 13 S. W. 699; Radcliffe *v.* Scruggs, 46 Ark. 96; Chandler *v.* Keeler, 46 Iowa 596; Spear *v.* Ditty, 8 Vt. 419.

The officer is protected in selling property for taxes on the day when, according to his interpretation of the statute, it should be done, process for such sale apparently in due form of law having been given. Mathers *v.* Bull, 9 Ohio S. & C. Pl. Dec. 408, 6 Ohio N. P. 45.

82. Stilwell *v.* People, 49 Ill. 45; Coleman *v.* Shattuck, 62 N. Y. 348.

83. Carne *v.* Peacock, 114 Ill. 347, 2 N. E. 165; Patterson *v.* Carruth, 13 Kan. 494; Jordan *v.* Kyle, 27 Kan. 190.

84. McConnell *v.* Day, 61 Ark. 464, 33 S. W. 731; Vernon *v.* Nelson, 33 Ark. 748; Shell *v.* Duncan, 31 S. C. 547, 10 S. E. 330, 5 L. R. A. 821; Roddy *v.* Purdy, 10 S. C. 137; Todd *v.* Werry, 15 U. C. Q. B. 614. In Taylor *v.* Allen, 67 N. C. 346, it was held that the sheriff's power to sell land for taxes being given on the condition that it shall be exercised within a certain time, the legislature cannot by a private act give him power to sell after the expiration of the time allowed by law. But *compare* Ford *v.* Delta, etc., Land Co., 43 Fed. 181 [*affirmed* in 164 U. S. 662, 17 S. Ct. 230, 41 L. ed. 590].

85. *California.*— Tully *v.* Bauer, 52 Cal. 487.

Connecticut.— Beacher *v.* Bray, 1 Root 459.

Minnesota.— Sheehy *v.* Hinds, 27 Minn. 259, 6 N. W. 781; Prindle *v.* Campbell, 9 Minn. 212.

Missouri.— Sullivan *v.* Donnell, 90 Mo. 278, 2 S. W. 264.

Ohio.— Wilkins *v.* Huse, 10 Ohio 139.

See 45 Cent. Dig. tit. "Taxation," § 1345.

86. *Colorado.*— Seymour *v.* Deisher, 33 Colo. 349, 80 Pac. 1038; Gomer *v.* Chaffee, 6 Colo. 314.

Louisiana.— Person *v.* O'Neal, 32 La. Ann. 228.

Maine.— Hobbs *v.* Clements, 32 Me. 67.

Michigan.—See Hooker *v.* Bond, 118 Mich. 255, 76 N. W. 404.

Minnesota.— See Everett *v.* Boyington, 29 Minn. 264, 13 N. W. 45.

Mississippi.— Davis *v.* Schmidt, 68 Miss. 736, 10 So. 64; Caston *v.* Caston, 60 Miss. 475; Harkreader *v.* Clayton, 56 Miss. 383, 31 Am. Rep. 369; McGehee *v.* Martin, 53 Miss. 519.

South Carolina.— Cooke *v.* Pennington, 15 S. C. 185.

Vermont.— Buzzell *v.* Johnson, 54 Vt. 90.

United States.— Moore *v.* Brown, 11 How. 414, 13 L. ed. 751.

Canada.— Connor *v.* McPherson, 18 Grant Ch. (U. C.) 607; Kelly *v.* Macklem, 14 Grant Ch. (U. C.) 29; Ford *v.* Proudfoot, 9 Grant Ch. (U. C.) 478; Bell *v.* McLean, 18 U. C. C. P. 416.

See 45 Cent. Dig. tit. "Taxation," § 1347.

Curing defect by statute.— Where the law requires that all tax-sales shall be made between the hours of twelve and five in the afternoon, and a sale is advertised and held at ten in the morning, the defect may be cured by a subsequent retroactive curative statute. Jones *v.* Landis Tp., 50 N. J. L. 374, 13 Atl. 251.

87. *Arkansas.*— Boehm *v.* Porter, 54 Ark. 665, 17 S. W. 1.

Maine.— Usher *v.* Taft, 33 Me. 199.

Massachusetts.— Noyes *v.* Haverhill, 11 Cush. 338; Pierce *v.* Benjamin, 14 Pick. 356, 25 Am. Dec. 396.

New Hampshire.— Mason *v.* Bilbruck, 62 N. H. 440. But *compare* Cahoon *v.* Coe, 52 N. H. 518.

New Jersey.— Johnson *v.* Van Horn, 45 N. J. L. 136; Field *v.* West Orange, 7 N. J. L. 348.

New York.— Dubois *v.* Poughkeepsie, 22 Hun 117.

North Carolina.— Taylor *v.* Allen, 67 N. C. 346.

United States.— Kelly *v.* Herrall, 20 Fed. 364.

Canada.— Hamilton *v.* McDonald, 22 U. C. Q. B. 136. See Cotter *v.* Sutherland, 18 U. C. C. P. 357.

See 45 Cent. Dig. tit. "Taxation," § 1347.

But *compare* Paden *v.* Akin, 7 Watts & S. (Pa.) 456; Little *v.* Gibbs, 8 Utah 261, 30 Pac. 986.

88. Picket *v.* Allen, 10 Conn. 146; Hadley *v.* Musselman, 104 Ind. 459, 3 N. E. 122 (tax-sale made on Christmas day is not invalid); Lynch *v.* Donnell, 104 Mo. 519, 15 S. W. 927 (no sale can lawfully be made on Thanksgiving day); Wood *v.* Meyer, 36 Wis. 308.

erty under these conditions for less than two thirds of its assessed or appraised value.[96]

b. Sale For Excessive Amount. If real property is offered at tax-sale for an amount exceeding the aggregate of taxes, costs, penalties, and charges for which the land is legally and actually liable, the sale, as a rule, is entirely void and passes no title.[97] But it will not be lightly assumed that the sale was made for an excessive amount; on the contrary, this must be clearly shown.[98] And in some states, in such a case, the owner of the property can have relief only on condition of paying or tendering what was justly due.[99]

c. Including Unauthorized Fees or Charges. The amount for which the land is offered may include costs and fees which are due and legally chargeable on the property up to the time of sale;[1] but the sale is invalid if such amount is made to include any fees, costs, commissions, or other charges which are illegal, excessive, unauthorized, or not yet accrued or due.[2]

S. W. 685; Blanton *v.* Nunley, (Civ. App. 1909) 119 S. W. 881.

United States.— Slater *v.* Maxwell, 6 Wall. (U. S.) 268, 18 L. ed. 796.

But gross inadequacy of price may justify the courts in laying stress on other matters, constituting in themselves only irregularities, which otherwise would not be sufficient to invalidate the sale, and so finding ground upon the whole case to set the sale aside. Davis *v.* McGee, 28 Fed. 867. And see Walters *v.* Herman, 99 Mo. 529, 12 S. W. 890; Younger *v.* Meadows, 63 W. Va. 275, 59 S. E. 1087.

96. See the statutes of the different states. And see Wooley *v.* Louisville, 114 Ky. 556, 71 S. W. 893, 24 Ky. L. Rep. 1357; Turner *v.* Smith, 18 Gratt. (Va.) 830.

97. *Arkansas.*— Sibley *v.* Thomas, 86 Ark. 578, 112 S. W. 210; Dickinson *v.* Arkansas City Imp. Co., 77 Ark. 570, 92 S. W. 21, 113 Am. St. Rep. 170; Cowling *v.* Muldrow, 71 Ark. 488, 76 S. W. 424; Cooper *v.* Freeman Lumber Co., 61 Ark. 36, 31 S. W. 981, 32 S. W. 494; Pack *v.* Crawford, 29 Ark. 489.

California.— Knox *v.* Higby, 76 Cal. 264, 18 Pac. 381; Boston Tunnel Co. *v.* McKenzie, 67 Cal. 485, 8 Pac. 22; Axtell *v.* Gerlach, 67 Cal. 483, 8 Pac. 34; Harper *v.* Rowe, 53 Cal. 233; Treadwell *v.* Patterson, 51 Cal. 637; Bucknall *v.* Story, 36 Cal. 67.

Georgia.—See Barnes *v.* Lewis, 98 Ga. 558, 25 S. E. 589.

Illinois.— Harland *v.* Eastman, 119 Ill. 22, 8 N. E. 810.

Kansas.— Glenn *v.* Stewart, 78 Kan. 608, 97 Pac. 863; Kansas State Agricultural College *v.* Linscott, 30 Kan. 240, 1 Pac. 81; Wilder *v.* Cockshutt, 25 Kan. 504; Genthner *v.* Lewis, 24 Kan. 309; Herzog *v.* Gregg, 23 Kan. 726; McQuesten *v.* Swope, 12 Kan. 32.

Kentucky.— Smith *v.* Ryan, 88 Ky. 636, 11 S. W. 647, 11 Ky. L. Rep. 128; Carlisle *v.* Cassady, 46 S. W. 490, 20 Ky. L. Rep. 562.

Louisiana.— The sale is not invalid if the taxes of any one of the years for which the sale was made are shown to have been legal and valid. Clifford *v.* Michiner, 49 La. Ann. 1511, 22 So. 811.

Massachusetts.— Loud *v.* Penniman, 19 Pick. 539.

Michigan.— Case *v.* Dean, 16 Mich. 12. But *compare* Smith *v.* Auditor-Gen., 138 Mich. 582, 101 N. W. 807.

Minnesota.— Prindle *v.* Campbell, 9 Minn. 212.

New Hampshire.— Wells *v.* Burbank, 17 N. H. 393.

New Jersey.— Landis *v.* Vineland, (Sup. 1899) 43 Atl. 569.

Texas.— Eustis *v.* Henrietta, 91 Tex. 325, 43 S. W. 259.

Utah.— Asper *v.* Moon, 24 Utah 241, 67 Pac. 409.

Wisconsin.—Pinkerton *v.* J. L. Gates Land Co., 118 Wis. 514, 95 N. W. 1089; Pierce *v.* Schutt, 20 Wis. 423; Warner *v.* Outagamie County, 19 Wis. 611; Kimball *v.* Ballard, 19 Wis. 601, 88 Am. Dec. 705.

Canada.— Cotter *v.* Sutherland, 18 U. C. C. P. 357; Allan *v.* Fisher, 13 U. C. C. P. 63; Doe *v.* Langton, 9 U. C. Q. B. 91.

See 45 Cent. Dig. tit. "Taxation," § 1350.

Contra.— Darling *v.* Purcell, 13 N. D. 288, 100 N. W. 726; Shuttuck *v.* Smith, 6 N. D. 56, 69 N. W. 5; Winder *v.* Sterling, 7 Ohio, Pt. II, 190; Peters *v.* Heasley, 10 Watts (Pa.) 208. But *compare* Lee *v.* Crawford, 10 N. D. 482, 88 N. W. 97.

98. Drennan *v.* Beierlein, 49 Mich. 272, 13 N. W. 587. And see Doland *v.* Mooney, 79 Cal. 137, 21 Pac. 436, holding that it will not be adjudged that a tax-sale was made for a sum exceeding the amount of the tax and legal costs, and is therefore void, merely because the recitals of the amount in the certificate and the deed differ.

99. Hansen *v.* Mauberret, 52 La. Ann. 1565, 28 So. 167; Pierce *v.* Schutt, 20 Wis. 423; Mills *v.* Johnson, 17 Wis. 598.

1. Trimble *v.* Allen-West Commission Co., 72 Ark. 72, 77 S. W. 898; Fish *v.* Genett, 56 S. W. 813, 22 Ky. L. Rep. 177; Nichols *v.* Roberts, 12 N. D. 193, 96 N. W. 298.

2. *Arkansas.*— Sibly *v.* Thomas, 86 Ark. 578, 112 S. W. 210; Kirker *v.* Daniels, 73 Ark. 263, 83 S. W. 912; Muskegon Lumber Co. *v.* Brown, 66 Ark. 539, 51 S. W. 1056; Darter *v.* Houser, 63 Ark. 475, 39 S. W. 358; Salinger *v.* Gunn, 61 Ark. 414, 33 S. W. 959; Goodrum *v.* Ayers, 56 Ark. 93, 19 S. W. 97.

California.—Axtell *v.* Gerlich, 67 Cal. 483, 8 Pac. 34.

Illinois.— Fuller *v.* Shedd, 161 Ill. 462, 44

assessments on the separate interests of tenants in common or other persons jointly interested, and where this is done the interest of one, although undivided, may be sold for his own default, without disturbing the title of the other.[7] But aside from these exceptions, it is the general rule that the tax collector has no authority to sell an undivided interest in land, but if the tract is to be divided the part sold must be a designated portion by metes and bounds.[8] It is also a general rule that the interest sold must be an estate in fee, not for years or any lesser estate.[9]

7. **Quantity of Land Which May Be Sold — a. In General.** According to the rule obtaining in most of the states, each particular tract of land is liable only for the taxes which have been assessed against itself, and consequently cannot be sold for the delinquency of taxes due on other lands of the same owner.[10] Under this rule, where a tract of land is assessed as an entirety, the sale of a portion of it for a part of the tax is voidable;[11] and conversely, the whole tract cannot be sold for the tax assessed on only a part of it or where the taxes on a part have

Gibson, 4 N. C. 480, 7 Am. Dec. 690. And see Pennell *v.* Monroe, 30 Ark. 661; Lawrence *v.* Miller, 86 Ill. 502; Fellows *v.* Denniston, 23 N. Y. 420.

7. Dyer *v.* Mobile Branch Bank, 14 Ala. 622; Payne *v.* Danley, 18 Ark. 441, 68 Am. Dec. 187; Townsend Sav. Bank *v.* Todd, 47 Conn. 190; Peirce *v.* Weare, 41 Iowa 378.

Applications of text.—As between life-estate and estate of remainder-man see Fenley *v.* Louisville, 119 Ky. 569, 84 S. W. 582, 27 Ky. L. Rep. 204; Woolley *v.* Louisville, 118 Ky. 897, 82 S. W. 608, 26 Ky. L. Rep. 872; Hellrigle *v.* Ould, 11 Fed. Cas. No. 6,344, 4 Cranch C. C. 72. As between two tenants in common see Payne *v.* Danley, 18 Ark. 441, 68 Am. Dec. 187; Ronkendorff *v.* Taylor, 4 Pet. (U. S.) 349, 7 L. ed. 882. As between two reversioners see Weaver *v.* Arnold, 15 R. I. 53, 23 Atl. 41. Mortgagor and mortgagee see Detroit *v.* Detroit Bd. of Assessors, 91 Mich. 78, 51 N. W. 787, 16 L. R. A. 59. Under N. H. Pub. St. (1901) c. 60, § 13, the tax collector has a prior lien on the land of a mortgagor for all taxes assessed against him, which may be foreclosed by sale if the mortgagor does not pay or expose personal property within fourteen days after notice. O'Donnell *v.* Meredith, 75 N. H. 272, 73 Atl. 32. Heir owning a half interest see Marti *v.* Wall, 51 La. Ann. 946, 26 So. 44.

Property of one person cannot be sold confusedly with that of another for taxes where there is no privity of estate between the parties. George *v.* Cole, 109 La. 816, 33 So. 784.

Effect on outstanding easement.—A private alley may be sold for non-payment of taxes thereon, although the easement of passage over it given to an adjoining owner may be thereby destroyed. Hill *v.* Williams, 104 Md. 595, 65 Atl. 413.

8. *California.*— Roberts *v.* Chan Tin Pen, 23 Cal. 259.

Connecticut.—Townsend Sav. Bank *v.* Todd, 47 Conn. 190.

Iowa.— Cragin *v.* Henry, 40 Iowa 158. *Compare* Jenswold *v.* Doran, 77 Iowa 692, 42 N. W. 465.

Kansas.—Auld *v.* McAllaster, 43 Kan. 162, 23 Pac. 165; Corbin *v.* Inslee, 24 Kan. 154.

Louisiana.— McDonough *v.* Elam, 1 La. 489, 20 Am. Dec. 284.

Massachusetts.— Sanford *v.* Sanford, 135 Mass. 314; Wall *v.* Wall, 124 Mass. 65; Loud *v.* Penniman, 19 Pick. 539.

Mississippi.— Stevenson *v.* Reed, 90 Miss. 341, 43 So. 433.

Rhode Island.—Weaver *v.* Arnold, 15 R. I. 53, 23 Atl. 41.

West Virginia.— Toothman *v.* Courtney, 62 W. Va. 167, 58 S. E. 915.

United States.— Clarke *v.* Strickland, 5 Fed. Cas. No. 2,864, 2 Curt. 439.

See 45 Cent. Dig. tit. "Taxation," § 1352.

City lots.—Under the laws of West Virginia, a separate part of a city, village, or town lot cannot be sold for taxes, but the sale must be of the whole lot or of an undivided interest therein. Old Dominion Bldg., etc., Assoc. *v.* Sohn, 54 W. Va. 101, 46 S. E. 222.

9. *In re* New York Protestant Episcopal Public School, 31 N. Y. 574. *Compare* Schatt *v.* Grosch, 31 N. J. Eq. 199.

10. Jodon *v.* Brenham, 57 Tex. 655; Edmonson *v.* Galveston, 53 Tex. 157; State *v.* Baker, 49 Tex. 763. And see State *v.* Sargeant, 76 Mo. 557.

11. *Kansas.*— Heil *v.* Redden, 38 Kan. 255, 16 Pac. 743; Kregelo *v.* Flint, 25 Kan. 695; Shaw *v.* Kirkwood, 24 Kan. 476.

Maine.—Allen *v.* Morse, 72 Me. 502.

Mississippi.— House *v.* Gumble, 78 Miss. 259, 29 So. 71.

North Dakota.— Roberts *v.* Fargo First Nat. Bank, 8 N. D. 504, 79 N. W. 1049.

United States.— Ballance *v.* Forsyth, 13 How. 18, 14 L. ed. 32.

See 45 Cent. Dig. tit. "Taxation," § 1353.

Exceptions to rule.—A part of a lot may be sold to pay taxes when they have accrued on that part. Ronkendorff *v.* Taylor, 4 Pet. (U. S.) 349, 7 L. ed. 882. And half of a piece of land can legally be sold under an advertisement of the whole, if there is legal cause for staying the sale as to the other half, as where the whole tract was advertised as belonging to unknown owners, but the owner of one half subsequently appears and pays his tax. Clay *v.* O'Brien, 24 La. Ann. 232.

tracts owned by one person are assessed as one whole,[29] where two or more lots, owned by the same person, are used and occupied as a whole or for one purpose,[30] where two distinct lots belonging to the same owner are offered separately and no bids are received,[31] and where the officer, in making the sale, obeys the directions of a judgment.[32] Conversely, where a tax of a single gross sum is assessed on several lots or parcels of land, grouped as an entirety, all the lots must be sold together for the payment of the tax, and the tax cannot be arbitrarily apportioned and the lots sold separately, each for the payment of its proportionate share.[33]

H. Persons Who May Purchase — 1. General Rule. Any person who owes a positive duty to the state or municipality to pay the taxes on a particular tract of land cannot become a purchaser at a sale of the property for such taxes, or if he does so purchase it is deemed merely a mode of paying the taxes and does not found a new title or affect the existing title in any way.[34]

28 S. W. 874; Keene *v.* Barnes, 29 Mo. 377; Smith *v.* H. D. Williams Cooperage Co., 100 Mo. App. 153, 73 S. W. 315.

Montana.— Casey *v.* Wright, 14 Mont. 315, 36 Pac. 191.

Nebraska.— Rohrer *v.* Fassler, 2 Nebr. (Unoff.) 262, 96 N. W. 523.

Nevada.— Wright *v.* Cradlebaugh, 3 Nev. 341.

New Jersey.— Hasbrouck Heights Co. *v.* Lodi Tp. Committee, 66 N. J. L. 102, 48 Atl. 517.

New York.— People *v.* Golding, 55 Misc. 425, 106 N. Y. Suppl. 821; National F. Ins. Co. *v.* McKay, 1 Sheld. 138, 5 Abb. Pr. N. C. 445.

North Dakota.— State Finance Co. *v.* Beck, 15 N. D. 374, 109 N. W. 357.

Oregon.— Brentano *v.* Brentano, 41 Oreg. 15, 67 Pac. 922.

Pennsylvania.— Woodburn *v.* Wireman, 27 Pa. St. 18; Morton *v.* Harris, 9 Watts 319; Cunningham *v.* White, 2 Pa. Dist. 531.

Tennessee.— Sheafer *v.* Mitchell, 109 Tenn. 181, 71 S. W. 86.

Texas.— Allen *v.* Courtney, 24 Tex. Civ. App. 86, 58 S. W. 200; Fant *v.* Brannin, 2 Tex. Unrep. Cas. 323.

Wisconsin.— Jenkins *v.* Rock County, 15 Wis. 11.

United States.— Walker *v.* Moore, 29 Fed. Cas. No. 17,080, 2 Dill. 256. *Compare* Springer *v.* U. S., 102 U. S. 586, 26 L. ed. 253.

Canada.— Christie *v.* Johnston, 12 Grant Ch. (U. C.) 534; Laughtenborough *v.* McLean, 14 U. C. C. P. 175; McDonald *v.* Robillard, 23 U. C. Q. B. 105; Munro *v.* Grey, 12 U. C. Q. B. 647.

See 45 Cent. Dig. tit. "Taxation," § 1354.

The grantee in good faith from the purchaser of lands sold in mass at tax-sale acquires a good title, if without notice of the irregularity. Martin *v.* Ragsdale, 49 Iowa 589.

Invalidity of tax deed see *infra*, XIII, D, 2, e.

29. *Iowa.*— Smith *v.* Easton, 37 Iowa 584; Bulkley *v.* Callanan, 32 Iowa 461; Ware *v.* Thompson, 29 Iowa 65; Corbin *v.* De Wolf, 25 Iowa 124.

Kansas.— Cross *v.* Herman, 74 Kan. 554, 87 Pac. 686; Dodge *v.* Emmons, 34 Kan. 732, 9 Pac. 951; McQuesten *v.* Swope, 12 Kan. 32.

Minnesota.— National Bond, etc., Co. *v.* Hennepin County, 91 Minn. 63, 97 N. W. 413; Moulton *v.* Doran, 10 Minn. 67.

Nebraska.— Pettibone *v.* Fitzgerald, 62 Nebr. 869, 88 N. W. 143.

Pennsylvania.— Woodburn *v.* Wireman, 27 Pa. St. 18.

Tennessee.— Brien *v.* O'Shaughnesy, 3 Lea 724.

See 45 Cent. Dig. tit. "Taxation," § 1354.

30. *Iowa.*— Greer *v.* Wheeler, 41 Iowa 85; Weaver *v.* Grant, 39 Iowa 294.

Kansas.— Cross *v.* Herman, 74 Kan. 554, 87 Pac. 686.

Missouri.— Roth *v.* Gabbert, 123 Mo. 21, 27 S. W. 528.

New Jersey.— Jones *v.* Landis Tp., 50 N. J. L. 374, 13 Atl. 251.

Rhode Island.— Howland *v.* Pettey, 15 R. I. 603, 10 Atl. 650.

Washington.— Swanson *v.* Hoyle, 32 Wash. 169, 72 Pac. 1011.

United States.— Land, etc., Imp. Co. *v.* Bardon, 45 Fed. 706.

See 45 Cent. Dig. tit. "Taxation," § 1354.

31. Biscoe *v.* Coulter, 18 Ark. 423; Douthett *v.* Kettle, 104 Ill. 356; Slater *v.* Maxwell, 6 Wall. (U. S.) 268, 18 L. ed. 796.

32. Knight *v.* Valentine, 34 Minn. 26, 24 N. W. 295; Wellshear *v.* Kelley, 69 Mo. 343; Howard *v.* Stevenson, 11 Mo. App. 410.

33. *Arkansas.*—Bonner *v.* St. Francis Levee Dist. Bd. of Directors, 77 Ark. 519, 92 S. W. 1124.

Iowa.— Cedar Rapids, etc., R. Co. *v.* Carroll County, 41 Iowa 153; Iowa R. Land Co. *v.* Sac County, 39 Iowa 124.

Kansas.— Kregelo *v.* Flint, 25 Kan. 695.

Michigan.— Wyman *v.* Baer, 46 Mich. 418, 9 N. W. 455.

North Dakota.— O'Neil *v.* Tyler, 3 N. D. 47, 53 N. W. 434.

Ohio.— Willey *v.* Scoville, 9 Ohio 43.

Tennessee.— Morristown *v.* King, 11 Lea 669.

Canada.— Reed *v.* Smith, 1 Manitoba 341.

But *compare* Fellows *v.* Denniston, 23 N. Y. 420.

34. *Alabama.*— Johnston *v.* Smith, 70 Ala. 108.

Arkansas.— Guynn *v.* McCauley, 32 Ark. 97; Jacks *v.* Dyer, 31 Ark. 334.

California.— Christy *v.* Fisher, 58 Cal. 256; Garwood *v.* Hastings, 38 Cal. 216; Cop-

2. **Owners and Others Liable.** In most jurisdictions the owner of land can neither add to nor strengthen his title by omitting to pay taxes on it for which he is liable and then buying at the tax-sale; such a transaction amounts to no more than a payment of the taxes.[35] And the same rule applies to any person

pinger *v.* Rice, 33 Cal. 408; McMinn *v.* Whelan, 27 Cal. 300; Kelsey *v.* Abbott, 13 Cal. 609.

Georgia.— Bourquin *v.* Bourquin, 120 Ga. 115, 47 S. E. 639.

Illinois.— Lewis *v.* Ward, 99 Ill. 525; Busch *v.* Huston, 75 Ill. 343; Higgins *v.* Crosby, 40 Ill. 260; Blakeley *v.* Bestor, 13 Ill. 708; Frye *v.* Illinois Bank, 11 Ill. 367.

Indiana.— Buckley *v.* Taggart, 62 Ind. 236.

Iowa.— Fallon *v.* Chidester, 46 Iowa 588, 26 Am. Rep. 164; Weare *v.* Van Meter, 42 Iowa 128, 20 Am. Rep. 616.

Kansas.— Morrill *v.* Douglass, 17 Kan. 291; Carithers *v.* Weaver, 7 Kan. 110; Bowman *v.* Cockrill, 6 Kan. 311.

Kentucky.— Oldhams *v.* Jones, 5 B. Mon. 458.

Maine.— Dunn *v.* Snell, 74 Me. 22; Haskell *v.* Putnam, 42 Me. 244; Matthews *v.* Light, 32 Me. 305; Varney *v.* Stevens, 22 Me. 331.

Michigan.— Sands *v.* Davis, 40 Mich. 14; Bertram *v.* Cook, 32 Mich. 518; Dubois *v.* Campau, 24 Mich. 360; Lacey *v.* Davis, 4 Mich. 140, 66 Am. Dec. 524.

Mississippi.—Allen *v.* Poole, 54 Miss. 323; McLaughlin *v.* Green, 48 Miss. 175.

Missouri.— McCune *v.* Goodwillie, 204 Mo. 306, 102 S. W. 997; Smith *v.* Phelps, 63 Mo. 585.

Nebraska.— Tolliver *v.* Stephenson, 83 Nebr. 747, 120 N. W. 450; Gibson *v.* Sexson, 82 Nebr. 475, 118 N. W. 77.

New Hampshire.— Brown *v.* Simons, 44 N. H. 475.

New York.— Williams *v.* Townsend, 31 N. Y. 411; Nellis *v.* Lathrop, 22 Wend. 121, 34 Am. Dec. 285; Sharpe *v.* Kelley, 5 Den. 431.

Ohio.— Douglas *v.* Dangerfield, 10 Ohio 152; Piatt *v.* St. Clair, 6 Ohio 227.

Oklahoma.— Brooks *v.* Garner, 20 Okla. 236, 94 Pac. 694, 97 Pac. 995.

Pennsylvania.— Reinboth *v.* Zerbe Run Imp. Co., 29 Pa. St. 139; Coxe *v.* Wolcott, 27 Pa. St. 154.

Vermont.— Downer *v.* Smith, 38 Vt. 464; Willard *v.* Strong, 14 Vt. 532, 39 Am. Dec. 240.

Virginia.— Miller *v.* Williams, 15 Gratt. 213.

West Virginia.— Williamson *v.* Russell, 18 W. Va. 612.

Wisconsin.— Frentz *v.* Klotsch, 28 Wis. 312; Edgerton *v.* Schneider, 26 Wis. 385; Smith *v.* Lewis, 20 Wis. 350.

See 45 Cent. Dig. tit. "Taxation," § 1358.

The mere fact that taxes on land are assessed against a particular person does not impose on him the duty of paying the taxes if in fact the land does not belong to him and he stands in no trust relation to the owner; such person may permit the lands to be sold for the taxes and acquire a valid title to them by purchase at the tax-sale. Fink *v.* Miller, 19 Pa. Super. Ct. 556. *Compare, however, infra*, note 36.

Stock-holders of corporation.— The fact that purchasers of property at a tax-sale were stock-holders in a corporation which then owned the legal title to the property is not sufficient to constitute such purchase a payment of the taxes, in favor of a subsequent purchaser of the property at a foreclosure sale. Jenks *v.* Brewster, 96 Fed. 625.

35. *Arkansas.*— Pleasants *v.* Scott, 21 Ark. 370, 76 Am. Dec. 403.

California.— Gates *v.* Lindley, 104 Cal. 451, 38 Pac. 311.

Connecticut.— Middletown Sav. Bank *v.* Bacharach, 46 Conn. 513.

Dakota.— Wambole *v.* Foote, 2 Dak. 1, 2 N. W. 239.

Florida.— Petty *v.* Mays, 19 Fla. 652.

Iowa.— Griffin *v.* Turner, 75 Iowa 250, 39 N. W. 294; Emmet County *v.* Griffin, 73 Iowa 163, 34 N. W. 792.

Kansas.— Pomeroy *v.* Graham County, 6 Kan. App. 401, 50 Pac. 1094.

Maine.— Burgess *v.* Robinson, 95 Me. 120, 49 Atl. 606.

Michigan.— Cooley *v.* Waterman, 16 Mich. 366.

Mississippi.— Gaskins *v.* Blake, 27 Miss. 675.

Nebraska.— Tolliver *v.* Stephenson, 83 Nebr. 747, 120 N. W. 450; Wygant *v.* Dahl, 26 Nebr. 562, 42 N. W. 735. But the owner of a definite portion of a city lot may purchase the lot at a sale for delinquent taxes assessed against the whole lot, and enforce his lien for taxes on the portion not owned by him. Towle *v.* Shelly, 19 Nebr. 632, 28 N. W. 292.

West Virginia.— State *v.* Eddy, 41 W. Va. 95, 23 S. E. 529.

See 45 Cent. Dig. tit. "Taxation," § 1358; and cases cited in the preceding note.

Contra.— In a few states it is held that the owner of land has the same right as a stranger to buy it at tax-sale, and he may thereafter rely on his original title or the tax title or both. Branham *v.* Bezanson, 33 Minn. 49, 21 N. W. 861; Neill *v.* Lacy, 110 Pa. St. 294, 1 Atl. 325; Coxe *v.* Gibson, 27 Pa. St. 160, 67 Am. Dec. 454; Stewart *v.* Taggart, 22 U. C. C. P. 284.

Land of purchaser sold jointly with land of another.— Where a party purchases at a tax-sale his own land, together with land of another, which he had listed in one tract as belonging to himself, he simply pays his own taxes and the sheriff's deed conveys no title. Griffith *v.* Silver, 125 N. C. 368, 34 S. E. 544. And see Lewis *v.* Ward, 99 Ill. 525; Cooley *v.* Waterman, 16 Mich. 366; State *v.* Williston, 20 Wis. 228. *Compare* Bennet *v.* North Colorado Springs Land, etc., Co., 23

interests of the tenants in common are separately assessed, or where the statute provides that either may relieve his undivided share from the lien of the assessment by paying a proportionate amount of the tax, it is considered that a cotenant who has paid his share may buy the other's interest when it is sold for taxes.[51] A partition effected before the assessment of the particular tax leaves either party free to purchase, but not so where the division is made after the assessment, although before the sale.[52] One who has parted with his interest and ceased to be connected with the title as a tenant in common may buy an outstanding tax title;[53] and if the purchase at the tax-sale is made by an entire stranger, and the title is held by him until it has become fixed and mature, either of the former cotenants may then buy from him without restoring the relation of cotenancy or

N. W. 780; Dickinson v. White, 64 Iowa 708, 21 N. W. 153; Conn v. Conn, 58 Iowa 747, 13 N. W. 51; Shell v. Walker, 54 Iowa 386, 6 N. W. 581; Sheean v. Shaw, 47 Iowa 411; Fallon v. Chidester, 46 Iowa 588, 26 Am. Rep. 164; Weare v. Van Meter, 42 Iowa 128, 20 Am. Rep. 616.

Kansas.— Delashmutt v. Parrent, 39 Kan. 548, 18 Pac. 712; Muthersbaugh v. Burke. 33 Kan. 260, 6 Pac. 252.

Kentucky.— Venable v. Beauchamp, 3 Dana 321, 28 Am. Dec. 74.

Michigan.— Richards v. Richards, 75 Mich. 408, 42 N. W. 954; Dubois v. Campau, 24 Mich. 360; Cooley v. Waterman, 16 Mich. 366; Butler v. Porter, 13 Mich. 292.

Minnesota.— Holterhoff v. Mead, 36 Minn. 42, 29 N. W. 675.

Mississippi.— Howell v. Shannon, 80 Miss. 598, 31 So. 965, 92 Am. St. Rep. 609; Ragsdale v. Alabama, etc., R. Co., 67 Miss. 106, 6 So. 630; Fox v. Coon, 64 Miss. 465, 1 So. 629; Harrison v. Harrison, 56 Miss. 174; Allen v. Poole, 54 Miss. 323.

New Hampshire.— Barker v. Jones, 62 N. H. 497, 13 Am. St. Rep. 413.

Ohio.— Piatt v. St. Clair, 6 Ohio 227.

Pennsylvania.— Davis v. King, 87 Pa. St. 261; Maul v. Rider, 51 Pa. St. 377; Lloyd v. Lynch, 28 Pa. St. 419, 70 Am. Dec. 137.

Vermont.— Downer v. Smith, 38 Vt. 464; Willard v. Strong, 14 Vt. 532, 39 Am. Dec. 240.

Wisconsin.— Perkins v. Wilkinson, 86 Wis. 538, 57 N. W. 371; Phelan v. Boylan, 25 Wis. 679; State v. Williston, 20 Wis. 228.

United States.— Bissell v. Foss, 114 U. S. 252, 5 S. Ct. 851, 29 L. ed. 126; Baker v. Whiting, 2 Fed. Cas. No. 787, 3 Sumn. 475.

See 29 Cent. Dig. tit. "Joint Tenancy," § 11; 45 Cent. Dig. tit. "Tenancy in Common," §§ 60, 61. And see JOINT TENANCY, 23 Cyc. 492; TENANCY IN COMMON.

Applications of rule.—The rule stated in the text applies to the husband of a tenant in common or coheiress; he cannot obtain title as against her cotenant by purchase at a tax-sale. Busch v. Huston, 75 Ill. 343; Burns v. Byrne, 45 Iowa 285; Austin v. Barrett, 44 Iowa 488; Robinson v. Lewis, 68 Miss. 69, 8 So. 258, 24 Am. St. Rep. 254, 10 L. R. A. 101; Chace v. Durfee, 16 R. I. 248, 14 Atl. 919. But see Broquet v. Warner, 43 Kan. 48, 22 Pac. 1004, 19 Am. St. Rep. 124. So a trustee holding the legal title to an undivided interest in the land cannot acquire a tax title adverse to the cotenants of his *cestui que trust*. Sorenson v. Davis, 83 Iowa 405, 49 N. W. 1004. And the grantee of a tenant in common cannot divest the interests of the cotenants of his grantor by buying at tax-sale. Tice v. Derby, 59 Iowa 312, 13 N. W. 301; Austin v. Barrett, 44 Iowa 488; Flinn v. McKinley, 44 Iowa 68. But *compare* Sands v. Davis, 40 Mich. 14. And see St. Mary's Power Co. v. Chandler-Dunbar Water Power Co., 133 Mich. 470, 95 N. W. 554. But on the other hand, the owner of mineral rights under a reservation in a deed of the surface of the lands may purchase the estate of the other at tax-sale, since they are not cotenants. Hutchinson v. Kline, 199 Pa. St. 564, 49 Atl. 312. And a purchaser at mortgage foreclosure sale, acquiring title to an undivided interest in the land, although he occupies in law the position of a tenant in common with the mortgagor, may take title to the remainder of the property by purchase of an outstanding tax title of the whole. Wright v. Sperry, 21 Wis. 331.

Title good against strangers.— A title thus acquired under a tax-sale by one of the cotenants will be good as against strangers. Burgett v. Williford, 56 Ark. 187, 19 S. W. 750, 35 Am. St. Rep. 96.

As foundation of claim of adverse possession.— Although a cotenant wrongfully purchases the property at tax-sale, yet if he takes out a tax deed and holds possession of the property for twenty years, claiming to be the exclusive owner, he may acquire a complete title by adverse possession. English v. Powell, 119 Ind. 93, 21 N. E. 458. But see Davis v. Chapman, 24 Fed. 674.

Remedy of cotenants.— Where the statute makes a tax deed *prima facie* evidence of title, the only remedy of the cotenants against one wrongfully taking a tax title to the whole estate is in equity; they have no title to support an action at law. Johns v. Johns, 93 Ala. 239, 9 So. 419.

51. Bennet v. North Colorado Springs Land, etc., Co., 23 Colo. 470, 48 Pac. 812, 58 Am. St. Rep. 281; Butler v. Porter, 13 Mich. 292; Willard v. Strong, 14 Vt. 532, 39 Am. Dec. 240.

52. Maul v. Rider, 51 Pa. St. 377.

53. Jonas v. Flanniken, 69 Miss. 577, 11 So. 319.

trine prevailing in some states, the second sale amounts to a waiver and relinquishment of all rights or titles acquired by the state or municipality under the first.[4] But on the other hand, where the original purchase is regarded as vesting in the state or municipality no more than a lien, or a right to hold the lands for redemption, it is not in any way affected by a second assessment and sale.[5] When property has passed absolutely to the state for taxes, the original owner is not concerned in the legality of tax-sales subsequently made.[6]

I. Bids and Terms of Sale — 1. Bids and Bidders. Any person competent to purchase the land may attend the tax-sale and bid,[7] and the sale, when required by law to be made to the highest bidder, must appear of record to have been so made.[8] But where the bid is for a certain quantity of land, instead of a sum in cash, it must be definite and precise or it may be rejected;[9] and under some statutes the property must be struck off to the bidder who will agree to accept the lowest rate of interest from the date of the sale on the amount of the tax.[10] There is no objection to requiring a deposit of a reasonable portion of the price as an evidence of good faith.[11] The successful bid at a tax-sale may be assigned by the bidder making it.[12]

2. Stifling Competition and Combinations Among Bidders. A tax-sale will be invalidated by any fraudulent conduct on the part of the successful bidder which tends to prevent competition or procure an undue advantage for himself,[13] as

4. *Florida.*— Orlando *v.* Giles, 51 Fla. 422, 40 So. 834.

Mississippi.— Sigman *v.* Lundy, 66 Miss. 522, 6 So. 245.

New Jersey.— Smith *v.* Specht, 58 N. J. Eq. 47, 42 Atl. 599. See Maginnis *v.* Rutherford, 73 N. J. L. 287, 63 Atl. 16.

North Dakota.— McHenry *v.* Kidder County, 8 N. D. 413, 79 N. W. 875.

Pennsylvania.— Schreiber *v.* Moynihan, 197 Pa. St. 578, 47 Atl. 851.

Texas.— League *v.* State, 93 Tex. 553, 57 S. W. 34.

United States.— Murphy *v.* Packer, 152 U. S. 398, 14 S. Ct. 636, 38 L. ed. 489; Clarke *v.* Strickland, 5 Fed. Cas. No. 2,864, 2 Curt. 439.

See 45 Cent. Dig. tit. "Taxation," § 1361.

5. *Louisiana.*— Reinach *v.* Duplantier, 46 La. Ann. 151, 15 So. 13.

Maine.— Hodgdon *v.* Wight, 36 Me. 326.

Minnesota.— Countryman *v.* Wasson, 78 Minn. 244, 80 N. W. 973, 81 N. W. 213; Berglund *v.* Graves, 72 Minn. 148, 75 N. W. 118.

New York.— Raquette Falls Land Co. *v.* International Paper Co., 94 N. Y. App. Div. 609, 87 N. Y. Suppl. 1146 [*affirmed* in 181 N. Y. 540, 73 N. E. 1131]; People *v.* Buffalo, 33 Misc. 170, 68 N. Y. Suppl. 409 [*affirmed* in 63 N. Y. App. Div. 563, 68 N. Y. Suppl. 409, 71 N. Y. Suppl. 1145].

Texas.— Traylor *v.* State, 19 Tex. Civ. App. 86, 46 S. W. 81.

6. Gounaux *v.* Beaullieu, 123 La. 684, 49 So. 285.

7. See *supra*, XI, H, 1. And see Shedd *v.* Disney, 139 Ind. 240, 38 N. E. 594 (statute forbidding acceptance of bid by non-resident except on certain conditions); Jury *v.* Day, 54 Iowa 573, 6 N. W. 893 (principal and agent both present and bidding); New Orleans Pac. R. Co. *v.* Kelly, 52 La. Ann. 1741, 28 So. 212 (holding that a sale to a firm was not invalid because the assessor of the taxes was a member).

8. Bean *v.* Thompson, 19 N. H. 290, 49 Am. Dec. 154; Cardigan *v.* Page, 6 N. H. 182. But if the record shows the terms of sale, viz., that the land would be sold to the highest bidder, and then shows that A was the purchaser, this is evidence that A was also the highest bidder. Smith *v.* Messer, 17 N. H. 420.

9. Poindexter *v.* Doolittle, 54 Iowa 52, 6 N. W. 136. As to bids in the form of an offer to take a certain part or quantity of the land for the amount of the taxes and charges see *supra*, XI, G, 7, b, c.

10. Youker *v.* Hobart, 17 N. D. 296, 115 N. W. 839, holding void on its face a tax deed showing that the sale was made under a repealed statute (Laws (1897), c. 126, § 76) for the smallest quantity of land that would sell for the amount of the tax, and not, as required by Laws (1901), c. 154, then in force, to the person offering to accept the lowest rate of interest from the date of the sale on the amount of the tax. See also King *v.* Lane, 21 S. D. 101, 110 N. W. 37.

11. Whelen *v.* Stilwell, 4 Nebr. (Unoff.) 24, 93 N. W. 189.

12. Dickson *v.* Burckmyer, 67 S. C. 526, 46 S. E. 343. But *compare* Keene *v.* Houghton, 19 Me. 368, holding that where the statute only authorizes the officer to make a deed to the highest bidder, he cannot legally substitute the name of another for that of the highest bidder, and an agreement with the officer to pay the amount bid by another and receive a deed by way of substitution is void for want of consideration.

13. *Alabama.*— Thorington *v.* Montgomery, 94 Ala. 266, 10 So. 634.

Iowa.— McCready *v.* Sexton, 29 Iowa 356, 4 Am. Rep. 214; Eldridge *v.* Kuehl, 27 Iowa 160.

to be made within a limited time after the sale, it must be strictly complied with, and it is a fatal defect if the report is made too late.[56]

b. Effect of Omission of Report or Return. It is generally held that the omission of the proper officer to make his report or return of the tax-sale is a fatal defect and one which invalidates the title founded on such sale,[57] although in some states this is considered only an irregularity, not fatal to the title, especially in view of constitutional or statutory provisions dispensing with the extreme strictness of the rule regarding tax titles.[58] And it should be noted that the loss of such a report or return once duly made, or the fact that it cannot be found in the proper office, will not necessarily affect the tax title, since here the presumption may be invoked that public officers have duly and regularly performed the duties with which they were charged.[59]

Reeds, 6 Mo. 64. See Wescott *v.* McDonald, 22 Me. 402. And it furnishes the proper official evidence of the amount for which each tract of land was sold, and hence is important as determining the amount required for redemption. Salinger *v.* Gunn, 61 Ark. 414, 33 S. W. 959; Cooper *v.* Freeman Lumber Co., 61 Ark. 36, 31 S. W. 981, 32 S. W. 494. And under the laws of some of the states, the treasurer has no power to sell land for taxes at a private sale, until after his report of the public tax-sale is made and filed. State *v.* Helmer, 10 Nebr. 25, 4 N. W. 367.

56. *Florida.*— Stieff *v.* Hartwell, 35 Fla. 606, 17 So. 899.

Maine.— Pinkham *v.* Morang, 40 Me. 587; Andrews *v.* Senter, 32 Me. 394; Shimmin *v.* Inman, 26 Me. 228.

Michigan.—Youngs *v.* Peters, 118 Mich. 45, 76 N. W. 138. Under a statute requiring the report of sale to be made "as soon as" the tax-sales are confirmed, ten or twelve days is not an unreasonable length of time to take in making such report. Youngs *v.* Peters, *supra*; Detroit F. & M. Ins. Co. *v.* Wood, 118 Mich. 31, 76 N. W. 136.

North Carolina.— Taylor *v.* Allen, 67 N. C. 346.

Vermont.— Lane *v.* James, 25 Vt. 481; Chandler *v.* Spear, 22 Vt. 388; Taylor *v.* French, 19 Vt. 49; Richardson *v.* Dorr, 5 Vt. 9; Mead *v.* Mallet, 1 D. Chipm. 239.

Virginia.— Bond *v.* Pettit, 89 Va. 474, 16 S. E. 666.

West Virginia.— State *v.* Harman, 57 W. Va. 447, 50 S. E. 828; McCallister *v.* Cottrille, 24 W. Va. 173; Barton *v.* Gilchrist, 19 W. Va. 223. But see State *v.* McEldowney, 54 W. Va. 695, 47 S. E. 650, as to effect of curative statute.

United States.— De Forest *v.* Thompson, 40 Fed. 375.

See 45 Cent. Dig. tit. "Taxation," § 1370.

Contra.— Langley *v.* Batchelder, 69 N. H. 566, 46 Atl. 1085; Hoitt *v.* Burnham, 61 N. H. 620; Brien *v.* O'Shaughnesy, 3 Lea (Tenn.) 724.

Sale of lands to state.—Where a sale of land by the county trustee to the treasurer of the state is void because of failure of the trustee to file in the office of the clerk of the circuit court a certified list of the land so sold by him, as required by Tenn. Acts (1897), p. 34, c. 1, § 63, the defect cannot be cured by the filing of such list after the property has been sold to an individual purchaser. Harris *v.* Mason, 120 Tenn. 668, 115 S. W. 1146, 25 L. R. A. N. S. 1011; Condon *v.* Galbraith, 106 Tenn. 14, 58 S. W. 916.

57. *District of Columbia.*— King *v.* District of Columbia, 4 MacArthur 36.

Florida.— Ellis *v.* Clark, 39 Fla. 714, 23 So. 410. But the failure of a city tax collector to forward a copy of his report of city tax-sales to the controller does not invalidate the sales. Orlando *v.* Equitable Bldg., etc., Assoc., 45 Fla. 507, 33 So. 986.

Maine.— Pinkham *v.* Morang, 40 Me. 587; Andrews *v.* Senter, 32 Me. 394; Shimmin *v.* Inman, 26 Me. 228.

Michigan.— Jenkinson *v.* Auditor-Gen., 104 Mich. 34, 62 N. W. 163; Millard *v.* Truax, 99 Mich. 157, 58 N. W. 70.

Mississippi.— Zingerling *v.* Henderson, (1895) 18 So. 432; National Bank of Republic *v.* Louisville, etc., R. Co., 72 Miss. 447, 17 So. 7; Ferrill *v.* Dickerson, 63 Miss. 210; Hopkins *v.* Sandidge, 31 Miss. 668. *Compare* Wolfe *v.* Murphy, 60 Miss. 1.

North Carolina.— Taylor *v.* Allen, 67 N. C. 346.

Oregon.—Ayers *v.* Lund, 49 Oreg. 303, 89 Pac. 806, 124 Am. St. Rep. 1046.

Tennessee.— Harris *v.* Mason, 120 Tenn. 668, 115 S. W. 1146, 25 L. R. A. N. S. 1011; Condon *v.* Galbraith, 106 Tenn. 14, 58 S. W. 916; *In re* Tax Title Cases, 105 Tenn. 243, 58 S. W. 259; Bloomstein *v.* Brien, 3 Tenn. Ch. 55. But *compare* Brien *v.* O'Shaughnesy, 3 Lea 724.

Vermont.— Lane *v.* James, 25 Vt. 481; Sumner *v.* Sherman, 13 Vt. 609.

West Virginia.— McCallister *v.* Cottrille, 24 W. Va. 173; Barton *v.* Gilchrist, 19 W. Va. 223; Orr *v.* Wiley, 19 W. Va. 150; Dequasie *v.* Harris, 16 W. Va. 345.

United States.— Martin *v.* Barbour, 140 U. S. 634, 11 S. Ct. 944, 35 L. ed. 546; Fay *v.* Crozer, 156 Fed. 486; Cook *v.* Lasher, 73 Fed. 701, 19 C. C. A. 654; De Forest *v.* Thompson, 40 Fed. 375.

See 45 Cent. Dig. tit. "Taxation," § 1372.

58. Vance *v.* Schuyler, 6 Ill. 160; Playter *v.* Cochran, 37 Iowa 258; Negus *v.* Yancey, 23 Iowa 417; Cahoon *v.* Coe, 52 N. H. 518; Smith *v.* Messer, 17 N. H. 420; Allen *v.* Allen, 114 Wis. 615, 91 N. W. 218

59. Scott *v.* Watkins, 22 Ark. 556; Church

sale of land for taxes after service of an injunction on the commissioners who levied the tax, enjoining them from "collecting or proceeding to collect" the tax on such land, is irregular and will be set aside.[32]

3. Payment or Tender. It will be made a condition to granting relief on an application to vacate a tax-sale that the owner of the property shall pay or tender to the holder of the tax certificate whatever sum he paid for his purchase with interest, or at least so much thereof as was for taxes justly and legally due.[33] And where plaintiff seeks to cancel a void sale of state tax lands and to purchase the land himself, he should be required to repay the amount paid on such void sale and subsequent taxes.[34]

4. Time For Proceedings. A proceeding to set aside a tax-sale and certificate must be brought within the time limited by law if there is a statute applicable to such actions,[35] and at any rate may be barred by complainant's laches if he delays for several years to seek relief.[36] But where a sale of state tax land is void, laches cannot be imputed to a stranger to the title in his delay of twelve years before seeking to cancel such sale and to purchase the land.[37]

5. Parties to Proceeding. The complainant in such a proceeding must show that he is the owner of the property, or at least that he has some title to it or interest in it,[38] and although several persons jointly interested in the premises

32. Williams v. Cammack, 27 Miss. 209, 61 Am. Dec. 508.

33. *Illinois.*— Gage v. Nichols, 112 Ill. 269; Peacock v. Carnes, 110 Ill. 99; Sankey v. Seipp, 27 Ill. App. 299; Durfee v. Murray, 7 Ill. App. 213.

Indiana.— McWhinney v. Brinker, 64 Ind. 360.

Iowa.— Corbin v. Woodbine, 33 Iowa 297.

Kansas.— Miller v. Ziegler, 31 Kan. 417, 2 Pac. 601.

New Jersey.— Under the maxim that he who seeks equity must do equity, a purchaser of land on mortgage foreclosure, charged with a tax lien, held by the mortgagee as a prior encumbrance, could not maintain a suit to vacate the tax lien without paying the amount represented by the tax certificate, with interest. Farmer v. Ward, 75 N. J. Eq. 33, 71 A. 401.

North Dakota.— Douglas v. Fargo, 13 N. D. 467, 101 N. W. 919.

Texas.— Crosby v. Terry, 41 Tex. Civ. App. 594, 91 S. W. 652.

West Virginia.— Lohr v. George, 65 W. Va. 241, 64 S. E. 609.

Wisconsin.— Hayes v. Douglas County, 92 Wis. 429, 65 N. W. 482, 53 Am. St. Rep. 926, 31 L. R. A. 213.

Canada.— Schultz v. Alloway, 10 Manitoba 221; Paul v. Ferguson, 14 Grant Ch. (U. C.) 230.

See 45 Cent. Dig. tit. "Taxation," § 1381 *et seq.*

Amount of legal taxes uncertain.— Where, in an action to set aside tax-sales and certificates for the illegality of a part of the taxes, the record discloses no means of determining what amount of the taxes levied upon plaintiff was valid, the court will not require payment of any amount as a condition of relief. Hebard v. Ashland County, 55 Wis. 145, 12 N. W. 437.

Action to impeach or vacate tax title see *infra*, XIV, B, 3, d.

34. Horton v. Salling, 155 Mich. 502, 119 N. W. 912.

35. Hall v. Miller, 150 Mich. 300, 113 N. W. 1104; Hayward v. O'Connor, 145 Mich. 52, 108 N. W. 366; Wisconsin Cent. R. Co. v. Lincoln County, 67 Wis. 478, 30 N. W. 619; Oberreich v. Fond du Lac County, 63 Wis. 216, 23 N. W. 421; Ruggles v. Fond du Lac County, 63 Wis. 205, 23 N. W. 416; Wisconsin Cent. R. Co. v. Lincoln County, 57 Wis. 137, 15 N. W. 121; Dalrymple v. Milwaukee, 53 Wis. 178, 10 N. W. 141; Farmers', etc., Loan Co. v. Conklin, 1 Manitoba 181. And see Shaaf v. O'Connor, 146 Mich. 504, 109 N. W. 1061, 117 Am. St. Rep. 652. See also *infra*, XIV, B, 4, d, (III).

Void judgment or certificate.— Some of the statutes of limitations have been construed as not applying where the tax judgment or certificate is void on its face. Babcock v. Johnson, 108 Minn. 217, 121 N. W. 909; Holmes v. Longhren, 97 Minn. 83, 105 N. W. 558; Williams v. St. Paul, 82 Minn. 273, 84 N. W. 1009; Burdick v. Bingham, 38 Minn. 482, 38 N. W. 489; Sanborn v. Cooper, 31 Minn. 307, 17 N. W. 856; Sheehy v. Hinds, 27 Minn. 259, 6 N. W. 781. See also *infra*, XIV, B, 4, a.

36. McFarlane v. Simpson, 153 Mich. 193, 116 N. W. 982; Scholfield v. Dickenson, 10 Grant Ch. (U. C.) 226.

37. Horton v. Salling, 155 Mich. 502, 119 N. W. 912.

38. Picquet v. Augusta, 64 Ga. 254.

Owner not in possession.—A suit to set aside a tax-sale on the ground of fraud may be maintained by the owner, although he is not in possession of the land, as it is not a suit to quiet title. Herr v. Martin, 90 Ky. 377, 14 S. W. 356, 12 Ky. L. Rep. 359.

Heirs and persons claiming through them. —That land was distributed by the probate court to the tax record owner's heirs, from whom plaintiffs derive title, shows sufficient title in plaintiffs to enable them to sue to set aside, for want of jurisdictional process,

XII. REDEMPTION FROM TAX-SALES.

A. Right to Redeem — 1. RIGHT AND NECESSITY IN GENERAL. A statutory right to redeem from tax-sales differs essentially from an equity of redemption proper; the former is self-executing and requires no judicial proceedings to make it effective; it is claimable as a matter of mere right by the owner of the property and is not founded on any special equities, and it is available not only where the sale was irregular or defective, but also, and especially, where the sale was perfectly regular and valid.[78] Indeed if the sale was void the owner is under no necessity of redeeming, but may have it vacated or set aside without redemption.[79] Such a statutory right of redemption is given by law in almost all the states, and is intended to afford the owner a last opportunity to save his property.[80] But it

Gage County, 67 Nebr. 6, 93 N. W. 194, 99 N. W. 524.

78. Lincoln *v.* Lincoln St. R. Co., 75 Nebr. 523, 106 N. W. 317; Carly *v.* Boner, 70 Nebr. 674, 102 N. W. 761; Logan County *v.* McKinley-Lanning L. & T. Co., 70 Nebr. 406, 101 N. W. 991.

Foreclosure of equity of redemption.— In some states the statutes provide for an action by the holder of a tax-sale certificate to foreclose the owner's equity of redemption. Such laws are valid and constitutional. Partridge *v.* Corkey, 4 Greene (Iowa) 383; Durbin *v.* Platto, 47 Wis. 484, 3 N. W. 30. As to action and proceedings under such statutes in general see *infra*, XII, A, 5.

Effect of confirming tax-sale.—A judicial decree confirming a tax-sale, although it precludes all further objection to the sale on account of informality or illegality, does not cut off the statutory right of redemption. Smith *v.* Thornton, 74 Ark. 572, 86 S. W. 1008. The right of redemption from sales of real estate for non-payment of taxes given by Nebr. Const. art. 9, § 3, applies to judicial as well as administrative sales, and the confirmation of such sales in no way adjudicates the right of redemption. Butler *v.* Libe, 81 Nebr. 740, 744, 116 N. W. 663, 117 N. W. 700. Even assuming that the court has jurisdiction, in confirming a judicial sale for taxes, to cut off the right of redemption, an order of confirmation which does not in terms deny to the owner such right will not be construed as having such effect. Smith *v.* Carnahan, 83 Nebr. 667, 120 N. W. 212.

In case of sale of lands to state.— The laws of Michigan do not prevent the sale or disposition of lands sold to the state at tax-sales, but give the owners the right of redemption after such lands have been sold to private purchasers from the state. Griffin *v.* Kennedy, 148 Mich. 583, 112 N. W. 756. *Compare* State *v.* Jackson, 56 W. Va. 558, 49 S. E. 465. Under Minn. Rev. Laws (1905), §§ 936–940, lands bid in to the state and not assigned to purchasers within three years are subject to redemption by the owner or other persons entitled to redeem. Minnesota Debenture Co. *v.* Scott, 106 Minn. 32, 119 N. W. 391.

Estoppel of purchaser to deny right of redemption.— In a suit by the person assessed with taxes against the purchaser at the tax-sale, to set aside a tax deed, the defendant, having bought plaintiff's title, is estopped to deny his right to redeem. Townshend *v.* Shaffer, 30 W. Va. 176, 3 S. E. 586.

The owner's failure to pay taxes on unimproved and unoccupied land does not necessarily defeat his right to redeem from the holder of an invalid tax title. Nicodemus *v.* Young, 90 Iowa 423, 57 N. W. 906.

79. Shoemaker *v.* Lacy, 45 Iowa 422; Stewart *v.* Crysler, 100 N. Y. 378, 3 N. E. 471; Simpson *v.* Meyers, 197 Pa. St. 522, 47 Atl. 868; French *v.* Edwards, 9 Fed. Cas. No. 5,098, 5 Sawy. 266.

Voluntary redemption from void sale.— If the owner of land, instead of resorting to litigation, seeks to redeem the same from an invalid tax-sale, he is required to pay the purchaser only the amount of his bid with common interest thereon, not the statutory rate of interest required on redemption from a valid sale. Roberts *v.* Merrill, 60 Iowa 166, 14 N. W. 235; Lynam *v.* Anderson, 9 Nebr. 367, 2 N. W. 732. *Compare* Jones *v.* Duras, 14 Nebr. 40, 14 N. W. 537. But if the owner, with full knowledge of the character of the sale and all the facts affecting its validity, pays the money required of him as the cost of redemption, the payment is voluntary and he cannot recover back the money from the county; the mere fact that a tax deed will be issued to the purchaser if he does not redeem does not put him under duress. Morris *v.* Sioux County, 42 Iowa 416; Shane *v.* St. Paul, 26 Minn. 543, 6 N. W. 349. But *compare* Brownlee *v.* Marion County, 53 Iowa 487, 5 N. W. 610; Marsh *v.* St. Croix County, 42 Wis. 355.

80. See the statutes of the different states. And see the following cases:

Iowa.— Henderson *v.* Robinson, 76 Iowa 603, 41 N. W. 371.

Kansas.— Where the holder of an invalid tax deed in possession sues to quiet title, and the tax deed is held void, but the lien of the taxes is preserved, and the land is sold to satisfy the same. Laws (1893), p. 188, c. 109 (Gen. St. (1901) §§ 4927 *et seq.*), providing for redemption on foreclosure of mortgage trust deeds, mechanics' liens, or other liens, has no application, and neither the defendant owner nor the holder of the mortgage lien has any right to redeem therefrom. Davidson *v.* Plummer, 76 Kan. 462, 92 Pac. 705.

Michigan.— G. F. Sanborn & Co. *v.* Alston,

If a person assumes without any authority to act as the owner's agent and pays the redemption money, the owner may accept and ratify his act, and the self-styled agent will not be permitted to deny the character in which he acted or to set up a claim of title in himself or assert any other claim to the land than as security for his reimbursement.[16]

e. Attempted Redemption by Stranger. A party having no interest in land, and not representing the owner, has no right to redeem it from a tax-sale, and if he tenders the redemption money to the holder of the tax-sale certificate the latter may refuse to receive it, or if the money is paid to the proper officer, the tax purchaser may repudiate it, and in either case the title of the latter is not divested, nor will the attempted redemption inure to the benefit of the real owner.[17] If, however, the tax purchaser consents to the redemption and accepts and retains the money, it is clear that he will be estopped to deny the effect of the transaction as a redemption,[18] and it seems that in such case the act of the stranger will inure to the benefit of the true owner of the land, at least if he chooses to ratify it and claim the advantage of it.[19]

f. Tenants in Common. As between joint tenants or tenants in common holding undivided interests in a tract of land sold *in solido* for taxes, either may redeem, but as a rule he must redeem the entire estate, not merely his undivided interest, and on so doing he will have a claim against his cotenant for reimbursement to the extent of his proportionate share.[20]

g. Persons Under Disabilities. An infant whose lands have been sold for non-payment of taxes has the same right as an adult to redeem them,[21] and indeed

see State *v.* Harper, 26 Nebr. 761, 42 N. W. 764.

16. Houston *v.* Buer, 117 Ill. 324, 7 N. E. 646; Schedda *v.* Sawyer, 21 Fed. Cas. No. 12,443, 4 McLean 181. And see State *v.* Register of Conveyances, 113 La. 93, 36 So. 900, holding that any one may, for the advantage of the owner of property sold for taxes, act as his agent and make payment of the redemption money, even without his knowledge.

17. *Iowa.*— Penn *v.* Clemens, 19 Iowa 372; Byington *v.* Bookwalter, 7 Iowa 512, 74 Am. Dec. 279.

Kentucky.— Bradford *v.* Walker, 5 S. W. 555, 8 Ky. L. Rep. 586.

Louisiana.— Staples *v.* Mayer, 44 La. Ann. 628, 11 So. 29.

Pennsylvania.— Laird *v.* Hiester, 24 Pa. St. 452; McBride *v.* Hoey, 2 Watts 436.

Wisconsin.— Rutledge *v.* Price County, 66 Wis. 35, 27 N. W. 819; Cousins *v.* Allen, 28 Wis. 232; Eaton *v.* North, 25 Wis. 514.

United States.— Halsted *v.* Buster, 140 U. S. 273, 11 S. Ct. 782, 35 L. ed. 484; Wood *v.* Welpton, 29 Fed. 405.

See 45 Cent. Dig. tit. "Taxation," § 1394.

But *compare* Jamison *v.* Thompson, 65 Miss. 516, 5 So. 107; Greene *v.* Williams, 58 Miss. 752.

18. Hunt *v.* Seymour, 76 Iowa 751, 39 N. W. 909; Orr *v.* Cunningham, 4 Watts & S. (Pa.) 294.

19. Sloan *v.* Cobb, 74 Ark. 393, 85 S. W. 1126; Alexander *v.* Ellis, 123 Pa. St. 81, 16 Atl. 770; Coxe *v.* Sartwell, 21 Pa. St. 480; Orr *v.* Cunningham, 4 Watts & S. (Pa.) 294. And see Harman *v.* Stearns, 95 Va. 58, 27 S. E. 601; Boulton *v.* Ruttan, 2 U. C. Q. B. (O. S.) 396.

20. *California.*— Quinn *v.* Kenney, 47 Cal. 147; Mayo *v.* Marshall, 23 Cal. 594; People *v.* McEwen, 23 Cal. 54.

Iowa.— Curl *v.* Watson, 25 Iowa 35, 95 Am. Dec. 763.

Maine.— Loomis *v.* Pingree, 43 Me. 299; Watkins *v.* Eaton, 30 Me. 529, 50 Am. Dec. 637.

Massachusetts.— Hurley *v.* Hurley, 148 Mass. 444, 19 N. E. 545, 2 L. R. A. 172.

Oregon.— Rich *v.* Palmer, 6 Oreg. 339.

Pennsylvania.— Halsey *v.* Blood, 29 Pa. St. 319.

Rhode Island.— Chace *v.* Durfee, 16 R. I. 248, 14 Atl. 919.

West Virginia.— Cain *v.* Brown, 54 W. Va. 656, 46 S. E. 579.

United States.— O'Reilly *v.* Holt, 18 Fed. Cas. No. 10,563, 4 Woods 645.

But *compare* People *v.* Detroit Treasurer, 8 Mich. 14, 77 Am. Dec. 433.

Minors see *infra*, XII, A, 4, e.

21. *Arkansas.*— Cowley *v.* Spradlin, 77 Ark. 190, 91 S. W. 550; Carroll *v.* Johnson, 41 Ark. 59.

Illinois.— Holloway *v.* Clark, 27 Ill. 483; Chapin *v.* Curtenius, 15 Ill. 427.

Kansas.— Douglass *v.* Lowell, 55 Kan. 574, 40 Pac. 917.

Michigan.— Foegan *v.* Carpenter, 117 Mich. 89, 75 N. W. 290.

Wisconsin.— Tucker *v.* Whittlesey, 74 Wis. 74, 41 N. W. 535, 42 N. W. 101; Karr *v.* Washburn, 56 Wis. 303, 14 N. W. 189.

See 45 Cent. Dig. tit. "Taxation," § 1396.

Estate of minor entitling him to redeem.— A minor may redeem who has either a vested or contingent remainder in the lands. Minnesota Debenture Co. *v.* Dean, 85 Minn. 473, 89 N. W. 848. He may redeem after execut-

is usually accorded a longer period for this purpose.[22] This right of redemption vested in a minor is a transferable interest and passes to his vendee.[23] So also a married woman may redeem her property from a tax-sale,[24] and so may the guardian or committee of an insane person.[25]

4. Time for Redemption — a. In General. Unless there are some special equities in the case giving the owner a right to maintain a suit for redemption from a tax-sale,[26] he must exercise his privilege of redeeming within the specific time limited by the constitution or statute for that purpose, or lose it finally. This time varies in the different states, but is usually one, two or three years from the time of the sale or execution of a tax deed, or a certain length of time after receiving notice from the purchaser.[27] Under some statutes the owner

ing and delivering a warranty deed. Hoffman *v.* Peterson, 123 Wis. 632, 102 N. W. 47.

Minor "heir."—Wash. Laws (1899), p. 298, c. 141, § 17 (Pierce Code, § 8696), providing for the redemption of real property of any "minor heir" from a sale for taxes, applies only to minors inheriting the property. Burdick *v.* Kimball, 53 Wash. 198, 101 Pac. 845.

22. See *infra*, XII, A, 4, e.

23. McConnell *v.* Swepston, 66 Ark. 141, 49 S. W. 566; Stout *v.* Merrill, 35 Iowa 47.

24. Anderson *v.* Batson, 37 S. W. 84, 18 Ky. L. Rep. 493; Plumb *v.* Robinson, 13 Ohio St. 298; Corbett *v.* Nutt, 18 Gratt. (Va.) 624.

25. Powell *v.* Smallwood, 48 W. Va. 298, 37 S. E. 551.

26. See *infra*, XII, A, 4, f; XII, D, 1.

27. See the statutes of the different states. And see the following cases:

Alabama.— Boyd *v.* Holt, 62 Ala. 296.

Arkansas.— Sibly *v.* Cason, 86 Ark. 32, 109 S. W. 1007; Thornton *v.* Smith, 36 Ark. 508.

Georgia.— Millen *v.* Howell, 81 Ga. 653, 8 S. E. 316.

Illinois.— Netterstrom *v.* Kemeys, 187 Ill. 617, 58 N. E. 609; Gage *v.* Parker, 103 Ill. 528; Eggleston *v.* Gage, 33 Ill. App. 184.

Iowa.— Cummings *v.* Wilson, 59 Iowa 14, 12 N. W. 747; Pearson *v.* Robinson, 44 Iowa 413.

Kansas.— Pierce *v.* Adams, 77 Kan. 46, 93 Pac. 594; Cable *v.* Coates, 36 Kan. 191, 12 Pac. 931.

Louisiana.—Winchester *v.* Cain, 1 Rob. 421.

Massachusetts.—Hawks *v.* Davis, 185 Mass. 119, 69 N. E. 1072; Perry *v.* Lancy, 179 Mass. 183, 60 N. E. 472.

Michigan.— Pike *v.* Richardson, 136 Mich. 414, 99 N. W. 398.

Minnesota.— State *v.* Halden, 75 Minn. 512, 78 N. W. 16; State *v.* McDonald, 26 Minn. 145, 1 N. W. 832.

Mississippi.— Le Blanc *v.* Illinois Cent. R. Co., 72 Miss. 669, 18 So. 381.

Nebraska.— Douglas *v.* Hayes County, 82 Nebr. 577, 118 N. W. 114; Wood *v.* Speck, 78 Nebr. 435, 110 N. W. 1001; Selby *v.* Pueppka, 73 Nebr. 179, 102 N. W. 263; Logan County *v.* Carnahan, 67 Nebr. 685, 92 N. W. 984, 95 N. W. 812. And see *infra*, this note.

New York.— Turner *v.* Boyce, 11 Misc. 502, 33 N. Y. Suppl. 433.

North Carolina.— Tiddy *v.* Graves, 126 N. C. 620, 36 S. E. 127.

Pennsylvania.— Russel *v.* Reed, 27 Pa. St. 166.

Texas.— Berry *v.* San Antonio, (Civ. App. 1898) 46 S. W. 273.

West Virginia.— Forqueran *v.* Donnally, 7 W. Va. 114.

See 45 Cent. Dig. tit. "Taxation," § 1402.

Judicial sale on foreclosure of tax lien.— In Nebraska, where there has been no valid administrative tax-sale, the owner has two years from and after the confirmation of the judicial sale in the action to foreclose the tax lien in which to redeem his land from such sale. Barker *v.* Hume, 84 Nebr. 235, 120 N. W. 1131; Smith *v.* Carnahan, 83 Nebr. 667, 120 N. W. 212; Douglas *v.* Hayes County, 82 Nebr. 577, 118 N. W. 114; Butler *v.* Libe, 81 Nebr. 740, 116 N. W. 663; Wood *v.* Speck, 78 Nebr. 435, 110 N. W. 1001; Logan County *v.* McKinley-Lanning L. & T. Co., 70 Nebr. 406, 101 N. W. 991; Logan County *v.* Carnahan, 66 Nebr. 685, 92 N. W. 984, 95 N. W. 812. Where a county before any administrative sale of real estate for taxes sues to foreclose a tax lien and obtains a decree, a sale thereunder is a judicial sale and does not become complete until confirmation; the time for redemption dating from such confirmation. Smith *v.* Carnahan, *supra.*

Sale under void decree.— But the limitation of two years within which a party may redeem from sale for taxes does not apply to a sale made under a void decree foreclosing a tax lien. Payne *v.* Anderson, 80 Nebr. 216, 114 N. W. 148.

Redemption by county.— The statute allowing two years for redemption from a tax-sale is not a statute of limitations within Miss. Const. § 104, providing that limitations shall not run against the state or any county, etc., and a county has not the right after the expiration of the two-year period to redeem land, which after the tax-sale it bought at a trustee's sale, to protect a loan made by it on the land prior to the tax-sale. Tallahatchie County *v.* Little, 94 Miss. 88, 46 So. 257.

Redemption of land sold to state.— Under Ky. St. (1909) § 4152, providing that, in the redemption of land sold to the state for taxes, the county clerk, at any time within two years after the sale, or until the revenue agent under the auditor's direction assumes charge of a collection by sale or otherwise, is vested with authority to collect the delinquent taxes, interest, and penalties, and

may redeem from taxes and tax-sales at any time before execution and delivery of a valid tax deed.[28]

b. Computation of Time. Where the statute provides that the owner shall have a certain length of time after the sale in which to redeem, this period begins to run from the day of the sale, and not from the time the purchaser takes a deed.[29] Under some statutes, however, the tax deed is to be issued directly after the sale, and not at the end of the redemption period, and where this is the case the time for redemption begins to run from the date of filing or recording the deed.[30] Under other statutes, again, the right of redemption is limited to a certain length of time after giving of notice of the sale or notice to redeem; and this is computed in the ordinary way, the requirements as to the fact and sufficiency of notice being applied with some strictness.[31]

c. When Time Expires. When the time for redemption is limited to a certain number of days after service of notice, or to one or more years from the sale, the day of giving the notice or the day of the sale is to be excluded, and the owner will be allowed the whole of the last day in which to redeem,[32] so that a tax deed

section 4154 allowing the revenue agent fifteen per cent for the collection and payment of delinquent taxes. interest, etc., it is held that, notwithstanding the fee-simple title to land sold to the state for taxes vests in the state on the expiration of the two-year redemption period, such title is subject to be divested by the payment of the taxes by the delinquent prior to the sale of the land by the revenue agent. James *v.* Blanton, 134 Ky. 803, 121 S. W. 951, 123 S. W. 328.

28. Stockand *v.* Hall, 54 Wash. 106, 102 Pac. 1037; Kahn *v.* Thorpe, 43 Wash. 463, 86 Pac. 855; State *v.* Cranney, 30 Wash. 594, 71 Pac. 50.

Void deed.— Limitations do not run in favor of a tax deed, void on its face. and under Rev. Pol. Code, § 2205, providing that the owner of land sold for taxes may redeem any time before the tax deed was issued, such a deed will not bar a redemption by the owner after the period of limitations. Battelle *v.* Wolven, 22 S. D. 39, 115 N. W. 99.

29. *Georgia.*—Wood *v.* Henry, 107 Ga. 389, 33 S. E. 410 (holding that a tax-sale, relative to the right of the owner to redeem, is not complete until payment of the purchase-money by the bidder); Boyd *v.* Wilson, 86 Ga. 379, 12 S. E. 744, 13 S. E. 428.

Kansas.— Doudna *v.* Harlan, 45 Kan. 484, 25 Pac. 883, rule applied where the land was bought in by the county for want of other bidders.

Louisiana.— Gonzales *v.* Saux, 119 La. 657, 44 So. 332; Geddes *v.* Cunningham, 104 La. 306, 29 So. 138.

Maine.— Millett *v.* Mullen, 95 Me. 400, 49 Atl. 871.

Oregon.— Hendershott *v.* Sagsvold, 49 Oreg. 592, 90 Pac. 1104.

Pennsylvania.— Rockland, etc., Coal, etc., Co. *v.* McCalmont, 72 Pa. St. 221.

See 45 Cent. Dig. tit. "Taxation," § 1404.

30. *Alabama.*— Pugh *v.* Youngblood, 69 Ala. 296.

Kansas.— Pierce *v.* Adams, 77 Kan. 46, 93 Pac. 594; Taylor *v.* Moise, 52 La. Ann. 2016, 28 So. 237, requisites of deed.

Washington.— State *v.* Maple, 16 Wash. 430, 47 Pac. 966.

Wisconsin.— Hiles *v.* Atlee, 90 Wis. 72, 62 N. W. 940 (defects in record of deed); Lander *v.* Bromley, 79 Wis. 372, 48 N. W. 594 (deed void on its face).

United States.—West *v.* Duncan, 42 Fed. 430; Berthold *v.* Hoskins, 38 Fed. 772.

31. *Iowa.*—Ashenfelter *v.* Seiling, 141 Iowa 512, 119 N. W. 984; Swope *v.* Prior, 58 Iowa 412, 10 N. W. 788.

Massachusetts.—Hawks *v.* Davis, 185 Mass. 119, 69 N. E. 1072; Barry *v.* Lancy, 179 Mass. 112, 60 N. E. 395; McGauley *v.* Sullivan, 174 Mass. 303, 54 N. E. 842; Keith *v.* Wheeler, 159 Mass. 161, 34 N. E. 174.

Michigan.— Escanaba Timber Land Co. *v.* Rusch, 147 Mich. 619, 111 N. W. 345.

Minnesota.— Patterson *v.* Grettum, 83 Minn. 69, 85 N. W. 907.

New York.— See Halsted *v.* Silberstein, 196 N. Y. 1, 89 N. E. 443.

Pennsylvania.—Arthurs *v.* Smathers, 38 Pa. St. 40.

See 45 Cent. Dig. tit. "Taxation," § 1404.

Report of return of service of notice.— Under Code (1897), § 1341, until written report of the return of service of notice of expiration of the time of redemption from a tax-sale is made by the treasurer to the auditor, as required by the statute. the auditor is justified in assuming that the right of redemption has not expired, and in accepting redemption at the hands of the owner or lien-holder, or at least from such as have not been served with notice in due time. Ashenfelter *v.* Seiling, 141 Iowa 512, 119 N. W. 984.

32. *Alabama.*— Pugh *v.* Youngblood, 69 Ala. 296.

Arkansas.— Hare *v.* Carnall, 39 Ark. 196.

Kansas.— Hicks *v.* Nelson, 45 Kan. 47. 25 Pac. 218, 23 Am. St. Rep. 709; Richards *v.* Thompson, 43 Kan. 209, 23 Pac. 106; Ireland *v.* George, 41 Kan. 751, 21 Pac. 776.

Massachusetts.— Clark *v.* Lancy, 178 Mass. 460, 59 N. E. 1034.

Minnesota.— Cole *v.* Lamm, 81 Minn. 463, 84 N. W. 329.

appeal,[77] and may be opened within the time limited by statute, when rendered on default, or set aside for cause.[78]

B. Notice to Redeem — 1. **Nature and Necessity.** It is required in several states that the purchaser at a tax-sale shall give notice to the owner of the property, within a designated reasonable time, of the expiration of the period allowed for redemption and of his intention thereupon to claim a deed. A law of this kind is to be construed liberally and beneficially in the interest of the owner,[79] and in some jurisdictions it may be made retroactive, so as to apply to sales made before its passage, provided the purchaser is accorded in each case a reasonable time to give the notice,[80] although on the other hand, the right of the owner to receive such a notice, vested at the time of the sale, cannot be taken away by a subsequent statute.[81] The tax purchaser must comply with such a statute so far as it is in his power to do so, although a notice may be dispensed with in cases where there is no person legally entitled to it, as where the land is unoccupied and was assessed to unknown owners; [82] and the notice must be such as the law requires and given as it directs, in order to preserve the purchaser's rights.[83]

Logan County *v.* McKinley-Lanning L. & T. Co., 70 Nebr. 399, 97 N. W. 642.

77. Brown *v.* Davis, 36 Wash. 135, 78 Pac. 779; Nolan *v.* Arnot, 36 Wash. 101, 78 Pac. 463.

78. McGahen *v.* Carr, 6 Iowa 331, 71 Am. Dec. 421; Williams *v.* Pittock, 35 Wash. 271, 77 Pac. 385; Whitney *v.* Knowlton, 33 Wash. 319, 74 Pac. 469.

79. Nelson *v.* Central Land Co., 35 Minn. 408, 29 N. W. 121; Merrill *v.* Dearing, 32 Minn. 479, 21 N. W. 721.

80. *California.*— Oullahan *v.* Sweeney, 79 Cal. 537, 21 Pac. 960, 12 Am. St. Rep. 172. But *compare* Rollins *v.* Wright, 93 Cal. 395, 29 Pac. 58; King *v.* Samuel, 7 Cal. App. 55, 93 Pac. 391.

Illinois.— Gage *v.* Stewart, 127 Ill. 207, 19 N. E. 702, 11 Am. St. Rep. 116.

Washington.— Herrick *v.* Niesz, 16 Wash. 74, 47 Pac. 414.

Wisconsin.—Curtis *v.* Morrow, 24 Wis. 664; State *v.* Hundhausen, 24 Wis. 196. *Compare* Kearns *v.* McCarville, 24 Wis. 457; State *v.* Hundhausen, 23 Wis. 508.

United States.— Curtis *v.* Whitney, 13 Wall. 68, 20 L. ed. 513.

See 45 Cent. Dig. tit. "Taxation," § 1410.

Contra.— Robinson *v.* Cedar Rapids First Nat. Bank, 48 Iowa 354; Curry *v.* Backus, 156 Mich. 342, 120 N. W. 796; Stein *v.* Hanson, 99 Minn. 387, 109 N. W. 821 (holding that a notice of expiration of the period for redemption of property sold for taxes in 1901, prepared and served in accordance with Gen. St. (1894) c. 11, § 1564, was sufficient); Kipp *v.* Johnson, 73 Minn. 34, 75 N. W. 736; Gaston *v.* Merriam, 33 Minn. 271, 22 N. W. 614; State *v.* McDonald, 26 Minn. 145, 1 N. W. 832. But *compare* Pigott *v.* O'Halloran, 37 Minn. 415, 35 N. W. 4. But a statute may change the time within which the redemption notice shall be given, as to sales made before its passage, provided a reasonable time is allowed. State *v.* Krahmer, 105 Minn. 422, 117 N. W. 780, 21 L. R. A. N. S. 157.

81. Cole *v.* Lamm, 81 Minn. 463, 84 N. W. 329. See People *v.* Hegeman, 4 N. Y. Suppl. 352 [*affirmed* in 115 N. Y. 653, 21 N. E. 1118].

82. Lawrence *v.* Hornick, 81 Iowa 193, 46 N. W. 987; Burdick *v.* Connell, 69 Iowa 458, 29 N. W. 416; Walker *v.* Sioux City, etc., Land Co., 65 Iowa 563, 22 N. W. 676; Garmoe *v.* Sturgeon, 65 Iowa 147, 21 N. W. 493; Meredith *v.* Phelps, 65 Iowa 118, 21 N. W. 156; Parker *v.* Cochran, 64 Iowa 757, 21 N. W. 13; Chambers *v.* Haddock, 64 Iowa 556, 21 N. W. 32; Tuttle *v.* Griffin, 64 Iowa 455, 20 N. W. 757; Fuller *v.* Armstrong, 53 Iowa 683, 6 N. W. 61. But *compare* Barnard *v.* Hoyt, 63 Ill. 341; Hoyt *v.* Clark, 64 Minn. 139, 66 N. W. 262.

Death of owner.— The fact that the owner of the lands is dead does not dispense with the necessity of notice, as in the case of an unknown owner. Kessey *v.* Connell, 68 Iowa 430, 27 N. W. 365.

83. G. F. Sanborn Co. *v.* Alston, 153 Mich. 456, 463, 116 N. W. 1099, 117 N. W. 625; Lawton *v.* Barker, 105 Minn. 102, 117 N. W. 249; Levy *v.* Newman, 50 Hun (N. Y.) 438, 3 N. Y. Suppl. 324 [*affirmed* in 130 N. Y. 11, 28 N. E. 660] (notice to an infant who has no guardian is invalid); Jackson *v.* Esty, 7 Wend. (N. Y.) 148 (not sufficient for purchaser to show a waiver of notice by an occupant having no interest in the property); Broughton *v.* Journeay, 51 Pa. St. 31 (discovery by the owner that his property has been sold for taxes is not equivalent to notice).

Issuance of notice.— A notice of expiration of time of redemption is not invalidated because it does not appear that the holder of the tax certificate presented it to the county auditor under Gen. St. (1894) § 1654, in order that the notice might issue. Slocum *v.* McLaren, 106 Minn. 386, 119 N. W. 406; Lawton *v.* Barker, 105 Minn. 102, 117 N. W. 249. Nor is such notice invalid because it does not appear that the auditor delivered the notice to the person applying therefor as required by statute. Slocum *v.* McLaren, *supra.*

Form and requisites of notice see *infra*, XII, B, 6.

Service and proof thereof see *infra*, XII, B, 7.

actual and not merely constructive possession is intended.[8] But this does not mean that the possession must be that of one who is living on the premises,[9] for it is sufficient if he manifests an intention to use and enjoy the property, in the character of one entitled to its possession, by building on it, fencing or otherwise improving it, or cultivating it systematically,[10] although no possession or occupancy, within the meaning of the law, can be predicated on an occasional or temporary use of the premises by one who does not claim an interest in them,[11] nor on such accidental intrusion upon the property as may result from a mistake as to the boundaries.[12] A tenant occupying under a lease is in possession of the premises and should be served with the notice,[13] but not so of mere laborers,

and even though the occupancy is not such as to constitute adverse possession. Smith *v.* Sanger, 3 Barb. (N. Y.) 360 [*reversed* on other grounds in 4 N. Y. 577]; Comstock *v.* Beardsley, 15 Wend. (N. Y.) 348.

The forest preserve commission in New York, which is by statute given the care, control, and supervision of the forest preserve, and which, through its wardens, foresters, and protectors actually occupies the preserve, is an "occupant" within the meaning of the statute relating to redemption notice. People *v.* Kelsey, 180 N. Y. 24, 72 N. E. 524 [*reversing* 96 N. Y. App. Div. 148, 89 N. Y. Suppl. 416].

Occupant under master's deed.— Under Ill. Revenue Law (Hurd Rev. St. (1908) c. 120) § 216, providing that a purchaser of land for taxes, before he is entitled to a deed, shall cause a notice to be served on the occupant of such land, and on the owners thereof, of the time of redemption, one claiming the land in good faith as owner thereof, under a master's deed purporting to convey to him the title, is entitled to notice as being the actual occupant, whether or not he is the actual owner. Kenealy *v.* Glos, 241 Ill. 15, 89 N. E. 289.

8. Taylor *v.* Wright, 121 Ill. 455, 13 N. E. 529.

Question for jury.— Whether given acts amount to an occupation or possession of property is a question of fact for the jury. Jones *v.* Chamberlain, 109 N. Y. 100, 16 N. E. 72.

9. Whities *v.* Farsons, 73 Iowa 137, 34 N. W. 782; People *v.* Gaus, 134 N. Y. App. Div. 80, 118 N. Y. Suppl. 756; and other cases in the note following.

10. Shelley *v.* Smith, 97 Iowa 259, 66 N. W. 172; Cahalan *v.* Van Sant, 87 Iowa 593, 54 N. W. 433; Callanan *v.* Raymond, 75 Iowa 307, 39 N. W. 511; Sapp *v.* Walker, 66 Iowa 497, 24 N. W. 13; People *v.* Wemple, 144 N. Y. 478, 39 N. E. 397; People *v.* Gaus, 134 N. Y. App. Div. 80, 118 N. Y. Suppl. 756.

Illustrations.— Such occupancy has been held to exist where the occupant had built a log house, cleared and fenced an acre of the land about it, and lived in the house and occupied the land as his home, keeping parts of it under cultivation, for a considerable number of years. People *v.* Wemple, 144 N. Y. 478, 39 N. E. 397. Additional land purchased to straighten boundary of preserve and used and controlled in connection with the same see People *v.* Gaus, 134 N. Y. App. Div. 80, 118 N. Y. Suppl. 756.

"Actual possession" by cultivation or improvement.— The failure of the holder of a tax title to serve notice of the expiration of redemption on one who, through another, had cultivated and cropped the land, and was therefore in actual possession, avoided the notice. Wallace *v.* Sache, 106 Minn. 123, 118 N. W. 360. An improvement of property was notice of possession, making it incumbent on the holder of a tax certificate to serve notice on such person of the expiration of redemption. Wallace *v.* Sache, *supra.*

Cutting timber.— Where the land was not fit for cultivation and was unoccupied, but was used by the owner, who lived in the same county, to cut timber therefrom, it was held that he was "in possession" so as to be entitled to personal notice to redeem. Ellsworth *v.* Low, 62 Iowa 178, 17 N. W. 450.

11. Hammond *v.* Carter, 155 Ill. 579, 40 N. E. 1019; Drake *v.* Ogden, 128 Ill. 603, 21 N. E. 511; Brown *v.* Pool, 81 Iowa 455, 46 N. W. 1069, 9 L. R. A. 767; Stoddard *v.* Sloan, 65 Iowa 680, 22 N. W. 924; People *v.* Turner, 145 N. Y. 451, 40 N. E. 400; People *v.* Campbell, 143 N. Y. 335, 38 N. E. 300.

Illustrations.— Building a stack or two of hay on a tract of land actually occupied by another and inclosing the stack with boards to protect it from the rain is not occupancy within a statute requiring the "occupant" to be notified of a tax-sale. Drake *v.* Ogden, 128 Ill. 603, 21 N. E. 511. Occupying, at irregular intervals, as a hunting camp, a log house located on an island within or near the property in question, without any use of the main land except to roam over it in pursuit of game, does not constitute "actual occupancy" under the statute (People *v.* Campbell, 143 N. Y. 335, 338, 38 N. E. 300); nor does the mowing of a portion of land erroneously included in a fence. It seems there must be a substantial occupancy with intention to enjoy the property either by right or by wrong (Smith *v.* Sanger, 4 N. Y. 577).

12. Hammond *v.* Carter, 155 Ill. 579, 40 N. E. 1019; Smith *v.* Sanger, 4 N. Y. 577.

13. Gage *v.* Lyons, 138 Ill. 590, 28 N. E. 832; Callanan *v.* Raymond, 75 Iowa 307, 39 N. W. 511; Bradley *v.* Brown, 75 Iowa 180, 39 N. W. 258; Bank of Utica *v.* Mersereau, 3 Barb. Ch. (N. Y.) 528; Gage *v.* Bani, 141 U. S. 344, 12 S. Ct. 22, 35 L. ed. 776. See Simmons *v.* McCarthy, 118 Cal. 622, 50 Pac.

held, however, that a very trifling inaccuracy in the statement of the amount will not vitiate the notice.[34] But if the error is substantial it cannot be disregarded, even though it consists in stating a smaller sum than is legally due, and so is apparently advantageous to the redemptioner.[35] If the notice includes several distinct parcels of land, it must state the amount required for the redemption of each, and not the aggregate sum.[36]

f. Time For Redemption. The time when the right of redemption will expire by law must be stated in the redemption notice and correctly given, and if the time is there stated earlier or later than the time fixed by law, although it be by a single day, the notice is void.[37] Where the last day of the statutory time for redemption falls upon a Sunday, and the notice appoints the same day as the last for redemption, the notice is void, because in that case the owner will have the whole of the succeeding day in which to redeem.[38] The notice must also state the time precisely and specifically; if there is any indefiniteness, ambiguity, or uncertainty in this respect, it will not be effective to foreclose the right of redemption.[39]

objectionable for failure to set out in figures the amount of the thirty-seven and one-half per cent penalty. Halsted *v.* Silberstein, 196 N. Y. 1, 89 N. E. 443 [*reversing* 122 N. Y. App. Div. 909, 107 N. Y. Suppl. 1129].

Amount paid for controller's deed.— Where a tax-sale redemption notice requires payment of ten cents for a controller's deed, it is not defective for failure to state in terms that that amount has been paid to the controller, for executing and delivering the deed. Halsted *v.* Silberstein, 196 N. Y. 1, 89 N. E. 443 [*reversing* 122 N. Y. App. Div. 909, 107 N. Y. Suppl. 1129].

Successive sales.—A notice of expiration of the time to redeem from a tax-sale need not include the amount necessary to redeem from a later tax-sale to the same purchaser, as payment of such amount is not necessary in order to redeem from the first sale. Brodie *v.* State, 102 Minn. 202, 113 N. W. 2.

34. Robert *v.* Western Land Assoc., 43 Minn. 3, 44 N. W. 668; Western Land Assoc. *v.* McComber, 41 Minn. 20, 42 N. W. 543. *Contra*, Reed *v.* Lyon, 96 Cal. 501, 31 Pac. 619. And see Salter *v.* Corbett, 80 Kan. 327, 102 Pac. 452.

35. State *v.* Scott, 92 Minn. 210, 99 N. W. 799. But *compare* Watkins *v.* Inge, 24 Kan. 612.

36. Haden *v.* Closser, 153 Mich. 182, 116 N. W. 1001; G. F. Sanborn Co. *v.* Johnson, 148 Mich. 405, 111 N. W. 1091.

37. *California.*— Landregan *v.* Peppin, 86 Cal. 122, 24 Pac. 859.

Illinois.— Benefield *v.* Albert, 132 Ill. 665, 24 N. E. 634; Gage *v.* Davis, (1887) 14 N. E. 36; Wisner *v.* Chamberlin, 117 Ill. 568, 7 N. E. 68; Gage *v.* Bailey, 100 Ill. 530.

Kansas.— Ireland *v.* George, 41 Kan. 751, 21 Pac. 776; Torrington *v.* Rickershauser, 41 Kan. 486, 21 Pac. 648; Hollenback *v.* Ess, 31 Kan. 87, 1 Pac. 275.

Minnesota.— Kipp *v.* Robinson, 75 Minn. 1, 77 N. W. 414; State *v.* Nord, 73 Minn. 1, 75 N. W. 760, 72 Am. St. Rep. 594.

New York.— Clason *v.* Baldwin, 152 N. Y. 204, 46 N. E. 322; Hennessey *v.* Volkening, 22 N. Y. Suppl. 528, 30 Abb. N. Cas. 100.

North Dakota.— State Finance Co. *v.* Beck, 15 N. D. 374, 109 N. W. 357.

See 45 Cent. Dig. tit. "Taxation," § 1423.

Notice sufficient.— Where a delinquent tax-sale is held Sept. 4, 1900, and the final redemption notice states that lands sold at that sale must be redeemed on or before Sept. 4, 1903, or they will be deeded to the purchasers, such notice gives full three years after the sale for redemption and is not void. Michner *v.* Ford, 78 Kan. 837, 98 Pac. 273; Ireland *v.* George, 41 Kan. 751, 21 Pac. 776.

38. Brophy *v.* Harding, 137 Ill. 621, 27 N. E. 523, 34 N. E. 253; Gage *v.* Davis, 129 Ill. 236, 21 N. E. 788, 16 Am. St. Rep. 260; Gage *v.* Davis, (Ill. 1887) 14 N. E. 36; Hill *v.* Timmermeyer, 36 Kan. 252, 13 Pac. 211. But when the notice gives the full statutory time for redemption and one day more, and the last day named in the notice is Sunday, the owner will not be permitted to set aside a tax deed following such notice without showing that he was misled by the notice and that he offered to redeem on the day after the last day named. Hicks *v.* Nelson, 45 Kan. 47, 25 Pac. 218, 23 Am. St. Rep. 709.

39. *California.*— California, etc., R. Co. *v.* Mecartney, 104 Cal. 616, 38 Pac. 448.

Illinois.— Wilson *v.* McKenna, 52 Ill. 43, notice fixing the day on which the right of redemption will expire as of the day of the sale is void.

Kansas.— Jackson *v.* Challis, 41 Kan. 247, 21 Pac. 87 (not sufficient to say that the land must be redeemed "before the day limited therefor"); Blackistone *v.* Sherwood, 31 Kan. 35, 2 Pac. 874 (statement that the land will be deeded, if not redeemed, "on and after September 5, 1879, or within three years from the day of sale" is insufficient).

Minnesota.— Gahre *v.* Berry, 82 Minn. 200, 84 N. W. 733; Clary *v.* O'Shea, 72 Minn. 105, 75 N. W. 115, 71 Am. St. Rep. 465 (notice stating two different dates is void for uncertainty); State *v.* Halden, 62 Minn. 246, 64 N. W. 568; Peterson *v.* Mast, 61 Minn. 118, 63 N. W. 168 (stating the time in the alternative is insufficient).

was struck off to the state or county, this is usually the amount of all taxes delinquent and unpaid; [68] but in the case of a private purchaser, it is ordinarily the amount paid by him at the tax-sale,[69] together with such interest and penalties as the law prescribes,[70] and the costs and expenses of advertising and selling the land,[71] to which may be added the value of improvements put upon the land by the tax purchaser after the sale,[72] but deducting the sum of rents and profits or the fair rental value of the land if the purchaser has been in possession.[73] Where a tract of land was divided into parcels for the purpose of assessment and sale, the owner of any one parcel may redeem it by paying the price which it brought; [74] but in the absence of a statute the owner of an undivided interest in a tract, or of a separate portion of a tract which was assessed and sold as an entirety, cannot redeem his part or interest by payment of a proportionate part of the entire amount, but must redeem the whole.[75] Where land is sold to a private purchaser

and pay a larger sum than the amount of taxes, damages, and costs, and the excess at redemption be in the collector's hands, it shall be refunded to the purchaser, and if only a part of the land be redeemed the excess shall be apportioned ratably to the amount of taxes due at the time of sale on the respective parts, and section 3853, providing that the owner of land sold for taxes may redeem any part of it, where it is separable by legal subdivisions of not less than forty acres. Moores *v.* Thomas, (Miss. 1909) 48 So. 1025.

68. Couts *v.* Cornell, 147 Cal. 560, 82 Pac. 194, 109 Am. St. Rep. 168; Statton *v.* People, 18 Colo. App. 85, 70 Pac. 157; Everson *v.* Woodbury County, 118 Iowa 99, 91 N. W. 900; Soper *v.* Espeset, 63 Iowa 326, 19 N. W. 232; Judd *v.* Driver, 1 Kan. 455.

69. *Colorado.*— Elder *v.* Chaffee County, 33 Colo. 475, 81 Pac. 244.

Louisiana.— Richards *v.* Fuller, 122 La. 847, 48 So. 285.

Michigan.— Haney *v.* Miller, 154 Mich. 337, 117 N. W. 71, 745.

Minnesota.— State *v.* Johnson, 83 Minn. 496, 86 N. W. 610.

Missouri.— State *v.* Tufts, (1891) 15 S. W. 954.

Nebraska.— Douglas *v.* Hayes County, 82 Nebr. 577, 118 N. W. 114; Butler *v.* Libe, 81 Nebr. 740, 116 N. W. 663, 81 Nebr. 744, 117 N. W. 700.

A very trifling difference between the amount paid or tendered in redemption from a sale for taxes and the correct amount, if it is such only as might result from different modes of calculation, will not invalidate the redemption. Wyatt *v.* Simpson, 8 W. Va. 394.

Addition of judgment lien.— Where the holder of a judgment procures a tax deed to lands of the judgment debtor, which he agrees shall be subject to redemption by payment of the judgment, other claimants of the land can redeem only on complying with the terms of the agreement. Jordan *v.* Brown, 56 Iowa 281, 9 N. W. 200. And see Clower *v.* Fleming, 81 Ga. 247, 7 S. E. 278.

Lands bid in to state and sold to purchasers.— Under Minn. Rev. Laws (1905), §§ 936–940, where lands are bid in to the state and not assigned to purchasers within three years from the sale at which they were offered to purchasers at the highest price are expressly subject to redemption by the owner or other person duly and properly entitled to redeem. Upon redemption the full consideration of the sale must be paid to the tax purchaser, but the person redeeming is entitled to a return from the state of the surplus above the amount due the state. Minnesota Debenture Co. *v.* Scott, 106 Minn. 32, 119 N. W. 391.

Deduction for illegal taxes not allowed on redemption from purchaser of state tax lands see Haney *v.* Miller, 154 Mich. 337, 117 N. W. 71, 745.

70. See *infra*, XII, C, 1, b.

71. State *v.* Bowker, 4 Kan. 114; State *v.* Harper, 26 Nebr. 761, 42 N. W. 764; Permanent Sav., etc., Co. *v.* Sennt, 7 Ohio S. & C. Pl. Dec. 224, 4 Ohio N. P. 346. See Ramsey *v.* State, 78 Tex. 602, 14 S. W. 793; Dooley *v.* Christian, 96 Va. 534, 32 S. E. 54.

72. Cowley *v.* Spradlin, 77 Ark. 190, 91 S. W. 550; Waterman *v.* Irby, 76 Ark. 551, 89 S. W. 844; Humphreys *v.* Hays, 85 Nebr. 239, 122 N. W. 987; Towle *v.* Holt, 14 Nebr. 221, 15 N. W. 203; Lynch *v.* Brudie, 63 Pa. St. 206.

73. Cornoy *v.* Wetmore, 92 Iowa 100, 60 N. W. 245; Elliott *v.* Parker, 72 Iowa 746, 32 N. W. 494; Strang *v.* Burris, 61 Iowa 375, 16 N. W. 285; Gaskins *v.* Blake, 27 Miss. 675; Van Landingham *v.* Buena Vista Imp. Co., 99 Va. 37, 37 S. E. 274. *Compare* Bender *v.* Bean, 52 Ark. 132, 12 S. W. 180, 241.

No rent on purchaser's improvements.— The owner is not in any case entitled to the rent of buildings and improvements put upon the land by the occupying claimant. Elliott *v.* Parker, 72 Iowa 746, 32 N. W. 494; Boatmen's Sav. Bank *v.* Grewe, 101 Mo. 625, 14 S. W. 708.

Redemption after the time.— If the owner has allowed the whole statutory period for redemption to elapse, and a tax deed has been issued and recorded, he cannot thereafter indirectly effect a redemption by charging the purchaser for rents and profits received before the recording of the deed. Spengin *v.* Forry, 37 Iowa 242.

74. People *v.* McEwen, 23 Cal. 54; Penn *v.* Clemans, 19 Iowa 372; Hewes *v.* Seal, 80 Miss. 437, 32 So. 55.

75. *California.*— Quinn *v.* Kenney, 47 Cal. 147; Mayo *v.* Marshall, 23 Cal. 594; People *v.* McEwen, 23 Cal. 54.

tions of the statute as to the establishment of his lien or the evidence of it.[85] But he cannot exact repayment of any taxes assessed against the land for years previous to the sale,[86] or of any taxes paid by him after the redemption.[87]

2. **Payment or Tender — a. In General.** When the person entitled to redeem from a sale for taxes duly offers the proper amount to the proper person, it is immaterial that the money is not accepted; for a sufficient tender will *ipso facto* work a redemption.[88] But to have this effect the tender must be of the full amount which the purchaser is entitled to receive,[89] and must be made in due time and

N. W. 365; Curl *v.* Watson, 25 Iowa 35, 95 Am. Dec. 763.

Kentucky.— Bleight *v.* Auditor, 2 T. B. Mon. 25.

Michigan.— G. F. Sanborn Co. *v.* Alston, 153 Mich. 436, 116 N. W. 1099, 153 Mich. 463, 117 N. W. 625; Cheever *v.* Flint Land Co., 134 Mich. 604, 96 N. W. 933.

Minnesota.— Jenswold *v.* Minnesota Canal Co., 93 Minn. 382, 101 N. W. 603; State *v.* Butler, 89 Minn. 220, 94 N. W. 688; State *v.* Peltier, 86 Minn. 181, 90 N. W. 375; McLachlan *v.* Carpenter, 75 Minn. 17, 77 N. W. 436; Berglund *v.* Graves, 72 Minn. 148, 75 N. W. 118. See Sprague *v.* Roverud, 34 Minn. 475, 26 N. W. 603.

Nebraska.— Hannold *v.* Valley County, 82 Nebr. 221, 117 N. W. 350; Butler *v.* Libe, 81 Nebr. 740, 116 N. W. 663, 81 Nebr. 744, 117 N. W. 700.

Pennsylvania.— Bannan's Appeal, 1 Walk. 461.

Tennessee.—Ayres *v.* Dozier, (Ch. App. 1899) 52 S. W. 662.

Virginia.— Parsons *v.* Newman, 99 Va. 298, 38 S. E. 186; Hale *v.* Penn, 25 Gratt. 261.

United States.— Harmon *v.* Steed, 49 Fed. 779; O'Reilly *v.* Holt, 18 Fed. Cas. No. 10,563, 4 Woods 645.

See 45 Cent. Dig. tit. "Taxation," § 1435.

Including municipal taxes.—A statute requiring the redemptioner to refund to the purchaser the amount of any taxes paid by him since the sale includes not only state and county taxes but also all municipal taxes paid by the purchaser. Cobb. *v.* Vary, 120 Ala. 263, 24 So. 442; Turner *v.* White, 97 Ala. 545, 12 So. 601. *Contra*, Byington *v.* Hampton, 13 Iowa 23; Byington *v.* Rider, 9 Iowa 566.

Not including personal taxes see San Diego, etc., R. Co. *v.* Shaffer, 137 Cal. 103, 69 Pac. 855; Buell *v.* Boylan, 10 S. D. 180, 72 N. W. 406.

Defective redemption notice.—Although a tax-sale purchaser's notice to the original owners of the sale and of their right to redeem is technically defective, the owners cannot redeem without reimbursing him for taxes paid subsequent to service of the notice, with interest on the sums paid. G. F. Sanborn Co. *v.* Alston, 153 Mich. 436, 116 N. W. 1099, 153 Mich. 463, 117 N. W. 625.

85. Kennedy *v.* Bigelow, 43 Iowa 74. But see Elliott *v.* Parker, 72 Iowa 746, 32 N. W. 494 (as to redemption in equity).

86. Sheppard *v.* Clark, 58 Iowa 371, 12 N. W. 316.

87. Byington *v.* Allen, 11 Iowa 3.

Effect of statute of limitations.— In a suit by the owner of land to redeem it from one claiming under a tax deed and under a decree quieting his title, it appeared that defendant's right of possession under the deed was barred by adverse possession before he actually gained the possession and before the date of the decree, and that the decree itself was void for want of jurisdiction. It was held that plaintiff could redeem on reimbursing defendant only for the taxes paid by him within five years before the commencement of the suit to redeem. Thode *v.* Spofford, 65 Iowa 294, 17 N. W. 561, 21 N. W. 647.

88. *Arkansas.*— Bender *v.* Bean, 52 Ark. 132, 12 S. W. 180, 241.

Georgia.— Bourquin *v.* Bourquin, 120 Ga. 115, 47 S. E. 639.

Kansas.—Wilson *v.* Reasoner, 37 Kan. 663, 16 Pac. 100.

Louisiana.— Bentley *v.* Cavallier, 121 La. 60, 46 So. 101; Spanier *v.* De Voe, 52 La. Ann. 581, 27 So. 174; Basso *v.* Benker, 33 La. Ann. 432; Brooks *v.* Hardwick, 5 La. Ann. 675.

Missouri.— Olmstead *v.* Tarsney, 69 Mo. 396.

Nebraska.— See Douglas *v.* Hayes County, 82 Nebr. 574, 118 N. W. 114.

Pennsylvania.— Deringer *v.* Coxe, 6 Pa. Cas. 283, 10 Atl. 412.

Texas.— Burns *v.* Ledbetter, 54 Tex. 374; Logan *v.* Logan, 31 Tex. Civ. App. 295, 72 S. W. 416.

West Virginia.— Koon *v.* Snodgrass, 18 W. Va. 320; Sperry *v.* Gibson, 3 W. Va. 522.

Canada.— Cunningham *v.* Markland, 5 U. C. Q. B. O. S. 645.

See 45 Cent. Dig. tit. "Taxation," § 1346.

Effect of tender.— The owner of land, having tendered the amount paid by the purchaser at the tax-sale, will be required to pay the same in order to redeem, although the tax deed is set aside as void. Chicago, etc., R. Co. *v.* Kelley, 105 Iowa 106, 74 N. W. 935.

Where tender unnecessary.—Where the tax deed was made without any authority of law, no tender or payment of the amount required to redeem need be proven. Adams *v.* Snow, 65 Iowa 435, 21 N. W. 765.

What effects redemption a question of law. —Whether the act of a person paying to the clerk of the county court the sum of money specified in his official receipt has operated as a redemption or not is a question of law for the court. Elliott *v.* Shaffer, 30 W. Va. 347, 4 S. E. 292.

89. Cowley *v.* Spradlin, 77 Ark. 190, 91 S. W. 550; Fitts *v.* Huff, 63 Miss. 594; Richards *v.* Fuller, 122 La. 847, 48 So. 285; Sanford *v.* Moore, 58 Nebr. 654, 79 N. W. 548.

ized by statute,[96] and provided he is still the holder of a valid and uncanceled certificate of purchase,[97] and has done all that is necessary on his part to entitle him to a conveyance,[98] and provided that the property has not been redeemed.[99] But if the purchaser was disqualified from bidding at the sale, as, where he was under a legal or moral obligation to pay the taxes or stood in such a relation to the owner of the property that it would be a fraud for him to acquire a tax title, he is not entitled to a deed and will not be assisted in procuring it.[1] If the original purchaser has assigned his certificate of purchase, the assignee succeeds to his rights and will be entitled to a deed if his assignor was;[2] and the executor of a deceased purchaser may be considered the "assign" of his decedent within this rule.[3]

2. Conditions and Prerequisites. A tax deed cannot be issued unless there has been a sale of the land.[4] Any provisions of the statute imposing on the tax purchaser the duty of complying with prescribed conditions or obligations before taking out his deed are to be considered mandatory and essential to the validity of the deed.[5] This is particularly the case where the purchaser is required to produce his certificate or give evidence of his right to a deed, to cause the land to be surveyed, to file an affidavit concerning the occupancy or possession of it, or to serve notice to redeem on the owner or others.[6]

does not affect the right of a purchaser of such lands at a tax-sale to demand and receive a deed therefor when entitled thereto under the state laws. Whitehead *v.* Farmers' L. & T. Co., 98 Fed. 10, 39 C. C. A. 34; Rice *v.* Jerome, 97 Fed. 719, 38 C. C. A. 388. *Compare*, however, Johnson *v.* Southern Bldg., etc., Assoc., 132 Fed. 540, holding that a tax deed executed after the property has passed into the custody of a court, by its appointment of a receiver in foreclosure proceedings, is void and does not cut off the receiver's right to redeem.

96. Doe *v.* Chunn, 1 Blackf. (Ind.) 336; Sibley *v.* Smith, 2 Mich. 486; Byrd *v.* Phillips, 120 Tenn. 14, 111 S. W. 1109; Smith *v.* Todd, 55 Wis. 459, 13 N. W. 488; Knox *v.* Peterson, 21 Wis. 247. And see Powell *v.* Jenkins, 11 Misc. (N. Y.) 83, 35 N. Y. Suppl. 265. See also *infra*, XIII, C, 1.

Implication.— The power to issue a tax deed is not implied from the power to sell for taxes. The principle that every grant of power carries with it the usual and necessary means for the exercise of that power, and that the power to convey is implied in the power to sell, does not apply in the construction of statutes which are in derogation of the common law, and the effect of which is to divest a citizen of his real estate. Doe *v.* Chunn, 1 Blackf. (Ind.) 336; Sibley *v.* Smith, 2 Mich. 486. *Compare*, however, Bruce *v.* Schuyler, 9 Ill. 221, 46 Am. Dec. 447, where it was said that an auditor, being authorized by statute to sell lands for taxes, and having executed that power, would have been authorized to execute deeds to the purchaser without any express provision on the subject.

97. Ogden *v.* Bemis, 125 Ill. 105, 17 N. E. 55, holding that a mere showing that a tax certificate was canceled as to a part of the property does not deprive the holder of the right to a deed for the balance.

98. Hoffman *v.* Silverthorn, 137 Mich. 60, 100 N. W. 183.

99. State *v.* Evans, 53 Mo. App. 663; People *v.* Hegeman, 14 N. Y. Suppl. 567.

1. *California.*— Mills *v.* Tukey, 22 Cal. 373, 83 Am. Dec. 74.

Florida.— Gamble *v.* Hamilton, 31 Fla. 401, 12 So. 229.

Kansas.— Bowman *v.* Cockrill, 6 Kan. 311.

Wisconsin.— Bennett *v.* Keehn, 57 Wis. 582, 15 N. W. 776; Lybrand *v.* Haney, 31 Wis. 230; Smith *v.* Lewis, 20 Wis. 350; State *v.* Williston, 20 Wis. 228.

United States.— Horner *v.* Dellinger, 18 Fed. 495.

See 45 Cent. Dig. tit. "Taxation," § 1493. And see *supra*, XI, H, 1, 2.

2. Smith *v.* Stephenson, 45 Iowa 645; McCauslin *v.* McGuire, 14 Kan. 234; Kerner *v.* Boston Cottage Co., 126 N. C. 356, 35 S. E. 590; Bell *v.* Orr, 5 U. C. Q. B. O. S. 433.

3. Blakemore *v.* Cooper, 15 N. D. 5, 106 N. W. 566, 125 Am. St. Rep. 574, 4 L. R. A. N. S. 1074. But *compare* Alexander *v.* Savage, 90 Ala. 383, 8 So. 93, holding that no tax deed can be issued to the administrator of a deceased purchaser where the statute only authorizes a deed to the original purchaser or to "the assignee, by written indorsement, of the certificate of purchase."

4. People *v.* Golding, 55 Misc. (N. Y.) 425, 106 N. Y. Suppl. 821, holding that where lands were withdrawn by the controller from sale in a statement that they belonged to the state, a conveyance given without any actual sale was a nullity.

5. Davis *v.* Jackson, 14 W. Va. 227.

Tax leases which show on their face that the statute authorizing their execution has not been complied with are void. Obermeyer *v.* Behn, 123 N. Y. App. Div. 440, 108 N. Y. Suppl. 289.

Foreclosure of certificate where land sold to county.—A deed from the county commissioners for land sold to the county for delinquent taxes without foreclosure of the certificate is a nullity. Smith *v.* Smith, 160 N. C. 81, 63 S. E. 177; Wilcox *v.* Leach, 123 N. C. 74, 31 S. E. 374.

6. Production or exhibition of tax certificate see Duggan *v.* McCullough, 27 Colo. 43,

where the tax-sale was invalidated by disobedience to the directions of the law as to its conduct, by selling for an excessive amount, or by fraudulent combinations preventing competition,[25] or where the conduct of the purchaser has been fraudulent, in deceiving or misleading the owner as to the fact or time of redemption.[26] Both the tax purchaser, or holder of the certificate, and the officer whose duty it is to execute the deed should be made parties to the injunction suit.[27]

b. Payment or Tender. On the principle of doing equity, the complainant in an action of this kind should as a rule offer to reimburse the *bona fide* purchaser to the extent of the taxes lawfully chargeable upon the land and all legal costs;[28] and the court may order such payment as a condition to granting the relief asked.[29]

6. Mandamus to Compel Execution of Deed. If the property has not been redeemed,[30] and the purchaser or holder of the tax certificate has done all that is required of him in the way of giving notice,[31] and otherwise has a clear right to receive a deed, mandamus may issue to compel the proper officer to execute such a deed,[32] or to issue a second and perfect deed where the one originally given was

Curative statute.— Under a statute providing that no "sale" of land for taxes shall be impeached because of the addition of interest to the taxes, a bill will not lie to prevent the execution of a tax deed in pursuance of a sale on the ground that such an addition had been made, as the statute is not confined in its operation to a sale completed by conveyance, but makes valid the sale itself. Schultz *v.* Winnipeg, 6 Manitoba 269.

25. Axtell *v.* Gerlach, 67 Cal. 483, 8 Pac. 34; Glos *v.* Swigart, 156 Ill. 229, 41 N. E. 42; Gage *v.* Graham, 57 Ill. 144. See Dudley *v.* Gilmore, 35 Kan. 555, 11 Pac. 398.

Failure to exhaust personalty.—An injunction to restrain the execution of a tax deed will not be granted merely because the owner of the premises had personal property at the time, out of which the tax could have been collected. St. Clair *v.* McClure, 111 Ind. 467, 12 N. E. 134; Harrison *v.* Haas, 25 Ind. 281.

26. Allen *v.* Evans, 7 Ariz. 359, 64 Pac. 412; Holt *v.* King, 54 W. Va. 441, 47 S. E. 362; Koon *v.* Snodgrass, 18 W. Va. 320.

27. Siegel *v.* Outagamie County, 26 Wis. 70.

Failure to join tax purchaser.—As a judgment binds only parties and privies, a tax purchaser who is not made a party to an action to enjoin the treasurer from issuing a tax deed, and does not appear in the action, is not bound by the decree. Helphrey *v.* Redick, 21 Nebr. 80, 31 N. W. 256.

28. *Arkansas.*— Hare *v.* Carnall, 39 Ark. 196.

California.— San Diego Realty Co. *v.* Cornell, 150 Cal. 637, 89 Pac. 603; Grant *v.* Cornell, 147 Cal. 565, 82 Pac. 193, 109 Am. St. Rep. 173.

Illinois.— Moore *v.* Wayman, 107 Ill. 192.

Indiana.— Logansport *v.* Case, 124 Ind. 254, 24 N. E. 88; Morrison *v.* Jacoby, 114 Ind. 84, 14 N. E. 546, 15 N. E. 806; Rowe *v.* Peabody, 102 Ind. 198, 1 N. E. 353.

Nebraska.— Iler *v.* Colson, 8 Nebr. 331, 1 N. W. 248.

Wisconsin.— Hart *v.* Smith, 44 Wis. 213; Mills *v.* Johnson, 17 Wis. 598; Bond *v.* Kenosha, 17 Wis. 284; Hersey *v.* Milwaukee County, 16 Wis. 185, 82 Am. Dec. 713.

See 45 Cent. Dig. tit. "Taxation," § 1502.

No taxes due.— It is not necessary that the bill shall contain an offer to pay the purchaser the amount paid by him at the sale, and subsequently for taxes and otherwise, where the bill shows that there are no legal arrears of taxes. Schultz *v.* Alloway, 10 Manitoba 221.

29. San Diego Realty Co. *v.* Cornell, 150 Cal. 637, 89 Pac. 603; Alexander *v.* Merrick, 121 Ill. 606, 13 N. E. 190; Harrigan *v.* Peoria County, 106 Ill. App. 218; Iler *v.* Colson, 8 Nebr. 331, 1 N. W. 248; Hart *v.* Smith, 44 Wis. 213.

30. State *v.* Harper, 26 Nebr. 761, 42 N. W. 764; State *v.* Cranney, 30 Wash. 594, 71 Pac. 50.

31. Hintrager *v.* Traut, 69 Iowa 746, 27 N. W. 807; State *v.* Gayhart, 34 Nebr. 192, 51 N. W. 746; People *v.* New York, 10 Wend. (N. Y.) 393.

32. *Florida.*— State *v.* Bradshaw, 35 Fla. 313, 17 So. 642.

Illinois.— Maxcy *v.* Clabaugh, 6 Ill. 26.

Iowa.— Jones *v.* Welsing, 52 Iowa 220, 2 N. W. 1106.

Kansas.— Ide *v.* Finneran, 29 Kan. 569; Clippinger *v.* Tuller, 10 Kan. 377.

South Carolina.— State *v.* Lancaster, 46 S. C. 282, 24 S. E. 198.

Washington.— State *v.* Cranney, 30 Wash. 594, 71 Pac. 50.

Wisconsin.— State *v.* Winn, 19 Wis. 304, 88 Am. Dec. 689.

See 45 Cent. Dig. tit. "Taxation," § 1503.

Purchaser rescinding sale.—A tax purchaser cannot have mandamus to compel the issuance of a deed to him where it is shown that the money paid by him was tendered back to him on the same day and was accepted, and that the lands were afterward conveyed to other persons before he again tendered the money. Aitcheson *v.* Huebner, 90 Mich. 643, 51 N. W. 634.

Purchaser's assignee.—An assignee of the certificate of purchase may be entitled to compel the execution of a deed by mandamus, but not where he neglected to file or record the assignment and meanwhile a tax deed

to law," or "in manner and form as directed by law," but the particular facts must be recited.[17] Especially it is necessary to recite enough of the previous proceedings to show authority to sell the land and authority in the officer making the sale,[18] and authority for the execution of the deed and the manner of its execution;[19] and the recitals in a tax deed of lands sold to a county must show affirmatively the right of the county to take the lands.[20] But these conditions being met, and the law being silent as to the incorporation of particular recitals, it is generally held that only so much of the previous history need be set out as is essential to the meaning and validity of the tax deed, standing by itself as an independent instrument of conveyance.[21] But of course, if it shows that it was made without any legal authority, or shows disobedience to any essential requirement of the law, it is void and inoperative for every purpose.[22] A tax deed need not state the address or residence of the grantee unless the statute so requires.[23]

b. Assessment and Delinquency of Tax. It is generally held essential to the validity of a tax deed that it shall recite the levy of the tax and its legal assessment on the land in question,[24] and it is void if it shows on its face an assessment

Dakota.— Wambole *v.* Foote, 2 Dak. 1, 2 N. W. 239.

Maine.— Skowhegan Sav. Bank *v.* Parsons, 86 Me. 514, 30 Atl. 110.

Missouri.— Atkison *v.* Butler Imp. Co., 125 Mo. 565, 28 S. W. 861; Burden *v.* Taylor, 124 Mo. 12, 27 S. W. 349; Western *v.* Flanagan, 120 Mo. 61, 25 S. W. 531.

Texas.— Henderson *v.* White, 69 Tex. 103, 5 S. W. 374.

West Virginia.— Buchanan *v.* Reynolds, 4 W. Va. 681.

See 45 Cent. Dig. tit. "Taxation," § 1507.

17. Duncan *v.* Gillette, 37 Kan. 156, 14 Pac. 479; Moore *v.* Harris, 91 Mo. 616, 4 S. W. 439; Yankee *v.* Thompson, 51 Mo. 234; Large *v.* Fisher, 49 Mo. 307; Spurlock *v.* Allen, 49 Mo. 178; Rush *v.* Lewis & Clark County, 36 Mont. 566, 93 Pac. 943, 37 Mont. 240, 95 Pac. 836. *Contra,* O'Grady *v.* Barnhisel, 23 Cal. 287.

18. *Louisiana.*— Reeves *v.* Towles, 10 La. 276. But *compare* Boyle *v.* West, 107 La. 347, 31 So. 794; Sims *v.* Walshe, 49 La. Ann. 781, 21 So. 861.

Michigan.— Upton *v.* Kennedy, 36 Mich. 215.

Minnesota.— Madland *v.* Benland, 24 Minn. 372.

Missouri.— State *v.* Mantz, 62 Mo. 258.

Ohio.— Woodward *v.* Sloan, 27 Ohio St. 592.

19. Hereford *v.* O'Connor, 5 Ariz. 258, 52 Pac. 471; Garner *v.* Wallace, 118 Mich. 387, 76 N. W. 758; Hunt *v.* Miller, 101 Wis. 583, 77 N. W. 874.

20. Rush *v.* Lewis & Clark County, 36 Mont. 566, 93 Pac. 943, 37 Mont. 240, 95 Pac. 836.

That county was not a competitive bidder see *infra,* XIII, D, 2, d, (I).

21. *Arkansas.*— Pleasants *v.* Scott, 21 Ark. 370, 76 Am. Dec. 403.

California.— Wetherbee *v.* Dunn, 32 Cal. 106; Moss *v.* Shear, 25 Cal. 38, 85 Am. Dec. 94.

Indiana.— Scarry *v.* Lewis, 133 Ind. 96, 30 N. E. 411.

Louisiana.— Jopling *v.* Chachere, 107 La. 522, 32 So. 243.

Missouri.— State *v.* Richardson, 21 Mo. 420.

Virginia.— Flanagan *v.* Grimmet, 10 Gratt. 421.

See 45 Cent. Dig. tit. "Taxation," § 1507 *et seq.*

22. Spain *v.* Johnson, 31 Ark. 314; Twombly *v.* Kimbrough, 24 Ark. 459; Hall *v.* Dowling, 18 Cal. 619; Cogel *v.* Raph, 24 Minn. 194. A statement in a tax deed of a fact showing that it was improperly issued is fatal to its validity, although occurring in the course of a recital not required by the statute. Price *v.* Barnhill, 79 Kan. 93, 98 Pac. 774.

23. And such requirement is not implied from the fact that in the statutory form blanks are left after the names of the purchaser and his assignee in which to insert the counties of their residence. Havel *v.* Decatur County Abstract Co., 76 Kan. 336, 91 Pac. 790. And see Nichols *v.* Trueman, 80 Kan. 89, 101 Pac. 633; Stevenson *v.* Carson, 77 Kan. 444, 94 Pac. 796; Lincoln Mortg., etc., Co. *v.* Davis, 76 Kan. 639, 92 Pac. 707, rule applies to a tax deed based on proceedings under the compromise act.

24. *Arizona.*— Seaverns *v.* Costello, 8 Ariz. 308, 71 Pac. 930.

Arkansas.— Lawrence *v.* Zimpleman, 37 Ark. 643; Jacks *v.* Dyer, 31 Ark. 334.

California.— Davis *v.* Pacific Imp. Co., 127 Cal. 245, 70 Pac. 15; Simmons *v.* McCarthy, 118 Cal. 622, 50 Pac. 761.

Colorado.— See Waddingham *v.* Dickson, 17 Colo. 223, 29 Pac. 177.

Kansas.— Where at a tax-sale land for want of bidders was taken by the county, and after five years the certificate was assigned, and a deed made pursuant to Gen. St. (1901) § 7672, the fact that the recitals showed that the taxes which accrued while the land was held by the county were charged on the tax roll in the month of September of each year, instead of November, did not render the deed void. Taylor *v.* Adams, 79 Kan. 360, 99 Pac. 597.

South Dakota.— Horswill *v.* Farnham, 16 S. D. 414, 92 N. W. 1082.

Tennessee.— Conrad *v.* Darden, 4 Yerg. 307.

that was illegal or erroneous because made to a wrong person.[25] The deed must also contain proper recitals to show that the taxes remained delinquent and unpaid at the time of the sale,[26] or, if the statute so requires, that they were not paid within a specified time after demand,[27] and for what year's taxes the sale was made.[28]

c. Proceedings Preliminary to Sale. The tax deed must recite the proceedings preliminary to the sale at least so far as to show the authority under which the officer acted.[29] A tax deed showing that certain essential preliminary steps have not been taken is void on its face.[30] In particular, it must recite a demand for payment, if that is required by law, and failure to comply therewith,[31] and the

See 45 Cent. Dig. tit. "Taxation," § 1508.

Contra.— McQuain *v.* Meline, 16 Fed. Cas. No. 8,923.

Sufficiency of recital.— See Madland *v.* Benland, 24 Minn. 372, holding that a recital in a tax deed that lands have been duly forfeited for non-payment of taxes is a sufficient recital of the levy, assessment, and delinquency of the tax.

Misrecital of person to whom assessed.—A tax deed based on an assessment to "Priscilla Durham," which recites that the land was assessed to "Petruella Durham," is not a substantial statement of the assessment within the requirements of Ballinger & C. Comp. St. Oreg. § 3127, defining the effect of tax deeds as evidence. Bradford *v.* Durham, 54 Oreg. 1, 101 Pac. 897.

25. Russ *v.* Crichton, 117 Cal. 695, 49 Pac. 1043; Jatunn *v.* O'Brien, 89 Cal. 57, 26 Pac. 635; Greenwood *v.* Adams, 80 Cal. 74, 21 Pac. 1134; Pearson *v.* Creed, 78 Cal. 144, 20 Pac. 302; Brady *v.* Dowden, 59 Cal. 51; Grimm *v.* O'Connell, 54 Cal. 522; Brown *v* Hartford, 173 Mo. 183, 73 S. W. 140. But *compare* Hickman *v.* Kempner, 35 Ark. 505, holding that a false recital in a tax deed that the land was assessed in the name of an unknown owner does not vitiate the sale.

26. Hubbard *v.* Johnson, 9 Kan. 632; Smith *v.* Bodfish, 27 Me. 289; Gilfillan *v.* Chatterton, 38 Minn. 335, 37 N. W. 583; Sherburne *v.* Rippe, 35 Minn. 540, 29 N. W. 322; O'Mulcahy *v.* Florer, 27 Minn. 449, 8 N. W. 166; Sheehy *v.* Hinds, 27 Minn. 259, 6 N. W. 781.

Sufficiency of recital.—A tax deed is not void on its face merely because of the omission of the word "remaining," where it should be stated that the land was sold for the payment of the "taxes, interest and costs then due and remaining unpaid." Heil *v.* Redden, 38 Kan. 255, 16 Pac. 743. A certificate of sale under which defendant claimed reciting that the taxes due were not paid and at the time of sale remained wholly unpaid, and that at the time of sale all the property assessed and delinquent as aforesaid was sold to the state, and a deed reciting that all the said property assessed and delinquent was by the sale vested in the state, substantially complied with Kan. Pol. Code, §§ 3776, 3785, providing that the certificate of sale of property for taxes and the deed thereof shall recite that the property was "sold for delinquent taxes." Phillips *v.* Cox, 7 Cal. App. 308, 94 Pac. 377.

Showing amount of delinquent taxes.—A tax deed from which it is impossible to determine the amount of the delinquent taxes is void. Finn *v.* Jones, 80 Kan. 431, 102 Pac. 479. A tax deed should show upon its face the amount of taxes, interest, and costs due upon each tract. Guffey *v.* O'Reiley, 88 Mo. 418, 57 Am. Rep. 424.

27. Harrington *v.* Worcester, 6 Allen (Mass.) 576. But see Cahoon *v.* Coe, 52 N. H. 518. And *compare* Gossett *v.* Kent, 19 Ark. 602.

28. *Arkansas.*— Spain *v.* Johnson, 31 Ark. 314.

California.— Simmons *v.* McCarthy, 118 Cal. 622, 50 Pac. 761.

Illinois.— Maxcy *v.* Clabaugh, 6 Ill. 26.

Louisiana.—Waddill *v.* Walton, 42 La. Ann. 763, 7 So. 737. And see Boyle *v.* West, 107 La. 347, 31 So. 794, holding that where the records show the year for which the property was sold, the deed is not invalidated by failure to recite such year.

Mississippi.— Bower *v.* Chess, etc., Co., 83 Miss. 218, 35 So. 444.

West Virginia.— Buchanan *v.* Reynolds, 4 W. Va. 681.

See 45 Cent. Dig. tit. "Taxation," §§ 1507, 1508.

But *compare* Utica Bank *v.* Mersereau, 3 Barb. Ch. (N. Y.) 528, 49 Am. Dec. 189; Marshall *v.* Benson, 48 Wis. 558, 4 N. W. 385, 762. A tax deed executed under Kan. Laws (1893), p. 195, c. 110, § 4, in substantial compliance with the requirements of that provision, and attacked more than five years after it was recorded, was not void on its face because the granting clause of such deed did not specify the particular years for the taxes of which the land was conveyed. Gibson *v.* Freeland, 77 Kan. 450, 94 Pac. 782. Omission of a tax deed which was not assailed for more than five years after being recorded to state in terms in what year the taxes accrued for the land which was sold, the sale having been made in 1895, was supplied by a recital that the total consideration of the deed was made up of the taxes of 1894 and subsequent years; it being inferable therefrom that the sale was made for the taxes of 1894. Gow *v.* Blackman, 78 Kan. 489, 96 Pac. 799.

29. See, generally, cases cited *infra*, this section. *Compare* Sibley *v.* Smith, 2 Mich. 486.

30. Whitehead *v.* Callahan, 44 Colo. 396, 99 Pac. 57.

31. Pixley *v.* Pixley, 164 Mass. 335, 41

h. Evidence to Explain, Supply, or Contradict Recitals.[69] Unless the statute makes the recitals of a tax deed conclusive evidence,[70] extrinsic evidence is admissible to explain these recitals for the purpose of supporting the validity of the deed,[71] as also to contradict or control them,[72] to supply defects and omissions in the deed,[73] and to correct misrecitals and clerical or other errors.[74]

3. DESCRIPTION OF PROPERTY — **a. Certainty and Sufficiency in General.** The description in the tax deed must be accurate enough to convey to the purchaser the precise land which he has bought and no other, and must be sufficiently clear and certain for all purposes of identification, both in support of the tax title and in order that it may not injuriously mislead parties interested in the land; if it fails in this it is void and passes no title.[75] Subject to this rule, and according

statutory form for a tax deed relating to the payment of subsequent taxes by the purchaser should be inserted in a deed, based on a sale to the county and an assignment of the certificate, only when the purchaser has paid taxes after the assignment of the certificate. Pierce *v.* Adams, 77 Kan. 46, 93 Pac. 594.

69. **Tax deeds as evidence** see *infra*, XIII, G.

Evidence to impeach deed or title see *infra*, XIII, G, 5.

70. Reckitt *v.* Knight, 16 S. D. 395, 92 N. W. 1077. And see Donohoe *v.* Veal, 19 Mo. 331. See *infra*, XIII, G, 2.

71. Greer *v.* Wheeler, 41 Iowa 85; John *v.* Young, 74 Kan. 865, 86 Pac. 295; Robbins *v.* Phillips, 74 Kan. 113, 85 Pac. 815. *Contra*, Greenwood *v.* Adams, 80 Cal. 74, 21 Pac. 1134; Preston *v.* Hirsch, 5 Cal. App. 485, 90 Pac. 965.

72. *Arkansas.*— Hickman *v.* Kempner, 35 Ark. 505.

California.— Landregan *v.* Peppin, 86 Cal. 122, 24 Pac. 859.

Illinois.— Billings *v.* Kankakee Coal Co., 67 Ill. 489.

Missouri.—Abbott *v.* Doling, 49 Mo. 302.

Pennsylvania.— Turner *v.* Waterson, 4 Watts & S. 171.

See 45 Cent. Dig. tit. "Taxation," § 1540 *et seq.*

73. Budd *v.* Bettison, 21 Ark. 582; Bonnell *v.* Roane, 20 Ark. 114; Moss *v.* Shear, 25 Cal. 38, 85 Am. Dec. 94; Clark *v.* Holton, 94 Ga. 542, 20 S. E. 429; John *v.* Young, 74 Kan. 865, 86 Pac. 295.

74. Klumpke *v.* Baker, 131 Cal. 80, 63 Pac. 137, 676; Knowles *v.* Martin, 20 Colo. 393, 38 Pac. 467; Kneeland *v.* Hull, 116 Mich. 55, 74 N. W. 300; Hardie *v.* Chrisman, 60 Miss. 671.

75. *Alabama.*—Francis *v.* Sandlin, 150 Ala. 583, 43 So. 829.

California.— Commercial Nat. Bank *v.* Schlitz, 6 Cal. App. 174, 91 Pac. 750. See Bosworth *v.* Danzien, 25 Cal. 296.

Colorado.— Lives *v.* Digges, 43 Colo. 166, 95 Pac. 341. See Halbouer *v.* Cuenin, 45 Colo. 507, 101 Pac. 763. Although Mills Annot. St. § 1901, prescribing the form of tax deeds, requires two descriptions of the property, one of the property assessed, and the other of the property sold, the second description need not be of the same particularity as the first, but any apt words which clearly indicate the property bid for and sold are sufficient, and hence, where the entire property assessed is sold the use of the words "said property," "the property above described," or "the whole of said property," is a sufficient compliance with the statute, being a description of the property bid for and sold by reference to the property described as taxed. Lines *v.* Digges, *supra.*

Indiana.— Sloan *v.* Sewell, 81 Ind. 180; Sharpe *v.* Dillman, 77 Ind. 280.

Iowa.— Martin *v.* Cole, 38 Iowa 141.

Kansas.— Robertson *v.* Lombard Liquidation Co., 73 Kan. 779, 85 Pac. 528; Kruse *v.* Fairchild, 73 Kan. 308, 85 Pac. 303; Ham *v.* Booth, 72 Kan. 429, 83 Pac. 24; Gibson *v.* Hammerburg, 72 Kan. 363, 83 Pac. 23; McDonough *v.* Merten, 53 Kan. 120, 35 Pac. 1117; Wood *v.* Nicholson, 43 Kan. 461, 23 Pac. 587; Wilkins *v.* Tourtellott, 28 Kan. 825; Hale *v.* Sweet, 7 Kan. App. 409, 53 Pac. 279.

Louisiana.— Levy *v.* Gause, 112 La. 789, 36 So. 684; Boyle *v.* West, 107 La. 347, 31 So. 794; Thibodaux *v.* Keller, 29 La. Ann. 508; Wills *v.* Auch, 8 La. Ann. 19.

Minnesota.— Kampfer *v.* East Side Syndicate, 95 Minn. 309, 104 N. W. 290; Bell *v.* McLaren, 89 Minn. 24, 93 N. W. 515.

Mississippi.— Cassidy *v.* Hartman, 93 Miss. 94, 46 So. 536; Boone *v.* Wells, 91 Miss. 799, 45 So. 571.

Missouri.—Where the proceedings for the sale of land for taxes and the deed pursuant thereto designated the landowner as "R. L. Hall," the deed was insufficient to convey the title of record of "Robert Lee Hall." Proctor *v.* Nance, 220 Mo. 104, 119 S. W. 409, 132 Am. St. Rep. 555.

New Hampshire.— Greely *v.* Steele, 2 N. H. 284, holding that a mistake as to the christian name of a former owner of the land will not avoid a tax deed.

New York.— People *v.* Golding, 55 Misc. 425, 106 N. Y. Suppl. 821; Utica Bank *v.* Mersereau, 3 Barb. Ch. 528, 49 Am. Dec. 189.

Ohio.— Marmet-Helm Coal, etc., Co. *v.* Cincinnati, etc., St. Ry., 28 Ohio Cir. Ct. 618.

Pennsylvania.— Norris *v.* Delaware, etc., R. Co., 218 Pa. St. 88, 56 Atl. 1122.

Texas.— Ozee *v.* Henrietta, 90 Tex. 334, 38 S. W. 768; Crumbley *v.* Busse, 11 Tex. Civ. App. 319, 32 S. W. 438.

Washington.— Miller *v.* Daniels, 47 Wash. 411, 92 Pac. 268.

Wisconsin.—Austin *v.* Holt, 32 Wis. 478.

to local usage, the description in the deed may be by metes and bounds,[76] or by giving the number of the lot and block,[77] or by giving the streets bounding the

United States.— Ontario Land Co. *v.* Wilfong, 162 Fed. 999 [*reversed* on other grounds in 171 Fed. 51, 96 C. C. A. 293.

Canada.—White *v.* Nelles, 11 Can. Sup. Ct. 587; Booth *v.* Girdwood, 32 U. C. Q. B. 23.

See 45 Cent. Dig. tit. "Taxation," §§ 1519, 1520.

Technical accuracy not required.—A tax deed is not void because the description is not technically accurate, where definite and certain enough to enable those familiar with it to readily recognize the land intended. Goodrow *v.* Stober, 80 Kan. 597, 102 Pac. 1089.

Exceptions and reservations see Abbott *v.* Coates, 62 Nebr. 247, 86 N. W. 1058; Day *v.* Needham, 2 Tex. Civ. App. 680, 22 S. W. 103; Pearson *v.* Mulholland, 17 Ont. 502.

Error as to one of several tracts.—An error in the description of one tract of land in a tax deed will not invalidate the deed as to other tracts included in it and properly described. Watkins *v.* Inge, 24 Kan. 612.

Application of recitals to several tracts.—In the case of a tax deed covering several tracts which has been of record for five years, failure to add to the statutory form, which includes but one description, words showing that the recitals apply to the tracts severally and not collectively, is not a fatal omission, but results at most in an ambiguity. Lincoln Mortg., etc., Co. *v.* Davis, 76 Kan. 639, 92 Pac. 707.

"Last hereinbefore described."—A tax deed which contains several distinct descriptions of real estate, and the granting clause of which provides that the real property "last hereinbefore described" is conveyed, is upon its face invalid as a conveyance of any tracts other than those included in the last description. Spicer *v.* Howe, 38 Kan. 465, 16 Pac. 825. A deed from a tax collector to the territory, which recites the assessment and levy of taxes for the year on property described as "Cabin and Lot 6 of Block 60 and Cabin and Lot 7 of Block 60" of a city and on personal property, and which states that the taxes were delinquent. and that the property was sold to the territory, and which conveys to the territory "all that lot . . . of land . . . above and last described in this deed," conveys only lot 7. Abell *v.* Swain, (Ariz. 1909) 100 Pac. 831.

Sale of least quantity bidder would take.—Where, under the statute, the sale was of the least quantity of the land which the bidder would take for the taxes, costs, etc., the deed, in addition to setting out this fact (see *supra*, XIII, D, 2, e), shows that the entire property assessed was sold, the use of the words "said property," "the property above described," or "the whole of said property," to indicate the property bid for and sold, describes with sufficient certainty the particular property sold, being a description of the property bid for and sold by reference to the property previously described as taxed. Lines *v.* Diggs, 43 Colo. 166, 95 Pac. 341. In Best *v.* Wohlford, 153 Cal. 17, 94 Pac. 98, a tax deed, having theretofore given a description of a parcel of land, and stated that the collector offered for sale the least quantity thereof to pay the assessment, etc., and that the grantee was the bidder who was willing to take the least quantity thereof, and pay the assessments etc., stated that the said least quantity or smallest portion of the land described was struck off to the grantee, and that the land was sold for assessments and subject to redemption. The granting clause stated that the collector thereby granted "all that lot, piece, or parcel of land so sold and hereinbefore and lastly described in this deed." It was held that the deed showed that the whole of the lot was the least quantity which any bidder was willing to take, and that such whole was in fact sold and conveyed by the deed, and that the deed was not open to the objection that it purported to convey the "least quantity or smallest portion," without designating what it was. *Compare*, however, Lines *v.* Digges, *supra*. A tax deed, reciting that a person named having offered to pay a certain sum, "being the whole amount of taxes, interest and costs then due and remaining unpaid on said property for 1889, to wit, NE[4] sec. 35-2-36, which was the least quantity bid for," is not open to the objection that the property is not described with sufficient certainty, in that the word "for" should have been used between the words "remaining unpaid" and "said property," instead of "on," as there immediately followed a description of the property, and the words "which was the least quantity bid for" removed any possible uncertainty. Howell *v.* Gruver, 78 Kan. 378, 97 Pac. 467.

76. *California.*— Brunn *v.* Murphy, 29 Cal. 326.

Kansas.— Dodge *v.* Emmons, 34 Kan. 732, 9 Pac. 951.

Louisiana.— Cooper *v.* Falk, 109 La. 474, 33 So. 567, holding insufficient the following description: "A certain tract of land assessed in the name of Robins and Cooper, containing six hundred and forty acres; boundaries unknown."

Massachusetts.—Hill *v.* Mowry, 6 Gray 551.

New York.— Zink *v.* McManus, 121 N. Y. 259, 24 N. E. 467; Oakley *v.* Healey, 38 Hun 244.

Wisconsin.— Scheiber *v.* Kaehler, 49 Wis. 291, 5 N. W. 817.

Canada.— McIntyre *v.* Great Western R. Co., 17 U. C. Q. B. 118.

See 45 Cent. Dig. tit. "Taxation," § 1520.

77. Gibson *v.* Shiner, 74 Kan. 728, 88 Pac. 259; Syer *v.* Bundy, 9 La. Ann. 540; Hubbard *v.* Arnold, 2 Tex. Unrep. Cas. 327; Wolf *v.* Gibbons, (Tex. Civ. App. 1902) 69 S. W. 238; Homes *v.* Henriette, (Tex. Civ. App.

b. Presumptions From Possession and Lapse of Time. As a general rule, and in the absence of a statute changing the common law in this respect, mere lapse of time will not of itself afford presumptive evidence of the regularity and validity of a tax-sale, if the purchaser and those claiming under him have not had pos-

91 Ind. 515; Farrar *v.* Clark, 85 Ind. 449; Smith *v.* Kyler, 74 Ind. 575; McEntire *v.* Brown, 28 Ind. 347; Ellis *v.* Kenyon, 25 Ind. 134; Gavin *v.* Shuman, 23 Ind. 32; Barnes *v.* Doe, 4 Ind. 132; Doe *v.* McQuilkin, 8 Blackf. 335; Mason *v.* Roe, 5 Blackf. 98; O'Brien *v.* Coulter, 2 Blackf. 421.

Iowa.— Blair Town Lot, etc., Co. *v.* Scott, 44 Iowa 143; McGahen *v.* Carr, 6 Iowa 331, 71 Am. Dec. 421; Gaylord *v.* Scarff, 6 Iowa 179; Laraby *v.* Reid, 3 Greene 419; Scott *v.* Babcock, 3 Greene 133; Fitch *v.* Casey, 2 Greene 300.

Kansas.— Ordway *v.* Cowles, 45 Kan. 447, 25 Pac. 862.

Kentucky.— Jones *v.* Miracle, 93 Ky. 639, 21 S. W. 241, 14 Ky. L. Rep. 639; Whipple *v.* Earick, 93 Ky. 121, 19 S. W. 237, 14 Ky. L. Rep. 85; Smith *v.* Ryan, 88 Ky. 636, 11 S. W. 647, 11 Ky. L. Rep. 128; Bishop *v.* Lovan, 4 B. Mon. 116; Craig *v.* Johnson, 3 T. B. Mon. 323; Terry *v.* Bleight, 3 T. B. Mon. 270, 16 Am. Dec. 101; Carlisle *v.* Cassady, 46 S. W. 490, 20 Ky. L. Rep. 562; Rice *v.* West, 42 S. W. 116, 19 Ky. L. Rep. 832; Pryor *v.* Hardwick, 22 S. W. 545, 15 Ky. L. Rep. 166. And see Griffin *v.* Sparks, 70 S. W. 30, 24 Ky. L. Rep. 849. *Compare* T. J. Moss Tie Co. *v.* Myers, (1909) 116 S. W. 255.

Louisiana.— Brady *v.* Offutt, 19 La. Ann. 184; Sutton *v.* Calhoun, 14 La. Ann. 209; Reeves *v.* Towles, 10 La. 276; Smith *v.* Corcoran, 7 La. 46; Nancarrow *v.* Weathersbee, 6 Mart. N. S. 347. And see Welsch *v.* Augusti, 52 La. Ann. 1949, 28 So. 363.

Maine.— McAllister *v.* Shaw, 69 Me. 348; French *v.* Patterson, 61 Me. 203; Worthing *v.* Webster, 45 Me. 270, 71 Am. Dec. 543; Matthews *v.* Light, 32 Me. 305; Brown *v.* Veazie, 25 Me. 359.

Maryland.— Dyer *v.* Boswell, 39 Md. 465; Beatty *v.* Mason, 30 Md. 409; Polk *v.* Rose, 25 Md. 153, 89 Am. Dec. 773; Alexander *v.* Walter, 8 Gill 239, 50 Am. Dec. 688.

Massachusetts.—Burke *v.* Burke, 170 Mass. 499, 49 N. E. 753; Blossom *v.* Cannon, 14 Mass. 177.

Michigan.— Norris *v.* Hall, 124 Mich. 170, 82 N. W. 832; Upton *v.* Kennedy, 36 Mich. 215.

Mississippi.— Sunflower Land, etc., Co. *v.* Watts, 77 Miss. 56, 25 So. 863; Chamberlain *v.* Lawrence County, 71 Miss. 949, 15 So. 40; Griffin *v.* Dogan, 48 Miss. 11; Natchez *v.* Minor, 10 Sm. & M. 246.

Missouri.— Nelson *v.* Goebel, 17 Mo. 161; Reeds *v.* Morton, 9 Mo. 878; Morton *v.* Reeds, 6 Mo. 64.

New Hampshire.— Cahoon *v.* Coe, 57 N. H. 556; Harvey *v.* Mitchell, 31 N. H. 575; Waldron *v.* Tuttle, 3 N. H. 340.

New Jersey.— Woodbridge Tp. *v.* State, 43 N. J. L. 262. And see Brooks *v.* Union Tp., 68 N. J. L. 133, 52 Atl. 238.

New York.— Westfall *v.* Preston, 49 N. Y. 349; Tallman *v.* White, 2 N. Y. 66; White *v.* Hill, 100 N. Y. App. Div. 207, 91 N. Y. Suppl. 623; Dever *v.* Haggerty, 43 N. Y. App. Div. 354, 60 N. Y. Suppl. 181 [*reversed* on other grounds in 169 N. Y. 481, 62 N. E. 586]; Hoyt *v.* Dillon, 19 Barb. 644; Varick *v.* Tallman, 2 Barb. 113; Stevens *v.* Palmer, 10 Bosw. 60; Sharp *v.* Speir, 4 Hill 76; Jackson *v.* Esty, 7 Wend. 148.

North Carolina.— Worth *v.* Simmons, 121 N. C. 357, 28 S. E. 528; Jordan *v.* Rouse, 46 N. C. 119; Pentland *v.* Stewart, 20 N. C. 521; Love *v.* Gates, 20 N. C. 498; Martin *v.* Lucey, 5 N. C. 311.

Ohio.— Rhodes *v.* Gunn, 35 Ohio St. 387; Thompson *v.* Gotham, 9 Ohio 170; Holt *v.* Hemphill, 3 Ohio 232; Clark *v.* Southard, 2 Ohio Dec. (Reprint) 612, 4 West. L. Month. 197.

Oregon.— Rafferty *v.* Davis, 54 Oreg. 77, 102 Pac. 305; Ayers *v.* Lund, 49 Oreg. 303, 89 Pac. 806, 124 Am. St. Rep. 1046.

Pennsylvania.— Stark *v.* Shupp, 112 Pa. St. 395, 3 Atl. 864; McReynolds *v.* Longenberger, 57 Pa. St. 13; Shearer *v.* Woodburn, 10 Pa. St. 511; Huston *v.* Foster, 1 Watts 477; Birch *v.* Fisher, 13 Serg. & R. 208; Blair *v.* Waggoner, 2 Serg. & R. 472; Blair *v.* Caldwell, 3 Yeates 284; Bernhard *v.* Allen, 10 Pa. Cas. 274, 14 Atl. 42; Canole *v.* Allen, 28 Pa. Super. Ct. 244.

Texas.— Dawson *v.* Ward, 71 Tex. 72, 9 S. W. 106; Clayton *v.* Rehm, 67 Tex. 52, 2 S. W. 45; Devine *v.* McCulloch, 15 Tex. 488; Robson *v.* Osborn, 13 Tex. 298; Yenda *v.* Wheeler, 9 Tex. 408; Hubbard *v.* Arnold, 2 Tex. Unrep. Cas. 327; Fant *v.* Brannin, 2 Tex. Unrep. Cas. 323; Lewright *v.* Walls, (Civ. App. 1909) 119 S. W. 721; Keenan *v.* Slaughter, 49 Tex. Civ. App. 180, 108 S. W. 703; Woody *v.* Strong, 45 Tex. Civ. App. 256, 100 S. W. 801; Lamberida *v.* Barnum, (Civ. App. 1905) 90 S. W. 698.

Utah.— Asper *v.* Moon, 24 Utah 241, 67 Pac. 409.

Vermont.— Brush *v.* Watson, 81 Vt. 43, 69 Atl. 141; Downer *v.* Tarbell, 61 Vt. 530, 17 Atl. 482; Cummings *v.* Holt, 56 Vt. 384; Wing *v.* Hall, 47 Vt. 182; Townsend *v.* Downer, 32 Vt. 183; Chandler *v.* Spear, 22 Vt. 388; Langdon *v.* Poor, 20 Vt. 13; Judevine *v.* Jackson, 18 Vt. 470; Carpenter *v.* Sawyer, 17 Vt. 121; May *v.* Wright, 17 Vt. 97, 42 Am. Dec. 481; Sumner *v.* Sherman, 13 Vt. 609; Bellows *v.* Elliot, 12 Vt. 569; Spear *v.* Ditty, 9 Vt. 282; Richardson *v.* Dorr, 5 Vt. 9; Hall *v.* Collins, 4 Vt. 316; Mix *v.* Whitlock, 1 Tyler 30.

Virginia.— Hobbs *v.* Shumates, 11 Gratt. 516; Chapman *v.* Doe, 2 Leigh 329; Nalle *v.* Fenwick, 4 Rand. 585.

West Virginia.— Columbia Finance, etc., Co. *v.* Fierbaugh, 59 W. Va. 334, 53 S. E. 468.

session under the deed; that is, the antiquity of a tax deed, if no possession has been taken under it, affords no presumption in its favor, but on the contrary operates the more strongly against the holder.[27] But on the other hand, an ancient tax deed and its recitals, together with long-continued and uninterrupted possession, are evidence from which compliance with the statute regulating tax-sales may be presumed.[28] In regard to the length of time during which possession must have continued in order to raise this presumption, no certain rule can be gathered from the authorities, but it is doubtful whether any time less than the full period prescribed by the statute of limitations will suffice.[29]

c. Effect of Tax Deed as Evidence. At common law, neither the tax deed nor its recitals can be accepted as evidence of the existence, legality, or validity of the prior proceedings, but these must be proved step by step as a necessary preliminary to the introduction of the deed as evidence of title.[30] Exceptions to this

Wisconsin.— Bridge *v.* Bracken, 3 Pinn. 73, 3 Chandl. 75.

United States.— Little *v.* Herndon, 10 Wall. 26, 19 L. ed. 878; Parker *v.* Overman, 18 How. 137, 15 L. ed. 318 [*affirming* 18 Fed. Cas. No. 10,623, Hempst. 692]; Pillow *v.* Roberts, 13 How. 472, 14 L. ed. 228; Games *v.* Dunn, 14 Pet. 322, 10 L. ed. 476 [*affirming* 8 Fed. Cas. No. 4,176, 1 McLean 321]; Boardman *v.* Reed, 6 Pet. 328, 8 L. ed. 415; Thatcher *v.* Powell, 6 Wheat. 119, 5 L. ed. 221; Williams *v.* Peyton, 4 Wheat. 77, 4 L. ed. 518; Parker *v.* Rule, 9 Cranch 64, 3 L. ed. 658 [*affirming* 20 Fed. Cas. No. 12,125, Brunn. Col. Cas. 239, Cooke (Tenn.) 365]; Stead *v.* Course, 4 Cranch 403, 2 L. ed. 660; Lamb *v.* Gillett, 14 Fed. Cas. No. 8,016, 6 McLean 365; Miner *v.* McLean, 17 Fed. Cas. No. 9,630, 4 McLean 138. *Compare* Ronkendorff *v.* Taylor, 4 Pet. 349, 7 L. ed. 882.

Canada.—Alloway *v.* Campbell, 7 Manitoba 506; Cameron *v.* Lee, 27 Quebec Super. Ct. 535.

See 45 Cent. Dig. tit. "Taxation," § 1559. And see the cases cited *infra*, XIII, G, 1, c, d.

Purchase by state.—A presumption can no more be indulged in favor of the validity of a tax-sale, where the state is the purchaser, than where an individual purchases. Lewright *v.* Walls, (Tex. Civ. App. 1909) 119 S. W. 721.

27. *Arkansas.*— Parr *v.* Matthews, 50 Ark. 390, 8 S. W. 22.

District of Columbia.—Keefe *v.* Bramhall, 3 Mackey 551.

Maine.— McAllister *v.* Shaw, 69 Me. 348; Worthing *v.* Webster, 45 Me. 270, 71 Am. Dec. 543. *Compare* Freeman *v.* Thayer, 33 Me. 76.

New Hampshire.— Waldron *v.* Tuttle, 3 N. H. 340.

New York.— Westbrook *v.* Willey, 47 N. Y. 457; Turner *v.* Boyce, 11 Misc. 502, 33 N. Y. Suppl. 433.

North Carolina.— Eastern Land, etc., Co. *v.* State Bd. of Education, 101 N. C. 35, 7 S. E. 573.

Pennsylvania.— Coxe *v.* Deringer, 78 Pa. St. 271; Alexander *v.* Bush, 46 Pa. St. 62; Shearer *v.* Woodburn, 10 Pa. St. 511; Deringer *v.* Coxe, 6 Pa. Cas. 283, 10 Atl. 412. But see Foust *v.* Ross, 1 Watts & S. 501. And *compare* Lackawanna Iron, etc., Co. *v.* Fales, 55 Pa. St. 90; Read *v.* Goodyear, 17 Serg. & R. 350.

Texas.— Telfener *v.* Dillard, 70 Tex. 139, 7 S. W. 847.

Vermont.— Downer *v.* Tarbell, 61 Vt. 530, 17 Atl. 482; Brown *v.* Wright, 17 Vt. 97, 42 Am. Dec. 481; Reed *v.* Field, 15 Vt. 672.

See 45 Cent. Dig. tit. "Taxation," § 1564.

Compare Keane *v.* Cannovan, 21 Cal. 291, 82 Am. Dec. 738; Colman *v.* Anderson, 10 Mass. 105.

28. *Arkansas.*— Pleasants *v.* Scott, 21 Ark. 370, 76 Am. Dec. 403.

Louisiana.— Gouaux *v.* Beaullieu, 123 La. 684, 49 So. 285; Corkran Oil, etc., Co. *v.* Arnaudet, 111 La. 563, 35 So. 747.

Maine.— Worthing *v.* Webster, 45 Me. 270, 71 Am. Dec. 543.

New Hampshire.— Waldron *v.* Tuttle, 3 N. H. 340.

Ohio.— Fitzpatrick *v.* Forsythe, 6 Ohio Dec. (Reprint) 682, 7 Am. L. Rec. 411.

Virginia.— Lennig *v.* White, (1894) 20 S. E. 831; Flanagan *v.* Grimmet, 10 Gratt. 421.

Wisconsin.— Sprecker *v.* Wakeley, 11 Wis. 432.

United States.— Williams *v.* William J. Athens Lumber Co., 62 Fed. 558.

See 45 Cent. Dig. tit. "Taxation," § 1564.

29. Phillips *v.* Sherman, 61 Me. 548; Townsend *v.* Downer, 32 Vt. 183; Richardson *v.* Dorr, 5 Vt. 9; Allen *v.* Smith, 1 Leigh (Va.) 231; Sprecker *v.* Wakeley, 11 Wis. 432. *Compare* Fitzpatrick *v.* Forsythe, 6 Ohio Dec. (Reprint) 682, 7 Am. L. Rec. 411.

30. *Alabama.*— Collins *v.* Robinson, 33 Ala. 91.

California.— Emeric *v.* Alvarado, 90 Cal. 444, 27 Pac. 356.

District of Columbia.—Keefe *v.* Bramhall, 3 Mackey 551.

Georgia.— Johnson *v.* Phillips, 89 Ga. 286, 15 S. E. 368; Butler *v.* Davis, 68 Ga. 173.

Illinois.— Glanz *v.* Ziabek, 233 Ill. 22, 84 N. E. 36; Glos *v.* Mulcahy, 210 Ill. 639, 71 N. E. 629; Anderson *v.* McCormick, 129 Ill. 308, 21 N. E. 803; Skinner *v.* Fulton, 39 Ill. 484; Goewey *v.* Urig, 18 Ill. 238; Doe *v.* Bean, 6 Ill. 302; Doe *v.* Leonard, 5 Ill. 140.

deed presumptive evidence of title which would not have been so at the time of the sale.[55] On the other hand it is competent to repeal a law of this kind, and it cannot be said that contractual rights are impaired, although the repeal affects deeds in existence at the time.[56]

4. EFFECT OF STATUTES MAKING TAX DEEDS EVIDENCE — **a. In General.** The effect of the statutes under consideration is to dispense with the necessity of proving the various steps in the tax proceedings, one by one, and to permit the introduction of the tax deed in evidence without preliminary proof.[57] If the statute enumerates the particular matters as to which it shall be presumptive evidence, all other essential steps must of course be proved;[58] but where, as is more usually the case, it makes the deed evidence of the facts recited in it, these need not be separately proved, in the first instance, but the deed will *prima facie* establish their existence and regularity;[59] and where the tax deed is made pre-

L. Rep. 1221; Heyward *v.* Christensen, 80 S. C. 146, 61 S. E. 399.

55. Wildharber *v.* Lunkenheimer, 128 Ky. 344, 108 S. W. 327, 32 Ky. L. Rep. 1221; Freeman *v.* Thayer, 33 Me. 76; Heyward *v.* Christensen, 80 S. C. 146, 61 S. E. 399. But see Keane *v.* Cannovan, 21 Cal. 291, 82 Am. Dec. 738; Norris *v.* Russell, 5 Cal. 249; Garrett *v.* Doe, 2 Ill. 335.

56. Emeric *v.* Alvarado, 90 Cal. 444, 27 Pac. 356; Gage *v.* Caraher, 125 Ill. 447, 17 N. E. 777. And see Madland *v.* Benland, 24 Minn. 372. But *compare* Fisher *v.* Betts, 12 N. D. 197, 96 N. W. 132.

57. *Alabama.*— Doe *v.* Moog, 150 Ala. 460, 43 So. 710.

Arkansas.— Jacks *v.* Kelley Trust Co., 90 Ark. 548, 120 S. W. 142; Morris *v.* Breedlove, 89 Ark. 296, 116 S. W. 223; Doniphan Lumber Co. *v.* Reid, 82 Ark. 31, 100 S. W. 69; Cracraft *v.* Meyer, 76 Ark. 450, 88 S. W. 1027; Thornton *v.* St. Louis Refrigerator, etc., Co., 69 Ark. 424, 65 S. W. 113; Alexander *v.* Bridgford, 59 Ark. 195, 27 S. W. 69; Scott *v.* Mills, 49 Ark. 266, 4 S. W. 908.

California.— Best *v.* Wohlford, 153 Cal. 17, 94 Pac. 98; Davis *v.* Pacific Imp. Co., 7 Cal. App. 452, 94 Pac. 595; Commercial Nat. Bank *v.* Schlitz, 6 Cal. App. 174, 91 Pac. 750. But *compare* Norris *v.* Russell, 5 Cal. 249.

Florida.— Saunders *v.* Collins, 56 Fla. 534, 47 So. 958; Stieff *v.* Hartwell, 35 Fla. 606, 17 So. 899.

Illinois.— Graves *v.* Bruen, 11 Ill. 431; Vance *v.* Schuyler, 6 Ill. 160.

Indiana.— May *v.* Dobbins, 166 Ind. 331, 77 N. E. 353; Bivens *v.* Henderson, 42 Ind. App. 562, 86 N. E. 426; Holbrook *v.* Kunz, 41 Ind. App. 260, 83 N. E. 730.

Iowa.— McCash *v.* Penrod, 131 Iowa 631, 109 N. W. 180; Allen *v.* Armstrong, 16 Iowa 508.

Kansas.— Bowman *v.* Cockrill, 6 Kan. 311.

Kentucky.— Wildharber *v.* Lunkenheimer, 128 Ky. 344, 108 S. W. 327, 32 Ky. L. Rep. 1221; Alexander *v.* Aud, 121 Ky. 10, 88 S. W. 1103, 28 Ky. L. Rep. 69.

Michigan.— Sibley *v.* Smith, 2 Mich. 486.

Minnesota.— Madland *v.* Benland, 24 Minn. 372; Broughton *v.* Sherman, 21 Minn. 431.

New York.— Baer *v.* McCullough, 176 N. Y. 97, 68 N. E. 129; Finlay *v.* Cook, 54 Barb. 9.

North Carolina.— Matthews *v.* Fry, 141 N. C. 582, 54 S. E. 379.

Ohio.— Stanbery *v.* Sillon, 13 Ohio St. 571; Turney *v.* Yeoman, 14 Ohio 207.

Pennsylvania.— Hubley *v.* Keyser, 2 Penr. & W. 496.

South Carolina.— Heyward *v.* Christensen, 80 S. C. 146, 61 S. E. 399.

South Dakota.— St. Paul, etc., R. Co. *v.* Howard, 23 S. D. 34, 119 N. W. 1032.

Virginia.— Smith *v.* Chapman, 10 Gratt. 445.

Washington.— Ward *v.* Huggins, 7 Wash. 617, 32 Pac. 740, 1015, 36 Pac. 285. See Tacoma Gas, etc., Co. *v.* Pauley, 49 Wash. 562, 95 Pac. 1103.

West Virginia.— Hogan *v.* Piggott, 60 W. Va. 541, 56 S. E. 189.

Wisconsin.— Whitney *v.* Marshall, 17 Wis. 174.

United States.— Lamb *v.* Gillett, 14 Fed. Cas. No. 8,016, 6 McLean 365; McQuain *v.* Meline, 16 Fed. Cas. No. 8,923.

See 45 Cent. Dig. tit. "Taxation," § 1557.

58. Parker *v.* Smith, 4 Blackf. (Ind.) 70; Cucullu *v.* Brakenridge Lumber Co., 49 La. Ann. 1445, 22 So. 409; Latimer *v.* Lovett, 2 Dougl. (Mich.) 204; King *v.* Cooper, 128 N. C. 347, 38 S. E. 924.

Proof that owner had no available personal property see Richard *v.* Carrie, 145 Ind. 49, 43 N. E. 949; Pitcher *v.* Dove, 99 Ind. 175; Earle *v.* Simons, 94 Ind. 573; Ellis *v.* Kenyon, 25 Ind. 134; Stewart *v.* Corbin, 25 Iowa 144; Doremus *v.* Cameron, 49 N. J. Eq. 1, 22 Atl. 802.

59. *Alabama.*— Riddle *v.* Messer, 84 Ala. 236, 4 So. 185.

Arkansas.— Bonnell *v.* Roane, 20 Ark. 114.

Illinois.— Ransom *v.* Henderson, 114 Ill. 528, 4 N. E. 141.

Kentucky.— Morton *v.* Waring, 18 B. Mon. 72.

Louisiana.— Welsch *v.* Augusti, 52 La. Ann. 1949, 28 So. 363.

Michigan.— Hoffman *v.* Silverthorn, 137 Mich. 60, 100 N. W. 183.

Mississippi.— Chamberlain *v.* Lawrence County, 71 Miss. 949, 15 So. 40.

Missouri.— Wall *v.* Holladay-Klotz Land, etc., Co., 175 Mo. 406, 75 S. W. 385.

New York.— See Jackson *v.* Esty, 7 Wend. 148.

(III) *Judgment and Precept or Order of Sale.* In some states where a tax-sale of land is founded on the judgment or decree of a court, it is necessary, before receiving the tax deed as evidence of title, that the party relying on it shall first show the judgment and the precept or order of sale thereon, these facts not being proved by the recitals of the deed.[84]

i. Effect of Such Statutes in Other States. A tax deed properly executed, and which is made presumptive evidence of title or of the regularity of the prior proceedings by a statute of the state where such proceedings were had, is admissible for the same purpose and has the same effect in the courts of any other state.[85]

5. Evidence to Impeach Deed or Title [86] — a. In General. Although a tax deed is by law made *prima facie* evidence of compliance with the provisions of the statute regulating tax-sales, yet it may be impeached by showing any substantial failure of such compliance; and when this is done its presumptive weight is overcome and the case thrown open.[87] Also it may be shown against the deed that

Co., 45 Minn. 66, 47 N. W. 453; Cogel *v.* Raph, 24 Minn. 194.

Nebraska.— Merriam *v.* Dovey, 25 Nebr. 618, 41 N. W. 550.

North Dakota.— State Finance Co. *v.* Trimble, 16 N. D. 199, 112 N. W. 984; State Finance Co. *v.* Beck, 15 N. D. 374, 109 N. W. 357.

Oregon.— Minter *v.* Durham, 13 Oreg. 470, 11 Pac. 231.

United States.— Daniels *v.* Case, 45 Fed. 843; Sonoma County Tax Case, 13 Fed. 789, 8 Sawy. 312; Roberts *v.* Pillow, 20 Fed. Cas. No. 11,909, 1 Hempst. 624.

Acknowledgment.—A tax deed void on its face because it was not acknowledged before the proper officer is inadmissible for the purpose of proving title in the purchaser, or his right to possession. Matthews *v.* Blake, 16 Wyo. 116, 92 Pac. 242, 27 L. R. A. N. S. 339.

Canceled deed.— Where a public officer, by statutory authority, issues a certificate canceling an existing tax deed, it is no longer evidence of title in the purchaser. Nowlen *v.* Hall, 128 Mich. 274, 87 N. W. 222.

84. *California.*— People *v.* Doe, 31 Cal. 220.

Georgia.— Sabattie *v.* Baggs, 55 Ga. 572.

Illinois.— Glanz *v.* Ziabek, 233 Ill. 22, 84 N. E. 36; Metropolitan West Side El. R. Co. *v.* Eschner, 232 Ill. 210, 83 N. E. 809; Blair *v.* Johnson, 215 Ill. 552, 74 N. E. 747; Gage *v.* Thompson, 161 Ill. 403, 43 N. E. 1062; Gilbreath *v.* Dilday, 152 Ill. 207, 38 N. E. 572; Perry *v.* Burton, 126 Ill. 599, 18 N. E. 653; Gage *v.* Caraher, 125 Ill. 447, 17 N. E. 777; Bell *v.* Johnson, 111 Ill. 374; Smith *v.* Hutchinson, 108 Ill. 662; Gage *v.* Lightburn, 93 Ill. 248; Cottingham *v.* Springer, 88 Ill. 90; Wilding *v.* Horner, 50 Ill. 50; Elston *v.* Kennicott, 46 Ill. 187; Charles *v.* Waugh, 35 Ill. 315; Baily *v.* Doolittle, 24 Ill. 577; Dukes *v.* Rowley, 24 Ill. 210; Marsh *v.* Chestnut, 14 Ill. 223; Spellman *v.* Curtenius, 12 Ill. 409; Lusk *v.* Harber, 8 Ill. 158; Atkins *v.* Hinman, 7 Ill. 437; Hinman *v.* Pope, 6 Ill. 131.

Indiana.— Burt *v.* Hasselman, 139 Ind. 196, 38 N. E. 598; Doe *v.* Himelick, 4 Blackf. 494.

Michigan.— McKinnon *v.* Meston, 104 Mich. 642, 62 N. W. 1014; Taylor *v.* Deveaux, 100 Mich. 581, 59 N. W. 250.

Nevada.— Bolan *v.* Bolan, 4 Nev. 150.

Tennessee.— Johnson *v.* Mills, 3 Hayw. 38; Castleman *v.* Phillipsburg Land Co., 1 Tenn. Ch. App. 9.

United States.—Little *v.* Herndon, 10 Wall. 26, 19 L. ed. 878, construing Illinois statute.

See 45 Cent. Dig. tit. "Taxation," § 1558.

Deed as evidence of collateral fact.— Although a tax deed is not evidence of title without proof of a valid judgment and precept, it may be offered in evidence to prove the *bona fides* of the purchaser. Sawyer *v.* Campbell, (Ill. 1885) 2 N. E. 660.

85. Watson *v.* Atwood, 25 Conn. 313; Bronson *v.* St. Croix Lumber Co., 44 Minn. 348, 46 N. W. 570. *Compare* Bisbee *v.* Torinus, 22 Minn. 555.

86. **Evidence to explain, supply, or contradict recitals in deed see** *supra*, XIII, D, 2, h.

87. *Arkansas.*— Morris *v.* Breedlove, 89 Ark. 296, 116 S. W. 223; Townsend *v.* Martin, 55 Ark. 192, 17 S. W. 875; Williamson *v.* Mimms, 49 Ark. 336, 5 S. W. 320; Hickman *v.* Kempner, 35 Ark. 505.

Florida.— Starks *v.* Sawyer, 56 Fla. 596, 47 So. 513.

Idaho.— McMasters *v.* Torsen, 7 Ida. 536, 51 Pac. 100.

Illinois.— Job *v.* Tebbetts, 10 Ill. 376.

Indiana.— Skelton *v.* Sharp, 161 Ind. 383, 67 N. E. 535; Wilson *v.* Lemon, 23 Ind. 433, 85 Am. Dec. 471; Brown *v.* Reeves, 31 Ind. App. 517, 68 N. E. 604.

Iowa.— Farmers' L. & T. Co. *v.* Wall, 129 Iowa 651, 106 N. W. 160; Long *v.* Burnett, 13 Iowa 28, 81 Am. Dec. 420; Rayburn *v.* Kuhl, 10 Iowa 92; Laraby *v.* Reid, 3 Greene 419.

Kansas.— City R. Co. *v.* Chesney, 30 Kan. 199, 1 Pac. 520.

Kentucky.— The statute requiring the original owner of land, in order to defeat a tax title, to show that the assessment, the levy, and sale were defective, shifted the burden to the owner, but did not change the rule that, before one can obtain a complete tax title, each legal step required by law to

the land in question was not subject to taxation at the time it was assessed,[88] or that the purchaser at the tax-sale was disqualified from acquiring the title by reason of a duty resting on him to pay the taxes.[89]

b. Levy and Assessment. Under the rule just stated, it is competent for the party seeking to impeach or invalidate a tax title, notwithstanding the recitals in the deed, to show that there was no levy of the tax in question,[90] that the levy was illegal or for an unlawful purpose,[91] that the land was never assessed for taxation,[92] or that the assessment was so erroneous, irregular, or defective as not to sustain the subsequent tax-sale founded thereon.[93]

c. Sale. Notwithstanding the effect given by statute to tax deeds as presumptive evidence, it is competent to show, in opposition to the title founded

subject land to sale must be complied with. Hamilton *v.* Steele, (1909) 117 S. W. 378.

Louisiana.— Tensas Delta Land Co. *v.* Sholars, 105 La. 357, 29 So. 908; Waddill *v.* Walton, 42 La. Ann. 763, 7 So. 737; State *v.* Herron, 29 La. Ann. 848; Winter *v.* Atkinson, 28 La. Ann. 650.

Michigan.—See Watts *v.* Bublitz, 99 Mich. 586, 58 N. W. 465.

Mississippi.— National Bank of the Republic *v.* Louisville, etc., R. Co., 72 Miss. 447, 17 So. 7; Hardie *v.* Chrisman, 60 Miss. 671; Caston *v.* Caston, 60 Miss. 475; Ray *v.* Murdock, 36 Miss. 692.

Missouri.— Kinney *v.* Forsythe, 96 Mo. 414, 9 S. W. 918; Ewart *v.* Davis, 76 Mo. 129.

New York.— Curtiss *v.* Follett, 15 Barb. 337.

North Dakota.— Cruser *v.* Williams, 13 N. D. 284, 100 N. W. 721.

Ohio.— Turney *v.* Yeoman, 16 Ohio 24. See Gwynne *v.* Neiswanger, 18 Ohio 400.

Pennsylvania.— Simpson *v.* Meyers, 197 Pa. St. 522, 47 Atl. 868.

South Carolina.— Bull *v.* Kirk, 37 S. C. 395, 16 S. E. 151.

Tennessee.—Randolph *v.* Metcalf, 6 Coldw. 400; Henderson *v.* Staritt, 4 Sneed 470.

West Virginia.— Dequasie *v.* Harris, 16 W. Va. 345.

Wisconsin.—Burrows *v.* Bashford, 22 Wis. 103; Delaplaine *v.* Cook, 7 Wis. 44.

United States.— Martin *v.* Barbour, 140 U. S. 634, 11 S. Ct. 944, 35 L. ed. 546; Gage *v.* Kaufman, 133 U. S. 471, 10 S. Ct. 406, 33 L. ed. 725; Kelly *v.* Herrall, 20 Fed. 364.

See 45 Cent. Dig. tit. "Taxation," § 1566 *et seq.*

Statute restricting defenses see Gibbs *v.* Dortch, 62 Miss. 671; Davis *v.* Vanarsdale, 59 Miss. 367; Greene *v.* Williams, 58 Miss. 752.

88. Treat *v.* Lawrence, 42 Wis. 330.

89. Blakeley *v.* Bestor, 13 Ill. 708.

90. Florida Sav. Bank *v.* Brittain, 20 Fla. 507; Hintrager *v.* Kiene, 62 Iowa 605, 15 N. W. 568, 17 N. W. 910.

91. Parr *v.* Matthews, 50 Ark. 390, 8 S. W. 22; Lufkin *v.* Galveston, 73 Tex. 340, 11 S. W. 340; Culbertson *v.* H. Whitbeck Co., 127 U. S. 326, 8 S. Ct. 1136, 32 L. ed. 134.

92. *Illinois.*— Schuyler *v.* Hull, 11 Ill. 462; Tibbetts *v.* Job, 11 Ill. 453; Graves *v.* Bruen, 11 Ill. 431.

Iowa.— Barrett *v.* Kevane, 100 Iowa 653, 69 N. W. 1036; Lathrop *v.* Irwin, 96 Iowa 713, 65 N. W. 972; Slocum *v.* Slocum, 70 Iowa 259, 30 N. W. 562; Easton *v.* Savery, 44 Iowa 654.

Louisiana.— *In re* Lake, 40 La. Ann. 142, 3 So. 479.

Washington.— Hurd *v.* Brisner, 3 Wash. 1, 28 Pac. 371, 28 Am. St. Rep. 17.

United States.— Parker *v.* Overman, 18 How. 137, 15 L. ed. 318.

See 45 Cent. Dig. tit. "Taxation," § 1567.

93. *California.*— Daly *v.* Ah Goon, 64 Cal. 512, 2 Pac. 401.

Florida.— Daniel *v.* Taylor, 33 Fla. 636, 15 So. 313; Brown *v.* Castellaw, 33 Fla. 204, 14 So. 822; Mundee *v.* Freeman, 23 Fla. 529, 3 So. 153; Donald *v.* McKinnon, 17 Fla. 746.

Illinois.— Hough *v.* Hastings, 18 Ill. 312; Grave *v.* Bruen, 6 Ill. 167.

Iowa.— Cassady *v.* Sapp, 64 Iowa 203, 19 N. W. 909; Sully *v.* Kuehl, 30 Iowa 275. But see Robinson *v.* Cedar Rapids First Nat. Bank, 48 Iowa 354.

Michigan.— Williams *v.* Mears, 61 Mich. 86, 27 N. W. 863.

Mississippi.— Gibbs *v.* Dortch, 62 Miss. 671; Davis *v.* Vanarsdale, 59 Miss. 367.

New York.— People *v.* Turner, 117 N. Y. 227, 22 N. E. 1022, 15 Am. St. Rep. 498; Colman *v.* Shattuck, 62 N. Y. 348; Ne-ha-sa-ne Park Assoc. *v.* Lloyd, 7 N. Y. App. Div. 359, 40 N. Y. Suppl. 58; Turner *v.* Boyce, 11 Misc. 502, 33 N. Y. Suppl. 433.

Oregon.— Strode *v.* Washer, 17 Oreg. 50, 16 Pac. 926.

Pennsylvania.— Miller *v.* McCullough, 104 Pa. St. 624.

Texas.— Meredith *v.* Coker, 65 Tex. 29.

Washington.— Baer *v.* Choir, 7 Wash. 631, 32 Pac. 776, 36 Pac. 286.

West Virginia.— Dequasie *v.* Harris, 16 W. Va. 345.

Wisconsin.— Marshall *v.* Benson, 48 Wis. 558, 4 N. W. 385, 762; Treat *v.* Lawrence, 42 Wis. 330; Orton *v.* Noonan, 25 Wis. 672; Eaton *v.* North, 20 Wis. 449.

United States.— Mathews *v.* Burdick, 48 Fed. 894.

See 45 Cent. Dig. tit. "Taxation," § 1567. And see *supra*, XI, C, 2.

Contra.— Burgett *v.* Williford, 56 Ark. 187, 19 S. W. 750, 35 Am. St. Rep. 96. And see Scott *v.* Mills, 49 Ark. 266, 4 S. W. 908;

without the consent of the former, it is a trespass,[26] although under some statutes the holder of the tax title is entitled to possession until the property is redeemed.[27] But when the purchaser has obtained his deed he is entitled to the possession, and to hold it against a mortgagee or *cestui que trust*.[28] He must, however, obtain the possession in fact, either peaceably or by the aid of judicial process,[29] the tax deed itself not being sufficient to give him a constructive possession.[30] But a purchaser of a tax title is not entitled to possession of the property where his purchase is only of an inchoate interest in the property.[31] Under some statutes the holder of a tax title is not entitled to possession as against subsequent tax titles, until he has acquired all of such subsequent titles.[32]

(II) *LOSS OF TITLE BY FAILURE OF POSSESSION OR BY ADVERSE POSSESSION.* In the absence of a statute to that effect, the purchaser at a tax-sale does not forfeit his rights by a failure to take possession of the premises.[33] But it is now provided by law in several states that this result shall follow if he fails to acquire the possession within a special limited time;[34] and either under these statutes or under the general rules of adverse possession and the limitation of actions, continued possession on the part of the owner, protracted for a sufficient length of time, will bar all claims of the tax purchaser under his deed.[35]

App. 421, 78 S. W. 704, 79 S. W. 40; Ryon *v.* Davis, 32 Tex. Civ. App. 500, 75 S. W. 59; Masterson *v.* State, 17 Tex. Civ. App. 91, 42 S. W. 1003.

Vermont.— Wing *v.* Hall, 47 Vt. 182.

Wisconsin.— Lacy *v.* Johnson, 58 Wis. 414, 17 N. W. 246.

See 45 Cent. Dig. tit. "Taxation," § 1474.

26. Ives *v.* Beeler, (Kan. App. 1900) 59 Pac. 726.

But possession under a tax or assessment lease for a term of years is not adverse to the title of the owner in fee, but is in subordination thereto. Miller *v.* Warren, 94 N. Y. App. Div. 192, 87 N. Y. Suppl. 1011 [*affirmed* in 182 N. Y. 539, 75 N. E. 1131].

27. Donohoe *v.* Veal, 19 Mo. 331; Hack *v.* Heffern, 19 Ohio Cir. Ct. 233, 10 Ohio Cir. Dec. 461, possession under deed. See also Pratt *v.* Roseland R. Co., 50 N. J. Eq. 150, 24 Atl. 1027. But see Thevenin *v.* Slocum, 16 Ohio 519.

28. Allen *v.* McCabe, 93 Mo. 138, 6 S. W. 62.

29. Mitchell *v.* Titus, 33 Colo. 385, 80 Pac. 1042; Welsch *v.* Augusti, 52 La. Ann. 1949, 28 So. 363; Martin *v.* Langenstein, 43 La. Ann. 789, 9 So. 507.

Recovery of possession by tax purchaser see *infra*, XIV, B, 1, a.

Where the holder of a tax title finds the premises unoccupied he may enter, and in doing so is not liable to the original owner. Steltz *v.* Morgan, 16 Ida. 368, 101 Pac. 1057, 28 L. R. A. N. S. 398.

30. Mitchell *v.* Titus, 33 Colo. 385, 80 Pac. 1042; Weir *v.* Cordz-Fisher Lumber Co., 186 Mo. 388, 85 S. W. 341. And see *supra*, XIII, F, 1.

31. Gitchell *v.* Messmer, 14 Mo. App. 83 [*affirmed* in 87 Mo. 131], holding that where land belonging to a wife is assessed to the husband and for non-payment of taxes on judgment against him sold on execution, the purchaser's right is only that of a tenant by the curtesy initiate, and he cannot disturb the wife's possession.

32. Sinclair *v.* Learned, 51 Mich. 335, 16 N. W. 672, holding also that the subsequent title which will preclude possession need not necessarily be a legal tax title, although the tax on which it is based must be one that is not merely arbitrary.

33. Koen *v.* Martin, 110 La. 242, 34 So. 429.

Possession taken of wrong tract.— If the tax purchaser takes possession of a wrong tract by a mistake as to its identity, he is not precluded, on discovering his mistake, from asserting his right to that which he purchased. Hiester *v.* Laird, 1 Watts & S. (Pa.) 245.

Forfeiture of title by county.— Title acquired by a county by purchase at a tax-sale is lost, if it thereafter taxes the same property and sells it for taxes, so that one to whom it thereafter conveys the land takes no title. Feltz *v.* Nathalie Anthracite Coal Co., 203 Pa. St. 166, 52 Atl. 82.

34. See the statutes of the several states. And see the following cases:

Colorado.— Halbouer *v.* Cuenin, 45 Colo. 507, 101 Pac. 763.

Iowa.— Hintrager *v.* Hennessy, 46 Iowa 600; Wallace *v.* Sexton, 44 Iowa 257; Laverty *v.* Sexton, 41 Iowa 435; Peck *v.* Sexton, 41 Iowa 566; Brown *v.* Painter, 38 Iowa 456.

North Dakota.— Beggs *v.* Paine, 15 N. D. 436, 109 N. W. 322.

Wisconsin.— Smith *v.* Ford, 48 Wis. 115, 2 N. W. 134, 4 N. W. 462.

United States.— Barrett *v.* Holmes, 102 U. S. 651, 26 L. ed. 291.

See 45 Cent. Dig. tit. "Taxation," § 1475.

35. *Illinois.*— Mickey *v.* Barton, 194 Ill. 446, 62 N. E. 802.

Iowa.— Clark *v.* Sexton, 122 Iowa 310, 98 N. W. 127.

Kansas.— Hollenback *v.* Ess, 31 Kan. 87, 1 Pac. 275.

Kentucky.— James *v.* Luscher, (1909) 121 S. W. 954; James *v.* Blanton, 134 Ky. 803, 121 S. W. 951, 123 S. W. 328.

corded deed from such former owner, provided the tax purchaser had no notice or knowledge of such deed or of facts which should have put him on inquiry.[59]

g. Separate Interests Separately Assessed. If the statute deals with particular interests in land, rather than the land itself, and directs their separate assessment to their respective owners,[60] the purchase of a particular estate or interest so assessed, and sold for the non-payment of the taxes on it, will not in general disturb or affect any other estates or interests in the land or liens upon it.[61]

4. Liens and Encumbrances — a. In General. It is competent for the legislature to make the lien of taxes on real estate paramount to all other existing liens and encumbrances; [62] and when this is done, and when the tax-sale is considered as creating a new and independent title, it destroys and extinguishes all existing liens, charges, and encumbrances of every kind, and gives the purchaser a clear and unencumbered title.[63] But on the other hand, if the tax lien is not made

Georgia.— Gross *v.* Taylor, 81 Ga. 86, 6 S. E. 179; Kile *v.* Fleming, 78 Ga. 1.

Illinois.— Hill *v.* Figley, 25 Ill. 156; Hulick *v.* Scovil, 9 Ill. 159.

Indiana.— Indianapolis *v.* City Bond Co., 42 Ind. App. 470, 84 N. E. 20.

Kentucky.— Oldhams *v.* Jones, 5 B. Mon. 458; Husbands *v.* Polivick, 96 S. W. 825, 29 Ky. L. Rep. 890; Furguson *v.* Clark, 52 S. W. 964, 21 Ky. L. Rep. 697.

Louisiana.— Coucy *v.* Cummings, 12 La. Ann. 748.

Mississippi.— Dunn *v.* Winston, 31 Miss. 135.

Missouri. — Harrison Mach. Works *v.* Bowers, 200 Mo. 219, 98 S. W. 770; Powell *v.* Greenstreet, 95 Mo. 13, 8 S. W. 176; Jasper County *v.* Wadlow, 82 Mo. 172; Watt *v.* Donnell, 80 Mo. 195.

North Carolina.—*In re* Macay, 84 N. C. 63.

Tennessee.— Anderson *v.* Post, (Ch. App. 1896) 38 S. W. 283; Cardwell *v.* Crumley, (Ch. App. 1895) 35 S. W. 767.

Texas.—Wheeler *v.* Yenda, 11 Tex. 562, 9 Tex. 408.

Virginia.— Gates *v.* Lawson, 32 Gratt. 12.

West Virginia.— Cain *v.* Fisher, 57 W. Va. 492, 50 S. E. 752, 1015; McGhee *v.* Sampselle, 47 W. Va. 352, 34 S. E. 815; Kanawha Valley Bank *v.* Wilson, 29 W. Va. 645, 2 S. E. 768; Summers *v.* Kanawha County, 26 W. Va. 159; Smith *v.* Lewis, 2 W. Va. 39. *Compare* State *v.* Harman, 57 W. Va. 447. 50 S. E. 828.

Wisconsin.— Chase *v.* Dearborn, 21 Wis. 57.

United States.— McDonald *v.* Hannah, 59 Fed. 977, 8 C. C. A. 426 [*affirming* 51 Fed. 73]; Blodget *v.* Brent, 3 Fed. Cas. No. 1,553, 3 Cranch C. C. 394.

See 45 Cent. Dig. tit. "Taxation," § 1549.

59. Harrison Mach. Works *v.* Bowers, 200 Mo. 219, 98 S. W. 770; Wilcox *v.* Phillips, 199 Mo. 288, 97 S. W. 886; Stuart *v.* Ramsey, 196 Mo. 404, 95 S. W. 382; Evarts *v.* Missouri Lumber, etc., Co., 193 Mo. 433, 92 S. W. 372; Lucas *v.* Current River Land, etc., Co., 186 Mo. 448, 85 S. W. 359; Vance *v.* Corrigan, 78 Mo. 94. *Compare* Wood *v.* Smith, 193 Mo. 484, 91 S. W. 85.

But the above rule is inapplicable to a purchaser under a judgment in a back tax suit brought against the apparent owner of the land, where the deed from such apparent owner has been recorded and the book containing the record is destroyed by fire before suit brought for the taxes. Manwaring *v.* Missouri Lumber, etc., Co., 200 Mo. 718, 98 S. W. 762; Weir *v.* Cordz-Fisher Lumber Co., 186 Mo. 388, 85 S. W. 341.

60. See *supra*, VI, C, 5, i.

61. Windmiller *v.* Leach, 194 Ill. 631, 62 N. E. 789; Brundige *v.* Maloney, 52 Iowa 218, 2 N. W. 1110; Cadmus *v.* Jackson, 52 Pa. St. 295; Allegheny City's Appeal, 41 Pa. St. 60; Pittsburgh's Appeal, 40 Pa. St. 455; Irwin *v.* U. S. Bank, 1 Pa. St. 349; Frum *v.* Fox, 58 W. Va. 334, 52 S. E. 178.

62. See *supra*, VIII, C, 2.

63. *Georgia.*— Verdery *v.* Dotterer, 69 Ga. 194.

Indiana.— Ellison *v.* Branstrattor, (App. 1909) 88 N. E. 963, 89 N. E. 513, except claim or lien of state. See also Indianapolis *v.* City Bond Co., 42 Ind. App. 470, 84 N. E. 20.

Kansas.— Douglass *v.* Lowell, 64 Kan. 533. 67 Pac. 1106.

Louisiana.— Fitzpatrick *v.* Leake, 49 La. Ann. 794, 21 So. 597. *Compare* Font *v.* Gulf State Land, etc., Co., 47 La. Ann. 272, 16 So. 828.

Massachusetts.—Hunt *v.* Boston, 183 Mass. 305, 67 N. E. 244.

Michigan.—Robbins *v.* Barron, 32 Mich. 36.

Nebraska.—Topliff *v.* Richardson, 76 Nebr. 114, 107 N. W. 114; Leigh *v.* Green, 64 Nebr. 533, 90 N. W. 255, 101 Am. St. Rep. 592.

Ohio.— Kahle *v.* Nisley, 74 Ohio St. 328, 78 N. E. 526. *Compare* Bouton *v.* Lord, 10 Ohio St. 453.

Virginia.— Stevenson *v.* Henkle, 100 Va. 591, 42 S. E. 672.

West Virginia. — Kendall *v.* Scott, 48 W. Va. 251, 37 S. E. 531. *Compare* Smith *v.* Lewis, 2 W. Va. 39.

See 45 Cent. Dig. tit. "Taxation," § 1465. See also *supra*, XIV, A, 3, c.

Merger of tax title in fee.—Where the purchaser of a tax title acquires the interest of the record owner by conveyance subsequent to the acquisition of the tax title and within the period allowed by statute for redemption, the tax title is merged in the title acquired from the owner of record, and the purchaser holds subject to existing liens and equities.

paramount by law, or if the tax-sale is considered as passing only the title of the person assessed, it does not divest valid liens previously attaching.[64]

b. Judgment and Execution Liens. If the tax lien is made paramount to all others, as just stated, the lien of a judgment or execution against the owner of the land will be divested by a tax-sale and the maturing of the title in the purchaser, and the only right of the creditor will be to come upon the surplus, if any, of the purchase-money or to redeem from the tax-sale.[65]

c. Mortgage Liens — (I) *In General.* As a general rule, where the tax is laid upon the land as such, irrespective of separate estates, liens, or interests, and is collected by a valid tax-sale, the purchaser will take a clear title, freed from the lien of a prior mortgage.[66] But the mortgagee will have a right to redeem the

Boucher *v.* Trembley, 140 Mich. 352, 103 N. W. 819. *Compare* Carson *v.* Fulbright, 80 Kan. 624, 103 Pac. 139.

64. Battelle *v.* McIntosh, 62 Nebr. 647, 87 N. W. 361 (subject to liens deducted from the appraisement); Bouton *v.* Lord, 10 Ohio St. 453; Smith *v.* Lewis, 2 W. Va. 39.

65. Merrick *v.* Hutt, 15 Ark. 331; Morgan *v.* Burks, 90 Ga. 287, 15 S. E. 821; Indianapolis First Nat. Bank *v.* Hendricks, 134 Ind. 361, 33 N. E. 110, 34 N. E. 218; Jenkins *v.* Newman, 122 Ind. 99, 23 N. E. 683.

Effect of redemption by owner.— The purchaser at a tax-sale acquires but an inchoate title, which does not divest liens against the land until the expiration of the time allowed for redemption; hence if, within that time, the owner redeems, the property remains subject to a previously attaching judgment lien. Singer's Appeal, 4 Pa. Cas. 430, 7 Atl. 800.

Purchase equivalent to redemption.— Where the purchaser at a tax-sale stands in such a relation to the land or the owner that his purchase is legally equivalent merely to a payment of the taxes or a redemption, existing judgment liens are not divested. Beacham *v.* Gurney, 91 Iowa 621, 60 N. W. 187.

Tax deed not acknowledged or not recorded.—Where a tax deed was executed but was not acknowledged or proved for record as required by law, and afterward the original owner still remaining in possession, a judgment was rendered against him, it was held that the lien of the judgment was superior to the tax deed, as such deed, although spread on the records, was not constructive notice to subsequent creditors. Hill *v.* Gordon, 45 Fed. 276.

66. *Georgia.*— Verdery *v.* Dotterer, 69 Ga. 194.

Indiana.— Peckham *v.* Millikan, 99 Ind. 352.

Kansas.— Carson *v.* Fulbright, 80 Kan. 624, 103 Pac. 139, holding that one not obliged to pay taxes, nor in privity with one so liable, may obtain a tax title and when in possession thereunder may accept a conveyance from the former owner without incurring the risk of losing his land for failure to pay a mortgage given by such former owner, outstanding when the tax became delinquent. See also Cones *v.* Gibson, 77 Kan. 425, 94 Pac. 998, 16 L. R. A. N. S. 121, holding that a guarantor of payment of a note secured by mortgage may take a tax title to the mortgaged premises good against all the world except the mortgagee, and that the mortgagee may impeach such title only so far as may be necessary to protect his lien.

Louisiana.— *In re* Douglas, 41 La. Ann. 765, 6 So. 675; Maumus *v.* Beynet, 31 La. Ann. 462. See also Fitzpatrick *v.* Leake, 47 La. Ann. 1643, 18 So. 649.

Maine.—Williams *v.* Hilton, 35 Me. 547, 58 Am. Dec. 729.

Massachusetts.—Abbott *v.* Frost, 185 Mass. 398, 70 N. E. 478; Coughlin *v.* Gray, 131 Mass. 56; Parker *v.* Baxter, 2 Gray 185.

Missouri.— Allen *v.* McCabe, 93 Mo. 138, 6 S. W. 62; Cowell *v.* Gray, 85 Mo. 169; Gitchell *v.* Kreidler, 84 Mo. 472; Stafford *v.* Fizer, 82 Mo. 393.

New Jersey.— Blackwell *v.* Pidcock, 43 N. J. L. 165; Doremus *v.* Cameron, 49 N. J. Eq. 1, 22 Atl. 802; Paterson *v.* O'Neill, 32 N. J. Eq. 386; Campbell *v.* Dewick, 20 N. J. Eq. 186. But *compare* Morrow *v.* Dows, 28 N. J. Eq. 459. And see Hopper *v.* Malleson, 16 N. J. Eq. 382.

New York.— Erie County Sav. Bank *v.* Schuster, 187 N. Y. 111, 79 N. E. 843 [*affirming* 107 N. Y. App. Div. 46, 94 N. Y. Suppl. 737]; Oliphant *v.* Burns, 146 N. Y. 218, 40 N. E. 980. See Ruyter *v.* Reid, 121 N. Y. 498, 24 N. E. 791. But a mortgagee's rights are not divested by a tax-sale of the mortgaged property where the assessment of the tax was invalid. Bennett *v.* Kovarick, 44 N. Y. App. Div. 629, 60 N. Y. Suppl. 1133 [*affirming* 23 Misc. 73, 51 N. Y. Suppl. 752].

North Carolina.— Lyman *v.* Hunter, 123 N. C. 508, 31 S. E. 827; Powell *v.* Sikes, 119 N. C. 231, 26 S. E. 38. See also Virginia L. Ins. Co. *v.* Day, 127 N. C. 133, 37 S. E. 158.

Pennsylvania.— Cadmus *v.* Jackson, 52 Pa. St. 295; Fager *v.* Campbell, 5 Watts 287.

South Carolina. — Interstate Bldg., etc., Assoc. *v.* Waters, 50 S. C. 459, 27 S. E. 948.

United States.— Greenwalt *v.* Tucker, 8 Fed. 792, 3 McCrary 166.

See 45 Cent. Dig. tit. "Taxation," §§ 1466, 1552.

But *compare* Kepley *v.* Jansen, 107 Ill. 79; Middleton *v.* Moore, 43 Oreg. 357, 73 Pac. 16; Smith *v.* Lewis, 2 W. Va. 39.

Priority of tax lien as against mortgages and other encumbrances in general see *supra*, VIII, C, 2, d.

County as purchaser.— The authorities of a county cannot buy in a tax title, for the use of the school fund, for the purpose of

the sale voidable at the instance of the injured owner, does not, like a jurisdictional defect, make the sale entirely null and void.[89]

b. Application of Doctrine of Bona Fide Purchasers. A purchaser of real property at a tax-sale is not entitled to protection as an innocent purchaser where he purchases for a grossly inadequate consideration; [90] or where he fraudulently causes the land to be assessed to himself and suffers it to be sold for taxes and buys it in through the agency of a third person; [91] but such a purchaser is not affected by fraud contemplated by the officer making the sale of which he had no notice.[92] Ordinarily such persons come strictly within the rule *caveat emptor*,[93] and as the proceedings for the collection of taxes are matters of public record, to which intending purchasers have access, they are chargeable with knowledge of defects which the records disclose.[94] Where the proceedings are based on the judgment or decree of a court, such a purchaser may generally rely on it to protect himself; [95] but his title is liable to be divested by the cancellation or setting aside of the tax-sale for cause, provided he has notice of the proceedings.[96]

c. Amendment of Records. The purchaser of a tax title takes it subject to the right to have the record amended or corrected to correspond with the actual facts; [97] but on the other hand, it is generally held that tax deeds or the proceedings in tax cases cannot be reformed or amended for the purpose of supporting or validating the tax title.[98]

6. LIABILITY OF PURCHASER.[99] Beyond his liability to pay the amount of his bid and his responsibility on the surplus bond, if any was given,[1] and in respect to existing liens or encumbrances on the property not discharged by the tax-sale,[2] the purchaser at such sale is not ordinarily subject to any special liabilities growing out of the peculiar nature of his title or the mode of its acquisition. Thus he is not responsible in damages for taking the proper steps to acquire possession of the premises, if his own conduct was entirely correct, although the tax title may prove to be invalid.[3] But where the former owner of land pays overdue

89. Ellis *v.* Peck, 45 Iowa 112; Slater *v.* Maxwell, 6 Wall. (U. S.) 268, 18 L. ed. 796.

90. Green *v.* Robertson, 30 Tex. Civ. App. 236, 70 S. W. 345; Huff *v.* Maroney, 23 Tex. Civ. App. 465, 56 S. W. 754.

91. Turner *v.* Ladd, 42 Wash. 274, 84 Pac. 866.

92. Boyd *v.* Wilson, 86 Ga. 379, 12 S. E. 744, 13 S. E. 428.

93. See *infra*, XIV, C, 1, a.

94. St. Paul *v.* Louisiana Cypress Lumber Co., 116 La. 585, 40 So. 906; Martin *v.* Kearney County, 62 Nebr. 538, 87 N. W. 351.

A patent from the government, like a deed, must be filed and recorded, and if by failure to so file and record the patent the rights of an innocent purchaser accrue, such rights must prevail. Wilcox *v.* Phillips, 199 Mo. 288, 97 S. W. 886.

A purchaser with knowledge that someone besides the owner of record paid taxes on the land is placed on inquiry as to the claim of such party; and if the purchaser had actual or constructive notice that the suit for taxes was not against the real owner, although against the record owner, the tax deed would be unavailing as between him and the latter. Zweigart *v.* Reed, 221 Mo. 33, 119 S. W. 960.

95. Evarts *v.* Missouri Lumber, etc., Co., 193 Mo. 433, 92 S. W. 372; Bagley *v.* Sligo Furnace Co., 120 Mo. 248, 25 S. W. 207; Schmidt *v.* Niemeyer, 100 Mo. 207, 13 S. W. 405; Jones *v.* Driskill, 94 Mo. 190, 7 S. W. 111; Williams *v.* Young, 41 Tex. Civ. App. 212, 90 S. W. 940.

96. People *v.* Wemple, 67 Hun (N. Y.) 495, 22 N. Y. Suppl. 497 [*reversed* on other grounds in 139 N. Y. 240, 34 N. E. 883]; Ostrander *v.* Darling, 53 Hun (N. Y.) 190, 6 N. Y. Suppl. 718 [*affirmed* in 127 N. Y. 70, 27 N. E. 353].

97. Cass *v.* Bellows, 31 N. H. 501, 64 Am. Dec. 347; Gibson *v.* Bailey, 9 N. H. 168.

98. Altes *v.* Hinckler, 36 Ill. 265, 85 Am. Dec. 406; Keepfer *v.* Force, 86 Ind. 81; Ramos Lumber, etc., Co. *v.* Labarre, 116 La. 559, 40 So. 898; Bowers *v.* Andrews, 52 Miss. 596. But *compare* Hickman *v.* Kempner, 35 Ark. 505; Davis *v.* Sawyer, 66 N. H. 34, 20 Atl. 100.

An entry upon the tax record by the treasurer, designating the sale as erroneous, cannot thereafter be rightfully erased by him and a deed issued to the tax-sale purchaser without notice or opportunity to the owner to protect his rights. Burckhardt *v.* Scofield, 141 Iowa 336, 117 N. W. 1061, 133 Am. St. Rep. 173.

99. **Liability of purchaser for:** Rents and profits see *supra*, XIV, A, 2, e. Taxes see *supra*, XIV, A, 4, d.

1. See *supra*, XI, J, 1, 2.

2. See *supra*, XIV, A, 4.

Ground-rent.— The purchaser takes the land subject to payment of reserved ground-rent. Irwin *v.* U. S. Bank, 1 Pa. St. 349.

3. Fernandez *v.* Smith, 43 La. Ann. 708, 9

times the case, it is essential to an assignment that it shall be acknowledged,[13] and recorded.[14]

(III) *WHO MAY TAKE ASSIGNMENT*. Any person who is disqualified from purchasing at a tax-sale, either by reason of his title to the property or his fiduciary relation to the owner,[15] is equally disqualified from taking an assignment of the certificate of purchase, and if he does so, it merely amounts to a redemption.[16] Where municipal corporations are prohibited by law from taking assignments of tax certificates, an assignment to a town or other municipality is absolutely void, and if it in turn assigns the certificate to a stranger, he acquires no title as against the owner of the land.[17]

(IV) *RIGHTS OF ASSIGNEES*. The assignee of a tax certificate becomes invested with all the rights and interests of his assignor; he becomes entitled to the redemption money, if the same is paid, or to a deed if it is not.[18] But he can acquire no greater interest than his assignor had at the time, and hence takes nothing as against a prior assignee of the certificate in good faith or against one claiming an interest in the land previously granted by the assignor.[19] More-

Mo. 571, 17 S. W. 641; Pitkin *v.* Reibel, 104 Mo. 505, 16 S. W. 244.

Wisconsin.— Smith *v.* Todd, 55 Wis. 459, 13 N. W. 488; Hyde *v.* Kenosha County, 43 Wis. 129.

See 45 Cent. Dig. tit. "Taxation," § 1481.

The word "indorsement" means the writing of the name of the holder on the back of the certificate, under a statute authorizing the assignment of tax certificates by indorsement. Jones *v.* Glos, 236 Ill. 178, 86 N. E. 282; Larson *v.* Glos, 235 Ill. 584, 85 N. E. 926 [*reversing* 138 Ill. App. 412]. But see Territory *v.* Perea, 6 N. M. 531, 30 Pac. 928.

Place of indorsement immaterial.—Although the statute authorizes the assignment of a tax certificate by an indorsement "on the back thereof," it is equally valid when written across the face. Potts *v.* Cooley, 56 Wis. 45, 13 N. W. 682.

13. Williamson *v.* Hitner, 79 Ind. 233; Mattocks *v.* McLain Land, etc., Co., 11 Okla. 433, 68 Pac. 501; Wilson *v.* Wood, 10 Okla. 279, 61 Pac. 1045.

14. Smith *v.* Stephenson, 45 Iowa 645; Territory *v.* Perea, 6 N. M. 531, 30 Pac. 928; White *v.* Brooklyn, 122 N. Y. 53, 25 N. E. 243. *Compare* Swan *v.* Whaley, 75 Iowa 623, 35 N. W. 440.

15. See *supra*, XI, H, 1, 2.

16. *Illinois*.— Busch *v.* Huston, 75 Ill. 343.

Iowa.— Bowman *v.* Eckstien, 46 Iowa 583.

Kansas.— Wiswell *v.* Simmons, 77 Kan. 622, 95 Pac. 407.

Missouri.— Kohle *v.* Hobson, 215 Mo. 213, 114 S. W. 952.

Wisconsin.— Bennett *v.* Keehn, 57 Wis. 582, 15 N. W. 776; Bassett *v.* Welch, 22 Wis. 175.

See 45 Cent. Dig. tit. "Taxation," § 1481. See also *supra*, XII, C, 6.

But *compare* Arthurs *v.* King, 95 Pa. St. 167.

A tenant in common cannot acquire an independent title against his cotenants, where the land held in common is sold for taxes, by taking an assignment of the purchaser's certificate before the time for redemption has expired. Lloyd *v.* Lynch, 28 Pa. St. 419, 70 Am. Dec. 137.

Merger of tax title in fee.—An assignment of a tax certificate to one who, subsequently to the sale, has become the owner of the patent title, will not discharge the land from the lien of prior delinquent taxes. Bowman *v.* Eckstien, 46 Iowa 583.

Purchase by county officer.— Although county officers are strictly prohibited from buying at tax-sales, this does not necessarily prevent them from taking assignments of the tax certificates from the original purchasers, if done in good faith. Coleman *v.* Hart, 37 Wis. 180. And see Guthrie *v.* Harker, 27 Fed. 586.

17. Irvin *v.* Smith, 60 Wis. 175, 18 N. W. 724; Wright *v.* Zettel, 60 Wis. 168, 18 N. W. 760; Jackson *v.* Jacksonport, 56 Wis. 310, 14 N. W. 296; Dreutzer *v.* Smith, 56 Wis. 292, 14 N. W. 465; Eaton *v.* Manitowoc County, 44 Wis. 489.

18. *Arkansas*.—Bird *v.* Jones, 37 Ark. 195.

Colorado.— Rio Grande County *v.* Whelen, 28 Colo. 435, 65 Pac. 38.

Iowa.— Smith *v.* Stephenson, 45 Iowa 645; Lloyd *v.* Bunce, 41 Iowa 660.

Kansas.— McCauslin *v.* McGuire, 14 Kan. 234; City Trust Co. *v.* Tilton, 6 Kan. App. 442, 40 Pac. 796.

Nebraska.— Green *v.* Hellman, 61 Nebr. 875, 86 N. W. 912.

See 45 Cent. Dig. tit. "Taxation," § 1481.

19. Smith *v.* Todd, 55 Wis. 459, 13 N. W. 488; Horn *v.* Garry, 49 Wis. 464, 5 N. W. 897.

Agreement not to take deed.—A purchaser of a tax-sale certificate containing an indorsement by a prior purchaser not to procure a treasurer's deed of the premises, which such person had sold by warranty deed to another, will be enjoined from taking a deed under it. Soukup *v.* Union Inv. Co., 84 Iowa 448, 51 N. W. 167, 35 Am. St. Rep. 317.

Assignment of original and of duplicate.— A purchaser of a duplicate certificate of tax-sale cannot acquire a title under it as against, or superior to, that of a subsequent assignee of the original certificate, who purchased it and obtained a deed thereon with-

is not changed by such a transfer, and the grantee must generally be prepared to maintain its validity, the same as the original purchaser.[29]

(II) *BONA FIDES AND NOTICE OF DEFECTS.* One who takes a conveyance of a tax title can claim no benefit from it if he had actual knowledge of facts which render it invalid,[30] or if the records show on their face fatal defects or irregularities.[31] But a purchaser in good faith and for value is protected against latent equities,[32] and against the consequences of fraud in the conduct of the tax-sale in which he did not participate and of which he had no knowledge,[33] and also against errors or irregularities in the proceedings of which he had no notice and of which the records give no hint.[34]

(III) *PURCHASE FROM STATE OR COUNTY.* Where the title to land under a tax-sale has become fully vested in the state or a municipality, one who thereafter purchases from the state or municipality must see to it that his deed is properly executed by the officers having authority for that purpose,[35] in the manner and with the formalities prescribed by law.[36] It is competent for the legislature

could not have purchased at the tax-sale); Wygant *v.* Dahl, 26 Nebr. 562, 42 N. W. 735 (merger of tax title on conveyance of it to owner of fee).

Purchase by tenant in common from purchaser at tax-sale as not amounting to a mere renunciation in favor of the estate of an undivided half interest see Duson *v.* Roos, 123 La. 835, 49 So. 590, 131 Am. St. Rep. 375.

29. *Illinois.*—Warden *v.* Glos, 236 Ill. 511, 86 N. E. 116, holding that a grantor claiming under a void tax deed can convey nothing as against the true owner.

Kansas.—Harris *v.* Curran, 32 Kan. 580, 4 Pac. 1044.

New Hampshire.—Wells *v.* Jackson Iron Mfg. Co., 47 N. H. 235, 90 Am. Dec. 575, holding that a quitclaim deed executed by a tax collector's grantee is color of title, although the collector's deed conveyed no title.

Pennsylvania.—Goettel *v.* Sage, 117 Pa. St. 298, 10 Atl. 889, rescission of contract of sale on failure of tax title.

Virginia.—Taylor *v.* Stringer, 1 Gratt. 158

United States.—Curts *v.* Cisna, 6 Fed. Cas. No. 3,507, 7 Biss. 260.

See 45 Cent. Dig. tit. "Taxation," § 1485.

A grantee of one who has conspired to eliminate competition in bidding at a tax-sale must deny notice of the misconduct of his grantor, whether alleged or not, and the burden of proof thereof is on the party seeking relief against him, but he must establish payment of consideration. Lohr *v.* George, 65 W. Va. 241, 64 S. E. 609.

30. Cooper *v.* Falk, 109 La. 474, 33 So. 567; Coney *v.* Timmons, 16 S. C. 378; Yancey *v.* Hopkins, 1 Munf. (Va.) 419.

Adverse possession as notice.—See Leas *v.* Garverich, 77 Iowa 275, 42 N. W. 194. But during the period allowed for redemption the continued possession of the owner is not inconsistent with the right of the tax purchaser, and hence is no notice, to one who purchases the tax title during that time, of any infirmity in the tax-sale. Jefferson Land Co. *v.* Grace, 57 Ark. 423, 21 S. W. 877; Major *v.* Brush, 7 Ind. 232.

Purchaser under quitclaim deed.—Where one by quitclaim deed purchases a defective tax title, he buys at his own risk and will be deemed to have notice of the defects in the title. Leland *v.* Isenbeck, 1 Ida. 469.

Neglect of tax title purchaser to record his deed see Billings *v.* Stark, 15 Fla. 297.

31. Sorenson *v.* Davis, 83 Iowa 405, 49 N. W. 1004; Simpson *v.* Edmiston, 23 W. Va. 675.

32. Jefferson Land Co. *v.* Grace, 57 Ark. 423, 21 S. W. 877; Morris *v.* Gregory, 80 Kan. 626, 103 Pac. 137.

33. St. Louis, etc., Lumber, etc., Co. *v.* Godwin, 85 Ark. 372, 108 S. W. 516; Jefferson Land Co. *v.* Grace, 57 Ark. 423, 21 S. W. 877; Lamb *v.* Davis, 74 Iowa 719, 39 N. W. 114; Martin *v.* Ragsdale, 49 Iowa 589; Huston *v.* Markley, 49 Iowa 162; Ellis *v.* Peck, 45 Iowa 112; Watson *v.* Phelps, 40 Iowa 482; Sibley *v.* Bullis, 40 Iowa 429; Van Shaack *v.* Robbins, 36 Iowa 201. But *compare* Merrett *v.* Poulter, 96 Mo. 237, 9 S. W. 586.

A deed acquired by a conspirator to prevent competition in bidding at a tax-sale will not be set aside as to his grantee, where the latter is a *bona fide* purchaser for a valuable consideration. Lohr *v.* George, 65 W. Va. 241, 64 S. E. 609.

34. *Arkansas.*—Jefferson Land Co. *v.* Grace, 57 Ark. 423, 21 S. W. 877.

Iowa.—Martin *v.* Ragsdale, 49 Iowa 589.

Pennsylvania.—Gamble *v.* Central Pennsylvania Lumber Co., 225 Pa. St. 288, 74 Atl. 69.

West Virginia.—Wingfield *v.* Neall, 60 W. Va. 106, 54 S. E. 47, 116 Am. St. Rep. 882.

United States.—Atlanta Nat. Bldg., etc., Assoc. *v.* Gilmer, 128 Fed. 293 [*reversed* on the facts in 136 Fed. 539, 69 C. C. A. 315].

See 45 Cent. Dig. tit. "Taxation," § 1487.

But *compare* Gonzalia *v.* Bartelsman, 143 Ill. 634, 32 N. E. 532.

35. Everett *v.* Boyington, 29 Minn. 264, 13 N. W. 45; Powell *v.* Jenkins, 14 Misc. (N. Y.) 83, 35 N. Y. Suppl. 265; Rice *v.* Ashland Real Estate, etc., Co., 72 Wis. 103, 38 N. W. 183; Haseltine *v.* Donahue, 42 Wis. 576.

36. Hier *v.* Rullman, 22 Kan. 606.

c. Payment or Tender as Condition to Right to Defend. In some of the states the laws are so framed as to require a tender or deposit of an amount sufficient to cover the taxes and costs, as a condition to the right to contest a tax title, and confirmation of title cannot be prevented unless such tender or deposit is made.[71] Statutes of this kind will not be construed retrospectively;[72] nor can they constitutionally apply to cases where the defense calls in question the validity of the tax or goes to the groundwork of the tax proceedings.[73] But as applied to merely technical defenses or such as are based only on irregularities in the proceedings, they are valid.[74] It has been held, however, that a law of this character does not apply to the defense of fraud in the conduct of the tax-sale;[75] or where the action is brought before the expiration of the time for redemption;[76] or where, from the confusion of different parcels of land in the sale, defendant cannot ascertain how much to tender.[77]

3. Actions to Impeach or Vacate Tax Titles — a. Right to Attack Tax Title — (I) *In General.* The owner of land sold for taxes, or those who have succeeded to his rights, may impeach and overturn the tax title[78] by an action to set aside

Doullut *v.* Smith, 117 La. 491, 41 So. 913 (previous payment of taxes); Lisso *v.* Unknown Owner, 114 La. 392, 38 So. 282; Boagni *v.* Pacific Imp. Co., 111 La. 1063, 36 So. 129; Fernandez *v.* Smith, 43 La. Ann. 708, 9 So. 482.

Mississippi.— Foote *v.* Dismukes, 71 Miss. 110, 13 So. 879; Osburn *v.* Hyde, 68 Miss. 45, 8 So. 514 (assessment roll not filed according to law); Chrisman *v.* Currie, 60 Miss. 858 (land not taxable); Bell *v.* Coates, 54 Miss. 538 (want of notice).

Missouri.— Brown *v.* Walker, 11 Mo. App. 226, sale of lots *en masse*.

New York.— People *v.* Ladew, 189 N. Y. 355, 82 N. E. 431 [*reversing* 108 N. Y. App. Div. 356, 95 N. Y. Suppl. 1151], 190 N. Y. 543, 82 N. E. 1092 (no notice to redeem); Andrus *v.* Wheeler, 29 Misc. 412, 61 N. Y. Suppl. 983 (wrong conduct of sale); Terrell *v.* Wheeler, 13 N. Y. Civ. Proc. 178 (inadequacy of price no defense).

North Dakota.— Beggs *v.* Paine, 15 N. D. 436, 109 N. W. 322.

Pennsylvania.— Iddings *v.* Carns, 2 Grant 88.

Texas.— Collins *v.* Fergurson, 22 Tex. Civ. App. 552, 56 S. W. 225, inadequacy of price.

Wisconsin.— Lain *v.* Shepardson, 23 Wis. 224; Wilson *v.* Jarvis, 19 Wis. 597, purchaser disqualified from buying at tax-sale.

See 45 Cent. Dig. tit. "Taxation," § 1576.

Waiver of objections.— A waiver by all persons interested in land sold by a collector of taxes of an informality in the sale, after the bringing of a writ of entry by the purchaser at the sale against a person claiming title as a disseisor, will operate, by estoppel, to make good defendant's title as against such persons, but it will not have that effect as against the tenant. Reed *v.* Crapo, 133 Mass. 201.

71. See the statutes of the several states. And see Carter *v.* Hadley, 59 Miss. 130; McMillan *v.* Hogan, 129 N. C. 314, 40 S. E. 63; McKinney *v.* Minnehaha County, 17 S. D. 407, 97 N. W. 15; Paine *v.* Germantown Trust Co., 136 Fed. 527, 69 C. C. A. 303. *Compare* Manwaring *v.* Missouri Lumber, etc., Co., 200 Mo. 718, 98 S. W. 762.

Sufficiency of tender see Cone *v.* Wood, 108 Iowa 260, 79 N. W. 86, 75 Am. St. Rep. 223; Nicodemus *v.* Young, 90 Iowa 423, 57 N. W. 906.

When tender necessary.— See Orono *v.* Veazie, 57 Me. 517, holding that defendant may contest the sufficiency of plaintiff's evidence to establish compliance with the law, without being required to pay or tender the taxes, but must do this if he wishes to introduce evidence on his own behalf.

72. Conway *v.* Cable, 37 Ill. 82, 87 Am. Dec. 240.

73. Immegart *v.* Gorgas, 41 Iowa 439; Eustis *v.* Henrietta, 91 Tex. 325, 43 S. W. 259; Tierney *v.* Union Lumbering Co., 47 Wis. 248, 2 N. W. 289; Philleo *v.* Hiles, 42 Wis 527; Call *v.* Chase, 21 Wis. 511.

Unnecessary tender and deposit regarded as voluntary payment.—Although the tax on which plaintiff's deed was based was void and it was therefore unnecessary for defendant to tender the amount, yet if he deposits it with the clerk of the court, it is a voluntary payment which cannot be recovered back. Powell *v.* St. Croix County, 46 Wis. 210, 50 N. W. 1013.

74. Knight *v.* Barnes, 25 Wis. 352; Smith *v.* Smith, 19 Wis. 615, 88 Am. Dec. 707; Wakeley *v.* Nicholas, 16 Wis. 588.

75. Corbin *v.* Beebee, 36 Iowa 336.

76. Dayton *v.* Relf, 34 Wis. 86.

77. Phillips *v.* Sherman, 61 Me. 548.

78. Cramer *v.* Armstrong, 28 Colo. 496, 66 Pac. 889; Iowa L. & T. Co. *v.* Pond, 128 Iowa 660, 105 N. W. 119; Burgson *v.* Jacobson, 124 Wis. 295, 102 N. W. 563.

Title necessary to maintain suit see *infra*, XIV, B, 3, a, (III).

The right of parties who have purchased timber cut from lands sold for taxes cannot be litigated in a proceeding by the original owner to set aside the tax-sale and deed issued thereon. Cook *v.* Hall, 123 Mich. 378, 82 N. W. 59.

Action by receiver.—Where property involved in a receivership is sold for taxes, the receiver, if he wishes to attack the sale for irregularities, must institute in the county where the property is situated such appro-

or by his unreasonable delay in the assertion of his rights.[91] But on the other hand the state is not estopped from selling and conveying land for the non-payment of taxes by a previous attempted tax-sale to another person which was null and void;[92] nor is the state or a county estopped from asserting title to its own non-taxable lands by the unauthorized acts of its officers in assessing and selling them.[93] In accordance with general principles, any party to an action of this kind is estopped from denying a title under which he claims or through which he must derive his rights,[94] but not by the acts or admissions of a party with whom he is not in privity.[95]

(III) *TITLE NECESSARY TO MAINTAIN SUIT* — (A) *In General.* In some states the statutes debar any claimant of land from disputing a tax title thereon unless he shows title acquired from the state or the United States.[96] And as a general rule no one will be permitted to contest a tax title without first showing title in himself or in those under whom he claims at the time of the tax-sale,[97]

91. Weir *v.* Cordez-Fisher Lumber Co., 186 Mo. 388, 85 S. W. 341. And see *infra*, XIV, B, 4, e.

That a deed is five years old is no ground for applying the doctrine of estoppel against a claim of its being void for not showing the amount of taxes or the amount for which the land is sold. Finn *v.* Jones, 80 Kan. 431, 102 Pac. 479.

Where notice to redeem is void because of the premature issue of the tax deed, the owners of the property are not barred from questioning the validity of the tax title, by reason of their neglecting to redeem under such notice. Fitschen *v.* Olson, 155 Mich. 320, 119 N. W. 3.

92. Dick *v.* Foraker, 155 U. S. 404, 15 S. Ct. 124, 39 L. ed. 201.

93. Howard County *v.* Bullis, 49 Iowa 519; Bixby *v.* Adams County, 49 Iowa 507; Buena Vista County *v.* Iowa Falls, etc., R. Co., 46 Iowa 226; Slattery *v.* Heilperin, 110 La. 86, 34 So. 139; Wells *v.* Johnston, 171 N. Y. 324, 63 N. E. 1095. *Compare* Austin *v.* Bremer County, 44 Iowa 155, holding that where a county has sold land for taxes it has assessed and levied thereon, it cannot subsequently set up title in itself upon the ground that such land was not subject to taxation.

94. Norwich *v.* Congden, 1 Root (Conn.) 222; Carlisle *v.* Cassady, 46 S. W. 490, 20 Ky. L. Rep. 562.

But a grantee of land under a deed subject to "all unpaid taxes and sales for the same" is not estopped thereby to deny the validity of a tax-sale, where the assessment on which the sale was based was wholly void. Blackburn *v.* Lewis, 45 Oreg. 422, 77 Pac. 746.

95. Miller *v.* Cook, 135 Ill. 190, 25 N. E. 756, 10 L. R. A. 292; Flanagan *v.* Dunne, 105 Fed. 828, 45 C. C. A. 81.

96. See the statutes of the several states. And see Rhea *v.* McWilliams, 73 Ark. 557, 84 S. W. 726; Hintrager *v.* Kiene, 62 Iowa 605, 15 N. W. 568, 17 N. W. 910; Chandler *v.* Keeler, 46 Iowa 596; Hoffman *v.* H. M. Loud, etc., Lumber Co., 138 Mich. 5, 100 N. W. 1010, 104 N. W. 424; Ruggles *v.* Sands, 40 Mich. 559; Hewitt, Jr. *v.* Butterfield, 52 Wis. 384, 9 N. W. 15.

Such a provision does not apply to one who shows a title *prima facie* sufficient under common-law rules. Gamble *v.* Horr, 40 Mich. 561.

97. *Arkansas.*— Meyer *v.* Snell, 89 Ark. 298, 116 S. W. 208; Osceola Land Co. *v.* Chicago Mill, etc., Co., 84 Ark. 1, 103 S. W. 609; St. Louis Refrigerator, etc., Co. *v.* Thornton, 74 Ark. 383, 86 S. W. 852; Rhodes *v.* Covington, 69 Ark. 357, 63 S. W. 799.

Illinois.— Lusk *v.* Harber, 8 Ill. 158; Bestor *v.* Powell, 7 Ill. 119.

Iowa.— Swan *v.* Harvey, 117 Iowa 58, 90 N. W. 489; State *v.* Havrah, 101 Iowa 486, 70 N. W. 618; Callanan *v.* Wayne County, 73 Iowa 709, 36 N. W. 654; Foster *v.* Ellsworth, 71 Iowa 262, 32 N. W. 314; Pitt's Sons Mfg. Co. *v.* Beed, 69 Iowa 546, 29 N. W. 458.

Michigan.— Seymour *v.* Peters, 67 Mich. 415, 35 N. W. 62.

Mississippi.—Wilkinson *v.* Hiller, 71 Miss. 678, 14 So. 442.

Missouri.— Cobb *v.* Griffith, etc., Sand, etc., Co., 12 Mo. App. 130.

New York.— People *v.* Bain, 60 Misc. 253, 113 N. Y. Suppl. 27; Andrus *v.* Wheeler, 18 Misc. 646, 42 N. Y. Suppl. 525.

North Carolina.— Eames *v.* Armstrong, 146 N. C. 1, 59 S. E. 165, 125 Am. St. Rep. 426.

West Virginia.— Despard *v.* Pearcy, 65 W. Va. 140, 63 S. E. 871.

United States.— Robinson *v.* Bailey, 26 Fed. 219.

See 45 Cent. Dig. tit. "Taxation," § 1580.

Mere failure to redeem land or neglect to pay taxes will not *per se* divest the title, so as to prevent the owner from maintaining an action against the claimant under a tax-sale. St. Anthony Falls Water Power Co. *v.* Greely, 11 Minn. 321.

Two tenants in common may sue jointly to set aside the sale of their land for taxes; and it is no defense that the contract between the two complainants, whereby one of them acquired his title, was champertous. Gage *v.* Du Puy, 134 Ill. 132, 24 N. E. 866, 137 Ill. 652, 24 N. E. 541, 26 N. E. 386.

Where both parties to a suit to quiet title claim under tax-sales which are shown to have been void, neither party is precluded from showing the invalidity of the other's title, and in such a case the position of defendant is the stronger. Meyer *v.* Snell, 89 Ark. 298, 116 S. W. 208.

for if a person is devoid of all interest in the land or cannot show that he was injured by the tax-sale, it would be against the policy of the law to permit him to impugn the validity of the sale.[98] But it is not necessary for one who shows a good title to show also possession of the premises; [99] nor is it necessary that the title shown as a foundation for maintaining the suit shall be a perfect title in fee simple, for generally any one who has such an interest as would give him the right to redeem from the tax-sale may contest its validity,[1] and his interest may therefore be in the nature of a lien,[2] or an inchoate title under an executory contract of sale.[3] Nor will he be debarred from his suit because his record title is not perfect, it being sufficient to show an adverse possession under a claim of title in good faith based on any instrument which constitutes color of title.[4] He will not be required, in the first instance, to prove his title completely, a *prima facie* showing of title being enough; [5] and the holder of the tax title cannot impeach the deed under which the record owner claims as having been made in fraud of creditors.[6]

(B) *Mortgagees.* A mortgagee of real property has such a title to the land, or at least such an interest in it, as will entitle him to maintain an action to set aside a tax-sale and deed thereof; [7] and the same is true of the purchaser at a sale on foreclosure of the mortgage.[8]

b. Suit to Set Aside Tax-Sale and Deed. A court of equity has jurisdiction of a suit to set aside, on proper grounds, a tax-sale and cancel the deed issued

98. McArthur *v.* Peacock, 93 Ga. 715, 20 S. E. 215; McCash *v.* Penrod, 131 Iowa 631, 109 N. W. 180; Citizens' Bank *v.* Marr, 120 La. 236, 45 So. 115; West *v.* Negrotto, 48 La. Ann. 922, 19 So. 819; Reinach *v.* Duplantier, 46 La. Ann. 151, 15 So. 13; Lacroix *v.* Camors, 34 La. Ann. 639; New Orleans Ins. Assoc. *v.* Labranche, 31 La. Ann. 839; Murphy *v.* Burke, 47 Minn. 99, 49 N. W. 387.

99. Herr *v.* Martin, 90 Ky. 377, 14 S. W. 356, 12 Ky. L. Rep. 359. But *compare* Steele *v.* Fish, 2 Minn. 153. And see Smith *v.* Newman, 62 Kan. 318, 62 Pac. 1011, 53 L. R. A. 934.

1. South Chicago Brewing Co. *v.* Taylor, 205 Ill. 132, 68 N. E. 732; Gerac *v.* Guilbeau, 36 La. Ann. 843; Ludeling *v.* McGuire, 35 La. Ann. 893; Despard *v.* Pearcy, 65 W. Va. 140, 63 S. E. 871; Hawkinberry *v.* Snodgrass, 39 W. Va. 332, 19 S. E. 417.

2. See *infra*, XIV, B, 3, a, (III), (B), as to right of mortgagee to impeach tax title. But see University Bank *v.* Athens Sav. Bank, 107 Ga. 246, 33 S. E. 34 (holding that one who has no interest in the land except for holding a judgment lien on it cannot attack the tax-sale); Robbins *v.* Barron, 34 Mich. 517 (laying down a similar rule as to one who only has a claim for taxes paid on the land).

3. Langlois *v.* Stewart, 156 Ill. 609, 41 N. E. 177; Jones *v.* Hollister, 51 Kan. 310, 32 Pac. 1115; Horton *v.* Helmholtz, 149 Mich. 227, 112 N. W. 930; Brown *v.* Lyon, 81 Miss. 438, 33 So. 284.

4. Curry *v.* Hinman, 11 Ill. 420; Shelley *v.* Smith, 97 Iowa 259, 66 N. W. 172; Callanan *v.* Wayne County, 73 Iowa 709, 36 N. W. 654; Frank *v.* Arnold, 73 Iowa 370, 35 N. W. 453; Keokuk, etc., R. Co. *v.* Lindley, 48 Iowa 11; Chandler *v.* Keeler, 46 Iowa 596; Long *v.* Stanley, 79 Miss. 298, 30 So. 823; Edwards *v.* Lyman, 122 N. C. 741, 30 S. E. 328.

Applications.—A deed from an administrator, regular on its face, and reciting the proceedings in the probate court, is sufficient evidence of title (Glos *v.* Ault, 221 Ill. 562, 77 N. E. 939), as is also a tax deed which is valid on its face (McQuity *v.* Doudna, 101 Iowa 144, 70 N. W. 99; Adams *v.* Burdick, 68 Iowa 666, 27 N. W. 911); but not a mere certificate of purchase at a tax-sale (Johns *v.* Griffin, 76 Iowa 419, 41 N. W. 59), nor any deed which is void on its face (Baird *v.* Law, 93 Iowa 742, 61 N. W. 1086). And a merely constructive possession will not answer (Towson *v.* Denson, 74 Ark. 302, 86 S. W. 661); nor a miner's mere entry on the lands of another for the purpose of following his own vein (Lebanon Min. Co. *v.* Rogers, 8 Colo. 34, 5 Pac. 661).

5. Baird *v.* Law, 93 Iowa 742, 61 N. W. 1086; Pitts *v.* Seavey, 88 Iowa 336, 55 N. W. 480; Hintrager *v.* Kiene, 62 Iowa 205, 15 N. W. 568, 17 N. W. 910; Murphy *v.* Williams, (Tex. Civ. App. 1900) 56 S. W. 695.

6. Clark *v.* Sexton, 122 Iowa 310, 98 N. W. 127; Boggess *v.* Scott, 48 W. Va. 316, 37 S. E. 661.

7. *Illinois.*— Burton *v.* Perry, 146 Ill. 71, 34 N. E. 60; Miller *v.* Cook, 135 Ill. 190, 25 N. E. 756, 10 L. R. A. 292; McAlpine *v.* Zitzer, 119 Ill. 273, 10 N. E. 901.

Iowa.— Blumenthal *v.* Culver, 116 Iowa 326, 89 N. W. 1116; Petersborough Sav. Bank *v.* Des Moines Sav. Bank, 110 Iowa 519, 81 N. W. 786.

Kansas.— Hoffman *v.* Groll, 35 Kan. 652, 12 Pac. 34.

Louisiana.— Beltram *v.* Villere, (1888) 4 So. 506; Villey *v.* Jarreau, 33 La. Ann. 291.

New York.— Cromwell *v.* MacLean, 123 N. Y. 474, 25 N. E. 932.

South Dakota.— Stoddard *v.* Lyon, 18 S. D. 207, 99 N. W. 1116.

Wisconsin.—Avery *v.* Judd, 21 Wis. 262.

See 45 Cent. Dig. tit. "Taxation," § 1581.

8. McManus *v.* Morgan, 38 Wash. 528, 80 Pac. 786.

statutes have generally been held valid and constitutional, in so far as they relate to the setting aside of tax titles on account of mere errors and irregularities, and do not impose on the landowner conditions or restrictions beyond what the principles of equity would ordinarily require of him.[30] **But they do not apply**

595, 35 N. W. 659; Gardner *v.* Early, 69 Iowa 42, 28 N. W. 427; White *v.* Smith, 68 Iowa 313, 25 N. W. 115, 27 N. W. 250; Taylor *v.* Ormsby, 66 Iowa 109, 23 N. W. 288; Corbin *v.* Woodbine, 33 Iowa 297.

Kansas.— Franz *v.* Krebs, 41 Kan. 223, 21 Pac. 99; Miller *v.* Ziegler, 31 Kan. 417, 2 Pac. 601; Wilder *v.* Cockshutt, 25 Kan. 504; Cartwright *v.* McFadden, 24 Kan. 662; Coe *v.* Farwell, 24 Kan. 566; Pritchard *v.* Madren, 24 Kan. 486; Millbank *v.* Ostertag, 24 Kan. 462; Herzog *v.* Gregg, 23 Kan. 726; Knox *v.* Dunn, 22 Kan. 683; Hagaman *v.* Cloud County Com'rs, 19 Kan. 394.

Louisiana.— State *v.* Judges of Ct. of Appeals, 49 La. Ann. 303, 21 So. 516; Prescott *v.* Payne, 44 La. Ann. 650, 11 So. 140; Blanton *v.* Ludeling, 30 La. Ann. 1232. See also State *v.* Cannon, 44 La. Ann. 734, 11 So. 86.

Maine.— Belfast Sav. Bank *v.* Kennebec Land, etc., Co., 73 Me. 404; Briggs *v.* Johnson, 71 Me. 235.

Maryland.— Steuart *v.* Meyer, 54 Md. 454.

Michigan.— Greenley *v.* Hovey, 115 Mich. 504, 73 N. W. 808.

Mississippi.— Ragsdale *v.* Alabama Great Southern R. Co., 67 Miss. 106, 6 So. 630.

Missouri — Burkham *v.* Manewal, 195 Mo. 500, 94 S. W. 520; Yeaman *v.* Lepp, 167 Mo. 61, 66 S. W. 957; Petring *v.* Current River Land, etc., Co., 111 Mo. App. 373, 85 S. W. 933.

Ohio.— Mathers *v.* Bull, 19 Ohio Cir. Ct. 657, 10 Ohio Cir. Dec. 515; Hack *v.* Heffern, 19 Ohio Cir. Ct. 233, 10 Ohio Cir. Dec. 461.

Oregon.— Brentano *v.* Brentano, 41 Oreg. 15, 67 Pac. 922.

Pennsylvania.— See Rogers *v.* Johnson, 67 Pa. St. 43.

Texas.— Eustis *v.* Henrietta, (Civ. App. 1897) 41 S. W. 720.

Virginia.—Mathews *v.* Glenn, 100 Va. 352, 41 S. E. 735.

Washington.—Nunn *v.* Stewart, 52 Wash. 513, 100 Pac. 1004; Ontario Land Co. *v.* Yordy, 44 Wash. 239, 87 Pac. 257; Young *v.* Droz, 38 Wash. 648, 80 Pac. 810; McManus *v.* Morgan, 38 Wash. 528, 80 Pac. 786; Denman *v.* Steinbach, 29 Wash. 179, 69 Pac. 751; Merritt *v.* Corey, 22 Wash. 444, 61 Pac. 171.

West Virginia.— Siers *v.* Wiseman, 58 W. Va. 340, 52 S. E. 460.

Wisconsin.—Van Ostrand *v.* Cole, 131 Wis. 446, 1[illegible] N. W. 891; Maxcy *v.* Simonson, 130 Wis. 650, 110 N. W. 803; Tucker *v.* Whittlesey, 74 Wis. 74, 41 N. W. 535, 42 N. W. 101; Wisconsin Cent. R. Co. *v.* Comstock, 71 Wis. 88, 36 N. W. 843; Kimball *v.* Ballard, 19 Wis. 601, 88 Am. Dec. 705; Wright *v.* Wing, 18 Wis. 45.

United States.— Whitehead *v.* Farmers' [illegible]. & T. Co., 98 Fed. 10, 39 C. C. A. 34; Smith *v.* Gage, 12 Fed. 32, 11 Biss. 217.

See 45 Cent. Dig. tit. "Taxation," § 1586.

In the federal courts, the payment or tender by the owner of land of the amount of taxes for which it was sold, together with the interest and penalties to which the holder of the tax certificate is entitled under the state laws, is an indispensable condition precedent to his right to maintain a bill in equity to cancel such certificate. Rice *v.* Jerome, 97 Fed. 719, 38 C. C. A. 388.

Form of action.— Such statutes apply notwithstanding the fact that the suit is in form of ejectment (Ward *v.* Huggins, 16 Wash. 530, 48 Pac. 240); but not where the proceeding is one to foreclose a mortgage (Mather *v.* Darst, 13 S. D. 75, 82 N. W. 407).

To what parties statutes apply.— Statutes such as those mentioned in the text apply to one holding a judgment lien on the land and suing to quiet title. Browning *v.* Smith, 139 Ind. 280, 37 N. E. 540; Gillett *v.* Webster, 15 Ohio 623. But not to an administrator who sues for an order to sell the lands of his decedent and to quiet title against a tax-sale (Hannah *v.* Collins, 94 Ind. 201); nor where it is the tax title claimant who takes the offensive and sues to quiet his title (Manwarring *v.* Missouri Lumber, etc., Co., 200 Mo. 718, 98 S. W. 762); nor where the holder of the tax title sues for partition, and the owner of the patent title pleads in bar a former adjudication declaring the tax title invalid (Thomsen *v.* McCormick, 136 Ill. 135, 26 N. E. 373); nor in a bill by the state to sell forfeited lands and to annul a tax deed constituting a title hostile to that of the state (State *v.* Harman, 57 W. Va. 447, 50 S. E. 828).

Sufficiency of tender.— A tender of the amount due on a tax certificate, with interest and costs, and requiring the holder to convey his title, is insufficient, since only conditions enjoined by law or arising out of a contract or trust relation between the parties can be attached to a tender. Glos *v.* Goodrich, 175 Ill. 20, 51 N. E. 643.

Where the sole requirement of the statute is a tender of all the taxes paid, the rule that one seeking the aid of equity to vacate a judgment must show that the former judgment was inequitable, and that he had a good defense, does not apply to an action to set aside a tax judgment, and a sale based thereon. Holly *v.* Munro, 55 Wash. 311, 104 Pac. 508.

30. *Alabama.*—Lassiter *v.* Lee, 68 Ala. 287 (holding that a statute requiring a deposit of double the amount of the purchase-money is unconstitutional as imposing an unreasonable condition); Whitworth *v.* Anderson, 54 Ala. 33.

Arkansas.— Coats *v.* Hill, 41 Ark. 149; Pope *v.* Macon, 23 Ark. 644; Craig *v.* Flanagin, 21 Ark. 319.

Kansas.—Belz *v.* Bird, 31 Kan. 139, 1 Pac.

otherwise where the objection goes to the legality of the tax or discloses a want of jurisdiction or faults rendering the proceedings entirely void.[41] If any definable portion of the tax was legal, although the balance may have been illegal, equity will not interfere unless that which is legal is first paid.[42] Where, however, it is impossible to determine what amount of the tax levied on the land was a just charge, the court will not require payment of any sum as a condition of relief.[43]

4. **Limitation of Actions and Laches — a. Statutes of Limitation** — (I) *In General.* In many states laws have been enacted prescribing a special short period of limitations for actions concerning the validity of tax titles,[44] as distinguished from titles founded in any other manner.[45] Provided the time allowed

Arkansas.—Hickman *v.* Kempner, 35 Ark. 505; Twombly *v.* Kimbrough, 24 Ark. 459. See also McCrary *v.* Joyner, 64 Ark. 547, 44 S. W. 79.

California.— Flannigan *v.* Towle, 8 Cal. App. 229, 96 Pac. 507.

Connecticut.— Adams *v.* Castle, 30 Conn. 404.

Georgia.— Picquet *v.* Augusta, 64 Ga. 516.

Illinois.— Gage *v.* Du Puy, 134 Ill. 132, 24 N. E. 866; Gage *v.* Caraher, 125 Ill. 447, 17 N. E. 777; Gage *v.* Nichols, 112 Ill. 269; Glos *v.* Dawson, 83 Ill. App. 197.

Indiana.— Skelton *v.* Sharp, 161 Ind. 383, 67 N. E. 535; Montgomery *v.* Trumbo, 126 Ind. 331, 26 N. E. 54; Peckham *v.* Millikan, 99 Ind. 352.

Kansas.— Black *v.* Johnson, 63 Kan. 47, 64 Pac. 988; Millbank *v.* Ostertag, 24 Kan. 462; Knox *v.* Dunn, 22 Kan. 683; Challiss *v.* Hekelnkaemper, 14 Kan. 474.

Minnesota.— Lewis *v.* Knowlton, 84 Minn. 53, 86 N. W. 875.

Nebraska.— Payne *v.* Anderson, 80 Nebr. 216, 114 N. W. 148 (holding that in an action to quiet title as against a sale for taxes under a void decree, an offer to pay such sum as the court may find due on account of any lien for taxes paid is a sufficient offer to do equity and a sufficient tender); Browne *v.* Finlay, 51 Nebr. 465, 71 N. W. 34; Dillon *v.* Merriam, 22 Nebr. 151, 34 N. W. 344; McNish *v.* Perrine, 14 Nebr. 582, 16 N. W. 837; Boeck *v.* Merriam, 10 Nebr. 199, 4 N. W. 962; Hunt *v.* Easterday, 10 Nebr. 165, 4 N. W. 952; Wood *v.* Helmer, 10 Nebr. 65, 4 N. W. 968.

North Dakota.— State Finance Co. *v.* Trimble, 16 N. D. 199, 112 N. W. 984; Powers *v.* Bottoneau First Nat. Bank, 15 N. D. 466, 109 N. W. 361; Fenton *v.* Minnesota Title Ins., etc., Co., 15 N. D. 365, 109 N. W. 363, 125 Am. St. Rep. 599.

West Virginia.—Lohr *v.* George, 65 W. Va. 241, 64 S. E. 609 (holding that equity will not set aside a tax-deed without providing for repayment of the taxes, interest, and costs paid by the purchaser, and that the bill should tender payment thereof or aver a willingness to pay the same; but that if such an offer is omitted the defect may be cured by a tender or offer before or on the entry of the decree); Toothman *v.* Courtney, 62 W. Va. 167, 58 S. E. 915.

United States.— Smith *v.* Gage, 12 Fed. 32, 11 Biss. 217.

See 45 Cent. Dig. tit. "Taxation," § 1586.

Form of decree.— It is not enough to decree that such repayment to the tax purchaser be made, but the court should make it a condition precedent to setting aside the tax deed. Gage *v.* Du Puy, 134 Ill. 132, 24 N. E. 866; Johnson *v.* Huling, 127 Ill. 14, 18 N. E. 786.

41. *Illinois.*— Eagan *v.* Connelly, 107 Ill. 458.

Iowa.— Miller *v.* Corbin, 46 Iowa 150.

Maine.— Wiggin *v.* Temple, 73 Me. 380.

North Carolina.— Warren *v.* Williford, 148 N. C. 474, 62 S. E. 697. See also Eames *v.* Armstrong, 146 N. C. 1, 59 S. E. 165, 125 Am. St. Rep. 436.

North Dakota.— State Finance Co. *v.* Trimble, 16 N. D. 199, 112 N. W. 984; State Finance Co. *v.* Beck, 15 N. D. 374, 109 N. W. 357; Eaton *v.* Bennett, 10 N. D. 346, 87 N. W. 188.

United States.— Gage *v.* Kaufman, 133 U. S. 471, 10 S. Ct. 406, 33 L. ed. 725.

See 45 Cent. Dig. tit. "Taxation," § 1586.

42. Orlando *v.* Equitable Bldg., etc., Assoc., 45 Fla. 507, 33 So. 986; Lawrence *v.* Killam, 11 Kan. 499.

43. Cahalan *v.* Van Sant, 87 Iowa 593, 54 N. W. 433; Anderson *v.* Douglas County, 98 Wis. 393, 74 N. W. 109; Hebard *v.* Ashland County, 55 Wis. 145, 12 N. W. 437.

44. See the statutes of the several states. And see the following cases:

Alabama.— Doe *v.* Moog, 150 Ala. 460, 43 So. 710.

Arkansas.— Helena *v.* Hornor, 58 Ark. 151, 23 S. W. 966.

Iowa.— Roth *v.* Munzenmaier, 118 Iowa 326, 91 N. W. 1072.

Kansas.— Long *v.* Wolf, 25 Kan. 522.

Louisiana.— Russell *v.* Lang, 50 La. Ann. 36, 23 So. 113.

Michigan.—St. Mary's Power Co. *v.* Chandler-Dunbar Water Power Co., 133 Mich. 470, 95 N. W. 554.

Minnesota.— Security Inv. Co. *v.* Buckler, 72 Minn. 251, 75 N. W. 107.

Pennsylvania.— Young *v.* Hosack, 2 Penr. & W. 162.

Washington.—Ward *v.* Huggins, 16 Wash. 530, 48 Pac. 240.

See 45 Cent. Dig. tit. "Taxation." § 1588.

What property affected.—Where the statute prescribes a period of time within which action must be brought for the recovery of "lands" held under a tax title, the term quoted includes town lots. Helena *v.* Hornor, 58 Ark. 151, 23 S. W. 966.

45. Worthen *v.* Fletcher, 64 Ark. 662, 42 S. W. 900, holding that a tax-sale is not a

under the various statutes may be the execution and recording of the tax deed; [68] or it may be the date of the sale, which means a sale completed by the delivery of a conveyance, and hence the statute begins to run from the time the purchaser becomes entitled to a deed,[69] or when the period of redemption has expired.[70] But it has been held that a statute of this kind does not apply to an action by the tax purchaser to quiet his title; [71] although, on the other hand, it is not limited to actions against the original owner, but applies as well to a suit against one claiming under a later tax-sale.[72] Independently of statutes of this kind, great and unreasonable delay on the part of the purchaser in asserting his rights may deprive him of the ordinary remedies.[73]

(II) *POSSESSION OR OCCUPATION OF LAND.* If the tax title claimant acquires and holds possession of the premises, the statute of limitations will not run against him.[74] And if the land has remained entirely vacant and unoccupied during the period limited by the statute, it is considered that the tax deed gives a constructive possession, and the same result follows.[75] But if the original owner remains in undisputed possession, or if he takes possession at any time during the period of limitations and holds it to the close thereof, the bar of the statute may then be interposed to prevent any action by the tax purchaser.[76]

632, 110 N. W. 785; Lain *v.* Shepardson, 23 Wis. 224; Falkner *v.* Dorman, 7 Wis. 388.

United States.— Barrett *v.* Holmes, 102 U. S. 651, 26 L. ed. 291.

See 45 Cent. Dig. tit. "Taxation," § 1591.

But *compare* Sullivan *v.* Collins, 20 Colo. 528, 39 Pac. 334, holding that Mills Annot. St. § 3904, so providing, does not apply to an action by a purchaser at a tax-sale, but only to an action by the prior owner whose title is sought to be divested by the tax-sale.

Relief in equity against operation of statute see Koen *v.* Martin, 110 La. 242, 34 So. 429; Union Mut. L. Ins. Co. *v.* Dice, 14 Fed. 523, 11 Biss. 373.

68. Cassady *v.* Sapp, 64 Iowa 203, 19 N. W. 909; Bowman *v.* Cockrill, 6 Kan. 311; Falkner *v.* Dorman, 7 Wis. 388.

Second deed on same sale.— Where the tax deed first issued is invalid and the purchaser procures a second and valid deed, the statute begins to run from the execution of the second deed. Adams *v.* Griffin, 66 Iowa 125, 23 N. W. 295. But one cannot have a second deed merely for the purpose of evading the statute of limitations, after the expiration of the time within which he should have sued for the land. Corbin *v.* Bronson, 28 Kan. 532.

Arrest of statute by recovery of judgment see Fulton *v.* Mathers, 75 Kan. 770, 90 Pac. 256.

69. Innes *v.* Drexel, 78 Iowa 253, 43 N. W. 201; Thode *v.* Spofford, 65 Iowa 294, 17 N. W. 561, 21 N. W. 647; Keokuk, etc., R. Co. *v.* Lindley, 48 Iowa 11; Thornton *v.* Jones, 47 Iowa 397; Hintrager *v.* Hennessy, 46 Iowa 600.

70. Smith *v.* Midland R. Co., 4 Ont. 494.

71. Francis *v.* Griffin, 72 Iowa 23, 33 N. W. 345; Wright *v.* Lacy, 52 Iowa 248, 3 N. W. 47; Lewis *v.* Soule, 52 Iowa 11, 2 N. W. 400; Walker *v.* Boh, 32 Kan. 354, 4 Pac. 272.

72. Smith *v.* Jones, 37 Kan. 292, 15 Pac. 185.

73. Slattery *v.* Heilperin, 110 La. 86, 34 So. 139. And see Hole *v.* Rittenhouse, 19 Pa. St. 305.

74. Gunnison *v.* Hoehne, 18 Wis. 268.

75. Dorweiler *v.* Callanan, 91 Iowa 299, 59 N. W. 74; Strabala *v.* Lewis, 80 Iowa 510, 45 N. W. 871; Maxwell *v.* Hunter, 65 Iowa 121, 21 N. W. 481; Goslee *v.* Tearney, 52 Iowa 455, 3 N. W. 502; Lewis *v.* Soule, 52 Iowa 11, 2 N. W. 400; Moingona Coal Co. *v.* Blair, 51 Iowa 447, 1 N. W. 768; Myers *v.* Coonradt, 28 Kan. 211; Austin *v.* Holt, 32 Wis. 478; Lawrence *v.* Kenney, 32 Wis. 281; Gunnison *v.* Hoehne, 18 Wis. 268. And see Warren *v.* Putnam, 63 Wis. 410, 24 N. W. 58. *Compare* Slattery *v.* Heilperin, 110 La. 86, 34 So. 139.

76. Griffith *v.* Carter, 64 Iowa 193, 19 N. W. 903; Monk *v.* Corbin, 58 Iowa 503, 12 N. W. 571; Barrett *v.* Love, 48 Iowa 103; Wallace *v.* Sexton, 44 Iowa 257; Peck *v.* Sexton, 41 Iowa 566; Brown *v.* Painter, 38 Iowa 456; Jones *v.* Collins, 16 Wis. 594; Parish *v.* Eager, 15 Wis. 532; Hintrager *v.* Nightingale, 36 Fed. 847.

In Kansas, where land is actually vacant and unoccupied for more than two years after the recording of the tax deed, the holder of such deed will have two years from the time when the original owner or other person took actual possession before being barred of his action to recover possession. Case *v.* Frazier, 30 Kan. 343, 2 Pac. 519.

Character of possession by owner.— The possession of land necessary to bar an action by a tax-title claimant against the occupant, by virtue of a patent, is not required to be of the adverse, hostile, and exclusive character required under the general statute of limitations. Griffith *v.* Carter, 64 Iowa 193, 19 N. W. 903. Cutting hay, by authority of the record owner, on wild prairie land sold for taxes, stacking it on the land, and plowing fire breaks around the stacks, indicate an intention to dispute the tax title, and are sufficient acts of possession by the record owner to satisfy the

except as the representatives of the state or county in cases where the latter was the purchaser.[25]

b. Process. Process in cases of this kind is governed by the ordinary rules, save for exceptions growing out of the peculiar nature of the proceedings.[26]

6. PLEADING — a. Pleading a Tax Title. Whenever a tax title is specially set forth in pleadings it is necessary that every fact should be averred which is requisite to show that each of the statutory provisions has been complied with;[27] and it is not enough to allege that the proceedings, or any of the proceedings, were taken "duly" or "according to the statute."[28] Furthermore it has been held that a statute declaring that tax deeds shall be *prima facie* evidence of certain facts essential to their validity does not dispense with the necessity of alleging such facts in a plea setting up a tax deed.[29] If plaintiff wishes to protect himself

Commercial Bank *v.* Sandford, 90 Fed. 154, holding that in a suit against a purchaser at a tax-sale to set aside such sale on the ground that the action of the sheriff who made it was illegal, such sheriff is a proper party defendant.

25. Sanders *v.* Saxton, 33 Misc. (N. Y.) 389, 67 N. Y. Suppl. 680.

In a suit by one entitled to a deed of the state's title to real estate, acquired by its purchasing the same at a tax-sale and to establish his interest therein, the auditor-general is a proper party, and complainant may ask that he execute a proper deed. Horton *v.* Helmholtz, 149 Mich. 227, 112 N. W. 930.

26. G. F. Sanborn Co. *v.* Johnson, 148 Mich. 405, 111 N. W. 1091 (holding that a notice of the expiration of the time for redemption of certain tax-sales reciting that, if payment was not made as required, the undersigned would institute proceedings for the possession of the land, is insufficient to confer jurisdiction upon the court, without further process, to issue a writ of assistance); Davis *v.* Cass, 72 Miss. 985, 18 So. 454 (publication of notice); Babcock *v.* Wolffarth, 35 Tex. Civ. App. 512, 80 S. W. 642 (notice to "unknown owner whose residence is unknown" is fatally defective).

27. *Arkansas.*— Blakeney *v.* Ferguson, 8 Ark. 272.

California.— Russell *v.* Mann, 22 Cal. 131.

Illinois.— Koch *v.* Hubbard, 85 Ill. 533.

Indiana.— Locke *v.* Catlett, 96 Ind. 291.

Iowa.— Stratton *v.* Drenan, 58 Iowa 571, 12 N. W. 602. See Mallory *v.* French, 44 Iowa 133.

Kentucky.— Com. *v.* Three Forks Coal Co., 95 Ky. 273, 25 S. W. 3, 15 Ky. L. Rep. 633; Durrett *v.* Stewart, 88 Ky. 665, 11 S. W. 773, 11 Ky. L. Rep. 172; Hundley *v.* Taylor, 25 S. W. 887, 15 Ky. L. Rep. 808. See also Packard *v.* Beaver Valley Land, etc., Co., 96 Ky. 249, 28 S. W. 779, 16 Ky. L. Rep. 451.

Mississippi.— Coffee *v.* Coleman, 85 Miss. 14, 37 So. 499; Brulie *v.* Cooney, (1893) 12 So. 463; Griffin *v.* Dogan, 48 Miss. 11. See also Belcher *v.* Mhoon, 47 Miss. 613.

Tennessee.— Reeves *v.* Brockman, (Ch. App. 1901) 62 S. W. 50.

Wisconsin.— Preston *v.* Thayer, 127 Wis. 123, 106 N. W. 672; Comstock *v.* Ludington, 47 Wis. 229, 2 N. W. 283. See also Hunt *v.* Miller, 101 Wis. 583, 77 N. W. 874; Manseau *v.* Edwards, 53 Wis. 457, 10 N. W. 554.

See 45 Cent. Dig. tit. "Taxation," §§ 1600, 1601.

But *compare* Blakemore *v.* Roberts, 12 N. D. 394, 96 N. W. 1029, holding that a complaint under Laws (1901), c. 5, p. 9, and based on a tax lien, need not allege that such tax lien was based on a regular assessment and levy of tax.

The year for which the tax was assessed must be averred; and moreover it is not sufficient to aver that in that year the assessor entered the levy on the assessment roll. Russell *v.* Mann, 22 Cal. 131.

Allegation as to possession.— In Louisiana it is not necessary that a tax purchaser suing to quiet title shall allege possession in himself or want of possession in defendant, but the fact of possession by defendant is a matter of defense. Slattery *v.* Kellum, 114 La. 282, 38 So. 170.

Admission of defendant's ownership.— Where, under the statute, a suit to foreclose a tax title can be brought only against the original owner, the bringing of the action is an admission that defendant was such owner, although the allegation of the fact is defective. Randall *v.* Dailey, 66 Wis. 285, 28 N. W. 352.

A complaint in an adversary suit to quiet title which alleges that plaintiff is the owner of the land which is unoccupied, claiming under a tax deed, and that defendant is asserting title thereto and paying taxes, states a cause of action to quiet title under the general equity jurisdiction of the court, irrespective of whether plaintiff is entitled to a general decree for confirmation of the tax-sale. Knauff *v.* National Cooperage Co., 87 Ark. 494, 113 S. W. 28.

28. Blakeney *v.* Ferguson, 8 Ark. 272; Carter *v.* Koezley, 9 Bosw. (N. Y.) 583, 14 Abb. Pr. 147. See also Chrisman *v.* Currie, 60 Miss. 858.

29. Gage *v.* Harbert, 145 Ill. 530, 32 N. E. 543; Smith *v.* Denny, 90 Miss. 434, 43 So. 479, holding that under such a statute a bill of complaint alleging that the land was sold and that the list of the land sold to the state at the time of the sale shows the lands in question were sold, and making the tax collector's deed an exhibit, states a perfect cause of action. But see Hibernia Sav., etc., Soc. *v.* Ordway, 38 Cal. 679, holding

against the consequences of his tax deed being held invalid, and to secure such compensation or reimbursement as the law allows in that case, he may do so by amendment to his bill or complaint, or, where he is attacked, by cross bill.[30]

b. Complaint or Answer Impeaching Tax Title. Where a pleading undertakes to impeach the validity of a tax title it is not sufficient to allege that the opposite party claims some interest in the premises under certain tax-sales or deeds but that the same are invalid;[31] but it is necessary to point out, clearly and specifically and in apt terms, the particular defect, illegality, or failure of compliance with the law which is supposed to invalidate the title and on which the pleader means to rely.[32] And in case the action is against a subsequent purchaser from the original holder of the tax title, there must be allegations to connect him with

that naming the instrument is sufficient to show an apparent validity.

30. Wartensleben *v.* Haithcock, 80 Ala. 565, 1 So. 38; Robinson *v.* Dunne, 45 Fla. 553, 33 So. 530; Preston *v.* Banks, 71 Miss. 601, 14 So. 258; Stephenson *v.* Doolittle, 123 Wis. 36, 100 N. W. 1041.

31. Smith *v.* Gilmer, 93 Ala. 224, 9 So. 588; Knudson *v.* Curley, 30 Minn. 433, 15 N. W. 873. But *compare* Gray *v.* Coan, 23 Iowa 344.

A bill to quiet title by a tax deed holder, under Mich. Comp. Laws, § 448, setting up a claim to property, must aver, where no record evidence of a cloud upon its title is asserted, that defendants have asserted title or some claim adverse to defendant's title. Triangle Land Co. *v.* Nessen, 155 Mich. 463, 119 N. W. 586; Jenks *v.* Hathaway, 48 Mich. 536, 12 N. W. 621.

32. *Alabama.*— Francis *v.* Sandlin, 150 Ala. 583, 43 So. 829.

Arkansas.— Shell *v.* Martin, 19 Ark. 139.

Colorado.— Webber *v.* Wannemaker, 39 Colo. 425, 89 Pac. 780.

Florida.—Robertson *v.* Dunne, 45 Fla. 553, 33 So. 530.

Illinois.— Glos. *v.* Hayes, 214 Ill. 372, 73 N. E. 802; Glos *v.* Stern, 213 Ill. 325, 72 N. E. 1057; Glos *v.* Hanford, 212 Ill. 261, 72 N. E. 439; Langlois *v.* People, 212 Ill. 75, 72 N. E. 28; Glos *v.* Kingman, 207 Ill. 26, 69 N. E. 632; Langlois *v.* McCullom, 184 Ill. 195, 54 N. E. 955; Gage *v.* Bailey, 102 Ill. 11; Gage *v.* McLaughlin, 101 Ill. 155.

Indiana.—Ethel *v.* Batchelder, 90 Ind. 520, Sohn *v.* Wood, 75 Ind. 17; Beatty *v.* Krauskopf, 7 Ind. 565.

Iowa.— Farmers' L. & T. Co. *v.* Wall, 129 Iowa 651, 106 N. W. 160; Grove *v.* Benedict, 69 Iowa 346, 28 N. W. 631; Plympton *v.* Sapp, 55 Iowa 195, 7 N. W. 498.

Kansas.— Taylor *v.* Adams, 79 Kan. 360, 99 Pac. 597; Crebbin *v.* Wever, 71 Kan. 445, 80 Pac. 977. See also Shinkle *v.* Meek, 69 Kan. 368, 76 Pac. 837.

Kentucky.— Stites *v.* Short, 76 S. W. 518, 25 Ky. L. Rep. 918.

Louisiana.— Edwards *v.* Fairex, 47 La. Ann. 170, 16 So. 736.

Michigan.— Flint Land Co. *v.* Godkin, 136 Mich. 668, 99 N. W. 1058; Wagar *v.* Bowley, 104 Mich. 38, 62 N. W. 293; Gamble *v.* East Saginaw, 43 Mich. 367, 5 N. W. 416.

Mississippi.— Byrd *v.* McDonald, (1900) 28 So. 847; Clarke *v.* Frank, 64 Miss. 827, 3 So. 531.

Montana.— Casey *v.* Wright, 14 Mont. 315, 36 Pac. 191.

Nebraska.— Weston *v.* Meyers, 45 Nebr. 95, 63 N. W. 117; Dillon *v.* Merriam, 22 Nebr. 151, 34 N. W. 344.

North Carolina.— Beck *v.* Meroney, 135 N. C. 532, 47 S. E. 613.

Oregon.— O'Hara *v.* Parker, 27 Oreg. 156, 39 Pac. 1004.

Texas.— Gulf, etc., R. Co. *v.* Poindexter, 70 Tex. 98, 7 S. W. 316.

Virginia.— Glenn *v.* Brown, 99 Va. 322, 38 S. E. 189.

Washington.— Kahn *v.* Thorp, 43 Wash. 463, 86 Pac. 855 (holding that in an action either of ejectment or to recover property or to remove a cloud, where the property has been sold for taxes, the petition must allege that the lands were not taxable or that the taxes, penalties, interest, and costs sustained by the purchaser at the tax-sale had been fully paid or tendered and tender rejected); Rowland *v.* Eskland, 40 Wash. 253, 82 Pac. 599; McManus *v.* Morgan, 38 Wash. 528, 80 Pac. 786.

West Virginia.— Hogan *v.* Piggott, 60 W. Va. 541, 56 S. E. 189; State *v.* McEldowney, 54 W. Va. 695, 47 S. E. 650.

Wisconsin.— Mitchell Iron, etc., Co. *v.* Flambeau Land Co., 120 Wis. 545, 98 N. W. 530; Anderson *v.* Douglas County, 98 Wis. 393, 74 N. W. 109; Prentice *v.* Ashland County, 56 Wis. 345, 14 N. W. 297; Lawrence *v.* Kenney, 32 Wis. 281; Sayles *v.* Davis, 22 Wis. 225; Johnston *v.* Oshkosh, 21 Wis. 184; Wilson *v.* Jarvis, 19 Wis. 597; Jarvis *v.* McBride, 18 Wis. 316; Wakeley *v.* Nicholas, 16 Wis. 588.

United States.— Meyer *v.* Kuhn, 65 Fed. 705, 13 C. C. A. 298; De Forest *v.* Thompson, 40 Fed. 375.

See 45 Cent. Dig. tit. "Taxation," §§ 1600, 1601.

But *compare* Owen *v.* Ruthruff, 81 Minn. 397, 84 N. W. 217 (holding that it is proper pleading to specify in the complaint, in a statutory action to test tax titles, the tax certificate or deed which is assailed as invalid); Lewis *v.* Bartleson, 39 Minn. 89, 38 N. W. 707; Jones *v.* Boykin, 70 S. C. 309, 49 S. E. 877.

Alleging cloud on title.— Where the statute makes a tax deed *prima facie* evidence of title, in an action to remove a cloud created by a tax deed, an allegation in the complaint that the deed is regular on its face

to assert his title and can receive no aid from prescription.[48] But statutes making tax deeds *prima facie* or conclusive evidence of title or of the regularity of the prior proceedings have the effect of shifting the burden of proof, so that it is incumbent on the party assailing the tax title to show the particular defect which is fatal to its validity.[49] But even with the help of such a statute, various matters may come in issue which are not covered by the recitals of the deed or the provisions of the statute, and as to these the party relying on the tax title must assume the burden of proof, such as, to identify the particular land affected,[50] to show an assignment of the tax certificate to himself,[51] to show that his purchase was fair and in good faith,[52] or that there has been no redemption; [53] or, if he means to claim reimbursement on the setting aside of the tax deed, to show the precise amount to which he is entitled.[54] Similarly it is a general rule that one shall not be permitted to impeach a tax title without first showing title in himself,[55] and in some jurisdictions he is required to prove that all taxes due on the land have been paid,[56] and his continued and adverse possession of the premises, if that is essential to his attack or defense.[57]

c. Admissibility.[58] As a general rule, all the books, papers, and records relating to the taxes, made by and in the custody of the proper officers, are admis-

48. Waddill *v.* Walton, 42 La. Ann. 763, 7 So. 737.

49. See *supra*, XIII, G, 4, b. See also Husbands *v.* Polivick, 96 S. W. 825, 29 Ky. L. Rep. 890; St. Paul, etc., R. Co. *v.* Howard, 23 S. D. 34, 119 N. W. 1032, holding that a railroad company attacking a tax deed on the ground that the land was "necessarily used in the operations of its lines," so as to be subject only to a mileage tax, has the burden of showing that the land was so used.

Action before issuance of deed.— In a suit to set aside a tax-sale, commenced before a deed is issued, the burden of proof is on the purchaser to show compliance with the law, and is not changed by the fact that a deed is recorded pending the suit. Columbia Finance, etc., Co. *v.* Fierbaugh, 59 W. Va. 334, 53 S. E. 468.

Where in an action to test the validity of a tax deed plaintiff owns the fee and defendant is in possession under the tax deed, which the court holds to be good on its face, the burden is on plaintiff to show facts which make the deed ineffective. Taylor *v.* Adams, 79 Kan. 360, 99 Pac. 597.

Where in ejectment defendant exhibits a title derived from a treasurer's sale for taxes assessed on the land as unseated, regular in form and long subsequent to the acquisition of the title exhibited by plaintiffs, derived from a like sale, the burden is on plaintiffs to prove the defect alleged in defendant's title. Floyd *v.* Kulp Lumber Co., 222 Pa. St. 257, 71 Atl. 15.

Where a complaint alleges that tax deeds were issued and recorded, it will be assumed, in the absence of averment to the contrary, that such tax deeds were in the form required by law, thus entitling them to a presumption in favor of the regularity of all prior proceedings and to the protection of the statute of limitations when the lands are vacant and unoccupied. Strange *v.* Oconto Land Co., 136 Wis. 516, 117 N. W. 1023.

Tax deed set aside.—Where, on account of irregularities connected with a tax-sale, the deed is set aside, it no longer possesses any evidential force, and the party relying on the tax title must prove the regularity of the tax proceedings. O'Neil *v.* Tyler, 3 N. D. 47, 53 N. W. 434. And see Wood *v.* Bigelow, 115 Mich. 123, 73 N. W. 129.

50. Chapman *v.* Zoberlein, 152 Cal. 216, 92 Pac. 188; Smith *v.* Bodfish, 27 Me. 289; Canole *v.* Allen, 28 Pa. Super. Ct. 244; Swanson *v.* Hoyle, 32 Wash. 169, 72 Pac. 1011.

51. Smith *v.* Harrow, 1 Bibb (Ky.) 97.

52. Morton *v.* Waring, 18 B. Mon. (Ky.) 72.

53. Goodman *v.* Sanger, 85 Pa. St. 37, holding that a presumption of redemption arising from lapse of time and non-claim may be rebutted by facts. But see Nind *v.* Myers, 15 N. D. 400, 109 N. W. 335, 8 L. R. A. N. S. 157, holding that a party claiming title under a tax-sale certificate need not prove that no redemption had been made.

54. Glos *v.* Kelly, 212 Ill. 314, 72 N. E. 378; Barrow *v.* Lapene, 30 La. Ann. 310.

55. Hilton *v.* Singletary, 107 Ga. 821, 33 S. E. 715; Glos *v.* Gleason, 209 Ill. 517, 70 N. E. 1045 (holding, however, that in a suit to set aside a tax deed as a cloud on title it is not necessary for complainant to prove his own title with the same strictness as in an action of ejectment); Glos *v.* Adams, 204 Ill. 546, 68 N. E. 398; Glos *v.* Randolph, 133 Ill. 197, 24 N. E. 426, 138 Ill. 268, 27 N. E. 941; Curry *v.* Hinman, 11 Ill. 420; Roth *v.* Munzenmaier, 118 Iowa 326, 91 N. W. 1072.

56. Curry *v.* Hinman, 11 Ill. 420; Maxwell *v.* Palmer, 73 Iowa 595, 35 N. W. 659; Lufkin *v.* Galveston, 73 Tex. 340, 11 S. W. 340.

57. Glos *v.* Perkins, 188 Ill. 467, 58 N. E. 971; Glos *v.* Beckman, 183 Ill. 158, 55 N. E. 636; Jones *v.* Sadler, 75 Kan. 380, 89 Pac. 1019; Boagni *v.* Pacific Imp. Co., 111 La. 1063, 36 So. 129; Lawrence *v.* Kenney, 32 Wis. 281.

58. Evidence to impeach deed or title see *supra*, XIII, G, 5.

costs, but may, on the other hand, be entitled to his own costs,[10] as he will be also when he is successful in an action to confirm or quiet his title or to foreclose the interest of the former owner.[11]

C. Reimbursement of Purchaser of Invalid Title — 1. Right to Relief in General — a. Application of Rule of Caveat Emptor. At common law the purchaser at a tax-sale assumes the risks of his purchase. The proceedings are of record, and he is chargeable with notice of any defect or irregularity which the records disclose. Moreover the power of the officer to sell is a naked power, statutory, and not coupled with an interest, and the purchaser is bound to inquire whether it is rightly exercised. Therefore, in the absence of special legislation to the contrary, he comes within the rule of *caveat emptor*, and if his title proves worthless, he cannot recover his money from the officer or the municipality,[12] although on equitable principles, and if he is free from fraud or bad faith,[13] it is

Iowa.— Springer *v.* Bartle, 46 Iowa 688.

Kansas.— Shinkle *v.* Meek, 69 Kan. 368, 76 Pac. 837.

Ohio.— Mathers *v.* Bull, 9 Ohio S. & C. Pl. Dec. 408, 6 Ohio N. P. 45.

Texas.— Rogers *v.* Moore, (Civ. App. 1906) 94 S. W. 114.

Washington.— Wheeler Co. *v.* Pates, 43 Wash. 247, 86 Pac. 625.

In Michigan where a bill to remove a cloud on title to land and to redeem from a tax-sale for delinquent drain taxes is in effect a suit to set aside the drain taxes, within the meaning of the statute which precludes costs against either party in an action to set aside any sale for delinquent taxes, the auditor-general, although a necessary party under General Tax Law, § 144 (Pub. Acts (1899), p. 140), is not entitled to costs on the dismissal of the bill. Haney *v.* Miller, 154 Mich. 337, 117 N. W. 71, 745.

10. Bauer *v.* Gloss, 236 Ill. 450, 86 N. E. 116; Glos *v.* Garrett, 219 Ill. 208, 76 N. E. 373; South Chicago Brewing Co. *v.* Taylor, 205 Ill. 132, 68 N. E. 732; Glos *v.* Adams, 204 Ill. 546, 68 N. E. 398. But *compare* Van Ostrand *v.* Cole, 131 Wis. 446, 110 N. W. 891; Stephenson *v.* Doolittle, 123 Wis. 36, 100 N. W. 1041.

Equitable grounds for awarding costs.—A decree for costs against one holding a tax certificate or a tax deed cannot be entered until after, by a valid tender, he has been placed in the position of refusing to do equity. Stearns *v.* Glos, 235 Ill. 290, 85 N. E. 335; Glos *v.* Collins, 110 Ill. App. 121. But a tender to a tax purchaser of the amount paid for a tax certificate, together with costs and interest, coupled with a condition that a quitclaim deed of the property should be given by him, is not a sufficient tender. Stearns *v.* Glos, *supra.*

Where deed absolutely void.— Where it is determined, in a suit to set aside a tax deed, that the deed is absolutely void on the ground that the property was not subject to the assessment in question, costs should not be allowed to either party. Barnes *v.* Bee, 138 Fed. 476.

11. Collins *v.* Bryan, 124 N. C. 738, 32 S. E. 975; State *v.* Hatch, 36 Wash. 164, 78 Pac. 796; Loomis *v.* Rice, 37 Wis. 262. See also Jarvis *v.* Mohr, 18 Wis. 188.

12. *Colorado.*— Mitchell *v.* Minnequa Town Co., 41 Colo. 367, 92 Pac. 678.

Illinois.— Miller *v.* Cook, 135 Ill. 190, 25 N. E. 756, 10 L. R. A. 292.

Indiana.— Worley *v.* Cicero, 110 Ind. 208, 11 N. E. 227; State *v.* Casteel, 110 Ind. 174, 11 N. E. 219; McWhinney *v.* Indianapolis, 98 Ind. 182; Indianapolis *v.* Langsdale, 29 Ind. 486.

Kansas.— Sullivan *v.* Davis, 29 Kan. 28.

Louisiana.— Lindner *v.* New Orleans, 116 La. 372, 40 So. 736.

Maryland.— Hamilton *v.* Valiant, 30 Md. 139; Polk *v.* Rose, 25 Md. 153, 89 Am. Dec. 773.

Michigan.— People *v.* Auditor-Gen., 30 Mich. 12.

Montana.— Larson *v.* Peppard, 38 Mont. 128, 99 Pac. 136, 129 Am. St. Rep. 630.

Nebraska.— Martin *v.* Kearney County, 62 Nebr. 538, 87 N. W. 351; McCague *v.* Omaha, 58 Nebr. 37, 78 N. W. 463; Norris *v.* Burt County, 56 Nebr. 295, 76 N. W. 551; Adams *v.* Osgood, 42 Nebr. 450, 60 N. W. 869; Pennock *v.* Douglas County, 39 Nebr. 293, 58 N. W. 117, 42 Am. St. Rep. 579, 27 L. R. A. 121.

North Dakota.— Tyler *v.* Cass County, 1 N. D. 369, 48 N. W. 232.

South Carolina.— Cooke *v.* Pennington, 15 S. C. 185.

South Dakota.—American Inv. Co. *v.* Beadle County, 5 S. D. 410, 59 N. W. 212.

Tennessee.— Ross *v.* Mabry, 1 Lea 226.

Virginia.— Hoge *v.* Currin, 3 Gratt. 201.

United States.— Stead *v.* Course, 4 Cranch 403, 2 L. ed. 660; Martin *v.* Barbour, 34 Fed. 701 [*affirmed* in 140 U. S. 634, 11 S. Ct. 944, 35 L. ed. 546].

See 45 Cent. Dig. tit. "Taxation," § 1619. See also *infra*, XIV, C, 2, a.

In Pennsylvania, under an act of 1856, the rule of *caveat emptor* did not apply to tax-sales in case of double assessment, or where the taxes had been paid, or where the lands did not lie within the county; and in such cases the money was to be refunded to the purchaser. Bredin *v.* Cranberry Tp. Road Com'rs, 87 Pa. St. 441; Siggins *v.* Forest County, 2 Chest. Co. Rep. 421.

13. West *v.* Negrotto, 52 La. Ann. 381, 27 So. 75.

right that he should be subrogated to the rights of the municipality in any tax he has paid in making his purchase or in its protection.[14]

b. Covenants and Liabilities of Officers. A public officer may be liable in damages to a tax purchaser for neglect or inaction which prevents such purchaser from securing his rights under a valid sale;[15] but he is not liable in damages for a failure of title, unless due to fraud or wilful neglect on his own part.[16] Even where a covenant of warranty is inserted in a tax deed, as required by the statute, it is regarded as an official and not a personal covenant, and the officer is not to be held personally liable for its breach.[17]

2. RECOVERY FROM STATE OR MUNICIPALITY — a. Right of Action at Common Law. Unless aided by express statutory authority, the purchaser at a tax-sale whose title proves to be invalid is not entitled to recover back his money in an action against the state, or its officers, or the city or county for whose taxes the land was sold.[18] Neither is it competent for the officers of a county to make a special contract with tax purchasers, agreeing to refund the money if the title fails, for unless such a contract is authorized by statute it will not be binding on the county, or give the purchaser a right of action.[19]

b. Statutes Giving Right of Action — (I) *IN GENERAL.* In many states the statutes now provide that the purchase-money paid at a tax-sale shall be refunded to the purchaser if the title conveyed proves to be invalid, with a right of action against the municipality if the refund is refused.[20] Such laws, however, are

14. Leavitt *v.* Bartholomew, 1 Nebr. (Unoff.) 756, 764, 93 N. W. 856.

15. Holden *v.* Eaton, 7 Pick. (Mass.) 15, holding that a tax collector was liable for a failure to make a proper return of the tax-sale, in consequence of which the purchaser could not procure a deed.

16. Harris *v.* Willard, Smith (N. H.) 63.

17. Stephenson *v.* Weeks, 22 N. H. 257; Wilson *v.* Cochran, 14 N. H. 397; Gibson *v.* Mussey, 11 Vt. 212. And see *supra*, XIII, D, 1, d. *Compare* Stubbs *v.* Page, 2 Me. 378.

18. *Arkansas.*— Nevada County *v.* Dickey, 68 Ark. 160, 56 S. W. 779.

California.— Loomis *v.* Los Angeles County, 59 Cal. 456.

Colorado.— Larimer County *v.* National State Bank, 11 Colo. 564, 19 Pac. 537.

Indiana.— Worley *v.* Cicero, 110 Ind. 208, 11 N. E. 227; State *v.* Casteel, 110 Ind. 174, 11 N. E. 219; Hilgenberg *v.* Marion County, 107 Ind. 494, 8 N. E. 294; McWhinney *v.* Indianapolis, 98 Ind. 182; Logansport *v.* Humphrey, 84 Ind. 467; Indianapolis *v.* Langsdale, 29 Ind. 486.

Iowa.— Lindsey *v.* Boone County, 92 Iowa 86, 60 N. W. 173.

Kansas.— Lyon County *v.* Goddard, 22 Kan. 389.

Louisiana.— Lindner *v.* New Orleans, 116 La. 372, 40 So. 736.

Maine.— Packard *v.* New Limerick, 34 Me. 266; Treat *v.* Orono, 26 Me. 217.

Massachusetts.— Lynde *v.* Melrose, 10 Allen 49.

Michigan.— People *v.* Auditor-Gen., 30 Mich. 12.

Nebraska.— Martin *v.* Kearney County, 62 Nebr. 538, 87 N. W. 351; Norris *v.* Burt County, 56 Nebr. 295, 76 N. W. 551.

New York.— Coffin *v.* Brooklyn, 116 N. Y. 159, 22 N. E. 227; Brevoort *v.* Brooklyn, 89 N. Y. 128.

North Dakota.— Tyler *v.* Cass County, 1 N. D. 369, 48 N. W. 232; Budge *v.* Grand Forks, 1 N. D. 309, 47 N. W. 390, 10 L. R. A. 165.

Oregon.— Dowell *v.* Portland, 13 Oreg. 248, 10 Pac. 308.

Pennsylvania.— Lackey *v.* Mercer County, 9 Pa. St. 318.

South Dakota.— Minnesota Loan, etc., Co. *v.* Beadle County, 18 S. D. 431, 101 N. W. 29; American Inv. Co. *v.* Beadle County, 5 S. D. 410, 59 N. W. 212.

Wisconsin.— See Jackson *v.* Jacksonport, 56 Wis. 310, 14 N. W. 296, holding that where a town, under the statutes, cannot legally purchase and hold tax certificates and therefore cannot sell them, a town making such a sale may be sued for the return of the money paid by the purchaser for the certificate.

Canada.—Austin *v.* Simcoe County Corp., 22 U. C. Q. B. 73.

See 45 Cent. Dig. tit. "Taxation," § 1621. See also *supra*, XIV, C, 1, a.

19. Hyde *v.* Kenosha County Sup'rs, 43 Wis. 129.

20. See the statutes of the several states. And see the following cases:

California.— Hayes *v.* Los Angeles County, 99 Cal. 74, 33 Pac. 766.

Illinois.— Joliet Stove Works *v.* Kiep, 230 Ill. 550, 82 N. E. 875 [*affirming* 132 Ill. App. 457], holding that the Revenue Act (Hurd Rev. St. (1905) c. 120), §§ 213, 214, modified the rule of *caveat emptor* applicable to tax-sales, in so far that when the sale is void for any of the specified defects the purchaser or his assignee is entitled to recover the money paid from the county.

Massachusetts.— Spring *v.* Cambridge, 199 Mass. 1, 85 N. E. 160.

Nebraska.— McCann *v.* Otoe County, 9 Nebr. 324, 2 N. W. 707.

construed with some strictness and confined to the specific cases mentioned.[21] They are not unconstitutional if they give a right of action against a county for a claim which it is morally or legally bound to recognize, but it is otherwise where the only basis for the action is attributable to the purchaser's own fault or neglect.[22] Such a statute, in force at the time of the sale, forms a part of the contract, and the rights vesting in the purchaser under it cannot be impaired or taken away by the repeal of the act.[23]

(II) *RETROACTIVE STATUTES.* A statute of this character may constitutionally be made to apply to tax-sales occurring before its enactment;[24] but such a law will not be construed as being retroactive unless the intention of the legislature to give it such an operation is clearly apparent.[25]

New York.— Wheeler *v.* State, 190 N. Y. 406, 83 N. E. 54, 132 Am. St. Rep. 555 [*affirming* 118 N. Y. App. Div. 913, 103 N. Y. Suppl. 1150].

South Dakota.— King *v.* Lane, 21 S. D. 101, 110 N. W. 37.

See 45 Cent. Dig. tit. "Taxation," § 1622.

Demand and refusal of refund.— Where a statute provides that any taxes erroneously or illegally collected may be refunded by the county treasurer by order of the board of supervisors, the word "may" means "shall," and the board have no discretion to allow or refuse a claim for refund, and if they refuse to allow it, an action then lies against the county. Hayes *v.* Los Angeles County, 99 Cal. 74, 33 Pac. 766.

Effect of refunding.— The state does not lose its lien on the property for the taxes refunded. Auditor-Gen. *v.* Patterson, 122 Mich. 39, 80 N. W. 884; Olmsted County *v.* Barber, 31 Minn. 256, 17 N. W. 473, 944.

Refunding by mistake and subsequent restoration of money.— Where a purchaser of land at a tax-sale, through a mistake of fact, applies to the county to refund the amount paid, which is done, but afterward, on discovering the mistake, he returns the money, this will not estop him to perfect and rely on the tax title, at least where the former owner was in no way misled or influenced thereby; nor will this operate as a cancellation of the tax purchaser's deed, which was in fact valid, the county board having no power to refund money received on a valid sale. Edwards *v.* Upham, 93 Wis. 455, 67 N. W. 728.

21. People *v.* Auditor-Gen., 30 Mich. 12; Roberts *v.* Fargo First Nat. Bank, 8 N. D. 504, 79 N. W. 1049.

Judgment annulling tax-sale.— Where the law provides for a refund of the purchase-money in case the tax title has been "annulled pursuant to law," this means that it must have been annulled by a judgment acting directly on the title in a proceeding analogous to a suit to quiet title, and does not apply where the tax title was merely introduced in evidence in an action of ejectment and there held defective. People *v.* Auditor-Gen., 30 Mich. 12. But *compare* Fleming *v.* Roverud, 30 Minn. 273, 15 N. W. 119.

Purchase from state.— The statute in Mississippi providing for refunding to the purchaser if the taxes were not due applies to the state's vendee as well as to the purchaser at a tax collector's sale. Wilkinson County *v.* Fitts, 63 Miss. 600.

Failure to recover possession.— Where the statute authorizes a refund in case the purchaser "shall be unable to recover possession" by reason of the invalidity of the tax-sale, he must show not only that the tax-sale was invalid but also that he has made some effort to recover possession of the land. Reid *v.* Albany County, 128 N. Y. 364, 28 N. E. 367.

Deed invalid but not sale.— Where the tax-sale and all proceedings preliminary thereto were regular and valid, the fact of an irregularity or error in the certificate or deed does not impair the sale, and therefore does not give the purchaser a right to recover his money. Clarke *v.* New York, 111 N. Y. 21, 19 N. E. 436. And see Ball *v.* Barnes, 123 Ind. 394, 24 N. E. 142, holding that where the sale is sufficient to pass the tax lien, although ineffectual to convey title, on account of a defective description, the purchaser must rely on his lien and cannot recover his money back from the county.

22. State *v.* Bruce, 50 Minn. 491, 52 N. W. 970.

23. St. Louis, etc., R. Co. *v.* Alexander, 49 Ark. 190, 4 S. W. 753; Morgan *v.* Miami County, 27 Kan. 89; Harding *v.* Auditor-Gen., 136 Mich. 358, 99 N. W. 275; Tillotson *v.* Saginaw Cir. Judge, 97 Mich. 585, 56 N. W. 945; Comstock *v.* Devlin, 99 Minn. 68, 108 N. W. 888.

In Minnesota Gen. Laws (1905), c. 271, relating to notice of the expiration of the time of redemption of any tax certificate, does not deprive the holder of such certificate of the right to refundment secured to him under the prior law on judicial determination of the invalidity of the certificate. State *v.* Krahmer, 105 Minn. 422, 117 N. W. 780, 21 L. R. A. N. S. 157.

24. Millikan *v.* Lafayette, 118 Ind. 323, 20 N. E. 847; School Dist. No. 15 *v.* Allen County, 22 Kan. 568; Schoonover *v.* Galarnault, 45 Minn. 174, 47 N. W. 654; Easton *v.* Hayes, 35 Minn. 418, 29 N. W. 59; Coles *v.* Washington County, 35 Minn. 124, 27 N. W. 497; State *v.* Cronkhite, 28 Minn. 197, 9 N. W. 681; Pier *v.* Oneida County, 102 Wis. 338, 78 N. W. 410. *Compare* State *v.* Bruce, 50 Minn. 491, 52 N. W. 970.

25. Shaw *v.* Morley, 89 Mich. 313, 50 N. W. 993; Norris *v.* Burt County, 56 Nebr. 295, 76

fails in his effort to recover possession of the land;[56] and if no clause of the statute applies explicitly to such a claim for reimbursement, it will be governed by a provision limiting the right of action "on a liability created by statute other than a penalty or forfeiture."[57] In this connection the statute of limitations should not be construed retrospectively.[58] Aside from the statute the purchaser's claim may be rejected on the ground of laches.[59]

f. Authority and Duty of Public Officers to Refund. In some states the laws provide for the reimbursement of the purchaser of an invalid tax title by authorizing the county treasurer or other proper officer to refund the money without suit,[60] on the surrender of the tax certificate or deed for cancellation,[61] and the presentation of proper proof of the applicant's right to a return of his money.[62] The decision of the officer on the question of refunding is so far judicial in its nature as to be immune against collateral impeachment;[63] but in a case where his duty is plain he may be required by mandamus to perform it,[64] or if he is restrained by the order of the county commissioners, forbidding him to pay over the money, the purchaser may then bring suit against the county.[65]

3. PURCHASER'S LIEN — a. Right to Lien in General. A mere purchase of land at a tax-sale gives no lien enforceable in equity for the reimbursement of the money paid;[66] but where the tax title proves defective, the statutes of many states now create a lien in favor of the purchaser for the amount of the price paid, or to the extent of the taxes paid, either generally or in special cases.[67] There is, however,

Vista County, 66 Iowa 128, 23 N. W. 297; White *v.* Brooklyn, 122 N. Y. 53, 25 N. E. 243. But *compare* Clapp *v.* Pinegrove Tp., 138 Pa. St. 35, 20 Atl. 836, 12 L. R. A. 618.

Until the grantee has clear and positive knowledge that the sale is invalid, the statute of limitations does not commence to run against his claim to have the purchase-money refunded by reason of the invalidity of the tax-sale. Hutchinson *v.* Sheboygan County, 26 Wis. 402.

56. Reid *v.* Albany County, 128 N. Y. 364, 28 N. E. 367.

57. Rork *v.* Douglas County, 46 Kan. 175, 26 Pac. 391.

58. Reid *v.* Albany County, 128 N. Y. 364, 28 N. E. 367.

59. Jefferson County *v.* Johnson, 23 Kan. 717; Harding *v.* Auditor-Gen., 136 Mich. 358, 99 N. W. 275.

60. See the statutes of the several states. And see the following cases:

Louisiana.— State *v.* Cannon, 44 La. Ann. 734, 11 So. 86.

Michigan.— Harding *v.* Auditor-Gen., 136 Mich. 358, 99 N. W. 275; O'Connor *v.* Auditor-Gen., 127 Mich. 553, 86 N. W. 1023; Auditor-Gen. *v.* Bay County, 106 Mich. 662, 64 N. W. 570.

New Mexico.— Stewart *v.* Bernalillo County, 11 N. M. 517, 70 Pac. 574.

New York.— People *v.* Campbell, 35 N. Y. App. Div. 103, 54 N. Y. Suppl. 725.

Wisconsin.— Pier *v.* Oneida County, 102 Wis. 338, 78 N. W. 410, 93 Wis. 463, 67 N. W. 702; State *v.* Sheboygan County, 29 Wis. 79.

Availability of funds for reimbursement of tax purchaser see Brown *v.* Pontchartrain Land Co., 49 La. Ann. 1779, 23 So. 292.

61. Warner *v.* Outagamie County, 19 Wis. 611.

62. Corbin *v.* Morrow, 46 Minn. 522, 49 N. W. 201. And see State *v.* Dunn, 88 Minn. 444, 93 N. W. 306, as to determination by the state auditor that a tax certificate is or is not invalid within the purport of previous decisions of the supreme court.

63. People *v.* Chapin, 104 N. Y. 96, 10 N. E. 141; People *v.* Land Office Com'rs, 90 Hun (N. Y.) 525, 36 N. Y. Suppl. 29. *Compare* State *v.* Dressel, 38 Minn. 90, 35 N. W. 580.

64. Curd *v.* Auditor-Gen., 122 Mich. 151, 80 N. W. 1005. See also Harding *v.* Auditor-Gen., 136 Mich. 358, 99 N. W. 275.

Action to compel issuance of warrant.—An action may be brought against a county auditor, by a person entitled to require him to issue his warrant upon the county treasurer for money paid on a tax-sale subsequently adjudged void, to compel him to issue it. Corbin *v.* Morrow, 46 Minn. 522, 49 N. W. 201.

65. Lincoln County *v.* Faulkner, 27 Kan. 164; Saline County *v.* Geis, 22 Kan. 381.

66. *California.*— Greenwood *v.* Adams, 80 Cal. 74, 21 Pac. 1134.

Iowa.— Smith *v.* Blackiston, 82 Iowa 240, 47 N. W. 1075.

Michigan.— Croskery *v.* Busch, 116 Mich. 288, 74 N. W. 464.

Missouri.— Burkham *v.* Manewal, 195 Mo. 500, 94 S. W. 520.

New Mexico.— Blackwell *v.* Albuquerque First Nat. Bank, 10 N. M. 555, 63 Pac. 43.

Tennessee.— Ross *v.* Mabry, 1 Lea 226.

But *compare* Pettit *v.* Black, 8 Nebr. 52; Kaighn *v.* Burgin, 56 N. J. L. 852, 42 Atl. 1117.

Equitable lien on interest of cotenants for taxes advanced see Niday *v.* Cochran, 42 Tex. Civ. App. 292, 93 S. W. 1027.

67. *Arkansas.*— Files *v.* Jackson, 84 Ark. 587, 106 S. W. 950; Hunt *v.* Curry, 37 Ark. 100.

California.— Harper *v.* Rowe, 53 Cal. 233.

sary for the purchaser to bring an action to test the validity of the title; he may proceed directly for the foreclosure of his lien,[86] and he may even assert his lien and secure its enforcement in any proceeding in which the tax title is directly in issue, whether it be ejectment or a bill to quiet or confirm title or to set aside the deed,[87] or even a mortgage foreclosure proceeding in which he is made a defendant.[88] To proceed for the enforcement of this lien it is necessary that the purchaser shall have taken out his deed,[89] but not that he shall give notice to the owner of the land.[90] The proper defendant is the person entitled to the equity of redemption, and others may be joined having interests to be affected by the lien.[91] The claimant is required to allege and prove the facts essential to his

Porter, 42 Mich. 569, 4 N. W. 306; Webb v. Bidwell, 15 Minn. 479.

In Alabama the lien conferred by statute upon the purchaser at an ineffectual tax-sale for the amounts paid thereon and for subsequent taxes paid does not arise except at the end, and as the result, of a judgment in ejectment for the land so sold, and where the lien is not so established, it cannot be enforced by defendant in a suit to quiet title to the land or by a bill in equity to enforce the same. Geo. E. Wood Lumber Co. v. Williams, 157 Ala. 73, 47 So. 202; Tradesmen's Nat. Bank v. Sheffield City Co., 137 Ala. 547, 34 So. 625; Sheffield City Co. v. Tradesmen's Nat. Bank, 131 Ala. 185, 32 So. 598.

Former judgment no bar.—A judgment declaring the invalidity of the tax title, even if not a condition precedent to the institution of a suit to foreclose the lien, as held by the cases cited above, is clearly no bar to such a suit. Harding v. Greene, 59 Kan. 202, 52 Pac. 436; Merriam v. Dovey, 25 Nebr. 618, 41 N. W. 550.

86. McClure v. Warner, 16 Nebr. 447, 20 N. W. 387; Bryant v. Estabrook, 16 Nebr. 217, 20 N. W. 245; Shelley v. Towle, 16 Nebr. 194, 20 N. W. 251; Miller v. Hurford, 11 Nebr. 377, 9 N. W. 477.

87. *Arkansas.*— Haney v. Cole, 28 Ark. 299.

Indiana.— Jones v. Foley, 121 Ind. 180, 22 N. E. 987; Millikan v. Ham, 104 Ind. 498, 4 N. E. 60; Reed v. Earhart, 88 Ind. 159; Jenkins v. Rice, 84 Ind. 342.

Iowa.— Buck v. Holt, 74 Iowa 294, 37 N. W. 377; Harper v. Sexton, 22 Iowa 442.

Kansas.— Lewis Academy v. Wilkinson, 79 Kan. 557, 100 Pac. 510; Rose v. Newman, 47 Kan. 18, 27 Pac. 181; Krutz v. Chandler, 32 Kan. 659, 5 Pac. 170; Russell v. Hudson, 28 Kan. 99; Arn v. Hoppin, 25 Kan. 707; Fairbanks v. Williams, 24 Kan. 16. *Compare* Corbin v. Young, 24 Kan. 198.

Kentucky.— Wheeler v. Bramel, 8 S. W. 199, 10 Ky. L. Rep. 301.

Nebraska.— Pettit v. Black, 8 Nebr. 52.

United States.— Hintrager v. Nightingale, 36 Fed. 847.

Canada.— *In re* Cameron, 14 Grant Ch. (U. C.) 612.

Contra.— Bidwell v. Webb, 10 Minn. 59, 88 Am. Dec. 56.

Provision in decree setting aside tax-sale or title for purchaser's lien for reimbursement see *supra*, XIV, B, 9, b, (II), (A).

Waiver by failure to assert lien.— Defendant, in an action to quiet title against a void tax-sale, need not be given judgment for the amount tendered as a condition precedent to setting aside the sale; but while the court will allow a person, who has paid taxes on land of another in the belief that title is in him, a lien on the land for the amount so paid, when he comes into court and asserts his lien, he may waive the right, and does waive it by failure to assert it. Cordiner v. Finch Inv. Co., 54 Wash. 574, 103 Pac. 829.

Action by assignee of tax purchaser.— Where one buys land from a purchaser thereof at tax-sale and sues to recover it from a third person in possession, if he fails to recover he is not entitled to a lien for the amount which he paid to the original holder of the tax title, although the tax execution may have been a lien on the land. Maddox v. Arthur, 122 Ga. 671, 50 S. E. 668.

88. Columbia Bank v. Jones, (N. J.) 17 Atl. 808. And see Dixon v. Eikenberry, (Ind. App. 1903) 65 N. E. 938.

89. Sharpe v. Dillman, 77 Ind. 280. But see Parker v. Matheson, 21 Nebr. 546, 32 N. W. 598, holding that an action to foreclose the tax lien may be maintained on the certificate of sale, when it is alleged in the petition that a deed would be invalid if issued.

Expiration of time for redemption.— The right of action in the tax purchaser to foreclose his lien does not accrue until after the expiration of the time allowed by law for the owner to redeem from the tax-sale. Peet v. O'Brien, 5 Nebr. 360.

90. Carman v. Harris, 61 Nebr. 635, 85 N. W. 848; Merrill v. Ijams, 58 Nebr. 706, 79 N. W. 734; McClure v. Lavender, 21 Nebr. 181, 31 N. W. 672; Helphrey v. Redick, 21 Nebr. 80, 31 N. W. 256; Lammers v. Comstock, 20 Nebr. 341, 30 N. W. 251; Bryant v. Estabrook, 16 Nebr. 217, 20 N. W. 245; Merrill v. Riverview Inv. Co., 1 Nebr. (Unoff.) 260, 95 N. W. 333.

91. Jenkins v. Rice, 84 Ind. 342; Carman v. Harris, 61 Nebr. 635, 85 N. W. 848; Alexander v. Thacker, 30 Nebr. 614, 46 N. W. 825; Moss. v. Rockport, (Tex. Civ. App. 1899) 51 S. W. 652.

The wife is not a necessary party to a suit to foreclose a tax lien against her husband's homestead. San Antonio v. Berry, 92 Tex. 319, 48 S. W. 496; Collins v. Ferguson, 22 Tex. Civ. App. 552, 56 S. W. 225.

Disability of owner.— The right of action

and also, in some jurisdictions, although not in all, any penalties prescribed for delinquency in the payment of taxes or granted by the statute to the purchaser.[15] The aggregate thus made up is not necessarily the price paid by the purchaser at the sale, nor will it ordinarily include the costs of the sale.[16] But there should be added the amount of subsequent taxes paid by the purchaser in the character of a claimant in good faith, and to the extent to which such payment has relieved the land from a legal charge,[17] except in cases where the tax-sale was absolutely void, as for want of jurisdiction or other such cause; for in this event the payment of subsequent taxes by the purchaser is voluntary and irrevocable.[18]

c. Action or Proceeding to Enforce Claim. The ultimate holder of the tax title [19] may maintain an action against the original owner of the land within the period limited by statute for that purpose,[20] in which, on pleading and proving the facts essential to establish his claim for reimbursement,[21] he may have a personal judgment for the amount found due; [22] or, where the statute so directs, provision for his reimbursement may be made in a judgment or decree setting aside the tax-sale or quieting the title in the original owner.[23]

15. Barke *v.* Early, 72 Iowa 273, 33 N. W. 677; Foreman *v.* Hinchcliffe, 106 La. 225, 30 So. 762. *Compare* Michigan Mut. L. Ins. Co. *v.* Kroh, 102 Ind. 515, 2 N. E. 733; Johnson *v.* Stewart, 29 Ohio St. 498.

16. Hopkins *v.* Daunoy, 33 La. Ann. 1423; Stafford *v.* Twitchell, 33 La. Ann. 520; Jacques *v.* Kopman, 6 La. Ann. 542; Carter *v.* Phillips, 49 Mo. App. 319. *Compare* Gage *v.* Consumers' Electric Light Co., 194 Ill. 30, 64 N. E. 653; Collins *v.* Reger, 62 W. Va. 195, 57 S. E. 743.

17. *Arkansas.*— Gregory *v.* Bartlett, 55 Ark. 30, 17 S. W. 344.

Illinois.— Joliet Stove Works *v.* Kiep, 230 Ill. 550, 82 N. E. 875 [*affirming* 132 Ill. App. 457], recovery of subsequent taxes authorized by statute.

Indiana.— Millikan *v.* Ham, 104 Ind. 498, 4 N. E. 60; Crecelius *v.* Mann, 84 Ind. 147.

Iowa.— Barke *v.* Early, 72 Iowa 273, 33 N. W. 677; Forey *v.* Bigelow, 56 Iowa 381, 9 N. W. 313; Thompson *v.* Savage, 47 Iowa 522; Sexton *v.* Henderson, 45 Iowa 160; Early *v.* Whittingham, 43 Iowa 162; Fenton *v.* Way, 40 Iowa 196; Curl *v.* Watson, 25 Iowa 35, 95 Am. Dec. 763; Harper *v.* Sexton, 22 Iowa 442; Orr *v.* Travacier, 21 Iowa 68.

Kansas.— Jackson *v.* Challiss, 41 Kan. 247, 21 Pac. 87; Belz *v.* Bird, 31 Kan. 139, 1 Pac. 246; Coonradt *v.* Myers, 31 Kan. 30, 2 Pac. 858; Arn. *v.* Hoppin, 25 Kan. 707.

Louisiana.— Guidry *v.* Broussard, 32 La. Ann. 924.

Nebraska.— Merriam *v.* Hemple, 17 Nebr. 345, 22 N. W. 775.

Ohio.—Younglove *v.* Hackman, 43 Ohio St. 69, 1 N. E. 230; Chapman *v.* Sollars, 38 Ohio St. 378.

Washington.—Wheeler Co. *v.* Pates, 43 Wash. 247, 86 Pac. 625.

Wisconsin.— Morrow *v.* Lander, 77 Wis. 77, 45 N. W. 956.

See 45 Cent. Dig. tit. "Taxation," § 1645.

Compare Broxson *v.* McDougal, 70 Tex. 64, 7 S. W. 591.

Apportionment according to value of land and of improvements.— Under Kan. Gen. St. (1901) § 7681, providing that the successful claimant in ejectment shall not be let into possession until the defeated tax title holder has been paid the full amount he has expended for taxes on the land, with interest, costs, and charges, and section 5088, providing that a defeated tax title holder shall not be evicted until he is paid the value of all lasting and valuable improvements he has placed on the land, and section 5091, allowing the successful claimant to elect to take the value of the land, apart from the value added by the improvements, and leave the tax title holder in possession. A tax deed holder in possession who is defeated in ejectment and who claims the benefit of the statute should be reimbursed for that portion only of the taxes paid, levied upon the assessed valuation of the land apart from the improvements, and not for the full amount of the taxes. Hills *v.* Allison, 79 Kan. 617, 100 Pac. 651.

Payment after redemption.— A purchaser of land at a tax-sale cannot demand from the original owner repayment of taxes paid after redemption. Byington *v.* Wood, 12 Iowa 479; Byington *v.* Allen, 11 Iowa 3.

Taxes paid subsequent to commencement of suit not recoverable see Roach *v.* Sanborn Land Co., 140 Wis. 435, 122 N. W. 1020.

18. Barke *v.* Early, 72 Iowa 273, 33 N. W. 677; Roberts *v.* Deeds, 57 Iowa 320, 10 N. W. 740; Croskery *v.* Busch, 116 Mich. 288, 74 N. W. 464; McHenry *v.* Brett, 9 N. D. 68, 81 N. W. 65; Phelps *v.* Tacoma, 15 Wash. 367, 46 Pac. 400.

19. Morton *v.* Shortridge, 38 Ind. 492.

20. Barke *v.* Early, 72 Iowa 273, 33 N. W. 677; Sexton *v.* Peck, 48 Iowa 250; Steel *v.* Pogue, 15 Ohio Cir. Ct. 149, 8 Ohio Cir. Ct. 255.

21. Hershey *v.* Thompson, 50 Ark. 484, 8 S. W. 689; Reid *v.* Yazoo, etc., R. Co., 74 Miss. 769, 21 So. 745; Chapman *v.* Sollars, 38 Ohio St. 378.

22. St. Louis, etc., R. Co. *v.* Alexander, 49 Ark. 190, 4 S. W. 753 (there may be a "personal judgment," although defendant is a railroad company); Phelps *v.* Brumback, 107 Mo. App. 16, 80 S. W. 678.

23. See *supra*, XIV, B, 9, b, (II). And see Heffern *v.* Hack, 65 Ohio St. 164, 61 N. E. 703.

taxes due and in arrear, together with interest, penalties, and costs.[39] Although a redemption of this kind is generally to be effected as a matter of office business, it is sometimes provided that the owner shall proceed by petition in equity and obtain a decree; [40] and, where the redemption proceedings are regular and complete, the person redeeming is invested with the paper title to the land.[41]

8. Setting Aside, Release, or Waiver. It is competent for the legislature to release or remit a forfeiture already incurred,[42] or it may be canceled or set aside for good cause shown in a judicial proceeding brought for that purpose.[43] If the theory is that the forfeiture vests a final and complete title in the state, subject to no further equities in the original owner, it would be inconsistent for the state to continue to assess taxes on the lands in the former owner's name after the forfeiture, and such an act would be a waiver of the forfeiture.[44] But if, after the forfeiture, a time is still given to the owner in which to redeem, the assessment and collection of state taxes for several successive years after the forfeiture is no waiver.[45]

9. Sale or Other Disposition of Forfeited Lands.[46] After forfeiture has become complete, the state, in disposing of the lands forfeited, acts as an owner and proprietor, rather than a creditor,[47] and, as it cannot sell that which it does not own,[48] it cannot sell the same land twice, unless, after the first sale, the lands have again become forfeited in the hands of the new owner.[49] To make a valid

39. Neff *v.* Smyth, 111 Ill. 100; Stamposki *v.* Stanley, 109 Ill. 210; Belleville Nail Co. *v.* People, 98 Ill. 399; People *v.* Smith, 94 Ill. 226; People *v.* Gale, 93 Ill. 127; State *v.* King, 47 W. Va. 437, 35 S. E. 30; Tebbetts *v.* Charleston, 33 W. Va. 705, 11 S. E. 23.

A tender of the amount of the taxes and the value of the improvements is impracticable and unnecessary, under the Arkansas statute, when redemption is sought by one claiming an undivided share of the land, and the rights of the parties must be determined upon equitable principles. Loudon *v.* Spellman, 80 Fed. 592, 26 C. C. A. 13.

Payment in behalf of party redeeming.— Payment of taxes in redemption will be presumed, in the absence of anything to the contrary, to have been made by or for someone entitled to redeem. Harman *v.* Stearns, 95 Va. 58, 27 S. E. 601.

40. Mills *v.* Henry Oil Co., 57 W. Va. 255, 50 S. E. 157; Yokum *v.* Fickey, 37 W. Va. 762, 17 S. E. 318; Simmons Creek Coal Co. *v.* Doran, 142 U. S. 417, 12 S. Ct. 239, 35 L. ed. 1063, effect of proceedings where true owner was not made a party or notified.

A decree allowing redemption is prima facie evidence of redemption as to third persons, and cannot be collaterally attacked for error in that the sum paid to redeem was less than the amount actually due (State *v.* Jackson, 56 W. Va. 558, 49 S. E. 465), or that the land was not within the jurisdiction of the court (Cecil *v.* Clark, 44 W. Va. 659, 30 S. E. 216).

41. Mitchell *v.* Bond, 84 Miss. 72, 36 So. 148; State *v.* Jackson, 56 W. Va. 558, 49 S. E. 465, holding that, under a decree declaring the owner redeeming should occupy the position of a purchaser, the owner took, not only the title redeemed, but any other title in the state at the time of the redemption.

42. Fagg *v.* Martin, 53 Ark. 449, 14 S. W. 647; Lewis *v.* Yates, 62 W. Va. 575, 59 S. E. 1073; Van Gunden *v.* Virginia Coal, etc., Co., 52 Fed. 838, 3 C. C. A. 294.

But a county board has no power to set aside a forfeiture of land to the state for the non-payment of taxes. Madison County *v.* Smith, 95 Ill. 328.

43. Madison County *v.* Smith, 95 Ill. 328; Surget *v.* Newman, 43 La. Ann. 873, 9 So. 561; Willard *v.* Redwood County, 22 Minn. 61; Hall *v.* Swann, 39 W. Va. 353, 19 S. E. 509.

44. Clarke *v.* Strickland, 5 Fed. Cas. No. 2,864, 2 Curt. 439, holding also that a subsequent act of the legislature giving further time for the payment of the taxes would likewise be a waiver of the forfeiture.

The mere retention, on the tax books, of the description of the lands, without charging any taxes against it or collecting any from the owner, does not affect a forfeiture incurred during a previous year. Hill *v.* Denton, 74 Ark. 463, 86 S. W. 402.

45. Hodgdon *v.* Wight, 36 Me. 326; Crane *v.* Reeder, 25 Mich. 303; State *v.* Sponaugle, 45 W. Va. 27, 32 S. E. 283, 43 L. R. A. 101.

46. **Form, contents, and effect of tax deeds** see *supra*, XIII. D.

47. Leathem, etc., Lumber Co. *v.* Nalty, 109 La. 325, 33 So. 354.

48. George *v.* Cole, 109 La. 816, 33 So. 784; State *v.* Garnett, 66 W. Va. 106, 66 S. E. 98; State *v.* Harman, 57 W. Va. 447, 50 S. E. 828.

49. State *v.* Garnett, 66 W. Va. 106, 66 S. E. 98; State *v.* King, 64 W. Va. 610, 63 S. E. 495; State *v.* Jackson, 56 W. Va. 558, 49 S. E. 465, holding, however, that where a senior title is forfeited and transferred to the holder of a junior title, and the junior title subsequently becomes forfeited, a sale by the state will pass both titles to the purchaser.

evidence in an action directly affecting it,[57] or in proceedings by the purchaser to obtain a confirmation of his title, if that is provided for by law.[58]

XVI. LEGACY AND INHERITANCE TAXES.[59]

A. Nature and Power to Impose — 1. NATURE OF SUCCESSION TAXES. An inheritance or legacy tax is not a tax on the property affected, real or personal, but on the privilege of succeeding to the inheritance or of becoming a beneficiary under the will, the privilege of acquiring property by will or by succession being a right created and regulated by the state.[60] Hence the right and power of the

57. *Arkansas.*— Henry *v.* Knod, 74 Ark. 390, 85 S. W. 1130.

Mississippi.— Mitchell *v.* Bond, 84 Miss. 72, 36 So. 148.

Virginia.— Hitchcox *v.* Rawson, 14 Gratt. 526; Smith *v.* Chapman, 10 Gratt. 445.

West Virginia.—Webb *v.* Ritter, 60 W. Va. 193, 54 S. E. 484; Bowman *v.* Dewing, 37 W. Va. 117, 16 S. E. 440; Strader *v.* Goff, 6 W. Va. 257; Twiggs *v.* Chevallie, 4 W. Va. 463.

United States.— Lasher *v.* McCreery, 66 Fed. 834.

See 45 Cent. Dig. tit. "Taxation," § 1672.

Where the title given by the state has failed, there can be no recovery from the county of the portion of the purchase-price which it received, in the absence of express statute for such refunding. Nevada County *v.* Dickey, 68 Ark. 160, 56 S. W. 779.

Valid sale bars dower rights.— Tullis *v.* Pierano, 9 Ohio Cir. Ct. 647, 9 Ohio Cir. Dec. 103.

58. Martin *v.* Hawkins, 62 Ark. 421, 35 S. W. 1104.

59. **Descent and distribution** see DESCENT AND DISTRIBUTION, 14 Cyc. 1.

Internal revenue tax see INTERNAL REVENUE, 22 Cyc. 1592, 1616.

Legacies and devises generally see EXECUTORS AND ADMINISTRATORS, 18 Cyc. 1; WILLS.

60. *Colorado.*— *In re* Macky, 46 Colo. 79, 102 Pac. 1075, 23 L. R. A. N. S. 1207.

Connecticut.— Hopkin's Appeal, 77 Conn. 644, 60 Atl. 657.

Iowa.— Lacy *v.* State Treasurer, (1909) 121 N. W. 179; *In re* Stone, 132 Iowa 136, 109 N. W. 455.

Kentucky.— Allen *v.* McElroy, 130 Ky. 111, 113 S. W. 66; Booth *v.* Com., 130 Ky. 88, 113 S. W. 61; Barrett *v.* Continental Realty Co., (1908) 113 S. W. 66, 130 Ky. 109, 114 S. W. 750.

Louisiana.—Kohn's Succession, 115 La. 71, 38 So. 898.

Maryland.— Tyson *v.* State, 28 Md. 577.

Massachusetts.— Minot *v.* Winthrop, 162 Mass. 113, 38 N. E. 512, 26 L. R. A. 259.

Michigan.— *In re* Fox, 154 Mich. 5, 117 N. W. 558.

Montana.— *In re* Touhy, 35 Mont. 431, 90 Pac. 170.

New Jersey.—Nelson *v.* Russell, 76 N. J. L. 27, 69 Atl. 476.

New York.— *In re* Keeney, 194 N. Y. 281, 87 N. E. 428; *In re* Davis, 149 N. Y. 539, 44 N. E. 185; *In re* Swift, 137 N. Y. 77, 32 N. E. 1096, 18 L. R. A. 709; *In re* Cooley, 113 N. Y. App. Div. 388, 98 N. Y. Suppl. 1006 [*reversed* on other grounds in 186 N. Y. 220, 78 N. E. 939]; Matter of Pell, 60 N. Y. App. Div. 286, 70 N. Y. Suppl. 196 [*reversed* on other grounds in 171 N. Y. 48, 63 N. E. 789, 89 Am. St. Rep. 791, 57 L. R. A. 545]; Matter of Wolfe, 15 N. Y. Suppl. 539, 2 Connoly Surr. 600; Matter of Swift, 16 N. Y. Suppl. 193, 2 Connoly Surr. 644.

Ohio.— State *v.* Ferris, 53 Ohio St. 314, 41 N. E. 579, 30 L. R. A. 218.

Utah.— See Dixon *v.* Ricketts, 26 Utah 215, 72 Pac. 947.

Virginia.— Eyre *v.* Jacob, 14 Gratt. 422, 73 Am. Dec. 367.

Wisconsin.— Beals *v.* State, 139 Wis. 544, 121 N. W. 347; Nunnemacher *v.* State, 129 Wis. 190, 108 N. W. 627, holding, however, that the taxation of inheritances is justifiable, not on the ground that the right to inherit is a creation of the law which can be given or withheld on such terms as the legislature may see fit to impose, but under the power reasonably to regulate and tax transfers of property. See also Black *v.* State, 113 Wis. 205, 89 N. W. 522, 90 Am. St. Rep. 853.

United States.— Plummer *v.* Coler, 178 U. S. 115, 20 S. Ct. 829, 44 L. ed. 998 [*affirming* 30 Misc. 19, 62 N. Y. Suppl. 1024]; U. S. *v.* Perkins, 163 U. S. 625, 16 S. Ct. 1073, 41 L. ed. 287; Scholey *v.* Rew, 23 Wall. 331, 23 L. ed. 99.

See 45 Cent. Dig. tit. "Taxation," § 1673.

A "death duty" is an exaction by the state, to be collected from the property left by a deceased person while in its custody, prescribed upon the occasion of his death, and the consequent devolution of his property, by force of its laws. The particular name given the duty in any statute — as probate, legacy, succession, transfer, or estate tax or duty — depends for its meaning upon the terms of that statute. A tax may be laid upon property immediately after it has devolved upon any person by will or inheritance, so as to be not easily distinguishable from a form of taxation sometimes called a "legacy tax." Hopkins' Appeal, 77 Conn. 644, 60 Atl. 657, 659.

The collateral inheritance tax is a specific tax and not *ad valorem*, notwithstanding it is based on the value of the property inherited. Union Trust Co. *v.* Wayne Prob. Judge, 125 Mich. 487, 84 N. W. 1101.

"Probate duty" see 32 Cyc. 404.

"A 'succession tax' as the words indicate and the history of such taxes clearly establishes, is an excise or duty upon the

legislature to impose burdens in the form of taxes on this privilege is not restricted by the constitutional provisions relating to the taxation of property as such.[61] And for the same reason the tax may be imposed on the transfer, by bequest or under the intestate laws, of securities which are not within the taxing power of the state, considered as property in themselves, such as United States bonds.[62]

2. CONSTITUTIONALITY OF STATUTES[63] — a. **In General.** The constitutional validity of legacy and inheritance taxes has generally been sustained both in principle and in detail.[64] The power to tax is incident to the legislative power, so

right of a person or corporation to receive property by devise or inheritance from another under the regulation of the State. Whenever properly laid, this is its distinguishing feature in contradistinction from a property tax." The mere calling of such a tax a "succession tax" does not make it different from an ordinary tax upon property, when the effect and operation are identical with an ordinary property tax. State *v.* Switzler, 143 Mo. 287, 328, 45 S. W. 245, 65 Am. St. Rep. 653, 40 L. R. A. 280. "The succession tax provided for, as defined by the terms of the Act in force when the testatrix died, is a death duty prescribed in view of the death of a domiciled resident of this State whose land within this State and whose personal property, wherever situate, is governed as to its disposition, distribution and succession, by the laws of this State, and of the death of a non-resident owning land within this State which is governed as to its distribution and succession by the same law; prescribed in respect to the beneficial interest which thus by force of our laws devolves upon all beneficiaries of the decedent; and fixed as to amount by a percentage upon the value of the whole interest thus devolving on the decedent's beneficial successors, based upon a valuation previously made of all the decedent's property inventoried by the administrator." Hopkins' Appeal, 77 Conn. 644, 649, 60 Atl. 657.

"The transfer tax . . . must be regarded as a tax, not upon the money which is the subject of the legacy, but upon the passing of that money under the will in possession or enjoyment." Matter of Wolfe, 89 N. Y. App. Div. 349, 350, 85 N. Y. Suppl. 949 [*affirmed* in 179 N. Y. 599, 72 N. E. 1152].

Such taxes are very ancient in origin, and have been long in use, especially in European states. The states of the Union have been singularly slow in adopting such laws, but the number of states to adopt and enforce them is increasing year by year. Black *v.* State, 113 Wis. 205, 210, 89 N. W. 522, 90 Am. St. Rep. 853.

61. *Kentucky.*— Allen *v.* McElroy, 130 Ky. 111, 113 S. W. 66; Booth *v.* Com., 130 Ky. 88, 113 S. W. 61; Barrett *v.* Continental Realty Co., (1908) 113 S. W. 66, 130 Ky. 109, 114 S. W. 750.

Michigan.— *In re* Fox, 154 Mich. 5, 117 N. W. 558.

Montana.— *In re* Touhy, 35 Mont. 431, 90 Pac. 170.

New Hampshire.— Thompson *v.* Kidder, 74 N. H. 89, 65 Atl. 392.

North Carolina.— *In re* Morris, 138 N. C. 259, 50 S. E. 682; Pullen *v.* Wake County, 66 N. C. 361.

Ohio.— State *v.* Guilbert, 70 Ohio St. 229, 71 N. E. 636.

In Missouri it is held that an excise upon the right to receive property by devise or inheritance is a "tax" within the meaning of the constitutional provision that taxes may be levied and collected for public purposes only. State *v.* Switzler, 143 Mo. 287, 45 S. W. 245, 65 Am. St. Rep. 653, 40 L. R. A. 280.

62. Levy's Succession, 115 La. 377, 39 So. 37, 8 L. R. A. N. S. 1180; Kohn's Succession, 115 La. 71, 38 So. 898 (state and municipal bonds); *In re* Sherman, 153 N. Y. 1, 46 N. E. 1032; Matter of Whiting, 2 N. Y. App. Div. 590, 38 N. Y. Suppl. 131 [*modified* in 150 N. Y. 27, 44 N. E. 715, 55 Am. St. Rep. 640, 34 L. R. A. 232]; Matter of Carver, 4 Misc. (N. Y.) 592, 25 N. Y. Suppl. 991 [*affirmed* in 28 N. Y. Suppl. 1126]; Matter of Tuigg, 15 N. Y. Suppl. 548, 2 Connoly Surr. 633; Matter of Howard, 5 Dem. Surr. (N. Y.) 483; Strode *v.* Com., 52 Pa. St. 181; Plummer *v.* Coler, 178 U. S. 115, 20 S. Ct. 829, 44 L. ed. 998 [*affirming* 30 Misc. (N. Y.) 19, 62 N. Y. Suppl. 1024] (holding that the impairment of the borrowing power of the government as the remote effect of a state statute imposing a tax upon the transfer of a decedent's property, when the statute is applied to property consisting of United States bonds, is not sufficient to render the statute unconstitutional); Wallace *v.* Myers, 38 Fed. 184, 4 L. R. A. 171. See also Matter of Schermerhorn, 50 Misc. (N. Y.) 233, 100 N. Y. Suppl. 480. But *compare* Matter of Coogan, 27 Misc. (N. Y.) 563, 59 N. Y. Suppl. 111.

63. Constitutional law generally see CONSTITUTIONAL LAW, 8 Cyc. 695 *et seq.*

64. *Connecticut.*— Nettleton's Appeal, 76 Conn. 235, 56 Atl. 565.

Illinois.— Walker *v.* People, 192 Ill. 106, 61 N. E. 489.

Louisiana.— Stauffer's Succession, 119 La. 66, 43 So. 928.

Minnesota.— State *v.* Vance, 97 Minn. 532, 106 N. W. 98; State *v.* Bazille, 97 Minn. 11, 106 N. W. 93, 6 L. R. A. N. S. 732.

New York.— *In re* Delano, 176 N. Y. 486, 68 N. E. 871, 64 L. R. A. 279; Matter of Kimberly, 27 N. Y. App. Div. 470, 50 N. Y. Suppl. 586.

Pennsylvania.— Lacey's Estate, 19 Pa. Co. Ct. 431. *Compare In re* Cope, 29 Pittsb. Leg. J. N. S. 379 [*affirmed* in 191 Pa. St. 1, 43 Atl. 79, 71 Am. St. Rep. 749, 45 L. R. A. 316].

imposed until the power of appointment is exercised.[52] Under statute it has been held that if the donee of the power fails to make any appointment, or appoints in favor of the same persons who were to succeed in default of an appointment, they are to be regarded as taking under the donee or appointor.[53]

c. Ante-Mortem Deeds and Gifts. In some states the laws impose a tax on all transfers of property by deed made or intended to take effect in possession or enjoyment after the death of the grantor, or, as it is sometimes expressed, on gifts or transfers made in contemplation of death.[54] These provisions are intended to prevent evasions of the inheritance tax by distributions of property among the members of a family or others just before the death of the owner.[55] Whether or not a transfer was made "in contemplation of death" is a question of fact, in the determination of which the donor's age, his physical condition at the time, and the length of time he actually survives should be taken into account.[56] Under these provisions the tax of course attaches to a gift *causa mortis*.[57] The provisions, however, do not apply to a purchase and sale of property,[58] although a part of the consideration may be the support and maintenance of the grantor during his life.[59] And generally a gift, assignment, or transfer to a man's wife or children or to

M. & W. 756; Vandiest *v.* Fynmore, 6 Sim. 570, 9 Eng. Ch. 570, 58 Eng. Reprint 707; Nail *v.* Punter, 5 Sim. 555, 9 Eng. Ch. 555, 58 Eng. Reprint 447; Palmer *v.* Whitmore, 5 Sim. 178, 9 Eng. Ch. 178, 58 Eng. Reprint 304.

52. *In re* Howe, 176 N. Y. 570, 68 N. E. 1118 [*affirming* 86 N. Y. App. Div. 286, 83 N. Y. Suppl. 825]. *Compare* Howe *v.* Howe, 179 Mass. 546, 61 N. E. 225, 55 L. R. A. 626; Matter of Le Brun, 39 Misc. (N. Y.) 516, 80 N. Y. Suppl. 486.

Remainders created in a trust fund by the exercise of a power of appointment by the beneficiary under the will creating the trust are subject to taxation at the time of the transfer where they are absolute and not subject to be divested or to fail in any contingency whatever, and their present value is determinable by the aid of the table of annuities. *In re* Dows, 167 N. Y. 227, 60 N. E. 439, 88 Am. St. Rep. 508, 52 L. R. A. 433.

53. *In re* Cooksey, 182 N. Y. 92, 74 N. E. 880; *In re* Langdon, 153 N. Y. 6, 46 N. E. 1034; Matter of Lewis, 60 Misc. (N. Y.) 643, 113 N. Y. Suppl. 1112 [*reversed* in 129 N. Y. App. Div. 905, 113 N. Y. Suppl. 1136]; Matter of Bartow, 30 Misc. (N. Y.) 27, 62 N. Y. Suppl. 1000. See also Matter of Lowndes, 60 Misc. (N. Y.) 506, 113 N. Y. Suppl. 1114; Atty.-Gen. *v.* Brackenbury, 1 H. & C. 782, 9 Jur. N. S. 257, 32 L. J. Exch. 108, 8 L. T. Rep. N. S. 822, 11 Wkly. Rep. 380. But *compare* *In re* Lansing, 182 N. Y. 238, 74 N. E. 882.

54. Emmons *v.* Shaw, 171 Mass. 410, 50 N. E. 1033; Matter of Miller, 77 N. Y. App. Div. 473, 78 N. Y. Suppl. 930; Matter of Cruger, 54 N. Y. App. Div. 405, 66 N. Y. Suppl. 636 [*affirmed* in 166 N. Y. 602, 59 N. E. 1121]; Matter of Hendricks, 3 N. Y. Suppl. 281, 1 Connoly Surr. 301; State *v.* Pabst, 139 Wis. 561, 121 N. W. 351.

55. Matter of Palmer, 117 N. Y. App. Div. 360, 102 N. Y. Suppl. 236; Matter of Birdsall, 22 Misc. (N. Y.) 180, 49 N. Y. Suppl. 450 [*affirmed* in 43 N. Y. App. Div. 624, 60 N. Y. Suppl. 1133].

56. Merrifield *v.* People, 212 Ill. 400, 72 N. E. 446; Rosenthal *v.* People, 211 Ill. 306, 71 N. E. 1121; Matter of Palmer, 117 N. Y. App. Div. 360, 102 N. Y. Suppl. 236; Matter of Bullard, 76 N. Y. App. Div. 207, 78 N. Y. Suppl. 491; Matter of Mahlstedt, 67 N. Y. App. Div. 176, 73 N. Y. Suppl. 818; *In re* Spaulding, 49 N. Y. App. Div. 541, 63 N. Y. Suppl. 694 [*affirmed* in 163 N. Y. 607, 57 N. E. 1124]; Matter of Birdsall, 22 Misc. (N. Y.) 180, 49 N. Y. Suppl. 450; State *v.* Pabst, 139 Wis. 561, 121 N. W. 351.

57. Matter of Cornell, 66 N. Y. App. Div. 162, 73 N. Y. Suppl. 32 [*modified* in 170 N. Y. 423, 63 N. E. 445]; Matter of Edgerton, 35 N. Y. App. Div. 125, 54 N. Y. Suppl. 700 [*affirmed* in 158 N. Y. 671, 52 N. E. 1124]; Matter of Edwards, 85 Hun (N. Y.) 436, 32 N. Y. Suppl. 901 [*affirmed* in 146 N. Y. 380, 41 N. E. 89].

Gifts in contemplation of death not confined to gifts causa mortis.— Gifts in contemplation of the death of the donor within the contemplation of the inheritance tax laws are not limited to gifts *causa mortis* but include gift *inter vivos*, made in view of such death. *In re* Benton, 234 Ill. 366, 84 N. E. 1026, 18 L. R. A. N. S. 458; Matter of Price, 62 Misc. (N. Y.) 149, 116 N. Y. Suppl. 283; Matter of Birdsall, 22 Misc. (N. Y.) 180, 49 N. Y. Suppl. 450; State *v.* Pabst, 139 Wis. 561, 121 N. W. 351. The object of the inheritance tax law, however, is not to prevent a parent from giving the whole or any portion of his property to his children during his lifetime, if he so desires, but only to subject such property to a tax if the gift is made in contemplation of the death of the donor. People *v.* Kelley, 218 Ill. 509, 75 N. E. 1038. And see Matter of Baker, 83 N. Y. App. Div. 530, 82 N. Y. Suppl. 390 [*affirmed* in 178 N. Y. 575, 70 N. E. 1094].

58. Matter of Hess, 110 N. Y. App. Div. 476, 96 N. Y. Suppl. 990 [*affirmed* in 187 N. Y. 554, 80 N. E. 1111]; Matter of Thorne, 44 N. Y. App. Div. 8, 60 N. Y. Suppl. 419; Hagerty *v.* State, 55 Ohio St. 613, 45 N. E. 1046; Garman's Estate, 3 Pa. Co. Ct. 550.

59. Matter of Hess, 110 N. Y. App. Div.

including estates for life or for years,[66] annuities or life incomes charged upon property,[67] and pecuniary legacies, although the payment of them may be postponed to a future time.[68]

b. Estates in Remainder. A vested estate in remainder created by a will is a taxable transfer of property,[69] and the fact that the prior estate is exempt from the inheritance tax will not relieve the remainder-man from the payment of such tax.[70] So also a contingent remainder absolute is taxable,[71] although it may not be immediately subject to the tax on account of the uncertainty of the person to whom it may eventually descend or because he is not yet *in esse*,[72] or because the life-tenant is given full control of the *corpus* of the property, with a right to use so much thereof as he may desire or as may be necessary, and the ultimate value of the remainder therefore cannot be determined.[73]

C. Exemptions — 1. Amount or Value of Estate. In Louisiana, property on which taxes have already been paid is exempt from the inheritance tax.[74] In other states no succession tax is imposed unless the estate exceeds a certain value; and this exemption is held valid if not unreasonable in amount.[75] In some jurisdictions the rule is that the "estate passing by will," which is exempt if below a certain sum, refers to the portion passing to the legatee or heir, and not to the whole estate of the decedent, so that a legacy or distributive share below that value is not taxable, although the estate to be distributed may in the aggregate exceed the statutory limit.[76] But in other states the rule is that an estate to be

66. Billings *v.* People, 189 Ill. 472, 59 N. E. 798; Ayers *v.* Chicago Title, etc., Co., 187 Ill. 42, 58 N. E. 318; Dow *v.* Abbott, 197 Mass. 283, 84 N. E. 96; *In re* Plum, 37 Misc. (N. Y.) 466, 75 N. Y. Suppl. 940; Matter of Eldridge, 29 Misc. (N. Y.) 734, 62 N. Y. Suppl. 1026.

67. People *v.* McCormick, 208 Ill. 437, 70 N. E. 350, 64 L. R. A. 775; *In re* De Hoghton, [1896] 1 Ch. 855, 65 L. J. Ch. 528, 74 L. T. Rep. N. S. 297, 44 Wkly. Rep. 550; Stow *v.* Davenport, 5 B. & Ad. 359, 2 N. & M. 805, 27 E. C. L. 156, 110 Eng. Reprint 823; Bryan *v.* Mansion, 3 Jur. N. S. 473, 26 L. J. Ch. 510, 5 Wkly. Rep. 483. See also Green *v.* Croft, 2 H. Bl. 30.

68. Matter of Cogswell, 4 Dem. Surr. (N. Y.) 248.

69. *In re* Rohan-Chabot, 167 N. Y. 280, 60 N. E. 598; *In re* Seaman, 147 N. Y. 69, 41 N. E. 401; Matter of Bushnell, 73 N. Y. App. Div. 325, 77 N. Y. Suppl. 4 [*affirmed* in 172 N. Y. 649, 65 N. E. 1115]; Knight *v.* Stevens, 66 N. Y. App. Div. 267, 72 N. Y. Suppl. 815 [*reversed* on other grounds in 171 N. Y. 40, 63 N. E. 787]; Matter of Cruger, 54 N. Y. App. Div. 405, 66 N. Y. Suppl. 636 [*affirmed* in 166 N. Y. 602, 59 N. E. 1121]; *In re* Hoyt, 37 Misc. (N. Y.) 720, 76 N. Y. Suppl. 504; Matter of Runcie, 36 Misc. (N. Y.) 607, 73 N. Y. Suppl. 1120; Matter of Sherman, 30 Misc. (N. Y.) 547, 63 N. Y. Suppl. 957; Matter of Bogert, 25 Misc. (N. Y.) 466, 55 N. Y. Suppl. 751; *In re* Lange, 55 N. Y. Suppl. 750; *In re* Vinot, 7 N. Y. Suppl. 517; Harrison *v.* Johnston, 109 Tenn. 245, 70 S. W. 414; Bailey *v.* Drane, 96 Tenn. 16, 33 S. W. 573.

70. Bailey *v.* Drane, 96 Tenn. 16, 33 S. W. 573.

71. Ayers *v.* Chicago Title, etc., Co., 187 Ill. 42, 58 N. E. 318; *In re* Dows, 167 N. Y. 227, 60 N. E. 439, 88 Am. St. Rep. 508, 52 L. R. A. 433; Matter of Hitchins, 43 Misc. (N. Y.) 485, 89 N. Y. Suppl. 472 [*affirmed* in 101 N. Y. App. Div. 612, 92 N. Y. Suppl. 1128 (*affirmed* in 181 N. Y. 553, 74 N. E. 1118)]; Matter of Forsyth, 10 Misc. (N. Y.) 477, 32 N. Y. Suppl. 175; Willing's Estate, 11 Phila. (Pa.) 119; Bailey *v.* Drane, 96 Tenn. 16, 33 S. W. 573.

72. See *infra*, XVI, D, 1, b.

73. See *infra*, XVI, D, 1, b.

74. Pritchard's Succession, 118 La. 883, 43 So. 537, holding that the constitutional provision exempting from the inheritance tax property which has borne its just proportion of taxes is restricted to the particular property inherited, and if taxes thereon have not been paid by the former owner, it is immaterial that he paid all the taxes assessed on other property which he sold, investing the proceeds in the property inherited, for the exemption is neither personal nor transmissible.

75. State *v.* Vance, 97 Minn. 532, 106 N. W. 98; State *v.* Bazille, 97 Minn. 11, 106 N. W. 93, 6 L. R. A. N. S. 732; Blight's Estate, 6 Pa. Dist. 459; Black *v.* State, 113 Wis. 205, 89 N. W. 522, 90 Am. St. Rep. 853.

76. People *v.* Koenig, 37 Colo. 283, 85 Pac. 1129; Booth *v.* Com., 130 Ky. 88, 113 S. W. 61; State *v.* Hamlin, 86 Me. 495, 30 Atl. 76, 41 Am. St. Rep. 569, 25 L. R. A. 632; State *v.* Hennepin County Probate Ct., 101 Minn. 485, 112 N. W. 878.

In New York the rule of the text obtains at present under statute. Laws (1910), c. 706. A different rule was declared by prior statutes. *In re* Costello, 189 N. Y. 288, 82 N. E. 139; *In re* Corbett, 171 N. Y. 516, 64 N. E. 209; *In re* Hoffman, 143 N. Y. 327, 38 N. E. 311; Matter of Fisher, 96 N. Y. App. Div. 133, 89 N. Y. Suppl. 102; Matter of McMurray, 96 N. Y. App. Div. 128, 89 N. Y. Suppl. 71; Matter of Garland, 88 N. Y. App. Div. 380, 84 N. Y. Suppl. 630; Matter

of relations by specific designation, as "brothers," "nephews," or the like, will not exempt their descendants.[86] But where the legacy or devise passes over the original legatee and vests in a third person, in consequence of the pre-decease of the original legatee, the exercise of a power of appointment, or the vesting of a remainder after a life-estate, it is regarded as passing directly from the testator to the final taker, and its taxability must be determined by the relationship of that taker to the testator, not by his relationship to the original legatee.[87] A legacy intended for the use and benefit of an exempt relative is not taxable because it is left to a third person in trust for him.[88] In addition to the usual exemptions of this kind, the laws of some states include legacies to the wife or widow of a son or the husband of a daughter.[89]

b. Adopted and Putative Children. Where an exemption is made in favor of the children or lineal descendants of the testator, it does not include adopted children,[90] unless specially so provided by statute, as is now the case in several states;[91] nor does it include illegitimate children unless legitimated by the subsequent marriage of their parents.[92] In New York an exemption is made where the testator and legatee have for a certain number of years "stood in the mutually acknowledged relation of parent and child."[93] The mutual acknowledgment here

St. 341. Nor does it include a grandmother. McDowell *v.* Addams, 45 Pa. St. 430.

Half brothers.— In Ohio, it has been held that bequests to half brothers are exempt from the payment of the collateral inheritance tax. Ormsby's Estate, 5 Ohio S. & C. Pl. Dec. 553, 7 Ohio N. P. 542.

Nephews and nieces.— The exemption of bequests to a decedent's nephews and nieces extends only to children of the decedent's brothers and sisters, and does not include nephews or nieces of a decedent's husband or wife. Bates' Estate, 5 Ohio S. & C. Pl. Dec. 547, 7 Ohio N. P. 625.

Widow of decedent.— Provision is usually made for special exemption in favor of the widow of a decedent. See the statutes of the several states. And see Connell *v.* Crosby, 210 Ill. 380, 71 N. E. 350; Memphis Trust Co. *v.* Speed, 114 Tenn. 677, 88 S. W. 321.

86. Matter of Moore, 90 Hun (N. Y.) 162, 35 N. Y. Suppl. 782; Matter of Bird, 11 N. Y. Suppl. 895, 2 Connoly Surr. 376; Simon's Estate, 5 Ohio S. & C. Pl. Dec. 548, 7 Ohio N. P. 667; Bates' Estate, 5 Ohio S. & C. Pl. Dec. 547, 7 Ohio N. P. 625.

87. *In re* Hulett, 121 Iowa 423, 96 N. W. 952; Dow *v.* Abbott, 197 Mass. 283, 84 N. E. 96; Parke's Estate, 3 Pa. Dist. 196; Com. *v.* Sharpless, 2 Chest. Co. (Pa.) 246; Com. *v.* Schumacher, 9 Lanc. Bar (Pa.) 195, 199. *Compare* Matter of Rogers, 71 N. Y. App. Div. 461, 75 N. Y. Suppl. 835 [*affirmed* in 172 N. Y. 617, 64 N. E. 1125]; Matter of Walworth, 66 N. Y. App. Div. 171, 72 N. Y. Suppl. 984; Matter of Seaver, 63 N. Y. App. Div. 283, 71 N. Y. Suppl. 544.

88. Matter of Murphy, 4 Misc. (N. Y.) 230, 25 N. Y. Suppl. 107; Matter of Farley, 15 N. Y. St. 727; Morris's Estate, 1 Pa. Dist. 818.

89. See the statutes of the several states.

In New York a legacy to the husband of the testator's daughter is exempt from taxation, although the daughter died before the testator (Matter of Woolsey, 19 Abb. N. Cas. 232; Matter of McGarvey, 6 Dem. Surr. 145), and even though the husband of the deceased daughter has remarried (Matter of Ray, 13 Misc. 480, 35 N. Y. Suppl. 481).

In Pennsylvania a legacy to a daughter-in-law who remarries is held to be taxable. Com. *v.* Powell, 51 Pa. St. 438.

90. Miller's Estate, 110 N. Y. 216, 18 N. E. 139; Com. *v.* Ferguson, 137 Pa. St. 595, 20 Atl. 870, 10 L. R. A. 240; Tharp *v.* Com., 58 Pa. St. 500; Com. *v.* Nancrede, 32 Pa. St. 389; Galbraith *v.* Com., 14 Pa. St. 258; Province's Estate, 4 Pa. Dist. 591; Wayne's Estate, 2 Pa. Co. Ct. 93.

91. See the statutes of the several states. And see *In re* Winchester, 140 Cal. 468, 74 Pac. 10; Frigala's Succession, 123 La. 71, 48 So. 652; Miller's Estate, 110 N. Y. 216, 18 N. E. 139; Matter of Duryea, 128 N. Y. App. Div. 205, 112 N. Y. Suppl. 611; Matter of Butler, 58 Hun (N. Y.) 400, 12 N. Y. Suppl. 201 [*affirmed* in 136 N. Y. 649, 32 N. E. 1016]; *In re* Cayuga County Surrogate, 46 Hun (N. Y.) 657 [*affirmed* in 111 N. Y. 343, 18 N. E. 866]; Matter of Thompson, 14 N. Y. St. 487; Warrimer *v.* People, 6 Dem. Surr. (N. Y.) 211.

Issue of adopted children.— These share the benefit of the exemption given to their ancestor, in inheriting from the adopting parent. *In re* Winchester, 140 Cal. 468, 74 Pac. 10; *In re* Cook, 187 N. Y. 253, 79 N. E. 991 [*modifying* 114 N. Y. App. Div. 718, 99 N. Y. Suppl. 1049, and *reversing* 50 Misc. 487, 100 N. Y. Suppl. 628]. See also Matter of Fisch, 34 Misc. (N. Y.) 146, 69 N. Y. Suppl. 493.

92. Com. *v.* Ferguson, 137 Pa. St. 595, 20 Atl. 870; Galbraith *v.* Com., 14 Pa. St. 258; Com. *v.* Gilkeson, 18 Pa. Super. Ct. 516, 9 Pa. Dist. 679, 24 Pa. Co. Ct. 289. *Compare* Com. *v.* Mackey, 222 Pa. St. 613, 72 Atl. 250, holding that an illegitimate child inheriting money from its mother is under no liability to pay a collateral inheritance tax thereon.

93. N. Y. Laws (1887), c. 713, § 25; Laws (1892), c. 399, § 2; Laws (1905), p. 829,

intended is not necessarily a formal act of adoption or any formal declaration of the parties as to their real or intended relationship;[94] but it may be established by pertinent facts, such as the care and maintenance of the legatee by the testator, that the latter supported and educated the former, that the legatee lived in the testator's home and as a member of his family, their mutually affectionate relations, and their style of address to each other.[95] On the other hand a presumption arising from circumstances of this kind may be rebutted by proof that the relationship of the parties was other than that of parent and child, as, for example, that of uncle and niece, and that they always addressed each other in terms appropriate to their actual relation.[96]

4. **Character of Donee — a. In General.** As the inheritance tax is not laid on the property but on the privilege of transferring it,[97] the state may lawfully tax a legacy given to the United States, and such a legacy is taxable if not specifically exempt by statute.[98] Nor is a bequest to a city or other public corporation exempt unless made so by law,[99] or unless the purpose of the gift brings it within the exemption of bequests for charitable and educational uses.[1] A statute imposing a tax on property of a decedent "which passes to any person" other than certain specified relatives, includes property devised to a private corporation.[2]

b. Charitable, Educational, and Religious Institutions. A legacy to a charitable, educational, or religious institution is not exempt from taxation merely because the property of the institution is exempt from general taxes.[3] But it is

c. 368, § 221. And see Matter of Harder, 124 N. Y. App. Div. 77, 108 N. Y. Suppl. 154, Matter of Wheeler, 115 N. Y. App. Div. 616, 100 N. Y. Suppl. 1044; Matter of Thomas, 3 Misc. (N. Y.) 388, 24 N. Y. Suppl. 713; *In re* Ryan, 3 N. Y. Suppl. 136.

Application of statute.— It was at first thought that the statute in question applied only to the illegitimate children of the testator. Matter of Beach, 19 N. Y. App. Div. 630, 46 N. Y. Suppl. 354 [*reversed* in 154 N. Y. 242, 48 N. E. 516]; Matter of Hunt, 86 Hun (N. Y.) 232, 33 N. Y. Suppl. 256. But the application of the statute has been very much broadened by construction. See Matter of Nichols, 91 Hun (N. Y.) 134, 36 N. Y. Suppl. 538, and cases cited *infra*, notes 94, 95.

94. Matter of Butler, 58 Hun (N. Y.) 400, 12 N. Y. Suppl. 201 [*affirmed* in 136 N. Y. 649, 32 N. E. 1016]; *In re* Stilwell, 34 N. Y. Suppl. 1123.

95. *In re* Beach, 154 N. Y. 242, 48 N. E. 516; Matter of Nichols, 91 Hun (N. Y.) 134, 36 N. Y. Suppl. 538; Matter of Birdsall, 22 Misc. (N. Y.) 180, 49 N. Y. Suppl. 450; Matter of Moulton, 11 Misc. (N. Y.) 694, 33 N. Y. Suppl. 578; Matter of Wheeler, 1 Misc. (N. Y.) 450, 22 N. Y. Suppl. 1075; Matter of Sweetland, 20 N. Y. Suppl. 310, 1 Pow. Surr. 200; *In re* Capron, 10 N. Y. Suppl. 23.

96. Matter of Deutsch, 107 N. Y. App. Div. 192, 95 N. Y. Suppl. 65. But see *In re* Davis, 184 N. Y. 299, 77 N. E. 259 [*reversing* 98 N. Y. App. Div. 546, 90 N. Y. Suppl. 244]; Matter of Spencer, 4 N. Y. Suppl. 395, 1 Connoly Surr. 208.

97. See *supra*, XVI, A, 1.

98. Matter of Cullom, 5 Misc. (N. Y.) 173, 25 N. Y. Suppl. 699 [*affirmed* in 76 Hun 610]; U. S. *v.* Perkins, 163 U. S. 625, 16 S. Ct. 1073, 41 L. ed. 287 [*affirming* 141 N. Y. 479, 36 N. E. 505]. See also Carter *v.* Whitcomb, 74 N. H. 482, 69 Atl. 779, 17 L. R. A. N. S. 733.

99. *In re* Hamilton, 148 N. Y. 310, 42 N. E. 717. But *compare In re* Macky, 46 Colo. 79, 102 Pac. 1075, 23 L. R. A. N. S. 1207.

1. *In re* Graves, 242 Ill. 23, 89 N. E. 672 (bequest to city to erect drinking fountain for horses); Essex *v.* Brooks, 164 Mass. 79, 41 N. E. 119 (bequest to establish public library); *In re* Thrall, 157 N. Y. 46, 51 N. E. 411 (bequest to city to establish and maintain public library).

2. Miller *v.* Com., 27 Gratt. (Va.) 110.

3. *Kentucky.*— Leavell *v.* Arnold, 131 Ky. 426, 115 S. W. 232.

New York.— Sherrill *v.* Christ Church, 121 N. Y. 701, 25 N. E. 50; Presbyterian Church Bd. of Foreign Missions, 58 Hun 116, 11 N. Y. Suppl. 310; *In re* Kavanagh, 6 N. Y. Suppl. 669; *In re* Keith, 5 N. Y. Suppl. 201, 1 Connoly Surr. 370.

North Carolina.— Barringer *v.* Cowan, 55 N. C. 436.

Ohio.— Simon's Estate, 5 Ohio S. & C. Pl. Dec. 548, 7 Ohio N. P. 667; Bates' Estate, 5 Ohio S. & C. Pl. Dec. 547, 7 Ohio N. P. 625.

Pennsylvania.— *In re* Finnen, 196 Pa. St. 72, 46 Atl. 269; Com. *v.* Gilpin, 3 Pa. Dist. 711; Gilpin's Estate, 14 Pa. Co. Ct. 122.

Virginia.— Miller *v.* Com., 27 Gratt. 110.

England.— Harris *v.* Howe, 29 Beav. 261, 7 Jur. N. S. 383, 30 L. J. Ch. 612, 9 Wkly. Rep. 404, 54 Eng. Reprint 627; *In re* Parker, 4 H. & N. 666, 5 Jur. N. S. 1058, 29 L. J. Exch. 66, 7 Wkly. Rep. 600; Atty.-Gen. *v.* Fitzgerald, 7 Jur. 569, 13 Sim. 83, 36 Eng. Ch. 83, 60 Eng. Reprint 33.

See 45 Cent. Dig. tit. "Taxation," § 1693.

Exemption of charitable, educational, and

price for this reason.[69] In the case of unlisted securities, their value is to be determined on the best available data, including prices established by actual sales, unofficial quotations or offers, earning capacity of the corporation as shown by current dividends, and the value of the real estate, plant, or other property in which its capital is invested.[70] In assessing the tax on the stock of a railroad corporation incorporated under the laws of various states, the tax should be assessed on such percentage of the value of the stock as the amount of property of the railroad within the state bears to the total property in the several states of the railroad's incorporation.[71]

d. Deductions — (I) *IN GENERAL.* In determining the taxable value of an entire estate or of a residuary estate, all valid and genuine debts due from the decedent should first be deducted,[72] mortgage debts, however, being deducted only from the real estate on which they rest, and not from personal estate.[73] There should also be deducted the proper costs and expenses of administering and settling the estate,[74] including the cost of litigation to sustain the will as against

69. Walker *v.* People, 192 Ill. 106, 61 N. E. 489; Matter of Gould, 19 N. Y. App. Div. 352, 46 N. Y. Suppl. 506 [*modified* on other grounds in 156 N. Y. 423, 51 N. E. 287]; Matter of Cook, 50 Misc. (N. Y.) 487, 100 N. Y. Suppl. 628 [*reversed* in 114 N. Y. App. Div. 718, 99 N. Y. Suppl. 1049 (*modified* in 187 N. Y. 253, 79 N. E. 991)].

70. *In re* Cooley, 186 N. Y. 220, 78 N. E. 939; *In re* Curtice, 185 N. Y. 543, 77 N. E. 1184; *In re* Palmer, 183 N. Y. 238, 76 N. E. 16; *In re* Jones, 172 N. Y. 575, 65 N. E. 570, 60 L. R. A. 476; Matter of Smith, 71 N. Y. App. Div. 602, 76 N. Y. Suppl. 185; Matter of Proctor, 41 Misc. (N. Y.) 79, 83 N. Y. Suppl. 643; Matter of Brandreth, 28 Misc. (N. Y.) 468, 59 N. Y. Suppl. 1092 [*reversed* in 58 N. Y. App. Div. 575, 69 N. Y. Suppl. 142 (*reversed* in 169 N. Y. 437, 62 N. E. 563, 58 L. R. A. 148)].

Compelling production of evidence.— In fixing the value of corporate stock belonging to a decedent's estate, the court has no power to compel the corporation to produce and exhibit its books and papers. State *v.* Carpenter, 129 Wis. 180, 108 N. W. 641, 8 L. R. A. N. S. 78.

71. Kingsbury *v.* Chapin, 196 Mass. 533, 82 N. E. 700; Gardiner *v.* Carter, 74 N. H. 507, 69 Atl. 939; *In re* Cooley, 186 N. Y. 220, 78 N. E. 939; Matter of Thayer, 58 Misc. (N. Y.) 117, 110 N. Y. Suppl. 751.

72. *Illinois.*— Connell *v.* Crosby, 210 Ill. 380, 71 N. E. 350.

Louisiana.— May's Succession, 120 La. 692, 45 So. 551; Levy's Succession, 115 La. 377, 39 So. 37, 8 L. R. A. N. S. 1180.

New York.— Matter of King, 71 N. Y. App. Div. 581, 76 N. Y. Suppl. 220 [*affirmed* in 172 N. Y. 616, 64 N. E. 1122]; Matter of Campbell, 50 Misc. 485, 100 N. Y. Suppl. 637; Matter of Burden, 47 Misc. 329, 95 N. Y. Suppl. 972; Matter of Morgan, 36 Misc. 753, 74 N. Y. Suppl. 478. See also Matter of Wormser, 28 Misc. 608, 59 N. Y. Suppl. 1088. *Compare* Matter of Westurn, 152 N. Y. 93, 46 N. E. 315 [*reversing* 8 N. Y. App. Div. 59, 40 N. Y. Suppl. 567]; Matter of Havemeyer, 32 Misc. 416, 66 N. Y. Suppl. 722; Matter of Millward, 6 Misc. 425, 27 N. Y. Suppl. 286.

Pennsylvania.— Commonwealth's Appeal, 127 Pa. St. 435, 17 Atl. 1094.

Tennessee.— Memphis Trust Co. *v.* Speed, 114 Tenn. 677, 88 S. W. 321; Shelton *v.* Campbell, 109 Tenn. 690, 72 S. W. 112.

Canada.— Receiver-Gen. *v.* Hayward, 35 N. Brunsw. 453.

See 45 Cent. Dig. tit. "Taxation," § 1719.

Debts barred by limitation.—Debts justly due by the decedent, but which are barred by the statute of limitations, are to be deducted from the gross assets of the estate, where neither legatees nor creditors desire to interpose the plea of the statute. McKee's Estate, 10 Pa. Dist. 538, 25 Pa. Co. Ct. 589.

Debts not yet proved.— The surrogate is not bound to wait until all debts are proved before proceeding to assess the tax, but has power to reserve an amount from the appraisal adequate to meet the probable debts, especially where the statute provides for the refunding of a proportionate part of the tax in case debts are allowed after its payment. *In re* Westurn, 152 N. Y. 93, 46 N. E. 315.

73. McCurdy *v.* McCurdy, 197 Mass. 248, 83 N. E. 881, 16 L. R. A. N. S. 329; *In re* Fox, 154 Mich. 5, 117 N. W. 558; Matter of Maresi, 74 N. Y. App. Div. 76, 77 N. Y. Suppl. 76; Matter of Offerman, 25 N. Y. App. Div. 94, 48 N. Y. Suppl. 993; Matter of Sutton, 3 N. Y. App. Div. 208, 38 N. Y. Suppl. 277 [*affirmed* in 149 N. Y. 618, 44 N. E. 1128]; Matter of Livingston, 1 N. Y. App. Div. 568, 37 N. Y. Suppl. 463; Matter of De Graaf, 24 Misc. (N. Y.) 147, 53 N. Y. Suppl. 591; Matter of Berry, 23 Misc. (N. Y.) 230, 51 N. Y. Suppl. 1132; Matter of Kene, 8 Misc. (N. Y.) 102, 29 N. Y. Suppl. 1078.

74. Hopkins' Appeal, 77 Conn. 644, 10 Atl. 657; *In re* Gihon, 169 N. Y. 443, 62 N. E. 561; Matter of Dimon, 82 N. Y. App. Div. 107, 81 N. Y. Suppl. 428; Matter of Gould, 19 N. Y. App. Div. 352, 46 N. Y. Suppl. 506 [*modified* in 156 N. Y. 423, 51 N. E. 287]; Matter of Rothschild, 63 Misc. (N. Y.) 615, 118 N. Y. Suppl. 654; Matter of Purdy, 24 Misc. (N. Y.) 301, 53 N. Y. Suppl. 735. See also Matter of Ludlow, 4 Misc. (N. Y.) 594, 25 N. Y. Suppl. 989; *In re* Miller, 182 Pa. St. 157, 37 Atl. 1000; Cullen's Estate, 8 Pa. Co. Ct. 234; Shelton *v.* Camp-

within which proceedings for this purpose may be taken is commonly limited by law.[98] In New York it is also provided that a person receiving a legacy and paying a tax therefor, who shall thereafter be compelled to refund a part of the legacy to pay debts proved against the estate after the payment of the legacy, shall be entitled to repayment of an equitable portion of the tax, by the executor if the tax has not yet been paid, or by the proper state or county officers if it has.[99]

3. **COLLECTION AND ENFORCEMENT — a. In General.** The collection of the inheritance tax is ordinarily made in and as a part of the proceedings for the administration of the estate, the executor or administrator being ordered to retain the amount of the tax from the funds in his hands, and being required, by rule if necessary, to pay it over to the proper officer.[1] The officers of the probate court are responsible for it if paid into that court.[2] But this does not exclude the maintenance of a suit by or on behalf of the state for the recovery of the tax where resort to such action becomes necessary;[3] and the state is not estopped from bringing such a suit for the unpaid tax on certain legacies by the fact that it has accepted payment of the tax on other legacies passing under the same will.[4]

b. Lien and Priority. In some states the inheritance tax rests as a lien upon the lands of the decedent,[5] but it is generally limited in time as against pur-

98. *In re* Hoople, 179 N. Y. 308, 72 N. E. 229; Matter of Mather, 90 N. Y. App. Div. 382, 85 N. Y. Suppl. 657 [*affirmed* in 179 N. Y. 526, 71 N. E. 1134]; Matter of Willets, 51 Misc. (N. Y.) 176, 100 N. Y. Suppl. 850 [*affirmed* in 119 N. Y. App. Div. 119, 104 N. Y. Suppl. 1150 (*affirmed* in 190 N. Y. 527, 83 N. E. 1134)]; Matter of Sherar, 25 Misc. (N. Y.) 138, 54 N. Y. Suppl. 930.

99. Matter of Park, 8 Misc. (N. Y.) 550, 29 N. Y. Suppl. 1081. See also Matter of Hamilton, 41 Misc. (N. Y.) 268, 84 N. Y. Suppl. 44; *In re* Taylor, 8 Exch. 384, 22 L. J. Exch. 211.

1. *In re* Mahoney, 133 Cal. 180, 65 Pac. 389, 85 Am. St. Rep. 155; *In re* Vivian, 1 Cromp. & J. 409, 1 Tyrw. 379; *In re* Pigott, 1 Cromp. & M. 827, 2 L. J. Exch. 298, 3 Tyrw. 859; *In re* Robinson, 5 Dowl. P. C. 609, 6 L. J. Exch. 158, M. & H. 71, 2 M. & W. 407; *In re* Evans, 3 H. & C. 562, 11 Jur. N. S. 182, 34 L. J. Exch. 87, 11 L. T. Rep. N. S. 717, 13 Wkly. Rep. 350.

Contempt proceedings to enforce order for payment of tax see *In re* Prout, 3 N. Y. Suppl. 831.

2. Com. *v.* Toms, 45 Pa. St. 408, liability of sureties on bond of register of wills for collateral inheritance taxes collected by him but not paid over.

3. *Illinois.*— Connell *v.* Crosby, 210 Ill. 380, 71 N. E. 350.

Kentucky.— Com. *v.* Gaulbert, 134 Ky. 157, 119 S. W. 779.

Louisiana.— Pargoud's Succession, 13 La. Ann. 367.

New York.— Matter of Blackstone, 69 N. Y. App. Div. 127, 74 N. Y. Suppl. 508 [*affirmed* in 171 N. Y. 682, 64 N. E. 1118 (*affirmed* in 188 U. S. 189, 23 S. Ct. 277, 47 L. ed. 439)]; Kissam *v.* People, 3 N. Y. Suppl. 135, 6 Dem. Surr. 171.

Tennessee.— Harrison *v.* Johnston, 109 Tenn. 245, 70 S. W. 414.

What law governs.— A proceeding to enforce a collateral inheritance tax is governed by the law in force at the time of decedent's death. Matter of Sterling, 9 Misc. (N. Y.) 224, 30 N. Y. Suppl. 385.

Parties.— It is unnecessary to appoint a special guardian to represent an infant heir, where the latter's interest is only in remainder and not presently taxable. Matter of Post, 5 N. Y. App. Div. 113, 38 N. Y. Suppl. 977.

Nature and form of remedy.— If the administrator pays over money to a distributee or legatee without deducting the inheritance tax, it becomes, to the extent of the tax, money had and received by him for the use of the state, and an action of assumpsit may be maintained against him therefor. Montague *v.* State, 54 Md. 481. See also Fidelity, etc., Co. *v.* Crenshaw, 120 Tenn. 606, 110 S. W. 1017. But see Atty.-Gen. *v.* Pierce, 59 N. C. 240, holding that the proper mode of suing for the inheritance tax is by a bill in equity in the nature of an information, in the name of the attorney-general.

Burden of proof.— The state has the burden of proving that property is subject to the inheritance tax. Matter of Miller, 77 N. Y. App. Div. 473, 78 N. Y. Suppl. 930. But where the government has made out a *prima facie* case for duty at a particular rate, if events have happened by which the duty would be less, the burden of proving such facts is on defendant. Solicitor-Gen. *v.* Law Reversionary Interest Soc., L. R. 8 Exch. 233, 42 L. J. Exch. 146, 28 L. T. Rep. N. S. 769, 21 Wkly. Rep. 854.

4. Matter of Smith, 23 N. Y. Suppl. 762, Pow. Surr. 150; Matter of Wolfe, 15 N. Y. Suppl. 539, 2 Connoly Surr. 600.

5. Kitching *v.* Shear, 26 Misc. (N. Y.) 436, 57 N. Y. Suppl. 464 (holding that the lien is not paramount to that of an existing mortgage); *In re* Wilcox, 118 N. Y. Suppl. 254.

Discharge of lien by judicial sale.—In Pennsylvania the lien of the state for a collateral inheritance tax will be deemed constructively discharged if, upon a judicial sale of the land, although for other purposes, which realizes more than enough to pay such lien, the

of the legislature, not only by appropriation bills but also by directions incorporated in the revenue laws, to regulate the disposition which shall be made of the taxes collected both by the state agencies and by the local authorities.[33]

B. Distribution of Taxes as Between State and Municipalities[34] — 1. TAXES COLLECTED BY STATE. Where the taxation of particular kinds of property, such as corporate franchises,[35] is withdrawn from the local authorities which otherwise would have jurisdiction, and committed to the state authorities under a general system, the state holds the taxes so collected as a trustee for the various municipalities affected,[36] and the apportionment to them of their distributive shares will be made in accordance with the provisions of the statute regulating the subject and according to the method of administration therein prescribed.[37]

2. GENERAL TAXES COLLECTED BY MUNICIPALITIES — **a. Rights of State in General.** There is nothing in the nature or the ordinary purposes and functions of a county to impose upon it the duty of collecting taxes for the state;[38] but such a duty may be laid upon counties or other municipalities by statute,[39] and in that case the county acts as the agent of the state in the collection of so much of the general taxes as belongs to the state.[40] It is also competent to give the state a preference and

Kansas.— Lawrence Nat. Bank *v.* Barber, 24 Kan. 534.

Michigan.— Chambe *v.* Durfee, 100 Mich. 112, 58 N. W. 661.

North Carolina.— Macon County Bd. of Education *v.* Macon County, 137 N. C. 310, 49 S. E. 353.

South Carolina.— State *v.* Smith, 8 S. C. 127; State *v.* Cobb, 8 S. C. 123.

Tennessee.— Nashville *v.* Towns, 5 Sneed 186.

See 45 Cent. Dig. tit. "Taxation," § 1738.

Application to bonded debt see *infra*, XVIII, D.

33. *Indiana.*— Florer *v.* State, 133 Ind. 453, 32 N. E. 829.

Kentucky.—Auditor *v.* Frankfort Common School, 81 Ky. 680.

Missouri.— State *v.* Ferguson, 62 Mo. 77; State *v.* Thompson, 41 Mo. 25.

Nebraska.— State *v.* Cobb, 44 Nebr. 434, 62 N. W. 867.

North Carolina.— Brown *v.* Hertford County, 100 N. C. 92, 5 S. E. 178.

Oregon.— Yamhill County *v.* Foster, 53 Oreg. 124, 99 Pac. 286.

See 45 Cent. Dig. tit. "Taxation," § 1738. See also COUNTIES, 11 Cyc. 582 text and notes 39–47; MUNICIPAL CORPORATIONS, 28 Cyc. 1729 text and note 73.

Compare State *v.* Smith, 8 S. C. 127; State *v.* Cobb, 8 S. C. 123.

Application to bonded debt see *infra*. XVIII, D.

Money collected as taxes by a county is public property, and within constitutional limits is subject to legislative control. Yamhill County *v.* Foster, 53 Oreg. 124, 99 Pac. 286.

Apportionment between city and county.— The legislature has authority to prescribe the division and apportionment of money raised by county taxes between the county and a city within its limits. Logan County *v.* Lincoln, 81 Ill. 156; Sangamon County *v.* Springfield, 63 Ill. 66; Hannibal *v.* Marion County, 69 Mo. 571; State *v.* St. Louis County Ct., 34 Mo. 546. It is otherwise, however, where constitutional limitations have been infringed. Sleight *v.* People, 74 Ill. 47; Nashville *v.* Towns, 5 Sneed (Tenn.) 186.

However, the state has no such control over the funds of a county that it may divert the money received from the citizens of one county by taxation for the benefit of citizens of another. Yamhill County *v.* Foster, 53 Oreg. 124, 99 Pac. 286.

34. **Liability for uncollected taxes** see *infra*, XVIII, F.

35. Worcester *v.* Board of Appeal, 184 Mass. 460, 69 N. E. 330.

36. Worcester *v.* Board of Appeal, 184 Mass. 460, 69 N. E. 330.

37. Strong *v.* Wright, 1 Conn. 459; Worcester *v.* Board of Appeal, 184 Mass. 460, 69 N. E. 330; Alcona County *v.* Auditor-Gen., 136 Mich. 130, 98 N. W. 975.

38. Com. *v.* Griffith, 1 Lanc. L. Rev. (Pa.) 201.

39. People *v.* Ontario County, 188 N. Y. 1, 80 N. E. 381 [*reversing* on other grounds 114 N. Y. App. Div. 915, 100 N. Y. Suppl. 1136]; Ulster County *v.* State, 79 N. Y. App. Div. 277, 80 N. Y. Suppl. 128 [*affirmed* in 177 N. Y. 189, 69 N. E. 370]; Yamhill County *v.* Foster, 53 Oreg. 124, 99 Pac. 286; State *v.* Stong, (Tenn. Ch. App. 1897) 47 S. W. 1103.

40. Washington County *v.* Clapp, 83 Minn. 512, 86 N. E. 775; Ulster County *v.* State, 79 N. Y. App. Div. 277, 80 N. Y. Suppl. 128 [*affirmed* in 177 N. Y. 189, 69 N. E. 370]; Chicago, etc., R. Co. *v.* State, 128 Wis. 553, 108 N. W. 557. *Compare* Yamhill County *v.* Foster, 53 Oreg. 124, 99 Pac. 286, where it is held that, although the general scheme of taxation creates the relation of debtor and creditor between the county and the state for the amount of state revenue apportioned to the county, to the extent of the county's liability therefor, for which an action may be maintained and for which the county may be charged, whether it collects the tax or not, the debt so created is not a contract obligation, but is a liability

and absolute,[67] and upon a presentation of its claims in appropriate form,[68] and within the time limited by law for such proceedings.[69] It is no defense to such an action that the money collected as taxes was paid under protest.[70]

D. Rights of Bond and Other Creditors. Where a tax is levied for the distinct purpose of paying interest on the public debt, and the constitution provides that money raised by taxation shall be applied to the object stated in the statute imposing the tax, this is a sufficient appropriation of it to that purpose.[71] Where the law provides that money raised by the taxation of particular property in a municipality shall be held by the county treasurer as a sinking fund for the redemption of bonds issued by that municipality in aid of a railroad, the money so raised is appropriated to the specific purpose mentioned and cannot be diverted to any other, and the obligation resting on the treasurer may be enforced by the municipality by appropriate action;[72] and such obligation resting upon the

See also Kilbourne *v.* Sullivan County, 137 N. Y. 170, 33 N. E. 159.

Oregon.— Eugene *v.* Lane County, 50 Oreg. 468, 93 Pac. 255.

Wisconsin.— Newbold *v.* Douglas, 123 Wis. 28, 100 N. W. 1040. *Compare* Milwaukee *v.* Whitefish Bay, 106 Wis. 25, 81 N. W. 989.

See 45 Cent. Dig. tit. "Taxation," § 1750.

Compare Atlantic County *v.* Weymouth Tp., 68 N. J. L. 652, 54 Atl. 458.

Extent of rule.— Where, under a city charter, taxes on property within the city, for road purposes within the city, should have been levied by the city, but the same were levied by the county, and the county collected them, as required by Ballinger & C. Comp. St. § 3094, and the taxes were voluntarily paid, the city was entitled to recover them from the county. Eugene *v.* Lane County, 50 Oreg. 468, 93 Pac. 255.

Form of remedy.— The fact that the county collector may be liable on his bond will not prevent the town from maintaining an action against the county for taxes collected for the town. Bridges *v.* Sullivan County, 27 Hun (N. Y.) 175 [*affirmed* in 92 N. Y. 570]. But *compare* Hart Tp. *v.* Oceana County, 44 Mich. 417, 6 N. W. 863. As to when a state officer acts judicially in apportioning taxes, so that his decision cannot be reviewed collaterally, but only by certiorari see Pittsfield *v.* Exeter, 69 N. H. 336, 41 Atl. 82. Common counts in assumpsit is the proper form of remedy. Sangamon County *v.* Springfield, 63 Ill. 66; Chicago *v.* Cook County, 136 Ill. App. 120. See also Kilbourne *v.* Sullivan County, 137 N. Y. 170, 33 N. E. 159.

Equity has no jurisdiction to determine a question as to what amount collected in taxes, if any, a county has illegally withheld from a city. Chicago *v.* Cook County, 136 Ill. App. 120.

Insufficiency of complaint see Iron River *v.* Bayfield County, 106 Wis. 587, 82 N. W. 559.

67. Millsaps *v.* Monroe, 37 La. Ann. 641.

68. Mountainhome *v.* Elmore County, 9 Ida. 410, 75 Pac. 65; Spooner *v.* Washburn County, 124 Wis. 24, 102 N. W. 325.

69. Mountainhome *v.* Elmore County, 9 Ida. 410, 75 Pac. 65.

Laches.— Where a county has collected taxes for road purposes, and a city claims under its charter the right to receive and disburse for street purposes a portion thereof, the claim will not be enforced in equity where the city has for several years neglected to demand its proportion of the tax until the same has been disbursed by the county under statutory authority. Sanford *v.* Orange County, 54 Fla. 577, 45 So. 479.

70. Ratterman *v.* State, 44 Ohio St. 641, 10 N. E. 678.

71. Morton *v.* Comptroller-Gen., 4 S. C. 430.

72. Woods *v.* Madison County, 136 N. Y. 403, 32 N. E. 1011; Spaulding *v.* Arnold, 125 N. Y. 194, 26 N. E. 295; Strough *v.* Jefferson County, 119 N. Y. 212, 23 N. E. 552; Clark *v.* Sheldon, 106 N. Y. 104, 12 N. E. 341; Bridges *v.* Sullivan County, 92 N. Y. 570; People *v.* Brown, 55 N. Y. 180; Ackerson *v.* Niagara County, 72 Hun (N. Y.) 616, 25 N. Y. Suppl. 196; People *v.* Cayuga County, 63 Hun (N. Y.) 636, 18 N. Y. Suppl. 808; Walsh *v.* Richards, 22 Misc. (N. Y.) 610, 50 N. Y. Suppl. 1114. See also Ulster County *v.* State, 79 N. Y. App. Div. 277, 80 N. Y. Suppl. 128 [*affirmed* in 177 N. Y. 189, 69 N. E. 370].

Applications of rule.— The fact that the predecessors of the present county treasurer failed to make the appropriation of the railroad taxes required by law, and paid them over to their successors in office, will not excuse the present treasurer from making the appropriation. Spaulding *v.* Arnold, 125 N. Y. 194, 26 N. E. 295. And it is the duty of the treasurer to set aside and invest the money in question, as the law directs, although by doing so a deficiency is left in other funds and he will not have money enough to pay the obligations of the county to the state. Clark *v.* Sheldon, 106 N. Y. 104, 12 N. E. 341. If the money is diverted by the county treasurer, by the payment of state taxes and ordinary county expenses, it may be recovered by the town from the county. Crowinshield *v.* Cayuga County, 124 N. Y. 583, 27 N. E. 242. And it is no defense for the county to allege that the taxes were not all paid into the county treasury, but part was used by the town collector to pay town expenses. Ackerson *v.* Niagara County, 72 Hun (N. Y.) 616, 25 N. Y. Suppl. 196. But *compare* as to the last point Peirson *v.* Wayne County, 87 Hun (N. Y.) 605, 34 N. Y. Suppl. 568 [*affirmed*

TAXATION OF COSTS. In practice, the process of ascertaining and charging up the amount of costs in an action to which a party is legally entitled, or which are legally chargeable. In English practice, the process of examining the items in an attorney's bill of costs and making the proper deductions, if any.[1] (Taxation of Costs: In General, see COSTS, 11 Cyc. 154. As Subject of Mandamus, see MANDAMUS, 26 Cyc. 217. In Admiralty, see ADMIRALTY, 1 Cyc. 910. In Garnishment Proceedings, see GARNISHMENT, 20 Cyc. 1125. In Proceedings — Before Arbitrators, see ARBITRATION AND AWARD, 3 Cyc. 724; To Establish Highway, see STREETS AND HIGHWAYS, *ante*, p. 150. On Accounting and Settlement by Executor, see EXECUTORS AND ADMINISTRATORS, 18 Cyc. 1218.)

TAX BILL. See TAXATION, *ante*, p. 1204.

TAX BOOK. See TAXATION, *ante*, p. 1046 *et seq.*

TAX CERTIFICATE. See TAXATION, *ante*, pp. 1169, 1370 *et seq.*

TAX COLLECTOR. See TAXATION, *ante*, p. 1190 *et seq.*

TAX DEED. See TAXATION, *ante*, p. 1422.

TAXED CART. A designation given by statute[2] to a particular kind of carriage described in the Act, namely, to a carriage with less than four wheels, constructed wholly of wood and iron, without any covering other than a tilted covering, and without any lining or springs, and with a fixed seat, without slings or braces, and without any ornament whatever other than paint of a dark colour for the preservation of the wood or iron only, and which should have the words "A taxed cart," and the christian and surname and address of the owner painted in letters of a given length and of a given colour upon the back panel, and which should not be of more than a given value.[3]

TAXICAB. A cab drawn or propelled by motor power, electricity, or other artificial means.[4]

TAXIMETER. Designation of the fare indicator and time and distance register which is affixed to a motor cab or horse-drawn vehicle for the purpose of automatically determining the charge for which the passenger becomes liable.[5]

TAXING-MASTER. At common law, an officer of the court by whom the costs in an action were taxed.[6]

TAX LEGISLATION. The making of laws that are to furnish the measure of every man's duty in support of the public burdens, and the means of enforcing it.[7]

TAX LIEN. See TAXATION, *ante*, p. 1138 *et seq.*

TAX LIST. See TAXATION, *ante*, p. 964 *et seq.*

TAXPAYER. A person owning property in the state subject to taxation, and on which he regularly pays taxes.[8] (Taxpayer: Qualification of as — Grand

587; Rahway Water Com'rs *v.* Brewster, 42 N. J. L. 125; Bayonne *v.* Kingsland, 41 N. J. L. 368.

State and county taxes are distinguished from other taxes in their object, destination, and amount. Pillsbury *v.* Humphrey, 26 Mich. 245.

Money or cash for this purpose has been held to include warrants but not bonds taken and received by a city treasurer in payment of taxes. Sheridan *v.* Rahway, 44 N. J. L. 587.

Taking part of a borough as a public park and thereby exempting it from taxation, after the fixing of the quota of state and county taxes to be levied and collected within the borough, does not excuse a borough collector from paying out of the first moneys collected the full quota of state and county taxes. Coe *v.* Englewood Cliffs, 68 N. J. L. 559, 53 Atl. 562.

1. Black L. Dict.

2. St. 43 Geo. III, c. 161 (2).

3. Williams *v.* Lear, L. R. 7 Q. B. 285, 287, 41 L. J. M. C. 76, 25 L. T. Rep. N. S. 906.

4. Lynch *v.* Robert P. Murphy Hotel Co., 112 N. Y. Suppl. 915, 917.

5. Lynch *v.* Robert P. Murphy Hotel Co., 112 N. Y. Suppl. 915, 917.

6. Hersey *v.* Hutchins, 71 N. H. 458, 459, 52 Atl. 862.

7. Philadelphia Assoc. *v.* Wood, 39 Pa. St. 73, 82.

Imposing on agents of foreign insurance companies the duty of paying two per cent on premiums received by them to an association for the relief of disabled firemen is not either in form or substance, tax legislation, but is a mere requisition that one class of men shall pay their money to another class, and is not legislation at all. Philadelphia Assoc. *v.* Wood, 39 Pa. St. 73, 82.

8. State *v.* Fasse, (Mo. App. 1903) 71 S. W. 745.

Statutory definition see Strang *v.* Cook, 47 Hun (N. Y.) 46, 48. See also Mentz *v.* Cook,

TECHNICALLY PURE. Pure in the ordinary acceptation of the terms of the art.[24]

TELEGRAM. See TELEGRAPHS AND TELEPHONES, *post*, p. 1607.

cation, than that which they suggest, can be affixed to it, unless upon the most positive declaration that a different meaning was designed); People *v.* May, 3 Mich. 598, 605.

24. Matheson *v.* Campbell, 69 Fed. 597, 608, where such was held to be the meaning of the term as used in reference to substances employed in chemical process.

CROSS-REFERENCES

For Matters Relating to:

Abatement of Action For Mental Suffering For Failure to Deliver Telegram by Death of Plaintiff, see ABATEMENT AND REVIVAL, 1 Cyc. 62.

Admissions of Accused Persons by Telephone, see CRIMINAL LAW, 12 Cyc. 423.

Appropriation of Property For Telegraph or Telephone Lines, see EMINENT DOMAIN, 15 Cyc. 592, 625, 627, 628.

Contracts in Furtherance of Gambling, see GAMING, 20 Cyc. 934.

ally,[58] and without discrimination,[59] and to conduct their business in a manner conducive to the public benefit.[60] Owing to their quasi-public character such companies are subject to legislative regulation and control.[61] While the franchise for conducting such a business may be exercised by an individual as well as by a corporation,[62] the fact that it is so exercised does not affect the public character of the business,[63] or the obligation owing to the public,[64] or its liability to legislative regulation and control.[65]

2. As Common Carriers. Telegraph and telephone companies have frequently been termed "common carriers," [66] or common carriers of news or information,[67] and in some jurisdictions have been declared to be common carriers by constitutional or statutory provisions; [68] but while they are in the nature of common carriers in regard to their quasi-public character,[69] and their duty to serve the public generally and without discrimination,[70] and in being subject to legislative

Union Tel. Co., 79 Me. 493, 10 Atl. 495, 1 Am. St. Rep. 353; State *v.* Nebraska Tel. Co., 17 Nebr. 126, 22 N. W. 237, 52 Am. Rep. 404.

58. Central Union Tel. Co. *v.* Bradbury, 106 Ind. 1, 5 N. E. 721; State *v.* Kinloch Tel. Co., 93 Mo. App. 349, 67 S. W. 684. See also *infra*, III.

59. Central Union Tel. Co. *v.* State, 118 Ind. 194, 19 N. E. 604, 10 Am. St. Rep. 114; Central Union Tel. Co. *v.* Bradbury, 106 Ind. 1, 5 N. E. 721; State *v.* Kinloch Tel. Co., 93 Mo. App. 349, 67 S. W. 684; State *v.* Nebraska Tel. Co., 17 Nebr. 126, 22 N. W. 237, 52 Am. Rep. 404; State *v.* Delaware, etc., Tel. Co., 47 Fed. 633 [*affirmed* in 50 Fed. 677, 2 C. C. A. 1]. See also *infra*, III.

60. Central Union Tel. Co. *v.* State, 118 Ind. 194, 19 N. E. 604, 10 Am. St. Rep. 114.

61. Central Union Tel. Co. *v.* Bradbury, 106 Ind. 1, 5 N. E. 721; Hockett *v.* State, 105 Ind. 250, 5 N. E. 178, 55 Am. Rep. 201; State *v.* Kinloch Tel. Co., 93 Mo. App. 349, 67 S. W. 684.

Regulation and control see *infra*, II, B.

62. See *infra*, I, D, 2, a.

63. State *v.* Cadwallader, 172 Ind. 619, 87 N. E. 644, 89 N. E. 319; Lowther *v.* Bridgeman, 57 W. Va. 306, 50 S. E. 410.

64. State *v.* Cadwallader, 172 Ind. 619, 87 N. E. 644, 89 N. E. 319.

65. Lowther *v.* Bridgeman, 57 W. Va. 306, 50 S. E. 410.

66. *California.*— Parks *v.* Alta California Tel. Co., 13 Cal. 422, 73 Am. Dec. 589.

Indiana.— Central Union Tel. Co. *v.* State, 118 Ind. 194, 19 N. E. 604, 10 Am. St. Rep. 114, 2 Am. Elec. Cas. 27; Western Union Tel. Co. *v.* Meek, 49 Ind. 53, 1 Am. Elec. Cas. 139.

Iowa.— Manville *v.* Western Union Tel. Co., 37 Iowa 214, 18 Am. Rep. 8, 1 Am. Elec. Cas. 94.

Kentucky.—Western Union Tel. Co. *v.* Eubanks, 100 Ky. 591, 38 S. W. 1068, 18 Ky. L. Rep. 995, 66 Am. St. Rep. 361, 36 L. R. A. 711, 6 Am. Elec. Cas. 770.

Maine.— True *v.* International Tel. Co., 60 Me. 9, 11 Am. Rep. 156, Allen Tel. Cas. 530.

Nebraska.— Western Union Tel. Co. *v.* Call Pub. Co., 44 Nebr. 326, 62 N. W. 506, 48 Am. St. Rep. 729, 27 L. R. A. 622, 5 Am. Elec. Cas. 673; Pacific Tel. Co. *v.* Underwood, 37 Nebr. 315, 55 N. W. 1057, 40 Am. St. Rep. 490; Kemp *v.* Western Union Tel. Co., 28 Nebr. 661, 44 N. W. 1064, 26 Am. St. Rep. 363.

Ohio.— Daily *v.* State, 51 Ohio St. 348, 37 N. E. 710, 46 Am. St. Rep. 578, 24 L. R. A. 724.

United States.— Muskogee Nat. Tel. Co. *v.* Hall, 118 Fed. 382, 55 C. C. A. 208, 8 Am. Elec. Cas. 64; State *v.* Delaware, etc., Tel. Co., 47 Fed. 633 [*affirmed* in 50 Fed. 677, 2 C. C. A. 1]; State *v.* Bell Tel. Co., 23 Fed. 539.

England.— MacAndrew *v.* Electric Tel. Co., 17 C. B. 3, 1 Jur. N. S. 1073, 25 L. J. C. P. 26, 4 Wkly. Rep. 7, 84 E. C. L. 3, 3 Allen Tel. Cas. 38.

Canada.— Bell Tel. Co. *v.* Montreal St. R. Co., 10 Quebec Super. Ct. 162.

67. State *v.* Cadwallader, 172 Ind. 619, 87 N. E. 644, 89 N. E. 319; Central Union Tel. Co. *v.* State, 118 Ind. 194, 19 N. E. 604, 10 Am. St. Rep. 114; Central Union Tel. Co. *v.* Bradbury, 106 Ind. 1, 5 N. E. 721; Hockett *v.* State, 105 Ind. 250, 5 N. E. 178, 55 Am. Rep. 201; State *v.* Nebraska Tel. Co., 17 Nebr. 126, 22 N. W. 237, 52 Am. Rep. 404; Muskogee Nat. Tel. Co. *v.* Hall, 118 Fed. 382, 55 C. C. A. 208. See also cases cited *supra*, note 66.

68. Western Union Tel. Co. *v.* Eubanks, 100 Ky. 591, 38 S. W. 1068, 18 Ky. L. Rep. 995, 66 Am. St. Rep. 361, 36 L. R. A. 711; Alabama, etc., R. Co. *v.* Cumberland Tel., etc., Co., 88 Miss. 438, 41 So. 258; Postal Tel., etc., Co. *v.* Wells, 82 Miss. 733, 35 So. 190; Blackwell Milling, etc., Co. *v.* Western Union Tel. Co., 17 Okla. 376, 89 Pac. 235.

69. Hockett *v.* State, 105 Ind. 250, 5 N. E. 178, 55 Am. Rep. 201; Central Union Tel. Co. *v.* Swoveland, 14 Ind. App. 341, 42 N. E. 1035; True *v.* International Tel. Co., 60 Me. 9, 11 Am. Rep. 156; State *v.* Nebraska Tel. Co., 17 Nebr. 126, 22 N. W. 237, 52 Am. Rep. 404.

70. Central Union Tel. Co. *v.* State, 118 Ind. 194, 19 N. E. 604, 10 Am. St. Rep. 114; Central Union Tel. Co. *v.* Bradbury, 106 Ind. 1, 5 N. E. 721; State *v.* Kinloch Tel. Co., 93 Mo. App. 349, 67 S. W. 684; State *v.* Nebraska Tel. Co., 17 Nebr. 126, 22 N. W. 237, 52 Am. Rep. 404; State *v.* Delaware, etc., Tel.

regulation and control,[71] they are not strictly speaking common carriers,[72] and their obligations and liabilities are not to be measured by the same rules as are

Co., 47 Fed. 633 [*affirmed* in 50 Fed. 677, 2 C. C. A. 1].

Duty as to furnishing services and facilities see *infra*, III.

71. Central Union Tel. Co. *v.* Bradbury, 106 Ind. 1, 5 N. E. 721; Hockett *v.* State, 105 Ind. 250, 5 N. E. 178, 55 Am. Rep. 201; State *v.* Kinloch Tel. Co., 93 Mo. App. 349, 67 S. W. 684.

72. *Arkansas.*—Western Union Tel. Co. *v.* Short, 53 Ark. 434, 14 S. W. 649, 9 L. R. A. 744.

California.— Coit *v.* Western Union Tel. Co., 130 Cal. 657, 63 Pac. 83, 80 Am. St. Rep. 153, 53 L. R. A. 678; Hart *v.* Western Union Tel. Co., 66 Cal. 579, 6 Pac. 637, 56 Am. Rep. 119, 1 Am. Elec. Cas. 734.

Georgia.— Stamey *v.* Western Union Tel. Co., 92 Ga. 613, 18 S. E. 1008, 44 Am. St. Rep. 95; Western Union Tel. Co. *v.* Fontaine, 58 Ga. 433, 1 Am. Elec. Cas. 229.

Illinois.— Western Union Tel. Co. *v.* Tyler, 74 Ill. 168, 24 Am. Rep. 279, 1 Am. Elec. Cas. 115.

Indiana.— Western Union Tel. Co. *v.* Meredith, 95 Ind. 93, 1 Am. Elec. Cas. 643; Central Union Tel. Co. *v.* Swoveland, 14 Ind. App. 341, 42 N. E. 1035.

Iowa.— Sweatland *v.* Illinois, etc., Tel. Co., 27 Iowa 433, 1 Am. Rep. 285.

Kentucky.— Smith *v.* Western Union Tel. Co., 83 Ky. 104, 4 Am. St. Rep. 126, 1 Am. Elec. Cas. 743; Camp *v.* Western Union Tel. Co., 1 Metc. 164, 71 Am. Dec. 461, Allen Tel. Cas. 85.

Maine.— Fowler *v.* Western Union Tel. Co., 80 Me. 381, 15 Atl. 29, 6 Am. St. Rep. 211, 2 Am. Elec. Cas. 607; Bartlett *v.* Western Union Tel. Co., 62 Me. 209, 16 Am. Rep. 437, 1 Am. Elec. Cas. 45.

Maryland.— Birney *v.* New York, etc., Tel. Co., 18 Md. 341, 81 Am. Dec. 607; Allen Tel. Cas. 195.

Massachusetts.—Grinnell *v.* Western Union Tel. Co., 113 Mass. 299, 18 Am. Rep. 485, 1 Am. Elec. Cas. 70; Ellis *v.* American Tel. Co., 13 Allen 226, Allen Tel. Cas. 306.

Michigan.— Jacob *v.* Western Union Tel. Co., 135 Mich. 600, 98 N. W. 402; Birkett *v.* Western Union Tel. Co., 103 Mich. 361, 61 N. W. 645, 50 Am. St. Rep. 374, 33 L. R. A. 404, 5 Am. Elec. Cas. 727; Western Union Tel. Co. *v.* Carew, 15 Mich. 525.

Missouri.— State *v.* St. Louis, 145 Mo. 551, 46 S. W. 981, 42 L. R. A. 113; Reed *v.* Western Union Tel. Co., 56 Mo. App. 168.

Nebraska.— Becker *v.* Western Union Tel. Co., 11 Nebr. 87, 7 N. W. 868, 38 Am. Rep. 356.

New York.— Kiley *v.* Western Union Tel. Co., 109 N. Y. 231, 16 N. E. 75; Elwood *v.* Western Union Tel. Co., 45 N. Y. 549, 6 Am. Rep. 140, Allen Tel. Cas. 594; Leonard *v.* New York, etc., Tel. Co., 41 N. Y. 544, 1 Am. St. Rep. 446, Allen Tel. Cas. 500; Hirsch *v.* American Dist. Tel. Co., 112 N. Y. App. Div. 265, 98 N. Y. Suppl. 371 [*reversing* 48 Misc. 370, 95 N. Y. Suppl. 562]; Wolfskehl *v.* Western Union Tel. Co., 46 Hun 542, 2 Am. Elec. Cas. 647; Schwartz *v.* Atlantic, etc., Tel. Co., 18 Hun 157, 1 Am. Elec. Cas. 284; Breese *v.* U. S. Telegraph Co., 45 Barb. 274, 31 How. Pr. 86 [*affirmed* in 48 N. Y. 132, 8 Am. Rep. 526]; MacPherson *v.* Western Union Tel. Co., 52 N. Y. Super. Ct. 232, 1 Am. Elec. Cas. 755; De Rutte *v.* New York, etc., Electro Magnetic Tel. Co., 1 Daly 547, 30 How. Pr. 403.

North Carolina.— Lassiter *v.* Western Union Tel. Co., 89 N. C. 334.

Ohio.— Western Union Tel. Co. *v.* Griswold, 37 Ohio St. 301, 41 Am. Rep. 500, 1 Am. Elec. Cas. 329.

Pennsylvania.—Passmore *v.* Western Union Tel. Co., 78 Pa. St. 238, 1 Am. Elec. Cas. 168; New York, etc., Tel. Co. *v.* Dryburg, 35 Pa. St. 298, 78 Am. Dec. 338, Allen Tel. Cas. 157.

South Carolina.— Pinckney *v.* Western Union Tel. Co., 19 S. C. 71, 45 Am. Rep. 765, 1 Am. Elec. Cas. 516; Aiken *v.* Western Union Tel. Co., 5 S. C. 358, 1 Am. Elec. Cas. 121.

Tennessee.— Western Union Tel. Co. *v.* Mellon, 96 Tenn. 66, 33 S. W. 725; Western Union Tel. Co. *v.* Munford, 87 Tenn. 190, 10 S. W. 318, 10 Am. St. Rep. 630, 2 L. R. A. 601; Marr *v.* Western Union Tel. Co., 85 Tenn. 529, 3 S. W. 496.

Texas.— Western Union Tel. Co. *v.* Hearne, 77 Tex. 83, 13 S. W. 970; Western Union Tel. Co. *v.* Neill, 57 Tex. 283, 44 Am. Rep. 589, 1 Am. Elec. Cas. 355.

Utah.— Wertz *v.* Western Union Tel. Co., 7 Utah 446, 27 Pac. 172, 13 L. R. A. 510.

Vermont.— Gillis *v.* Western Union Tel. Co., 61 Vt. 461, 17 Atl. 736, 15 Am. St. Rep. 917, 4 L. R. A. 611.

Virginia.— Western Union Tel. Co. *v.* Reynolds, 77 Va. 173, 46 Am. Rep. 715, 1 Am. Elec. Cas. 487.

Wisconsin.— Thompson *v.* Western Union Tel. Co., 64 Wis. 531, 25 N. W. 789, 54 Am. Rep. 644; Hibbard *v.* Western Union Tel. Co., 33 Wis. 558, 14 Am. Rep. 775, 1 Am. Elec. Cas. 62.

United States.— Primose *v.* Western Union Tel. Co., 154 U. S. 1, 14 S. Ct. 1098, 38 L. ed. 883, 5 Am. Elec. Cas. 809; Western Union Tel. Co. *v.* Coggin, 68 Fed. 137, 15 C. C. A. 231; Western Union Tel. Co. *v.* Cook, 61 Fed. 624, 9 C. C. A. 680, 5 Am. Elec. Cas. 799; Abraham *v.* Western Union Tel. Co., 23 Fed. 315, 1 Am. Elec. Cas. 728.

England.— Playford *v.* United Kingdom Electric Tel. Co., L. R. 4 Q. B. 706, 10 B. & S. 759, 38 L. J. Q. B. 249, 21 L. T. Rep. N. S. 21, 17 Wkly. Rep. 968, Allen Tel. Cas. 437; Dickson *v.* Reuter's Tel. Co., 3 C. P. D. 1, 47 L. J. C. P. 1, 37 L. T. Rep. N. S. 370, 26 Wkly. Rep. 23 [*affirming* 2 C. P. D. 62, 46 L. J. C. P. 197, 35 L. T. Rep. N. S 842, 25 Wkly. Rep. 272].

tional or statutory provision such municipal consent is necessary;[91] but this doctrine has been questioned,[92] and the term "franchise" is frequently used in this connection;[93] and it has been held even where the right to occupy public streets is termed a license and not a franchise, that such right, since it can only be granted pursuant to legislative authority, may be inquired into by information in the nature of quo warranto.[94] The fact that the incorporation of a telephone company is incomplete at the time a privilege is granted to it by a municipality does not affect its right thereto;[95] nor can a municipality which has granted rights and privileges to a telephone company organized under the laws of the state question the validity of the company's incorporation in a suit to restrain the municipality from interfering with the exercise of the rights which it has granted.[96] A grant by a municipality of rights, franchises, or privileges to a telegraph or telephone company and their acceptance by such company constitute a contract,[97] which is binding upon the municipality so that it cannot be revoked or rescinded without cause,[98] or the rights granted be nullified or materially impaired,[99] or made subject to new and burdensome conditions not justifiable under the municipality's police powers;[1] and it is also binding upon the company as to the conditions imposed,[2] and estops the company to repudiate any of the provisions of such

91. Dakota Cent. Tel. Co. *v.* Huron, 165 Fed. 226.

Where municipal consent not necessary.— If a telegraph or telephone company is authorized by statute to occupy public streets and the consent of the municipality is not necessary, the franchise is derived from the legislature, although the municipality may have the right to regulate and control the manner in which it is exercised. Barhite *v.* Home Tel. Co., 50 N. Y. App. Div. 25, 63 N. Y. Suppl. 659.

92. See CORPORATIONS, 10 Cyc. 1086.

93. See Mt. Pleasant Tel. Co. *v.* Ohio, etc., Tel. Co., 140 Ill. App. 27; Cumberland Tel., etc., Co. *v.* Cartwright Creek Tel. Co., 128 Ky. 395, 108 S. W. 875, 32 Ky. L. Rep. 1357; Old Colony Trust Co. *v.* Wichita, 123 Fed. 762 [*affirmed* in 132 Fed. 641, 66 C. C. A. 19].

94. People *v.* Chicago Tel. Co., 220 Ill. 238, 77 N. E. 245.

Although a municipality cannot grant a franchise, if the telegraph or telephone company accepts the ordinance and exercises the franchise attempted to be conferred, quo warranto is a proper proceeding to oust it from exercising the same. State *v.* Milwaukee Independent Tel. Co., 133 Wis. 588, 114 N. W. 108, 315.

95. State *v.* Citizens' Tel. Co., 9 N. J. L. J. 210.

96. Old Colony Trust Co. *v.* Wichita, 123 Fed. 762 [*affirmed* in 132 Fed. 641, 66 C. C. A. 19].

97. *Illinois.*— Chicago *v.* Chicago Tel. Co., 230 Ill. 157, 82 N. E. 607, 13 L. R. A. N. S. 1084; London Mills *v.* White, 208 Ill. 289, 70 N. E. 313; People *v.* Central Union Tel. Co., 192 Ill 307, 61 N. E. 428, 85 Am. St. Rep. 338; Rock Island *v.* Central Union Tel. Co., 132 Ill. App. 248.

Kentucky.— Cumberland Tel., etc., Co. *v.* Cartwright Creek Tel. Co., 128 Ky. 395, 108 S. W. 875, 32 Ky. L. Rep. 1357.

Maryland.— Chesapeake, etc., Tel. Co. *v.* Baltimore, 90 Md. 638, 45 Atl. 446; Chesapeake, etc., Tel. Co. *v.* Baltimore, 89 Md. 689, 43 Atl. 784, 44 Atl. 1033.

New York.— Western Union Tel. Co. *v.* Syracuse, 24 Misc. 338, 53 N. Y. Suppl. 690 [*modified* in 35 N. Y. App. Div. 631, 55 N. Y. Suppl. 1151].

North Dakota.— Northwestern Tel. Exch. Co. *v.* Anderson, 12 N. D. 585, 98 N. W. 706, 102 Am. St. Rep. 580, 65 L. R. A. 771.

United States.— Southern Bell Tel., etc., Co. *v.* Mobile, 162 Fed. 523; Cumberland Tel., etc., Co. *v.* Evansville, 143 Fed. 238, 74 C. C. A. 368 [*affirming* 127 Fed. 187]; Morristown *v.* East Tennessee Tel. Co., 115 Fed. 304, 53 C. C. A. 132.

98. London Mills *v.* White, 208 Ill. 289, 70 N. E. 313; People *v.* Central Union Tel. Co., 192 Ill. 307, 61 N. E. 428, 85 Am. St. Rep. 338; Rock Island *v.* Central Union Tel. Co., 132 Ill. App. 248; Hudson Tel. Co. *v.* Jersey City, 49 N. J. L. 303, 8 Atl. 123, 60 Am. Rep. 619; Morristown *v.* East Tennessee Tel. Co., 115 Fed. 304, 53 C. C. A. 132.

99. Chesapeake, etc., Tel. Co. *v.* Baltimore, 89 Md. 689, 43 Atl. 784, 44 Atl. 1033; Western Union Tel. Co. *v.* Syracuse, 24 Misc. (N. Y.) 338, 53 N. Y. Suppl. 690 [*modified* in 35 N. Y. App. Div. 631, 55 N. Y. Suppl. 1151]; Northwestern Tel. Exch. Co. *v.* Anderson, 12 N. D. 585, 98 N. W. 706, 102 Am. St. Rep. 580, 65 L. R. A. 771; Southern Bell Tel., etc., Co. *v.* Mobile, 162 Fed. 523.

A municipality will be enjoined from illegally interfering with or destroying the property of a telephone company which is conducting a telephone system pursuant to an ordinance which it has accepted and acted upon. Rock Island *v.* Central Union Tel. Co., 132 Ill. App. 248; Southern Bell Tel., etc., Co. *v.* Mobile, 162 Fed. 523.

1. Chesapeake, etc., Tel. Co. *v.* Baltimore, 89 Md. 689. 43 Atl. 784, 44 Atl. 1033.

2. Jamestown *v.* Home Tel. Co., 125 N. Y. App. Div. 1, 109 N. Y. Suppl. 297; Cumberland Tel., etc., Co. *v.* Evansville, 143 Fed. 238, 74 C. C. A. 368 [*affirming* 127 Fed. 187].

contract;[3] but where pursuant to statute the designation of streets or manner of constructing the line is made by a court, the court cannot insert requirements not authorized by the statute, although assented to by the company.[4] An ordinance granting rights to a telegraph or telephone company will be strictly construed against the grantee,[5] and one company under a grant of the right to use streets cannot under its franchise confer a similar right upon a separate and distinct company without the consent of the municipality;[6] but the limitations or conditions imposed must be construed as coterminous with the franchise which the municipality was authorized to grant.[7] A right or franchise granted by a municipality to a telephone company for a certain period cannot be arbitrarily terminated by the municipality prior to the expiration of such period unless the right to do so is expressly reserved,[8] and if reserved the municipality must in enforcing such right proceed in accordance with the provisions of the ordinance reserving it,[9] although the grant may be revoked for an abuse of the powers granted or failure to comply with the conditions imposed,[10] and will terminate at the expiration of the time limited.[11] Where a municipality by ordinance has granted certain rights and privileges to a telegraph or telephone company, a subsequent ordinance granting other or additional rights to such company does not necessarily repeal the former ordinance;[12] but under some circumstances an acceptance by the company of the second ordinance may estop it to claim any further rights under the original ordinance.[13]

b. Right to Alienate Franchise or Property. The general rule that corporations having public duties to perform cannot without legislative authority disable themselves from discharging such duties[14] applies to telegraph and telephone

Rates.— A municipality may legally annex to the grant of a telephone franchise a condition limiting the rates to be charged to its citizens. Moberly *v.* Richmond Tel. Co., 126 Ky. 369, 103 S. W. 714, 31 Ky. L. Rep. 783.

Mandamus will not lie to enforce the contract between a municipality and a telephone company growing out of an ordinance authorizing the company to occupy its streets and imposing conditions accepted by the company, although mandamus would lie to compel the performance of a duty owing to the public growing out of such ordinance and acceptance as distinguished from a duty owing merely to the municipality. Chicago *v.* Chicago Tel. Co., 230 Ill. 157, 82 N. E. 607, 13 L. R. A. N. S. 1084.

3. Cumberland Tel., etc., Co. *v.* Cartwright Creek Tel. Co., 128 Ky. 395, 108 S. W. 875, 32 Ky. L. Rep. 1357.

Reasonableness of terms.— Where a telegraph company accepts an ordinance granting it the right to maintain poles and wires in city streets in consideration of an annual payment of a certain sum, it cannot thereafter contest the reasonableness of such charge. Postal Tel. Cable Co. *v.* Newport, 76 S. W. 159, 25 Ky. L. Rep. 635.

4. State *v.* Lord, 61 N. J. L. 136, 38 Atl. 752.

5. State *v.* Thief River Falls, 102 Minn. 425, 113 N. W. 1057, holding that an ordinance granting to a long distance telephone company authority to construct its line within and through a city will be construed as referring to the company's long distance system only and will not authorize the establishment of a local telephone exchange.

6. Western Union Tel. Co. *v.* Toledo, 103 Fed. 746.

7. Moberly *v.* Richmond Tel. Co., 126 Ky. 369, 103 S. W. 714, 31 Ky. L. Rep. 783, holding that as a city can only grant a telephone franchise operative within the city, a condition of the grant limiting the rates to be charged does not apply to the county service of such company outside of the city.

8. Old Colony Trust Co. *v.* Wichita, 123 Fed. 762 [*affirmed* in 132 Fed. 641, 66 C. C. A. 19].

9. Wichita *v.* Old Colony Trust Co., 132 Fed. 641, 66 C. C. A. 19 [*affirming* 123 Fed. 762].

Who may raise question.— Whether a telephone company has strictly observed all the conditions of a franchise ordinance is a question which can only be raised by the municipality granting the same. Mt. Pleasant Tel. Co. *v.* Ohio, etc., Tel. Co., 140 Ill. App. 27.

10. Western Union Tel. Co. *v.* Toledo, 103 Fed. 746.

11. Mutual Union Tel. Co. *v.* Chicago, 16 Fed. 309, 11 Biss. 539, holding, however, that, although the ordinance provides that the rights and privileges granted shall terminate upon a particular date, the municipal authorities have no right, without notice to the company, to cut down and remove the wires after the expiration of such time.

12. Wichita *v.* Old Colony Trust Co., 132 Fed. 641, 66 C. C. A. 19 [*affirming* 123 Fed. 762].

13. Cumberland Tel., etc., Co. *v.* Evansville, 143 Fed. 238, 74 C. C. A. 368 [*affirming* 127 Fed. 187].

14. See CORPORATIONS, 10 Cyc. 1090.

b. Right to Make Rules and Regulations.[47] Telegraph and telephone companies have a right to make reasonable rules and regulations in regard to the conduct of their business,[48] which persons desiring to avail themselves of the services and facilities furnished by such companies must comply with,[49] such as rules and regulations in regard to their office hours,[50] requiring telegraphic messages to be presented in writing,[51] and at one of the company's transmitting offices,[52] and requiring transient persons sending telegrams requiring answers to make a deposit to pay for the expected answer;[53] and they may also establish reasonable free delivery limits.[54] Telephone companies may also make reasonable regulations,[55] such as requiring rentals to be paid in advance or by a certain date and providing for a discontinuance of the service in case of non-payment,[56] or prohibiting the use of profane or indecent language and making such use a ground for discontinuing the service.[57] It is well settled, however, that any rule

47. **Limitation of liability** see *infra*, V.

48. *Georgia.*— Stamey *v.* Western Union Tel. Co., 92 Ga. 613, 18 S. E. 1008, 44 Am. St. Rep. 95.

Indiana.— Western Union Tel. Co. *v.* McGuire, 104 Ind. 130, 2 N. E. 201, 54 Am. Rep. 296; Western Union Tel. Co. *v.* Harding, 103 Ind. 505, 3 N. E. 172.

Kentucky.— McDaniel *v.* Faubush Tel. Co., 106 S. W. 825, 32 Ky. L. Rep. 572; Roche *v.* Western Union Tel. Co., 70 S. W. 39, 24 Ky. L. Rep. 845.

Maryland.— Birney *v.* New York, etc., Tel. Co., 18 Md. 341, 81 Am. Dec. 607.

Ohio.— Pugh *v.* City, etc., Tel. Assoc., 8 Ohio Dec. (Reprint) 644, 9 Cinc. L. Bul. 104 [*affirmed* in 13 Cinc. L. Bul. 190].

Texas.— Western Union Tel. Co. *v.* Neel, 86 Tex. 368, 25 S. W. 15, 40 Am. St. Rep. 847; Western Union Tel. Co. *v.* McMillan, (Civ. App. 1895) 30 S. W. 298.

West Virginia.— Davis *v.* Western Union Tel. Co., 46 W. Va. 48, 32 S. E. 1026.

United States.— Howlett *v.* Western Union Tel. Co., 28 Fed. 181.

Knowledge of rule or regulation.— Reasonable rules and regulations made by a telegraph company for the management of its business are binding upon its patrons, whether they have knowledge of the existence of such rules or not. Western Union Tel. Co. *v.* Neel, 86 Tex. 368, 25 S. W. 15, 40 Am. St. Rep. 847; Western Union Tel. Co. *v.* McMillan, (Tex. Civ. App. 1895) 30 S. W. 298. But see State *v.* Kinloch Tel. Co., 93 Mo. App. 349, 67 S. W. 684.

49. Pugh *v.* City, etc., Tel. Assoc., 8 Ohio Dec. (Reprint) 644, 9 Cinc. L. Bul. 104 [*affirmed* in 13 Cinc. L. Bul. 190]; Gardner *v.* Providence Tel. Co., 23 R. I. 262, 49 Atl. 1004.

50. *Indiana.*— Western Union Tel. Co. *v.* Harding, 103 Ind. 505, 3 N. E. 172.

Kentucky.— Western Union Tel. Co. *v.* Van Cleave, 107 Ky. 464, 54 S. W. 827, 22 Ky. L. Rep. 53, 92 Am. St. Rep. 366; Roche *v.* Western Union Tel. Co., 70 S. W. 39, 24 Ky. L. Rep. 845.

North Carolina.— Suttle *v.* Western Union Tel. Co., 148 N. C. 480, 62 S. E. 593, 128 Am. St. Rep. 631.

Rhode Island.— Sweet *v.* Postal Tel., etc., Co., 22 R. I. 344, 47 Atl. 881, 53 L. R. A. 732.

Texas.— Western Union Tel. Co. *v.* Neel, 86 Tex. 368, 25 S. W. 15, 40 Am. St. Rep. 847; Western Union Tel. Co. *v.* Wingate, 6 Tex. Civ. App. 394, 32 So. 430.

West Virginia.— Davis *v.* Western Union Tel. Co., 46 W. Va. 48, 32 So. 1026.

The reasonableness depends upon the location and size of the place and amount and character of business transacted there. Western Union Tel. Co. *v.* Van Cleave, 107 Ky. 464, 54 S. W. 827, 22 Ky. L. Rep. 53, 92 Am. St. Rep. 366; Davis *v.* Western Union Tel. Co., 46 W. Va. 48, 32 So. 1026.

Different hours at different places.— A telegraph company need not observe the same office hours at all places where it maintains offices but may regulate the same according to the necessities of its business at the different points. Western Union Tel. Co. *v.* Harding, 103 Ind. 505, 3 N. E. 172.

51. People *v.* Western Union Tel. Co., 166 Ill. 15, 46 N. E. 731, 36 L. R. A. 637. See also Western Union Tel. Co. *v.* Wilson, 93 Ala. 32, 9 So. 414, 30 Am. St. Rep. 23.

52. Stamey *v.* Western Union Tel. Co., 92 Ga. 613, 18 S. E. 1008, 44 Am. St. Rep. 95.

53. Western Union Tel. Co. *v.* McGuire, 104 Ind. 130, 2 N. E. 201, 54 Am. Rep. 296; Hewlett *v.* Western Union Tel. Co., 28 Fed. 181.

54. Roche *v.* Western Union Tel. Co., 70 S. W. 39, 24 Ky. L. Rep. 845; Western Union Tel. Co. *v.* Ayers, 41 Tex. Civ. App. 627, 93 S. W. 199. See also *infra*, IV, C, 4, b.

55. McDaniel *v.* Faubush Tel. Co., 106 S. W. 825, 32 Ky. L. Rep. 572; People *v.* Hudson River Tel. Co., 19 Abb. N. Cas. (N. Y.) 466; Pugh *v.* City, etc., Tel. Assoc., 8 Ohio Dec. (Reprint) 644, 9 Cinc. L. Bul. 104 [*affirmed* in 13 Cinc. L. Bul. 190].

Rates and charges.— A telephone company may, in the absence of statute, prescribe the rates which it will charge for its services or facilities, and individual subscribers cannot complain if such rates are reasonable and uniform. McDaniel *v.* Faubush Tel. Co., 106 S. W. 825, 32 Ky. L. Rep. 572.

56. Irvin *v.* Rushville Co-operative Tel. Co., 161 Ind. 524, 69 N. E. 258; Malochee *v.* Great Southern Tel., etc., Co., 49 La. Ann. 1090, 22 So. 922.

57. Pugh *v.* City, etc., Tel. Assoc., 8 Ohio Dec. (Reprint) 644, 9 Cinc. L. Bul. 104 [*affirmed* in 13 Cinc. L. Bul. 190].

with the carrying on of interstate commerce.[92] It may, however, as a police measure impose a license fee or tax to cover the cost of police regulation and supervision, provided the amount of the fee or tax is reasonably commensurate with such cost.[93] Under the rights of ownership and control with regard to their streets vested in certain municipalities by their charters or by statute, it has been held that they might exact from telegraph or telephone companies a charge in the nature of a rental for the occupancy and use of the streets;[94] but under other charter and statutory provisions this right has been denied.[95] A municipality having power to demand compensation for the privilege of maintaining a telephone system may fix the charge by means of competitive bidding,[96] and award the franchise or privilege to the bidder offering the largest percentage of its gross receipts.[97]

4. Place and Mode of Construction and Maintenance — a. In General. While a municipality cannot exclude from its streets a telegraph or telephone company having authority from the legislature to occupy and use the same,[98] it may make reasonable and proper regulations as to the manner in which such right shall be exercised.[99] The general powers possessed by municipal corporations with regard to the control and regulation of their streets extend as a rule to the deter-

92. See Commerce, 7 Cyc. 450, 482.

93. Philadelphia *v.* Postal Tel. Cable Co., 67 Hun (N. Y.) 21, 21 N. Y. Suppl. 556; Allentown *v.* Western Union Tel. Co., 148 Pa. St. 117, 23 Atl. 1070, 33 Am. St. Rep. 820; Schellsburg *v.* Western Union Tel. Co., 26 Pa. Super. Ct. 343; Kittanning Borough *v.* Western Union Tel. Co., 26 Pa. Super. Ct. 346; Atlantic, etc., Tel. Co. *v.* Philadelphia, 190 U. S. 160, 23 S. Ct. 817, 47 L. ed. 995; Western Union Tel. Co. *v.* New Hope, 187 U. S. 419, 23 S. Ct. 204, 47 L. ed. 240. See also Commerce, 7 Cyc. 450, 482; Municipal Corporations, 28 Cyc. 720, 722, 726, 749.

Where police supervision is necessary a municipality is not bound to furnish it for nothing, although the company is engaged in interstate commerce, but may require the company to pay a reasonable license-fee to cover the cost of such supervision. Atlantic, etc., Tel. Co. *v.* Philadelphia, 190 U. S. 160, 23 S. Ct. 817, 47 L. ed. 995.

The use of streets for a telephone business is a proper and legal use, but the exercise of the right to such use is subject to municipal regulation, and the power to regulate carries with it the power to impose a money charge as a condition to the enjoyment of the right. Lancaster *v.* Briggs, 118 Mo. App. 570, 96 S. W. 314.

If the fee is unreasonable in amount the ordinance imposing it is invalid. Collingdale Borough *v.* Keystone State Tel., etc., Co., 33 Pa. Super. Ct. 351; Postal Tel. Cable Co. *v.* New Hope, 192 U. S. 55, 24 S. Ct. 204, 48 L. ed. 338; Postal Tel. Cable Co. *v.* Taylor, 192 U. S. 64, 24 S. Ct. 208, 48 L. ed. 342. See also as to reasonableness of fee Licenses, 25 Cyc. 611; Municipal Corporations, 28 Cyc. 749.

94. Postal Tel. Cable Co. *v.* Baltimore, 79 Md. 502, 29 Atl. 819, 24 L. R. A. 161 [*affirmed* in 156 U. S. 210, 15 S. Ct. 356, 39 L. ed. 399]; Nebraska Tel. Co. *v.* Lincoln, 82 Nebr. 59, 117 N. W. 284; St. Louis *v.* Western Union Tel. Co., 149 U. S. 465, 13 S. Ct. 990, 37 L. ed. 810; St. Louis *v.* Western Union Tel. Co., 148 U. S. 92, 13 S. Ct. 485, 37 L. ed. 380; Memphis *v.* Postal Tel. Cable Co., 145 Fed. 602, 76 C. C. A. 292 [*reversing* 139 Fed. 707].

Such charge is not a tax but is in the nature of a rental. St. Louis *v.* Western Union Tel. Co., 148 U. S. 92, 13 S. Ct. 485, 37 L. ed. 380; Memphis *v.* Postal Tel. Cable Co., 145 Fed. 602, 76 C. C. A. 292.

The federal statute of 1866 does not affect the right of a municipality to exact such a rental. St. Louis *v.* Western Union Tel. Co., 148 U. S. 92, 13 S. Ct. 485, 37 L. ed. 380. And see *supra*, II, A, 1, a.

Reasonableness of charge.— A charge by a city of three dollars per pole as rental for the occupancy and use of its streets by a telegraph company is reasonable. Memphis *v.* Postal Tel., etc., Co., 164 Fed. 600, 91 C. C. A. 135.

95. Hodges *v.* Western Union Tel. Co., 72 Miss. 910, 18 So. 84, 29 L. R. A. 770.

96. California *v.* Bunceton Tel. Co., 112 Mo. App. 722, 87 S. W. 604; Plattsburg *v.* Peoples' Tel. Co., 88 Mo. App. 306.

Under the Kentucky constitution providing that a city may sell telephone franchises at public sale to the highest bidder for a term not exceeding twenty years, a city has no power to grant such a franchise without offering the same at public sale. Moberly *v.* Richmond Tel. Co., 126 Ky. 369, 103 S. W. 714, 31 Ky. L. Rep. 783.

97. Plattsburg *v.* People's Tel. Co., 88 Mo. App. 306.

Payment cannot be avoided by a telephone company which has obtained its right by offering a certain percentage of its gross receipts at a competitive bidding on the ground that others have been granted a like privilege without charge. California *v.* Bunceton Tel. Co., 112 Mo. App. 722, 87 S. W. 604.

98. See *supra*, II, A, 3.

99. Barhite *v.* Home Tel. Co., 50 N. Y. App. Div. 25, 63 N. Y. Suppl. 659; Philadelphia *v.* Western Union Tel. Co., 11 Phila. (Pa.) 327, 2 Wkly. Notes Cas. 455; State

and pay the expense incident to such change,[33] and the legislature may delegate to a municipal corporation the power to make such requirements,[34] and of regulating the manner in which the work of excavation and construction shall be done.[35] So also the legislature, or municipality pursuant to legislative authority, may authorize the construction by independent companies of subways or conduits to be used by telegraph, telephone, and other companies using electrical conductors,[36] and may require telegraph or telephone companies to remove their wires into such conduits,[37] and pay a reasonable rental therefor,[38] or to remove them into conduits constructed by the municipality,[39] and may refuse such companies permission to construct their own conduits,[40] provided the other conduits already constructed or provided are adequate and suitable.[41] The legislature may also require that companies constructing underground conduits shall submit to the local authorities for approval plans and specifications of the system proposed, and that the work of excavation and construction shall be done under the supervision and control of such authorities.[42] Where a telegraph or telephone company has legislative authority to construct its lines upon city streets, without the consent of the municipality, and subject only to its regulation and control, the municipality cannot require that in constructing such line it shall place its wires in underground conduits;[43] and it has also been held that in such case the municipality cannot without express legislative authority subsequently require overhead wires to be removed into underground conduits;[44] but on the contrary it has been held that a municipality has this power,[45] although it cannot exercise it arbitrarily where no reasonable necessity for such change exists.[46] The duty of making such removal may, however, be imposed upon the company by agree-

ground conduits (American Rapid Tel. Co. *v.* Hess, 125 N. Y. 641, 26 N. E. 919, 21 Am. St. Rep. 764, 13 L. R. A. 454. See also *supra*, II, A, 1, a); although in one case the court, in sustaining the right to require the removal of wires from poles into underground conduits, held that the right to require such removal from the structure of an elevated railroad, where at the time the wires did not cause any public inconvenience, was so doubtful that it should be submitted to the court of last resort and the doubt temporarily be resolved in favor of the telegraph company (Western Union Tel. Co. *v.* New York, 38 Fed. 552, 3 L. R. A. 449).

33. American Rapid Tel. Co. *v.* Hess, 125 N. Y. 641, 26 N. E. 919, 21 Am. St. Rep. 764, 13 L. R. A. 454; People *v.* Squire, 107 N. Y. 593, 14 N. E. 820, 1 Am. St. Rep. 893 [*affirmed* in 145 U. S. 175, 12 S. Ct. 880, 36 L. ed. 666]; Western Union Tel. Co. *v.* New York, 38 Fed. 552, 3 L. R. A. 449.

34. People *v.* Squire, 107 N. Y. 593, 14 N. E. 820, 1 Am. St. Rep. 893 [*affirmed* in 145 U. S. 175, 12 S. Ct. 880, 36 L. ed. 666]; Geneva *v.* Geneva Tel. Co., 30 Misc. (N. Y.) 236, 62 N. Y. Suppl. 172.

35. People *v.* Squire, 107 N. Y. 593, 14 N. E. 820, 1 Am. St. Rep. 893 [*affirmed* in 145 U. S. 175, 12 S. Ct. 880, 36 L. ed. 666].

36. State *v.* St. Louis, 145 Mo. 551, 46 S. W. 981, 42 L. R. A. 113; American Rapid Tel. Co. *v.* Hess, 125 N. Y. 641, 26 N. E. 919, 21 Am. St. Rep. 764, 13 L. R. A. 454; Western Union Tel. Co. *v.* New York, 38 Fed. 552, 3 L. R. A. 449.

Public use.— A subway for telegraph and telephone wires is for a public use and may properly be permitted to be constructed under the streets of a city. State *v.* St. Louis, 145 Mo. 551, 46 S. W. 981, 42 L. R. A. 113 [*overruling* State *v.* Murphy, 134 Mo. 548, 31 S. W. 784, 34 S. W. 51, 35 S. W. 1132, 56 Am. St. Rep. 515, 34 L. R. A. 369].

37. American Rapid Tel. Co. *v.* Hess, 125 N. Y. 641, 26 N. E. 919, 21 Am. St. Rep. 764, 13 L. R. A. 454; Western Union Tel. Co. *v.* New York, 38 Fed. 552, 3 L. R. A. 449.

38. See Western Union Tel. Co. *v.* New York, 38 Fed. 552, 3 L. R. A. 449.

39. Geneva *v.* Geneva Tel. Co., 30 Misc. (N. Y.) 236, 62 N. Y. Suppl. 172.

40. Geneva *v.* Geneva Tel. Co., 30 Misc. (N. Y.) 236, 62 N. Y. Suppl. 172.

41. Rochester *v.* Bell Tel. Co., 52 N. Y. App. Div. 6, 64 N. Y. Suppl. 804; Geneva *v.* Geneva Tel. Co., 30 Misc. (N. Y.) 236, 62 N. Y. Suppl. 172.

42. People *v.* Squire, 107 N. Y. 593, 14 N. E. 820, 1 Am. St. Rep. 893 [*affirmed* in 145 U. S. 175, 12 S. Ct. 880, 36 L. ed. 666].

43. State *v.* Red Lodge, 30 Mont. 338, 76 Pac. 758.

44. Carthage *v.* Central New York Tel., etc., Co., 185 N. Y. 448, 78 N. E. 165, 113 Am. St. Rep. 932 [*reversing* 110 N. Y. App. Div. 625, 96 N. Y. Suppl. 919 (*reversing* 48 Misc. 423, 96 N. Y. Suppl. 917)].

45. Northwestern Tel. Exch. Co. *v.* Minneapolis, 81 Minn. 140, 83 N. W. 527, 86 N. W. 69, 53 L. R. A. 175.

46. Northwestern Tel. Exch. Co. *v.* Minneapolis, 81 Minn. 140, 83 N. W. 527, 86 N. W. 69, 53 L. R. A. 175. See also Hudson River Tel. Co. *v.* Johnstown, 37 Misc. (N. Y.) 41, 74 N. Y. Suppl. 767.

in making any necessary repairs and maintaining its line in a safe and proper condition;[58] and for failure to do so it will be liable for injuries to persons or property caused by such negligent or improper construction or maintenance.[59]

D. Injuries From Construction or Maintenance — 1. LIABILITY FOR INJURIES — a. Personal Injuries. A telegraph or telephone company will be liable for injuries to persons caused by the negligent or improper manner of constructing its lines,[60] as in the case of injuries caused by wires being strung too low,[61] or improperly located,[62] poles placed in the traveled part of a street or highway,[63] lack of proper safeguards against lighting,[64] failure to provide proper

must exercise care to prevent injury to travelers on the street, and the care must be proportionate to the danger that may be reasonably apprehended from the location and nature of the appliances used. The greater the danger, the greater must be the care. Davidson *v.* Utah Independent Tel. Co., 34 Utah 249, 97 Pac. 124.

58. *Alabama.*— Postal Tel. Cable Co. *v.* Jones, 133 Ala. 217, 32 So. 500.

Iowa.— Crawford *v.* Standard Tel. Co., 139 Iowa 331, 115 N. W. 878.

Kentucky.— West Kentucky Tel. Co. *v.* Pharis, 78 S. W. 917, 25 Ky. L. Rep. 1838.

New York.— Walther *v.* American Dist. Tel. Co., 11 Misc. 71, 32 N. Y. Suppl. 751.

North Carolina.— Harton *v.* Forest City Tel. Co., 146 N. C. 429, 59 S. E. 1022, 14 L. R. A. N. S. 956.

The duty of inspection in regard to its frequency cannot be definitely stated, as it depends upon the condition of the weather, season of the year, character of the soil, and other conditions. Harton *v.* Forest City Tel. Co., 146 N. C. 429, 59 S. E. 1022, 14 L. R. A. N. S. 956. It cannot be said, however, that so long as a telegraph or telephone wire will carry messages there is no duty to inspect it to ascertain if it is hanging loose or otherwise in a dangerous condition. Crawford *v.* Standard Tel. Co., 139 Iowa 331, 115 N. W. 878.

A telephone company must exercise ordinary care to maintain its line in good working order but is not liable for interruptions in the service not preventable by ordinary care. Eastern Kentucky Tel., etc., Co. *v.* Hardwick, 106 S. W. 307, 32 Ky. L. Rep. 582.

59. See *infra*, II, D, 1.

60. *Alabama.*— Postal Tel. Cable Co. *v.* Jones, 133 Ala. 217, 32 So. 500.

Kentucky.— Bevis *v.* Vanceburg Tel. Co., 121 Ky. 177, 89 S. W. 126, 28 Ky. L. Rep. 142.

Missouri.— Politowitz *v.* Citizens' Tel. Co., 123 Mo. App. 77, 99 S. W. 756.

New Hampshire.— Ela *v.* Postal Tel. Cable Co., 71 N. H. 1, 51 Atl. 281, failure to provide proper guards and brackets on curve.

New York.— Ensign *v.* Central New York Tel., etc., Co., 79 N. Y. App. Div. 244, 79 N. Y. Suppl. 799 [*affirmed* in 179 N. Y. 539, 71 N. E. 1130].

Pennsylvania.— Little *v.* Central Dist., etc., Tel. Co. 213 Pa. St. 229, 62 Atl. 848.

Utah.— Davidson *v.* Utah Independent Tel. Co., 34 Utah 249, 97 Pac. 124.

61. *Alabama.*— Postal Tel. Cable Co. *v.* Jones, 133 Ala. 217, 32 So. 500, wire sagging because attached to rotten cross arm.

Colorado.— Western Union Tel. Co. *v.* Eyser, 2 Colo. 141 [*reversed* on other grounds in 91 U. S. 495, 23 L. ed. 377].

Maine.— Dickey *v.* Maine Tel. Co., 46 Me. 483.

Massachusetts.— Thomas *v.* Western Union Tel. Co., 100 Mass. 156.

Michigan.— Hovey *v.* Michigan Tel. Co., 124 Mich. 607, 83 N. W. 600.

Nebraska.— Weaver *v.* Dawson County Mut. Tel. Co., 82 Nebr. 696, 118 N. W. 650, 22 L. R. A. N. S. 1189.

Pennsylvania.— Pennsylvania Tel. Co. *v.* Varnau, (1888) 15 Atl. 624.

Texas.— Commercial Tel. Co. *v.* Davis, 43 Tex. Civ. App. 547, 96 S. W. 939; Adams *v.* Weakley, 35 Tex. Civ. App. 371, 80 S. W. 411.

West Virginia.— Hannum *v.* Hill, 52 W. Va. 166, 43 S. E. 223.

Wisconsin.— Chant *v.* Clinton Tel. Co., 130 Wis. 533, 110 N. W. 423.

See 45 Cent. Dig. tit. "Telegraphs and Telephones," § 9.

62. Ensign *v.* Central New York Tel., etc., Co., 79 N. Y. App. Div. 244, 79 N. Y. Suppl. 799 [*affirmed* in 179 N. Y. 539, 71 N. E. 1130], wire strung so near decayed tree as to be broken down by a falling limb.

63. *Illinois.*— Illinois Terminal R. Co. *v.* Thompson, 210 Ill. 226, 71 N. E. 328, brakeman on car colliding with pole located too near track.

Kentucky.— Bevis *v.* Vanceburg Tel. Co., 121 Ky. 177, 89 S. W. 126, 28 Ky. L. Rep. 142.

Massachusetts.— Riley *v.* New England Tel., etc., Co., 184 Mass. 150, 68 N. E. 17, irrespective of negligence under Massachusetts statute.

Nebraska.— Nebraska Tel. Co. *v.* Jones, 60 Nebr. 396, 83 N. W. 197, stump of pole in middle of road.

Pennsylvania.— Little *v.* Central Dist. etc., Tel. Co., 213 Pa. St. 229, 62 Atl. 848.

Texas.— Alice, etc., Tel. Co. *v.* Billingsley, 33 Tex. Civ. App. 452, 77 S. W. 255.

Virginia.— Watts *v.* Southern Bell Tel., etc., Co., 100 Va. 45, 40 S. E. 107.

United States.— Moore *v.* East Tennessee Tel. Co., 142 Fed. 965, 74 C. C. A. 227.

Canada.— Wells *v.* Western Union Tel. Co., 40 Nova Scotia 81 (brace against pole); Bonn *v.* Bell Tel. Co., 30 Ont. 696.

64. *Alabama.*— Southern Bell Tel., etc., Co.

uniformly held that a telegraph or telephone company will be liable in damages to an abutting landowner for any unnecessary or wanton injury to trees which overhang or are growing upon a sidewalk, street, or highway in front of his premises;[88] but as to its liability where there is no more cutting or trimming than is reasonably necessary for the proper construction or maintenance of its line, the authorities are directly conflicting,[89] it being held in some cases that the abutting owner is entitled to damages,[90] and in others that he is not;[91] the question, according to some of the cases, being in the absence of statute dependent upon whether the use of the street by the telegraph or telephone company is to be considered as a proper and ordinary use or as an additional servitude,[92] as to which there is a direct conflict of authority in different jurisdictions.[93] The fact that an abutting owner is entitled to damages does not, however, necessarily entitle him to an injunction.[94] Telegraph and telephone companies are also within the applica-

88. *Alabama.*— See Southern Bell Tel. Co. *v.* Francis, 109 Ala. 224, 19 So. 1, 55 Am. St. Rep. 930, 131 L. R. A. 193.

Louisiana.— Tissot *v.* Great Southern Tel., etc., Co., 39 La. Ann. 996, 3 So. 261, 4 Am. St. Rep. 248.

Michigan.— See Wyant *v.* Central Tel. Co., 123 Mich. 51, 81 N. W. 928, 81 Am. St .Rep. 155, 47 L. R. A. 497.

Nebraska.— Bronson *v.* Albion Tel. Co., 67 Nebr. 111, 93 N. W. 201, 60 L. R. A. 426.

New York.— Van Siclen *v.* Jamaica Electric Light Co., 45 N. Y. App. Div. 1, 61 N. Y. Suppl. 210 [*affirmed* in 168 N. Y. 650, 61 N. E. 1135.

Tennessee.— Memphis Bell Tel. Co. *v.* Hunt, 16 Lea 456, 1 S. W. 159, 57 Am. Rep. 237.

Canada.— Gilchrist *v.* Dominion Tel. Co., 19 N. Brunsw. 553.

Even if he is not the owner, if he has planted the trees in front of his premises with the acquiescence of the city he may recover for their wrongful or wilful cutting. Osborne *v.* Auburn Tel. Co., 111 N. Y. App. Div. 702, 97 N. Y. Suppl. 874.

89. See Bronson *v.* Albion Tel. Co., 67 Nebr. 111, 93 N. W. 201, 60 L. R. A. 426, and cases cited *infra*, notes 90–92.

90. *Connecticut.*— Bradley *v.* Southern New England Tel. Co., 66 Conn. 559, 34 Atl. 499, 32 L. R. A. 280, under statutory provision.

Illinois.— Board of Trade Tel. Co. *v.* Barnett, 107 Ill. 507, 47 Am. Rep. 453.

Mississippi.— Cumberland Tel., etc., Co. *v.* Cassedy, 78 Miss. 666, 29 So. 762.

Missouri.— Cartwright *v.* Liberty Tel. Co., 205 Mo. 126, 103 S. W. 982, 12 L. R. A. N. S. 1125; State *v.* Graeme, 130 Mo. App. 138, 108 S. W. 1131; McAntire *v.* Joplin Tel. Co., 75 Mo. App. 535.

Nebraska.— Bronson *v.* Albion Tel. Co., 67 Nebr. 111, 93 N. W. 201, 60 L. R. A. 426.

New York.— Osborne *v.* Auburn Tel. Co., 111 N. Y. App. Div. 702, 97 N. Y. Suppl. 874.

Ohio.— See Daily *v.* State, 51 Ohio St. 348, 37 N. E. 710, 46 Am. St. Rep. 578, 24 L. R. A. 724, injury to ornamental trees in highway under Ohio statutes.

Pennsylvania.— Marshall *v.* American Tel., etc., Co., 16 Pa. Super. Ct. 615, under statutory provision.

Canada.— See O'Connor *v.* Nova Scotia Tel. Co., 22 Can. Sup. Ct. 276; Gilchrist *v.* Dominion Tel. Co., 19 N. Brunsw. 553; Hodgins *v.* Toronto, 19 Ont. App. 537. *Compare* O'Connor *v.* Nova Scotia Tel. Co., 23 Nova Scotia 509.

In Canada a telegraph company if authorized by statute may, without liability to an abutting owner, cut off overhanging branches which interfere with the working of its line, provided it does not go upon his land and thus commit a trespass in so doing. Roy *v.* Great Northwestern Tel. Co., 2 Quebec Super. Ct. 135.

91. Southern Bell Tel. Co. *v.* Francis, 109 Ala. 224, 19 So. 1, 55 Am. St. Rep. 930, 31 L. R. A. 193; Wyant *v.* Central Tel. Co., 123 Mich. 51, 81 N. W. 928, 81 Am. St. Rep. 155, 47 L. R. A. 497; Southern Bell Tel., etc., Co. *v.* Constantine, 61 Fed. 61, 9 C. C. A. 359, 4 Am. Elec. Cas. 219. See also Western Union Tel. Co. *v.* Rich, 19 Kan. 517, 27 Am. Rep. 159, 1 Am. Elec. 271.

If a telephone company is required by ordinance to move its poles and wires from a street to the adjoining sidewalk, and in so doing it is necessary to trim trees, the company is not liable in trespass therefor to an abutting owner. Southern Bell Tel. Co. *v.* Francis, 109 Ala. 224, 19 So. 1, 55 Am. St. Rep. 930, 31 L. R. A. 193; Southern Bell Tel., etc., Co. *v.* Constantine, 61 Fed. 61, 9 C. C. A. 359.

The company need not give the owner an opportunity to cut or trim the trees himself unless required to do so by statute. Wyant *v.* Central Tel. Co., 123 Mich. 51, 81 N. W. 928, 81 Am. St. Rep. 155, 47 L. R. A. 497.

92. Wyant *v.* Central Tel. Co., 123 Mich. 51, 81 N. W. 928, 81 Am. St. Rep. 155, 47 L. R. A. 497; Bronson *v.* Albion Tel. Co., 67 Nebr. 111, 93 N. W. 201, 60 L. R. A. 426. But see Southern Bell Tel. Co. *v.* Francis, 109 Ala. 224, 19 So. 1, 55 Am. St. Rep. 930, 31 L. R. A. 193; McAntire *v.* Joplin Tel. Co., 75 Mo. App. 535, holding that an abutting owner is entitled to damages for injuries to trees growing inside of the curb line of the street, although the company is proceeding pursuant to lawful authority, and conceding that such use of the street is not an additional servitude.

93. See EMINENT DOMAIN, 15 Cyc. 681, 682.

94. Bronson *v.* Albion Tel. Co., 67 Nebr.

furnish facilities to persons who refuse to comply with such rules,[84] or may discontinue facilities furnished in case of a substantial violation thereof.[85] In such cases the rule or regulation must be reasonable; [86] but if reasonable the fact that it has not been enforced in particular cases does not necessarily make its enforcement in other cases an unjust discrimination.[87] Such companies may also require payment for their services or facilities in advance,[88] or require rentals to be paid on a certain day of the month,[89] and the fact that credit has been extended to one person does not require that it should be extended to others,[90] nor does the fact that such a company is indebted to a subscriber prevent it from enforcing against him its proper rules as to payment.[91] Such companies may in good faith determine for themselves the limits within which they will carry on their business,[92] and the character of such business.[93] So a telephone company doing business

84. *Indiana.*— Western Union Tel. Co. *v.* McGuire, 104 Ind. 130, 2 N. E. 201, 54 Am. Rep. 296.

Ohio.— Pugh *v.* City, etc., Tel. Assoc., 8 Ohio Dec. (Reprint) 644, 9 Cinc. L. Bul. 104 [*affirmed* in 13 Cinc. L. Bul. 190].

Rhode Island.— Gardner *v.* Providence Tel. Co., 23 R. I. 262, 49 Atl. 1004.

South Dakota.— Kirby *v.* Western Union Tel. Co., 7 S. D. 623, 65 N. W. 37, 46 Am. St. Rep. 765, 30 L. R. A. 612, 621, 624.

United States.—Hewlett *v.* Western Union Tel. Co., 28 Fed. 181.

85. Irvin *v.* Rushville Co-operative Tel. Co., 161 Ind. 524, 69 N. E. 258 (failure to pay telephone rentals by a certain day of the month); Pugh *v.* City, etc., Tel. Assoc., 8 Ohio Dec. (Reprint) 644, 9 Cinc. L. Bul. 104 [*affirmed* in 13 Cinc. L. Bul. 190] (use of profane or indecent language over telephone); Gardner *v.* Providence Tel. Co., 23 R. I. 262, 49 Atl. 1004 (regulation forbidding the use by telephone subscribers in connection with the telephone company's wires of extension instruments not furnished by such company).

86. See *supra*, I, D, 3, b.

87. People *v.* Western Union Tel. Co., 166 Ill. 15, 46 N. E. 731, 36 L. R. A. 637 (regulation requiring telegraph messages to be in writing); Irvin *v.* Rushville Co-operative Tel. Co., 161 Ind. 524, 69 N. E. 258 (rule requiring telephone rentals to be paid by a certain day of the month on pain of having the service discontinued). But see Plummer *v.* Hattelsted, (Iowa 1908) 117 N. W. 680 (holding that a patron of a telephone company may be unjustly discriminated against in the use of the telephone exchange by the mere enforcement against him of a just and proper rule, it being ignored in favor of others in like situation); Atlantic, etc., Tel. Co. *v.* Western Union Tel. Co., 4 Daly (N. Y.) 527 (holding that a telegraph company cannot enforce a regulation against another telegraph company alone, the effect of which is to place the latter company at a disadvantage and defeat the object of a statute requiring one telegraph company to transmit messages for other telegraph companies impartially and in good faith for the usual rates charged to individuals).

88. Yancey *v.* Batesville Tel. Co., 81 Ark. 486, 99 S. W. 679; Western Union Tel. Co. *v.* McGuire, 104 Ind. 130, 2 N. E. 201, 54 Am. Rep. 296; Rushville Co-operative Tel. Co. *v.* Irvin, 27 Ind. App. 62, 59 N. E. 327; Buffalo County Tel. Co. *v.* Turner, 82 Nebr. 841, 118 N. W. 1064, 130 Am. St. Rep. 699, 19 L. R. A. N. S. 693; Nebraska Tel. Co. *v.* State, 55 Nebr. 627, 76 N. W. 171, 45 L. R. A. 113. See also Ashley *v.* Rocky Mountain Bell Tel. Co., 25 Mont. 286, 64 Pac. 765.

Reasonableness of rule.— A rule of a rural telephone company that telephone rentals must be paid six months in advance is reasonable; and a subscriber, refusing to comply therewith, is not entitled to service. Buffalo County Tel. Co. *v.* Turner, 82 Nebr. 841, 118 N. W. 1064, 130 Am. St. Rep. 699, 19 L. R. A. N. S. 693.

89. Irvin *v.* Rushville Co-operative Tel. Co., 161 Ind. 524, 69 N. E. 258, holding that where a telephone company has made a rule requiring telephone rentals to be paid by a certain day of the month on pain of discontinuance of the service, and such rule is known to a subscriber, the company may in case of non-payment discontinue the service without informing the subscriber at the exact time of such discontinuance as to the reasons therefor.

90. Irvin *v.* Rushville Co-operative Tel. Co., 161 Ind. 524, 69 N. E. 258.

91. Irvin *v.* Rushville Co-operative Tel. Co., 161 Ind. 524, 69 N. E. 258, holding that, where a telephone company has made a rule unknown to its subscribers requiring rentals to be paid by a certain day of the month, it may discontinue the service for non-payment although it is indebted to the subscriber.

A counter-claim by a rural telephone subscriber against the company for faulty services or for insignificant acts performed for its benefit, a large part of which is exorbitant and illegal, does not justify him in demanding that he be given a service without a prepayment of such rent as other subscribers pay. Buffalo County Tel. Co. *v.* Turner, 82 Nebr. 841, 118 N. W. 1064, 130 Am. St. Rep. 699, 19 L. R. A. N. S. 693.

92. Cumberland Tel., etc., Co. *v.* Kelly, 160 Fed. 316, 87 C. C. A. 268; Delaware, etc., Tel., etc., Co. *v.* Delaware, 50 Fed. 677, 2 C. C. A. 1 [*affirming* 47 Fed. 633].

93. Delaware, etc., Tel., etc., Co. *v.* Delaware, 50 Fed. 677, 2 C. C. A. 1 [*affirming* 47 Fed. 633].

more than it charges others for the performance of a similar service under similar conditions;[6] and in the application of this rule it is not material that the higher rate charged to one customer is not in itself unreasonable, since the rates charged must not only be reasonable in themselves but relatively reasonable.[7] It is not, however, every discrimination which is illegal but only such a discrimination as is under the circumstances unreasonable and unjust;[8] and in some cases different rates may be charged to different customers where there are substantial differences in the character of the services rendered or facilities furnished or a difference in conditions affecting the inconvenience and expense thereof to the company.[9] Even in such cases, however, the difference in rates must be reasonably proportionate to the difference in the conditions justifying a discrimination;[10] and the difference in conditions must not be due to the wrongful or improper conduct of the company, as by sending messages of one customer by a direct route and those of another by a longer and more expensive route,[11] although if a difference in conditions is shown justifying a discrimination, the burden is upon the party complaining to show the injustice of the amount thereof.[12] A discrimination in rates is not justified merely because one customer transacts a larger amount of business with the company than another.[13]

4. Character or Quality of Services and Facilities. A telegraph or telephone company cannot discriminate between different patrons in regard to the character and quality of the services or facilities furnished.[14] Such companies doing business within a certain place or territory must provide themselves with sufficient operatives and equipment reasonably to supply the public demand,[15] and there-

181 U. S. 92, 21 S. Ct. 561, 45 L. ed. 765 [*affirming* 58 Nebr. 192, 78 N. W. 519].

Statutory regulation of rates see *supra*, II, B, 2.

6. Western Union Tel. Co. *v.* Call Pub. Co., 44 Nebr. 326, 62 N. W. 506, 48 Am. St. Rep. 729, 27 L. R. A. 622; Leavell *v.* Western Union Tel. Co., 116 N. C. 211, 21 S. E. 391, 47 Am. St. Rep. 798, 27 L. R. A. 843; Western Union Tel. Co. *v.* Call Pub. Co., 181 U. S. 92, 21 S. Ct. 561, 45 L. ed. 765 [*affirming* 58 Nebr. 192, 78 N. W. 519].

7. Western Union Tel. Co. *v.* Call Pub. Co., 44 Nebr. 326, 62 N. W. 506, 48 Am. St. Rep. 729, 27 L. R. A. 622.

8. Western Union Tel. Co. *v.* Call Pub. Co., 44 Nebr. 326, 62 N. W. 506, 48 Am. St. Rep. 729, 27 L. R. A. 622; Western Union Tel. Co. *v.* Call Pub. Co., 181 U. S. 92, 21 S. Ct. 561, 45 L. ed. 765 [*affirming* 58 Nebr. 192, 78 N. W. 519.

Statutory provisions prohibiting discriminations do not prohibit the charging of different rates for services rendered under materially different conditions. Western Union Tel. Co. *v.* Call Pub. Co., 44 Nebr. 326, 62 N. W. 506, 48 Am. St. Rep. 729, 27 L. R. A. 622.

9. Western Union Tel. Co. *v.* Call Pub. Co., 44 Nebr. 326, 62 N. W. 506, 48 Am. St. Rep. 729, 27 L. R. A. 622.

Application of rule.— A telegraph company may discriminate in rates for news despatches between different newspapers in the same place where one is a morning paper receiving its news at night, when the amount of ordinary commercial business is small, and the other an afternoon paper receiving its news during the day, when the amount of ordinary commercial business is large. Western Union Tel. Co. *v.* Call Pub. Co., 44 Nebr. 326, 62 N. W. 506, 48 Am. St. Rep. 729, 27 L. R. A. 622. A telegraph company may establish reasonable limits within which it will make free deliveries of telegrams, and it is not a discrimination to exact from persons living outside of such limits extra compensation approximately commensurate with the distance traveled and the expense incurred in making such delivery. State *v.* Western Union Tel. Co., 172 Ind. 20, 87 N. E. 641.

10. Western Union Tel. Co. *v.* Call Pub. Co., 181 U. S. 92, 21 S. Ct. 561, 45 L. ed. 765 [*affirming* 58 Nebr. 192, 78 N. W. 519].

11. Leavell *v.* Western Union Tel. Co., 116 N. C. 211, 21 S. E. 391, 47 Am. St. Rep. 798, 27 L. R. A. 843.

12. Western Union Tel. Co. *v.* Call Pub. Co., 44 Nebr. 326, 62 N. W. 506, 48 Am. St. Rep. 729, 27 L. R. A. 622.

13. Western Union Tel. Co. *v.* Call Pub. Co., 44 Nebr. 326, 62 N. W. 506, 48 Am. St. Rep. 729, 27 L. R. A. 622.

14. *Indiana.*— State *v.* Cadwallader, 172 Ind. 619, 87 N. E. 644, 89 N. E. 319; Central Union Tel. Co. *v.* State, 118 Ind. 194, 19 N. E. 604, 10 Am. St. Rep. 114.

Iowa.— Plummer *v.* Hattelsted, (1908) 117 N. W. 680.

Missouri.— State *v.* Kinlock Tel. Co., 93 Mo. App. 349, 67 S. W. 684.

Nebraska.— State *v.* Nebraska Tel. Co., 17 Nebr. 126, 22 N. W. 237, 52 Am. Rep. 404.

North Carolina.— Leavell *v.* Western Union Tel. Co., 116 N. C. 211, 21 S. E. 391, 47 Am. St. Rep. 798, 27 L. R. A. 843.

15. Leavell *v.* Western Union Tel. Co., 116 N. C. 211, 21 S. E. 391, 47 Am. St. Rep. 798, 27 L. R. A. 843; Gwynn *v.* Citizens' Tel. Co.,

company is also liable in an action at law for damages;[43] and, in some jurisdictions, where the refusal to furnish service has amounted to a wilful and conscious invasion of plaintiff's rights, for punitive damages,[44] although there can be no recovery of punitive damages for mere negligence or honest mistake without any conscious invasion of plaintiff's rights,[45] or where the failure to furnish facilities demanded was due merely to the inadequacy of the company's equipment.[46] In some jurisdictions such companies are also liable for statutory penalties.[47]

IV. DUTIES AND LIABILITIES IN REGARD TO MESSAGES.

A. Duty to Accept — 1. IN GENERAL. Generally speaking telegraph companies are bound to accept and contract to transmit, at a reasonable rate,[48] all messages offered to them by any member of the public, on compliance with their reasonable conditions.[49] A telegraph company may, however, make and insist

43. *Georgia.*— Southern Bell Tel., etc., Co. *v.* Earle, 118 Ga. 506, 45 S. E. 319; Atlanta Standard Tel. Co. *v.* Porter, 117 Ga. 124, 43 S. E. 441, bad service pleaded in action for rentals.

Kentucky.— Cumberland Tel., etc., Co. *v.* Hendon, 114 Ky. 501, 71 S. W. 435, 24 Ky. L. Rep. 1271, 102 Am. St. Rep. 290, 60 L. R. A. 849 (where no proof of pecuniary loss, measure of damages is amount paid for service during time instrument was disconnected, calculated at contract rate); Owensboro-Harrison Tel. Co. *v.* Wisdom, 62 S. W. 529, 23 Ky. L. Rep. 97 (substantial damages sustained, where removal of telephone practically destroyed one branch of plaintiff's business, and jury allowed to consider profits which would have been made).

Louisiana.— Barton *v.* Cumberland Tel., etc., Co., 116 La. 125, 40 So. 590.

Mississippi.— Cumberland Tel., etc., Co. *v.* Hobart, 89 Miss. 252, 42 So. 349; Cumberland Tel., etc., Co. *v.* Baker, 85 Miss. 486, 37 So. 1012.

Montana.— Ashley *v.* Rocky Mountain Bell Tel. Co., 25 Mont. 286, 64 Pac. 765, offer to restore telephone on payment of certain sum provable in mitigation, since plaintiff must use efforts to reduce his loss.

South Carolina.— Gwynn *v.* Citizens' Tel. Co., 69 S. C. 434, 48 S. E. 460, holding that the fact that defendant's switchboard was full may be shown in mitigation of damages, but that such fact will not preclude a recovery.

Damages for annoyance and inconvenience as well as actual loss sustained may be allowed in cases of wrongful removal or refusal to install a telephone. Cumberland Tel., etc., Co. *v.* Hobart, 89 Miss. 252, 42 So. 349.

A physician cannot, in an action for cutting off his telephone service, recover for loss of practice proved only by his own testimony that certain persons told him that they had tried to reach him by telephone to secure his services. Cumberland Tel., etc., Co. *v.* Hicks, 89 Miss. 270, 42 So. 285.

Liability of purchasing company.— Where a telephone company makes a contract to furnish perpetual service to a subscriber and thereafter sells its system to another company without any provision as to the carrying out of such contract, there is no privity of contract between the subscriber and the purchasing company and he cannot maintain an action against such company for damages for removing the telephone. Southern Bell Tel., etc., Co. *v.* Jacoway, 131 Ga. 483, 62 S. E. 640.

44. See Southern Bell Tel., etc., Co. *v.* Earle, 118 Ga. 506, 45 S. E. 319 (verdict for one thousand dollars sustained, telephone having been wantonly removed from premises of grocer, whereby he was humiliated on account of impression conveyed to customers that he was without capital sufficient for his business); Barton *v.* Cumberland Tel., etc., Co., 116 La. 125, 40 So. 590.

45. Cumberland Tel., etc., Co. *v.* Hendon, 114 Ky. 501, 71 S. W. 435, 24 Ky. L. Rep. 1271, 102 Am. St. Rep. 290, 60 L. R. A. 849; Cumberland Tel., etc., Co. *v.* Baker, 85 Miss. 486, 37 So. 1012; Gwynn *v.* Citizens' Tel. Co., 69 S. C. 434, 48 S. E. 460, 104 Am. St. Rep. 819, 67 L. R. A. 111.

46. Gwynn *v.* Citizens' Tel. Co., 69 S. C. 434, 48 S. E. 460, 104 Am. St. Rep. 819, 67 L. R. A. 111.

47. See *infra*, VII.

48. Western Union Tel. Co. *v.* Call Pub. Co., 44 Nebr. 326, 62 N. W. 506, 48 Am. St. Rep. 729, 27 L. R. A. 622.

Regulation of rates see *supra*, II, B, 2.

49. *Georgia.*— Gray *v.* Western Union Tel. Co., 87 Ga. 350, 13 S. E. 562, 27 Am. St. Rep. 259, 14 L. R. A. 95; Jeffries *v.* Western Union Tel. Co., 2 Ga. App. 853, 59 S. E. 192; Dunn *v.* Western Union Tel. Co., 2 Ga. App. 845, 59 S. E. 189.

Illinois.— Tyler *v.* Western Union Tel. Co., 60 Ill. 421, 14 Am. Rep. 38.

Indiana.— Western Union Tel. Co. *v.* Ferguson, 57 Ind. 495; Central Union Tel. Co. *v.* Swoveland, 14 Ind. App. 341, 42 N. E. 1035.

Kentucky.— Com. *v.* Western Union Tel. Co., 112 Ky. 355, 67 S. W. 59, 23 Ky. L. Rep. 1633, 99 Am. St. Rep. 299, 57 L. R. A. 614.

Maine.— Fowler *v.* Western Union Tel. Co., 80 Me. 381, 15 Atl. 29, 6 Am. St. Rep. 211.

Michigan.— Western Union Tel. Co. *v.* Carew, 15 Mich. 525.

Nebraska.— Nebraska Tel. Co. *v.* State, 55 Nebr. 627, 76 N. W. 171, 45 L. R. A. 113; Western Union Tel. Co. *v.* Call Pub. Co., 44

communicated to him over a telephone;[60] but it is the duty of such a company to exercise reasonable care to transmit only genuine and authorized messages and to avoid being made an instrument of fraud or deception;[61] and if there are facts and circumstances reasonably calculated to arouse suspicion the company should not receive and transmit the message without investigating and ascertaining the identity or authority of the sender,[62] or should at least communicate such circumstances, inquiry, or suspicions to the addressee at or before the time of delivering the message.[63]

3. Obscene Messages. A telegraph company need not accept a message unless it is couched in decent language,[64] although if such a message is accepted and transmitted, there would seem to be no liability at common law on the part of the company for transmitting it, unless it is libelous.[65]

4. Libelous Messages.[66] A telegraph company need not and should not accept a message which is obviously libelous;[67] but if the message is reasonably capable of an innocent construction, or might reasonably be supposed to be a privileged communication, the telegraph company cannot refuse it on the ground that it may possibly be libelous.[68]

5. Messages For Illegal or Immoral Purposes. A telegraph company is not permitted to act as a censor of public or private morals,[69] or a judge of the good or

Western Union Tel. Co. *v.* Totten, 141 Fed. 533, 72 C. C. A. 591.

The presumption is that a message presented for transmission is genuine and authorized, and an operator has the right to rely and act upon such presumption in the absence of suspicious facts or circumstances. Havelock Bank *v.* Western Union Tel. Co., 141 Fed. 522, 72 C. C. A. 580.

Transmission of money by telegraph.— Where a person presents for transmission a telegram wherein another is requested to transmit money by telegraph to the sender, the telegraph company, in the absence of anything calculated to excite suspicion, is not required before sending the message or delivering to the sender the money received in reply to require the sender to identify himself as being the person whose name is signed to the telegram. Western Union Tel. Co. *v.* Meyer, 61 Ala. 158, 32 Am. Rep. 1.

60. Havelock Bank *v.* Western Union Tel. Co., 141 Fed. 522, 72 C. C. A. 580. See also Western Union Tel. Co. *v.* Totten, 141 Fed. 533, 72 C. C. A. 591.

61. Elwood *v.* Western Union Tel. Co., 45 N. Y. 549, 6 Am. Rep. 140; Western Union Tel. Co. *v.* Totten, 141 Fed. 533, 72 C. C. A. 591.

62. Elwood *v.* Western Union Tel. Co., 45 N. Y. 549, 6 Am. Rep. 140; Western Union Tel. Co. *v.* Totten, 141 Fed. 533, 72 C. C. A. 591. See also Havelock Bank *v.* Western Union Tel. Co., 141 Fed. 522, 72 C. C. A. 580.

The character of the message itself may be such that it should arouse suspicion and require investigation. Western Union Tel. Co. *v.* Totten, 141 Fed. 533, 72 C. C. A. 591.

63. Western Union Tel. Co. *v.* Totten, 141 Fed. 533, 72 C. C. A. 591.

64. See Western Union Tel. Co. *v.* Lillard, 86 Ark. 208, 110 S. W. 1035, 17 L. R. A. N. S. 836; Gray *v.* Western Union Tel. Co., 87 Ga. 350, 13 S. E. 562, 27 Am. St. Rep. 259, 14 L. R. A. 95; Western Union Tel. Co. *v.* Ferguson, 57 Ind. 495, 1 Am. Elec. Cas. 266; Nye *v.* Western Union Tel. Co., 104 Fed. 628.

65. Stockman *v.* Western Union Tel. Co., (Kan. App. 1900) 63 Pac. 658.

Libelous messages see *infra*, IV, A, 4; VI, A.

66. **Liability of company for transmission** of libelous messages see *infra*, VI, A.

67. *Kansas.*— See Stockman *v.* Western Union Tel. Co., (App. 1900) 63 Pac. 658.

Minnesota.— Peterson *v.* Western Union Tel. Co., 65 Minn. 18, 67 N. W. 646, 33 L. R. A. 302, "Slippery Sam, your name is pants. [Signed] Many Republicans."

Wisconsin.— Monson *v.* Lathrop, 96 Wis. 386, 71 N. W. 596, 65 Am. St. Rep. 54, "The citizens of Wisconsin demonstrated you are an unscrupulous liar. A Marshfield Democrat."

United States.— Western Union Tel. Co. *v.* Cashman, 149 Fed. 367, 81 C. C. A. 5, 9 L. R. A. N. S. 140 ("Your article in issue of Thursday is a dirty lie as you know. Who is responsible? You nasty dog. Answer."); Nye *v.* Western Union Tel. Co., 104 Fed. 628.

Canada.— Dominion Tel. Co. *v.* Silver, 10 Can. Sup. Ct. 238 ("John Silver & Company . . . have failed, liabilities heavy." But this was a news despatch sent under a special contract, and one therefore which the telegraph company might have refused); Archambault *v.* Great Northwestern Tel. Co., 14 Quebec 8.

68. Stockman *v.* Western Union Tel. Co., (Kan. App. 1900) 63 Pac. 658; Nye *v.* Western Union Tel. Co., 104 Fed. 628, "Judge Vanderburgh . . . stated distinctly in my presence that Charlie Pillsbury bought you up in 1896, otherwise you would have been for Bryan." See also Peterson *v.* Western Union Tel. Co., 65 Minn. 18, 67 N. W. 646, 33 L. R. A. 302.

69. Western Union Tel. Co. *v.* Ferguson, 57 Ind. 495; Com. *v.* Western Union Tel. Co.,

payment is a privilege which the company may waive,[2] and if it undertakes to render a dead-head[3] or collect[4] service, or to extend credit therefor, charging the tolls for the same at the regular tariff rates to the account of the sender,[5] or agreeing to accept payment at a later date,[6] it is held in the absence of contract to the same degree of care and diligence as though the charges had been fully prepaid.[7]

11. **Unstamped Messages.** Where a statute or act of congress provides for a stamp tax on telegraph messages the duty of affixing such stamp and paying such tax is on the person sending the message, and the telegraph company is not bound to accept for transmission a message which is not properly stamped.[8]

B. Duty to Transmit — 1. In General. Where a telegraph company has duly received a message for transmission, it is its duty to transmit the same, and it will be liable for a failure to do so,[9] notwithstanding it is a message which the company might have refused to accept,[10] unless it is also one which it would be unlawful for the company to transmit.[11] It is no justification for failure to transmit a message that it was written in cipher,[12] or that the operator mistakenly thought that the addressee was not at the place stated in the address.[13] A telegraph company by receiving a message for transmission does not, however, abso-

ciple it has been held that a regulation requiring a deposit from transient persons sending telegrams which require answers is reasonable. Western Union Tel. Co. *v.* McGuire, 104 Ind. 130, 2 N. E. 201, 54 Am. Rep. 296, 1 Am. Elec. Cas. 77; Hewlett *v.* Western Union Tel. Co., 28 Fed. 181, 2 Am. Elec. Cas. 851.

Telephone rentals see *supra*, III, B, 1.

2. Western Union Tel. Co. *v.* Cunningham, 99 Ala. 314, 14 So. 579; Western Union Tel. Co. *v.* Henley, 157 Ind. 90, 60 N. E. 682.

3. Western Union Tel. Co. *v.* Snodgrass, 94 Tex. 284, 60 S. W. 308, 86 Am. St. Rep. 851.

4. Western Union Tel. Co. *v.* Cunningham, 99 Ala. 314, 14 So. 579; Western Union Tel. Co. *v.* Yopst, 118 Ind. 248, 20 N. E. 222, 3 L. R. A. 224; Cogdell *v.* Western Union Tel. Co., 135 N. C. 431, 47 S. E. 490.

5. Western Union Tel. Co. *v.* Henley, 157 Ind. 90, 60 N. E. 682.

6. Western Union Tel. Co. *v.* Cunningham, 99 Ala. 314, 14 So. 579.

7. Western Union Tel. Co. *v.* Henley, 157 Ind. 90, 60 N. E. 682. See also cases cited *supra*, notes 2-6.

8. Western Union Tel. Co. *v.* Waters, 139 Ala. 652, 36 So. 773; Western Union Tel. Co. *v.* Young, 138 Ala. 240, 36 So. 374 (subsequent repeal of the act does not make the company liable where no stamp was originally affixed); Kirk *v.* Western Union Tel. Co., 90 Fed. 809.

9. *Georgia.*— Baldwin *v.* Western Union Tel. Co., 93 Ga. 692, 21 S. E. 212, 44 Am. St. Rep. 194.

Maryland.— Birney *v.* New York, etc., Printing Tel. Co., 18 Md. 341, 81 Am. Dec. 607.

Mississippi.— Western Union Tel. Co. *v.* Jones, 69 Miss. 658, 13 So. 471, 30 Am. St. Rep. 579.

Missouri.— Burnett *v.* Western Union Tel. Co., 39 Mo. App. 599.

North Carolina.—Hocutt *v.* Western Union Tel. Co., 147 N. C. 186, 60 S. E. 980.

Pennsylvania.— U. S. Tel. Co. *v.* Wenger, 55 Pa. St. 262, 93 Am. Dec. 751.

Virginia.— Western Union Tel. Co. *v.* Reynolds, 77 Va. 173, 46 Am. Rep. 715.

See 45 Cent. Dig. tit. "Telegraphs and Telephones," § 31.

If a telegraph company makes no effort to transmit a message which it has received, as where the operator forgets and entirely neglects to transmit the same, it will be liable for all damages resulting from such neglect regardless of any rule or regulation limiting its liability in the case of unrepeated messages. Birney *v.* New York, etc., Printing Tel., Co., 18 Md. 341, 81 Am. Dec. 607.

Message stopped at intermediate point.— If a message is received at one point to be transmitted to another point on the company's line and is transmitted from the first point but never goes beyond an intermediate point on the line, and no reason is shown for the failure to transmit it to its destination, the company will be liable for the damages sustained. U. S. Telegraph Co. *v.* Wenger, 55 Pa. St. 262, 93 Am. Dec. 751.

10. Western Union Tel. Co. *v.* Cunningham, 99 Ala. 314, 14 So. 579 (charges not prepaid); Western Union Tel. Co. *v.* Jones, 69 Miss. 658, 13 So. 471, 30 Am. St. Rep. 579 (message not on regular blank); Western Union Tel. Co. *v.* Reynolds, 77 Va. 173, 46 Am. Rep. 715.

11. Western Union Tel. Co. *v.* Young, 138 Ala. 240, 36 So. 374; Kirk *v.* Western Union Tel. Co., 90 Fed. 809, under statute making telegraph company liable for a penalty for transmitting unstamped messages.

12. Western Union Tel. Co. *v.* Reynolds, 77 Va. 173, 46 Am. Rep. 715, holding that the fact that a message is in cipher so that its meaning is not intelligible to the company is no justification for a failure to transmit it, where it is expressed in a series of letters which could readily be transmitted.

13. Hocutt *v.* Western Union Tel. Co., 147 N. C. 186, 60 S. E. 980.

messages it has been held that, although the company receives a message on Sunday, it is not liable for failure to transmit it on the same day if it does not relate to a matter of charity or necessity;[26] but if the message is of such character the company will be liable for failure to transmit the same.[27]

b. Excuses For Delay — (I) *IN GENERAL.* In addition to the general rule requiring that ordinarily messages are to be transmitted in the order in which they are received,[28] various circumstances or conditions may exist which will justify or excuse a delay in transmission,[29] or justify a refusal to accept a message for transmission unless it is taken subject to delay.[30] If, however, the message is accepted for transmission and circumstances arise making a prompt transmission impossible, the sender of the message should be notified.[31]

(II) *WIRE TROUBLE.* Inasmuch as a telegraph company is liable only for negligence and does not insure prompt transmission,[32] it follows that it is not responsible for delays due to unavoidable interruptions in the working of its lines, such as those due to storms or atmospheric disturbances or other causes over which it has no control and against which, in the exercise of ordinary prudence and foresight, it was not reasonably practicable to guard.[33] Wire trouble, however, is no legal excuse where its existence and extent were known to the company's operator when the message was accepted, and the facts not communicated by him to the sender;[34] nor is it an excuse when the trouble arises because of the

ment to transmit the message and receive payment on the following day.

26. Willingham *v.* Western Union Tel. Co., 91 Ga. 449, 18 S. E. 298; Western Union Tel. Co. *v.* Yopst, 118 Ind. 248, 20 N. E. 222, 3 L. R. A. 224 (not liable for statutory penalty); Rogers *v.* Western Union Tel. Co., 78 Ind. 169, 41 Am. Rep. 558 (not liable for statutory penalty). See also *supra*, IV, A, 6.

27. Burnett *v.* Western Union Tel. Co., 39 Mo. App. 599.

28. See *infra*, IV, B, 2, c.

29. See Glover *v.* Western Union Tel. Co., 78 S. C. 502, 59 S. E. 526; Behm *v.* Western Union Tel. Co., 3 Fed. Cas. No. 1,234, 8 Biss. 131, 7 Reporter 710; Dorgan *v.* Western Union Tel. Co., 7 Fed. Cas. No. 4,004; Stevenson *v.* Montreal Tel. Co., 16 U. C. Q. B. 530.

30. Petze *v.* Western Union Tel. Co., 128 N. Y. App. Div. 192, 112 N. Y. Suppl. 516, holding that where a message is presented to a telegraph company for transmission during a strike of its operators, the company is not liable for a statutory penalty because it refuses to receive the message except subject to delay.

31. Swan *v.* Western Union Tel. Co., 129 Fed. 318, 63 C. C. A. 550, 67 L. R. A. 153. See also Buchanan *v.* Western Union Tel. Co., (Tex. Civ. App. 1907) 100 S. W. 974. But see Stevenson *v.* Montreal Tel. Co., 16 U. C. Q. B. 530.

In case of wire trouble see *infra*, IV, B, 2, b, (II).

32. See *supra*, IV, B, 2, a.

33. *Georgia.*— Western Union Tel. Co. *v.* Davis, 95 Ga. 522, 22 S. E. 642.

Indiana.— Bierhaus *v.* Western Union Tel. Co., 8 Ind. App. 246, 34 N. E. 581.

Michigan.— Jacob *v.* Western Union Tel. Co., 135 Mich. 600, 98 N. W. 402.

Missouri.— Taylor *v.* Western Union Tel. Co., 107 Mo. App. 105, 80 S. W. 697; Smith *v.* Western Union Tel. Co., 57 Mo. App. 259.

New York.— Leonard *v.* New York, etc., Electro Magnetic Tel. Co., 41 N. Y. 544, 1 Am. Rep. 446.

South Carolina.— Glover *v.* Western Union Tel. Co., 78 S. C. 502, 59 S. E. 526.

South Dakota.— Kirby *v.* Western Union Tel. Co., 4 S. D. 105, 55 N. W. 759, 46 Am. St. Rep. 765, 30 L. R. A. 612, 621, 624.

Texas.— Western Union Tel. Co. *v.* McGown, 42 Tex. Civ. App. 565, 93 S. W. 710; Faubion *v.* Western Union Tel. Co., 36 Tex. Civ. App. 98, 81 S. W. 56; Western Union Tel. Co. *v.* Birge-Forbes Co., 29 Tex. Civ. App. 526, 69 S. W. 181; Western Union Tel. Co. *v.* Stiles, (Civ. App. 1896) 35 S. W. 76.

United States.— Beasley *v.* Western Union Tel. Co., 39 Fed. 181; Behm *v.* Western Union Tel. Co., 3 Fed. Cas. No. 1,234, 8 Biss. 131, 7 Reporter 710; Dorgan *v.* Western Union Tel. Co., 7 Fed. Cas. No. 4,004.

Canada.— Stevenson *v.* Montreal Tel. Co., 16 U. C. Q. B. 530.

See 45 Cent. Dig. tit. "Telegraphs and Telephones," § 33.

34. Bierhaus *v.* Western Union Tel. Co., 8 Ind. App. 246, 34 N. E. 581, 12 Ind. App. 17, 39 N. E. 881; Western Union Tel. Co. *v.* Birge-Forbes Co., 29 Tex. Civ. App. 526, 69 S. W. 181; Swan *v.* Western Union Tel. Co., 129 Fed. 318, 63 C. C. A. 550, 67 L. R. A. 153; Fleischner *v.* Pacific Postal Tel. Co., 55 Fed. 738 [*affirmed* on this point in 66 Fed. 899, 14 C. C. A. 166]. But see Stevenson *v.* Montreal Tel. Co., 16 U. C. Q. B. 530.

Time or place of delay.— It is the duty of a telegraph company to notify the sender of a message of its inability promptly to transmit the same, whether the cause of the delay exists at the time the message is received or arises subsequently before the message is transmitted. Swan *v.* Western Union Tel. Co., 129 Fed. 318, 63 C. C. A. 550, 67 L. R. A. 153.

such free-delivery limits, unless an additional charge covering the cost of such service is prepaid or satisfactorily guaranteed.[47] Free-delivery limits, however, are no defense where such limits exist merely on paper, without being observed in practice;[48] where the addressee, although he resides without the limits, could by reasonable diligence have been found within;[49] where with full notice as to the distance at which the addressee resided the company has made a special contract with the sender to deliver at all events;[50] or where the message has never been transmitted to the point of destination, or where its delay in reaching that point, and not the delay in delivery thereafter, is the subject of complaint.[51] It is *prima facie* the duty of the sender to ascertain where the addressee resides and to provide for the delivery of the message by paying or guaranteeing the charges for special delivery, if such charges are required;[52] and it has been held that handing in a message for transmission without explanation imposes no duty upon the transmitting operator other than to forward it accurately and promptly, or upon the terminal operator other than to copy it accurately and deliver it with reasonable promptness if the addressee resides within the free-delivery limits,[53]

47. *Alabama.*— Western Union Tel. Co. *v.* Whitson, 145 Ala. 426, 41 So. 405; Western Union Tel. Co. *v.* Henderson, 89 Ala. 510, 7 So. 419, 18 Am. St. Rep. 148.

Arkansas.— Arkansas, etc., R. Co. *v.* Stroude. 82 Ark. 117, 100 S. W. 760.

Georgia.— Western Union Tel. Co. *v.* Smith, 93 Ga. 635, 21 S. E. 166.

Illinois.— Western Union Tel. Co. *v.* Trotter, 55 Ill. App. 659.

Kansas.— Western Union Tel. Co. *v.* Harvey, 67 Kan. 729, 74 Pac. 250.

Kentucky.— Cumberland Tel., etc., Co. *v.* Atherton, 122 Ky. 154, 91 S. W. 257, 28 Ky. L. Rep. 1100; Western Union Tel. Co. *v.* Cross, 116 Ky. 5, 74 S. W. 1098, 76 S. W. 162, 25 Ky. L. Rep. 268, 646; Western Union Tel. Co. *v.* Matthews, 113 Ky. 188, 67 S. W. 849, 24 Ky. L. Rep. 3; Western Union Tel. Co. *v.* Mathews, 107 Ky. 663, 55 S. W. 427, 21 Ky. L. Rep. 1405; Western Union Tel. Co. *v.* Scott, 87 S. W. 289, 27 Ky. L. Rep. 975; Roche *v.* Western Union Tel. Co., 70 S. W. 39, 24 Ky. L. Rep. 845.

Missouri.— Reynolds *v.* Western Union Tel. Co., 81 Mo. App. 223.

Tennessee.— Western Union Tel. Co. *v.* McCaul, 115 Tenn. 99, 90 S. W. 856; McCaul *v.* Western Union Tel. Co., 114 Tenn. 661, 88 S. W. 325.

Texas.— Western Union Tel. Co. *v.* Jennings, 98 Tex. 465, 84 S. W. 1056; Western Union Tel. Co. *v.* Swearingen, 95 Tex. 420, 67 S. W. 767 [*reversing* (Civ. App. 1901) 65 S. W. 1080]; Anderson *v.* Western Union Tel. Co., 84 Tex. 17, 19 S. W. 285; Western Union Tel. Co. *v.* Ayers, 41 Tex. Civ. App. 627, 93 S. W. 199; Western Union Tel. Co. *v.* Bryant, 35 Tex. Civ. App. 442, 80 S. W. 406; Western Union Tel. Co. *v.* Byrd, 34 Tex. Civ. App. 594, 79 S. W. 40; Western Union Tel. Co. *v.* Christensen, (Civ. App. 1904) 78 S. W. 744; Hargrave *v.* Western Union Tel. Co., (Civ. App. 1901) 60 S. W. 687; Western Union Tel. Co. *v.* Redinger, 22 Tex. Civ. App. 362, 54 S. W. 417; Western Union Tel. Co. *v.* Teague, 8 Tex. Civ. App. 444, 27 S. W. 958; Western Union Tel. Co. *v.* Taylor, 3 Tex. Civ. App. 310, 22 S. W. 532.

United States.— Whittemore *v.* Western Union Tel. Co., 71 Fed. 651; Given *v.* Western Union Tel. Co., 24 Fed. 119.

The free delivery limits must be reasonable in order to protect the company for failing to deliver. Western Union Tel. Co. *v.* Ayers, 41 Tex. Civ. App. 627, 93 S. W. 199.

Determination of free delivery limits.— Where the free delivery limits of a telegraph office extend to a radius of half a mile, if the addressee's residence is within that radius he is entitled to free delivery, although the usual route in going from the office to his residence is more than half a mile. Western Union Tel. Co. *v.* Benson, 159 Ala. 254, 48 So. 712.

48. Western Union Tel. Co. *v.* Robinson, 97 Tenn. 638, 37 S. W. 545, 34 L. R. A. 431; Western Union Tel. Co. *v.* Davis, 24 Tex. Civ. App. 427, 59 S. W. 46; Western Union Tel. Co. *v.* Cain, (Tex. Civ. App. 1897) 40 S. W. 624.

49. Western Union Tel. Co. *v.* Benson, 159 Ala. 254, 48 So. 712; Arkansas, etc., R. Co. *v.* Stroude, 82 Ark. 117, 100 S. W. 760; Rosser *v.* Western Union Tel. Co., 130 N. C. 251, 41 S. E. 378; Western Union Tel. Co. *v.* Davis, 30 Tex. Civ. App. 590, 71 S. W. 313.

50. Western Union Tel. Co. *v.* Matthews, 113 Ky. 188, 67 S. W. 849, 24 Ky. L. Rep. 3; Western Union Tel. Co. *v.* Robinson, 97 Tenn. 638, 37 S. W. 545, 34 L. R. A. 431; Western Union Tel. Co. *v.* Carter, 24 Tex. Civ. App. 80, 58 S. W. 198. See also Western Union Tel. Co. *v.* McIlvoy, 107 Ky. 633, 55 S. W. 428, 21 Ky. L. Rep. 1393; Gainey *v.* Western Union Tel. Co., 136 N. C. 261, 48 S. E. 653.

51. Western Union Tel. Co. *v.* Merrill, 144 Ala. 618, 39 So. 121, 113 Am. St. Rep. 66; Western Union Tel. Co. *v.* Scott, 87 S. W. 289, 27 Ky. L. Rep. 975; Western Union Tel. Co. *v.* Lyles, (Tex. Civ. App. 1897) 42 S. W. 636.

52. Western Union Tel. Co. *v.* Henderson, 89 Ala. 510, 7 So. 419, 18 Am. St. Rep. 148.

53. Western Union Tel. Co. *v.* Henderson, 89 Ala. 510, 7 So. 419, 18 Am. St. Rep. 148.

the addressee is improper unless such person is authorized by the addressee to receive the same.[67] If, however, the addressee is absent the telegraph company may deliver the message to any other person who is expressly [68] or impliedly authorized to receive the same,[69] and it is its duty to do so, so that the message may be forwarded or the addressee notified by such person.[70] So it has been held that in the absence of the addressee a message may be delivered to his wife,[71] or to the clerk at his hotel.[72] It is not, however, the duty of a telegraph company, although the addressee is absent, to deliver the message to a person not authorized to receive the same;[73-74] and it has been held that there is no such implied authority growing out of the relation between the parties as makes it the duty of a telegraph company, in the absence of the addressee, to deliver a message to his wife,[75] unless the message relates to a family matter in which the wife is directly interested.[76]

b. Person in Whose Care Message Is Addressed. Where a message is addressed to one person in care of another, it may be delivered either to the addressee or to

67. Glover *v.* Western Union Tel. Co., 78 S. C. 502, 59 S. E. 526; Western Union Tel. Co. *v.* Cobb, 95 Tex. 333, 67 S. W. 87, 93 Am. St. Rep. 862.

Instances of improper delivery.— A hotel clerk has no authority as a matter of law to receive telegrams for guests, and in the absence of any showing of a custom to this effect the delivery of a telegram to the clerk of the hotel where the addressee resides, without any attempt to find the addressee, is not sufficient. Western Union Tel. Co. *v.* Cobb, 95 Tex. 333, 67 S. W. 87, 93 Am. St. Rep. 862. The delivery of a telegram to the addressee's minor son while passing the telegraph office is improper and makes such person the agent of the company so as to render it liable for any delay in delivering the telegram to the addressee. Mott *v.* Western Union Tel. Co., 142 N. C. 532, 55 S. E. 363. Where a telegram is addressed to a certain person at the freight yards of a railroad company, the telegraph company is not justified in leaving it with a yard master at such place who does not know the addressee, without any further effort to find the addressee. Western Union Tel. Co. *v.* Newhouse, 6 Ind. App. 422, 33 N. E. 800. If a telegraph company delivers a telegram to a neighbor of the addressee, it will be liable for damages caused by a delay on the part of such person in delivering it to the addressee. Western Union Tel. Co. *v.* Belew, 32 Tex. Civ. App. 338, 74 S. W. 799. The delivery of a telegram to the captain of a steamboat on which the addressee is a passenger is not sufficient. Davies *v.* Eastern Steamboat Co., 94 Me. 379, 47 Atl. 896, 53 L. R. A. 239. A business partner has no authority, as such, to receive his copartner's private or social telegrams. Glover *v.* Western Union Tel. Co., 78 S. C. 502, 59 S. E. 526.

Agreement to deliver to third person.— If the addressee, anticipating the receipt of a telegram, directs the agent of the telegraph company to deliver the same to a third person living near the telegraph office, by whom it is to be taken to the addressee, and the agent agrees to do so, the telegraph company will be liable for a failure to do so, such agreement being within the scope of the agent's authority. Western Union Tel. Co. *v.* Evans, 5 Tex. Civ. App. 55, 23 S. W. 998.

68. Western Union Tel. Co. *v.* Barefoot, 97 Tex. 159, 76 S. W. 914, 64 L. R. A. 491, holding that where a person directs a hotel clerk to forward telegrams for him, he thereby expressly constitutes such person his agent to receive telegrams, so that a delivery by the company to such agent is a sufficient delivery to the addressee.

69. Western Union Tel. Co. *v.* Trissal, 98 Ind. 566, holding that the authority of one person to receive telegrams for another need not be express but may be implied.

70. Western Union Tel. Co. *v.* Woods, 56 Kan. 737, 44 Pac. 989; Western Union Tel. Co. *v.* Clark, 14 Tex. Civ. App. 563, 38 S. W. 225. See *infra*, note 76, and *infra*, note 75.

71. Given *v.* Western Union Tel. Co., 24 Fed. 119.

72. Western Union Tel. Co. *v.* Trissal, 98 Ind. 566; Western Union Tel. Co. *v.* Barefoot, 97 Tex. 159, 76 S. W. 914, 64 L. R. A. 491. See *supra*, note 67.

73–74. Western Union Tel. Co. *v.* Mitchell, 91 Tex. 454, 44 S. W. 274, 66 Am. St. Rep. 906, 40 L. R. A. 209; Western Union Tel. Co. *v.* Moseley, 28 Tex. Civ. App. 562, 67 S. W. 1059; Western Union Tel. Co. *v.* Redinger, (Tex. Civ. App. 1901) 63 S. W. 156.

75. Western Union Tel. Co. *v.* Mitchell, 91 Tex. 454, 44 S. W. 274, 66 Am. St. Rep. 906, 40 L. R. A. 209 (no duty to deliver business telegrams to addressee's wife); Western Union Tel. Co. *v.* Moseley, 28 Tex. Civ. App. 562, 67 S. W. 1059 (no duty to deliver to wife a message relating to death of husband's brother). *Compare* Western Union Tel. Co. *v.* Woods, 56 Kan. 737, 44 Pac. 989.

Applying this rule to a delivery to the clerk of a hotel see Western Union Tel. Co. *v.* Redinger, (Tex. Civ. App. 1901) 63 S. W. 156. *Compare* Western Union Tel. Co. *v.* Trissal, 98 Ind. 566.

76. Western Union Tel. Co. *v.* Hendricks, 29 Tex. Civ. App. 413, 68 S. W. 720, holding that while it is not the duty of a telegraph company, in the absence of the addressee, to deliver business telegrams to his wife, she

to some other person who has been expressly authorized by the addressee to receive the same.[86]

6. Mode of Delivery. It is ordinarily the duty of a telegraph company to make delivery of a message by writing out a copy thereof and actually delivering such copy to the addressee or person authorized to receive the same,[87] and in the absence of agreement to the contrary a different mode of delivery, as by telephone, is insufficient.[88] The addressee may, however, agree to accept delivery by telephone,[89] in which case it has been held that if an error is made in telephoning the message the company will not be liable either to the addressee or to the sender of the message.[90] Where a telegram is received for a person living beyond the free-delivery limits of the company,[91] and no arrangement has been made for extra charges for delivery, it has been held sufficient for the company to mail the message to the addressee;[92] and under some circumstances this may be sufficient even where it is held that ordinarily the company should in such cases wire back for the payment or guarantee of delivery charges.[93] It is not the duty of the telegraph company under its ordinary contract to telephone a telegraphic message, particularly as it would impair the confidential relations assumed;[94] but it is competent for it to agree to deliver a message in this manner.[95] It is also within the apparent scope of an agent's authority to agree on accepting a message that it shall be transmitted by wire to a point where the company has an office and thence by mail to a different point and specially delivered to the addressee from the latter point.[96]

86. Western Union Tel. Co. *v.* Barefoot, 97 Tex. 159, 76 S. W. 914, 64 L. R. A. 491, holding that a telegram addressed to A in care of B may in the absence of A be delivered to C, if C has been expressly authorized by A to receive the same, and that in such case the company will not be liable for making such delivery instead of delivering the message to B.

87. Brashears *v.* Western Union Tel. Co., 45 Mo. App. 433; Western Union Tel. Co. *v.* Pearce, 95 Tex. 578, 68 S. W. 771; Barnes *v.* Western Union Tel. Co., 120 Fed. 550. *Compare* Norman *v.* Western Union Tel. Co., 31 Wash. 577, 72 Pac. 474.

88. Brashears *v.* Western Union Tel. Co., 45 Mo. App. 433 (holding that where a message is delivered to the addressee by telephone, and the operator makes a mistake in telephoning the message, the company will be liable to the sender of the message for a statutory penalty); Barnes *v.* Western Union Tel. Co., 120 Fed. 550.

A person in whose care a message is addressed cannot by receiving the same over a telephone waive the duty owing by the company to the addressee of the message to make an actual delivery thereof. Western Union Tel. Co. *v.* Pearce, 95 Tex. 578, 68 S. W. 771 [*reversing* (Civ. App. 1902) 67 S. W. 920].

89. Norman *v.* Western Union Tel. Co., 31 Wash. 577, 72 Pac. 474.

90. Norman *v.* Western Union Tel. Co., 31 Wash. 577, 72 Pac. 474, holding that where the addressee directs a messenger of a telegraph company to telephone a message, the messenger in so doing acts as the agent of the addressee, and that if an error is made in telephoning the message, it is in effect an error of the addressee, so that while he may be liable to the sender of the message the telegraph company will not. But see Brashears *v.* Western Union Tel. Co., 45 Mo. App. 433, holding that while an addressee may waive his own rights by accepting a message by telephone, he cannot, by so doing, waive the rights of the sender, and that if an error is made in telephoning the message to the addressee the company will be liable therefor to the sender.

91. Rules as to free delivery limits generally see *supra*, IV, C, 4, b.

92. King *v.* Western Union Tel. Co., 89 Ark. 402, 117 S. W. 521, where the message was for a person living six or eight miles in the country and nothing had been said by the sender of the message in regard to the payment or guarantee of delivery charges.

93. Gainey *v.* Western Union Tel. Co., 136 N. C. 261, 48 S. E. 653, holding that ordinarily where a message is received for a person beyond the free delivery limits, the company should wire back for a payment or guarantee of delivery charges, but where the message was addressed "Mr. Noel Gainey, (P. O. Idaho), Fayetteville, N. C.," and did not show any necessity for immediate delivery, the company was justified in assuming from the character of the address and other circumstances that the parties contemplated a delivery by mail.

94. Hellams *v.* Western Union Tel. Co., 70 S. C. 83, 49 S. E. 12. See also Lyles *v.* Western Union Tel. Co., 77 S. C. 174, 57 S. E. 725, 12 L. R. A. N. S. 534.

95. Lyles *v.* Western Union Tel. Co., 77 S. C. 174, 57 S. E. 725, 12 L. R. A. N. S. 534, holding that where such agreement is made the company will be liable for failing to comply therewith.

96. Western Union Tel. Co. *v.* Carter, 24 Tex. Civ. App. 80, 58 S. W. 198, holding that under such agreement the company will be liable, although the message is duly trans-

can there be a recovery for subjects of damage not included in the claim presented,[47] although it is not necessary that the claim should accurately state the amount of the loss,[48] and plaintiff will not be limited in his recovery to the amount of damages stated in his claim.[49]

c. Condition Precedent or Subsequent. In some cases it has been held that the stipulation requiring claims to be presented within a certain time is a condition precedent to a right of action,[50] and that if such claim is not presented an action cannot be maintained, although the action is brought within the time stipulated for presenting claims.[51] In other cases, however, it is held that the condition is not a condition precedent, but a condition subsequent,[52] merely operating, in cases where no claim is presented within the time limited, to defeat a cause of action which has already accrued,[53] and that it is sufficient, although no other claim is presented, if suit is instituted within the time limited.[54] These decisions seem to be based upon the ground that the suit is equivalent to a written presentation of claim, and therefore a sufficient compliance with the stipulation,[55] it being stated that while it is sufficient if the process or complaint sufficiently informs defendant of the different facts which a written claim should set out,[56] a mere summons to answer is not sufficient.[57]

d. Waiver. Like any other contractual stipulation, the requirement in the contract of transmission that a written claim for damages shall be presented within a specified time may be waived by the party for whose benefit it was inserted in the contract — that is, the telegraph company;[58-59] and it is held that

Union Tel. Co. *v.* Beck, 58 Ill. App. 564; Brockelsby *v.* Western Union Tel. Co., (Iowa 1910) 126 N. W. 1105; Younker *v.* Western Union Tel. Co., (Iowa 1910) 125 N. W. 577; Swain *v.* Western Union Tel. Co., 12 Tex. Civ. App. 385, 34 S. W. 783; Western Union Tel Co. *v.* Kinsley, 8 Tex. Civ. App. 527, 28 S. W. 831.

47. Western Union Tel. Co. *v.* Nelson, 86 Ark. 336, 111 S. W. 274; Western Union Tel. Co. *v.* Moxley, 80 Ark. 554, 98 S. W. 112; Western Union Tel. Co. *v.* Murray, 29 Tex. Civ. App. 207, 68 S. W. 549.

There can be no recovery for mental anguish where plaintiff in his claim expressly limited the same to compensation for loss "sustained in actual money." Western Union Tel. Co. *v.* Nelson, 86 Ark. 336, 111 S. W. 274.

48. Western Union Tel. Co. *v.* Lehman, 106 Md. 318, 67 Atl. 241.

49. Western Union Tel. Co. *v.* Murray, 29 Tex. Civ. App. 207, 68 S. W. 549.

50. Western Union Tel. Co. *v.* Yopst, (Ind. 1887) 11 N. E. 16; Western Union Tel Co. *v.* McKinney, 2 Tex. App. Civ. Cas. § 644.

51. Western Union Tel. Co. *v.* Yopst, (Ind. 1887) 11 N. E. 16; Western Union Tel. Co. *v.* Hays, (Tex. Civ. App. 1901) 63 S. W. 171; Western Union Tel. Co. *v.* Ferguson, (Tex. Civ. App. 1894) 27 S. W. 1048; Western Union Tel. Co. *v.* McKinney, 2 Tex. App. Civ. Cas. § 644.

52. Western Union Tel. Co. *v.* Way, 83 Ala. 542, 4 So. 844; Western Union Tel. Co. *v.* Piner, 9 Tex. Civ. App. 152, 29 S. W. 66.

53. Western Union Tel. Co. *v.* Trumbull, 1 Ind. App. 121, 27 N. E. 313; Phillips *v.* Western Union Tel. Co., 95 Tex. 638, 69 S. W. 63; Western Union Tel. Co. *v.* Piner, 9 Tex. Civ. App. 152, 29 S. W. 66.

54. *Alabama.*—Western Union Tel. Co. *v.* Henderson, 89 Ala. 510, 7 So. 419, 18 Am. St. Rep. 148.

Indiana.—Western Union Tel. Co. *v.* Trumbull, 1 Ind. App. 121, 27 N. E. 313.

North Carolina.—Bryan *v.* Western Union Tel. Co., 133 N. C. 603, 45 S. E. 938; Sherrill *v.* Western Union Tel. Co., 109 N. C. 527, 14 S. E. 94.

South Carolina.—Smith *v.* Western Union Tel. Co., 77 S. C. 378, 58 S. E. 6.

Tennessee.—Western Union Tel. Co. *v.* Mellon, 96 Tenn. 66, 33 S. W. 725.

Texas.—Phillips *v.* Western Union Tel. Co., 95 Tex. 638, 69 S. W. 63; Western Union Tel. Co. *v.* Crawford, (Civ. App. 1903) 75 S. W. 843; Phillips *v.* Western Union Tel. Co., (Civ. App. 1902) 69 S. W. 997; Western Union Tel. Co. *v.* Piner, 9 Tex. Civ. App. 152, 29 S. W. 66.

See 45 Cent. Dig. tit. "Telegraphs and Telephones," § 42.

55. See Smith *v.* Western Union Tel. Co., 77 S. C. 378, 58 S. E. 6; Western Union Tel. Co. *v.* Mellon, 96 Tenn. 66, 33 S. W. 725; Phillips *v.* Western Union Tel. Co., (Tex. Civ. App. 1902) 69 S. W. 997.

56. Postal Tel.-Cable Co. *v.* Moss, 5 Ga. App. 503, 63 S. E. 590; Western Union Tel. Co. *v.* Greer, 115 Tenn. 368, 89 S. W. 327, 1 L. R. A. N. S. 525; Western Union Tel. Co. *v.* Courtney, 113 Tenn. 482, 82 S. W. 484; Phillips *v.* Western Union Tel. Co., 95 Tex. 638, 69 S. W. 63.

Requisites of claim see *supra*, V, A, 4, b.

57. Western Union Tel. Co. *v.* Courtney, 113 Tenn. 482, 82 S. W. 484. But see Bryan *v.* Western Union Tel. Co., 133 N. C. 603, 45 S. E. 938, holding that the service of a summons puts defendant upon inquiry and is therefore sufficient.

58-59. *Alabama.*—Western Union Tel. Co. *v.* Heathcoat, 149 Ala. 623, 43 So. 117.

the message is necessarily transferred;[70] but such a stipulation does not protect the original transmitting company against its own negligence prior to the transfer of the message to the connecting company,[71] or affect the liability of the latter company for its own negligence after the message has been transferred to it.[72] Such a stipulation does not authorize the transfer of a message to a telephone company if there is a connecting telegraph company;[73] nor does it require a telegraph company, where the addressee of a message lives at a distance from its office, to deliver the message by telephone.[74]

B. How Such Contracts Made — 1. PROOF OF SENDER'S ASSENT — a. Message Written on Usual Blank — (I) *BY SENDER.* A person who writes a telegram on one of the blank forms in common use by telegraph companies, and delivers it, so written, to the company for transmission, is bound by the stipulations printed on the form, to the extent that the same are reasonable and valid;[75] and in such cases, in the absence of fraud, he must be held to have assented to the contract signed, whether as a matter of fact he read or knew of the stipulations contained therein or not.[76] It is also immaterial in the application of the

70. *Indiana.*— Western Union Tel. Co. *v.* Stratemeier, 6 Ind. App. 125, 32 N. E. 871.

Louisiana.— La Grange *v.* Southwestern Tel. Co., 25 La. Ann. 383.

Michigan.— Western Union Tel. Co. *v.* Carew, 15 Mich. 525.

Nebraska.— Pacific Tel. Co. *v.* Underwood, 37 Nebr. 315, 55 N. W. 1057, 40 Am. St. Rep. 490.

New York.— Baldwin *v.* U. S. Tel. Co., 45 N. Y. 744, 6 Am. Rep. 165 [*reversing* 54 Barb. 505, 6 Abb. Pr. N. S. 405]; De Rutte *v.* New York, etc., Electric Magnetic Tel. Co., 1 Daly 547, 30 How. Pr. 403.

Ohio.— Western Union Tel. Co. *v.* Griswold, 37 Ohio St. 301, 41 Am. Rep. 500.

South Carolina.— Hellams *v.* Western Union Tel. Co., 70 S. C. 83, 49 S. E. 12.

Tennessee.— Western Union Tel. Co. *v.* Mumford, 87 Tenn. 190, 10 S. W. 318, 10 Am. St. Rep. 630, 2 L. R. A. 601; Marr *v.* Western Union Tel. Co., 85 Tenn. 529, 3 S. W. 496.

Texas.— Smith *v.* Western Union Tel. Co., 84 Tex. 359, 19 S. W. 441, 31 Am. St. Rep. 59; Western Union Tel. Co. *v.* Jones, 81 Tex. 271, 16 S. W. 1006; Western Union Tel. Co. *v.* McDonald, 42 Tex. Civ. App. 229, 95 S. W. 691; Western Union Tel. Co. *v.* Sorsby, 29 Tex. Civ. App. 345, 69 S. W. 122 (but initial company must notify sender if terminal line down); Gulf, etc., R. Co. *v.* Geer, 5 Tex. Civ. App. 349, 24 S. W. 86; Western Union Tel. Co. *v.* McLeod, (Civ. App. 1893) 22 S. W. 988; Western Union Tel. Co. *v.* Taylor, 3 Tex. Civ. App. 310, 22 S. W. 532.

Canada.—See Baxter *v.* Dominion Tel. Co., 37 U. C. Q. B. 470; Stevenson *v.* Montreal Tel. Co., 16 U. C. Q. B. 530.

71. Western Union Tel. Co. *v.* Seals, (Tex. Civ. App. 1898) 45 S. W. 964; Weatherford, etc., R. Co. *v.* Seals, (Tex. Civ. App. 1897) 41 S. W. 841.

72. Squire *v.* Western Union Tel. Co., 98 Mass. 232, 93 Am. Dec. 157; Smith *v.* Western Union Tel. Co., 84 Tex. 359, 19 S. W. 441, 31 Am. St. Rep. 59.

73. Western Union Tel. Co. *v.* McLeod, (Tex. Civ. App. 1894) 24 S. W. 815.

74. Hellams *v.* Western Union Tel. Co., 70 S. C. 83, 49 S. E. 12.

75. *Alabama.*—Western Union Tel. Co. *v.* Prevatt, 149 Ala. 106, 43 So. 106.

Georgia.— Hill *v.* Western Union Tel. Co., 85 Ga. 425, 11 S. E. 874, 21 Am. St. Rep. 166.

Massachusetts.—Grinnell *v.* Western Union Tel. Co., 113 Mass. 299, 18 Am. Rep. 485; Redpath *v.* Western Union Tel. Co., 112 Mass. 71, 17 Am. Rep. 69.

Michigan.— Jacob *v.* Western Union Tel. Co., 135 Mich. 600, 98 N. W. 402; Western Union Tel. Co. *v.* Carew, 15 Mich. 525.

Minnesota.— Cole *v.* Western Union Tel. Co., 33 Minn. 227, 22 N. W. 385.

New York.— Kiley *v.* Western Union Tel. Co., 109 N. Y. 231, 16 N. E. 75; Young *v.* Western Union Tel. Co., 65 N. Y. 163; Breese *v.* U. S. Telegraph Co., 48 N. Y. 132, 8 Am. Rep. 526.

Pennsylvania.— Wolf *v.* Western Union Tel. Co., 62 Pa. St. 83, 1 Am. Rep. 387.

Tennessee.— Western Union Tel. Co. *v.* Courtney, 113 Tenn. 482, 82 S. W. 484.

Texas.— Womack *v.* Western Union Tel. Co., 58 Tex. 176, 44 Am. Rep. 614.

United States.— Primrose *v.* Western Union Tel. Co., 154 U. S. 1, 14 S. Ct. 1098, 38 L. ed. 883; Postal Tel. Cable Co. *v.* Nichols, 159 Fed. 643, 89 C. C. A. 585, 16 L. R. A. N. S. 870; Beasley *v.* Western Union Tel. Co., 39 Fed. 181.

See 45 Cent. Dig. tit. "Telegraphs and Telephones," § 45.

Although the blank was torn and mutilated if there was sufficient to show that it contained certain agreements the sender must be held to be bound by the stipulations contained in a perfect blank. Kiley *v.* Western Union Tel. Co., 109 N. Y. 231, 16 N. E. 75.

76. *Alabama.*—Western Union Tel. Co. *v.* Prevatt, 149 Ala. 617, 43 So. 106.

Massachusetts.— Grinnell *v.* Western Union Tel. Co., 113 Mass. 299, 18 Am. Rep. 485.

Minnesota.— Cole *v.* Western Union Tel. Co., 33 Minn. 227, 22 N. W. 385.

New York.— Kiley *v.* Western Union Tel. Co., 109 N. Y. 231, 16 N. E. 75; Breese *v.*

rule that the sender of the message may have been an infant, the stipulation if valid being as binding upon infants as adults.[77]

(II) *By Operator.* Where the message is written on the blank by one of the company's messengers or operators at the dictation and request of the sender, the messenger or operator is, for this purpose, the sender's agent, and the latter is bound by the stipulations as though he had written the message himself;[78] and in such cases it is not material, in the absence of fraud or misrepresentation, that the sender did not read such stipulations,[79] or even that he was unable to read or write,[80] or did not know of the existence of such stipulations.[81]

b. Message on Other Company's Blank. Where a message as delivered to and accepted by a telegraph company for transmission is written not on a form issued by that company, but on a form issued by another company containing certain stipulations, such stipulations are a part of the contract and the sender is bound thereby to the same extent that he would have been bound had he delivered the message to the company whose name appeared on the blank;[82] although it seems that if the transmitting operator, without the knowledge of the sender, rewrites the message upon a blank of his own company, the sender will not be bound by stipulations upon that blank which he never saw, signed, or agreed to.[83]

c. Message on Plain Paper. Where a message as delivered to the telegraph company is written on paper containing no contract stipulations, the sender is not ordinarily bound by the stipulations printed on the usual blank,[84] and this rule is not affected by the fact that the operator may, without the sender's knowledge or consent, subsequently attach it to or copy it upon one of such blanks.[85]

U. S. Telegraph Co., 48 N. Y. 132, 8 Am. Rep. 526.

Texas.— Western Union Tel. Co. *v.* Edsall, 63 Tex. 668.

United States.— Postal Tel. Cable Co. *v.* Nichols, 159 Fed. 643, 89 C. C. A. 585, 16 L. R. A. N. S. 870; Beasley *v.* Western Union Tel. Co., 39 Fed. 181.

See 45 Cent. Dig. tit. "Telegraphs and Telephones," § 45.

But see Tyler *v.* Western Union Tel. Co., 60 Ill. 421, 14 Am. Rep. 38; Western Union Tel. Co. *v.* Fairbanks, 15 Ill. App. 600.

In Illinois it is held that the condition must have been known or assented to and that while slight evidence of assent may suffice yet there must be something more than the mere fact that the condition was to be found in the printed matter appearing upon the blank used (Western Union Tel. Co. *v.* Lycan, 60 Ill. App. 124); and that in an action by the addressee of a message the condition is not binding unless assented to by him notwithstanding he had knowledge of the condition (Webbe *v.* Western Union Tel. Co., 169 Ill. 610, 48 N. E. 670, 6 Am. St. Rep. 207 [*reversing* 64 Ill. App. 331]).

77. Western Union Tel. Co. *v.* Greer, 115 Tenn. 368, 89 S. W. 327, 1 L. R. A. N. S. 525.

78. Western Union Tel. Co. *v.* Benson, 159 Ala. 254, 48 So. 712; Western Union Tel. Co. *v.* Prevatt, 149 Ala. 617, 43 So. 106; Western Union Tel. Co. *v.* Foster, 64 Tex. 220, 53 Am. Rep. 754; Western Union Tel. Co. *v.* Edsall, 63 Tex. 668; Gulf, etc., R. Co. *v.* Geer, 5 Tex. Civ. App. 349, 24 S. W. 86. See also Western Union Tel. Co. *v.* Simms, 30 Tex. Civ. App. 32, 69 S. W. 464.

79. Western Union Tel. Co. *v.* Edsall, 63 Tex. 668.

80. Western Union Tel. Co. *v.* Prevatt, 149 Ala. 617, 43 So. 106.

81. Western Union Tel. Co. *v.* Prevatt, 149 Ala. 617, 43 So. 106. But see Mims *v.* Western Union Tel. Co., 82 S. C. 247, 64 S. E. 236.

82. *Georgia.*—Western Union Tel. Co. *v.* Waxelbaum, 113 Ga. 1017, 39 S. E. 443, 56 L. R. A. 741.

Maryland.— U. S. Telegraph Co. *v.* Gildersleve, 29 Md. 232, 96 Am. Dec. 519.

Massachusetts.— Clement *v.* Western Union Tel. Co., 137 Mass. 463.

Michigan.— Jacob *v.* Western Union Tel. Co., 135 Mich. 600, 98 N. W. 402.

South Carolina.— Young *v.* Western Union Tel. Co., 65 S. C. 93, 43 S. E. 448.

It is not material what company's name appears upon the blank since the intention of the sender is to contract with the company to which the message is delivered for transmission, and the stipulations on the blank used constitute the contract, and being assented to are binding upon the sender. Western Union Tel. Co. *v.* Waxelbaum, 113 Ga. 1017, 39 S. E. 443, 56 L. R. A. 741; Young *v.* Western Union Tel. Co., 65 S. C. 93, 43 S. E. 448.

83. See Western Union Tel. Co. *v.* Uvalde Nat. Bank, (Tex. Civ. App. 1903) 72 S. W. 232.

84. Harris *v.* Western Union Tel. Co., 121 Ala. 519, 25 So. 910, 77 Am. St. Rep. 70; Pearsall *v.* Western Union Tel. Co., 124 N. Y. 256, 26 N. E. 534, 21 Am. St. Rep. 662; Anderson *v.* Western Union Tel. Co., 84 Tex. 17, 19 S. W. 285; Western Union Tel. Co. *v.* Pruett, (Tex. Civ. App. 1896) 35 S. W. 78. See also Western Union Tel. Co. *v.* McMillan, (Tex. Civ. App. 1894) 25 S. W. 821.

85. Harris *v.* Western Union Tel. Co., 121

do so it will be liable for damages resulting from the delivery of a forged, fraudulent, or unauthorized message;[3] but as the company is not absolutely bound to ascertain that messages offered for transmission are not of this character, it will not, in the absence of any facts or circumstances reasonably calculated to arouse suspicion, be liable merely because a message is not genuine.[4] The company may, however, be liable whether the message was one accepted from an impostor in the ordinary course of business, but under such peculiar circumstances that the company is chargeable with negligence either in accepting it or in failing to communicate the suspicious facts to the addressee,[5] or a forged message placed on the wires by a wire tapper, if such tapping of the line is contributed to by some affirmative negligence on the part of the company, or by lack of reasonable care to safeguard its lines against such interference;[6] or a message forged by one of the company's own operators, acting within the scope of his employment.[7] In such cases the company has been held liable in tort to the person whose name was forged as the apparent sender of the message,[8] or to the addressee to whom the message was delivered,[9] although not to an undisclosed principal of the addressee[10] or a mere stranger,[11] for the damages actually sustained,[12] as a proximate consequence of its wrongful act,[13] and without contributory negligence on the part of plaintiff.[14]

C. Ticker or Market Quotation Service. Telegraph companies are in some cases organized for or engage in the business of furnishing stock or market quotations or other information, usually by means of instruments known as

N. Y. 549, 6 Am. Rep. 140, Allen Tel. Cas. 594; Western Union Tel. Co. *v.* Uvalde Nat. Bank, (Tex. Civ. App. 1903) 72 S. W. 232 [*affirmed* in 97 Tex. 219, 77 S. W. 603, 65 L. R. A. 805]; Pacific Postal Tel. Cable Co. *v.* Palo Alto Bank, 109 Fed. 369, 48 C. C. A. 413, 54 L. R. A. 711.

Duty as to acceptance, where message may not be genuine see *supra*, IV, A, 2.

3. *California.*— State Bank *v.* Western Union Tel. Co., 52 Cal. 280.

Minnesota.— McCord *v.* Western Union Tel. Co., 39 Minn. 181, 39 N. W. 315, 12 Am. St. Rep. 636, 1 L. R. A. 143, 2 Am. Elec. Cas. 629.

Mississippi.— Magouirk *v.* Western Union Tel. Co., 79 Miss. 632, 31 So. 206, 89 Am. St. Rep. 663.

New York.— Elwood *v.* Western Union Tel. Co., 45 N. Y. 549, 6 Am. Rep. 140, Allen Tel. Cas. 594.

Texas.— Western Union Tel. Co. *v.* Uvalde Nat. Bank, (Civ. App. 1903) 72 S. W. 232 [*affirmed* in 97 Tex. 219, 77 S. W. 603, 65 L. R. A. 805].

United States.— Western Union Tel. Co. *v.* Schriver, 141 Fed. 538, 72 C. C. A. 596, 4 L. R. A. N. S. 678; Pacific Postal Tel. Cable Co. *v.* Palo Alto Bank, 109 Fed. 369, 48 C. C. A. 413, 54 L. R. A. 711; Strause *v.* Western Union Tel. Co., 23 Fed. Cas. No. 13,531, 8 Biss. 104.

4. Western Union Tel. Co. *v.* Meyer, 61 Ala. 158, 32 Am. St. Rep. 1, 1 Am. Elec. Cas. 282; Havelock Bank *v.* Western Union Tel. Co., 141 Fed. 522, 72 C. C. A. 580.

5. Elwood *v.* Western Union Tel. Co., 45 N. Y. 549, 6 Am. Rep. 140, Allen Tel. Cas. 594; Western Union Tel. Co. *v.* Schriver, 141 Fed. 538, 72 C. C. A. 596, 4 L. R. A. N. S. 678.

6. Western Union Tel. Co. *v.* Uvalde Nat. Bank, (Tex. Civ. App. 1903) 72 S. W. 232 [*affirmed* in 97 Tex. 219, 77 S. W. 603, 65 L. R. A. 805].

7. California Bank *v.* Western Union Tel. Co., 52 Cal. 280; McCord *v.* Western Union Tel. Co., 39 Minn. 181, 39 N. W. 315, 12 Am. St. Rep. 636, 1 L. R. A. 143, 2 Am. Electric Cas. 629; Magouirk *v.* Western Union Tel. Co., 79 Miss. 632, 31 So. 206, 89 Am. St. Rep. 663; Pacific Postal Tel. Cable Co. *v.* Palo Alto, 109 Fed. 369, 48 C. C. A. 413, 54 L. R. A. 711.

8. Magouirk *v.* Western Union Tel. Co., 79 Miss. 632, 31 So. 206, 89 Am. St. Rep. 663.

9. California Bank *v.* Western Union Tel. Co., 52 Cal. 280; McCord *v.* Western Union Tel. Co., 39 Minn. 181, 39 N. W. 315, 12 Am. St. Rep. 636, 1 L. R. A. 143; Elwood *v.* Western Union Tel. Co., 45 N. Y. 549, 6 Am. Rep. 140.

10. Western Union Tel. Co. *v.* Schriver, 141 Fed. 538, 72 C. C. A. 596, 4 L. R. A. N. S. 678.

11. McCormick *v.* Western Union Tel. Co., 79 Fed. 449, 25 C. C. A. 35, 38 L. R. A. 684, not liable to a stranger who had merely seen the telegram and acted thereon to his injury.

12. McCord *v.* Western Union Tel. Co., 39 Minn. 181, 39 N. W. 315, 12 Am. St. Rep. 636, 1 L. R. A. 143; Strause *v.* Western Union Tel. Co., 23 Fed. Cas. No. 13,531, 8 Biss. 104.

13. McCord *v.* Western Union Tel. Co., 39 Minn. 181, 39 N. W. 315, 12 Am. St. Rep. 636, 1 L. R. A. 143, 2 Am. Elec. Cas. 629; Western Union Tel. Co. *v.* Uvalde Nat. Bank, (Tex. Civ. App. 1903) 72 S. W. 232 [*affirmed* in 97 Tex. 219, 77 S. W. 603, 65 L. R. A. 805].

14. See California Bank *v.* Western Union Tel. Co., 52 Cal. 280; Western Union Tel. Co. *v.* Uvalde Nat. Bank, (Tex. Civ. App.

tickers,[15] and while ordinary telegraph companies not regularly engaged in such a business will not be required to do so for the benefit of a particular applicant,[16] yet where they do engage in such a business they are subject to the general rule previously stated,[17] that they must without partiality or discrimination furnish such service to all members of the public desiring the same, upon payment of their usual charges and compliance with their ordinary and reasonable regulations,[18] and under such circumstances they may be compelled by mandamus to furnish such service,[19] or enjoined from discontinuing the same or removing their instruments from a subscriber's office or place of business.[20] Such companies may, however, make reasonable rules and regulations for the conduct of their business,[21] such as that subscribers shall not communicate the information received to other persons,[22] and they will not be required to furnish or continue to furnish their service to persons who refuse to comply with or who violate such regulations,[23] nor are such companies required to furnish or continue to furnish such service for the use of a bucket shop or gambling house.[24] A distinction has also been made between cases where the telegraph company itself collects or purchases and distributes such information, and cases where it merely transmits reports or quotations which are the property of and furnished by a stock exchange or board of trade, under an agreement to furnish such information only to subscribers designated or approved by the board or exchange,[25] it being held that in the latter case the company cannot be required to furnish or continue to furnish such information to persons other than those designated or approved by

1903) 72 S. W. 232 [*affirmed* in 97 Tex. 219, 77 S. W. 603, 65 L. R. A. 805].

15. See Western Union Tel. Co. *v.* State, 165 Ind. 492, 76 N. E. 100, 3 L. R. A. N. S. 153; Friedman *v.* Gold, etc., Tel. Co., 32 Hun (N. Y.) 4, 1 Am. Elec. Cas. 621; Davis *v.* Electric Reporting Co., 19 Wkly. Notes Cas. (Pa.) 567, 2 Am. Elec. Cas. 375.

The information gathered and transmitted in such a business is property of the telegraph company and entitled to protection as such. Illinois Commission Co. *v.* Cleveland Tel. Co., 119 Fed. 301, 56 C. C. A. 205; National Tel. News Co. *v.* Western Union Tel. Co., 119 Fed. 294, 56 C. C. A. 198, 60 L. R. A. 805.

16. See Smith *v.* Gold, etc., Tel. Co., 42 Hun (N. Y.) 454, 2 Am. Electric Cas. 373; Bradley *v.* Western Union Tel. Co., 8 Ohio Dec. (Reprint) 707, 9 Cinc. L. Bul. 223; Sterrett *v.* Philadelphia Local Tel. Co., 18 Wkly. Notes Cas. (Pa.) 77; Metropolitan Grain, etc., Co. *v.* Chicago Bd. of Trade, 15 Fed. 847, 11 Biss. 531.

17. See *supra*, III, A.

18. Western Union Tel. Co. *v.* State, 165 Ind. 492, 76 N. E. 100, 3 L. R. A. N. S. 153; Smith *v.* Gold, etc., Tel. Co., 42 Hun (N. Y.) 454; Friedman *v.* Gold, etc., Tel. Co., 32 Hun (N. Y.) 4, 1 Am. Elec. Cas. 621; Davis *v.* Electric Reporting Co., 19 Wkly. Notes Cas. (Pa.) 567, 2 Am. Elec. Cas. 375. See also Metropolitan Grain, etc., Co. *v.* Chicago Bd. of Trade, 15 Fed. 847, 11 Biss. 531.

News service.— The rule as stated in the text applies to the furnishing of news service such as that furnished by the Associated Press. Inter-Ocean Pub. Co. *v.* Associated Press, 184 Ill. 438, 56 N. E. 822, 71 Am. St. Rep. 184, 48 L. R. A. 568.

19. Davis *v.* Electric Reporting Co., 19 Wkly. Notes Cas. (Pa.) 567, 2 Am. Elec. Cas. 375.

20. Smith *v.* Gold, etc., Tel. Co., 42 Hun (N. Y.) 454, 2 Am. Elec. Cas. 373; Friedman *v.* Gold, etc., Tel. Co., 32 Hun (N. Y.) 4.

21. Western Union Tel. Co. *v.* State, 165 Ind. 492, 76 N. E. 100, 3 L. R. A. N. S. 153.

It is a reasonable regulation that a person furnished with the special service in question shall not communicate the information to non-subscribers. Shepard *v.* Gold, etc., Tel Co., 38 Hun (N. Y.) 338, 1 Am. Elec. Cas. 584.

But it is not a reasonable regulation that the company shall be authorized to remove its instrument whenever, in its judgment, there has been any violation of the conditions of the contract by the subscriber. Smith *v.* Gold, etc., Tel. Co., 42 Hun (N. Y.) 454, 2 Am. Elec. Cas. 373.

22. Shepard *v.* Gold, etc., Tel. Co., 38 Hun (N. Y.) 338, 1 Am. Elec. Cas. 854.

23. Shepard *v.* Gold, etc., Tel. Co., 38 Hun (N. Y.) 338, 1 Am. Elec. Cas. 854.

24. Western Union Tel. Co. *v.* State, 165 Ind. 492, 76 N. E. 100, 3 L. R. A. N. S. 153; Smith *v.* Western Union Tel. Co., 84 Ky. 664, 2 S. W. 483, 8 Ky. L. Rep. 672, 2 Am. Elec. Cas. 289; Bradley *v.* Western Union Tel. Co., 8 Ohio Dec. (Reprint) 707, 9 Cinc. L. Bul. 223; Bryant *v.* Western Union Tel. Co., 17 Fed. 825. But see Sterrett *v.* Philadelphia Local Tel. Co., 18 Wkly. Notes Cas. (Pa.) 77.

25. Matter of Renville, 46 N. Y. App. Div. 37, 61 N. Y. Suppl. 549; Cain *v.* Western Union Tel. Co., 10 Ohio Dec. (Reprint) 72, 18 Cinc. L. Bul. 267. See also Davis *v.* Electric Reporting Co., 19 Wkly. Notes Cas. (Pa.) 567.

accrue, which were not communicated to it by the first company or apparent from the message itself.[47] If the original transmitting company expressly undertakes to send a message to its destination, it will be liable for a failure to do so, although such failure was due to the default of a connecting line,[48] and one company may also be liable for the acts of another on the ground that in the particular case there was an agency or partnership relation;[49] but the existence of such a relation cannot be inferred merely from the fact that the two companies have a common terminus and are in the habit of receiving messages from each other,[50] even if it further appears that, for convenience, an arrangement exists between them whereby the initial company collects from the sender in each case the tolls for both lines, accounting afterward to the connecting company for the latter's proportion.[51] If there is more than one connecting line to which it is possible to transfer the message the sender may determine which one shall be selected, and the initial company will be liable if it transfers to the other and the other is negligent;[52] but it will be relieved from liability if it transfers to the one selected by the sender, whether the latter company is negligent or not.[53] In case there is negligence or default on both the line of the initial and the line of the connecting company, and each default contributes to the ultimate damage, both companies are liable.[54]

F. Telephone Companies.[55] Ordinarily it is not the duty of a telephone company, although conducting a long distance business, to transmit messages, but merely to furnish a means of communication and to find and notify persons for whom calls are made,[56] in which case it will not be liable for refusing to transmit a message;[57] but it will be liable for a negligent failure or delay in regard to notifying persons for whom calls are made,[58] or negligently bringing in response to such a call a different person from the one for whom the call is made.[59] If,

47. Baldwin *v.* U. S. Telegraph Co., 45 N. Y. 744, 6 Am. Rep. 165 [*reversing* 54 Barb. 505, 6 Abb. Pr. N. S. 405]. See also Sabine Valley Tel. Co. *v.* Oliver, 46 Tex. Civ. App. 428, 102 S. W. 925, applying the same rule to calls in the case of connecting long distance telephones.

48. Western Union Tel. Co. *v.* Stratemeier, 6 Ind. App. 125, 32 N. E. 871. See also Western Union Tel. Co. *v.* Carter, 24 Tex. Civ. App. 80, 58 S. W. 198.

Estoppel.—Where the sender of a message inquires if the company has an office at the place of destination and is informed that it has, and thereupon delivers the message and pays for its transmission to such point, the company is estopped in an action for non-delivery to assert that it had no office at such place and that the non-delivery was due to the negligence of a connecting line. Western Union Tel. Co. *v.* Stratemeier, 6 Ind. App. 125, 32 N. E. 871.

49. Western Union Tel. Co. *v.* Craven, (Tex. Civ. App. 1906) 95 S. W. 633. See also Sabine Val. Tel. Co. *v.* Oliver, 46 Tex. Civ. App. 428, 102 S. W. 925, telephone companies.

50. Baldwin *v.* U. S. Telegraph Co., 45 N. Y. 744, 6 Am. Rep. 165 [*reversing* 54 Barb. 505, 6 Abb. Pr. N. S. 405]; Western Union Tel. Co. *v.* Lovely, (Tex. Civ. App. 1899) 52 S. W. 563.

51. Western Union Tel. Co. *v.* Lovely, (Tex. Civ. App. 1899) 52 S. W. 563.

52. Western Union Tel. Co. *v.* Turner, 94 Tex. 304, 60 S. W. 432.

53. Western Union Tel. Co. *v.* Simms, 30 Tex. Civ. App. 32, 69 S. W. 464.

54. Weatherford, etc., R. Co. *v.* Seals, (Tex. Civ. App. 1897) 41 S. W. 841.

55. **Duty to furnish services and facilities** see *supra*, III.

56. Southwestern Tel., etc., Co. *v.* Gotcher, 93 Tex. 114, 53 S. W. 686; Southwestern Tel., etc., Co. *v.* Flood, (Tex. Civ. App. 1908) 111 S. W. 1064.

57. Southwestern Tel., etc., Co. *v.* Gotcher, 93 Tex. 114, 53 S. W. 686.

58. McLeod *v.* Pacific Tel. Co., 52 Oreg. 22, 94 Pac. 568, 95 Pac. 1009, 15 L. R. A. N. S. 810, 18 L. R. A. N. S. 954; Southwestern Tel., etc., Co. *v.* Owens, (Tex. Civ. App. 1909) 116 S W. 89; Southwestern Tel., etc., Co. *v.* McCoy, (Tex. Civ. App. 1908) 114 S. W. 387; Southwestern Tel., etc., Co. *v.* Flood, (Tex. Civ. App. 1908) 111 S. W. 1064; Southwestern Tel., etc., Co. *v.* Taylor, 26 Tex. Civ. App. 79, 63 S. W. 1076.

It is a question for the jury whether a telephone company has exercised due care and diligence to find and notify the person for whom a call is made. Southwestern Tel., etc., Co. *v.* McCoy, (Tex. Civ. App. 1908) 114 S. W. 387.

59. McLeod *v.* Pacific Tel. Co., 52 Oreg. 22, 94 Pac. 568, 95 Pac. 1009, 15 L. R. A. N. S. 810, 18 L. R. A. N. S. 954, holding that where a telephone company negligently summons the wrong person in response to a long distance call it will be liable for any resulting damages to the person for whom the call was in fact made.

however, a telephone company undertakes to transmit and deliver messages, its duties and liabilities in this regard are similar to those of telegraph companies.[60] Where a request is made for a particular number or telephone, the company discharges its duty by making the proper connection, and is not responsible for the identity of the person answering,[61] although it might be liable for negligently giving a wrong connection.[62]

VII. STATUTORY PENALTIES.

A. In General. In a number of jurisdictions there are statutes imposing penalties upon telegraph companies for violations of their public duties,[63] which statutes in some cases expressly include telephone companies also,[64] and such statutes are not unconstitutional,[65] except in so far as they attempt to regulate or interfere with interstate commerce.[66] The statutes vary both as to their terms and their objects, some being designed merely to prevent partiality or discrimination,[67] or applying only to wilful or intentional acts,[68] and others including

60. See Cumberland Tel., etc., Co. *v.* Atherton, 122 Ky. 154, 91 S. W. 257, 28 Ky. L. Rep. 1100.

61. See McLeod *v.* Pacific Tel. Co., 52 Oreg. 22, 94 Pac. 568, 95 Pac. 1009, 15 L. R. A. N. S. 810, 18 L. R. A. N. S. 954.

62. See McLeod *v.* Pacific Tel. Co., 52 Oreg. 22, 94 Pac. 568, 95 Pac. 1009, 15 L. R. A. N. S. 810, 18 L. R. A. N. S. 954.

63. *Arkansas.*— State *v.* Western Union Tel. Co., 76 Ark. 124, 88 S. W. 834.

California.— Thurn *v.* Alta Tel. Co., 15 Cal. 472.

Georgia.— Western Union Tel. Co. *v.* Rountree, 92 Ga. 611, 18 S. E. 979, 44 Am. St. Rep. 93.

Indiana.— Western Union Tel. Co. *v.* Braxton, 165 Ind. 165, 74 N. E. 985; Western Union Tel. Co. *v.* Ferguson, 157 Ind. 37, 60 N. E. 679.

Michigan.— Weaver *v.* Grand Rapids, etc., R. Co., 107 Mich. 300, 65 N. W. 225.

Missouri.— Connell *v.* Western Union Tel. Co., 108 Mo. 459, 18 S. W. 883; Pollard *v.* Missouri, etc., Tel. Co., 114 Mo. App. 533, 90 S. W. 121.

New York.— Gifford *v.* Glenn Tel. Co., 54 Misc. 468, 106 N. Y. Suppl. 53; Hearn *v.* Western Union Tel. Co., 36 Misc. 557, 73 N. Y. Suppl. 1077.

North Carolina.— Mayo *v.* Western Union Tel. Co., 112 N. C. 343, 16 S. E. 1006.

Virginia.— Western Union Tel. Co. *v.* Hughes, 104 Va. 240, 51 S. E. 225; Western Union Tel. Co. *v.* Powell, 94 Va. 268, 26 S. E. 828.

United States.— Stafford *v.* Western Union Tel. Co., 73 Fed. 273, California statute.

See 45 Cent. Dig. tit. "Telegraphs and Telephones," §§ 79, 80.

In Mississippi the statute imposing a penalty for delay in the delivery of messages was omitted from the enrolled bill of the code of 1906 and was therefore repealed by section 13 thereof, which expressly repeals all laws of a general nature not brought forward and embodied in such code. Postal Tel. Cable Co. *v.* Shannon, 91 Miss. 476, 44 So. 809. See also Western Union Tel. Co. *v.* Morgan, 92 Miss. 108, 45 So. 427.

64. *Arkansas.*— Phillips *v.* Southwestern Tel., etc., Co., 72 Ark. 478, 81 S. W. 605.

Indiana.— Central Union Tel. Co. *v.* Fehring, 146 Ind. 189, 45 N. E. 64.

Mississippi.— Cumberland Tel., etc., Co. *v.* Sanders, 83 Miss. 357, 35 So. 653.

Missouri.— Pollard *v.* Missouri, etc., Tel. Co., 114 Mo. App. 533, 90 S. W. 121.

United States.— Cumberland Tel., etc., Co. *v.* Kelly, 160 Fed. 316, 87 C. C. A. 268, Tennessee statute.

The Indiana statute, in its application to telephones, applies not only to the furnishing of instruments and their connection with the exchange, but also to subsequent connections and facilities for the use of such instruments for conversing with particular persons. Central Union Tel. Co. *v.* Fehring, 146 Ind. 189, 45 N. E. 64.

65. Western Union Tel. Co. *v.* Ferguson, 157 Ind. 37, 60 N. E. 679; Central Union Tel. Co. *v.* Fehring, 146 Ind. 189, 45 N. E. 64; Marshall *v.* Western Union Tel. Co., 79 Miss. 154, 27 So. 614, 89 Am. St. Rep. 585; Western Union Tel. Co. *v.* Hughes, 104 Va. 240, 51 S. E. 225; Western Union Tel. Co. *v.* Powell, 94 Va. 268, 26 S. E. 828.

66. Western Union Tel. Co. *v.* Pendleton, 122 U. S. 347, 7 S. Ct. 1126, 30 L. ed. 1187 [*reversing* 95 Ind. 12, 48 Am. Rep. 692]. See also COMMERCE, 7 Cyc. 450–452.

67. State *v.* Western Union Tel. Co., 76 Ark. 124, 88 S. W. 834; Weaver *v.* Grand Rapids, etc., R. Co., 107 Mich. 300, 65 N. W. 225; Hearn *v.* Western Union Tel. Co., 36 Misc. (N. Y.) 557, 73 N. Y. Suppl. 1077; Wichelman *v.* Western Union Tel. Co., 30 Misc. (N. Y.) 450, 62 N. Y. Suppl. 491. See also *infra*, VII, B, 2.

68. State *v.* Western Union Tel. Co., 76 Ark. 124, 88 S. W. 834; Frauenthal *v.* Western Union Tel. Co., 50 Ark. 78, 6 S. W. 236.

In Arkansas the act of 1885, repealing a former statute applying in terms to every "neglect or refusal" to transmit or receive messages, omits the word "neglect," and it is held that the latter statute applies only to wilful or intentional acts, and not to such as are merely negligent. State *v.* Western Union Tel. Co., 76 Ark. 124, 88 S. W. 834.

"correctly" does not require absolute literal accuracy, but only that they shall be substantially correct.[99]

2. Statutes Relating to Discrimination. Penal statutes merely directing in substance that telegraph companies shall receive and transmit messages without discrimination, and with impartiality and in good faith, and in the order received, without any express requirement that the transmission shall be correct or prompt, are ordinarily construed as intended merely to prevent partiality and discrimination between different patrons,[1] and as applying only to intentional or wilful acts,[2] not including merely negligent acts or omissions,[3] such as a negligent failure to transmit,[4] delay in transmission or delivery,[5] error in transmission,[6] or even a positive refusal to accept a message for transmission, due merely to negligence on the part of the operator in ascertaining whether the company has an office at the point of destination;[7] but in some cases it has been held that if the act or omission complained of is within the terms of the statute, it is not material whether it was intentional or merely negligent.[8]

3. No Extraterritorial Effect. Statutes imposing penalties upon telegraph companies have no extraterritorial effect,[9] and so there can be no recovery in one

99. Western Union Tel. Co. *v.* Clarke, 71 Miss. 157, 14 So. 452.

1. State *v.* Western Union Tel. Co., 76 Ark. 124, 88 S. W. 834; Weaver *v.* Grand Rapids, etc., R. Co., 107 Mich. 300, 65 N. W. 225; Petze *v.* Western Union Tel. Co., 128 N. Y. App. Div. 192, 112 N. Y. Suppl. 516; Gifford *v.* Glen Tel. Co., 54 Misc. (N. Y.) 468, 106 N. Y. Suppl. 53; Hearn *v.* Western Union Tel. Co., 36 Misc. (N. Y.) 557, 73 N. Y. Suppl. 1077; Wichelman *v.* Western Union Tel. Co., 30 Misc. (N. Y.) 450, 62 N. Y. Suppl. 491.

Use of slot telephone at pay station.— Under the New York statute which is designed to prevent partiality and discrimination, if a person, contrary to the printed instructions, deposits his money in the slot while the receiver is hung up, so that the operator cannot hear the coins register, the company is not liable for the penalty in case the operator refuses to make the connection unless another deposit is made with the receiver down. Gifford *v.* Glen Tel. Co., 54 Misc. (N. Y.) 468, 106 N. Y. Suppl. 53.

Where the company's operators are on a strike, a refusal to accept a message for transmission except subject to delay is not an act of partiality, bad faith, or discrimination, and does not subject the company to the statutory penalty. Petze *v.* Western Union Tel. Co., 128 N. Y. App. Div. 192, 112 N. Y. Suppl. 516.

2. State *v.* Western Union Tel. Co., 76 Ark. 124, 88 S. W. 834; Weaver *v.* Grand Rapids, etc., R. Co., 107 Mich. 300, 65 N. W. 225; Wichelman *v.* Western Union Tel. Co., 30 Misc. (N. Y.) 450, 62 N. Y. Suppl. 491.

3. State *v.* Western Union Tel. Co., 76 Ark. 124, 88 S. W. 834; Frauenthal *v.* Western Union Tel. Co., 50 Ark. 78, 6 S. W. 236; Weaver *v.* Grand Rapids, etc., R. Co., 107 Mich. 300, 65 N. W. 225; Hearn *v.* Western Union Tel. Co., 36 Misc. (N. Y.) 557, 73 N. Y. Suppl. 1077.

In Indiana the same construction was formerly placed upon a similar statute (Western Union Tel. Co. *v.* Jones, 116 Ind. 361, 18 N. E. 529; Hadley *v.* Western Union Tel. Co., 115 Ind. 191, 15 N. E. 845; Western Union Tel. Co. *v.* Swain, 109 Ind. 405, 9 N. E. 927; Western Union Tel. Co. *v.* Steele, 108 Ind. 163, 9 N. E. 78); but later cases construe it as applying to mere negligence if within the terms of the statute (Western Union Tel. Co. *v.* Braxton, 165 Ind. 165, 74 N. E. 985; Western Union Tel. Co, *v.* Ferguson, 157 Ind. 37, 60 N. E. 679).

4. Frauenthal *v.* Western Union Tel. Co., 50 Ark. 78, 6 S. W. 236.

5. Hearn *v.* Western Union Tel. Co., 36 Misc. (N. Y.) 557, 73 N. Y. Suppl. 1077.

6. Wichelman *v.* Western Union Tel. Co., 30 Misc. (N. Y.) 450, 62 N. Y. Suppl. 491.

7. State *v.* Western Union Tel. Co., 76 Ark. 124, 88 S. W. 834.

8. Western Union Tel. Co. *v.* Braxtan, 165 Ind. 165, 74 N. E. 985; Western Union Tel. Co. *v.* Ferguson, 157 Ind. 37, 60 N. E. 679 [*disapproving* Western Union Tel. Co. *v.* Jones, 116 Ind. 361, 18 N. E. 529; Western Union Tel. Co. *v.* Swain, 109 Ind. 405, 9 N. E. 927; Western Union Tel. Co. *v.* Steele, 108 Ind. 163, 9 N. E. 78]; Wood *v.* Western Union Tel. Co., 59 Mo. App. 236; Burnett *v.* Western Union Tel. Co., 39 Mo. App. 599.

Under the Indiana statute it is held that telegraph companies are required, under penalty, to receive and transmit messages: (1) With impartiality and in good faith; (2) in the order of time in which they are received; and (3) without discrimination in rates or conditions of service; and that even conceding that the first and third requirements can be violated only by intentional acts, the second may be by negligence as well as by design. Western Union Tel. Co. *v.* Ferguson, 157 Ind. 37, 60 N. E. 679.

9. Western Union Tel. Co. *v.* Carter, 156 Ind. 531, 60 N. E. 305; Western Union Tel. Co. *v.* Reed, 96 Ind. 195; Carnahan *v.* Western Union Tel. Co., 89 Ind. 526, 46 Am. Rep. 175; Taylor *v.* Western Union Tel. Co., 95 Iowa 740, 64 N. W. 660; Connell *v.* Western Union Tel. Co., 108 Mo. 459, 18 S. W. 883.

state of a penalty incurred under the laws of another state,[10] or for an act or omission occurring beyond the borders of the state where the action is brought and by the laws of which the penalty is provided.[11]

C. Who May Recover. The question as to what person or persons may sue to recover a statutory penalty depends upon the terms of the statute.[12] Under some of the statutes imposing penalties upon telegraph companies, the right to recover is limited to the sender of the message and does not include the addressee,[13] and some statutes have been so construed, although applying in terms to "any party aggrieved;"[14] but under other statutes the action may

10. Taylor *v.* Western Union Tel. Co., 95 Iowa 740, 64 N. W. 660, South Dakota penalty not recoverable in Iowa.

11. *Indiana.*—Western Union Tel. Co. *v.* Carter, 156 Ind. 531, 60 N. E. 305; Rogers *v.* Western Union Tel. Co., 122 Ind. 395, 24 N. E. 157, 17 Am. St. Rep. 373; Western Union Tel. Co. *v.* Reed, 96 Ind. 195; Carnahan *v.* Western Union Tel. Co., 89 Ind. 526, 47 Am. Rep. 175. But see Western Union Tel. Co. *v.* Hamilton, 50 Ind. 181.

Mississippi.— See Alexander *v.* Western Union Tel. Co., 66 Miss. 161, 5 So. 397, 14 Am. St. Rep. 556, 3 L. R. A. 71.

Missouri.— Connell *v.* Western Union Tel. Co., 108 Mo. 459, 18 S. W. 883; Rixke *v.* Western Union Tel. Co., 96 Mo. App. 406, 70 S. W. 265.

New York.— Hearn *v.* Western Union Tel. Co., 36 Misc. 557, 73 N. Y. Suppl. 1077.

Oklahoma.— Butner *v.* Western Union Tel. Co., 2 Okla. 234, 37 Pac. 1087.

United States.— Western Union Tel. Co. *v.* James, 162 U. S. 650, 16 S. Ct. 934, 40 L. ed. 1105; Western Union Tel. Co. *v.* Pendleton, 122 U. S. 347, 7 S. Ct. 1126, 30 L. ed. 1187 [*reversing* 95 Ind. 12, 48 Am. Rep. 692].

See 45 Cent. Dig. tit. "Telegraphs and Telephones," §§ 79, 80.

Application of rule.—A telegraph company is not subject to a penalty provided by the laws of one state for failing to transmit a message to that state from a point in another state (Western Union Tel. Co. *v.* Reed, 96 Ind. 195); or for failing to deliver in another state a message transmitted from a point in the state imposing the penalty (Western Union Tel. Co. *v.* Carter, 156 Ind. 531, 60 N. E. 305; Connell *v.* Western Union Tel. Co., 108 Mo. 459, 18 S. W. 883).

Interference with interstate commerce.—As the telegraph is an instrument of commerce (see COMMERCE, 7 Cyc. 450), any attempt on the part of one state to penalize a telegraph company in regard to the conduct of its business in another state, as by attempting to regulate the delivery of messages in another state, would be in conflict with the commerce clause of the federal constitution (Western Union Tel. Co. *v.* Pendleton, 122 U. S. 347, 7 S. Ct. 1126, 30 L. ed. 1187 [*reversing* 95 Ind. 12, 48 Am. Rep. 692]); but such a statute is not invalid, even in regard to interstate messages, in so far as it applies only to defaults occurring within the state imposing the penalty, provided it imposes no new burden or duty (Western Union Tel. Co. *v.* James, 162 U. S. 650, 16 S. Ct. 934, 40 L. ed. 1105. See also COMMERCE, 7 Cyc. 452 text and note 6).

12. Thompson *v.* Western Union Tel. Co., 40 Misc. (N. Y.) 443, 82 N. Y. Suppl. 675.

Statutes strictly construed see *supra*, VII, B, 1.

13. Thurn *v.* Alta Tel. Co., 15 Cal. 472 (statute reading, "the person or persons sending or desiring to send" messages); Western Union Tel. Co. *v.* Brown, 108 Ind. 538, 8 N. E. 171 (statute reading, "the person whose dispatch is neglected or postponed"); Western Union Tel. Co. *v.* Kinney, 106 Ind. 468, 7 N. E. 191; Western Union Tel. Co. *v.* Reed, 96 Ind. 195; Thompson *v.* Western Union Tel. Co., 40 Misc. (N. Y.) 443, 82 N. Y. Suppl. 675 (statute reading, "the person or persons sending or desiring to send").

One who directs a message to be forwarded to him at another address does not thereby make himself the sender of the message forwarded. Western Union Tel. Co. *v.* Kinney, 106 Ind. 468, 7 N. E. 191.

Message transferred to other line.— Under a statute imposing a penalty for the benefit of "the person or persons sending or desiring to send" messages, it has been held that where a message is filed for transmission with the A company for a point not on its line, and is transferred by it to the B company, and the B company is guilty of a breach of duty, the proper plaintiff in an action against the B company is not the original sender of the message, but the A company. Thurn *v.* Alta Tel. Co., 15 Cal. 472.

Another telegraph company which desires to forward a message to a point beyond the terminus of its own line, over the line of another company, is the party desiring to send the message and may sue the connecting company for a failure or refusal to transmit the same. The words "person or persons," as used in the statute, include corporations. U. S. Telegraph Co. *v.* Western Union Tel. Co., 56 Barb. (N. Y.) 46.

14. Western Union Tel. Co. *v.* Ferguson, 157 Ind. 37, 60 N. E. 679; Hadley *v.* Western Union Tel. Co., 115 Ind. 191, 15 N. E. 845.

The reason for this construction of the Indiana statute is that it is designed merely to prevent partiality and discrimination between different patrons of the company, and that only those giving or offering business to the company can rightly be called its patrons. Hadley *v.* Western Union Tel. Co., 115 Ind. 191, 15 N. E. 845.

which would be available in case the action was brought by the agent,[43] and the addressee may be entitled to sue as an undisclosed principal of the sender.[44] In the application of the rule a distinction has, however, been made between cases relating to business messages and cases where damages are claimed for mental anguish,[45] it being held that there can be no recovery of damages for mental anguish by the undisclosed principal;[46] but this rule is said not to involve any denial of the general right of an undisclosed principal to sue but merely a question of the character of damages recoverable,[47] it being held that the principal can recover only what the agent if suing in his own name might recover,[48] and that damages for mental anguish to a person whose existence and whose interest in the message was not disclosed cannot be said to have been within the contemplation of the parties;[49] but that, although he cannot recover for mental anguish, he may recover nominal damages or the price paid for the transmission of the message.[50] It has, however, been held that the addressee may recover for mental anguish where he sues on the contract as the principal of the sender, although the agency was not disclosed.[51]

Am. St. Rep. 23; Kennon v. Western Union Tel. Co., 92 Ala. 399, 9 So. 200].

Georgia.— Propeller Tow-Boat Co. v. Western Union Tel. Co., 124 Ga. 478, 52 S. E. 766; Dodd Grocery Co. v. Postal Tel. Cable Co., 112 Ga. 685, 37 S. E. 981.

Iowa.— Harkness v. Western Union Tel. Co., 73 Iowa 190, 34 N. W. 811, 5 Am. St. Rep. 672.

New York.— Milliken v. Western Union Tel. Co., 110 N. Y. 403, 18 N. E. 251, 1 L. R. A. 281; Leonard v. New York, etc., Electro Magnetic Tel. Co., 41 N. Y. 544, 1 Am. Rep. 446.

Tennessee.— See Western Union Tel. Co. v. Potts, 120 Tenn. 37, 113 S. W. 789, 127 Am. St. Rep. 991, 19 L. R. A. N. S. 479.

Texas.—Western Union Tel. Co. v. Broesche, 72 Tex. 654, 10 S. W. 734, 13 Am. St. Rep. 843; Gulf Coast, etc., R. Co. v. Todd, (App. 1892) 19 S. W. 761.

United States.— Purdom Naval Stores Co. v. Western Union Tel. Co., 153 Fed. 327. See also Western Union Tel. Co. v. Schriver, 141 Fed. 538, 72 C. C. A. 596, 4 L. R. A. N. S. 678.

If the agent was not authorized to send the message which was sent, as where he was instructed to send a certain message prepared by plaintiff but instead of so doing wrote out and sent a different message, and plaintiff's interest therein was not disclosed to defendant, plaintiff cannot recover for negligence in regard to its transmission or delivery. Elliott v. Western Union Tel. Co., 75 Tex. 18, 12 S. W. 954, 16 Am. St. Rep. 872.

Sender not acting as agent.— Where a merchant at the request of a customer telegraphs for certain goods desired by the latter, but in sending the message does not act as agent of the customer, but is merely seeking to supply himself with the goods in order subsequently to sell the same to the customer at a profit, there is no privity between the telegraph company and the customer which will authorize an action by the latter for negligence in regard to the delivery of the message. Deslottes v. Baltimore, etc., Tel. Co., 40 La. Ann. 183, 3 So. 566.

43. See Harkness v. Western Union Tel. Co., 73 Iowa 190, 34 N. W. 811, 5 Am. St. Rep. 672; Western Union Tel. Co. v. Kerr, 4 Tex. Civ. App. 280, 23 S. W. 564.

44. Western Union Tel. Co. v. Manker, 145 Ala. 418, 41 So. 850; Manker v. Western Union Tel. Co., 137 Ala. 292, 34 So. 839 [*overruling* Western Union Tel. Co. v. Allgood, 125 Ala. 712, 27 So. 1024, and *disapproving* on this point Western Union Tel. Co. v. Wilson, 93 Ala. 32, 9 So. 414, 30 Am. St. Rep. 23; Kennon v. Western Union Tel. Co., 92 Ala. 399, 9 So. 200].

Right of addressee to sue generally see *supra*, VIII, B, 2.

45. Western Union Tel. Co. v. Potts, 120 Tenn. 37, 113 S. W. 789, 127 Am. St. Rep. 991, 19 L. R. A. N. S. 479.

46. Helms v. Western Union Tel. Co., 143 N. C. 386, 55 S. E. 831, 8 L. R. A. N. S. 249 [*disapproving* Cashion v. Western Union Tel. Co., 124 N. C. 459, 32 S. E. 746, 45 L. R. A. 160]; Western Union Tel. Co. v. Potts, 120 Tenn. 37, 113 S. W. 789, 127 Am. St. Rep. 991, 19 L. R. A. N. S. 479; Western Union Tel. Co. v. Fore, (Tex. Civ. App. 1894) 26 S. W. 783; Western Union Tel. Co. v. Kerr, 4 Tex. Civ. App. 280, 23 S. W. 564. See also *supra*, VIII, B, 1. *Compare* Western Union Tel. Co. v. Broesche, 72 Tex. 654, 10 S. W. 734, 13 Am. St. Rep. 843, where, however, it seems that defendant was informed of the agency of the sender.

47. Western Union Tel. Co. v. Potts, 120 Tenn. 37, 113 S. W. 789, 127 Am. St. Rep. 991, 19 L. R. A. N. S. 479; Western Union Tel. Co. v. Kerr, 4 Tex. Civ. App. 280, 23 S. W. 564.

48. Western Union Tel. Co. v. Kerr, 4 Tex. Civ. App. 280, 23 S. W. 564.

49. Western Union Tel. Co. v. Potts, 120 Tenn. 37, 113 S. W. 789, 127 Am. St. Rep. 991, 19 L. R. A. N. S. 479; Western Union Tel. Co. v. Kerr, 4 Tex. Civ. App. 280, 23 S. W. 564.

50. Western Union Tel. Co. v. Potts, 120 Tenn. 37, 113 S. W. 789, 127 Am. St. Rep. 991, 19 L. R. A. N. S. 479. See also Helms v. Western Union Tel. Co., 143 N. C. 386, 55 S. E. 831, 8 L. R. A. N. S. 249.

51. Western Union Tel. Co. v. Manker, 145

to apprise defendant of the nature and amount of the damages claimed;[88] but, although the special damages claimed are defectively pleaded or are too remote or otherwise not recoverable, the complaint is not subject to general demurrer if it would warrant a recovery of general or of nominal damages.[89] If plaintiff seeks to increase his measure of damages by proof that at the time the message was accepted by the company the latter had notice from some source other than the language of the message itself of its importance and of the consequences which would result from a failure duly to deliver it,[90] he must allege such special notice;[91] but it is not necessary to allege such notice where the complaint sets out the message and the language of the message is sufficient to charge the company with notice of its urgency and importance.[92]

(II) *EXEMPLARY DAMAGES.*[93] While it has been held that the complaint should state whether the damages claimed therein are actual or exemplary,[94]

(physical suffering, and expenses for medicine and nursing, in mental anguish case); Mood *v.* Western Union Tel. Co., 40 S. C. 524, 19 S. E. 67 (loss of contract of employment).

Texas.— Western Union Tel. Co. *v.* Turner, (Civ. App. 1904) 78 S. W. 362; Western Union Tel. Co. *v.* Partlow, 30 Tex. Civ. App. 599, 71 S. W. 584 (action for loss of employment; expense of securing another position not provable unless alleged); Western Union Tel. Co. *v.* Bell, 24 Tex. Civ. App. 572, 59 S. W. 918.

See 45 Cent. Dig. tit. "Telegraphs and Telephones," § 55; and, generally, DAMAGES, 13 Cyc. 176.

In an action before a justice of the peace the rule that special damages must be specially pleaded does not apply. Lee *v.* Western Union Tel. Co., 51 Mo. App. 375.

88. Bashinsky *v.* Western Union Tel. Co., 1 Ga. App. 761, 58 S. E. 91; Ferguson *v.* Anglo-American Tel. Co., 151 Pa. St. 211, 25 Atl. 40; Purdom Naval Stores Co. *v.* Western Union Tel. Co., 153 Fed. 327.

Loss of commissions.—Where the complaint is based upon the non-delivery of a message relating to a contract, on which if consummated plaintiff would have earned commissions, the complaint must show the nature and terms of the contract and the amount of the commissions contracted for or what would have accrued to plaintiff upon the completion of the contract. Bashinsky *v.* Western Union Tel. Co., 1 Ga. App. 761, 58 S. E. 91.

Message accepting offer.— Where a telegraph company failed to deliver a message, accepting an offer for the sale of the addressee's business, possession to be delivered on completion of the addressee's business year, a complaint for damages, failing to definitely allege the time when possession and delivery were to be accomplished, was defective. Purdom Naval Stores Co. *v.* Western Union Tel. Co., 153 Fed. 327.

Allegations held sufficient.— In an action for a loss on a shipment of cattle to a certain market due to the non-delivery of a message to plaintiff notifying him not to make the shipment, a complaint alleging the market value of the cattle at the time and place of shipment, the cost of shipment and the amount realized on a sale at the place of destination, is sufficient to show plaintiff's damages. Western Union Tel. Co. *v.* Linney, (Tex. Civ. App. 1894) 28 S. W. 234. Allegations held sufficient as to damages due to a loss of profits on an exchange of property which was prevented by the non-delivery of a message see Western Union Tel. Co. *v.* Wilhelm, 48 Nebr. 910, 67 N. W. 870.

89. *Alabama.*— Western Union Tel. Co. *v.* McMorris, 158 Ala. 563, 48 So. 349, 132 Am. St. Rep. 46.

Florida.— Western Union Tel. Co. *v.* Merritt, 55 Fla. 462, 46 So. 1024, 127 Am. St. Rep. 169.

Georgia.—Trigg *v.* Western Union Tel. Co., 4 Ga. App. 416, 61 S. E. 855.

Indiana.— Western Union Tel. Co. *v.* Hopkins, 49 Ind. 223.

Kentucky.— Taliferro *v.* Western Union Tel. Co., 54 S. W. 825, 21 Ky. L. Rep. 1290.

Mississippi.— Alexander *v.* Western Union Tel. Co., 66 Miss. 161, 5 So. 397, 14 Am. St. Rep. 556, 3 L. R. A. 71.

North Carolina.— Hall *v.* Western Union Tel. Co., 139 N. C. 369, 52 S. E. 50.

United States.— Stafford *v.* Western Union Tel. Co., 73 Fed. 273.

See 45 Cent. Dig. tit. "Telegraphs and Telephones," § 55; and, generally, DAMAGES, 13 Cyc. 174, 178.

90. See *infra*, IX, B, 1, a, (I).

91. Taylor *v.* Western Union Tel. Co., 101 S. W. 969, 31 Ky. L. Rep. 240; Graddy *v.* Western Union Tel. Co., 43 S. W. 468, 19 Ky. L. Rep. 1455; Fass *v.* Western Union Tel. Co., 82 S. C. 461, 64 S. E. 235; Western Union Tel. Co. *v.* Steele, (Tex. Civ. App. 1908) 110 S. W. 546; Western Union Tel. Co. *v.* Turner, (Tex. Civ. App. 1904) 78 S. W. 362.

Cipher message.— In order to recover damages for negligence in the transmission of a cipher message the complaint must allege that defendant when it received the message was notified of its value and importance. Harrison *v.* Western Union Tel. Co., 3 Tex. App. Civ. Cas. § 43.

92. Western Union Tel. Co. *v.* Eskridge, 7 Ind. App. 208, 33 N. E. 238.

93. **Right to recover exemplary damages** see *infra*, IX, C.

94. McAllen *v.* Western Union Tel. Co., 70 Tex. 243, 7 S. W. 715.

2. Admissibility — a. In General. As in other civil actions any evidence if justified by the pleadings,[61] and otherwise competent, is admissible if it is relevant to any of the material matters in issue;[62] but evidence which is immaterial or irrelevant is not admissible.[63] The message itself wherever relevant is admissible in evidence,[64] and in an action for delay in delivery the message delivered to the addressee is admissible,[65] it being unnecessary to produce the original message filed for transmission by the sender;[66] and in an action for delay in delivery the delivery sheet is also admissible after proof of the genuineness of the signature.[67] The general rules as to best and secondary evidence[68] apply in regard to the admission of copies of messages or of records relating thereto,[69] secondary evidence of the contents of a message being admissible if the original is shown to have been lost or destroyed.[70] While it has been held that the general rule applies[71] that parol evidence is not admissible to contradict or vary the written contract of transmission,[72] evidence is not inadmissible on this ground that defendant's transmitting agent was informed by the sender as to the character and importance of the message or the whereabouts of the addressee;[73] and it has also been held that parol evidence is admissible of an understanding between the sender and defendant's transmitting agent as to the words "care of" in the address,[74] or of the purpose of writing the word "day" across the stipulations

61. See *supra*, VIII, D.

62. Whitten *v.* Western Union Tel. Co., 141 N. C. 361, 54 S. E. 289; Western Union Tel. Co. *v.* James, 31 Tex. Civ. App. 503, 73 S. W. 79; Western Union Tel. Co. *v.* Karr, 5 Tex. Civ. App. 60, 24 S. W. 302.

Message requesting addressee to meet sender.— In an action for non-delivery of a message requesting the addressee to meet plaintiff at a railroad station, plaintiff may show that he was not met (Western Union Tel. Co. *v.* Westmoreland, 150 Ala. 654, 43 So. 790); and also that he had an agreement with the addressee that the latter should meet him when notified (Western Union Tel. Co. *v.* Westmoreland, *supra*); and the addressee may testify that if the message had been delivered he would have met plaintiff (Western Union Tel. Co. *v.* Karr, 5 Tex. Civ. App. 60, 24 S. W. 302).

63. Western Union Tel. Co. *v.* Way, 83 Ala. 542, 4 So. 844; Grinnell *v.* Western Union Tel. Co., 113 Mass. 299, 18 Am. Rep. 485; Western Union Tel. Co. *v.* Mellon, 96 Tenn. 66, 33 S. W. 725; Western Union Tel. Co. *v.* Waller, 96 Tex. 589, 74 S. W. 751, 97 Am. St. Rep. 936 [*reversing* (Civ. App. 1903) 72 S. W. 264]; Western Union Tel. Co. *v.* Stiles, 89 Tex. 312, 34 S. W. 438; Western Union Tel. Co. *v.* Jackson, 35 Tex. Civ. App. 419, 80 S. W. 649; Western Union Tel. Co. *v.* McMillan, (Tex. Civ. App. 1894) 25 S. W. 821.

Evidence held inadmissible.— Where the contract of transmission contains valid stipulations limiting the liability of the company and the message was written by plaintiff on such a blank, testimony that he did not read such stipulations is inadmissible. Grinnell *v.* Western Union Tel. Co., 113 Mass. 299, 18 Am. Rep. 485.

64. Western Union Tel. Co. *v.* Northcutt, 158 Ala. 539, 48 So. 553, 132 Am. St. Rep. 38; Western Union Tel. Co. *v.* Bennett, 1 Tex. Civ. App. 558, 21 S. W. 699.

65. Western Union Tel. Co. *v.* Northcutt, 158 Ala. 539, 48 So. 553, 132 Am. St. Rep. 38; Western Union Tel. Co. *v.* Westmoreland, 150 Ala. 654, 43 So. 790; Western Union Tel. Co. *v.* Bates, 93 Ga. 352, 20 S. E. 639; Western Union Tel. Co. *v.* Bennett, 1 Tex. Civ. App. 558, 21 S. W. 699.

66. Western Union Tel. Co. *v.* Bates, 93 Ga. 352, 20 S. E. 639; Western Union Tel. Co. *v.* Bennett, 1 Tex. Civ. App. 558, 21 S. W. 699.

67. Western Union Tel. Co. *v.* Northcutt, 158 Ala. 539, 48 So. 553, 132 Am. St. Rep. 38.

68. See Evidence, 17 Cyc. 512, 515 text and note 54.

69. Cason *v.* Western Union Tel. Co., 77 S. C. 157, 57 S. E. 722 (copy of message not admissible in the absence of evidence that it is an authorized copy); Southwestern Tel., etc., Co. *v.* Owens, (Tex. Civ. App. 1909) 116 S. W. 89 (copy of long distance telephone company's ticket record not admissible where the absence of the original is not sufficiently accounted for); Buchanan *v.* Western Union Tel. Co., (Tex. Civ. App. 1907) 100 S. W. 974 (copy of message not admissible where original is not properly accounted for).

70. Western Union Tel. Co. *v.* Williford, (Tex. Civ. App. 1894) 27 S. W. 700.

71. See Evidence, 17 Cyc. 567.

72. Grinnell *v.* Western Union Tel. Co., 113 Mass. 299, 18 Am. Rep. 485.

73. Western Union Tel. Co. *v.* O'Fiel, 47 Tex. Civ. App. 40, 104 S. W. 406.

Evidence of information as to whereabouts of addressee see *infra*, VIII, E, 2, c.

Evidence of notice as to importance of message see *infra*, VIII, E, 2, d.

74. Western Union Tel. Co. *v.* Bryant, 35 Tex. Civ. App. 442, 80 S. W. 406, holding that parol evidence of an understanding between the sender and defendant's agent that the words "care of" in a message addressed to B care of K were intended merely as a matter of reference to enable defendant's agent at the place of destination to ascertain

of a blank used for night messages.[75] So also where the message itself contains abbreviated expressions or technical or trade terms parol evidence is admissible to translate and explain its meaning.[76] One of defendant's regular blanks containing stipulations limiting its liability is not admissible where it is not shown that the message in question was written on one of such blanks.[77]

b. Declarations and Admissions. The general rules as to the admissibility of such evidence in other civil actions [78] apply in determining whether declarations and admissions of defendant's agents are [79] or are not [80] admissible against defendant.

where B resided, is admissible to show that defendant did not agree and was not bound to deliver the message to K.

75. Western Union Tel. Co. *v.* Piner, 9 Tex. Civ. App. 152, 29 S. W. 66, holding that parol evidence is admissible to show that the word "day" written across the printed stipulations on a blank used for night messages was intended to cancel such stipulations in so far as applicable to night messages.

76. Western Union Tel. Co. *v.* Merritt, 55 Fla. 462, 46 So. 1024, 127 Am. St. Rep. 169.

Evidence is admissible to show that a message reading "Buy three May" meant three thousand bushels of wheat for May delivery. Carland *v.* Western Union Tel. Co., 118 Mich. 369, 76 N. W. 762, 74 Am. St. Rep. 394, 43 L. R. A. 280.

77. Western Union Tel. Co. *v.* McMillan, (Tex. Civ. App. 1894) 25 S. W. 821.

78. See EVIDENCE, 16 Cyc. 1003 *et seq.*

79. *Alabama.*— Western Union Tel. Co. *v.* Rowell, 153 Ala. 295, 45 So. 73, holding that evidence is admissible of a telephone conversation between plaintiff, the addressee, and defendant's agent tending to show that due diligence was not exercised in delivering the message.

Iowa.— Evans *v.* Western Union Tel. Co., 102 Iowa 219, 71 N. W. 219, statement made to sender of message on calling for an answer that the message had not been sent, admissible as a part of the same transaction.

Michigan.— Carland *v.* Western Union Tel. Co., 118 Mich. 369, 76 N. W. 762, 74 Am. St. Rep. 394, 43 L. R. A. 280, statement of transmitting operator made two days after the message should have been sent that it had never been received at the office of destination, admissible to show non-delivery.

South Carolina.— Fail *v.* Western Union Tel. Co., 80 S. C. 207, 60 S. E. 697, 61 S. E. 258 (declaration by defendant's agent that he had sent the message in question); Glover *v.* Western Union Tel. Co., 78 S. C. 502, 59 S. E. 526 (evidence of declarations of defendant's messenger when delivering a message to a person other than the addressee, admissible as part of the *res gestæ* as tending to show whether the delivery to such person was negligent or in wilful disregard of duty).

Texas.— Western Union Tel. Co. *v.* Simmons, (Civ. App. 1906) 93 S. W. 686 (statement made by operator on refusing to accept the message for transmission, admissible as evidence of the motive actuating him); Western Union Tel. Co. *v.* Cooper, 29 Tex. Civ. App. 591, 69 S. W. 427 (statement of agent on delivering message that he had received it the day before); Western Union Tel. Co. *v.* Davis, 24 Tex. Civ. App. 427, 59 S. W. 46 (evidence that defendant's agent when consulted as to the advisability of sending a second message said that it was an important death message and would be delivered, admissible to show defendant's knowledge of the nature and importance of the message); Western Union Tel. Co. *v.* Reeves, 8 Tex. Civ. App. 37, 27 S. W. 318 (evidence that plaintiff after sending a message and receiving no reply suggested that it be repeated and was informed by defendant's agent that it had gone through all right); Western Union Tel. Co. *v.* Bennett, 1 Tex. Civ. App. 558, 21 S. W. 699 (evidence of declarations of defendant's messenger as to his inability to find plaintiff, admissible against defendant in action for delay in delivery).

See 45 Cent. Dig. tit. "Telegraphs and Telephones," § 62.

To explain conduct of plaintiff.— Evidence of a declaration by defendant's transmitting agent made to the sender after the transmission of the message that it had been delivered is admissible to explain the subsequent conduct of plaintiff. Western Union Tel. Co. *v.* Lydon, 82 Tex. 364, 18 S. W. 701.

80. *Alabama.*— Western Union Tel. Co. *v.* Henderson, 89 Ala. 510, 7 So. 419, 18 Am. St. Rep. 148 (holding that a declaration by defendant's operator at the terminal office made to plaintiff the day after the message was received as to his reason for not delivering the message as soon as received is not admissible against defendant); Western Union Tel. Co. *v.* Way, 83 Ala. 542, 4 So. 844 (statements of defendant's agent not made in the performance of any duty relating to the transmission of the message, not admissible against defendant).

Iowa.— Sweatland *v.* Illinois, etc., Tel. Co., 27 Iowa 433, 1 Am. Rep. 285, declarations of defendant's agent several days after the message had been delivered inadmissible as being narrative of a past occurrence and not a part of the *res gestæ*.

Kentucky.— Graddy *v.* Western Union Tel. Co., 43 S. W. 468, 19 Ky. L. Rep. 1455.

Massachusetts.—Grinnell *v.* Western Union Tel. Co., 113 Mass. 299, 18 Am. Rep. 485, subsequent declarations of defendant's agent not connected with the transmission of the message.

South Carolina.— Aiken *v.* Western Union Tel. Co., 5 S. C. 358, admission by receiving

c. Evidence as to Negligence.[81] Subject to the general rules above stated,[82] any evidence is admissible which tends to establish the negligence relied on,[83] such as evidence that defendant's agent or messenger was informed where the addressee could be found,[84] or was directed to a person who could give such information,[85] and that the information if requested would have been given,[86] that

operator of an error in transcribing a message, the admission being made several days subsequently, not a part of the *res gestæ*.

Texas.— Southwestern Tel., etc., Co. *v.* Gotcher, 93 Tex. 114, 53 S. W. 686 (statement made by agent several days after the transaction in question); Western Union Tel. Co. *v.* Wofford, (Civ. App. 1897) 42 S. W. 119 (statement made by agent several days subsequently as to why message was not delivered).

See 45 Cent. Dig. tit. "Telegraphs and Telephones," § 62.

Rule stated.— The declarations or admissions of an agent of a telegraph company are not admissible against the company unless made within the scope of the agent's authority and while in the performance of his duty or so near in point of time to the main fact as to form a part of the *res gestæ*. Western Union Tel. Co. *v.* Way, 83 Ala. 542, 4 So. 844.

81. See, generally, NEGLIGENCE, 29 Cyc. 606.

82. See *supra*, VIII, E, 2, a, b.

83. Woods *v.* Western Union Tel. Co., 148 N. C. 1, 61 S. E. 653, 128 Am. St. Rep. 581; Western Union Tel. Co. *v.* Cooper, 71 Tex. 507, 9 S. W. 598, 10 Am. St. Rep. 772, 1 L. R. A. 728; Western Union Tel. Co. *v.* James, 31 Tex. Civ. App. 503, 73 S. W. 79; Western Union Tel. Co. *v.* Drake, 14 Tex. Civ. App. 601, 38 S. W. 632; Western Union Tel. Co. *v.* Hearne, 7 Tex. Civ. App. 67, 26 S. W. 478.

Evidence held admissible.— In an action for non-delivery a city directory giving the addressee's name and address is admissible as evidence to show negligence. Woods *v.* Western Union Tel. Co., 148 N. C. 1, 61 S. E. 653, 128 Am. St. Rep. 581. Where defendant seeks to excuse non-delivery on the ground that plaintiff was an obscure person and little known evidence is admissible of the business plaintiff was engaged in and the means employed to advertise the same, and he may introduce printed cards, letter-heads, and envelopes used by him in such business. Gulf, etc., R. Co. *v.* Wilson, 69 Tex. 739, 7 S. W. 653. Where the message is addressed to a third party and requests him to notify plaintiff, proof of the whereabouts of plaintiff is relevant. Western Union Tel. Co. *v.* Crawford, (Tex. Civ. App. 1903) 75 S. W. 843. Where defendant received and agreed to transmit a message, knowing that its wires were down and not informing the sender of the fact, plaintiff may show that previously and under similar circumstances defendant had caused messages to be sent over the wires of another company, which it did not attempt to do in this case. Pacific Postal Tel. Cable Co. *v.* Fleischner, 66 Fed. 899, 14 C. C. A. 166. In case of an error in transmitting a word in the message, where it appears that there was some difficulty in the reading of the message as written by plaintiff, plaintiff may testify what word was intended where it was so read by him to the transmitting agent. Western Union Tel. Co. *v.* Hearne, 7 Tex. Civ. App. 67, 26 S. W. 478. In an action for non-delivery of a telegram to plaintiff, the court properly permitted the sender of the telegram to testify that, if it had been reported to him that the message could not be delivered to plaintiff, because the initials in the address were not the same as plaintiff's, he would have had the initials changed. Arkansas, etc., R. Co. *v.* Stroude, 82 Ark. 117, 100 S. W. 760. Evidence is also admissible of the habits and reputation of defendant's agent to whom the message was delivered for transmission (Western Union Tel. Co. *v.* Hearne, *supra*. But see NEGLIGENCE, 29 Cyc. 610); of the time which it would take to deliver the message to the addressee at the place where he was at work (Western Union Tel. Co. *v.* Drake, 14 Tex. Civ. App. 601, 38 S. W. 632); of precautionary measures taken by plaintiff, the addressee, to secure a prompt delivery of the expected message (Western Union Tel. Co. *v.* Drake, *supra*); that plaintiff's employees were authorized to and did receive messages addressed to him (Western Union Tel. Co. *v.* Moran, (Tex. Civ. App. 1908) 113 S. W. 625); that defendant's agent was informed that a message was expected and requested to deliver it at once (Bailey *v.* Western Union Tel. Co., 150 N. C. 316, 63 S. E. 1044); that a second message was sent to defendant's operator requesting that the first message be promptly delivered (Western Union Tel. Co. *v.* Frith, 105 Tenn. 167, 58 S. W. 118); that plaintiff after waiting for two days for an answer to his message sent another message to a different person at the same place and received a reply in less than twenty-four hours (Western Union Tel. Co. *v.* Lydon, 82 Tex. 364, 18 S. W. 701); and that plaintiff gave instructions as to where he could be found if a telegram came for him to a man whom he saw using the telegraph instrument, although he did not know his name or that he was defendant's agent (Bolton *v.* Western Union Tel. Co., 76 S. C. 529, 57 S. E. 543).

84. Western Union Tel. Co. *v.* Benson, 159 Ala. 254, 48 So. 712; Western Union Tel. Co. *v.* Cooper, 71 Tex. 507, 9 S. W. 598, 10 Am. St. Rep. 772, 1 L. R. A. 728; Western Union Tel. Co. *v.* O'Fiel, 47 Tex. Civ. App. 40, 104 S. W. 406.

85. Western Union Tel. Co. *v.* Bell, 48 Tex. Civ. App. 359, 107 S. W. 570; Western Union Tel. Co. *v.* Waller, 37 Tex. Civ. App. 515, 84 S. W. 695.

86. Western Union Tel. Co. *v.* Waller, (Tex. Civ. App. 1903) 72 S. W. 264.

applies that ordinarily questions not raised in the trial court will not be considered on appeal,[92] and that a verdict based upon conflicting evidence will not ordinarily be disturbed on appeal,[93] if there is any evidence legally sufficient to sustain it; [94] but only where it is unsupported by evidence or is clearly and manifestly contrary to the great weight of evidence.[95] So also a judgment will not be reversed *in toto* where the only error is in the amount of damages which can be corrected by computation.[96]

IX. DAMAGES.

A. Nominal Damages or Cost of Transmission. Where an actionable breach of duty in regard to the transmission or delivery of a message is shown, plaintiff is entitled to recover at least nominal damages, although no actual damages are shown; [97] but if no actual recoverable damages are shown, plaintiff can recover only nominal damages.[98] Plaintiff has generally been allowed, however, to recover as actual damages [99] the amount paid for the transmission of the message,[1] provided he has actually paid the same; [2] but if no other actual

Texas.— Southwestern Tel., etc., Co. *v.* Owens, (Civ. App. 1909) 116 S. W. 89; Western Union Tel. Co. *v.* Edmonson, (Civ. App. 1897) 40 S. W. 622; Western Union Tel. Co. *v.* Stephens, 2 Tex. Civ. App. 129, 21 S. W. 148.

92. Western Union Tel. Co. *v.* De Golyer, 27 Ill. App. 489; Western Union Tel. Co. *v.* Hopkins, 49 Ind. 223. See also, generally, APPEAL AND ERROR, 2 Cyc. 660 *et seq.*

Whether the damages are excessive will not be considered on appeal where the question was not raised by a motion for a new trial in the court below. Western Union Tel. Co. *v.* Hopkins, 49 Ind. 223.

93. Western Union Tel. Co. *v.* Jones, 81 Tex. 271, 16 S. W. 1006. See also, generally, APPEAL AND ERROR, 3 Cyc. 348.

94. Harper *v.* Western Union Tel. Co., 92 Mo. App. 304; Western Union Tel. Co. *v.* Jones, 81 Tex. 271, 16 S. W. 1006; Gulf, etc., R. Co. *v.* Miller, 69 Tex. 739, 7 S. W. 653. See also, generally, APPEAL AND ERROR, 3 Cyc. 348.

95. Gulf, etc., R. Co. *v.* Miller, 69 Tex. 739, 7 S. W. 653. See also, generally, APPEAL AND ERROR, 3 Cyc. 351, 352.

Excessive damages see *infra*, IX, D.

96. Pacific Postal Tel. Cable Co. *v.* Fleischner, 66 Fed. 899, 14 C. C. A. 166.

97. *Alabama.*—Western Union Tel. Co. *v.* Westmoreland, 150 Ala. 654, 43 So. 790; Western Union Tel. Co. *v.* Haley, 143 Ala. 586, 39 So. 386.

Georgia.— Richmond Hosiery Mills *v.* Western Union Tel. Co., 123 Ga. 216, 51 S. E. 290; Glenn *v.* Western Union Tel. Co., 1 Ga. App. 821, 58 S. E. 83.

Indiana.— Western Union Tel. Co. *v.* Bryant, 17 Ind. App. 70, 46 N. E. 358.

Kentucky.—Denham *v.* Western Union Tel. Co., 87 S. W. 788, 27 Ky. L. Rep. 999.

Missouri.— Reynolds *v.* Western Union Tel. Co., 81 Mo. App. 223.

North Carolina.—Gerock *v.* Western Union Tel. Co., 147 N. C. 1, 60 S. E. 637; Hall *v.* Western Union Tel. Co., 139 N. C. 369, 52 S. E. 50.

Texas.— Western Union Tel. Co. *v.* Hendricks, 26 Tex. Civ. App. 366, 63 S. W. 341.

Wisconsin.— Hibbard *v.* Western Union Tel. Co., 33 Wis. 558, 14 Am. Rep. 775.

98. *Kentucky.*— Smith *v.* Western Union Tel. Co., 83 Ky. 104, 4 Am. St. Rep. 126.

Maine.— Merrill *v.* Western Union Tel. Co., 78 Me. 97, 2 Atl. 847.

North Carolina.— Cherokee Tanning Extract Co. *v.* Western Union Tel. Co., 143 N. C. 376, 55 S. E. 777; Walser *v.* Western Union Tel. Co., 114 N. C. 440, 19 S. E. 366.

West Virginia.— Beatty Lumber Co. *v.* Western Union Tel. Co., 52 W. Va. 410, 44 S. E. 309.

United States.— Western Union Tel. Co. *v.* Williams, 163 Fed. 513, 90 C. C. A. 143.

See 45 Cent. Dig. tit. "Telegraphs and Telephones," § 66.

99. Western Union Tel. Co. *v.* Lawson, 66 Kan. 660, 72 Pac. 283, holding that the charges of transmission constitute actual and not nominal damages.

1. *Alabama.*—Western Union Tel. Co. *v.* Crumpton, 138 Ala. 632, 36 So. 517.

Kansas.— Western Union Tel. Co. *v.* Lawson, 66 Kan. 660, 72 Pac. 283.

Kentucky.— Taliferro *v.* Western Union Tel. Co., 54 S. W. 825, 21 Ky. L. Rep. 1290, nominal damages, including the price of the telegram.

Minnesota.— Beaupré *v.* Pacific, etc., Tel. Co., 21 Minn. 155.

Missouri.— Abeles *v.* Western Union Tel. Co., 37 Mo. App. 554.

North Carolina.— Kennon *v.* Western Union Tel. Co., 126 N. C. 232, 35 S. E. 468.

Texas.— Western Union Tel. Co. *v.* Adams, 75 Tex. 531, 12 S. W. 857, 16 Am. St. Rep. 920, 6 L. R. A. 844.

See 45 Cent. Dig. tit. "Telegraphs and Telephones," § 73.

Whether the action is in contract or in tort if the company has negligently failed to deliver a message the sender is entitled to recover as actual damage the amount paid for its transmission. Western Union Tel. Co. *v.* Westmoreland, 150 Ala. 654, 43 So. 790.

2. Bass *v.* Postal Tel.-Cable Co., 127 Ga. 423, 56 S. E. 465, holding that if no charges were actually paid, plaintiff cannot recover the same on the ground that he had assumed

tinction should be made between messages which are wholly unintelligible and those which disclose their importance and general character or purpose,[21] particularly where they show that they relate to a business transaction,[22] it being held that notice of the main purpose is sufficient to charge the company with notice of attendant details.[23]

(IV) *MESSAGES RELATING TO BUSINESS TRANSACTIONS.* It has frequently been held that if a message shows that it relates to a business transaction it is not necessary, in order to render the company liable for more than nominal damages, that the company should be advised of the details of the transaction to which the message relates,[24] it being sufficient if it discloses its general character and purpose,[25] and the fact that trade terms and abbreviations are used does not make it a cipher message.[26] So it has been held that the actual loss as far as it is the proximate result of the company's negligence is recoverable if the message contains sufficient, when read in the light of well-known usage in commercial correspondence, to apprise the telegraph company that it is an order to buy or to sell or to close a pending trade or option, or an offer of a definite contract, or the acceptance of such an offer.[27] It will be observed, however, that a

So. 746 ("Send Eckford on first train this evening. Am here. Answer"). See also Western Union Tel. Co. *v.* Pearce, 82 Miss. 487, 34 So. 152.

Missouri.— Melson *v.* Western Union Tel. Co., 72 Mo. App. 111. "If possible come to Shelbina in the morning."

New York.— Baldwin *v.* U. S. Telegraph Co., 45 N. Y. 744, 6 Am. Rep. 165 ("Telegraph me at Rochester what that well is doing"); Landsberger *v.* Magnetic Tel. Co., 32 Barb. 530 ("Get ten thousand dollars of the Mail Company"); McColl *v.* Western Union Tel. Co., 44 N. Y. Super. Ct. 487, 7 Abb. N. Cas. 151, 1 Am. Elec. Cas. 280 ("Can close Valkyria and Othere twenty-two, twenty net Montreal. Ans. immediately").

Oklahoma.— Western Union Tel. Co. *v.* Pratt, 18 Okla. 274, 89 Pac. 237, "High water, expense heavy, send ten dollars; funds low."

Texas.— Western Union Tel. Co. *v.* True, 101 Tex. 236, 106 S. W. 315 [*reversing* (Civ. App. 1907) 103 S. W. 1180] ("Parties failed arrange deal. If you want cattle come here"); Elliott *v.* Western Union Tel. Co., 75 Tex. 18, 12 S. W. 954, 16 Am. St. Rep. 872 (message directing immediate shipment of saw; plaintiff's mill idle); Western Union Tel. Co. *v.* Twaddell, 47 Tex. Civ. App. 51, 103 S. W. 1120.

United States.— Primrose *v.* Western Union Tel. Co., 154 U. S. 1, 14 S. Ct. 1098, 38 L. ed. 883 ("Despot am exceedingly busy bay all kinds quo perhaps bracken half of it mince moment promptly of purchase"); Western Union Tel. Co. *v.* Coggin, 68 Fed. 137, 15 C. C. A. 231 ("Be on hand evening of third. I got early"); Behm *v.* Western Union Tel. Co., 3 Fed. Cas. No. 1,234, 8 Biss. 131, 7 Reporter 710 ("Take separate deed to Marks for White Fountaine, Tippecanoe and Iowa, 4, and meet me at office at 9 to-night").

See 45 Cent. Dig. tit. "Telegraphs and Telephones," § 65.

21. Postal Tel.-Cable Co. *v.* Lathrop, 33 Ill. App. 400 [*affirmed* in 131 Ill. 575, 23 N. E. 583, 19 Am. St. Rep. 55, 7 L. R. A. 474]; Western Union Tel. Co. *v.* Nagle, 11 Tex. Civ. App. 539, 32 S. W. 707.

22. See *infra*, IX, B, 1, a, (IV).

23. Western Union Tel. Co. *v.* Edsall, 74 Tex. 329, 12 S. W. 41, 15 Am. St. Rep. 835; Western Union Tel. Co. *v.* Nagle, 11 Tex. Civ. App. 539, 32 S. W. 707.

24. Western Union Tel. Co. *v.* Merritt, 55 Fla. 462, 46 So. 1024, 127 Am. St. Rep. 169; Postal Tel.-Cable Co. *v.* Lathrop, 33 Ill. App. 400 [*affirmed* in 131 Ill. 575, 23 N. E. 583, 19 Am. St. Rep. 55, 7 L. R. A. 474]; Texas, etc., Tel., etc., Co. *v.* Mackenzie, 36 Tex. Civ. App. 178, 81 S. W. 581; Western Union Tel. Co. *v.* Nagle, 11 Tex. Civ. App. 539, 32 S. W. 707.

It is sufficient under some of the authorities if there is enough on the face of the message to show that it is a commercial message of value. Western Union Tel. Co. *v.* Blanchard, 68 Ga. 299, 45 Am. Rep. 480.

25. Postal Tel.-Cable Co. *v.* Lathrop, 33 Ill. App. 400 [*affirmed* in 131 Ill. 575, 23 N. E. 583, 19 Am. St. Rep. 55, 7 L. R. A. 474]; Pepper *v.* Western Union Tel. Co., 87 Tenn. 554, 11 S. W. 783, 10 Am. St. Rep. 699, 4 L. R. A. 660; Western Union Tel. Co. *v.* Edsall, 74 Tex. 429, 12 S. W. 41, 15 Am. St. Rep. 835; Texas, etc., Tel., etc., Co. *v.* Mackenzie, 36 Tex. Civ. App. 178, 81 S. W. 581; Western Union Tel. Co. *v.* Nagle, 11 Tex. Civ. App. 539, 32 S. W. 707.

26. Pepper *v.* Western Union Tel. Co., 87 Tenn. 554, 11 S. W. 783, 10 Am. St. Rep. 699, 4 L. R. A. 660.

27. *District of Columbia.*— Fererro *v.* Western Union Tel. Co., 9 App. Cas. 455, "Fifty-five cents, usual terms, quick acceptance."

Florida.— Western Union Tel. Co. *v.* Merritt, 55 Fla. 462, 46 So. 1024, 127 Am. St. Rep. 169.

Georgia.— Western Union Tel. Co. *v.* Blanchard, 68 Ga. 299, 45 Am. Rep. 480, "Cover two hundred September and one hundred August."

plaintiff's broker to buy or to sell short is delayed and the transaction directed is never entered into;[44] but where there is an actual purchase at a higher price than plaintiff would have had to pay if the message had been promptly delivered, there is an actual loss for which a recovery may be had.[45]

(III) *INTERVENING EFFICIENT CAUSES.* If, notwithstanding the negligence of the telegraph company, the loss would not have occurred had it not been for the subsequent operation of a new intervening efficient cause for which the telegraph company is not responsible and over which it has no control,[46] such as a storm or flood,[47] or the felonious,[48] fraudulent,[49] or negligent [50] act of another party, the telegraph company's breach of duty is not the proximate cause of the loss.[51]

(IV) *LOSSES WHICH PLAINTIFF MIGHT HAVE PREVENTED.* It is the duty of plaintiff on learning of the negligence of the telegraph company to make reasonable efforts to render the resulting damage as light as possible,[52] and he cannot recover damages which by such care and diligence he could have avoided.[53]

Where a message notifying plaintiff of a purchase of stocks for him by his brokers is not delivered and the market subsequently declines beyond the amount of his margin and he is closed out, he cannot recover actual damages on the theory that if he had been notified of the purchase he would have sold earlier or put up more margin. Smith *v.* Western Union Tel. Co., 83 Ky. 104, 4 Am. St. Rep. 126.

44. Western Union Tel. Co. *v.* Fellner, 58 Ark. 29, 22 S. W. 917, 41 Am. St. Rep. 81; Hibbard *v.* Western Union Tel. Co., 33 Wis. 558, 14 Am. Rep. 775; Western Union Tel. Co. *v.* Hall, 124 U. S. 444, 8 S. Ct. 577, 31 L. ed. 479; Cahn *v.* Western Union Tel. Co., 48 Fed. 810, 1 C. C. A. 107.

Although there is an advance in the market price so that plaintiff if the purchase had been made might have resold at a profit, there is no presumption that he would have done so. Western Union Tel. Co. *v.* Fellner, 58 Ark. 29, 22 S. W. 917, 41 Am. St. Rep. 81.

45. Pearsall *v.* Western Union Tel. Co., 124 N. Y. 256, 26 N. E. 534, 21 Am. St. Rep. 662; U. S. Telegraph Co. *v.* Wenger, 55 Pa. St. 262, 93 Am. Dec. 751; Swan *v.* Western Union Tel. Co., 129 Fed. 318, 63 C. C. A. 550, 67 L. R. A. 153.

46. Lowery *v.* Western Union Tel. Co., 60 N. Y. 198, 19 Am. Rep. 154; Ross *v.* Western Union Tel. Co., 81 Fed. 676, 26 C. C. A. 564; Bodkin *v.* Western Union Tel. Co., 31 Fed. 134.

47. Bodkin *v.* Western Union Tel. Co., 31 Fed. 134.

48. Lowery *v.* Western Union Tel. Co., 60 N. Y. 198, 19 Am. Rep. 154; Ross *v.* Western Union Tel. Co., 81 Fed. 676, 26 C. C. A. 564.

49. Strahorn-Hutton-Evans Commission Co. *v.* Western Union Tel. Co, 101 Mo. App. 500, 74 S. W. 876; Lowery *v.* Western Union Tel. Co., 60 N. Y. 198, 19 Am. Rep. 154.

50. Western Union Tel. Co. *v.* Briscoe, 18 Ind. App. 22, 47 N. E. 473; Higdon *v.* Western Union Tel. Co., 132 N. C. 726, 44 S. E. 558.

51. Ross *v.* Western Union Tel. Co., 81 Fed. 676, 26 C. C. A. 564; Bodkin *v.* Western Union Tel. Co., 31 Fed. 134. And see cases cited *supra*, notes 46–50.

52. Western Union Tel. Co. *v.* Reid, 83 Ga. 401, 10 S. E. 919; Postal Tel. Cable Co. *v.* Schaefer, 110 Ky. 907, 62 S. W. 1119, 23 Ky. L. Rep. 344; Jones *v.* Western Union Tel. Co., 75 S. C. 208, 55 S. E. 318; Western Union Tel. Co. *v.* Jeanes, 88 Tex. 230, 31 S. W. 186. See also, generally, DAMAGES, 13 Cyc. 71.

53. *Alabama.*—Western Union Tel. Co. *v.* Way, 83 Ala. 542, 4 So. 844; Daughtery *v.* American Union Tel. Co., 75 Ala. 168, 51 Am. Rep. 435.

Arkansas.— Brewster *v.* Western Union Tel. Co., 65 Ark. 537, 47 S. W. 560.

California.— Germain Fruit Co. *v.* Western Union Tel. Co., 137 Cal. 598, 70 Pac. 658, 59 L. R. A. 575.

District of Columbia.— Fererro *v.* Western Union Tel. Co., 9 App. Cas. 455, 35 L. R. A. 548.

Georgia.— Western Union Tel. Co. *v.* Reid, 83 Ga. 401, 10 S. E. 919. See also Haber, etc., Hat Co. *v.* Southern Bell Tel., etc., Co., 118 Ga. 874, 45 S. E. 696; Western Union Tel. Co. *v.* Bailey, 115 Ga. 725, 42 S. E. 89, 61 L. R. A. 933.

Illinois.— Western Union Tel. Co. *v.* North Packing, etc., Co., 188 Ill. 366, 58 N. E. 958, 52 L. R. A. 274; Western Union Tel. Co. *v.* Hart, 62 Ill. App. 120.

Indiana.— Western Union Tel. Co. *v.* Briscoe, 18 Ind. App. 22, 47 N. E. 473.

Iowa.— Hasbrouck *v.* Western Union Tel. Co., 107 Iowa 160, 77 N. W. 1034, 70 Am. St. Rep. 181.

Kentucky.— Western Union Tel. Co. *v.* Matthews, 113 Ky. 188, 67 S. W. 849, 24 Ky. L. Rep. 3; Postal Tel. Cable Co. *v.* Schaefer, 110 Ky. 907, 62 S. W. 1119, 23 Ky. L. Rep. 344.

Mississippi.— Shingleur *v.* Western Union Tel. Co., 72 Miss. 1030, 18 So. 425, 48 Am. St. Rep. 604, 30 L. R. A. 444.

Missouri.— Reynolds *v.* Western Union Tel. Co., 81 Mo. App. 223.

New York.— Rittenhouse *v.* Independent Tel. Line, 44 N. Y. 263, 4 Am. Rep. 673; Leonard *v.* New York, etc., Electro Magnetic Tel. Co., 41 N. Y. 544, 1 Am. Rep. 446.

Plaintiff is, however, required only to incur a reasonable amount of trouble and expense according to the circumstances of the particular case,[54] and it is not incumbent upon him to enter into litigation to rescind a contract which had already been entered into before the company's negligence was discovered.[55]

(v) *LOSSES WHICH MIGHT HAVE OCCURRED AT ALL EVENTS.* The loss is not, in the eye of the law, the proximate consequence of the telegraph company's negligence in a case where, even if the company had performed its duty, there can be no legal certainty that the loss would not still have occurred or the object of the message have been defeated.[56] Thus if the happening or preventing of the loss, even though the telegraph company had performed its duty, would still have been dependent on a speculative or contingent future event,[57] or on the voluntary action or inaction of the other party to the message,[58] or of plaintiff himself,[59] or of a third party,[60] where there was no obligation on the part of such party to act or not to act, it cannot be said with legal certainty that the loss was the result of the telegraph company's negligence.[61]

North Carolina.— Hocutt *v.* Western Union Tel. Co., 147 N. C. 186, 60 S. E. 980; Cranford *v.* Western Union Tel. Co., 138 N. C. 162, 50 S. C. 585.

Ohio.— Postal Tel. Cable Co. *v.* Akron Cereal Co., 23 Ohio Cir. Ct. 516.

South Carolina.— Cason *v.* Western Union Tel. Co., 77 S. C. 157, 57 S. E. 722; Key *v.* Western Union Tel. Co., 76 S. C. 301, 56 S. E. 962; Jones *v.* Western Union Tel. Co., 75 S. C. 208, 55 S. E. 318; Mitchiner *v.* Western Union Tel. Co., 75 S. C. 182, 55 S. E. 222; Willis *v.* Western Union Tel. Co., 69 S. C. 531, 48 S. E. 538, 104 Am. St. Rep. 828.

Tennessee.— Marr *v.* Western Union Tel. Co., 85 Tenn. 529, 3 S. W. 496.

Texas.— Western Union Tel. Co. *v.* Jeanes, 88 Tex. 230, 31 S. W. 186; Womack *v.* Western Union Tel. Co., 58 Tex. 176, 44 Am. Rep. 614; Mitchell *v.* Western Union Tel. Co., 23 Tex. Civ. App. 445, 56 S. W. 439; Western Union Tel. Co. *v.* Hearne, 7 Tex. Civ. App. 67, 26 S. W. 478. See also Western Union Tel. Co. *v.* Salter, (Civ. App. 1906) 95 S. W. 549.

Virginia.— Washington, etc., Tel. Co. *v.* Hobson, 15 Gratt. 122.

United States.— Western Union Tel. Co. *v.* Baker, 140 Fed. 315, 72 C. C. A. 87.

Allowance for expenses.— It being the duty of the addressee of a telegram to minimize the damages resulting from a telegraph company's negligent delay in delivery, he may recover for his expense in lessening such damage. Postal Tel. Co. *v.* Levy, (Tex. Civ. App. 1907) 102 S. W. 134.

54. Western Union Tel. Co. *v.* Witt, 110 S. W. 889, 33 Ky. L. Rep. 685.

55. Hasbrouck *v.* Western Union Tel. Co., 107 Iowa 160, 77 N. W. 1034, 70 Am. St. Rep. 181; Reed *v.* Western Union Tel. Co., 135 Mo. 661, 37 S. W. 904, 58 Am. St. Rep. 609, 34 L. R. A. 492.

56. Bashinsky *v.* Western Union Tel. Co., 1 Ga. App. 761, 58 S. E. 91; Cherokee Tanning Extract Co. *v.* Western Union Tel. Co., 143 N. C. 376, 55 S. E. 777; Clio Gin Co. *v.* Western Union Tel. Co., 82 S. C. 405, 64 S. E. 426; Bird *v.* Western Union Tel. Co., 76 S. C. 345, 56 S. E. 973; Beatty Lumber Co. *v.* Western Union Tel. Co., 52 W. Va. 410, 44 S. E. 309.

57. Western Union Tel. Co. *v.* Crall, 39 Kan. 580, 18 Pac. 719 (whether P's horse would have won a trotting race); Chapman *v.* Western Union Tel. Co., 90 Ky. 265, 13 S. W. 880, 12 Ky. L. Rep. 265 (whether P's father would have given him a note); Rich Grain Distilling Co. *v.* Western Union Tel. Co., 13 Ky. L. Rep. 256 (what profits, if any, would have been made by the operation of a plant); Barnesville First Nat. Bank *v.* Western Union Tel. Co., 30 Ohio St. 555, 27 Am. Rep. 475 (whether personal property parted with under mistake could have been recovered); Martin *v.* Sunset Tel., etc., Co., 18 Wash. 260, 51 Pac. 376 (whether P would have succeeded in a lawsuit).

58. *Kentucky.*—Taliferro *v.* Western Union Tel. Co., 54 S. W. 825, 21 Ky. L. Rep. 1290.

New York.— Kiley *v.* Western Union Tel. Co., 39 Hun 158 [*affirmed* in 109 N. Y. 231, 16 N. E. 75].

North Carolina.— Newsome *v.* Western Union Tel. Co., 137 N. C. 513, 50 S. E. 279.

South Carolina.—Capers *v.* Western Union Tel. Co., 71 S. C. 29, 50 S. E. 537.

United States.— Western Union Tel. Co. *v.* Hall, 124 U. S. 444, 8 S. Ct. 577, 31 L. ed. 479.

59. *Alabama.*— Frazer *v.* Western Union Tel. Co., 84 Ala. 487, 4 So. 831.

Georgia.—Haber, etc., Hat Co. *v.* Southern Bell Tel., etc., Co.. 118 Ga. 874, 45 S. E. 696.

Kentucky.— Smith *v.* Western Union Tel. Co., 83 Ky. 104, 4 Am. St. Rep. 126.

New York.— Baldwin *v.* U. S. Telegraph Co., 45 N. Y. 744, 6 Am. Rep. 165; McColl *v.* Western Union Tel. Co., 44 N. Y. Super. Ct. 487, 7 Abb. N. Cas. 151, 1 Am. Elec. Cas. 280.

United States.— Alexander *v.* Western Union Tel. Co., 126 Fed. 445.

Message an offer see *infra*, **IX, B, 2, b.**

60. Kenyon *v.* Western Union Tel. Co., 100 Cal. 454, 35 Pac. 75; Postal Tel. Cable Co. *v.* Barwise, 11 Colo. App. 328, 53 Pac. 252; Walser *v.* Western Union Tel. Co., 114 N. C. 440, 19 S. E. 366.

61. Walser *v.* Western Union Tel. Co., 114 N. C. 440, 19 S. E. 366; Western Union Tel. Co. *v.* Connelly, 2 Tex. App. Civ. Cas. § 113.

proximate result of the failure duly to deliver the message.[4] Since, however, where a contract is made by an exchange of telegrams, the contract is ordinarily regarded as complete and binding on both parties from the instant the message of acceptance is delivered to the company for transmission,[5] it would seem that in the ordinary case of offer and acceptance by telegram the offeree, whose message of acceptance is delayed, has suffered no loss, since, notwithstanding the delay, the offerer is liable to him and must, on demand, perform the contract.[6] If the message of acceptance is not in all respects an unconditional acceptance it is, at best, no more than a counter offer, and is to be treated according to the principles which apply in the case of an original offer.[7]

d. Loss of a Mere Chance.[8] Plaintiff cannot recover on the theory that, if it had not been for the telegraph company's negligence, he might, and probably would, have reaped a benefit, when such benefit is in the nature of things speculative and contingent, and where it is impossible to show with legal certainty that plaintiff would have received the benefit had the message been duly delivered,[9] or in other words where he has lost only the mere chance or possibility of making something.[10] Thus it has been held that plaintiff cannot ask the jury to speculate as to whether, had it not been for the telegraph company's negligence, his horse would have won a prize purse at a trotting race;[11] whether his father, had he reached him before death, would have given him a note;[12] whether, had he received a message from his failing debtor inviting him to come, the debtor would voluntarily have given him security;[13] or whether, had he received the information contained in the message at the time it should have been received, he would have been able to recover money previously paid out,[14] or property delivered.[15]

e. Loss of a Sale. Where within the principles previously discussed the neg-

4. *Alabama.*—Western Union Tel. Co. *v.* Way, 83 Ala. 542, 4 So. 844, 2 Am. Elec. Cas. 467.

Arkansas.—Western Union Tel. Co. *v.* Hoyt, 89 Ark. 118, 115 S. W. 941.

Georgia.—Dodd Grocery Co. *v.* Postal Tel. Co., 112 Ga. 685, 37 S. E. 981.

Illinois.—Western Union Tel. Co. *v.* Kemp, 55 Ill. App. 583.

Iowa.—Lucas *v.* Western Union Tel. Co., 131 Iowa 669, 109 N. W. 191, 6 L. R. A. N. S. 1016.

Maine.—True *v.* International Tel. Co., 60 Me. 9, 11 Am. Rep. 156.

Massachusetts.—Squire *v.* Western Union Tel. Co., 98 Mass. 232, 93 Am. Dec. 157.

Missouri.—Elam *v.* Western Union Tel. Co., 113 Mo. App. 538, 88 S. W. 115.

Texas.—Western Union Tel. Co. *v.* Turner, 94 Tex. 304, 60 S. W. 452; Western Union Tel. Co. *v.* Bowen, 84 Tex. 476, 19 S. W. 554. See also Western Union Tel. Co. *v.* T. H. Thompson Milling Co., 41 Tex. Civ. App. 223, 91 S. W. 307.

United States.—Purdom Naval Stores Co. *v.* Western Union Tel. Co., 153 Fed. 327.

An order for goods made pursuant to an offer previously made by the addressee to sell the same constitutes an acceptance of the offer. Elam *v.* Western Union Tel. Co., 113 Mo. App. 538, 88 S. W. 115.

5. See CONTRACTS, 9 Cyc. 295.

6. Western Union Tel. Co. *v.* Davis, (Tex. Civ. App. 1902) 70 S. W. 784. See also Western Union Tel. Co. *v.* Turner, 94 Tex. 304, 60 S. W. 432, holding, however, that the telegraph company has no right to suppose that the filing of the message of acceptance will close the trade so that no damage will result from a failure to deliver it, and if by the terms of the contract a delivery of the message of acceptance is necessary to complete the same the company will be liable in case of a non-delivery.

Where an offer made by letter is accepted by telegram, neither party is bound until the telegram is delivered, and the delay of the telegram therefore may be the proximate cause of the failure of the contract. Lucas *v.* Western Union Tel. Co., 131 Iowa 669, 109 N. W. 191, 6 L. R. A. N. S. 1016.

7. Cherokee Tanning Extract Co. *v.* Western Union Tel. Co., 143 N. C. 376, 55 S. E. 777; Western Union Tel. Co. *v.* Burns, (Tex. Civ. App. 1902) 70 S. W. 784. See also Fisher *v.* Western Union Tel. Co., 119 Wis. 146, 96 N. W. 545; Kinghorne *v.* Montreal Tel. Co., 18 U. C. Q. B. 60.

Message a definite offer see *supra*, IX, B, 2, b.

8. See also *supra*, IX, B, 1, b.

9. Western Union Tel. Co. *v.* Crall, 39 Kan. 580, 18 Pac. 719; Chapman *v.* Western Union Tel. Co., 90 Ky. 265, 13 S. W. 880, 12 Ky. L. Rep. 265.

10. Clay *v.* Western Union Tel. Co., 81 Ga. 285, 6 S. E. 813, 12 Am. St. Rep. 316.

11. Western Union Tel. Co. *v.* Crall, 39 Kan. 580, 18 Pac. 719.

12. Chapman *v.* Western Union Tel. Co., 90 Ky. 265, 13 S. W. 880, 12 Ky. L. Rep. 265.

13. Hartstein *v.* Western Union Tel. Co., 89 Wis. 531, 62 N. W. 412.

14. Barnesville First Nat. Bank *v.* Western Union Tel. Co., 30 Ohio St. 555, 27 Am. Rep. 485, 1 Am. Elec. Cas. 221.

15. Western Union Tel. Co. *v.* Cornwell, 2 Colo. App. 491, 31 Pac. 393.

with the expense, if any, of keeping it in the meanwhile;[23] but where plaintiff resells to a different purchaser and seeks to recover the difference between the amount so received and the original contract price, it must appear that he resold for the best price obtainable under the circumstances.[24]

f. Loss of a Purchase. If by reason of the negligence of a telegraph company in regard to the transmission or delivery of a message a purchase is defeated resulting in a loss to plaintiff, the company will be liable.[25] The general rule is that the measure of damages is the difference between the contract price and the market value of the goods at the time and place of delivery;[26] and where as the result of the telegraph company's negligence the purchase is not lost but delayed, there may as a general rule be a recovery for the rise in market value of the subject-matter of the sale during the delay.[27] Where the message is from plaintiff to his agent, instructing him to purchase, and there is a negligent delay in transmission, plaintiff is entitled to recover the difference between the market price at the time when the message should have been delivered and the price at which the order was in fact executed;[28] and where such a message to an agent is never delivered at all, the measure of damages is the difference between the price mentioned in the message, at which the purchase could have been made had the message been promptly delivered, and the market price at the time plaintiff learned of the non-delivery;[29] but where the message is not a positive direction to the agent to purchase, but leaves the matter to his discretion, or where in fact the agent does not purchase when the message is actually received, and no transaction takes place, there can ordinarily be no recovery beyond nominal damages or the amount paid for transmitting the message.[30]

g. Loss of an Exchange. Where, instead of a sale or a purchase, the telegraph company's negligence causes plaintiff to lose a contract for the exchange of property, the measure of damages is the difference between the value of the property

23. *Arkansas.*— Hoyt *v.* Western Union Tel. Co., 85 Ark. 473, 108 S. W. 1056.

Georgia.—Western Union Tel. Co. *v.* James, 90 Ga. 254, 16 S. E. 83.

Iowa.— Herron *v.* Western Union Tel. Co., 90 Iowa 129, 57 N. W. 696.

Kentucky.— Blackburn *v.* Kentucky Cent. R. Co., 15 Ky. L. Rep. 303.

South Carolina.— Wallingford *v.* Western Union Tel. Co., 53 S. C. 410, 31 S. E. 275.

Utah.— Brooks *v.* Western Union Tel. Co., 26 Utah 147, 72 Pac. 499.

See 45 Cent. Dig. tit. "Telegraphs and Telephones," § 72.

24. Brooks *v.* Western Union Tel. Co., 26 Utah 147, 72 Pac. 499.

25. Alexander *v.* Western Union Tel. Co., 67 Miss. 386, 7 So. 280. See also cases cited *infra*, notes 26–29.

26. True *v.* International Tel. Co., 60 Me. 9, 11 Am. Rep. 156; Squire *v.* Western Union Tel. Co., 98 Mass. 232, 93 Am. Dec. 157; Alexander *v.* Western Union Tel. Co., 66 Miss. 161, 5 So. 397, 14 Am. St. Rep. 556, 3 L. R. A. 71; Western Union Tel. Co. *v.* Hall, 124 U. S. 444, 8 S. Ct. 577, 31 L. ed. 479; Purdom Naval Stores Co. *v.* Western Union Tel. Co., 153 Fed. 327. See also Western Union Tel. Co. *v.* Pells, 2 Tex. App. Civ. Cas. § 41. In Western Union Tel. Co. *v.* Hirsch, (Tex. Civ. App. 1904) 84 S. W. 394, a message offered plaintiffs an option on one hundred bales of cotton. Not receiving the message they bought the cotton in question, fifty bales at a higher price and the other fifty bales on the following day at a price still higher. Recovery was allowed only for the difference between the contract price and the market price at the time plaintiffs bought the first fifty bales, it being held that the subsequent fluctuations of the market could neither increase nor diminish the liability of defendant.

27. Gulf, etc., R. Co. *v.* Loonie, 82 Tex. 323, 18 S. W. 221, 27 Am. St. Rep. 891; Swan *v.* Western Union Tel. Co., 129 Fed. 318, 63 C. C. A. 550, 67 L. R. A. 153.

28. Dodd Grocery Co. *v.* Postal Tel.-Cable Co., 112 Ga. 685, 37 S. E. 981; Western Union Tel. Co. *v.* North Packing, etc., Co., 89 Ill. App. 301 [*affirmed* in 188 Ill. 366, 58 N. E. 958, 52 L. R. A. 274]; Pearsall *v.* Western Union Tel. Co., 124 N. Y. 256, 26 N. E. 534, 21 Am. St. Rep. 662]; Rittenhouse *v.* Independent Tel. Line, 44 N. Y. 263, 4 Am. Rep. 673; U. S. Telegraph Co. *v.* Wenger, 55 Pa. St. 262, 93 Am. Dec. 751.

29. Western Union Tel. Co. *v.* Carver, 15 Tex. Civ. App. 547, 39 S. W. 1021.

30. Western Union Tel. Co. *v.* Fellner, 58 Ark. 29, 22 S. W. 917, 41 Am. St. Rep. 81; Hibbard *v.* Western Union Tel. Co., 33 Wis. 558, 14 Am. Rep. 775; Western Union Tel. Co. *v.* Hall, 124 U. S. 444, 8 S. Ct. 577, 31 L. ed. 479. See also Brewster *v.* Western Union Tel. Co., 65 Ark. 537, 47 S. W. 560.

The damages are too remote, speculative, and contingent in such cases to authorize a recovery of more than nominal damages.

being recoverable unless an actual loss was sustained.[63] Where in a message quoting a price to plaintiff the price is changed to a larger amount, which is paid by plaintiff, it has been held that the measure of damages is the difference between the price as stated in the original message and the higher price paid by plaintiff;[64] but on the contrary it has been held that while plaintiff cannot recover more than this difference, he is not necessarily entitled to recover this amount,[65] his actual loss being the difference between the price paid and the market value of the property purchased.[66] Plaintiff is also entitled to recover the loss actually sus-

Where defendant agreed to furnish plaintiff correct market reports and furnished incorrect reports upon the faith of which he directed the purchase of grain to fill a contract for future delivery, the measure of damages has been held to be the difference between the price actually paid and the price as represented in the report. Turner *v.* Hawkeye Tel. Co., 41 Iowa 458, 20 Am. Rep. 605. But see Western Union Tel. Co. *v.* Bradford, (Tex. Civ. App. 1908) 114 S. W. 686, holding that the measure of damages in such a case is the difference between the incorrect price quoted and the correct market price on the day when the price was furnished. Where plaintiff, who was engaged in buying cattle for the Chicago market, had an arrangement with the dealers there through whom he sold, to furnish him market prices on request unless there was no change in prices since their last report, in which case no answer to his inquiry was to be sent, and on a failure to receive a reply to a request for prices he bought on the basis of the prices last quoted, it was held that the measure of damages was the difference between the Chicago market prices last quoted and the market price on the day of such purchase. Garrett *v.* Western Union Tel. Co., 92 Iowa 449, 58 N. W. 1064, 60 N. W. 644. Where by reason of an error in a message from plaintiff to his agent directing the purchase of a certain amount of cotton, the agent purchases a larger amount, the measure of damages is the amount lost on resale of the excess at the market price including the commissions of the agent who purchased it. Washington, etc., Tel. Co. *v.* Hobson, 15 Gratt. (Va.) 122. Where in a message ordering goods the telegraph company changed the name of the addressee and delivered the message to plaintiff, who filled the order, whereupon the sender of the message refused to accept the goods, which being perishable were entirely lost, the measure of plaintiff's damages is the value of the goods and the amount paid for transportation. Elsey *v.* Postal Tel. Co., 15 Daly (N. Y.) 58, 3 N. Y. Suppl. 117.

63. Mickelwait *v.* Western Union Tel. Co., 113 Iowa 177, 84 N. W. 1038.

No damages.—Where a message addressed to plaintiff offering twenty and one-half cents for grain was changed in transmission to twenty-one and one-half cents, and after the order was filled the sender refused to pay over twenty and one-half cents, and it was delivered to him at that price, it was held that plaintiff was not damaged if he procured the grain and filled the order at less than twenty and one-half unless the work of procuring it was worth more than this margin of profit. Mickelwait *v.* Western Union Tel. Co., 113 Iowa 177, 84 N. W. 1038. Where an incorrect transmission of a message induced plaintiff to sell shares of stock but he received the full market value therefor, it was held that he could not recover more than the cost of the message, the market value of stock, nothing else appearing, being the actual value thereof. Hughes *v.* Western Union Tel. Co., 114 N. C. 70, 19 S. E. 100, 41 Am. St. Rep. 782. Where a message directing plaintiff's broker to purchase a certain number of bales of July cotton was changed so as to direct a purchase of January cotton, which was made, and plaintiff elected to stand upon the contract as made and afterward closed out at a profit, it was held that he could not recover any damages, having made an actual profit, and any additional profits that might have been made on July cotton being too remote, speculative, and contingent to authorize a recovery. James *v.* Western Union Tel. Co., 86 Ark. 339, 111 S. W. 276.

64. Western Union Tel. Co. *v.* Dubois, 128 Ill. 248, 21 N. E. 4, 15 Am. St. Rep. 109; Bowie *v.* Western Union Tel. Co., 78 S. C. 424, 59 S. E. 65 (where a message quoting flour to plaintiff at four dollars and thirty cents per barrel was changed to four dollars and sixty cents, which plaintiff paid, and he was allowed to recover on the basis of the difference between these prices, although he had resold the flour at four dollars and forty cents); Hays *v.* Western Union Tel. Co., 70 S. C. 16, 48 S. E. 608, 106 Am. St. Rep. 731, 67 L. R. A. 481. See also Western Union Tel. Co. *v.* McCants, (Miss. 1908) 46 So. 535, where a message directing plaintiff's agent to purchase at a certain price was changed so as to authorize a purchase at a higher price, no recovery, however, being allowed on any excess of quantity purchased by the agent over that authorized.

65. Western Union Tel. Co. *v.* Spivey, 98 Tex. 308, 83 S. W. 364, holding that the difference between the price quoted in the original message and the higher price paid is the proper measure of damages only where it happens that the price so paid is the exact value of the goods bought. See also Western Union Tel. Co. *v.* Bell, 24 Tex. Civ. App. 572, 59 S. W. 918, holding that a complaint which does not allege that plaintiff has resold the goods or that they are not worth as much as he paid for them does not show that plaintiff has sustained any loss.

66. Western Union Tel. Co. *v.* Spivey, 98 Tex. 308, 83 S. W. 364. See also Western

r. Money Transfer Messages. Where the telegraph company undertakes, for a consideration, to pay a sum of money to a person at a distant point, and fails to perform its contract, the measure of damages ordinarily is interest on the money from the time of default until tender.[95] There can be no recovery for mental distress, even in a mental anguish state;[96] nor can there be a recovery of special damages based on the fact that as a result of the failure to receive the money in due time plaintiff was evicted from home,[97] or was injured in reputation,[98] or lost credit,[99] such special damages as a rule being deemed too remote, and not within the contemplation of the parties at the time the contract for the transfer of the money was made;[1] but the company may have notice of facts and circumstances such as to render it liable for special damages.[2]

3. Mental Anguish — a. In General. At common law there can as a rule be no recovery of compensatory damages for mental suffering unaccompanied by physical injury,[3] unless resulting from the wilful or malicious wrong of defendant,[4] and in opposition to a doctrine now recognized in some jurisdictions,[5] it has been vigorously maintained that there is no sufficient reason or justification for making an exception to the common-law rule in the case of actions against telegraph companies.[6] It is accordingly held in most jurisdictions that in such cases there can be no recovery for mental anguish, although by reason of the company's negligence or default in regard to the transmission or delivery of a message plaintiff is prevented from seeing a near relative before death or from being present at the funeral.[7] Even in these jurisdictions, however, there may be a recovery for

Co. *v.* Powell, (Tex. Civ. App. 1909) 118 S. W. 226.

95. Robinson *v.* Western Union Tel. Co., 68 S. W. 656, 24 Ky. L. Rep. 452, 57 L. R. A. 611; Smith *v.* Western Union Tel. Co., 150 Pa. St. 561, 24 Atl. 1049; De Voegler *v.* Western Union Tel. Co., 10 Tex. Civ. App. 229, 30 S. W. 1107; Ricketts *v.* Western Union Tel. Co., 10 Tex. Civ. App. 226, 30 S. W. 1105; Stansell *v.* Western Union Tel. Co., 107 Fed. 668. See also Gooch *v.* Western Union Tel. Co., 90 S. W. 587, 28 Ky. L. Rep. 828; Cason *v.* Western Union Tel. Co., 77 S. C. 157, 57 S. E. 722.

96. See *infra*, IX, B, 3, d, (I).

97. Stansell *v.* Western Union Tel. Co., 107 Fed. 668.

98. Capers *v.* Western Union Tel. Co., 71 S. C. 29, 50 S. E. 537; Stansell *v.* Western Union Tel. Co., 107 Fed. 668.

99. Smith *v.* Western Union Tel. Co., 150 Pa. St. 561, 24 Atl. 1049.

1. Stansell *v.* Western Union Tel. Co., 107 Fed. 668. See also cases cited *supra*, notes 97–99.

2. Western Union Tel. Co. *v.* Wells, 50 Fla. 474, 39 So. 838, 111 Am. St. Rep. 129, 2 L. R. A. N. S. 1072.

3. Francis *v.* Western Union Tel. Co., 58 Minn. 252, 59 N. W. 1078, 49 Am. St. Rep. 507, 25 L. R. A. 406; Western Union Tel. Co. *v.* Rogers, 68 Miss. 748, 9 So. 823, 24 Am. St. Rep. 300, 13 L. R. A. 859; Connelly *v.* Western Union Tel. Co., 100 Va. 51, 40 S. E. 618, 93 Am. St. Rep. 919, 56 L. R. A. 663; Western Union Tel. Co. *v.* Sklar, 126 Fed. 295, 61 C. C. A. 281. See also Damages, 13 Cyc. 39–46.

4. See Western Union Tel. Co. *v.* Rogers, 68 Miss. 748, 9 So. 823, 24 Am. St. Rep. 300, 13 L. R. A. 859; and, generally, **Damages**, 13 Cyc. 44.

5. See *infra*, IX, B, 3, b.

6. *Georgia*.— Chapman *v.* Western Union Tel. Co., 88 Ga. 763, 15 S. E. 901, 30 Am. St. Rep. 183, 17 L. R. A. 430.

Indiana.— Western Union Tel. Co. *v.* Ferguson, 157 Ind. 64, 60 N. E. 674, 1080, 54 L. R. A. 846.

Minnesota.— Francis *v.* Western Union Tel. Co., 58 Minn. 252, 59 N. W. 1078, 49 Am. St. Rep. 507, 25 L. R. A. 406.

Mississippi.— Western Union Tel. Co. *v.* Rogers, 68 Miss. 748, 9 So. 823, 24 Am. St. Rep. 300, 13 L. R. A. 859.

Virginia.— Connelly *v.* Western Union Tel. Co., 100 Va. 51, 40 S. E. 618, 93 Am. St. Rep. 919, 56 L. R. A. 663.

United States.— Western Union Tel. Co. *v.* Sklar, 126 Fed. 295, 61 C. C. A. 281.

See 45 Cent. Dig. tit. "Telegraphs and Telephones," §§ 69, 70.

7. *Arkansas*.— Peay *v.* Western Union Tel. Co., 64 Ark. 538, 43 S. W. 965, 39 L. R. A. 463. Rule changed by statute see *infra*, IX, B, 3, b.

Dakota.— Russell *v.* Western Union Tel. Co., 3 Dak. 315, 19 N. W. 408.

Florida.— International Ocean Tel. Co. *v.* Saunders, 32 Fla. 434, 14 So. 148, 21 L. R. A. 810.

Georgia.— Seifert *v.* Western Union Tel. Co., 129 Ga. 181, 58 S. E. 699, 121 Am. St. Rep. 210, 11 L. R. A. N. S. 1149; Chapman *v.* Western Union Tel. Co., 88 Ga. 763, 15 S. E. 901, 30 Am. St. Rep. 183, 17 L. R. A. 430; Glenn *v.* Western Union Tel. Co., 1 Ga. App. 821, 58 S. E. 83.

Illinois.— Western Union Tel. Co. *v.* Haltom, 71 Ill. App. 63.

Indiana.— Western Union Tel. Co. *v.* Ferguson, 157 Ind. 64, 60 N. E. 674, 1080, 54 L. R. A. 846 [*overruling* Reese *v.* Western Union Tel. Co., 123 Ind. 294, 24 N. E. 163,

in regard to its application,[23] which in recent cases they have expressed a disinclination to extend beyond the limitations established by the earlier decisions.[24] Some of these rules and limitations grow out of the general principles previously stated,[25] requiring that the damages recoverable must be the proximate result of the negligence or default complained of,[26] and reasonably within the contemplation of the parties,[27] while others are of a more or less arbitrary character.[28] The cases are not entirely uniform in the different states, or even in the same state, as to the proper applications and limitation of the doctrine,[29] and applications or limitations recognized in some states have been expressly disapproved in others.[30] So in some cases it has been said that the doctrine should be limited to cases where the message related to a matter of sickness or death,[31] and, even in cases of this character, to cases where there was a close family relationship between the parties,[32] and where plaintiff was prevented from being present at the last illness or funeral of his relative.[33] In other cases it is held that the doctrine is not limited to messages relating to sickness or death,[34] but should be restricted

23. *Alabama.*—Western Union Tel. Co. *v.* Ayers, 131 Ala. 391, 31 So. 78, 90 Am. St. Rep. 92.

Arkansas.—Western Union Tel. Co. *v.* Shenep, 83 Ark. 476, 104 S. W. 154, 12 L. R. A. N. S. 886.

Indiana.—Western Union Tel. Co. *v.* Stratemeier, 6 Ind. App. 125, 32 N. E. 871.

Kentucky.—Lee *v.* Western Union Tel. Co., 130 Ky. 202, 113 S. W. 55; Robinson *v.* Western Union Tel. Co., 68 S. W. 656, 24 Ky. L. Rep. 452.

South Carolina.—Capers *v.* Western Union Tel. Co., 71 S. C. 29, 50 S. E. 537.

Tennessee.—Western Union Tel. Co. *v.* McCaul, 115 Tenn. 99, 90 S. W. 856.

Texas.—Western Union Tel. Co. *v.* Arnold, 96 Tex. 493, 73 S. W. 1043; Western Union Tel. Co. *v.* Edmondson, 91 Tex. 206, 42 S. W. 549; Rowell *v.* Western Union Tel. Co., 75 Tex. 26, 12 S. W. 534; Western Union Tel. Co. *v.* Reed, 37 Tex. Civ. App. 445, 84 S. W. 296.

24. Western Union Tel. Co. *v.* Ayers, 131 Ala. 391, 31 So. 78, 90 Am. St. Rep. 92; Western Union Tel. Co. *v.* Stratemeier, 6 Ind. App. 125, 32 N. E. 871; Western Union Tel. Co. *v.* McCaul, 115 Tenn. 99, 90 S. W. 856; Western Union Tel. Co. *v.* Edmondson, 91 Tex. 206, 42 S. W. 549; Western Union Tel. Co. *v.* Reed, 37 Tex. Civ. App. 445, 84 S. W. 296.

25. See *supra*, IX, B, 1.

26. See *infra*, IX, B, 3, d, (IV).

27. See *infra*, IX, B, 3, d, (III).

28. Western Union Tel. Co. *v.* Ayers, 131 Ala. 391, 31 So. 78, 90 Am. St. Rep. 92; Lee *v.* Western Union Tel. Co., 130 Ky. 202, 113 S. W. 55; Robinson *v.* Western Union Tel. Co., 68 S. W. 656, 24 Ky. L. Rep. 452; Western Union Tel. Co. *v.* McCaul, 115 Tenn. 99, 90 S. W. 856.

In Tennessee the rule has been stated, in a recent case, that mental anguish may be recovered for being deprived of the privilege of attending the bedside of a near relative during his last hours, or of superintending the preparations for his interment or of being present at the burial, but in no other cases. Western Union Tel. Co. *v.* McCaul, 115 Tenn. 99, 90 S. W. 856.

29. See Western Union Tel. Co. *v.* Henderson, 89 Ala. 510, 7 So. 419, 18 Am. St. Rep. 148; Western Union Tel. Co. *v.* Hollingsworth, (Ark. 1907) 102 S. W. 681, 11 L. R. A. N. S. 497; Western Union Tel. Co. *v.* Reid, 120 Ky. 231, 85 S. W. 1171, 27 Ky. L. Rep. 659, 70 L. R. A. 289.

30. Western Union Tel. Co. *v.* Ayers, 131 Ala. 391, 31 So. 78, 90 Am. St. Rep. 92; Western Union Tel. Co. *v.* Hollingsworth, (Ark. 1907) 102 S. W. 681, 11 L. R. A. N. S. 497; Western Union Tel. Co. *v.* Moxley, 80 Ark. 554, 98 S. W. 112; Western Union Tel. Co. *v.* Arnold, 96 Tex. 493, 73 S. W. 1043.

31. Western Union Tel. Co. *v.* Sledge, 153 Ala. 291, 45 So. 59; Western Union Tel. Co. *v.* Westmoreland, 151 Ala. 319, 44 So. 382; Western Union Tel. Co. *v.* McCaul, 115 Tenn. 99, 90 S. W. 856.

32. Western Union Tel. Co. *v.* Ayers, 131 Ala. 391, 31 So. 78, 90 Am. St. Rep. 92; Lee *v.* Western Union Tel. Co., 130 Ky. 202, 113 S. W. 55.

Relationship between parties see *infra*, IX, B, 3, d, (VI).

33. Western Union Tel. Co. *v.* McCaul, 115 Tenn. 99, 90 S. W. 856.

If plaintiff was not prevented from being present at the funeral, he cannot recover for mental anguish suffered from the uncertainty as to whether the funeral would be postponed in order to permit him to be present. Western Union Tel. Co. *v.* Reed, 37 Tex. Civ. App. 445, 84 S. W. 296.

34. Western Union Tel. Co. *v.* Hanley, 85 Ark. 263, 107 S. W. 1168; Thurman *v.* Western Union Tel. Co., 127 Ky. 137, 105 S. W. 155, 32 Ky. L. Rep. 26, 14 L. R. A. N. S. 499; Postal Tel. Cable Co. *v.* Terrell, 124 Ky. 822, 100 S. W. 292, 14 L. R. A. N. S. 927; Dayvis *v.* Western Union Tel. Co., 139 N. C. 79, 51 S. E. 898; Green *v.* Western Union Tel. Co., 136 N. C. 489, 49 S. E. 165, 103 Am. St. Rep. 955, 67 L. R. A. 985; Western Union Tel. Co. *v.* Burgess, (Tex. Civ. App. 1900) 56 S. W. 237.

Recovery allowed.—Where plaintiff was expecting the arrival of his wife and children on a certain train, it was held that he might recover for mental anguish due to the nondelivery of a telegram from his wife notify-

body or funeral preparations.[75] In such cases it has been held that there may be a recovery if the relationship between the parties is close, such as that of husband and wife, parent and child, or brother and sister,[76] or even that of grandparent and grandchild; [77] but that there can be no recovery where the relationship is merely by marriage or a remote blood relationship,[78] or the parties are merely engaged to be married; [79] and while in some cases the rule is stated that there can be no recovery in cases of a remote family relationship unless the company had notice of some special relations between the parties from which mental anguish would be likely to result,[80] in others the rule seems to be applied arbitrarily,[81] regardless of any special relations of intimacy or affection.[82] In other cases, however, it is held that the right of recovery does not depend upon the technical relationship or legal status of the parties, but upon the actual relations and state of feeling between them,[83] and that while there is no presumption of mental anguish in the case of a remote family relationship,[84] yet if such suffering does in fact result it may be shown and damages recovered therefor.[85] As to whether the company must have notice of the relationship there is some conflict of authority,[86] it being held in some cases that if the message shows that it is urgent, as where

75. Western Union Tel. Co. *v.* McMorris, 158 Ala. 563, 48 So. 349, 132 Am. St. Rep. 46. See also *infra*, IX, B, 3, d, (x), (c).

76. Western Union Tel. Co. *v.* Benson, 159 Ala. 254, 48 So. 712; Western Union Tel. Co. *v.* McMorris, 158 Ala. 563, 48 So. 349, 132 Am. St. Rep. 46; Western Union Tel. Co. *v.* Heathcoat, 149 Ala. 623, 43 So. 117; Western Union Tel. Co. *v.* De Andrea, 45 Tex. Civ. App. 395, 100 S. W. 977.

If the deceased is plaintiff's child, even though an infant, a recovery is allowed. Western Union Tel. Co. *v.* De Andrea, 45 Tex. Civ. App. 395, 100 S. W. 977.

77. Western Union Tel. Co. *v.* Prevatt, 149 Ala. 617, 43 So. 106; Doster *v.* Western Union Tel. Co., 77 S. C. 56, 57 S. E. 671; Western Union Tel. Co. *v.* Porterfield, (Tex. Civ. App. 1904) 84 S. W. 850.

78. Western Union Tel. Co. *v.* Ayers, 131 Ala. 391, 31 So. 78, 90 Am. St. Rep. 92 (brother-in-law); Lee *v.* Western Union Tel. Co., 130 Ky. 202, 113 S. W. 55 (plaintiff nephew of deceased); Western Union Tel. Co. *v.* Steenbergen, 107 Ky. 469, 54 S. W. 829, 21 Ky. L. Rep. 1289 (plaintiff father-in-law of addressee); Denham *v.* Western Union Tel. Co., 87 S. W. 788, 27 Ky. L. Rep. 999 (plaintiff aunt of deceased); Davidson *v.* Western Union Tel. Co., 54 S. W. 830, 21 Ky. L. Rep. 1292 (plaintiff son-in-law of deceased); Western Union Tel. Co. *v.* Wilson, 97 Tex. 22, 75 S. W. 482 (plaintiff uncle of deceased).

79. Randall *v.* Western Union Tel. Co., 107 S. W. 235, 32 Ky. L. Rep. 859, 15 L. R. A. N. S. 277, holding that an action will not lie by the addressee of a telegram, to recover damages for mental anguish due to a negligent failure of defendant to deliver a telegram, announcing the death of his fiancée, in time to enable him to attend her funeral.

80. Butler *v.* Western Union Tel. Co., 77 S. C. 148, 57 S. E. 757 (plaintiff brother-in-law of addressee); Western Union Tel. Co. *v.* Coffin, 88 Tex. 94, 30 S. W. 896 (plaintiff brother-in-law of deceased); Rich *v.* Western Union Tel. Co., (Tex. Civ. App. 1908) 110 S. W. 93; Western Union Tel. Co. *v.* Gibson, (Tex. Civ. App. 1896) 39 S. W. 198 (plaintiff father-in-law of deceased); Western Union Tel. Co. *v.* Garrett, (Tex. Civ. App. 1896) 34 S. W. 649 (plaintiff stepson of deceased); Western Union Tel. Co. *v.* McMillan, (Tex. Civ. App. 1895) 30 S. W. 298 (sister-in-law).

81. Western Union Tel. Co. *v.* Ayers, 131 Ala. 391, 31 So. 78, 90 Am. St. Rep. 92; Lee *v.* Western Union Tel. Co., 130 Ky. 202, 113 S. W. 55; Western Union Tel. Co. *v.* Steenbergen, 107 Ky. 469, 54 S. W. 829, 21 Ky. L. Rep. 1289; Randall *v.* Western Union Tel. Co., 107 S. W. 235, 32 Ky. L. Rep. 859, 15 L. R. A. N. S. 277.

In Kentucky the right of recovery is said to be arbitrarily limited to cases where the relationship between the parties is that of parent and child, husband and wife, sister and brother, or grandparent and grandchild. Lee *v.* Western Union Tel. Co., 130 Ky. 202, 113 S. W. 55.

82. Randall *v.* Western Union Tel. Co., 107 S. W. 235, 32 Ky. L. Rep. 859, 15 L. R. A. N. S. 277.

83. Hunter *v.* Western Union Tel. Co., 135 N. C. 458, 47 S. E. 745; Bright *v.* Western Union Tel. Co., 132 N. C. 317, 43 S. E. 841.

84. Foreman *v.* Western Union Tel. Co., 141 Iowa 32, 116 N. W. 724, 19 L. R. A. N. S. 374; Harrison *v.* Western Union Tel. Co., 136 N. C. 381, 48 S. E. 772; Cashion *v.* Western Union Tel. Co., 123 N. C. 267, 31 S. E. 493.

85. Western Union Tel. Co. *v.* Moxley, 80 Ark. 554, 98 S. W. 112 (plaintiff son-in-law of person who was sick); Foreman *v.* Western Union Tel. Co., 141 Iowa 32, 116 S. W. 724, 19 L. R. A. N. S. 374 (plaintiff son-in-law of addressee); Hunter *v.* Western Union Tel. Co., 135 N. C. 458, 47 S. E. 745 (second cousin); Bright *v.* Western Union Tel. Co., 132 N. C. 317, 43 S. E. 841 (husband's uncle); Bennett *v.* Western Union Tel. Co., 128 N. C. 103, 38 S. E. 294 (father-in-law).

86. See Western Union Tel. Co. *v.* Moxley, 80 Ark. 554, 98 S. W. 112; and cases cited *infra*, notes 87–90.

CPSIA information can be obtained
at www.ICGtesting.com
Printed in the USA
LVHW010013260920
667178LV00027B/2042